Fundamentals of Financial Management,
11th edition

Van Horne * Wachowicz

The Finance Center

www.prenhall.com/financecenter

One-stop shopping for all of your textbook needs, including:

- Stock updates
- Technology demos
- PowerPoint slides
- Excel spreadsheets
- Text-specific on-line study guide

- Headline news
- Supplements
- Virtual textbook tours
- Other related titles available
- Current events

Fundamentals of Financial Management

PRENTICE HALL FINANCE SERIES

Personal Finance

Keown, *Personal Finance: Turning Money into Wealth*
Trivoli, *Personal Portfolio Management: Fundamentals & Strategies*
Winger/Frasca, *Personal Finance: An Integrated Planning Approach*

Investments

Alexander/Sharpe/Bailey, *Fundamentals of Investments*
Fabozzi, *Investment Management*
Fischer/Jordan, *Security Analysis and Portfolio Management*
Haugen, *Modern Investment Management*
Haugen, *The New Finance: The Case Against Efficient*
Haugen, *The Beast on Wall Street*
Haugen, *The Inefficient Stock Market*
Sharpe/Alexander/Bailey, *Investments*
Taggart, *Quantitative Analysis for Investment Management*
Winger/Frasca, *Investments*

Portfolio Analysis

Alexander/Sharpe/Bailey, *Fundamentals of Investments*
Fischer/Jordan, *Security Analysis and Portfolio Management*
Haugen, *Modern Investment Theory*
Sharpe/Alexander/Bailey, *Investments*

Options/Futures/Derivatives

Hull, *Introduction to Futures and Options Markets*
Hull, *Options, Futures, and Other Derivatives*

Risk Management/Financial Engineering

Hull, *Financial Engineering and Risk Management*
Mason/Merton/Perold/Tufano, *Cases in Financial Engineering*

Fixed Income Securities

Van Horne, *Financial Market Rates and Flows*
Handa, *FinCoach: Fixed Income* (Software)

Bond Markets

Fabozzi, *Bond Markets, Analysis and Strategies*
Van Horne, *Financial Market Rates and Flows*

Capital Markets

Fabozzi/Modigliani, *Capital Markets: Institutions and Instruments*
Van Horne, *Financial Market Rates and Flows*

Corporate Finance, Survey of Finance, & Financial Economics

Bodie/Merton, *Finance*
Emery/Finnerty/Stowe, *Principles of Financial Managment*
Emery/Finnerty, *Corporate Financial Management*
Gallagher/Andrew, *Financial Management: Principles and Practice*
Haugen, *The New Finance: The Case Against Efficient Markets*
Keown/Martin/Petty/Scott, *Basic Financial Management*
Keown/Martin/Petty/Scott, *Foundations of Finance: The Logic and Practice of Financial Management*
Shapiro/Balbirer, *Modern Corporate Finance: A Multidisciplinary Approach to Value Creation*
Van Horne, *Financial Management and Policy*
Van Horne/Wachowicz, *Fundamentals of Financial Management*

International Finance

Baker, *International Finance: Management, Markets, and Institutions*
Grabbe, *International Financial Markets*
Rivera-Batiz/Rivera-Batiz, *International Finance and Open Economy Macroeconomics*

Capital Budgeting

Aggarwal, *Capital Budgeting Under Uncertainty*
Bierman/Smidt, *The Capital Budgeting Decision*

Mergers/Acquisitions/Takeovers

Hill/Sartoris, *Short Term Financial Management*
Weston/Chung/Siu, *Takeovers, Restructuring and Corporate Governance*

Short-Term Finance

Hill/Sartoris, *Short Term Financial Management*

Taxes and Corporate Financial Decision Making

Scholes/Wolfson, *Taxes and Business Strategy: A Global Planning Approach*

Insurance

Black/Skipper, *Life and Health Insurance*
Dorfman, *Introduction to Risk Management and Insurance*
Rejda, *Social Insurance and Economic Security*

Financial Markets and Institutions

Arshadi/Karels, *Modern Financial Intermediaries and Markets*
Dietrich, *Financial Services and Financial Institutions*
Fabozzi/Modigliani/Ferri/Jones, *Foundations of Financial Markets and Institutions*
Kaufman, *The U.S. Financial System*
Van Horne, *Financial Market Rates and Flows*

Commercial Banking

Arshadi/Karels, *Modern Financial Intermediaries and Markets*
Dietrich, *Financial Services and Financial Institutions*
Sinkey, *Commercial Bank Financial Management*

Entrepreneurial Finance

Adelman/Marks, *Entrepreneurial Finance*
Vaughn, *Financial Planning for the Entrepreneur*

Cases in Finance

May/May/Andrew, *Effective Writing: A Handbook for Finance People*

Financial Statement Analysis

Fraser/Ormiston, *Understanding Financial Statements*

Finance Center

for downloadable supplements and much more . . . visit us at
www.prenhall.com/financecenter

Fundamentals
of Financial Management

ELEVENTH EDITION

James C. Van Horne
Stanford University

John M. Wachowicz Jr.
The University of Tennessee

Prentice
Hall

Upper Saddle River, New Jersey 07458

Library of Congress Cataloging-in-Publication Data
Van Horne, James C.
    Fundamentals of financial management / James C. Van Horne,
John M. Wachowicz.—11 ed.
      p. cm.
    Includes bibliographical references and index.
    ISBN 0-13-018377-6
    1. Corporations—Finance. 2. Business enterprises—Finance.
I. Wachowicz, John Martin. II. Title.

HG4026.V36 2001
658.15—dc21

                                     00-026317

Senior Editor: Maureen Riopelle
Managing Editor (Editorial): Gladys Soto
Editor-in-Chief: PJ Boardman
Editorial Assistant: Cheryl Clayton
Assistant Editor: Holly Brown
Media Project Manager: Bill Minick
Senior Marketing Manager: Lori Braumberger
Production/Manufacturing Manager: Gail Steier de Acevedo
Production Coordinator: Maureen Wilson
Manufacturing Buyer: Natacha St. Hill Moore
Senior Prepress/Manufacturing Manager: Vincent Scelta
Cover Design: Kiwi Design
Cover Image: Silvestra Machado/Tony Stone Images
Composition: Impressions Book and Journal Services, Inc.

10 9 8 7 6 5 4 3 2

ISBN 0-13-018377-6

To Mimi, Drew, Stuart, and Stephen
James C. Van Horne

To Emerson, John, June, Lien, and Patricia
John M. Wachowicz Jr.

BRIEF CONTENTS

PART I: INTRODUCTION TO FINANCIAL MANAGEMENT

Chapter 1   The Role of Financial Management   1

Chapter 2   The Business, Tax, and Financial Environments   13

PART II: VALUATION

Chapter 3   The Time Value of Money   37

Chapter 4   The Valuation of Long-Term Securities   69

Chapter 5   Risk and Return   93

PART III: TOOLS OF FINANCIAL ANALYSIS AND PLANNING

Chapter 6   Financial Statement Analysis   125

Chapter 7   Funds Analysis, Cash-Flow Analysis, and Financial Planning   169

PART IV: WORKING CAPITAL MANAGEMENT

Chapter 8   Overview of Working Capital Management   209

Chapter 9   Cash and Marketable Securities Management   225

Chapter 10   Accounts Receivable and Inventory Management   253

Chapter 11   Short-Term Financing   287

PART V: INVESTMENT IN CAPITAL ASSETS

Chapter 12   Capital Budgeting and Estimating Cash Flows   315

Chapter 13   Capital Budgeting Techniques   333

Chapter 14   Risk and Managerial Options in Capital Budgeting   361

PART VI: THE COST OF CAPITAL, CAPITAL STRUCTURE, AND DIVIDEND POLICY

Chapter 15   Required Returns and the Cost of Capital   393

Chapter 16   Operating and Financial Leverage   433

Chapter 17   Capital Structure Determination   467

Chapter 18   Dividend Policy   491

PART VII: INTERMEDIATE AND LONG-TERM FINANCING

Chapter 19   The Capital Market   523

Chapter 20   Long-Term Debt, Preferred Stock, and Common Stock   545

Chapter 21   Term Loans and Leases   571

PART VIII: SPECIAL AREAS OF FINANCIAL MANAGEMENT

Chapter 22   Convertibles, Exchangeables, and Warrants   597

Chapter 23   Mergers and Other Forms of Corporate Restructuring   623

Chapter 24   International Financial Management   667

Appendix   701

Glossary   711

Commonly Used Symbols   725

Index   727

CONTENTS

Preface XIII

PART I: INTRODUCTION TO FINANCIAL MANAGEMENT

CHAPTER 1   The Role of Financial Management   1

Introduction   2

What Is Financial Management?   2

The Goal of the Firm   3

Organization of the Financial Management Function   6

Organization of the Book   8

Summary   10

Questions   11

Selected References   11

CHAPTER 2   The Business, Tax, and Financial Environments   13

The Business Environment   14

The Tax Environment   17

The Financial Environment   23

Summary   32

Questions   32

Self-Correction Problems   33

Problems   34

Solutions to Self-Correction Problems   35

Selected References   36

PART II: VALUATION

CHAPTER 3   The Time Value of Money   37

The Interest Rate   38

Simple Interest   39

Compound Interest   39

Compounding More Than Once a Year   56

Amortizing a Loan   59

Summary Table of Key Compound Interest Formulas   60

Summary   61

Questions   61

Self-Correction Problems   62

Problems   63

Solutions to Self-Correction Problems   66

Selected References   68

CHAPTER 4   The Valuation of Long-Term Securities   69

Distinctions Among Valuation Concepts   70

Bond Valuation   71

Bonds with a Finite Maturity   72

Preferred Stock Valuation   74

Common Stock Valuation   75

Rates of Return (or Yields)   80

Summary Table of Key Present Value Formulas for Valuing Long-Term Securities   85

Summary   85

Questions   86

Self-Correction Problems   87

Problems   88

Solutions to Self-Correction Problems   90

Selected References   92

CHAPTER 5   Risk and Return   93

Defining Risk and Return   94

Using Probability Distributions to Measure Risk   95

Attitudes Toward Risk   98

Risk and Return in a Portfolio Context   99

Diversification   101

The Capital-Asset Pricing Model (CAPM)   103

Efficient Financial Markets   112

Summary   113

Appendix A: Measuring Portfolio Risk   114

Appendix B: Arbitrage Pricing Theory   116

Questions   119

Self-Correction Problems   119

Problems   120

Solutions to Self-Correction Problems   123

Selected References   124

**PART III: TOOLS OF FINANCIAL ANALYSIS
            AND PLANNING**

CHAPTER 6   Financial Statement Analysis   125

Financial Statements   126

A Possible Framework for Analysis   130

Balance Sheet Ratios   134

Income Statement and Income Statement/Balance Sheet Ratios 138

Trend Analysis 149

Common-Size and Index Analysis 150

Summary 154

Summary of Key Ratios 154

Appendix: Deferred Taxes and Financial Analysis 156

Questions 157

Self-Correction Problems 158

Problems 160

Solutions to Self-Correction Problems 164

Selected References 167

CHAPTER 7   Funds Analysis, Cash-Flow Analysis, and Financial Planning 169

Flow of Funds (Sources and Uses) Statement 170

Accounting Statement of Cash Flows 177

Cash-Flow Forecasting 181

Range of Cash-Flow Estimates 186

Forecasting Financial Statements 188

Summary 192

Appendix: Sustainable Growth Modeling 193

Questions 197

Self-Correction Problems 198

Problems 200

Solutions to Self-Correction Problems 203

Selected References 207

PART IV: WORKING CAPITAL MANAGEMENT

CHAPTER 8   Overview of Working Capital Management 209

Introduction 210

Working Capital Issues 211

Financing Current Assets: Short-Term and Long-Term Mix 214

Combining Liability Structure and Current Asset Decisions 219

Summary 220

Questions 221

Self-Correction Problem 221

Problems 222

Solutions to Self-Correction Problem 223

Selected References 224

CHAPTER 9   Cash and Marketable Securities Management 225

Motives for Holding Cash 226

Speeding Up Cash Receipts 227

S-l-o-w-i-n-g D-o-w-n Cash Payouts   232

Electronic Commerce   234

Outsourcing   235

Cash Balances to Maintain   237

Investment in Marketable Securities   238

Summary   247

Questions   247

Self-Correction Problems   248

Problems   249

Solutions to Self-Correction Problems   250

Selected References   250

CHAPTER 10   Accounts Receivable and Inventory Management   253

Credit and Collection Policies   254

Analyzing the Credit Applicant   262

Inventory Management and Control   267

Summary   278

Questions   279

Self-Correction Problems   279

Problems   280

Solutions to Self-Correction Problems   283

Selected References   285

CHAPTER 11   Short-Term Financing   287

Spontaneous Financing   288

Negotiated Financing   293

Factoring Accounts Receivable   305

Composition of Short-Term Financing   307

Summary   308

Questions   209

Self-Correction Problems   310

Problems   311

Solutions to Self-Correction Problems   313

Selected References   314

PART V: INVESTMENT IN CAPITAL ASSETS

CHAPTER 12   Capital Budgeting and Estimating Cash Flows   315

The Capital Budgeting Process: An Overview   316

Generating Investment Project Proposals   316

Estimating Project "After-Tax Incremental Operating Cash Flows"   317

Summary   326

Questions   327

Contents

Self-Correction Problems   327
Problems   328
Solutions to Self-Correction Problems   330
Selected References   331

CHAPTER 13   Capital Budgeting Techniques   333
Project Evaluation and Selection: Alternative Methods   334
Potential Difficulties   340
Project Monitoring: Progress Reviews and Post-Completion Audits   349
Summary   349
Appendix A: Multiple Internal Rates of Return   350
Appendix B: Replacement Chain Analysis   352
Questions   354
Self-Correction Problems   355
Problems   356
Solutions to Self-Correction Problems   358
Selected References   359

CHAPTER 14   Risk and Managerial Options in Capital Budgeting   361
The Problem of Project Risk   362
Total Project Risk   366
Contribution to Total Firm Risk: Firm-Portfolio Approach   373
Managerial Options   378
Summary   383
Questions   384
Self-Correction Problems   384
Problems   386
Solutions to Self-Correction Problems   389
Selected References   391

PART VI: THE COST OF CAPITAL, CAPITAL STRUCTURE, AND DIVIDEND POLICY

CHAPTER 15   Required Returns and the Cost of Capital   393
Creation of Value   394
Overall Cost of Capital of the Firm   395
The CAPM: Project-Specific and Group-Specific Required Rates of Return   408
Evaluation of Projects on the Basis of Their Total Risk   414
Summary   418
Appendix A: Adjusting the Beta for Financial Leverage   419
Appendix B: Adjusted Present Value   420
Questions   423

Self-Correction Problems   424

Problems   425

Solutions to Self-Correction Problems   428

Selected References   430

CHAPTER 16   Operating and Financial Leverage   433

Operating Leverage   434

Financial Leverage   441

Total Leverage   450

Cash-Flow Ability to Service Debt   451

Other Methods of Analysis   455

Combination of Methods   457

Summary   457

Questions   458

Self-Correction Problems   459

Problems   461

Solutions to Self-Correction Problems   463

Selected References   466

CHAPTER 17   Capital Structure Determination   467

A Conceptual Look   468

The Total-Value Principle   472

Presence of Market Imperfections and Incentive Issues   475

The Effect of Taxes   478

Taxes and Market Imperfections Combined   480

Financial Signaling   482

Summary   482

Questions   483

Self-Correction Problems   484

Problems   484

Solutions to Self-Correction Problems   487

Selected References   488

CHAPTER 18   Dividend Policy   491

Passive versus Active Dividend Policy   492

Factors Influencing Dividend Policy   497

Dividend Stability   500

Stock Dividends and Stock Splits   503

Stock Repurchase   508

Administrative Considerations   512

Summary   513

Questions   515

Self-Correction Problems   515

Problems   516

Solutions to Self-Correction Problems   519

Selected References   521

PART VII: INTERMEDIATE AND LONG-TERM FINANCING

CHAPTER 19   The Capital Market   523

Déjà Vu All Over Again   524

Public Issue   524

Privileged Subscription   527

Regulation of Security Offerings   531

Private Placement   534

Initial Financing   536

Signaling Effects   538

The Secondary Market   539

Summary   540

Questions   541

Self-Correction Problems   542

Problems   542

Solutions to Self-Correction Problems   543

Selected References   544

CHAPTER 20   Long-Term Debt, Preferred Stock, and Common Stock   545

Bonds and Their Features   546

Types of Long-Term Debt Instruments   547

Retirement of Bonds   551

Preferred Stock and Its Features   553

Common Stock and Its Features   556

Rights to Common Shareholders   558

Dual-Class Common Stock   560

Summary   561

Appendix: Refunding a Bond Issue   562

Questions   564

Self-Correction Problems   565

Problems   566

Solutions to Self-Correction Problems   568

Selected References   569

CHAPTER 21   Term Loans and Leases   571

Term Loans   572

Provisions of Loan Agreements   574

Equipment Financing   576

Lease Financing   577

Evaluating Lease Financing in Relation to Debt Financing   581

Summary   586

Appendix: Accounting Treatment of Leases   587

Questions   589

Self-Correction Problems   590

Problems   590

Solutions to Self-Correction Problems   592

Selected References   594

PART VIII: SPECIAL AREAS OF FINANCIAL MANAGEMENT

CHAPTER 22   Convertibles, Exchangeables, and Warrants   597

Convertible Securities   598

Value of Convertible Securities   601

Exchangeable Bonds   605

Warrants   606

Summary   609

Appendix: Option Pricing   610

Questions   616

Self-Correction Problems   617

Problems   618

Solutions to Self-Correction Problems   620

Selected References   621

CHAPTER 23   Mergers and Other Forms of Corporate Restructuring   623

Sources of Value   624

Strategic Acquisitions Involving Common Stock   628

Acquisitions and Capital Budgeting   635

Closing the Deal   637

Takeovers, Tender Offers, and Defenses   640

Strategic Alliances   643

Divestiture   644

Ownership Restructuring   646

Leveraged Buyouts   648

Summary   650

Appendix: Remedies for a Failing Company   651

Questions   655

Self-Correction Problems   656

Problems   658

Solutions to Self-Correction Problems   662

Selected References   665

CHAPTER 24   International Financial Management   667

   Some Background   668

   Types of Exchange-Rate Risk Exposure   672

   Management of Exchange-Rate Risk Exposure   677

   Structuring International Trade Transactions   688

   Summary   691

   Questions   692

   Self-Correction Problems   693

   Problems   695

   Solutions to Self-Correction Problems   697

   Selected References   698

Appendix

   Table I: Future value interest factor   701

   Table II: Present value interest factor   704

   Table III: Future value interest factor of an (ordinary) annuity   706

   Table IV: Present value interest factor of an (ordinary) annuity   708

   Table V: Area of normal distribution that is Z standard deviations
                 to the left or right of the mean   710

Glossary   711

Commonly Used Symbols   725

Index   727

PREFACE

Financial management continues to change rapidly. Advancements are occurring not only in the theory of financial management but also in its real-world practice. One result has been for financial management to take on a greater strategic focus as managers struggle to create value within a corporate setting. Conflicting stakeholder claims, a downsized corporate environment, information and financial signaling effects, the globalization of finance, the growth of e-commerce, strategic alliances, outsourcing and the emergence of virtual corporations, and a host of other considerations now permeate the landscape of financial decision making. It is an exciting time, and we hope to convey a sense of this excitement to our readers.

The purpose of the eleventh edition of *Fundamentals of Financial Management* is to enable you to understand the financial decision-making process and to interpret the impact that financial decisions will have on value creation. The book therefore introduces you to the three major decision-making areas in financial management: the investment, financing, and asset management decisions.

We explore finance, including its frontiers, in an easy-to-understand, user-friendly manner. Although the book is designed for an introductory course in financial management, it can be used as a reference tool as well. For example, participants in management development programs, candidates preparing for various professional exams, and practicing finance professionals will find it useful. And because of the extensive material available through the text's Web site (which we will discuss shortly) the book is ideal for Web-based training and distance learning.

There are many important changes in this new edition. Rather than list them all, we will explain some essential themes that governed our revisions and, in the process, highlight some of the changes. The institutional material—necessary for understanding the environment in which financial decisions are made—was updated. The book continues to grow more international in scope. New sections, examples, and boxed features have been added that focus on the international dimensions of financial management. Attention was also given to streamlining coverage and better expressing fundamental ideas in every chapter.

Chapter 3, The Time Value of Money, and Chapter 5, Risk and Return, have benefited from expanded coverage. A discussion of economic value added (EVA) has been incorporated into Chapter 15, Required Returns and the Cost of Capital. Chapter 19, The Capital Market, addresses new SEC proposals for streamlining the registration procedures, and looks for the first time at registration rights and underwritten Rule 144a private placements. Chapter 21, Term Loans and Leases, shows major improvements in the discussion of leasing. Finally, we continued our efforts to make the book more user-friendly. New boxed items appear, including tips, Q&As, and special features, to capture the reader's interest and illustrate underlying concepts. Many of these boxed features come from new, first-time contributors to the text—The Motley Fool (www.fool.com); *CFO Asia, Exec, Strategic Finance,* and *Business Finance* magazines; and Lloyds TSB, Wit Capital, and First Tennessee corporations.

The order of the chapters reflects a common sequence for teaching the course, but the instructor may reorder many chapters without causing the students any difficulty.

For example, some instructors prefer covering Part III, Tools of Financial Analysis and Planning, before Part II, Valuation. Extensive selected references at the ends of chapters give the reader direct access to relevant literature utilized in preparing the chapters. The appendices at the ends of some chapters invite the reader to go into certain topics in greater depth, but the book's continuity is maintained even if this material is not covered.

A number of materials supplement the text. For the teacher, a comprehensive *Instructor's Manual* contains suggestions for organizing the course, answers to chapter questions, and solutions to chapter problems. Another aid is a Test-Item File of extensive questions and problems, prepared by Professor Gregory A. Kuhlemeyer, Carroll College. This supplement is available both in printed form and as a custom computerized test bank (for Windows) through your Prentice Hall sales representative. In addition, Professor Kuhlemeyer has done a wonderful job preparing an extensive collection of Microsoft PowerPoint slides as outlines (with examples) to go along with this text. The PowerPoint presentation graphics are available for downloading through the following Prentice Hall site: www.prenhall.com/financecenter. All text figures and tables are available as transparency masters through this same site listed above. Computer application software prepared by Craig W. Holden of Indiana University, which can be used in conjunction with specially identified end-of-chapter problems is available in Microsoft Excel format on the same site. The companion Web site also contains an Online Study Guide prepared by Gregory A. Kuhlmeyer. Designed to help the student familiarize himself with chapter material, each chapter of the Online Study Guide is comprised of multiple choice, true/false, and short answer questions.

For the student, self-correction problems appear at the end of each chapter in the textbook. These are in addition to the regular questions and problems and give students immediate feedback on their understanding of the chapter.

Learning finance is like learning a foreign language. Part of the difficulty is simply learning the vocabulary. Therefore, we provide an extensive glossary of close to 400 business terms in two formats—a running glossary (appears alongside the textual material in the margins) and an end-of-book cumulative glossary.

Take Note

> We purposely have made limited use of Internet addresses (i.e., the address you type into your browser window that usually begins "http://www.") in the body of this text. Web sites are extremely transient—any Web site that we mention in print could change substantially, alter its address, or even disappear entirely by the time you read this. Therefore, we use our Web site to flag other sites that should be of interest to you. We then constantly update our listings and check for any broken or dead links. We strongly encourage you to make use of our text's Web site as you read each chapter. Although the text's Web site was created with students uppermost in mind, we are pleased to report that it has found quite a following among business professionals. In fact, the Web site has received favorable reviews in a number of business publications, including *The Financial Times* newspaper and both *Corporate Finance* and *CFO Asia* magazines.

To help harness the power of the Internet as a financial management learning device, students (and instructors) are invited to visit the text's award-winning Web site, **Wachowicz's Web World,** for which a link can be found at www.prenhall.com /wachowicz. This Web site provides links to hundreds of financial management Web sites grouped to correspond with the major headings in the text (e.g., Valuation, Tools of Financial Analysis and Planning, and so on). In addition, the Web site contains interactive true/false and multiple-choice quizzes, more than 1,000 PowerPoint slides, and interactive Web-based exercises.

The authors are grateful for the comments, suggestions, and assistance given by a number of business and government professionals. In particular we would like to thank Judy Ames and Selena Maranjian, The Motley Fool; Michael Annin, Ibbotson Associates; Jennifer Banner, Pershing Yoakley and Associates, CPAs and Consultants; John Goff, *CFO Asia* magazine; Sue Harris, Federal Reserve System; John Markese, American Association of Individual Investors; David Montgomery, Morningstar; Rhee Rosenman, Wit Capital; and Annette Winston, Knoxville Area Chamber Partnership. Finally, we want to thank Natacha St. Hill Moore, Maureen Riopelle, Gail Steier, and Maureen Wilson at Prentice Hall and the individuals at Impressions Book and Journal Services, and Steel/Katigbak Indexing, who helped with the production of this edition.

We hope that *Fundamentals of Financial Management*, eleventh edition, contributes to your understanding of finance and imparts a sense of excitement in the process. You, the reader, are the final judge. We thank you for choosing our textbook and welcome your comments and suggestions (please e-mail: jwachowi@utk.edu).

JAMES C. VAN HORNE   *Palo Alto, California*
JOHN M. WACHOWICZ JR.   *Knoxville, Tennessee*

Chapter 1

The Role of Financial Management

INTRODUCTION
WHAT IS FINANCIAL MANAGEMENT?
    Investment Decision • Financing Decision • Asset Management
    Decision
THE GOAL OF THE FIRM
    Value Creation • Agency Problems • Social Responsibility
ORGANIZATION OF THE FINANCIAL MANAGEMENT FUNCTION
ORGANIZATION OF THE BOOK
    The Underpinnings • Managing and Acquiring Assets • Financing
    Assets • A Mixed Bag
SUMMARY
QUESTIONS
SELECTED REFERENCES

> *Increasing shareholder value over time is the bottom line of
> every move we make.*

> —ROBERTO GOIZUETA
> *Former CEO, The Coca-Cola Company*

1

The financial manager plays a dynamic role in a modern company's development. This has not always been the case. Until around the first half of the 1900s financial managers primarily raised funds and managed their firms' cash positions—and that was pretty much it. In the 1950s, the increasing acceptance of present value concepts encouraged financial managers to expand their responsibilities and to become concerned with the selection of capital investment projects.

Today, external factors have an increasing impact on the financial manager. Heightened corporate competition, technological change, volatility in inflation and interest rates, worldwide economic uncertainty, fluctuating exchange rates, tax law changes, and ethical concerns over certain financial dealings must be dealt with almost daily. As a result, finance is required to play an ever more vital strategic role within the corporation. The financial manager has emerged as a team player in the overall effort of a company to create value. The "old ways of doing things" simply are not good enough in a world where old ways quickly become obsolete. Thus, today's financial manager must have the flexibility to adapt to the changing external environment if his or her firm is to survive.

If you become a financial manager, your ability to adapt to change, raise funds, invest in assets, and manage wisely will affect the success of your firm and, ultimately, the overall economy as well. To the extent that funds are misallocated, the growth of the economy will be slowed. When economic wants are unfulfilled, this misallocation of funds may work to the detriment of society. In an economy, efficient allocation of resources is vital to optimal growth in that economy; it is also vital to ensuring that individuals obtain satisfaction of their highest levels of personal wants. Thus, through efficiently acquiring, financing, and managing assets, the financial manager contributes to the firm and to the vitality and growth of the economy as a whole.

WHAT IS FINANCIAL MANAGEMENT?

Financial management concerns the acquisition, financing, and management of assets with some overall goal in mind.

Financial management is concerned with the acquisition, financing, and management of assets with some overall goal in mind. Thus, the decision function of financial management can be broken down into three major areas: the investment, financing, and asset management decisions.

Investment Decision

The investment decision is the most important of the firm's three major decisions when it comes to value creation. It begins with a determination of the total amount of assets needed to be held by the firm. Picture the firm's balance sheet in your mind for a moment. Imagine liabilities and owners' equity being listed on the right side of the balance sheet and its assets on the left. The financial manager needs to determine the dollar amount that appears above the double lines on the left-hand side of the balance sheet—that is, the size of the firm. Even when this number is known, the composition of the assets must still be decided. For example, how much of the firm's total assets should be devoted to cash or to inventory? Also, the flip side of investment—disinvestment—must not be ignored. Assets that can no longer be economically justified may need to be reduced, eliminated, or replaced.

Financing Decision

The second major decision of the firm is the financing decision. Here the financial manager is concerned with the makeup of the right-hand side of the balance sheet. If you look at the mix of financing for firms across industries, you will see marked differences. Some firms have relatively large amounts of debt, whereas others are almost debt free. Does the type of financing employed make a difference? If so, why? And, in some sense, can a certain mix of financing be thought of as best?

In addition, dividend policy must be viewed as an integral part of the firm's financing decision. The dividend-payout ratio determines the amount of earnings that can be retained in the firm. Retaining a greater amount of current earnings in the firm means that fewer dollars will be available for current dividend payments. The value of the dividends paid to stockholders must therefore be balanced against the opportunity cost of retained earnings lost as a means of equity financing.

Once the mix of financing has been decided, the financial manager must still determine how best to physically acquire the needed funds. The mechanics of getting a short-term loan, entering into a long-term lease arrangement, or negotiating a sale of bonds or stock must be understood.

Asset Management Decision

The third important decision of the firm is the asset management decision. Once assets have been acquired and appropriate financing provided, these assets must still be managed efficiently. The financial manager is charged with varying degrees of operating responsibility over existing assets. These responsibilities require that the financial manager be more concerned with the management of current assets than with that of fixed assets. A large share of the responsibility for the management of fixed assets would reside with the operating managers who employ these assets.

THE GOAL OF THE FIRM

Efficient financial management requires the existence of some objective or goal because judgment as to whether or not a financial decision is efficient must be made in light of some standard. Although various objectives are possible, we assume in this book that the goal of the firm is to maximize the wealth of the firm's present owners.

Shares of common stock give evidence of ownership in a corporation. Shareholder wealth is represented by the market price per share of the firm's common stock, which, in turn, is a reflection of the firm's investment, financing, and asset management decisions. The idea is that the success of a business decision should be judged by the effect that it ultimately has on share price.

Profit maximization Maximizing a firm's earnings after taxes (EAT).

Earnings per share (EPS) Earnings after taxes (EAT) divided by the number of common shares outstanding.

Value Creation

Frequently, **profit maximization** is offered as the proper objective of the firm. However, under this goal a manager could continue to show profit increases by merely issuing stock and using the proceeds to invest in Treasury bills. For most firms, this would result in a decrease in each owner's share of profits—that is, **earnings per share** would fall. Maximizing earnings per share, therefore, is often advocated as an improved version of profit maximization. However, maximization of earnings per share is not a fully appropriate goal because it does not specify the timing or duration

What Companies Say About Their Corporate Goal

of expected returns. Is the investment project that will produce a $100,000 return five years from now more valuable than the project that will produce annual returns of $15,000 in each of the next five years? An answer to this question depends on the time value of money to the firm and to investors at the margin. Few existing stockholders would think favorably of a project that promised its first return in 100 years, no matter how large this return. Therefore, our analysis must take into account the time pattern of returns.

Another shortcoming of the objective of maximizing earnings per share—a shortcoming shared by other traditional return measures, such as return on investment—is that risk is not considered. Some investment projects are far more risky than others. As a result, the prospective stream of earnings per share would be more risky if these projects were undertaken. In addition, a company will be more or less risky depending on the amount of debt in relation to equity in its capital structure. This financial risk also contributes to the overall risk to the investor. Two companies may have the same expected earnings per share, but if the earnings stream of one is subject to considerably more risk than the earnings stream of the other, the market price per share of its stock may well be less.

Finally, this objective does not allow for the effect of dividend policy on the market price of the stock. If the only objective were to maximize earnings per share, the firm would never pay a dividend. It could always improve earnings per share by retaining earnings and investing them at any positive rate of return, however small. To the extent that the payment of dividends can affect the value of the stock, the maximization of earnings per share will not be a satisfactory objective by itself.

For the reasons just given, an objective of maximizing earnings per share may not be the same as maximizing market price per share. The market price of a firm's stock represents the focal judgment of all market participants as to the value of the particular firm. It takes into account present and expected future earnings per share; the timing, duration, and risk of these earnings; the dividend policy of the firm; and other factors that bear on the market price of the stock. The market price serves as a barometer for business performance; it indicates how well management is doing on behalf of its shareholders.

Management is under continuous review. Shareholders who are dissatisfied with management performance may sell their shares and invest in another company. This action, if taken by other dissatisfied shareholders, will put downward pressure on market price per share. Thus, management must focus on creating value for shareholders. This requires management to judge alternative investment, financing, and asset management strategies in terms of their effect on shareholder value (share price). In addition, management should pursue product-market strategies, such as building market share or increasing customer satisfaction, only if they too will increase shareholder value.

Agency Problems

It has long been recognized that the separation of ownership and control in the modern corporation results in potential conflicts between owners and managers. In particular, the objectives of management may differ from those of the firm's shareholders. In a large corporation, stock may be so widely held that shareholders cannot even make known their objectives, much less control or influence management. Thus, this separation of ownership from management creates a situation in which management may act in its own best interests rather than those of the shareholders.

Agent(s) Individual(s) authorized by another person, called the principal, to act in the latter's behalf.

Agency (theory) A branch of economics relating to the behavior of principals (such as owners) and their agents (such as managers).

We may think of management as the **agents** of the owners. Shareholders, hoping that the agents will act in the shareholders' best interests, delegate decision-making authority to them. Jensen and Meckling were the first to develop a comprehensive theory of the firm under **agency** arrangements.[1] They showed that the principals, in our case the shareholders, can assure themselves that the agents (management) will make optimal decisions only if appropriate incentives are given and only if the agents are monitored. Incentives include stock options, bonuses, and perquisites ("perks," such as company automobiles and expensive offices), and these must be directly related to how close management decisions come to the interests of the shareholders. Monitoring is done by bonding the agent, systematically reviewing management perquisites, auditing financial statements, and limiting management decisions. These monitoring activities necessarily involve costs, an inevitable result of the separation of ownership and control of a corporation. The less the ownership percentage of the managers, the less the likelihood that they will behave in a manner consistent with maximizing shareholder wealth and the greater the need for outside shareholders to monitor their activities.

Some people suggest that the primary monitoring of managers comes not from the owners but from the managerial labor market. They argue that efficient capital markets provide signals about the value of a company's securities and, thus, about the performance of its managers. Managers with good performance records should have an easier time finding other employment (if they need to) than managers with poor performance records. Thus, if the managerial labor market is competitive both within and outside the firm, it will tend to discipline managers. In that situation, the signals given by changes in the total market value of the firm's securities become very important.

Social Responsibility

Maximizing shareholder wealth does not mean that management should ignore social responsibility, such as protecting the consumer, paying fair wages to employees, maintaining fair hiring practices and safe working conditions, supporting education,

---

[1]Michael C. Jensen and William H. Meckling, "Theory of the Firm: Managerial Behavior, Agency Costs and Ownership Structure," *Journal of Financial Economics* 3 (October 1976), 305–60.

Incentive Compensation Programs Can Be Used to Align Chief Executive Officer's and Shareholders' Interests

Harvard Business Review

Shareholders rely on CEOs to adopt policies that maximize the value of their shares. Like other human beings, however, CEOs tend to engage in activities that increase their own well-being. One of the most critical roles of the board of directors is to create incentives that make it in the CEO's best interest to do what's in the shareholders' best interests. Conceptually this is not a difficult challenge. Some combination of three basic policies will create the right monetary incentives for CEOs to maximize the value of their companies:

1. Boards can require that CEOs become substantial owners of company stock.

2. Salaries, bonuses, and stock options can be structured so as to provide big rewards for superior performance and big penalties for poor performance.

3. The threat of dismissal for poor performance can be made real.

Stakeholders All constituencies with a stake in the fortunes of the company. They include shareholders, creditors, customers, employees, suppliers, and local communities.

and becoming involved in such environmental issues as clean air and water. It is appropriate for management to consider the interests of **stakeholders** other than shareholders. These stakeholders include creditors, employees, customers, suppliers, communities in which a company operates, and others. Only through attention to the legitimate concerns of the firm's various stakeholders can the firm attain its ultimate goal of maximizing shareholder wealth.

Many people feel that a firm has no choice but to act in socially responsible ways. They argue that shareholder wealth and, perhaps, the corporation's very existence depend on its being socially responsible. Because the criteria for social responsibility are not clearly defined, however, formulating consistent policies is difficult. When society, acting through various representative bodies, establishes the rules governing the trade-off between social goals and economic efficiency, the task for the corporation is clearer. We can then view the company as producing both private and social goods, and the maximization of shareholder wealth remains a viable corporate objective.

ORGANIZATION OF THE FINANCIAL MANAGEMENT FUNCTION

Whether your business career takes you in the direction of manufacturing, marketing, finance, or accounting, it is important for you to understand the role that financial management plays in the operations of the firm. Figure 1-1 is an organization chart for a typical manufacturing firm that gives special attention to the finance function.

As the head of one of the three major functional areas of the firm, the vice president of finance, or chief financial officer (CFO), generally reports directly to the president, or chief executive officer (CEO). In large firms, the financial operations overseen by the CFO will be split into two branches, with one headed by a treasurer and the other by a controller.

FIGURE 1-1
Financial Management on the Organization Chart

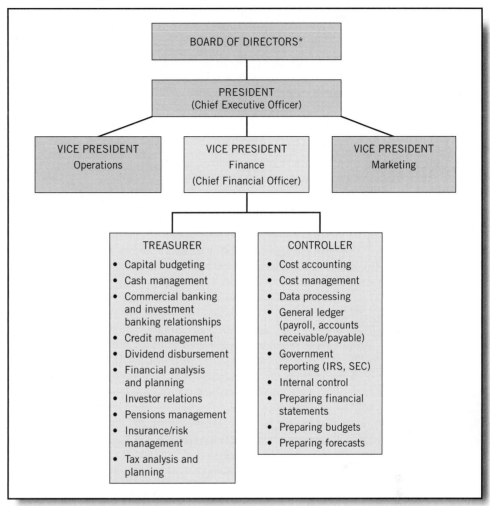

*In response to heightened concern over shareholders' interests, a growing number of companies have placed stockholders in a box above the board of directors on their organization chart.

The controller's responsibilities are primarily accounting in nature. Cost accounting, as well as budgets and forecasts, concerns internal consumption. External financial reporting is provided to the IRS, the Securities and Exchange Commission (SEC), and the stockholders.

The treasurer's responsibilities fall into the decision areas most commonly associated with financial management: investment (capital budgeting, pension management), financing (commercial banking and investment banking relationships, investor relations, dividend disbursement), and asset management (cash management, credit management). The organization chart may give you the false impression that a clear split exists between treasurer and controller responsibilities. In a well-functioning firm, information will flow easily back and forth between both branches. In small firms the treasurer and controller functions may be combined into one position with a resulting commingling of activities.

We began this chapter by offering the warning that today's financial manager must have the flexibility to adapt to the changing external environment if his or her firm is to survive. The recent past has witnessed the production of sophisticated new technology-driven techniques for raising and investing money that offer only a hint of things to come. But, take heart. Although the techniques of financial management change, the principles do not.

As we introduce you to the most current techniques of financial management, our focus will be on the underlying principles or fundamentals. In this way, we feel that we can best prepare you to adapt to change over your entire business career.

The Underpinnings

In Part I, Chapter 1 we define financial management, advocate maximization of shareholder wealth as the goal of the firm, and look at the position that financial management holds on the firm's organization chart. Our next aim is to arm you with certain background material and some of the basic tools of financial analysis. Therefore, in Chapter 2 we examine the legal setting for financial management as it relates to organizational form and to taxes. The function of financial markets and institutions, as well as of interest rates, is also included as pertinent background information. In particular, we will focus on how business firms interact with financial markets. The time value of money, valuation, and the twin concepts of risk and return are explored in Part II, Chapters 3, 4, and 5, because an understanding of these fundamentals is essential to sound financial decisions. Indeed, the foundation for maximizing shareholder wealth lies in valuation and in an understanding of the trade-offs between risk and return. As a result, we explore these topics early on.

Lloyds TSB Speaks Out on Value Creation and Society

Companies everywhere that want to attract capital have to ensure that they are responsive to shareholders' interests. Lloyds TSB, a leading United Kingdom–based financial services group, is one such firm that views maximizing shareholder value as its governing objective. Putting value creation in the forefront does not mean, however, that its customers, employees, or society in general will take a back seat. Here is what Lloyds TSB Chairman, Sir Brian Pitman, has to say about "putting value creation first":

Putting value creation first can bring huge benefits, not only to the company, but to society as a whole. No company can survive for long unless it creates wealth. A sick company is a drag on society. It cannot sustain jobs, much less widen the opportunities available to its employees. It cannot adequately serve customers. It cannot give to philanthropic causes.

As businessmen and businesswomen, we believe that there is no better way for us to serve all our stakeholders—not just our shareholders and customers, but our fellow employees, our business partners and our communities—than by creating value over time for those who employ us. It is our success in value creation that has also enabled the Lloyds TSB Group to become a leader in charitable giving, a leader in the community and a leader in sponsorship of education, enterprise, the arts and sports. The Lloyds TSB Foundations will receive some £27 million in 1999 for distribution to charities, with a particular focus on disabled and disadvantaged people.

Source: Lloyds TSB Group Annual Report & Accounts 1998, p. 3. Reproduced with permission of Lloyds TSB Group plc.

If I have no intention of becoming a financial manager, why do I need to understand financial management?

One good reason is "to prepare yourself for the workplace of the future." More and more businesses are reducing management jobs and squeezing together the various layers of the corporate pyramid. This is being done to reduce costs and boost productivity. As a result, the responsibilities of the remaining management positions are being broadened. The successful manager will need to be much more of a team player who has the knowledge and ability to move not just vertically within an organization but horizontally as well. Developing cross-functional capabilities will be the rule, not the exception. Thus, a mastery of basic financial management skills is a key ingredient that will be required in the workplace of your not-too-distant future.

To invest in, finance, and manage assets efficiently, financial managers must plan carefully. For one thing, they must project future cash flows and then assess the likely effect of these flows on the financial condition of the firm. On the basis of these projections, they also must plan for adequate liquidity to pay bills and other debts as they come due. These obligations may make it necessary to raise additional funds. In order to control performance, the financial manager needs to establish certain norms. These norms are then used to compare actual performance with planned performance. Because financial analysis, planning, and control underlie a good deal of the discussion in this book, we examine these topics in Part III, Chapters 6 and 7.

Managing and Acquiring Assets

Decisions regarding the management of assets must be made in accordance with the underlying objective of the firm: to maximize shareholder wealth. In Part IV, we examine cash, marketable securities, accounts receivable, and inventories. We shall explore ways of efficiently managing these current assets in order to maximize profitability relative to the amount of funds tied up in the assets. Determining a proper level of liquidity is very much a part of this asset management. The optimal level of a current asset depends on the profitability and flexibility associated with that level in relation to the cost involved in maintaining it. In the past, the management of working capital (current assets and their supporting financing) dominated the role of financial managers. Although this traditional function continues to be vital, expanded attention is now being paid to the management of longer-term assets and liabilities.

In Part V, under capital budgeting, we consider the acquisition of fixed assets. Capital budgeting involves selecting investment proposals whose benefits are expected to extend beyond one year. When a proposal requires an increase or decrease in working capital, this change is treated as part of the capital budgeting decision and not as a separate working capital decision. Because the expected future benefits from an investment proposal are uncertain, risk is necessarily involved. Changes in the business-risk complexion of the firm can have a significant influence on the firm's value in the marketplace. Because of this important effect, attention is devoted to the problem of measuring risk for a capital investment project. In addition to risk, an investment project sometimes embodies options for management to alter previous decisions. Therefore, the effect of managerial options on project desirability is studied. Capital is apportioned according to an acceptance criterion. The return required of the project must be in accord with the objective of maximizing shareholder wealth.

Financing Assets

A major facet of financial management involves providing the financing necessary to support assets. A wide variety of financing sources is available. Each has certain characteristics as to cost, maturity, availability, claims on assets, and other terms imposed by the suppliers of capital. On the basis of these factors, the financial manager must determine the best mix of financing for the firm. Implications for shareholder wealth must be considered when these decisions are made.

In Part VI, we discuss the capital structure (or permanent long-term financing makeup) of a firm. We look at the concept of financial leverage from a number of different angles in an effort to understand financial risk and how this risk is interrelated with business (or operating) risk. In addition, we analyze the retention of earnings as a source of financing. Because this source represents dividends forgone by stockholders, dividend policy very much impinges on financing policy and vice versa. While in Part IV, previously discussed, we examine the various sources of short-term financing, in Part VII the sources of long-term financing are explored. Both parts reveal the features, concepts, and problems associated with alternative methods of financing.

A Mixed Bag

In Part VIII we cover some of the specialized areas of financial management in detail. Some of the more exotic financing instruments—convertibles, exchangeables, and warrants—are discussed. Mergers, strategic alliances, divestitures, restructurings, and remedies for a failing company are explored. Growth of a company can be internal, external, or both, and domestic or international in flavor. Finally, because the multinational firm has come into prominence, it is particularly relevant that we study growth through international operations.

Financial management, then, involves the acquisition, financing, and management of assets. These three decision areas are all interrelated: the decision to acquire an asset necessitates the financing and management of that asset, whereas financing and management costs affect the decision to invest. The focus of this book is on the investment, financing, and asset management decisions of the firm. Together, these decisions determine the value of the firm to its shareholders. Mastering the concepts involved is the key to understanding the role of financial management.

SUMMARY

- *Financial management* is concerned with the acquisition, financing, and management of assets with some overall goal in mind.
- The decision function of financial management can be broken down into three major areas: the investment, financing, and asset management decisions.
- We assume in this book that the *goal of the firm* is to maximize the wealth of the firm's present owners (or shareholders). Shareholder wealth is represented by the market price per share of the firm's common stock, which, in turn, is a reflection of the firm's investment, financing, and asset management decisions.
- The market price of a firm's stock represents the focal judgment of all market participants as to the value of the particular firm. It takes into account present and prospective future earnings per share; the timing, duration, and risk of these earnings; the dividend policy of the firm; and

other factors that bear on the market price of the stock.

- *Agency theory* suggests that managers (the agents), particularly those of large, publicly owned firms, may have different objectives from those of the shareholders (the principals). The shareholders can assure themselves that the managers will make shareholder wealth–maximizing decisions only if management receives appropriate incentives and only if management is monitored.
- Maximizing shareholder wealth does *not* relieve the firm of the responsibility to act in socially responsible ways.
- In large firms, the finance function is the responsibility of the vice president of finance, or chief financial officer (CFO), who generally reports directly to the president, or chief executive officer (CEO). The financial operations overseen by the CFO will be split into two branches, with one headed by a treasurer and the other by a controller. The controller's responsibilities are primarily accounting in nature, while the treasurer's responsibilities fall into the decision areas most commonly associated with financial management.

QUESTIONS

1. If all companies had an objective of maximizing shareholder wealth, would people overall tend to be better or worse off?
2. Contrast the objective of maximizing earnings with that of maximizing wealth.
3. What is financial management all about?
4. Is the goal of zero profits for some finite period (three to five years, for example) ever consistent with the maximization-of-wealth objective?
5. Explain why judging the efficiency of any financial decision requires the existence of a goal.
6. What are the three major functions of the financial manager? How are they related?
7. Should the managers of a company own sizable amounts of common stock in the company? What are the pros and cons?
8. During the last few decades, a number of environmental, hiring, and other regulations have been imposed on businesses. In view of these regulatory changes, is maximization of shareholder wealth any longer a realistic objective?
9. As an investor, do you think that some managers are paid too much? Do their rewards come at your expense?
10. How does the notion of risk and reward govern the behavior of financial managers?
11. Compare and contrast the roles that a firm's treasurer and controller have in the operation of the firm.

SELECTED REFERENCES

Barfield, Richard. "Shareholder Value: Managing for the Long Term." *Accountancy* 108 (October 1991), 100–101.

Barnea, Amir, Robert A. Haugen, and Lemma W. Senbet. "Management of Corporate Risk," in *Advances in Financial Planning and Forecasting.* New York: JAI Press, 1985.

———. *Agency Problems and Financial Contracting.* Englewood Cliffs, NJ: Prentice Hall, 1985.

Birchard, Bill. "How Many Masters Can You Serve?" *CFO* 11 (July 1995), 48–54.

Brennan, Michael. "Corporate Finance Over the Past 25 Years." *Financial Management* 24 (Summer 1995), 9–22.

Chambers, Donald R., and Nelson J. Lacey. "Corporate Ethics and Shareholder Wealth Maximization." *Financial Practice and Education* 6 (Spring–Summer 1996), 93–96.

Copeland, Tom, Tim Koller, and Jack Murrin. *Valuation: Measuring and Managing the Value of Companies,* 2nd ed. New York: John Wiley, 1994.

Cornell, Bradford, and Alan C. Shapiro. "Corporate Stakeholders and Corporate Finance." *Financial Management* 16 (Spring 1987), 5–14.

Donaldson, Gordon. "Financial Goals: Management vs. Stockholders." *Harvard Business Review* 41 (May–June 1963), 116–29.

Friedman, Milton. "The Social Responsibility of Business Is to Increase Its Profits." *New York Times Magazine* (September 13, 1970).

Jensen, Michael C., and William H. Meckling. "Theory of the Firm: Managerial Behavior, Agency Costs and

Ownership Structure." *Journal of Financial Economics* 3 (October 1976), 305–60.

Jensen, Michael C., and Clifford W. Smith Jr. "Stockholder, Manager, and Creditor Interests: Applications of Agency Theory." In *Recent Advances in Corporate Finance,* ed. Edward I. Altman and Marti G. Subrahmanyam, 93–132. Homewood, IL: Richard D. Irwin, 1985.

McTaggart, James M., Peter W. Kontes, and Michael C. Mankins. *The Value Imperative: Managing for Superior Shareholder Returns.* New York: Free Press, 1994. Chapters 1 and 2 offer an especially good discussion concerning the goal of the firm.

Rappaport, Alfred. *Creating Shareholder Value: A Guide for Managers and Investors,* rev. ed. New York: Free Press, 1997.

Seitz, Neil. "Shareholder Goals, Firm Goals and Firm Financing Decisions." *Financial Management* 11 (Autumn 1982), 20–26.

Shleifer, Andrei, and Robert W. Vishney. "A Survey of Corporate Governance." *Journal of Finance* 52 (June 1997), 737–83.

Statement on Management Accounting No. 1C (revised), Standards of Ethical Conduct for Practitioners of Management Accounting and Financial Management. Montvale, NJ: Institute of Management Accountants, April 30, 1997.

Stewart, G. Bennett. *The Quest for Value.* New York: Harper Business, 1991.

Treynor, Jack L. "The Financial Objective in the Widely Held Corporation." *Financial Analysts Journal* 37 (March–April 1981), 68–71.

Williamson, Oliver E. "Corporate Finance and Corporate Governance." *Journal of Finance* 43 (July 1988), 567–92.

Chapter 2

The Business, Tax, and Financial Environments

THE BUSINESS ENVIRONMENT
  Sole Proprietorships • Partnerships • Corporations • Limited
    Liability Companies (LLCs)
THE TAX ENVIRONMENT
  Corporate Income Taxes • Personal Income Taxes
THE FINANCIAL ENVIRONMENT
  The Purpose of Financial Markets • Financial Markets • Financial
    Intermediaries • Financial Brokers • The Secondary Market
    • Allocation of Funds and Interest Rates
SUMMARY
QUESTIONS
SELF-CORRECTION PROBLEMS
PROBLEMS
SOLUTIONS TO SELF-CORRECTION PROBLEMS
SELECTED REFERENCES

> *Corporation, n. An ingenious device for obtaining individual profit
> without individual responsibility.*
>
> —AMBROSE BIERCE
> *The Devil's Dictionary*

To understand better the role of financial managers, you must be familiar with the environments in which they operate. The form of business organization that a firm chooses is one aspect of the business setting in which it must function. We will explore the advantages and disadvantages of the various alternative forms of business organization. Next, we will look at the tax environment in order to gain a basic understanding of how tax implications may impact various financial decisions. Finally, we investigate the financial system and the ever-changing environment in which capital is raised.

THE BUSINESS ENVIRONMENT

In the United States there are four basic forms of business organization: sole proprietorships (one owner), partnerships (general and limited), corporations, and limited liability companies (LLCs). Sole proprietorships outnumber the others combined by over 2 to 1, but corporations rank first by far when measured by sales, assets, profits, and contribution to national income. As this section unfolds, you will discover some of the pluses and minuses of each alternative form of business organization.

Sole Proprietorships

Sole proprietorship A business form for which there is one owner. This single owner has unlimited liability for all debts of the firm.

The **sole proprietorship** is the oldest form of business organization. As the title suggests, a single person owns the business, holds title to all its assets, and is personally responsible for all of its debts. A proprietorship pays no separate income taxes. The owner merely adds any profits or subtracts any losses from the business when determining personal taxable income. This business form is widely used in service industries. Because of its simplicity, a sole proprietorship can be established with few complications and little expense. Simplicity is its greatest virtue.

Its principal shortcoming is that the owner is personally liable for all business obligations. If the organization is sued, the proprietor as an individual is sued and has unlimited liability, which means that much of his or her personal property, as well as the assets of the business, may be seized to settle claims. Another problem with a sole proprietorship is the difficulty in raising capital. Because the life and success of the business is so dependent on a single individual, a sole proprietorship may not be as attractive to lenders as another form of organization. Moreover, the proprietorship has certain tax disadvantages. Fringe benefits, such as medical coverage and group insurance, are not regarded by the Internal Revenue Service as expenses of the firm and therefore are not fully deductible for tax purposes. A corporation often deducts these benefits, but the proprietor must pay for a major portion of them from income left over after paying taxes. In addition to these drawbacks, the proprietorship form makes the transfer of ownership more difficult than does the corporate form. In estate planning, no portion of the enterprise can be transferred to members of the family during the proprietor's lifetime. For these reasons, this form of organization does not afford the flexibility that other forms do.

Partnerships

Partnership A business form in which two or more individuals act as owners. In a *general partnership* all partners have unlimited liability for the debts of the firm; in a *limited partnership* one or more partners may have limited liability.

A **partnership** is similar to a proprietorship, except there is more than one owner. A partnership, like a proprietorship, pays no income taxes. Instead, individual partners include their share of profits or losses from the business as part of their personal taxable income. One potential advantage of this business form is that, relative to a proprietorship, a greater amount of capital can often be raised. More than one owner may now be providing personal capital, and lenders may be more agreeable to providing funds given a larger owner investment base.

In *general partnership* all partners have unlimited liability; they are jointly liable for the obligations of the partnership. Because each partner can bind the partnership with obligations, general partners should be selected with care. In most cases a formal arrangement, or partnership agreement, sets forth the powers of each partner, the distribution of profits, the amounts of capital to be invested by the partners, procedures for admitting new partners, and procedures for reconstituting the partnership in the case of the death or withdrawal of a partner. Legally, the partnership is dissolved if one of the partners dies or withdraws. In such cases, settlements are invariably "sticky," and reconstitution of the partnership can be a difficult matter.

Limited partner Member of a limited partnership not personally liable for the debts of the partnership.

In *limited partnerships,* **limited partners** contribute capital and have liability confined to that amount of capital; they cannot lose more than they put in. There must, however, be at least one **general partner** in the partnership, whose liability is unlimited. Limited partners do not participate in the operation of the business; this is left to the general partner(s). The limited partners are strictly investors, and they share in the profits or losses of the partnership according to the terms of the partnership agreement. This type of arrangement is frequently used in financing real estate ventures.

General partner Member of a partnership with unlimited liability for the debts of the partnership.

Corporations

Corporation A business form legally separate from its owners. Its distinguishing features include limited liability, easy transfer of ownership, unlimited life, and an ability to raise large sums of capital.

Because of the importance of the corporate form in the United States, the focus of this book is on corporations. A **corporation** is an "artificial entity" created by law. It can own assets and incur liabilities. In the famous Dartmouth College decision in 1819, Justice Marshall concluded that

> a corporation is an artificial being, invisible, intangible, and existing only in contemplation of the law. Being a mere creature of law, it possesses only those properties which the charter of its creation confers upon it, either expressly or as incidental to its very existence.[1]

The principal feature of this form of business organization is that the corporation exists legally separate and apart from its owners. An owner's liability is limited to his or her investment. Limited liability represents an important advantage over the proprietorship and general partnership. Capital can be raised in the corporation's name without exposing the owners to unlimited liability. Therefore, personal assets cannot be seized in the settlement of claims. Ownership itself is evidenced by shares of stock, with each stockholder owning that proportion of the enterprise represented by his or her shares in relation to the total number of shares outstanding. These shares are easily transferable, representing another important advantage of the corporate form. Moreover, corporations have found what the explorer Ponce de Leon could only dream of finding—unlimited life. Because the corporation exists apart from its owners, its life is not limited by the lives of the owners (unlike proprietorships and partnerships). The corporation can continue even though individual owners may die or sell their stock.

Because of the advantages associated with limited liability, easy transfer of ownership through the sale of common stock, unlimited life, and the ability of the corporation to raise capital apart from its owners, the corporate form of business

---

[1]*The Trustees of Dartmouth College* v. *Woodward,* 4 Wheaton 636 (1819).

organization has grown enormously in the twentieth century. With the large demands for capital that accompany an advanced economy, the proprietorship and partnership have proven unsatisfactory, and the corporation has emerged as the most important organizational form.

A possible disadvantage of the corporation is tax related. Corporate profits are subject to *double taxation.* The company pays tax on the income it earns, and the stockholder is also taxed when he or she receives income in the form of a cash dividend. (We will take a closer look at taxes in the next section.[2]) Minor disadvantages include the length of time to incorporate and the red tape involved, as well as the incorporation fee that must be paid to the state in which the firm is incorporated. Thus, a corporation is more difficult to establish than either a proprietorship or a partnership.

Limited Liability Companies (LLCs)

Limited liability company (LLC) A business form that provides its owners (called "members") with corporate-style limited personal liability and the federal-tax treatment of a partnership.

A **limited liability company (LLC)** is a hybrid form of business organization that combines the best aspects of both a corporation and a partnership. It provides its owners (called "members") with corporate-style limited personal liability and the federal-tax treatment of a partnership.[3] Especially well suited for small and medium-sized firms, it has fewer restrictions and greater flexibility than an older hybrid business form—the *S corporation* (which we discuss in the section on taxes).

Until 1990 only two states, Wyoming and Florida, allowed the formation of LLCs. A 1988 Internal Revenue Service (IRS) ruling that any Wyoming LLC would be treated as a partnership for federal-tax purposes opened the floodgates for the remaining states to start enacting LLC statutes. Though new to the United States, LLCs have been a long-accepted form of business organization in Europe and Latin America.

Limited liability companies generally possess no more than two of the following four (desirable) standard corporate characteristics: (1) limited liability, (2) centralized management, (3) unlimited life, and (4) the ability to transfer ownership interest without prior consent of the other owners. LLCs (by definition) have limited liability. Thus, members are not personally liable for any debts that may be incurred by the LLC. Most LLCs choose to maintain some type of centralized management structure. One drawback to an LLC, however, is that it generally lacks the corporate feature of "unlimited life," although most states do allow an LLC to continue if a member's ownership interest is transferred or terminated. Another drawback is that complete transfer of an ownership interest is usually subject to the approval of at least a majority of the other LLC members.

Although the LLC structure is applicable to most businesses, service-providing professionals in many states who want to form an LLC must resort to a parallel structure. In those states, accountants, lawyers, doctors, and other professionals are allowed to form a *professional LLC (PLLC)* or *limited liability partnership (LLP)*, a PLLC look-alike. One indication of the popularity of the PLLC/LLP structure among professionals can be found in the fact that all of the "Big Five" accounting firms in the United States are LLPs.

---

[2]An *S corporation,* named for a subchapter of the Internal Revenue Code, is a special type of corporate structure only open to qualifying "small corporations." Since its reason for being is entirely tax motivated, we defer its discussion until the section on taxes.

[3]Many states permit single-member LLCs. Qualified single-member LLCs are taxed as sole proprietorships.

THE TAX ENVIRONMENT

Most business decisions are affected either directly or indirectly by taxes. Through their taxing power, federal, state, and local governments have a profound influence on the behavior of businesses and their owners. What might prove to be an outstanding business decision in the absence of taxes may prove to be very inferior with taxes (and sometimes, vice versa). In this section we introduce you to some of the fundamentals of taxation. A basic understanding of this material will be needed for later chapters when we consider specific financial decisions.

We begin with the corporate income tax. Then we briefly consider personal income taxes. We must be mindful that tax laws frequently change.

Corporate Income Taxes

A corporation's taxable income is found by deducting all allowable expenses, including depreciation and interest, from revenues. This taxable income is then subjected to the following graduated tax structure:

CORPORATE TAXABLE INCOME

AT LEAST	BUT LESS THAN	TAX RATE (%)	TAX CALCULATION
$ 0	$ 50,000	15	.15 × (income over $0)
50,000	75,000	25	$ 7,500 + .25 × (income over 50,000)
75,000	100,000	34	13,750 + .34 × (income over 75,000)
100,000	335,000	39[a]	22,250 + .39 × (income over 100,000)
335,000	10,000,000	34	113,900 + .34 × (income over 335,000)
10,000,000	15,000,000	35	3,400,000 + .35 × (income over 10,000,000)
15,000,000	18,333,333	38[b]	5,150,000 + .38 × (income over 15,000,000)
18,333,333	—	35	6,416,667 + .35 × (income over 18,333,333)

[a]Between $100,000 and $335,000, there is a built-in surtax of 5% over the 34% rate. This results in corporations with taxable income between $335,000 and $10,000,000 "effectively" paying a flat 34% rate on all of their taxable income.

[b]Between $15,000,000 and $18,333,333, there is a built-in surtax of 3% over the 35% rate. This results in corporations with taxable income over $18,333,333 "effectively" paying a flat 35% rate on all of their taxable income.

The tax rate—the percent of taxable income that must be paid in taxes—that is applied to each income bracket is referred to as a *marginal rate*. For example, each additional dollar of taxable income above $50,000 is taxed at the marginal rate of 25 percent until taxable income reaches $75,000. At that point, the new marginal rate becomes 34 percent. The *average tax rate* for a firm is measured by dividing taxes actually paid by taxable income. For example, a firm with $100,000 of taxable income pays $22,250 in taxes and, therefore, has an average tax rate of $22,250/$100,000, or 22.25 percent. For small firms (i.e., firms with less than $335,000 of taxable income), the distinction between the average and marginal tax rates may prove important. However, the average and marginal rates converge at 34 percent for firms with taxable income between $335,000 and $10 million and, finally, converge again, this time to the 35 percent rate, for firms with taxable income above $18,333,333.

Alternative Minimum Tax. Companies dislike paying taxes and will take advantage of all the deductions and credits that the law allows. Therefore, the Internal Revenue Service has devised a special tax to ensure that large firms that benefit from the

Ask the Fool

Q I read somewhere that dividends are taxed twice. Is this really true?

A It's true. Consider Whee Press-On Socks Inc. Let's say it rakes in $100 million in sales one year, and after subtracting expenses, retains $20 million as its operating profit. Well, Uncle Sam doesn't just pat the company on the back. He demands his share, in taxes. Corporate income tax rates can reach 35 percent or higher. So perhaps $13 million will remain after taxes as net profit.

The firm has many things it can do with that money. It can buy back some of its own shares (increas-ing the value of remaining shares), build more facto-ries, hire more workers and so on. If it pays out some of these earnings as dividends to shareholders, though, the shareholders will recognize them as income. Which means Uncle Sam will claim a chunk of that personal income in taxes. Voilà—that money has now been taxed twice.

This is one reason why investors might prefer to see a company using its money to build more value for shareholders without paying out dividends. It's also why some companies are reducing dividends, opting instead to repurchase shares and reward shareholders in a tax-free way.

---

tax laws pay at least a minimum amount of tax. This special tax is called the *alternative minimum tax (AMT)*. The tax—20 percent of *alternative minimum taxable income (AMTI)*—applies only when the AMT would be greater than the firm's normally computed tax. To broaden the base of taxable income, AMTI is calculated by applying adjustments to items that had previously received some tax preference.

Quarterly Tax Payments. Corporations of any significant size are required to make quarterly tax payments. Specifically, calendar-year corporations are required to pay 25 percent of their estimated taxes in any given year on or before April 15, June 15, September 15, and December 15. When actual income differs from that which has been estimated, adjustments are made. A company that is on a calendar-year basis of accounting must make final settlement by March 15 of the subsequent year.

Depreciation. **Depreciation** is the systematic allocation of the cost of a capital asset over a period of time for financial reporting purposes, tax purposes, or both. Depreciation deductions taken on a firm's tax return are treated as expense items. Thus, depreciation lowers taxable income. Everything else being equal, the greater the depreciation charges, the lower the tax. There are a number of alternative procedures for depreciating capital assets, including **straight-line depreciation** and various **accelerated depreciation** methods. The depreciation methods chosen may differ for tax reporting versus financial reporting. Most firms with taxable income prefer to use an accelerated depreciation method for tax reporting purposes—one that allows for a more rapid write-off and, hence, a lower taxable income figure.

Depreciation The systematic allocation of the cost of a capital asset over a period of time for financial reporting purposes, tax purposes, or both.

Straight-line depreciation A method of depreciation that allocates expenses evenly over the depreciable life of the asset.

Accelerated depreciation Methods of depreciation that write off the cost of a capital asset faster than under straight-line depreciation.

The Tax Reform Act of 1986 allows companies to use a particular type of accelerated depreciation for tax purposes; it is known as the Modified Accelerated Cost Recovery System (MACRS, pronounced "makers").[4] Under MACRS, machinery, equipment, and real estate are assigned to one of eight classes for purposes of determining a prescribed life, called a cost recovery period, and a depreciation method. The property class in which an asset falls determines its cost recovery period or prescribed life for tax purposes—a life that may differ from the asset's useful or economic life. A general description of the property classes is provided in Table 2-1. (The reader should refer to the Internal Revenue Code for more detail.)

To illustrate some of the various methods of depreciation, let's first consider straight-line depreciation. If the fully installed acquisition cost of a five-year property class asset is $10,000, annual depreciation charges using straight-line depreciation would be $10,000/5, or $2,000. (For tax purposes, expected salvage value does not affect depreciation charges.)

Declining-balance depreciation, on the other hand, calls for an annual charge that is a "fixed percentage" of the asset's net book value (acquisition cost minus accumulated depreciation) at the beginning of the year to which the depreciation charge applies. For example, when using the *double-declining-balance (DDB) method*, we compute a rate by dividing 1 by the number of years of depreciable life for the asset. Then we double that rate. (Other declining-balance methods use other multiples.) Under the declining-balance methods the general formula for determining the depreciation charge in any period is

$$m(1/n)NBV \hspace{4cm} (2\text{-}1)$$

Declining-balance depreciation Methods of depreciation calling for an annual charge based on a fixed percentage of the asset's depreciated book value at the beginning of the year for which the depreciation charge applies.

---

[4]The term "Modified Accelerated Cost Recovery System" (MACRS) is used to distinguish the deductions computed under post-1986 rules from deductions prescribed under pre-1987 rules of the Accelerated Cost Recovery System (ACRS).

TABLE 2-1
Property classes under MACRS

- *3-Year 200% Class.* Includes property with a midpoint life of 4 years or less, except automobiles and light trucks. Under the Asset Depreciation Range (ADR) system, assets are grouped within classes and a guideline (midpoint) life is determined by the Treasury Department.
- *5-Year 200% Class.* Includes property with an ADR midpoint life of more than 4 to less than 10 years. Also included are automobiles, light trucks, most technological and semiconductor manufacturing equipment, switching equipment, small power production facilities, research and experimental equipment, high technology medical equipment, computers, and certain office equipment.
- *7-Year 200% Class.* Includes property with ADR midpoints of 10 to less than 16 years and single-purpose agricultural structures. Also includes office furniture and any other property for which no class life is specified by law.
- *10-Year 200% Class.* Includes property with ADR midpoints of 16 to less than 20 years.
- *15-Year 150% Class.* Includes property with ADR midpoints of 20 to less than 25 years, sewage treatment plants, and telephone distribution plants.
- *20-Year 150% Class.* Includes property with ADR midpoints of 25 years or more, other than real property described below.
- *27.5-Year Straight-Line Class.* Includes residential rental property.
- *39-Year Straight-Line Class.* Includes other real estate.

where m is the multiple, n is the depreciable life of the asset, and NBV is the asset's net book value at the start of the year. For a $10,000 asset, with a five-year life, the depreciation charge in the first year using the DDB method would be

$$2(1/5)\$10,000 = \textbf{\$4,000}$$

For our example, 2(1/5) determines the "fixed percentage," or 40 percent, that is applied against the declining net book value each year. The depreciation charge in the second year is based on the depreciated net book value of $6,000. We arrive at the $6,000 by subtracting the first year's depreciation charge, $4,000, from the asset's original acquisition cost. The depreciation charge in the second year would be

$$2(1/5)\$6,000 = \textbf{\$2,400}$$

The third year's charge would be

$$2(1/5)\$3,600 = \textbf{\$1,440}$$

and so on.

Modified Accelerated Cost Recovery System. For the 3-, 5-, 7-, and 10-year property classes, the double-declining-balance (also called *200%-declining-balance*) depreciation method is used. This method then switches to straight-line depreciation for the remaining undepreciated book value in the first year that the straight-line method yields an equal or greater deduction than the declining-balance method. Assets in the 15- and 20-year classes are depreciated using the 150-percent-declining-balance method, again switching to straight-line at the optimal time. The straight-line method must be used for all real estate.

Normally, the *half-year convention* must be applied to all declining-balance methods. This calls for a half year of depreciation in the year an asset is acquired, regardless of the date of purchase. There is also a half year of depreciation in the year an asset is sold or retired from service. If property is held for longer than its recovery period, a half year of depreciation is allowed for the year following the end of the recovery period. Thus, 5-year property class assets held for 6 years or longer have depreciation spread over 6 years.

To illustrate for the 5-year 200 percent property class, assume that an asset costing $10,000 is acquired in February. For our example, the declining-balance formula yields $2(1/5) = 40\%$ as the fixed percentage annual depreciation. However, in the first year the half-year convention is employed, so first-year depreciation is 20 percent, or $2,000. In the fourth year, it is favorable to switch to straight-line depreciation. Thus, the depreciation schedule is as follows:

YEAR	DEPRECIATION CALCULATION	DEPRECIATION CHARGE	NET BOOK VALUE (END OF YEAR)
0	—	—	$10,000
1	(.2)$10,000	$2,000	8,000
2	(.4)$8,000	3,200	4,800
3	(.4)$4,800	1,920	2,880
4	$2,880/2.5 years	1,152	1,728
5	$2,880/2.5 years	1,152	576
6	(.5)$2,880/2.5 years	576	0

At the beginning of the fourth year, the net book value at the end of the third year is divided by the remaining life to get straight-line depreciation. The remaining

Part I Introduction to Financial Management

life is 2.5 years, owing to the half-year convention in the sixth year. Finally, in the sixth year the remaining balance is $576, or one-half the yearly straight-line amount.

Take Note

Instead of making such calculations (which as you can see can be quite a chore), one can use depreciation percentages of original cost for each property class (see Table 2-1) published by the Treasury. The first four property categories are seen in the following table.

RECOVERY YEAR	PROPERTY CLASS			
	3-YEAR	5-YEAR	7-YEAR	10-YEAR
1	33.33%	20.00%	14.29%	10.00%
2	44.45	32.00	24.49	18.00
3	14.81	19.20	17.49	14.40
4	7.41	11.52	12.49	11.52
5		11.52	8.93	9.22
6		5.76	8.92	7.37
7			8.93	6.55
8			4.46	6.55
9				6.56
10				6.55
11				3.28
Totals	100.00%	100.00%	100.00%	100.00%

These percentages correspond to the principles on which our previous calculations are based, and they are used for determining depreciation deductions.

Interest Expense versus Dividends Paid. Interest paid on outstanding corporate debt is treated as an expense and is tax deductible. However, dividends paid to preferred or common stockholders are not tax deductible. Thus, for a profitable, tax-paying company, the use of debt (e.g., bonds) in its financing mix results in a significant tax advantage relative to the use of preferred or common stock. Given a marginal tax rate of 35 percent, a firm that pays out $1 in interest lowers its tax bill by 35 cents because of its ability to deduct the $1 of interest from taxable income. The after-tax cost of $1 of interest for this firm is really only 65 cents—$1 × (1 − tax rate). On the other hand, the after-tax cost of $1 of dividends paid by the firm is still $1— there is no tax advantage here. Therefore, there are tax advantages associated with using debt financing that are simply not present with either preferred or common stock financing.

Cash dividend Cash distribution of earnings to stockholders, usually on a quarterly basis.

Dividend Income. A corporation may own stock in another company. If it receives a **cash dividend** on this stock, normally 70 percent of the dividend is tax exempt.[5] The tax laws allow this tax break for corporations (not individuals) to help reduce the

---

[5]For any dividend income to be tax exempt, however, the corporation must have owned the stock for at least 45 days. If a corporation owns 20 percent or more of another corporation's stock, however, 80 percent of any dividend received is tax exempt. Also, if a corporation owns 80 percent or more of the stock of another firm, it can file a consolidated tax return. In this way, any funds transferred between the two entities are generally not considered dividends for tax purposes, and no tax is paid on such transfers.

effects of multiple taxation of the same earnings. The remaining 30 percent is taxed at the corporate income tax rate. A firm that receives $10,000 in dividend income pays taxes on only $3,000 of this income. At a marginal tax rate of 35 percent, taxes would amount to $1,050, as opposed to $3,500 if the entire dividend income were treated as taxable income.

Carryback and Carryforward.   If a corporation sustains a net operating loss, this loss may generally be carried back 2 years and forward up to 20 years to offset taxable income in those years.[6] Any loss carried back must first be applied to the earliest preceding year. If a firm sustained an operating loss of $400,000 in 2001, it would first carry this loss back to 1999. If the company had net profits of $400,000 in that year and paid taxes of $136,000, it would recompute its taxes for 1999 to show zero profit for tax purposes. Consequently, the company would be eligible for a tax refund of $136,000. If the 2001 operating loss was greater than operating profits in 1999, the residual would be carried back to 2000 and taxes recomputed for that year. However, if the net operating loss was greater than the net operating income in both years, the residual would be carried forward in sequence to future profits in 2002 to 2021. Profits in each of these years would be reduced for tax purposes by the amount of the unused loss carried forward. This feature of the tax laws is designed to avoid penalizing companies that have sharply fluctuating net operating income.

Capital gain (loss) The amount by which the proceeds from the sale of a capital asset exceeds (is less than) the asset's original cost.

Capital Gains and Losses.   When a capital asset (as defined by the Internal Revenue Service) is sold, a **capital gain or loss** is generally incurred. Often in the history of our tax laws there has been a differential tax treatment of capital gains income and operating income, with capital gains being treated more favorably. Under the Revenue Reconciliation Act of 1993, however, capital gains are taxed at the ordinary income tax rates for corporations, or a maximum of 35 percent. Capital losses are deductible only against capital gains.

Personal Income Taxes

The subject of personal taxes is extremely complex, but our main concern here is with the personal taxes of individuals who own businesses—proprietors, partners, members (of LLCs), and shareholders. Any income reported by a sole proprietorship, partnership, or properly structured LLC becomes income of the owner(s) and is taxed at the personal rate. For individuals there are four progressive tax brackets: 15 percent, 28 percent, 31 percent, and 36 percent. The 15 percent marginal tax rate applies up to a certain level of taxable income that varies depending on the individual's filing status, that is, single, married filing a joint return, married filing separately, or head of household. Even within a filing category, however, the taxable income levels that trigger the 28 percent, 31 percent, and 36 percent marginal tax rates will generally increase from year to year because they are indexed to account for inflation. There are also standard deductions (which vary by filing status and are indexed for inflation) that enable those with very low income to pay no taxes. In addition, certain high-income taxpayers are subject to a 10 percent surtax. It is computed by applying a 39.6 percent rate—.36 + (.36 × .10)—to taxable income in excess of a certain level that varies with filing status and is indexed for inflation.

---

[6]A corporation has the option, however, of forgoing the carryback and simply carrying the loss forward up to 20 years. For example, a corporation might elect to forgo the loss carryback if it anticipated a significant increase in tax rates in future years. Prior to 1998, the loss carryback was 3 years and the carryforward was up to 15 years.

Interest, Dividends, and Capital Gains. For the individual, interest received on corporate and Treasury securities is fully taxable at the federal level. (Interest on Treasury securities is not taxable at the state level.) However, interest received on most municipal securities is exempt from federal taxation. Taxable interest and cash dividends received are subject to the ordinary income tax rates. Realized capital gains are taxed at a variety of rates depending on how long an individual holds a particular asset and on that individual's marginal tax bracket.

Subchapter S. Subchapter S of the Internal Revenue Code allows the owners of small corporations to elect to be taxed as an *S corporation*. In making this election, the company gets to use the corporate organization form but is taxed as though the firm were a partnership. Thus, the owners are able to avail themselves of the legal advantages extended to corporations, but they are able to avoid any tax disadvantages that might result. They simply declare any corporate profits as personal income on a pro rata basis and pay the appropriate tax on this income. This treatment eliminates the double taxation normally associated with dividend income—that is, the corporation paying dividends from after-tax income, and shareholders paying taxes on the dividend income they receive. In addition, stockholders active in the business may deduct any operating losses on a pro rata basis against their personal income.

As discussed earlier, a limited liability company (LLC) provides similar benefits of an S corporation, but with fewer limitations (e.g., no restriction as to the number and type of owners). Many predict that the LLC form of business will grow in numbers to surpass the S corporation form.

THE FINANCIAL ENVIRONMENT

In varying degrees, all businesses operate within the financial system, which consists of a number of institutions and markets serving business firms, individuals, and governments. When a firm invests temporarily idle funds in marketable securities, it has direct contact with **financial markets.** More important, most firms use financial markets to help finance their investment in assets. In the final analysis, the market price of a company's securities is the test of whether the company is a success or a failure. While business firms compete with each other in the product markets, they must continually interact with the financial markets. Because of the importance of this environment to the financial manager, as well as to the individual as a consumer of financial services, this section is devoted to exploring the financial system and the ever-changing environment in which capital is raised.

Financial markets All institutions and procedures for bringing buyers and sellers of financial instruments together.

The Purpose of Financial Markets

Financial assets exist in an economy because the savings of various individuals, corporations, and governments during a period of time differ from their investment in real assets. By real assets, we mean such things as houses, buildings, equipment, inventories, and durable goods. If savings equaled investment in real assets for all economic units in an economy over all periods of time, there would be no external financing, no financial assets, and no money or capital markets. Each economic unit would be self-sufficient. Current expenditures and investment in real assets would be paid for out of current income. A financial asset is created only when the investment of an economic unit in real assets exceeds its savings and it finances this excess by borrowing or issuing stock. Of course, another economic unit must be willing to lend. This interaction of borrowers with lenders determines interest rates. In the economy as a whole, savings-surplus units (those whose savings exceed their investment in real assets) provide funds to savings-deficit units (those whose investments in real assets exceed their savings). This exchange of funds is evidenced by investment instruments, or securities, representing financial assets to the holders and financial liabilities to the issuers.

The purpose of financial markets in an economy is to allocate savings efficiently to ultimate users. If those economic units that saved were the same as those that engaged in capital formation, an economy could prosper without financial markets. In modern economies, however, most nonfinancial corporations use more than their total savings for investing in real assets. Most households, on the other hand, have total savings in excess of total investment. Efficiency entails bringing the ultimate investor in real assets and the ultimate saver together at the least possible cost and inconvenience.

Financial Markets

Financial markets are not so much physical places as they are mechanisms for channeling savings to the ultimate investors in real assets. Figure 2-1 illustrates the role of financial markets and financial institutions in moving funds from the savings sector (savings-surplus units) to the investment sector (savings-deficit units). From the figure, we can also note the prominent position held by certain financial institutions in channeling the flow of funds in the economy. The *secondary market, financial intermediaries,* and *financial brokers* are the key institutions that enhance funds flows. We will study their unique roles as this section unfolds.

Money market The market for short-term (less than one year original maturity) government and corporate debt securities. It also includes government securities originally issued with maturities of more than one year but that now have a year or less until maturity.

Capital market The market for relatively long-term (greater than one year original maturity) financial instruments (e.g., bonds and stocks).

Primary market A market where new securities are bought and sold for the first time (a "new issues" market).

Secondary market A market for existing (used) securities rather than new issues.

Money and Capital Markets.   Financial markets can be broken into two classes—the money market and the capital market. The **money market** is concerned with the buying and selling of short-term (less than one year original maturity) government and corporate debt securities. The **capital market,** on the other hand, deals with relatively long-term (greater than one year original maturity) debt and equity instruments (e.g., bonds and stocks). This section gives special attention to the market for long-term securities—the capital market. The money market and the securities that form its lifeblood are covered in Part IV of this book.

Primary and Secondary Markets.   Within money and capital markets there exist both primary and secondary markets. A **primary market** is a "new issues" market. Here, funds raised through the sale of new securities flow from the ultimate savers to the ultimate investors in real assets. In a **secondary market,** existing securities are bought and sold. Transactions in these already existing securities do *not* provide additional funds to finance capital investment. (*Note:* On Fig. 2-1 there is no line directly connecting the secondary market with the investment sector.) An analogy can be made to the market for automobiles. The sale of new cars provides cash to the auto manufacturers; the sale of used cars in the used-car market does not. In a real sense, a secondary market is a "used-car lot" for securities.

The existence of used-car lots makes it easier for you to consider buying a new car because you have a mechanism at hand to sell the car when you no longer want it. In a similar fashion, the existence of a secondary market encourages the purchase of new securities by individuals and institutions. With a viable secondary market, a purchaser of financial securities achieves marketability. If the buyer needs to sell a security in the future, he or she will be able to do so. Thus, the existence of a strong secondary market enhances the efficiency of the primary market.

Part I Introduction to Financial Management

FIGURE 2-1

Flow of Funds in the Economy and the Mechanism Financial Markets Provide for Channeling Savings to the Ultimate Investors in Real Assets

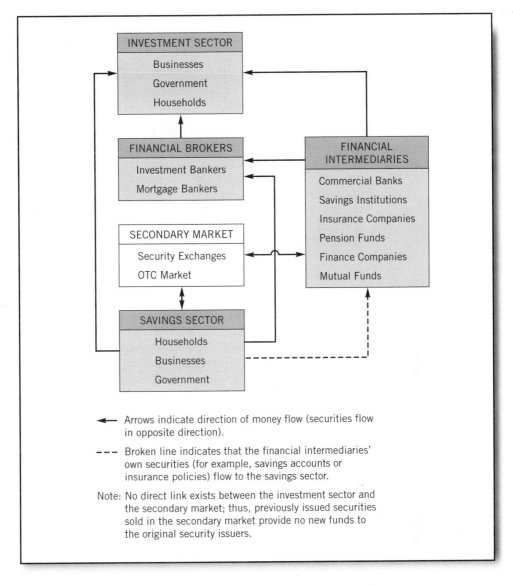

← Arrows indicate direction of money flow (securities flow in opposite direction).

--- Broken line indicates that the financial intermediaries' own securities (for example, savings accounts or insurance policies) flow to the savings sector.

Note: No direct link exists between the investment sector and the secondary market; thus, previously issued securities sold in the secondary market provide no new funds to the original security issuers.

Financial Intermediaries

Financial intermediaries
Financial institutions that accept money from savers and use those funds to make loans and other financial investments in their own name. They include commercial banks, savings institutions, insurance companies, pension funds, finance companies, and mutual funds.

The flow of funds from savers to investors in real assets can be direct; if there are financial intermediaries in an economy, the flow can also be indirect. **Financial intermediaries** consist of financial institutions, such as commercial banks, savings institutions, insurance companies, pension funds, finance companies, and mutual funds. These intermediaries come between ultimate borrowers and lenders by transforming direct claims into indirect claims. Financial intermediaries purchase *direct* (or *primary*) *securities* and, in turn, issue their own *indirect* (or *secondary*) *securities* to the public. For example, the direct security that a savings and loan association purchases is a mortgage; the indirect claim issued is a savings account or a certificate of deposit. A life insurance company, on the other hand, purchases corporate bonds, among other things, and issues life insurance policies.

Financial intermediation is the process of savers depositing funds with financial intermediaries (rather than directly buying stocks and bonds) and letting the intermediaries do the lending to the ultimate investors. We usually think of financial intermediation making the markets more efficient by lowering the cost and/or inconvenience to consumers of financial services.

Among the various financial intermediaries, some institutions invest much more heavily in the securities of business firms than others. In what follows, we concentrate on those institutions involved in buying and selling corporate securities.

Deposit Institutions. *Commercial banks* are the most important source of funds for business firms in the aggregate. Banks acquire demand (checking) and time (savings) deposits from individuals, companies, and governments and, in turn, make loans and investments. Among the loans made to business firms are seasonal and other short-term loans, intermediate-term loans of up to five years, and mortgage loans. Besides performing a banking function, commercial banks affect business firms through their trust departments, which invest in corporate bonds and stocks. They also make mortgage loans available to companies and manage pension funds.

Other deposit institutions include *savings and loan associations, mutual savings banks,* and *credit unions.* These institutions are primarily involved with individuals, acquiring their savings and making home and consumer loans.

Insurance Companies. There are two types of insurance companies: property and casualty companies and life insurance companies. These are in the business of collecting periodic payments from those they insure in exchange for providing payouts should events, usually adverse, occur. With the funds received in premium payments, insurance companies build reserves. These reserves and a portion of the insurance companies' capital are invested in financial assets.

Property and casualty companies insure against fires, thefts, car accidents, and similar unpleasantness. Because these companies pay taxes at the full corporate income tax rate, they invest heavily in municipal bonds, which offer tax-exempt interest income. To a lesser extent they also invest in corporate stocks and bonds.

Life insurance companies insure against the loss of life. Because the mortality of a large group of individuals is highly predictable, these companies are able to invest in long-term securities. Also, the income of these institutions is partially exempt from taxes owing to the buildup of reserves over time. They, therefore, seek taxable investments with yields higher than those of tax-exempt municipal bonds. As a result, life insurance companies invest heavily in corporate bonds. Also important are mortgages, some of which are granted to business firms.

Other Financial Intermediaries. *Pension funds* and other *retirement funds* are established to provide income to individuals when they retire. During their working lives, employees usually contribute to these funds, as do employers. Funds invest these contributions and either pay out the cumulative amounts periodically to retired workers or arrange annuities. In the accumulation phase, monies paid into a fund are not taxed. When the benefits are paid out in retirement, taxes are paid by the recipient. Commercial banks, through their trust departments, and insurance companies offer pension funds, as do the federal government, local governments, and certain other noninsurance organizations. Because of the long-term nature of their liabilities, pension funds are able to invest in longer-term securities. As a result, they invest heavily in corporate stocks and bonds. In fact, pension funds are the largest single institutional investors in corporate stocks.

Mutual investment funds also invest heavily in corporate stocks and bonds. These funds accept monies contributed by individuals and invest them in specific types of financial assets. The mutual fund is connected with a management company, to which the fund pays a fee (frequently 0.5 percent of total assets per annum) for professional investment management. Each individual owns a specified percentage of the mutual fund, which depends on that person's original investment. Individuals can sell their shares at any time as the mutual fund is required to redeem them. Though many mutual funds invest only in common stocks, others specialize in corporate bonds; money market instruments, including commercial paper issued by corporations; or municipal securities. Various stock funds have different investment philosophies, ranging from investing for income and safety to a highly aggressive pursuit of growth. In all cases, the individual obtains a diversified portfolio managed by professionals. Unfortunately, there is no evidence that such management results in consistently superior performance.

Finance companies make consumer installment loans, personal loans, and secured loans to business enterprises. These companies raise capital through stock issues as well as through borrowings, some of which are long term but most of which come from commercial banks. In turn, the finance company makes loans.

Financial Brokers

Certain financial institutions perform a necessary brokerage function. When brokers bring together parties who need funds with those who have savings, they are not performing a direct lending function but rather are acting as matchmakers, or middlemen.

Investment banker A financial institution that underwrites (purchases at a fixed price on a fixed date) new securities for resale.

Investment bankers are middlemen involved in the sale of corporate stocks and bonds. When a company decides to raise funds, an investment banker will often buy the issue (at wholesale) and then turn around and sell it to investors (at retail). Because investment bankers are continually in the business of matching users of funds with suppliers, they can sell issues more efficiently than can the issuing companies. For this service investment bankers receive fees in the form of the difference between the amounts received from the sale of the securities to the public and the amounts paid to the companies. Much more will be said about the role of investment bankers in Part VII, when we consider long-term financing.

Mortgage banker A financial institution that originates (buys) mortgages primarily for resale.

Mortgage bankers are involved in acquiring and placing mortgages. These mortgages come either directly from individuals and businesses or, more typically, through builders and real estate agents. In turn, the mortgage banker locates institutional and other investors for the mortgages. Although mortgage bankers do not typically hold mortgages in their own portfolios for very long, they usually service mortgages for the ultimate investors. This involves receiving payments and following through on delinquencies. For this service they receive fees.

The Secondary Market

Various security exchanges and markets facilitate the smooth functioning of the financial system. Purchases and sales of existing financial assets occur in the *secondary market*. Transactions in this market do not increase the total amount of financial assets outstanding, but the presence of a viable secondary market increases the liquidity of financial assets and therefore enhances the primary or direct market for securities. In this regard, *organized exchanges,* such as the New York Stock Exchange, the American Stock Exchange, and the New York Bond Exchange, provide a means by which buy and sell orders can be efficiently matched. In this matching, the forces of supply and demand determine price.

In addition, the *over-the-counter (OTC) market* serves as part of the secondary market for stocks and bonds not listed on an exchange as well as for certain listed securities. It is composed of brokers and dealers who stand ready to buy and sell securities at quoted prices. Most corporate bonds, and a growing number of stocks, are traded OTC as opposed to being traded on an organized exchange. The OTC market has become highly mechanized, with market participants linked together by a telecommunications network. They do not come together in a single place as they would on an organized exchange. The National Association of Securities Dealers Automated Quotation Service (NASDAQ, pronounced "nas-dac") maintains this network, and price quotations are instantaneous. Whereas once it was considered a matter of prestige, as well as necessity in many cases, for a company to list its shares on a major exchange, the electronic age has changed that. Many companies now prefer to have their shares traded OTC, despite the fact that they qualify for listing, because they feel that they get as good or sometimes better execution of buy and sell orders.

Although there are a number of other financial institutions, we have looked only at those interacting with business firms. As the book continues, we will become better acquainted with many of those discussed. Our purpose here was only to introduce you briefly to them; further explanation will come later.

Allocation of Funds and Interest Rates

The allocation of funds in an economy occurs primarily on the basis of price, expressed in terms of expected return. Economic units in need of funds must outbid others for their use. Although the allocation process is affected by capital rationing, government restrictions, and institutional constraints, expected return constitutes the primary mechanism by which supply and demand are brought into balance for a particular financial instrument across financial markets. If risk is held constant, economic units willing to pay the highest expected return are the ones entitled to the use of funds. If people are rational, the economic units bidding the highest prices will have the most promising investment opportunities. As a result, savings will tend to be allocated to the most efficient uses.

It is important to recognize that the process by which savings are allocated in an economy occurs not only on the basis of expected return but on the basis of risk as well. Different financial instruments have different degrees of risk. In order for them to compete for funds, these instruments must provide different expected returns, or yields. Figure 2-2 illustrates the idea of the market-imposed "trade-off" between risk and return for securities—that is, the higher the risk of a security, the higher the expected return that must be offered to the investor. If all securities had exactly the same risk characteristics, they would provide the same expected returns if markets were in balance. Because of differences in default risk, marketability, maturity, taxability, and embedded options, however, different instruments pose different degrees of risk and provide different expected returns to the investor.

Default The failure to meet the terms of a contract, such as failure to make interest or principal payments when due on a loan.

Default Risk.   When we speak of **default** risk, we mean the danger that the borrower may not meet payments due on principal or interest. Investors demand a risk premium (or extra expected return) to invest in securities that are not default free. The greater the possibility that the borrower will default, the greater the default risk and the premium demanded by the marketplace. Because Treasury securities are usually regarded as default free, risk and return are judged in relation to them. The greater the default risk of a security issuer, the greater the expected return or yield of the security, all other things the same.[7]

---

[7]For an extended discussion of the influence of default risk on yields, as well as a review of the various empirical studies, see Van Horne, *Financial Market Rates and Flows,* Chap. 8. This book also presents a detailed examination of the other major security attributes that affect expected return.

Part I Introduction to Financial Management

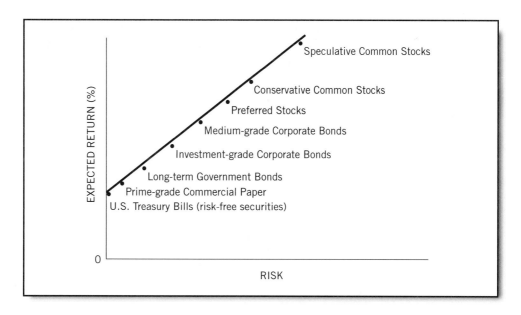

FIGURE 2-2
Risk–Expected
Return Profile for
Securities Showing
the Greater the Risk
of a Given Security,
the Higher the
Expected Return

For the typical investor, default risk is not judged directly but rather in terms of quality ratings assigned by the principal rating agencies, Moody's Investors Service and Standard & Poor's. These investment agencies assign and publish letter grades for the use of investors. In their ratings, the agencies attempt to rank issues in order of the perceived probability of default. The ratings used by the two agencies are shown in Table 2-2. The highest-grade securities, judged to have negligible default risk, are rated triple-A.

Credit ratings in the top four categories (for Moody's, Aaa to Baa; for Standard and Poor's, AAA to BBB) are considered "investment grade quality." This term is used by regulatory agencies to identify securities that are eligible for investment by financial institutions such as commercial banks and insurance companies. Securities rated below the top four categories are referred to as "speculative grade." Because of the limited institutional demand for these securities and their higher default risk, they must offer considerably higher expected returns than investment-grade securities.

Marketability (or **liquidity**) The ability to sell a significant volume of securities in a short period of time in the secondary market without significant price concession.

Marketability. The **marketability** (or **liquidity**) of a security relates to the owner's ability to convert it into cash. There are two dimensions to marketability: the price realized and the amount of time required to sell the asset. The two are interrelated in that it is often possible to sell an asset in a short period if enough price concession is given. For financial instruments, marketability is judged in relation to the ability to sell a significant volume of securities in a short period of time without significant price concession. The more marketable the security, the greater the ability to execute a large transaction near the quoted price. In general, the lower the marketability of a security, the greater the yield necessary to attract investors. Thus, the yield differential between different securities of the same maturity is caused not by differences in default risk alone, but also by differences in marketability.

Maturity The life of a security; the amount of time before the principal amount of a security becomes due.

Maturity. Securities with about the same default risk, having similar marketability, and not faced with different tax implications can still trade at different yields. Why? "Time" is the answer. The **maturity** of a security can often have a powerful effect on expected return, or yield. The relationship between yield and maturity for securities

TABLE 2-2
Ratings by invest-
ment agencies

MOODY'S INVESTORS SERVICE		STANDARD & POOR'S	
Aaa	Best quality	AAA	Highest grade
Aa	High quality	AA	High grade
A	Upper medium grade	A	Higher medium grade
Baa	Medium grade	BBB	Medium grade
Ba	Possess speculative elements	BB	Speculative
B	Generally lack characteristics of desirable investment	B	Very speculative
Caa	Poor standing; may be in default	CCC–CC	Outright speculation
Ca	Highly speculative; often in default	C	Reserved for income bonds on which no interest is being paid
C	Lowest guide	D	In default

Note: The top four categories indicate "investment grade quality" securities; the categories below the dashed line are reserved for securities below investment grade.

Term structure of interest rates The relationship between yield and maturity for securities *differing only in the length of time (or term) to maturity.*

Yield curve A graph of the relationship between yields and term to maturity for particular securities.

differing only in the length of time (or term) to maturity is called the **term structure of interest rates.** The graphical representation of this relationship at a moment in time is called a **yield curve.** An example of the yield-maturity relationship for default-free Treasury securities on a particular date is shown in Figure 2-3. Maturity is plotted on the horizontal axis and yield on the vertical. What results is a line, or yield curve, fitted to the observations.

The most commonly observed yield pattern is the *positive* (i.e., upward-sloping) *yield curve*—where short-term yields are lower than long-term yields. Most economists attribute the tendency for positive yield curves to the presence of risk for those who invest in long-term securities as opposed to short-term securities. In general, the longer the maturity, the greater the risk of fluctuation in the market value of the security. Consequently, investors need to be offered risk premiums to induce them to invest in long-term securities. Only when interest rates are expected to fall significantly are they willing to invest in long-term securities yielding less than short- and intermediate-term securities.

Taxability. Another factor affecting the observed differences in market yields is the differential impact of taxes. The most important tax, and the only one that we will consider here, is the income tax. The interest income on all but one category of securities is taxable to taxable investors. Interest income from state and local government securities is tax exempt. Therefore, state and local issues sell in the market at lower yields to maturity than Treasury and corporate securities of the same maturity. For corporations located in states with income taxes, interest income on Treasury securities is exempt from state income taxes. Therefore, such instruments may hold an advantage over the debt instruments issued by corporations or banks because the interest they pay is fully taxable at the state level. Under present law, capital gains arising from the sale of any security at a profit are taxed at the ordinary tax rates for corporations, or at a maximum of 35 percent.

Option Features. Another consideration is whether a security contains any option features, such as a conversion privilege or warrants, which upon exercise allow the

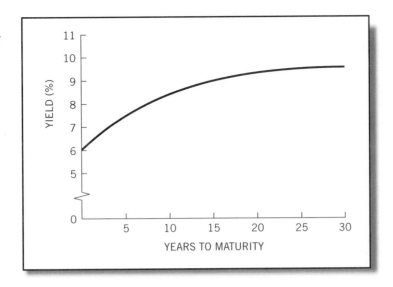

FIGURE 2-3
Example of Treasury
Positive Yield Curve

investor to obtain common stock. Other options include the call feature, which enables a company to prepay its debt, and a sinking-fund provision, which allows a company to retire bonds periodically with cash payments or by buying bonds in the secondary market. If the investors receive options, the issuing company should be able to borrow at a lower interest cost. Conversely, if the issuing company receives an option, such as a call feature, the investors must be compensated with a higher yield. The valuation principles behind options are complex. Chapter 22 covers these principles in detail.

Inflation A rise in the average level of prices of goods and services.

Inflation. In addition to the preceding factors, which affect the yield of one security relative to that of another, **inflation** expectations have a substantial influence on interest rates overall. It is generally agreed that the nominal (observed) rate of interest on a security embodies a premium for inflation. The higher the expected inflation, the higher the nominal yield on the security; and the lower the expected inflation, the lower the nominal yield. Many years ago Irving Fisher expressed the nominal rate of interest on a bond as the sum of the real rate of interest (i.e., the interest rate in the absence of price level changes) and the rate of price change *expected* to occur over the life of the instrument.[8] If the annual real rate of interest in the economy was 4 percent for low-risk securities and inflation of 6 percent per annum was *expected* over the next 10 years, this would imply a yield of 10 percent for 10-year, high-grade bonds. (*Note:* It is the expected rate of inflation, not the observed or reported rate of inflation, that is added to the real rate of interest.) This states merely that lenders require a nominal rate of interest high enough for them to earn the real rate of interest after being compensated for the *expected* decrease in the buying power of money caused by inflation.

Behavior of Yields on Corporate Securities. Differences in default risk, marketability, maturity, taxability, and option features affect the yield of one security relative to another *at a point in time.* In addition, the security yields themselves (and

---

[8]*Appreciation and Interest* (New York: Macmillan, 1896).

hence the cost of funds to business firms) will vary *over time*. Fluctuations in supply and demand pressures in financial markets, as well as changing inflation expectations, help explain this variability in yields.

SUMMARY

- The four basic forms of business organization are the *sole proprietorship*, the *partnership*, the *corporation*, and the *limited liability company (LLC)*.
- The corporation has emerged as the most important organizational form due to certain advantages that it has over the other organizational forms. These advantages include limited liability, easy transfer of ownership, unlimited life, and an ability to raise large sums of capital.
- Most firms with taxable income prefer to use an *accelerated depreciation method* for tax reporting purposes in order to lower their taxes. A firm that is profitable for financial reporting purposes may, in fact, show losses for tax purposes.
- Interest paid by corporations is considered a tax-deductible expense; however, dividends paid are not tax deductible.
- Financial assets (securities) exist in an economy because an economic unit's investment in real assets (such as buildings and equipment) frequently differs from its savings. In the economy as a whole, savings-surplus units (those whose savings exceed their investment in real assets) provide funds to savings-deficit units (those whose investments in real assets exceed their savings). This exchange of funds is evidenced by investment instruments, or securities, representing financial assets to the holders and financial liabilities to the issuers.
- The purpose of financial markets in an economy is to allocate savings efficiently to ultimate users.
- *Financial intermediaries* help make the financial markets more efficient. Intermediaries come between ultimate borrowers and lenders by transforming direct claims into indirect claims. Finan-

cial intermediaries purchase *direct* (or *primary*) *securities* and, in turn, issue their own *indirect* (or *secondary*) *securities* to the public.
- Financial brokers, such as *investment bankers* and *mortgage bankers*, bring together parties who need funds with those who have savings. These brokers are not performing a direct lending function but rather are acting as matchmakers, or middlemen.
- Financial markets can be broken into two classes—the money market and the capital market. The *money market* is concerned with the buying and selling of short-term government and corporate debt securities. The *capital market* deals with relatively long-term debt and equity instruments.
- Within the money and capital markets there exist both primary and secondary markets. A *primary market* is a "new issues" market, and a *secondary market* is a "used issues" market.
- The *secondary market* for long-term securities, comprised of the *organized exchanges* and the *OTC market*, increases the liquidity (marketability) of financial assets and, therefore, enhances the *primary market* for long-term securities.
- The allocation of savings in an economy occurs primarily on the basis of expected return and risk.
- Differences in default risk, marketability, maturity, taxability, and option features affect the yield of one security relative to another *at a point in time*. Fluctuations in supply and demand pressures in financial markets, as well as changing inflation expectations, help explain variability in yields *over time*.

QUESTIONS

1. What is the principal advantage of the corporate form of business organization? Discuss the importance of this advantage to the owner of a small family restaurant. Discuss the importance of this advantage to a wealthy entrepreneur who owns several businesses.
2. How does being a limited partner in a business enterprise differ from being a stockholder, assuming the same percentage of ownership?

Part I Introduction to Financial Management

3. What are some of the disadvantages of (a) a sole proprietorship? (b) a partnership? (c) a limited liability company (LLC)?
4. What kind of corporation benefits from the graduated income tax?
5. In general, what are the principles on which the Modified Accelerated Cost Recovery System (MACRS) is based?
6. Interest on Treasury securities is not taxable at the state level, whereas interest on municipal securities is not taxable at the federal level. What is the reason for this feature?
7. Are individual tax rates progressive or regressive in the sense of increasing or decreasing with income levels?
8. If capital gains were to be taxed at a lower rate than ordinary income, as has been the case in the past, what types of investments would be favored?
9. The method of depreciation does not alter the total amount deducted from income during the life of an asset. What does it alter and why is that important?
10. If the owners of a new corporation are very few in number, does becoming an S corporation make sense for tax purposes? Explain.
11. Tax laws have become extremely complex. In addition, there is little theoretical or moral justification for a substantial number of tax incentives (loopholes). Why and how are these incentives created? In your opinion, is there any indication that these incentives will be eliminated?
12. What is the purpose of the *carryback* and the *carryforward* provisions in the tax laws?
13. What is the purpose of financial markets? How can this purpose be accomplished efficiently?
14. Discuss the functions of financial intermediaries.
15. A number of factors give rise to different interest rates or yields being observed for different types of debt instruments. What are these factors?
16. What is meant by making the financial markets more efficient? More complete?
17. What is the purpose of stock market exchanges such as the New York Stock Exchange?
18. In general, what would be the likely effect of the following occurrences on the money and capital markets?
   a. The savings rate of individuals in the country declines.
   b. Individuals increase their savings at savings and loan associations and decrease their savings at banks.
   c. The government taxes capital gains at the ordinary income tax rate.
   d. Unanticipated inflation of substantial magnitude occurs, and price levels rise rapidly.
   e. Savings institutions and lenders increase transaction charges for savings and for making loans.
19. Pick a financial intermediary with which you are familiar and explain its economic role. Does it make the financial markets more efficient?
20. What is the distinction between the money market and the capital market? Is the distinction real or artificial?
21. How do transaction costs affect the flow of funds and the efficiency of financial markets?
22. What are the major sources of external financing for business firms?
23. In addition to financial intermediaries, what other institutions and arrangements facilitate the flow of funds to and from business firms?

SELF-CORRECTION PROBLEMS

1. John Henry has a small housecleaning business that presently is a sole proprietorship. The business has nine employees, annual sales of $480,000, total liabilities of $90,000, and total assets of $263,000. Including the business, Henry has a

personal net worth of $467,000 and nonbusiness liabilities of $42,000, represented by a mortgage on his home. He would like to give one of his employees, Tori Kobayashi, an equity interest in the business. Henry is considering either the partnership form or the corporate form, where Kobayashi would be given some stock. Kobayashi has a personal net worth of $36,000.

    a. What is the extent of Henry's exposure under the sole proprietorship in the case of a large lawsuit (say, $600,000)?

    b. What is his exposure under a partnership form? Do the partners share the risk?

    c. What is his exposure under the corporate form?

2. Bernstein Tractor Company has just invested in new equipment costing $16,000. The equipment falls in the five-year property class for cost recovery (depreciation) purposes. What depreciation charges can it claim on the asset for each of the next six years?

3. Wallopalooza Financial, Inc., believes that it can successfully "intermediate" in the mortgage market. Presently, borrowers pay 7 percent on adjustable rate mortgages. The deposit interest rate necessary to attract funds to lend is 3 percent, also adjustable with market conditions. Wallopalooza's administrative expenses, including information costs, are $2 million per annum on a base business of $100 million in loans.

    a. What interest rates on mortgage loans and on deposits would you recommend to obtain business?

    b. If $100 million in loans and an equal amount of deposits are attracted with a mortgage rate of 6.5 percent and a deposit interest rate of 3.5 percent, what would be Wallopalooza's annual before-tax profit on the new business? (Assume that interest rates do not change.)

4. Suppose that 91-day Treasury bills currently yield 6 percent to maturity and that 25-year Treasury bonds yield 7.25 percent. Lopez Pharmaceutical Company recently has issued long-term, 25-year bonds that yield 9 percent to maturity.

    a. If the yield on Treasury bills is taken to be the short-term, risk-free rate, what premium in yield is required for the default risk and lower marketability associated with the Lopez bonds?

    b. What premium in yield above the short-term, risk-free rate is attributable to maturity?

PROBLEMS

1. Zaharias-Liras Wholesalers, a partnership, owes $418,000 to various shipping companies. Armand Zaharias has a personal net worth of $1,346,000, including a $140,000 equity interest in the partnership. Nick Liras has a personal net worth of $893,000, including the same equity interest in the business as his partner. The partners have kept only a moderate equity base of $280,000 in the business, with earnings being taken out as partner withdrawals. They wish to limit their risk exposure and are considering the corporate form.

    a. What is their liability now for the business? What would it be under the corporate form?

    b. Will creditors be more or less willing to extend credit with a change in organization form?

2. The Loann Le Milling Company is going to purchase a new piece of testing equipment for $28,000 and a new machine for $53,000. The equipment falls in the three-year property class, and the machine is in the five-year class. What annual depreciation will the company be able to take on the two assets?

3. Tripex Consolidated Industries owns $1.5 million in 12 percent bonds of Solow Electronics Company. It also owns 100,000 shares of preferred stock of Solow, which constitutes 10 percent of all outstanding Solow preferred shares. In the past year, Solow paid the stipulated interest on its bonds and dividends of $3 per share on its preferred stock. The marginal tax rate of Tripex is 34 percent. What taxes must Tripex pay on this interest and dividend income?

4. The Castle Cork Company was founded in 20X1 and had the following taxable income through 20X5:

20X1	20X2	20X3	20X4	20X5
$0	$35,000	$68,000	−$120,000	$52,000

Compute the corporate income tax or tax refund in each year, assuming the graduated tax rates discussed in the chapter.

5. Loquat Foods Company is able to borrow at an interest rate of 9 percent for one year. For the year, market participants expect 4 percent inflation.
   a. What approximate real rate of return does the lender expect? What is the inflation premium embodied in the nominal interest rate?
   b. If inflation proves to be 2 percent for the year, does the lender suffer? Does the borrower suffer? Why?
   c. If inflation proves to be 6 percent, who gains and who loses?

6. From a recent Monday *Wall Street Journal,* collect yield information on yields for a long-term Treasury bond, a public utility bond (probably AA in quality), municipal bonds as described by the municipal bond index, Treasury bills, and commercial paper. (This information appears at the back of the paper under the Bond Market section, the Money Market Rates section, and the Treasury Issues section.) What reasons can you give for the differences in yield on these various instruments?

SOLUTIONS TO SELF-CORRECTION PROBLEMS

1. a. Henry is responsible for all liabilities, book as well as contingent. If the lawsuit were lost, he would lose all his net assets, as represented by a net worth of $467,000. Without the lawsuit, he still is responsible for $90,000 in liabilities if for some reason the business is unable to pay them.
   b. He still could lose all his net assets because Kobayashi's net worth is insufficient to make a major dent in the lawsuit: $600,000 − $36,000 = $564,000. As the two partners have substantially different net worths, they do not share equally in the risk. Henry has much more to lose.
   c. Under the corporate form, he could lose the business, but that is all. The net worth of the business is $263,000 − $90,000 = **$173,000,** and this represents Henry's personal financial stake in the business. The remainder of his net worth, $467,000 − $173,000 = $294,000, would be protected under the corporate form.

2. Depreciation charges for the equipment:

YEAR	PERCENT	AMOUNT
1	20.00%	$ 3,200.00
2	32.00	5,120.00
3	19.20	3,072.00
4	11.52	1,843.20
5	11.52	1,843.20
6	5.76	921.60
Total		$16,000.00

3. a. At $2 million in expenses per $100 million in loans, administrative costs come to 2 percent. Therefore, just to break even, the firm must set rates so

that (at least) a 2 percent difference exists between the deposit interest rate and the mortgage rate. In addition, market conditions dictate that 3 percent is the floor for the deposit rate, and 7 percent is the ceiling for the mortgage rate. Suppose that Wallopalooza wished to increase the current deposit rate and lower the current mortgage rate by equal amounts while earning a before-tax return spread of 1 percent. It would then offer a deposit rate of 3.5 percent and a mortgage rate of 6.5 percent. Of course, other answers are possible, depending on your profit assumptions.

    b. Before-tax profit of 1 percent on $100 million in loans equals **$1 million.**

4. a. The premium attributable to default risk and to lower marketability is $9\% - 7.25\% = \mathbf{1.75\%}.$

    b. The premium attributable to maturity is $7.25\% - 6\% = \mathbf{1.25\%}.$ In this case, default risk is held constant, and marketability, for the most part, is also held constant.

SELECTED REFERENCES

Choosing a Business Entity in the 1990's. Washington, D.C.: Coopers & Lybrand, LLP, 1994.

Fabozzi, Frank J., and Franco Modigliani. *Capital Markets: Institutions and Instruments,* 2nd ed. Upper Saddle River, NJ: Prentice Hall, 1995.

Friedman, Samuel J., and Steven D. Goldberg. "Selecting a Form of Business: The Trend Toward Limited Liability Companies." *The Small Business Controller* 8 (Spring 1995), 11–16.

A Guide to Limited Liability Companies, 3rd ed. Chicago: CCH Incorporated, 1995.

Kidwell, David S., Richard L. Peterson, and David Blackwell. *Financial Institutions, Markets, and Money,* 7th ed. Fort Worth, TX: Harcourt, 2000.

Rexner, Christian, and Timothy J. Sheehan. "Organizing the Firm: Choosing the Right Business Entity." *Journal of Applied Corporate Finance* 7 (Spring 1994), 59–65.

Rose, Peter. *Money and Capital Markets,* 7th ed. New York: McGraw-Hill, 2000.

Van Horne, James C. "Of Financial Innovations and Excesses," *Journal of Finance* 40 (July 1985).

———. *Financial Market Rates and Flows,* 6th ed. Upper Saddle River, NJ: Prentice Hall, 2001.

Chapter 3

The Time Value of Money

THE INTEREST RATE
SIMPLE INTEREST
COMPOUND INTEREST
    Single Amounts • Annuities • Mixed Flows
COMPOUNDING MORE THAN ONCE A YEAR
    Semiannual and Other Compounding Periods • Continuous
        Compounding • Effective Annual Interest Rate
AMORTIZING A LOAN
SUMMARY TABLE OF KEY COMPOUND INTEREST FORMULAS
SUMMARY
QUESTIONS
SELF-CORRECTION PROBLEMS
PROBLEMS
SOLUTIONS TO SELF-CORRECTION PROBLEMS
SELECTED REFERENCES

The chief value of money lies in the fact that one lives in a world in which it is overestimated.

—H. L. MENCKEN
From *A Mencken Chrestomathy.*
© 1949. Reprinted by permission of Alfred A. Knopf, Inc.

THE INTEREST RATE

Interest Money paid (earned) for the use of money.

Which would you prefer—$1,000 today or $1,000 ten years from today? Common sense tells us to take the $1,000 today because we recognize that there is a *time value to money*. The immediate receipt of $1,000 provides us with the *opportunity* to put our money to work and earn **interest**. In a world in which all cash flows are certain, the *rate of interest* can be used to express the time value of money. As we will soon discover, the rate of interest will allow us to adjust the value of cash flows, whenever they occur, to a particular point in time. Given this ability, we will be able to answer more difficult questions, such as: which should you prefer—$1,000 today or $2,000 ten years from today? To answer this question, it will be necessary to position *time-adjusted* cash flows at a single point in time so that a fair comparison can be made.

If we allow for uncertainty surrounding cash flows to enter into our analysis, it will be necessary to add a risk premium to the interest rate as compensation for uncertainty. In later chapters we will study how to deal with uncertainty (risk). But for now, our focus is on the time value of money and the ways in which the rate of interest can be used to adjust the value of cash flows to a single point in time.

Most financial decisions, personal as well as business, involve time value of money considerations. In Chapter 1, we learned that the objective of management should be to maximize shareholder wealth and that this depends, in part, on the timing of cash flows. Not surprisingly, one important application of the concepts stressed in this chapter will be to value a stream of cash flows. Indeed, much of the development of this book depends on your understanding of this chapter. You will never really understand finance until you understand the time value of money. Although the discussion that follows cannot avoid being mathematical in nature, we focus on only a handful of formulas so that you can more easily grasp the fundamentals. We start with a discussion of *simple interest* and use this as a springboard to develop the concept of *compound interest*. Also, to observe more easily the effect of compound interest, most of the examples in this chapter assume an 8 percent annual interest rate.

Take Note

Before we begin, it is important to sound a few notes of caution. The examples in the chapter frequently involve numbers that must be raised to the *n*th power—for example, (1.05) to the third power equals $(1.05)^3$ equals $[(1.05) \times (1.05) \times (1.05)]$. However, this operation is easy to do with a calculator, and tables are provided in which this calculation has already been done for you. Although the tables provided are a useful aid, you cannot rely on them for solving *every* problem. Not every interest rate or time period can possibly be represented in each table. Therefore, you will need to become familiar with the operational formulas on which the tables are based. (As a reminder, the appropriate formula is included at the top of every table.) Those of you possessing a business calculator may feel the urge to bypass both the tables and formulas and head straight for the various function keys designed to deal with time value of money problems. However, we urge you to master first the logic behind the procedures outlined in this chapter. Even the best of calculators cannot overcome a faulty sequence of steps programmed in by the user.

SIMPLE INTEREST

Simple interest Interest paid (earned) on only the original amount, or principal, borrowed (lent).

Simple interest is interest that is paid (earned) on only the original amount, or *principal*, borrowed (lent). The dollar amount of simple interest is a function of three variables: the original amount borrowed (lent), or principal; the interest rate per time period; and the number of time periods for which the principal is borrowed (lent). The formula for calculating simple interest is

$$SI = P_0(i)(n) \tag{3-1}$$

where SI = simple interest in dollars
P_0 = principal, or original amount borrowed (lent) at time period 0
i = interest rate per time period
n = number of time periods

For example, assume that you deposit $100 in a savings account paying 8 percent simple interest and keep it there for 10 years. At the end of 10 years, the amount of interest accumulated is determined as follows:

$$\$80 = \$100(.08)(10)$$

Future value (terminal value) The value at some future time of a present amount of money, or a series of payments, evaluated at a given interest rate.

To solve for the **future value** (also known as the **terminal value**) of the account at the end of 10 years (FV_{10}), we add the interest earned on the principal only to the original amount invested. Therefore

$$FV_{10} = \$100 + [\$100(.08)(10)] = \$180$$

For any simple interest rate, the future value of an account at the end of n periods is

$$FV_n = P_0 + SI = P_0 + P_0(i)(n)$$

or, equivalently,

$$FV_n = P_0[1 + (i)(n)] \tag{3-2}$$

Sometimes we need to proceed in the opposite direction. That is, we know the future value of a deposit at i percent for n years, but we don't know the principal originally invested—the account's **present value** ($PV_0 = P_0$). A rearrangement of Eq. (3-2), however, is all that is needed.

Present value The current value of a future amount of money, or a series of payments, evaluated at a given interest rate.

$$PV_0 = P_0 = FV_n/[1 + (i)(n)] \tag{3-3}$$

Now that you are familiar with the mechanics of simple interest, it is perhaps a bit cruel to point out that most situations in finance involving the time value of money do not rely on simple interest at all. Instead, *compound interest* is the norm; however, an understanding of simple interest will help you appreciate (and understand) compound interest all the more.

COMPOUND INTEREST

The distinction between *simple* and *compound interest* can best be seen by example. Table 3-1 illustrates the rather dramatic effect that compound interest has on an investment's value over time when compared to the effect of simple interest. From the table it is clear to see why some people have called compound interest the greatest of human inventions.

TABLE 3-1
Future value of $1
invested for various
time periods at an
8% annual interest
rate

YEARS	AT SIMPLE INTEREST	AT COMPOUND INTEREST
2	$ 1.16	$ 1.17
20	2.60	4.66
200	17.00	4,838,949.59

Compound interest Interest paid (earned) on any previous interest earned, as well as on the principal borrowed (lent).

The notion of **compound interest** is crucial to understanding the mathematics of finance. The term itself merely implies that interest paid (earned) on a loan (an investment) is periodically added to the principal. As a result, interest is earned on interest as well as the initial principal. It is this interest-on-interest, or *compounding*, effect that accounts for the dramatic difference between simple and compound interest. As we will see, the concept of compound interest can be used to solve a wide variety of problems in finance.

Single Amounts

Future (or Compound) Value. To begin with, consider a person who deposits $100 into a savings account. If the interest rate is 8 percent, compounded annually, how much will the $100 be worth at the end of a year? Setting up the problem, we solve for the *future value* (which in this case is also referred to as the *compound value*) of the account at the end of the year (FV_1).

$$FV_1 = P_0(1 + i)$$

$$= \$100(1.08) = \textbf{\$108}$$

Interestingly, this first-year value is the same number that we would get if simple interest were employed. But, this is where the similarity ends.

What if we leave $100 on deposit for two years? The $100 initial deposit will have grown to $108 at the end of the first year at 8 percent compound annual interest. Going to the end of the second year, $108 becomes $116.64, as $8 in interest is earned on the initial $100, and $.64 is earned on the $8 in interest credited to our account at the end of the first year. In other words, interest is earned on previously earned interest, hence the name *compound interest*. Therefore, the future value at the end of the second year is

$$FV_2 = FV_1(1 + i) = P_0(1 + i)(1 + i) = P_0(1 + i)^2$$
$$= \$108(1.08) = \$100(1.08)(1.08) = \$100(1.08)^2$$
$$= \textbf{\$116.64}$$

At the end of three years, the account would be worth

$$FV_3 = FV_2(1 + i) = FV_1(1 + i)(1 + i) = P_0(1 + i)^3$$
$$= \$116.64(1.08) = \$108(1.08)(1.08) = \$100(1.08)^3$$
$$= \textbf{\$125.97}$$

In general, FV_n, the future (compound) value of a deposit at the end of n periods, is

$$FV_n = P_0(1 + i)^n \tag{3-4}$$

or

$$FV_n = P_0(FVIF_{i,n}) \tag{3-5}$$

TABLE 3-2
Illustration of compound interest with $100 initial deposit and 8% annual interest rate

YEAR	BEGINNING AMOUNT	INTEREST EARNED DURING PERIOD (8% of beginning amount)	ENDING AMOUNT (FV_n)
1	$100.00	$ 8.00	$108.00
2	108.00	8.64	116.64
3	116.64	9.33	125.97
4	125.97	10.08	136.05
5	136.05	10.88	146.93
6	146.93	11.76	158.69
7	158.69	12.69	171.38
8	171.38	13.71	185.09
9	185.09	14.81	199.90
10	199.90	15.99	215.89

where we let $FVIF_{i,n}$ (i.e., the *future value interest factor at i% for n periods*) equal $(1 + i)^n$. Table 3-2, showing the future values for our example problem at the end of years 1 to 3 (and beyond), illustrates the concept of interest being earned on interest.

A calculator makes Eq. (3-4) very simple to use. In addition, tables have been constructed for values of $(1 + i)^n$—$FVIF_{i,n}$—for wide ranges of *i* and *n*. These tables, called (appropriately) Future Value Interest Factor (or Terminal Value Interest Factor) Tables, are designed to be used with Eq. (3-5). Table 3-3 is one example covering various interest rates ranging from 1 to 15 percent. The *Interest Rate (i)* headings and *Period (n)* designations on the table are similar to map coordinates. They help us locate the appropriate interest factor. For example, the future value interest factor at 8 percent for nine years ($FVIF_{8\%,9}$) is located at the intersection of the *8% column* with the *9-period row* and equals 1.999. This 1.999 figure means that $1 invested at 8 percent compound interest for nine years will return roughly $2—consisting of initial principal *plus* accumulated interest. (For a more complete table, see Table I in the Appendix at the end of this book.)

TABLE 3-3
Future value interest factor of $1 at *i*% at the end of *n* periods ($FVIF_{i,n}$)

$(FVIF_{i,n}) = (1 + i)^n$

PERIOD (n)	INTEREST RATE (i)					
	1%	3%	5%	8%	10%	15%
1	1.010	1.030	1.050	**1.080**	1.100	1.150
2	1.020	1.061	1.102	**1.166**	1.210	1.322
3	1.030	1.093	1.158	**1.260**	1.331	1.521
4	1.041	1.126	1.216	**1.360**	1.464	1.749
5	1.051	1.159	1.276	**1.469**	1.611	2.011
6	1.062	1.194	1.340	**1.587**	1.772	2.313
7	1.072	1.230	1.407	**1.714**	1.949	2.660
8	1.083	1.267	1.477	**1.851**	2.144	3.059
9	**1.094**	**1.305**	**1.551**	1.999	2.358	3.518
10	1.105	1.344	1.629	2.159	2.594	4.046
25	1.282	2.094	3.386	6.848	10.835	32.919
50	1.645	4.384	11.467	46.902	117.391	1,083.657

FIGURE 3-1
Future Values with
$100 Initial Deposit
and 5%, 10%, and
15% Compound
Annual Interest
Rates

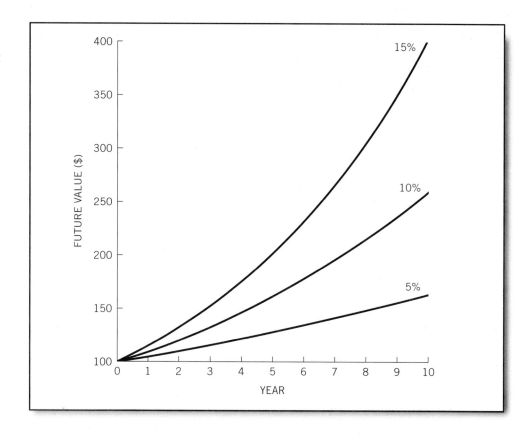

If we take the *FVIFs* for $1 in the *8% column* and multiply them by $100, we get figures (aside from some rounding) that correspond to our calculations for $100 in the final column of Table 3-2. Notice, too, that in rows corresponding to two or more years, the proportional increase in future value becomes greater as the interest rate rises. A picture may help make this point a little clearer. Therefore, in Figure 3-1 we graph the growth in future value for a $100 initial deposit with interest rates of 5, 10, and 15 percent. As can be seen from the graph, the greater the interest rate, the steeper the growth curve by which future value increases. Also, the greater the number of years during which compound interest can be earned, obviously the greater the future value.

Compound Growth. Although our concern so far has been with interest rates, it is important to realize that the concept involved applies to compound growth of any sort—for example, in gas prices, tuition fees, corporate earnings, and dividends. Suppose that a corporation's most recent dividend was $10 per share but that we expect this dividend to grow at a 10 percent compound annual rate. For the next five years we would expect dividends to look as shown in the table.

YEAR	GROWTH FACTOR	EXPECTED DIVIDEND/SHARE
1	$(1.10)^1$	$11.00
2	$(1.10)^2$	12.10
3	$(1.10)^3$	13.31
4	$(1.10)^4$	14.64
5	$(1.10)^5$	16.11

In 1790 John Jacob Astor bought approximately an acre of land on the east side of Manhattan Island for $58. Astor, who was considered a shrewd investor, made many such purchases. How much would his descendants have in 2001, if instead of buying the land, Astor had invested the $58 at 5 percent compound annual interest?

In Table I we won't find the *FVIF* of $1 in 211 years at 5 percent. But, notice that we can find the *FVIF* of $1 in 50 years—11.467—and the *FVIF* of $1 in 11 years—1.710. So what, you might ask. Being a little creative, we can express our problem as follows:[1]

$$FV_{211} = P_0 \times (1 + i)^{211}$$
$$= P_0 \times (1 + i)^{50} \times (1 + i)^{50} \times (1 + i)^{50} \times (1 + i)^{50} \times (1 + i)^{11}$$
$$= \$58 \times 11.467 \times 11.467 \times 11.467 \times 11.467 \times 1.710$$
$$= \$58 \times 29,566.19 = \mathbf{\$1,714,839.02}$$

Given the current price of land in New York City, Astor's one-acre purchase seems to have passed the test of time as a wise investment. It is also interesting to note that with a little reasoning we can get quite a bit of mileage out of even a basic table.

Similarly, we can determine the future levels of other variables that are subject to compound growth. This principle will prove especially important when we consider certain valuation models for common stock, which we do in the next chapter.

Present (or Discounted) Value. We all realize that a dollar today is worth more than a dollar to be received one, two, or three years from now. Calculating the *present value* of future cash flows allows us to place all cash flows on a current footing so that comparisons can be made in terms of today's dollars.

An understanding of the present value concept should enable us to answer a question that was posed at the very beginning of this chapter: which should you prefer—$1,000 today or $2,000 ten years from today?[2] Assume that both sums are completely certain and your opportunity cost of funds is 8 percent per annum (i.e., you could borrow or lend at 8 percent). The present worth of $1,000 received today is easy—it is worth $1,000. However, what is $2,000 received at the end of 10 years worth to you today? We might begin by asking what amount (today) would grow to be $2,000 at the end of 10 years at 8 percent compound interest. This amount is called the *present value* of $2,000 payable in 10 years, *discounted* at 8 percent. In present value problems such as this, the interest rate is also known as the **discount rate** (or **capitalization rate**).

Discount rate (capitalization rate) Interest rate used to convert *future values* to *present values*.

Finding the present value (or *discounting*) is simply the reverse of *compounding*. Therefore, let's first retrieve Eq. (3-4):

$$FV_n = P_0(1 + i)^n$$

Rearranging terms, we solve for present value

$$PV_0 = P_0 = FV_n/(1 + i)^n$$
$$= FV_n[1/(1 + i)^n] \tag{3-6}$$

---

[1]We make use of one of the rules governing exponents. Specifically, $A^{m+n} = A^m \times A^n$

[2]Alternatively, we could treat this as a future value problem. To do this, we would compare the future value of $1,000, compounded at 8 percent annual interest for 10 years, to a future $2,000.

Note that the term $[1/(1 + i)^n]$ is simply the reciprocal of the *future value interest factor at i% for n periods* ($FVIF_{i,n}$). This reciprocal has its own name—the *present value interest factor at i% for n periods* ($PVIF_{i,n}$)—and allows us to rewrite Eq. (3-6) as

$$PV_0 = FV_n(PVIF_{i,n}) \qquad (3\text{-}7)$$

A present value table containing $PVIFs$ for a wide range of interest rates and time periods relieves us of making the calculations implied by Eq. (3-6) every time we have a present value problem to solve. Table 3-4 is an abbreviated version of one such table. (Table II in the Appendix found at the end of the book is a more complete version.)

We can now make use of Eq. (3-7) and Table 3-4 to solve for the present value of $2,000 to be received at the end of 10 years, discounted at 8 percent. In Table 3-4, the intersection of the *8% column* with the *10-period row* pinpoints $PVIF_{8\%,10}$—.463. This tells us that $1 received 10 years from now is worth roughly 46 cents to us today. Armed with this information, we get

$$PV_0 = FV_{10}(PVIF_{8\%,10})$$
$$= \$2,000(.463) = \textbf{\$926}$$

Finally, if we compare this present value amount ($926) to the promise of $1,000 to be received today, we should prefer to take the $1,000. In present value terms we would be better off by $74 ($1,000 − $926).

Discounting future cash flows turns out to be very much like the process of *handicapping*. That is, we put future cash flows at a mathematically determined disadvantage relative to current dollars. For example, in the problem just addressed, every future dollar was handicapped to such an extent that each was worth only about 46 cents. The greater the disadvantage assigned to a future cash flow, the smaller the corresponding present value interest factor (*PVIF*). Figure 3-2 illustrates how both time and discount rate combine to affect present value; the present value of $100 received from 1 to 10 years in the future is graphed for discount rates of 5, 10, and 15 percent. The graph shows that the present value of $100 decreases by a decreasing rate the further in the future that it is to be received. The greater the interest rate, of course, the lower the present value but also the more pronounced the curve. At a 15 percent discount rate, $100 to be received 10 years hence is worth only $24.70 today—or roughly 25 cents on the (future) dollar.

TABLE 3-4
Present value interest factor of $1 at *i%* for *n* periods ($PVIF_{i,n}$)

$(PVIF_{i,n}) = 1/(1 + i)^n$

	INTEREST RATE (*i*)					
PERIOD (*n*)	1%	3%	5%	8%	10%	15%
1	.990	.971	.952	**.926**	.909	.870
2	.980	.943	.907	**.857**	.826	.756
3	.971	.915	.864	**.794**	.751	.658
4	.961	.888	.823	**.735**	.683	.572
5	.951	.863	.784	**.681**	.621	.497
6	.942	.837	.746	**.630**	.564	.432
7	.933	.813	.711	**.583**	.513	.376
8	.923	.789	.677	**.540**	.467	.327
9	.914	.766	.645	**.500**	.424	.284
10	.905	.744	.614	**.463**	.386	.247

Part II Valuation

FIGURE 3-2
Present Values with $100 Cash Flow and 5%, 10%, and 15% Compound Annual Interest Rates

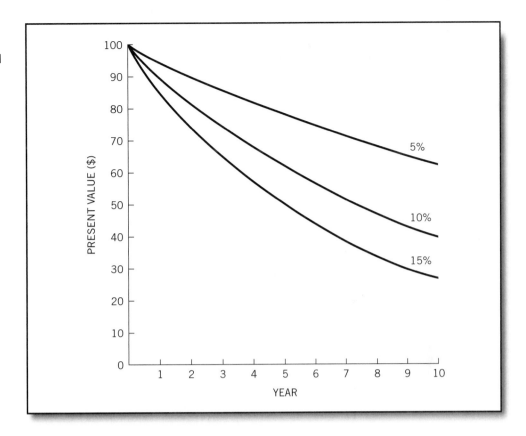

QUESTION•ANSWER•QUESTION•ANSWER

How do you determine the future value (present value) of an investment over a time span that contains a fractional period (e.g., 1¼ years)?

Simple. All you do is alter the future value (present value) formula to include the fraction in decimal form. Let's say that you invest $1,000 in a savings account that compounds annually at 6 percent and want to withdraw your savings in 15 months (i.e., 1.25 years). Since $FV_n = P_0(1 + i)^n$, you could withdraw the following amount 15 months from now:

$$FV_{1.25} = \$1,000(1 + .06)^{1.25} = \mathbf{\$1,075.55}$$

Unknown Interest (or Discount) Rate. Sometimes we are faced with a time-value-of-money situation in which we know both the future and present values, as well as the number of time periods involved. What is unknown, however, is the compound interest rate (i) implicit in the situation.

Let's assume that if you invest $1,000 today, you will receive $3,000 in exactly 8 years. The compound interest (or discount) rate implicit in this situation can be found by rearranging either a basic future value or present value equation. For example, making use of future value Eq. (3-5), we have

$$FV_8 = P_0(FVIF_{i,8})$$
$$\$3,000 = \$1,000(FVIF_{i,8})$$
$$FVIF_{i,8} = \$3,000/\$1,000 = \mathbf{3}$$

Reading across the *8-period row* in Table 3-3, we look for the future value interest factor (*FVIF*) that comes closest to our calculated value of 3. In our table, that interest factor is 3.059 and is found in the *15% column*. Because 3.059 is slightly larger than 3, we conclude that the interest rate implicit in the example situation is actually slightly less than 15 percent.

For a more accurate answer, we simply recognize that $FVIF_{i,8}$ can also be written as $(1 + i)^8$, and solve directly for i as follows:

$$(1 + i)^8 = 3$$
$$(1 + i) = 3^{1/8} = 3^{.125} = 1.1472$$
$$i = .1472$$

(*Note:* Solving for i, we first have to raise both sides of the equation to the 1/8 or .125 power. To raise "3" to the ".125" power, we use the **[y^x]** key on a handheld calculator—entering "3," pressing the **[y^x]** key, entering ".125," and finally pressing the **[=]** key.)

Unknown Number of Compounding (or Discounting) Periods. At times we may need to know how long it will take for a dollar amount invested today to grow to a certain future value given a particular compound rate of interest. For example, how long would it take for an investment of $1,000 to grow to $1,900 if we invested it at a compound annual interest rate of 10 percent? Because we know both the investment's future and present value, the number of compounding (or discounting) periods (n) involved in this investment situation can be determined by rearranging either a basic future value or present value equation. Using future value Eq. (3-5), we get

$$FV_n = P_0(FVIF_{10\%,n})$$
$$\$1,900 = \$1,000(FVIF_{10\%,n})$$
$$FVIF_{10\%,n} = \$1,900/\$1,000 = 1.9$$

Reading down the *10% column* in Table 3-3, we look for the future value interest factor (*FVIF*) in that column that is closest to our calculated value. We find that 1.949 comes closest to 1.9, and that this number corresponds to the *7-period row*. Because 1.949 is a little larger than 1.9, we conclude that there are slightly less than 7 annual compounding periods implicit in the example situation.

For greater accuracy, simply rewrite $FVIF_{10\%,n}$ as $(1 + .10)^n$, and solve for n as follows:

$$(1 + .10)^n = 1.9$$
$$n(\ln 1.1) = \ln 1.9$$
$$n = (\ln 1.9)/(\ln 1.1) = 6.73 \text{ years}$$

To solve for n, which appeared in our rewritten equation as an exponent, we employed a little trick. We took the natural logarithm (ln) of both sides of our equation. This allowed us to solve explicitly for n. (*Note:* To divide (ln 1.9) by (ln 1.1), we use the **[LN]** key on a handheld calculator as follows: enter "1.9"; press the **[LN]** key; then press the **[÷]** key; now enter "1.1"; press the **[LN]** key one more time; and finally, press the **[=]** key.)

Annuity A series of equal payments or receipts occurring over a specified number of periods. In an *ordinary annuity*, payments or receipts occur at the end of each period; in an *annuity due*, payments or receipts occur at the beginning of each period.

Annuities

Ordinary Annuity. An **annuity** is a series of equal payments or receipts occurring over a specified number of periods. In an *ordinary annuity*, payments or receipts occur at the end of each period. Figure 3-3 shows the cash-flow sequence for an ordinary annuity on a time line.

Part II Valuation

Psst! Want to Double Your Money? The "Rule of 72" Tells You How.

Bill Veeck once bought the Chicago White Sox for $10 million and then sold it 5 years later for $20 million. In short, he doubled his money in 5 years. What compound rate of return did Veeck earn on his investment?

A quick way to handle compound interest problems involving doubling your money makes use of the "Rule of 72." This rule states that if the number of years, n, that an investment will be held is divided into the value 72, we will get the approximate interest rate, i, required for the investment to double in value. In Veeck's case, the rule gives

$$72/n = i$$
or
$$72/5 = \textbf{14.4\%}$$

Alternatively, if Veeck had taken his initial investment and placed it in a savings account earning 6 per-

cent compound interest, he would have had to wait approximately 12 years for his money to have doubled:

$$72/i = n$$
or
$$72/6 = \textbf{12 years}$$

Indeed, for most interest rates we encounter, the "Rule of 72" gives a good approximation of the interest rate—or the number of years—required to double your money. But the answer is not exact. For example, money doubling in 5 years would have to earn at a 14.87 percent compound annual rate $[(1 + .1487)^5 = 2]$; the "Rule of 72" says 14.4 percent. Also, money invested at 6 percent interest would actually require only 11.9 years to double $[(1 + .06)^{11.9} = 2]$; the "Rule of 72" suggests 12. However, for ballpark-close money-doubling approximations that can be done in your head, the "Rule of 72" comes in pretty handy.

Assume that Figure 3-3 represents your receiving $1,000 a year for three years. Now let's further assume that you deposit each annual receipt in a savings account earning 8 percent compound annual interest. How much money will you have at the end of three years? Figure 3-4 provides the answer (the long way)—using only the tools that we have discussed so far.

Expressed algebraically, with FVA_n defined as the future (compound) value of an annuity, R the periodic receipt (or payment), and n the length of the annuity, the formula for FVA_n is

$$FVA_n = R(1 + i)^{n-1} + R(1 + i)^{n-2} + \cdots + R(1 + i)^1 + R(1 + i)^0$$
$$= R[FVIF_{i,n-1} + FVIF_{i,n-2} + \cdots + FVIF_{i,1} + FVIF_{i,0}]$$

As you can see, FVA_n is simply equal to the periodic receipt (R) times the "sum of the future value interest factors at i percent for time periods 0 to $n - 1$." Luckily, we have two shorthand ways of stating this mathematically:

$$FVA_n = R\left[\sum_{t=1}^{n}(1 + i)^{n-t}\right] = R([(1 + i)^n - 1]/i) \tag{3-8}$$

or equivalently,

$$FVA_n = R(FVIFA_{i,n}) \tag{3-9}$$

where $FVIFA_{i,n}$ stands for the *future value interest factor of an annuity at i% for n periods.*

FIGURE 3-3
Time Line Showing the Cash-Flow Sequence for an Ordinary Annuity of $1,000 per Year for 3 Years

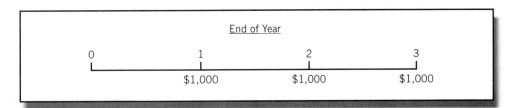

End of Year

0	1	2	3
	$1,000	$1,000	$1,000

FIGURE 3-4
Time Line for Calculating the Future (Compound) Value of an (Ordinary) Annuity [Periodic Receipt = R = $1,000; i = 8%; and n = 3 Years]

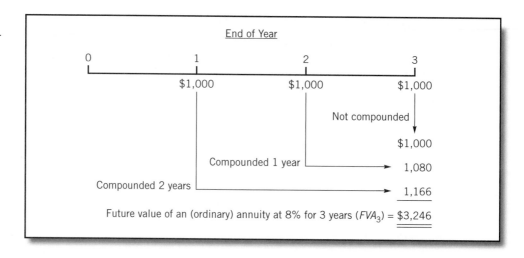

An abbreviated listing of *FVIFA*s appears in Table 3-5. A more complete listing appears in Table III in the Appendix.

Making use of Table 3-5 to solve the problem described in Figure 3-4, we get

$$FVA_3 = \$1,000(FVIFA_{8\%,3})$$

$$= \$1,000(3.246) = \textbf{\$3,246}$$

TABLE 3-5
Future value interest factor of an (ordinary) annuity of $1 per period at i% for n periods ($FVIFA_{i,n}$)

$$(FVIFA_{i,n}) = \sum_{t=1}^{n}(1 + i)^{n-t} = [(1 + i)^n - 1]/i$$

PERIOD (n)	INTEREST RATE (i)					
	1%	3%	5%	8%	10%	15%
1	1.000	1.000	1.000	**1.000**	1.000	1.000
2	2.010	2.030	2.050	**2.080**	2.100	2.150
3	**3.030**	**3.091**	**3.153**	3.246	3.310	3.473
4	4.060	4.184	4.310	4.506	4.641	4.993
5	5.101	5.309	5.526	5.867	6.105	6.742
6	6.152	6.468	6.802	7.336	7.716	8.754
7	7.214	7.662	8.142	8.923	9.487	11.067
8	8.286	8.892	9.549	10.637	11.436	13.727
9	9.369	10.159	11.027	12.488	13.579	16.786
10	10.462	11.464	12.578	14.487	15.937	20.304

This answer is identical to that shown in Figure 3-4. (*Note:* Use of a table rather than a formula subjects us to some slight rounding error. Had we used Eq. (3-8), our answer would have been 40 cents more. Therefore, when extreme accuracy is called for, use formulas rather than tables.)

Return for the moment to Figure 3-3. Only now let's assume the cash flows of $1,000 a year for three years represent withdrawals from a savings account earning 8 percent compound annual interest. How much money would you have to place in the account right now (time period 0) such that you would end up with a zero balance after the last $1,000 withdrawal? Figure 3-5 shows the long way to find the answer.

As can be seen from Figure 3-5, solving for the present value of an annuity boils down to determining the sum of a series of individual present values. Therefore, we can write the general formula for the present value of an (ordinary) annuity for n periods (PVA_n) as

$$PVA_n = R[1/(1 + i)^1] + R[1/(1 + i)^2] + \cdots + R[1/(1 + i)^n]$$

$$= R[PVIF_{i,1} + PVIF_{i,2} + \cdots + PVIF_{i,n}]$$

Notice that our formula reduces to PVA_n being equal to the periodic receipt (R) times the "sum of the present value interest factors at i percent for time periods 1 to n." Mathematically, this is equivalent to

$$PVA_n = R\left[\sum_{t=1}^{n} 1/(1 + i)^t\right] = R\left[(1 - [1/(1 + i)^n])/i\right] \qquad \textbf{(3-10)}$$

and can be expressed even more simply as

$$PVA_n = R(PVIFA_{i,n}) \qquad \textbf{(3-11)}$$

where $PVIFA_{i,n}$ stands for the *present value interest factor of an (ordinary) annuity at i percent for n periods*. Table IV in the Appendix to this book holds $PVIFA$s for a wide range of values for i and n, and Table 3-6 contains excerpts from it.

We can make use of Table 3-6 to solve for the present value of the $1,000 annuity for three years at 8 percent shown in Figure 3-5. The $PVIFA_{8\%,3}$ is found from the table to be 2.577. (Notice this figure is nothing more than the sum of the first three numbers under the *8% column* in Table 3-4, which gives *PVIFs.*) Employing Eq. (3-11), we get

$$PVA_3 = \$1,000(PVIFA_{8\%,3})$$

$$= \$1,000(2.577) = \mathbf{\$2,577}$$

FIGURE 3-5
Time Line for Calculating the Present (Discounted) Value of an (Ordinary) Annuity [Periodic Receipt = R = $1,000; i = 8%; and n = 3 Years]

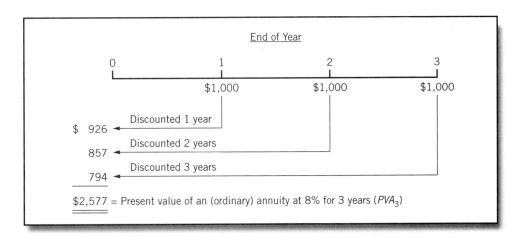

TABLE 3-6
Present value interest factor of an (ordinary) annuity of $1 per period at i% for n periods $(PVIFA_{i,n})$

$$(PVIFA_{i,n}) = \sum_{t=1}^{n} 1/(1+i)^t = (1 - [1/(1+i)^n])/i$$

	INTEREST RATE (i)					
PERIOD (n)	1%	3%	5%	8%	10%	15%
1	.990	.971	.952	**.926**	.909	.870
2	1.970	1.913	1.859	**1.783**	1.736	1.626
3	**2.941**	**2.829**	**2.723**	2.577	2.487	2.283
4	3.902	3.717	3.546	3.312	3.170	2.855
5	4.853	4.580	4.329	3.993	3.791	3.352
6	5.795	5.417	5.076	4.623	4.355	3.784
7	6.728	6.230	5.786	5.206	4.868	4.160
8	7.652	7.020	6.463	5.747	5.335	4.487
9	8.566	7.786	7.108	6.247	5.759	4.772
10	9.471	8.530	7.722	6.710	6.145	5.019

Unknown Interest (or Discount) Rate. A rearrangement of the basic future value (present value) of an annuity equation can be used to solve for the compound interest (discount) rate implicit in an annuity if we know: (1) the annuity's future (present) value, (2) the periodic payment or receipt, and (3) the number of periods involved. Suppose that you need to have at least $9,500 at the end of 7 years in order to send your parents on a luxury cruise. To accumulate this sum, you have decided to deposit $1,000 at the end of each of the next 7 years in a bank savings account. If the bank compounds interest annually, what minimum compound annual interest rate must the bank offer for your savings plan to work?

To solve for the compound annual interest rate (i) implicit in this annuity problem, we make use of future value of an annuity Eq. (3-9) as follows:

$$FVA_7 = R(FVIFA_{i,7})$$
$$\$9,500 = \$1,000(FVIFA_{i,7})$$
$$FVIFA_{i,7} = \$9,500/\$1,000 = \mathbf{9.5}$$

Reading across the *8-period row* in Table 3-5, we look for the future value interest factor of an annuity (*FVIFA*) that comes closest to our calculated value of 9.5. In our table, that interest factor is 9.549 and is found in the *5% column*. Because 9.549 is slightly larger than 9.5, we conclude that the interest rate implicit in the example situation is actually slightly less than 5 percent. (For a more accurate answer, you would need to rely on trial-and-error testing of different interest rates, interpolation, or a financial calculator.)

Unknown Periodic Payment (or Receipt). When dealing with annuities, one frequently encounters situations in which either the future (or present) value of the annuity, the interest rate, and the number of periodic payments (or receipts) are known. What needs to be determined, however, is the size of each equal payment or receipt. In a business setting, we most frequently encounter the need to determine periodic annuity payments in *sinking fund* (i.e., building up a fund through equal-dollar payments) and *loan amortization* (i.e., extinguishing a loan through equal-dollar payments) problems.

Rearrangement of either the basic present or future value annuity equation is necessary to solve for the periodic payment or receipt implicit in an annuity. Because we devote an entire section at the end of this chapter to the important topic of loan amortization, we will illustrate how to calculate the periodic payment with a sinking fund problem.

How much must one deposit each year end in a savings account earning 5 percent compound annual interest to accumulate $10,000 at the end of 8 years? We compute the payment (R) going into the savings account each year with the help of future value of an annuity Eq. (3-9). In addition, we use Table 3-5 to find the value corresponding to $FVIFA_{5\%,8}$ and proceed as follows:

$$FVA_8 = R(FVIFA_{5\%,8})$$

$$\$10,000 = R(9.549)$$

$$R = \$10,000/9.549 = \mathbf{\$1,047.23}$$

Therefore, by making 8 year-end deposits of $1,047.23 each into a savings account earning 5 percent compound annual interest, we will build up a sum totaling $10,000 at the end of 8 years.

Perpetuity An *ordinary annuity* whose payments or receipts continue forever.

Perpetuity. A **perpetuity** is an *ordinary annuity* whose payments or receipts continue forever. The ability to determine the present value of this special type of annuity will be required when we value perpetual bonds and preferred stock in the next chapter. A look back to PVA_n Eq. (3-10) should help us to make short work of this type of task. Replacing n in Eq. (3-10) with the value *infinity* (∞) gives us

$$PVA_\infty = R[(1 - [1/(1 + i)^\infty])/i] \qquad \textbf{(3-12)}$$

Because the bracketed term—$[1/(1 + i)^\infty]$—approaches zero, we can rewrite Eq. (3-12) as follows

$$PVA_\infty = R[(1 - 0)/i] = R(1/i)$$

or simply

$$PVA_\infty = R/i \qquad \textbf{(3-13)}$$

Thus, the present value of a perpetuity is simply the periodic receipt (payment) divided by the interest rate per period. For example, if $100 is received each year forever and the interest rate is 8 percent, the present value of this perpetuity is $1,250 (that is, $100/.08).

Annuity Due. In contrast to an ordinary annuity where payments or receipts occur at the *end* of each period, an *annuity due* calls for a series of equal payments occurring at the *beginning* of each period. Luckily, only a slight modification to the procedures already outlined for the treatment of ordinary annuities will allow us to solve annuity due problems.

Figure 3-6 compares and contrasts the calculation for the future value of a $1,000 ordinary annuity for three years at 8 percent (FVA_3) to that of the future value of a $1,000 annuity due for three years at 8 percent ($FVAD_3$). Notice that the cash flows for the ordinary annuity are *perceived* to occur at the *end* of periods 1, 2, and 3, and those for the annuity due are *perceived* to occur at the *beginning* of periods 2, 3, and 4.

Notice that the future value of the three-year annuity due is simply equal to the future value of a comparable three-year ordinary annuity compounded for one more period. Thus, the future value of an annuity due at i percent for n periods ($FVAD_n$) is determined as

$$FVAD_n = R(FVIFA_{i,n})(1 + i) \qquad \textbf{(3-14)}$$

FIGURE 3-6
Time Lines for Calcu-
lating the Future
(Compound) Value
of an (Ordinary)
Annuity and an
Annuity Due [Peri-
odic Receipt = R
= \$1,000; i = 8%;
and n = 3 Years]

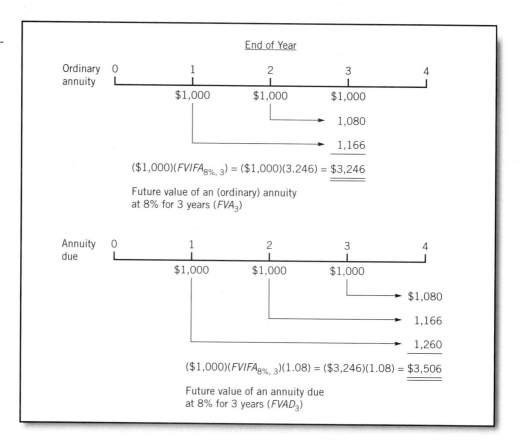

Take Note

Whether a cash flow appears to occur at the beginning or end of a period often depends on your perspective, however. (In a similar vein, is midnight the end of one day or the beginning of the next?) Therefore, the real key to distinguishing between the future value of an ordinary annuity and an annuity due is the point at which the future value is calculated. For an ordinary annuity, future value is calculated as of the last cash flow. For an annuity due, future value is calculated as of one period after the last cash flow.

The determination of the present value of an annuity due at i percent for n periods ($PVAD_n$) is best understood by example. Figure 3-7 illustrates the calculations necessary to determine both the present value of a \$1,000 ordinary annuity at 8 percent for three years (PVA_3), as well as the present value of a \$1,000 annuity due at 8 percent for three years ($PVAD_3$).

As can be seen in Figure 3-7, the present value of a three-year annuity due is equal to the present value of a two-year ordinary annuity plus one nondiscounted periodic receipt or payment. This can be generalized as follows:

$$PVAD_n = R(PVIFA_{i,n-1}) + R$$

$$= R(PVIFA_{i,n-1} + 1) \qquad \text{(3-15)}$$

Alternatively, we could view the present value of an annuity due as the present value of an ordinary annuity that had been brought back one period too far. That is, we

FIGURE 3-7

FIGURE 3-7
Time Lines for Calculating the Present (Discounted) Value of an (Ordinary) Annuity and an Annuity Due [Periodic Receipt = $R = \$1,000$; $i = 8\%$; and $n = 3$ Years]

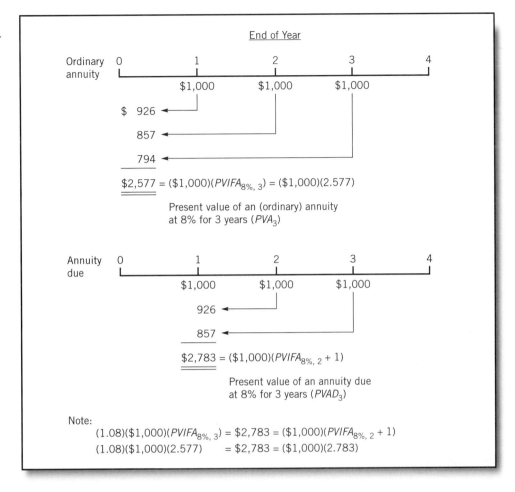

want the present value *one period later* than the ordinary annuity approach provides. Therefore, we could calculate the present value of an n-period annuity and then compound it one period forward. The general formula for this approach to determining $PVAD_n$ is

$$PVAD_n = (1 + i)(R)(PVIFA_{i,n}) \qquad \textbf{(3-16)}$$

Figure 3-7 proves by example that both approaches to determining $PVAD_n$ work equally well. However, the use of Eq. (3-15) seems to be the more obvious approach. The time-line approach taken in Figure 3-7 also helps us recognize the major differences between the present value of an ordinary annuity and an annuity due.

Take Note

In solving for the present value of an ordinary annuity, we consider the cash flows as occurring at the *end* of periods (in our Figure 3-7 example, the end of periods 1, 2, and 3) *and* calculate the present value as of one period before the first cash flow. Determination of the present value of an annuity due calls for us to consider the cash flows as occurring at the *beginning* of periods (in our example, the beginning of periods 1, 2, and 3) *and* to calculate the present value as of the first cash flow.

Mixed Flows

Many time value of money problems that we face involve neither a single cash flow nor a single annuity. Instead, we may encounter a mixed (or uneven) pattern of cash flows.

QUESTION•QUESTION•QUESTION•QUESTION

Assume that you are faced with the following problem—on an *exam* (arghh!), perhaps. What is the present value of $5,000 to be received annually at the end of years 1 and 2, followed by $6,000 annually at the end of years 3 and 4, and concluding with a final payment of $1,000 at the end of year 5, all discounted at 5 percent?

The first step in solving the boxed question above, or any similar problem, is to draw a time line, position the cash flows, and draw arrows indicating the direction and position to which you are going to adjust the flows. Second, make the necessary calculations as indicated by your diagram. (You may think that drawing a picture of what needs to be done is somewhat "childlike." However, consider that most *successful* home builders work from blueprints—why shouldn't you?)

Figure 3-8 illustrates that mixed flow problems can always be solved by adjusting each flow individually and then summing the results. This is time-consuming, but it works.

Often we can recognize certain patterns within mixed cash flows that allow us to take some calculation shortcuts. Thus, the problem that we have been working on could be solved in a number of alternative ways. One such alternative is shown in Figure 3-9. Notice how our two-step procedure continues to lead us to the correct solution:

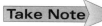

- Step 1: Draw a time line, position cash flows, and draw arrows to indicate direction and position of adjustments.
- Step 2: Perform calculations as indicated by your diagram.

A wide variety of mixed (uneven) cash-flow problems could be illustrated. To appreciate this variety and to master the skills necessary to determine solutions, be

The Magic of Compound Interest

Each year, on your birthday, you invest $2,000 in a tax-free retirement investment account. By age 65 you will have accumulated:*

COMPOUND ANNUAL INTEREST RATE (i)	STARTING AGE			
	21	31	41	51
6%	$ 425,487	$222,870	$109,730	$46,552
8	773,011	344,634	146,212	54,304
10	1,437,810	542,048	196,694	63,544
12	2,716,460	863,326	266,668	74,560

*From the table, it looks like the time to start saving is *now!*

FIGURE 3-8
(Alternative 1) Time Line for Calculating the Present (Discounted) Value of Mixed Cash Flows [$FV_1 = FV_2 = \$5,000$; $FV_3 = FV_4 = \$6,000$; $FV_5 = \$1,000$; $i = 5\%$; and $n = 5$ Years]

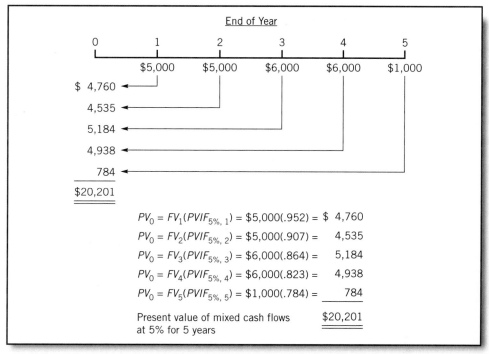

$$PV_0 = FV_1(PVIF_{5\%, 1}) = \$5,000(.952) = \$\ 4,760$$
$$PV_0 = FV_2(PVIF_{5\%, 2}) = \$5,000(.907) = \ \ 4,535$$
$$PV_0 = FV_3(PVIF_{5\%, 3}) = \$6,000(.864) = \ \ 5,184$$
$$PV_0 = FV_4(PVIF_{5\%, 4}) = \$6,000(.823) = \ \ 4,938$$
$$PV_0 = FV_5(PVIF_{5\%, 5}) = \$1,000(.784) = \ \ \ \ 784$$

Present value of mixed cash flows $20,201
at 5% for 5 years

FIGURE 3-9
(Alternative 2) Time Line for Calculating the Present (Discounted) Value of Mixed Cash Flows [$FV_1 = FV_2 = \$5,000$; $FV_3 = FV_4 = \$6,000$; $FV_5 = \$1,000$; $i = 5\%$; and $n = 5$ Years]

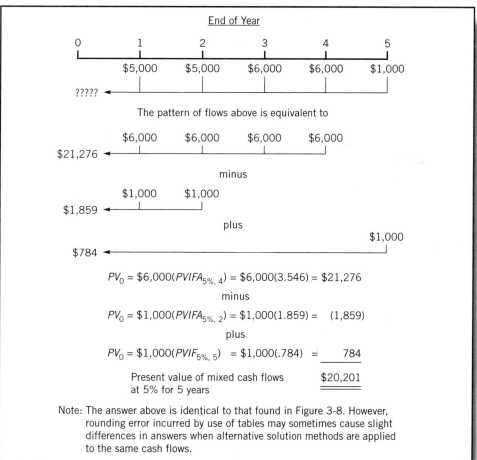

$$PV_0 = \$6,000(PVIFA_{5\%, 4}) = \$6,000(3.546) = \$21,276$$
minus
$$PV_0 = \$1,000(PVIFA_{5\%, 2}) = \$1,000(1.859) = \ \ (1,859)$$
plus
$$PV_0 = \$1,000(PVIF_{5\%, 5}) \ \ = \$1,000(.784) \ = \ \ \ \ \ 784$$

Present value of mixed cash flows $20,201
at 5% for 5 years

Note: The answer above is identical to that found in Figure 3-8. However, rounding error incurred by use of tables may sometimes cause slight differences in answers when alternative solution methods are applied to the same cash flows.

sure to do the problems at the end of this chapter. Don't be too bothered if you make some mistakes at first. Time value of money problems can be tricky. Mastering this material is a little bit like learning to ride a bicycle. You expect to fall and get bruised a bit until you pick up the necessary skills. But, practice makes perfect.

COMPOUNDING MORE THAN ONCE A YEAR

Semiannual and Other Compounding Periods

Future (or Compound) Value. Up to now, we have assumed that interest is paid annually. It is easiest to get a basic understanding of the time value of money with this assumption. Now, however, it is time to consider the relationship between future value and interest rates for different compounding periods. To begin, suppose that interest is paid semiannually. If you then deposit $100 in a savings account at a **nominal**, or **stated**, 8 percent annual **interest rate**, the future value at the end of six months would be

Nominal (stated) interest rate A rate of interest quoted for a year that has not been adjusted for frequency of compounding. If interest is compounded more than once a year, the *effective interest rate* will be higher than the *nominal rate*.

$$FV_{.5} = \$100(1 + [.08/2]) = \textbf{\$104}$$

In other words, at the end of one-half year you would receive 4 percent in interest, not 8 percent. At the end of a year the future value of the deposit would be

$$FV_1 = \$100(1 + [.08/2])^2 = \textbf{\$108.16}$$

This amount compares with $108 if interest is paid only once a year. The $.16 difference is caused by interest being earned in the second six months on the $4 in interest paid at the end of the first six months. The more times during the year that interest is paid, the greater the future value at the end of a given year.

The general formula for solving for the future value at the end of n years where interest is paid m times a year is

$$FV_n = PV_0(1 + [i/m])^{mn} \qquad \textbf{(3-17)}$$

To illustrate, suppose that now interest is paid quarterly and that you wish to know the future value of $100 at the end of one year where the stated annual rate is 8 percent. The future value would be

$$FV_1 = \$100(1 + [.08/4])^{(4)(1)}$$
$$= \$100(1 + .02)^4 = \textbf{\$108.24}$$

which, of course, is higher than it would be with either semiannual or annual compounding.

The future value at the end of three years for the example with quarterly compounding is

$$FV_3 = \$100(1 + [.08/4])^{(4)(3)}$$
$$= \$100(1 + .02)^{12} = \textbf{\$126.82}$$

compared to a future value with semiannual compounding of

$$FV_3 = \$100(1 + [.08/2])^{(2)(3)}$$
$$= \$100(1 + .04)^6 = \textbf{\$126.53}$$

and with annual compounding of

$$FV_3 = \$100(1 + [.08/1])^{(1)(3)}$$
$$= \$100(1 + .08)^3 = \textbf{\$125.97}$$

Thus, the more frequently interest is paid each year, the greater the future value. When m in Eq. (3-17) approaches infinity, we achieve *continuous compounding*. Shortly, we will take a special look at continuous compounding and discounting.

Present (or Discounted) Value. When interest is compounded more than once a year, the formula for calculating present value must be revised along the same lines as for the calculation of future value. Instead of dividing the future cash flow by $(1 + i)^n$ as we do when annual compounding is involved, we determine the present value by

$$PV_0 = FV_n/(1 + [i/m])^{mn} \qquad \textbf{(3-18)}$$

where, as before, FV_n is the future cash flow to be received at the end of year n, m is the number of times a year interest is compounded, and i is the discount rate. We can use Eq. (3-18), for example, to calculate the present value of $100 to be received at the end of year 3 for a nominal discount rate of 8 percent compounded quarterly:

$$PV_0 = \$100/(1 + [.08/4])^{(4)(3)}$$
$$= \$100/(1 + .02)^{12} = \textbf{\$78.85}$$

If the discount rate is compounded only annually, we have

$$PV_0 = \$100/(1 + .08)^3 = \textbf{\$79.38}$$

Thus, the fewer times a year that the nominal discount rate is compounded, the greater the present value. This relationship is just the opposite of that for future values.

Continuous Compounding

In practice, interest is sometimes compounded continuously. Therefore, it is useful to consider how this works. Recall that the general formula for solving for the future value at the end of year n, Eq. (3-17), is

$$FV_n = PV_0(1 + [i/m])^{mn}$$

As m, the number of times a year that interest is compounded, approaches infinity (∞), we get continuous compounding, and the term $(1 + [i/m])^{mn}$ approaches e^{in}, where e is approximately 2.71828. Therefore, the future value at the end of n years of an initial deposit of PV_0 where interest is compounded continuously at a rate of i percent is

$$FV_n = PV_0(e)^{in} \qquad \textbf{(3-19)}$$

For our earlier example problem, the future value of a $100 deposit at the end of three years with continuous compounding at 8 percent would be

$$FV_3 = \$100(e)^{(.08)(3)}$$
$$= \$100(2.71828)^{(.24)} = \textbf{\$127.12}$$

This compares with a future value with annual compounding of

$$FV_3 = \$100(1 + .08)^3 = \textbf{\$125.97}$$

Continuous compounding results in the maximum possible future value at the end of n periods for a given nominal rate of interest.

By the same token, when interest is compounded continuously, the formula for the present value of a cash flow received at the end of year n is

$$PV_0 = FV_n/(e)^{in} \qquad \textbf{(3-20)}$$

Thus, the present value of $1,000 to be received at the end of 10 years with a discount rate of 20 percent, compounded continuously, is

$$PV_0 = \$1,000/(e)^{(.20)(10)}$$
$$= \$1,000/(2.71828)^2 = \mathbf{\$135.34}$$

We see then that present value calculations involving continuous compounding are merely the reciprocals of future value calculations. Also, although continuous compounding results in the maximum possible future value, it results in the minimum possible present value.

QUESTION•ANSWER•QUESTION•ANSWER

When a bank quotes you an annual percentage yield (APY) on a savings account or certificate of deposit, what does that mean?

Based on a congressional act, the Federal Reserve requires that banks and thrifts adopt a standardized method of calculating the effective interest rates they pay on consumer accounts. It is called the *annual percentage yield (APY)*. The APY is meant to eliminate confusion caused when savings institutions apply different methods of compounding and use various terms, such as *effective yield, annual yield,* and *effective rate.* The APY is similar to the *effective annual interest rate.* The APY calculation, however, is based on the actual number of days that the money is deposited in an account in a 365-day year (366 days in a leap year).

In a similar vein, the Truth-in-Lending Act mandates that all financial institutions report the effective interest rate on any loan. This rate is called the *annual percentage rate (APR).* However, the financial institutions are not required to report the "true" effective annual interest rate as the APR. Instead, they may report a noncompounded version of the effective annual interest rate. For example, assume that a bank makes a loan for less than a year or interest is to be compounded more frequently than annually. The bank would determine an *effective periodic interest rate*—based on usable funds (i.e., the amount of funds the borrower can actually use)—and then simply multiply this rate by the number of such periods in a year. The result is the APR.

Effective Annual Interest Rate

Effective annual interest rate The actual rate of interest earned (paid) after adjusting the *nominal rate* for factors such as the number of compounding periods per year.

Different investments may provide returns based on various compounding periods. If we want to compare alternative investments that have different compounding periods, we need to state their interest on some common, or standardized, basis. This leads us to make a distinction between nominal, or stated, interest and the **effective annual interest rate.** The effective annual interest rate is the interest rate compounded annually that provides the same annual interest as the nominal rate does when compounded m times per year.

By definition then,

$$(1 + \text{effective annual interest rate}) = (1 + [i/m])^{(m)(1)}$$

Therefore, given the nominal rate i and the number of compounding periods per year m, we can solve for the effective annual interest rate as follows:[3]

$$\text{effective annual interest rate} = (1 + [i/m])^m - 1 \tag{3-21}$$

---

[3]The "special case" formula for effective annual interest rate when there is continuous compounding is as follows:

$$\text{effective annual interest rate} = (e)^i - 1$$

Part II Valuation

TABLE 3-7
Effects of different
compounding peri-
ods on future values
of $1,000 invested at
an 8% nominal inter-
est rate

INITIAL AMOUNT	COMPOUNDING PERIODS	FUTURE VALUE AT END OF 1 YEAR	EFFECTIVE ANNUAL INTEREST RATE*
$1,000	Annually	$1,080.00	8.000%
1,000	Semiannually	1,081.60	8.160
1,000	Quarterly	1,082.43	8.243
1,000	Monthly	1,083.00	8.300
1,000	Daily (365 days)	1,083.28	8.328
1,000	Continuously	1,083.29	8.329

Note: $1,000 invested for a year at these rates compounded annually would provide the same future values as those found in Column 3.

For example, if a savings plan offered a nominal interest rate of 8 percent compounded quarterly on a one-year investment, the effective annual interest rate would be

$$(1 + [.08/4])^4 - 1 = (1 + .02)^4 - 1 = .08243$$

Only if interest had been compounded annually would the effective annual interest rate have equaled the nominal rate of 8 percent.

Table 3-7 contains a number of *future values at the end of one year* for $1,000 earning a *nominal rate* of 8 percent for several different compounding periods. The table illustrates that the more numerous the compounding periods, the greater the future value of (and interest earned on) the deposit, and the greater the *effective annual interest rate*.

AMORTIZING A LOAN

An important use of present value concepts is in determining the payments required for an installment-type loan. The distinguishing feature of this loan is that it is repaid in equal periodic payments that include both interest and principal. These payments can be made monthly, quarterly, semiannually, or annually. Installment payments are prevalent in mortgage loans, auto loans, consumer loans, and certain business loans.

To illustrate with the simplest case of annual payments, suppose you borrow $22,000 at 12 percent compound annual interest to be repaid over the next six years. Equal installment payments are required at the end of each year. In addition, these payments must be sufficient in amount to repay the $22,000 together with providing the lender with a 12 percent return. To determine the annual payment, R, we set up the problem as follows:

$$\$22,000 = R\left[\sum_{t=1}^{6} 1/(1 + .12)^t\right]$$

$$= R(PVIFA_{12\%,6})$$

In Table IV in the Appendix at the end of the book, we find that the discount factor for a six-year annuity with a 12 percent interest rate is 4.111. Solving for R in the problem above, we have

$$\$22,000 = R(4.111)$$
$$R = \$22,000/4.111 = \mathbf{\$5,351}$$

Thus, annual payments of $5,351 will completely amortize (extinguish) a $22,000 loan in six years. Each payment consists partly of interest and partly of principal

TABLE 3-8
Amortization schedule for illustrated loan

END OF YEAR	(1) INSTALLMENT PAYMENT	(2) ANNUAL INTEREST $(4)_{t-1} \times .12$	(3) PRINCIPAL PAYMENT $(1) - (2)$	(4) PRINCIPAL AMOUNT OWING AT YEAR END $(4)_{t-1} - (3)$
0	—	—	—	$22,000
1	$ 5,351	$ 2,640	$ 2,711	19,289
2	5,351	2,315	3,036	16,253
3	5,351	1,951	3,400	12,853
4	5,351	1,542	3,809	9,044
5	5,351	1,085	4,266	4,778
6	5,351	573	4,778	0
	$32,106	$10,106	$22,000	

Amortization schedule
A table showing the repayment schedule of interest and principal necessary to pay off a loan by maturity.

repayment. The **amortization schedule** is shown in Table 3-8. We see that annual interest is determined by multiplying the principal amount outstanding at the beginning of the year by 12 percent. The amount of principal payment is simply the total installment payment minus the interest payment. Notice that the proportion of the installment payment composed of interest declines over time, whereas the proportion composed of principal increases. At the end of six years, a total of $22,000 in principal payments will have been made and the loan will be completely amortized. The breakdown between interest and principal is important because only interest is deductible as an expense for tax purposes.

SUMMARY TABLE OF KEY COMPOUND INTEREST FORMULAS

FLOW(S)	EQUATION	END OF BOOK TABLE
Single Amounts:		
$FV_n = P_0(1 + i)^n$	(3-4)	
$\quad = P_0(FVIF_{i,n})$	(3-5)	I
$PV_0 = FV_n[1/(1 + i)^n]$	(3-6)	
$\quad = FV_n(PVIF_{i,n})$	(3-7)	II
Annuities:		
$FVA_n = R([(1 + i)^n - 1]/i)$	(3-8)	
$\quad = R(FVIFA_{i,n})$	(3-9)	III
$PVA_n = R[(1 - [1/(1 + i)^n]/i]$	(3-10)	
$\quad = R(PVIFA_{i,n})$	(3-11)	IV
$FVAD_n = R(FVIFA_{i,n})(1 + i)$	(3-14)	III (adjusted)
$PVAD_n = R(PVIFA_{i,n-1} + 1)$	(3-15)	
$\quad = (1 + i)(R)(PVIFA_{i,n})$	(3-16)	IV (adjusted)

Part II Valuation

SUMMARY

- Most financial decisions, personal as well as business, involve the *time value of money*. We use the *rate of interest* to express the *time value of money*.
- *Simple interest* is interest paid (earned) on only the original amount, or principal, borrowed (lent).
- *Compound interest* is interest paid (earned) on any previous interest earned, as well as on the principal borrowed (lent). The concept of compound interest can be used to solve a wide variety of problems in finance.
- Two key concepts—*future value* and *present value*—underlie all compound interest problems. *Future value* is the value at some future time of a present amount of money, or a series of payments, evaluated at a given interest rate. *Present value* is the current value of a future amount of money, or a series of payments, evaluated at a given interest rate.
- It is very helpful to begin solving time value of money problems by first drawing a time line on which you position the relevant cash flows.
- An *annuity* is a series of equal payments or receipts occurring over a specified number of periods.
- There are some characteristics that should help you to identify and solve the various types of annuity problems:
  1. Present value of an ordinary annuity—cash flows occur at the *end* of each period, and *present value is calculated as of one period before the first cash flow*.
  2. Present value of an annuity due—cash flows occur at the *beginning* of each period, and *present value is calculated as of the first cash flow*.
  3. Future value of an ordinary annuity—cash flows occur at the *end* of each period, and *future value is calculated as of the last cash flow*.
  4. Future value of an annuity due—cash flows occur at the *beginning* of each period, and *future value is calculated as of one period after the last cash flow*.
- Various formulas were presented for solving for future values and present values of single amounts and of annuities. Mixed (uneven) cash-flow problems can always be solved by adjusting each flow individually and then summing the results. The ability to recognize certain patterns within mixed cash flows will allow you to take calculation shortcuts.
- To compare alternative investments having different compounding periods, it is often necessary to calculate their effective annual interest rates. The *effective annual interest rate* is the interest rate compounded annually that provides the same annual interest as the nominal rate does when compounded *m* times per year.
- Amortizing a loan involves determining the periodic payment necessary to reduce the principal amount to zero at maturity, while providing interest payments on the unpaid principal balance. The principal amount owed decreases at an increasing rate as payments are made.

QUESTIONS

1. What is simple interest?
2. What is compound interest? Why is it important?
3. What kinds of personal financial decisions have you made that involve compound interest?
4. What is an annuity? Is an annuity worth more or less than a lump sum payment received now that would be equal to the sum of all the future annuity payments?
5. What type of compounding would you prefer in your savings account? Why?
6. Contrast the calculation of future (terminal) value with the calculation of present value. What is the difference?
7. What is the advantage of using present value tables rather than formulas?
8. If you are scheduled to receive a certain sum of money five years from now but wish to sell your contract for its present value, which type of compounding would you prefer to be used in the calculation? Why?

9. The "Rule of 72" suggests that an amount will double in 12 years at a 6 percent compound annual rate or double in 6 years at a 12 percent annual rate. Is this a useful rule, and is it an accurate one?

10. Does present value decrease at a linear rate, at an increasing rate, or at a decreasing rate with the discount rate? Why?

11. Does present value decrease at a linear rate, at an increasing rate, or at a decreasing rate with the length of time in the future the payment is to be received? Why?

12. Sven Smorgasbord is 35 years old and is presently experiencing the "good" life. As a result, he anticipates that he will increase his weight at a rate of 3 percent a year. Presently he weighs 200 pounds. What will he weigh at age 60?

SELF-CORRECTION PROBLEMS

1. The following cash-flow streams need to be analyzed:

CASH-FLOW STREAM	END OF YEAR				
	1	2	3	4	5
W	$100	$200	$200	$300	$ 300
X	600	—	—	—	—
Y	—	—	—	—	1,200
Z	200	—	500	—	300

    a. Calculate the future (terminal) value of each stream at the end of year 5 with a compound annual interest rate of 10 percent.

    b. Compute the present value of each stream if the discount rate is 14 percent.

2. Muffin Megabucks is considering two different savings plans. The first plan would have her deposit $500 every six months, and she would receive interest at a 7 percent annual rate, compounded semiannually. Under the second plan she would deposit $1,000 every year with a rate of interest of 7.5 percent, compounded annually. The initial deposit with Plan 1 would be made six months from now and with Plan 2, one year hence.

    a. What is the future (terminal) value of the first plan at the end of 10 years?

    b. What is the future (terminal) value of the second plan at the end of 10 years?

    c. Which plan should Muffin use, assuming that her only concern is with the value of her savings at the end of 10 years?

    d. Would your answer change if the rate of interest on the second plan were 7 percent?

3. On a contract you have a choice of receiving $25,000 six years from now or $50,000 twelve years from now. At what implied compound annual interest rate should you be indifferent between the two contracts?

4. Emerson Cammack wishes to purchase an annuity contract that will pay him $7,000 a year for the rest of his life. The Philo Life Insurance Company figures that his life expectancy is 20 years, based on its actuary tables. The company imputes a compound annual interest rate of 6 percent in its annuity contracts.

    a. How much will Cammack have to pay for the annuity?

    b. How much would he have to pay if the interest rate were 8 percent?

5. You borrow $10,000 at 14 percent compound annual interest for four years. The loan is repayable in four equal annual installments payable at the end of each year.

    a. What is the annual payment that will completely *amortize* the loan over four years? (You may wish to round to the nearest dollar.)

    b. Of each equal payment, what is the amount of interest? The amount of loan principal? (*Hint:* In early years, the payment is composed largely of interest, whereas at the end it is mainly principal.)

6. Your late Uncle Vern's will entitles you to receive $1,000 at the end of every other year for the next two decades. The first cash flow is two years from now. At a 10 percent compound annual interest rate, what is the present value of this unusual cash-flow pattern? (Try to solve this problem in as few steps as you can.)

7. A bank offers you a seven-month certificate of deposit (CD) at a 7.06 percent annual rate that would provide a 7.25 percent effective annual yield. For the seven-month CD, is interest being compounded daily, weekly, monthly, or quarterly? And, by the way, having invested $10,000 in this CD, how much money would you receive when your CD matures in seven months? That is, what size check would the bank give you if you closed your account at the end of seven months?

8. A Dillonvale, Ohio, man saved pennies for 65 years. When he finally decided to cash them in, he had roughly 8 million of them (or $80,000 worth), filling 40 trash cans. On average, the man saved $1,230 worth of pennies a year. If he had deposited the pennies saved each year, at each year's end, into a savings account earning 5 percent compound annual interest, how much would he have had in this account after 65 years of saving? How much more "cents" (sense) would this have meant for our "penny saver" compared to simply putting his pennies into trash cans?

9. Xu Lin recently obtained a 10-year, $50,000 loan. The loan carries an 8 percent compound annual interest rate and calls for annual installment payments of $7,451.47 at the end of each of the next 10 years.
   a. How much (in dollars) of the first year's payment is *principal*?
   b. How much total interest will be paid over the life of the loan? (*Hint:* You do not need to construct a loan amortization table to answer this question. Some simple math is all you need.)

PROBLEMS

1. The following are exercises in future (terminal) values:
   a. At the end of three years, how much is an initial deposit of $100 worth, assuming a compound annual interest rate of (i) 100 percent? (ii) 10 percent? (iii) 0 percent?
   b. At the end of five years, how much is an initial $500 deposit followed by five year-end, annual $100 payments worth, assuming a compound annual interest rate of (i) 10 percent? (ii) 5 percent? (iii) 0 percent?
   c. At the end of six years, how much is an initial $500 deposit followed by five year-end, annual $100 payments worth, assuming a compound annual interest rate of (i) 10 percent? (ii) 5 percent? (iii) 0 percent?
   d. At the end of three years, how much is an initial $100 deposit worth, assuming a quarterly compounded annual interest rate of (i) 100 percent? (ii) 10 percent?
   e. Why do your answers to Part (d) differ from those to Part (a)?
   f. At the end of 10 years, how much is a $100 initial deposit worth, assuming an annual interest rate of 10 percent compounded (i) annually? (ii) semi-annually? (iii) quarterly? (iv) continuously?

2. The following are exercises in present values:
   a. $100 at the end of three years is worth how much today, assuming a discount rate of (i) 100 percent? (ii) 10 percent? (iii) 0 percent?
   b. What is the aggregate present value of $500 received at the end of each of the next three years, assuming a discount rate of (i) 4 percent? (ii) 25 percent?
   c. $100 is received at the end of one year, $500 at the end of two years, and $1,000 at the end of three years. What is the aggregate present value of these receipts, assuming a discount rate of (i) 4 percent? (ii) 25 percent?

d. $1,000 is to be received at the end of one year, $500 at the end of two years, and $100 at the end of three years. What is the aggregate present value of these receipts assuming a discount rate of (i) 4 percent? (ii) 25 percent?

e. Compare your solutions in Part (c) with those in Part (d) and explain the reason for the differences.

3. Joe Hernandez has inherited $25,000 and wishes to purchase an annuity that will provide him with a steady income over the next 12 years. He has heard that the local savings and loan association is currently paying 6 percent compound interest on an annual basis. If he were to deposit his funds, what year-end equal-dollar amount (to the nearest dollar) would he be able to withdraw annually such that he would have a zero balance after his last withdrawal 12 years from now?

4. You need to have $50,000 at the end of 10 years. To accumulate this sum, you have decided to save a certain amount at the *end* of each of the next 10 years and deposit it in the bank. The bank pays 8 percent interest compounded annually for long-term deposits. How much will you have to save each year (to the nearest dollar)?

5. Same as Problem 4 above, except that you deposit a certain amount at the *beginning* of each of the next 10 years. Now, how much will you have to save each year (to the nearest dollar)?

6. Vernal Equinox wishes to borrow $10,000 for three years. A group of individuals agrees to lend him this amount if he contracts to pay them $16,000 at the end of the three years. What is the implicit compound annual interest rate implied by this contract (to the nearest whole percent)?

7. You have been offered a note with four years to maturity, which will pay $3,000 at the end of each of the four years. The price of the note to you is $10,200. What is the implicit compound annual interest rate you will receive (to the nearest whole percent)?

8. Sales of the P.J. Cramer Company were $500,000 this year, and they are expected to grow at a compound rate of 20 percent for the next six years. What will be the sales figure at the end of each of the next six years?

9. The H & L Bark Company is considering the purchase of a debarking machine that is expected to provide cash flows as follows:

	END OF YEAR				
	1	2	3	4	5
Cash flow	$1,200	$2,000	$2,400	$1,900	$1,600

	END OF YEAR				
	6	7	8	9	10
Cash flow	$1,400	$1,400	$1,400	$1,400	$1,400

If the appropriate annual discount rate is 14 percent, what is the present value of this cash-flow stream?

10. Suppose you were to receive $1,000 at the end of 10 years. If your opportunity rate is 10 percent, what is the present value of this amount if interest is compounded (a) annually? (b) quarterly? (c) continuously?

11. In connection with the United States Bicentennial, the Treasury once contemplated offering a savings bond for $1,000 that would be worth $1 million in 100 years. Approximately what compound annual interest rate is implied by these terms?

12. Selyn Cohen is 63 years old and recently retired. He wishes to provide retirement income for himself and is considering an annuity contract with the Philo Life Insurance Company. Such a contract pays him an equal-dollar amount each year that he lives. For this cash-flow stream, he must put up a specific amount of money at the beginning. According to actuary tables, his life expectancy is

15 years, and that is the duration on which the insurance company bases its calculations regardless of how long he actually lives.

    a. If Philo Life uses a compound annual interest rate of 5 percent in its calculations, what must Cohen pay at the outset for an annuity to provide him with $10,000 per year? (Assume that the expected annual payments are at the end of each of the 15 years.)

    b. What would be the purchase price if the compound annual interest rate is 10 percent?

    c. Cohen had $30,000 to put into an annuity. How much would he receive each year if the insurance company uses a 5 percent compound annual interest rate in its calculations? A 10 percent compound annual interest rate?

13. The Happy Hang Glide Company is purchasing a building and has obtained a $190,000 mortgage loan for 20 years. The loan bears a compound annual interest rate of 17 percent and calls for equal annual installment payments at the end of each of the 20 years. What is the amount of the annual payment?

14. Establish loan amortization schedules for the following loans to the nearest cent (see Table 3-8 for an example):

    a. A 36-month loan of $8,000 with equal installment payments at the end of each month. The interest rate is 1 percent per month.

    b. A 25-year mortgage loan of $184,000 at a 10 percent compound annual interest rate with equal installment payments at the end of each year.

15. You have borrowed $14,300 at a compound annual interest rate of 15 percent. You feel that you will be able to make annual payments of $3,000 per year on your loan. (Payments include both principal and interest.) How long will it be before the loan is entirely paid off (to the nearest year)?

16. Lost Dutchman Mines, Inc., is considering investing in Peru. It makes a bid to the government to participate in the development of a mine, the profits of which will be realized at the end of five years. The mine is expected to produce $5 million in cash to Lost Dutchman Mines at that time. Other than the bid at the outset, no other cash flows will occur, as the government will reimburse the company for all costs. If Lost Dutchman requires a nominal annual return of 20 percent (ignoring any tax consequences), what is the maximum bid it should make for the participation right if interest is compounded (a) annually? (b) semiannually? (c) quarterly? (d) continuously?

17. Earl E. Bird has decided to start saving for his retirement. Beginning on his twenty-first birthday, Earl plans to invest $2,000 each birthday into a savings investment earning a 7 percent compound annual rate of interest. He will continue this savings program for a total of 10 years and then stop making payments. But his savings will continue to compound at 7 percent for 35 more years, until Earl retires at age 65. Ivana Waite also plans to invest $2,000 a year, on each birthday, at 7 percent, and will do so for a total of 35 years. However, she will not begin her contributions until her thirty-first birthday. How much will Earl's and Ivana's savings programs be worth at the retirement age of 65? Who is better off financially at retirement, and by how much?

18. When you were born, your dear old Aunt Minnie promised to deposit $1,000 in a savings account for you on each and every one of your birthdays, beginning with your first. The savings account bears a 5 percent compound annual rate of interest. You have just turned 25 and want all the cash. However, it turns out that dear old (forgetful) Aunt Minnie made no deposits on your fifth, seventh, and eleventh birthdays. How much is in the account now—on your twenty-fifth birthday?

19. Assume that you will be opening a savings account today by depositing $100,000. The savings account pays 5 percent compound annual interest, and this rate is assumed to remain in effect for all future periods. Four years from today you will withdraw **R** dollars. You will continue to make additional annual withdrawals of **R** dollars for a while longer—making your last withdrawal at the end of year 9—to achieve the following pattern of cash flows over time. (*Note:* Today is time period zero; one year from today is the end of time period 1; etc.)

Cash withdrawals at the END of year . . .

How large must **R** be to leave you with exactly a zero balance after your final **R** withdrawal is made at the end of year 9? (*Tip:* making use of an annuity table or formula will make your work a lot easier!)

20. Suppose that an investment promises to pay a nominal 9.6 percent annual rate of interest. What is the *effective annual interest rate* on this investment assuming that interest is compounded (a) annually? (b) semiannually? (c) quarterly? (d) monthly? (e) daily (365 days)? (f) continuously? (*Note:* Report your answers accurate to four decimal places—e.g., .0987 or 9.87%.)

21. "Want to win a million dollars? Here's how. . . . One winner, chosen at random from all entries, will win a $1,000,000 annuity." That was the statement announcing a contest on the World Wide Web. The contest rules described the "million-dollar prize" in greater detail: "40 annual payments of $25,000 each, which will result in a total payment of $1,000,000. The first payment will be made January 1; subsequent payments will be made each January thereafter." Using a compound annual interest rate of 8 percent, what is the present value of this "million-dollar prize" as of the first installment on January 1?

22. It took roughly 14 years for the Dow Jones Average of 30 Industrial Stocks to go from 1,000 to 2,000. To double from 2,000 to 4,000 took only 8 years, and to go from 4,000 to 8,000 required roughly 2 years. To the nearest whole percent, what compound annual growth rates are implicit in these three index-doubling milestones?

SOLUTIONS TO SELF-CORRECTION PROBLEMS

1. **a.** Future (terminal) value of each cash flow and total future value of each stream are as follows (using Table I in the end-of-book Appendix):

CASH-FLOW STREAM	FV_5 FOR INDIVIDUAL CASH FLOWS RECEIVED AT END OF YEAR					TOTAL FUTURE VALUE
	1	2	3	4	5	
W	$146.40	$266.20	$242.00	$330.00	$ 300.00	**$1,284.60**
X	878.40	—	—	—	—	**878.40**
Y	—	—	—	—	1,200.00	**1,200.00**
Z	292.80	—	605.00	—	300.00	**1,197.80**

b. Present value of each cash flow and total present value of each stream (using Table II in the end-of-book Appendix):

CASH-FLOW STREAM	PV_0 FOR INDIVIDUAL CASH FLOWS RECEIVED AT END OF YEAR					TOTAL PRESENT VALUE
	1	2	3	4	5	
W	$ 87.70	$153.80	$135.00	$177.60	$155.70	**$709.80**
X	526.20	—	—	—	—	**526.20**
Y	—	—	—	—	622.80	**622.80**
Z	175.40	—	337.50	—	155.70	**668.60**

2. a. FV_{10} Plan 1 $= \$500(FVIFA_{3.5\%,20})$
$$= \$500([(1 + .035)^{20} - 1]/[.035]) = \mathbf{\$14,139.84}$$

b. FV_{10} Plan 2 $= \$1,000(FVIFA_{7.5\%,10})$
$$= \$1,000\{[(1 + .075)^{10} - 1]/[.075]\} = \mathbf{\$14,147.09}$$

c. Plan 2 would be preferred by a slight margin—$7.25.

d. FV_{10} Plan 2 $= \$1,000(FVIFA_{7\%,10})$
$$= \$1,000\{[(1 + .07)^{10} - 1]/[.07]\} = \mathbf{\$13,816.45}$$

Now, Plan 1 would be preferred by a nontrivial $323.37 margin.

3. Indifference implies that you could reinvest the $25,000 receipt for 6 years at X% to provide an equivalent $50,000 cash flow in year 12. In short, $25,000 would double in 6 years. Using the "Rule of 72," 72/6 = **12%**.

Alternatively, note that $50,000 = \$25,000(FVIF_{X\%,6})$. Therefore, $(FVIF_{X\%,6})$ $= \$50,000/\$25,000 = 2$. In Table I in the Appendix at the end of the book, the interest factor for 6 years at 12 percent is 1.974 and that for 13 percent is 2.082. Interpolating, we have

$$X\% = 12\% + \frac{2.000 - 1.974}{2.082 - 1.974} = \mathbf{12.24\%}$$

as the interest rate implied in the contract.

For an even more accurate answer, recognize that $FVIF_{X\%,6}$ can also be written as $(1 + i)^6$. Then, we can solve directly for i (and $X\% = i[100]$) as follows:

$$(1 + i)^6 = 2$$
$$(1 + i) = 2^{1/6} = 2^{0.1667} = 1.1225$$
$$i = .1225 \text{ or } X\% = \mathbf{12.25\%}$$

4. a. $PV_0 = \$7,000(PVIFA_{6\%,20}) = \$7,000(11.470) = \mathbf{\$80,290}$

b. $PV_0 = \$7,000(PVIFA_{8\%,20}) = \$7,000(19.818) = \mathbf{\$68,726}$

5. a. $PV_0 = \$10,000 = R(PVIFA_{14\%,4}) = R(2.914)$

Therefore, $R = \$10,000/2.914 = \mathbf{\$3,432}$ (to the nearest dollar).

b.

END OF YEAR	(1) INSTALLMENT PAYMENT	(2) ANNUAL INTEREST $(4)_{t-1} \times .14$	(3) PRINCIPAL PAYMENT $(1) - (2)$	(4) PRINCIPAL AMOUNT OWING AT YEAR END $(4)_{t-1} - (3)$
0	—	—	—	$10,000
1	$ 3,432	**$1,400**	$ 2,032	7,968
2	3,432	1,116	2,316	5,652
3	3,432	791	2,641	3,011
4	3,432	421	3,011	0
	$13,728	**$3,728**	**$10,000**	

6. When we draw a picture of the problem, we get $1,000 at the end of every even-numbered year for years 1 through 20:

Tip: Convert $1,000 every 2 years into an *equivalent annual annuity* (i.e., an annuity that would provide an equivalent present or future value to the actual cash flows) pattern. Solving for a 2-year annuity that is equivalent to a future $1,000 to be received at the end of year 2, we get

$$FVA_2 = \$1{,}000 = R(FVIFA_{10\%,2}) = R(2.100)$$

Therefore, $R = \$1{,}000/2.100 = \$476.19$. Replacing every $1,000 with an equivalent two-year annuity gives us $476.19 for 20 years.

| | 0 | 1 | 2 | 3 | 4 | 19 | 20 |

$476.19 $476.19 $476.19 $476.19 $476.19 $476.19

$$PVA_{20} = \$476.19(PVIFA_{10\%,20}) = \$476.19(8.514) = \textbf{\$4{,}054.28}$$

7. Effective annual interest rate $= (1 + [i/m])^m - 1$
$$= (1 + [.0706/4])^4 - 1 = .07249 \text{ (approximately 7.25\%)}$$

   Therefore, we have *quarterly compounding*. And, investing $10,000 at 7.06 percent compounded quarterly for seven months (*Note:* Seven months equals $2\frac{1}{3}$ quarter periods), we get

$$\$10{,}000(1 + [.0706/4])^{2.3\bar{3}} = \$10{,}000(1.041669) = \textbf{\$10{,}416.69}$$

8. $FVA_{65} = \$1{,}230(FVIFA_{5\%,65}) = \$1{,}230[([1 + .05]^{65} - 1)/(.05)]$
$$= \$1{,}230(456.798) = \textbf{\$561{,}861.54}$$

   Our "penny saver" would have been better off by ($561,861.54 − $80,000) = **$481,861.54**—or **48,186,154 pennies**—by depositing the pennies saved each year into a savings account earning 5 percent compound annual interest.

9. **a.** $50,000(.08) = $4,000 interest payment
   $7,451.47 − $4,000 = **$3,451.47 principal payment**

   b. Total installment payments − total principal payments = total interest payments

   | $74,514.70 | − | $50,000 | = | **$24,514.70** |

SELECTED REFERENCES

Rich, Steven P., and John T. Rose. "Interest Rate Concepts and Terminology in Introductory Finance Textbooks." *Financial Practice and Education* 7 (Spring–Summer 1997), 113–21.

Shao, Stephen P., and Lawrence P. Shao. *Mathematics for Management and Finance,* 8th ed. Cincinnati, OH: South-Western, 1998.

Trainer, Richard D.C. *The Arithmetic of Interest Rates.* Federal Reserve Bank of New York. (Available free of charge from the Public Information Department, Federal Reserve Bank of New York, 33 Liberty Street, New York, NY 10045.)

Chapter 4

The Valuation of Long-Term Securities

DISTINCTIONS AMONG VALUATION CONCEPTS
Liquidation Value versus Going-Concern Value • Book Value
versus Market Value • Market Value versus Intrinsic Value
BOND VALUATION
Perpetual Bonds • Bonds with a Finite Maturity
PREFERRED STOCK VALUATION
COMMON STOCK VALUATION
Are Dividends the Foundation? • Dividend Discount Models
RATES OF RETURN (OR YIELDS)
Yield to Maturity (YTM) on Bonds • Yield on Preferred
Stock • Yield on Common Stock
SUMMARY TABLE OF KEY PRESENT VALUE FORMULAS
FOR VALUING LONG-TERM SECURITIES
SUMMARY
QUESTIONS
SELF-CORRECTION PROBLEMS
PROBLEMS
SOLUTIONS TO SELF-CORRECTION PROBLEMS
SELECTED REFERENCES

> *What is a cynic? A man who knows the price of everything
> and the value of nothing.*
>
> —OSCAR WILDE

In the last chapter we discussed the *time value of money* and explored the wonders of compound interest. We are now able to apply these concepts to determining the value of different securities. In particular, we are concerned with the valuation of the firm's long-term securities—bonds, preferred stock, and common stock (though the principles discussed apply to other securities as well). Valuation will, in fact, underlie much of the later development of the book. Because the major decisions of a company are all interrelated in their effect on valuation, we must understand how investors value the financial instruments of a company.

DISTINCTIONS AMONG VALUATION CONCEPTS

The term *value* can mean different things to different people. Therefore, we need to be precise in how we both use and interpret this term. Let's look briefly at the differences that exist among some of the major concepts of value.

Liquidation Value versus Going-Concern Value

Liquidation value is the amount of money that could be realized if an asset or a group of assets (e.g., a firm) is sold separately from its operating organization. This value is in marked contrast to the **going-concern value** of a firm, which is the amount the firm could be sold for as a continuing operating business. These two values are rarely equal, and sometimes a company is actually worth more dead than alive.

The security valuation models that we will discuss in this chapter will generally assume that we are dealing with *going concerns*—operating firms able to generate positive cash flows to security investors. In instances where this assumption is not appropriate (e.g., impending bankruptcy), the firm's liquidation value will have a major role in determining the value of the firm's financial securities.

Liquidation value The amount of money that could be realized if an asset or a group of assets (e.g., a firm) is sold separately from its operating organization.

Going-concern value The amount a firm could be sold for as a continuing operating business.

Book Value versus Market Value

The **book value** of an *asset* is the accounting value of the asset—the asset's cost minus its accumulated depreciation. The book value of a *firm*, on the other hand, is equal to the dollar difference between the firm's total assets and its liabilities and preferred stock as listed on its balance sheet. Because *book value* is based on historical values, it may bear little relationship to an asset's or firm's *market value*.

In general, the **market value** of an asset is simply the market price at which the asset (or a similar asset) trades in an open marketplace. For a firm, market value is often viewed as being the higher of the firm's liquidation or going-concern value.

Book value (1) An *asset:* the accounting value of an asset—the asset's cost minus its accumulated depreciation; (2) a *firm:* total assets minus liabilities and preferred stock as listed on the balance sheet.

Market value The market price at which an asset trades.

Market Value versus Intrinsic Value

Based on our general definition for market value, the market value of a security is the market price of the security. For an actively traded security, it would be the last reported price at which the security was sold. For an inactively traded security, an estimated market price would be needed.

The **intrinsic value** of a security, on the other hand, is what the price of a security *should be* if properly priced based on all factors bearing on valuation—assets, earnings, future prospects, management, and so on. In short, the intrinsic value of a security is its economic value. If markets are reasonably efficient and informed, the current market price of a security should fluctuate closely around its intrinsic value.

Intrinsic value The price a security "ought to have" based on all factors bearing on valuation.

The valuation approach taken in this chapter is one of determining a security's *intrinsic value*—what the security ought to be worth based on hard facts. This value is the present value of the cash-flow stream provided to the investor, discounted at a required rate of return appropriate for the risk involved. With this general valuation concept in mind, we are now able to explore in more detail the valuation of specific types of securities.

BOND VALUATION

Bond A long-term debt instrument issued by a corporation or government.

A **bond** is a security that pays a stated amount of interest to the investor, period after period, until it is finally retired by the issuing company. Before we can fully understand the valuation of such a security, certain terms must be discussed. For one thing, a bond has a **face value.**[1] This value is usually $1,000 per bond. The bond almost always has a stated *maturity*, which is the time when the company is obligated to pay the bondholder the face value of the instrument. Finally, the **coupon rate,** or nominal annual rate of interest, is stated on the bond's face.[2] If, for example, the coupon rate is 12 percent on a $1,000-face-value bond, the company pays the holder $120 each year until the bond matures.

Face value The stated value of an asset. In the case of a bond, the face value is usually $1,000.

Coupon rate The stated rate of interest on a bond; the annual interest payment divided by the bond's face value.

In valuing a bond, or any security for that matter, we are primarily concerned with discounting, or capitalizing, the cash-flow stream that the security holder would receive over the life of the instrument. The terms of a bond establish a legally binding payment pattern at the time the bond is originally issued. This pattern consists of the payment of a stated amount of interest over a given number of years coupled with a final payment, when the bond matures, equal to the bond's face value. The discount, or capitalization, rate applied to the cash-flow stream will differ among bonds depending on the risk structure of the bond issue. In general, however, this rate can be thought to be composed of the risk-free rate plus a premium for risk. (You may remember that we introduced the idea of a market-imposed "trade-off" between risk and return in Chapter 2. We will have more to say about risk and required rates of return in the next chapter.)

Perpetual Bonds

Consol A bond that never matures; a perpetuity in the form of a bond.

The first (and easiest) place to start determining the value of bonds is with a unique class of bonds that never matures. These are indeed rare, but they help illustrate the valuation technique in its simplest form. Originally issued by Great Britain after the Napoleonic Wars to consolidate debt issues, the British **consol** (short for *consolidated annuities*) is one such example. This bond carries the obligation of the British government to pay a fixed interest payment in perpetuity.

The present value of a perpetual bond would simply be equal to the capitalized value of an infinite stream of interest payments. If a bond promises a fixed annual payment of I forever, its present (intrinsic) value, V, at the investor's required rate of return for this debt issue, k_d, is

---

[1]Much like criminals, many of the terms used in finance are also known under a number of different aliases. Thus, a bond's *face value* is also known as its *par value,* or *principal*. Like a good detective, you need to become familiar with the basic terms used in finance as well as their aliases.

[2]The term *coupon rate* comes from the detachable coupons that are affixed to *bearer bond* certificates, which, when presented to a paying agent or the issuer, entitle the holder to receive the interest due on that date. Nowadays, *registered bonds*, whose ownership is registered with the issuer, allow the registered owner to receive interest by check through the mail.

$$V = \frac{I}{(1 + k_d)^1} + \frac{I}{(1 + k_d)^2} + \cdots + \frac{I}{(1 + k_d)^\infty} \tag{4-1}$$

$$= \sum_{t=1}^{\infty} \frac{I}{(1 + k_d)^t}$$

$$= I(PVIFA_{k_d,\infty}) \tag{4-2}$$

which, from Chapter 3's discussion of perpetuities, we know should reduce to

$$V = I/k_d \tag{4-3}$$

Thus, the present value of a perpetual bond is simply the periodic interest payment divided by the appropriate discount rate per period. Suppose you could buy a bond that paid $50 a year forever. Assuming that your required rate of return for this type of bond is 12 percent, the present value of this security would be

$$V = \$50/.12 = \mathbf{\$416.67}$$

This is the amount that you would be willing to pay for this bond. If the market price is greater than this amount, however, you would not want to buy it.

BONDS WITH A FINITE MATURITY

Nonzero Coupon Bonds.　If a bond has a finite maturity, then we must consider not only the interest stream but also the terminal or maturity value (face value) in valuing the bond. The valuation equation for such a bond that pays interest at the end of each year is

$$V = \frac{I}{(1 + k_d)^1} + \frac{I}{(1 + k_d)^2} + \cdots + \frac{I}{(1 + k_d)^n} + \frac{MV}{(1 + k_d)^n}$$

$$= \sum_{t=1}^{n} \frac{I}{(1 + k_d)^t} + \frac{MV}{(1 + k_d)^n} \tag{4-4}$$

$$= I(PVIFA_{k_d,n}) + MV(PVIF_{k_d,n}) \tag{4-5}$$

where n is the number of years until final maturity and MV is the maturity value of the bond.

We might wish to determine the value of a $1,000-par-value bond with a 10 percent coupon and nine years to maturity. The coupon rate corresponds to interest payments of $100 a year. If our required rate of return on the bond is 12 percent, then

$$V = \frac{\$100}{(1.12)^1} + \frac{\$100}{(1.12)^2} + \cdots + \frac{\$100}{(1.12)^9} + \frac{\$1,000}{(1.12)^9}$$

$$= \$100(PVIFA_{12\%,9}) + \$1,000(PVIF_{12\%,9})$$

Referring to Table IV in the Appendix at the back of the book, we find that the present value interest factor of an annuity at 12 percent for nine periods is 5.328. Table II in the Appendix reveals under the 12 percent column that the present value interest factor for a single payment nine periods in the future is .361. Therefore, the value, V, of the bond is

$$V = \$100(5.328) + \$1,000(.361)$$

$$= \$532.80 + \$361.00 = \mathbf{\$893.80}$$

The interest payments have a present value of $532.80, whereas the principal payment at maturity has a present value of $360.00. (*Note:* All of these figures are *approximate* because the present value tables used are rounded to the third decimal place; the true present value of the bond is $893.44.)

If the appropriate discount rate is 8 percent instead of 12 percent, the valuation equation becomes

$$V = \frac{\$100}{(1.08)^1} + \frac{\$100}{(1.08)^2} + \dots + \frac{\$100}{(1.08)^9} + \frac{\$1,000}{(1.08)^9}$$

$$= \$100(PVIFA_{8\%,9}) + \$1,000(PVIF_{8\%,9})$$

Looking up the appropriate interest factors in Tables II and IV in the Appendix, we determine that

$$V = \$100(6.247) + \$1,000(.500)$$
$$= \$624.70 + \$500.00 = \mathbf{\$1,124.70}$$

In this case, the present value of the bond is in excess of its $1,000 par value because the required rate of return is less than the coupon rate. Investors would be willing to pay a *premium* to buy the bond. In the previous case, the required rate of return was greater than the coupon rate. As a result, the bond has a present value less than its par value. Investors would be willing to buy the bond only if it sold at a *discount* from par value. Now if the required rate of return equals the coupon rate, the bond has a present value equal to its par value, $1,000. More will be said about these concepts shortly when we discuss the behavior of bond prices.

Zero-coupon bond A bond that pays no interest but sells at a deep discount from its face value; it provides compensation to investors in the form of price appreciation.

Zero-Coupon Bonds.   A **zero-coupon bond** makes no periodic interest payments but instead is sold at a deep discount from its face value. Why buy a bond that pays no interest? The answer lies in the fact that the buyer of such a bond does receive a return. This return consists of the gradual increase (or appreciation) in the value of the security from its original, *below-face-value* purchase price until it is redeemed *at face value* on its maturity date.

The valuation equation for a zero-coupon bond is a truncated version of that used for a normal interest-paying bond. The "present value of interest payments" component is lopped off, and we are left with value being determined solely by the "present value of principal payment at maturity," or

$$V = \frac{MV}{(1 + k_d)^n} \tag{4-6}$$

$$= MV(PVIF_{k_d,n}) \tag{4-7}$$

Suppose that Pace Enterprises issues a zero-coupon bond having a 10-year maturity and a $1,000 face value. If your required return is 12 percent, then

$$V = \frac{\$1,000}{(1.12)^{10}}$$

$$= \$1,000 \, (PVIF_{12\%,10})$$

Using Table II in the Appendix, we find that the present value interest factor for a single payment 10 periods in the future at 12 percent is .322. Therefore,

$$V = \$1,000(.322) = \mathbf{\$322}$$

If you could purchase this bond for $322 and redeem it 10 years later for $1,000, your initial investment would thus provide you with a 12 percent compound annual rate of return.

Semiannual Compounding of Interest. Although some bonds (typically those issued in European markets) make interest payments once a year, most bonds issued in the United States pay interest twice a year. As a result, it is necessary to modify our bond valuation equations to account for compounding twice a year.[3] For example, Eqs. (4-4) and (4-5) would be changed as follows

$$V = \sum_{t=1}^{2n} \frac{I/2}{(1 + k_d/2)^t} + \frac{MV}{(1 + k_d/2)^{2n}} \tag{4-8}$$

$$= (I/2)(PVIFA_{k_d/2,2n}) + MV(PVIF_{k_d/2,2n}) \tag{4-9}$$

where k_d is the nominal annual required rate of interest, $I/2$ is the semiannual coupon payment, and $2n$ is the number of semiannual periods until maturity.

Take Note

> Notice that semiannual discounting is applied to both the semiannual interest payments *and* the lump-sum maturity value payment. Though it may seem inappropriate to use semiannual discounting on the maturity value, it isn't. The assumption of semiannual discounting, once taken, applies to all inflows.

To illustrate, if the 10 percent coupon bonds of U.S. Blivet Corporation have 12 years to maturity and our nominal annual required rate of return is 14 percent, the value of one $1,000-par-value bond is

$$V = (\$50)(PVIFA_{7\%,24}) + \$1,000(PVIF_{7\%,24})$$

$$= (\$50)(11.469) + \$1,000(.197) = \textbf{\$770.45}$$

Rather than having to solve for value by hand, professional bond traders often turn to bond value tables. Given the maturity, coupon rate, and required return, one can look up the present value. Similarly, given any three of the four factors, one can look up the fourth. Also, some specialized calculators are programmed to compute bond values and yields, given the inputs mentioned. In your professional life you may very well end up using these tools when working with bonds.

TIP•TIP•TIP•TIP•TIP•TIP•TIP•TIP•TIP•TIP•TIP

> Remember, when you use bond Eqs. (4-4), (4-5), (4-6), (4-7), (4-8), and (4-9), the variable *MV* is equal to the bond's *maturity value,* **not** its current *market value.*

PREFERRED STOCK VALUATION

Preferred stock A type of stock that promises a (usually) fixed dividend, but at the discretion of the board of directors. It has preference over common stock in the payment of dividends and claims on assets.

Most **preferred stock** pays a fixed dividend at regular intervals. The features of this financial instrument are discussed in Chapter 20. Preferred stock has no stated maturity date and, given the fixed nature of its payments, is similar to a perpetual bond. It is not surprising, then, that we use the same general approach applied to valuing a

---

[3]Even with a zero-coupon bond, the pricing convention among bond professionals is to use semiannual rather than annual compounding. This provides consistent comparisons with interest-bearing bonds.

perpetual bond to the valuation of preferred stock.[4] Thus, the present value of preferred stock is

$$V = D_p/k_p \qquad \text{(4-10)}$$

where D_p is the stated annual dividend per share of preferred stock and k_p is the appropriate discount rate. If Margana Cipher Corporation had a 9 percent, $100-par-value preferred stock issue outstanding and your required return was 14 percent on this investment, its value per share to you would be

$$V = \$9/.14 = \textbf{\$64.29}$$

COMMON STOCK VALUATION

Common stock Securities that represent the ultimate ownership (and risk) position in a corporation.

The theory surrounding the valuation of **common stock** has undergone profound change during the last few decades. It is a subject of considerable controversy, and no one method for valuation is universally accepted. Still, in recent years there has

---

[4]Virtually all preferred stock issues have a call feature (a provision that allows the company to force retirement), and many are eventually retired. When valuing a preferred stock that is expected to be called, we can apply a modified version of the formula used for valuing a bond with a finite maturity; the periodic preferred dividends replace the periodic interest payments and the "call price" replaces the bond maturity value in Eqs. (4-4) and (4-5), and all the payments are discounted at a rate appropriate to the preferred stock in question.

emerged growing acceptance of the idea that individual common stocks should be analyzed as part of a total portfolio of common stocks that the investor might hold. In other words, investors are not as concerned with whether a particular stock goes up or down as they are with what happens to the overall value of their portfolios. This concept has important implications for determining the required rate of return on a security. We shall explore this issue in the next chapter. First, however, we need to focus on the size and pattern of the returns to the common stock investor. Unlike bond and preferred stock cash flows, which are contractually stated, much more uncertainty surrounds the future stream of returns connected with common stock.

Are Dividends the Foundation?

When valuing bonds and preferred stock, we determined the discounted value of all the cash distributions made by the firm to the investor. In a similar fashion, the value of a share of common stock can be viewed as the discounted value of all expected cash dividends provided by the issuing firm until the end of time.[5] In other words,

$$V = \frac{D_1}{(1 + k_e)^1} + \frac{D_2}{(1 + k_e)^2} + \dots + \frac{D_\infty}{(1 + k_e)^\infty} \tag{4-11}$$

$$= \sum_{t=1}^{\infty} \frac{D_t}{(1 + k_e)^t} \tag{4-12}$$

where D_t is the cash dividend at the end of time period t and k_e is the investor's required return, or capitalization rate, for this equity investment. This seems consistent with what we have been doing so far.

But what if we plan to own the stock for only two years? In this case, our model becomes

$$V = \frac{D_1}{(1 + k_e)^1} + \frac{D_2}{(1 + k_e)^2} + \frac{P_2}{(1 + k_e)^2}$$

where P_2 is the expected sales price of our stock at the end of two years. This assumes that investors will be willing to buy our stock two years from now. In turn, these future investors will base their judgments of what the stock is worth on expectations of future dividends and a future selling price (or terminal value). And so the process goes through successive investors.

Note that it is the expectation of future dividends and a future selling price, which itself is based on expected future dividends, that gives value to the stock. Cash dividends are all that stockholders, as a whole, receive from the issuing company. Consequently, the foundation for the valuation of common stock must be dividends. These are construed broadly to mean any cash distribution to shareholders, including share repurchases. (See Chapter 18 for a discussion of share repurchase as part of the overall dividend decision.)

The logical question to raise at this time is, why do the stocks of companies that pay no dividends have positive, often quite high, values? The answer is that investors expect to sell the stock in the future at a price higher than they paid for it. Instead of dividend income plus a terminal value, they rely only on the terminal value. In turn, terminal value depends on the expectations of the marketplace viewed from this terminal point. The ultimate expectation is that the firm will eventually pay dividends, either regular or liquidating, and that future investors will

---

[5]This model was first developed by John B. Williams, *The Theory of Investment Value* (Cambridge, MA: Harvard University Press, 1938). And, as Williams so aptly put it in poem form, "A cow for her milk/A hen for her eggs/And a stock, by heck/For her dividends."

receive a company-provided cash return on their investment. In the interim, investors are content with the expectation that they will be able to sell their stock at a subsequent time, because there will be a market for it. In the meantime, the company is reinvesting earnings and, everyone hopes, enhancing its future earning power and ultimate dividends.

Dividend Discount Models

Dividend discount models are designed to compute the intrinsic value of a share of common stock under specific assumptions as to the expected growth pattern of future dividends and the appropriate discount rate to employ. Merrill Lynch, CS First Boston, and a number of other investment banks routinely make such calculations based on their own particular models and estimates. What follows is an examination of such models, beginning with the simplest one.

Constant Growth. Future dividends of a company could jump all over the place; but, if dividends are expected to grow at a constant rate, what implications does this hold for our basic stock valuation approach? If this constant rate is g, then Eq. (4-11) becomes

$$V = \frac{D_0(1 + g)}{(1 + k_e)^1} + \frac{D_0(1 + g)^2}{(1 + k_e)^2} + \ldots + \frac{D_0(1 + g)^\infty}{(1 + k_e)^\infty} \qquad \textbf{(4-13)}$$

where D_0 is the present dividend per share. Thus, the dividend expected at the end of period n is equal to the most recent dividend times the compound growth factor, $(1 + g)^n$. This may not look like much of an improvement over Eq. (4-11). However, assuming that k_e is greater than g (a reasonable assumption because a dividend growth rate that is always greater than the capitalization rate would imply an infinite stock value), Eq. (4-13) can be reduced to[6]

$$V = D_1/(k_e - g) \qquad \textbf{(4-14)}$$

Rearranging, the investor's required return can be expressed as

$$k_e = (D_1/V) + g \qquad \textbf{(4-15)}$$

The critical assumption in this valuation model is that dividends per share are expected to grow perpetually at a compound rate of g. For many companies this

---

[6]If we multiply both sides of Eq. (4-13) by $(1 + k_e)/(1 + g)$ and subtract Eq. (4-13) from the product, we get

$$\frac{V(1 + k_e)}{(1 + g)} - V = D_0 - \frac{D_0(1 + g)^\infty}{(1 + k_e)^\infty}$$

Because we assume that k_e is greater than g, the second term on the right-hand side approaches zero. Consequently,

$$V\left[\frac{(1 + k_e)}{(1 + g)} - 1\right] = D_0$$

$$V\left[\frac{(1 + k_e) - (1 + g)}{(1 + g)}\right] = D_0$$

$$V(k_e - g) = D_0(1 + g) = D_1$$

$$V = D_1/(k_e - g)$$

This model is sometimes called the "Gordon Dividend Valuation Model" after Myron J. Gordon, who developed it from the pioneering work done by John Williams. See Myron J. Gordon, *The Investment, Financing, and Valuation of the Corporation* (Homewood, IL: Richard D. Irwin, 1962).

assumption may be a fair approximation of reality. To illustrate the use of Eq. (4-14), suppose that LKN, Inc.'s dividend per share at $t = 1$ is expected to be $4, that it is expected to grow at a 6 percent rate forever, and that the appropriate discount rate is 14 percent. The value of one share of LKN stock would be

$$V = \$4/(.14 - .06) = \textbf{\$50}$$

For companies in the mature stage of their life cycle, the perpetual growth model is often reasonable.

TIP•TIP•TIP•TIP•TIP•TIP•TIP•TIP•TIP•TIP•TIP

A common mistake made in using Eqs. (4-14) and (4-15) is to use, incorrectly, the firm's most recent annual dividend for the variable D_1 instead of the annual dividend expected by the end of the coming year.

Conversion to an Earnings Multiplier Approach   With the constant growth model, we can easily convert from dividend valuation, Eq. (4-14), to valuation based on an earnings multiplier approach. The idea is that investors often think in terms of how many dollars they are willing to pay for a dollar of future expected earnings. Assume that a company retains a constant proportion of its earnings each year; call it b. The dividend-payout ratio (dividends per share divided by earnings per share) would also be constant. Therefore,

$$(1 - b) = D_1/E_1 \tag{4-16}$$

and

$$(1 - b)E_1 = D_1$$

where E_1 is expected earnings per share in period 1. Equation (4-14) can then be expressed as

$$V = [(1 - b)E_1]/(k_e - g) \tag{4-17}$$

where value is now based on expected earnings in period 1. In our earlier example, suppose that LKN, Inc., has a retention rate of 40 percent and earnings per share for period 1 are expected to be $6.67. Therefore,

$$V = [(.60)\$6.67]/(.14 - .06) = \textbf{\$50}$$

Rearranging Eq. (4-17), we get

$$\text{Earnings multiplier} = V/E_1 = (1 - b)/(k_e - g) \tag{4-18}$$

Equation (4-18) thus gives us the highest multiple of expected earnings that the investor would be willing to pay for the security. In our example,

$$\text{Earnings multiplier} = (1 - .40)/(.14 - .06) = \textbf{7.5 times}$$

Thus, expected earnings of $6.67 coupled with an earnings multiplier of 7.5 values our common stock at $50 a share ($6.67 × 7.5 = $50). But remember, the foundation for this alternative approach to common stock valuation was nevertheless our constant growth dividend discount model.

No Growth.   A special case of the constant growth dividend model calls for an expected dividend growth rate, g, of zero. Here the assumption is that dividends will be maintained at their current level forever. In this case, Eq. (4-14) reduces to

$$V = D_1/k_e \qquad \text{(4-19)}$$

Not many stocks can be expected simply to maintain a constant dividend forever. However, when a stable dividend is expected to be maintained for a long period of time, Eq. (4-19) can provide a good approximation of value.[7]

Growth Phases. When the pattern of expected dividend growth is such that a constant growth model is not appropriate, modifications of Eq. (4-13) can be used. A number of valuation models are based on the premise that firms may exhibit above-normal growth for a number of years (g may even be larger than k_e during this phase), but eventually the growth rate will taper off. Thus, the transition might well be from a presently above-normal growth rate to one that is considered normal. If dividends per share are expected to grow at a 10 percent compound rate for five years and thereafter at a 6 percent rate, Eq. (4-13) becomes

$$V = \sum_{t=1}^{5} \frac{D_0(1.10)^t}{(1+k_e)^t} + \sum_{t=6}^{\infty} \frac{D_5(1.06)^{t-5}}{(1+k_e)^t} \qquad \text{(4-20)}$$

Note that the growth in dividends in the second phase uses the expected dividend in period 5 as its foundation. Therefore, the growth-term exponent is $t - 5$, which means that the exponent in period 6 equals 1, in period 7 it equals 2, and so forth. This second phase is nothing more than a constant growth model following a period of above-normal growth. We can make use of that fact to rewrite Eq. (4-20) as follows:

$$V = \sum_{t=1}^{5} \frac{D_0(1.10)^t}{(1+k_e)^t} + \left[\frac{1}{(1+k_e)^5}\right]\left[\frac{D_6}{(k_e - .06)}\right] \qquad \text{(4-21)}$$

---

[7]AT&T is one example of a firm that maintained a stable dividend for an extended period of time. For 36 years, from 1922 until December 1958, AT&T paid $9 a year in dividends.

TABLE 4-1
Two-phase growth and common stock valuation calculations

PHASE 1: PRESENT VALUE OF DIVIDENDS TO BE RECEIVED OVER FIRST 5 YEARS					
END OF YEAR	PRESENT VALUE CALCULATION (DIVIDEND	$\times$	$PVIF_{14\%,t}$)		PRESENT VALUE OF DIVIDEND
1	$2(1.10)^1 = $2.20	$\times$	.877	=	$1.93
2	$2(1.10)^2 = $ 2.42	$\times$	.769	=	1.86
3	$2(1.10)^3 = $ 2.66	$\times$	.675	=	1.80
4	$2(1.10)^4 = $ 2.93	$\times$	.592	=	1.73
5	$2(1.10)^5 = $ 3.22	$\times$	.519	=	1.67
	or $\left[\sum_{t=1}^{5} \dfrac{\$2(1.10)^t}{(1.14)^t}\right]$			=	**$8.99**

PHASE 2: PRESENT VALUE OF CONSTANT GROWTH COMPONENT	
Dividend at the end of year 6	= $3.22(1.06) = $3.41
Value of stock at the end of year 5	= $D_6/(k_e - g) = $3.41/(.14 - .06) = $42.63
Present value of $42.63 at end of year 5	= ($42.63)($PVIF_{14\%,5}$)
	= ($42.63)(.519) = **$22.13**

PRESENT VALUE OF STOCK
$V = $8.99 + $22.13 = **$31.12**

If the current dividend, D_0, is \$2 per share and the required rate of return, k_e, is 14 percent, we could solve for V. (See Table 4-1 for specifics.)

$$V = \sum_{t=1}^{5} \frac{\$2(1.10)^t}{(1.14)^t} + \left[\frac{1}{(1.14)^5}\right]\left[\frac{\$3.41}{(.14 - .06)}\right]$$

$$= \$8.99 + \$22.13 = \textbf{\$31.12}$$

The transition from an above-normal rate of dividend growth could be specified as more gradual than the two-phase approach just illustrated. We might expect dividends to grow at a 10 percent rate for five years, followed by an 8 percent rate for the next five years and a 6 percent growth rate thereafter. The more growth segments that are added, the more closely the growth in dividends will approach a curvilinear function. But no firm can grow at an above-normal rate forever. Typically, companies tend to grow at a very high rate initially, after which their growth opportunities slow down to a rate that is normal for companies in general. If maturity is reached, the growth rate may stop altogether.

RATES OF RETURN (OR YIELDS)

So far, this chapter has illustrated how the valuation of any long-term financial instrument involves a capitalization of that security's income stream by a discount rate (or *required rate of return*) appropriate for that security's risk. If we replace intrinsic value (V) in our valuation equations with the market price (P_0) of the security, we can then solve for the *market required rate of return*. This rate, which sets the discounted value of the expected cash inflows equal to the security's current market price, is also referred to as the security's (market) *yield*. Depending on the security being analyzed, the expected cash inflows may be interest payments, repayment of principal, or dividend payments. It is important to recognize that only when the intrinsic value of a security to an investor equals the security's market value (price) would the investor's required rate of return equal the security's (market) yield.

Market yields serve an essential function by allowing us to compare, on a uniform basis, securities that differ in cash flows provided, maturities, and current prices. In future chapters we will see how security yields are related to the firm's future financing costs and overall cost of capital.

Yield to Maturity (YTM) on Bonds

Yield to maturity (YTM)
The expected rate of return on a bond if bought at its current market price and held to maturity.

The market required rate of return on a bond (k_d) is more commonly referred to as the bond's yield to maturity. **Yield to maturity (YTM)** is the expected rate of return on a bond if bought at its current market price and held to maturity; it is also known as the bond's *internal rate of return (IRR)*. Mathematically, it is the discount rate that equates the present value of all expected interest payments and the payment of principal (face value) at maturity with the bond's current market price. For an example, let's return to Eq. (4-4), the valuation equation for an interest-bearing bond with a finite maturity. Replacing intrinsic value (V) with current market price (P_0) gives us

$$P_0 = \sum_{t=1}^{n} \frac{I}{(1 + k_d)^t} + \frac{MV}{(1 + k_d)^n} \tag{4-22}$$

If we now substitute actual values for I, MV, and P_0, we can solve for k_d, which in this case would be the bond's yield to maturity. However, the precise calculation for yield to maturity is rather complex and either requires bond value tables, a sophisticated handheld calculator, or a computer.

Interpolation. If all we have to work with are present value tables, we can still determine an approximation of the yield to maturity by making use of a trial-and-error procedure. To illustrate, consider a $1,000-par-value bond with the following characteristics: a current market price of $761; 12 years until maturity, and an 8 percent coupon rate (with interest paid annually). We want to determine the discount rate that sets the present value of the bond's expected future cash-flow stream equal to the bond's current market price. Suppose that we start with a 10 percent discount rate and calculate the present value of the bond's expected future cash flows. For the appropriate present value interest factors, we make use of Tables II and IV in the Appendix at the end of the book.

$$V = \$80(PVIFA_{10\%,12}) + \$1,000(PVIF_{10\%,12})$$
$$= \$80(6.814) + \$1,000(.319) = \textbf{\$864.12}$$

A 10 percent discount rate produces a resulting present value for the bond that is greater than the current market price of $761. Therefore, we need to try a higher discount rate to handicap further the future cash flows and drive their present value down to $761. Let's try a 15 percent discount rate.

$$V = \$80(PVIFA_{15\%,12}) + \$1,000(PVIF_{15\%,12})$$
$$= \$80(5.421) + \$1,000(.187) = \textbf{\$620.68}$$

This time the chosen discount rate was too large. The resulting present value is less than the current market price of $761. The rate necessary to discount the bond's expected cash flows to $761 must fall somewhere between 10 and 15 percent.

Interpolate Estimate an unknown number that lies somewhere between two known numbers.

To approximate this discount rate, we **interpolate** between 10 and 15 percent as follows:[8]

$$.05\begin{bmatrix} X\begin{bmatrix} .10 & \$864.12 \\ YTM & \$761.00 \end{bmatrix}\$103.12 \\ .15 & \$620.68 \end{bmatrix}\$243.44$$

$$\frac{X}{.05} = \frac{\$103.12}{\$243.44} \qquad \text{Therefore,} \qquad X = \frac{(.05) \times (\$103.12)}{\$243.44} = \textbf{.0212}$$

In this example $X = YTM - .10$. Therefore, $YTM = .10 + X = .10 + .0212 = .1212$, or **12.12 percent.** The use of a computer provides a precise yield to maturity of 11.82 percent. It is important to keep in mind that interpolation gives only an approximation of the exact percentage; the relationship between the two discount rates is not linear with respect to present value. However, the tighter the range of discount rates that we use in interpolation, the closer the resulting answer will be to the mathematically correct one. For example, had we used 11 and 12 percent, we would have come even closer to the "true" yield to maturity.

---

[8]Mathematically, we can generalize our discount-rate interpolation as follows:

$$\text{Interpolated discount rate} = i_L + \frac{(i_H - i_L)(PV_L - PV_{YTM})}{PV_L - PV_H}$$

where i_L = discount rate that is somewhat lower than the investment's YTM (or IRR), i_H = discount rate that is somewhat higher than the investment's YTM, PV_L = present value of the investment at a discount rate equal to i_L, PV_H = present value of the investment at a discount rate equal to i_H, PV_{YTM} = present value of the investment at a discount rate equal to the investment's YTM, which (by definition) must equal the investment's current price.

Behavior of Bond Prices. On the basis of an understanding of Eq. (4-22), a number of observations can be made concerning bond prices:

1. When the market required rate of return is *more* than the stated coupon rate, the price of the bond will be *less* than its face value. Such a bond is said to be selling at a *discount* from face value. The amount by which the face value exceeds the current price is the **bond discount.**
2. When the market required rate of return is *less* than the stated coupon rate, the price of the bond will be *more* than its face value. Such a bond is said to be selling at a *premium* over face value. The amount by which the current price exceeds the face value is the **bond premium.**
3. When the market required rate of return *equals* the stated coupon rate, the price of the bond will *equal* its face value. Such a bond is said to be selling at *par.*

TIP•TIP•TIP•TIP•TIP•TIP•TIP•TIP•TIP•TIP•TIP

If a bond sells at a *discount,* then P_0 < par and YTM > coupon rate.
If a bond sells at *par,* then P_0 = par and YTM = coupon rate.
If a bond sells at a *premium,* then P_0 > par and YTM < coupon rate.

4. If interest rates *rise* so that the market required rate of return *increases,* the bond's price will *fall.* If interest rates *fall,* the bond's price will *increase.* In short, interest rates and bond prices move in opposite directions.

From the last observation, it is clear that variability in interest rates should lead to variability in bond prices. This variation in the market price of a security caused by changes in interest rates is referred to as **interest-rate** (or **yield**) **risk.** It is important to note that an investor incurs a loss due to interest-rate (or yield) risk only if a security is sold prior to maturity *and* the level of interest rates has increased since time of purchase.

A further relationship, not as apparent as the previous four observations, needs to be illustrated separately.

5. For a given change in market required return, the price of a bond will change by a greater amount, the longer its maturity.

In general, the longer the maturity, the greater the price fluctuation associated with a given change in market required return. The closer in time that you are to this relatively large maturity value being realized, the less important are interest payments in determining the market price, and the less important is a change in market required return on the market price of the security. In general, then, the longer the maturity of a bond, the greater the risk of price change to the investor when changes occur in the overall level of interest rates.

Figure 4-1 illustrates our discussion by comparing two bonds that differ only in maturity. The price sensitivities of a 5-year bond and a 15-year bond are shown relative to changes in market required rate of return. As expected, the bond with the longer term to maturity shows a greater change in price for any given change in market yield. [All points on the two curves are based on the use of pricing Eq. (4-22).]

One last relationship also needs to be addressed separately, and it is known as the *coupon effect.*

6. For a given change in market required rate of return, the price of a bond will change by proportionally more, the lower the coupon rate. In other words, bond price volatility is *inversely* related to coupon rate.

Part II Valuation

FIGURE 4-1
Price–Yield Relation-
ship for Two Bonds
Where Each
Price–Yield Curve
Represents a Set
of Prices for That
Bond for Different
Assumed Market
Required Rates of
Return (Market
Yields)

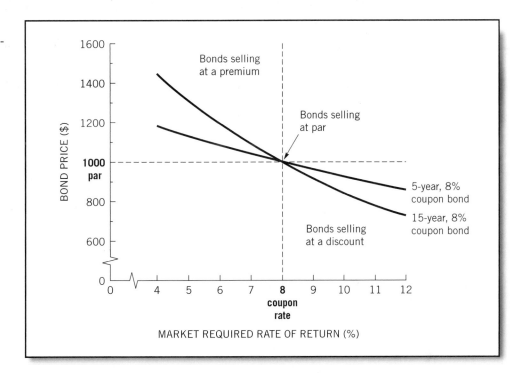

The reason for this effect is that the lower the coupon rate, the more return to the investor is reflected in the principal payment at maturity as opposed to interim interest payments. Put another way, investors realize their returns later with a low-coupon-rate bond than with a high-coupon-rate bond. In general, the further in the future the bulk of the payment stream, the greater the present value effect caused by a change in required return.[9] Even if high- and low-coupon-rate bonds have the same maturity, the price of the low-coupon-rate bond tends to be more volatile.

YTM and Semiannual Compounding. As previously mentioned, most domestic bonds pay interest twice a year, not once. This real-world complication is often ignored in an attempt to simplify discussion. We can take semiannual interest payments into account, however, when determining yield to maturity by replacing intrinsic value (V) with current market price (P_0) in bond valuation Eq. (4-8). The result is

$$P_0 = \sum_{t=1}^{2n} \frac{I/2}{(1 + k_d/2)^t} + \frac{MV}{(1 + k_d/2)^{2n}} \qquad \textbf{(4-23)}$$

Solving for $k_d/2$ in this equation would give us the semiannual yield to maturity.

The practice of doubling the semiannual YTM has been adopted by convention in bond circles to provide the "annualized" (nominal annual) YTM or what bond traders would call the *bond-equivalent yield.* The appropriate procedure, however, would be to square "1 plus the semiannual YTM" and then subtract 1, that is,

$$(1 + \text{semiannual YTM})^2 - 1 = (\text{effective annual}) \text{ YTM}$$

---

[9]The interested reader is referred to James C. Van Horne, *Financial Market Rates and Flows,* 6th ed. (Upper Saddle River, NJ: Prentice Hall, 2001), Chap. 6.

Chapter 4 The Valuation of Long-Term Securities

As you may remember from Chapter 3, the (effective annual) YTM just calculated is the *effective annual interest rate*.

Yield on Preferred Stock

Substituting current market price (P_0) for intrinsic value (V) in preferred stock valuation Eq. (4-10), we have

$$P_0 = D_p/k_p \qquad \text{(4-24)}$$

where D_p is still the stated annual dividend per share of preferred stock, but k_p is now the market required return for this stock, or simply the yield on preferred stock. Rearranging terms allows us to solve directly for the yield on preferred stock.

$$k_p = D_p/P_0 \qquad \text{(4-25)}$$

To illustrate, assume that the current market price per share of Acme Zarf Company's 10 percent, $100-par-value preferred stock is $91.25. Acme's preferred stock is, therefore, priced to provide a yield of

$$k_p = \$10/\$91.25 = \textbf{10.96\%}$$

Yield on Common Stock

The rate of return that sets the discounted value of the expected cash dividends from a share of common stock equal to the share's current market price is the yield on that common stock. If, for example, the constant dividend growth model was appropriate to apply to the stock of a particular company, the current market price (P_0) could be said to be

$$P_0 = D_1/(k_e - g) \qquad \text{(4-26)}$$

Solving for k_e, which in this case is the market-determined yield on a company's common stock, we get

$$k_e = D_1/P_0 + g \qquad \text{(4-27)}$$

From this last expression, it becomes clear that the yield on common stock comes from two sources. The first source is the expected *dividend yield*, D_1/P_0; whereas the second source, g, is the expected *capital gains yield*. Yes, g wears a number of hats. It is the expected compound annual growth rate in dividends. But given this model, it is also the expected annual percent change in stock price (that is, $P_1/P_0 - 1 = g$) and, as such, is referred to as the capital gains yield.

QUESTION•ANSWER•QUESTION•ANSWER

What market yield is implied by a share of common stock currently selling for $40 whose dividends are expected to grow at a rate of 9 percent per year and whose dividend next year is expected to be $2.40?

The market yield, k_e, is equal to the dividend yield, D_1/P_0, plus the capital gains yield, g, as follows:

$$k_e = \$2.40/\$40 + .09 = .06 + .09 = \textbf{15\%}$$

SUMMARY TABLE OF KEY PRESENT VALUE FORMULAS FOR VALUING LONG-TERM SECURITIES (ANNUAL CASH FLOWS ASSUMED)

SECURITIES	EQUATION

BONDS

1. Perpetual

$$V = \sum_{t=1}^{\infty} \frac{I}{(1 + k_d)^t} = \frac{I}{k_d} \qquad\qquad (4\text{-}1), (4\text{-}3)$$

2. Finite maturity, nonzero coupon

$$V = \sum_{t=1}^{n} \frac{I}{(1 + k_d)^t} + \frac{MV}{(1 + k_d)^n} \qquad\qquad (4\text{-}4)$$

$$= I(PVIFA_{k_d,n}) + MV(PVIF_{k_d,n}) \qquad\qquad (4\text{-}5)$$

3. Zero coupon

$$V = \frac{MV}{(1 + k_d)^n} \qquad\qquad (4\text{-}6)$$

$$= MV(PVIF_{k_d,n}) \qquad\qquad (4\text{-}7)$$

PREFERRED STOCK

1. No call expected

$$V = \sum_{t=1}^{\infty} \frac{D_p}{(1 + k_p)^t} = \frac{D_p}{k_p} \qquad\qquad (4\text{-}10)$$

2. Call expected at n

$$V = \sum_{t=1}^{n} \frac{D_p}{(1 + k_p)^t} + \frac{\text{call price}}{(1 + k_p)^n} \qquad\qquad (\text{see footnote 4})$$

$$= D_p(PVIFA_{k_p,n}) + (\text{call price})(PVIF_{k_p,n})$$

COMMON STOCK

Constant growth

$$V = \sum_{t=1}^{\infty} \frac{D_0(1 + g)^t}{(1 + k_e)^t} = \frac{D_1}{(k_e - g)} \qquad\qquad (4\text{-}14)$$

SUMMARY

- The concept of value includes *liquidation value, going-concern value, book value, market value,* and *intrinsic value.*
- The valuation approach taken in this chapter is one of determining a security's *intrinsic value*— what the security ought to be worth based on hard facts. This value is the present value of the cash-flow stream provided to the investor, discounted at a required rate of return appropriate for the risk involved.
- The intrinsic value of a *perpetual bond* is simply the capitalized value of an infinite stream of interest payments. This present value is the periodic interest payment divided by the investor's required rate of return.
- The intrinsic value of an *interest-bearing bond* with a finite maturity is equal to the present value of the interest payments plus the present value of principal payment at maturity, all discounted at the investor's required rate of return.
- The intrinsic value of a *zero-coupon bond* (a bond that makes no periodic interest payments) is the present value of the principal payment at maturity, discounted at the investor's required rate of return.

- The intrinsic value of *preferred stock* is equal to the stated annual dividend per share divided by the investor's required rate of return.
- Unlike bonds and preferred stock for which the future cash flows are contractually stated, much more uncertainty surrounds the future stream of returns connected with common stock.
- The intrinsic value of a share of *common stock* can be viewed as the discounted value of all the cash dividends provided by the issuing firm.
- Dividend discount models are designed to compute the intrinsic value of a share of stock under specific assumptions as to the expected growth pattern of future dividends and the appropriate discount rate to employ.
- If dividends are expected to grow at a constant rate, the formula used to calculate the intrinsic value of a share of common stock is

$$V = D_1/(k_e - g) \qquad \textbf{(4-14)}$$

- In the case of no expected dividend growth, the equation above reduces to

$$V = D_1/k_e \qquad \textbf{(4-19)}$$

- Finally, when dividend growth is expected to differ during various phases of a firm's development, the present value of dividends for various growth phases can be determined and summed to produce the stock's intrinsic value.
- If intrinsic value (V) in our valuation equations is replaced with the security's market price (P_0), we can then solve for the *market required rate of return*. This rate, which sets the discounted value of the expected cash inflows equal to the security's market price, is also referred to as the security's (market) *yield*.
- *Yield to maturity (YTM)* is the expected rate of return on a bond if bought at its current market price and held to maturity. It is also known as the bond's *internal rate of return*.
- Interest rates and bond prices move in opposite directions.
- In general, the longer the maturity for a bond, the greater the bond's price fluctuation associated with a given change in market required return.
- The lower the coupon rate, the more sensitive that relative bond price changes are to changes in market yields.
- The yield on common stock comes from two sources. The first source is the expected *dividend yield*, and the second source is the expected *capital gains yield*.

QUESTIONS

1. What connection, if any, does a firm's *market value* have with its *liquidation* and/or *going-concern value?*
2. Could a security's *intrinsic value* to an investor ever differ from the security's *market value?* If so, under what circumstances?
3. In what sense is the treatment of bonds and preferred stock the same when it comes to valuation?
4. Why do bonds with long maturities fluctuate more in price than do bonds with short maturities, given the same change in yield to maturity?
5. A 20-year bond has a coupon rate of 8 percent, and another bond of the same maturity has a coupon rate of 15 percent. If the bonds are alike in all other respects, which will have the greater relative market price decline if interest rates increase sharply? Why?
6. Why are dividends the basis for the valuation of common stock?
7. Suppose that the controlling stock of IBM Corporation was placed in a perpetual trust with an irrevocable clause that cash or liquidating dividends would never be paid out of this trust. Earnings per share continued to grow. What would be the value of the company to the stockholders? Why?
8. Why is the growth rate in earnings and dividends of a company likely to taper off in the future? Could the growth rate increase as well? If it did, what would be the effect on stock price?
9. Using the constant perpetual growth dividend valuation model, could you have a situation in which a company grows at 30 percent per year (after subtracting out inflation) forever? Explain.

10. Tammy Whynot, a classmate of yours, suggests that when the constant growth dividend valuation model is used to explain a stock's current price, the quantity $(k_e - g)$ represents the expected dividend yield. Is she right or wrong? Explain.

11. **"$1,000 U.S. Government Treasury Bond FREE! with any $999 Purchase"** shouted the headline of an ad from a local furniture company. "*Wow!* Like, for sure, this is like getting the furniture like free," said your friend Heather Dawn Tiffany. What Heather overlooked was the fine print in the ad where you learned that the "free" bond was a zero-coupon issue with a 30-year maturity. Explain to Heather why the "free" $1,000 bond is more in the nature of an advertising "come-on" rather than something of large value.

$1000

U.S. GOVERNMENT
TREASURY BOND

FREE!

WITH ANY $999 PURCHASE
ANY COMBINATION OF ANY ITEMS TOTALLING
$999 OR MORE AND YOU
GET A $1000 U.S. GOVERNMENT BOND FREE.

SELF-CORRECTION PROBLEMS

1. Fast and Loose Company has outstanding an 8 percent, four-year, $1,000-par-value bond on which interest is paid annually.
   a. If the market required rate of return is 15 percent, what is the market value of the bond?
   b. What would be its market value if the market required return dropped to 12 percent? To 8 percent?
   c. If the coupon rate were 15 percent instead of 8 percent, what would be the market value [under Part (a)]? If the required rate of return dropped to 8 percent, what would happen to the market price of the bond?

2. James Consol Company presently pays a dividend of $1.60 per share on its common stock. The company expects to increase the dividend at a 20 percent annual rate the first four years and at a 13 percent rate the next four years and then grow the dividend at a 7 percent rate thereafter. This phased-growth pattern is in keeping with the expected life cycle of earnings. You require a 16 percent return to invest in this stock. What value should you place on a share of this stock?

3. A $1,000-face-value bond has a current market price of $935, an 8 percent coupon rate, and 10 remaining years until maturity. Interest payments are made semiannually. Before you do any calculations, decide if the yield to maturity is above or below the coupon rate. Why?
   a. What is the implied market-determined semiannual discount rate (i.e., semiannual yield to maturity) on this bond?
   b. Using your answer to Part (a), what is the bond's (i) (nominal annual) yield to maturity? (ii) (effective annual) yield to maturity?

4. A zero-coupon, $1,000-par-value bond is currently selling for $312 and matures in exactly 10 years.
   a. What is the implied market-determined semiannual discount rate (i.e., semiannual yield to maturity) on this bond? (Remember, the bond pricing convention in the United States is to use semiannual compounding—even with a zero-coupon bond.)
   b. Using your answer to Part (a), what is the bond's (i) (nominal annual) yield to maturity? (ii) (effective annual) yield to maturity?

5. Just today, Acme Rocket, Inc.'s common stock paid a $1 annual dividend per share and had a closing price of $20. Assume that the market expects this company's annual dividend to grow at a constant 6 percent rate forever.
   a. Determine the implied *yield* on this common stock.
   b. What is the expected *dividend yield*?
   c. What is the expected *capital gains yield*?

6. Peking Duct Tape Company has outstanding a $1,000-face-value bond with a 14 percent coupon rate and 3 years remaining until final maturity. Interest payments are made semiannually.
   a. What value should you place on this bond if your nominal annual required rate of return is (i) 12 percent? (ii) 14 percent? (iii) 16 percent?
   b. Assume that we are faced with a bond similar to the one described above, except that it is a zero-coupon, pure discount bond. What value should you place on this bond if your nominal annual required rate of return is (i) 12 percent? (ii) 14 percent? (iii) 16 percent? (Assume semiannual discounting.)

PROBLEMS

1. Gonzalez Electric Company has outstanding a 10 percent bond issue with a face value of $1,000 per bond and three years to maturity. Interest is payable annually. The bonds are privately held by Suresafe Fire Insurance Company. Suresafe wishes to sell the bonds and is negotiating with another party. It estimates that in current market conditions, the bonds should provide a (nominal annual) return of 14 percent. What price per bond should Suresafe be able to realize on the sale?

2. What would be the price per bond in Problem 1 if interest payments were made semiannually?
3. Superior Cement Company has an 8 percent preferred stock issue outstanding, with each share having a $100 face value. Currently, the yield is 10 percent. What is the market price per share? If interest rates in general should rise so that the required return becomes 12 percent, what will happen to the market price per share?
4. The stock of the Health Corporation is currently selling for $20 a share and is expected to pay a $1 dividend at the end of the year. If you bought the stock now and sold it for $23 after receiving the dividend, what rate of return would you earn?
5. Delphi Products Corporation currently pays a dividend of $2 per share, and this dividend is expected to grow at a 15 percent annual rate for three years, then at a 10 percent rate for the next three years, after which it is expected to grow at a 5 percent rate forever. What value would you place on the stock if an 18 percent rate of return was required?
6. North Great Timber Company will pay a dividend of $1.50 a share next year. After this, earnings and dividends are expected to grow at a 9 percent annual rate indefinitely. Investors presently require a rate of return of 13 percent. The company is considering several business strategies and wishes to determine the effect of these strategies on the market price per share of its stock.
   a. Continuing the present strategy will result in the expected growth rate and required rate of return stated above.
   b. Expanding timber holdings and sales will increase the expected dividend growth rate to 11 percent but will increase the risk of the company. As a result, the rate of return required by investors will increase to 16 percent.
   c. Integrating into retail stores will increase the dividend growth rate to 10 percent and increase the required rate of return to 14 percent.
   From the standpoint of market price per share, which strategy is best?
7. A share of preferred stock for the Buford Pusser Baseball Bat Company just sold for $100 and carries an $8 annual dividend.
   a. What is the yield on this stock?
   b. Now assume that this stock has a call price of $110 in five years, when the company intends to call the issue. (*Note:* The preferred stock in this case should not be treated as a perpetual—it will be bought back in five years for $110.) What is this preferred stock's *yield to call?*

8. Wayne's Steaks, Inc., has a 9 percent, noncallable, $100-par-value preferred stock issue outstanding. On January 1 the market price per share is $73. Dividends are paid annually on December 31. If you require a 12 percent annual return on this investment, what is this stock's intrinsic value to you (on a per share basis) on January 1?

9. The 9-percent-coupon-rate bonds of the Melbourne Mining Company have exactly 15 years remaining to maturity. The current market value of one of these $1,000-par-value bonds is $700. Interest is paid semiannually. Melanie Gibson places a nominal annual required rate of return of 14 percent on these bonds. What dollar intrinsic value should Melanie place on one of these bonds (assuming semiannual discounting)?

10. Just today, Fawlty Foods, Inc.'s common stock paid a $1.40 annual dividend per share and had a closing price of $21. Assume that the market's required return, or capitalization rate, for this investment is 12 percent and that dividends are expected to grow at a constant rate forever.
    a. Calculate the implied growth rate in dividends.
    b. What is the expected *dividend yield?*
    c. What is the expected *capital gains yield?*

11. The Great Northern Specific Railway has noncallable, perpetual bonds outstanding. When originally issued, the perpetual bonds sold for $955 per bond; today (January 1) their current market price is $1,120 per bond. The company pays a semiannual interest payment of $45 per bond on June 30 and December 31 each year.
    a. As of today (January 1), what is the implied semiannual yield on these bonds?
    b. Using your answer to Part (a), what is the (nominal annual) yield on these bonds? the (effective annual) yield on these bonds?

12. Assume that everything stated in Problem 11 remains the same except that the bonds are not perpetual. Instead, they have a $1,000 par value and mature in 10 years.
    a. Determine the implied semiannual yield to maturity (YTM) on these bonds. (*Tip:* If all you have to work with are present value tables, you can still determine an approximation of the semiannual YTM by making use of a trial-and-error procedure coupled with interpolation. In fact, the answer to Problem 11, Part (a)—rounded to the nearest percent—gives you a good starting point for a trial-and-error approach.)
    b. Using your answer to Part (a), what is the (nominal annual) YTM on these bonds? the (effective annual) YTM on these bonds?

13. Red Frog Brewery has $1,000-par-value bonds outstanding with the following characteristics: currently selling at par; 5 years until final maturity; and a 9 percent coupon rate (with interest paid semiannually). Interestingly, Old Chicago Brewery has a very similar bond issue outstanding. In fact, every bond feature is the same as for the Red Frog bonds, except that Old Chicago's bonds mature in exactly 15 years. Now, assume that the market's nominal annual required rate of return for both bond issues suddenly fell from 9 percent to 8 percent.
    a. Which brewery's bonds would show the greatest price change? Why?
    b. At the market's new, lower required rate of return for these bonds, determine the per bond price for each brewery's bonds. Which bond's price fell the most, and by how much?

14. Burp-Cola Company just finished making an annual dividend payment of $2 per share on its common stock. Its common stock dividend has been growing at an annual rate of 10 percent. Kelly Scott requires a 16 percent annual return on this stock. What intrinsic value should Kelly place on one share of Burp-Cola common stock under the following three situations?
    a. Dividends are expected to continue growing at a constant 10 percent annual rate.

b. The annual dividend growth rate is expected to decrease to 9 percent and to remain constant at that level.

c. The annual dividend growth rate is expected to increase to 11 percent and to remain constant at the level.

SOLUTIONS TO SELF-CORRECTION PROBLEMS

1. a, b.

END OF YEAR	PAYMENT	DISCOUNT FACTOR, 15%	PRESENT VALUE, 15%	DISCOUNT FACTOR, 12%	PRESENT VALUE, 12%
1–3	$ 80	2.283	$182.64	2.402	$192.16
4	1,080	.572	617.76	.636	686.88
	Market value		$800.40		$879.04

Note: Rounding error incurred by use of tables may sometimes cause slight differences in answers when alternative solution methods are applied to the same cash flows.

The market value of an 8 percent bond yielding 8 percent is its face value, of **$1,000.**

c. The market value would be **$1,000** if the required return were 15 percent.

END OF YEAR	PAYMENT	DISCOUNT FACTOR, 8%	PRESENT VALUE, 8%
1–3	$ 150	2.577	$ 386.55
4	1,150	.735	845.25
	Market value		$1,231.80

2.

PHASES 1 AND 2: PRESENT VALUE OF DIVIDENDS TO BE RECEIVED OVER FIRST 8 YEARS

END OF YEAR	PRESENT VALUE CALCULATION			PRESENT VALUE OF DIVIDEND
	(DIVIDEND	$\times$	$PVIF_{16\%,t}$)	
Phase 1 1	$1.60(1.20)^1 = \$1.92$	$\times$	.862	=	$ 1.66
2	$1.60(1.20)^2 = 2.30$	$\times$	.743	=	1.71
3	$1.60(1.20)^3 = 2.76$	$\times$	.641	=	1.77
4	$1.60(1.20)^4 = \mathbf{3.32}$	$\times$	.552	=	1.83
Phase 2 5	$\mathbf{3.32}(1.13)^1 = 3.75$	$\times$	.476	=	1.79
6	$3.32(1.13)^2 = 4.24$	$\times$	.410	=	1.74
7	$3.32(1.13)^3 = 4.79$	$\times$	.354	=	1.70
8	$3.32(1.13)^4 = 5.41$	$\times$	.305	=	1.65

$$\text{or} \left[\sum_{t=1}^{8} \frac{D_t}{(1.16)_t} \right] = \mathbf{\$13.85}$$

PHASE 3: PRESENT VALUE OF CONSTANT GROWTH COMPONENT

Dividend at the end of year 9 $= \$5.41(1.07) = \$5.79$

Value of stock at the end of year 8 $= \dfrac{D_9}{(k_e - g)} = \dfrac{\$5.79}{(.16 - .07)} = \$64.33$

Present value of $64.33 at end of year 8 $= (\$64.33)(PVIF_{16\%,8})$

$$= (\$64.33)(.305) = \mathbf{\$19.62}$$

PRESENT VALUE OF STOCK

$V = \$13.85 + \$19.62 = \mathbf{\$33.47}$

3. The yield to maturity is higher than the coupon rate of 8 percent because the bond sells at a discount from its face value. The (nominal annual) yield to maturity as reported in bond circles is equal to $(2 \times$ semiannual YTM). The (effective annual) YTM is equal to $(1 +$ semiannual YTM$)^2 - 1$. The problem is set up as follows:

$$\$935 = \sum_{t=1}^{20} \frac{\$40}{(1 + k_d/2)^t} + \frac{\$1,000}{(1 + k_d/2)^{20}}$$

$$= (\$40)(PVIFA_{k_d/2,20}) + MV(PVIF_{k_d/2,20})$$

   a. Solving for $k_d/2$ (the semiannual YTM) in this expression using a calculator, a computer routine, or present value tables yields **4.5 percent.**

   b. **(i)** The (nominal annual) YTM is then 2×4.5 percent = **9 percent.**

   (ii) The (effective annual) YTM is $(1 + .045)^2 - 1 =$ **9.2025 percent.**

4. **a.** $P_0 = FV_{20}(PVIF_{k_d}/2,20)$

   $(PVIF_{k_d/2,20}) = P_0/FV_{20} = \$312/\$1,000 = .312$

   From Table II in the end-of-book Appendix, the interest factor for 20 periods at 6 percent is .312; therefore, the bond's semiannual yield to maturity (YTM) is **6 percent.**

   b. **(i)** (nominal annual) YTM = $2 \times$ (semiannual YTM)

   $$= 2 \times (.06) = \textbf{12 percent}$$

   (ii) (effective annual) YTM = $(1 +$ semiannual YTM$)^2 - 1$

   $$= (1 + .06)^2 - 1 = \textbf{12.36 percent}$$

5. **a.** $k_e = (D_1/P_0 + g) = ([D_0(1 + g)]/P_0) + g$

   $= ([\$1(1 + .06)]/\$20) + .06$

   $= .053 + .06 = \textbf{.113}$

   b. Expected dividend yield $= D_1/P_0 = \$1(1 + .06)/\$20 = \textbf{.053}$

   c. Expected capital gains yield $= g = \textbf{.06}$

6. **a.** **(i)** $V = (\$140/2)(PVIFA_{.06,6}) + \$1,000(PVIF_{.06,6})$

   $= \quad \$70(4.917) \quad + \quad \$1,000(.705)$

   $= \quad \$344.19 \quad + \quad \$705$

   $= \textbf{\$1,049.19}$

   (ii) $V = (\$140/2)(PVIFA_{.07,6}) + \$1,000(PVIF_{.07,6})$

   $= \quad \$70(4.767) \quad + \quad \$1,000(.666)$

   $= \quad \$333.69 \quad + \quad \$666$

   $= \textbf{\$999.69}$ or **\$1,000**

   (Value should equal \$1,000 when the nominal annual required return equals the coupon rate; our answer differs from \$1,000 only because of rounding in the Table values used.)

   (iii) $V = (\$140/2)(PVIFA_{.08,6}) + \$1,000(PVIF_{.08,6})$

   $= \quad \$70(4.623) \quad + \quad \$1,000(.630)$

   $= \quad \$323.61 \quad + \quad \$630$

   $= \textbf{\$953.61}$

   b. The value of this type of bond is based on simply discounting to the present the maturity value of each bond. We have already done that in answering Part (a) and those values are: (i) **\$705;** (ii) **\$666;** and (iii) **\$630.**

SELECTED REFERENCES

Bauman, W. Scott. "Investment Returns and Present Values." *Financial Analysts Journal* 25 (November–December 1969), 107–18.

Chew, I. Keong, and Ronnie J. Clayton. "Bond Valuation: A Clarification." *The Financial Review* 18 (May 1983), 234–36.

Fuller, Russell J., and Chi-Cheng Hsia. "A Simplified Model for Estimating Stock Prices of Growth Firms." *Financial Analysts Journal* 40 (September–October 1984), 49–56.

Gordon, Myron J. *The Investment, Financing, and Valuation of the Corporation.* Homewood, IL: Richard D. Irwin, 1962.

Haugen, Robert A. *Modern Investment Theory,* 4th ed. Upper Saddle River, NJ: Prentice Hall, 1997.

Reilly, Frank K., and Keith C. Brown. *Investment Analysis and Portfolio Management,* 6th ed. Orlando, FL: Dryden Press, 2000.

Rusbarsky, Mark, and David B. Vicknair. "Accounting for Bonds with Accrued Interest in Conformity with Brokers' Valuation Formulas." *Issues in Accounting Education* 14 (May 1999), 233–53.

Shao, Stephen P., and Lawrence P. Shao. *Mathematics for Management and Finance,* 8th ed. Cincinnati, OH: South-Western, 1998.

Sharpe, William F., Gordon J. Alexander, and Jeffrey V. Bailey. *Investments,* 6th ed. Upper Saddle River, NJ: Prentice Hall, 1999.

Siegel, Jeremy J. "The Application of the DCF Methodology for Determining the Cost of Equity Capital." *Financial Management* 14 (Spring 1985), 46–53.

Van Horne, James C. *Financial Market Rates and Flows,* 6th ed. Upper Saddle River, NJ: Prentice Hall, 2001.

White, Mark A., and Janet M. Todd. "Bond Pricing between Coupon Payment Dates Using a 'No-Frills' Financial Calculator." *Financial Practice and Education* 5 (Spring–Summer, 1995), 148–51.

Williams, John B. *The Theory of Investment Value.* Cambridge, MA: Harvard University Press, 1938.

Chapter 5

Risk and Return

DEFINING RISK AND RETURN
   Return • Risk
USING PROBABILITY DISTRIBUTIONS TO MEASURE RISK
   Expected Return and Standard Deviation • Coefficient of
      Variation
ATTITUDES TOWARD RISK
RISK AND RETURN IN A PORTFOLIO CONTEXT
   Portfolio Return • Portfolio Risk and the Importance of
      Covariance
DIVERSIFICATION
   Systematic and Unsystematic Risk
THE CAPITAL-ASSET PRICING MODEL (CAPM)
   The Characteristic Line • Beta: An Index of Systematic Risk
      • Unsystematic (Diversifiable) Risk Revisited • Required Rates
      of Return and the Security Market Line (SML) • Returns and
      Stock Prices • Challenges to the CAPM
EFFICIENT FINANCIAL MARKETS
   Three Forms of Market Efficiency • Does Market Efficiency
      Always Hold?
SUMMARY
APPENDIX A: MEASURING PORTFOLIO RISK
APPENDIX B: ARBITRAGE PRICING THEORY
QUESTIONS
SELF-CORRECTION PROBLEMS
PROBLEMS
SOLUTIONS TO SELF-CORRECTION PROBLEMS
SELECTED REFERENCES

Risk is like pornography. It's hard to define, but you know it when you see it.

—JOHN WACHOWICZ

In Chapter 2 we briefly introduced the concept of a market-imposed "trade-off" between risk and return for securities—that is, the higher the risk of a security, the higher the expected return that must be offered the investor. We made use of this concept in Chapter 3. There we viewed the value of a security as the present value of the cash-flow stream provided to the investor, discounted at a required rate of return appropriate for the risk involved. We have, however, purposely postponed until now a more detailed treatment of risk and return. We wanted you first to have an understanding of certain valuation fundamentals before tackling this more difficult topic.

Most everyone recognizes that risk must be considered in determining value and making investment choices. In fact, valuation and an understanding of the trade-off between risk and return form the foundation for maximizing shareholder wealth. And yet, there is controversy over what is risk and how it should be measured.

In this chapter we will focus our discussion on risk and return for common stock for an individual investor. The results, however, can be extended to other assets and classes of investors. In fact, in later chapters we will take a close look at the firm as an investor in assets (projects) when we take up the topic of capital budgeting.

DEFINING RISK AND RETURN

Return

Return Income received on an investment plus any change in market price, usually expressed as a percent of the beginning market price of the investment.

The **return** from holding an investment over some period—say, a year—is simply any cash payments received due to ownership, plus the change in market price, divided by the beginning price.[1] You might, for example, buy for $100 a security that would pay $7 in cash to you and be worth $106 one year later. The return would be ($7 + $6)/$100 = 13%. Thus, return comes to you from two sources: income plus any price appreciation (or loss in price).

For common stock we can define one-period return as

$$R = \frac{D_t + (P_t - P_{t-1})}{P_{t-1}}$$ (5-1)

where R is the actual (expected) return when t refers to a particular time period in the past (future); D_t is the cash dividend at the end of time period t; P_t is the stock's price at time period t; and P_{t-1} is the stock's price at time period $t - 1$. Notice that this formula can be used to determine both actual one-period returns (when based on historical figures) as well as expected one-period returns (when based on future expected dividends and prices). Also note that the term in parentheses in the numerator of Eq. (5-1) represents the capital gain or loss during the period.

Risk

Most people would be willing to accept our definition of return without much difficulty. Not everyone, however, would agree on how to define risk, let alone how to measure it.

---

[1]This holding period return measure is useful with an investment horizon of one year or less. For longer periods, it is better to calculate rate of return as an investment's *yield* (or *internal rate of return*), as we did in the last chapter. The yield calculation is present-value-based and thus considers the time value of money.

To begin to get a handle on risk, let's first consider a couple of examples. Assume that you buy a one-year Treasury bill (T-bill) to yield 8 percent.[2] If you hold it for the full year, you will realize a government-guaranteed 8 percent return on your investment—not more, not less. Now, buy a share of common stock in any company and hold it for one year. The cash dividend that you anticipate receiving may or may not materialize as expected. And, what is more, the year-end price of the stock might be much lower than expected—maybe even less than you started with. Thus, your *actual* return on this investment may differ substantially from your *expected* return. If we define **risk** as the variability of returns from those that are expected, the T-bill would be a risk-free security while the common stock would be a risky security. The greater the variability, the riskier the security is said to be.

Risk The variability of returns from those that are expected.

USING PROBABILITY DISTRIBUTIONS TO MEASURE RISK

As we have just noted, for all except risk-free securities the return we expect may be different from the return we receive. For risky securities, the actual rate of return can be viewed as a random variable subject to a **probability distribution.** Suppose, for example, that an investor believed that the possible one-year returns from investing in a particular common stock were as shown in the shaded section of Table 5-1, which represents the probability distribution of one-year returns. This probability distribution can be summarized in terms of two parameters of the distribution: (1) the *expected return* and (2) the *standard deviation.*

Probability distribution A set of possible values that a random variable can assume and their associated probabilities of occurrence.

Expected Return and Standard Deviation

The **expected return,** $\bar{R}$, is

Expected return The weighted average of possible returns, with the weights being the probabilities of occurrence.

$$\bar{R} = \sum_{i=1}^{n} (R_i)(P_i) \tag{5-2}$$

where R_i is the return for the ith possibility, P_i is the probability of that return occurring, and n is the total number of possibilities. Thus, the expected return is simply a weighted average of the possible returns, with the weights being the probabilities of occurrence. For the distribution of possible returns shown in Table 5-1, the expected return is shown to be **9 percent.**

To complete the two-parameter description of our return distribution, we need a measure of the dispersion, or variability, around our expected return. The conventional measure of dispersion is the **standard deviation.** The greater the standard deviation of returns, the greater the variability of returns, and the greater the risk of the investment. The standard deviation, σ, can be expressed mathematically as

Standard deviation A statistical measure of the variability of a distribution around its mean. It is the square root of the *variance.*

$$\sigma = \sqrt{\sum_{i=1}^{n} (R_i - \bar{R})^2 (P_i)} \tag{5-3}$$

where $\sqrt{}$ represents the square root. The square of the standard deviation, σ^2, is known as the *variance* of the distribution. Operationally, we generally first calculate a distribution's variance, or the weighted average of squared deviations of possible

---

[2]T-bills do not pay interest. Instead, they are sold at a discount and redeemed at face value. The difference between the discount price paid and the face value received at maturity provides your return.

TABLE 5-1

Illustration of the use of a probability distribution of possible one-year returns to calculate expected return and standard deviation of return

POSSIBLE RETURN, R_i	PROBABILITY OF OCCURRENCE, P_i	EXPECTED RETURN ($\bar{R}$) CALCULATION $(R_i)(P_i)$	VARIANCE (σ^2) CALCULATION $(R_i - \bar{R})^2(P_i)$
−.10	.05	−.005	$(-.10 - .09)^2(.05)$
−.02	.10	−.002	$(-.02 - .09)^2(.10)$
.04	.20	.008	$(.04 - .09)^2(.20)$
.09	.30	.027	$(.09 - .09)^2(.30)$
.14	.20	.028	$(.14 - .09)^2(.20)$
.20	.10	.020	$(.20 - .09)^2(.10)$
.28	.05	.014	$(.28 - .09)^2(.05)$
	$\Sigma = 1.00$	$\Sigma = .090 = \bar{R}$	$\Sigma = .00703 = \sigma^2$

Standard deviation $= (.00703)^{.5} = .0838 = \sigma$

occurrences from the mean value of the distribution, with the weights being the probabilities of occurrence. Then, the square root of this figure provides us with the standard deviation. Table 5-1 reveals our example distribution's variance to be **.00703.** Taking the square root of this value, we find that the distribution's standard deviation is **8.38 percent.**

Use of Standard Deviation Information. So far we have been working with a *discrete* (noncontinuous) probability distribution, one where a random variable, like return, can take on only certain values within an interval. In such cases we do not have to calculate the standard deviation in order to determine the probability of specific outcomes. To determine the probability of the actual return in our example being less than zero, we look at the shaded section of Table 5-1 and see that the probability is .05 + .10 = **15%.** The procedure is slightly more complex when we deal with a *continuous* distribution, one where a random variable can take on any value within an interval. And, for common stock returns, a continuous distribution is a more realistic assumption, as any number of possible outcomes ranging from a large loss to a large gain are possible.

Assume that we are facing a *normal* (continuous) probability distribution of returns. It is symmetrical and bell-shaped, and 68 percent of the distribution falls within one standard deviation (right or left) of the expected return; 95 percent falls within two standard deviations; and over 99 percent falls within three standard deviations. By expressing differences from the expected return in terms of standard deviations, we are able to determine the probability that the actual return will be greater or less than any particular amount.

We can illustrate this process with a numerical example. Suppose that our return distribution had been approximately normal with an expected return equal to 9 percent and a standard deviation of 8.38 percent. Let's say that we wish to find the probability that the actual future return will be less than zero. We first determine how many standard deviations 0 percent is from the mean (9 percent). To do this we take the difference between these two values, which happens to be −9 percent, and divide it by the standard deviation. In this case the result is −.09/.0838 = −1.07 standard deviations. (The *negative* sign reminds us that we are looking to the *left* of the mean.) In general, we can make use of the formula

$$Z = \frac{R - \bar{R}}{\sigma}$$

$$= \frac{0 - .09}{.0838} = -1.07 \qquad \textbf{(5-4)}$$

where R is the return range limit of interest and where Z (the Z-score) tells us how many standard deviations R is from the mean.

Table V in the Appendix at the back of the book can be used to determine the proportion of the area under the normal curve that is Z standard deviations to the left or right of the mean. This proportion corresponds to the probability that our return outcome would be Z standard deviations away from the mean.

Turning to (Appendix) Table V, we find that there is approximately a 14 percent probability that the actual future return will be zero or less. The probability distribution is illustrated in Figure 5-1. The shaded area is located 1.07 standard deviations left of the mean, and as indicated, this area represents approximately 14 percent of the total distribution.

As we have just seen, a return distribution's standard deviation turns out to be a rather versatile risk measure. It can serve as an absolute measure of return variability—the higher the standard deviation, the greater the uncertainty concerning the actual outcome. In addition, we can use it to determine the likelihood that an actual outcome will be greater or less than a particular amount. However, there are those who suggest that our concern should be with "downside" risk—occurrences less than expected—rather than variability both above and below the mean. Those people have a good point. But, as long as the return distribution is relatively symmetric—a mirror image above and below the mean—standard deviation still works. The greater the standard deviation, the greater the possibility for large disappointments.

Coefficient of Variation

The standard deviation can sometimes be misleading in comparing the risk, or uncertainty, surrounding alternatives if they differ in size. Consider two investment

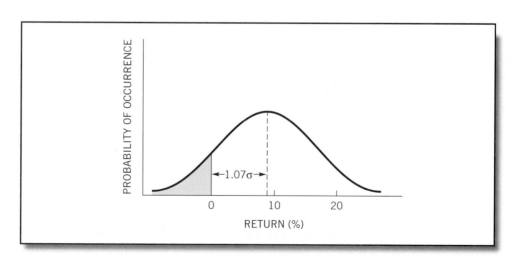

FIGURE 5-1
Normal Probability Distribution of Possible Returns for Example Highlighting Area 1.07 Standard Deviations Left of the Mean

opportunities, A and B, whose normal probability distributions of one-year returns have the following characteristics:

	INVESTMENT A	INVESTMENT B
Expected return, $\bar{R}$	.08	.24
Standard deviation, σ	.06	.08
Coefficient of variation, CV	.75	.33

Can we conclude that because the standard deviation of B is larger than that of A, it is the riskier investment? With standard deviation as our risk measure, we would have to. However, relative to the size of expected return, investment A has greater variation. This is similar to recognizing that a $10,000 standard deviation of annual income to a multimillionaire is really less significant than an $8,000 standard deviation in annual income would be to you. To adjust for the size, or scale, problem, the standard deviation can be divided by the expected return to compute the **coefficient of variation (CV)**

$$\text{Coefficient of variation (CV)} = \sigma/\bar{R} \qquad \text{(5-5)}$$

Thus, the coefficient of variation is a measure of *relative dispersion (risk)*—a measure of risk "per unit of expected return." The larger the CV, the larger the relative risk of the investment. Using the CV as our risk measure, investment A with a return distribution CV of .75 is viewed as being more risky than investment B, whose CV equals only .33.

Coefficient of variation (CV) The ratio of the standard deviation of a distribution to the mean of that distribution. It is a measure of *relative* risk.

ATTITUDES TOWARD RISK

Just when you thought that you were safely immersed in the middle of a finance chapter, you find yourself caught up in a time warp, and you are a contestant on the television game show *Let's Make a Deal*. The host, Monty Hall, explains that you get to keep whatever you find behind either door #1 or door #2. He tells you that behind one door is $10,000 in cash, but behind the other door is a "zonk," a used tire with a current market value of zero. You choose to open door #1 and claim your prize. But before you can make a move, Monty says that he will offer you a sum of money to call off the whole deal.

"Will it be door #1, or door #2?"

(Before reading any further, decide for yourself what dollar amount would make you indifferent between taking what is behind the door or taking the money. That is, determine an amount such that one dollar more would prompt you to take the money; one dollar less and you would keep the door. Write this number down on a sheet of paper. In a moment, we will predict what that number will look like.)

Let's assume that you decide that if Monty offers you $2,999 or less, you will keep the door. At $3,000 you can't quite make up your mind. But at $3,001, or more, you would take the cash offered and give up the door. Monty offers you $3,500, so you take the cash and give up the door. (By the way, the $10,000 was behind door #1, so you blew it.)

What does any of this have to do with this chapter on risk and return? Everything. We have just illustrated the fact that the average investor is averse to risk. Let's see why. You had a 50/50 chance of getting $10,000 or nothing by keeping a door. The expected value of keeping a door is $5,000 (.50 × $10,000 plus .50 × $0). In our example, you found yourself *indifferent* between a risky (uncertain) $5,000 expected return and a certain return of $3,000. In other words, this certain or riskless amount, your **certainty equivalent (CE)** to the risky gamble, provided you with the same utility or satisfaction as the risky expected value of $5,000.

Certainty equivalent (CE) The amount of cash someone would require with certainty at a point in time to make the individual indifferent between that certain amount and an amount expected to be received with risk at the same point in time.

It would be amazing if your actual certainty equivalent in this situation was exactly $3,000, the number that we used in the example. But, take a look at the number that we asked you to write down. It is probably less than $5,000. Studies have shown that the vast majority of individuals, if placed in a similar situation, would have a certainty equivalent less than the expected value (i.e., less than $5,000). We can, in fact, use the relationship of an individual's certainty equivalent to the expected monetary value of a risky investment (or opportunity) to define their attitude toward risk. In general, if the

- Certainty equivalent < expected value, *risk aversion* is present.
- Certainty equivalent = expected value, *risk indifference* is present.
- Certainty equivalent > expected value, *risk preference* is present.

Thus, in our *Let's Make a Deal* example, any certainty equivalent less than $5,000 indicates risk aversion. For risk-averse individuals, the difference between the certainty equivalent and the expected value of an investment constitutes a *risk premium;* this is additional expected return that the risky investment must offer to the investor for this individual to accept the risky investment. Notice that in our example the risky investment's expected value had to exceed the sure-thing offer of $3,000 by $2,000 or more for you to be willing to accept it.

Risk averse Term applied to an investor who demands a higher expected return, the higher the risk.

In this book we will take the generally accepted view that investors are, by and large, **risk averse.** This implies that risky investments must offer higher expected returns than less risky investments in order for people to buy and hold them. (Keep in mind, however, that we are talking about *expected* returns; the *actual* return on a risky investment could be much less than the *actual* return on a less risky alternative.) And, to have low risk, you must be willing to accept investments having lower expected returns. In short, there is no free lunch when it comes to investments. Any claims for high returns produced by low-risk investments should be viewed skeptically.

RISK AND RETURN IN A PORTFOLIO CONTEXT

So far, we have focused on the risk and return of single investments held in isolation. Investors rarely place their entire wealth into a single asset or investment. Rather, they construct a **portfolio** or group of investments. Therefore, we need to extend our analysis of risk and return to include portfolios.

Portfolio A combination of two or more securities or assets.

Portfolio Return

The expected return of a portfolio is simply a weighted average of the expected returns of the securities comprising that portfolio. The weights are equal to the proportion of total funds invested in each security (the weights must sum to 100 percent). The general formula for the expected return of a portfolio, $\bar{R}_p$, is as follows:

$$\bar{R}_p = \sum_{j=1}^{m} W_j \bar{R}_j \qquad \text{(5-6)}$$

where W_j is the proportion, or *weight*, of total funds invested in security j; $\bar{R}_j$ is the expected return for security j; and m is the total number of different securities in the portfolio.

The expected return and standard deviation of the probability distribution of possible returns for two securities are shown below.

	SECURITY A	SECURITY B
Expected return, $\bar{R}_j$	14.0%	11.5%
Standard deviation, σ_j	10.7	1.5

If equal amounts of money are invested in the two securities, the expected return of the portfolio is $(.5)14.0\% + (.5)11.5\% = \mathbf{12.75\%}$.

Portfolio Risk and the Importance of Covariance

Although the portfolio expected return is a straightforward, weighted average of returns on the individual securities, the portfolio standard deviation is *not* the simple, weighted average of individual security standard deviations. To take a weighted average of individual security standard deviations would be to ignore the relationship, or **covariance,** between the returns on securities. This covariance, however, does not affect the portfolio's expected return.

Covariance A statistical measure of the degree to which two variables (e.g., securities' returns) move together. A positive value means that, on average, they move in the same direction.

Covariance is a statistical measure of the degree to which two variables (e.g., securities' returns) move together. Positive covariance shows that, on average, the two variables move together. Negative covariance suggests that, on average, the two variables move in opposite directions. Zero covariance means that the two variables show no tendency to vary together in either a positive or negative linear fashion. Covariance between security returns complicates our calculation of portfolio standard deviation. Still, this dark cloud of mathematical complexity contains a silver lining—covariance between securities provides for the possibility of eliminating some risk *without reducing potential return.*

The calculation of a portfolio's standard deviation, σ_p, is complicated and requires illustration.[3] We therefore address it in detail in Appendix A at the end of this chapter. As explained in Appendix A, for a large portfolio, the standard deviation depends primarily on the "weighted" covariances among securities. The "weights" refer to the proportion of funds invested in each security, and the covariances are those determined between security returns for all pairwise combinations of securities.

An understanding of what goes into the determination of a portfolio's standard deviation leads to a startling conclusion. The riskiness of a portfolio depends much

---

[3]The standard deviation of a probability distribution of possible portfolio returns, σ_p, is

$$\sigma_p = \sqrt{\sum_{j=1}^{m} \sum_{k=1}^{m} W_j W_k \sigma_{j,k}}$$

where m is the total number of different securities in the portfolio, W_j is the proportion of total funds invested in security j, W_k is the proportion of total funds invested in security k, and $\sigma_{j,k}$ is the covariance between possible returns for securities j and k.

Part II Valuation

more on the paired security covariances than on the riskiness (standard deviations) of the separate security holdings. This means that a combination of *individually* risky securities could still comprise a moderate- to low-risk portfolio as long as securities do not move in lockstep with each other. In short, low covariances lead to low portfolio risk.

DIVERSIFICATION

The concept of diversification makes such common sense that our language even contains everyday expressions that exhort us to diversify ("Don't put all your eggs in one basket."). The idea is to spread your risk across a number of assets or investments. While pointing us in the right direction, this is a rather naive approach to diversification. It would seem to imply that investing $10,000 evenly across 10 different securities makes you more diversified than the same amount of money invested evenly across 5 securities. The catch is that naive diversification ignores the covariance (or correlation) between security returns. The portfolio containing 10 securities could represent stocks from only one industry and have returns that are highly correlated. The 5-stock portfolio might represent various industries whose security returns might show low correlation and, hence, low portfolio return variability.

Meaningful diversification, combining securities in a way that will reduce risk, is illustrated in Figure 5-2. Here the returns over time for security A are cyclical in that they move with the economy in general. Returns for security B, however, are mildly countercyclical. Thus, the returns for these two securities are negatively correlated. Equal amounts invested in both securities will reduce the dispersion of return, σ_p, on the portfolio of investments. This is because some of each individual security's variability is offsetting. Benefits of diversification, in the form of risk reduction, occur as long as the securities are not perfectly, positively correlated.

Investing in world financial markets can achieve greater diversification than investing in securities from a single country. As we will discuss in Chapter 24, the economic cycles of different countries are not completely synchronized, and a weak economy in one country may be offset by a strong economy in another. Moreover, exchange-rate risk and other risks discussed in Chapter 24 add to the diversification effect.

FIGURE 5-2
Effect of Diversification on Portfolio Risk

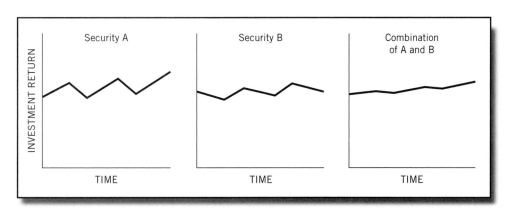

Systematic and Unsystematic Risk

We have stated that combining securities that are not perfectly, positively correlated helps to lessen the risk of a portfolio. How much risk reduction is reasonable to expect, and how many different security holdings in a portfolio would be required? Figure 5-3 helps provide answers.

Research studies have looked at what happens to portfolio risk as randomly selected stocks are combined to form equally weighted portfolios. When we begin with a single stock, the risk of the portfolio is the standard deviation of that one stock. As the number of randomly selected stocks held in the portfolio is increased, the total risk of the portfolio is reduced. Such a reduction is at a decreasing rate, however. Thus, a substantial proportion of the portfolio risk can be eliminated with a relatively moderate amount of diversification, say, 15 to 20 randomly selected stocks in equal-dollar amounts. Conceptually, this is illustrated in Figure 5-3.

As the figure shows, total portfolio risk is comprised of two components:

$$\text{Total risk} = \begin{matrix}\text{Systematic risk} \\ \text{(nondiversifiable} \\ \text{or unavoidable)}\end{matrix} + \begin{matrix}\text{Unsystematic risk} \\ \text{(diversifiable} \\ \text{or avoidable)}\end{matrix} \qquad (5\text{-}7)$$

The first part, **systematic risk,** is due to risk factors that affect the overall market—such as changes in the nation's economy, tax reform by Congress, or a change in the world energy situation. These are risks that affect securities overall and, consequently, cannot be diversified away. In other words, even an investor who holds a well-diversified portfolio will be exposed to this type of risk.

The second risk component, **unsystematic risk,** is risk unique to a particular company or industry; it is independent of economic, political, and other factors that affect all securities in a systematic manner. A wildcat strike may affect only one

Systematic risk The variability of return on stocks or portfolios associated with changes in return on the market as a whole.

Unsystematic risk The variability of return on stocks or portfolios not explained by general market movements. It is avoidable through diversification.

FIGURE 5-3
Relationship of Total, Systematic, and Unsystematic Risk to Portfolio Size

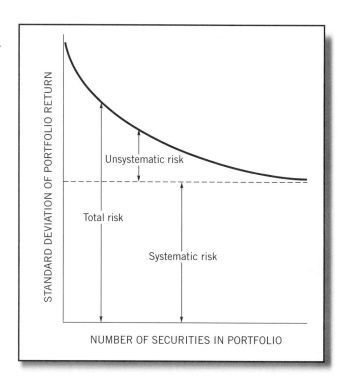

company; a new competitor may begin to produce essentially the same product; or a technological breakthrough can make an existing product obsolete. For most stocks, unsystematic risk accounts for around 50 percent of the stock's total risk or standard deviation. However, by diversification this kind of risk can be reduced and even eliminated if diversification is efficient. Therefore, not all of the risk involved in holding a stock is relevant because part of this risk can be diversified away. The important risk of a stock is its unavoidable or systematic risk. Investors can expect to be compensated for bearing this systematic risk. They should not, however, expect the market to provide any extra compensation for bearing avoidable risk. It is this logic that lies behind the *capital-asset pricing model.*

THE CAPITAL-ASSET PRICING MODEL (CAPM)

Capital-asset pricing model (CAPM) A model that describes the relationship between risk and expected (required) return; in this model, a security's expected (required) return is the risk-free rate plus a premium based on the systematic risk of the security.

Based on the behavior of risk-averse investors, there is an implied equilibrium relationship between risk and expected return for each security. In market equilibrium, a security is supposed to provide an expected return commensurate with its *systematic risk*—the risk that cannot be avoided by diversification. The greater the systematic risk of a security, the greater the return that investors will expect from the security. The relationship between expected return and systematic risk, and the valuation of securities that follows, is the essence of Nobel laureate William Sharpe's **capital-asset pricing model (CAPM).** This model was developed in the 1960s, and it has had important implications for finance ever since. Though other models also attempt to capture market behavior, the CAPM is simple in concept and has real-world applicability.

Like any model, this one is a simplification of reality. Nevertheless, it allows us to draw certain implications about risk and the size of the risk premium necessary to compensate for bearing risk. We shall concentrate on the general aspects of the model and its important implications. Certain corners have been cut in the interest of simplicity.

As with any model, there are assumptions to be made. First, we assume that capital markets are efficient in that investors are well informed, transactions costs are low, there are negligible restrictions on investment, and no investor is large enough to affect the market price of a stock. We also assume that investors are in general agreement about the likely performance of individual securities and that their expectations are based on a common holding period, say, one year. There are two types of investment opportunities with which we will be concerned. The first is a risk-free security whose return over the holding period is known with certainty. Frequently, the rate on short- to intermediate-term Treasury securities is used as a surrogate for the risk-free rate. The second is the *market portfolio* of common stocks. It is represented by all available common stocks and weighted according to their total aggregate market values outstanding. As the market portfolio is a somewhat unwieldy thing with which to work, most people use a surrogate, such as the **Standard & Poor's 500 Stock Price Index (S&P 500 Index).** This broad-based, market-value-weighted index reflects the performance of 500 major common stocks.

Standard & Poor's 500 Stock Index (S&P 500 Index) A market-value-weighted index of 500 large-capitalization common stocks selected from a broad cross section of industry groups. It is used as a measure of overall market performance.

Earlier we discussed the idea of unavoidable risk—risk that cannot be avoided by efficient diversification. Because one cannot hold a more diversified portfolio than the market portfolio, it represents the limit to attainable diversification. Thus, all the risk associated with the market portfolio is unavoidable, or systematic.

The Characteristic Line

We are now in a position to compare the expected return for an individual stock with the expected return for the market portfolio. In our comparison, it is useful to deal with returns in excess of the risk-free rate, which acts as a benchmark against which the risky asset returns are contrasted. The *excess* return is simply the expected return less the risk-free return. Figure 5-4 shows an example of a comparison of expected excess returns for a specific stock with those for the market portfolio. The dark blue line is known as the security's **characteristic line;** it depicts the expected relationship between excess returns for the stock and excess returns for the market portfolio. The expected relationship may be based on past experience, in which case actual excess returns for the stock and for the market portfolio would be plotted on the graph, and a regression line best characterizing the historical relationship would be drawn. Such a situation is illustrated by the scatter diagram shown in the figure. Each point represents the excess return of the stock and that of the S&P 500 Index for a given month in the past (60 months in total). The monthly returns are calculated as

$$\frac{(\text{Dividends paid}) + (\text{Ending price} - \text{Beginning price})}{\text{Beginning price}}$$

From these returns the monthly risk-free rate is subtracted to obtain excess returns.

For our example stock, we see that when returns on the market portfolio are high, returns on the stock tend to be high as well. Instead of using historical return relationships, one might obtain future return estimates from security analysts who follow the stock. Because this approach is usually restricted to investment organizations with a number of security analysts, we illustrate the relationship assuming the use of historical data.

Characteristic line A line that describes the relationship between an individual security's returns and returns on the market portfolio. The slope of this line is *beta.*

FIGURE 5-4
Relationship Between Excess Returns for a Stock and Excess Returns for the Market Portfolio Based on 60 Pairs of Excess Monthly Return Data

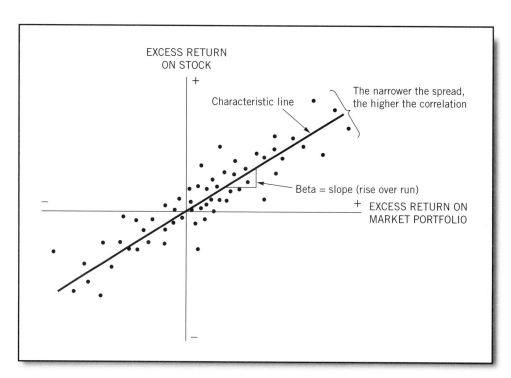

Beta: An Index of Systematic Risk

A measure that stands out in Figure 5-4, and the most important one for our purposes, is **beta.** Beta is simply the slope (i.e., the change in the excess return on the stock over the change in excess return on the market portfolio) of the characteristic line. If the slope is 1.0, it means that excess returns for the stock vary proportionally with excess returns for the market portfolio. In other words, the stock has the same systematic risk as the market as a whole. If the market goes up and provides an excess return of 5 percent for a month, we would expect, on average, the stock's excess return to be 5 percent as well. A slope steeper than 1.0 means that the stock's excess return varies more than proportionally with the excess return of the market portfolio. Put another way, it has more unavoidable risk than the market as a whole. This type of stock is often called an "aggressive" investment. A slope less than 1.0 means that the stock's excess return varies less than proportionally with the excess return of the market portfolio. This type of stock is often called a "defensive" investment. Examples of the three types of relationships are shown in Figure 5-5.

The greater the slope of the characteristic line for a stock, as depicted by its beta, the greater its systematic risk. This means that for both upward and downward movements in market excess returns, movements in excess returns for the individual stock are greater or less depending on its beta. With the beta of the market portfolio equal to 1.0 by definition, beta is thus an index of a stock's systematic or unavoidable risk relative to that of the market portfolio. This risk cannot be diversified away by investing in more stocks, because it depends on such things as changes in the economy and in the political atmosphere, which affect all stocks.

FIGURE 5-5
Examples of Characteristic Lines with Different Betas

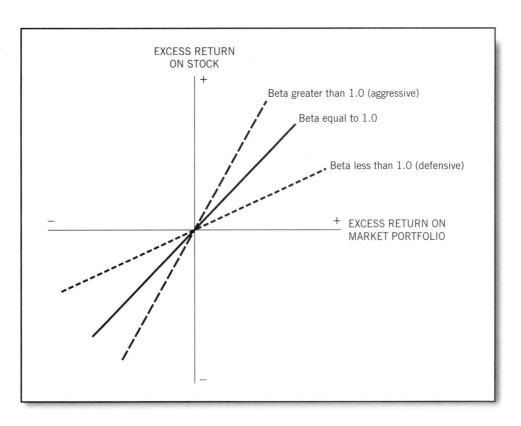

In addition, a portfolio's beta is simply a weighted average of the individual stock betas in the portfolio, with the weights being the proportion of total portfolio market value represented by each stock. Thus, the beta of a stock represents its contribution to the risk of a highly diversified portfolio of stocks.

Unsystematic (Diversifiable) Risk Revisited

Before moving on, we need to mention an additional feature of Figure 5-4. The dispersion of the data points about the characteristic line is a measure of the unsystematic risk of the stock. The wider the relative distance of the points from the line, the greater the unsystematic risk of the stocks; this is to say that the stock's return has increasingly lower correlation with the return on the market portfolio. The narrower the dispersion, the higher the correlation and the lower the unsystematic risk. From before, we know that unsystematic risk can be reduced or even eliminated through efficient diversification. For a portfolio of 20 carefully selected stocks, the data points would hover closely around the characteristic line for the portfolio.

Required Rates of Return and the Security Market Line (SML)

If we assume that financial markets are efficient and that investors as a whole are efficiently diversified, unsystematic risk is a minor matter. The major risk associated with a stock becomes its systematic risk. The greater the beta of a stock, the greater the relevant risk of that stock, and the greater the return required. If we assume that unsystematic risk is diversified away, the required rate of return for stock j is

$$\bar{R}_j = R_f + (\bar{R}_m - R_f)\beta_j \qquad \textbf{(5-8)}$$

where R_f is the risk-free rate, $\bar{R}_m$ is the expected return for the market portfolio, and β_j is the beta coefficient for stock j as defined earlier.

Put another way, the required rate of return for a stock is equal to the return required by the market for a riskless investment plus a risk premium. In turn, the risk premium is a function of (1) the expected market return less the risk-free rate, which represents the risk premium required for the typical stock in the market; and (2) the beta coefficient. Suppose that the expected return on Treasury securities is 8 percent, the expected return on the market portfolio is 13 percent, and the beta of Savance Corporation is 1.3. The beta indicates that Savance has more systematic risk than the typical stock (i.e., a stock with a beta of 1.0). Given this information and using Eq. (5-8), we find that the required return on Savance stock would be

$$\bar{R}_j = .08 + (.13 - .08)(1.3) = \textbf{14.5\%}$$

What this tells us is that on average the market expects Savance to show a 14.5 percent annual return. Because Savance has more systematic risk, this return is higher than that expected of the typical stock in the marketplace. For the typical stock, the expected return would be

$$\bar{R}_j = .08 + (.13 - .08)(1.0) = \textbf{13.0\%}$$

Suppose now that we are interested in a defensive stock whose beta coefficient is only .7. Its expected return is

$$\bar{R}_j = .08 + (.13 - .08)(.7) = \textbf{11.5\%}$$

The Security Market Line. Equation (5-8) describes the relationship between an individual security's expected return and its systematic risk, as measured by beta. This linear relationship is known as the **security market line (SML)** and is illustrated in Figure 5-6. The expected one-year return is shown on the vertical axis. Beta, our index of systematic risk, is on the horizontal axis. At zero risk, the security market line has an intercept on the vertical axis equal to the risk-free rate. Even when no risk is involved, investors still expect to be compensated for the time value of money. As risk increases, the required rate of return increases in the manner depicted.

Obtaining Information for the Model. If the past is thought to be a good surrogate for the future, one can use past data on excess returns for the stock and for the market to calculate the beta. Several services provide betas on companies whose stocks are actively traded; these betas are usually based on weekly or monthly returns for the past three to five years. Services providing beta information include the Value Line Investment Survey, Market Guide (www.marketguide.com), and Standard & Poor's Stock Reports. The obvious advantage is that one can obtain the historical beta for a stock without having to calculate it. See Table 5-2 for a sample of companies, their

identifying **ticker symbols,** and their stock betas. The betas of most stocks range from .4 to 1.4. If one feels that the past systematic risk of a stock is likely to prevail in the future, the historical beta can be used as a proxy for the expected beta coefficient.

In addition to beta, the numbers used for the market return and for the risk-free rate must be the best possible estimates of the future. The past may or may not be a good proxy. If the past was represented by a period of relative economic stability but considerable inflation is expected in the future, averages of past market returns and past risk-free rates would be biased, low estimates of the future. In this case, it would be a mistake to use historical average returns in the calculation of the required return for a security. In another situation, realized market returns in the recent past might be very high and not expected to continue. As a result, the use of the historical past would result in an estimate of the future market return that is too high.

In situations of this sort, direct estimates of the risk-free rate and of the market return must be made. The risk-free rate is easy; one simply looks up the current rate of return on an appropriate Treasury security. The market return is more difficult, but

FIGURE 5-6
The Security Market Line (SML)

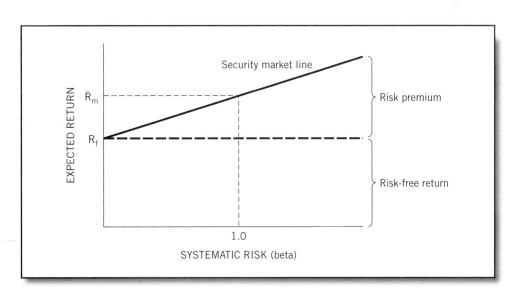

TABLE 5-2
Betas for selected stocks (August 11, 1999)

COMMON STOCK (Ticker Symbol)	BETA
Amazon.com (AMZN)	3.31
Apple Computer (AAPL)	.72
Boeing (BA)	.96
Bristol-Myers Squibb (BMY)	.86
The Coca-Cola Company (KO)	.96
Dow Chemical (DOW)	.86
The Gap (GPS)	1.09
General Electric (GE)	1.13
Georgia-Pacific Group (GP)	1.11
Hewlett-Packard (HWP)	1.34
The Limited (LTD)	.84
Microsoft (MSFT)	1.33
Nike (NKE)	1.01
Yahoo! (YHOO)	3.32

Source: Market Guide (www.marketguide.com).

even here forecasts are available. These forecasts might be consensus estimates of security analysts, economists, and others who regularly predict such returns. Estimates in recent years of the return on common stocks overall have been in the 12 to 17 percent range.

Use of the Risk Premium. The excess return of the market portfolio (over the risk-free rate) is known as the *market risk premium*. It is represented by $(\bar{R}_m - R_f)$ in Eq. (5-8). The expected excess return for the S&P 500 Index has generally ranged from 5 to 8 percent. Instead of estimating the market portfolio return directly, one might simply add a risk premium to the prevailing risk-free rate. To illustrate, suppose that we feel we are in a period of uncertainty and there is considerable risk aversion in the market. Therefore, our estimated market return is $\bar{R}_m = .08 + .07 = 15\%$, where .08 is the risk-free rate and .07 is our market risk premium estimate. If, on the other hand, we feel that there is substantially less risk aversion in the market, we might use a risk premium of 5 percent, in which case the estimated market return is 13 percent.

The important thing is that the expected market return on common stocks and the risk-free rate employed in Eq. (5-8) be current market estimates. Blind adherence to historical rates of return may result in faulty estimates of these data inputs to the capital-asset pricing model.

Returns and Stock Prices

The capital-asset pricing model provides us a means by which to estimate the required rate of return on a security. This return can then be used as the discount rate in a dividend valuation model. You will recall that the intrinsic value of a share of stock can be expressed as the present value of the stream of expected future dividends. That is

$$V = \sum_{t=1}^{\infty} \frac{D_t}{(1 + k_e)^t}$$

(5-9)

where D_t is the expected dividend in period t, k_e is the required rate of return for the stock, and Σ is the sum of the present value of future dividends going from period 1 to infinity.

Suppose that we wished to determine the value of the stock of Savance Corporation and that the perpetual dividend growth model was appropriate. This model is

$$V = \frac{D_1}{k_e - g} \tag{5-10}$$

where g is the expected annual future growth rate in dividends per share. Furthermore, assume that Savance Corporation's expected dividend in period 1 is $2 per share and that the expected annual growth rate in dividends per share is 10 percent. A few pages ago, we determined that the required rate of return for Savance was 14.5 percent. On the basis of these expectations, the value of the stock is

$$V = \frac{\$2.00}{(.145 - .10)} = \textbf{\$44.44}$$

If this value equaled the current market price, the *expected return* on the stock and the *required return* would be equal. The $44.44 figure would represent the *equilibrium price* of the stock, based on investor expectations about the company, about the market as a whole, and about the return available on the riskless asset.

These expectations can change, and when they do, the value (and price) of the stock changes. Suppose that inflation in the economy has diminished and we enter a period of relatively stable growth. As a result, interest rates decline, and investor risk aversion lessens. Moreover, the growth rate of the company's dividends also declines somewhat. The variables, both before and after these changes, are as listed below.

	BEFORE	AFTER
Risk-free rate, R_f	.08	.07
Expected market return, $\bar{R}_m$	.13	.11
Savance beta, β_j	1.30	1.20
Savance dividend growth rate, g	.10	.09

The required rate of return for Savance stock, based on systematic risk, becomes

$$\bar{R}_j = .07 + (.11 - .07)(1.20) = \textbf{11.8\%}$$

Using this rate as k_e, the new value of the stock is

$$V = \frac{\$2.00}{.118 - .09} = \textbf{\$71.43}$$

Thus, the combination of these events causes the value of the stock to increase from $44.44 to $71.43 per share. If the expectation of these events represented the market consensus, $71.43 would also be the equilibrium price. Thus, the equilibrium price of a stock can change very quickly as expectations in the marketplace change.

Underpriced and Overpriced Stocks. We just finished saying that in market equilibrium the required rate of return on a stock equals its expected return. That is, all stocks will lie on the security market line. What happens when this is not so? Suppose that in Figure 5-7 the security market line is drawn on the basis of what investors as a whole know to be the approximate relationship between the required rate of return and systematic or unavoidable risk. For some reason, two stocks—call them X and Y—are improperly priced. Stock X is underpriced relative to the security market line, whereas stock Y is overpriced.

FIGURE 5-7
Underpriced and
Overpriced Stocks
During Temporary
Market Disequilib-
rium

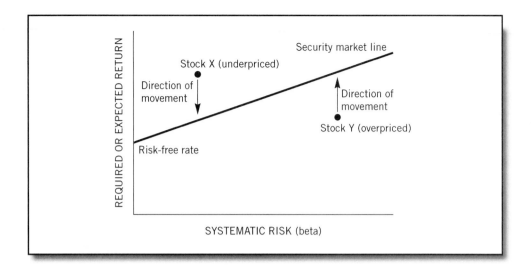

As a result, stock X is expected to provide a rate of return greater than that required, based on its systematic risk. In contrast, stock Y is expected to provide a lower return than that required to compensate for its systematic risk. Investors, seeing the opportunity for superior returns by investing in stock X, should rush to buy it. This action would drive the price up and the expected return down. How long would this continue? It would continue until the market price was such that the expected return would now lie on the security market line. In the case of stock Y, investors holding this stock would sell it, recognizing that they could obtain a higher return for the same amount of systematic risk with other stocks. This selling pressure would drive Y's market price down and its expected return up until the expected return was on the security market line.

When the expected returns for these two stocks return to the security market line, market equilibrium will again prevail. As a result, the expected returns for the two stocks will then equal their required returns. Available evidence suggests that disequilibrium situations in stock prices do not long persist and that stock prices adjust rapidly to new information. With the vast amount of evidence indicating market efficiency, the security market line concept becomes a useful means for determining the expected and required rate of return for a stock.[4] This rate can then be used as the discount rate in the valuation procedures described earlier.

Challenges to the CAPM

The CAPM has not gone unchallenged. As we know, the key ingredient in the model is the use of beta as a measure of risk. Early empirical studies showed beta to have reasonable predictive power about return, particularly the return on a portfolio of common stocks. No one claimed the model was perfect; as if anything were! However, it is fairly easy to understand and apply. Such market imperfections as bankruptcy costs, taxes, and institutional restraints have been recognized, and

---

[4]It is difficult in practice to derive satisfactory beta information for fixed-income securities. Therefore, most of the work on the CAPM has involved common stocks. The concept of the relationship between systematic risk and the required return is important, however, for both fixed-income securities and common stocks.

refinements can be made to account for their effects. Some of these refinements are explored in subsequent chapters when we deal with applications of the CAPM.

Anomalies. When scholars have tried to explain actual security returns, several anomalies have become evident. One is a *small-firm, or size, effect.* It has been found that common stocks of firms with small market capitalizations (price per share times the number of shares outstanding) provide higher returns than common stocks of firms with high capitalizations, holding other things constant. Another irregularity is that common stocks with low *price/earnings* and *market-to-book-value ratios* do better than common stocks with high ratios. Still other anomalies exist. For example, holding a common stock from December to January often produces a higher return than is possible for other similar-length periods. This anomaly is known as the *January effect.* Although these January effects have been found for many years, they do not occur every year.

Fama and French Study. In a provocative article, Eugene Fama and Kenneth French looked empirically at the relationship among common stock returns and a firm's market capitalization (size), market-to-book-value ratio, and beta.[5] Testing stock returns over the 1963–1990 period, they found that the size and market-to-book-value variables are powerful predictors of average stock returns. When these variables were used first in a regression analysis, the added beta variable was found to have little additional explanatory power. This led Professor Fama, a highly respected researcher, to claim that beta—as sole variable explaining returns—is "dead." Thus, Fama and French launched a powerful attack on the ability of the CAPM to explain common stock returns, suggesting that a firm's market value (size) and market-to-book-value ratio are the appropriate proxies for risk.

However, the authors tried to explain market value returns with two variables that are based on market value. The fact that the correlation between the explained variable and the explaining variables is high is not surprising. Fama and French did not focus on risk, but rather on realized returns. No theoretical foundation is offered for the findings they discovered. Though beta may not be a good indicator of the returns to be *realized* from investing in common stocks, beta remains a reasonable measure of risk. To the extent that investors are risk averse, beta gives information about the underlying minimum return that one should expect to earn. This return may or may not be realized by investors. However, for purposes of corporate finance it is a helpful guide for allocating capital to investment projects.

The CAPM and Multifactor Models. Although the CAPM remains useful for our purposes, it does not give a precise measurement of the market equilibration process or of the required return for a particular stock. *Multifactor models*—that is, models which claim that the return on a security is sensitive to movements of multiple factors, or indices, and not just to overall market movements—give added dimension to risk and certainly have more explanatory power than a single-factor model like the CAPM. In Appendix B to this chapter we take up multifactor models and a specific model called the *arbitrage pricing theory.* Our view is that the CAPM remains a practical way to look at risk and returns that might be required in capital markets. It also serves as a general framework for understanding unavoidable (systematic) risk, diversification, and the risk premium above the risk-free rate that is necessary in order to attract capital. This framework is applicable to all valuation models in finance.

---

[5]Eugene F. Fama and Kenneth R. French, "The Cross-Section of Expected Stock Returns," *Journal of Finance* 47 (June 1992), 427–65. See also Eugene F. Fama and Kenneth R. French, "Common Risk Factors in the Returns on Stocks and Bonds," *Journal of Financial Economics* 33 (February 1993), 3–56.

Efficient financial market A financial market in which current prices fully reflect all available relevant information.

Throughout this chapter we have implicitly considered the efficiency of financial markets. An **efficient financial market** exists when security prices reflect all available public information about the economy, about financial markets, and about the specific company involved. The implication is that market prices of individual securities adjust very rapidly to new information. As a result, security prices are said to fluctuate randomly about their "intrinsic" values. The driving force behind market efficiency is self-interest, as investors seek under- and overvalued securities either to buy or to sell. The more market participants and the more rapid the release of information, the more efficient a market should be.

New information can result in a change in the intrinsic value of a security, but subsequent security price movements will not follow any predictable pattern, so that one cannot use past security prices to predict future prices in such a way as to profit on average. Moreover, close attention to news releases will be for naught. Alas, by the time you are able to take action, security price adjustments already will have occurred, according to the efficient market notion. Unless they are lucky, investors will on average earn a "normal" or "expected" rate of return given the level of risk assumed.

Three Forms of Market Efficiency

Eugene Fama, a pioneer in efficient markets research, has described three levels to market efficiency:

- *Weak-form efficiency:* current prices fully reflect the *historical sequence of prices*. In short, knowing past price patterns will not help you improve your forecast of future prices.

- *Semistrong-form efficiency:* current prices fully reflect *all publically available information*, including such things as annual reports and news items.

- *Strong-form efficiency:* current prices fully reflect *all information*, both public and private (i.e., information known only to insiders).

On balance, the evidence indicates that the market for common stocks, particularly those listed on the New York Stock Exchange (NYSE), is reasonably efficient. Security prices appear to be a good reflection of available information, and market prices adjust quickly to new information. About the only way one can consistently profit is to have insider information, that is, information about a company known to officers and directors but not to the public. And, even here, SEC regulations act to limit attempts by insiders to profit unduly from information not generally available to the public. If security prices impound all available public information, they tell us a good deal about the future. In efficient markets, one can hope to do no better.

Stock market efficiency presents us with a curious paradox: The hypothesis that stock markets are efficient will be true only if a sufficiently large number of investors *disbelieve* its efficiency and behave accordingly. In other words, the theory requires that there be a sufficiently large number of market participants who, in their attempts to earn profits, promptly receive and analyze all information that is publically available concerning companies whose securities they follow. Should this considerable effort devoted to data accumulation and evaluation cease, financial markets would become markedly less efficient.

Does Market Efficiency Always Hold?

Anyone who remembers the stock market crash on October 19, 1987—when it went into a free fall, losing 20 percent in a few hours—is inclined to question the efficiency of financial markets. We know that stock market levels tend to increase over time in relatively small increments, but when they decline it is often with a vengeance. Still, the 1987 crash was huge by any standard. A number of explanations have been offered, but none is particularly compelling.

We are left with the uneasy feeling that although market efficiency is a good explainer of market behavior most of the time and securities seem to be efficiently priced relative to each other, there are exceptions. These exceptions call into question market prices embodying all available information and, therefore, whether they can be completely trusted. Not only are there some extreme events, like the 1987 stock market crash, but there are also some seemingly persistent anomalies. Perhaps these anomalies, some of which we discussed earlier, are merely the result of an inadequate measurement of risk. But perhaps they are due to things that we really do not understand. Although the concept of financial market efficiency underlies a good deal of our thinking, we must be mindful of the evidence that suggests exceptions.

SUMMARY

- The (holding period) *return* from an investment is the change in market price, plus any cash payments received due to ownership, divided by the beginning price.
- The *risk* of a security can be viewed as the variability of returns from those that are expected.
- The *expected return* is simply a weighted average of the possible returns, with the weights being the probabilities of occurrence.
- The conventional measure of dispersion, or variability, around an expected value is the *standard deviation, σ*. The square of the standard deviation, σ^2, is known as the *variance*.
- The standard deviation can sometimes be misleading in comparing the risk, or uncertainty, surrounding alternative investments if they differ in size. To adjust for the size, or scale, problem, the standard deviation can be divided by the expected return to compute the *coefficient of variation (CV)*—a measure of "risk per unit of expected return."
- Investors are, by and large, *risk averse*. This implies that they demand a higher expected return, the higher the risk.
- The *expected return from a portfolio* (or group) of investments is simply a weighted average of the expected returns of the securities comprising that portfolio. The weights are equal to the proportion of total funds invested in each security. (The weights must sum to 100 percent.)

- The *covariance* of the possible returns of two securities is a measure of the extent to which they are expected to vary together rather than independently of each other.
- For a large portfolio, total variance and, hence, standard deviation depend primarily on the weighted covariances among securities.
- Meaningful diversification involves combining securities in a way that will reduce risk. Risk reduction occurs as long as the securities combined are not perfectly, positively correlated.
- Total security (or portfolio) risk is comprised of two components—systematic risk and unsystematic risk. The first component, sometimes known as *unavoidable* or *nondiversifiable risk,* is *systematic* in the sense that it affects all securities, although to different degrees.
- *Unsystematic risk* is company specific in that it does not depend on general market movements. This risk is *avoidable* through proper diversification of one's portfolio.
- In market equilibrium, a security is supposed to provide an expected return commensurate with its systematic risk, the risk that cannot be avoided with diversification. The *capital-asset pricing model (CAPM)* formally describes this relationship between risk and return.
- The degree of systematic risk that a security possesses can be determined by drawing a *characteristic line.* This line depicts the relationship

between a stock's excess expected returns (returns in excess of the risk-free rate) and the market's excess expected returns. The slope (rise over run) of this line, known as *beta*, is an index of systematic risk. The greater the beta, the greater the unavoidable risk of the security involved.

- The relationship between the required rate of return for a security and its beta is known as the *security market line*. This line reflects the linear, positive relationship between the return investors require and systematic risk. The required return is the risk-free rate plus a risk premium for systematic risk that is proportional to beta.
- Although the CAPM has proved useful in estimating rates of return in capital markets, it has been seriously challenged in recent years. Anomalies such as the *small-firm effect, price/earnings ratio effect,* and the *January effect* have detracted from it. Professors Fama and French claim that a firm's market capitalization (size) and market-to-book-value ratio are better predictors of average stock returns than is beta. Still, the CAPM serves as a useful theoretical framework for understanding risk and leads naturally to multiple-factor models and the arbitrage pricing theory described in the Appendix to this chapter.
- Financial markets are said to be *efficient* when security prices fully reflect all available information. In such a market, security prices adjust very rapidly to new information.

Appendix A

Measuring Portfolio Risk

The total risk of a portfolio is measured by the standard deviation of the probability distribution of possible security returns, σ_p. The portfolio standard deviation, σ_p, is

$$\sigma_p = \sqrt{\sum_{j=1}^{m} \sum_{k=1}^{m} W_j W_k \sigma_{j,k}} \qquad \text{(5A-1)}$$

where m is the total number of different securities in the portfolio, W_j is the proportion of total funds invested in security j, W_k is the proportion of total funds invested in security k, and $\sigma_{j,k}$ is the covariance between possible returns for securities j and k. (The covariance term will be explained shortly.)

This rather intimidating formula needs some further explanation. The double summation signs, $\Sigma\Sigma$, mean that we sum across rows and columns all the elements within a square (m by m) matrix—in short, we sum m^2 items. The matrix consists of weighted covariances between every possible pairwise combination of securities, with the weights consisting of the product of the proportion of funds invested in each of the two securities forming each pair. For example, suppose that m equals 4. The matrix of weighted covariances for possible pairwise combinations would be

	COLUMN 1	COLUMN 2	COLUMN 3	COLUMN 4
Row 1	$W_1 W_1 \sigma_{1,1}$	$W_1 W_2 \sigma_{1,2}$	$W_1 W_3 \sigma_{1,3}$	$W_1 W_4 \sigma_{1,4}$
Row 2	$W_2 W_1 \sigma_{2,1}$	$W_2 W_2 \sigma_{2,2}$	$W_2 W_3 \sigma_{2,3}$	$W_2 W_4 \sigma_{2,4}$
Row 3	$W_3 W_1 \sigma_{3,1}$	$W_3 W_2 \sigma_{3,2}$	$W_3 W_3 \sigma_{3,3}$	$W_3 W_4 \sigma_{3,4}$
Row 4	$W_4 W_1 \sigma_{4,1}$	$W_4 W_2 \sigma_{4,2'}$	$W_4 W_3 \sigma_{4,3}$	$W_4 W_4 \sigma_{4,4}$

The combination in the upper left-hand corner is 1,1, which means that $j = k$ and our concern is with the weighted covariance of security 1 with itself, or simply security 1's weighted variance. That is because $\sigma_{1,1} = \sigma_1 \sigma_1 = \sigma^2_1$ in Eq. (5A-1) or the standard deviation squared. As we trace down the main diagonal from upper left to lower right, there are four situations in all where $j = k$, and we would be concerned with the weighted variances in all four. The second combination in row 1 is $W_1W_2\sigma_{1,2}$, which signifies the weighted covariance between returns for securities 1 and 2. Note, however, that the first combination in row 2 is $W_2W_1\sigma_{2,1}$, which signifies the weighted covariance between possible returns for securities 2 and 1. In other words, we count the weighted covariance between securities 1 and 2 twice. Similarly, we count the weighted covariances between all other combinations not on the diagonal twice. This is because all elements above the diagonal have a mirror image, or twin, below the diagonal. In short, we sum all of the weighted variances and covariances in our matrix of possible pairwise combinations. In our example matrix, we have 16 elements, represented by 4 weighted variances and 6 weighted covariances counted twice. The matrix, itself, is appropriately referred to as a *variance-covariance matrix*.

Equation (5A-1) makes a very fundamental point. The standard deviation for a portfolio depends not only on the variance of the individual securities but also on the covariances between various securities that have been paired. As the number of securities in a portfolio increases, the covariance terms become more important relative to the variance terms. This can be seen by examining the variance-covariance matrix. In a two-security portfolio, there are two weighted variance terms and two weighted covariance terms. For a large portfolio, however, total variance depends primarily on the covariances among securities. For example, with a 30-security portfolio, there are 30 weighted variance terms in the matrix and 870 weighted covariance terms. As a portfolio expands further to include all securities, covariance clearly becomes the dominant factor.

The *covariance* of the possible returns of two securities is a measure of the extent to which they are expected to vary together rather than independently of each other. More formally, the covariance term in Eq. (5A-1) is

$$\sigma_{j,k} = r_{j,k}\sigma_j\sigma_k \qquad \text{(5A-2)}$$

Correlation coefficient
A standardized statistical measure of the linear relationship between two variables. Its range is from -1.0 (perfect negative correlation), through 0 (no correlation), to $+1.0$ (perfect positive correlation).

where $r_{j,k}$ is the expected **correlation coefficient** between possible returns for securities j and k, σ_j is the standard deviation for security j, and σ_k is the standard deviation for security k. When $j = k$ in Eq. (5A-1), the correlation coefficient is 1.0 as a variable's movements correlate perfectly with itself, and $r_{j,j}\sigma_j\sigma_j$ becomes σ_j^2. Once again, we see that our concern along the diagonal of the matrix is with each security's own variance.

The correlation coefficient always lies in the range from -1.0 to $+1.0$. A positive correlation coefficient indicates that the returns from two securities generally move in the same direction, whereas a negative correlation coefficient implies that they generally move in opposite directions. The stronger the relationship, the closer the correlation coefficient is to one of the two extreme values. A 0 correlation coefficient implies that the returns from two securities are uncorrelated; they show no tendency to vary together in either a positive or negative linear fashion. Most stock returns tend to move together, but not perfectly. Therefore, the correlation coefficient between two stocks is generally positive, but less than 1.0.

Illustration of Calculations. To illustrate the determination of the standard deviation for a portfolio using Eq. (5A-1), consider a stock for which the expected value of annual return is 16 percent, with a standard deviation of 15 percent. Suppose further that another stock has an expected value of annual return of 14 percent and a standard deviation of 12 percent and that the expected correlation coefficient between the two stocks is .40. By investing equal-dollar amounts in each of the two stocks, the expected return for the portfolio would be

$$\bar{R}_p = (.5)16\% + (.5)14\% = \textbf{15\%}$$

In this case, the expected return is an equally weighted average of the two stocks comprising the portfolio. As we will see next, the standard deviation for the probability distribution of possible returns for the new portfolio will *not* be an equally weighted average of the standard deviations for two stocks in our portfolio; in fact, it will be less.

The standard deviation for the portfolio is found by summing up all the elements in the following variance-covariance matrix and then taking the sum's square root.

	Stock 1	Stock 2
Stock 1	$(.5)^2(1.0)(.15)^2$	$(.5)(.5)(.4)(.15)(.12)$
Stock 2	$(.5)(.5)(.4)(.12)(.15)$	$(.5)^2(1.0)(.12)^2$

Therefore,

$$\sigma_p = [(.5)^2(1.0)(.15)^2 + 2(.5)(.5)(.4)(.15)(.12)$$
$$+ (.5)^2(1.0)(.12)^2]^{.5}$$

$$= [.012825]^{.5} = \mathbf{11.3\%}$$

From Eq. (5A-1) we know that the covariance between the two stocks must be counted twice. Therefore, we multiply the covariance by 2. When $j = 1$ and $k = 1$ for stock 1, the proportion invested (.5) must be squared, as must the standard deviation (.15). The correlation coefficient, of course, is 1.0. The same thing applies to stock 2 when $j = 2$ and $k = 2$.

The important principle to grasp is that as long as the correlation coefficient between two securities is less than 1.0, the standard deviation of the portfolio will be less than the weighted average of the two individual standard deviations. [Try changing the correlation coefficient in this example to 1.0, and see what standard deviation you get by applying Eq. (5A-1)—it should, in this special case, be equal to a weighted average of the two standard deviations (.5)15% + (.5)12% = 13.5%.] In fact, for any size portfolio, as long as the correlation coefficient for even one pair of securities is less than 1.0, the portfolio's standard deviation will be less than the weighted average of the individual standard deviations.

The example suggests that, everything else being equal, risk-averse investors may want to diversify their holdings to include securities that have less-than-perfect, positive correlation $(r_{j,k} < 1.0)$ among themselves. To do otherwise would be to expose oneself to needless risk.

Appendix B

Arbitrage Pricing Theory

Arbitrage pricing theory (APT) A theory where the price of an asset depends on multiple factors and arbitrage efficiency prevails.

Perhaps the most important challenge to the capital-asset pricing model (CAPM) is the **arbitrage pricing theory (APT).** Originally developed by Stephen A. Ross, this theory is based on the idea that in competitive financial markets *arbitrage* will assure equilibrium pricing according to risk and return.[6] *Arbitrage* simply means finding two things that are essentially the same and buying the cheaper and selling the more expensive. How do you know which security is cheap and which is dear? According to the APT, you look at a small number of common risk factors.

Two-Factor Model

To illustrate with a simple two-factor model, suppose that the actual return on a security, R_j, can be explained by the following:

$$R_j = a + b_{1j}F_1 + b_{2j}F_2 + e_j \tag{5B-1}$$

---

[6]Stephen A. Ross, "The Arbitrage Theory of Capital Asset Pricing." *Journal of Economic Theory* 13 (December 1976), 341–60.

where a is the return when the two factors have zero values, F_1 and F_2 are the (uncertain) values of factors 1 and 2, b_{1j} and b_{2j} are the reaction coefficients depicting the change in the security's return to a one-unit change in a factor, and e_j is the error term.

For the model, the factors represent systematic, or unavoidable, risk. The constant term, denoted by a, corresponds to the risk-free rate. The error term is security specific and represents unsystematic risk. This risk can be diversified away by holding a broad-based portfolio of securities. These notions are the same as we discussed for the capital-asset pricing model, with the exception that there now are two risk factors as opposed to only one, the stock's beta. Risk is represented by an unanticipated change in a factor.

The expected return on a security, in contrast to the actual return in Eq. (5B-1), is

$$\bar{R}_j = \lambda_0 + b_{1j}(\lambda_1) + b_{2j}(\lambda_2) \tag{5B-2}$$

The λ_0 parameter corresponds to the return on a risk-free asset. The other λ (lambda) parameters represent risk premiums for the types of risk associated with particular factors. For example, λ_1 is the expected excess return (above the risk-free rate) when $b_{1j} = 1$ and $b_{2j} = 0$. The parameters can be positive or negative. A positive λ reflects risk aversion by the market to the factor involved. A negative parameter indicates value being associated with the factor, in the sense of a lesser return being required.

Suppose Torquay Resorts Limited's common stock is related to two factors where the reaction coefficients, b_{1j} and b_{2j}, are 1.4 and .8, respectively. If the risk-free rate is 8 percent, λ_1 is 6 percent, and λ_2 is -2 percent, the stock's expected return is

$$\bar{R} = \lambda_0 + b_{1j}(\lambda_1) + b_{2j}(\lambda_2)$$
$$= .08 + 1.4(.06) - .8(.02) = \mathbf{14.8\%}$$

The first factor reflects risk aversion and must be compensated for with a higher expected return, whereas the second is a thing of value to investors and lowers the expected return. Thus, the lambdas represent market prices associated with factor risks.

Thus, Eq. (5B-2) simply tells us that a security's expected return is the risk-free rate, λ_0, plus risk premiums for each of the factors. To determine the expected return, we simply multiply the market prices of the various factor risks, the lambdas, by the reaction coefficients for a particular security, the bs, and sum them. This weighted product represents the total risk premium for the security, to which we add the risk-free rate to obtain its expected return.

Multifactor Model

The same principles hold when we go to more than two factors. We simply extend Eq. (5B-1) by adding factors and their reaction coefficients. Factor models are based on the idea that security prices move together or apart in reaction to common forces as well as by chance (the error term). The idea is to isolate the chance element in order to get at the common forces (factors.) One way to do so is with a statistical technique called *factor analysis*, which, unfortunately, is beyond the scope of this book.

Another approach is to specify various factors on the basis of theory and then proceed to test them. For example, Richard Roll and Stephen A. Ross believe that there are five factors of importance.[7] These factors are (1) changes in expected inflation; (2) unanticipated changes in inflation; (3) unanticipated changes in industrial production; (4) unanticipated changes in the yield differential between low-grade and high-grade bonds (the default-risk premium); and (5) unanticipated changes in the yield differential between long-term and short-term bonds (the

---

[7]Richard Roll and Stephen A. Ross, "The Arbitrage Pricing Theory Approach to Strategic Portfolio Planning." *Financial Analysis Journal* 40 (May–June 1984), 14–26. For testing of the five factors, see Nai-Fu Chen, Richard Roll, and Stephen A. Ross, "Economic Forces and the Stock Market." *Journal of Business* 59 (July 1986), 383–403.

term structure of interest rates). The first three factors primarily affect the cash flow of the company and, hence, its dividends and growth in dividends. The last two factors affect the market capitalization, or discount, rate.

Different investors may have different risk attitudes. For example, some may want little inflation risk but be willing to tolerate considerable default risk and productivity risk. Several stocks may have the same beta, but greatly different factor risks. If investors are, in fact, concerned with these factor risks the CAPM beta would not be a good predictor of the expected return for a stock.

The Means to Producing Equilibrium—Arbitrage

How does a factor model of the Roll-Ross (or some other) type produce equilibrium security prices? The answer is, it produces them through individuals arbitraging across multiple factors, as mentioned at the outset. According to the APT, two securities with the same reaction coefficients (the bs in Eq. (5B-2)) should provide the same expected return. What happens if this is not the case? Investors rush in to buy the security with the higher expected return and sell the security with the lower expected return.

Suppose that returns required in the markets by investors are a function of two factors where the risk-free rate is 7 percent, as in

$$\bar{R}_j = .07 + b_{1j}(.04) - b_{2j}(.01)$$

Quigley Manufacturing Company and Zolotny Basic Products Corporation both have the same reaction coefficients to the factors, such that $b_{1j} = 1.2$ and $b_{2j} = .9$. Therefore, the required return for both securities is

$$\bar{R}_j = .07 + 1.3(.04) - .9(.01) = \textbf{11.3\%}$$

However, Quigley's stock is depressed, so its expected return is 12.8 percent. Zolotny's share price, on the other hand, is relatively high and has an expected return of only 10.6 percent. A clever arbitrager should buy Quigley and sell Zolotny (or sell Zolotny short). If the arbitrager has things right and the only risks of importance are captured by factors 1 and 2, the two securities have the same overall risk. Yet because of mispricing, one security provides a higher expected return than its risk would dictate, and the other provides a lower expected return than the facts would imply. This is a money game, and our clever arbitrager will want to exploit the opportunity as long as possible.

Price adjustments will occur as arbitragers recognize the mispricing and engage in the transactions suggested. The price of Quigley stock will rise, and its expected return will fall. Conversely, the price of Zolotny stock will fall, and its expected return will rise. This will continue until both securities have an expected return of 11.3 percent.

According to the APT, rational market participants will exhaust all opportunities for arbitrage profits. Market equilibrium will occur when expected returns for all securities bear a linear relationship to the various reaction coefficients, the bs. Thus, the foundation for equilibrium pricing is arbitrage. The APT implies that market participants act in a manner consistent with general agreement as to what are the relevant risk factors that move security prices.

Whether this assumption is a reasonable approximation of reality is a subject of much debate. There is disagreement as to which factors are important, and empirical testing has not produced parameter stability and consistency from test to test and over time. Because multiple risks are considered, the APT is intuitively appealing. We know that different stocks may be affected differently by different risks. Despite its appeal, the APT has not displaced the CAPM in use. However, it holds considerable future promise for corporate finance, and for this reason we have presented it to you.

QUESTIONS

1. If investors were not risk averse on average, but rather were either risk indifferent (neutral) or even liked risk, would the risk-return concepts presented in this chapter be valid?
2. Define the *characteristic line* and its *beta*.
3. Why is *beta* a measure of *systematic risk?* What is its meaning?
4. What is the required rate of return of a stock? How can it be measured?
5. Is the *security market line* constant over time? Why or why not?
6. What would be the effect of the following changes on the market price of a company's stock, all other things the same?
   a. Investors demand a higher required rate of return for stocks in general.
   b. The covariance between the company's rate of return and that for the market decreases.
   c. The standard deviation of the probability distribution of rates of return for the company's stock increases.
   d. Market expectations of the growth of future earnings (and dividends) of the company are revised downward.
7. Suppose that you are highly risk averse but that you still invest in common stocks. Will the betas of the stocks in which you invest be more or less than 1.0? Why?
8. If a security is undervalued in terms of the *capital-asset pricing model,* what will happen if investors come to recognize this undervaluation?

SELF-CORRECTION PROBLEMS

1. Suppose that your estimates of the possible one-year returns from investing in the common stock of the A. A. Eye-Eye Corporation were as follows:

Probability of occurrence	.1	.2	.4	.2	.1
Possible return	−10%	5%	20%	35%	50%

   a. What are the expected return and standard deviation?
   b. Assume that the parameters that you just determined [under Part (a)] pertain to a *normal* probability distribution. What is the probability that return will be zero or less? Less than 10 percent? More than 40 percent? (Assume a normal distribution.)
2. Sorbond Industries has a beta of 1.45. The risk-free rate is 8 percent and the expected return on the market portfolio is 13 percent. The company presently pays a dividend of $2 a share, and investors expect it to experience a growth in dividends of 10 percent per annum for many years to come.
   a. What is the stock's required rate of return according to the CAPM?
   b. What is the stock's present market price per share, assuming this required return?
   c. What would happen to the required return and to market price per share if the beta were .80? (Assume that all else stays the same.)

Appendix A Self-Correction Problem

3. The common stocks of companies A and B have the expected returns and standard deviations given below; the expected correlation coefficient between the two stocks is −.35.

	$\bar{R}_j$	σ_j
Common stock A	.10	.05
Common stock B	.06	.04

Compute the risk and return for a portfolio comprised of 60 percent invested in the stock of company A and 40 percent invested in the stock of company B.

PROBLEMS

1. Jerome J. Jerome is considering investing in a security that has the following distribution of possible one-year returns:

Probability of occurrence	.10	.20	.30	.30	.10
Possible return	−.10	.00	.10	.20	.30

   a. What is the expected return and standard deviation associated with the investment?
   b. Is there much "downside" risk? How can you tell?

2. Summer Storme is analyzing an investment. The expected one-year return on the investment is 20 percent. The probability distribution of possible returns is approximately normal with a standard deviation of 15 percent.
   a. What are the chances that the investment will result in a negative return?
   b. What is the probability that the return will be greater than 10 percent? 20 percent? 30 percent? 40 percent? 50 percent?

3. Suppose that you were given the following data for past excess quarterly returns for Markese Imports, Inc., and for the market portfolio:

QUARTER	EXCESS RETURNS MARKESE	EXCESS RETURNS MARKET PORTFOLIO
1	.04	.05
2	.05	.10
3	−.04	−.06
4	−.05	−.10
5	.02	.02
6	.00	−.03
7	.02	.07
8	−.01	−.01
9	−.02	−.08
10	.04	.00
11	.07	.13
12	−.01	.04
13	.01	−.01
14	−.06	−.09
15	−.06	−.14
16	−.02	−.04
17	.07	.15

QUARTER	EXCESS RETURNS MARKESE	EXCESS RETURNS MARKET PORTFOLIO
18	.02	.06
19	.04	.11
20	.03	.05
21	.01	.03
22	−.01	.01
23	−.01	−.03
24	.02	.04

On the basis of this information, graph the relationship between the two sets of excess returns and draw a *characteristic line*. What is the approximate *beta*? What can you say about the *systematic risk* of the stock, based on past experience?

4. Assuming that the CAPM approach is appropriate, compute the required rate of return for each of the following stocks, given a risk-free rate of .07 and an expected return for the market portfolio of 1.13:

Stock	A	B	C	D	E
Beta	1.5	1.0	.6	2.0	1.3

What implications can you draw?

5. On the basis of an analysis of past returns and of inflationary expectations, Marta Gomez feels that the expected return on stocks in general is 12 percent. The risk-free rate on short-term Treasury securities is now 7 percent. Gomez is particularly interested in the return prospects for Kessler Electronics Corporation. Based on monthly data for the past five years, she has fitted a characteristic line to the responsiveness of excess returns of the stock to excess returns of the S&P 500 Index and has found the slope of the line to be 1.67. If financial markets are believed to be efficient, what return can she expect from investing in Kessler Electronics Corporation?

6. Presently, the risk-free rate is 10 percent and the expected return on the market portfolio is 15 percent. Market analysts' return expectations for four stocks are listed here, together with each stock's expected beta.

STOCK	EXPECTED RETURN	EXPECTED BETA
1. Stillman Zinc Corporation	17.0%	1.3
2. Union Paint Company	14.5	.8
3. National Automobile Company	15.5	1.1
4. Parker Electronics, Inc.	18.0	1.7

a. If the analysts' expectations are correct, which stocks (if any) are overvalued? Which (if any) are undervalued?

b. If the risk-free rate were suddenly to rise to 12 percent and the expected return on the market portfolio to 16 percent, which stocks (if any) would be overvalued? Which (if any) undervalued? (Assume that the market analysts' return and beta expectations for our four stocks stay the same.)

7. Selena Maranjian invests the following sums of money in common stocks having expected returns as follows:

COMMON STOCK (Ticker Symbol)	AMOUNT INVESTED	EXPECTED RETURN
One-Legged Chair Company (WOOPS)	$ 6,000	.14
Acme Explosives Company (KBOOM)	11,000	.16
Ames-to-Please, Inc. (JUDY)	9,000	.17
Sisyphus Transport Corporation (UPDWN)	7,000	.13
Excelsior Hair Growth, Inc. (SPROUT)	5,000	.20
In-Your-Face Telemarketing, Inc. (RINGG)	13,000	.15
McDonald Farms, Ltd. (EIEIO)	9,000	.18

  a. What is the expected return (percentage) on her portfolio?

  b. What would be her expected return if she quadrupled her investment in Excelsior Hair Growth, Inc., while leaving everything else the same?

8. Salt Lake City Services, Inc., provides maintenance services for commercial buildings. Presently, the beta on its common stock is 1.08. The risk-free rate is now 10 percent, and the expected return on the market portfolio is 15 percent. It is January 1, and the company is expected to pay a $2 per share dividend at the end of the year, and the dividend is expected to grow a compound annual rate of 11 percent for many years to come. Based on the CAPM and other assumptions you might make, what dollar value would you place on one share of this common stock?

9. The following common stocks are available for investment:

COMMON STOCK (Ticker Symbol)	BETA
Nanyang Business Systems (NBS)	1.40
Yunnan Garden Supply, Inc. (YUWHO)	.80
Bird Nest Soups Company (SLURP)	.60
Wacho.com! (WACHO)	1.80
Park City Cola Company (BURP)	1.05
Oldies Records, Ltd. (SHABOOM)	.90

  a. If you invest 20 percent of your funds in each of the first four securities, and 10 percent in each of the last two, what is the beta of your portfolio?

  b. If the risk-free rate is 8 percent and the expected return on the market portfolio is 14 percent, what will be the portfolio's expected return?

Appendix A Problem

10. Common stocks D, E, and F have the following characteristics with respect to expected return, standard deviation, and correlation between them:

	$\bar{R}_j$	σ_j		$r_{j,k}$
Common stock D	.08	.02	between D and E	.40
Common stock E	.15	.16	between D and F	.60
Common stock F	.12	.08	between E and F	.80

What is the expected return and standard deviation of a portfolio comprised of 20 percent of funds invested in stock D, 30 percent of funds in stock E, and 50 percent of funds in stock F?

Part II Valuation

SOLUTIONS TO SELF-CORRECTION PROBLEMS

1. a.

POSSIBLE RETURN, R_i	PROBABILITY OF OCCURRENCE, P_i	$(R_i)(P_i)$	$(R_i - \bar{R})^2(P_i)$
−.10	.10	−.010	$(-.10 - .20)^2(.10)$
.05	.20	.010	$(.05 - .20)^2(.20)$
.20	.40	.080	$(.20 - .20)^2(.40)$
.35	.20	.070	$(.35 - .20)^2(.20)$
.50	.10	.050	$(.50 - .20)^2(.10)$
	$\Sigma = 1.00$	$\Sigma = .200 = \bar{R}$	$\Sigma = .027 = \sigma^2$
			$(.027)^{.5} = 16.43\% = \sigma$

b. For a return that will be zero or less, standardizing the deviation from the expected return, we obtain $(0\% - 20\%)/16.43\% = -1.217$ standard deviations. Turning to Table V in the Appendix at the back of the book, 1.217 falls between standard deviations of 1.20 and 1.25. These standard deviations correspond to areas under the curve of .1151 and .1056, respectively. This means that there is *approximately an 11 percent probability* that actual return will be zero or less.

For a return that will be 10 percent or less, standardizing the deviation we obtain $(10\% - 20\%)/16.43\% = -.609$ standard deviations. Referring to Table V, we see that this corresponds to *approximately 27 percent*.

For a return of 40 percent or more, standardizing the deviation we obtain $(40\% - 20\%)/16.43\% = 1.217$ standard deviations. This is the same as in our first instance involving a zero return or less, except that it is to the right, as opposed to the left, of the mean. Therefore, the probability of a return of 40 percent or more is *approximately 11 percent*.

2. a. $\bar{R} = 8\% + (13\% - 8\%)1.45 = \textbf{15.25\%}$

b. If we use the perpetual dividend growth model, we would have

$$P_0 = \frac{D_1}{k_e - g} = \frac{\$2(1.10)}{.1525 - .10} = \textbf{\$41.90}$$

c. $\bar{R} = 8\% + (13\% - 8\%).80 = \textbf{12\%}$

$$P_0 = \frac{\$2(1.10)}{.12 - .10} = \textbf{\$110}$$

Solution to Appendix A Self-Correction Problem

3. $\bar{R}_p = (.60)(.10) + (.40)(.06) = \textbf{8.4\%}$

$\sigma_p = [(.6)^2(1.0)(.05)^2 + 2(.6)(.4)(-.35)(.05)(.04) + (.4)^2(1.0)(.04)^2]^{.5}$

In the above expression, the middle term denotes the covariance $(-.35)(.05)(.04)$ times the weights of .6 and .4, all of which is counted twice—hence, the two in front. For the first and last terms, the correlation coefficients for these weighted variance terms are 1.0. This expression reduces to

$$\sigma_p = [.00082]^{.5} = \textbf{2.86\%}$$

SELECTED REFERENCES

Evans, Jack, and Stephen H. Archer. "Diversification and the Reduction of Dispersion: An Empirical Analysis." *Journal of Finance* 23 (December 1968), 761–67.

Fabozzi, Frank J. *Investment Management*, 2nd ed., Upper Saddle River, NJ: Prentice Hall, 1999.

Fama, Eugene F. "Efficient Capital Markets: A Review of Theory and Empirical Work." *Journal of Finance* 25 (May 1970), 384–87.

———. "Components of Investment Performance." *Journal of Finance* 27 (June 1972), 551–67.

———, and Kenneth R. French. "The Cross-Section of Expected Stock Returns." *Journal of Finance* 47 (June 1992), 427–65.

———, and Kenneth R. French. "Common Risk Factors in the Returns on Stocks and Bonds." *Journal of Financial Economics* 33 (February 1993), 3–56.

———, and Kenneth French. "Multifactor Explanations of Asset Pricing Anomalies." *Journal of Finance* 51 (March 1996), 55–84.

Ferson, Wayne, and Robert A. Korajczyk. "Do Arbitrage Pricing Models Explain the Predictability of Stock Returns?" *Journal of Business* 68 (1995), 309–49.

Grundy, Kevin, and Burton G. Malkiel. "Reports of Beta's Death Have Been Greatly Exaggerated." *Journal of Portfolio Management* 22 (Spring 1996), 36–44.

Haugen, Robert A. *Modern Investment Theory*, 4th ed. Upper Saddle River, NJ: Prentice Hall, 1997.

Horim, M. Ben, and H. Levy. "Total Risk, Diversifiable Risk and Nondiversifiable Risk: A Pedagogic Note." *Journal of Financial and Quantitative Analysis* 15 (June 1980), 289–97.

Jagannathan, Ravi, and Ellen R. McGrattan. "The CAPM Debate." Federal Reserve Bank of Minneapolis, *Quarterly Review* 19 (Fall 1995), 1–17.

Kothari, S. P., and Jay Shanken. "In Defense of Beta." *Journal of Applied Corporate Finance* 8 (Spring 1995), 53–58.

Levy, Haim, Deborah Gunthorpe, and John Wachowicz Jr. "Beta and an Investor's Holding Period." *Review of Business* 15 (Spring 1994), 32–35.

Lindahl, Mary, and John Wachowicz Jr. "Judging Your Portfolio's Return, Given its Risk." *Review of Business* (forthcoming).

Modigliani, Franco, and Gerald A. Pogue. "An Introduction to Risk and Return." *Financial Analysts Journal* 30 (March–April 1974), 68–80, and (May–June 1974), 69–86.

Mullins, David W., Jr. "Does the Capital Asset Pricing Model Work?" *Harvard Business Review* 60 (January–February 1982), 105–14.

Reilly, Frank K., and Keith C. Brown. *Investment Analysis and Portfolio Management*, 6th ed. Orlando, FL: Dryden Press, 2000.

Roll, Richard. "Performance Evaluation and Benchmark Errors," *Journal of Portfolio Management* 6 (Summer 1980), 5–12.

———, and Stephen A. Ross. "The Arbitrage Pricing Theory Approach to Strategic Portfolio Planning." *Financial Analysts Journal* 40 (May–June 1984), 14–26.

Rosenberg, Barr. "The Capital Asset Pricing Model and the Market Model." *Journal of Portfolio Management* 7 (Winter 1981), 5–16.

Ross, Stephen A. "The Arbitrage Theory of Capital Asset Pricing." *Journal of Economic Theory* 13 (December 1976), 341–60.

Shanken, Jay, and Clifford W. Smith. "Implications of Capital Markets Research for Corporate Finance." *Financial Management* 25 (Spring 1996), 98–104.

Sharpe, William. "Capital Asset Prices: A Theory of Market Equilibrium Under Conditions of Risk." *Journal of Finance* 19 (September 1964), 425–42.

———, Gordon J. Alexander, and Jeffrey V. Bailey. *Investments*, 6th ed. Upper Saddle River, NJ: Prentice Hall, 1999.

Shrieves, Ronald E., and John M. Wachowicz Jr. "A Utility Theoretic Basis for 'Generalized' Mean-Coefficient of Variation (MCV) Analysis." *Journal of Financial and Quantitative Analysis* 16 (December 1981), 671–83.

Siegel, Jeremy J. "The Application of the DCF Methodology for Determining the Cost of Equity Capital." *Financial Management* 14 (Spring 1985), 46–53.

Stocks, Bonds, Bills and Inflation: Valuation Edition 1999 Yearbook. Chicago: Ibbotson Associates, 1999.

Wachowicz, John M., Jr., and Ronald E. Shrieves. "An Argument for 'Generalized' Mean-Coefficient of Variation Analysis." *Financial Management* 9 (Winter 1980), 51–58.

Chapter 6

Financial Statement Analysis

FINANCIAL STATEMENTS
  Balance Sheet Information • Income Statement Information
A POSSIBLE FRAMEWORK FOR ANALYSIS
  Use of Financial Ratios • Types of Ratios
BALANCE SHEET RATIOS
  Liquidity Ratios • Financial Leverage (Debt) Ratios
INCOME STATEMENT AND INCOME STATEMENT/BALANCE SHEET
  RATIOS
  Coverage Ratios • Activity Ratios • Profitability Ratios
TREND ANALYSIS
COMMON-SIZE AND INDEX ANALYSIS
  Financial Statement Items as Percentages of Totals • Financial
    Statement Items as Indexes Relative to a Base Year
SUMMARY
SUMMARY OF KEY RATIOS
APPENDIX: DEFERRED TAXES AND FINANCIAL ANALYSIS
QUESTIONS
SELF-CORRECTION PROBLEMS
PROBLEMS
SOLUTIONS TO SELF-CORRECTION PROBLEMS
SELECTED REFERENCES

Financial statements are like a fine perfume—to be sniffed but not swallowed.

—ABRAHAM BRILLOFF

To make rational decisions in keeping with the objectives of the firm, the financial manager must have analytical tools. Some of the more useful tools of financial analysis and planning are the subjects of this and the next chapter.

The firm itself and outside providers of capital—creditors and investors—all undertake financial statement analysis. The type of analysis varies according to the specific interests of the party involved. Trade creditors (suppliers owed money for goods and services) are primarily interested in the liquidity of a firm. Their claims are short term, and the ability of the firm to pay these claims quickly is best judged by an analysis of the firm's liquidity. The claims of bondholders, on the other hand, are long term. Accordingly, bondholders are more interested in the cash-flow ability of the firm to service debt over a long period of time. They may evaluate this ability by analyzing the capital structure of the firm, the major sources and uses of funds, the firm's profitability over time, and projections of future profitability.

Investors in a company's common stock are principally concerned with present and expected future earnings as well as with the stability of these earnings about a trend line. As a result, investors usually focus on analyzing profitability. They would also be concerned with the firm's financial condition insofar as it affects the ability of the firm to pay dividends and avoid bankruptcy.

Internally, management also employs financial analysis for the purpose of internal control and to better provide what capital suppliers seek in financial condition and performance from the firm. From an internal control standpoint, management needs to undertake financial analysis in order to plan and control effectively. To plan for the future, the financial manager must assess the firm's present financial position and evaluate opportunities in relation to this current position. With respect to internal control, the financial manager is particularly concerned with the return on investment provided by the various assets of the company and in the efficiency of asset management. Finally, to bargain effectively for outside funds, the financial manager needs to be attuned to all aspects of financial analysis that outside suppliers of capital use in evaluating the firm. We see, then, that the type of financial analysis undertaken varies according to the particular interests of the analyst.

FINANCIAL STATEMENTS

Balance sheet A summary of a firm's financial position on a given date that shows total assets = total liabilities + owners' equity.

Income statement A summary of a firm's revenues and expenses over a specified period, ending with net income or loss for the period.

Financial analysis involves the use of various financial statements. These statements do several things. First, the **balance sheet** summarizes the assets, liabilities, and owners' equity of a business at a moment in time, usually the end of a year or a quarter. Next, the **income statement** summarizes the revenues and expenses of the firm over a particular period of time, again usually a year or a quarter. Though the balance sheet represents a snapshot of the firm's financial position *at a moment in time*, the income statement depicts a summary of the firm's profitability *over time*. From these two statements (plus, in some cases, a little additional information), certain derivative statements can be produced, such as a statement of retained earnings, a sources and uses of funds statement, and a statement of cash flows. (We consider the latter two in the next chapter.)

In analyzing financial statements, you may want to use a computer spreadsheet program. For repetitive analyses, such a program permits changes in assumptions and simulations to be done with ease. Analyzing various scenarios allows richer insight than otherwise would be the case. In fact, financial statements are an ideal application for these powerful programs, and their use for financial statement analysis (both external and internal) is quite common.

Balance Sheet Information

Table 6-1 shows the balance sheets of Aldine Manufacturing Company for the fiscal years ending March 31, 20X2, and March 31, 20X1. The assets are listed in the upper panel according to their relative degree of liquidity (that is, their closeness to cash). Cash and **cash equivalents** are the most liquid of assets, and they appear first. The further an asset is removed from cash, the less liquid it is. Accounts receivable are one step from cash, and inventories are two steps. Accounts receivable represent IOUs from customers, which should convert into cash within a given billing period, usually 30 to 60 days. Inventories are used in the production of a product. The product must first be sold and a receivable generated before it can go the next step and be converted into cash. Because fixed assets, long-term investment, and other long-term assets are the least liquid, they appear last.

The bottom panel of the table shows the liabilities and **shareholders' equity** of the company. These items are ordered according to the nearness with which they are likely to be paid. All current liabilities are payable within one year, whereas the long-term debt is payable beyond one year. Shareholders' equity will be "paid" only through regular cash dividends and, perhaps, a final liquidation dividend. Shareholders' equity, or *net worth* as it is sometimes called, consists of several subcategories. *Common stock* (at par) and *additional paid-in capital* together represent the total amount of money paid into the company in exchange for shares of common stock. As we discuss in Chapter 20, a par value is usually assigned to the stock. In this case the par value is $1 per share, which means that on March 31, 20X2, there were roughly 421,000 shares of common stock outstanding. The additional paid-in capital section represents money paid in excess of par value for shares sold. For example, if the company were to sell an additional share of stock for $6, there would be a $1 increase in the common stock section and a $5 increase in the additional paid-in capital section. *Retained earnings* represent a company's cumulative profits after dividends since the firm's inception; thus, these are earnings that have been retained (or reinvested) in the firm.

> **Take Note**
>
> It is common to hear people say that a company pays dividends "out of retained earnings." Wrong. A company pays dividends out of "cash," while incurring a corresponding reduction in the retained earnings account. Retained earnings are not a pile of cash (or any other asset) but merely an accounting entry used to describe one source of financing for the firm's assets.

We see in the table that total assets equal total liabilities plus shareholders' equity. Indeed, that is an accounting identity. Also, it follows that assets minus liabilities equal shareholders' equity. For the most part, the liabilities of the firm are known with certainty. Most accounting questions concerning the balance sheet have to do with the numbers attached to the assets. We must remember that the figures are accounting numbers as opposed to estimates of the economic value of the assets. The accounting value of fixed assets (land, buildings, equipment) is based on their actual (historical) costs, not on what they would cost today (the replacement value). Inventories are stated at the lower of cost or market value. The receivable figure implies

---

Cash equivalents Highly liquid, short-term marketable securities that are readily convertible to known amounts of cash and generally have remaining maturities of three months or less at the time of acquisition.

Shareholders' equity Total assets minus *total liabilities.* Alternatively, the book value of a company's common stock (at par) plus additional paid-in capital and retained earnings.

TABLE 6-1
Aldine Manufacturing Company balance sheets (in thousands)[1]

ASSETS[2]	MARCH 31 20X2	MARCH 31 20X1	EXPLANATIONS
Cash and cash equivalents	$ 178	$ 175	1. Shows how Company stands at close of business on a given date.
Accounts receivable[3]	678	740	2. What Aldine owned.
Inventories, at lower of cost or market[4]	1,329	1,235	3. Amounts owed to Company by customers.
Prepaid expenses[5]	21	17	4. Raw materials, work-in-process, and finished goods.
Accumulated tax prepayments	35	29	5. Future expense items (e.g., insurance premiums) that have already been paid.
Current assets[6]	$2,241	$2,196	
Fixed assets at cost[7]	1,596	1,538	
Less: Accumulated depreciation[8]	(857)	(791)	6. Cash and items likely convertible to cash within 1 year.
Net fixed assets	$ 739	$ 747	7. Original amount paid for land, buildings, and equipment.
Investment, long term	65	—	8. Accumulated deductions for wear and tear on fixed assets.
Other assets, long term	205	205	
Total assets[9]	$3,250	$3,148	9. Assets = liabilities + shareholders' equity.

LIABILITIES AND SHAREHOLDERS' EQUITY[10,11]	MARCH 31 20X2	MARCH 31 20X1	
Bank loans and notes payable	$ 448	$ 356	10. What Aldine owed.
Accounts payable[12]	148	136	11. Ownership interest of shareholders.
Accrued taxes[13]	36	127	12. Due to suppliers for goods and services.
Other accrued liabilities[14]	191	164	
Current liabilities[15]	$ 823	$ 783	13. "Accrued" refers to an obligation incurred but payment not yet made.
Long-term debt[16]	631	627	
Shareholders' equity			14. Unpaid wages, salaries, etc.
Common stock, $1 par value[17]	421	421	15. Debts payable within 1 year.
Additional paid-in capital	361	361	16. Debt that need not be paid until after 1 year (e.g., bonds).
Retained earnings[18]	1,014	956	
Total shareholders' equity	$1,796	$1,738	17. Amount originally invested in the business by the shareholders.
Total liabilities and shareholders' equity[19]	$3,250	$3,148	18. Earnings retained (i.e., reinvested) in the business.
			19. Liabilities + shareholders' equity = assets.

that all of these receivables will be collected. This may or may not be the case. Often it is necessary to go beyond the reported figures to properly analyze the financial condition of the firm. Depending on the analysis, the shareholders' equity figure shown on the balance sheet, which is a residual amount, may or may not be a reasonable approximation of the true value of the firm to the shareholders.

Income Statement Information

The income (earnings, or profit and loss) statement in Table 6-2 shows Aldine's revenues, expenses, and net profits for the two fiscal years under discussion. The **cost of goods sold** represents the cost of actually producing the products that were sold

Cost of goods sold Product costs (inventoriable costs) that become period expenses only when the products are sold; equals *beginning inventory* plus *cost of goods purchased* or *manufactured* minus *ending inventory.*

TABLE 6-2
Aldine Manufacturing Company statements of earnings (in thousands)[1]

	YEARS ENDED MARCH 31		EXPLANATIONS
	20X2	20X1	
Net sales[2]	$3,992	$3,721	1. Measures profitability over a period of time.
Cost of goods sold[3]	2,680	2,500	
Gross profit	$1,312	$1,221	2. Amount received, or receivable, from customers.
Selling, general, and administrative expenses[4]	912	841	3. Directly related to operating levels: wages, raw materials, supplies, and manufacturing overhead.
Earnings before interest and taxes[5]	$ 400	$ 380	
Interest expense[6]	85	70	
Earnings before taxes[7]	$ 315	$ 310	4. Salesmen's commissions, advertising, officers' salaries, etc.
Income taxes (federal and state)	114	112	
Earnings after taxes[8]	$ 201	$ 198	5. Operating income.
Cash dividends	143	130	6. Cost of borrowed funds.
Increase in retained earnings	$ 58	$ 68	7. Taxable income.
			8. Amount earned for stockholders.

Note: Depreciation expenses for 20X1 and 20X2 were $114 and $112, respectively.

during the period. Included here are the cost of raw materials, labor costs associated with production, and manufacturing overhead related to products sold. Selling, general, and administrative expenses as well as interest expense are shown separately from the cost of goods sold because they are viewed as period expenses rather than product costs.

Ask the Fool

Q Can you explain the "accrual" method of recognizing sales?

A With pleasure. It's an important concept to understand, because under this system, the "revenues" on a company's income statement may not have actually been received by the company.

Revenues, sometimes reported as "sales," don't necessarily represent the receipt of cash in a sale. Many firms "accrue" revenues, booking sales when goods are shipped, when services are rendered, or as a long-term contract proceeds through stages of completion.

Imagine the Beehive Wig Co. (ticker: WHOAA). With the accrual method, if it has shipped off a thousand crates of wigs but hasn't yet received payment for them, those sales still appear on the income statement. The checks "in the mail" get reported as "accounts receivable" on the balance sheet.

Keep an eye on receivables, to make sure the company isn't booking as sales that which it cannot collect. Also, make sure it's not packing sales into this quarter that really belong in the next quarter.

Source: The Motley Fool (www.fool.com). Reproduced with the permission of The Motley Fool.

For a manufacturing company, as in this case, depreciation expense is generally considered one component of the cost of goods manufactured and thus becomes part of the cost of goods sold. For a merchandising firm (wholesaler or retailer), depreciation is generally listed separately as another period expense (like interest expense) *below* the gross profit figure. Depreciation was discussed in Chapter 2, but remember that it is based on historical costs, which in a period of inflation may not correspond with economic costs.

The last three rows of the income statement shown in Table 6-2 represent a simplified *statement of retained earnings.* Dividends are deducted from earnings after taxes to give the increase in retained earnings. The increase of $58,000 in fiscal year 20X2 should agree with the balance sheet figures in Table 6-1. At fiscal year end for two consecutive periods, retained earnings were $956,000 and $1,014,000, the difference being $58,000. Therefore, there is agreement between the two balance sheets and the most recent income statement. With this background in mind, we are now ready to examine financial statement analysis.

A POSSIBLE FRAMEWORK FOR ANALYSIS

A number of different approaches might be used in analyzing a firm. Many analysts have a favorite procedure for coming to some generalizations about the firm being analyzed. At the risk of treading on some rather sacred ground, we present a conceptual framework that lends itself to situations in which external financing is contemplated. The factors to be considered are shown in Figure 6-1.

Taking them in order, our concern in the first case is with the trend and seasonal component of a firm's funds requirements. How much funding will be required in the future, and what is the nature of these needs? Is there a seasonal component to the needs? Analytical tools used to answer these questions include sources and uses of funds statements, statements of cash flow, and cash budgets, all of which are considered in Chapter 7. The tools used to assess the financial condition and performance of

FIGURE 6-1
Framework for
Financial Analysis

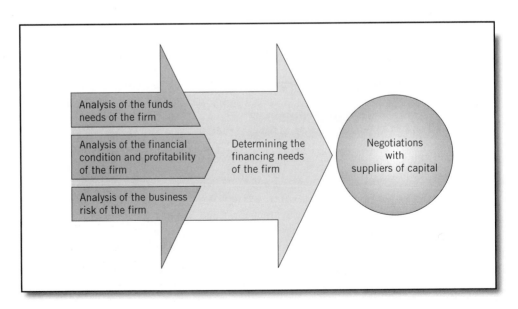

Analysis of the funds needs of the firm

Analysis of the financial condition and profitability of the firm

Analysis of the business risk of the firm

Determining the financing needs of the firm

Negotiations with suppliers of capital

the firm are financial ratios, a topic taken up in this chapter. The financial analyst uses these ratios much like a skilled physician uses lab-test results. In combination, and over time, these data offer valuable insight into the health of a firm—its financial condition and profitability. Completing our first set of three factors is an analysis of the business risk of the firm. *Business risk* relates to the risk inherent in the operations of the firm. Some companies are in highly volatile lines of business and/or may be operating close to their break-even point. Other companies are in very stable lines of business and/or find themselves operating far from their break-even point. A machine tool company might fall in the first category, whereas a profitable electric utility would probably fall in the latter. The analyst needs to estimate the degree of business risk of the firm being analyzed.

All three of these factors should be used in determining the financial needs of the firm. Moreover, they should be considered jointly. The greater the funds requirements, of course, the greater the total financing that will be necessary. The nature of the needs for funds influences the type of financing that should be used. If there is a seasonal component to the business, this component lends itself to short-term financing, bank loans in particular. The firm's level of business risk also strongly affects the type of financing that should be used. The greater the business risk, the less desirable debt financing usually becomes relative to common stock financing. In other words, equity financing is safer in that there is no contractual obligation to pay interest and principal, as there is with debt. A firm with a high degree of business risk is generally ill-advised to take on considerable financial risk as well.[1] The financial condition and performance of the firm also influence the type of financing that should be used. The greater the firm's liquidity, the stronger the overall financial condition; and the greater the profitability of the firm, the more risky the type of financing that can be incurred. That is, debt financing becomes more attractive with improvements in liquidity, financial condition, and profitability. The circled item in Figure 6-1 indicates that it is not sufficient to determine the best financing plan from the viewpoint of the firm and simply assume that it can be achieved. The plan needs to be sold to outside suppliers of capital. The firm may determine that it needs $1 million in short-term financing, but lenders may not go along with either the amount or the type of financing requested by management. In the end, the firm may have to compromise its plan to meet the realities of the marketplace. The interaction of the firm with these suppliers of capital determines the amount, terms, and price of financing. These negotiations are often not too far removed from the type of haggling one may witness in an oriental bazaar—although usually at a lower decibel level. In any event, the fact that the firm must negotiate with outside suppliers of capital serves as a feedback mechanism to the other factors in Figure 6-1. Analysis cannot be undertaken in isolation from the fact that ultimately an appeal will have to be made to suppliers of capital. Similarly, suppliers of capital must keep an open mind to a company's approach to financing, even if it is different from their own.

As we have just seen, there are a number of facets to financial analysis. Presumably, analysis will be in relation to some structural framework similar to that presented here. Otherwise, the analysis is likely to be loose and not lend itself to answering the questions for which it was intended. As we shall see, an integral part of financial analysis is the analysis of financial ratios—a topic that fills most of the remainder of this chapter.

---

[1] In Chapter 16 we discuss business risk in some detail, especially as it relates to the firm's willingness to take on financial risk.

Use of Financial Ratios

Financial ratio An index that relates two accounting numbers and is obtained by dividing one number by the other.

To evaluate a firm's financial condition and performance, the financial analyst needs to perform "checkups" on various aspects of a firm's financial health. A tool frequently used during these checkups is a **financial ratio,** or index, which relates two pieces of financial data by dividing one quantity by the other.

Why bother with a ratio? Why not simply look at the raw numbers themselves? We calculate ratios because in this way we get a *comparison* that may prove more useful than the raw numbers by themselves. For example, suppose that a firm had a net profit figure this year of $1 million. That looks pretty profitable. But, what if the firm has $100 million invested in total assets? Dividing net profit by total assets, we get $1M/$100M = .01, the firm's return on total assets. The .01 figure means that each dollar of assets invested in the firm earned a 1 percent return. A savings account provides a better return on investment than this, and with less risk. In this example, the ratio proved quite informative. But be careful. You need to be cautious in your choice and interpretation of ratios. Take *inventory* and divide it by *additional paid-in capital.* You have a ratio, but we challenge you to come up with any meaningful interpretation of the resulting figure.

Internal Comparisons. The analysis of financial ratios involves two types of comparison. First, the analyst can compare a present ratio with past and expected future ratios for the same company. The current ratio (the ratio of current assets to current liabilities) for the present year could be compared with the current ratio for the previous year end. When financial ratios are arrayed over a period of years (on a spreadsheet, perhaps), the analyst can study the composition of change and determine whether there has been an improvement or deterioration in the firm's financial condition and performance over time. In short, we are not so much concerned with one ratio at one point in time, but rather, that ratio over time. Financial ratios can also be computed for projected, or pro forma, statements and compared with present and past ratios.

External Comparisons and Sources of Industry Ratios. The second method of comparison involves comparing the ratios of one firm with those of similar firms or with industry averages at the same point in time. Such a comparison gives insight into the *relative* financial condition and performance of the firm. It also helps us identify any significant deviations from any applicable industry average (or standard). Financial ratios are published for various industries by Robert Morris Associates, Dun & Bradstreet, Prentice Hall (*Almanac of Business and Industrial Financial Ratios*), the Federal Trade Commission/the Securities and Exchange Commission, and by various credit agencies and trade associations.[2] Industry-average ratios should not, however, be treated as targets or goals. Rather, they provide general guidelines.

The analyst should also avoid using "rules of thumb" indiscriminately for all industries. The criterion that all companies have at least a 1.5 to 1 current ratio is inappropriate. The analysis must be in relation to the type of business in which the

---

[2]Robert Morris Associates, an association of bank credit and loan officers, publishes industry averages based on financial statements supplied to banks by borrowers. Sixteen ratios are computed annually for over 360 industries. In addition, each industry is divided into asset-size and sales-volume categories. Dun & Bradstreet annually calculates 14 important ratios for more than 800 industries. The *Almanac of Business and Industrial Financial Ratios* (Upper Saddle River, NJ: Prentice Hall, annual) shows industry averages for some 22 financial ratios. Approximately 180 businesses and industries are listed, covering the complete spectrum. The data for this publication come from United States corporate tax filings with the Internal Revenue Service. The *Quarterly Financial Report for Manufacturing Corporations* is published jointly by the Federal Trade Commission and the Securities and Exchange Commission. This publication contains balance sheet and income statement information by industry groupings and by asset-size categories.

firm is engaged and to the firm itself. The true test of liquidity is whether a company has the ability to pay its bills on time. Many sound companies, including electric utilities, have this ability despite current ratios substantially below 1.5 to 1. It depends on the nature of the business. Failure to consider the nature of the business (and the firm) may lead one to misinterpret ratios. We might end up with a situation similar to one in which a student with a 3.5 grade point average from Ralph's Home Correspondence School of Cosmetology is perceived as being a better scholar than a student with a 3.4 grade point average from Harvard Law School just because one index number is higher than the other. Only by comparing the financial ratios of one firm with those of similar firms can one make a realistic judgment.

To the extent possible, accounting data from different companies should be standardized (i.e., adjusted to achieve comparability).[3] Apples cannot be compared with oranges. Even with standardized figures, the analyst should use caution in interpreting the comparisons.

Types of Ratios

The commonly used financial ratios are of essentially two kinds. The first kind summarizes some aspect of the firm's "financial condition" at a point in time—the point at which a balance sheet has been prepared. We call these *balance sheet ratios*, quite appropriately, because both the numerator and denominator in each ratio come directly from the balance sheet. The second kind of ratio summarizes some aspect of a firm's performance over a period of time, usually a year. These ratios are called either *income statement* or *income statement/balance sheet ratios*. Income statement ratios compare one "flow" item from the income statement to another flow item from the income statement. Income statement/balance sheet ratios compare a flow (income statement) item in the numerator to a "stock" (balance sheet) item in the denominator. Comparing a flow item to a stock item poses a potential problem for the analyst. We run the risk of a possible mismatch of variables. The stock item, being a snapshot taken from the balance sheet, may not be representative of how this variable looked over the period during which the flow occurred. (Would a photograph of you taken at midnight on New Year's Eve be representative of how you look, on average?) Therefore, where appropriate, we may need to use an "average" balance sheet figure in the denominator of an income statement/balance sheet ratio to make the denominator more representative of the entire period. (We will have more to say on this later.)

TIP•TIP•TIP•TIP•TIP•TIP•TIP•TIP•TIP•TIP•TIP

Benchmarking—measuring a company's operations and performance against those of world-class firms—can be applied to ratio analysis. Therefore, in addition to comparing a firm's ratios to industry averages over time, you may also want to compare the firm's ratios to those of a "benchmark," or world-class, competitor in the firm's industry.

Additionally, we can further subdivide our financial ratios into five distinct types: liquidity, financial leverage (or debt), coverage, activity, and profitability ratios. (See Fig. 6-2.) No one ratio gives us sufficient information by which to judge

---

[3]Firms, even within the same industry, may apply different accounting procedures, thus contributing to a confusion between perceived and real differences among firms. For example, one firm may use FIFO inventory valuation, while another firm uses LIFO, and still a third firm uses average cost.

FIGURE 6-2
Types of Ratios

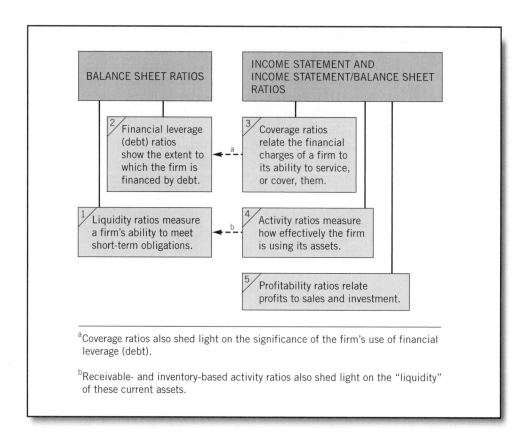

FIGURE 6-2
Types of Ratios

the financial condition and performance of the firm. Only when we analyze a group of ratios are we able to make reasonable judgments. We must be sure to take into account any seasonal character of a business. Underlying trends may be assessed only through a comparison of raw figures and ratios at the same time of year. We should not compare a December 31 balance sheet with a May 31 balance sheet but rather compare December 31 with December 31.

Although the number of financial ratios that might be compared increases geometrically with the amount of financial data, only the more important ratios are considered in this chapter. Actually, the ratios needed to assess the financial condition and performance of a company are relatively few.

BALANCE SHEET RATIOS

Liquidity Ratios

Liquidity ratios Ratios that measure a firm's ability to meet short-term obligations.

Liquidity ratios are used to measure a firm's ability to meet short-term obligations. They compare short-term obligations to short-term (or current) resources available to meet these obligations. From these ratios, much insight can be obtained into the present cash solvency of the firm and the firm's ability to remain solvent in the event of adversity.

Current ratio Current assets divided by current liabilities. It shows a firm's ability to cover its current liabilities with its current assets.

Current Ratio. One of the most general and frequently used of these liquidity ratios is the **current ratio**:

$$\frac{\text{Current assets}}{\text{Current liabilities}} \tag{6-1}$$

For Aldine Manufacturing Company, this ratio for year-end 20X2 is

$$\frac{\$2,241,000}{\$823,000} = \mathbf{2.72}$$

Aldine is engaged in making household electrical appliances. Its current ratio is somewhat above the median ratio for the industry of 2.1. (The median—or middle value—for the industry is taken from Robert Morris Associates, *Statement Studies.*[4]) Although comparisons with industry averages do not always reveal financial strength or weakness, they are meaningful in identifying companies that are out of line. Where a significant deviation occurs, the analyst will want to determine the reasons. Perhaps the industry itself is overly liquid, and the company being examined is basically sound despite a lower current ratio. In another situation, the company being analyzed may be too liquid, relative to the industry, with the result that it forgoes additional profitability. Whenever a financial "red flag" is raised, the analyst must search out the reasons behind it.

---

[4]The use of a median average eliminates the influence that extreme values from "unusual" statements would have on a simple arithmetic average.

Window Dressing: Taking steps, just before financial statements are prepared, to create a more favorable-looking situation than really exists

To illustrate, assume that it is March 30, the auditors are soon to arrive, we hope to make a short-term loan next week, and the bank will be very concerned with our current position as a sign of our short-term solvency.

We could postpone some purchases and use available cash (or sell marketable securities) to pay some current creditors. The current and quick ratios may thus be temporarily improved.

Let's see how Aldine Manufacturing Company might have tried this gambit. Assume, on March 30, 20X2, we find:

Current Assets	Current Liabilities	Current Ratio
$2,918,000	$1,500,000	1.95

If we pay off $677,000 worth of accounts payable from cash and marketable securities, we get

$2,241,000	$ 823,000	2.72

The current ratio has shown a healthy improvement. However, if we go back to business as usual, has our liquidity position really been improved by this one-time early payment to creditors?

It should be noted that year-end financial statements may paint a more rosy financial-condition picture than those at any other time in the year even when no deliberate steps have been taken to artificially enhance financial position. For example, a firm that has adopted a fiscal year ending in a seasonal low point (Red flag: note Aldine's March 31 fiscal-year closing date) may have done so not to deceive but to make inventory counting easier. However, cash may also be at a yearly high in anticipation of inventory purchases while accounts payable may be at a yearly low; the result may be higher than normal current and quick ratios.

Therefore, as a manager you may want to look at an average of monthly or quarterly liquidity ratios. This would give you a feel for the firm's *average* liquidity position. The idea here is that even if others who look at your annual data get fooled—don't fool yourself.

Liquidity The ability of an asset to be converted into cash without a significant price concession.

Supposedly, the higher the current ratio, the greater the ability of the firm to pay its bills; however, this ratio must be regarded as a crude measure because it does not take into account the **liquidity** of the individual components of the current assets. A firm having current assets composed principally of cash and nonoverdue receivables is generally regarded as more liquid than a firm whose current assets consist primarily of inventories.[5] Consequently, we turn to a more critical, or severe, test of the firm's liquidity—the acid-test ratio.

Acid-Test (or Quick) Ratio. A more conservative measure of liquidity is the **acid-test,** or **quick, ratio:**

Acid-test (quick) ratio Current assets less inventories divided by current liabilities. It shows a firm's ability to meet current liabilities with its most liquid (quick) assets.

$$\frac{\text{Current assets} - \text{Inventories}}{\text{Current liabilities}} \qquad (6\text{-}2)$$

For Aldine, this ratio for 20X2 year end is

$$\frac{\$2,241,000 - \$1,329,000}{\$823,000} = \textbf{1.11}$$

This ratio serves as a supplement to the current ratio in analyzing liquidity. This ratio is the same as the current ratio except that it excludes inventories—presumably the least liquid portion of current assets—from the numerator. The ratio concentrates primarily on the more liquid current assets—cash, marketable securities, and receivables—in relation to current obligations. Thus, this ratio provides a more penetrating measure of liquidity than does the current ratio. Aldine's acid-test ratio is slightly above the industry median average of 1.1, indicating that it is in line with the industry.

Summary of Aldine's Liquidity (So Far). Comparisons of Aldine's current and acid-test ratios with medians for the industry are favorable. However, these ratios don't tell us whether accounts receivable and/or inventory might actually be too high. If they are, this should affect our initial favorable impression of the firm's liquidity. Thus, we need to go behind the ratios and examine the size, composition, and quality of these two important current assets. We will look more closely at accounts receivable and inventory when we discuss activity ratios. We will reserve a final opinion on liquidity until then.

Financial Leverage (Debt) Ratios

Debt-to-Equity Ratio. To assess the extent to which the firm is using borrowed money, we may use several different **debt ratios.** The *debt-to-equity ratio* is computed by simply dividing the total debt of the firm (including current liabilities) by its shareholders' equity:

Debt ratios Ratios that show the extent to which the firm is financed by debt.

$$\frac{\text{Total debt}}{\text{Shareholders' equity}} \qquad (6\text{-}3)$$

For Aldine, at year-end 20X2 this ratio is

$$\frac{\$1,454,000}{\$1,796,000} = \textbf{.81}$$

---

[5]*Liquidity* has two dimensions: (1) the time required to convert the asset into cash, and (2) the certainty of the price realized. Even if the price realized on receivables were as predictable as that realized on inventories, receivables would be a more liquid asset than inventories, owing to the shorter time required to convert the asset into cash. If the price realized on receivables were more certain than that on inventories, receivables would be regarded as being even more liquid.

The ratio tells us that creditors are providing 81 cents of financing for each $1 being provided by shareholders. Creditors would generally like this ratio to be low. The lower the ratio, the higher the level of the firm's financing that is being provided by shareholders, and the larger the creditor cushion (margin of protection) in the event of shrinking asset values or outright losses. The median debt-to-equity ratio for the electrical appliance industry is .80, so Aldine is right in line with the industry. Presumably, it would not experience difficulty with creditors because of an excessive debt ratio.

Depending on the purpose for which the ratio is used, preferred stock is sometimes included as debt rather than as equity when debt ratios are calculated. Preferred stock represents a prior claim from the standpoint of the investors in common stock; consequently, investors might include preferred stock as debt when analyzing a firm. The ratio of debt to equity will vary according to the nature of the business and the variability of cash flows. An electric utility, with very stable cash flows, will usually have a higher debt-to-equity ratio than will a machine tool company, whose cash flows are far less stable. A comparison of the debt-to-equity ratio for a given company with those of similar firms gives us a general indication of the creditworthiness and financial risk of the firm.

Debt-to-Total-Assets Ratio. The *debt-to-total-assets ratio* is derived by dividing a firm's total debt by its total assets:

$$\frac{\text{Total debt}}{\text{Total assets}} \tag{6-4}$$

For Aldine, at the end of 20X2 this ratio is

$$\frac{\$1,454,000}{\$3,250,000} = .45$$

This ratio serves a similar purpose to the debt-to-equity ratio. It highlights the relative importance of debt financing to the firm by showing the percentage of the firm's assets that is supported by debt financing. Thus, 45 percent of the firm's assets are financed with debt (of various types), and the remaining 55 percent of the financing comes from shareholders' equity. Theoretically, if the firm were liquidated right now, assets could be sold to net as little as 45 cents on the dollar before creditors would face a loss. Once again, this points out that the greater the percentage of financing provided by shareholders' equity, the larger the cushion of protection afforded the firm's creditors. In short, the higher the debt-to-total-assets ratio, the greater the financial risk; the lower this ratio, the lower the financial risk.

In addition to the two previous debt ratios, we may wish to compute the following ratio, which deals with only the long-term capitalization of the firm:

$$\frac{\text{Long-term debt}}{\text{Total capitalization}} \tag{6-5}$$

where *total capitalization* represents all long-term debt and shareholders' equity. For Aldine, the most recent year-end *long-term-debt-to-total-capitalization ratio* is

$$\frac{\$631,000}{\$2,427,000} = .26$$

This measure tells us the relative importance of long-term debt to the capital structure (long-term financing) of the firm. Again, this ratio is in line with the median ratio of .24 for the industry. The debt ratios just computed have been based on accounting, book value, figures; it is sometimes useful to calculate these ratios using market values. In summary, debt ratios tell us the relative proportions of capital contribution by creditors and by owners.

INCOME STATEMENT AND INCOME STATEMENT/BALANCE SHEET RATIOS

We now turn our attention to three new types of ratios—coverage, activity, and profitability ratios—that are derived from either income statement or income statement/balance sheet data. The significance is that we are no longer talking about just stock (balance sheet) relationships. Now, each ratio relates a flow (income statement) item to another flow item or a mixture of a flow to a stock item. (And, to compare a flow to a stock item correctly, we may need to make some minor adjustments.)

Coverage Ratios

Coverage ratios Ratios that relate the financial charges of a firm to its ability to service, or cover, them.

Coverage ratios are designed to relate the financial charges of a firm to its ability to service, or cover, them. Bond rating services, such as Moody's Investors Service and Standard & Poor's, make extensive use of these ratios. One of the most traditional of the coverage ratios is the **interest coverage ratio,** or *times interest earned*. This ratio is simply the ratio of earnings before interest and taxes for a particular reporting period to the amount of interest charges for the period; that is,

Interest coverage ratio Earnings before interest and taxes divided by interest charges. It indicates a firm's ability to cover interest charges.

$$\frac{\text{Earnings before interest and taxes (EBIT)}}{\text{Interest expense}} \qquad \textbf{(6-6)}$$

For Aldine, in fiscal-year 20X2 this ratio is

$$\frac{\$400,000}{\$85,000} = \textbf{4.71}$$

This ratio serves as one measure of the firm's ability to meet its interest payments and thus avoid bankruptcy. In general, the higher the ratio, the greater the likelihood that the company could cover its interest payments without difficulty. It also sheds some light on the firm's capacity to take on new debt. With an industry median average of 4.0, Aldine's ability to cover annual interest 4.71 times with operating income (EBIT) appears to provide a good margin of safety.

A broader type of analysis would evaluate the ability of the firm to cover all charges of a fixed nature. In addition to interest payments, we could include principal payments on debt obligations, preferred stock dividends, lease payments, and possibly even certain essential capital expenditures. As we will see in Chapter 16, an analysis of this type is a far more realistic gauge than a simple interest coverage ratio in determining whether a firm has the ability to meet its long-term obligations.

In assessing the financial risk of a firm, then, the financial analyst should first compute debt ratios as a rough measure of financial risk. Depending on the payment schedule of the debt and the average interest rate, debt ratios may or may not give an accurate picture of the firm's ability to meet its financial obligations. Therefore, we augment debt ratios with an analysis of coverage ratios. Additionally, we realize that interest and principal payments are not really met out of earnings per se, but out of cash. Therefore, it is also necessary to analyze the cash-flow ability of the firm to service debt (and other financial charges as well). The topics addressed in the following chapter, as well as Chapter 16, will aid us in that task.

Activity Ratios

Activity ratios Ratios that measure how effectively the firm is using its assets.

Activity ratios, also known as *efficiency* or *turnover ratios,* measure how effectively the firm is using its assets. As we will see, some aspects of activity analysis are closely related to liquidity analysis. In this section, we will primarily focus our attention on how effectively the firm is managing two specific asset groups—receivables and inventories—and its total assets in general.

In computing activity ratios for the Aldine Company, we will use year-end asset levels from the balance sheet. However, an average of monthly, quarterly, or beginning and year-end asset levels is often employed with these income statement/ balance sheet ratios. As we mentioned earlier in the chapter, the use of an average balance sheet figure is an attempt to better match the income statement flow item with a balance sheet stock figure more representative of the *entire* period, not just year end.

Receivables Activity. The *receivable turnover (RT) ratio* provides insight into the quality of the firm's receivables and how successful the firm is in its collections. This ratio is calculated by dividing receivables into annual net credit sales:

$$\frac{\text{Annual net credit sales}}{\text{Receivables}} \tag{6-7}$$

If we assume that all 20X2 sales for Aldine are credit sales, this ratio is

$$\frac{\$3,992,000}{\$678,000} = \textbf{5.89}$$

This ratio tells us the number of times accounts receivable have been turned over (turned into cash) during the year. The higher the turnover, the shorter the time between the typical sale and cash collection. For Aldine, receivables turned over 5.89 times during 20X2.

When credit sales figures for a period are not available, we must resort to using total sales figures. When sales are seasonal or have grown considerably over the year, using the year-end receivable balance may not be appropriate. With seasonality, an average of the monthly closing balances may be the most appropriate to use. With growth, the receivable balance at the end of the year will be deceptively high in relation to sales. The result is that the receivable turnover calculated is a biased and low estimate of the number of times receivables turned over during the course of the year. In this case, an average of receivables at the beginning and end of the year might be appropriate if the growth in sales was steady throughout the year.

The median industry receivable turnover ratio is 8.1, which tells us that Aldine's receivables are considerably slower in turning over than is typical for the industry. This might be an indication of a lax collection policy and a number of past-due accounts still on the books. In addition, if receivables are far from being current, we may have to reassess the firm's liquidity. To regard all receivables as liquid, when in fact a sizable portion may be past due, overstates the liquidity of the firm being analyzed. Receivables are liquid only insofar as they can be collected in a reasonable amount of time. In an attempt to determine whether there is cause for concern, the analyst may reformulate the receivable turnover ratio to produce receivable turnover in days (RTD), or average collection period.

Receivable turnover in days (RTD), or *average collection period*, is calculated as

$$\frac{\text{Days in the year}}{\text{Receivable turnover}} \qquad \text{(6-8)}$$

or equivalently

$$\frac{\text{Receivables} \times \text{Days in the year}}{\text{Annual credit sales}} \qquad \text{(6-9)}$$

For Aldine, whose receivable turnover we calculated to be 5.89, the average collection period is

$$\frac{365}{5.89} = \textbf{62 days}$$

This figure tells us the average number of days that receivables are outstanding before being collected. Since the median industry receivable turnover ratio is 8.1, the average collection period for the industry is $365/8.1 =$ **45 days.** The disparity between the industry's receivable collection performance and Aldine's is once again highlighted.

However, before concluding that a collections problem exists, we should check the credit terms offered by Aldine to its customers. If the average collection period is 62 days and the credit terms are "2/10, net 30,"[6] a sizable proportion of the receivables are past the final due date of 30 days. On the other hand, if the terms are "net 60," the typical receivable is being collected only two days after the final due date.

Although too high an average collection period is usually bad, a very low average collection period may not necessarily be good. A very low average collection period may be a symptom of a credit policy that is excessively restrictive. The few receivables on the books may be of prime quality, yet sales may be curtailed unduly—and profits less than they might be—because of the restrictive issuance of credit to customers. In this situation, perhaps credit standards used to determine an acceptable credit account should be relaxed somewhat.

Aging accounts receivable The process of classifying accounts receivable by their age outstanding as of a given date.

Aging Accounts Receivable. Another means by which we can obtain insight into the liquidity of receivables and management's ability to enforce its credit policy is through **aging accounts receivable.** With this method, we categorize the receivables on a given date according to the percentages billed in previous months. We might have the following hypothetical aging schedule of accounts receivable at December 31:

Aging schedule for accounts receivable as of December 31

MONTH OF CREDIT SALE	DEC	NOV	OCT	SEPT	AUG AND BEFORE	
MONTHS PAST DUE	CURRENT	0–1	1–2	2–3	3 OR MORE	TOTAL
Percent of total accounts receivable balance outstanding	67	19	7	2	5	100

If the credit terms are "2/10, net 30," this aging schedule tells us that 67 percent of the receivables outstanding at December 31 are current, 19 percent are up to one month past due, 7 percent are one to two months past due, and so on. Depending on the conclusions drawn from our analysis of the aging schedule, we may want to

---

[6]The notation means that the supplier gives a 2 percent discount if the receivable invoice is paid within 10 days and total payment is due within 30 days if the discount is not taken.

examine more closely the company's credit and collection policies. In this example, we might be prompted to investigate the individual receivables that were billed in August and before to determine if any should be charged off as bad debts. The receivables shown on the books are only as good as the likelihood that they will be collected. An aging of accounts receivable gives us considerably more information than does the calculation of the average collection period, because it pinpoints the trouble spots more specifically.

Payables Activity.   There may be occasions when a firm wants to study its own promptness of payment to suppliers or that of a potential credit customer. In such cases, it may be desirable to obtain an *aging of accounts payable,* much like that just illustrated for accounts receivable. This method of analysis, combined with the less exact *payable turnover (PT) ratio* (annual credit purchases divided by accounts payable), allows us to analyze payables in much the same manner as we analyze receivables. Also, we can compute the *payable turnover in days (PTD)* or *average payable period* as

$$\frac{\text{Days in the year}}{\text{Payable turnover}} \qquad \text{(6-10)}$$

or, equivalently,

$$\frac{\text{Accounts payable} \times \text{Days in the year}}{\text{Annual credit purchases}} \qquad \text{(6-11)}$$

where accounts payable is the ending (or perhaps, average) balance outstanding for the year and annual credit purchases are the external purchases during the year. This figure yields the average age of a firm's accounts payable.

When information on purchases is not available, one can occasionally use instead the "cost of goods sold plus (minus) any increase (decrease) in inventory" in determining these ratios. A department store chain, for example, typically does no manufacturing. As a result, the "cost of goods sold plus the change in inventory" consists primarily of purchases.[7] However, in situations where sizable value is added, as with a manufacturer, the "cost of goods sold plus the change in inventory" is an inappropriate proxy for purchases. One must have the actual dollar amount of purchases if the ratio is to be used. Another caveat relates to growth. As with receivables, the use of a year-end payable balance will result in a biased and high estimate of the time it will take a company to make payment on its payables if there is strong underlying growth. In this situation, it may be better to use an average of payables at the beginning and end of the year.

The average payable period is valuable information in evaluating the probability that a credit applicant will pay on time. If the average age of payables is 48 days and the terms in the industry are "net 30," we know that a portion of the applicant's payables is not being paid on time. A credit check of the applicant's other suppliers will give insight into the severity of the problem.

Inventory Activity.   To help determine how effectively the firm is managing inventory (and also to gain an indication of the liquidity of inventory), we compute the *inventory turnover (IT) ratio:*

$$\frac{\text{Cost of goods sold}}{\text{Inventory}} \qquad \text{(6-12)}$$

---

[7]Typically, for a retail firm we have

(Beginning inventory) + (Purchases) − (Cost of goods sold) = Ending inventory

Therefore,

(Cost of goods sold) + [(Ending inventory) − (Beginning inventory)] = Purchases

For Aldine, this ratio for 20X2 is

$$\frac{\$2,680,000}{\$1,329,000} = \textbf{2.02}$$

The figure for cost of goods sold used in the numerator is for the period being studied—usually a year; the inventory figure used in the denominator, though a year-end figure in our example, might represent an average value. For a situation involving simple growth, an average of beginning and ending inventories for the period might be used. As is true with receivables, however, it may be necessary to compute a more sophisticated average when there is a strong seasonal element. The inventory turnover ratio tells us how many times inventory is turned over into receivables through sales during the year. This ratio, like other ratios, must be judged in relation to past and expected future ratios of the firm and in relation to ratios of similar firms, the industry average, or both.

Generally, the higher the inventory turnover, the more efficient the inventory management of the firm and the "fresher," more liquid, the inventory. However, sometimes a high inventory turnover indicates a hand-to-mouth existence. It therefore might actually be a symptom of maintaining too low a level of inventory and incurring frequent **stockouts.** Relatively low inventory turnover is often a sign of excessive, slow-moving, or obsolete items in inventory. Obsolete items may require substantial write-downs, which, in turn, would tend to negate the treatment of at least a portion of the inventory as a liquid asset. Because the inventory turnover ratio is a somewhat crude measure, we would want to investigate further any perceived inefficiency in inventory management. In this regard, it is helpful to compute the turnover of the major categories of inventory to see if there are imbalances, which may indicate excessive investment in specific components of the inventory.

Stockout Not having enough items in inventory to fill an order.

Aldine's inventory turnover of 2.02 is in marked contrast to an industry median turnover ratio of 3.3. This unfavorable comparison suggests that the company is less efficient in inventory management than is average for the industry and that Aldine holds excessive inventory stock. A question also arises as to whether the inventory on the books is worth its stated value. If not, the liquidity of the firm is less than the current ratio or quick ratio alone suggests. Once we have a hint of an inventory problem, we must investigate it more specifically to determine its cause.

An alternative measure of inventory activity is *inventory turnover in days (ITD):*

$$\frac{\text{Days in the year}}{\text{Inventory turnover}} \qquad \textbf{(6-13)}$$

or, equivalently,

$$\frac{\text{Inventory} \times \text{Days in the year}}{\text{Cost of goods sold}} \qquad \textbf{(6-14)}$$

For Aldine, whose inventory turnover we calculated to be 2.02, the inventory turnover in days (ITD) is

$$\frac{365}{2.02} = \textbf{181 days}$$

This figure tells us how many days, on average, before inventory is turned into accounts receivable through sales. Transforming the industry's median inventory turnover of 3.3 into an inventory turnover in days figure, we get 365/3.3 = **111 days.** Thus, Aldine is, on average, 70 days slower in "turning" its inventory than is typical for the industry.

Operating cycle The length of time from the *commitment* of cash for purchases until the collection of receivables resulting from the sale of goods or services.

Operating Cycle versus Cash Cycle.   A direct result of our interest in both liquidity and activity ratios is the concept of a firm's **operating cycle.** A firm's operating cycle is the length of time from the *commitment* of cash for purchases until the collection of receivables resulting from the sale of goods or services. It is as if we start a stopwatch when we purchase raw materials and stop the watch only when we receive cash after the finished goods have been sold. The time appearing on our watch (usually in days) is the firm's operating cycle. Mathematically, a firm's *operating cycle* is equal to

$$\text{Inventory turnover in days (ITD)} + \text{Receivable turnover in days (RTD)} \qquad \text{(6-15)}$$

We stress the fact that our stopwatch starts at the *commitment* of cash for purchases rather than from the actual cash outlay itself. The reason for this subtle distinction is that most firms do not pay for raw materials immediately but rather buy on credit and incur an account payable. However, if we want to measure the length of time from the actual outlay of cash for purchases until the collection of cash resulting from sales, it is a simple matter. We would subtract the firm's payable turnover in days (PTD) from its operating cycle and thus produce the firm's **cash cycle:**

Cash cycle The length of time from the *actual outlay* of cash for purchases until the collection of receivables resulting from the sale of goods or services.

$$\text{Operating cycle (ITD + RTD)} - \text{Payable turnover in days (PTD)} \qquad \text{(6-16)}$$

Figure 6-3 illustrates the operating cycle and cash cycle for the firm—and highlights their differences.[8]

---

[8]For more information on the firm's operating and cash cycles, see Verlyn D. Richards and Eugene J. Laughlin, "A Cash Conversion Cycle Approach to Liquidity Analysis." *Financial Management* 9 (Spring 1980), 32–38.

FIGURE 6-3
Operating Cycle versus Cash Cycle

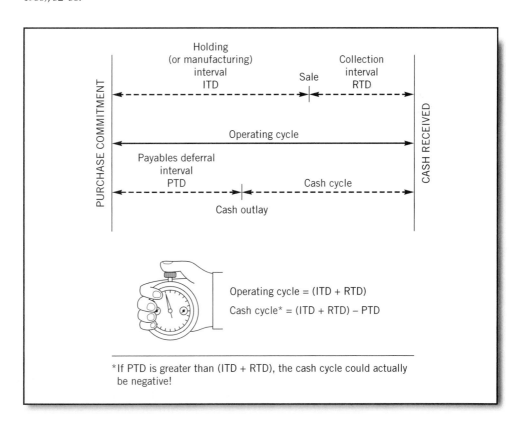

Why even worry about the firm's operating cycle? The length of the operating cycle is an important factor in determining a firm's current asset needs. A firm with a very short operating cycle can operate effectively with a relatively small amount of current assets and relatively low current and acid-test ratios. This firm is relatively liquid in a "dynamic" sense—it can produce a product, sell it, and collect cash for it, all in a relatively short period of time. It does not have to rely so heavily on high "static" levels of liquidity as measured by the current or acid-test ratio. This is very similar to judging the "liquidity" of a garden hose. This liquidity depends not only on the "static" amount of water in the hose at any one time but also the velocity with which the water moves through the hose.

The operating cycle, by focusing on ITD and RTD, provides a summary activity measure. For example, a relatively short operating cycle generally indicates effectively managed receivables and inventory. But, as we have just discussed, this measure provides supplementary information on a firm's liquidity as well. A relatively short operating cycle would thus also reflect favorably on a firm's liquidity. In contrast, a relatively long operating cycle might be a warning sign of excessive receivables and/or inventory and would reflect negatively on the firm's true liquidity.

Comparing Aldine's operating cycle to that of the median industry average, we have:

	Aldine	Median Industry Average
Operating cycle	**243 days**	**156 days**

The cumulative effect of both a sluggish inventory turnover and receivable turnover for Aldine is clearly apparent; relative to the typical firm in the industry, it takes Aldine an extra 87 days to manufacture a product, sell it, and collect cash from sales. The length of the firm's operating cycle should also cause us to to have second thoughts about the firm's liquidity.

We have not said very much, so far, about the firm's cash cycle. One reason is that one must be extremely careful in trying to analyze this measure. On the surface, it would seem that a relatively short cash cycle would be a sign of good management. Such a firm is quick to collect cash from sales once it pays for purchases. The catch is that this measure reflects both operating and financing decisions of the firm, and mismanagement in one or both of these decision areas might be overlooked. For example, one way to arrive at a short cash cycle is simply never to pay your bills on time (a poor financing decision). Your payable turnover in days figure will become large, and subtracted from your operating cycle, it will produce a low (perhaps even negative!) cash cycle. The operating cycle, by focusing strictly on the effects of operating decisions on inventory and receivables, provides clearer signals for the analyst to consider.

A Second Look at Aldine's Liquidity.   As you may remember, Aldine's current and acid-test ratios compared favorably to industry median ratios. However, we decided to reserve a final opinion on liquidity until we had performed a more detailed examination of the firm's receivables and inventory. The turnover ratios for both of these assets, and the resulting operating cycle, are significantly worse than the industry median values for these same measures. These findings suggest that the two assets are not entirely current, and this factor detracts from the favorable current and quick ratios. A sizable portion of receivables is slow, and there appear to be inefficiencies in inventory management. On the basis of our analysis, we conclude that these assets are not particularly liquid in the sense of turning over into cash in a reasonable period of time (see the boxed feature on page 145).

Total Asset (or Capital) Turnover. The relationship of net sales to total assets is known as the *total asset turnover,* or *capital turnover, ratio:*

$$\frac{\text{Net sales}}{\text{Total assets}} \tag{6-17}$$

Aldine's total asset turnover for fiscal-year 20X2 is

$$\frac{\$3,992,000}{\$3,250,000} = \textbf{1.23}$$

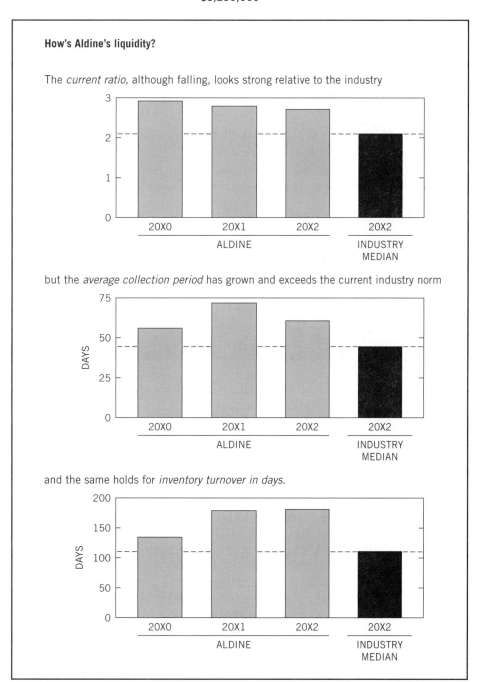

How's Aldine's liquidity?

The *current ratio*, although falling, looks strong relative to the industry

but the *average collection period* has grown and exceeds the current industry norm

and the same holds for *inventory turnover in days.*

The median total asset turnover for the industry is 1.66, so it is clear that Aldine generates less sales revenue per dollar of asset investment than does the industry, on average. The total asset turnover ratio tells us the relative efficiency with which a firm utilizes its total assets to generate sales. Aldine is less efficient than the industry in this regard. From our previous analysis of Aldine's receivables and inventory activity, we suspect that excessive investments in receivables and inventories may be responsible for a large part of the problem. If Aldine could generate the same sales revenue with fewer dollars invested in receivables and inventories, total asset turnover would improve.

Profitability Ratios

Profitability ratios Ratios that relate profits to sales and investment.

Profitability ratios are of two types—those showing profitability in relation to sales and those showing profitability in relation to investment. Together, these ratios indicate the firm's overall effectiveness of operation.

Profitability in Relation to Sales. The first ratio we consider is the *gross profit margin:*

$$\frac{\text{Net sales} - \text{Cost of goods sold}}{\text{Net sales}} \tag{6-18}$$

or simply gross profit divided by net sales. For Aldine, the gross profit margin for fiscal-year 20X2 is

$$\frac{\$1,312,000}{\$3,992,000} = 32.9\%$$

This ratio tells us the profit of the firm relative to sales, after we deduct the cost of producing the goods. It is a measure of the efficiency of the firm's operations, as well as an indication of how products are priced. Aldine's gross profit margin is significantly above the median of 23.8 percent for the industry, indicating that it is relatively more effective at producing and selling products above cost.

A more specific measure of sales profitability is the *net profit margin:*

$$\frac{\text{Net profit after taxes}}{\text{Net sales}} \tag{6-19}$$

For Aldine, this ratio for fiscal-year 20X2 is

$$\frac{\$201,000}{\$3,992,000} = 5.04\%$$

The net profit margin is a measure of the firm's profitability of sales after taking account of all expenses and income taxes. It tells us a firm's net income per dollar of sales. For Aldine, roughly 5 cents out of every sales dollar constitutes after-tax profits. Aldine's net profit margin is above the median net profit margin (4.7 percent) for the industry, which indicates that it has a higher relative level of "sales profitability" than most other firms in the industry.

By considering both ratios jointly, we are able to gain considerable insight into the operations of the firm. If the gross profit margin is essentially unchanged over a period of several years but the net profit margin has declined over the same period, we know that the cause is either higher selling, general, and administrative (SG&A) expenses relative to sales or a higher tax rate. On the other hand, if the gross profit margin falls, we know that the cost of producing goods relative to sales has increased. This occurrence, in turn, may be due to lower prices or to lower operating efficiency in relation to volume.

Profitability in Relation to Investment. The second group of profitability ratios relates profits to investment. One of these measures is the rate of *return on investment (ROI)*, or *return on assets:*

$$\frac{\text{Net profit after taxes}}{\text{Total assets}} \qquad (6\text{-}20)$$

For Aldine, ROI for fiscal-year 20X2 is

$$\frac{\$201,000}{\$3,250,000} = \mathbf{6.18\%}$$

This ratio compares unfavorably to a median value of 7.8 percent for the industry. Higher profitability per dollar of sales but a slightly lower return on investment confirm that Aldine employs more assets to generate a dollar of sales than does the typical firm in the industry.

ROI and the Du Pont Approach. In about 1919, the Du Pont Company began to use a particular approach to ratio analysis to evaluate the firm's effectiveness. One variation of this Du Pont approach has special relevance to understanding a firm's return on investment. As shown in Figure 6-4, when we multiply the net profit margin of the firm by the total asset turnover, we obtain the return on investment, or *earning power* on total assets.

For Aldine, we have

Earning power	=	Sales profitability	×	Asset efficiency
ROI	=	Net profit margin	×	Total asset turnover
6.20%	=	5.04%	×	1.23

Neither the net profit margin nor the total asset turnover ratio by itself provides an adequate measure of overall effectiveness. The net profit margin ignores the utilization of assets, and the total asset turnover ratio ignores profitability on sales. The return on investment ratio, or *earning power,* resolves these shortcomings. An improvement in the earning power of the firm will result if there is an increase in turnover on assets, an increase in the net profit margin, or both. Two firms with different net profit margins and total asset turnovers may have the same earning power. Geraldine Lim's Oriental Grocery, with a net profit margin of only 2 percent and a

FIGURE 6-4
Earning Power and the Du Pont Approach

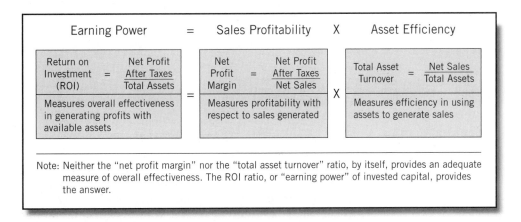

Note: Neither the "net profit margin" nor the "total asset turnover" ratio, by itself, provides an adequate measure of overall effectiveness. The ROI ratio, or "earning power" of invested capital, provides the answer.

DILBERT. United Feature Syndicate. Reprinted by Permission.

total asset turnover of 10, has the same earning power—20 percent—as the Megawatt Power Supply Company, with a net profit margin of 20 percent and a total asset turnover of 1. For each firm, every dollar invested in assets returns 20 cents in after-tax profit per year.

Return on Equity (ROE).   Another summary measure of overall firm performance is return on equity. *Return on equity (ROE)* compares net profit after taxes (minus preferred stock dividends, if any) to the equity that shareholders have invested in the firm:

$$\frac{\text{Net profit after taxes}}{\text{Shareholders' equity}} \qquad \text{(6-21)}$$

For Aldine, ROE is

$$\frac{\$201,000}{\$1,796,000} = \textbf{11.19}\%$$

This ratio tells us the earning power on shareholders' book value investment and is frequently used in comparing two or more firms in an industry. A high return on equity often reflects the firm's acceptance of strong investment opportunities and effective expense management. However, if the firm has chosen to employ a level of debt that is high by industry standards, a high ROE might simply be the result of assuming excessive financial risk. Aldine's ROE is below the median return (14.04 percent) for the industry.

To investigate this return more fully, we can utilize a Du Pont approach—that is, break this return measure into its components:

$$\frac{\text{Net profit after taxes}}{\text{Shareholders' equity}} = \frac{\text{Net profit after taxes}}{\text{Net sales}} \times \frac{\text{Net sales}}{\text{Total assets}} \times \frac{\text{Total assets}}{\text{Shareholders' equity}}$$

$$\text{ROE} = \text{Net profit margin} \times \text{Total asset turnover} \times \text{Equity multiplier}$$

For, Aldine, we have

$$11.2\% = 5.04\% \times 1.23 \times 1.81$$

This Du Pont approach to ROE helps to explain "why" Aldine's ROE is less than the industry's median ROE. Although Aldine's net profit margin is higher than average

Part III Tools of Financial Analysis and Planning

and its equity multiplier is about at the industry norm,[9] its lower-than-average total asset turnover pulls its ROE down below that of the typical firm in the industry. This suggests that Aldine's use of a relatively greater proportion of assets to produce sales than most other firms in the industry is the root cause of its below-average ROE.

With all of the profitability ratios discussed, comparing one company to similar companies and industry standards is extremely valuable. Only by comparisons are we able to judge whether the profitability of a particular company is good or bad, and why. Absolute figures provide some insight, but it is relative performance that is most revealing.

TREND ANALYSIS

Until now, our concern has been with introducing the various financial ratios, explaining their uses in analysis, and comparing the ratios computed for our sample company with industry averages. As we pointed out earlier, it is important to compare the financial ratios for a given company over time. In this way, the analyst is able to detect any improvement or deterioration in a firm's financial condition and performance.

To illustrate, Table 6-3 shows selected financial ratios for Aldine Manufacturing Company over the 20X0–20X2 period along with industry median figures for 20X2.

---

[9]The "equity multiplier" is yet another measure of financial leverage. Since it is equivalent to (1 + debt-to-equity ratio), the higher the debt-to-equity ratio, the higher the multiplier. For Aldine, the multiplier is 1 + .81 = 1.81, while for the industry we have 1 + .80 = 1.80.

TABLE 6-3
Selected financial ratios of Aldine Manufacturing Company for fiscal years 20X0–X2

	20X0	20X1	20X2	INDUSTRY MEDIAN 20X2
Liquidity				
Current ratio	2.95	2.80	2.72	**2.10**
Acid-test ratio	1.30	1.23	1.11	**1.10**
Leverage				
Debt-to-equity ratio	.76	.81	.81	**.80**
Total-debt-to-total-assets ratio	.43	.45	.45	**.44**
Coverage				
Interest coverage ratio	5.95	5.43	4.71	**4.00**
Activity				
Average collection period[a]	55 days	73 days	62 days	**45 days**
Inventory turnover in days[a]	136 days	180 days	181 days	**111 days**
Total asset turnover[a]	1.25	1.18	1.23	**1.66**
Profitability				
Gross profit margin	30.6%	32.8%	32.9%	**23.8%**
Net profit margin	4.90%	5.32%	5.04%	**4.70%**
Return on investment[a]	6.13%	6.29%	6.19%	**7.80%**
Return on equity[a]	10.78%	11.36%	11.19%	**14.04%**

[a]In computing "income statement/balance sheet"-type ratios, year-end balance sheet figures were used.

As can be seen, the current and acid-test ratios have fallen off somewhat over time but still exceed industry norms in 20X2. The average collection period and inventory turnover in days figures have grown since 20X0 and exceed the current industry median levels. The trends here tell us that there has been a relative buildup in receivables and inventories. The turnover of each has slowed, which raises questions as to the quality and liquidity of these assets. When a trend analysis of receivables and inventory is coupled with a comparison to median ratios for the industry, the only conclusion possible is that a problem exists. The analyst would want to investigate the credit policies of Aldine, the company's collection experience, and its bad-debt losses. Moreover, one should investigate inventory management, obsolescence of inventory, and any imbalances in the makeup of inventory (i.e., raw material versus work-in-process versus finished goods). Thus, despite above average levels of current and acid-test ratios, the apparent deterioration in receivables and inventory is a matter of concern and needs to be investigated in depth.

The stability of the firm's leverage (debt) ratios coupled with a present relative debt level typical of the industry would be viewed favorably by creditors. The gross profit margin and net profit margin have generally shown improvement over the recent past, and current levels are stronger than for the typical firm in the industry. Return on investment has been relatively stable over time, but at a level below the industry standard. Sluggish asset turnover over time has dampened any positive effects of above average sales profitability. From our analysis of activity ratios, we know that the primary cause has been the large and growing relative amounts of receivables and inventory.

We see, then, that the analysis of the trend of financial ratios over time, coupled with a comparison to industry averages, can give the analyst valuable insight into changes that have occurred in a firm's financial condition and performance. Additional insight can be provided if we extend our analysis to include comparisons with similar competitors in the industry.

COMMON-SIZE AND INDEX ANALYSIS

Common-size analysis An analysis of *percentage* financial statements where all balance sheet items are divided by *total assets* and all income statement items are divided by *net sales* or *revenues*.

Index analysis An analysis of *percentage* financial statements where all balance sheet or income statement figures for a base year equal 100.0 (percent) and subsequent financial statement items are expressed as percentages of their values in the base year.

In addition to financial ratio analysis over time, it is often useful to express balance sheet and income statement items as percentages. The percentages can be related to totals, such as total assets or total net sales, or to some base year. Called **common-size analysis** and **index analysis,** respectively, the evaluation of levels and trends in financial statement percentages over time affords the analyst insight into the underlying improvement or deterioration in financial condition and performance. Though a good portion of this insight is revealed in the analysis of financial ratios, a broader understanding of the trends is possible when the analysis is extended to include the foregoing considerations. Also, these two new types of analysis are extremely helpful in comparing firms whose data differ significantly in size because every item on the financial statements gets placed on a relative, or standardized, basis.

Financial Statement Items as Percentages of Totals

In common-size analysis, we express the various components of a balance sheet as percentages of the total assets of the company. In addition, this can be done for the income statement, but here items are related to net sales. The gross and net profit margins, taken up earlier, are examples of this type of expression, and the procedure

Part III Tools of Financial Analysis and Planning

can be extended to include all the items on the income statement. The expression of individual financial statement items as percentages of total helps the analyst spot trends with respect to the relative importance of these items over time. To illustrate, common-size balance sheets and income statements are shown alongside regular statements in Tables 6-4 and 6-5 for R. B. Harvey Electronics Company for 20X0 through 20X2. In Table 6-4 we see that over the three-year span, the percentage of current assets increased and that this was particularly true for cash. In addition, we see that accounts receivable showed a relative increase from 20X1 to 20X2. On the liability and equity portion of the balance sheet, the debt of the company declined on a relative (and absolute) basis from 20X0 to 20X1. However, with the large absolute increase in assets that occurred in 20X1 and 20X2, the debt ratio increased from 20X1 to 20X2. The rebound in the importance of debt financing is particularly apparent in accounts payable, which increased substantially in both absolute and relative terms in 20X2.

The common-size income statement shown in Table 6-5 shows the gross profit margin fluctuating from year to year. An improved 20X2 gross profit margin, coupled with better relative control over selling, general, and administrative expenses, caused 20X2 profitability to sharply improve over 20X0 and 20X1.

TABLE 6-4
R. B. Harvey Electronics Company balance sheets (at December 31)

ASSETS	REGULAR (IN THOUSANDS)			COMMON-SIZE (%)		
	20X0	20X1	20X2	20X0	20X1	20X2
Cash	$ 2,507	$ 11,310	$ 19,648	1.0	3.8	5.1
Accounts receivable	70,360	85,147	118,415	29.3	28.9	30.9
Inventory	77,380	91,378	118,563	32.2	31.0	31.0
Other current assets	6,316	6,082	5,891	2.6	2.1	1.5
Current assets	$156,563	$193,917	$262,517	65.1	65.8	68.5
Fixed assets, net	79,187	94,652	115,461	32.9	32.2	30.1
Other long-term assets	4,695	5,899	5,491	2.0	2.0	1.4
Total assets	$240,445	$294,468	$383,469	100.0	100.0	100.0
LIABILITIES AND SHAREHOLDERS' EQUITY						
Accounts payable	$ 35,661	$ 37,460	$ 62,725	14.8	12.7	16.4
Notes payable	20,501	14,680	17,298	8.5	5.0	4.5
Other current liabilities	11,054	8,132	15,741	4.6	2.8	4.1
Current liabilities	$ 67,216	$ 60,272	$ 95,764	27.9	20.5	25.0
Long-term debt	888	1,276	4,005	.4	.4	1.0
Total liabilities	$ 68,104	$ 61,548	$ 99,769	28.3	20.9	26.0
Common stock	12,650	20,750	24,150	5.3	7.0	6.3
Additional paid-in capital	37,950	70,350	87,730	15.8	23.9	22.9
Retained earnings	121,741	141,820	171,820	50.6	48.2	44.8
Total shareholders' equity	$172,341	$232,920	$283,700	71.7	79.1	74.0
Total liabilities and shareholders' equity	$240,445	$294,468	$383,469	100.0	100.0	100.0

	REGULAR (IN THOUSANDS)			COMMON-SIZE (%)		
	20X0	20X1	20X2	20X0	20X1	20X2
Net sales	$323,780	$375,088	$479,077	100.0	100.0	100.0
Cost of goods sold	148,127	184,507	223,690	45.8	49.2	46.7
Gross profit	$175,653	$190,581	$255,387	54.2	50.8	53.3
Selling, general, and administrative expenses	131,809	140,913	180,610	40.7	37.6	37.7
Depreciation	7,700	9,595	11,257	2.4	2.5	2.3
Interest expense	1,711	1,356	1,704	.5	.4	.4
Earnings before taxes	$ 34,433	$ 38,717	$ 61,816	10.6	10.3	12.9
Taxes	12,740	14,712	23,490	3.9	3.9	4.9
Earning after taxes	$ 21,693	$ 24,005	$ 38,326	6.7	6.4	8.0

Financial Statement Items as Indexes Relative to a Base Year

The common-size balance sheets and income statements can be supplemented by the expression of items relative to a base year. For Harvey Electronics, the base year is 20X0, and all financial statement items are 100.0 (percent) for that year. Items for subsequent years are expressed as an index relative to that year. For example, comparing Harvey Electronics' accounts receivable in 20X1 ($85,147,000) to its receivables in the base year, 20X0 ($70,360,000), the index would be 121.0 (i.e., [$85,147,000/ $70,360,000] × 100). Tables 6-6 and 6-7 show indexed balance sheets and income statements alongside regular statements. In Table 6-6 the buildup in cash from the base year is particularly apparent, and this agrees with our previous assessment. Also, note the large increase in accounts receivable and inventory from 20X1 to 20X2. This latter change was not apparent in the common-size analysis. (We would want to follow up on this information by checking the firm's receivable turnover and inventory turnover to see how well the firm is managing these growing asset accounts.) To a lesser extent, there was a sizable increase in fixed assets. On the liability portion of the balance sheet, we note the large increase in accounts payable and in other current liabilities that occurred from 20X1 to 20X2. This, coupled with increases in retained earnings and the sale of stock, financed the large increase in assets that occurred between these two points in time.

The indexed income statement in Table 6-7 gives much the same picture as the common-size income statement, namely, fluctuating behavior. The sharp improvement in 20X2 profitability is more easily distinguished. Moreover, the indexed statements give us information on the magnitude of absolute changes in profits and expenses. With common-size statements, we have no information about how the absolute amounts change over time.

In summary, the standardization of balance sheet and income statement items as percentages of totals and as indexes to a base year often gives us insights additional to those obtained from the analysis of financial ratios. Common-size and index analysis is much easier when a computer spreadsheet program, such as Excel, is employed. The division calculations by rows or columns can be done quickly and accurately with such a program—but it is up to you, the analyst, to interpret the results.

TABLE 6-6
R. B. Harvey Electronics Company balance sheets (at December 31)

ASSETS	REGULAR (IN THOUSANDS)			INDEXED (%)		
	20X0	20X1	20X2	20X0	20X1	20X2
Cash	$ 2,507	$ 11,310	$ 19,648	100.0	451.1	783.7
Accounts receivable	70,360	85,147	118,415	100.0	121.0	168.3
Inventory	77,380	91,378	118,563	100.0	118.1	153.2
Other current assets	6,316	6,082	5,891	100.0	96.3	93.3
Current assets	$156,563	$193,917	$262,517	100.0	123.9	167.7
Fixed assets, net	79,187	94,652	115,461	100.0	119.5	145.8
Other long-term assets	4,695	5,899	5,491	100.0	125.6	117.0
Total assets	$240,445	$294,468	$383,469	100.0	122.5	159.5
LIABILITIES AND SHAREHOLDERS' EQUITY						
Accounts payable	$ 35,661	$ 37,460	$ 62,725	100.0	105.0	175.9
Notes payable	20,501	14,680	17,298	100.0	71.6	84.4
Other current liabilities	11,054	8,132	15,741	100.0	73.6	142.4
Current liabilities	$ 67,216	$ 60,272	$ 95,764	100.0	89.7	142.5
Long-term debt	888	1,276	4,005	100.0	143.7	451.0
Total liabilities	$ 68,104	$ 61,548	$ 99,769	100.0	90.4	146.5
Common stock	12,650	20,750	24,150	100.0	164.0	190.9
Additional paid-in capital	37,950	70,350	87,730	100.0	185.4	231.2
Retained earnings	121,741	141,820	171,820	100.0	116.5	141.1
Total shareholders' equity	$172,341	$232,920	$283,700	100.0	135.2	164.6
Total liabilities and shareholders' equity	$240,445	$294,468	$383,469	100.0	122.5	159.5

TABLE 6-7
R. B. Harvey Electronics Company income statements (for years ending December 31)

	REGULAR (IN THOUSANDS)			INDEXED (%)		
	20X0	20X1	20X2	20X0	20X1	20X2
Net sales	$323,780	$375,088	$479,077	100.0	115.8	148.0
Cost of goods sold	148,127	184,507	223,690	100.0	124.6	151.0
Gross profit	$175,653	$190,581	$255,387	100.0	108.5	145.4
Selling, general, and administrative expenses	131,809	140,913	180,610	100.0	106.9	137.0
Depreciation	7,700	9,595	11,257	100.0	124.6	146.2
Interest expense	1,711	1,356	1,704	100.0	79.3	99.6
Earnings before taxes	$ 34,433	$ 38,717	$ 61,816	100.0	112.4	179.5
Taxes	12,740	14,712	23,490	100.0	115.5	184.4
Earnings after taxes	$ 21,693	$ 24,005	$ 38,326	100.0	110.7	176.7

SUMMARY

- Financial analysis, though varying according to the particular interests of the analyst, always involves the use of various financial statements—primarily the balance sheet and income statement.
- The *balance sheet* summarizes the assets, liabilities, and owners' equity of a business at a point in time, and the *income statement* summarizes revenues and expenses of a firm over a particular period of time.
- A conceptual framework for financial analysis provides the analyst with an interlocking means for structuring the analysis. For example, in the analysis of external financing, one is concerned with the firm's funds needs, its financial condition and performance, and its business risk. Upon analysis of these factors, one is able to determine the firm's financing needs and to negotiate with outside suppliers of capital.
- Financial ratios are the tools used to analyze financial condition and performance. We calculate ratios because in this way we get a *comparison* that *may* prove more useful than the raw numbers by themselves.
- Financial ratios can be divided into five basic types: liquidity, leverage (debt), coverage, activ-

ity, and profitability. No one ratio is itself sufficient for realistic assessment of the financial condition and performance of a firm. With a group of ratios, however, reasonable judgments can be made. The number of key ratios needed for this purpose is not particularly large—about a dozen or so.
- The usefulness of ratios depends on the ingenuity and experience of the financial analyst who employs them. By themselves, financial ratios are fairly meaningless; they must be analyzed on a comparative basis. Comparing one company to similar companies and industry standards over time is crucial. Such a comparison uncovers leading clues in evaluating changes and trends in the firm's financial condition and profitability. This comparison may be historical, but it may also include an analysis of the future based on projected financial statements.
- Additional insights can be gained by *common-size* and *index* analysis. In the former, we express the various balance sheet items as a percentage of total assets and the income statement items as a percentage of net sales. In the latter, balance sheet and income statement items are expressed as an index relative to an initial base year.

SUMMARY OF KEY RATIOS

	LIQUIDITY	
CURRENT	$= \dfrac{\text{Current assets}}{\text{Current liabilities}}$	Measures ability to meet current debts with current assets.
ACID-TEST (QUICK)	$= \dfrac{\text{Current assets less inventories}}{\text{Current liabilities}}$	Measures ability to meet current debts with most-liquid (quick) current assets.
	LEVERAGE	
DEBT-TO-EQUITY	$= \dfrac{\text{Total debt}}{\text{Shareholders' equity}}$	Indicates the extent to which debt financing is used relative to equity financing.
DEBT-TO-TOTAL-ASSETS	$= \dfrac{\text{Total debt}}{\text{Total assets}}$	Shows the relative extent to which the firm is using borrowed money.

Part III Tools of Financial Analysis and Planning

INTEREST COVERAGE	$= \dfrac{EBIT^*}{\text{Interest expense}}$	Indicates ability to cover interest charges; tells number of times interest is earned.

RECEIVABLE TURNOVER (RT)	$= \dfrac{\text{Annual net credit sales}}{\text{Receivables}^{**}}$	Measures how many times the receivables have been turned over (into cash) during the year; provides insight into quality of the receivables.
RECEIVABLE TURNOVER IN DAYS (RTD) (Average collection period)	$= \dfrac{365}{RT}$	Average number of days receivables are outstanding before being collected.
INVENTORY TURNOVER (IT)	$= \dfrac{\text{Cost of goods sold}}{\text{Inventory}^{**}}$	Measures how many times the inventory has been turned over (sold) during the year; provides insight into liquidity of inventory and tendency to overstock.
INVENTORY TURNOVER IN DAYS (ITD)	$= \dfrac{365}{IT}$	Average number of days the inventory is held before it is turned into accounts receivable through sales.
TOTAL ASSET TURNOVER (Capital turnover)	$= \dfrac{\text{Net sales}}{\text{Total assets}^{**}}$	Measures relative efficiency of total assets to generate sales.

NET PROFIT MARGIN	$= \dfrac{\text{Net profit after taxes}}{\text{Net sales}}$	Measures profitability with respect to sales generated; net income per dollar of sales.
RETURN ON INVESTMENT (ROI) (Return on assets)	$= \dfrac{\text{Net profit after taxes}}{\text{Total assets}^{**}}$	Measures overall effectiveness in generating profits with available assets; earning power of invested capital.
	$=$ NET PROFIT MARGIN $\times$ TOTAL ASSET TURNOVER	
	$= \dfrac{\text{Net profit after taxes}}{\text{Net sales}} \times \dfrac{\text{Net sales}}{\text{Total assets}^{**}}$	
RETURN ON EQUITY (ROE)	$= \dfrac{\text{Net profit after taxes}}{\text{Shareholders' equity}^{**}}$	Measures earning power on shareholders' book-value investment.
	$=$ NET PROFIT MARGIN $\times$ TOTAL ASSET TURNOVER $\times$ EQUITY MULTIPLIER	
	$= \dfrac{\text{Net profit after taxes}}{\text{Net sales}} \times \dfrac{\text{Net sales}}{\text{Total assets}^{**}} \times \dfrac{\text{Total assets}^{**}}{\text{Shareholders' equity}^{**}}$	

*Earnings before interest and taxes.
**An average, rather than an ending, balance may be needed.

Appendix

Deferred Taxes and Financial Analysis

Deferred taxes A "liability" that represents the accumulated difference between the income tax expense reported on the firm's books and the income tax actually paid. It arises principally because depreciation is calculated differently for financial reporting than for tax reporting.

Deferred taxes[10]—an item that often appears in the long-term liability portion of a firm's balance sheet—pose some real problems for the financial analyst attempting to do ratio analysis. Though its position on the balance sheet would make it appear to be a long-term debt item, analysts (and especially accountants) can't agree on whether to treat the deferred taxes account as debt or equity, or neither, in ratio and other analyses. Why the confusion?

WHERE DO DEFERRED TAXES COME FROM?

Deferred taxes most commonly arise when a firm determines depreciation expense in its published financial statements on a different basis than in its tax returns. Most likely, a company chooses straight-line depreciation for its published income statement but uses a type of accelerated depreciation (MACRS) for tax purposes. (See Table 6A-1 for an example.) This action "temporarily" defers the payment of taxes by making *tax-return* profits less than *book* profits. When a higher tax expense is reported on the firm's books than is actually paid, the firm's books won't balance. To solve this problem, accountants create a deferred tax account in the long-term liability section of the balance sheet to maintain a running total of these differences between taxes reported and taxes actually due. If the firm slows or ceases buying new assets, there will eventually be a reversal—reported taxes will be less than actual taxes due—and the deferred taxes account will need to be reduced to keep the balance sheet in balance. In this particular situation, our deferred tax liability item is truly a "debt" that eventually comes due. On the other hand, if the firm continues to invest in depreciable assets, payment of the deferred tax may continue to be delayed indefinitely.

---

[10]*Deferred taxes* is not the same thing as *taxes payable*. *Taxes payable* are tax payments due within the year, whereas deferred taxes are "due" at some indefinite long-term date.

TABLE 6A-1
Income statements highlighting deferred taxes for year ending December 31, 20X2 (in millions)

	FINANCIAL REPORTING	TAX REPORTING
Net sales	$100.0	$100.0
Costs and expenses, except for depreciation	45.0	45.0
Depreciation		
Straight-line	15.0	
Accelerated (MACRS)		20.0
Earnings before taxes	$ 40.0	$ 35.0
Taxes (40%)	$ 16.0*	$ 14.0
Earnings after taxes	$ 24.0	$ 21.0

*Taxes	
Current (involves cash payment)	$14.0
Deferred (noncash charge added to deferred taxes account on balance sheet)	2.0
Total tax shown	$16.0

SO WHAT'S THE PROBLEM?

The catch is that for stable or growing firms there is no foreseeable reversal, and the deferred taxes account balance continues to grow. For many firms, a growing, never-reversing, deferred taxes account is the norm. Faced with this reality, the analyst may decide to modify the financial statements for purposes of analysis.

Depending on the situation (for example, the nature and magnitude of the tax deferrals, whether the account has been growing, and the likelihood of a reversal), the analyst may decide to make one or both of the following adjustments to the firm's financial statements:

- The current period's deferred tax expense (a noncash charge) is added back to net income—the argument is that profits were understated because taxes were, in effect, overstated.
- The deferred taxes reported on the firm's balance sheet are added to equity—here the argument is that because this amount is not a definite, legal obligation requiring payment in the foreseeable future, it overstates the debt position of the firm. In short, it is more like equity than debt.

Such adjustment will, of course, affect the calculation of the firm's debt and profitability ratios.

Still another school of thought rejects both of the previous adjustments. Called the "net-of-tax" approach, this viewpoint calls for most deferred taxes to be treated as adjustments to the amounts at which the related assets are carried on the firm's books. An analyst subscribing to this approach would make the following financial statement adjustment:

- The deferred taxes on the firm's balance sheet are subtracted from net fixed assets—the reason is that when there is an excess of tax depreciation over book depreciation, an asset's value is decreased, rather than a liability created. Accelerated depreciation, in effect, uses up an additional part of an asset's tax-reducing capacity relative to straight-line depreciation. The immediate loss of the future tax-reducing (i.e., tax-shield) benefit should be deducted from the related asset account.

This adjustment will affect the calculation of various leverage, activity, and profitability ratios.

QUESTIONS

1. What is the purpose of a balance sheet? An income statement?
2. Why is the analysis of trends in financial ratios important?
3. Auxier Manufacturing Company has a current ratio of 4 to 1 but is unable to pay its bills. Why?
4. Can a firm generate a 25 percent return on assets and still be technically insolvent (unable to pay its bills)? Explain.
5. The traditional definitions of *collection period* and *inventory turnover* are criticized because in both cases balance sheet figures that are a result of approximately the last month of sales are related to annual sales (in the former case) or annual cost of goods sold (in the latter case). Why do these definitions present problems? Suggest a solution.
6. Explain why a long-term creditor should be interested in liquidity ratios.
7. Which financial ratios would you be most likely to consult if you were the following? Why?
   a. A banker considering the financing of seasonal inventory
   b. A wealthy equity investor
   c. The manager of a pension fund considering the purchase of a firm's bonds
   d. The president of a consumer products firm
8. In trying to judge whether a company has too much debt, what financial ratios would you use and for what purpose?

9. Why might it be possible for a company to make large operating profits, yet still be unable to meet debt payments when due? What financial ratios might be employed to detect such a condition?

10. Does increasing a firm's inventory turnover ratio increase its profitability? Why should this ratio be computed using cost of goods sold (rather than sales, as is done by some compilers of financial statistics)?

11. Is it appropriate to insist that a financial ratio, such as the current ratio, exceed a certain absolute standard (e.g., 2:1)? Why?

12. Which firm is more profitable—Firm A with a total asset turnover of 10.0 and a net profit margin of 2 percent, or Firm B with a total asset turnover of 2.0 and a net profit margin of 10 percent? Provide examples of both types of firms.

13. Why do short-term creditors, such as banks, emphasize balance sheet analysis when considering loan requests? Should they also analyze projected income statements? Why?

14. How can index analysis be used to reinforce the insight gained from a trend analysis of financial ratios?

SELF-CORRECTION PROBLEMS

1. Barnaby Cartage Company has current assets of $800,000 and current liabilities of $500,000. What effect would the following transactions have on the firm's current ratio (and state the resulting figures)?
   a. Two new trucks are purchased for a total of $100,000 in cash.
   b. The company borrows $100,000 short term to carry an increase in receivables of the same amount.
   c. Additional common stock of $200,000 is sold and the proceeds invested in the expansion of several terminals.
   d. The company increases its accounts payable to pay a cash dividend of $40,000 out of cash.

2. Acme Plumbing Company sells plumbing fixtures on terms of *2/10, net 30*. Its financial statements over the last three years are as follows:

	20X1	20X2	20X3
Cash	$ 30,000	$ 20,000	$ 5,000
Accounts receivable	200,000	260,000	290,000
Inventory	400,000	480,000	600,000
Net fixed assets	800,000	800,000	800,000
	$1,430,000	$1,560,000	$1,695,000
Accounts payable	$ 230,000	$ 300,000	$ 380,000
Accruals	200,000	210,000	225,000
Bank loan, short term	100,000	100,000	140,000
Long-term debt	300,000	300,000	300,000
Common stock	100,000	100,000	100,000
Retained earnings	500,000	550,000	550,000
	$1,430,000	$1,560,000	$1,695,000
Sales	$4,000,000	$4,300,000	$3,800,000
Cost of goods sold	3,200,000	3,600,000	3,300,000
Net profit	300,000	200,000	100,000

Using the ratios discussed in the chapter, analyze the company's financial condition and performance over the last three years. Are there any problems?

3. Using the following information, complete the balance sheet:

Long-term debt to equity	.5 to 1
Total asset turnover	2.5 times
Average collection period*	18 days
Inventory turnover	9 times
Gross profit margin	10%
Acid-test ratio	1 to 1

*Assume a 360-day year and all sales on credit.

Cash	$_____	Notes and payables	$100,000
Accounts receivable	_____	Long-term debt	_____
Inventory	_____	Common stock	$100,000
Plant and equipment	_____	Retained earnings	$100,000
Total assets		Total liabilities and	
	$_____	shareholders' equity	$_____

4. Kedzie Kord Company had the following balance sheets and income statements over the last three years (in thousands):

	20X1	20X2	20X3
Cash	$ 561	$ 387	$ 202
Receivables	1,963	2,870	4,051
Inventories	2,031	2,613	3,287
Current assets	$ 4,555	$ 5,870	$ 7,540
Net fixed assets	2,581	4,430	4,364
Total assets	$ 7,136	$10,300	$11,904
Payables	$ 1,862	$ 2,944	$ 3,613
Accruals	301	516	587
Bank loan	250	900	1,050
Current liabilities	$ 2,413	$ 4,360	$ 5,250
Long-term debt	500	1,000	950
Shareholder's equity	4,223	4,940	5,704
Total liabilities and shareholder's equity	$ 7,136	$10,300	$11,904
Sales	$11,863	$14,952	$16,349
Cost of goods sold	8,537	11,124	12,016
Selling, general, and administrative expenses	2,276	2,471	2,793
Interest	73	188	200
Profit before taxes	$ 977	$ 1,169	$ 1,340
Taxes	390	452	576
Profit after taxes	$ 587	$ 717	$ 764

Using common-size and index analysis, evaluate trends in the company's financial condition and performance.

PROBLEMS

1. The data for various companies in the same industry are as follows:

	COMPANY					
	A	B	C	D	E	F
Sales (in millions)	$10	$20	$8	$5	$12	$17
Total assets (in millions)	8	10	6	2.5	4	8
Net income (in millions)	.7	2	.8	.5	1.5	1

Determine the total asset turnover, net profit margin, and earning power for each of the companies.

2. Cordillera Carson Company has the following balance sheet and income statement for 20X2 (in thousands):

BALANCE SHEET		INCOME STATEMENT	
Cash	$ 400	Net sales (all credit)	$12,680
Accounts receivable	1,300	Cost of goods sold	8,930
Inventories	2,100	Gross profit	$ 3,750
Current assets	$3,800	Selling, general, and	
Net fixed assets	3,320	administration expenses	2,230
Total assets	$7,120	Interest expense	460
		Profit before taxes	$ 1,060
Accounts payable	$ 320	Taxes	390
Accruals	260	Profit after taxes	$ 670
Short-term loans	1,100		
Current liabilities	$1,680		
Long-term debt	2,000		
Net worth	3,440		
Total liabilities and net worth	$7,120		

Notes: (i) current period's depreciation is $480; (ii) ending inventory for 20X1 was $1,800.

On the basis of this information, compute (a) the current ratio, (b) the acid-test ratio, (c) the average collection period, (d) the inventory turnover ratio, (e) the debt-to-net-worth ratio, (f) the long-term debt-to-total-capitalization ratio, (g) the gross profit margin, (h) the net profit margin, and (i) the return on equity.

Part III Tools of Financial Analysis and Planning

3. Selected financial ratios for RMN, Incorporated, are as follows:

	20X1	20X2	20X3
Current ratio	4.2	2.6	1.8
Acid-test ratio	2.1	1.0	.6
Debt-to-total-assets	23%	33%	47%
Inventory turnover	8.7×	5.4×	3.5×
Average collection period	33 days	36 days	49 days
Total asset turnover	3.2×	2.6×	1.9×
Net profit margin	3.8%	2.5%	1.4%
Return on investment (ROI)	12.1%	6.5%	2.8%
Return on equity (ROE)	15.7%	9.7%	5.4%

a. Why did return on investment decline?
b. Was the increase in debt a result of greater current liabilities or of greater long-term debt? Explain.

4. The following information is available on the Vanier Corporation:

BALANCE SHEET AS OF DECEMBER 31, 20X6 (IN THOUSANDS)

Cash and marketable securities	$500	Accounts payable		$ 400
Accounts receivable	?	Bank loan		?
Inventories	?	Accruals		200
Current assets	?	Current liabilities		?
		Long-term debt		2,650
Net fixed assets	?	Common stock and retained earnings		3,750
Total assets	?	Total liabilities and equity		?

INCOME STATEMENT FOR 20X6 (IN THOUSANDS)

Credit sales	$8,000
Cost of goods sold	?
Gross profit	?
Selling and administrative expenses	?
Interest expense	400
Profit before taxes	?
Taxes (44% rate)	?
Profit after taxes	?

OTHER INFORMATION

Current ratio	3 to 1
Depreciation	$500
Net profit margin	7%
Total liabilities/shareholders' equity	1 to 1
Average collection period	45 days
Inventory turnover ratio	3 to 1

Assuming that sales and production are steady throughout a 360-day year, complete the balance sheet and income statement for Vanier Corporation.

5. A company has total annual sales (all credit) of $400,000 and a gross profit margin of 20 percent. Its current assets are $80,000; current liabilities, $60,000; inventories, $30,000; and cash, $10,000.
   a. How much average inventory should be carried if management wants the inventory turnover to be 4?
   b. How rapidly (in how many days) must accounts receivable be collected if management wants to have an average of $50,000 invested in receivables? (Assume a 360-day year.)

6. Stoney Mason, Inc., has sales of $6 million, a total asset turnover ratio of 6 for the year, and net profits of $120,000.
   a. What is the company's return on assets or earning power?
   b. The company is considering the installation of new point-of-sales cash registers throughout its stores. This equipment is expected to increase efficiency in inventory control, reduce clerical errors, and improve record keeping throughout the system. The new equipment will increase the investment in assets by 20 percent and is expected to increase the net profit margin from 2 to 3 percent. No change in sales is expected. What is the effect of the new equipment on the return on assets ratio or earning power?

7. The long-term debt section of the balance sheet of the Queen Anne's Lace Corporation appears as follows:

$9\frac{1}{4}$% mortgage bonds	$2,500,000
$12\frac{3}{8}$% second mortgage bonds	1,500,000
$10\frac{1}{4}$% debentures	1,000,000
$14\frac{1}{2}$% subordinated debentures	1,000,000
	$6,000,000

If the average earnings before interest and taxes of the company is $1.5 million and all debt is long term, what is the overall interest coverage?

8. Tic-Tac Homes has had the following balance sheet statements the past four years (in thousands):

	20X1	20X2	20X3	20X4
Cash	$ 214	$ 93	$ 42	$ 38
Receivables	1,213	1,569	1,846	2,562
Inventories	2,102	2,893	3,678	4,261
Net fixed assets	2,219	2,346	2,388	2,692
Total assets	$5,748	$6,901	$7,954	$9,553
Accounts payable	$1,131	$1,578	$1,848	$2,968
Notes payable	500	650	750	750
Accruals	656	861	1,289	1,743
Long-term debt	500	800	800	800
Common stock	200	200	200	200
Retained earnings	2,761	2,812	3,067	3,092
Total liabilities and shareholders' equity	$5,748	$6,901	$7,954	$9,553

Using index analysis, what are the major problems in the company's financial condition?

9.

U.S. REPUBLIC CORPORATION BALANCE SHEET, DECEMBER 31, 20X3

ASSETS		LIABILITIES AND SHAREHOLDERS' EQUITY	
Cash	$ 1,000,000	Notes payable, bank	$ 4,000,000
Accounts receivable	5,000,000	Accounts payable	2,000,000
Inventory	7,000,000	Accrued wages and taxes	2,000,000
Fixed assets, net	17,000,000	Long-term debt	12,000,000
		Preferred stock	4,000,000
		Common stock	2,000,000
		Retained earnings	4,000,000
		Total liabilities and	
Total assets	$30,000,000	shareholders' equity	$30,000,000

U.S. REPUBLIC CORPORATION STATEMENT OF INCOME AND RETAINED EARNINGS,
YEAR ENDED DECEMBER 31, 20X3

Net sales		
Credit		$16,000,000
Cash		4,000,000
Total		$20,000,000
Cost and Expenses		
Cost of goods sold	$12,000,000	
Selling, general, and administrative expenses	2,200,000	
Depreciation	1,400,000	
Interest	1,200,000	$16,800,000
Net income before taxes		$ 3,200,000
Taxes on income		1,200,000
Net income after taxes		$ 2,000,000
Less: Dividends on preferred stock		240,000
Net income available to common shareholders		$ 1,760,000
Add: Retained earnings at 1/1/X3		2,600,000
Subtotal		$ 4,360,000
Less: Dividends paid on common stock		360,000
Retained earnings 12/31/X3		$ 4,000,000

a. Fill in the 20X3 column in the table that follows.

U.S. REPUBLIC CORPORATION

RATIO	20X1	20X2	20X3	INDUSTRY NORMS
1. Current ratio	250%	200%		225%
2. Acid-test ratio	100%	90%		110%
3. Receivable turnover	5.0×	4.5×		6.0×
4. Inventory turnover	4.0×	3.0×		4.0×
5. Long-term debt/total capitalization	35%	40%		33%
6. Gross profit margin	39%	41%		40%
7. Net profit margin	17%	15%		15%
8. Return on equity	15%	20%		20%
9. Return on investment	15%	12%		12%
10. Total asset turnover	.9x	.8x		1.0x
11. Interest coverage ratio	5.5x	4.5x		5.0x

b. Evaluate the position of the company using information from the table. Cite specific ratio levels and trends as evidence.

c. Indicate which ratios would be of most interest to you and what your decision would be in each of the following situations:

(i) U.S. Republic wants to buy $500,000 worth of merchandise inventory from you, with payment due in 90 days.

(ii) U.S. Republic wants you, a large insurance company, to pay off its note at the bank and assume it on a 10-year maturity basis at a current rate of 14 percent.

(iii) There are 100,000 shares outstanding, and the stock is selling for $80 a share. The company offers you 50,000 additional shares at this price.

SOLUTIONS TO SELF-CORRECTION PROBLEMS

1. Present current ratio = $800/$500 = **1.60.**
   a. $700/$500 = **1.40.** Current assets decline, and there is no change in current liabilities.
   b. $900/$600 = **1.50.** Current assets and current liabilities each increase by the same amount.
   c. $800/$500 = **1.60.** Neither current assets nor current liabilities are affected.
   d. $760/$540 = **1.41.** Current assets decline, and current liabilities increase by the same amount.

2.

	20X1	20X2	20X3
Current ratio	1.19	1.25	1.20
Acid-test ratio	.43	.46	.40
Average collection period	18	22	27
Inventory turnover	8.0	7.5	5.5
Total debt/equity	1.38	1.40	1.61
Long-term debt/total capitalization	.33	.32	.32
Gross profit margin	.200	.163	.132
Net profit margin	.075	.047	.026
Total asset turnover	2.80	2.76	2.24
Return on assets	.21	.13	.06

The company's profitability has declined steadily over the period. As only $50,000 is added to retained earnings, the company must be paying substantial dividends. Receivables are growing at a slower rate, although the average collection period is still very reasonable relative to the terms given. Inventory turnover is slowing as well, indicating a relative buildup in inventories. The increase in receivables and inventories, coupled with the fact that shareholders' equity has increased very little, has resulted in the total-debt-to-equity ratio increasing to what would have to be regarded on an absolute basis as quite a high level.

The current and acid-test ratios have fluctuated, but the current ratio is not particularly inspiring. The lack of deterioration in these ratios is clouded by the relative buildup in both receivables and inventories, evidencing a deterioration in the liquidity of these two assets. Both the gross profit and net profit margins have declined substantially. The relationship between the two suggests that the company has reduced relative expenses in 20X3 in particular. The buildup in inventories and receivables has resulted in a decline in the asset turnover ratio and this, coupled with the decline in profitability, has resulted in a sharp decrease in the return on assets ratio.

3. $\dfrac{\text{Long-term debt}}{\text{Equity}} = .5 = \dfrac{\text{Long-term debt}}{\$200,000}$ Long-term debt = **$100,000**

Total liabilities and shareholders' equity = **$400,000**

Total assets = **$400,000**

$\dfrac{\text{Sales}}{\text{Total assets}} = 2.5 = \dfrac{\text{Sales}}{\$400,000}$ Sales = **$1,000,000**

Cost of goods sold = $(1 - \text{Gross profit margin})(\text{Sales})$
$$= (.9)(\$1,000,000) = \textbf{\$900,000}$$

$\dfrac{\text{Cost of goods sold}}{\text{Inventory}} = \dfrac{\$900,000}{\text{Inventory}} = 9$ Inventory = **$100,000**

$\dfrac{\text{Receivables} \times 360 \text{ days}}{\$1,000,000} = 18 \text{ days}$ Receivables = **$50,000**

$\dfrac{\text{Cash} + \$50,000}{\$100,000} = 1$ Cash = **$50,000**

Plant and equipment (plug figure on left-hand side of the balance sheet) = **$200,000**

BALANCE SHEET			
Cash	$ 50,000	Notes and payables	$100,000
Accounts receivable	50,000	Long-term debt	100,000
Inventory	100,000	Common stock	100,000
Plant and equipment	200,000	Retained earnings	100,000
Total	$400,000	Total	$400,000

4.

COMMON-SIZE ANALYSIS (%)	20X1	20X2	20X3
Cash	7.9	3.8	1.7
Receivables	27.5	27.8	34.0
Inventories	28.4	25.4	27.6
Current assets	63.8	57.0	63.3
Net fixed assets	36.2	43.0	36.7
Total assets	100.0	100.0	100.0
Payables	26.1	28.6	30.4
Accruals	4.2	5.0	4.9
Bank loan	3.5	8.7	8.8
Current liabilities	33.8	42.3	44.1
Long-term debt	7.0	9.7	8.0
Shareholders' equity	59.2	48.0	47.9
Total liabilities and shareholders' equity	100.0	100.0	100.0
Sales	100.0	100.0	100.0
Cost of goods sold	72.0	74.4	73.5
Selling, general, and administrative expenses	19.2	16.5	17.1
Interest	.6	1.3	1.2
Profit before taxes	8.2	7.8	8.2
Taxes	3.3	3.0	3.5
Profit after taxes	4.9	4.8	4.7

INDEX ANALYSIS (%)	20X1	20X2	20X3
Cash	100.0	69.0	36.0
Receivables	100.0	146.2	206.4
Inventories	100.0	128.7	161.8
Current assets	100.0	128.9	165.5
Net fixed assets	100.0	171.6	169.1
Total assets	100.0	144.3	166.8
Payables	100.0	158.1	194.0
Accruals	100.0	171.4	195.0
Bank loan	100.0	360.0	420.0
Current liabilities	100.0	180.7	217.6
Long-term debt	100.0	200.0	190.0
Shareholders' equity	100.0	117.0	135.1
Total liabilities and shareholders' equity	100.0	144.3	166.8
Sales	100.0	126.0	137.8
Cost of goods sold	100.0	130.3	140.8
Selling, general, and administrative expenses	100.0	108.6	122.7
Interest	100.0	257.5	273.9
Profit before taxes	100.0	119.7	137.2
Taxes	100.0	115.9	147.7
Profit after taxes	100.0	122.2	130.2

The common-size analysis shows that cash declined dramatically relative to other current assets and total assets in general. Net fixed assets surged in 20X2 but then fell back as a percentage of the total to almost the 20X1 percentage. The absolute amounts suggest that the company spent less than its depreciation on fixed assets in 20X3. With respect to financing, shareholders' equity has not kept up, so the company has had to use somewhat more debt percentage-wise. It appears to be leaning more on trade credit as a financing source as payables increased percentage-wise. Bank loans and long-term debt also increased sharply in 20X2, no doubt to finance the bulge in net fixed assets. The bank loan remained about the same in 20X3 as a percentage of total liabilities and shareholders' equity, while long-term debt declined as a percentage. Profit after taxes slipped slightly as a percentage of sales over the three years. In 20X2, this decline was a result of the cost of goods sold and interest expense, as other expenses and taxes declined as a percentage of sales. In 20X3, cost of goods sold declined as a percentage of sales, but this was more than offset by increases in other expenses and taxes as percentages of sales.

Index analysis shows much the same picture. Cash declined faster than total assets and current assets, and receivables increased faster than these two benchmarks. Inventories fluctuated but were about the same percentage-wise relative to total assets in 20X3 as they were in 20X1. Net fixed assets increased more sharply than total assets in 20X2 and then fell back into line in 20X3. The sharp increase in bank loans in 20X2 and 20X3 and the sharp increase in long-term debt in 20X2, along with the accompanying increases in interest expenses, are evident. The percentage increases in shareholders' equity were less than those for total assets, so debt increased by larger percentages than for either of the other two items. With respect to profitability, net profits increased less than sales, for the reasons indicated earlier.

SELECTED REFERENCES

Almanac of Business and Industrial Ratios. Upper Saddle River, NJ: Prentice Hall, annual.

Altman, Edward I. "Financial Ratios, Discriminant Analysis and the Prediction of Corporate Bankruptcy." *Journal of Finance* 23 (September 1968), 589–609.

———, Robert G. Haldeman, and P. Narayanan. "Zeta Analysis: A New Model to Identify Bankruptcy Risk of Corporations." *Journal of Banking and Finance* 1 (June 1977), 29–54.

Chen, Kung H., and Thomas A. Shimerda. "An Empirical Analysis of Useful Financial Ratios." *Financial Management* 10 (Spring 1991), 51–69.

Cunningham, Donald F., and John T. Rose. "Industry Norms in Financial Statement Analysis: A Comparison of RMA and D&B Benchmark Data." *The Credit and Financial Management Review* (1995), 42–48.

Fraser, Lyn M., and Aileen Ormiston. *Understanding Financial Statements,* 6th ed. Upper Saddle River, NJ: Prentice Hall, 2001.

Gombola, Michael J., and J. Edward Ketz. "Financial Ratio Patterns in Retail and Manufacturing Organizations." *Financial Management* 12 (Summer 1983), 45–56.

Harrington, Diana R. *Corporate Financial Analysis,* 5th ed. Cincinnati, OH: South-Western, 1998.

Helfert, Erich A. *Techniques of Financial Analysis,* 10th ed. Burr Ridge, IL: Irwin, 2000.

Higgins, Robert C. *Analysis for Financial Management,* 5th ed. Burr Ridge, IL: Irwin, 1997.

Lewellen, W. G., and R. O. Edmister. "A General Model for Accounts Receivable Analysis and Control." *Journal of Financial and Quantitative Analysis* 8 (March 1973), 195–206.

Matsumoto, Keishiro, Melkote Shivaswamy, and James P. Hoban Jr. "Security Analysts' Views of the Financial Ratios of Manufacturers and Retailers." *Financial Practice and Education* 5 (Fall/Winter 1995), 44–55.

Richards, Verlyn D., and Eugene J. Laughlin. "A Cash Conversion Cycle Approach to Liquidity Analysis." *Financial Management* 9 (Spring 1980), 32–38.

Statement of Financial Accounting Standard No. 95. Stamford, CT: Financial Accounting Standards Board, 1987.

Stone, Bernell K. "The Payments-Pattern Approach to the Forecasting of Accounts Receivable." *Financial Management* 5 (Autumn 1976), 65–82.

Chapter 7

Funds Analysis, Cash-Flow Analysis, and Financial Planning

FLOW OF FUNDS (SOURCES AND USES) STATEMENT
Alternative "Funds" Definitions • What Are Sources? Uses?
• Adjustments • Analyzing the Sources and Uses of Funds
Statement
ACCOUNTING STATEMENT OF CASH FLOWS
Content and Alternative Forms of the Statement • Analyzing the
Statement of Cash Flows
CASH-FLOW FORECASTING
The Sales Forecast• Collections and Other Cash Receipts • Cash
Disbursements • Net Cash Flow and Cash Balance
RANGE OF CASH-FLOW ESTIMATES
Deviations from Expected Cash Flows • Use of Probabilistic
Information
FORECASTING FINANCIAL STATEMENTS
Forecast Income Statement • Forecast Balance Sheet • Use of
Ratios and Implications
SUMMARY
APPENDIX: SUSTAINABLE GROWTH MODELING
QUESTIONS
SELF-CORRECTION PROBLEMS
PROBLEMS
SOLUTIONS TO SELF-CORRECTION PROBLEMS
SELECTED REFERENCES

Forecasting is very difficult, especially if it is about the future.

—ANONYMOUS

The second portion of our examination of the tools of financial analysis and planning deals with the analysis of funds flows and cash flows and with financial forecasting. A flow of funds statement (also known as *sources and uses of funds statement* or a *statement of changes in financial position*) is a valuable aid to a financial manager or a creditor in evaluating the uses of funds by a firm and in determining how the firm finances those uses. In addition to studying past flows, the financial manager can evaluate future flows by means of a funds statement based on forecasts. Until 1989, all U.S. corporate annual reports were required to present a flow of funds statement in addition to a balance sheet and income statement. The cash flow statement now officially replaces the flow of funds statement in annual reports. The purpose of the cash flow statement is to report a firm's cash inflows and outflows—not its flow of funds—segregated into three categories: operating, investing, and financing activities. Although this statement certainly serves as an aid for analyzing cash receipts and disbursements, important current period investing and financing noncash transactions are omitted. Therefore, the analyst will still want to prepare a flow of funds statement in order to more fully understand the firm's funds flows.

Another major tool, the cash budget, is indispensable to the financial manager in determining the short-term cash needs of the firm and, accordingly, in planning its short-term financing. When cash budgeting is extended to include a range of possible outcomes, the financial manager can evaluate the business risk and liquidity of the firm and plan for a realistic margin of safety. The financial manager can adjust the firm's liquidity cushion, rearrange the maturity structure of its debt, arrange a line of credit with a bank, or do some combination of the three.

The preparation of forecast balance sheets and income statements enables the financial manager to analyze the effects of various policy decisions on the future financial condition and performance of the firm. Such statements may derive from the cash budget or be based on past or projected financial ratios and/or other assumptions. We examine each of these tools in turn.

The final method of analysis, contained in an Appendix to this chapter, involves sustainable growth modeling. Here we determine whether the sales growth objectives of the company are consistent with its operating efficiency and with its financial ratios. This powerful tool of analysis allows us to simulate the likely effects of changes in target ratios when we move from a steady-state environment.

Cash budgeting, the preparation of forecast statements, and even sustainable growth modeling are made easier through use of a computer spreadsheet program. Such programs are readily available for financial analysis and planning.

FLOW OF FUNDS
(SOURCES AND USES) STATEMENT

The financial manager makes decisions to ensure that the firm has sufficient funds to meet financial obligations when they are due and to take advantage of investment opportunities. To help the analyst appraise these decisions (made over a period of time), we need to study the firm's *flow of funds*. By arranging a company's flow of funds in a systematic fashion, the analyst can better determine whether the decisions made for the firm resulted in a reasonable flow of funds or in questionable flows, which warrant further inspection.

Alternative "Funds" Definitions

Just what do we mean by "funds"? The first definition that comes to mind is that funds are cash (and cash equivalents). So defined, we should be concerned with transactions that affect the cash accounts. These transactions, affecting inflows and outflows of cash, are extremely important (and, in fact, help to explain the prominence afforded the statement of cash flows). But, defining funds as cash is somewhat limiting. A flow of funds analysis in which funds are defined strictly as cash would fail to consider transactions that did not directly affect "cash," and these transactions could be critical to a complete evaluation of a business. Major end-of-period purchases and sales on credit, the acquisition of property in exchange for stock or bonds, and the exchange of one piece of property for another are just a few examples of transactions that would not be reported on a totally cash-based flow of funds statement. Broadening our conception of funds to include all of the firm's *investments and claims (against those investments)* allows us to capture all of these transactions as both sources and uses of funds.

Accepting "investments and claims" as our definition of funds, we turn our attention to the firm's balance sheet. The balance sheet is a statement of financial position (or "funds position"). On it we have arrayed all of the firm's investments (assets) and claims (liabilities and shareholders' equity) against these investments by creditors and by the owners. The firm's flow of funds is therefore comprised of the individual changes in balance sheet items between two points in time. These points conform to beginning and ending balance sheet dates for whatever period of examination is relevant—a quarter, a year, or five years. The differences in the individual balance sheet account items represent the various "net" funds flows resulting from decisions made by management during the period.

Take Note

Balance sheet = Stock of funds
Changes in balance sheet items = "Net" flow of funds

Flow of funds statement
A summary of a firm's changes in financial position from one period to another; it is also called a *sources and uses of funds statement* or a *statement of changes in financial position.*

We must emphasize that the **flow of funds statement** portrays *net* rather than *gross* changes between two comparable balance sheets at different dates. For example, gross changes might be thought to include all changes that occur between two statement dates, rather than the sum of these changes—the net change as defined. Although an analysis of the gross funds flow of a firm over time would be much more revealing than an analysis of net funds flow, we are usually constrained by the financial information available, namely, the basic financial statements. Though generally taking a broad view of funds, resulting funds statements will often focus on the firm's change in cash position over a period of time or its change in net working capital (current assets minus current liabilities). As you will see, our funds flow statement will ultimately focus on the firm's change in cash.

What Are Sources? Uses?

We prepare a basic, bare-bones funds statement by (1) determining the amount and direction of net balance sheet changes that occur between two balance sheet dates, (2) classifying net balance sheet changes as either sources or uses of funds, and (3) consolidating this information in a sources and uses of funds statement format. In the first of these steps, we simply place one balance sheet beside the other, compute the changes in the various accounts, note the direction of change—an increase (+) or decrease (−) in amount. In step 2, each balance sheet item change is classified as either a source or use of funds, as follows:

Sources of Funds	Uses of Funds
• Any **decrease** (−) in an **asset** item	• Any **increase** (+) in an **asset** item
• Any **increase** (+) in a **claim** item (i.e., a liability or shareholders' equity item)	• Any **decrease** (−) in a **claim** item (i.e., a liability or shareholders' equity item)

For example, a *reduction* in inventory (an asset) would be a source of funds, as would an *increase* in short-term loans (a claim). An *increase* in accounts receivable (assets) would be a use of funds, and a *reduction* in shareholders' equity (claims)—through, for example, a share repurchase—would also be a use of funds.

Table 7-1 walks us through the first two steps necessary to produce a funds statement for the Aldine Manufacturing Company, our example in the preceding chapter. The amount and direction of balance sheet changes are determined. Notice that total sources of funds ($263,000) equals total uses of funds ($263,000). Because total sources must always equal total uses, it provides a check on our work.

TIP•TIP•TIP•TIP•TIP•TIP•TIP•TIP•TIP•TIP•TIP

The following device should help you to remember what constitutes a source or use of funds:

The letters labeling the box stand for **U**ses, **S**ources, **A**ssets, and Liabilities (broadly defined). The pluses (minuses) indicate increases (decreases) in assets or liabilities. You might find it easier to remember the order of the letters by thinking—**U**nited **S**tates of **A**merica, **L**ucille.

Once all sources and uses are computed, they may be arranged in statement form so that we can analyze them better. Table 7-2 shows a "basic" sources and uses of funds statement for the Aldine Manufacturing Company for the fiscal year ended March 31, 20X2.

QUESTION•ANSWER•QUESTION•ANSWER

Is an increase in cash a source or use of funds?
One's first inclination is to answer, "a source." But, if you did, you would be wrong. Remember, because cash is an asset, if it increases, it is (by definition) a use. The real source might have been increased borrowing that could have gone to increase inventory but instead went to increase the cash account.

TABLE 7-1
Aldine Manufacturing Company balance sheets (in thousands)

ASSETS	MARCH 31 20X2	MARCH 31 20X1	DIRECTION OF CHANGE	CHANGES SOURCES	CHANGES USES
Cash and cash equivalents	$ 178	$ 175	+		$ 3
Accounts receivable	678	740	−	$ 62	
Inventories, at lower of cost or market	1,329	1,235	+		94
Prepaid expenses	21	17	+		4
Accumulated tax prepayments	35	29	+		6
Current assets	$2,241	$2,196		N/A	
Fixed assets at cost	1,596	1,538		N/A	
Less: Accumulated depreciation	(857)	(791)		N/A	
Net fixed assets	$ 739	$ 747	−	8	
Investment, long term	65	—	+		65
Other assets, long term	205	205	—	—	—
Total assets	$3,250	$3,148			

LIABILITIES AND SHAREHOLDERS' EQUITY					
Bank loans and notes payable	$ 448	$ 356	+	92	
Accounts payable	148	136	+	12	
Accrued taxes	36	127	−		91
Other accrued liabilities	191	164	+	27	
Current liabilities	$ 823	$ 783		N/A	
Long-term debt	631	627	+	4	
Shareholders' equity					
Common stock, $1 par value	421	421		—	—
Additional paid-in capital	361	361		—	—
Retained earnings	1,014	956	+	58	
Total shareholders' equity	$1,796	$1,738		N/A	
Total liabilities and shareholders' equity	$3,250	$3,148		$263	$263

Note: N/A = not applicable; we do not focus here on changes in subtotals or the components of "net fixed assets."

Adjustments

Although we could begin to analyze our "basic" sources and uses statement right now, a few minor adjustments will provide us with an even more useful statement with which to work. We will want to better explain the change in retained earnings and that in net fixed assets. We purposely separated these two items from all the rest in Table 7-2. Once we give a more detailed explanation of these two net changes, the rest of Table 7-2 will remain virtually untouched.

But to adjust these two items, we will have to go beyond the firm's balance sheets and get some additional information from the firm's statement of earnings, *Table 6-2 in Chapter 6.*

SOURCES		USES	
Increase, retained earnings	$ 58		
Decrease, net fixed assets	8		
Decrease, accounts receivable	62	Increase, inventories	$ 94
Increase, bank loans	92	Increase, prepaid expenses	4
Increase, accounts payable	12	Increase, tax prepayments	6
Increase, other accruals	27	Increase, long-term investment	65
Increase, long-term debt	4	Decrease, accrued taxes	91
		Increase, cash and cash equivalents	**3**
	$263		$263

Recognize Profits and Dividends.   So far our funds statement reflects only the net change in the retained earnings account. Profits earned and dividends paid have netted out to produce this figure. The individual components are important funds flows and need to be shown separately, however. Making use of the firm's earnings statement to get the needed figures, we simply delete the net change in retained earnings and substitute its components in our funds statement—net profit as a source of funds and cash dividends as a use of funds.

Source: *Net profit*	$201
Less Use: *Cash dividends*	143
(Net) Source: Increase, retained earnings	$ 58

Giving individual recognition to profits (or losses) and dividends paid provides important added funds detail with a minimum of effort.

Recognize Depreciation and Gross Change in Fixed Assets.   Depreciation is a bookkeeping entry that allocates the cost of assets against income but does not involve any movement of capital. This noncash expense actually helps conceal the full operating funds flow from us. What we really want to know is something called *funds provided by operations*—something usually not expressed directly on the income statement. To find it, we must add back depreciation to net profit.[1] We should keep in mind that depreciation does not really create funds; funds are generated from operations. But we need to add it back to net income to reverse the effect of the accounting entry that originally removed it. So although we will list depreciation as a source under net income, it is there more as a reversing entry than as a real source of funds in its own right.

Besides helping us derive *funds provided by operations,* adding back depreciation as a source of funds allows us to explain the *gross additions* (or *reductions*) to fixed assets as opposed to merely the *change* in net fixed assets. First, we need the change in net fixed assets from the "basic" sources and uses statement (Table 7-2). Then we need to retrieve the depreciation figure found on Aldine's earnings statement

---

[1]Amortization expense and any change in deferred taxes would also be added back to net profit in order to establish funds provided by operations. However, Aldine does not have these accounts.

(Table 6-2 in Chapter 6). From this data we compute gross additions (or reductions) to fixed assets in the following manner:

$$\begin{array}{ccc} \text{Gross additions} \\ \text{to fixed assets} \end{array} = \begin{array}{c} \text{Increase (decrease)} \\ \text{in net fixed assets} \end{array} + \begin{array}{c} \text{Depreciation} \\ \text{during period} \end{array} \qquad \textbf{(7-1)}$$

Therefore, for Aldine we have (in thousands)

$$\text{Gross additions to fixed assets} = -\$8 + \$112 = \textbf{\$104}$$

So we conclude:

Source: *Depreciation*	$112
Less Use: *Additions to fixed assets*	104
(Net) Source: Decrease, net fixed assets	$ 8

Once depreciation is added to the funds statement as a source and additions to fixed assets is shown as a use, we can remove the change in net fixed assets because it is no longer needed. The decrease in net fixed assets of $8,000 has been more fully explained as being the net result of the addition of $104,000 in new assets and depreciation charges of $112,000.

Table 7-3 shows a finalized sources and uses of funds statement for the Aldine Company. When we compare it to Table 7-2, the funds statement based solely on balance sheet changes, we see that changes in two balance sheet items—retained earnings and net fixed assets—have been replaced by their earnings-statement-derived components. And, as a result of this full explanation, the sources and uses totals, though still in balance, have increased to $510,000.

Analyzing the Sources and Uses of Funds Statement

In Table 7-3 we see that the principal uses of funds for the 20X2 fiscal year were dividends, additions to fixed assets, increases in inventories and long-term investment, and a sizable decrease in taxes payable. These were financed primarily by funds

TABLE 7-3
Aldine Manufacturing Company sources and uses of funds statement for March 31, 20X1 to March 31, 20X2 (in thousands)

SOURCES		USES	
Funds provided by operations			
Net profit	$201	Dividends	$143
Depreciation	112	Additions to fixed assets	104
Decrease, accounts receivable	62	Increase, inventories	94
Increase, bank loans	92	Increase, prepaid expenses	4
Increase, accounts payable	12	Increase, tax prepayments	6
Increase, other accruals	27	Increase, long-term investment	65
Increase, long-term debt	4	Decrease, accrued taxes	91
		Increase, cash and cash equivalents	3
	$510		$510

provided by operations, a decrease in accounts receivable, and an increase in bank loans. Also of note is the fact that the firm has increased its cash balance by $3,000. In a sources and uses of funds analysis, it is useful to place cash dividends opposite net profits and additions to fixed assets opposite depreciation. Doing this allows the analyst to easily evaluate both the amount of the dividend payout and the net increase (decrease) in fixed assets.

In Aldine's case, having the source of dividend payment being net profit rather than an increase in debt or a decrease in fixed assets is a healthy sign. However, having more of the firm's assets worn away (depreciated) rather than replaced (through additions) may not be such a good sign. The difference for now is small, but this could pose a problem if allowed to continue and grow.

Implications of Funds Statement Analysis. The analysis of funds statements gives us insight into the financial operations of a firm that will be especially valuable to you if you assume the role of a financial manager examining past and future expansion plans of the firm and their impact on liquidity. Imbalances in the uses of funds can be detected and appropriate actions undertaken. For example, an analysis spanning the past several years might reveal a growth in inventories out of proportion with the growth of other assets or with sales. Upon analysis, you might find that the problem was due to inefficiencies in inventory management. Thus, a funds statement alerts you to problems that you can analyze in detail and take proper actions to correct.

Another use of funds statements is in the evaluation of the firm's financing. An analysis of the major sources of funds in the past reveals what portions of the firm's growth were financed internally and externally. In evaluating the firm's financing, you will want to evaluate the ratio of dividends to earnings relative to the firm's total need for funds.

Funds statements are also useful in judging whether the firm has expanded at too fast a rate and whether the firm's financing capability is strained. You can determine if trade credit from suppliers (accounts payable) has increased out of proportion to increases in current assets and to sales. If trade credit has increased at a significantly faster rate, you would wish to evaluate the consequences of increased slowness in trade payments on the credit standing of the firm and its ability to finance in the future. It is also revealing to analyze the mix of short- and long-term financing in relation to the funds needs of the firm. If these needs are primarily for fixed assets and permanent increases in current assets, you might be disturbed if a significant portion of total financing came from short-term sources.

An analysis of a funds statement for the future will be extremely valuable to you as the financial manager in planning intermediate- and long-term financing of the firm. It reveals the firm's total prospective need for funds, the expected timing of these needs, and their nature—that is, whether the increased investment is primarily for inventories, fixed assets, and so forth. Given this information, along with the expected changes in trade payables and the various accruals, you can arrange the firm's financing more effectively. In addition, you can determine the expected closing cash position of the firm simply by adjusting the beginning cash balance for the change in cash reflected on the projected sources and uses statement. In essence, the projected change in cash is a residual. Alternatively, you can forecast future cash positions of the firm through a cash budget, where direct estimates of the future cash flows are made.

Accounting Statement of Cash Flows

Statement of cash flows
A summary of a firm's cash receipts and cash payments during a period of time.

The purpose of the **statement of cash flows** is to report a firm's cash inflows and outflows, during a period of time, segregated into three categories: operating, investing, and financing activities. This statement is required under Statement of Financial Accounting Standards (SFAS) No. 95. When used with the information contained in the other two basic financial statements and their related disclosures, it should help the financial manager to assess and identify

- A company's ability to generate future net cash inflows from operations to pay debts, interest, and dividends
- A company's need for external financing
- The reasons for differences between net income and net cash flow from operating activities
- The effects of cash and noncash investing and financing transactions[2]

Content and Alternative Forms of the Statement

The statement of cash flows explains changes in cash (and cash equivalents, such as Treasury bills) by listing the activities that increased cash and those that decreased cash. Each activity's cash inflow or outflow is segregated according to one of three broad category types: operating, investing, or financing activity. Table 7-4 lists the activities found most often in a typical statement of cash flows grouped according to the three required major categories.

The cash flow statement may be presented using either a "direct method" (which is encouraged by the Financial Accounting Standards Board because it is easier to understand) or an "indirect method" (which is likely to be the method followed by a good majority of firms because it is easier to prepare). Making use of both methods, alternative cash flow statements for the Aldine Manufacturing Company are presented in Table 7-5. (In addition, we share with you a worksheet—Table 7-6—that we used to determine some of the operating activity cash flows required under the direct method. Hopefully, this will help remove any confusion concerning where those particular cash-flow figures originated.)

The only difference between the direct and indirect methods of presentation concerns the reporting of operating activities; the investing and financing activity sections would be identical under either method. Under the direct method, operating cash flows are reported (directly) by major classes of operating cash receipts (from customers) and payments (to suppliers and employees). A separate (indirect) reconciliation of net income to net cash flow from operating activities must be provided. (For the Aldine Company, this reconciliation appears in Table 7-5 as the last section of the statement of cash flows in Frame A.) This reconciliation starts with reported net income and adjusts this figure for noncash income statement items and related changes in balance sheet items to determine cash provided by operating activities.

---

[2]The cash flow statement's biggest shortcoming is that important current period noncash transactions that may impact cash flow in future periods are omitted from the statement itself. For example, obtaining an asset by entering a capital lease would not be reported on a cash flow statement but would appear on a sources and uses statement. Only through disclosures (notes) to the financial statements and the preparation of a funds statement will users be able to round out the cash flow statement to get an understanding of the full scope of a company's investing and financing transactions.

TABLE 7-4
Operating, investing, and financing activities

CASH INFLOWS AND OUTFLOWS*	EXPLANATION
Operating Activities	Shows impact of transactions not defined as investing or financing activities. **These cash flows are generally the cash effects of transactions that enter into the determination of net income.** Thus, we see items that not all statement users might think of as "operating" flows—items such as dividends and interest received, as well as interest paid.
Cash Inflows	
From sales of goods or services	
From returns on loans (interest income) and equity securities (dividend income)**	
Cash Outflows	
To pay suppliers for inventory	
To pay employees for services	
To pay lenders (interest)**	
To pay government for taxes	
To pay other suppliers for other operating expenses	
Investing Activities	Shows impact of buying and selling fixed assets and debt or equity securities of other entities.
Cash Inflows	
From sale of fixed assets (property, plant, equipment)	
From sale of debt or equity securities (other than cash equivalents) of other entities	
Cash Outflows	
To acquire fixed assets (property, plant, equipment)	
To purchase debt or equity securities (other than cash equivalents) of other entities	
Financing Activities	Shows impact of all cash transactions with shareholders and the borrowing and repaying transactions with lenders.
Cash Inflows	
From borrowing	
From the sale of the firm's own equity securities	
Cash Outflows	
To repay amounts borrowed (principal)	
To repurchase the firm's own equity securities	
To pay shareholders dividends	

*These inflows and outflows are typical for a nonfinancial firm and are classified according to the operating, investing, and financing activity definitions of SFAS No. 95.

**It would seem logical to classify interest and dividends "received" as investing inflows, whereas interest "paid" certainly looks like a financing outflow. In fact, three out of seven Financial Accounting Standards Board members dissented from classifying interest and dividends received and interest paid as cash flows from operating activities—but the majority ruled.

Do the figures used in the reconciliation in Frame A of Table 7-5 look familiar? They should. They consist of the firm's "funds provided by operations" plus all of Aldine's balance sheet changes in current assets and current liabilities except for the changes in cash and bank loans. All of these figures can be found on the finalized sources and uses statement for Aldine, Table 7-3. The need for the figures used in the

TABLE 7-5
Alternate cash flow statements showing direct versus indirect methods

FRAME A — DIRECT METHOD

ALDINE MANUFACTURING COMPANY
STATEMENT OF CASH FLOWS
FOR THE YEAR ENDED MARCH 31, 20X2
(IN THOUSANDS)

CASH FLOW FROM OPERATING ACTIVITIES	
Cash received from customers[a]	$4,054
Cash paid to suppliers and employees[b]	(3,539)
Interest paid	(85)
Taxes paid[c]	(211)
Net cash provided (used) by operating activities	$ 219
CASH FLOW FROM INVESTING ACTIVITIES	
Additions to fixed assets	$ (104)
Payment for long-term investment	(65)
Net cash provided (used) by investing activities	$ (169)
CASH FLOW FROM FINANCING ACTIVITIES	
Increase in short-term borrowings	$ 92
Additions to long-term borrowing	4
Dividends paid	(143)
Net cash provided (used) by financing activities	$ (47)
Increase (decrease) in cash and cash equivalents	$ 3
Cash and cash equivalents, March 31, 20X1	175
Cash and cash equivalents, March 31, 20X2	$ 178

Supplementary Schedule: A reconciliation of net income to net cash provided by operating activities

Net income	$ 201
Depreciation	112
Cash provided (used) by current assets and operating-related current liabilities	
Decrease, accounts receivable	62
Increase, inventories	(94)
Increase, prepaid expenses	(4)
Increase, tax prepayments	(6)
Increase, accounts payable	12
Decrease, accrued taxes	(91)
Increase, other accrued liabilities	27
Net cash provided (used) by operating activities	$ 219

FRAME B — INDIRECT METHOD

ALDINE MANUFACTURING COMPANY
STATEMENT OF CASH FLOWS
FOR THE YEAR ENDED MARCH 31, 20X2
(IN THOUSANDS)

CASH FLOW FROM OPERATING ACTIVITIES	
Net income	$ 201
Depreciation	112
Cash provided (used) by current assets and operating-related liabilities	
Decrease, accounts receivable	62
Increase, inventories	(94)
Increase, prepaid expenses	(4)
Increase, tax prepayments	(6)
Increase, accounts payable	12
Decrease, accrued taxes	(91)
Increase, other accrued liabilities	27
Net cash provided (used) by operating activities	$ 219
CASH FLOW FROM INVESTING ACTIVITIES	
Additions to fixed assets	$(104)
Payment for long-term investment	(65)
Net cash provided (used) by investing activities	$(169)
CASH FLOW FROM FINANCING ACTIVITIES	
Increase in short-term borrowings	$ 92
Additions to long-term borrowing	4
Dividends paid	$(143)
Net cash provided (used) by financing activities	$ (47)
Increase (decrease) in cash and cash equivalents	$ 3
Cash and cash equivalents, March 31, 20X1	175
Cash and cash equivalents, March 31, 20X2	$ 178

Supplemental cash-flow disclosures

Interest paid	$ 85
Taxes paid[c]	211

[a,b,c] See Table 7-6 (Worksheet for Preparing Statement of Cash Flows) for details.

TABLE 7-6
Aldine Manufactur-
ing Company work-
sheet for preparing
statement of cash
flows (in thousands)

	Sales	$3,992
+(−)	Decrease (increase) in accounts receivable	62
=	Cash received from customers[a]	$4,054
	Cost of goods sold (minus depreciation for the year)	$2,568
+(−)	Increase (decrease) in inventory	94
+(−)	Decrease (increase) in accounts payable	(12)
+(−)	Increase (decrease) in prepaid expenses	4
+	Selling, general, and administrative expenses	912
+(−)	Decrease (increase) in other accrued liabilities	(27)
=	Cash paid to suppliers and employees[b]	$3,539
	Income taxes (federal and state)	$ 114
+(−)	Increase (decrease) in accumulated tax prepayments	6
+(−)	Decrease (increase) in accrued taxes	91
=	Taxes paid[c]	$ 211

[a,b,c] See Statement of Cash Flows for the year ended March 31, 20X2.

reconciliation provides another reason why we cannot simply forget about the "replaced" sources and uses statement.

Under the indirect method shown in Frame B of Table 7-5, the reconciliation of net income to net cash flow from operating activities moves up to *replace* the direct method's operating activity cash-flow section. In effect, then, the indirect method is just a reduced version of the direct method of presentation.

Analyzing the Statement of Cash Flows

In Table 7-5 we see that while Aldine's reported net income for 20X2 was $201,000, its cash flow from operating activities was $219,000. Interestingly, the company spent $169,000—slightly more than 75 percent of its entire operating cash flow—on new fixed assets and long-term investments. (Only the additions to fixed assets, however, would seem to be a recurring annual expenditure.) This left only $50,000 of operating cash flow to cover dividend payments of $143,000. Increased borrowings, mostly short term, provided the additional financing to cover dividend payments and provide for a small increase in cash and cash equivalents. When we consider that about half of Aldine's operating cash flow goes to replace depreciating assets, the firm's ability to maintain its current dividend seems to depend on its ability to continue to borrow funds. We may, therefore, be witnessing a signal that the firm will be encountering difficulty in maintaining its current dividend into the future.

From the reconciliation (net income to net cash provided by operating activities) section in Frame A of Table 7-5, we see that a decrease in receivables helped increase cash provided by operating activities, while an increase in inventories and a large decrease in taxes payable helped use up cash from operations. You may have noticed by now that the cash flow statement gives you much of the same information gathered from an analysis of the sources and uses of funds statement. However, with the direct method of cash-flow presentation, you do get some added details not necessarily derivable from an analysis of simple balance sheet changes.

Implications of Cash Flow Statement Analysis. A major benefit of the statement of cash flows (especially under the direct method) is that the user gets a reasonably detailed picture of a company's operating, investing, and financing transactions involving cash. This three-part breakdown of cash flow aids the user in assessing the company's current and potential future strengths and weaknesses. Strong internal generation of operating cash, over time, would be considered a positive sign. Poor operating cash flow should prompt the analyst to check for unhealthy growth in receivables and/or inventory. Even strong operating cash flow, however, is not enough to ensure success. Statement users need to see the extent to which operating cash is funding needed investments, debt reductions, and dividends. Too much reliance on external financing sources to meet recurring needs may be a danger signal. In short, the cash flow statement is a rich source of information. The difficulty with this statement (as with the other financial statements) is that it must be used in conjunction with other statements and disclosures in order to attain any real depth of understanding.

QUESTION•ANSWER•QUESTION•ANSWER

The signs (positive or negative) of a firm's net cash provided (used) by operating, investing, and financing activities form a particular *cash-flow pattern*. What type of pattern(s) should we "generally" expect to find?

For a healthy, growing firm "generally" expect:

- *Positive* cash flow from operating activities
- *Negative* cash flow from investing activities
- *Positive* or *negative* cash flow from financing activities (which may move back and forth over time).

CASH-FLOW FORECASTING

Cash budget A forecast of a firm's future cash flows arising from collections and disbursements, usually on a monthly basis.

A **cash budget** is arrived at through a projection of future cash receipts and cash disbursements of the firm over various intervals of time. It reveals the timing and amount of expected cash inflows and outflows over the period studied. With this information, the financial manager is better able to determine the future cash needs of the firm, plan for the financing of these needs, and exercise control over the cash and liquidity of the firm. Though cash budgets may be prepared for almost any interval of time, monthly projections for a year are most common. This enables analysis of seasonal variations in cash flows. When cash flows are volatile, however, weekly projections may be necessary.

The Sales Forecast

The key to the accuracy of most cash budgets is the sales forecast. This forecast can be based on an internal analysis, an external one, or both. With an internal approach, sales representatives are asked to project sales for the forthcoming period. The product sales managers screen these estimates and consolidate them into sales estimates for product lines. The estimates for the various product lines are then combined into an overall sales estimate for the firm. The basic problem with an internal approach is

Ask the Fool

Q How do I make sense of the Statement of Cash Flows?

A Let's say that Otis the postal carrier has just delivered the investor's package you requested from Coca-Cola. You've been thinking of buying stock in Coke, but good Fool that you are, you want to research it first. You flip through the glossy photos of happy people drinking Coke. Then you bear down and scrutinize the three main financial statements. The easiest of the three statements is the income statement, which shows how much money the company made over the last year. Next up is the balance sheet, revealing how much cash, inventories and debt Coke has. The third and most complex of all financial statements is the statement of cash flows.

The cash flow statement shows how much money Coke is really making, as it works through operations, makes investments, and borrows money. It breaks cash inflows and outflows into three categories: operations, investments and financing. Some operating activities include purchases or sales of supplies and changes in payments expected and payments due. Investing activities include the purchase or sale of equipment, plants, property, companies, and securities like stocks or bonds. Financing activities include issuing or repurchasing stock and issuing or reducing debt.

If the bottom-line number is positive, the company is "cash flow positive." That's a good thing. But it's not the only thing you should look at on this statement. Check to see where most of the moolah is coming from. You'd rather see more greenbacks generated from operations than financing. Examine the various line items and see how they have changed over past years.

For example, under financing activities, Coke's "payments of debt" jump from $212 million in 1995 to $751 million in 1997. This shows the firm increasingly paying off debt. In each of the last few years, Coke has repurchased more than $1 billion dollars' worth of its own stock. Coke is actively increasing its stock share value by reducing the number of shares outstanding. "Net cash provided by operating activities" in 1997 is a hefty $4.03 billion, about eight times more than was needed for investing activities. This is where the money to pay down debt and buy back stock came from.

Scouring the cash flow statement can be profitable.

Source: The Motley Fool (www.fool.com). Reproduced with the permission of The Motley Fool.

---

that it can be too myopic. Often, significant trends in the economy and in the industry are overlooked.

For this reason, many companies use an external analysis as well. With an external approach, economic analysts make forecasts of the economy and of industry sales for several years to come. They may use regression analysis to estimate the association between industry sales and the economy in general. After these basic predictions of business conditions and industry sales, the next step is to estimate market share by individual products, prices that are likely to prevail, and the expected reception of new products. Usually, these estimates are made in conjunction with marketing managers, even though the ultimate responsibility should lie with the economic forecasting department. From this information, an external sales forecast can be prepared.

When the internal sales forecast differs from the external one, as it is likely to do, a compromise must be reached. Past experience will show which of the two forecasts is likely to be more accurate. In general, the external forecast should serve as a foundation for the final sales forecast, often modified by the internal forecast. A final sales forecast based on both internal and external analyses is usually more accurate than either an internal or an external forecast by itself. The final sales forecast should be based on prospective demand, not modified initially by internal constraints, such as physical capacity. The decision to remove these constraints will depend on the forecast. The value of accurate sales forecasts cannot be overestimated because most of the other forecasts, in some measure, are based on expected sales.

Collections and Other Cash Receipts

The sales forecast out of the way, the next job is to determine the cash receipts from these sales. For cash sales, cash is received at the time of the sale; for credit sales, the receipts come later. How much later depends on the billing terms, the type of customer, and the credit and collection policies of the firm. Pacific Jams Company offers terms of "net 30," meaning that payment is due within 30 days after the invoice date. Also assume that in the company's experience, an average of 90 percent of receivables are collected one month from the date of sale and the remaining 10 percent are collected two months from sale date if no bad-debt losses occur. Moreover, on the average, 10 percent of total sales are cash sales.

If the sales forecasts are those shown in Frame A of Table 7-7, we can compute a schedule of the expected sales receipts based on the foregoing assumptions. This schedule appears as Frame B in Table 7-7. For January, we see that total sales are estimated to be $250,000, of which $25,000 are cash sales. Of the $225,000 in credit sales, 90 percent, or $202,500, is expected to be collected in February, and the remaining 10 percent, or $22,500, is expected to be collected in March. Similarly, collections in other months are estimated according to the same percentages. The firm should be ready, however, to change its assumptions with respect to collections when there is an underlying shift in the payment habits of its customers.

From this example, it is easy to see the effect of a variation in sales on the magnitude and timing of cash receipts, all other things held constant. For most firms, there is a degree of correlation between sales and collection experience. In times of recession and sales decline, the average collection period is likely to lengthen, and bad-debt losses are likely to increase. Thus, the collection experience of a firm may reinforce a decline in sales, magnifying the downward impact on total sales receipts.

Cash receipts may arise from the sale of assets, as well as from product sales. If Pacific Jams intends to sell $40,000 of fixed assets in February, total cash receipts that

TABLE 7-7
Schedules of projected sales and collections for January to June (in thousands)

	NOV.	DEC.	JAN.	FEB.	MAR.	APR.	MAY	JUNE
Frame A: *Sales*								
Credit sales, 90%	$270.0	$315.0	$225.0	$180.0	$225.0	$270.0	$315.0	$342.0
Cash sales, 10%	30.0	35.0	25.0	20.0	25.0	30.0	35.0	38.0
Total sales, 100%	$300.0	$350.0	$250.0	$200.0	$250.0	$300.0	$350.0	$380.0
Frame B: *Cash Collections*								
Cash sales, this month			$ 25.0	$ 20.0	$ 25.0	$ 30.0	$ 35.0	$ 38.0
90% of last month's credit sales			283.5	202.5	162.0	202.5	243.0	283.5
10% of 2-month-old credit sales			27.0	31.5	22.5	18.0	22.5	27.0
Total sales receipts			$355.5	$254.0	$209.5	$250.5	$300.5	$348.5

month would be $294,000. For the most part, the sale of assets is planned in advance and easily predicted for purposes of cash budgeting. In addition, cash receipts may arise from external financing as well as investment income.

Cash Disbursements

Next comes a forecast of cash disbursements. Given the sales forecast, management may choose to gear production closely to seasonal sales, to produce at a relatively constant rate over time, or to have mixed production strategy.

Production Outlays. Once a production schedule has been established, estimates can be made of the needs for materials, labor, and additional fixed assets. As with receivables, there is a lag between the time a purchase is made and the time of actual cash payment. If suppliers give average billing terms of "net 30" and the firm's policy is to pay its bills at the end of this period, there is approximately a one-month lag between a purchase and the payment. If the production program of Pacific Jams calls for the manufacture of goods in the month preceding forecasted sales, we might have a schedule of disbursements for purchases and operating expenses like that in Table 7-8. As we see, there is a one-month lag between the time of purchase and the payment for the purchase. As with the collection of receivables, payment for purchases can be lagged for other average payable periods. The setup is similar to that illustrated for collections. With a computer-based spreadsheet program, it is an easy matter to set up a lagged disbursement schedule (and a lagged collections schedule as well).

Wages are assumed to vary with the amount of production—but not perfectly. Generally, wages are more stable over time than are purchases. When production dips slightly, workers are usually not laid off. When production picks up, labor becomes more efficient with relatively little increase in total wages. Only after a certain point is overtime work required or are new workers needed to meet the increased production schedule. Other expenses include general, administrative, and selling costs; property taxes; interest; power, light, and heat; maintenance; and indirect labor and material. All of these expenses tend to be reasonably predictable over the short run.

Other Disbursements. In addition to cash operating expenses, we must take into account capital expenditures, dividends, federal income taxes, and any other cash

TABLE 7-8
Schedule of projected disbursements for purchases and operating expenses for January to June (in thousands)

	DEC.	JAN.	FEB.	MAR.	APR.	MAY	JUNE
Frame A: *Purchases*	$100	$ 80	$100	$120	$140	$150	$150
Frame B: *Cash Disbursements for Purchases and Operating Expenses*							
100% of last month's purchases		$100	$ 80	$100	$120	$140	$150
Wages paid		80	80	90	90	95	100
Other expenses paid		50	50	50	50	50	50
Total disbursements for purchases and operating expenses		$230	$210	$240	$260	$285	$300

TABLE 7-9
Schedule of projected total cash disbursements for January to June (in thousands)

	JAN.	FEB.	MAR.	APR.	MAY	JUNE
Total disbursements for purchases and operating expenses	$230	$210	$240	$260	$285	$300
Capital expenditures		150	50			
Dividend payments			20			20
Income taxes	30			30		
Total cash disbursements	$260	$360	$310	$290	$285	$320

outflows not already accounted for. Because capital expenditures are planned in advance, they are usually predictable for the short-term cash budget. As the forecast becomes more distant, however, prediction of these expenditures becomes less certain. Dividend payments for most companies are stable and are paid on specific dates. Federal income tax estimates must be based on projected profits for the period under review. Other cash outlays might consist of the repurchase of common stock or payment of long-term debt. These outlays are combined with total disbursements for purchases and operating expenses to obtain the schedule of total cash disbursements shown in Table 7-9.

Net Cash Flow and Cash Balance

Once we are satisfied that we have taken all foreseeable cash inflows and outflows into account, we combine the cash receipts and disbursements schedules to obtain the net cash inflow or outflow for each month. The net cash flow may then be added to beginning cash in January, which is assumed to be $100,000, and the projected cash position computed month by month for the period under review. This final schedule is shown in Table 7-10.

The cash budget shown there indicates that the firm is expected to have a cash deficit in April and May. These deficits are caused by a decline in collections through March, capital expenditures totaling $200,000 spread over February and March, and cash dividends of $20,000 in March and June. With the increase in collections in May and June, the cash balance without additional financing rises to $13,500 in June. The cash budget indicates that peak cash requirements occur in April. If the firm has a

TABLE 7-10
Schedule of projected net cash flows and cash balances for January to June (in thousands)

	JAN.	FEB.	MAR.	APR.	MAY	JUNE
Beginning cash balance, without additional financing	$100.0	$175.5	$ 109.5	$ 9.0	$(30.5)	$(15.0)
Total cash receipts	335.5	294.0*	209.5	250.5	300.5	348.5
Total cash disbursements	260.0	360.0	310.0	290.0	285.0	320.0
Net cash flow	$ 75.5	$ (66.0)	$(100.5)	$(39.5)	$ 15.5	$ 28.5
Ending cash balance, without additional financing	$175.5	$109.5	$ 9.0	$(30.5)	$(15.0)	$ 13.5

*Includes sales receipts of $254,000 and cash sale of fixed assets of $40,000.

policy of maintaining a minimum cash balance of $75,000 and of borrowing from its bank to maintain this minimum, it will need to borrow an additional $66,000 in March. Additional borrowings will peak at $105,500 in April, after which they will decline to $61,500 in June, if all goes according to prediction.

Alternative means of meeting the cash deficits are available. The firm may be able to delay its capital expenditures or its payments for purchases. Indeed, one of the principal purposes of a cash budget is to determine the timing and magnitude of prospective financing needs so that the most appropriate method of financing can be arranged. A decision to obtain long-term financing should be based on long-range funds requirements and on considerations apart from a cash forecast. In addition to helping the financial manager plan for short-term financing, the cash budget is valuable in managing the firm's cash position. On the basis of a cash budget, the manager can plan to invest excess funds in marketable securities. The result is an efficient transfer of funds from cash to marketable securities and back.

RANGE OF CASH-FLOW ESTIMATES

Often there is a tendency to place considerable faith in the cash budget simply because it is expressed in impressive-looking figures—perhaps even on a computer printout. We stress again that a cash budget merely represents an *estimate* of future cash flows. Depending on the care devoted to preparing the budget and the volatility of cash flows resulting from the nature of the business, actual cash flows will deviate more or less widely from those that are expected. In the face of uncertainty, we must provide information about the range of possible outcomes. Analyzing cash flows under only one set of assumptions, as is the case with conventional cash budgeting, can result in a faulty perspective of the future.

Deviations from Expected Cash Flows

To take into account deviations from expected cash flows, it is desirable to work out additional cash budgets. We might want to base one cash forecast on the assumption of a maximum probable decline in business and another on the assumption of the maximum probable increase in business. With a spreadsheet program, it is a simple matter to change assumptions and display a new cash budget in seconds.

The final product might be a series of distributions of end-of-month cash without additional financing. Figure 7-1 shows relative frequency distributions for the months of January through June, using bar graphs. The most likely values of ending cash balances are depicted by the highest bar; these conform with the values shown in Table 7-10. We note that while several of the distributions are reasonably symmetrical, others are skewed. In particular, the distributions for March and April are skewed to the left. As a result, the need for cash during these months might be considerably greater than that depicted in Table 7-10. It is clear that the type of information portrayed in Figure 7-1 better enables management to plan for contingencies than does information giving only single-point estimates of monthly cash flows.

Use of Probabilistic Information

The expected cash position plus the distribution of possible outcomes give us a considerable amount of information. We can see the additional funds required or the funds released under various possible outcomes. This information enables us to

FIGURE 7-1
Distributions of Ending Cash Balances for January through June

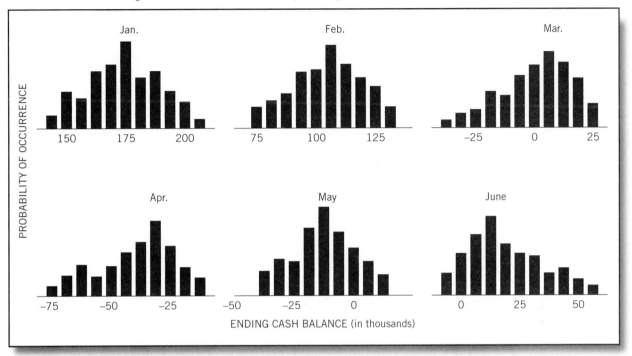

determine more accurately the minimum cash balance, maturity structure of debt, and borrowing levels necessary to give the firm a margin of safety.

We can also analyze the firm's ability to adjust to deviations from the expected outcomes. If sales should fall off, how flexible are our expenses? What can be cut? By how much? How quickly? How much effort should be devoted to the collection of receivables? If there is an unexpected increase in business, what additional purchases will be required, and when? Can labor be expanded? Can the present plant handle the additional demand? How much in funds will be needed to finance the buildup? Answers to these questions provide valuable insight into the efficiency and flexibility of the firm under a variety of conditions.

From the standpoint of internal planning, it is far better to allow for a range of possible outcomes than to rely solely on the expected outcome. This allowance is particularly necessary for firms whose business is relatively unstable in character. If the firm bases its plans on expected cash flows only, it is likely to be caught flat-footed if there is a significant deviation from the expected outcome. An unforeseen deficit in cash may be difficult to finance on short notice. Therefore, it is essential for the firm to be honest with itself and attempt to minimize the costs associated with deviations from expected outcomes. It may do this by taking the steps necessary to ensure accuracy and by preparing additional cash budgets to take into account the range of possible outcomes.

It is a good idea to compare each month's forecasted cash-flow figures with actual performance figures. Significant discrepancies between forecasted and actual numbers are a signal to revise assumptions and estimates. One may also need to make some operating and/or financing adjustments in response to these discrepancies (e.g., delay a capital expenditure or increase a bank line of credit).

FORECASTING FINANCIAL STATEMENTS

Forecast financial statements Expected future financial statements based on conditions that management expects to exist and actions it expects to take.

In addition to forecasting the cash flow of a firm over time, it is often useful to prepare prospective, or **forecast, financial statements** for selected future dates. A cash budget gives us information about only the prospective future cash positions of the firm, whereas forecast statements embody expected estimates of all assets and liabilities as well as of income statement items. Much of the information that goes into the preparation of the cash budget can be used to derive a forecast income statement. In fact, the forecast income statement usually precedes the cash budget. In this way the financial manager is able to use the tax estimates from the forecast income statement when preparing the cash budget.

Forecast Income Statement

The forecast income statement is a summary of a firm's expected revenues and expenses over some future period, ending with the net income (loss) for the period. As was true with our cash budget, the sales forecast is the key to scheduling production and estimating production costs. The analyst may wish to evaluate each component of the cost of goods sold. A detailed analysis of purchases, production-based wages, and overhead costs is likely to produce the most accurate forecasts. Often, however, costs of goods sold are estimated on the basis of past ratios of cost of goods sold to sales.

Selling, general, and administrative expenses are estimated next. Because these expenses are usually budgeted in advance, estimates of them are fairly accurate. Typically, these expenses are not overly sensitive to changes in sales, particularly to reductions in sales in the very short run. Next, we estimate other income and expenses as well as interest expenses to obtain net income before taxes. Income taxes are then computed—based on the applicable tax rate(s)—and deducted to arrive at estimated net income after taxes. All of these estimates are then combined into an income statement. To illustrate, suppose that estimated sales for January through June for Pacific Jams Company total $1,730,000, as reflected in Frame A of our cash budget in Table 7-7. In the cash budget, the cost of goods sold is not depicted directly. Rather than construct a detailed analysis of estimated components of cost of goods sold, we decide instead to rely on the recent historical relationship of the cost of goods sold to sales. Multiplying a three-year average of cost-of-goods-sold-to-sales ratios of 75.4 percent times our six-month net sales estimate of $1,730,000 yields a forecast figure for cost of goods sold of $1,305,000. Other expenses (selling, general, and administrative) are expected to be $50,000 a month and are shown in Table 7-8. For the six-month period they total $300,000. Finally, let us assume an income tax rate (federal plus state) of 48 percent. Given this information, we can derive a forecast income statement for the January-to-June period (in thousands):

		ASSUMPTIONS AND/OR SOURCES OF INFORMATION
Net sales	$1,730	• Based on sales budget in Frame A of Table 7-7.
Cost of goods sold	1,305	• Forecast at 75.4% of net sales; based on a 3-year
Gross profit	$ 425	average of cost-of-goods-sold-to-net-sales ratios.
Selling, general, and administrative expenses	300	• See Table 7-8.
Profit before taxes	$ 125	
Taxes	60	• Forecast at 48%.
Profit after taxes	$ 65	
Dividends	40	• See Table 7-9.
Increase in retained earnings	$ 25	• Carried to forecast balance sheet.

The last three lines of the income statement shown above represent a simplified forecast statement of retained earnings. Anticipated dividends are deducted from profit after taxes to give the expected increase in retained earnings. The anticipated increase of $25,000 should agree with the forecast balance sheet figures that we develop next.

Forecast Balance Sheet

To illustrate the preparation of a forecast balance sheet, suppose that we wish to prepare one for Pacific Jams for June 30 and that the company had the following balance sheet the previous December 31:

ASSETS (IN THOUSANDS)		LIABILITIES (IN THOUSANDS)	
Cash	$ 100	Bank borrowings	$ 50
Receivables	342	Accounts payable	100
Inventory	350	Accrued wages and expenses	150
		Accrued income taxes	70
Current assets	$ 792	Current liabilities	$ 370
Net fixed assets	800	Shareholders' equity	1,222
Total assets	$1,592	Total liabilities and shareholders' equity	$1,592

Receivables at June 30 can be estimated by adding to the receivable balance at December 31 the total projected credit sales from January through June, less total projected credit collections for the period. On the basis of the information in the cash budget, receivables at June 30 would be $342,000 + $1,557,000 − $1,525,500, or $373,500. Alternatively, for Pacific Jams this figure should be equal to estimated June credit sales plus 10 percent of May credit sales ($342,000 + $31,500 = $373,500).

Forecasting Assets. If a cash budget is not available, the receivable balance may be estimated on the basis of a receivable turnover ratio. This ratio, which depicts the relationship between credit sales and receivables, should be based on past experience. To obtain the estimated level of receivables, projected credit sales are simply divided by the turnover ratio. If the sales forecast and turnover ratio are realistic, the method will produce a reasonable approximation of the receivable balance. The estimated investment in inventories at June 30 may be based on the production schedule, which, in turn, is based on the sales forecast. This schedule should show expected purchases, the expected use of inventory in production, and the expected level of finished goods. On the basis of this information, together with the beginning inventory level, an inventory forecast can be made.

Rather than use the production schedule, estimates of future inventory can be based on an inventory turnover ratio. This ratio is applied in the same manner as for receivables, except that now we solve for the ending inventory position. We have

$$\frac{\text{Cost of goods sold}}{\text{(ending) Inventory}} = \begin{array}{c}\text{Inventory} \\ \text{turnover} \\ \text{ratio}\end{array}$$

Given an assumed *annual* turnover ratio and an assumed *six-month* figure for cost of goods sold and knowing the beginning inventory, we rearrange the equation to solve for the unknown ending inventory figure.

$$\text{(ending) Inventory} = \frac{2 \times (\text{6-month cost of goods sold})}{\text{Inventory turnover ratio}}$$

If the estimated inventory turnover ratio in our example is 6.2143 for a 12-month period and the estimated cost of goods sold for the upcoming 6-month period is $1,305,000, we have

$$\text{(ending) Inventory} = \frac{2 \times (\$1,305,000)}{6.2143} = \textbf{\$420,000}$$

In keeping with the buildup in sales, our estimate of inventory on June 30 would be $420,000, a figure that represents a moderate increase over the inventory level of December 31.

Future net fixed assets are estimated by adding planned expenditures to existing net fixed assets and subtracting from this sum the book value of any fixed assets sold along with depreciation during the period. From the cash budget, we note that capital expenditures are estimated at $200,000 over the period and that $40,000 in fixed assets will be sold at what we assume to be their depreciated book values. If depreciation for the period is expected to be $110,000, the expected net additions to fixed assets would be $50,000 ($200,000 − $40,000 − $110,000). Projected net fixed assets at June 30 would be $850,000. Because capital expenditures are planned in advance, fixed assets are fairly easy to forecast.

Forecasting Liabilities and Shareholders' Equity.   Turning now to the liabilities, accounts payable are estimated by adding projected purchases for January through June, less total projected cash payments for purchases for the period, to the December 31 balance. Our estimate of accounts payable, therefore, is $740,000 − $690,000 + $100,000, or $150,000—which, as we would expect with a one-month lag between the time of purchase and the payment, is equal to the June purchases amount. The calculation of accrued wages and expenses is based on the production schedule and the historical relationship between these accruals and production. We assume the estimate of accrued wages and expenses to be $140,000. Accrued income taxes are estimated by adding the taxes due on forecasted income for the six-month period to the December 31 balance and subtracting the actual payment of taxes. With a December 31 balance of $70,000, income taxes for the period forecast at $60,000 (as shown in the forecast income statement), and the firm scheduled to make $60,000 in actual payments (as shown in Table 7-9), estimated accrued income taxes at June 30 would be $70,000.

Shareholders' equity at June 30 would be equity at December 31 plus profits after taxes for the period, less the amount of dividends paid. If profits after taxes are estimated at $65,000 in the forecast income statement, shareholders' equity at June 30 would be $1,222,000 plus $65,000 minus dividends of $40,000, or $1,247,000. Two items remain: cash and bank loans. We see from the cash budget that estimated cash

Part III Tools of Financial Analysis and Planning

at June 30 would be $13,500 without additional financing. If the firm has the policy of maintaining a minimum cash balance of $75,000 and borrowing from its bank to maintain this balance, cash at June 30 would be $75,000; bank borrowings would therefore increase by $61,500 to produce an ending balance of $111,500. In general, cash and notes payable (short-term bank borrowings) serve as balancing factors in the preparation of forecast balance sheets, whereby assets and liabilities plus shareholders' equity are brought into balance.

Once we have estimated all the components of the forecast balance sheet, they are combined into a balance sheet format. Table 7-11 contains the forecast balance sheet for Pacific Jams at June 30. Notice that we provide some additional detail so that the reader might have some confidence in our estimates.

Use of Ratios and Implications

As we have seen, the information that goes into a cash budget can be used to prepare forecast financial statements. Instead, ratios could be used to produce these forecast statements. For example, one would make direct estimates of all the items on the

TABLE 7-11
Pacific Jams Company forecast balance sheet at June 30, 20X2 (in thousands)

ASSETS	ACTUAL 12-31-X1	CHANGE	FORECAST 6-30-X2	ASSUMPTIONS
Cash	$ 100	− 25.0	$ 75.0	• Set at estimated minimum balance.
Receivables	342	+ 31.5	373.5	• 100% June credit sales plus 10% May credit sales.
Inventory	350	+ 70.0	420.0	• Based on inventory turnover ratio of 6.2143 and cost of goods sold of $1,305.
Current assets	$ 792	+ 76.5	$ 868.5	
Net fixed assets	800	+ 50.0	850.0	• Capital expenditures of $200, sale of fixed assets with book value of $40, and depreciation of $110.
Total assets	$1,592	+126.5	$1,718.5	
LIABILITIES				
Bank borrowings	$ 50	+ 61.5	$ 111.5	• Previous balance plus additional financing needed.
Accounts payable	100	+ 50.0	150.0	• 100% June purchases.
Accrued wages and expenses	150	− 10.0	140.0	• Based on the production schedule and past experience.
Accrued income taxes	70	—	70.0	• Change equals new accruals less payments ($60–$60).
Current liabilities	$ 370	+101.5	$ 471.5	
Shareholders' equity	1,222	+ 25.0	1,247.0	• Change in retained earnings per forecast income statement.
Total liabilities and shareholders' equity	$1,592	+126.5	$1,718.5	

balance sheet by projecting financial ratios into the future and then making estimates on the basis of these ratios. Receivables, inventories, accounts payable, and accrued wages and expenses are frequently based on historical relationships to sales and production when a cash budget is not available. For example, if the average collection period is 45 days, receivable turnover would be eight times a year. If receivables were $500,000 but the firm was predicting a $2 million increase in sales for the coming year, receivables would increase by $2 million/8 = $250,000. Thus, the level of receivables one year from now might be forecast at $750,000.

Forecast statements allow us to study the composition of expected future balance sheets and income statements. Financial ratios may be computed for analysis of the statements; these ratios and the raw figures may be compared with those for present and past financial statements. Using this information, the financial manager can analyze the direction of change in the financial condition and performance of the firm over the past, the present, and the future. If the firm is accustomed to making accurate estimates, the preparation of a cash budget, forecast statements, or both literally forces it to plan ahead and to coordinate policy in the various areas of operation. Continual revision of these forecasts keeps the firm alert to changing conditions in its environment and in its internal operations. In addition, forecast statements can even be constructed with selected items taking on a range of probable values rather than single-point estimates.

SUMMARY

- The *sources and uses of funds statement* is a summary of a firm's changes in financial position from one period to another. An understanding of this statement gives the analyst considerable insight into the uses of funds and how these uses are financed over a specific period of time. Flow of funds analysis is valuable in analyzing the commitments of funds to assets and in planning the firm's intermediate- and long-term financing. The flow of funds studied, however, represents *net* rather than *gross* transactions between two points in time.

- The statement of cash flows has replaced the flow of funds statement when the firm is required to present a complete set of financial statements. However, unlike the cash flow statement, the flow of funds statement does not omit the net effects of important noncash transactions. In addition, the flow of funds statement is easy to prepare and is often preferred by managers over the more complex cash flow statement.

- An *accounting statement of cash flows* reports a firm's cash inflows and outflows during a period of time segregated into three categories: operating, investing, and financing activities. When used with other financial statements and disclo-

sures, the statement of cash flows should help the analyst to assess a firm's ability to generate cash for dividends and investments, identify a firm's needs for external financing, and understand the differences between net income and net cash flow from operating activities.

- A *cash budget* is a forecast of a firm's future cash receipts and disbursements. This forecast is particularly useful to the financial manager in determining the probable cash balances of the firm over the near future and in planning prospective cash needs. In addition to analyzing expected cash flows, the financial manager should take into account possible deviations from the expected outcome. An analysis of the range of possible outcomes enables management to better assess the efficiency and flexibility of the firm and to determine the appropriate margin of safety.

- *Forecast financial statements* are expected future financial statements based on conditions that management expects to exist and actions it expects to take. These statements offer financial managers insight into the prospective future financial condition and performance of their firms.

Appendix

Sustainable Growth Modeling

The management of growth requires careful balancing of the sales objectives of the firm with its operating efficiency and financial resources. Many a company overreaches itself financially at the altar of growth; the bankruptcy courts are filled with such cases. The trick is to determine what sales growth rate is consistent with the realities of the company and of the financial marketplace. In this regard, sustainable growth modeling is a powerful planning tool that has found enthusiastic use in companies like Hewlett-Packard. In the way of definition, the *sustainable growth rate (SGR)* is the maximum annual percentage increase in sales that can be achieved based on target operating, debt, and dividend-payout ratios. If actual growth exceeds the sustainable growth rate, something must give, and frequently it is the debt ratio. By modeling the process of growth, we are able to plan for intelligent trade-offs.

A STEADY-STATE MODEL

To illustrate the calculation of a sustainable growth rate, we begin with a steady-state model where the future is exactly like the past with respect to balance sheet and performance ratios. We also assume that the firm engages in no external equity financing; the equity account builds only through retaining earnings. Both of these assumptions will be relaxed later when we consider sustainable growth modeling under changing assumptions.

Variables Employed

In a steady-state environment, the variables necessary to determine the sustainable growth rate are

A/S = total-assets-to-sales ratio

NP/S = net profit margin (net profits divided by sales)

b = retention rate of earnings ($1 - b$ is the dividend-payout ratio)

D/Eq = debt-to-equity ratio

S_0 = most recent annual sales (beginning sales)

ΔS = absolute change in sales from the most recent annual sales

The first four variables are target variables. The total-assets-to-sales ratio, the reciprocal of the traditional total asset turnover ratio, is a measure of operating efficiency. The lower the ratio, the more efficient the utilization of assets. In turn, this ratio is a composite of (1) receivable management, as depicted by the average collection period; (2) inventory management, as indicated by the inventory turnover ratio; (3) fixed assets management, as reflected by the throughput of product through the plant; and (4) liquidity management, as suggested by the proportion of and return on liquid assets. For purposes of illustration, we assume liquid assets are kept at moderate levels.[3]

The net profit margin is a relative measure of operating efficiency, after taking account of all expenses and income taxes. Although both the total-assets-to-sales ratio and the net profit margin are affected by the external product markets, they largely capture internal management efficiency. The earnings retention rate and the debt-to-equity ratio should be determined in keeping

---

[3]If this is not the case, it may be better to use an operating-assets-to-sales ratio.

with dividend and capital structure theory and practice. They are importantly influenced by the external financial markets. Our purpose is not to touch on how they are established, because that is done elsewhere in this book, but to incorporate them in the planning model presented.

Sustainable Growth Rate (SGR)

With these six variables we can derive the sustainable growth rate (SGR). The idea is that an increase in assets (a use of funds) must equal the increase in liabilities and shareholders' equity (a source of funds). The increase in assets can be expressed as $\Delta S(A/S)$, the change in sales times the total-assets-to-sales ratio. The increase in shareholders' equity (through retaining earnings) is $b(NP/S)(S_0 + \Delta S)$, or the retention rate times the net profit margin times total sales. Finally, the increase in total debt is simply the shareholders' equity increase multiplied by the target debt-to-equity ratio, or $[b(NP/S)(S_0 + \Delta S)]D/Eq$. Putting these things together, we have

$$\underset{\substack{\text{Assets}\\\text{increase}}}{} = \underset{\substack{\text{Retained}\\\text{earnings}\\\text{increase}}}{} + \underset{\substack{\text{Debt}\\\text{increase}}}{}$$

$$\Delta S \left(\frac{A}{S}\right) = b\left(\frac{NP}{S}\right)(S_0 + \Delta S) + \left[b\left(\frac{NP}{S}\right)(S_0 + \Delta S)\right]\frac{D}{Eq} \tag{7A-1}$$

By rearrangement, this equation can be expressed as

$$\frac{\Delta S}{S_0} \quad \text{or} \quad SGR = \frac{b\left(\frac{NP}{S}\right)\left(1 + \frac{D}{Eq}\right)}{\left(\frac{A}{S}\right) - \left[b\left(\frac{NP}{S}\right)\left(1 + \frac{D}{Eq}\right)\right]} \tag{7A-2}$$

This is the maximum rate of growth in sales that is consistent with the target ratios. Whether or not this growth rate can be achieved, of course, depends on the external product markets and on the firm's marketing efforts. A particular growth rate may be financially feasible, but the product demand may simply not be there. Implicit in the formulations presented is that depreciation charges are sufficient to maintain the value of operating assets. A final caveat has to do with interest on new borrowings. The implicit assumption is that all interest expenses are incorporated in the target net profit margin.

An Illustration

Suppose that a company is characterized by the data shown in Table 7A-1. The sustainable growth rate would be computed as follows and is consistent with the steady-state variables shown in Table 7A-1.

$$SGR = \frac{.70(.04)(1.8)}{.60 - [.70(.04)(1.80)]} = \mathbf{9.17\%}$$

TABLE 7A-1
Initial inputs and variables used to illustrate sustainable growth rates

SYMBOL	INITIAL INPUT AND/OR VARIABLE	
Eq_0	Beginning equity capital (in millions)	$100
$Debt_0$	Beginning debt (in millions)	$ 80
$Sales_0$	Sales the previous year (in millions)	$300
b	Target earnings retention rate	.70
NP/S	Target net profit margin	.04
D/Eq	Target debt-to-equity ratio	.80
A/S	Target assets-to-sales ratio	.60

Part III Tools of Financial Analysis and Planning

It can be demonstrated that initial equity increases by 9.17 percent to $109.17 million and that debt grows by 9.17 percent to $87.34 million, as everything increases in stable equilibrium. If the actual growth rate is other than 9.17 percent, however, one or more of the variables must change. In other words, operating efficiency, leverage, or earnings retention must change, or there must be the sale or repurchase of common stock.

TIP•TIP•TIP•TIP•TIP•TIP•TIP•TIP•TIP•TIP•TIP

Multiplying both the numerator and denominator in Eq. (7A-2) by the quantity (S/A), and rearranging terms slightly, produces a much shortened, alternative SGR formula:

$$SGR = \frac{b(NP/Eq)}{1 - [b(NP/Eq)]}$$

This formula spotlights the fact that—reduced to its most basic elements—a firm's SGR is positively related to its target earnings retention rate (b) and its target return on equity (NP/Eq).

MODELING UNDER CHANGING ASSUMPTIONS

To see what happens when we move from a steady state and variables change from year to year, we must model sustainable growth in a different way. In effect, the growth in equity base and the growth in sales are unbalanced over time. More specifically, we must bring in beginning sales, S_0, and beginning equity capital, Eq_0, as foundations on which to build. Additionally, we express dividend policy in terms of the absolute amount of dividends a company wishes to pay, as opposed to a payout ratio. Finally, we allow for the sale of common stock in a given year, although this can be specified as zero.

With these variables, the sustainable growth rate in sales for the next year, SGR in decimal form, becomes

$$SGR = \left[\frac{(Eq_0 + New\ Eq - Div)\left(1 + \frac{D}{Eq}\right)\left(\frac{S}{A}\right)}{1 - \left[\left(\frac{NP}{S}\right)\left(1 + \frac{D}{Eq}\right)\left(\frac{S}{A}\right)\right]} \right]\left[\frac{1}{S_0}\right] - 1 \qquad (7A\text{-}3)$$

where New Eq is the amount of new equity capital raised, Div is the absolute amount of annual dividend, and S/A is the sales-to-total-assets ratio. The latter is simply the reciprocal of the total-assets-to-sales ratio that we used before. Intuitively, the numerator in the first bracket in Eq. (7A-3) represents the sales that could occur on the basis of existing capital plus any change occasioned by sale of new common stock or dividends. The equity base is expanded by the debt employed and then multiplied by the sales-to-assets ratio. The denominator in the first bracket is one minus the target earning power of the company, (NP/S)(S/A), as magnified by the proportion of debt employed. When the numerator is divided by the denominator, we obtain the new level of sales that can be achieved. In the last bracket we divided this new level by beginning sales to determine the change in sales that is sustainable for the next year.

To illustrate, suppose that the target dividend were $3.93 million, that no new equity issuance was planned, and that the other variables in Table 7A-1 held. The sustainable growth rate, using Eq. (7A-3), is

$$SGR = \left[\frac{(100 - 3.93)(1.80)(1.6667)}{1 - [(.04)(1.80)(1.6667)]} \right]\left[\frac{1}{300}\right] - 1 = \mathbf{9.17\%}$$

TABLE 7A-2
Thirteen different simulations using sustainable growth modeling

VARIABLE	1	2	3	4	5	6	7	8	9	10	11	12	13
A/S	.60	.60	.55	.50	.65	.70	.50	.4292	.5263	.60	.5882	.60	.60
NP/S	.04	.04	.05	.05	.035	.03	.05	.04	.0623	.0538	.05	.04	.04
D/E	.80	.80	1.00	.50	.80	.80	.50	.50	.60	1.00	.7682	1.0272	1.1659
Div	4.00	4.00	4.00	4.00	4.00	4.00	4.00	4.00	4.00	4.00	4.00	4.00	4.00
New Eq	0	10.00	0	0	5.00	0	10.00	10.00	0	0	10.00	0	0
SGR	.0909	.2046	.4222	.1294	.0325	−.1083	.25	.30	.20	.30	.25	.25	.35

Note: Beginning sales = $300; beginning equity = $100.

This is exactly the same as that computed with the steady-state model because a dividend of $3.93 million corresponds to an earnings retention rate of .70. Note also that a total-assets-to-sales ratio of .60 corresponds to a sales-to-total-assets ratio of 1.6667.

Suppose now that the target total-assets-to-sales ratio is .55 (a sales-to-assets ratio of 1.8182) instead of .60. Moreover, the target net profit margin is also better, .05 instead of .04. Finally, the target debt-to-equity ratio is moved up from .80 to 1.00. Assuming a dividend of $4 million, the sustainable growth rate for next year becomes

$$SGR = \left[\frac{(100 - 4)(2.00)(1.8182)}{1 - [(.05)(2.00)(1.8182)]} \right]\left[\frac{1}{300} \right] - 1 = \mathbf{42.22\%}$$

This substantial increase in SGR is due to improved operating efficiency, which generates more retained earnings, and a higher debt ratio. It is important to recognize that the sales growth rate possible is for one year only. Even if operating efficiency continues on an improved basis, the debt ratio would have to increase continually in order to generate a SGR of 42.22 percent. The change in debt ratio affects all assets, not just the growth component.

To illustrate, suppose the debt-to-equity ratio were to remain at 1.00 and the other ratios also stayed the same. At the end of the year, we would be building from higher equity and sales bases:

$$S_1 = \$300(1.4222) = \mathbf{\$426.66}$$
$$Eq_1 = \$300(1.4222).05 - \$4 + 100 = \mathbf{\$117.333}$$

The sustainable growth rate for year 2 becomes

$$SGR_2 = \left[\frac{(117.333 - 4)(2.00)(1.8182)}{1 - [(.05)(2.00)(1.8182)]} \right]\left[\frac{1}{426.66} \right] - 1$$
$$= \mathbf{18.06\%}$$

Thus, the model produces the sustainable growth rate year by year in a changing environment. Just because a high SGR is possible one year does not mean that this growth rate is sustainable in the future. In fact, it will not be sustainable unless further variable changes in the same direction occur. In this sense it represents a one-time occurrence.

SOLVING FOR OTHER VARIABLES AND IMPLICATIONS

With any five of the original six variables, together with beginning equity and beginning sales, it is possible to solve for the sixth. In Table 7A-2, we present certain simulations, where the missing variables for which we solve are shown in the shaded boxes.

By putting things into a sustainable growth model, we are able to check the consistency of various growth plans. Often in corporate planning the company wants a number of good things: high sales growth, manufacturing flexibility, moderate use of debt, and high dividends. However, these things may be inconsistent with one another.

Sustainable growth modeling enables one to check for such inconsistency. In this way, more informed and wiser marketing, finance, and manufacturing decisions can be reached. Sustainable growth modeling provides an integrative tool for helping the decision-making process. With the current emphasis in corporations on return on assets and on asset management, such modeling can play an integral part.

Questions

1. Contrast flow of funds (sources and uses) statements with cash budgets as planning tools.
2. What is the purpose of a statement of cash flows?
3. In constructing a cash budget, which variable is most important in order to arrive at accurate projections? Explain.
4. Discuss the benefits that can be derived by the firm from cash budgeting.
5. Explain why a decrease in cash constitutes a source of funds while an increase in cash is a use of funds in the sources and uses of funds statement.
6. Explain why selling inventory to credit customers is considered a source of funds when in fact no "funds" were generated.
7. Why do most audited financial reports to the shareholders include a statement of cash flows in addition to the balance sheet and income statement?
8. Why might some managers actually prefer to work with a flow of funds statement rather than the cash flow statement?
9. Is depreciation a source of funds? Under what conditions might the "source" dry up?
10. Why do bankers closely analyze cash flow statements and/or sources and uses of funds statements in considering credit applications?
11. Which of the following are sources of funds and which are uses of funds?
    a. Sale of land
    b. Dividend payments
    c. Decrease in accrued taxes
    d. Decrease in raw materials inventory
    e. Depreciation charges
    f. Sale of government bonds
    Now, go back and identify which items would appear under either the operating, investing, or financing activities sections of a cash flow statement prepared using the indirect method.
12. What are the major points of difference between a cash budget and the sources and uses of funds statement?
13. On what items should the financial manager concentrate in order to improve the accuracy of the cash budget? Explain your reasoning.
14. Is the cash budget a better measure of liquidity than traditional measures, such as the current ratio and quick ratio?
15. Why is the sales forecast so important in preparing the cash budget?
16. What is the principal purpose of forecast statements? Being a projection of the future, how do they differ from the cash budget?
17. What are the two principal ways by which one can prepare forecast financial statements?

18. What is a sustainable growth rate for a company? Of what value is sustainable growth modeling?
19. Explain the differences between steady-state sustainable growth modeling and year-by-year modeling.
20. List the variables used in sustainable growth modeling. Which variables usually have the most effect on the growth rate in sales?

SELF-CORRECTION PROBLEMS

1. a. Dana-Stallings, Inc., had the following financial statements for 20X1 and 20X2. Prepare a sources and uses of funds statement, and evaluate your findings.

ASSETS	20X1	20X2
Cash and equivalents	$ 53,000	$ 31,000
Marketable securities	87,000	0
Accounts receivable	346,000	528,000
Inventories	432,000	683,000
Current assets	$ 918,000	$1,242,000
Net fixed assets	1,113,000	1,398,000
Total	$2,031,000	$2,640,000

LIABILITIES AND EQUITY	20X1	20X2
Accounts payable	$ 413,000	$ 627,000
Accrued expenses	226,000	314,000
Bank borrowings	100,000	235,000
Current liabilities	$ 739,000	$1,176,000
Common stock	100,000	100,000
Retained earnings	1,192,000	1,364,000
Total	$2,031,000	$2,640,000

Note: For 20X2, depreciation was $189,000; interest paid was $21,000; taxes paid amounted to $114,000; and no dividends were paid.

b. Using the information provided plus your sources and uses of funds statement from Part (a), prepare a statement of cash flows using the indirect method and evaluate your findings. (Was your analysis based on the cash flow statement much different from that based on the flow of funds statement?)
2. At December 31, the balance sheet of Rodriguez Malting Company was the following (in thousands):

Cash	$ 50	Accounts payable	$ 360
Accounts receivable	530	Accrued expenses	212
Inventories	545	Bank loan	400
Current assets	$1,125	Current liabilities	$ 972
Net fixed assets	1,836	Long-term debt	450
		Common stock	100
		Retained earnings	1,439
		Total liabilities and	
Total assets	$2,961	shareholders' equity	$2,961

The company has received a large order and anticipates the need to go to its bank to increase its borrowings. As a result, it needs to forecast its cash requirements for January, February, and March.

Typically, the company collects 20 percent of its sales in the month of sale, 70 percent in the subsequent month, and 10 percent in the second month after the sale. All sales are credit sales.

Purchases of raw materials to produce malt are made in the month prior to the sale and amount to 60 percent of sales in the subsequent month. Payments for these purchases occur in the month after the purchase. Labor costs, including overtime, are expected to be $150,000 in January, $200,000 in February, and $160,000 in March. Selling, administrative, tax, and other cash expenses are expected to be $100,000 per month for January through March. Actual sales in November and December and projected sales for January through April are as follows (in thousands):

November	$500	February	$1,000
December	600	March	650
January	600	April	750

On the basis of this information,

a. Prepare a cash budget for the months of January, February, and March.
b. Determine the amount of additional bank borrowings necessary to maintain a cash balance of $50,000 at all times. (Ignore interest on such borrowings.)
c. Prepare a forecast balance sheet for March 31. (It should be noted that the company maintains a safety stock of inventory and that depreciation for the three-month period is expected to be $24,000.)

3. Margaritaville Nautical Company expects sales of $2.4 million next year and the same amount the following year. Sales are spread evenly throughout the year. On the basis of the following information, prepare a forecast income statement and balance sheet for year end:
   - *Cash:* Minimum of 4 percent of annual sales.
   - *Accounts receivable:* 60-day average collection period based on annual sales.
   - *Inventories:* Turnover of eight times a year.
   - *Net fixed assets:* $500,000 now. Capital expenditures equal to depreciation.
   - *Accounts payable:* One month's purchases.
   - *Accrued expenses:* 3 percent of sales.
   - *Bank borrowings:* $50,000 now. Can borrow up to $250,000.
   - *Long-term debt:* $300,000 now, payable $75,000 at year end.
   - *Common stock:* $100,000. No additions planned.
   - *Retained earnings:* $500,000 now.
   - *Net profit margin:* 8 percent of sales.
   - *Dividends:* None.
   - *Cost of goods sold:* 60 percent of sales.
   - *Purchases:* 50 percent of cost of goods sold.
   - *Income taxes:* 50 percent of before-tax profits.

APPENDIX SELF-CORRECTION PROBLEM

4. Kidwell Industries has equity capital of $12 million, total debt of $8 million, and sales last year of $30 million.
   a. It has a target assets-to-sales ratio of .6667, a target net profit margin of .04, a target debt-to-equity ratio of .6667, and a target earnings retention rate of .75. In steady state, what is its sustainable growth rate?

b. Suppose the company has established for next year a target assets-to-sales ratio of .62, a target net profit margin of .05, and a target debt-to-equity ratio of .80. It wishes to pay an annual dividend of $.3 million and raise $1 million in equity capital next year. What is its sustainable growth rate for next year? Why does it differ from that in Part (a)?

PROBLEMS

1. Shmenge Brothers Accordion Company reports the following changes from the previous year end. Categorize these items as either a source of funds or a use of funds.

ITEM		ITEM	
Cash	−$ 100	Accounts payable	+$300
Accounts receivable	+ 700	Accrued expenses	− 100
Inventory	− 300	Long-term debt	− 200
Dividends paid	+ 400	Net profit	+ 600
Depreciation	+1,000	Additions to fixed assets	+ 900

2.

Svoboda Corporation comparative balance sheets at December 31 (in millions)

ASSETS	20X1	20X2	LIABILITIES AND SHAREHOLDERS' EQUITY	20X1	20X2
Cash & equivalents	$ 5	$ 3	Notes payable	$20	$ 0
Accounts receivable	15	22	Accounts payable	5	8
Inventories	12	15	Accrued wages	2	2
Fixed assets, net	50	55	Accrued taxes	3	5
Other assets	8	5	Long-term debt	0	15
			Common stock	20	26
			Retained earnings	40	44
Total assets	$90	$100	Total liabilities and shareholders' equity	$90	$100

Svoboda Corporation statement of income and retained earnings, year ended December 31, 20X2 (in millions)

Net sales		$48
Expenses		
Cost of goods sold	$25	
Selling, general, and administrative expenses	5	
Depreciation	5	
Interest	2	37
Net income before taxes		$11
Less: Taxes		4
Net income		$ 7
Add: Retained earnings at 12/31/X1		40
Subtotal		$47
Less: Dividends		3
Retained earnings at 12/31/X2		$44

a. Prepare a flow of funds (sources and uses of funds) statement for 20X2 for the Svoboda Corporation.

b. Prepare a statement of cash flows for 20X2 using the indirect method for the Svoboda Corporation.

3. Financial statements for the Begalla Corporation follow.

Begalla Corporation comparative balance sheets at December 31 (in millions)

ASSETS	20X1	20X2	LIABILITIES	20X1	20X2
Cash and equivalents	$ 4	$ 5	Accounts payable	$ 8	$10
Accounts receivable	7	10	Notes payable	5	5
Inventory	12	15	Accrued wages	2	3
			Accrued taxes	3	2
Total current assets	$23	$30	Total current liabilities	$18	$20
Net fixed assets	40	40	Long-term debt	20	20
			Common stock	10	10
			Retained earnings	15	20
Total	$63	$70	Total	$63	$70

Begalla Corporation income statement 20X2 (in millions)

Sales		$95
Cost of goods sold	$50	
Selling, general, and administrative expenses	15	
Depreciation	3	
Interest	2	70
Net income before taxes		$25
Taxes		10
Net income		$15

a. Prepare a sources and uses of funds statement for Begalla Corporation.

b. Prepare a cash flow statement using the indirect method for Begalla Corporation.

4. Prepare a cash budget for the Ace Manufacturing Company, indicating receipts and disbursements for May, June, and July. The firm wishes to maintain at all times a minimum cash balance of $20,000. Determine whether or not borrowing will be necessary during the period, and if it is, when and for how much. As of April 30, the firm had a balance of $20,000 in cash.

ACTUAL SALES		FORECASTED SALES	
January	$50,000	May	$ 70,000
February	50,000	June	80,000
March	60,000	July	100,000
April	60,000	August	100,000

- *Accounts receivable:* 50 percent of total sales are for cash. The remaining 50 percent will be collected equally during the following two months (the firm incurs a negligible bad-debt loss).
- *Cost of goods manufactured:* 70 percent of sales: 90 percent of this cost is paid the following month and the remaining 10 percent one more month later.

- *Selling, general, and administrative expenses:* $10,000 per month plus 10 percent of sales. All of these expenses are paid during the month of incurrence.
- *Interest payments:* A semiannual interest payment on $150,000 of bonds outstanding (12 percent coupon) is paid during July. An annual $50,000 sinking-fund payment is also made at that time.
- *Dividends:* A $10,000 dividend payment will be declared and made in July.
- *Capital expenditures:* $40,000 will be invested in plant and equipment in June.
- *Taxes:* Income tax payments of $1,000 will be made in July.

5. Given the information that follows, prepare a cash budget for the Central City Department Store for the first six months of 20X2.
   a. All prices and costs remain constant.
   b. Sales are 75 percent for credit and 25 percent for cash.
   c. With respect to credit sales, 60 percent are collected in the month after the sale, 30 percent in the second month, and 10 percent in the third. Bad-debt losses are insignificant.
   d. Sales, actual and estimated, are

October 20X1	$300,000	March 20X2	$200,000
November 20X1	350,000	April 20X2	300,000
December 20X1	400,000	May 20X2	250,000
January 20X2	150,000	June 20X2	200,000
February 20X2	200,000	July 20X2	300,000

   e. Payments for purchases of merchandise are 80 percent of the following month's anticipated sales.
   f. Wages and salaries are

January	$30,000	March	$50,000	May	$40,000
February	40,000	April	50,000	June	35,000

   g. Rent is $2,000 a month.
   h. Interest of $7,500 is due on the last day of each calendar quarter, and no quarterly cash dividends are planned.
   i. A tax prepayment of $50,000 for 20X2 income is due in April.
   j. A capital investment of $30,000 is planned in June, to be paid for then.
   k. The company has a cash balance of $100,000 at December 31, 20X1, which is the minimum desired level for cash. Funds can be borrowed in multiples of $5,000. (Ignore interest on such borrowings.)

6. Use the cash budget worked out in Problem 5 and the following additional information to prepare a forecast income statement for the first half of 20X2 for the Central City Department Store. (Note that the store maintains a safety stock of inventory.)
   a. Inventory at 12/31/X1 was $200,000.
   b. Depreciation is taken on a straight-line basis on $250,000 of assets with an average remaining life of 10 years and no salvage value.
   c. The tax rate is 50 percent.

7. Given the following information and that contained in Problems 5 and 6, construct a forecast balance sheet as of June 30, 20X2, for the Central City Department Store. (Assume that accounts payable stay the same as at December 31, 20X1.)

Central City Department Store balance sheet at December 31, 20X1

ASSETS		LIABILITIES AND EQUITY	
Cash	$100,000	Accounts payable	$130,000
Accounts receivable	427,500	Bonds	500,000
Inventory	200,000	Common stock and	
Fixed assets, net	250,000	retained earnings	347,500
	$977,500		$977,500

APPENDIX PROBLEMS

8. Liz Clairorn Industries has $40 million in shareholders' equity and sales of $150 million last year.
   a. Its target ratios are assets to sales, .40; net profit margin, .07; debt to equity, .50; and earnings retention, .60. If these ratios correspond to steady state, what is its sustainable growth rate?
   b. What would be the sustainable growth rate next year if the company moved from steady state and had the following targets? Assets-to-sales ratio, .42; net profit margin, .06; debt-to-equity ratio, .45; dividend of $5 million; and no new equity financing.
9. Herb I. Vore Hydroponics Corporation wishes to achieve a 35 percent increase in sales next year. Sales last year were $30 million, and the company has equity capital of $12 million. It intends to raise $.5 million in new equity by the sale of common stock to officers. No dividend is planned. Tentatively, the company has set the following target ratios: assets to sales, .67; net profit margin, .08; and debt to equity, .60. The company has determined that these ratios are not sufficient to produce a growth in sales of 35 percent.
   a. Holding the other two target ratios constant, what assets-to-sales ratio would be necessary to attain the 35 percent sales increase?
   b. Holding the other two ratios constant, what net profit margin would be necessary?
   c. Holding the other two ratios constant, what debt-to-equity ratio would be necessary?

SOLUTIONS TO SELF-CORRECTION PROBLEMS

1. a.

Sources and uses of funds statement for Dana-Stallings, Inc. (in thousands)

SOURCES		USES	
Funds provided by operations			
Net profit	$172		
Depreciation	189	Additions to fixed assets	$474
	$361		
Decrease, marketable securities	87	Increase, accounts receivable	182
Increase, accounts payable	214	Increase, inventories	251
Increase, accrued expenses	88		
Increase, bank borrowings	135		
Decrease, cash and equivalents	**22**		
	$907		$907

The company has had substantial capital expenditures and increases in current assets. This growth has far outstripped the growth in retained earnings. To finance this growth, the company has reduced its marketable securities to zero, has leaned heavily on trade credit (accounts payable), and has increased its accrued expenses and bank borrowings. All of this is short-term financing of mostly long-term buildups in assets.

b.

Statement of cash flows for Dana-Stallings, Inc. (in thousands)

CASH FLOW FROM OPERATING ACTIVITIES	
Net income	$ 172
Depreciation	189
Cash provided (used) by current assets and operating-related current liabilities	
Increase, accounts payable	214
Increase, accrued expenses	88
Increase, accounts receivable	(182)
Increase, inventories	(251)
Net cash provided (used) by operating activities	$ 230
CASH FLOW FROM INVESTING ACTIVITIES	
Additions to fixed assets	$(474)
Decrease, marketable securities	87
Net cash provided (used) by investing activities	$(387)
CASH FLOW FROM FINANCING ACTIVITIES	
Increase in short-term bank borrowings	$ 135
Net cash provided (used) by financing activities	$ 135
Increase (decrease) in cash and cash equivalents	$ (22)
Cash and cash equivalents, December 31, 20X1	53
Cash and cash equivalents, December 31, 20X2	$ 31
Supplemental cash flow disclosures	
Interest paid	$ 21
Taxes paid	114

In addition to the same points raised by an analysis of the sources and uses of funds statement, we see that all of the firm's cash flow from operating activities (and then some) went toward additions to fixed assets. By and large, the cash flow statement prepared using the indirect method gives you much the same information gathered from an analysis of the sources and uses of funds statement.

2. a.

Cash budget (in thousands)

	NOV.	DEC.	JAN.	FEB.	MAR.	APR.
Sales	$500	$600	$600	$1,000	$650	$750
Cash collections						
20% of current month sales			$120	$ 200	$130	
70% of last month's sales			420	420	700	
10% of 2-month-old sales			50	60	60	
Total cash receipts			$590	$ 680	$890	
Purchases		$360	$600	$ 390	$450	

	NOV.	DEC.	JAN.	FEB.	MAR.	APR.
Cash disbursements for purchases and operating expenses						
100% of last month's purchases			$360	$ 600	$390	
Labor costs			150	200	160	
Other expenses paid			100	100	100	
Total cash disbursements			$610	$ 900	$650	
Cash receipts less cash disbursements			$ (20)	$ (220)	$240	

b.

	DEC.	JAN.	FEB.	MAR.
Beginning bank borrowings		$400	$420	$640
Additional borrowings		20	220	(240)
Ending bank borrowings	$400	$420	$640	$400

The amount of financing peaks in February owing to the need to pay for purchases made the previous month and higher labor costs. In March, substantial collections are made on the prior month's billings, causing a large net cash inflow sufficient to pay off the additional borrowings.

c.

Forecast balance sheet at March 31 (in thousands)

ASSETS	ACTUAL 12–31	CHANGE	FORECAST 3–31	ASSUMPTIONS
Cash	$ 50	0	$ 50	• Set at estimated minimum balance.
Receivables	530	+ 90	620	• 80% Mar sales plus 10% Feb sales.
Inventory	545	+ 90	635	• Based on $545 plus $1,985 in purchases (Jan–Mar) minus .6 times $2,250 in sales (Jan–Mar).
Current assets	$1,125	+180	$1,305	
Net fixed assets	1,836	− 24	1,812	• Depreciation expected to be $24.
Total assets	$2,961	+156	$3,117	

LIABILITIES	ACTUAL 12–31	CHANGE	FORECAST 3–31	ASSUMPTIONS
Bank borrowings	$ 400	0	$ 400	• Previous balance plus zero additional financing needed.
Accounts payable	360	+ 90	450	• 100% Mar purchases.
Accrued expenses	212	0	212	• No change expected.
Current liabilities	$ 972	+ 90	$1,062	
Long-term debt	450	0	450	• No change expected.
Common stock	100	0	100	• No change expected.
Retained earnings	1,439	+ 66	1,505	• Change in retained earnings equals sales, minus payment for purchases, minus labor costs, depreciation, and
Total liabilities and shareholders' equity	$2,961	+156	$3,117	other expenses, for Jan–Mar.

3.

Forecast income statement (in thousands)

		ASSUMPTIONS
Net sales	$2,400	• Based on sales forecast.
Cost of goods sold	1,440	• Forecast at 60% of net sales.
Gross profit	$ 960	
Expenses	576	• 24% of net sales; required to produce 16% before-tax profit margin (see below).
Profit before taxes	$ 384	• 16% of net sales; based on an 8% net profit margin and 50% tax rate.
Taxes	192	• Forecast at 50%.
Profit after taxes	**$ 192**	• Forecast at 8% of net sales.
Dividends	0	• None expected.
Increase in retained earnings	$ 192	• Carried to forecast balance sheet.

Forecast balance sheet (in thousands)

ASSETS	END OF YEAR	ASSUMPTIONS
Cash	$ 96	• Set at estimated minimum balance; 4% of annual sales of $2.4M.
Receivables	400	• Based on 60-day average collection period; (net sales of $2.4M)/(360/60).
Inventory	180	• Based on an annual turnover of 8; (cost of goods sold of $1.44M)/8.
Current assets	$ 676	
Net fixed assets	500	• $500,000 at beginning of year and capital expenditures expected to equal depreciation charge for the year.
Total assets	$1,176	

LIABILITIES	END OF YEAR	ASSUMPTIONS
Bank borrowings	$ 27	• *Plug figure* equal to total assets minus all the individual items listed below.
Accounts payable	60	• 1 month's purchases; (.5)(cost of goods sold of $1.44M)/12.
Accrued expenses	72	• Estimated at 3% of sales of $2.4M.
Current liabilities	$ 159	
Long-term debt	225	• $300,000 minus year-end $75,000 principal payment.
Common stock	100	• No change expected.
Retained earnings	692	• $500,000 plus $192,000 change in retained earnings per forecast income statement.
Total liabilities and shareholders' equity	$1,176	

SOLUTION TO APPENDIX SELF-CORRECTION PROBLEM

4. a. $SGR = \dfrac{.75(.04)(1.6667)}{.6667 - [.75(.04)(1.6667)]} = \mathbf{8.11\%}$

b. $SGR = \left[\dfrac{(12 + 1 - 0.3)(1.80)(1.6129)}{1 - [(.05)(1.80)(1.6129)]}\right]\left[\dfrac{1}{30}\right] - 1 = \mathbf{43.77\%}$

The company has moved from steady state with higher target operating efficiency, a higher debt ratio, and the sale of common stock. All of these things permit a high rate of growth in sales next year. Unless further changes in these directions occur, the SGR will decline.

SELECTED REFERENCES

Chambers, John C., Satinder K. Mullick, and Donald D. Smith. "How to Choose the Right Forecasting Technique." *Harvard Business Review* 49 (July–August 1971), 45–74.

Gahlon, James M., and Robert L. Vigeland. "An Introduction to Corporate Cash Flow Statements." *AAII Journal* 11 (January 1989), 14–18.

Gup, Benton E., William D. Samson, Michael T. Dugan, Myung J. Kim, and Thawatchai Jittrapanun. "An Analysis of Patterns from the Statement of Cash Flows." *Financial Practice and Education* 3 (Fall 1993), 73–79.

Helfert, Erich A. *Techniques of Financial Analysis*, 10th ed. Burr Ridge, IL: Richard D. Irwin, 2000, Chaps. 1–4.

Higgins, Robert C. "How Much Growth Can a Firm Afford?" *Financial Management* 6 (Fall 1977), 7–16.

———. "Sustainable Growth under Inflation." *Financial Management* 10 (Autumn 1981), 36–40.

———. *Analysis for Financial Management*, 5th ed. Homewood, IL: Richard D. Irwin, 1997.

Nurnberg, Hugo. "Inconsistencies and Ambiguities in Cash Flow Statements under FASB Statement No. 95." *Accounting Horizons* 7 (June 1993), 60–75.

Statement of Cash Flows: Understanding and Implementing FASB Statement No. 95. Ernst & Whinney, January 1988.

Van Horne, James C. "Sustainable Growth Modeling." *Journal of Corporate Finance* 1 (Winter 1988), 19–25.

Chapter 8

Overview of Working Capital Management

INTRODUCTION
    Working Capital Concepts • Significance of Working Capital
        Management • Profitability and Risk
WORKING CAPITAL ISSUES
    Optimal Amount (or Level) of Current Assets • Detour:
        Classification of Working Capital
FINANCING CURRENT ASSETS: SHORT-TERM AND LONG-TERM
    MIX
    Hedging (Maturity Matching) Approach • Short- versus
        Long-Term Financing
COMBINING LIABILITY STRUCTURE AND CURRENT ASSET
    DECISIONS
    Uncertainty and the Margin of Safety • Risk and Profitability
SUMMARY
QUESTIONS
SELF-CORRECTION PROBLEM
PROBLEMS
SOLUTIONS TO SELF-CORRECTION PROBLEM
SELECTED REFERENCES

> *Every noble acquisition is attended with risks; he who fears to*
> *encounter the one must not expect to obtain the other.*

—PIETRO METASTASIO

INTRODUCTION

Net working capital Current assets minus current liabilities.

Gross working capital The firm's investment in current assets (like cash and marketable securities, receivables, and inventory).

Working capital management The administration of the firm's current assets and the financing needed to support current assets.

Working Capital Concepts

There are two major concepts of working capital—*net* working capital and *gross* working capital. When accountants use the term *working capital*, they are generally referring to **net working capital,** which is the dollar difference between current assets and current liabilities. This is one measure of the extent to which the firm is protected from liquidity problems. From a management viewpoint, however, it makes little sense to talk about trying to actively manage a net difference between current assets and current liabilities, particularly when that difference is continually changing.

Financial analysts, on the other hand, mean current assets when they speak of working capital. Therefore, their focus is on **gross working capital.** Because it does make sense for the financial manager to be involved with providing the correct amount of current assets for the firm at all times, we will adopt the concept of gross working capital. As the discussion of **working capital management** unfolds, our concern will be to consider the administration of the firm's current assets—namely, cash and marketable securities, receivables, and inventory—and the financing (especially current liabilities) needed to support current assets.

Significance of Working Capital Management

The management of working capital, which is taken up in this and the subsequent three chapters, is important for several reasons. For one thing, the current assets of a typical manufacturing firm account for over half of its total assets. For a distribution company, they account for even more. Excessive levels of current assets can easily result in a firm realizing a substandard return on investment. However, firms with too few current assets may incur shortages and difficulties in maintaining smooth operations.

For small companies, current liabilities are the principal source of external financing. These firms do not have access to the longer-term capital markets, other than to acquire a mortgage on a building. The fast-growing but larger company also makes use of current liability financing. For these reasons, the financial manager and staff devote a considerable portion of their time to working capital matters. The management of cash, marketable securities, accounts receivable, accounts payable, accruals, and other means of short-term financing is the *direct* responsibility of the financial manager; only the management of inventories is not. Moreover, these management responsibilities require continuous, day-to-day supervision. Unlike dividend and capital structure decisions, you cannot study the issue, reach a decision, and set the matter aside for many months to come. Thus, working capital management is important, if for no other reason than the proportion of the financial manager's time that must be devoted to it. More fundamental, however, is the effect that working capital decisions have on the company's risk, return, and share price.

Profitability and Risk

Underlying sound working capital management lie two fundamental decision issues for the firm. They are the determination of

- The optimal level of investment in current assets
- The appropriate mix of short-term and long-term financing used to support this investment in current assets

In turn, these decisions are influenced by the trade-off that must be made between profitability and risk. Lowering the level of investment in current assets, while still being able to support sales, would lead to an increase in the firm's return on total assets. To the extent that the explicit costs of short-term financing are less than those of intermediate- and long-term financing, the greater the proportion of short-term debt to total debt, the higher is the profitability of the firm.

Although short-term interest rates sometimes exceed long-term rates, generally they are less. Even when short-term rates are higher, the situation is likely to be only temporary. Over an extended period of time, we would expect to pay more in interest cost with long-term debt than we would with short-term borrowings, which are continually rolled over (refinanced) at maturity. Moreover, the use of short-term debt as opposed to longer-term debt is likely to result in higher profits because debt will be paid off during periods when it is not needed.

These profitability assumptions suggest maintaining a low level of current assets and a high proportion of current liabilities to total liabilities. This strategy will result in a low, or conceivably negative, level of *net* working capital. Offsetting the profitability of this strategy, however, is the increased risk to the firm. Here, risk means jeopardy to the firm for not maintaining sufficient current assets to

- Meet its cash obligations as they occur
- Support the proper level of sales (e.g., running out of inventory)

In this chapter, we study the trade-off between risk and profitability as it relates to the level and financing of current assets.

WORKING CAPITAL ISSUES

Optimal Amount (or Level) of Current Assets

In determining the appropriate amount, or level, of current assets, management must consider the trade-off between profitability and risk. To illustrate this trade-off, suppose that, with existing fixed assets, a firm can produce up to 100,000 units of output a year.[1] Production is continuous throughout the period under consideration, in which there is a particular level of output. For each level of output, the firm can have a number of different levels of current assets. Let's assume, initially, three different current asset policy alternatives. The relationship between output and current asset level for these alternatives is illustrated in Figure 8-1. We see from the figure that the greater the output, the greater the need for investment in current assets to support that output (and sales). However, the relationship is not linear; current assets increase at a decreasing rate with output. This relationship is based on the notion that it takes a greater proportional investment in current assets when only a few units of output are produced than it does later on, when the firm can use its current assets more efficiently.

If we equate liquidity with "conservativeness," Policy A is the most conservative of the three alternatives. At all levels of output, Policy A provides for more current assets than any other policy. The greater the level of current assets, the greater the liquidity of the firm, all other things equal. Policy A is seen as preparing the firm for

---

[1]This illustration holds constant the amount of the firm's fixed assets. This is actually a rather fair assumption. A firm's fixed assets are generally determined by its scale of production. Once established, the fixed assets remain invested (at least in the short run) regardless of production levels.

FIGURE 8-1
Current Asset Levels for Three Alternative Working Capital Policies

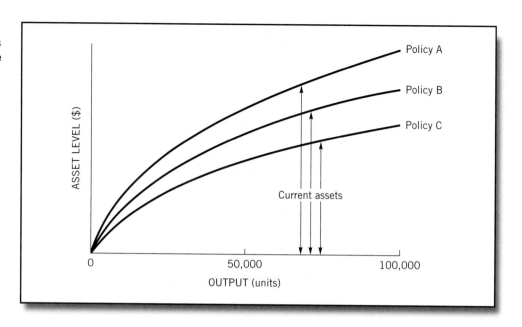

almost any conceivable current asset need; it is the financial equivalent to wearing a belt and suspenders. Policy C is least liquid and can be labeled "aggressive." This "lean and mean" policy calls for low levels of cash and marketable securities, receivables, and inventories. We should keep in mind that for every output level there is a minimum level of current assets that the firm needs just to get by. There is a limit to how "lean and mean" a firm can get. We can now summarize the rankings of the alternative working capital policies in respect to liquidity as follows:

	HIGH ←――――――――――――――→ LOW		
Liquidity	Policy A	Policy B	Policy C

Though policy A clearly provides the highest liquidity, how do the three alternative policies rank when we shift our attention to expected profitability? To answer this question, we need to recast the familiar return on investment (ROI) equation as follows:

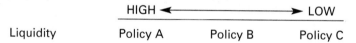

$$ROI = \frac{\text{Net profit}}{\text{Total assets}} = \frac{\text{Net profit}}{(\text{Cash} + \text{Receivables} + \text{Inventory}) + \text{Fixed assets}}$$

From the equation above we can see that decreasing the amounts of current assets held (for example, a movement from Policy A toward Policy C) will increase our potential profitability. If we can reduce the firm's investment in current assets while still being able to properly support output and sales, ROI will increase. Lower levels of cash, receivables, and inventory would reduce the denominator in the equation; and net profits, our numerator, would remain roughly the same or perhaps even increase. Policy C, then, provides the highest profitability potential as measured by ROI.

However, a movement from Policy A toward Policy C results in other effects besides increased profitability. Decreasing cash reduces the firm's ability to meet financial obligations as they come due. Decreasing receivables, by adopting stricter credit terms and a tougher enforcement policy, may result in some lost customers and sales. Decreasing inventory may also result in lost sales due to products being out of stock. Therefore, more aggressive working capital policies lead to increased risk. Clearly, Policy C is the most risky working capital policy. It is also a policy that emphasizes profitability over liquidity. In short, we can now make the following generalizations:

	HIGH ◄─────────────────────► LOW		
Liquidity	Policy A	Policy B	Policy C
Profitability	Policy C	Policy B	Policy A
Risk	Policy C	Policy B	Policy A

Interestingly, our discussion of working capital policies has just illustrated the two most basic principles in finance:

1. *Profitability varies inversely with liquidity.* Notice that for our three alternative working capital policies, the liquidity rankings are the exact opposite of those for profitability. Increased liquidity generally comes at the expense of reduced profitability.
2. *Profitability moves together with risk (i.e., there is a trade-off between risk and return).* In search of higher profitability, we must expect to take greater risks. Notice how the profitability and risk rankings for our alternative working capital policies are identical. You might say that risk and return walk hand in hand.

Ultimately, the optimal level of each current asset (cash, marketable securities, receivables, and inventory) will be determined by management's attitude to the trade-off between profitability and risk. For now, we continue to restrict ourselves to some broad generalities. In subsequent chapters, we will deal more specifically with the optimal levels of these assets, taking into consideration both profitability and risk.

Detour: Classification of Working Capital

Before turning our attention to the way working capital should be financed, we need to take a slight detour and classify working capital. Having defined working capital as current assets, it can now be classified according to

- *Components,* such as cash, marketable securities, receivables, and inventory (subsequent chapters will focus on these components), or
- *Time,* as either permanent or temporary.

Permanent working capital The amount of current assets required to meet a firm's long-term minimum needs.

Temporary working capital The amount of current assets that varies with seasonal requirements.

Though the *components* of working capital are self-explanatory, classification by *time* requires some explanation. A firm's **permanent working capital** is the amount of current assets required to meet long-term minimum needs. You might call this "bare bones" working capital. **Temporary working capital,** on the other hand, is the investment in current assets that varies with seasonal requirements. Figure 8-2 illustrates the firm's changing needs for working capital over time while highlighting both the temporary and permanent nature of those needs.

Permanent working capital is similar to the firm's fixed assets in two important respects. First, the dollar investment is long term, despite the seeming contradiction that the assets being financed are called "current." Second, for a growing firm, the level of permanent working capital needed will increase over time in the same way that a firm's fixed assets will need to increase over time. However, permanent working capital is different from fixed assets in one very important respect—it is constantly changing. Take a can of red paint and paint some of the firm's fixed assets (like plant and equipment). If you come back in a month, these same assets are there

FIGURE 8-2
Working Capital
Needs over Time

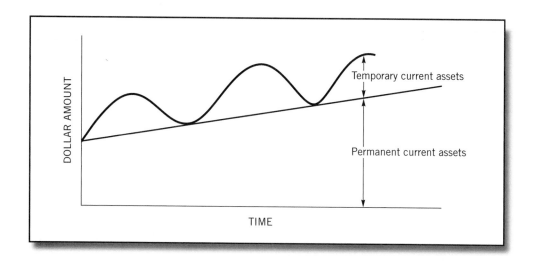

and they are still red. Now, paint the firm's cash, receivable invoices, and inventory green. If you come back in a month, you may still find some green items, but many, if not most, will have been replaced by new, unpainted items. Thus, permanent working capital does not consist of particular current assets staying permanently in place, but is a permanent level of investment in current assets, whose individual items are constantly turning over. Viewed still another way, permanent working capital is similar to the level of water that you find in a bay at low tide.

Like permanent working capital, temporary working capital also consists of current assets in a constantly changing form. However, because the need for this portion of the firm's total current assets is seasonal, we may want to consider financing this level of current assets from a source which can itself be seasonal or temporary in nature. Let us now direct our attention to the problem of how to finance current assets.

FINANCING CURRENT ASSETS: SHORT-TERM AND LONG-TERM MIX

The way in which the assets of a company are financed involves a trade-off between risk and profitability. For purposes of analysis, we initially assume that the company has an established policy with respect to payment for purchases, labor, taxes, and other expenses. Thus, the amounts of accounts payable and of accruals included in current liabilities are not active decision variables.[2] These current liabilities are **Spontaneous financing** regarded as **spontaneous financing** and are a topic in Chapter 11. They finance a portion of the current assets of the firm and tend to fluctuate with the production schedule and, in the case of accrued taxes, with profits. As the underlying investment in current assets grows, accounts payable and accruals also tend to grow, in part

Spontaneous financing
Trade credit, and other payables and accruals, that arise spontaneously in the firm's day-to-day operations.

---

[2]Delaying the payment of accounts payable can be an active decision variable for financing purposes. However, there are limits to the extent to which a firm can "s-t-r-e-t-c-h" its payables. For simplicity, we assume in this analysis that the firm has a definite policy for paying bills, such as taking advantage of all cash discounts and paying all other bills at the end of the credit period. See Chapter 11 for a discussion of trade credit as a means of financing.

financing the buildup in assets. Our concern is the way in which assets not supported by spontaneous financing are handled. This residual financing requirement pertains to the net investment in assets after spontaneous financing is deducted.

Hedging (Maturity Matching) Approach

If the firm adopts a **hedging (maturity matching) approach** to financing, each asset would be offset with a financing instrument of the same approximate maturity. Short-term or seasonal variations in current assets would be financed with short-term debt; the permanent component of current assets and all fixed assets would be financed with long-term debt or with equity. This policy is illustrated in Figure 8-3. If total funds requirements behave in the manner shown, only the short-term fluctuations shown at the top of the figure would be financed with short-term debt. The rationale for this is that if long-term debt is used to finance short-term needs, the firm will be paying interest for the use of funds during times when these funds are not needed. This occurrence can be illustrated by drawing a straight line across the seasonal humps in Figure 8-3 to represent the total amount of long-term financing. It is apparent that financing would be employed in periods of seasonal lulls—when it is not needed. With a hedging approach to financing, the borrowing and payment schedule for short-term financing would be arranged to correspond to the expected swings in current assets, less spontaneous financing. (Note again that some of the current assets are financed by payables and accruals but that we deduct such spontaneous financing, and equivalent amounts of current assets, in creating Figure 8-3.)

A hedging (maturity matching) approach to financing suggests that apart from current installments on long-term debt, a firm would show no current borrowings at the seasonal troughs for asset needs shown in Figure 8-3. As the firm moved into a period of seasonal asset needs, it would borrow on a short-term basis, paying off the

FIGURE 8-3
Financing (and Asset) Needs over Time: Hedging (Maturity Matching) Financing Policy

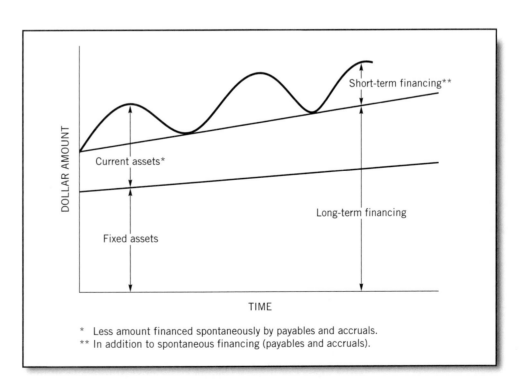

borrowings with the cash released as the recently financed temporary assets were eventually reduced. For example, a seasonal expansion in inventory (and receivables) for the Christmas selling season would be financed with a short-term loan. As the inventory was reduced through sales, receivables would be built up. The cash needed to repay the loan would come from the collection of these receivables. All of this would occur within a matter of a few months. In this way, financing would be employed only when it was needed. This loan to support a seasonal need would be following a *self-liquidating* principle. That is, the loan is for a purpose that will generate the funds necessary for repayment in the normal course of operations. (In fact, we have just described the "ideal bank loan"—short-term, inherently self-liquidating, referred to as "STISL.") Permanent asset requirements would be financed with long-term debt and equity. In this situation, it would be the long-term profitability of the financed assets that would be counted on to cover the long-term financing costs. In a growth situation, permanent financing would be increased in keeping with increases in permanent asset requirements.

Short- versus Long-Term Financing

Although an exact matching of the firm's schedule of future net cash flows and the debt payment schedule is appropriate under conditions of certainty, it is usually not appropriate when uncertainty exists. Net cash flows will deviate from expected flows in keeping with the firm's business risk. As a result, the schedule of maturities of the debt is very significant in assessing the risk-profitability trade-off. The question is: What margin of safety should be built into the maturity schedule to allow for adverse fluctuations in cash flows? This depends on management's attitude to the trade-off between risk and profitability.

The Relative Risks Involved. In general, the shorter the maturity schedule of a firm's debt obligations, the greater the risk that the firm will be unable to meet principal and interest payments. Suppose a company borrows on a short-term basis in order to build a new plant. The cash flows from the plant would not be sufficient in the short run to pay off the loan. As a result, the company bears the risk that the lender may not roll over (renew) the loan at maturity. This refinancing risk could be reduced in the first place by financing the plant on a long-term basis—the expected long-term future cash flows being sufficient to retire the debt in an orderly manner. Thus, committing funds to a long-term asset and borrowing short term carries the risk that the firm may not be able to renew its borrowings. If the company should fall on hard times, creditors might regard renewal as too risky and demand immediate payment. In turn, this would cause the firm either to retrench, perhaps by selling off assets to get cash, or to declare bankruptcy.

In addition to refinancing risk, there is also the uncertainty associated with interest costs. When the firm finances with long-term debt, it knows precisely its interest costs over the period of time that it needs the funds. If it finances with short-term debt, it is uncertain of interest costs on refinancing. In a real sense, then, the uncertainty of interest costs represents risk to the borrower. We know that short-term interest rates fluctuate far more than long-term rates. A firm forced to refinance its short-term debt in a period of rising interest rates may pay an overall interest cost on short-term debt that is higher than it would have been originally on long-term debt. Therefore, not knowing the cost of future short-term borrowing represents risk to a company.

The Risks versus Costs Trade-Off. Differences in risk between short- and long-term financing must be balanced against differences in interest costs. The longer the maturity schedule of a firm's debt, the more costly the financing is likely to be. In addition to the generally higher costs of long-term borrowings, the firm may well end up paying interest on debt over periods of time when the funds are not needed. Thus, there are cost inducements to finance funds requirements on a short-term basis.

Consequently, we have a trade-off between risk and profitability. We have seen that, in general, short-term debt has greater risk than long-term debt but also less cost. The margin of safety provided by the firm can be thought of as the lag between the firm's expected net cash flow and the contractual payments on its debt. This margin of safety will depend on the risk preferences of management. In turn, management's decision on the maturity composition of the firm's debt will determine the portion of current assets financed by current liabilities and the portion financed on a long-term basis.

To allow for a margin of safety, management might decide on the proportion of short-term and long-term financing shown in Figure 8-4. Here we see that the firm finances a portion of its expected seasonal funds requirement, less payables and accruals, on a long-term basis. If the expected net cash flows do occur as forecast, it will pay interest on excess debt (the shaded area in Figure 8-4) during seasonal troughs when these particular funds are not needed. In the extreme, peak requirements might be financed entirely on a long-term basis, as would be the case if we drew the long-term financing line across the seasonal humps at the top of Figure 8-4. The higher the long-term financing line, the more conservative the financing policy of the firm, and the higher the cost.

In contrast to a conservative (longer maturity schedule) financing policy, an aggressive policy might look like that shown in Figure 8-5. Here we see that there is a *negative* margin of safety. The firm has financed part of its permanent current assets

FIGURE 8-4
Financing (and Asset) Needs over Time: Conservative Financing Policy

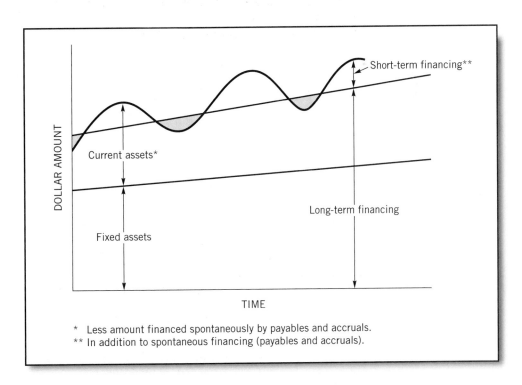

* Less amount financed spontaneously by payables and accruals.
** In addition to spontaneous financing (payables and accruals).

FIGURE 8-5
Financing (and Asset) Needs over Time: Aggressive Financing Policy

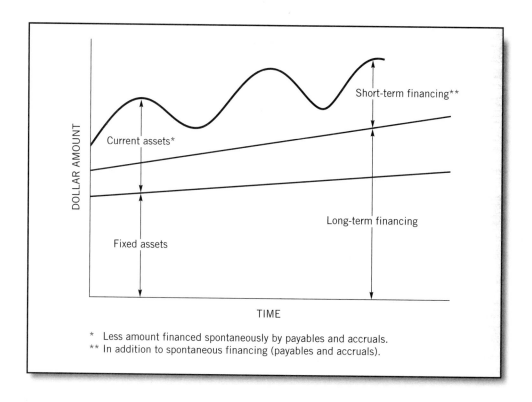

* Less amount financed spontaneously by payables and accruals.
** In addition to spontaneous financing (payables and accruals).

with short-term debt.[3] As a result, it must refinance this debt at maturity, and this involves an element of risk. The greater the portion of the permanent asset needs financed with short-term debt, the more aggressive the financing is said to be. Therefore, the expected margin of safety associated with a firm's policy regarding its short- and long-term financing mix can be either positive, negative, or zero. Zero would be the case in a hedging policy, illustrated in Figure 8-3.

As we have already seen in the earlier section, the firm can also create a margin of safety by increasing its liquid assets. Thus, the firm can reduce the risk of cash insolvency by either increasing the maturity schedule of its debt or by carrying greater amounts of short-lived (current) assets. Shortly, we will explore the interdependence of these two facets. But before we do, we need to take a look at Table 8-1.

Table 8-1 summarizes our discussion of short- versus long-term financing as it relates to the trade-off between risk and profitability. Notice that maintaining a policy of short-term financing for short-term, or temporary, asset needs (Box #1) and long-term financing for long-term, or permanent, asset needs (Box #3) would comprise a set of moderate risk-profitability strategies—what we have been calling a hedging (maturity matching) approach to financing. Other strategies are possible, however, and should not necessarily be considered wrong. But, what you gain by following alternative strategies (like those represented by Box #2 or Box #4) needs to be weighed against what you give up. For example, the low-risk strategy of using long-term financing to support short-term asset needs comes at the expense of curtailed

[3]Smaller companies are often forced to finance a portion of their permanent asset needs with short-term debt because of their difficulties in attracting long-term debt financing. Often this takes the form of a bank line of credit, rolled over again and again. For an informative, readable article on the special financing problems of the small but growing firm, see Jerry A. Viscione, "How Long Should You Borrow Short Term?" *Harvard Business Review* (March–April 1986), 20–24.

TABLE 8-1
Short- versus long-term financing

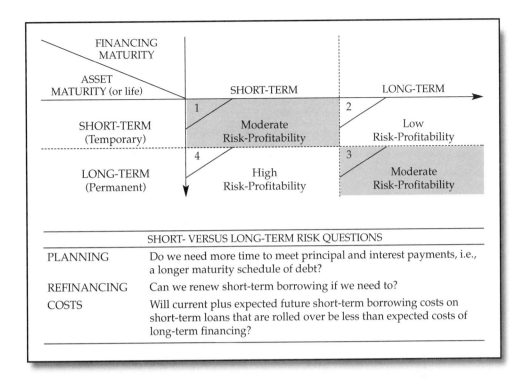

FINANCING MATURITY			
ASSET MATURITY (or life)		SHORT-TERM	LONG-TERM
SHORT-TERM (Temporary)	1	Moderate Risk-Profitability	2 Low Risk-Profitability
LONG-TERM (Permanent)	4	High Risk-Profitability	3 Moderate Risk-Profitability

SHORT- VERSUS LONG-TERM RISK QUESTIONS	
PLANNING	Do we need more time to meet principal and interest payments, i.e., a longer maturity schedule of debt?
REFINANCING	Can we renew short-term borrowing if we need to?
COSTS	Will current plus expected future short-term borrowing costs on short-term loans that are rolled over be less than expected costs of long-term financing?

profits. How management answers questions like those posed in the bottom panel of Table 8-1 will help them determine which strategies are best to employ (and when).

COMBINING LIABILITY STRUCTURE AND CURRENT ASSET DECISIONS

In the preceding sections, we examined two broad aspects of working capital management: what level of current assets to maintain and how to finance current assets. These two facets are interdependent. All other things equal, a firm that follows a conservative policy of maintaining high levels of current assets should be in a better position to successfully utilize short-term borrowing than a firm that maintains aggressively low levels of current assets. On the other hand, a firm that finances its current assets entirely with equity will be in a better risk position to take a more aggressive stance when it comes to maintaining low ("lean and mean") levels of current assets. Because of their interdependence, these two aspects of working capital management must be considered jointly.

Uncertainty and the Margin of Safety

If the firm knows with certainty its future sales demand, resulting receivable collections, and production schedule, it will be able to arrange its debt maturity schedule to correspond exactly to the schedule of future net cash flows. As a result, profits will be maximized, for there will be no need to hold excessive (and relatively low-yielding) levels of current assets nor to have more long-term financing than is absolutely necessary. When sales and resulting cash flows are subject to uncertainty, however, the situation is changed. The greater the dispersion of the probability distribution of possible net cash flows, the greater the margin of safety that management will wish to provide.

Assume initially that the firm cannot borrow on short notice to meet unexpected cash drains. As a result, it can provide a margin of safety only by (1) increasing the level of current assets (especially cash and marketable securities), or (2) lengthening the maturity schedule of financing. Both of these actions affect profitability. In the first choice, funds are committed to relatively low-yielding assets. In the second, the firm may pay interest on borrowings over periods of time when the funds are not needed. In addition, long-term debt has a higher expected interest cost than does short-term debt.

Risk and Profitability

A decision on the appropriate margin of safety will be governed by considerations of risk and profitability and by management's attitude toward bearing risk. Each solution (increasing liquidity, lengthening the maturity schedule, or a combination of the two), will cost the firm something in profit-making ability. For a given risk tolerance, management may determine which solution is least costly and then implement that solution. On the other hand, management might determine the least costly solution for various levels of risk. Then management could formulate risk tolerances on the basis of the cost involved in providing a margin of safety. Presumably, these tolerances would be in keeping with an objective of maximizing shareholder wealth.

If the firm can borrow in times of emergency, the foregoing analysis needs to be modified. The greater the ability of the firm to borrow on short notice, the less it needs to provide for a margin of safety by the means previously discussed. Certain companies can arrange for lines of credit or revolving credits that enable them to borrow on short notice.[4] When a company has access to such credit, it must compare the cost of these arrangements with the cost of other solutions. There are, of course, limits on how much a firm may borrow on short notice. Consequently, it must provide for some margin of safety on the basis of the considerations discussed in this chapter.

---

[4]For a discussion of these methods, see Chapter 11.

SUMMARY

- There are two major concepts of working capital—*net* working capital (current assets minus current liabilities) and *gross* working capital (current assets).
- In finance, *working capital* is synonymous with *current assets. Working capital management* concerns the administration of the firm's current assets along with the financing (especially current liabilities) needed to support current assets.
- In determining the appropriate amount, or level, of current assets, management must consider the trade-off between profitability and risk. The greater the level of current assets, the greater the liquidity of the firm, all other things equal. With greater liquidity comes less risk, but also less

profitability. In the management of working capital, we see the two most basic principles of finance in operation:

1. Profitability varies inversely with liquidity.
2. Profitability moves together with risk.

- We can classify working capital by *components*— cash, marketable securities, receivables, and inventory. In addition, working capital can be classified by *time*, as either permanent or temporary. *Permanent working capital* is the amount of current assets required to meet a firm's long-term minimum needs. *Temporary working capital*, on the other hand, is the amount of current assets that varies with seasonal needs.

- If the firm adopts a *hedging (maturity matching) approach* to financing, each asset would be offset with a financing instrument of the same approximate maturity. Short-term or seasonal variations in current assets would be financed with short-term debt. The permanent component of current assets and all fixed assets would be financed with long-term debt or equity.
- In general, the longer the composite maturity schedule of the financing used by the firm, the less risky is that financing. However, the longer this maturity schedule, the more costly the financing is likely to be. Consequently, we have yet another trade-off between risk and profitability.
- The two key facets of working capital management—what level of current assets to maintain and how to finance current assets—are interdependent. Because of their interdependence, these two facets must be considered jointly.

QUESTIONS

1. What does *working capital management* encompass? What functional decisions are involved, and what underlying principle or trade-off influences the decision process?
2. A firm is currently employing an "aggressive" working capital policy with regard to the level of current assets it maintains (relatively low levels of current assets for each possible level of output). The firm has decided to switch to a more "conservative" working capital policy. What effect will this decision probably have on the firm's profitability and risk?
3. Utilities hold 10 percent of total assets in current assets; retail trade industries hold 60 percent of total assets in current assets. Explain how industry characteristics account for this difference.
4. Distinguish between "temporary" and "permanent" working capital.
5. If the firm adopts a *hedging (maturity matching) approach* to financing, how would it finance its current assets?
6. Some firms finance their permanent working capital with short-term liabilities (commercial paper and short-term notes). Explain the impact of this decision on the profitability and risk of these firms.
7. Suppose that a firm finances its seasonal (temporary) current assets with long-term funds. What is the impact of this decision on the profitability and risk of this firm?
8. Risk associated with the amount of current assets is *generally* assumed to decrease with increased levels of current assets. Is this assumption *always* correct for *all* levels of current assets—in particular, for an excessively high level of current assets relative to the firm's needs? Explain.
9. At times, long-term interest rates are lower than short-term rates, yet the discussion in the chapter suggests that long-term financing is more expensive. If long-term rates are lower, should the firm finance itself entirely with long-term debt?
10. How does shortening the maturity composition of outstanding debt increase the firm's risk? Why does increasing the liquidity of the firm's assets reduce the risk?
11. What are the costs of maintaining too large a level of working capital? Too small a level of working capital?
12. How is a margin of safety provided for in working capital management?

SELF-CORRECTION PROBLEM

1. Zzzz Worst Company presently has total assets of $3.2 million, of which current assets comprise $.2 million. Sales are $10 million annually, and the before-tax net profit margin (the firm currently has no interest-bearing debt) is 12 percent.

Given renewed fears of potential cash insolvency, an overly strict credit policy, and imminent stockouts, the company is considering higher levels of current assets as a buffer against adversity. Specifically, levels of $.5 million and $.8 million are being considered instead of the $.2 million presently held. Any additions to current assets would be financed with new equity capital.

a. Determine the total asset turnover, before-tax return on investment, and before-tax net profit margin under the three alternative levels of current assets.

b. If the new additions to current assets were financed with long-term debt at 15 percent interest, what would be the before-tax interest "cost" of the two new policies?

PROBLEMS

1. The Anderson Corporation (an all-equity-financed firm) has a sales level of $280,000 with a 10 percent profit margin before interest and taxes. To generate this sales volume, the firm maintains a fixed-asset investment of $100,000. Currently, the firm maintains $50,000 in current assets.

a. Determine the total asset turnover for the firm and compute the rate of return on total assets before taxes.

b. Compute the before-tax rate of return on assets at different levels of current assets starting with $10,000 and increasing in $15,000 increments to $100,000.

c. What implicit assumption is being made about sales in Part (b)? Appraise the significance of this assumption along with the policy to choose the level of current assets that will maximize the return on total assets as computed in Part (b).

2. The Malkiel Corporation has made the three-year projection of its asset investment given in the following table. It has found that payables and accruals tend to equal one-third of current assets. It currently has $50 million in equity, and the remainder of its financing is provided by long-term debt. The earnings retained amount to $1 million per quarter.

DATE	FIXED ASSETS (in millions)	CURRENT ASSETS (in millions)
3/31/X1 (now)	$50	$21
6/30/X1	51	30
9/30/X1	52	25
12/31/X1	53	21
3/31/X2	54	22
6/30/X2	55	31
9/30/X2	56	26
12/31/X2	57	22
3/31/X3	58	23
6/30/X3	59	32
9/30/X3	60	27
12/31/X3	61	23

a. Graph the time path of (i) fixed assets and (ii) total assets (less amount financed spontaneously by payables and accruals).

b. Devise a financing plan, assuming that your objective is to use a *hedging (maturity matching) approach*.

222   **Part IV Working Capital Management**

3. Mendez Metal Specialties, Inc., has a seasonal pattern to its business. It borrows under a line of credit from Central Bank at 1 percent over prime. Its total asset requirements now (at year end) and estimated requirements for the coming year are (in millions):

	NOW	1ST QUARTER	2ND QUARTER	3RD QUARTER	4TH QUARTER
Total asset requirements	$4.5	$4.8	$5.5	$5.9	$5.0

Assume that these requirements are level throughout the quarter. Presently, the company has $4.5 million in equity capital plus long-term debt plus the permanent component of current liabilities, and this amount will remain constant throughout the year.

The prime rate presently is 11 percent, and the company expects no change in this rate for the next year. Mendez Metal Specialties is also considering issuing intermediate-term debt at an interest rate of 13.5 percent. In this regard, three alternative amounts are under consideration: zero, $500,000, and $1 million. All additional funds requirements will be borrowed under the company's bank line of credit.

a. Determine the total dollar borrowing costs for short- and intermediate-term debt under each of the three alternatives for the coming year. (Assume that there are no changes in current liabilities other than borrowings.) Which alternative is lowest in cost?

b. Is there a consideration other than expected cost that deserves our attention?

SOLUTIONS TO SELF-CORRECTION PROBLEM

1. a.

	POLICY		
	EXISTING	2	3
Sales (millions)	$10.0	$10.0	$10.0
EBIT (millions)	1.2	1.2	1.2
Total assets (millions)	3.2	3.5	3.8
Total asset turnover	3.125	2.857	2.632
Before-tax return on assets	37.5%	34.3%	32.6%
Before-tax net profit margin	12.0%	12.0%	12.0%

The before-tax net profit margin is unchanged, as sales and earnings before interest and taxes (EBIT) are the same regardless of the liquidity policy employed.

b.

	POLICY	
	2	3
Additional debt	$300,000	$600,000
Additional interest	45,000	90,000

The "cost" of financing additional current assets could be reduced by the amount that could be earned on any additional investment of cash in marketable securities. Also, more lenient credit terms may lead to increased sales and profits. A hidden cost is that part of the debt capacity of the firm is used up by virtue of financing increased levels of current assets with debt.

SELECTED REFERENCES

Gilmer, R. H., Jr. "The Optimal Level of Liquid Assets: An Empirical Test." *Financial Management* 14 (Winter 1985), 39–43.

Hawawini, Gabriel, Claude Viallet, and Ashok Vora. "Industry Influence on Corporate Working Capital Decisions." *Sloan Management Review* 27 (Summer 1986), 15–24.

Hill, Ned C., and William L. Sartoris. *Short-Term Financial Management,* 3rd ed. Englewood Cliffs, NJ: Prentice Hall, 1995.

Maness, Terry S., and John T. Zietlow. *Short-Term Financial Management.* Fort Worth, TX: Dryden Press, 1998.

Morris, James R. "The Role of Cash Balances in Firm Valuation." *Journal of Financial and Quantitative Analysis* 18 (December 1983), 533–46.

Petty, J. William, and David F. Scott. "The Analysis of Corporate Liquidity." *Journal of Economics and Business* 32 (Spring–Summer 1980), 206–18.

Sartoris, William L., and Ned C. Hill. "A Generalized Cash Flow Approach to Short-Term Financial Decisions." *Journal of Finance* 38 (May 1983), 349–60.

Van Horne, James C. "A Risk-Return Analysis of a Firm's Working-Capital Position." *Engineering Economist* 14 (Winter 1969), 71–89.

Viscione, Jerry A. "How Long Should You Borrow Short Term?" *Harvard Business Review* (March–April 1986), 20–24.

Walker, Ernest W. "Towards a Theory of Working Capital." *Engineering Economist* 9 (January–February 1964), 21–35.

Chapter 9

Cash and Marketable Securities Management

MOTIVES FOR HOLDING CASH
SPEEDING UP CASH RECEIPTS
    Collections • Concentration Banking
S-L-O-W-I-N-G D-O-W-N CASH PAYOUTS
    "Playing the Float" • Control of Disbursements • Remote and
        Controlled Disbursing
ELECTRONIC COMMERCE
    Electronic Data Interchange • Costs and Benefits of Electronic
        Data Interchange
OUTSOURCING
CASH BALANCES TO MAINTAIN
    Compensating Balances and Fees
INVESTMENT IN MARKETABLE SECURITIES
    The Marketable Securities Portfolio: Three Segments • Variables
        in Marketable Securities Selection • Common Money Market
        Instruments • Selecting Securities for the Portfolio Segments
SUMMARY
QUESTIONS
SELF-CORRECTION PROBLEMS
PROBLEMS
SOLUTIONS TO SELF-CORRECTION PROBLEMS
SELECTED REFERENCES

Money is like muck, not good except it be spread.

—FRANCIS BACON

In the previous chapter, we were occupied with questions concerning the optimal level of current assets for the firm. By examining the trade-off between profitability and risk, we were able to determine, generally, the proper level of current assets that the firm should carry. Once the overall level of current assets is determined, other questions remain. How much should be carried in cash? How much should be carried in marketable securities? We are going to find out how to answer these questions. We will also find out how to improve the efficiency of cash management and how to invest funds in marketable securities.

MOTIVES FOR HOLDING CASH

John Maynard Keynes suggested three reasons for individuals to hold cash.[1] Keynes labeled these motives as follows: transactions, speculative, and precautionary. Shifting the emphasis away from individuals, we can use these three categories to describe the motives for corporations to hold cash.

- *Transactions motive:* to meet payments, such as purchases, wages, taxes, and dividends, arising in the ordinary course of business.
- *Speculative motive:* to take advantage of temporary opportunities, such as a sudden decline in the price of a raw material.
- *Precautionary motive:* to maintain a safety cushion or buffer to meet unexpected cash needs. The more predictable the inflows and outflows of cash for a firm, the less cash that needs to be held for precautionary needs. Ready borrowing power to meet emergency cash drains also reduces the need for this type of cash balance.

It is important to point out that not all of the firm's needs for cash call for holding cash balances exclusively. Indeed, a portion of these needs may be met by holding marketable securities—cash-equivalent assets. For the most part, firms do not hold cash for the purpose of speculation. Consequently, we concentrate only on the transactions and precautionary motives of the firm, with these needs being met with balances held both in cash and in marketable securities.

Cash management involves the efficient collection, disbursement, and temporary investment of cash. The treasurer's department of a company is usually responsible for the firm's cash management system. A cash budget, instrumental in the process (see Chapter 7), tells us how much cash we are likely to have, when we are likely to have it, and for how long. Thus, it serves as a foundation for cash forecasting and control. In addition to the cash budget, the firm needs systematic information on cash as well as some kind of control system. (See Fig. 9-1.) For a large firm, the information is usually computer based. It is necessary to obtain frequent reports, generally daily, on cash balances in each of the company's bank accounts, on cash disbursements, on average daily balances, and on the marketable security position of the firm as well as a detailed report on changes in this position. It is also useful to have information on major anticipated cash receipts and cash disbursements. All of this information is essential if a firm is to manage its cash in an efficient manner—one that provides for safe and convenient cash availability and for reasonable investment income on temporary investments of cash.

---

[1]John Maynard Keynes, *The General Theory of Employment, Interest, and Money* (New York: Harcourt Brace Javonovich, 1936), pp. 170–74.

Part IV Working Capital Management

FIGURE 9-1
Cash Management
System

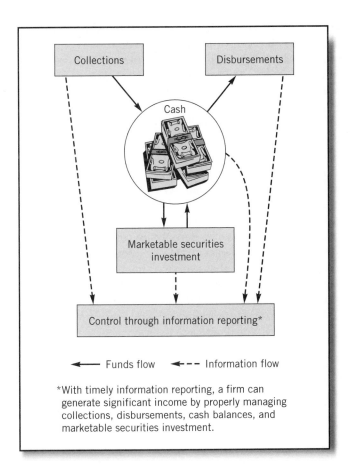

The figure shows:

Collections → Cash ← Disbursements

Cash → Marketable securities investment

Control through information reporting*

◄——— Funds flow   ◄-- - Information flow

*With timely information reporting, a firm can generate significant income by properly managing collections, disbursements, cash balances, and marketable securities investment.

SPEEDING UP CASH RECEIPTS

The various collection and disbursement methods that a firm employs to improve its cash management efficiency constitute two sides of the same coin. They exercise a joint impact on the overall efficiency of cash management. The general idea is that *the firm will benefit by "speeding up" cash receipts and "s-l-o-w-i-n-g d-o-w-n" cash payouts.* The firm wants to speed up the collection of accounts receivable so that it can have the use of money sooner. Conversely, it wants to pay accounts payable as late as is consistent with maintaining the firm's credit standing with suppliers so that it can make the most use of the money it already has. Today, most companies of reasonable size use sophisticated techniques to speed up collections and tightly control disbursements. Let's see how they do it.

Collections

Invoice Bill prepared by a seller of goods or services and submitted to the purchaser. It lists the items bought, prices, and terms of sale.

We consider first the acceleration of collections, which includes the steps taken by the firm from the time a product or service is sold until the customers' checks are collected and become usable funds for the firm. A number of methods are designed to speed up this collection process by doing one or more of the following: (1) expedite preparing and mailing the **invoice;** (2) accelerate the mailing of payments from customers to the firm; and (3) reduce the time during which payments received by the firm remain uncollected funds.

Collection Float. The second and third items in the preceding list collectively represent *collection float,* the total time between the mailing of a check by a customer and the availability of cash to the receiving firm. (See Fig. 9-2.) The second item, by itself, refers to *mail float,* or the time that the check is in the mail. The third item, representing *deposit float,* has two aspects. The first aspect, *processing float,* is the time it takes a company to process checks internally. This interval extends from the moment a check is received until the moment it is deposited with a bank for credit to the company's account. The second aspect of deposit float is *availability float;* it involves the time consumed in clearing the check through the banking system. A check becomes collected funds when it is presented to the payor's bank and is actually paid by that bank. To streamline the availability of credit, the Federal Reserve System has established a schedule specifying availability for all checks deposited with it for collection. This schedule is based on the average time required for a check deposited with a particular Federal Reserve Bank to be collected in a particular geographic area of the country. For business accounts, the maximum period for which credit is deferred is two days. This means that even if a check is not actually collected through the Federal Reserve System in two days, it becomes collected funds because the Federal Reserve carries the remaining float in the system.

Collection float is important to the financial manager because a company usually must wait until a check mailed by a customer finally clears the banking system before the cash becomes available to the firm. Because the name of the game is to turn mailed checks into cash more quickly, the financial manager wants to reduce collection float as much as possible. In what follows, we examine various ways to speed up the collection process to have more usable funds.

Earlier Billing. An obvious but easily overlooked way to speed up the collection of receivables is to get invoices to customers earlier. Customers have different payment

FIGURE 9-2
A Time-Line Explanation of Collection Float and its Components

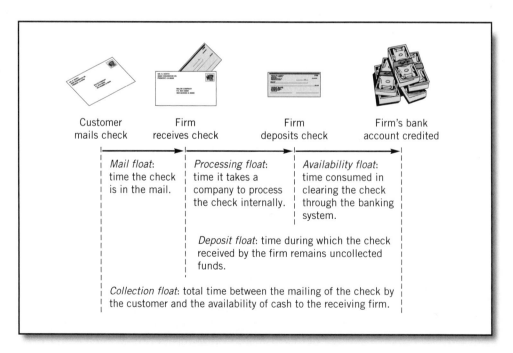

habits. Some pay their bills on the discount date or the final due date (or later), and others pay immediately on receipt of an invoice. In any event, accelerated preparation and mailing of invoices will result in faster payment because of the earlier invoice receipt and resulting earlier discount and due dates. Computerized billing could be used to accomplish this. In addition, some companies find it advantageous to enclose invoices with shipped merchandise, send invoices by fax, or even request advance payment.

Billing can be eliminated entirely through the use of a **preauthorized debit.** A customer signs an agreement with a firm allowing the firm to automatically debit the customer's bank account on a specified date and transfer funds from the customer's bank to the firm's bank. Insurance and mortgage payments are often handled this way, as they both involve recurring payments of a fixed amount.

Lockbox System. The single most important tool for accelerating the collection of remittances in the United States is the **lockbox.** A company rents a local post office box and authorizes its bank to pick up remittances in the box. Customers are billed with instructions to mail their remittances to the lockbox. The bank picks up the mail several times a day and deposits the checks directly into the company's account. The checks are recorded and cleared for collection. The company receives a deposit slip and a list of payments, together with any material in the envelopes. Often, the remittance material and checks are first scanned and converted into digital images. These images can then be transmitted to the company or supplied on a CD-ROM. The benefit of this system is that checks are deposited before, rather than after, any processing and accounting work is done. In short, the lockbox arrangement eliminates *processing float* (the time between the receipt of remittances by the company and their deposit in the bank). Today, because of modern technology, lockbox system users also benefit from improvements in data entry efficiency and the automation of information flows.

Many businesses have multiple collection locations in the form of a lockbox network. With a lockbox network, mail float and availability float are reduced by locating lockboxes close to customers' mailing points. This type of lockbox arrangement is usually on a regional basis, with the company choosing regional banks according to its billing patterns. Before determining the regions to be used and the number of collection points, a feasibility study is made of the availability of checks that would be deposited under alternative plans. Generally, the best collection points are cities that have a high volume of air traffic, since most mail travels by air.

The main advantage of a lockbox arrangement, once again, is that checks are deposited at a bank sooner and become collected balances sooner than if they were processed by the company prior to deposit. The principal disadvantage of a lockbox arrangement is the cost. Because the bank is providing a number of services in addition to the usual clearing of checks, it requires compensation for them. Because the cost is almost directly proportional to the number of checks deposited, lockbox arrangements are usually not profitable for the firm if the average remittance is small.

The appropriate rule for deciding whether or not to use a lockbox system is simply to compare the added cost of the more efficient system with the marginal income that can be generated from the accelerated funds availability. If costs are less than income, the system is profitable; if not, the system is not worth implementing. The degree of profitability depends primarily on the geographic dispersion of customers, the size of the typical remittance, and the earnings rate on the released funds.

Preauthorized debit The transfer of funds from a payor's bank account on a specified date to the payee's bank account; the transfer is initiated by the payee with the payor's advance authorization.

Lockbox A post office box maintained by a firm's bank that is used as a receiving point for customer remittances. *Retail lockbox* systems cater to the receipt and processing of low- to moderate-dollar, high-volume remittances, whereas *wholesale lockbox* systems are designed to handle high-dollar, low-volume remittances.

In any business, it is important to quickly convert outstanding receivables into cash. First Tennessee's Wholesale Lockbox service achieves that objective in a cost-effective way by reducing mail and check clearing times.

Our Wholesale Lockbox service speeds up the receivables process by allowing businesses to collect payments quickly and efficiently. We maintain a unique ZIP code at the post office for lockbox clients, and we pick up from the post office every two hours, thus dramatically reducing mail float time. In addition, we have a unique alliance with Federal Express, giving us the ability to clear checks faster than most banks throughout the country.

For those companies that can receive computer transmissions, invoice information can be entered into First Tennessee's computer system and transmitted on a same-day basis. This option is especially useful for those companies that need immediate invoice information prior to releasing shipments or need to monitor a credit limit very carefully.

"The procedure is simple," says a First Tennessee cash management specialist. "Clients mail in their remittance through a post office box with First Tennessee's unique lockbox ZIP code. We collect the mail, open and process the remittances according to the company's instructions, and deposit the checks directly into the company's account. On the same day of receipt, we notify the business of the total deposit and forward support data needed for accounts receivable posting."

This unique cash management product greatly improves availability of funds, decreases collection time and credit risk, provides quicker access to receivables and eliminates company processing prior to deposit.

Reprinted with permission, *First Tennessee Business Review*, Vol. 9:2 (Spring 1999), p. 4. © Copyright 1999, First Tennessee Bank.

Concentration Banking

The firm that uses a lockbox network as well as the one having numerous sales outlets that receive funds over the counter have something in common. Both firms will find themselves with deposit balances at a number of regional banks. Each firm may find it advantageous to move part or all of these deposits to one central location, which is known as a *concentration bank*. This process of **cash concentration**

Cash concentration The movement of cash from lockbox or field banks into the firm's central cash pool residing in a concentration bank.

- *Improves control* over inflows and outflows of corporate cash. The idea is to put all of your eggs (or in this case, cash) into one basket and then to watch the basket.

- *Reduces idle balances*—that is, keeps deposit balances at regional banks no higher than necessary to meet transactions needs (or alternatively, minimum **compensating balance** requirements). Any excess funds would be moved to the concentration bank.

Compensating balance Non-interest-bearing demand deposits maintained by a firm to compensate a bank for services provided, credit lines, or loans.

- *Allows for more effective investments.* Pooling excess balances provides the larger cash amounts needed for some of the higher yielding, short-term investment opportunities that require a larger minimum purchase. For example, some marketable securities are sold in blocks of $100,000 or more.

Concentration Services for Transferring Funds. The concentration process is dependent on the timely transfer of funds between financial institutions. There are three principal methods employed to move funds between banks: (1) depository transfer checks, (2) electronic transfer checks through automated clearinghouses, and (3) wire transfers.

Depository transfer check (DTC) A non-negotiable check payable to a single company account at a concentration bank.

The **depository transfer check (DTC)** arrangement moves funds through the use of a preprinted depository check drawn on a local bank and payable to a single company account at a concentration bank. Funds are not immediately available on receipt of the DTC, however, because the check must still be collected through the usual channels. Today, more and more companies are transmitting deposit information via telephone to their concentration banks, which prepare and deposit the DTCs into the firms' accounts. Of course, any savings that result from the use of the DTCs must be measured and compared to the costs of using this arrangement.

Automated clearinghouse (ACH) electronic transfer This is essentially an electronic version of the depository transfer check.

Another alternative is the **automated clearinghouse (ACH) electronic transfer.** This item is an electronic check image version of the depository transfer check, which can be used between banks that are members of the automated clearinghouse system. Transferred funds become available one business day later. As the cost is not significant, ACH electronic transfers have been replacing many mail-based DTC transfers.

Wire transfer A generic term for electronic funds transfer using a two-way communications system, like Fedwire.

The fastest way to move money between banks is with a **wire transfer.** A wire transfer is simply a telephone-like communication, which, via bookkeeping entries, removes funds from a payor bank account and deposits them in an account of a payee bank. Wire transfers may be made through the Federal Reserve Wire System (Fedwire) or through a private wire system. Funds are considered available upon receipt of the wire transfer. Though a DTC costs only 50 cents or so for processing, sending, and receiving, charges for a wire transfer typically range around $15. As a result of their relatively high cost, wire transfers are generally reserved for moving only large sums of money or when speed is of the essence.

The Check's Still in the Mail

Reports of the check's death are greatly exaggerated. Fortunately, innovations in imaging systems continue to keep check processing manageable.

It was decades ago that banking experts first predicted a shift from paper checks to electronic transactions. They were a bit ahead of their time. "We were supposed to become a checkless society by 1980," says Mike Thomas, vice president & general manager, Payment Systems, for Unisys. "But the world still processes about 85 billion checks a year, and check volume is growing by about 3 percent per year."

Checks have remained popular for several reasons. Although many consumers use credit and debit cards to replace cash, they still rely on checks for paying bills—presumably out of habit and an unwilling-

ness to give up "float," the time between when they write the check and when it's cashed. In addition, says Thomas, U.S. banks employ check-centric business practices that make checks hard to eliminate. "Banks have made the check a revenue-producing instrument through account fees, nonsufficient funds fees, and so on. In fact, checking accounts are often the lead product that draws customers to the institution."

A large bank's operations center might handle millions of checks each day. For many banks that incredible volume is managed by imaging systems, which capture digital pictures of checks—scanning up to 30 images a second—and process that electronic information rather than the checks themselves. Such systems slash processing time, enable operations centers to better manage workflow and allow customers the convenience of managing their accounts electronically.

Reprinted from the May 1999 issue of *Exec*. Copyright © 1999 Unisys Corp. Used by permission.

Whereas one of the underlying objectives of cash management is to accelerate collections, still another objective is to slow down cash disbursements as much as possible. The combination of fast collections and slow disbursements will result in increased availability of cash.

"Playing the Float"

Net float The dollar difference between the balance shown in a firm's (or individual's) checkbook balance and the balance on the bank's books.

The cash figure shown on a firm's books seldom represents the available amount of cash that the firm has in the bank. In fact, the funds available in the bank are generally greater than the balance shown on the company's books. The dollar difference between the company's bank balance and its book balance of cash is called **net float** (or sometimes, just plain *float*). Net float is the result of delays between the time checks are written and their eventual clearing by the bank. It is very possible for a company to have a negative cash balance on its books and a positive bank balance, because checks just written by the company may still be outstanding. If the size of net float can be estimated accurately, bank balances can be reduced and the funds invested to earn a positive return. This activity has been referred to by corporate treasurers as "playing the float."

Control of Disbursements

Essential to good cash management is a company's control of disbursements that will slow down cash outflows and minimize the time that cash deposits are idle. A company with multiple banks should be able to shift funds quickly to banks from which disbursements are made to prevent excess balances from temporarily building up in a particular bank. The idea is to have adequate cash at the various banks, but not to let excess balances build up. This requires daily information on collected balances. Excess funds may then be transferred to disbursement banks, either to pay bills or to invest in marketable securities. Many companies have developed sophisticated computer systems to provide the necessary information and to transfer excess funds automatically. Instead of developing one's own system, a firm can hire outside computer services to provide the described functions.

One procedure for tightly controlling disbursements is to centralize payables into a single account (or a small number of accounts), presumably at the company's headquarters. In this way, disbursements can be made at the precise time they are desired. Operating procedures for disbursements should be well established. If cash discounts are taken on accounts payable, the firm should send payment at the end of the cash discount period.[2] But, if a discount is not taken, the firm should not pay until the final due date in order to have maximum use of cash. (We will have more to say on whether or not to take a cash discount for prompt payment in Chapter 11.)

Payable through draft (PTD) A check-like instrument that is drawn against the payor and not against a bank as is a check. After a PTD is presented to a bank, the payor gets to decide whether to honor or refuse payment.

Payable Through Draft (PTD). A means for delaying disbursements is through the use of **payable through drafts (PTDs)**. Unlike an ordinary check, the payable through draft is not payable on demand. When it is presented to the issuer's bank for collection, the bank must present it to the issuer for acceptance. The funds are then deposited by the issuing firm to cover payment of the draft. The advantage of the draft arrangement is that it delays the time the firm actually has to have funds on

---

[2]Shortly after a creditor puts a check in the mail, an invoice is considered paid. The "mailbox rule," a custom since 1818, sets the postmark on the envelope as the date of payment.

deposit to cover the draft. Consequently, it allows the firm to maintain smaller balances at its banks. A disadvantage of a draft system is that certain suppliers may prefer checks. Also, banks do not like to process drafts because they often require special manual attention. As a result, banks typically impose a higher service charge to process drafts than they do to process checks.

Payroll and Dividend Disbursements. Many companies maintain a separate account for payroll disbursements. To minimize the balance in this account, the firm must predict when the payroll checks issued will be presented for payment. If payday falls on a Friday, not all of the checks will be cashed on that day. Consequently, the firm does not need to have funds on deposit to cover its entire payroll. Even on Monday, some checks will not be presented because of delays in their deposit. Based on its experience, the firm should be able to construct a distribution of when, on the average, checks are presented for collection. An example is shown in Figure 9-3. With this information, the firm can approximate the funds it needs to have on deposit to cover payroll checks. Many firms also establish a separate account for dividend payments, similar to the one used for payroll. Here, too, the idea is to predict when dividend checks will be presented for payment so that the firm can minimize the cash balance in the account.

Zero balance account (ZBA) A corporate checking account in which a zero balance is maintained. The account requires a master (parent) account from which funds are drawn to cover negative balances or to which excess balances are sent.

Zero Balance Account (ZBA). The use of a **zero balance account (ZBA)** system, which is offered by many major banks, eliminates the need to accurately estimate and fund each individual disbursement account. Under such a system, one master disbursing account services all other subsidiary accounts. When checks are cleared at the end of each day, the bank automatically transfers just enough funds from the master account to each disbursement account (e.g., one for payroll, one for payables, etc.) to just cover checks presented.[3] Thus a zero ending balance is maintained each day in all but the master account. Besides improving control over disbursements, a zero balance account system eliminates idle cash balances from all subsidiary accounts. The firm's cash manager still needs to forecast anticipated check-clearing times so that the master account will have sufficient cash to service the subsidiary disbursement accounts. But, by the law of large numbers, multiple errors tend to cancel each other out, and a fair approximation of the cash needed to be maintained in the master account can be made.

---

[3]Alternatively, zero balance accounts at one or more banks could be funded through wire transfers from a central account at another bank (often a concentration bank).

FIGURE 9-3
Percentage of Payroll Checks Collected

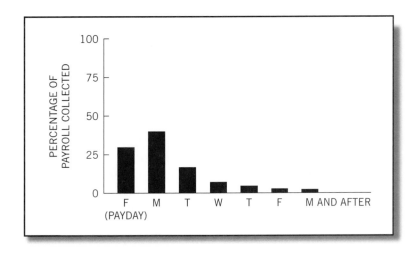

Remote and Controlled Disbursing

Disbursement float Total time between the mailing of a check by a firm and the check's clearing the firm's checking account.

Remote disbursement A system in which the firm directs checks to be drawn on a bank that is geographically remote from its customer so as to maximize check-clearing time.

Taking advantage of inefficiencies in the check-clearing processes of the Federal Reserve System and of certain commercial banks, as well as inefficiencies in the postal system, a firm may maximize the time the checks it writes remain outstanding. Various models have been proposed to maximize **disbursement float** through the selection of geographically optimal disbursing banks. The idea is to locate disbursing banks and to draw checks on them in a way that will maximize the time a check will remain outstanding. A firm using **remote disbursement** might, for example, mail a check to a supplier in Maine that was drawn on a bank in Helena, Montana.

By maximizing disbursement float, the firm can reduce the amount of cash it holds and employ these unused funds in more profitable ways. One firm's gain, however, is another's loss. Maximizing disbursement float means that suppliers will not have collectible funds as early as would otherwise be the case. To the extent that suppliers look with disfavor on such payment habits, supplier relations may be hurt by remote disbursing.

On May 2, 1985, E. F. Hutton, the nation's fifth largest brokerage firm at that time, pleaded guilty to 2,000 felony counts of mail and wire fraud. Hutton had been engaging in "extreme" float-creating practices—a number involving remote disbursing. This case prompted many companies to review all of their cash management practices. In many cases, these reviews led companies to adopt formal cash management policies and codes of conduct. In some cases, remote disbursing was considered to be unethical in that it was a cash management technique designed expressly to delay normal check clearing.

Controlled disbursement A system in which the firm directs checks to be drawn on a bank (or branch bank) that is able to give early or mid-morning notification of the total dollar amount of checks that will be presented against its account that day.

A practice related to remote disbursement, but having fewer negative connotations, is called **controlled disbursement.** It too may make use of small, out of-the-way disbursement banks (or branches of large banks). However, the primary reason for choosing these particular disbursement banks is that late presentments (checks received after the initial daily shipment of checks from the Federal Reserve) are minimal. This fact allows the firm to better predict disbursements on a day-to-day basis.

ELECTRONIC COMMERCE

Electronic commerce (EC) The exchange of business information in an electronic (nonpaper) format, including over the Internet.

Currently, most business documents and payments in the United States are in paper form and exchange generally takes place through the U.S. mail. **Electronic commerce (EC)**—the exchange of business information in an electronic format—offers an alternative to this paper-based system. At one end of the electronic commerce spectrum, we find unstructured electronic messaging such as facsimile transmission (fax) and electronic mail (e-mail). At the other end, the highly structured messaging known as *electronic data interchange (EDI)* is found. Our focus in this section is on EDI, especially how EDI relates to a company's collections and disbursements.

Electronic Data Interchange

Electronic data interchange (EDI) The movement of business data electronically in a structured, computer-readable format.

Electronic data interchange (EDI) involves the transfer of business information (e.g., invoices, purchase orders, and shipping information) in a computer-readable format. EDI not only involves direct, computer-to-computer data movement via communication links but also the physical delivery among businesses of electronic data storage items such as computer tapes, disks, and CD-ROMs.

Electronic funds transfer (EFT) The electronic movements of information between two depository institutions resulting in a value (money) transfer.

Society for Worldwide Interbank Financial Telecommunication (SWIFT) The major international financial telecommunications network that transmits international payment instructions as well as other financial messages.

Clearing House Interbank Payments System (CHIPS) An automated clearing system used primarily for international payments. The British counterpart is known as CHAPS.

Financial EDI (FEDI) The movement of financially related electronic information between a company and its bank or between banks.

Electronic funds transfer (EFT) forms an important subset of EDI. The distinguishing feature of EFT is that a transfer of value (money) occurs in which depository institutions (primarily banks) send and receive electronic payments. Examples of domestic EFT include automated clearinghouse (ACH) transfers and wire transfers. Internationally, EFT may involve instructions and transfers by way of the **Society for Worldwide Interbank Financial Telecommunication (SWIFT)** and the **Clearing House Interbank Payments System (CHIPS).**

A major boost to EFT in the United States came in January 1999, when a new regulation went into effect requiring that all federal government payments—except for tax refunds and situations where waivers are granted—be made electronically. Direct deposit of payments through EFT should prove more secure than paper checks and, typically, be more convenient. EFT payments are also expected to provide cost savings for the government.

A second major subset of EDI is known as **financial EDI (FEDI).** FEDI involves the exchange of electronic business information (non value transfer) between a firm and its bank or between banks. Examples include lockbox remittance information and bank balance information.

Even for businesses that have implemented electronic data interchange and funds transfer techniques, many of their transactions will still be at least partially paper-based. For example, a company could transact all of its business activities using EDI and yet make some payments with paper checks. Alternatively, some of a firm's *data interchange* may be paper-based, whereas ACH and wire transfers might handle all of its *payments*.

Costs of Benefits of Electronic Data Interchange

A host of benefits have been attributed to the application of electronic data interchange in its various forms. For example, information and payments move faster and with greater reliability. This benefit, in turn, leads to improved cash forecasting and cash management. The company's customers also benefit from faster and more reliable service. In addition, the company is able to reduce mail, paper, and document storage costs.

These benefits, however, come with a cost. The movement of electronic data requires computer hardware and software. The company must train personnel to utilize the EDI system. In addition, time, money, and effort often are expended convincing suppliers and customers to do business electronically with the company. Of course, the speed of an electronic funds transfer eliminates *float*. For some corporations, the loss of the favorable float in disbursements is a high price to pay.

Whether the benefits of adopting an electronic business document and payment system outweigh the costs must be decided on a company-by-company basis. However, even for those firms that embrace such an electronic system, it may be necessary (for legal, marketing, and other reasons) to maintain a dual system—both electronic and paper-based—for some time to come.

OUTSOURCING

In recent years, firms have increasingly focused on the core processes of their businesses—those *core competencies* they possess to create and sustain a competitive advantage. All other essential, but noncore areas of business are candidates for *outsourcing*.

CORPORATE FINANCE

Dell Computers is the world's leading direct computer systems company selling direct to customers. It uses no retailers, resellers and other intermediaries. It is the third-largest and the fastest growing major computer-systems company in the world, trading in 42 countries around the world and with revenue of $13.6 billion in the past four quarters.

WEB SITE

Dell started selling direct on the Internet in July 1996. Its web site, within which Dell maintains 42 country-specific sites, now has 1.5 million visits a week.

COLLECTING PAYMENTS

Dell offers a wide range of payment and financing methods to meet the different needs of its customers, all of which can be set up and initiated on the web site.

To ensure the privacy and security of the information that Dell receives from customers on the Internet, Dell encrypts all data transmitted to them and uses positive identification of the store each time the customer communicates; it has also built secure firewalls throughout its internal systems.

On its web site Dell provides the following payment options to be used after an order has been placed electronically:

- Business line of credit for the repeat-purchase customer.
- Checks drawn on local banks in each of the 42 countries.
- Locally issued credit and debit cards in each of the 42 countries.
- Credit transfers through the local country's automated clearing house.
- Personal financing deals available over 24 or 36 months.
- Leasing rental and purchase facilities for a 2–5 year period.

Source: Adapted from Jack Large, "Pick it up from the Dell Store," *Corporate Finance* (July 1998), p. 20. © Euromoney Publications plc, 1998. Used by permission. All rights reserved.

Outsourcing Subcontracting a certain business operation to an outside firm instead of doing it "in-house."

Outsourcing—shifting an ordinarily "in-house" operation to an outside firm—is not a "new" idea when it comes to cash management. Think back to our earlier discussion of lockboxes. Next to a firm's checking account, a lockbox service is the oldest corporate cash management service. The use of a lockbox is but one example of the outsourcing of a critical but noncore financial process. In fact, all the major areas of cash management—collections, disbursements, and marketable-securities investment—are ripe for outsourcing consideration.

Outsourcing has the potential to reduce a company's costs. The outsourcer (subcontractor) can use economies of scale and their specialized expertise to perform an outsourced business operation. As a result, the firm may get the service it needs at both a lower cost and a higher quality than it could have provided by itself. In addition, outsourcing may free up time and personnel so that the company can focus more on its core business. So, although cutting costs is an important consideration in the outsourcing decision, it is not the only one. Indeed, when The Outsourcing Institute asked outsourcing end users in a 1998 survey to list the reasons why they outsourced, "reducing and controlling operating costs" ranked first, "improving company focus" ranked second, and "gaining access to world-class capabilities" came in third.

We have already seen outsourcing applied to collections (i.e., a lockbox system). The growing interest shown by firms in electronic commerce makes the area of disbursements especially well suited for outsourcing. Most likely, a bank would manage this outsourced operation. For example, a firm might deliver a single file of all payment instructions to a bank in EDI format. The bank would then separate the payments by type (check, ACH, or wire) and make the payments. This service would be especially helpful to a firm needing to make international payments. A major, money-center bank would have the technical expertise necessary to handle the many currencies and clearing systems involved.

Europe Embraces Outsourcing

With the global business process outsourcing market expected to double in size to $200 billion over the next five years, top corporate decision makers in Europe are turning to this strategy as never before. They're outsourcing applications processing, payroll, real estate management, and tax compliance the most. Why? To access world-class services and technology in hopes of enhancing shareholder value.

These were some of the results of a major study conducted for PricewaterhouseCoopers by Yankelovich Partners market research firm. Over six months the firm interviewed senior executives at more than 100 European companies with an average of $5 billion in revenues and 16,000 employees. Here are some of the other key findings: More than half (55%) of the

executives said their companies have outsourced one or more business processes to external service providers, and nine out of 10 are satisfied with the results. Of those who outsource, the majority believe that:

- Business process outsourcing lets companies focus on their critical core competencies (84%).
- BPO enables companies to increase efficiency without having to invest in people and technology (71%).
- BPO helps companies become more profitable, leading to increases in shareholder value (70%).
- Maintaining a competitive edge is an important benefit of BPO (66%) as is increasing shareholder value (61%).

Source: Kathy Williams, Editor, "Europe Embraces Outsourcing," *Strategic Finance* (July 1999), p. 19. (www.strategicfinance.com) © IMA, 1999. Used by permission. All rights reserved.

CASH BALANCES TO MAINTAIN

Most business firms establish a target level of cash balances to maintain. They do not want to maintain excess cash balances because interest can be earned when these funds are invested in marketable securities. The greater the interest rate available on marketable securities, of course, the greater the opportunity cost to maintaining idle cash balances. The optimal level of cash should be the larger of (1) the transactions balances required when cash management is efficient, or (2) the compensating balance requirements of commercial banks with which the firm has deposit accounts.

Transactions balances are determined in keeping with considerations taken up earlier in the chapter. Also, the higher the interest rate, the greater the opportunity cost of holding cash, and the greater the corresponding desire to reduce the firm's cash holdings, all other things the same. A number of cash management models have been developed for determining an optimal split between cash and marketable securities.[4]

---

[4]See James C. Van Horne, *Financial Management and Policy,* 11th ed. (Upper Saddle River, NJ: Prentice Hall, 1998), Chapter 12, for a discussion of cash management models.

Compensating Balances and Fees

Establishing a minimum level of cash balances depends, in part, on the compensating balance requirements of banks. The requirements for the firm to maintain a certain amount of non-interest-bearing demand deposits to compensate a bank for services provided are based on the profitability of the account. A bank begins by calculating the average collected balance shown on its books over a period of time. As we have already noted, this balance is often higher than the cash balance shown on the company's books. From the average collected balance, the bank subtracts the percentage of deposits it is required to maintain as a reserve requirement—currently 10 percent. The residual constitutes the earnings base on which income is generated. Total income is determined by multiplying the base times the earnings rate of the bank. This rate fluctuates with money market conditions.

Once the income from an account is determined, the costs of servicing the account must be computed. Most banks have a schedule of costs on a per-item basis for such transactions as wire transfers and processing checks. The account is analyzed for a typical month, during which all transactions are multiplied by the per-item cost and then totaled. If the cost is less than the total income from the account, the account is profitable. The minimum average level of cash balances required is the point at which the account is just profitable. Because banks differ in the earnings rate they use as well as in their costs and method of account analysis, the determination of compensating balances varies. The firm, therefore, may be wise to shop around and find the bank that requires the lowest compensating balances for a given level of activity. If a firm has a lending arrangement with a bank, the firm may well be required to maintain balances in excess of those required to compensate the bank for the activity in its account. Because we consider compensation for a lending arrangement in Chapter 11, no discussion of this form of compensation will be undertaken at this time.

In recent years, there has been a marked trend toward paying cash for services rendered by a bank instead of maintaining compensating balances. The advantage to the firm is that it may be able to earn more on funds used for compensating balances than the fee for the services. The higher the interest rate in the money market, the greater the opportunity cost of compensating balances, and the greater the advantage of service charges. It is an easy matter to determine if the firm would be better off with service charges as opposed to maintaining compensating balances. One simply compares the charges with the earnings on the funds released. Where a service offered can better be paid for by a fee, the firm should be alert to take advantage of the situation and to reduce its compensating balances.

INVESTMENT IN MARKETABLE SECURITIES

In general, firms try to maintain some target level of cash to meet their needs for transactions and/or compensating balances requirements. But beyond that we often find firms investing in short-term marketable securities. In this section we explore the firm's use of marketable securities as near-cash investments. Before we begin, we should mention that for accounting purposes marketable securities (and time deposits) are shown on the balance sheet as "cash equivalents" if their remaining maturities are three months or less at the time of acquisition. Other marketable securities, assuming that their remaining maturities are less than one year, are shown as "short-term investments."

The Marketable Securities Portfolio: Three Segments

It is useful to think of the firm's portfolio of short-term marketable securities as if it were a pie cut into three (not necessarily equal) pieces.[5] (See Fig. 9-4.) One portion of the pie would consist of marketable securities acting as a reserve for the company's cash account. That is, if the firm found that its daily opening cash balance was less than desired, some of these particular securities could be sold quickly to build up cash. Unless a firm's cash inflows were *always* greater than or equal to its cash outflows each day, the firm would probably need to cash in some securities from time to time—but exactly when and in what amount would be difficult to forecast with certainty. In this segment, a major requirement is instant liquidity. Because these securities are intended to provide the first line of defense against unforeseen operating needs of the firm, these securities may have to be liquidated on very short notice. We could label that portion of the firm's total marketable securities portfolio held to meet these needs as the *ready cash segment (R$)*.

In addition to holding marketable securities to meet some unforeseen cash needs, securities are also held to meet "controllable" (or knowable) outflows as well. The firm knows in advance, and has quite a bit of control over, its quarterly dividend and tax payments, for example. Still other controllable outflows would be loans coming due and interest payments. The firm can prepare for these controllable outflows by gradually accumulating funds. This gradual accumulation could remain in the cash account but could just as easily be earning interest if invested temporarily in marketable securities instead. Thus, another portion of the firm's securities portfolio, the *controllable cash segment (C$)*, could be earmarked for meeting controllable (knowable) outflows, such as taxes and dividends.

Finally, we have the *free cash segment (F$)*. This is an amount of marketable securities that is set aside to service neither the cash account nor the firm's controllable

---

[5]We base this discussion on an approach suggested by James M. Stancill, *The Management of Working Capital* (Scranton, PA: Intext Educational Publishers, 1971), Chapters 2 and 3.

FIGURE 9-4
The Firm's Portfolio of Short-Term Marketable Securities Can Be Thought of as a Pie Cut into Three (Not Necessarily Equal) Pieces

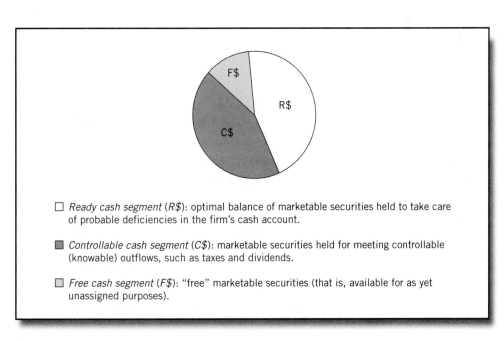

☐ *Ready cash segment (R$):* optimal balance of marketable securities held to take care of probable deficiencies in the firm's cash account.

◼ *Controllable cash segment (C$):* marketable securities held for meeting controllable (knowable) outflows, such as taxes and dividends.

◻ *Free cash segment (F$):* "free" marketable securities (that is, available for as yet unassigned purposes).

outlays. It is basically extra cash that the firm has simply invested short term. Because the firm has no immediate use for these funds, it is better to keep these funds invested than to have them lie idle in the cash account.

Before deciding which marketable securities are most appropriate for the three portfolio segments, we need to become acquainted with the variables that must be considered in the process of selecting marketable securities. We also need to become familiar with the alternative securities themselves.

Variables in Marketable Securities Selection

When considering the purchase of marketable securities, the firm's portfolio manager must first understand how each potential security purchase relates to certain key variables. Among the most important of these variables are safety, marketability, yield, and maturity.

Safety (of principal)
Refers to the likelihood of getting back the same number of dollars you originally invested (principal).

Safety. The most basic test that marketable securities must pass concerns **safety** of principal. This refers to the likelihood of getting back the same number of dollars originally invested. Safety is judged relative to U.S. Treasury securities, which are considered certain if held to maturity. For securities other than Treasury issues, the safety of these securities will vary depending on the issuer and the type of security issued. A relatively high degree of safety is a must for a security to be seriously considered for inclusion in the firm's short-term marketable securities portfolio.

Marketability (or liquidity) The ability to sell a significant volume of securities in a short period of time in the secondary market without significant price concession.

Marketability. The **marketability** (or **liquidity**) of a security relates to the owner's ability to convert it into cash on short notice. Although it is possible that a security could be quite "safe" if held to maturity, this does not necessarily mean that it is always possible to easily sell the security *before* maturity without incurring a loss. If your instructor (a very honest person, we might add) gave you a personal, one-week IOU in exchange for your providing a $10 loan, rest assured that you would get your money back at the end of a week. However, try to sell that IOU in your local shopping mall, and see how well you do. It would be a difficult, time-consuming task. Even if successful, you might have to accept a substantial price concession. In general, a large, active secondary market—that is, a secondhand market where a security can be traded after issuance—is necessary for a security to have high marketability.

Yield. The yield, or return, on a security is related to the interest and/or appreciation of principal provided by the security. Some securities, notably Treasury bills, do not pay interest. Instead, they are sold at a discount and redeemed at face value.

Take Note

Example

A $1,000 one-year Treasury bill (the minimum amount that can be sold) might be purchased for $926. In this case, the yield (or appreciation) of $74 might be expressed as a yearly return of 8 percent ($74/$926).

Interest-rate (or yield) risk The variability in the market price of a security caused by changes in interest rates.

You may remember that in Chapter 2 we discussed how the price of a debt security varies inversely with the interest rate or yield. The firm's marketable securities portfolio manager, therefore, needs to be alert to **interest-rate** (or **yield) risk.** The fact is that a loss can be incurred if a marketable security is sold prior to maturity *and* the level of interest rates has increased.

Example

Assume that we have just purchased the one-year Treasury bill described in the previous example. Further assume that we suddenly have a need to cash in this investment and that for some reason interest rates have risen such that investors now demand a 9 percent return before they will purchase a one-year Treasury bill.

	Market price	Face amount	Yield to maturity
This morning	$926.00	$1,000	$74.00/$926.00 = .08
Later the same day	**$917.50**	$1,000	$82.50/$917.50 = .09

If we sold our Treasury bill later that day—after interest rates had risen—we would experience a loss of $8.50 ($926.00 − $917.50). Now you should better understand that when security prices are volatile (due to changing interest rates), the firm's marketable securities portfolio manager may try to avoid having to sell securities before they mature.

Maturity. Maturity simply refers to the life of the security. Some marketable securities have a specific life. Treasury bills, for example, have original lives of 13, 26, or 52 weeks. Other securities, like commercial paper and negotiable certificates of deposit, can have lives tailored to meet specific needs. Usually, the longer the maturity, the greater the yield, but also the more exposure to yield risk.

Common Money Market Instruments

Money market instruments (Broadly defined). All government securities and short-term corporate obligations.

The firm's marketable securities portfolio manager usually restricts securities purchases to **money market instruments.** These instruments are generally short-term (original maturity of less than one year), high-quality government and corporate debt issues. In addition, government securities originally issued with maturities of more than one year but now having a year or less until maturity would also qualify as money market instruments. In what follows we will explore the most common types of money market instruments available to the company as near-cash investments.

Treasury bills (T-bills) Short-term, non-interest-bearing obligations of the U.S. Treasury issued at a discount and redeemed at maturity for full face value.

Treasury Securities. Treasury securities are direct obligations of the U.S. government and carry its full faith and credit. Bills, notes, and bonds are the principal securities issued. **Treasury bills (T-bills)** with maturities of 13 and 26 weeks are auctioned weekly by the Treasury. (All sales by the Treasury are by auction.) In addition, one-year bills are sold every four weeks. Smaller investors can enter a "noncompetitive" bid, which is filled at the market clearing price. Treasury bills carry no coupon but are sold on a discount basis. Bills are sold in minimum amounts of $1,000 and multiples of $1,000 above the minimum. These securities are very popular with companies, in part because of the large and active market in them. In addition, transactions costs involved in the sale of Treasury bills in the secondary market are small.

Treasury notes Medium-term (2–10 years' original maturity) obligations of the U.S. Treasury.

Treasury bonds Long-term (more than 10 years' original maturity) obligations of the U.S. Treasury.

The original maturity on **Treasury notes** is 2 to 10 years, whereas the original maturity on **Treasury bonds** is over 10 years. With the passage of time, of course, a number of these securities have maturities of less than one year and serve the needs of short-term investors. Notes and bonds are coupon issues, and there is an active market for them. Overall, Treasury securities are the safest and most marketable money market investments. Therefore, they provide the lowest yield for a given maturity of the various instruments that we consider. (Once again, we see the trade-off between risk and return.) The interest income on these securities is taxed at the federal level, but it is exempt from state and local income taxes.

Repurchase Agreements.   In an effort to finance their inventories of securities, government security dealers offer **repurchase agreements (RPs; repos)** to corporations. The repurchase agreement, or *repo*, is the sale of short-term securities by the dealer to the investor whereby the dealer agrees to repurchase the securities at an established higher price at a specified future time. The investor thereby receives a given yield while holding the securities. The length of the holding period itself is tailored to the needs of the investor. Thus, repurchase agreements give the investor a great deal of flexibility with respect to maturity. Rates on repurchase agreements are related to rates on Treasury bills, federal funds, and loans to government security dealers by commercial banks. There is limited marketability to repurchase agreements, but the most common maturities run from overnight to only a few days. Because the underlying instruments involved are generally Treasury securities, the safety of the arrangement depends solely on the reliability and financial condition of the dealer.

Federal Agency Securities.   **Federal agencies** issue securities directly, or indirectly through the Federal Financing Bank. Principal agencies include the Federal Housing Administration, the Government National Mortgage Association (GNMA, "Ginnie Mae"), and the Tennessee Valley Authority (TVA). In addition, a number of *government-sponsored enterprises (GSEs)*, which are privately owned, publicly chartered entities, issue their own securities. Major GSEs include the Federal Farm Credit Banks (FFCBs), Federal National Mortgage Association (FNMA, "Fannie Mae"), and Federal Home Loan Mortgage Corporation (FHLMC, "Freddie Mac"). Debt securities issued by federal agencies and GSEs are collectively referred to as *federal agency securities*.

Obligations of the various agencies of the federal government are guaranteed by the agency issuing the security and sometimes by the U.S. government. The federal government does not guarantee GSE securities; nor is there any stated "moral" obligation, but there is an implied backing. It would be hard to imagine the federal government allowing them to fail. Agency and GSE securities typically provide a fairly high degree of marketability and are sold in the secondary market through the same dealers that sell Treasury securities. Although interest income on these securities is subject to federal income taxes, for many issues it is not subject to state and local income taxes. About half of the outstanding securities mature in less than a year.

Bankers' Acceptances. Bankers' **acceptances (BAs)** are time drafts (short-term promissory notes) drawn on a bank by a firm to help finance foreign and domestic trade.[6] By "accepting" the draft, a bank promises to pay the holder of the draft a stated amount of money at maturity. The bank ends up substituting its own credit for that of a borrower. Therefore, the creditworthiness of bankers' acceptances is primarily judged relative to the bank accepting the draft. However, the drawer of the draft remains secondarily liable to the holder in case the bank defaults. Accepted drafts are negotiable instruments that generally have maturities of less than six months and are of very high quality. They are traded in an over-the-counter market. The rates on bankers' acceptances tend to be slightly higher than rates on Treasury bills of like maturity, and both are sold on a discount basis. Bankers' acceptances can be on domestic banks and on large foreign banks, where the yield tends to be higher.

Repurchase agreements (RPs; repos) Agreements to buy securities (usually Treasury bills) and to resell them at a specified higher price at a later date.

Federal agency An executive department, an independent federal establishment, a corporation, or other entity established by Congress that is owned in whole or in part by the United States.

Bankers' acceptances (BAs) Short-term promissory trade notes for which a bank (by having "accepted" them) promises to pay the holder the face amount at maturity.

---

[6]For an example, showing how a banker's acceptance can be used to help finance foreign trade, see the further discussion of bankers' acceptances in the "Money Market Credit" section of Chapter 11.

Commercial paper Short-term, unsecured promissory notes, generally issued by large corporations (unsecured corporate IOUs).

Commercial Paper.

Commercial paper consists of short-term, unsecured promissory notes issued by finance companies and certain industrial firms. It constitutes the largest dollar-volume instrument in the money market. Commercial paper can be sold by the issuing firm directly or through dealers acting as intermediaries. Because of the volume, a number of large finance companies have found it cheaper to sell their paper directly to investors, thus bypassing dealers. Among companies selling paper on this basis are General Electric Capital Corporation, Ford Motor Credit Company, General Motors Acceptance Corporation (GMAC), and Sears, Roebuck Acceptance Corporation. Paper sold through dealers is issued by industrial companies and smaller finance companies. Dealers carefully screen the creditworthiness of potential issuers. In a sense, dealers stand behind the paper they place with investors.

Usually, commercial paper is sold on a discount basis. Maturities generally run up to 270 days, and when directly placed, commercial paper is often tailored to mature on a specific date specified by the purchaser.[7] Most paper is held to maturity, and there is no formal secondary market. However, direct sellers of commercial paper will often repurchase the paper on request. Arrangements may also be made through dealers for repurchase of paper sold through them. Because of the absence of an active secondary market and the slight (but present) credit risk involved in corporate issuers, commercial paper has a somewhat higher yield than Treasury issues of similar maturity—or, about the same yield as available on similar maturity bankers' acceptances. Paper sold directly generally commands a lower yield than does paper sold through dealers. Commercial paper is sold only in fairly large denominations, usually at least $100,000.

Commercial paper issued in the United States by foreign corporations is called *Yankee commercial paper.* For instance, Mercedes-Benz AG might issue commercial paper in the United States to help finance working capital needs for its U.S. assembly plant. Commercial paper issued and sold outside the country in whose currency the security is denominated is called *Euro-commercial paper (Euro CP).* Dutch-guilder denominated commercial paper issued by General Motors in Germany would be an example. Euro-commercial paper gives the issuer the added flexibility to borrow in a variety of currencies. Though Euro-commercial paper is similar to domestic (U.S.) commercial paper, there are some differences. For instance, although U.S. commercial paper usually matures in less than 270 days, the maturity of Euro-commercial paper can be considerably longer due to its freedom from certain U.S. securities regulations. Also, because of the generally longer maturity of Euro-commercial paper versus U.S. commercial paper, a more active secondary market has developed for Euro-commercial paper than for U.S. commercial paper.

Negotiable certificate of deposit (CD) A large-denomination investment in a negotiable time deposit at a commercial bank or savings institution paying a fixed or variable rate of interest for a specified time period.

Negotiable Certificates of Deposit.

A short-term investment that originated in 1961, the **negotiable certificate of deposit (CD)** is a large-denomination, negotiable time deposit at a commercial bank or savings institution paying a fixed or variable rate of interest for a specified time. Original maturities usually range from 30 days to 12 months. To be negotiable (able to be sold in the secondary market), most money-center banks require a minimum denomination of $100,000. A secondary market for CDs issued by large money-center banks does exist. However, this market is not as liquid as that for Treasury issues, because CDs are more heterogeneous than Treasury issues. For example, CDs differ widely with respect to the quality of the issuing

---

[7]Companies rarely issue commercial paper with maturities longer than 270 days because these securities would then have to be registered with the Securities and Exchange Commission, which entails added time and expense.

bank, the maturity of the instrument, and the stated interest rate. Because of less liquidity and slightly higher risk, yields on CDs are greater than those on Treasury bills of similar maturity, but about the same as those on bankers' acceptances and commercial paper.

So far, our discussion of CDs has primarily focused on *domestic* CDs—those issued by domestic U.S. banks. There are, however, three other types of large CDs:

- *Eurodollar CDs (or Euro CDs)*—dollar-denominated CDs issued by foreign branches of U.S. banks and foreign banks, primarily in London (see the *Eurodollar* discussion that follows)
- *Yankee CDs*—CDs issued by U.S. branches of foreign banks
- *Thrift CDs*—CDs issued by savings and loan associations, savings banks, and credit unions

Thus, the firm's securities portfolio manager has quite a selection of CDs to choose from when it comes to making a short-term investment.

Eurodollars A U.S. dollar-denominated deposit—generally in a bank located outside the United States—not subject to U.S. banking regulations.

Eurodollars. **Eurodollars** are bank deposits, denominated in U.S. dollars, not subject to U.S. bank regulations. Although most Eurodollars are deposited in banks in Europe, the term applies to any dollar deposit in foreign banks or in foreign branches of U.S. banks. Eurodollars generally take the form of either *Eurodollar time deposits (Euro TDs)* or *Eurodollar certificates of deposit (Euro CDs)*. Although Euro TDs are nonnegotiable, most have relatively short maturities ranging from overnight to a few months. The Euro CD, on the other hand, is a negotiable instrument like its domestic counterpart. For the large corporation having ready access to international money centers, the Eurodollar deposit is usually an important investment option.

Short-Term Municipals. Increasingly, state and local governments are providing securities tailored to the short-term investor. One is a commercial paper type of instrument, where the interest rate is reset every week. That is, the security has a floating rate, and the weekly reset ensures that market price will scarcely vary. Some corporations invest in longer-term municipal securities, but the maturity is usually kept within one or two years. A problem with longer-term instruments is that they are not highly marketable. Shorter-term instruments designed for the corporate treasurer and for municipal money market mutual funds have much better marketability and greater price stability.

Money Market Preferred Stock. Beginning in 1982, a special type of preferred stock began to be issued, and it found considerable favor in the marketable securities portfolios of corporations. As we shall see in Chapter 20, straight preferred stock is a perpetual security paying a fixed dividend. However, the dividend can be omitted by the issuing firm if its financial condition deteriorates. For these reasons, we do not usually think of preferred stock as being suitable for the marketable security portfolio of a corporation. However, the corporate investor gains a considerable tax advantage, in that generally 70 percent of the preferred stock dividend is exempt from federal taxation. (The full dividend is subject to state income taxes.)

Money market preferred stock (MMP) Preferred stock having a dividend rate that is reset at auction every 49 days.

This tax advantage, together with regulatory changes, prompted the innovation of various floating-rate preferred stock products. One of the largest in use today is **money market preferred stock (MMP).** With MMP, an auction is held every 49 days, a period that is beyond the minimum holding period required for a corporate investor to benefit from the federal corporate dividend tax exclusion. The auction process provides the investor with liquidity and relative price stability. It does not protect the investor against default risk. The new auction rate is set by the forces of supply and demand in keeping with interest rates in the money market. Corporations already holding MMPs on auction day have three options. They can (1) rebid, (2) enter a sell order, or (3) enter a hold order, in which case they retain their shares, which yield the new rate.

In a failed auction where there is an insufficient number of bidders, a default dividend rate for one period at 110 percent of the commercial paper rate, together with an option to the holder to have the instrument redeemed at its face value, usually applies. These provisions protect the investor only so long as the issuing corporation is solvent and can provide the required cash flows to the investor. To date, there have been only a few instances of failed auctions and defaults.

Selecting Securities for the Portfolio Segments

The decision to invest cash in marketable securities involves not only the amount to invest but also the type of security in which to invest. Our earlier partitioning of the firm's marketable securities portfolio into three segments helps us in making these determinations. An evaluation of the firm's expected future cash-flow patterns and the degree of uncertainty associated with them is needed to help determine the size of the securities balances to be found in each segment. For securities comprising the firm's *ready cash segment (R$)*, safety and an ability to convert quickly into cash are primary concerns. Because they are both the safest and most marketable of all money market instruments, Treasury bills make an ideal choice to meet the firm's unexpected needs for ready cash. Short-term, high-quality repos and certain highly liquid, short-term municipals can also play a role. If, for example, overnight repos are secured by Treasury securities and continually rolled over (reinvested into other repos), funds can remain invested while providing continuing liquidity and safety of principal.

The second segment of the firm's securities portfolio, the *controllable cash segment (C$)*, holds securities earmarked for meeting controllable (knowable) outflows, such as payroll, payables, taxes, and dividends. Here the presumption is that the required conversion date to cash is known (or, at least, can be forecast to fall within very narrow limits). Thus, securities in this segment would not necessarily have to meet the same strict requirement for immediate marketability as those in the ready cash segment. The portfolio manager may attempt to choose securities whose maturities more accurately coincide with particular known cash needs—like a quarterly dividend payment or a large bill due on the 15th of the month. For this segment, federal agency issues, CDs, commercial paper, repos, bankers' acceptances, Eurodollar deposits, and MMPs would warrant consideration. Also, though safety and marketability would still be important issues of concern, the portfolio manager would place more emphasis on the yield of the securities in this segment than would be placed on securities in the ready cash segment.

Finally, for securities forming the firm's *free cash segment (F$)* of its securities portfolio, the date of needed conversion into cash is not known in advance—just like for the ready cash segment—but there is no overriding need for quick conversion. The portfolio manager may feel that yield is the most important characteristic of securities to be considered for this segment. Higher yields can generally be achieved by investing in longer-term, less marketable securities with greater default risk. Although the firm should always be concerned with marketability, some possibility of loss of principal is tolerable, provided the expected return is high enough. Thus, in this segment (as in the other two), the firm faces the familiar trade-off between risk

FIGURE 9-5
Determination of the Firm's Portfolio of Short-Term Marketable Securities

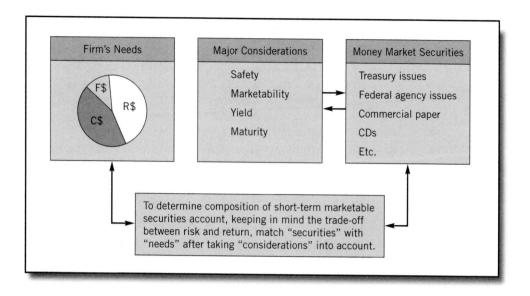

and return. (See Fig. 9-5 for a summary of our approach to determining the firm's portfolio of short-term marketable securities.)

Portfolio Management. The larger the firm's short-term marketable securities portfolio, the more chance there is for specialization and economies of scale in its operation. A large security portfolio may justify a staff solely responsible for managing it. Such a staff can undertake research, plan diversification, keep abreast of market conditions, and continually analyze and improve the firm's portfolio position. When portfolio management is a specialized function in a firm, it is likely that a large number of diverse securities will be considered for investment. Moreover, continual effort can be devoted to achieving the highest yield possible in keeping with the cash needs and the safety, marketability, and maturity requirements of the firm. For companies with modest security positions, there may be no economic justification for a separate staff. Indeed, a single individual may handle investments on a part-time basis. Alternatively, part or all of the portfolio management function may be outsourced.

Money Market Mutual Funds. Because of transactions costs and the large minimum cash amounts needed to purchase some of the higher-yielding marketable securities, the small firm has often felt that holding a short-term marketable securities portfolio was out of the question. In the early 1970s the creation of **money market mutual funds (MMFs)** made it possible for even small firms (and individuals) to hold a well-diversified portfolio of marketable securities. Money market funds sell shares to raise cash, and by pooling the funds of a large number of small investors they can invest in large-denomination money market instruments. Unlike other mutual funds, money market funds declare daily dividends (which for tax purposes are treated like interest income), which may be reinvested automatically or withdrawn in cash. Many of these funds allow an account to be started with as little as a $500 initial investment. Most of these funds have a check-writing privilege, usually with a stated check minimum. Money market funds thus provide many small firms with greater liquidity, diversification, and yield (net of expenses) than they could possibly obtain by managing their own marketable securities portfolio.

Money market mutual funds (MMFs) Mutual funds that utilize pools of investors' funds to invest in large-denomination money market instruments.

SUMMARY

- Firms, as well as individuals, hold cash to meet transactions, as well as for speculative and precautionary motives.
- Cash management involves the efficient collection and disbursement of cash and any temporary investment of cash while it resides with the firm.
- The firm will generally benefit by "speeding up" cash receipts and "s-l-o-w-i-n-g d-o-w-n" cash payouts. The firm wants to speed up the collection of accounts receivable so that it can have the use of money sooner. It wants to pay accounts payable as late as is consistent with maintaining the firm's credit standing with suppliers so that it can make the most use of the money it already has.
- To accelerate collections, the firm may utilize a number of methods, including computerized billing, preauthorized debits, and lockboxes.
- Large firms are likely to engage in the process of *cash concentration* to improve control over corporate cash, reduce idle cash balances, and provide for more effective short-term investing.
- The concentration process depends on three principal methods to move funds between banks: (1) *depository transfer checks (DTCs)*, (2) *automated clearinghouse (ACH) transfers*, and (3) *wire transfers*.
- Methods used by corporations to control disbursements include the use of *payable through drafts (PTDs)*, the maintenance of separate disbursement accounts, *zero balance accounts (ZBAs)*, and *controlled* (or possibly *remote*) *disbursing*.
- *Electronic data interchange (EDI)*, and two of its subsets, *electronic funds transfer (EFT)* and *financial EDI (FEDI)*, are all key elements of *electronic commerce (EC)*.
- All the major areas of cash management—collections, disbursements, and marketable-securities management—are candidates for *outsourcing*.
- The optimal level of cash should be the larger of (1) the transactions balances required when cash management is efficient or (2) the compensating balance requirements of commercial banks with which the firm has deposit accounts.
- It is useful to think of the firm's portfolio of short-term marketable securities as if it were a pie cut into three (not necessarily equal) pieces:
  1. *Ready cash segment (R$):* optimal balance of marketable securities held to take care of probable deficiencies in the firm's cash account.
  2. *Controllable cash segment (C$):* marketable securities held for meeting controllable (knowable) outflows, such as taxes and dividends.
  3. *Free cash segment (F$):* "free" marketable securities (i.e., available for as yet unassigned purposes).
- When considering the purchase of marketable securities, the firm's portfolio manager must understand how each potential security relates to *safety* of principal, *marketability*, *yield*, and *maturity*.
- The firm's marketable securities portfolio manager usually restricts purchases to *money market instruments*. Common money market instruments include *Treasury securities, repurchase agreements, federal agency securities, bankers' acceptances (BAs), commercial paper, negotiable certificates of deposit (CDs), Eurodollars, short-term municipals*, and *money market preferred stock (MMP)*.
- In selecting securities for the various marketable securities portfolio segments (R$, C$, and F$), the portfolio manager tries to match alternative money market instruments with the specific needs relating to each segment, after taking into account such considerations as safety, marketability, yield, and maturity. In short, the composition of the firm's short-term marketable securities account is determined while keeping in mind the trade-off that exists between risk and return.
- *Money market mutual funds (MMFs)* make it possible for even small firms (and individuals) to hold a well-diversified portfolio of marketable securities.

QUESTIONS

1. Define the function of *cash management*.
2. Explain the concept of *concentration banking*.
3. Explain how the *lockbox system* can improve the efficiency of cash management.
4. Money market instruments are used as investment vehicles for otherwise idle cash. Discuss the most important criterion for asset selection in investing temporarily idle cash.

5. Discuss the impact of *lockbox banking* on corporate cash balances.
6. A firm desires to maintain a certain portion of its marketable securities portfolio to meet unforeseen cash needs. Would *commercial paper* or *Treasury bills* be better suited as short-term investments in this *ready cash segment*? Why?
7. What are *compensating bank balances,* and why are they not the same for all depositors?
8. What is *net float?* How might a company "play the float" in its disbursements?
9. Assuming that the return on real assets of a company exceeds the return on marketable securities, why should a company hold any marketable securities?
10. Under what conditions would it be possible for a company to hold no cash or marketable securities? Are these conditions realistic?
11. What are the three motives for holding cash?
12. Compare and contrast *bankers' acceptances* and *Treasury bills* as marketable security investments for the corporation.
13. Compare and contrast *electronic commerce (EC), electronic data interchange (EDI), electronic funds transfer (EFT),* and *financial EDI (FEDI).*
14. What is *outsourcing?* Why might a company *outsource* some or all of its cash management processes?

SELF-CORRECTION PROBLEMS

1. The Zindler Company currently has a centralized billing system. Payments are made by all customers to the central billing location. It requires, on the average, four days for customers' mailed payments to reach the central location. An additional day and a half is required to process payments before a deposit can be made. The firm has a daily average collection of $500,000. The company has recently investigated the possibility of initiating a lockbox system. It has estimated that with such a system customers' mailed payments would reach the receipt location two and one-half days sooner. Further, the processing time could be reduced by an additional day because each lockbox bank would pick up mailed deposits twice daily.
   a. Determine how much cash would be freed up (released) through the use of a lockbox system.
   b. Determine the annual gross dollar benefit of the lockbox system, assuming the firm could earn a 5 percent return on the released funds in Part(a) by investing in short-term instruments.
   c. If the annual cost of the lockbox system will be $75,000, should such a system be initiated?

2. Over the next year, El Pedro Steel Company, a California corporation, expects the following returns on continual investment in the following marketable securities:

Treasury bills	8.00%
Commercial paper	8.50%
Money market preferred stock	7.00%

The company's marginal tax rate for federal income tax purposes is 30 percent (after allowance for the payment of state income taxes), and its marginal, incremental tax rate with respect to California income taxes is 7 percent. On the basis of after-tax returns, which is the most attractive investment? Are there other considerations?

PROBLEMS

1. Speedway Owl Company franchises "Gas and Go" stations in North Carolina and Virginia. All payments by franchisees for gasoline and oil products, which average $420,000 a day, are by check. Presently, the overall time between the mailing of the check by the franchisee to Speedway Owl and the time the company has collected or available funds at its bank is six days.
   a. How much money is tied up in this interval of time?
   b. To reduce this delay, the company is considering daily pickups from the stations. In all, three cars would be needed and three additional people hired. This daily pickup would cost $93,000 on an annual basis, and it would reduce the overall delay by two days. Currently, the opportunity cost of funds is 9 percent, that being the interest rate on marketable securities. Should the company inaugurate the pickup plan? Why?
   c. Rather than mail checks to its bank, the company could deliver them by messenger service. This procedure would reduce the overall delay by one day and cost $10,300 annually. Should the company undertake this plan? Why?

2. The List Company, which can earn 7 percent on money market instruments, currently has a lockbox arrangement with a New Orleans bank for its Southern customers. The bank handles $3 million a day in return for a compensating balance of $2 million.
   a. The List Company has discovered that it could divide the Southern region into a southwestern region (with $1 million a day in collections, which could be handled by a Dallas bank for a $1 million compensating balance) and a southeastern region (with $2 million a day in collections, which could be handled by an Atlanta bank by a $2 million compensating balance). In each case, collections would be one-half day quicker than with the New Orleans arrangement. What would be the annual savings (or cost) of dividing the Southern region?
   b. In an effort to retain the business, the New Orleans bank has offered to handle the collections strictly on a fee basis (no compensating balance). What would be the maximum fee the New Orleans bank could charge and still retain List's business?

3. The Franzini Food Company has a weekly payroll of $150,000 paid on Friday. On average, its employees cash their checks in the following manner:

DAY CHECK CLEARED ON COMPANY'S ACCOUNT	PERCENTAGE OF CHECKS CASHED
Friday	20
Monday	40
Tuesday	25
Wednesday	10
Thursday	5

As treasurer of the company, how would you arrange your payroll account? Are there any problems?

4. Sitmore and Dolittle, Inc., has 41 retail clothing outlets scattered throughout the country. Each outlet sends an average of $5,000 daily to the head office in South Bend, Indiana, through checks drawn on local banks. On average, it takes six days before the company's South Bend bank collects the checks. Sitmore and Dolittle is considering an electronic funds transfer arrangement that would completely eliminate the float.

a. What amount of funds will be released?

b. What amount will be released on a net basis if each local bank requires an increase in compensating balances of $15,000 to offset the loss of float?

c. Suppose that the company could earn 10 percent interest on the net released funds in Part (b). If the cost per electronic transfer were $7 and each store averaged 250 transfers per year, would the proposed arrangement be worthwhile? (Assume that the cost of issuing checks on local banks is negligible.)

5. In the *Wall Street Journal,* or some other financial paper, determine in the money-rate section the rate of interest on Treasury bills, commercial paper, certificates of deposit, and bankers' acceptances. Do the differentials in return have to do with marketability and default risk? If you were a corporate treasurer of a company with considerable business risk, in what security or securities would you invest? How would you arrange the maturities?

SOLUTIONS TO SELF-CORRECTION PROBLEMS

1. a.   Total time savings = 2.5 + 1 = **3.5 days**

$$\text{Time savings} \times \text{daily average collection} = \text{cash released}$$
$$3.5 \quad \times \quad \$500{,}000 \quad = \quad \$1{,}750{,}000$$

b. 5% × $1,750,000 = $87,500

c. Since the dollar gross benefit of the lockbox system ($87,500) exceeds the annual cost of the lockbox system ($75,000), the system should be initiated.

2.

SECURITY	FEDERAL TAX RATE	STATE TAX RATE	COMBINED EFFECT	AFTER-TAX EXPECTED RETURN
Treasury bills	.30	.00	.30	(1 − .30)8.00% = 5.60%
Commercial paper	.30	.07	.37	(1 − .37)8.50% = 5.36%
Money market preferred stock	.09*	.07	.16	(1 − .16)7.00% = 5.88%

*(1 − .70)(.30) = .09.

The money market preferred is the most attractive after taxes, owing to the 70 percent exemption for federal income tax purposes. Commercial paper is less attractive than Treasury bills because of the state income tax from which Treasury bills are exempt. (In states with no income taxes, the after-tax yield on commercial paper would be higher.)

Preferred stock may not be the most attractive investment when risk is taken into account. There is the danger that interest rates will rise above the ceiling and the market value will fall. There also is default risk with respect to dividend payment, whereas Treasury bills have no default risk.

SELECTED REFERENCES

Adam, Peter S., and William A. Harrison, eds. *Essentials of Cash Management,* 6th ed. Bethesda, MD: Treasury Management Association, 1998.

Arvizu, Benjamin. "Using Your Bank as a Cash Management Tool." *The Small Business Controller* 4 (Summer 1991), 42–47.

Batlin, C. A., and Susan Hinko. "Lockbox Management and Value Maximization." *Financial Management* 10 (Winter 1981), 39–44.

Bort, Richard. "Lockboxes: The Original Outsource." *The Small Business Controller* 8 (Fall 1995), 44–47.

————. "What Every Financial Manager Needs to Know About Controlled Disbursing." *The Small Business Controller* 9 (Winter 1996), 47–50.

Gitman, Lawrence J., D. Keith Forrester, and John R. Forrester Jr. "Maximizing Cash Disbursement Float." *Financial Management* 5 (Summer 1976), 15–24.

Hahn, Thomas K. "Commercial Paper." Federal Reserve Bank of Richmond *Economic Quarterly* 79 (Spring 1993), 45–67.

Hill, Ned C., and William L. Sartoris. *Short-Term Financial Management,* 3rd ed. Englewood Cliffs, NJ: Prentice Hall, 1995.

Kamath, Ravindra R., Shahriar Khaksari, Heidi Hylton Meier, and John Winkleplectk. "Management of Excess Cash: Practices and Developments." *Financial Management* 14 (Autumn 1985), 70–77.

Kim, Chang-Soo, David C. Mauer, and Ann E. Sherman. "The Determinants of Corporate Liquidity: Theory and Evidence." *Journal of Financial and Quantitative Analysis* 33 (September 1998), 335–59.

Lacker, Jeffrey M. "The Check Float Puzzle." *Economic Quarterly of the Federal Reserve Bank of Richmond* 83 (Summer 1997), 1–25.

Maier, Steven F., and James H. Vander Weide. "What Lockbox and Disbursement Models Really Do." *Journal of Finance* 38 (May 1983), 361–71.

Maness, Terry S., and John T. Zietlow. *Short-Term Financial Management.* Fort Worth, TX: Dryden Press, 1998.

Miller, Merton H., and Daniel Orr. "The Demand for Money by Firms: Extension of Analytic Results." *Journal of Finance* 23 (December 1968), 735–59.

Moss, James D. "Campbell Soup's Cutting-Edge Cash Management." *Financial Executive* 8 (September/October 1992), 39–42.

Nauss, Robert M., and Robert E. Markland. "Solving Lock Box Location Problems." *Financial Management* 8 (Spring 1979), 21–31.

Phillips, Aaron L. "Migration of Corporate Payments from Check to Electronic Format: A Report on the Current Status of Payments." *Financial Management* 27 (Winter 1998), 92–105.

Ricci, Cecilia W., and Gail Morrison. "International Working Capital Practices of the Fortune 200." *Financial Practice and Education* 6 (Fall/Winter 1996), 7–20.

Stancill, James M. *The Management of Working Capital.* Scranton, PA: Intext Educational Publishers, 1971.

Stone, Bernell K. "Design of a Receivable Collection System." *Management Science* 27 (August 1981), 866–80.

————. "The Design of a Company's Banking System." *Journal of Finance* 38 (May 1983), 373–85.

————. "Corporate Trade Payments: Hard Lessons in Product Design." *Economic Review of Fed of Atlanta* 71 (April 1986), 9–21.

————, and Ned C. Hill. "Cash Transfer Scheduling for Efficient Cash Concentration." *Financial Management* 9 (Autumn 1980), 35–43.

U.S. Treasury Securities Cash Market. Chicago: Chicago Board of Trade, 1998.

Van Horne, James C. *Financial Market Rates and Flows,* 6th ed. Upper Saddle River, NJ: Prentice Hall, 2001.

Chapter 10

Accounts Receivable and Inventory Management

CREDIT AND COLLECTION POLICIES
   Credit Standards • Credit Terms • Default Risk • Collection Policy and Procedures • Credit and Collection Policies—Summary
ANALYZING THE CREDIT APPLICANT
   Sources of Information • Credit Analysis • Credit Decision and Line of Credit • Outsourcing Credit and Collections
INVENTORY MANAGEMENT AND CONTROL
   Classification: What to Control? • Economic Order Quantity: How Much to Order? • Order Point: When to Order? • Safety Stock • Just-in-Time • Inventory and the Financial Manager
SUMMARY
QUESTIONS
SELF-CORRECTION PROBLEMS
PROBLEMS
SOLUTIONS TO SELF-CORRECTION PROBLEMS
SELECTED REFERENCES

IN GOD WE TRUST. All others must pay cash.

—ANONYMOUS

Accounts receivable
Amounts of money owed to a firm by customers who have bought goods or services on credit. A current asset, the accounts receivable account is also called *receivables*.

In Chapter 8, we saw that the investment of funds in **accounts receivable** involves a trade-off between profitability and risk. The optimum investment is determined by comparing benefits to be derived from a particular level of investment with the costs of maintaining that level. This chapter will reveal the key variables involved in managing receivables efficiently, and it will show how these variables can be changed to obtain the optimal investment. We consider first the credit and collection policies of the firm as a whole and then discuss credit and collection procedures for the individual account. The last part of the chapter investigates techniques for efficiently managing the final major current asset account for the typical firm—inventories.

CREDIT AND COLLECTION POLICIES

Credit standard The minimum quality of creditworthiness of a credit applicant that is acceptable to the firm.

Economic conditions, product pricing, product quality, and the firm's credit policies are the chief influences on the level of a firm's accounts receivable. All but the last of these influences are largely beyond the control of the financial manager. As with other current assets, however, the manager can vary the level of receivables in keeping with the trade-off between profitability and risk. Lowering **credit standards** may stimulate demand, which, in turn, should lead to higher sales and profits. But there is a cost to carrying the additional receivables, as well as a greater risk of bad-debt losses. It is this trade-off that we wish to examine.

The policy variables we consider include the quality of the trade accounts accepted, the length of the credit period, the cash discount (if any) for early payment, and the collection program of the firm. Together, these elements largely determine the *average collection period* and the proportion of credit sales that result in bad-debt losses. We analyze each element in turn, holding constant certain of the others as well as all external variables that affect the average collection period and the ratio of bad debts to credit sales. In addition, we assume that the evaluation of risk is sufficiently standardized so that degrees of risk for different accounts can be compared objectively.

Credit and Collection Policy Formulation—Done Right—Helps Break Down Barriers Between Marketing and Finance

Credit and collection policies share a relationship with marketing (sales and customer service) policies. For example, processing credit orders efficiently affects sales and customer satisfaction. In fact, it is useful to think of a company's credit and collection policies as part of the product or service that a business is selling. Therefore, the marketing manager and financial manager should actively cooperate in developing credit and collection policies. Usually, the financial manager is subsequently responsible for carrying out these policies. However, permanent, cross-functional teams involving finance and marketing personnel are becoming quite common—especially when it comes to implementing collection policies.

Credit Standards

Credit policy can have a significant influence on sales. If our competitors extend credit liberally and we do not, our policy may have a dampening effect on our firm's marketing effort. Credit is one of the many factors that influence the demand for a firm's product. Consequently, the degree to which credit can promote demand depends on what other factors are being employed. In theory, the firm should lower its quality standard for accounts accepted as long as the profitability of sales generated exceeds the added costs of the receivables. What are the costs of relaxing credit standards? Some arise from an enlarged credit department, the clerical work involved in checking additional accounts, and servicing the added volume of receivables. We assume that these costs are deducted from the profitability of additional sales to give a net profitability figure for computational purposes. Another cost comes from the increased probability of bad-debt losses. We postpone consideration of this cost to a subsequent section and assume, for now, that there are no bad-debt losses.

Finally, there is the *opportunity cost* of committing funds to the investment in additional receivables instead of to some other investment. The additional receivables result from (1) increased sales and (2) a longer average collection period. If new customers are attracted by the relaxed credit standards, collecting from these less-creditworthy customers is likely to be slower than collecting from existing customers. In addition, a more liberal extension of credit may cause certain existing customers to be less conscientious about paying their bills on time.

An Example of the Trade-off.   To assess the profitability of a more liberal extension of credit, we must know the profitability of additional sales, the added demand for products arising from the relaxed credit standards, the increased length of the average collection period, and the required return on investment. Suppose that a firm's product sells for $10 a unit, of which $8 represents variable costs before taxes, including credit department costs. The firm is operating at less than full capacity, and an increase in sales can be accommodated without any increase in fixed costs. Therefore, the *contribution margin per unit* for each additional unit sold is the selling price less variable costs involved in producing an additional unit, or $10 − $8 = **$2.**

Presently, annual credit sales are running at a level of $2.4 million, and there is no underlying growth trend in such credit sales. The firm may liberalize credit, which will result in an average collection period of two months for new customers. Existing customers are not expected to alter their payment habits. The relaxation in credit standards is expected to produce a 25 percent increase in sales, to $3 million annually. The $600,000 increase represents 60,000 additional units if we assume that the price per unit stays the same. Finally, assume that the firm's opportunity cost of carrying the additional receivables is 20 percent before taxes.

This information reduces our evaluation to a trade-off between the added expected profitability on the additional sales and the opportunity cost of the increased investment in receivables. The increased investment arises solely from new, slower-paying customers. We have assumed that existing customers continue to pay in 1 month. With additional sales of $600,000 and a receivable turnover of six times a year for new customers (12 months divided by the average collection period of 2 months), the additional receivables are $600,000/6 = **$100,000.** For these additional receivables, the firm invests the variable costs tied up in them. For our example, $.80 of every $1 in sales represents variable costs. Therefore, the added investment in receivables is .80 × $100,000 = **$80,000.** With these inputs, we are able to make the calculations shown in Table 10-1. Inasmuch as the profitability on additional sales, $2 × 60,000 = **$120,000,** far exceeds the required return on the additional investment in receivables, .20 × $80,000 = **$16,000,** the firm would be well advised to relax its credit standards. An optimal policy would involve extending credit more liberally until the marginal profitability on additional sales equals the required return on the additional investment in receivables necessary to generate those sales. However, as we take on poorer credit risks, we also increase the risk of the firm, as

TABLE 10-1
Profitability versus
required return in
evaluating a credit
standard change

Profitability of additional sales	= (Contribution margin per unit) × (Additional units sold) $2 × 60,000 units = **$120,000**
Additional receivables	= (Additional sales revenue)/(Receivable turnover for new customers) $600,000/6 = **$100,000**
Investment in additional receivables	= (Variable cost per unit/Sales price per unit) × (Additional receivables) .80 × $100,000 = **$80,000**
Required before-tax return on additional investment	= (Opportunity cost) × (Investment in additional receivables) .20 × $80,000 = **$16,000**

reflected in the variance of the firm's expected cash-flow stream. This increase in risk also manifests itself in additional bad-debt losses, a subject we deal with shortly.

Credit Terms

Credit Period. *Credit terms* specify the length of time over which credit is extended to a customer and the discount, if any, given for early payment. For example, one firm's credit terms might be expressed as "2/10, net 30." The term "2/10" means that a 2 percent discount is given if the bill is paid within 10 days of the invoice date. The term "net 30" implies that if a discount is not taken, the full payment is due by the 30th day from invoice date. Thus, the **credit period** is 30 days. Although the customs of the industry frequently dictate the credit terms given, the credit period is another means by which a firm may be able to increase product demand. As before, the trade-off is between the profitability of additional sales and the required return on the additional investment in receivables.

Credit period The total length of time over which credit is extended to a customer to pay a bill.

Let us say that the firm in our example changes its credit terms from "net 30" to "net 60"—thus increasing its credit period from 30 to 60 days. The average collection period for existing customers goes from one month to two months. The more liberal credit period results in increased sales of $360,000, and these new customers also pay, on average, in two months. The total additional receivables are composed of two parts. The first part represents the receivables associated with the increased sales. In our example, there are $360,000 in additional sales. With a new receivable turnover of six times a year, the additional receivables associated with the new sales are $360,000/6 = **$60,000.** For these additional receivables, the investment by the firm consists of the variable costs tied up in them. For our example, we have ($8/$10) × ($60,000) = **$48,000.**

The second part of the total additional receivables is caused by the slowing in collections associated with sales to original customers. Receivables due from original customers are now collected in a slower manner resulting in a higher receivable level. With $2.4 million in original sales, the level of receivables with a turnover of 12 times a year is $2,400,000/12 = **$200,000.** The new level with a turnover of 6 times a year is $2,400,000/6 = **$400,000.** Thus, there are $200,000 in additional receivables associated with sales to original customers. For this addition, the relevant investment using marginal analysis is the full $200,000. *In other words, the use of variable costs tied* *up in receivables pertains only to new sales.* The incremental $200,000 in receivables related to sales to original customers would have been collected in cash had it not been for the change in credit period. Therefore, the firm must increase its investment in receivables by $200,000.[1]

Based on these inputs, our calculations are shown in Table 10-2. The appropriate comparison is the profitability of additional sales with the opportunity cost of the additional investment in receivables. Inasmuch as the profitability on additional sales, $72,000, exceeds the required return on the investment in additional receivables, $49,600, the change in credit period from 30 to 60 days is worthwhile. The profitability of the additional sales more than offsets the opportunity cost associated with the added investment in receivables. The bulk of this added investment in receivables comes from existing customers slowing their payments.

Cash discount period
The period of time during which a cash discount can be taken for early payment.

Cash Discount Period and Cash Discount. The **cash discount period** represents the period of time during which a cash discount can be taken for early payment. Though technically a credit policy variable, like the credit period, it usually stays at

---

[1]For the first 30 days after the credit period change, original customers will be paying bills incurred before the change in credit policy. Since sales to original customers remain unchanged, the level of receivables related to original customers remains unchanged. During the next 30 days, however, no payments from these customers will be received as they will now wait to pay until 60 days have passed. Receivables will build up until, at the end of 60 days from the policy change, we have double the level of receivables that we began with. Thus, the firm is left *without* one month's worth of receipts from original customers ($200,000 less cash than would have flowed in without the change in policy) and *with* $200,000 more in receivables on the books.

TABLE 10-2
Profitability versus required return in evaluating a credit period change

Profitability of additional sales	= (Contribution margin per unit) × (Additional units sold) $2 × 36,000 units = **$72,000**
Additional receivables associated with new sales	= (New sales revenue)/(New receivable turnover) $360,000/6 = **$60,000**
Investment in additional receivables associated with new sales	= (Variable cost per unit/Sales price per unit) × (Additional receivables) .80 × $60,000 = **$48,000**
Level of receivables before credit period change	= (Annual credit sales)/(Old receivable turnover) $2,400,000/12 = **$200,000**
New level of receivables associated with original sales	= (Annual credit sales)/(New receivable turnover) $2,400,000/6 = **$400,000**
Investment in additional receivables associated with original sales	= $400,000 − $200,000 = **$200,000**
Total investment in additional receivables	= $48,000 + $200,000 = **$248,000**
Required before-tax return on additional investment	= (Opportunity cost) × (Total investment in additional receivables) .20 × $248,000 = **$49,600**

some standard length. For many firms, 10 days is about the minimum time they could expect between when an invoice is mailed to the customer and when the customer could put a check in the mail.

Cash discount A percent (%) reduction in sales or purchase price allowed for early payment of invoices. It is an incentive for credit customers to pay invoices in a timely fashion.

Varying the **cash discount** involves an attempt to speed up the payment of receivables. Here we must determine whether a speedup in collections would more than offset the cost of an increase in the discount. If it would, the present discount policy should be changed. Suppose that the firm has annual credit sales of $3 million and an average collection period of two months. Also, assume that sales terms are "net 45," with no cash discount given. Consequently, the average receivables balance is $3,000,000/6 = **$500,000.** By initiating terms of "2/10, net 45," the average collection period can be reduced to one month, as 60 percent of the customers (in dollar volume) take advantage of the 2 percent discount. The opportunity cost of the discount to the firm is .02 × .6 × $3 million, or **$36,000** annually. The turnover of receivables has improved to 12 times a year, so that average receivables are reduced from $500,000 to $250,000 (i.e., $3,000,000/12 = **$250,000**).

Thus, the firm realizes $250,000 from accelerated collections. The value of the funds released is their opportunity cost. If we assume a 20 percent before-tax rate of return, the opportunity saving is $50,000. (See Table 10-3 for step-by-step calculations.) In this case the opportunity saving arising from a speedup in collections is greater than the cost of the discount. The firm should adopt a 2 percent discount. If the speedup in collections had not resulted in sufficient opportunity savings to offset the cost of the cash discount, the discount policy would not be changed. It is possible, of course, that discounts other than 2 percent may result in an even greater difference between the opportunity saving and the cost of the discount.

Seasonal dating Credit terms that encourage the buyer of seasonal products to take delivery before the peak sales period and to defer payment until after the peak sales period.

Seasonal Datings. During periods of slack sales, firms will sometimes sell to customers without requiring payment for some time to come. This **seasonal dating** can be tailored to the cash flow of the customer and may stimulate demand from customers who cannot pay until later in the season. Again, we should compare the profitability of

TABLE 10-3
Cost versus savings in evaluating a cash discount change

Level of receivables before cash discount change	= (Annual credit sales) / (Old receivable turnover) $3,000,000/6 = **$500,000**
New level of receivables associated with cash discount change	= (Annual credit sales) / (New receivable turnover) $3,000,000/12 = **$250,000**
Reduction of investment in accounts receivable	= (Old receivable level) − (New receivable level) $500,000 − $250,000 = **$250,000**
Before-tax cost of cash discount change	= (Cash discount) × (Percentage taking discount) × (Annual credit sales) = .02 × .60 × $3,000 = **$36,000**
Before-tax opportunity savings on reduction in receivables	= (Opportunity cost) × (Reduction in receivables) = .20 × $250,000 = **$50,000**

Part IV Working Capital Management

additional sales with the required return on the additional investment in receivables to determine whether datings are appropriate terms by which to stimulate demand.

Seasonal datings can also be used to avoid inventory carrying costs. If sales are seasonal and production is steady throughout the year, there will be buildups in finished-goods inventory during certain times of the year. Storage involves warehousing costs that might be avoided by giving datings. If warehousing costs plus the required return on investment in inventory exceed the required return on the additional receivables, datings are worthwhile.

Default Risk

In the foregoing examples we assumed no bad-debt losses. Our concern in this section is not only with the slowness of collection but also with the portion of the receivables in default. Different credit standard policies will involve both of these factors. The optimum credit standard policy, as we shall see, will not necessarily be the one that minimizes bad-debt losses.

Suppose that we are considering the present credit standard policy (resulting in sales of $2.4 million) together with two, increasingly more liberal, new ones. These alternative policies are expected to produce the following results:

	PRESENT POLICY	POLICY A	POLICY B
Demand (credit sales)	$2,400,000	$3,000,000	$3,300,000
Incremental sales		$ 600,000	$ 300,000
Default losses			
Original sales	2%		
Incremental sales		10%	18%
Average collection period			
Original sales	1 month		
Incremental sales		2 months	3 months

We assume that after six months an account is turned over to a collection agency, and, on average, 2 percent of the original sales of $2.4 million is never received by the firm, 10 percent is never received on the $600,000 in additional sales under Policy A, and 18 percent on the $300,000 in additional sales under Policy B is never received. Similarly, the one-month average collection period pertains to the original sales, two months to the $600,000 in additional sales under Policy A, and three months to the $300,000 in additional sales under Policy B. These numbers of months correspond to annual receivable turnovers of 12 times, 6 times, and 4 times, respectively.

The incremental profitability calculations associated with these two new credit standard policies are shown in Table 10-4. We would want to adopt Policy A but would not want to go as far as Policy B in relaxing our credit standards. The marginal benefit is positive in moving from the present policy to Policy A but negative in going from Policy A to Policy B. It is possible, of course, that a relaxation of credit standards that fell on one side or the other of Policy A would provide an even greater marginal benefit. The optimal policy is the one that provides the greatest incremental benefit.

Collection Policy and Procedures

The firm determines its overall collection policy by the combination of collection procedures it undertakes. These procedures include such things as letters, phone calls, personal visits, and legal action. One of the principal policy variables is the

TABLE 10-4
Profitability versus
required return in
evaluating credit pol-
icy changes

	POLICY A	POLICY B
1. Additional sales	$600,000	$300,000
2. Profitability of additional sales: (20% contribution margin) × (Additional sales)	120,000	60,000
3. Additional bad-debt losses: (Additional sales) × (Bad-debt percentage)	60,000	54,000
4. Additional receivables: (Additional sales/New receivable turnover)	100,000	75,000
5. Investment in additional receivables: (.80) × (Additional receivables)	80,000	60,000
6. Required before-tax return on additional investment: (20%)	16,000	12,000
7. Additional bad-debt losses plus additional required return: Line (3) + Line (6)	76,000	66,000
8. **Incremental profitability: Line (2) − Line (7)**	**44,000**	**(6,000)**

amount of money spent on collection procedures. Within a range, the greater the relative amount expended, the lower the proportion of bad-debt losses, and the shorter the average collection period, all other things being the same.

The relationships are not linear, however. Initial collection expenditures are likely to cause little reduction in bad-debt losses. Additional expenditures begin to have a significant effect up to a point—then they tend to have little effect in further reducing these losses. The hypothesized relationship between collection expenditures and bad-debt losses is shown in Figure 10-1. The relationship between the average collection period and the level of collection expenditure is likely to be similar to that shown in the figure.

FIGURE 10-1
Relationship
Between Amount of
Bad-Debt Losses and
Collection Expendi-
tures

If sales are independent of the collection effort, the appropriate level of collection expenditures again involves a trade-off—this time between the level of expenditure on the one hand and the reduction in the cost of bad-debt losses and savings due to the reduction in investment in receivables on the other. Calculations are the same as for the cash discount given and for default losses illustrated earlier. The reader can easily verify the trade-off.

Because a receivable is only as good as the likelihood that it will be paid, a firm cannot afford to wait too long before initiating collection procedures. On the other hand, if it initiates procedures too soon, it may anger reasonably good customers who, for some reason, fail to make payments by the due date. Whatever they are, procedures should be firmly established. Initially, a telephone call is usually made to ask why payment has not been made. Next, a letter is often sent and followed, perhaps, by additional letters that become more serious in tone. A phone call or letter from the company's attorney may then prove necessary. Some companies have collection personnel who make visits to a customer about an overdue account.

If all else fails, the account may be turned over to a collection agency. The agency's fees are quite substantial—frequently one-half the amount of the receivable—but such a procedure may be the only feasible alternative, particularly for a small account. Direct legal action is costly, sometimes serves no real purpose, and may only force the account into bankruptcy. When payments cannot be collected, compromise settlements may provide a higher percentage of collection.

Credit and Collection Policies—Summary

We see that the credit and collection policies of a firm involve several decisions: (1) the quality of the account accepted; (2) the length of the credit period; (3) the size of the cash discount given; (4) any special terms, such as seasonal datings; and (5) the level of collection expenditures. In each case, the decision should involve a comparison of possible gains from a change in policy with the cost of the change. Optimal credit and collection policies would be those that resulted in the marginal gains equaling the marginal costs.

To maximize profits arising from credit and collection policies, the firm should vary these policies jointly until it achieves an optimal solution. That solution will determine the best combination of credit standards, credit period, cash discount policy, special terms, and level of collection expenditures. For most policy variables, profits increase at a decreasing rate up to a point and then decrease as the policy is varied from no effort to an extreme effort. Figure 10-2 depicts this relationship with the quality of accounts rejected. When there are no credit standards (that is, when all credit applicants are accepted), sales are maximized, but they are offset by large bad-debt losses as well as by the opportunity cost of carrying a very large receivables position. The latter is due to a long average collection period. As credit standards are initiated and applicants rejected, revenues from sales decline, but so do the average collection period and bad-debt losses. Because the last two decline initially at a faster rate than sales, profits increase. As credit standards are increasingly tightened, sales revenue declines at an increasing rate. At the same time, the average collection period and bad-debt losses decrease at a decreasing rate. Fewer and fewer bad credit risks are eliminated. Because of the combination of these influences, total profits of the firm increase at a diminishing rate with stricter credit standards up to a point, after which they decline. The optimal policy with respect to credit standards is represented by point X in the figure. In turn, this policy determines the level of accounts receivable held by the firm.

FIGURE 10-2
Relationship of
Sales, Average Col-
lection Period, Bad-
Debt Losses, and
Profits to the Quality
of Account Rejected

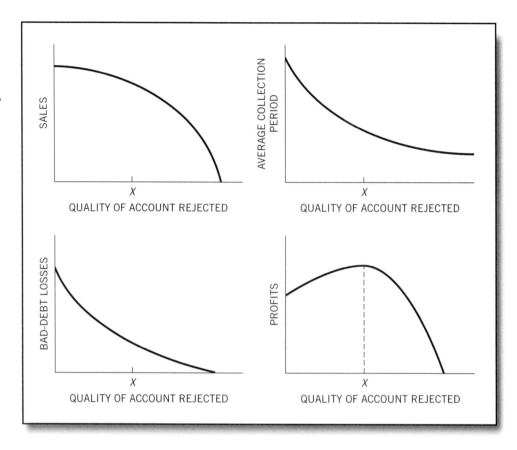

The analysis in the last several sections has purposely been rather general to provide insight into the primary concepts of credit and collection policies. Obviously, a
policy decision should be based on a far more specific evaluation than that contained
in the examples. Estimating the increased demand and increased slowness of collections that might accompany a relaxation of credit standards is difficult. Nevertheless,
management must make estimates of these relationships if it is to realistically
appraise existing policies.

ANALYZING THE CREDIT APPLICANT

Having established the terms of sale to be offered, the firm must evaluate individual
credit applicants and consider the possibilities of a bad debt or slow payment. The
credit evaluation procedure involves three related steps: (1) obtaining information
on the applicant, (2) analyzing this information to determine the applicant's creditworthiness, and (3) making the credit decision. The credit decision, in turn, establishes
whether credit should be extended and what the maximum amount of credit should be.

Sources of Information

A number of services supply credit information on businesses, but for some
accounts, especially small ones, the cost of collecting this information may outweigh
the potential profitability of the account. The firm extending credit may have to be

satisfied with a limited amount of information on which to base a decision. In addition to cost, the firm must consider the time it takes to investigate a credit applicant. A shipment to a prospective customer cannot be delayed unnecessarily pending an elaborate credit investigation. Thus, the amount of information collected needs to be considered in relation to the time and expense required. Depending on these considerations, the credit analyst may use one or more of the following sources of information.

Financial Statements. At the time of the prospective sale, the seller may request financial statements, one of the most desirable sources of information for credit analysis. Frequently, there is a correlation between a company's refusal to provide statements and a weak financial position. Audited statements are preferable. When possible, it is helpful to obtain interim statements in addition to year-end ones, particularly for companies having seasonal patterns of sales.

Credit Ratings and Reports. In addition to financial statements, credit ratings are available from various credit reporting agencies. Dun & Bradstreet (D&B) is perhaps the best known and most comprehensive of these agencies. It provides credit ratings to subscribers for a vast number of business firms. Figure 10-3 shows a D&B reference book's composite rating of "BB1" for Beaumont & Hunt, Inc., and provides a key to D&B's individual ratings. As we can see from the key to ratings, D&B ratings give the credit analyst an indication of the estimated size of net worth (labeled "estimated financial strength") and a credit appraisal for companies of a particular size, ranging from "high = 1" to "limited = 4."[2] D&B also indicates when the information available is insufficient to provide a rating for a given business. In addition to its rating service, D&B provides credit reports containing a brief history of a company and its principal officers; the nature of the business; certain financial information; and a trade check of suppliers, including the length of their experience with the company and whether payments are discount, prompt, or past due. The quality of the D&B report varies with the information available externally and the willingness of the company being checked to cooperate with the D&B reporter. The report itself can be accessed via a computer terminal if so desired.

Bank Checking. Another source of credit information for the credit analyst checking on a particular firm is the firm's bank. Most banks have credit departments that will provide information on their commercial customers as a service to those customers seeking to acquire trade credit (credit granted from one business to another). By calling or writing a bank in which the credit applicant has an account, the analyst can obtain information, such as average cash balance carried, loan accommodations, experience, and sometimes more extensive financial information. What is provided is determined by the extent of the permission given by the bank's customer. In exchanging credit information, most banks follow guidelines adopted by Robert Morris Associates (RMA), the national association of bank loan and credit officers. Both the RMA *Code of Ethics* and the *Statement of Principles* describe how to respond to requests for commercial credit information, whether they are received in writing, by telephone, or by fax.

Trade Checking. Credit information is frequently exchanged among companies selling to the same customer. Through various credit organizations, credit people in a particular area become a closely knit group. A company can ask other suppliers about their experiences with an account.

---

[2]The two letters, BB, in Beaumont & Hunt's "BB1" rating indicate that the company's net worth falls between $200,000 and $300,000. The number 1 following BB indicates that the firm has a "high" composite credit appraisal relative to other firms with a similar level of net worth.

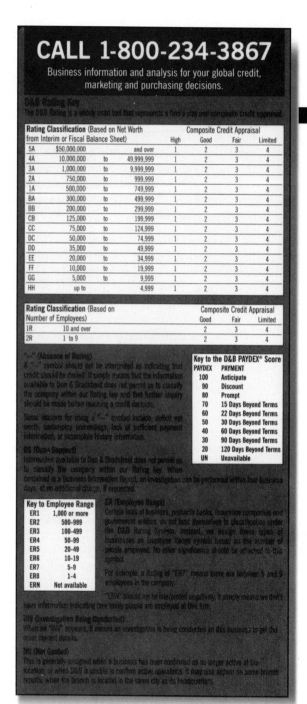

17	61	Asendorf Tin Shop	FF2
76	22	Austen Wes TV Service	EE2
55	41	Backers Service Station	HH2
57	12	Barber Furniture Co Inc.	CC1
50	13	Beasleys Automotive	FF4
53	**11**	**Beaumont & Hunt, Inc.**	**BB1**
59	41	Bedlans Sporting Goods	DC3
51	91	Bervin Distrg Inc of Beatrice	— —
51	91	Bervin Distributing Inc.	CC2
15	21	Blackwell Trenching Service	DD2
15	21	Boeckner Brothers Inc.	DC2
54	14	Boogaarts Fairbury Inc.	

FIGURE 10-3
Dun & Bradstreet Composite Rating from
a Reference Book and a Key to Ratings
Reprinted by permission, Dun & Bradstreet,
a company of The Dun & Bradstreet Corporation, 1998

The Company's Own Experience. A study of the promptness of past payments, including any seasonal patterns, is very useful. Frequently, the credit department will make written assessments of the quality of the management of a company to whom credit may be extended. These assessments are very important, for they pertain to the original "three Cs" of credit analysis: *character* (creditor's willingness to honor obligations), *capacity* (creditor's ability to generate cash to meet obligations), and *capital* (creditor's net worth and the relationship of net worth to debt). The person who made the sale to a prospective customer can frequently offer useful impressions of management and operations. Caution is necessary in interpreting this information because a salesperson has a natural bias toward granting credit and making the sale.

Credit Analysis

Having collected credit information, the firm must make a credit analysis of the applicant. In practice, the collection of information and its analysis are closely related. If, on the basis of initial credit information, a large account appears to be relatively risky, the credit analyst will want to obtain further information. Presumably, the expected value of the additional information will exceed the cost of acquiring it. Given the financial statements of a credit applicant, the credit analyst should undertake a ratio analysis, as described in Chapter 6. The analyst will be particularly interested in the applicant's liquidity and ability to pay bills on time. Such ratios as the quick ratio, receivable and inventory turnovers, the average payable period, and debt-to-equity ratio are particularly relevant.

In addition to analyzing financial statements, the credit analyst will consider the character of the company and its management, the financial strength of the firm, and various other matters. Then the analyst attempts to determine the ability of the applicant to service credit and the probability of an applicant's not paying on time and of a bad-debt loss. On the basis of this information, together with information about the profit margin on the product or service being sold, a decision is reached on whether or not to extend credit.

Sequential Investigation Process. The amount of information collected should be determined in relation to the expected profit from an order and the cost of investigation. More sophisticated analysis should be undertaken only when there is a chance that a credit decision based on the previous stage of investigation will be changed. If an analysis of a Dun & Bradstreet report resulted in an extremely unfavorable picture of the applicant, an investigation of the applicant's bank and trade suppliers might have little prospect of changing the reject decision. Therefore, the added cost associated with this stage of investigation would not be worthwhile. Each incremental stage of investigation has a cost, which can be justified only if the information obtained has value in changing a prior decision.[3]

Figure 10-4 is a flowchart example of a sequential approach to credit analysis. The first stage consists of simply consulting past experience to see if the firm has sold previously to the account and if it has, whether that experience has been satisfactory. Stage two might involve ordering a Dun & Bradstreet report on the applicant and evaluating it. The third and last stage could be credit checks of the applicant's bank and creditors—coupled, perhaps, with a financial statement analysis. Each stage adds to the cost. The expected profit from accepting an order will depend on the size of the order, as will the opportunity cost associated with its rejection. Rather than perform all stages of investigation regardless of the size of the order and the firm's past experience, the firm should investigate in stages and go to a new stage only when the expected net benefits of the additional information exceed the cost of acquiring it. When past experience has been favorable, there may be little need for further investigation. In general, the riskier the applicant, the greater the desire for

---

[3]For such an analysis, see Dileep Mehta, "The Formulation of Credit Policy Models." *Management Science* 15 (October 1968), 35–50.

FIGURE 10-4
Sequential Investigation Process: Who Should We Accept as a Credit Customer?

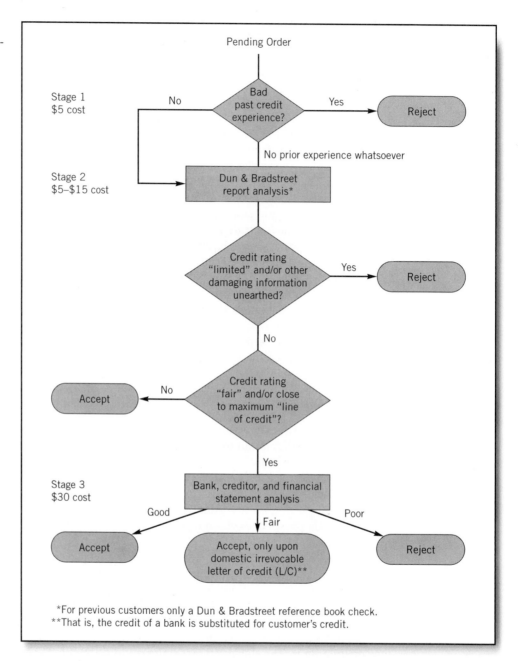

*For previous customers only a Dun & Bradstreet reference book check.
**That is, the credit of a bank is substituted for customer's credit.

more information. By balancing the costs of information with the likely profitability of the order, as well as with information from the next stage of investigation, added sophistication is introduced only when it is beneficial.

Credit-Scoring Systems. Quantitative approaches have been developed to estimate the ability of businesses to service credit granted to them; however, the final decision for most companies extending *trade credit* (credit granted from one business to another) rests on the credit analyst's judgment in evaluating available information. Strictly numerical evaluations have been successful in determining the granting of credit to retail customers (*consumer credit*), where various characteristics of an individual are quantitatively rated and a credit decision is made on the basis of the total score. The plastic credit cards many of us hold are often given out on the basis of a **credit-scoring system** in which such things as occupation, duration of employment, home ownership, years of residence, and annual income are taken into account. Numerical rating systems are also being used by some companies extending trade credit. With the overall growth of trade credit, a number of companies are finding it worthwhile to use numerical credit-scoring systems to identify clearly unacceptable and acceptable applicants. Credit analysts can then devote their energies to evaluating marginal applicants.

Credit-scoring system A system used to decide whether to grant credit by assigning numerical scores to various characteristics related to creditworthiness.

Credit Decision and Line of Credit

Once the credit analyst has marshaled the necessary evidence and analyzed it, a decision must be reached about the disposition of the account. In an initial sale, the first decision to be made is whether or not to ship the goods and extend credit. If repeat sales are likely, the company will probably want to establish procedures so that it does not have to fully evaluate the extension of credit each time an order is received. One means of streamlining the procedure is to establish a **line of credit** for an account. A line of credit is a maximum limit on the amount the firm will permit to be owed at any one time. In essence, it represents the maximum risk exposure that the firm will allow itself to undergo for an account.[4] The establishment of a credit line streamlines the procedure for shipping goods, but the line must be reevaluated on a regular basis to keep abreast of developments in the account. What was a satisfactory risk exposure today may be more or less satisfactory a year from today. Despite comprehensive credit procedures, there will always be special cases that must be dealt with individually. Here, too, a firm can streamline the operation by defining responsibilities clearly.

Line of credit A limit to the amount of credit extended to an account. Purchaser can buy on credit up to that limit.

Outsourcing Credit and Collections

The entire credit/collection function can be outsourced (i.e., subcontracted to an outside firm). A number of third-party companies, like Dun & Bradstreet, offer complete or partial services to corporations. Credit scoring systems, together with other information, are used in deciding whether credit will be granted. Ledger accounts are maintained, payments processed, and collection efforts on tardy accounts are initiated. As with the outsourcing of any business function, it often comes down to a question of core competence. Where such internal competency does not exist or is inefficient, the decision—even for large companies—may be to buy the service on the outside. For small- and medium-sized companies, credit and collections may simply prove too costly to do on one's own.

INVENTORY MANAGEMENT AND CONTROL

Inventories form a link between the production and sale of a product. A manufacturing company must maintain a certain amount of inventory, known as work-in-process, during production. Although other types of inventory—in-transit, raw-materials, and

---

[4]One credit agency offers the following "rule of thumb" for setting the dollar limit to the amount of credit extended—pick the *lesser* of (a) 10 percent of the applicant's net worth, or (b) 20 percent of the applicant's net working capital.

finished-goods inventories—are not necessary in the strictest sense, they allow the firm to be flexible. Inventory in transit—that is, inventory between various stages of production or storage—permits efficient production scheduling and utilization of resources. Without this type of inventory, each stage of production would have to wait for the preceding stage to complete a unit. The possibility of resultant delays and idle time gives the firm an incentive to maintain in-transit inventory.

Raw-materials inventory gives the firm flexibility in its purchasing. Without it, the firm must exist on a hand-to-mouth basis, buying raw materials strictly in keeping with its production schedule. Finished-goods inventory allows the firm flexibility in its production scheduling and in its marketing. Production does not need to be geared directly to sales. Large inventories allow efficient servicing of customer demands. If a certain product is temporarily out of stock, present as well as future sales to the customer may be lost. Thus, there is an incentive to maintain stocks of all types of inventory.

The traditionally extolled advantages of increased inventories, then, are several. The firm can effect economies of production and purchasing and can fill orders more quickly. In short, the firm is said to be more flexible. The obvious disadvantages are the total cost of holding the inventory, including storage and handling costs, and the required return on capital tied up in inventory. An additional disadvantage is the danger of obsolescence. Because of the benefits, however, the sales manager and production manager are often biased toward relatively large inventories. Moreover, the purchasing manager can often achieve quantity discounts with large orders, and there may be a bias here as well. It falls on the financial manager to dampen the temptation for large inventories. This is done by forcing consideration of the cost of funds necessary to carry inventories as well as perhaps of the handling and storage costs.

In recent years, additional support for the financial manager's questioning of the maintenance of large inventories has come from an understanding of a Japanese-inspired inventory control system called *Just-in-Time*, or *JIT* for short. JIT breaks with the conventional wisdom of maintaining large inventory stocks as buffers against uncertainties. The basic objective of JIT is to produce (or receive) a required item at the exact time needed, or "just in time." Inventories of all types would thus be reduced to a bare minimum (in some cases, zero). Reductions in inventory carrying costs is one of the more obvious results of the JIT system. However, additional hoped-for results include improvements in productivity, product quality, and flexibility.

Like accounts receivable, inventories should be increased as long as the resulting savings exceed the total cost of holding the added inventory. The balance finally reached depends on the estimates of actual savings, the cost of carrying additional inventory, and the efficiency of inventory control. Obviously, this balance requires coordination of the production, marketing, and finance areas of the firm in keeping with an overall objective. Our purpose is to examine various principles of inventory control by which an appropriate balance might be achieved.

Classification: What to Control?

We have already noted the different types of inventory that exist for a typical manufacturing firm—raw-materials, work-in-process, in-transit, and finished-goods inventories. Another way to classify inventory is by the dollar value of the firm's investment. If a firm were to rank inventory items by decreasing value per item, we might get a cumulative distribution that looks like Figure 10-5. For the firm described by Figure 10-5, we find that, as a group, "A" items reflect the fact that roughly 15 percent of the items in inventory account for 70 percent of inventory value. The next 30 percent

FIGURE 10-5
Distribution of Inventory by Inventory Value

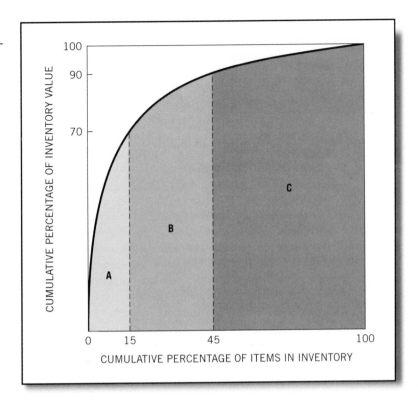

of the items, group "B," account for 20 percent of inventory value. And, more than half, or 55 percent, of the items explain only 10 percent of total inventory value.

Based on this typical breakdown, in which a relatively small proportion of items account for most of the total inventory value, it seems reasonable for the firm to devote more care and attention to controlling the more valuable items. This can be accomplished by assigning them an "A" classification and reviewing these items more frequently. "B" and "C" items might warrant increasingly less rigorous, less timely reviews. This system is often referred to, appropriately enough, as the **ABC method of inventory control.** Factors other than dollar value may also need to be considered when developing a classification plan—for example, whether something is a critical, or bottleneck, item or may soon become obsolete. The bottom line, however, is to classify inventory items in such a fashion that we ensure that the most important inventory items are reviewed most often.[5] Thus, a valid method of inventory classification forms the first leg in the construction of a solid inventory control system.

ABC method of inventory control Method that controls expensive inventory items more closely than less expensive items.

Economic Order Quantity: How Much to Order?

To be a successful contestant on the television quiz show *Jeopardy,* you must be able to provide the questions to answers that are given in various categories. Thus, if the category was inventory theory, you might run across the following answer: the EOQ

---

[5]Those of you familiar with the classic television series *M*A*S*H** may remember the doctors and nurses performing triage on arriving groups of wounded soldiers—that is, classifying the wounded according to who warrants more immediate attention. The firm, in essence, is performing a type of triage on its inventory as it classifies it into "A," "B," and "C" categories.

amount. Hopefully, by the time you finish reading this section you will understand why the correct "question" to this "answer" is, How much should we order?

The **economic order quantity (EOQ)** is an important concept in the purchase of raw materials and in the storage of finished-goods and in-transit inventories. In our analysis, we determine the optimal order quantity for a particular item of inventory, given its forecast usage, ordering cost, and carrying cost. *Ordering can mean either the purchase of the item or its production.* Assume for the moment that the usage of a particular item of inventory is known with certainty. This usage is at a steady rate throughout the period of time being analyzed. In other words, if usage is 2,600 items for a six-month period, 100 items are used each week.

We assume that ordering costs per order, O, are constant regardless of the size of the order. In the purchase of raw materials or other items, these costs represent the clerical costs involved in placing an order as well as certain costs of receiving and checking the goods once they arrive. For finished-goods inventories, ordering costs involve scheduling a production run. When setup costs are large—as they are in producing a machined piece of metal, for example—ordering costs can be quite significant. For in-transit inventories, ordering costs are likely to involve nothing more than record keeping. The total ordering cost for a period is simply the cost per order times the number of orders for that period.

Carrying costs per unit, C, represent the cost of inventory storage, handling, and insurance, together with the required return on the investment in inventory over the period. These costs are assumed to be constant per unit of inventory, per period of time. Thus, the total carrying cost for a period is the carrying cost per unit times the average number of units of inventory for the period. In addition, we assume that inventory orders are filled when needed, without delay. Because out-of-stock items can be replaced immediately, there is no need to maintain a buffer or safety stock. Though the assumptions made up to now may seem overly restrictive, they are necessary for an initial understanding of the conceptual framework that follows. Subsequently, we will relax some of them, and you may be surprised at how robust our original approach will prove itself to be.

If usage of an inventory item is at a steady rate over a period of time and there is no safety stock, average inventory (in units) can be expressed as

$$\text{Average inventory} = Q/2 \tag{10-1}$$

where Q is the quantity ordered and is assumed to be constant for the planning period. This situation is illustrated in Figure 10-6. Although the quantity demanded is a step function, we assume for analytical purposes that it can be approximated by a straight line. We see that when a zero level of inventory is reached, a new order of Q items arrives.

Once again, the carrying cost of inventory is the average number of units of inventory times the carrying cost per unit, or $C(Q/2)$. The total number of orders over a period of time is simply the total usage (in units) of an item of inventory for that period, S, divided by Q, the quantity ordered. Consequently, total ordering costs are represented by the ordering cost per order times the number of orders, or $O(S/Q)$. Total inventory costs, then, are the sum of the total carrying costs plus total ordering costs, or

$$\text{Total inventory cost } (T) = C(Q/2) + O(S/Q) \tag{10-2}$$

We see from Eq. (10-2) that the higher the order quantity, Q, the higher the total carrying costs, but the lower the total ordering costs. The lower the order quantity, the lower the total carrying costs, but the higher the total ordering costs. We are, therefore,

FIGURE 10-6
Order Quantity
Example with Cer-
tain, Steady Demand
and No Safety Stock

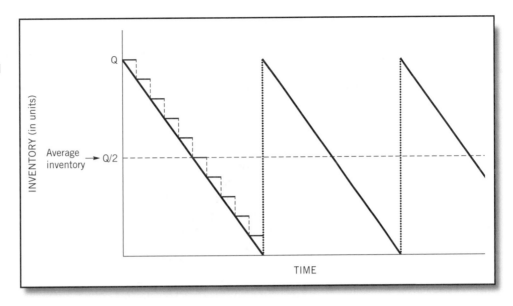

concerned with the trade-off between the economies of increased order size and the added cost of carrying additional inventory.

Optimal Order Quantity. The optimal quantity of an inventory item to order at any one time is that quantity, Q^*, that minimizes total inventory costs over our planning period. We can use calculus to find the lowest point on the total inventory cost curve described by Eq. (10-2) and then solve for Q.[6] The resulting optimal quantity, or EOQ, is

$$Q^* = \sqrt{\frac{2(O)(S)}{C}}$$

To illustrate the use of this EOQ equation, suppose that usage of an inventory item is 2,000 during a 100-day planning period, ordering costs are $100 per order, and carrying costs are $10 per unit per 100 days. The EOQ amount, then, is

$$Q^* = \sqrt{\frac{2(\$100)(2,000)}{\$10}} = \textbf{200 units} \tag{10-3}$$

With an order quantity of 200 units, the firm would order $(2,000/200) = \textbf{10 times}$ during the period under consideration or, in other words, every 10 days. We see from Eq. (10-3) that Q^* varies directly with usage, S, and order cost, O, and inversely with carrying cost, C. However, the relationship is dampened by the square-root sign in both cases. As usage increases, then, the optimal order size and the average level of inventory increase by a lesser percentage. In other words, economies of scale are possible. For example, if we double usage in our example to 4,000 units, we get a new optimal order quantity that is only 40 percent higher than the old one, that is,

---

[6]Taking the first derivative of Eq. (10-2) with respect to Q and setting the result equal to zero, we obtain
$$dT/dQ = (C/2) - O(S/Q^2) = 0$$
Now, solving for Q, we get
$$O(S/Q^2) = C/2$$
$$Q = \sqrt{\frac{2(O)(S)}{C}} = Q^*$$

280 units. This new order quantity results in a new average inventory level ($Q/2$) that is likewise only 40 percent higher—140 units versus 100 units.

The EOQ function is shown in Figure 10-7. In the figure, we plot total ordering costs; total carrying costs; and total inventory costs, which are the sum of the first two costs. We see that whereas total carrying costs vary directly with the size of the order, total ordering costs vary inversely with order size. The total inventory costs line declines at first as the fixed costs of ordering are incurred less often as fewer but larger orders are placed. However, the total inventory costs line then begins to rise when the decrease in total ordering costs is more than offset by the additional carrying costs caused by maintaining a larger average inventory. Point Q^*, then, represents the economic order quantity, which minimizes the total cost of inventory.[7] The EOQ formula taken up in this section is a useful tool for inventory control. In purchasing raw materials or other items of inventory, it tells us the amount to order. For finished goods, it enables us to exercise better control over the size of production runs. In general, the EOQ model gives us a rule for deciding the amount of inventory to replenish.

---

[7]As shown in Figure 10-7, the total carrying costs and total ordering costs lines intersect at the order-size level where the total inventory costs curve has its minimum, point Q^*. To see why this *always* holds true for our model, set total carrying costs (TCC) equal to total ordering costs (TOC) and solve for order quantity Q:

$$TCC = TOC$$
$$C(Q/2) = O(S/Q)$$
$$C(Q^2) = O(S/Q)$$
$$Q = \sqrt{\frac{2(O)(S)}{C}} = Q^* = EOQ$$

FIGURE 10-7
Economic Order Quantity Relationships

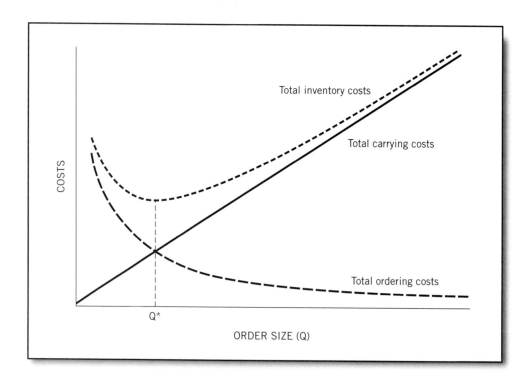

Part IV Working Capital Management

Order Point: When to Order?

In addition to knowing how much to order, the firm also needs to know when to order. "When," in this case, means the quantity to which inventory must fall in order to signal a reorder of the EOQ amount. In our previous example, we have assumed that inventory can be ordered and received without delay. Usually there is a time lapse between placement of a purchase order and receipt of the inventory, or in the time it takes to manufacture an item after an order is placed. This **lead time** must be considered.

Lead time The length of time between the placement of an order for an inventory item and when the item is received in inventory.

Suppose that demand for inventory is known with certainty, but that it takes 5 days between the placement and receipt of an order. In our previous illustration of the EOQ formula, we found that the EOQ for our example firm was 200 units, resulting in an order being placed (and filled) every 10 days. This firm thus had a zero lead time and a daily usage of 20 units. If usage remains at a steady rate, the firm would now need to order 5 days before it ran out of stock, or at 100 units of stock on hand. The **order point** may be expressed as

Order point The quantity to which inventory must fall in order to signal that an order must be placed to replenish an item.

$$\text{Order point (OP)} = \text{Lead time} \times \text{Daily usage} \qquad (10\text{-}4)$$

Thus, the order point is now

$$5 \text{ days} \times 20 \text{ units per day} = \textbf{100 units}$$

When the new order is received 5 days later, the firm will just have exhausted its existing stock. This example, involving an order point, is illustrated in Figure 10-8.

Safety Stock

In practice, the demand or usage of inventory is generally not known with certainty; usually, it fluctuates during a given period of time. Typically, the demand for finished-goods inventory is subject to the greatest uncertainty. In general, the usage of raw-materials inventory and in-transit inventory, both of which depend on the production scheduling, is more predictable. In addition to demand, the lead time required to receive delivery of inventory once an order is placed is usually subject to

FIGURE 10-8
Order Point When
Lead Time Is
Nonzero and Certain

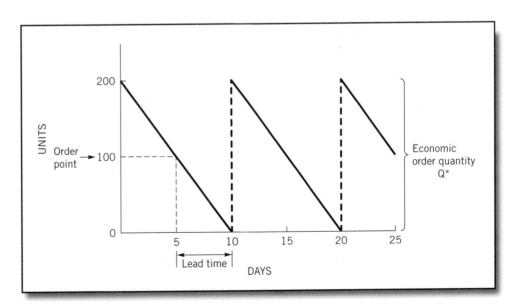

some variation. Owing to these fluctuations, it is not usually feasible to allow expected inventory to fall to zero before a new order is anticipated, as the firm could do when usage and lead time were known with certainty.

Therefore, when we allow for uncertainty in demand for inventory as well as in lead time, a **safety stock** becomes advisable. The concept of a safety stock is illustrated in Figure 10-9. Frame A of the figure shows what would happen if the firm had a safety stock of 100 units and if expected demand of 200 units every 10 days and expected lead time of 5 days were to occur. However, treating lead time and daily usage as average, or expected, values, rather than as constants, causes us to modify our original order point equation as follows:

$$\text{Order point (OP)} = (\textit{Average lead time} \times \textit{Average daily usage}) + \textit{Safety stock} \quad \textbf{(10-5)}$$

Note that with a safety stock of 100 units, the order point must be set at (5 days × 20 units) + 100 units = **200 units** of inventory on hand as opposed to the previous

Safety stock Inventory stock held in reserve as a cushion against uncertain demand (or usage) and replenishment lead time.

FIGURE 10-9
Safety Stock and Order Point When Demand and Lead Time Are Uncertain

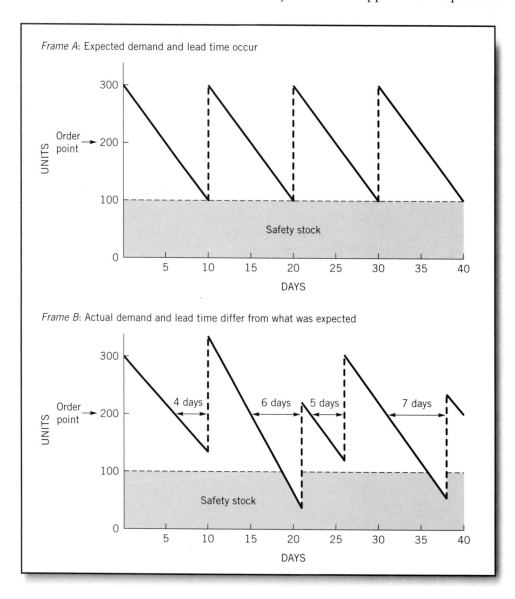

Part IV Working Capital Management

100 units. In other words, the order point determines the amount of safety stock held. Thus, by varying the order point, one can vary the safety stock that is held.

Frame B of the figure shows the actual experience for our hypothetical firm. In the first segment of demand, we see that actual usage is somewhat less than expected. (The slope of the line is less than that for the expected demand line in frame A.) At the order point of 200 remaining units, an order is placed for 200 units of additional inventory. Instead of taking the expected 5 days for the inventory to be replenished, we see that it takes only 4 days. The second segment of usage is much greater than expected, and, as a result, inventory is rapidly used up. At 200 units of remaining inventory, a 200-unit order is again placed, but here it takes 6 days for the inventory to be received. As a result of both of these factors, heavy inroads are made into the safety stock.

In the third segment of demand, usage is about the same as expected; that is, the slopes of the expected and actual usage lines are about the same. Because inventory was so low at the end of the previous segment of usage, an order is placed almost immediately. The lead time turns out to be 5 days. In the last segment of demand, usage is slightly greater than expected. The lead time necessary to receive an order is 7 days—much longer than expected. The combination of these two factors again causes the firm to go into its safety stock. The example illustrates the importance of safety stock in absorbing random fluctuations in usage and lead times. Without such a buffer stock, the firm would have run out of inventory on two occasions.

The Amount of Safety Stock. The proper amount of safety stock to maintain depends on several factors. The greater the uncertainty associated with forecasted demand for inventory, the greater the safety stock the firm will wish to carry, all other things being the same. Put another way, the greater the risk of running out of stock, the larger the unforeseen fluctuations in usage. Similarly, the greater the uncertainty of lead time to replenish stock, the greater the risk of running out of stock, and the more safety stock the firm will wish to maintain, all other things being equal. Another factor influencing the safety stock decision is the cost of running out of inventory. The cost of being out of raw-materials and in-transit inventories is a delay in production. How much does it cost when production closes down temporarily? Where fixed costs are high, this cost will be quite high, as, for example, in the case of an aluminum extrusion plant. The cost of running out of finished goods comes from lost sales and customer dissatisfaction. Not only will the immediate sale be lost but future sales will be endangered if customers take their business elsewhere. Although this opportunity cost is difficult to measure, it must be recognized by management and incorporated into the safety stock decision. The greater the costs of running out of stock, of course, the greater the safety stock that management will wish to maintain, all other things staying the same.

The final factor is the cost of carrying additional inventory. If it were not for this cost, a firm could maintain whatever safety stock was necessary to avoid all possibility of running out of inventory. The greater the cost of carrying inventory, the more costly it is to maintain a safety stock, all other things being equal. Determination of the proper amount of safety stock involves balancing the probability and cost of a stockout against the cost of carrying enough safety stock to avoid this possibility. Ultimately, the question reduces to the probability of inventory stockout that management is willing to tolerate. In a typical situation, this probability is reduced at a decreasing rate as more safety stock is added. A firm may be able to reduce the probability of inventory stockout by 20 percent if it adds 100 units of safety stock, but only by an additional 10 percent if it adds another 100 units. There comes a point when it becomes very expensive to further reduce the probability of stockout. Management will not wish to add safety stock beyond the point at which incremental carrying costs exceed the incremental benefits to be derived from avoiding a stockout.

Just-in-Time

In certain industries, the production process lends itself to **just-in-time (JIT)** inventory control. As the name implies, the idea is that inventories are acquired and inserted in production at the exact times they are needed. The JIT management philosophy thus focuses on *pulling* inventory through the production process on an "as-needed" basis, rather than *pushing* inventory through the process on an "as-produced" basis. This requires a very accurate production and inventory information system, highly efficient purchasing, very reliable suppliers, and an efficient inventory-handling system. Although raw-materials inventory and in-transit inventory can never be reduced to zero, the notion of "just in time" is one of extremely tight control so as to cut back on inventories. The goal of a JIT system, however, is not only to reduce inventories but to continuously improve productivity, product quality, and manufacturing flexibility.

EOQ in a JIT World. At first glance, it might seem that a JIT system—in which inventories would be reduced to a bare minimum and the EOQ for a particular item might approach one unit—would be in direct conflict with our EOQ model. However, it is not. A JIT system, on the other hand, rejects the notion that ordering costs (clerical, receiving, inspecting, scheduling, and/or setup costs) are necessarily fixed at their current levels. As part of a JIT system, steps are continuously taken to drive these costs down. For example,

- Small-sized delivery trucks, with predetermined unloading sequences, are used to facilitate economies in receiving time and costs.
- Pressure is placed on suppliers to produce raw materials with "no defects," thus reducing (or eliminating) inspection costs.
- Products, equipment, and procedures are modified to reduce setup time and costs.

By successfully reducing these ordering-related costs, the firm is able to flatten the total ordering cost curve in Figure 10-7. This causes the optimal order quantity, Q^*, to shift to the left, thus approaching the JIT ideal of one unit. Additionally, continuous efforts to reduce supplier delays, production inefficiencies, and sales forecasting errors allow safety stocks to be cut back or eliminated. How close a company comes to the JIT ideal depends on the type of production process and the nature of the supplier industries, but it is a worthy objective for most companies.

Inventory and the Financial Manager

Although inventory management is usually not the direct operating responsibility of the financial manager, the investment of funds in inventory is a very important aspect of financial management. Consequently, the financial manager must be familiar with ways to control inventories effectively so that capital may be allocated efficiently. The greater the opportunity cost of funds invested in inventory, the lower the optimal level of average inventory, and the lower the optimal order quantity, all other things held constant. This statement can be verified by increasing the carrying

What is needed to make a "just-in-time" system work

(According to General Motors Corp. vice president Robert B. Stone, who is overseeing implementation of "just-in-time" systems at GM.)

1. Geographic concentration.
Relatively short transit times from vendor plants to customer plants—less than one day—are necessary if customer production operation (using process) is to get the parts it requires "just-in-time." Toyota, in Japan, for example, has most of its suppliers located within 60 miles of its plants.

2. Dependable quality.
The using process must always be able to rely on receiving only good parts from its suppliers. The Japanese concept is that every operation must regard the next operation as the ultimate customer. Quality control efforts are aimed at controlling the production process, not on inspection to weed out the bad.

3. Manageable supplier network.
A minimum number of suppliers—and long-term contracts with them—helps make "just-in-time" systems work. Most Japanese auto companies use fewer than 250 parts suppliers. By contrast, General Motors Corp. uses about 3500 suppliers for assembly operations alone.

4. Controlled transportation system.
Key to this is short, reliable transit lines between suppliers and users. Japanese auto companies use only trucks (their own or under contract to them) to have parts shipped. Deliveries occur several times a day from each supplier at pre-scheduled times.

5. Manufacturing flexibility.
In the factory, the supplying process must be able to react quickly to produce whatever parts are taken by the using process. Key to this is quick tool-change capability. In Japan, for example, automated press lines are changed in under 6 minutes.

6. Small lot sizes.
Most Japanese companies that use "just-in-time" systems require lot sizes to be less than 10 pct of a day's usage. The idea is to achieve a lot size of one piece, so that every time one vehicle is produced, one of each part of the vehicle is also produced.

7. Efficient receiving and material handling.
Most Japanese companies, for example, have eliminated formal receiving operations. Whole sides of plants act as receiving areas and parts are delivered as close as possible to the points of use. Special design trucks are used to eliminate need for truck wells.

8. Strong management commitment.
"Just-in-time" system is plant-wide. Management must make available company resources to assure that the system works—and it must stand firm during conversion periods to "just-in-time" systems when the going can be very rough and prolonged.

Reprinted by permission, Iron Age.

costs, C, in Eq. (10-3). The EOQ model can also be used by the financial manager in planning for inventory financing.

When demand or usage of inventory is uncertain, the financial manager may try to effect policies that will reduce the average lead time required to receive inventory once an order is placed. The lower the average lead time, the lower the safety stock needed, and the lower the total investment in inventory, all other things held constant. The greater the opportunity cost of funds invested in inventory, the greater the incentive to reduce this lead time. The purchasing department may try to find new vendors that promise quicker delivery, or it may pressure existing vendors to deliver faster. The production department may be able to deliver finished goods faster by producing a smaller run. In either case, there is a trade-off between the added cost involved in reducing the lead time and the opportunity cost of funds tied up in inventory. This discussion serves to point out the value of inventory management to the financial manager.

SUMMARY

- Credit and collection policies encompass several decisions: (1) the quality of accounts accepted; (2) the length of the credit period; (3) the size of the cash discount (if any) for early payment; (4) any special terms, such as seasonal datings; and (5) the level of collection expenditures. In each case, the decision involves a comparison of the possible gains from a change in policy with the cost of the change. To maximize profits arising from credit and collection policies, the firm should vary these policies jointly until it achieves an optimal solution.
- The firm's credit and collection policies, together with its credit and collection procedures, determine the magnitude and quality of its receivable position.
- In evaluating a credit applicant, the credit analyst (1) obtains information on the applicant, (2) analyzes this information to determine the applicant's creditworthiness, and (3) makes the credit decision. The credit decision, in turn, establishes whether credit should be extended and what the maximum amount of credit, or *line of credit*, should be.
- Inventories form a link between the production and sale of a product. Inventories give the firm flexibility in its purchasing, production scheduling, and servicing of customer demands.
- In evaluating the level of inventories, management must balance the benefits of economies of production, purchasing, and marketing against the cost of carrying the additional inventory. Of particular concern to the financial manager is the cost of funds invested in inventory.
- Firms often classify inventory items into groups in such a fashion as to ensure that the most important items are reviewed most often. One such approach is called the *ABC method of inventory control.*
- The optimal order quantity for a particular item of inventory depends on the item's forecasted usage, ordering cost, and carrying cost. Ordering can mean either the purchase of the item or its production. *Ordering costs* include the costs of placing, receiving, and checking an order. *Carrying costs* represent the cost of inventory storage, handling, and insurance and the required return on the investment in inventory.
- The *economic order quantity (EOQ) model* affirms that the optimal quantity of an inventory item to order at any one time is that quantity that minimizes total inventory costs over our planning period.
- An inventory item's *order point* is that quantity to which inventory must fall to signal a reorder of the EOQ amount.
- Under conditions of uncertainty, the firm must usually provide for a *safety stock*, owing to fluctuations in demand for inventory and in *lead times*. By varying the point at which orders are placed, one varies the safety stock that is held.
- *Just-in-time (JIT) inventory control* is the result of a new emphasis by firms on continuous process improvement. The idea is that inventories are acquired and inserted in production at the exact times they are needed.

QUESTIONS

1. Is it always good policy to reduce the firm's bad debts by "getting rid of the deadbeats?"
2. What are the probable effects on sales and profits of each of the following credit policies?
   a. A high percentage of bad-debt loss but normal receivable turnover and credit rejection rate.
   b. A high percentage of past-due accounts and a low credit rejection rate.
   c. A low percentage of past-due accounts but high credit rejection and receivable turnover rates.
   d. A low percentage of past-due accounts and a low credit rejection rate but a high receivable turnover rate.
3. Is an increase in the collection period necessarily bad? Explain.
4. What are the various sources of information you might use to analyze a credit applicant?
5. What are the principal factors that can be varied in setting credit policy?
6. If credit standards for the quality of accounts accepted are changed, what things are affected?
7. Why is the *saturation point* reached in spending money on collections?
8. What is the purpose of establishing a *line of credit* for an account? What are the benefits of this arrangement?
9. The analysis of inventory policy is analogous to the analysis of credit policy. Propose a measure to analyze inventory policy that is analogous to the *aging of accounts receivable*.
10. What are the principal implications to the financial manager of ordering costs, storage costs, and cost of capital as they relate to inventory?
11. Explain how efficient inventory management affects the liquidity and profitability of the firm.
12. How can the firm reduce its investment in inventories? What costs might the firm incur from a policy of very low inventory investment?
13. Explain how a large seasonal demand complicates inventory management and production scheduling.
14. Do inventories represent an investment in the same sense as fixed assets?
15. Should the required rate of return for investment in inventories of raw materials be the same as that for finished goods?

SELF-CORRECTION PROBLEMS

1. Kari-Kidd Corporation presently gives credit terms of "net 30 days." It has $60 million in credit sales, and its average collection period is 45 days. To stimulate demand, the company may give credit terms of "net 60 days." If it does instigate these terms, sales are expected to increase by 15 percent. After the change, the average collection period is expected to be 75 days, with no difference in payment habits between old and new customers. Variable costs are $.80 for every $1.00 of sales, and the company's before-tax required rate of return on investment in receivables is 20 percent. Should the company extend its credit period? (Assume a 360-day year.)
2. Matlock Gauge Company makes wind and current gauges for pleasure boats. The gauges are sold throughout the Southeast to boat dealers, and the average order size is $50. The company sells to all registered dealers without a credit analysis. Terms are "net 45 days," and the average collection period is 60 days,

which is regarded as satisfactory. Sue Ford, vice president of finance, is now uneasy about the increasing number of bad-debt losses on new orders. With credit ratings from local and regional credit agencies, she feels she would be able to classify new orders into one of three risk categories. Past experience shows the following:

	ORDER CATEGORY		
	LOW RISK	MEDIUM RISK	HIGH RISK
Bad-debt loss	3%	7%	24%
Category orders to total orders	30%	50%	20%

The cost of producing and shipping the gauges and of carrying the receivables is 78 percent of sales. The cost of obtaining credit information and of evaluating it is $4 per order. Surprisingly, there does not appear to be any association between the risk category and the collection period; the average for each of the three risk categories is around 60 days. Based on this information, should the company obtain credit information on new orders instead of selling to all new accounts without credit analysis? Why?

3. Vostick Filter Company is a distributor of air filters to retail stores. It buys its filters from several manufacturers. Filters are ordered in lot sizes of 1,000, and each order costs $40 to place. Demand from retail stores is 20,000 filters per month, and carrying cost is $.10 a filter per month.

   a. What is the optimal order quantity with respect to so many lot sizes (that is, what multiple of 1,000 units should be ordered)?

   b. What would be the optimal order quantity if the carrying cost were cut in half to $.05 a filter per month?

   c. What would be the optimal order quantity if ordering costs were reduced to $10 per order?

4. To reduce production start-up costs, Bodden Truck Company may manufacture longer runs of the same truck. Estimated savings from the increase in efficiency are $260,000 per year. However, inventory turnover will decrease from eight times a year to six times a year. Cost of goods sold is $48 million on an annual basis. If the required before-tax rate of return on investment in inventories is 15 percent, should the company instigate the new production plan?

PROBLEMS

1. To increase sales from their present annual $24 million, Kim Chi Company, a wholesaler, may try more liberal credit standards. Currently, the firm has an average collection period of 30 days. It believes that with increasingly liberal credit standards, the following will result:

	CREDIT POLICY			
	A	B	C	D
Increase in sales from previous level (in millions)	$2.8	$1.8	$1.2	$.6
Average collection period for incremental sales (days)	45	60	90	144

The prices of its products average $20 per unit, and variable costs average $18 per unit. No bad-debt losses are expected. If the company has a pre-tax opportunity cost of funds of 30 percent, which credit policy should be pursued? Why? (Assume a 360-day year.)

2. Upon reflection, Kim Chi Company has estimated that the following pattern of bad-debt losses will prevail if it initiates more liberal credit terms:

	CREDIT POLICY			
	A	B	C	D
Bad-debt losses on incremental sales	3%	6%	10%	15%

Given the other assumptions in Problem 1, which credit policy should be pursued? Why?

3. Recalculate Problem 2, assuming the following pattern of bad-debt losses:

	CREDIT POLICY			
	A	B	C	D
Bad-debt losses on incremental sales	1.5%	3.0%	5.0%	7.5%

Which policy now would be best? Why?

4. The Acme Aglet Corporation has a 12 percent opportunity cost of funds and currently sells on terms of "net/10, EOM." (This means that goods shipped before the end of the month must be paid for by the tenth of the following month.) The firm has sales of $10 million a year, which are 80 percent on credit and spread evenly over the year. The average collection period is currently 60 days. If Acme offered terms of "2/10, net 30," 60 percent of its credit customers would take the discount, and the average collection period would be reduced to 40 days. Should Acme change its terms from "net/10, EOM" to "2/10, net 30"? Why?

5. Porras Pottery Products, Inc., spends $220,000 per annum on its collection department. The company has $12 million in credit sales, its average collection period is 2.5 months, and the percentage of bad-debt losses is 4 percent. The company believes that if it were to double its collection personnel, it could bring down the average collection period to 2 months and bad-debt losses to 3 percent. The added cost is $180,000, bringing total collection expenditures to $400,000 annually. Is the increased effort worthwhile if the before-tax opportunity cost of funds is 20 percent? If it is 10 percent?

6. The Pottsville Manufacturing Corporation is considering extending trade credit to the San Jose Company. Examination of the records of San Jose has produced the following financial statements:

San Jose Company balance sheets (in millions)

ASSETS	20X1	20X2	20X3
Current assets			
Cash and cash equivalents	$ 1.5	$ 1.6	$ 1.6
Receivables	1.3	1.8	2.5
Inventories (at lower of cost or market)	1.3	2.6	4.0
Other	.4	.5	.4
Total current assets	$ 4.5	$ 6.5	$ 8.5
Fixed assets			
Building (net)	2.0	1.9	1.8
Machinery and equipment (net)	7.0	6.5	6.0
Total fixed assets	$ 9.0	$ 8.4	$ 7.8
Other assets	1.0	.8	.6
Total assets	$14.5	$15.7	$16.9

Continued on next page

LIABILITIES

Current liabilities			
Notes payable (8.5%)	$ 2.1	$ 3.1	$ 3.8
Trade payables	.2	.4	.9
Other payables	.2	.2	.2
Total current liabilities	$ 2.5	$ 3.7	$ 4.9
Term loan (8.5%)	4.0	3.0	2.0
Total liabilities	$ 6.5	$ 6.7	$ 6.9
Net worth			
Preferred stock (6.5%)	1.0	1.0	1.0
Common stock	5.0	5.0	5.0
Retained earnings	2.0	3.0	4.0
Total liabilities and net worth	$14.5	$15.7	$16.9

San Jose Company income statements (in millions)

	20X1	20X2	20X3
Net credit sales	$15.0	$15.8	$16.2
Cost of goods sold	11.3	12.1	13.0
Gross profit	$ 3.7	$ 3.7	$ 3.2
Operating expenses	1.1	1.2	1.0
Net profit before taxes	$ 2.6	$ 2.5	$ 2.2
Tax	1.3	1.2	1.2
Profit after taxes	$ 1.3	$ 1.3	$ 1.0
Dividends	.3	.3	.0
To retained earnings	$ 1.0	$ 1.0	$ 1.0

The San Jose Company has a Dun & Bradstreet rating of *4A2*. Inquiries into its banking disclosed balances generally in the low millions. Five suppliers to San Jose revealed that the firm takes its discounts from the three suppliers offering "2/10, net 30" terms, though it is about 15 days slow in paying the two firms offering terms of "net 30."

Analyze the San Jose Company's application for credit. What positive factors are present? What negative factors are present?

7. A college bookstore is attempting to determine the optimal order quantity for a popular book on psychology. The store sells 5,000 copies of this book a year at a retail price of $12.50, and the cost to the store is 20 percent less, which represents the discount from the publisher. The store figures that it costs $1 per year to carry a book in inventory and $100 to prepare an order for new books.
   a. Determine the total inventory costs associated with ordering 1, 2, 5, 10, and 20 times a year.
   b. Determine the economic order quantity.
   c. What implicit assumptions are being made about the annual sales rate?

8. The Hedge Corporation manufactures only one product: planks. The single raw material used in making planks is the dint. For each plank manufactured, 12 dints are required. Assume that the company manufactures 150,000 planks per year, that demand for planks is perfectly steady throughout the year, that it costs $200 each time dints are ordered, and that carrying costs are $8 per dint per year.
   a. Determine the economic order quantity of dints.
   b. What are total inventory costs for Hedge (total carrying costs plus total ordering costs)?
   c. How many times per year would inventory be ordered?

9. A firm that sells 5,000 blivets per month is trying to determine how many blivets to keep in inventory. The financial manager has determined that it costs $200 to place an order. The cost of holding inventory is 4 cents per month per average blivet in inventory. A five-day lead time is required for delivery of goods ordered. (This lead time is known with certainty.)

    a. Develop the algebraic expression for determining the total cost of holding and ordering inventory.

    b. Plot the total holding costs and the total ordering costs on a graph where the horizontal axis represents size of order and the vertical axis represents costs.

    c. Determine the EOQ from the graph.

10. Common Scents, Inc., makes various scents for use in the manufacture of food products. Although the company does maintain a safety stock, it has a policy of maintaining "lean" inventories, with the result that customers sometimes must be turned away. In an analysis of the situation, the company has estimated the cost of being out of stock associated with various levels of safety stock:

	LEVEL OF SAFETY STOCK (in gallons)	ANNUAL COST OF STOCKOUTS
Present safety stock level	5,000	$26,000
New safety stock level 1	7,500	14,000
New safety stock level 2	10,000	7,000
New safety stock level 3	12,500	3,000
New safety stock level 4	15,000	1,000
New safety stock level 5	17,500	0

Carrying costs are $.65 per gallon per year. What is the best level of safety stock for the company?

SOLUTIONS TO SELF-CORRECTION PROBLEMS

1. Old receivable turnover	= 360/45	= 8 times
New receivable turnover	= 360/75	= 4.8 times
Profitability of additional sales	= .2 × $9,000,000	= **$1,800,000**
Additional receivables associated with the new sales	= $9,000,000/4.8	= $1,875,000
Investment in additional receivables associated with the new sales	= .8 × $1,875,000	= $1,500,000
Level of receivables before credit period change	= $60,000,000/8	= $7,500,000
New level of receivables associated with original sales	= $60,000,000/4.8	= $12,500,000
Investment in additional receivables associated with original sales	= $12.5M − $7.5M	= $5,000,000
Total investment in additional receivables	= $1.5M + $5.0M	= $6,500,000
Required before-tax return on additional investment	= .20 × $6.5M	= **$1,300,000**

Because the profitability on additional sales, $1,800,000, exceeds the required return on the investment in additional receivables, $1,300,000, the company should lengthen its credit period from 30 to 60 days.

2. Because the bad-debt loss ratio for the high-risk category exceeds the profit margin of 22 percent, it would be desirable to reject orders from this risk class if such orders could be identified. However, the cost of credit information as a percentage of the average order, is $4/$50 = 8%, and this cost is applicable to all new orders. Because the high-risk category is one-fifth of sales, the comparison would be 5 × 8% = 40% relative to the bad-debt loss of 24%. Therefore, the company should not undertake credit analysis of new orders.

An example can better illustrate the solution. Suppose that new orders were $100,000. The following would then hold:

	ORDER CATEGORY		
	LOW RISK	MEDIUM RISK	HIGH RISK
Total orders	$30,000	$50,000	$20,000
Bad-debt loss	900	3,500	4,800

$$\text{Number of orders} = \$100,000/\$50 = 2,000$$

$$\text{Credit analysis cost} = 2,000 \times \$4 = \$8,000$$

To save $4,800 in bad-debt losses by identifying the high-risk category of new orders, the company must spend $8,000. Therefore, it should not undertake the credit analysis of new orders. This is a case where the size of order is too small to justify credit analysis. After a new order is accepted, the company will gain experience and can reject subsequent orders if its experience is bad.

3.

a.

$$Q^* = \sqrt{\frac{2(O)(S)}{C}} = \sqrt{\frac{2(\$40)(20)}{\$100}} = \textbf{4 (thousand-unit) lots}$$

The optimal order size would be 4,000 filters, which represents five orders a month.
(*Note:* Carrying costs (C) per 1,000-unit lot = $.10 × 1,000 = $100)

b.

$$Q^* = \sqrt{\frac{2(O)(S)}{C}} = \sqrt{\frac{2(\$40)(20)}{\$50}} = \textbf{5.66 (thousand-unit) lots}$$

Since the lot size is 1,000 filters, the company would order 6,000 filters each time. The lower the carrying cost, the more important ordering costs become relatively, and the larger the optimal order size.

c.

$$Q^* = \sqrt{\frac{2(O)(S)}{C}} = \sqrt{\frac{2(\$10)(20)}{\$100}} = \textbf{2 (thousand-unit) lots}$$

The lower the order cost, the more important carrying costs become relatively, and the smaller the optimal order size.

4. Inventories after change = \$48 million/6 = \$8 million

Present inventories = \$48 million/8 = <u>\$6 million</u>

Additional inventories = \$2 million

Opportunity cost = \$2 million × .15 = \$300,000

The opportunity cost, \$300,000, is greater than the potential savings of \$260,000. Therefore, the new production plan should not be undertaken.

SELECTED REFERENCES

Dyl, Edward A. "Another Look at the Evaluation of Investment in Accounts Receivable." *Financial Management* 6 (Winter 1977), 67–70.

Hill, Ned C., and Kenneth D. Riener. "Determining the Cash Discount in the Firm's Credit Policy." *Financial Management* 8 (Spring 1979), 68–73.

Hill, Ned C., and William L. Sartoris. *Short-Term Financial Management*, 3rd ed. Englewood Cliffs, NJ: Prentice Hall, 1995.

Johnson, Gene H., and James D. Stice. "Not Quite Just In Time Inventories." *The National Public Accountant* 38 (March 1993), 26–29.

Kallberg, Jarl G., and Kenneth L. Parkinson. *Corporate Liquidity: Management and Measurement*. Homewood, IL: Irwin, 1993.

Magee, John F. "Guides to Inventory Policy," I–III, *Harvard Business Review* 34 (January–February 1956), 49–60; 34 (March–April 1956), 103–16; and 34 (May–June 1956), 57–70.

Maness, Terry S., and John T. Zietlow. *Short-Term Financial Management*. Fort Worth, TX: Dryden Press, 1998.

Mehta, Dileep. "The Formulation of Credit Policy Models." *Management Science* 15 (October 1968), 30–50.

Mester, Loretta J. "What's the Point of Credit Scoring?" *Business Review*, Federal Reserve Bank of Philadelphia (September–October 1997), 3–16.

Mian, Shehzad L., and Clifford W. Smith Jr. "Extending Trade Credit and Financing Receivables." *Journal of Applied Corporate Finance* 7 (Spring 1994), 75–84.

Oh, John S. "Opportunity Cost in the Evaluation of Investment in Accounts Receivable." *Financial Management* 5 (Summer 1976), 32–36.

Parkinson, Kenneth L., and Joyce R. Ochs. "Using Credit Screening to Manage Credit Risk." *Business Credit* 100 (March 1998), 22–27.

Sartoris, William L., and Ned C. Hill. "A Generalized Cash Flow Approach to Short-Term Financial Decisions." *Journal of Finance* 38 (May 1983), 349–60.

Scherr, Frederick C. "Optimal Trade Credit Limits." *Financial Management* 25 (Spring 1996), 71–85.

Stojanovic, Dusan, and Mark D. Vaughan. "The Commercial Paper Market: Who's Minding the Shop?" *The Regional Economist*, Federal Reserve Bank of St. Louis (April 1998), 5–9.

Tiernan, Frank M., and Dennis A. Tanner. "How Economic Order Quantity Controls Inventory Expense." *Financial Executive* 51 (July 1983), 46–52.

Wrightsman, D. W. "Optimal Credit Terms for Accounts Receivable." *Quarterly Review of Economics and Business* 9 (Summer 1969), 59–66.

Chapter 11

Short-Term Financing

SPONTANEOUS FINANCING
   Accounts Payable (Trade Credit from Suppliers) • Accrued
      Expenses
NEGOTIATED FINANCING
   Money Market Credit • Unsecured Loans • Detour: Cost of
      Borrowing • Secured (or Asset-Based) Loans
FACTORING ACCOUNTS RECEIVABLE
   Factoring Costs • Flexibility
COMPOSITION OF SHORT-TERM FINANCING
SUMMARY
QUESTIONS
SELF-CORRECTION PROBLEMS
PROBLEMS
SOLUTIONS TO SELF-CORRECTION PROBLEMS
SELECTED REFERENCES

> *Creditors have better memories than debtors, and creditors are a
> superstitious sect—great observers of set days and times.*

—BENJAMIN FRANKLIN

Short-term financing can be categorized according to whether or not the source is *spontaneous*. Accounts payable and accrued expenses are classified as spontaneous because they arise naturally from the firm's day-to-day transactions. Their magnitude is primarily a function of a company's level of operations. As operations expand, these liabilities typically increase and finance a part of the buildup in assets. Though all spontaneous sources of financing behave in this manner, there still remains a degree of discretion on the part of a company as to the exact magnitude of this financing. In this chapter, we consider the methods of spontaneous financing and how such discretion might be used.

In addition, we examine negotiated (or external) sources of short-term financing—consisting of certain money market credit and both *unsecured* and *secured* (or asset-based) loans. Such financing is not spontaneous or automatic. It must be arranged on a formal basis.

SPONTANEOUS FINANCING

Accounts Payable (Trade Credit from Suppliers)

Trade liabilities Money owed to suppliers.

Trade liabilities are a form of short-term financing common to almost all businesses. In fact, they are collectively the largest source of short-term funds for business firms. In an advanced economy, most buyers are not required to pay for goods on delivery but are allowed a short deferment period before payment is due. During this period the seller of goods extends credit to the buyer. Because suppliers are more liberal in the extension of credit than are financial institutions, companies—especially small ones—rely heavily on this **trade credit.**

Trade credit Credit granted from one business to another

Of the three types of trade credit—open accounts, notes payable, and trade acceptances—the open-account arrangement is by far the most common kind. With this arrangement the seller ships goods to the buyer and sends an invoice that specifies the goods shipped, the total amount due, and the terms of the sale. Open-account credit derives its name from the fact that the buyer does not sign a formal debt instrument evidencing the amount owed the seller. The seller generally extends credit based on a credit investigation of the buyer (see Chapter 10). Open-account credit appears on the buyer's balance sheet as *accounts payable*.

In some situations promissory notes are employed instead of open-account credit. The buyer signs a note that evidences a debt to the seller. The note calls for the payment of the obligation at some specified future date. This arrangement is employed when the seller wants the buyer to acknowledge the debt formally. For example, a seller might request a promissory note from a buyer if the buyer's open account became past due.

Draft A signed, written order by which the first party (drawer) instructs a second party (drawee) to pay a specified amount of money to a third party (payee). The drawer and payee are often one and the same.

A trade acceptance is another arrangement by which the indebtedness of the buyer is formally recognized. Under this arrangement, the seller draws a **draft** on the buyer, ordering the buyer to pay the draft at some future date. The seller will not release the goods until the buyer accepts the *time draft*.[1] Accepting the draft, the buyer designates a bank at which the draft will be paid when it comes due. At that time, the draft becomes a *trade acceptance,* and depending on the creditworthiness of the buyer, it may possess some degree of marketability. If the trade acceptance is

---

[1] If the instrument is a *sight draft*, the buyer is ordered to pay the draft on presentation. Under this arrangement, trade credit is not extended.

Part IV Working Capital Management

marketable, the seller of the goods can sell it at a discount and receive immediate payment for the goods. At final maturity, the holder of the acceptance presents it to the designated bank for collection.

Terms of Sale.   Because the use of promissory notes and trade acceptances is rather limited, the subsequent discussion will be confined to open-account trade credit. The terms of the sale make a great deal of difference in this type of credit. These terms, specified in the invoice, may be placed in several broad categories according to the "net period" within which payment is expected and according to the terms of the cash discount, if any.

1. *COD and CBD—No Trade Credit.* COD means *cash on delivery* of goods. The only risk the seller undertakes is that the buyer may refuse the shipment. Under such circumstances, the seller will be stuck with the shipping costs. Occasionally a seller might ask for *cash before delivery (CBD)* to avoid all risk. Under either COD or CBD terms, the seller does not extend credit.
2. *Net Period—No Cash Discount.* When credit is extended, the seller specifies the period of time allowed for payment. For example, the terms "net 30" indicate that the invoice or bill must be paid within 30 days. If the seller bills on a monthly basis, it might require such terms as "net 15, EOM," which means that all goods shipped before the *end of the month* must be paid for by the 15th of the following month.
3. *Net Period—Cash Discount.* In addition to extending credit, the seller may offer a cash discount if the bill is paid during the early part of the net period. The terms "2/10, net 30" indicate that the seller offers a 2 percent discount if the bill is paid within 10 days; otherwise, the buyer must pay the full amount within 30 days. Usually, a cash discount is offered as an incentive to the buyer to pay early. In Chapter 10, we discussed the optimal cash discount the seller might offer. A cash discount differs from a *trade discount* and from a *quantity discount*. A trade discount is greater for one class of customers (wholesalers) than for others (retailers). A quantity discount is offered on large shipments.
4. *Seasonal Dating.* In a seasonal business, sellers frequently use datings to encourage customers to place their orders before a heavy selling period. A manufacturer of lawn mowers, for example, may give *seasonal datings* specifying that any shipment to a dealer in the winter or spring does not have to be paid for until summer. (This topic is discussed in more detail in Chapter 10.)

Trade Credit as a Means of Financing.   We have seen that trade credit is a source of funds to the buyer because the buyer does not have to pay for goods until after they are delivered. If the firm automatically pays its bills a certain number of days after the invoice date, trade credit becomes a spontaneous (or built-in) source of financing that varies with the production cycle. As the firm increases its production and corresponding purchases, accounts payable increase and provide part of the funding needed to finance the increase in production. For example, suppose that, on average, a firm purchases $5,000 worth of goods a day from its suppliers on terms of "net 30." The firm will thus be provided with $150,000 worth of financing from accounts payable (30 days $\times$ $5,000 per day = $150,000) if it always pays at the end of the net period. Now, if purchases from suppliers should increase to $6,000 per day, $30,000 of additional financing will be provided as the level of accounts payable ultimately rises to $180,000 (30 days $\times$ $6,000 per day). Similarly, as production decreases, accounts payable tend to decrease. Under these circumstances, trade credit is not a discretionary source of financing. It is entirely dependent on the purchasing plans of the firm, which, in turn, are dependent on the firm's production cycle. In examining trade credit as a discretionary form of financing, we want to specifically consider situations in which (1) a firm does not take a cash discount but pays on the last day of the net period, and (2) a firm pays its bills beyond the net period.

Payment on the Final Due Date.   In this section we assume that the firm forgoes a cash discount but does pay its bill on the final due date of the net period. If no cash discount is offered, there is no cost for the use of credit during the net period. On the other hand, if a firm takes a discount, there is no cost for the use of trade credit during the discount period. If a cash discount is offered but not taken, however, there is a definite opportunity cost. If the terms of sale are "2/10, net 30," the firm has the use of funds for an additional 20 days if it does not take the cash discount but pays on the final day of the net period. For a $100 invoice, it would have the use of $98 for 20 days, and for this privilege it pays $2. (This is the result of paying $100 thirty days after the sale, rather than $98 ten days after the sale.) Treating this situation as equivalent to a loan of $98 for 20 days at a $2 interest cost, we can solve for the approximate *annual* interest rate ($X\%$) as follows:

$$\$2 = \$98 \times X\% \times (20 \text{ days}/365 \text{ days})$$

Therefore,

$$X\% = (2/98) \times (365/20) = \mathbf{37.2\%}$$

Thus, we see that trade credit can be a very expensive form of short-term financing when a cash discount is offered but not accepted.

The cost, on an annual percentage basis, of not taking a cash discount can be generalized as[2]

$$\begin{array}{c}\text{Approximate} \\ \text{annual interest} \\ \text{cost}\end{array} = \frac{\% \text{ discount}}{(100\% - \% \text{ discount})} \times \frac{365 \text{ days}}{(\text{payment date} - \text{discount period})} \quad \textbf{(11-1)}$$

Making use of Eq. (11-1), we can see that the cost of not taking a discount declines as the payment date becomes longer in relation to the discount period. Had the terms in our example been "2/10, net 60," the approximate annual percentage cost of not taking the discount, but rather paying at the end of the credit period, would have been

$$(2/98) \times (365/50) = \mathbf{14.9\%}$$

The relationship between the annualized implicit interest cost of trade credit and the number of days between the end of the discount period and the end of the net period is shown in Figure 11-1. We assume "2/10" discount terms. For situations in which payment is made on the final due date, we see that the cost of trade credit decreases at a decreasing rate as the net period increases. The point is that if a firm does not take a cash discount, its cost of trade credit declines with the length of time it is able to postpone payment.

S-t-r-e-t-c-h-i-n-g Accounts Payable.   In the preceding section we assumed that payment was made at the end of the net period; however, a firm may postpone payment beyond this period. We call this postponement "s-t-r-e-t-c-h-i-n-g" accounts payable or "leaning on the trade." Stretching accounts payable generates additional short-term financing for the firm by way of the additional buildup in a liability

---

[2]The simple formula presented does not take account of compound interest.

Part IV Working Capital Management

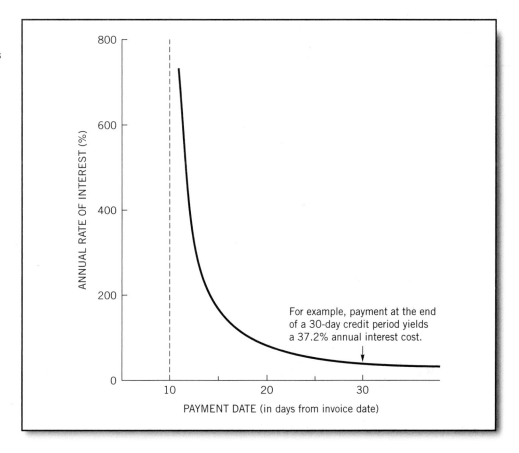

FIGURE 11-1
Annual Rate of
Interest on Accounts
Payable with
Credit Terms of
"2/10, Net _____"

account. However, this "benefit" must be weighed against the associated costs. The possible costs of stretching accounts payable include

- The cost of the cash discount (if any) forgone.
- Late payment penalties or interest that "may" be charged, depending on the industry practice.
- The possible deterioration in credit rating, along with the firm's ability to obtain future credit.

In Chapter 10 we discussed the rating system of credit agencies such as Dun & Bradstreet. If a firm stretches its payables excessively, so that payables are significantly delinquent, its credit rating will suffer. Suppliers will view the firm with apprehension and may insist on rather strict terms of sale if, indeed, they sell at all. In assessing a company, banks and other lenders do not favorably regard patterns of excessively slow payment. Although it is difficult to quantify, there is certainly an opportunity cost to a deterioration in a firm's credit reputation.

Notwithstanding the possibility of a deteriorating credit rating, it may be possible to postpone certain payables beyond the net period without severe consequences. Suppliers are in business to sell goods, and trade credit may increase sales. A supplier may be willing to go along with stretching payables, particularly if the risk of bad-debt loss is negligible. If the funds requirement of the firm is seasonal, suppliers may not view the stretching of payables in an unfavorable light during periods of peak requirements, provided that the firm is current in the trade during the rest of the year. There may be an indirect charge for this extension of credit, in the form of higher prices, a possibility that the firm should carefully consider in evaluating the cost of stretching accounts payable.

Periodic and reasonable stretching of payables is not necessarily bad, per se. It should be evaluated objectively in relation to alternative sources of short-term credit. When a firm does stretch its payables, it should make efforts to keep suppliers fully informed of its situation. A large number of suppliers will allow a firm to stretch payables if the firm is honest with the supplier and consistent in its payments.

Advantages of Trade Credit. The firm must balance the advantages of trade credit against the cost of forgoing a possible cash discount, any possible late payment penalties, the opportunity cost associated with a possible deterioration in credit reputation, and the possible increase in selling price the seller imposes on the buyer. There are several advantages of trade credit as a form of short-term financing. Probably the major advantage is its ready availability. The accounts payable of most firms represent a *continuous form of credit*. There is no need to formally arrange financing—it is already there. As old bills are paid and new credit purchases made, new accounts payable replace old, and the amount of trade credit financing fluctuates accordingly. If the firm is now taking cash discounts, additional credit is readily available by not paying existing accounts payable until the end of the net period. There is no need to negotiate with the supplier; the decision is entirely up to the firm. In stretching accounts payable, the firm will find it necessary, after a certain degree of postponement, to negotiate with the supplier.

In most other types of short-term financing, it is necessary to negotiate formally with the lender over the terms of a loan. The lender may impose restrictions on the firm and seek a secured position. Restrictions are possible with trade credit, but they are not nearly as likely. With other sources of short-term financing, there may be a lead time between the time the need for funds is recognized and the time the firm is able to borrow. Trade credit is a more flexible means of financing. The firm does not have to sign a note, pledge collateral, or adhere to a strict payment schedule on a note. A supplier views an occasional delinquent payment with a far less critical eye than does a banker or other lender.

The advantages of using trade credit must be weighed against the cost. As we have seen, the cost may be high when all factors are considered. Many firms utilize other sources of short-term financing to be able to take advantage of cash discounts. The savings in cost over other forms of short-term financing, however, must offset the loss of flexibility and convenience associated with trade credit. For certain firms, there are no alternative sources of short-term credit.

Who Bears the Cost? We should recognize that trade credit involves a cost for the use of funds over time. This use is not free. The burden may fall on the supplier, the buyer, or both parties. The supplier may be able to pass the cost on to the buyer in the form of higher prices.

The supplier of a product for which demand may slow dramatically if prices are raised may be reluctant to increase prices. This supplier may, therefore, end up absorbing most of the cost of trade credit. Under other circumstances the supplier is able to pass the cost on to the buyer. The buyer should determine who is bearing the cost of trade credit. A buyer who is bearing the cost may shop around for a better deal. The buyer should recognize that the cost of trade credit changes over time. In periods of rising interest rates and tight money, suppliers may raise the price of their products to take account of the rising cost of carrying receivables. This rise in price should not be confused with other rises caused by changing supply and demand conditions in the product markets.

Accrued Expenses

Perhaps even more than accounts payable, **accrued expenses** represent a spontaneous source of financing. The most common accrued expenses are for wages and taxes. For both accounts, the expense is incurred, or accrued, but not yet paid. Usually a date is specified when the accrued expense must be paid. Income taxes are paid quarterly; property taxes are paid semiannually. Wages are typically paid weekly, every other week, semimonthly, or monthly. Like accounts payable, accrued expenses tend to rise and fall with the level of the firm's operations. For example, as sales increase, labor costs usually increase, and with them, accrued wages also increase. And as profits increase, accrued taxes increase.

In a sense, accrued expenses represent costless financing. Services are rendered for wages, but employees are not paid and do not expect to be paid until the end of the pay period. Similarly, taxes are not expected to be paid until their due date. Thus, accrued expenses represent an interest-free source of financing.

Unfortunately for the company, they do not represent truly discretionary financing. For taxes, the government is the creditor, and it likes to be paid on time. A company in extreme financial difficulty can postpone a tax payment for a short while, but there are penalties and interest charges. It may postpone the payment of wages only at the expense of employees and morale. Employees may respond with absenteeism or reduced efficiency, or they may even seek employment elsewhere. A company must be extremely careful in postponing wages. It must inform employees and set a firm date for payment. Such a measure is one of last resort, but, nevertheless, many a company on the brink of cash-flow disaster finds itself having to postpone wages as well as all other payments.

NEGOTIATED FINANCING

From two of the main sources of short-term financing, trade credit from suppliers and accrued expenses, we turn to methods of negotiated (or external) short-term financing in the public or private market. In the public market, certain money market instruments provide corporations with financing when they are sold to investors, either directly by the issuer or indirectly through dealers. The principal sources of short-term loans are commercial banks and finance companies. With both money market credit and short-term loans, financing must be arranged on a formal basis.

Money Market Credit

Commercial Paper. Large, well-established companies sometimes borrow on a short-term basis through commercial paper and other money market instruments. **Commercial paper** represents an unsecured, short-term, negotiable promissory note sold in the money market. Because these notes are a money market instrument, only the most creditworthy companies are able to use commercial paper as a source of short-term financing.

The commercial paper market is composed of two parts: the dealer market and the direct-placement market.[3] Industrial firms, utilities, and medium-sized finance companies sell commercial paper through dealers. The dealer organization is composed of a half-dozen major dealers who purchase commercial paper from the issuer and, in turn, sell it to investors. The typical commission a dealer earns is 1/8 percent, and maturities on dealer-placed paper generally range from 30 to 90 days. The market is highly organized and sophisticated; paper is generally sold in minimum denominations of $100,000. Although the dealer market has been characterized in the past by the significant number of issuers who borrowed on a seasonal basis, the trend is definitely toward financing on a revolving or more permanent basis.

A number of large finance companies, such as General Motors Acceptance Corporation (GMAC), bypass the dealer organization in favor of selling their paper directly to investors. These issuers tailor both the maturity and the amount of the notes to the needs of investors, mostly large corporations with excess cash. Maturities on directly placed domestic paper can range from as little as a few days up to 270 days. Unlike many industrial issuers, finance companies use the commercial paper market as a permanent source of funds. Both dealer-placed and directly placed paper is rated according to its quality by one or more of the independent rating agencies—Moody's, Standard & Poor's, Duff & Phelps, and Fitch's. The top ratings are P-1, A-1, D-1, and F-1 for the four agencies, respectively. Only grade-1 and grade-2 paper find favor in the market.

The principal advantage of commercial paper as a source of short-term financing is that it is generally cheaper than a short-term business loan from a commercial bank. Depending on the interest-rate cycle, the rate on commercial paper may be as much as several percent lower than the prime rate for bank loans to the highest-quality borrowers. For most companies, commercial paper is a supplement to bank credit. In fact, commercial paper dealers require borrowers to maintain lines of credit at banks in order to backstop the use of commercial paper. This provides added assurance that commercial paper borrowings can be paid off. On the whole, however, the growth of the commercial paper and other money markets has been at the expense of bank borrowings. The market share of total corporate financing enjoyed by banks has declined over time.

Instead of issuing "stand-alone" paper, some corporations issue what is known as "bank-supported" commercial paper. For a fee, a bank provides a **letter of credit (L/C)** guaranteeing the investor that the company's obligation will be paid. The quality of the investment then depends on the creditworthiness of the bank, and the paper is rated accordingly by the rating agencies. A bank-supported arrangement makes sense for companies that are not well known, such as those which are privately held, as well as for companies that would be rated somewhat less than prime quality if they were to issue stand-alone paper. It affords access to the commercial paper market at times when the cost is less than direct borrowings at the bank.

Bankers' Acceptances.   For a company engaged in foreign trade or the domestic shipment of certain marketable goods, **bankers' acceptances** can be a meaningful source of financing. When an American company wishes to import $100,000 worth of electronic components from a company in Japan, the two companies agree that a 90-day time draft will be used in settlement of the trade. The American company arranges a letter of credit with its bank, whereby the bank agrees to honor drafts drawn on the company as presented through a Japanese bank. The Japanese company

Letter of credit (L/C) A promise from a third party (usually a bank) for payment in the event that certain conditions are met. It is frequently used to guarantee payment of an obligation.

Bankers' acceptances (BAs) Short-term promissory trade notes for which a bank (by having "accepted" them) promises to pay the holder the face amount at maturity.

---

[3]For a discussion of commercial paper from the standpoint of a short-term investor, see Chapter 9.

ships the goods and at the same time draws a draft ordering the American company to pay in 90 days. It then takes the draft to its Japanese bank. By prearrangement, the draft is sent to the American bank and is "accepted" by that bank. At that time it becomes a bankers' acceptance. In essence, the bank accepts responsibility for payment, thereby substituting its creditworthiness for that of the drawee, the American company.

If the bank is large and well known—and most banks accepting drafts are—the instrument becomes highly marketable upon acceptance. As a result, the drawer (the Japanese company) does not have to hold the draft until the final due date; it can sell the draft in the market for less than its face value. The discount involved represents the interest payment to the investor. At the end of 90 days the investor presents the acceptance to the accepting bank for payment and receives $100,000. At this time the American company is obligated to have funds on deposit to cover the draft. Thus, it has financed its import for a 90-day period. Presumably, the Japanese exporter would have charged a lower price if payment were to be made on shipment. In this sense the American company is the "borrower."

The presence of an active and viable bankers' acceptance market makes possible the financing of foreign trade at interest rates approximating those on commercial paper. Although the principles by which the acceptance is created are the same for foreign and domestic trade, a smaller portion of the total bankers' acceptances outstanding is domestic. In addition to trade, domestic acceptance financing is used in connection with the storage of such things as grain.

Unsecured Loans

Unsecured loans A form of debt for money borrowed that is not backed by the pledge of specific assets.

For explanatory purposes it is useful to separate business loans into two categories: **unsecured loans** and **secured loans.** Almost without exception, finance companies do not offer unsecured loans, simply because a borrower who deserves unsecured credit can borrow at a lower cost from a commercial bank. Consequently, our discussion of unsecured loans will involve only commercial banks.

Secured loans A form of debt for money borrowed in which specific assets have been pledged to guarantee payment.

Short-term, unsecured bank loans are typically regarded as "self-liquidating" in that the assets purchased with the proceeds generate sufficient cash flows to pay off the loan. At one time, banks confined their lending almost exclusively to this type of loan, but they now provide a wide variety of business loans tailored to the specific needs of the borrower. Still, the short-term, self-liquidating loan is a popular source of business financing, particularly in financing seasonal buildups in accounts receivable and inventories. Unsecured short-term loans may be extended under a line of credit, under a revolving credit agreement, or on a transaction basis. The debt itself is formally evidenced by a promissory note signed by the borrower, stating the interest to be paid along with how and when the loan will be repaid.

Line of credit (with a bank) An informal arrangement between a bank and its customer specifying the maximum amount of unsecured credit the bank will permit the firm to owe at any one time.

Line of Credit.   A **line of credit** is an informal arrangement between a bank and its customer specifying the maximum amount of unsecured credit the bank will permit the firm to owe at any one time. Usually, credit lines are established for a one-year period and are set for renewal after the bank receives the latest annual report and has had a chance to review the progress of the borrower. If the borrower's year-end statement date is December 31, a bank may set its line to expire sometime in March. At that time, the bank and the company would meet to discuss the credit needs of the firm for the coming year in light of its past year's performance. The amount of the line is based on the bank's assessment of the creditworthiness and the credit needs of the borrower. Depending on changes in these conditions, a line of credit may be adjusted at the renewal date or before, if conditions necessitate a change.

The cash budget often gives the best insight into the borrower's short-term credit needs. If maximum or peak borrowing needs over the forthcoming year are estimated at $800,000, a company might seek a line of credit of $1 million to give it a margin of safety. Whether the bank will go along with the request will depend, of course, on its evaluation of the creditworthiness of the firm. If the bank agrees, the firm then may borrow on a short-term basis—usually through a series of specific promissory notes whose average maturity is around 90 days—up to the full $1 million line. Because certain banks regard borrowing under lines of credit as seasonal or temporary financing, they may impose a *"cleanup" provision*. Under a cleanup provision, the borrower would be required to clean up bank debt—that is, to owe the bank nothing—for a period of time during the year. The cleanup period is usually one to two months. The cleanup itself is evidence to the bank that the loan is truly seasonal in nature and not part of the permanent financing of the firm. (Otherwise, the bank might end up providing, in essence, long-term financing at short-term rates.) If the interval during which a profitable firm were out of bank debt decreased from four months two years ago, to two months last year, and to no cleanup this year, the trend would suggest the use of bank credit to finance permanent funds requirements.

Despite its many advantages to the borrower, it is important to note that a line of credit does not constitute a legal commitment on the part of the bank to extend credit. The borrower is usually informed of the line by means of a letter indicating that the bank is willing to extend credit up to a certain amount. An example of such a letter (containing a cleanup provision) is shown in Figure 11-2. This letter is not a legal obligation of the bank to extend credit. If the creditworthiness of the borrower should deteriorate over the year, the bank might not want to extend credit and would not be required to do so. Under most circumstances, however, a bank feels bound to honor a line of credit.

Revolving credit agreement A formal, legal commitment to extend credit up to some maximum amount over a stated period of time.

Commitment fee A fee charged by the lender for agreeing to hold credit available.

Revolving Credit Agreement. A **revolving credit agreement** is a formal, legal commitment by a bank to extend credit up to a maximum amount. While the commitment is in force, the bank must extend credit whenever the borrower wishes to borrow, provided that total borrowings do not exceed the maximum amount specified. If the revolving credit is for $1 million and $700,000 is already owing, the borrower can borrow up to an additional $300,000 at any time. For the privilege of having this formal commitment, the borrower is usually required to pay a **commitment fee** on the unused portion of the revolving credit, in addition to interest on any loaned amount. If the revolving credit is for $1 million and borrowing for the year averages $400,000, the borrower could be required to pay a commitment fee on the $600,000 unused (but available) portion. If the commitment fee is .5 percent, the cost of this privilege will be $3,000 for the year.

Revolving credit agreements frequently extend beyond one year. Because lending agreements of more than a year must be regarded as intermediate- rather than short-term credit, we will examine revolving credits more extensively in Chapter 21.

Transaction Loan. Borrowing under a line of credit or under a revolving credit agreement is not appropriate when the firm needs short-term funds for only one specific purpose. A contractor may borrow from a bank in order to complete a job. When the contractor receives payment for the job, the loan is paid off. For this type of loan, a bank evaluates each request by the borrower as a separate transaction. In these evaluations, the cash-flow ability of the borrower to pay the loan is usually of paramount importance.

FIGURE 11-2
Sample Letter
Extending a Line
of Credit

First National Bank
Knoxville, Tennessee

March 23, 2001

Ms. Jean Proffitt
Vice President & Treasurer
Acme Aglet Corporation
11235 Fibonacci Circle
Maryville, Tennessee 37801

Dear Ms. Proffitt:

Based upon our analysis of your year-end audited statements, we are pleased
to renew your $1 million unsecured line of credit for the forthcoming year.
Borrowings under this line will be at a rate of one-half percent (1/2 %)
over the prime rate.

This line is subject to only the understanding that your company will maintain
its financial position and that it will be out of bank debt for at least 45 days
during the fiscal year.

Sincerely yours,

Annette E. Winston

Annette E. Winston
Vice President

Detour: Cost of Borrowing

Before turning our attention to secured loans, we need to take a slight detour and discuss a number of important factors that affect the cost of borrowing on a short-term
basis. These factors—which include "stated" interest rates, compensating balances,
and commitment fees—help determine the "effective" rate of interest on short-term
borrowing.

Interest Rates.   The stated (nominal) interest rates on most business loans are determined through negotiation between the borrower and the lender. In some measure,
banks try to vary the interest rate charged according to the creditworthiness of the
borrower—the lower the creditworthiness, the higher the interest rate. Interest rates
charged also vary in keeping with money market conditions. One measure that
changes with underlying market conditions, for example, is the **prime rate.** The
prime rate is the rate charged on short-term business loans to financially sound companies. The rate itself is usually set by large money market banks and is relatively
uniform throughout the country.

Prime rate Short-term
interest rate charged by
banks to large, creditworthy
customers. It is also called
simply *prime.*

Although the term *prime rate* would seem to imply the rate of interest a bank charges its most creditworthy customers, this has not been the recent practice. With banks becoming more competitive for corporate customers and facing extreme competition from the commercial paper market, the well-established, financially sound company often is able to borrow at a rate of interest below prime. The rate charged is based on the bank's marginal cost of funds, as typically reflected by the **London interbank offered rate (LIBOR),** or the rate paid on money market certificates of deposit. An interest-rate margin is added to the cost of funds, and this sum becomes the rate charged the customer. This rate is changed daily with changes in money market rates. The margin over the cost of funds depends on competitive conditions and on the relative bargaining power of the borrower, but it will usually be in excess of 1 percent.

Other borrowers will pay either the prime rate or a rate above prime, the bank's pricing of the loan being stated relative to the prime rate. Thus, the prime often serves as a benchmark rate. For example, with "prime-plus" pricing, a bank might extend a line of credit to a company at the prime rate plus .5 percent—"prime plus .5." If the prime rate is 10 percent, the borrower is charged an interest rate of 10.5 percent. If the prime rate changes to 8 percent, the borrower will pay 8.5 percent. Among the various bank customers, interest-rate differentials from prime supposedly should reflect only differences in creditworthiness.

Other factors, however, also influence the differential. Among them are the cash balances maintained and other business the borrower has with a bank (such as trust business). Also, the cost of servicing a loan is a factor determining the differential from prime. Certain collateralized loans are costly to administer, and this cost must be passed on to the borrower, either in the form of the interest rate charged or in a special fee.

Thus, the interest rate charged on a short-term loan will depend on the prevailing cost of funds to banks, the existing benchmark rate (often the prime rate), the creditworthiness of the borrower, the present and prospective relationships of the borrower with the bank, and sometimes other considerations as well. In addition, because of the fixed costs involved in credit investigation and in the processing of a loan, we would expect the interest rate on small loans to be higher than the rate on large loans.

Methods of Computing Interest Rates. Two common ways in which interest on a short-term business loan may be paid are on a *collect basis* and on a *discount basis*. When paid on a collect basis, the interest is paid at the maturity of the note; when paid on a discount basis, interest is deducted from the initial loan. On a $10,000 loan at 12 percent stated interest for one year, the effective rate of interest on a collect note is simply the stated rate:

$$\frac{\$1{,}200 \text{ in interest}}{\$10{,}000 \text{ in usable funds}} = \textbf{12.00}\%$$

On a discount basis, however, the effective rate of interest is higher than 12 percent:

$$\frac{\$1{,}200 \text{ in interest}}{\$8{,}800 \text{ in usable funds}} = \textbf{13.64}\%$$

When we pay on a discount basis, we have the "use" of only $8,800 for the year but must pay back $10,000 at the end of that time. Thus, the effective rate of interest is

Part IV Working Capital Management

higher on a discount note than on a collect note. We should point out that most bank loans are paid on a collect basis.

Compensating balance
Non-interest-bearing demand deposits maintained by a firm to compensate a bank for services provided, credit lines, or loans.

Compensating Balances. In addition to charging interest on loans, commercial banks may require the borrower to maintain non-interest-bearing demand deposit balances at the bank in direct proportion to either the amount of funds borrowed or the amount of the commitment. These minimum balances are known as **compensating balances.** The amount required in the compensating balance varies according to competitive conditions in the market for loans and specific negotiations between the borrower and the lender. Banks generally would like to obtain balances equal to at least 10 percent of a line of credit. If the line is $2 million, the borrower would be required to maintain average balances of at least $200,000 during the year. Another arrangement might be for the bank to require average balances of 5 percent on the line and 5 percent more on the amount owing when the line is in use. If a firm's line were $2 million and its borrowings averaged $600,000, it would be required to maintain $130,000 in compensating balances.

The result of compensating balance requirements is to raise the effective cost of borrowing if the borrower is required to maintain cash balances above the amount the firm would ordinarily maintain. If we borrow $1 million at 12 percent and are required to maintain $100,000 more in balances than we would ordinarily, we will then have the use of only $900,000 of the $1 million loan. The effective annual interest cost is then not equal to the stated rate of 12 percent, but rather

$$\frac{\$120,000 \text{ in interest}}{\$900,000 \text{ in usable funds}} = \textbf{13.33}\%$$

The notion of compensating balances for loans may be weakening. Increasingly, banks are becoming oriented toward "profits" as opposed to "deposits." Accordingly, they are fine-tuning profitability analyses of customer relationships. With the rapid and significant fluctuations in the cost of funds to banks in recent years, as well as the accelerated competition among financial institutions, banks are increasingly making loans without compensating balance requirements. The interest rate charged, however, is more in line with the bank's incremental cost of obtaining funds. The movement toward sophisticated profitability analyses has driven banks to direct compensation for loans through interest rates and fees as opposed to indirect compensation through deposit balances.

Commitment Fees. We have already discussed why a commitment fee is usually required under the terms of a revolving credit agreement. Now, let's see how the presence of this fee can affect the cost of borrowing. Assume that Acme Aglet Company has a revolving credit agreement with a bank. It can borrow up to $1 million at 12 percent interest but is required to maintain a 10 percent compensating balance on any funds borrowed under the agreement. In addition, it must pay a .5 percent commitment fee on the unused portion of the formal credit line. If the firm borrows $400,000 for an entire year under this agreement, makes all payments at note maturity, and would not otherwise maintain cash deposits at this particular bank, the effective cost of borrowing is

$$\frac{\$48,000 \text{ in interest} + \$3,000 \text{ in commitment fees}}{\$360,000 \text{ in usable funds}} = \textbf{14.17}\%$$

Secured (or Asset-Based) Loans

QUESTION•ANSWER•QUESTION•ANSWER

Two firms each seek a $100,000, three-month, short-term loan from the same financial institution. One firm walks away with an unsecured loan, and the other leaves with a secured loan. Which firm's loan is probably more expensive?

The secured loan will probably be more expensive. There are two reasons for this. First, short-term, unsecured loans generally carry a lower interest rate because only borrowers with high creditworthiness can acquire funds on an unsecured basis. Secondly, the lender will pass the administrative costs of monitoring collateral on to the secured borrower in the form of higher interest payments. In fact, the secured borrower's goal should be to eventually become an unsecured borrower. In this way the borrower may be able to save from 1 to 5 percent in short-term borrowing costs.

Many firms cannot obtain credit on an unsecured basis, either because they are new and unproven or because bankers do not have high regard for the firm's ability to service the amount of debt sought. To make loans to such firms, lenders may require **security (collateral)** that will reduce their risk of loss. With security, lenders have two sources of loan repayment: the cash-flow ability of the firm to service the debt and, if that source fails for some reason, the collateral value of the security. Most lenders will not make a loan unless the firm has sufficient expected cash flows to make proper servicing of debt highly probable. To reduce their risk, however, they may require security.

Security (collateral)
Asset(s) pledged by a borrower to ensure repayment of a loan. If the borrower defaults, the lender may sell the security to pay off the loan.

Collateral. The excess of the market value of the security pledged over the amount of the loan determines the lender's margin of safety. If the borrower is unable to meet an obligation, the lender can sell the security to satisfy the claim. If the security is sold for an amount exceeding the amount of the loan and interest owed, the difference is remitted to the borrower. If the security is sold for less, the lender becomes a general, or unsecured, creditor for the amount of the difference. Because secured lenders do not wish to become general creditors, they usually seek security with a market value sufficiently above the amount of the loan to minimize the likelihood of their not being able to sell the security in full satisfaction of the loan. The degree of security protection a lender seeks varies with the creditworthiness of the borrower, the security the borrower has available, and the financial institution making the loan.

The value of the collateral to the lender varies according to several factors. Perhaps the most important is marketability. If the collateral can be sold quickly in an active market without depressing the price, the lender is likely to be willing to lend an amount that represents a fairly high percentage of the collateral's stated value. On the other hand, if the collateral is a special-purpose machine designed specifically for a company and has no viable secondary market, the lender may choose to lend nothing at all. The life of the collateral also matters. If the collateral has a cash-flow life that closely parallels the life of the loan, it will be more valuable to the lender than collateral that has a much longer cash-flow life. As the collateral's economic use generates cash flow, these proceeds may be used to pay down the loan. Still another important factor is the basic riskiness associated with the collateral. The greater the fluctuation in its market value or the more uncertain the lender is concerning market value, the less desirable the collateral from the standpoint of the lender. Thus, marketability, life, and riskiness determine the attractiveness of various types of collateral to a lender and, in turn, the amount of potential financing available to a company. Before taking up specific, short-term, secured lending arrangements, we take a brief look at how lenders protect themselves under the **Uniform Commercial Code.**

Uniform Commercial Code Model state legislation related to many aspects of commercial transactions that went into effect in Pennsylvania in 1954. It has been adopted with limited changes by most state legislatures.

Article 9 of the Code deals with security interests of lenders, the specific aspect with which we are concerned. A lender who requires collateral of a borrower obtains a *security interest* in the collateral. The collateral may be accounts receivable, inventory, equipment, or other assets of the borrower. The security interest in the collateral is created by a *security agreement*, also known as a *security device.* This agreement is signed by the borrower and lender and contains a description of the collateral. To "perfect" a security interest in the collateral, the lender must file a copy of the security agreement, or a financing statement, with a public office of the state in which the collateral is located. Frequently, this office is that of the secretary of state. The filing gives public notice to other parties that the lender has a security interest in the collateral described. Before accepting collateral as security for a loan, a lender will search the public notices to see if the collateral has been pledged previously in connection with another loan. Only the lender with a valid security interest in the collateral has a prior claim on the assets and can sell the collateral in settlement of the loan.

Technically, a secured (or asset-based) loan is any loan secured by any of the borrower's assets. However, when the loan involved is "short-term," the assets most commonly used as security are accounts receivable and inventories.

Accounts-Receivable-Backed Loans. Accounts receivable are one of the most liquid assets of the firm. Consequently, they make desirable security for a short-term loan. From the standpoint of the lender, the major difficulties with this type of security are the cost of processing the collateral and the risk of fraud due to the borrower pledging nonexistent accounts. A company may seek a receivable loan from either a commercial bank or a finance company. Because a bank usually charges a lower interest rate than a finance company does, the firm will generally try to first borrow from a bank.

In evaluating the loan request, the lender will analyze the quality of the firm's receivables to determine how much to lend against them. The higher the quality of the accounts the firm maintains, the higher the percentage the lender is willing to advance against the face value of the receivables pledged. A lender does not have to accept all of the borrower's accounts receivable. Usually, accounts from creditors who have a low credit rating or who are unrated will be rejected. Based on an *aging schedule* analysis (see Chapter 6), accounts more than, say, one month overdue may be rejected. Also, government and foreign accounts are usually ineligible unless special arrangements are made. Depending on the quality of the receivables accepted, a lender typically advances between 50 and 80 percent of their face value.

The lender is concerned not only with the quality of receivables but also with their size. The lender must keep records on each account receivable that is pledged. Therefore, the smaller the average size of the accounts, the more it costs per dollar of loan to process them. Consequently, a firm that sells low-priced items on open account will generally be unable to obtain a receivable loan regardless of the quality of the accounts—the cost of processing the loan is simply too high. Sometimes a pledge of receivables "in general," also known as a "bulk" or "blanket" pledge, will be used to circumvent the cost involved with examining each account separately to determine acceptability. With such an arrangement, the lender does not keep track of the individual accounts but records only the total amounts of the pledged accounts and the payments received. Because preventing fraud is difficult with a "blanket" pledge of receivables, the percentage advance against face value of receivables is likely to be quite low, perhaps 25 percent.

Suppose a lender has decided to extend credit to a firm on the basis of a 75 percent advance against the face of specifically pledged accounts receivable. The borrower then sends the lender a schedule of accounts showing the names of the accounts, the dates of billing, and the amounts owed. The lender will sometimes require evidence of shipment, such as an invoice. Having received the schedule of accounts, the lender has the borrower sign a promissory note and a security agreement. The borrowing firm then receives 75 percent of the face value of the receivables shown on the schedule of accounts.

A receivable loan can be on either a *nonnotification* or a *notification basis*. Under the former arrangement, customers of the firm are not notified that their accounts have been pledged to the lender. When the firm receives payment on an account, it forwards this payment, together with other payments, to the lender. The lender checks the payments against its record of accounts outstanding and reduces the amount the borrower owes by 75 percent of the total payment. The other 25 percent is credited against the borrower's account. With a nonnotification arrangement, the lender must take precautions to make sure that the borrower does not withhold a payment check. With a notification arrangement, the account is notified of the assignment, and remittances are made directly to the lender. Under this arrangement, the borrower cannot withhold payments. Most firms naturally prefer to borrow on a nonnotification basis; however, the lender reserves the right to place the arrangement on a notification basis.

An accounts receivable loan is a more or less "continuous financing arrangement." As the firm generates new receivables that are acceptable to the lender, they are pledged, adding to the security base against which the firm is able to borrow. New receivables replace the old, and the security base and the amount of the loan fluctuate accordingly. A receivable loan is a very flexible means of securing financing. As receivables build up, the firm is able to borrow additional funds against them to help finance this buildup. Thus, the firm has access to "built-in" financing.

Inventory-Backed Loans.   Basic raw-material and finished-goods inventories represent reasonably liquid assets and are therefore suitable as security for short-term loans. As with a receivable loan, the lender determines a percentage advance against the market value of the collateral. This percentage varies according to the quality and type of inventory. Certain inventories, such as grains, are very marketable and, when properly stored, resist physical deterioration. The margin of safety required by the lender on a loan of this sort is fairly small, and the advance may be as high as 90 percent. (However, even this type of inventory is subject to misrepresentation, as you will soon see when we highlight "The Great Salad Oil Swindle.") On the other hand, the market for a highly specialized piece of equipment may be so narrow that a lender is unwilling to make any advance against its reported market value. Thus, not every kind of inventory can be pledged as security for a loan. The best collateral is inventory that is relatively standard and for which a ready market exists apart from the marketing organization of the borrower.

Lenders determine the percentage that they are willing to advance by considering marketability, perishability, market price stability, and the difficulty and expense of selling the inventory to satisfy the loan. The cost of selling some inventory may be very high. Lenders do not want to be in the business of liquidating collateral, but they do want to assure themselves that collateral has adequate value in case the borrower defaults in the payment of principal or interest. As is true with most secured, short-term loans, however, the actual decision to make the loan will primarily depend on the cash-flow ability of the borrower to service debt. There are a number of different ways a lender can obtain a secured interest in inventories, and we consider each in turn. In the first three methods (floating lien, chattel mortgage, and trust receipt), the inventory remains in the possession of the borrower. In the last two methods (terminal warehouse and field warehouse receipts), the inventory is in the possession of a third party.

1. *Floating lien.* Under the Uniform Commercial Code the borrower may pledge inventories "in general" without specifying the specific property involved. Under this arrangement the lender obtains a **floating lien** on all of the borrower's inventory. This *lien* allows for the legal seizure of the pledged assets in the event of loan default. By its very nature, the floating lien is a loose arrangement, and the lender may find it difficult to police. Frequently, a floating lien is requested only as additional protection and does not play a major role in determining whether or not the loan will be made. Even if the collateral is valuable, the lender is usually willing to make only a moderate advance because of the difficulty in exercising tight control over the collateral. The floating lien can be made to cover both receivables and inventories, as well as the collection of receivables. This modification gives the lender a lien on a major portion of a firm's current assets. In addition, the lien can be made to encompass almost any length of time so that it includes future as well as present inventory as security.

2. *Chattel mortgage.* With a **chattel mortgage,** inventories are identified by serial number or some other means. While the borrower holds title to the goods, the lender has a lien on inventory. This inventory cannot be sold unless the lender consents. Because of the rigorous identification requirements, chattel mortgages are ill-suited for inventory with rapid turnover or inventory that is not easy to identify specifically. Chattel mortgages are well suited, however, for certain finished-goods inventories of capital goods such as machine tools.

3. *Trust receipt.* Under a **trust receipt** arrangement, the borrower holds the inventory and the proceeds from its sale in trust for the lender. This type of lending arrangement, also known as *floor planning,* has been used extensively by automobile dealers, equipment dealers, and consumer durable goods dealers. An automobile manufacturer will ship cars to a dealer who, in turn, may finance the payment for these cars through a finance company. The finance company pays the manufacturer for the cars shipped. The dealer signs a trust receipt security agreement, which specifies what can be done with the inventory. The car dealer is allowed to sell the cars but must turn the proceeds of the sale over to the lender in payment of the loan. Inventory in trust, unlike inventory under a floating lien, is specifically identified by serial number or other means. In our example, the finance company periodically audits the cars the dealer has on hand. The serial numbers of these cars are checked against those shown in the security agreement. The purpose of the audit is to see if the dealer has sold cars without remitting the proceeds of the sale to the finance company.

   As the dealer buys new cars from the automobile manufacturer, a new trust receipt security agreement is signed, reflecting the new inventory. The dealer then borrows against this new collateral, holding it in trust. Although there is tighter control over collateral with a trust receipt agreement than with a floating

Floating lien A general, or blanket, lien against a group of assets, such as inventory or receivables, without the assets being specifically identified.

Chattel mortgage A lien on specifically identified *personal property* (assets other than real estate) backing a loan.

Trust receipt A security device acknowledging that the borrower holds specifically identified inventory and proceeds from its sale in trust for the lender.

lien, there is still the risk of inventory being sold without the proceeds being turned over to the lender. Consequently, the lender must exercise judgment in deciding to lend under this arrangement. A dishonest dealer can devise numerous ways to fool the lender.

Many durable goods manufacturers finance the inventories of their distributors or dealers. Their purpose is to encourage dealers or distributors to carry reasonable stocks of goods. It is reasoned that the greater the stock, the more likely the dealer or distributor is to make a sale. Because the manufacturer is interested in selling its product, financing terms are often more attractive than they would be with an "outside" lender.

Terminal warehouse receipt A receipt for the deposit of goods in a public warehouse that a lender holds as collateral for a loan.

4. *Terminal warehouse receipt.* A borrower secures a **terminal warehouse receipt** loan by storing inventory with a public, or terminal, warehousing company. The warehouse company issues a warehouse receipt, which evidences title to specific goods that are located in the warehouse. The warehouse receipt gives the lender a security interest in the goods, against which a loan can be made to the borrower. Under such an arrangement, the warehouse can release the collateral to the borrower only when authorized to do so by the lender. Consequently, the lender is able to maintain strict control over the collateral and will release collateral only when the borrower pays a portion of the loan. For protection, the lender usually requires the borrower to take out an insurance policy with a "loss-payable" clause in favor of the lender.

    Warehouse receipts may be either nonnegotiable or negotiable. A nonnegotiable warehouse receipt is issued in favor of a specific party—in this case, the lender—who is given title to the goods and has sole authority to release them. A negotiable warehouse receipt can be transferred by endorsement. Before goods can be released, the negotiable receipt must be presented to the warehouse operator. A negotiable receipt is useful when title to the goods is transferred from one party to another while the goods are in storage. With a nonnegotiable receipt, the release of goods can be authorized only in writing. Most lending arrangements are based on nonnegotiable receipts.

Field warehouse receipt A receipt for goods segregated and stored on the borrower's premises (but under the control of an independent warehousing company) that a lender holds as collateral for a loan.

5. *Field warehouse receipt.* In a terminal warehouse receipt loan, the pledged goods are located in a public warehouse. In a **field warehouse receipt** loan, the pledged inventory is located on the borrower's premises. Under this arrangement, a field warehousing company (an independent company that operates a borrower's warehouse) reserves a designated area on the borrower's premises for the inventory pledged as collateral. The field warehousing company has sole access to this area and is supposed to maintain strict control over it. (The goods that serve as collateral are segregated from the borrower's other inventory.) The field warehouse company issues a warehouse receipt as described in the previous section, and the lender extends a loan based on the collateral value of the inventory. The field warehouse arrangement is a useful means of financing when it is not desirable to place the inventory in a public warehouse—either because of the expense or because of the inconvenience. Field warehouse receipt lending is particularly appropriate when a borrower must make frequent use of inventory. Because of the need to pay the field warehouse company's expenses, the cost of this method of financing can be relatively high.

    The warehouse receipt, as evidence of collateral, is only as good as the issuing warehousing company. When administered properly, a warehouse receipt loan affords the lender a high degree of control over the collateral. However, sufficient examples of fraud show that the warehouse receipt does not always provide concrete evidence of value.

The Great Salad Oil Swindle

The most famous case of warehouse receipt fraud came to light in the early 1960s. Over 50 banks and other lenders made loans of roughly $200 million to the Allied Crude Vegetable Refining Corporation. These loans were secured by warehouse receipts for close to 2 billion pounds of vegetable oil. At first, cursory inspections failed to uncover the fact that a network of interconnecting pipes could move the same oil from tank to tank and that a thin layer of oil often covered a tankful of sea water or sludge.

A shortfall of 1.85 billion pounds of oil was eventually uncovered. The end result was that the field warehousing company went bankrupt, the lenders lost most of their $200 million in loans, and the president of Allied Crude, Antonio "Tino" DeAngelis, entered the *Guinness Book of World Records*. (What world record did "Tino" set? At the time, the highest amount ever demanded as bail was the $46,500,000 million against DeAngelis in a civil-damaged suit stemming from the Great Salad Oil Swindle.*)

For a more detailed account, see N. C. Miller, The Great Salad Oil Swindle (Baltimore: Penguin Books, 1965). For more on this and other frauds that have taken place against secured lenders, see Monroe R. Lazere, "Swinging Swindles and Creepy Frauds," Journal of Commercial Bank Lending 60 (September 1977), 44–52.

FACTORING ACCOUNTS RECEIVABLE

Factoring The selling of receivables to a financial institution, the *factor* usually "without recourse."

As we saw earlier, accounts receivable can be pledged to a lender as security against a loan. Instead of pledging receivables, however, a firm may engage in **factoring** receivables to acquire cash. In pledging accounts receivable, the firm still retains title to the receivables. When a firm *factors* its receivables, it transfers title to the receivables by actually selling them to a *factor* (often a subsidiary of a bank holding company). The sale is usually "without recourse," meaning that the selling firm would not be liable for any receivables not collected by the factor. The factor maintains a credit department and makes credit checks on accounts. Based on its credit investigation, the factor may refuse to buy certain accounts that it deems too risky. By factoring, a firm frequently relieves itself of the expense of maintaining a credit department and making collections. Thus, factoring can serve as a vehicle for *outsourcing* credit and collection responsibilities. Any account that the factor is unwilling to buy is an unacceptable credit risk unless, of course, the firm wants to assume this risk on its own and ship the goods.

Factoring arrangements are governed by a contract between the factor and the client. The contract is frequently for one year with an automatic provision for renewal and can be canceled only with prior notice of 30 to 60 days. Although it is customary in a factoring arrangement to notify customers that their accounts have been sold and that payments on the account should be sent directly to the factor, in many instances notification is not made. Customers continue to remit payments to the firm, which, in turn, endorses them to the factor. These endorsements are frequently camouflaged to prevent customers from learning that their accounts have been sold.

For many of you, factoring may still seem to be a rather foreign concept. You may, therefore, be surprised to learn that you have probably been a party to numerous factoring transactions without even realizing it. Every time that you make a purchase using a bank credit card you are involved in a factoring arrangement. The account receivable created by your credit purchase is being sold to a bank.

Factoring Costs

For bearing credit risk and servicing the receivables, the factor receives a commission, which for trade accounts is typically somewhat less than 1 percent of the face value of the receivables. The commission varies according to the size of the individual accounts, the volume of receivables sold, and the quality of the accounts. The factor generally does not pay the firm immediately on the purchase of accounts receivable. Rather, cash payment is usually made on the actual or average due date of the accounts receivable involved. If the factor advances money before it is due from customers, the firm must pay the factor interest on the advance. Advancing payment is a lending function of the factor in addition to risk bearing and servicing the receivables. For this additional function, the factor requires compensation. If the factored receivables total $10,000 and the factoring fee is 2 percent, the factor will credit the firm's account with $9,800. If the firm wants to draw on this account before the receivables become due, it will have to pay an interest charge—say, 1.5 percent a month—for the use of funds. If it wishes a cash advance and the receivables are due, on the average, in one month, the interest cost will be approximately .015 × $9,800 = **$147.**[4] Thus, the

---
[4]The actual cash advance would be $9,800 less the $147 interest cost, or $9,653.

Factoring Exports

Export factoring is catching on in a big way thanks to booming U.S. export sales and a growing demand on the part of foreign customers for shipments on open account. These days, export factoring is becoming commonplace for products as diverse as aircraft parts, surgical tools, and photo equipment.

For U.S. exporters, factoring foreign receivables has advantages over asking the buyer to open a letter of credit. The biggest is the ability to ship goods on open account without running the risk of not getting paid. By paying a fee of less than 2 percent of the value of the overseas shipment, U.S. exporters can avail themselves of an array of services, including credit checks, bill collection, bookkeeping, and cash advances of up to 90 percent of the shipment's value.

But factoring is not the answer for every exporter. Besides the transaction fee, which the exporter may not be able to pass along to the buyer, getting paid can sometimes take one or two weeks longer than with a letter of credit, exporters say.

What's more, factoring companies are reluctant to finance small shipments, generally insisting that their customers let them handle at least $2 million in transactions a year.

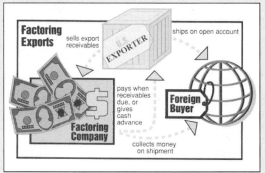

Export factoring typically works like this: The U.S. exporter sells or transfers title to its accounts receivable to a factoring company. The factor then assumes the credit risk and takes responsibility for all customer credit checks, billing and collection. If the factor discovers the prospective buyer's credit is no good, the exporter will often back out of the deal or insist on cash in advance.

Despite factoring's main advantages, the financing technique has its limitations. Since factors make their money by assessing credit risk, they generally avoid doing business in developing nations and in countries on shaky economic or political ground. Another drawback is timely payment. Getting paid is usually faster if the company uses a letter of credit.

All this considered, for established exporters seeking the competitive advantage of selling on open account or the peace of mind of trusting collections to a company with international contacts and experience, export factoring is a financing technique that should not be overlooked.

Source: Adapted from Rosalind Resnick, "Taking the Bite Out of Exporting," International Business *(April 1992), pp. 17–18.*

total cost of factoring is composed of a factoring fee plus an interest charge if the firm takes a cash advance. If the firm does not take a cash advance, there is no interest charge. In a third alternative, the firm may leave its funds with the factor beyond the receivables' due date and receive interest on the account from the factor.

Flexibility

The typical factoring arrangement is continuous. As new receivables are acquired, they are sold to the factor, and the firm's account is credited. The firm then draws on this account as it needs funds. Sometimes the factor will allow the firm to overdraw its account during periods of seasonal needs and thereby borrow on an unsecured basis. Under other arrangements, the factor may withhold a reserve from the firm's account as a protection against possible returns and allowances. The principal sources of factoring are commercial banks, factoring subsidiaries of bank holding companies, and certain old-line factors. Although some people attach a stigma to the company that factors its receivables, many others regard factoring as a perfectly acceptable method of financing. Its principal shortcoming is that it can be expensive. We must bear in mind, however, that the factor often relieves the firm of credit checking, the cost of processing receivables, collection expenses, and bad-debt expenses. For a small firm especially, the savings may be quite substantial.

COMPOSITION OF SHORT-TERM FINANCING

In this chapter we considered various sources of short-term financing. Because the total amount of short-term financing needed was assumed to have been determined according to the framework presented in Chapter 8, only the determination of the best combination of short-term financing need be considered in this chapter. The appropriate mix, or weighting, of alternative sources depends on considerations of cost, availability, timing, flexibility, and the degree to which the assets of the firm are encumbered (burdened with legal claims). Central to any meaningful analysis of alternative sources of funds is a comparison of their costs and the problem of timing. Cost differentials among the various short-term financing alternatives are not necessarily constant over time. Indeed, they fluctuate in keeping with changing market conditions. Thus, timing bears heavily on the question of the most appropriate mix of short-term financing.

Naturally, the availability of financing is important. If a firm cannot borrow through commercial paper or through a bank loan because of its low credit standing, it must turn to alternative sources. The lower the credit standing of the firm, of course, the fewer the sources of short-term financing available to it. Flexibility with respect to short-term financing pertains to the firm's ability to pay off a loan as well as to its ability to renew or even increase it. With short-term loans, the firm can pay off the debt when it has surplus funds and thereby reduce its overall interest costs. With factoring, advances can be taken only when needed, and interest costs incurred only as necessary. For commercial paper, the firm must wait until final maturity before paying off the loan.

Flexibility also relates to how easily the firm can increase its borrowing on short notice. With a line of credit or revolving credit at a bank, it is an easy matter to increase borrowings, assuming the maximum limit has not been reached. With other forms of short-term financing, the firm is less flexible. Finally, the degree to which assets are encumbered impacts the decision. With secured loans, lenders obtain a lien on the various assets of the firm. This secured position puts constraints on the firm's future financing possibilities. When receivables are actually sold under a factoring arrangement, the principle remains the same. In this case, the firm is selling one of its most liquid assets, thus reducing its creditworthiness in the minds of many creditors.

All of these factors influence the firm in deciding on the appropriate mix of short-term financing. Because cost is perhaps the key factor, differences in other factors should be compared with differences in cost. The cheapest source of financing from the standpoint of explicit costs may not be the cheapest source when flexibility, timing, and the degree to which assets are encumbered are considered. Although it would be desirable to express sources of short-term financing in terms of both explicit and implicit costs, the latter are hard to quantify. A more practical approach is to rank sources according to their explicit costs and then consider the other factors to see if they change the rankings as they relate to total desirability. Because the financing needs of the firm change over time, multiple sources of short-term financing should be explored on a continuous basis.

SUMMARY

- *Trade credit* from suppliers can be a significant source of short-term financing for the firm. If the firm has a strict policy regarding its promptness in paying bills, trade credit becomes a spontaneous (or built-in) source of financing that varies with the production cycle.

- When a cash discount for prompt payment is offered but not taken, the cash discount forgone becomes a cost of trade credit. The longer the period between the end of the discount period and the time the bill is paid, the less the annualized percentage opportunity cost incurred.

- "S-t-r-e-t-c-h-i-n-g" accounts payable involves postponement of payment beyond the due date. Although stretching payables generates additional short-term financing, this "benefit" must be weighed against associated costs, such as (1) the cost of the cash discount (if any) forgone, (2) any possible late payment penalties or interest charges, and (3) the possible deterioration in credit rating, along with the firm's ability to obtain future credit.

- Like accounts payable (trade credit from suppliers), *accrued expenses* represent a spontaneous source of financing. The principal accrued expenses are wages and taxes, and both are expected to be paid on established dates.

- Until accrued expenses are paid, interest-free financing is being provided to the company. For an ongoing firm, this financing is continuous. As old accrued expenses are paid, new expenses are incurred, and the amount of accrued expenses fluctuates accordingly. A company in dire financial straits will sometimes postpone tax and wage payments, but the consequences of such postponement can be severe.

- Money market credit and short-term loans are forms of negotiated (or external) short-term financing in the public or private market.

- Large, well-established, high-quality companies sometimes borrow on a short-term basis through *commercial paper*. Commercial paper represents an unsecured, short-term promissory note that is sold in the money market. Commercial paper is sold either through dealers or directly to investors. Rather than issue "stand-alone" paper, a firm may issue "bank-supported" paper, in which case a bank guarantees that the obligation will be paid. The principal advantage of commercial paper is that it is generally cheaper than a short-term business loan from a commercial bank.

- *Bankers' acceptance* financing is another type of money market credit. Usually associated with a foreign trade transaction, the acceptance is highly marketable and can be a very desirable source of short-term funds.

- Short-term loans can be divided into two types: *unsecured* and *secured*.

- Unsecured, short-term lending is generally confined to commercial bank loans under a *line of credit*, a *revolving credit agreement*, or a *transaction* basis.

- Often, banks require firms to maintain cash balances to compensate for a lending arrangement. If the borrowing firm is required to maintain balances above those that it would ordinarily maintain, the effective cost of borrowing is increased. Interest rates on short-term business loans are a function of the cost of funds to banks, the existing prime rate, the creditworthiness of the borrower, and the profitability of the relationship for the bank.
- Many firms unable to obtain unsecured credit are required by the lender to pledge *security.* In giving a secured loan, the lender has two sources of loan repayment: the cash-flow ability of the firm to service the debt and, if that source fails for some reason, the collateral value of the security. To provide a margin of safety, a lender will usually advance somewhat less than the market value of the collateral.

- Accounts receivable and inventory are the principal assets used to secure short-term business loans.
- There are a number of ways in which a lender can obtain a secured interest in inventories. With a *floating lien, chattel mortgage,* or *trust receipt* arrangement, the inventory remains in the possession of the borrower. Under a *terminal warehouse receipt* or a *field warehouse receipt* method, the inventory is in the possession of an independent third party.
- Instead of *pledging* receivables, a firm may engage in *factoring* (selling) receivables to acquire cash. Factoring often relieves the firm of credit checking, the cost of processing receivables, collection expenses, and bad-debt expenses.
- The best combination of alternative sources of short-term financing depends on considerations of cost, availability, timing, flexibility, and the degree to which the assets of the firm are encumbered (burdened with legal claims).

QUESTIONS

1. Explain why trade credit from suppliers is a "spontaneous source of funds."
2. Trade credit from suppliers is a very costly source of funds when discounts are lost. Explain why many firms rely on this source of funds to finance their temporary working capital.
3. Stretching payables provides "free" funds to customers for a short period. The supplier, however, can face serious financial problems if all of its customers stretch their accounts. Discuss the nature of the problems the supplier may face, and suggest different approaches to cope with stretching.
4. Suppose that a firm elected to tighten its trade credit policy from "2/10, net 90" to "2/10, net 30." What effect could the firm expect this change to have on its liquidity?
5. Why are accrued expenses a more spontaneous source of financing than trade credit from suppliers?
6. Why is the rate on commercial paper usually less than the prime rate charged by bankers and more than the Treasury bill rate?
7. Why would a firm borrow bank funds at higher rates instead of issuing commercial paper?
8. Who is able to issue commercial paper and for what purpose?
9. How do bankers' acceptances differ from commercial paper as a means of financing?
10. Compare and contrast a line of credit and a revolving credit agreement.
11. Would you rather have your loan on a "collect basis" or a "discount basis" if you were a borrower, all other things being the same? If you were a lender?
12. What determines whether a lending arrangement is unsecured or secured?
13. As a lender, how would you determine the percentage you are willing to advance against a particular type of collateral?
14. As a financial consultant to a company, how would you go about recommending whether to use an assignment of accounts receivable or a factoring arrangement?

15. List assets that you would accept as collateral on a short-term loan in your order of preference. Justify your priorities.
16. Which of the methods of short-term financing considered in this chapter would be most likely to be used by the following? Explain your reasoning.
    a. A raw-materials processor, such as a mining or lumber company
    b. A retail sales concern, such as an appliance retailer or stereo equipment dealer
    c. An international company
    d. A dealer in consumer durable goods, such as an automobile sales agency
17. In choosing the composition of short-term financing, what factors should be considered?

SELF-CORRECTION PROBLEMS

1. In Parts (a)–(h), determine the effective annualized cost of financing for the following credit terms, assuming that (i) discounts are not taken, (ii) accounts are paid at the end of the credit period, and (iii) a year has 365 days.
    a. 1/10, net/30   e. 3/10, net/60
    b. 2/10, net/30   f. 2/10, net/90
    c. 3/10, net/30   g. 3/10, net/90
    d. 10/30, net/60   h. 5/10, net/100
2. The Pawlowski Supply Company needs to increase its working capital by $4.4 million. The following three financing alternatives are available (assume a 365-day year):
    a. Forgo cash discounts (granted on a basis of "3/10, net 30") and pay on the final due date.
    b. Borrow $5 million from a bank at 15 percent interest. This alternative would necessitate maintaining a 12 percent compensating balance.
    c. Issue $4.7 million of six-month commercial paper to net $4.4 million. Assume that new paper would be issued every six months. (*Note:* Commercial paper has no stipulated interest rate. It is sold at a discount, and the amount of the discount determines the interest cost to the issuer.)
    Assuming that the firm would prefer the flexibility of bank financing, provided the additional cost of this flexibility was no more than 2 percent per annum, which alternative should Pawlowski select? Why?
3. The Barnes Corporation has just acquired a large account. As a result, it will soon need an additional $95,000 in working capital. It has been determined that there are three feasible sources of funds:
    a. *Trade credit:* The Barnes company buys about $50,000 of materials per month on terms of "3/30, net 90." Discounts currently are taken.
    b. *Bank loan:* The firm's bank will loan $106,000 at 13 percent. A 10 percent compensating balance will be required.
    c. *Factoring:* A factor will buy the company's receivables ($150,000 per month), which have an average collection period of 30 days. The factor will advance up to 75 percent of the face value of the receivables at 12 percent on an annual basis. The factor also will charge a 2 percent fee on all receivables purchased. It has been estimated that the factor's services will save the company $2,500 per month—consisting of both credit department expenses and bad-debts expenses.
    Which alternative should Barnes select on the basis of annualized percentage cost?
4. The Kedzie Cordage Company needs to finance a seasonal bulge in inventories of $400,000. The funds are needed for six months. The company is considering the following possibilities:

a. A terminal warehouse receipt loan is obtained from a finance company. Terms are 12 percent annualized with an 80 percent advance against the value of the inventory. The warehousing costs are $7,000 for the six-month period. The residual financing requirement ($80,000), which is $400,000 less the amount advanced, will need to be financed by forgoing some cash discounts on its payables. Standard terms are "2/10, net 30"; however, the company feels that it can postpone payment until the 40th day without adverse effect.

b. A floating lien arrangement is obtained from the supplier of the inventory at an effective interest rate of 20 percent. The supplier will advance the full value of the inventory.

c. A field warehouse loan is obtained from another finance company at an interest rate of 10 percent annualized. The advance is 70 percent, and field warehousing costs amount to $10,000 for the six-month period. The residual financing requirement will need to be financed by forgoing cash discounts on payables as in the first alternative.

What is the least costly method of financing the inventory needs of the firm? (*Tip:* Compare the total six-month financing costs under each alternative.)

PROBLEMS

1. The Dud Company purchases raw materials on terms of "2/10, net 30." A review of the company's records by the owner, Ms. Dud, revealed that payments are usually made 15 days after purchases are received. When asked why the firm did not take advantage of its discounts, the bookkeeper, Mr. Blunder, replied that it costs only 2 percent for these funds, whereas a bank loan would cost the firm 12 percent.
   a. What mistakes is Mr. Blunder making?
   b. What is the real cost of not taking advantage of the discount?
   c. If the firm could not borrow from the bank and were forced to resort to the use of trade credit funds, what suggestion might be made to Mr. Blunder that would reduce the annual interest cost?

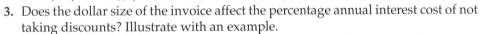

2. Determine the annual percentage interest cost for each of the following terms of sale, assuming that the firm does not take the cash discount but pays on the final day of the net period (assume a 365-day year):
   a. 1/20, net 30 ($500 invoice)   c. 2/5, net 10 ($100 invoice)
   b. 2/30, net 60 ($1,000 invoice)   d. 3/10, net 30 ($250 invoice)

3. Does the dollar size of the invoice affect the percentage annual interest cost of not taking discounts? Illustrate with an example.

4. Recompute Problem 2, assuming a 10-day stretching of the payment date.

5. Hayleigh Mills Company has a $5 million revolving credit agreement with First State Bank of Arkansas. Being a favored customer, the rate is set at 1 percent over the bank's cost of funds, where the cost of funds is approximated as the rate on negotiable certificates of deposit (CDs). In addition, there is a ½ percent commitment fee on the unused portion of the revolving credit. If the CD rate is expected to average 9 percent for the coming year and if the company expects to utilize, on average, 60 percent of the total commitment, what is the expected annual dollar cost of this credit arrangement? What is the percentage cost when both the interest rate and the commitment fee paid are considered? What happens to the percentage cost if, on average, only 20 percent of the total commitment is utilized?

6. Bork Corporation wishes to borrow $100,000 for one year. It has the following alternatives available to it.

a. An 8 percent loan on a discount basis with 20 percent compensating balances required.

b. A 9 percent loan on a discount basis with 10 percent compensating balances required.

c. A 10.5 percent loan on a collect basis with no compensating balance requirement.

Which alternative should the Bork Corporation choose if it is concerned with the effective interest rate?

7. The Shelby Gaming Manufacturing Company has experienced a severe cash squeeze and needs $200,000 over the next 90 days. The company has already pledged its receivables in support of a loan. However, it does have $570,000 in unencumbered inventories. Determine the best financing alternative from the following two that are available.

a. The Cody National Bank of Reno will lend against finished goods provided that they are placed in a public warehouse under its control. As the finished goods are released for sale, the loan will be reduced by the proceeds of the sale. The company currently has $300,000 in finished-goods inventory and would expect to replace finished goods that are sold out of the warehouse with new finished goods, so that it could borrow the full $200,000 for 90 days. The interest rate will be 10 percent, and the company will pay quarterly warehousing costs of $3,000. Finally, it will experience a reduction in efficiency as a result of this arrangement. Management estimates that the lower efficiency will reduce quarterly before-tax profits by $4,000.

b. The Vigorish Finance Company will lend the company the money under a floating lien on all of its inventories. The rate will be 23 percent, but no additional expenses will be incurred.

8. The Bone Company has been factoring its accounts receivable for the past 5 years. The factor charges a fee of 2 percent and will lend up to 80 percent of the volume of receivables purchased for an additional 1.5 percent per month. The firm typically has sales of $500,000 per month, 70 percent of which are on credit. By using the factor, two savings would be effected:

a. $2,000 per month that would be required to support a credit department

b. A bad-debt expense of 1 percent on credit sales

The firm's bank has recently offered to lend the firm up to 80 percent of the face value of the receivables shown on the schedule of accounts. The bank would charge 15 percent per annum interest plus a 2 percent monthly processing charge per dollar of receivables lending. The firm extends terms of "net 30," and all customers who pay their bills do so by the 30th day. Should the firm discontinue its factoring arrangement in favor of the bank's offer if the firm borrows, on the average, $100,000 per month on its receivables?

9. Solid-Arity Corporation is a chain of appliance stores in Chicago. It needs to finance all of its inventories, which average the following during the four quarters of the year:

| | QUARTER | | | |
	1	2	3	4
Inventory level (in thousands)	$1,600	$2,100	$1,500	$3,200

Solid-Arity presently utilizes a loan from a finance company secured by a floating lien. The interest rate is the prime rate plus 7.5 percent, but no additional expenses are incurred. The Boundary Illinois National Bank of Chicago is bidding for the

Solid-Arity business. It has proposed a trust receipt financing arrangement. The interest rate will be 2.5 percent above the prime rate, with servicing costs of $20,000 each quarter. Should the company switch financing arrangements? Why?

SOLUTIONS TO SELF-CORRECTION PROBLEMS

1. a. 1/10, net/30   (1/99)(365/20) =   18.4%
   b. 2/10, net/30   (2/98)(365/20) =   37.2%
   c. 3/10, net/30   (3/97)(365/20) =   56.4%
   d. 10/30, net/60   (10/90)(365/30) = 135.2%
   e. 3/10, net/60   (3/97)(365/50) =   22.6%
   f. 2/10, net/90   (2/98)(365/80) =   9.3%
   g. 3/10, net/90   (3/97)(365/80) =   14.1%
   h. 5/10, net/100   (5/95)(365/90) =   21.3%

2. Annualized costs are as follows:
   a. Trade credit:

   $$(3/97)(365/20) = \textbf{56.44\%}$$

   b. Bank financing:

   $$(\$5,000,000 \times .15)/(\$4,400,000) = \textbf{17.05\%}$$

   c. Commercial paper:

   $$(\$300,000/\$4,400,000) \times 2 = \textbf{13.64\%}$$

   The bank financing is approximately 3.4 percent more expensive than the commercial paper; therefore, commercial paper should be issued.

3. Annualized costs are as follows:
   a. *Trade credit:* If discounts are not taken, up to $97,000 (97% × $50,000 per month × 2 months) can be raised after the second month. The cost would be

   $$(3/97)(365/60) = \textbf{18.8\%}$$

   b. *Bank loan:* Assuming that the compensating balance would not otherwise be maintained, the cost would be

   $$(\$106,000 \times .13)/(\$106,000 \times .90) = \textbf{14.4\%}$$

   c. *Factoring:* Factor fee for the year would be

   $$2\% \times (\$150,000 \times 12) = \textbf{\$36,000}$$

   The savings effected, however, would be $30,000, giving a net factoring cost of $6,000. Borrowing $95,000 on the receivables would thus cost approximately

   $$([.12 \times \$95,000] + \$6,000)/\$95,000 = \textbf{18.3\%}$$

   Bank borrowing would thus be the cheapest source of funds.

4. a. 12% of 80% of $400,000 for 6 months $19,200
   Terminal warehousing cost for 6 months   7,000
   6-month cost of cash discount forgone to extend
   payables from 10 days to 40 days:
   (2/98)(365/30)($80,000)(1/2 year) = .2483 × $80,000 × .5   9,932
   Total 6-month cost   **$36,132**
   b. $400,000 × 20% × 1/2 year $40,000

c. 10% of 70% of $400,000 for 6 months	$14,000
Field warehousing cost for 6 months	10,000
6-month cost of cash discount forgone to extend payables from 10 days to 40 days:	
(2/98)(365/30)($120,000)(1/2 year) = .2483 × $120,000 × .5	14,898
Total 6-month cost	**$38,898**

The terminal warehouse receipt loan results in the lowest cost.

SELECTED REFERENCES

ABCs of Figuring Interest. Chicago, IL: Federal Reserve Bank of Chicago, 1994.

Duchessi, Peter, Hany Shawky, and John P. Seagle. "A Knowledge-Engineered System for Commercial Loan Decisions." *Financial Management* 17 (Autumn 1988), 57–65.

Edwards, Mace. "Factoring for Cash Flow: An Option." *The Small Business Controller* 7 (Fall 1994), 12–16.

Farragher, Edward J. "Factoring Accounts Receivable." *Journal of Cash Management* (March–April 1986), 38–42.

GE Capital: Guide to Asset Based Lending. Stamford, CT: GE Capital Corporation, 1999.

Hahn, Thomas K. "Commercial Paper." Federal Reserve Bank of Richmond *Economic Quarterly* 79 (Spring 1993), 45–67.

Hill, Ned C., and William L. Sartoris. *Short-Term Financial Management*, 3rd ed. Englewood Cliffs, NJ: Prentice Hall, 1995.

Lazere, Monroe R. "Swinging Swindles and Creepy Frauds." *Journal of Commercial Bank Lending* 60 (September 1977), 44–52.

Maness, Terry S., and John T. Zietlow. *Short-Term Financial Management.* Fort Worth, TX: Dryden Press, 1998.

Mian, Shehzad L., and Clifford W. Smith Jr. "Extending Trade Credit and Financing Receivables." *Journal of Applied Corporate Finance* 7 (Spring 1994), 75–84.

Miller, N. C. *The Great Salad Oil Swindle.* Baltimore: Penguin Books, 1965.

Shaw, Michael J., and James A. Gentry. "Using an Expert System with Inductive Learning to Evaluate Business Loans." *Financial Management* 17 (Autumn 1988), 45–56.

Shockley, Richard L., and Anjan V. Thakor. "Bank Loan Commitment Contracts." *Journal of Money, Credit and Banking* 33 (November 1997), 515–34.

Chapter

12

Capital Budgeting and Estimating Cash Flows

THE CAPITAL BUDGETING PROCESS: AN OVERVIEW
GENERATING INVESTMENT PROJECT PROPOSALS
ESTIMATING PROJECT "AFTER-TAX INCREMENTAL OPERATING
    CASH FLOWS"
    Cash-Flow Checklist • Tax Considerations • Calculating the
        Incremental Cash Flows • Example of Asset Expansion
        • Example of Asset Replacement • End of the Beginning
SUMMARY
QUESTIONS
SELF-CORRECTION PROBLEMS
PROBLEMS
SOLUTIONS TO SELF-CORRECTION PROBLEMS
SELECTED REFERENCES

"Data! data! data!" he cried impatiently.
"I can't make bricks without clay."

—SHERLOCK HOLMES IN *THE COPPER BEECHES*

THE CAPITAL BUDGETING PROCESS: AN OVERVIEW

Having just explored ways to efficiently manage working capital (current assets and their supporting financing), we now turn our attention to decisions that involve long-lived assets. These decisions involve both investment and financing choices, the first of which takes up the next three chapters.

When a business makes a capital investment, it incurs a current cash outlay in the expectation of future benefits. Usually, these benefits extend beyond one year in the future. Examples include investment in assets, such as equipment, buildings, and land, as well as the introduction of a new product, a new distribution system, or a new program for research and development. In short, the firm's future success and profitability depend on long-term decisions currently made.

An investment proposal should be judged in relation to whether or not it provides a return equal to, or greater than, that required by investors.[1] To simplify our investigation of the methods of **capital budgeting** in this and the following chapter, we assume that the required return is given and is the same for all investment projects. This assumption implies that the selection of any investment project does not alter the operating, or business-risk, complexion of the firm as perceived by financing suppliers. In Chapter 15 we investigate how to determine the required rate of return, and in Chapter 14 we allow for the fact that different investment projects have different degrees of business risk. As a result, the selection of an investment project may affect the business-risk complexion of the firm, which, in turn, may affect the rate of return required by investors. For purposes of introducing capital budgeting in this and the next chapter, however, we hold risk constant.

Capital budgeting The process of identifying, analyzing, and selecting investment projects whose returns (cash flows) are expected to extend beyond one year.

> Take Note
>
> Capital budgeting involves
>
> - Generating investment project proposals consistent with the firm's strategic objectives
> - Estimating after-tax incremental operating cash flows for investment projects
> - Evaluating project incremental cash flows
> - Selecting projects based on a value-maximizing acceptance criterion
> - Reevaluating implemented investment projects continually and performing postaudits for completed projects

In this chapter, we restrict ourselves to a discussion of the first two items on this list.

GENERATING INVESTMENT PROJECT PROPOSALS

Investment project proposals can stem from a variety of sources. For purposes of analysis, projects may be classified into one of five categories:

1. New products or expansion of existing products
2. Replacement of equipment or buildings

---

[1]The development of the material on capital budgeting assumes that the reader understands the concepts covered in Chapter 3 on the time value of money.

3. Research and development
4. Exploration
5. Other (for example, safety-related or pollution-control devices)

For a new product, the proposal usually originates in the marketing department. A proposal to replace a piece of equipment with a more sophisticated model, however, usually arises from the production area of the firm. In each case, efficient administrative procedures are needed for channeling investment requests. All investment requests should be consistent with corporate strategy to avoid needless analysis of projects incompatible with this strategy. (McDonald's probably would not want to sell cigarettes in its restaurants, for example.)

Most firms screen proposals at multiple levels of authority. For a proposal originating in the production area, the hierarchy of authority might run (1) from section chiefs, (2) to plant managers, (3) to the vice president for operations, (4) to a capital expenditures committee under the financial manager, (5) to the president, and (6) to the board of directors. How high a proposal must go before it is finally approved usually depends on its cost. The greater the capital outlay, the greater the number of "screens" usually required. Plant managers may be able to approve moderate-sized projects on their own, but only higher levels of authority approve larger ones. Because the administrative procedures for screening investment proposals vary from firm to firm, it is not possible to generalize. The best procedure will depend on the circumstances. It is clear, however, that companies are becoming increasingly sophisticated in their approach to capital budgeting.

ESTIMATING PROJECT "AFTER-TAX INCREMENTAL OPERATING CASH FLOWS"

Cash-Flow Checklist

One of the most important tasks in capital budgeting is estimating future cash flows for a project. The final results we obtain from our analysis are no better than the accuracy of our cash-flow estimates. Because cash, not accounting income, is central to all decisions of the firm, we express whatever benefits we expect from a project in terms of *cash flows* rather than income flows. The firm invests cash now in the hope of receiving even greater cash returns in the future. Only cash can be reinvested in the firm or paid to shareholders in the form of dividends. In capital budgeting, good guys may get credit, but effective managers get cash. In setting up the cash flows for analysis, a computer spreadsheet program is invaluable. It allows one to change assumptions and quickly produce a new cash-flow stream.

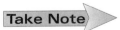

For each investment proposal we need to provide information on *operating*, as opposed to financing, cash flows. Financing flows, such as interest payments, principal payments, and cash dividends, are excluded from our cash-flow analysis. However, the need for an investment's return to cover capital costs is not ignored. The use of a discount (or hurdle) rate equal to the required rate of return of capital suppliers will capture the financing cost dimension. We will discuss the mechanics of this type of analysis in the next chapter.

Cash flows should be determined on an *after-tax* basis. The initial investment outlay, as well as the appropriate discount rate, will be expressed in after-tax terms. Therefore, all forecasted flows need to be stated on an equivalent, after-tax basis.

In addition, the information must be presented on an *incremental* basis, so that we analyze only the difference between the cash flows of the firm with and without the project. For example, if a firm contemplates a new product that is likely to compete with existing products, it is not appropriate to express cash flows in terms of estimated total sales of the new product. We must take into account the probable "cannibalization" of existing products and make our cash-flow estimates on the basis of incremental sales. When continuation of the status quo results in loss of market share, we must take this into account when analyzing what happens if we do not make a new investment. That is, if cash flows will erode if we do not invest, we must factor this into our analysis. The key is to analyze the situation with and without the new investment and where all relevant costs and benefits are brought into play. Only incremental cash flows matter.

In this regard, **sunk costs** must be ignored. Our concern lies with incremental costs and benefits. Unrecoverable past costs are irrelevant and should not enter into the decision process. Also, we must be mindful that certain relevant costs do not necessarily involve an actual dollar outlay. If we have allocated plant space to a project and this space can be used for something else, its **opportunity cost** must be included in the project's evaluation. If a presently unused building needed for a project can be sold for $300,000, that amount (net of any taxes) should be treated *as if it were a cash outlay* at the outset of the project. Thus, in deriving cash flows we need to consider any appropriate opportunity costs.

When a capital investment contains a current asset component, this component (net of any spontaneous changes in current liabilities) is treated as part of the capital investment and not as a separate working capital decision. For example, with the acceptance of a new project it is sometimes necessary to carry additional cash, receivables, or inventories. This investment in working capital should be treated as a cash outflow at the time it occurs. At the end of a project's life, the working capital investment is presumably returned in the form of an additional cash inflow.

In estimating cash flows, *anticipated inflation must be taken into account*. Often there is a tendency to assume erroneously that price levels will remain unchanged throughout the life of a project. If the required rate of return for a project to be accepted embodies a premium for inflation (as it usually does), then estimated cash flows must also reflect inflation. Such cash flows are affected in several ways. If cash inflows ultimately arise from the sale of a product, expected future prices affect these inflows. As for cash outflows, inflation affects both expected future wages and material costs.

Table 12-1 summarizes the major concerns to keep in mind as we prepare to actually determine project "after-tax incremental operating cash flows." It provides us with a "checklist" for determining cash-flow estimates.

Tax Considerations

Method of Depreciation. As you may remember from Chapter 2, *depreciation* is the systematic allocation of the cost of a capital asset over a period of time for financial reporting purposes, tax purposes, or both. Because depreciation deductions taken on a firm's tax return are treated as expense items, depreciation lowers taxable income. Everything else being equal, the greater the depreciation charges, the lower the taxes

Sunk costs Unrecoverable past outlays that, since they cannot be recovered, should not affect present actions or future decisions.

Opportunity cost What is lost by not taking the next-best investment alternative.

TABLE 12-1
Cash-flow checklist

BASIC CHARACTERISTICS OF RELEVANT PROJECT FLOWS

☑ *Cash* (not accounting income) flows

☑ *Operating* (not financing) flows

☑ *After-tax flows*

☑ *Incremental flows*

BASIC PRINCIPLES THAT MUST BE ADHERED TO
IN ESTIMATING "AFTER-TAX INCREMENTAL OPERATING CASH FLOWS"

☑ Ignore *sunk costs*

☑ Include *opportunity costs*

☑ Include project-driven *changes in working capital* net of spontaneous changes in current liabilities

☑ Include effects of *inflation*

paid. Although depreciation itself is a noncash expense, it does affect the firm's cash flow by directly influencing the cash outflow of taxes paid.

There are a number of alternative procedures that may be used to depreciate capital assets. These include straight-line and various accelerated depreciation methods. Most profitable firms prefer to use an accelerated depreciation method *for tax purposes*—one that allows for a more rapid write-off and, therefore, a lower tax bill.

The Tax Reform Act of 1986 allows companies to use a particular type of accelerated depreciation for tax purposes known as the Modified Accelerated Cost Recovery System (MACRS). Under MACRS, machinery, equipment, and real estate are assigned to one of eight classes for cost recovery (depreciation) purposes. As described in Chapter 2, the property category in which an asset falls determines its depreciable life for tax purposes. As also described in that chapter, the *half-year convention* must generally be applied to all machinery and equipment. There is a half-year of depreciation in the year an asset is acquired and in the final year that depreciation is taken on the asset. The Treasury publishes depreciation percentages of original cost for each property class, which incorporate the half-year conventions. Table 12-2 presents the depreciation percentages for the first four property classes. These percentages correspond to the principles taken up in Chapter 2, and they should be used for determining depreciation.

QUESTION•ANSWER•QUESTION•ANSWER

Can MACRS depreciation be utilized by U.S. companies on equipment used outside the United States?

No. Generally, MACRS depreciation is not allowed for equipment that is used predominantly outside the United States during the taxable year. For such equipment, the Alternative Depreciation System (ADS) is required. ADS is a straight-line method of depreciation (determined without regard to estimated future salvage value).

TABLE 12-2
MACRS depreciation
percentages

RECOVERY YEAR	PROPERTY CLASS			
	3-YEAR	5-YEAR	7-YEAR	10-YEAR
1	33.33%	20.00%	14.29%	10.00%
2	44.45	32.00	24.49	18.00
3	14.81	19.20	17.49	14.40
4	7.41	11.52	12.49	11.52
5		11.52	8.93	9.22
6		5.76	8.92	7.37
7			8.93	6.55
8			4.46	6.55
9				6.56
10				6.55
11				3.28
Totals	100.00%	100.00%	100.00%	100.00%

Take Note

Depreciable basis In tax accounting, the fully installed cost of an asset. This is the amount that, by law, may be written off over time for tax purposes.

Capitalized expenditures Expenditures that may provide benefits into the future and therefore are treated as capital outlays and not as expenses of the period in which they were incurred.

Depreciable Basis. Computing depreciation for an asset requires a determination of the asset's **depreciable basis.** This is the amount that taxing authorities allow to be written off for tax purposes over a period of years. The cost of the asset, including any other **capitalized expenditures**—such as shipping and installation—that are incurred to prepare the asset for its intended use, constitutes the asset's depreciable basis under MACRS. Notice that under MACRS the asset's depreciable basis is *not* reduced by the estimated salvage value of the asset.

Sale or Disposal of a Depreciable Asset.   In general, if a depreciable asset used in business is sold for more than its depreciated (tax) book value, any amount realized in excess of book value but less than the asset's depreciable basis is considered a "recapture of depreciation" and is taxed at the firm's ordinary income tax rate. This effectively reverses any positive tax benefits of having taken "too much" depreciation in earlier years—that is, reducing (tax) book value below market value. If the asset happens to sell for more than its depreciable basis (which, by the way, is not too likely), the portion of the total amount in excess of the depreciable basis is taxed at the capital gains tax rate (which currently is equal to the firm's ordinary income tax rate, or a maximum of 35 percent).

If the asset sells for less than (tax) book value, a loss is incurred equal to the difference between sales price and (tax) book value. In general, this loss is deducted from the firm's ordinary income. In effect, an amount of taxable income equal to the loss is "shielded" from being taxed. The net result is a tax-shield savings equal to the firm's ordinary tax rate multiplied by the loss on the sale of the depreciable asset. Thus, a "paper" loss is cause for a "cash" savings.

Our discussion on the tax consequences of the sale of a depreciable asset has assumed no additional complicating factors. In actuality, a number of complications can and often do occur. Therefore, the reader is cautioned to refer to the tax code and/or a tax specialist when faced with the tax treatment of a sale of an asset. In examples and problems, for ease of calculation we will generally use a 40 percent marginal ordinary income tax rate.

Calculating the Incremental Cash Flows

We now face the task of identifying the specific components that determine a project's relevant cash flows. We need to keep in mind both the concerns enumerated in our "Cash-Flow Checklist" (Table 12-1) as well as the various tax considerations just discussed. It is helpful to place project cash flows into three categories based on timing:

1. *Initial cash outflow:* the initial net cash investment.
2. *Interim incremental net cash flows:* those net cash flows occurring after the initial cash investment but not including the final period's cash flow.
3. *Terminal-year incremental net cash flow:* the final period's net cash flow. (This period's cash flow is singled out for special attention because a particular set of cash flows often occurs at project termination.)

Initial Cash Outflow. In general, the initial cash outflow for a project is determined as follows in Table 12-3. As seen, the cost of the asset is subject to adjustments to reflect the totality of cash flows associated with its acquisition. These cash flows include installation costs, changes in net working capital, sale proceeds from the disposition of any assets replaced, and tax adjustments.

Interim Incremental Net Cash Flows. After making the initial cash outflow that is necessary to begin implementing a project, the firm hopes to benefit from the future cash inflows generated by the project. Generally, these future cash flows can be determined by following the step-by-step procedure outlined in Table 12-4.

TABLE 12-3
Basic format for determining initial cash outflow

(a)		Cost of "new" asset(s)
(b)	+	Capitalized expenditures (for example, installation costs, shipping expenses, etc.)*
(c)	+(−)	Increased (decreased) level of "net" working capital**
(d)	−	Net proceeds from sale of "old" asset(s) if the investment is a replacement decision
(e)	+(−)	Taxes (tax savings) due to the sale of "old" asset(s) if the investment is a replacement decision
(f)	=	Initial cash outflow

*Asset cost plus capitalized expenditures form the basis on which tax depreciation is computed.

**Any change in working capital should be considered "net" of any spontaneous changes in current liabilities that occur because the project is implemented.

TABLE 12-4
Basic format for
determining interim
incremental net cash
flow (per period)

(a)		Net increase (decrease) in operating revenue less (plus) any net increase (decrease) in operating expenses, excluding depreciation
(b)	$-(+)$	Net increase (decrease) in tax depreciation charges
(c)	$=$	Net change in income before taxes
(d)	$-(+)$	Net increase (decrease) in taxes
(e)	$=$	Net change in income after taxes
(f)	$+(-)$	Net increase (decrease) in tax depreciation charges
(g)	$=$	Incremental net cash flow for the period

Notice that we first deduct any increase (add any decrease) in incremental tax depreciation related to project acceptance—see step (b)—in determining the "net change in income before taxes." However, a few steps later we add back any increase (deduct any decrease) in tax depreciation—see step (f)—in determining "incremental net cash flow for the period." What is going on here? Well, tax depreciation itself, as you may remember, is a noncash charge against operating income that lowers taxable income. So we need to consider it as we determine the incremental effect that project acceptance has on the firm's taxes. However, we ultimately need to add back any increase (subtract any decrease) in tax depreciation to our resulting "net change in income after taxes" figure so as not to understate the project's effect on cash flow.

Take Note

Project-related changes in working capital are more likely to occur at project inception and termination. Therefore, Table 12-4 does not show a separate, recurring adjustment for working capital changes. However, for any interim period in which a material change in working capital occurs, we would need to adjust our basic calculation. We should, therefore, include an additional step in the "interim incremental net cash flow" determination. The following line item would then appear right after step (f): $+ (-)$ *Decreased (increased) level of "net" working capital*—with any change in working capital being considered "net" of any spontaneous changes in current liabilities caused by the project in this period.

Terminal-Year Incremental Net Cash Flow. Finally, we turn our attention to determining the project's incremental cash flow in its final, or terminal, year of existence. We apply the same step-by-step procedure for this period's cash flow as we did to those in all the interim periods. In addition, we give special recognition to a few cash flows that are often connected only with project termination. These potential project windup cash flows are (1) the salvage value (disposal/reclamation costs) of any sold or disposed assets, (2) taxes (tax savings) related to asset sale or disposal, and (3) any project-termination-related change in working capital—generally, any initial working capital investment is now returned as an additional cash inflow. Table 12-5 summarizes all the necessary steps and highlights those steps that are reserved especially for project termination.

TABLE 12-5
Basic format for determining terminal year incremental net cash flow

(a)		Net increase (decrease) in operating revenue less (plus) any net increase (decrease) in operating expenses, excluding depreciation
(b)	−(+)	Net increase (decrease) in tax depreciation charges
(c)	=	Net change in income before taxes
(d)	−(+)	Net increase (decrease) in taxes
(e)	=	Net change in income after taxes
(f)	+(−)	Net increase (decrease) in tax depreciation charges
(g)	=	Incremental cash flow for the terminal year before project windup considerations
(h)	+(−)	Final salvage value (disposal/reclamation costs) of "new" asset(s)
(i)	−(+)	Taxes (tax savings) due to sale or disposal of "new" asset(s)
(j)	+(−)	Decreased (increased) level of "net" working capital*
(k)	=	Terminal year incremental net cash flow

*Any change in working capital should be considered "net" of any spontaneous changes in current liabilities that occur because the project is terminated.

Example of Asset Expansion

To illustrate the information needed for a capital budgeting decision, we examine the following situation. The Faversham Fish Farm is considering the introduction of a new fish-flaking facility. To launch the facility, it will need to spend $90,000 for special equipment. The equipment has a useful life of four years and is in the three-year property class for tax purposes. Shipping and installation expenditures equal $10,000, and the machinery has an expected final salvage value, four years from now, of $16,500. The machinery is to be housed in an abandoned warehouse next to the main processing plant. The old warehouse has no alternative economic use. No additional "net" working capital is needed. The marketing department envisions that use of the new facility will generate additional net operating revenue cash flows, before consideration of depreciation and taxes, as follows:

	END OF YEAR			
	1	2	3	4
Net cash flows	$35,167	$36,250	$55,725	$32,258

Assuming that the marginal tax rate equals 40 percent, we now need to estimate the project's relevant incremental cash flows.

The first step is to estimate the project's initial cash outflow:

	Step A: Estimating initial cash outflow	
	Cost of "new" asset(s)	$ 90,000
+	Capitalized expenditures (shipping and installation)	10,000
=	Initial cash outflow	$100,000

The next steps involve calculating the incremental future cash flows.

		END OF YEAR			
		1	2	3	4
	Step B: Calculating interim incremental net cash flows (years 1 to 3)				
	Net change in operating revenue, excluding depreciation	$35,167	$36,250	$55,725	$32,258
−	Net increase in tax depreciation charges[a]	(33,330)	(44,450)	(14,810)	(7,410)
=	Net change in income before taxes	$ 1,837	$ (8,200)	$40,915	$24,848
−(+)	Net increase (decrease) in taxes (40% rate)	(735)	3,280[b]	(16,366)	(9,939)
=	Net change in income after taxes	$ 1,102	$ (4,920)	$24,549	$14,909
+	Net increase in tax depreciation charges	33,330	44,450	14,810	7,410
=	Incremental net cash flow for years 1 to 3	$34,432	$39,530	$39,359	

	Step C: Calculating terminal-year incremental net cash flow	
=	Incremental cash flow for the terminal year before project windup considerations	$22,319
+	Final salvage value of "new" asset(s)	16,500
−	Taxes due to sale or disposal of "new" asset(s)	(6,600)[c]
=	Terminal-year incremental net cash flow	$32,219

[a]MACRS depreciation percentages for 3-year property class asset applied against asset with a depreciable basis of $100,000.
[b]Assumes that tax loss shields other income of the firm.
[c]Assumes salvage value is recapture of depreciation and taxed at ordinary income rate of 40 percent— $16,500(.40) = $6,600.

The expected incremental net cash flows from the project are

	END OF YEAR				
	0	1	2	3	4
Net cash flows	($100,000)	$34,432	$39,530	$39,359	$32,219

Thus, for an initial cash outflow of $100,000, the firm expects to generate net cash flows of $34,432, $39,530, $39,359, and $32,219 over the next four years. This data represents the relevant cash-flow information that we need to judge the attractiveness of the project.

By now, you are probably dying to know whether the Faversham Fish Farm should favor the fish-flaking facility. However, we will leave the analysis of these cash flows until the next chapter. Our concern here has been simply to determine the relevant cash-flow information needed. For the time being then, this expansion example must remain "to be continued in Chapter 13."

Example of Asset Replacement

To go to a somewhat more complicated example, we suppose that we are considering the purchase of a new automotive-glass mold to replace an old mold and that we need to obtain cash-flow information to evaluate the attractiveness of this project.

The purchase price of the new mold is $18,500, and it will require an additional $1,500 to install, bringing the total cost to $20,000. The old mold, which has a remaining useful life of four years, can be sold for its depreciated (tax) book value of $2,000. The old mold would have no salvage value if held to the end of its useful life. Notice that since salvage value equals tax book value, taxes due to the sale of the old asset are zero. The initial cash outflow for the investment project, therefore, is $18,000 as follows:

	Cost of "new" asset	$18,500
+	Capitalized expenditures (shipping and installation)	1,500
−	Net proceeds from sale of "old" asset	(2,000)
+	Taxes (tax savings) due to sale of "old" asset	0
=	Initial cash outflow	$18,000

The new machine should cut labor and maintenance costs and produce other cash savings totaling $7,100 a year before taxes for each of the next four years, after which it will probably not provide any savings nor have a salvage value. These savings represent the net operating revenue savings to the firm if it replaces the old mold with the new one. Remember, we are concerned with the differences in the cash flows resulting from continuing to use the old mold versus replacing it with a new one.

Suppose that the new mold we are considering falls into the three-year property category for MACRS depreciation. Moreover, assume the following in regards to the old mold:

1. The original depreciable basis was $9,000.
2. The mold fell into the three-year property class.
3. The remaining depreciable life is two years.

Because we are interested in the incremental impact of the project, we must subtract depreciation charges on the old mold from depreciation charges on the new one to obtain the incremental depreciation charges associated with the project. Given the information provided plus the appropriate MACRS depreciation percentages, we are able to calculate the difference in depreciation charges resulting from the acceptance of the project. The necessary calculations are as follows:

		YEAR			
		1	2	3	4
(a)	New mold's depreciable basis	$20,000	$20,000	$20,000	$20,000
(b) ×	MACRS depreciation (%)	× .3333	× .4445	× .1481	× .0741
(c) =	New mold's periodic depreciation	$ 6,666	$ 8,890	$ 2,962	$ 1,482
(d)	Old mold's depreciable basis	$ 9,000	$ 9,000	$ 9,000	$ 9,000
(e) ×	MACRS depreciation (%)	× .1481	× .0741	× 0	× 0
(f) =	Old mold's *remaining* periodic depreciation	$ 1,333	$ 667	$ 0	$ 0
(g)	Net increase in tax depreciation charges Line (c) − Line (f)	$ 5,333	$ 8,223	$ 2,962	$ 1,482

We can now calculate the future incremental cash flows as follows:

		END OF YEAR			
		1	2	3	4
	Interim incremental net cash flows (years 1 to 3)				
	Net change in operating revenue, excluding depreciation	$7,100	$ 7,100	$7,100	$7,100
−	Net increase in tax depreciation charges	(5,333)	(8,223)	(2,962)	(1,482)
=	Net change in income before taxes	$1,767	$(1,123)	$4,138	$5,618
−(+)	Net increase (decrease) in taxes (40% rate)	(707)	(449)[a]	(1,655)	(2,247)
=	Net change in income after taxes	$1,060	$ (674)	$2,483	$3,371
+	Net increase in tax depreciation charges	5,333	8,223	2,962	1,482
=	Incremental net cash flow for years 1 to 3	$6,393	$ 7,549	$5,445	

	Terminal-year incremental net cash flow	
=	Incremental cash flow for the terminal year before project windup considerations	$4,853
+	Final salvage value of "new" asset	0
−	Taxes (tax savings) due to sale or disposal of "new" asset	0
=	Terminal-year incremental net cash flow	$4,853

[a]Assumes that tax loss shields other income of the firm.

The expected incremental net cash flows from the replacement project are:

	END OF YEAR				
	0	1	2	3	4
Net cash flows	($18,000)	$6,393	$7,549	$5,445	$4,853

For an initial cash outflow of $18,000, then, we are able to replace an old glass mold with a new one that is expected to result in net cash flows of $6,393, $7,549, $5,445, and $4,853 over the next four years. As in the previous example, the relevant cash-flow information for capital budgeting purposes is expressed on an incremental, after-tax basis.

END OF THE BEGINNING

In this chapter we considered how to generate investment project proposals and how to estimate the relevant cash-flow information needed to evaluate investment proposals. In the next chapter we continue our discussion of the capital budgeting process. There you will learn how to evaluate project incremental cash flows and how to determine which projects should be accepted.

SUMMARY

- *Capital budgeting* is the process of identifying, analyzing, and selecting investment projects whose returns (cash flows) are expected to extend beyond one year.

- Specifically, capital budgeting involves (1) generating investment project proposals consistent with the firm's strategic objectives; (2) estimating after-tax incremental operating cash flows for the investment projects; (3) evaluating project incremental cash flows; (4) selecting projects based on a value-maximizing acceptance criterion; and (5) continually reevaluating implemented investment projects and performing postaudits for completed projects.

- Because cash, not accounting income, is central to all decisions of the firm, we express the benefits we expect to receive from a project in terms of *cash flows* rather than income flows.
- Cash flows should be measured on an *incremental, after-tax* basis. In addition, our concern is with *operating*, not financing, flows.

- Tax depreciation under the Modified Accelerated Cost Recovery System (1986 Tax Reform Act) has a significant effect on the size and pattern of cash flows. Also affecting the size and pattern of cash flows is the presence of salvage value (disposal/reclamation costs) and project-driven changes in working capital requirements.
- It is helpful to place project cash flows into three categories based on timing: (1) the initial cash outflow, (2) interim incremental net cash flows, and (3) the terminal-year incremental net cash flow.

QUESTIONS

1. When relevant project cash flows are examined, why is an increase in tax depreciation at first deducted and then later added back in determining incremental net cash flow for a period?
2. In capital budgeting, should the following be ignored, or rather added or subtracted from the new machine's purchase price when estimating initial cash outflow? When estimating the machine's depreciable basis?
   a. The market value of the old machine is $500, the old machine has a remaining useful life, and the investment is a replacement decision.
   b. An additional investment in inventory of $2,000 is required.
   c. $200 is required to ship the new machine to the plant site.
   d. A concrete foundation for the new machine will cost $250.
   e. Training of the machine operator will cost $300.
3. In determining the expected cash flows from a new investment project, why should past sunk costs be ignored in the estimates?
4. Discuss the adjustments in the capital budgeting process that should be made to compensate for expected inflation.
5. What is the purpose of requiring more levels of management approval, the larger the proposed capital expenditure? Is more information also required in support of the request?
6. What is the difference between a product expansion and an equipment replacement investment?

SELF-CORRECTION PROBLEMS

1. Pilsudski Coal Company is considering the replacement of two machines that are three years old with a new, more efficient machine. The two old machines could be sold currently for a total of $70,000 in the secondary market, but they would have a zero final salvage value if held to the end of their remaining useful life. Their original depreciable basis totaled $300,000. They have a depreciated tax book value of $86,400, and a remaining useful life of eight years. MACRS depreciation is used on these machines, and they are five-year property class assets. The new machine can be purchased and installed for $480,000. It has a useful life of eight years, at the end of which a salvage value of $40,000 is expected. The machine falls into the five-year property class for accelerated cost recovery (depreciation) purposes. Due to its greater efficiency, the new machine is expected to result in incremental annual

operating savings of $100,000. The company's corporate tax rate is 40 percent, and if a loss occurs in any year on the project, it is assumed that the company can offset the loss against other company income.

What are the incremental cash inflows over the eight years, and what is the incremental cash outflow at time 0?

2. The Fresno Finial Fabricating Works is considering automating its existing finial casting and assembly department. The plant manager, Mel Content, has accumulated the following information for you:
   - The automation proposal would result in reduced labor costs of $150,000 per year.
   - The cost of defects is expected to remain at $5,000 even if the new automation proposal is accepted.
   - New equipment costing $500,000 would need to be purchased. For financial reporting purposes, the equipment will be depreciated on a straight-line basis over its useful four-year life. For tax purposes, however, the equipment falls into the three-year property class and will be depreciated using the MACRS depreciation percentages. The estimated final salvage value of the new equipment is $50,000.
   - Annual maintenance costs will increase from $2,000 to $8,000 if the new equipment is purchased.
   - The company is subject to a marginal tax rate of 40 percent.
   What are the relevant incremental cash inflows over the proposal's useful life, and what is the incremental cash outflow at time 0?

PROBLEMS

1. Thoma Pharmaceutical Company may buy DNA-testing equipment costing $60,000. This equipment is expected to reduce labor costs of the clinical staff by $20,000 annually. The equipment has a useful life of five years but falls in the three-year property class for cost recovery (depreciation) purposes. No salvage value is expected at the end. The corporate tax rate for Thoma (combined federal and state) is 38 percent, and its required rate of return is 15 percent. (If profits after taxes on the project are negative in any year, the firm will offset the loss against other firm income for that year.) On the basis of this information, what are the relevant cash flows?

2. In Problem 1, suppose that 6 percent inflation in savings from labor costs is expected over the last four years, so that savings in the first year are $20,000, savings in the second year are $21,200,and so forth.
   a. On the basis of this information, what are the relevant cash flows?
   b. If working capital of $10,000 were required in addition to the cost of the equipment and this additional investment were needed over the life of the project,what would be the effect on the relevant cash flows? (All other things are the same as in Problem 2, Part (a).)

3. The City of San Jose must replace a number of its concrete-mixer trucks with new trucks. It has received two bids and has evaluated closely the performance characteristics of the various trucks. The Rockbuilt truck, which costs $74,000, is top-of-the-line equipment. The truck has a life of eight years, assuming that the engine is rebuilt in the fifth year. Maintenance costs of $2,000 a year are expected in the first four years, followed by total maintenance and rebuilding costs of $13,000 in the fifth

year. During the last three years, maintenance costs are expected to be $4,000 a year. At the end of eight years the truck will have an estimated scrap value of $9,000.

A bid from Bulldog Trucks, Inc., is for $59,000 a truck. Maintenance costs for the truck will be higher. In the first year they are expected to be $3,000, and this amount is expected to increase by $1,500 a year through the eighth year. In the fourth year the engine will need to be rebuilt, and this will cost the company $15,000 in addition to maintenance costs in that year. At the end of eight years the Bulldog truck will have an estimated scrap value of $5,000.

a. What are the relevant cash flows related to the trucks of each bidder? Ignore tax considerations because the City of San Jose pays no taxes.

b. Using the figures determined in Part (a), what are the cash-flow savings each year that can be obtained by going with the more expensive truck rather than the less expensive one? (That is, calculate the periodic cash-flow differences between the two cash-flow streams—assume that any net cost savings are positive benefits.)

4. U.S. Blivet is contemplating the purchase of a more advanced blivet-extrusion machine to replace the machine currently being used in its production process. The firm's production engineers contend that the newer machine will turn out the current volume of output more efficiently. They note the following facts in support of their contention.

- The old machine can be used for four more years. It has a *current* salvage value of $8,000; but if held to the end of its useful life, the old machine would have an estimated *final* salvage value of $2,000. This is the final year that tax depreciation will be taken on the machine, and the amount of depreciation is equal to the machine's remaining depreciated (tax) book value of $4,520.

- The new, advanced blivet-extrusion machine costs $60,000. Its final salvage value is projected to be $15,000 at the end of its four-year useful life. The new machine falls into the three-year property category for MACRS depreciation.

- The new machine will reduce labor and maintenance usage by $12,000 annually.

- Income taxes on incremental profits are paid at a 40 percent rate.

Calculate the expected annual incremental cash flows for years 1 through 4, as well as the estimated initial cash outflow.

5. In Problem 4, suppose that you just discovered that the production engineers had slipped up twice in their statement of the relevant facts concerning the potential purchase of the new machine:

- The engineers failed to note that in addition to the $60,000 invoice price for the new machine, $2,000 must be paid for installation.

- The *current* salvage value of the old machine is not $8,000, but rather only $3,000.

On the basis of this new information, what are the relevant cash flows for this replacement problem?

SOLUTIONS TO SELF-CORRECTION PROBLEMS

1. Incremental cash inflows:

	END OF YEAR			
	1	2	3	4
1. Savings	$100,000	$100,000	$100,000	$100,000
2. Depreciation, new	96,000	153,600	92,160	55,296
3. Depreciation, old	34,560	34,560	17,280	0
4. Incremental depreciation Line (2) − Line (3)	61,440	119,040	74,880	55,296
5. Profit change before tax Line (1) − Line (4)	38,560	(19,040)	25,120	44,704
6. Taxes Line (5) × (40%)	15,424	(7,616)	10,048	17,882
7. Profit change after tax Line (5) − Line (6)	23,136	(11,424)	15,072	26,822

	END OF YEAR			
	1	2	3	4
8. Operating cash-flow change Line (7) + Line (4) *or* Line (1) − Line (6)	84,576	107,616	89,952	82,118
9. Salvage value × (1 − .40)	0	0	0	0
10. Net cash flow Line (8) + Line (9)	**$ 84,576**	**$107,616**	**$ 89,952**	**$ 82,118**

	END OF YEAR			
	5	6	7	8
1. Savings	$100,000	$100,000	$100,000	$100,000
2. Depreciation, new	55,296	27,648	0	0
3. Depreciation, old	0	0	0	0
4. Incremental depreciation Line (2) − Line (3)	55,296	27,648	0	0
5. Profit change before tax Line (1) − Line (4)	44,704	72,352	100,000	100,000
6. Taxes Line (5) × (40%)	17,882	28,941	40,000	40,000
7. Profit change after tax Line (5) − Line (6)	26,822	43,411	60,000	60,000
8. Operating cash-flow change Line (7) + Line (4) *or* Line (1) − Line (6)	82,118	71,059	60,000	60,000
9. Salvage value × (1 − .40)	0	0	0	24,000
10. Net cash flow Line (8) + Line (9)	**$ 82,118**	**$ 71,059**	**$ 60,000**	**$ 84,000**

Incremental cash outflow at time 0 (initial cash outflow)

Cost − Sale of old machines − Tax savings on book loss
$480,000 − $70,000 − (.40)($86,400 − $70,000) = **$403,440**

2. Incremental cash inflows:

	END OF YEAR			
	1	2	3	4
1. Labor savings	$150,000	$150,000	$150,000	$150,000
2. Incremental maintenance	6,000	6,000	6,000	6,000
3. Depreciation	166,650	222,250	74,050	37,050
4. Profit change before tax Line (1) − Line (2) − Line (3)	(22,650)	(78,250)	69,950	106,950
5. Taxes Line (4) × (40%)	(9,060)	(31,300)	27,980	42,780
6. Profit change after tax Line (4) − Line (5)	(13,590)	(46,950)	41,970	64,170
7. Operating cash-flow change Line (6) + Line (3) *or* Line (1) − Line (2) − Line (5)	153,060	175,300	116,020	101,220
8. Salvage value × (1 − .40)	0	0	0	30,000
9. Net cash flow Line (7) + Line (8)	**$153,060**	**$175,300**	**$116,020**	**$131,220**

Incremental cash outflow at time 0 (initial cash outflow) = **$500,000** (in this case, simply the cost of the project).

SELECTED REFERENCES

Aggarwal, Raj. *Capital Budgeting Under Uncertainty.* Englewood Cliffs, NJ: Prentice Hall, 1993.

Barwise, Patrick, Paul R. Marsh, and Robin Wensley. "Must Finance and Strategy Clash?" *Harvard Business Review* 67 (September–October 1989), 85–90.

Bierman, Harold, Jr., and Seymour Smidt. *The Capital Budgeting Decision: Economic Analysis of Investment Projects,* 8th ed. New York: Macmillan, 1993.

Hong, Hai. "Inflation and the Market Value of the Firm: Theory and Tests." *Journal of Finance* 32 (September 1977), 1031–48.

Kim, Suk H. "A Summary of Empirical Studies on Capital Budgeting Practices." *Business and Public Affairs* 13 (Fall 1986), 21–25.

Levy, Haim, and Marshall Sarnat. *Capital Investment and Financial Decisions,* 5th ed. Englewood Cliffs, NJ:Prentice Hall, 1994.

Marshuetz, Richard J. "How American Can Allocates Capital." *Harvard Business Review* 63 (January–February 1985), 82–91.

Rappaport, Alfred, and Robert A. Taggart Jr. "Evaluation of Capital Expenditure Proposals Under Inflation." *Financial Management* 11 (Spring 1982), 5–13.

Seitz, Neil, and Mitch Ellison. *Capital Budgeting and Long-Term Financing Decisions,* 3rd ed. Fort Worth, TX: Dryden, 1998.

Shapiro, Alan C. "Corporate Strategy and the Capital Budgeting Decision." *Midland Corporate Finance Journal* 3 (Spring 1985), 22–36.

Van Horne, James C. "A Note on Biases in Capital Budgeting Introduced by Inflation." *Journal of Financial and Quantitative Analysis* 6 (January 1971), 653–58.

Chapter 13

Capital Budgeting Techniques

PROJECT EVALUATION AND SELECTION: ALTERNATIVE METHODS
   Payback Period • Internal Rate of Return • Net Present
      Value • Profitability Index
POTENTIAL DIFFICULTIES
   Dependency and Mutual Exclusion • Ranking Problems • Multiple
      Internal Rates of Return • Capital Rationing
PROJECT MONITORING: PROGRESS REVIEWS AND
   POST-COMPLETION AUDITS
SUMMARY
APPENDIX A: MULTIPLE INTERNAL RATES OF RETURN
APPENDIX B: REPLACEMENT CHAIN ANALYSIS
QUESTIONS
SELF-CORRECTION PROBLEMS
PROBLEMS
SOLUTIONS TO SELF-CORRECTION PROBLEMS
SELECTED REFERENCES

"These hieroglyphics have evidently a meaning. If it is a purely arbitrary one, it may be impossible for us to solve it. If, on the other hand, it is systematic, I have no doubt that we shall yet get to the bottom of it."

—SHERLOCK HOLMES
IN *THE ADVENTURE OF THE DANCING MEN*

Once we have determined the relevant cash-flow information necessary to make capital budgeting decisions, we need to evaluate the attractiveness of the various investment proposals under consideration. The investment decision will be to either accept or reject each proposal. In this chapter we study alternative methods of project evaluation and selection. In addition, we address some of the potential difficulties encountered in trying to implement these methods.

PROJECT EVALUATION AND SELECTION: ALTERNATIVE METHODS

In this section, we evaluate four alternative methods of project evaluation and selection used in capital budgeting:

1. Payback period
2. Internal rate of return
3. Net present value
4. Profitability index

Discounted cash flow (DCF) Any method of investment project evaluation and selection that adjusts cash flows over time for the time value of money.

The first is a simple additive method for assessing the worth of a project. The remaining methods are more complicated **discounted cash flow (DCF)** techniques. For simplicity, we assume throughout that the expected cash flows are realized at the end of each year. In addition, we carry over our assumption from Chapter 12 that the acceptance of any investment proposal would not change the total business-risk complexion of the firm. This assumption allows us to use a single required rate of return in judging whether or not to accept a project under the various discounted cash flow techniques. In Chapter 14 we allow for the possibility that different investment projects may have different degrees of business risk.

Payback Period

Payback period (PBP) The period of time required for the cumulative expected cash flows from an investment project to equal the initial cash outflow.

The **payback period (PBP)** of an investment project tells us the number of years required to recover our initial cash investment based on the project's expected cash flows. Suppose that we wish to determine the payback period for the new fish-flaking facility discussed in the last chapter. We determined, at that time, that for an initial cash outflow of $100,000, the Faversham Fish Farm expected to generate net cash flows of $34,432, $39,530, $39,359, and $32,219 over the next 4 years. Recording the cash flows in a column, and following a few simple steps, will help you calculate the paypack period.

YEAR	CASH FLOWS	CUMULATIVE INFLOWS
0	($100,000)(−b)	
1	34,432	$ 34,432
2(a)	39,530	73,962(c)
3	39,359(d)	113,321
4	32,219	145,540

Note: $PBP = a + (b − c)/d = 2.66$ years.

Steps:

1. Accumulate the cash flows occurring after the initial outlay in a "cumulative inflows" column.

2. Look at the "cumulative inflows" column and note the last year (a whole figure) for which the cumulative total does not exceed the initial outlay. (In our example, that would be year 2.)

3. Compute the fraction of the following year's cash inflow needed to "payback" the initial cash outlay as follows: Take the initial outlay minus the cumulative total from step 2, then divide this amount by the following year's cash inflow. [For our example, we have ($100,000 − $73,962)/$39,359 = .66.]

4. To get the payback period in years, take the whole figure determined in step 2, and add to it the fraction of a year determined in step 3. (Thus, our payback period is 2 plus .66, or **2.66 years.**)

Acceptance Criterion.   If the payback period calculated is less than some maximum acceptable payback period, the proposal is accepted; if not, it is rejected. If the required payback period were three years, our project would be accepted.

Problems.   A major shortcoming of the payback method is that it fails to consider cash flows occurring after the expiration of the payback period; consequently, it cannot be regarded as a measure of profitability. Two proposals costing $10,000 each would have the same payback period if they both had annual net cash inflows of $5,000 in the first two years. But one project might be expected to provide no cash flows after two years, whereas the other might be expected to provide cash flows of $5,000 in each of the next three years. Thus, the payback method can be deceptive as a yardstick of profitability.

In addition to this shortcoming, the method ignores the time value of money. It simply adds cash flows without regard to the timing of these flows. Finally, the maximum acceptable payback period, which serves as the cutoff standard, is a purely subjective choice.

Although a poor gauge of profitability, the payback period does give a rough indication of the liquidity of a project. Many managers also use it as a crude measure of project risk; but, as we shall see in the next chapter, other analytical approaches do a much better job of capturing risk. The payback period may provide useful insights, but it is best employed as a supplement to discounted cash flow methods.

Internal Rate of Return

Because of the various shortcomings in the payback method, it is generally felt that discounted cash flow methods provide a more objective basis for evaluating and selecting investment projects. These methods take account of both the magnitude and the timing of expected cash flows in each period of a project's life. Stockholders, for example, place a higher value on an investment project that promises cash returns over the next five years than on a project that promises identical cash flows for years 6 through 10. Consequently, the timing of expected cash flows is extremely important in the investment decision.

Discounted cash flow methods enable us to capture differences in the timing of cash flows for various projects through the discounting process. In addition, through our choice of the discount (or hurdle rate), we can also account for project risk. The three major discounted cash flow methods are the internal rate of return (IRR), the net present value (NPV), and the profitability index (PI). We consider each method in turn. This presentation builds on the foundations established in Chapter 3 when we covered the time value of money and in Chapter 4 when we took up security returns.

The **internal rate of return (IRR)** for an investment proposal is the discount rate that equates the present value of the expected net cash flows (CFs) with the initial

Internal rate of return (IRR) The discount rate that equates the present value of the future net cash flows from an investment project with the project's initial cash outflow.

cash outflow (ICO). If the initial cash outflow or cost occurs at time 0, it is represented by that rate, IRR, such that

$$ICO = \frac{CF_1}{(1 + IRR)^1} + \frac{CF_2}{(1 + IRR)^2} + \cdots + \frac{CF_n}{(1 + IRR)^n} \qquad \text{(13-1)}$$

Thus, IRR is the interest rate that discounts the stream of future net cash flows—CF_1 through CF_n—to equal in present value the initial cash outflow (ICO) at time 0. For our fish-flaking facility, the problem can be expressed as

$$\$100,000 = \frac{\$34,432}{(1 + IRR)^1} + \frac{\$39,530}{(1 + IRR)^2} + \frac{\$39,359}{(1 + IRR)^3} + \frac{\$32,219}{(1 + IRR)^4}$$

Interpolation. Solving for the internal rate of return, IRR, sometimes involves a trial-and-error procedure using present value tables. Fortunately, there are computer programs and programmed calculators for solving for the internal rate of return. These aids eliminate the arduous computations involved in the trial-and-error procedure. Still, there are times when, by necessity, one must resort to the trial-and-error method. To illustrate, again consider our example. We want to determine the discount rate that sets the present value of the future net cash-flow stream equal to the initial cash outflow. Suppose that we start with a 15 percent discount rate and calculate the present value of the cash-flow stream. For the appropriate present value interest factors, we use Table II in the Appendix at the end of the book. (Alternatively, we could make repeated use of the equation $PVIF_{i,n} = 1/(1 + i)^n$.)

YEAR	NET CASH FLOWS		PVIF AT 15%		PRESENT VALUES
1	$34,432	×	.870	=	$ 29,955.84
2	39,530	×	.756	=	29,884.68
3	39,359	×	.658	=	25,898.22
4	32,219	×	.572	=	18,429.27
					$104,168.01

A 15 percent discount rate produces a resulting present value for the project that is greater than the initial cash outflow of $100,000. Therefore, we need to try a higher discount rate to further handicap the future cash flows and force their present value down to $100,000. How about a 20 percent discount rate?

YEAR	NET CASH FLOWS		PVIF AT 20%		PRESENT VALUES
1	$34,432	×	.833	=	$28,681.86
2	39,530	×	.694	=	27,433.82
3	39,359	×	.579	=	22,788.86
4	32,219	×	.482	=	15,529.56
					$94,434.10

This time the discount rate chosen was too large. The resulting present value is less than the hoped-for $100,000 figure. The discount rate necessary to discount the cash-flow stream to $100,000 must, therefore, fall somewhere between 15 and 20 percent.

Present value at 15% > ICO > Present value at 20%

$104,168.01 > $100,000 > $94,434.10

Interpolate Estimate an unknown number that lies somewhere between two known numbers.

To approximate the actual rate, we **interpolate** between 15 and 20 percent as follows:

$$.05 \begin{bmatrix} X \begin{bmatrix} .15 & \$104,168.01 \\ IRR & \$100,000.00 \end{bmatrix} \$4,168.01 \\ .20 & \$\ 94,434.10 \end{bmatrix} \$9,733.91$$

$$\frac{X}{.05} = \frac{\$4,168.01}{\$9,733.91} \qquad \text{Therefore,} \qquad X = \frac{(.05) \times (\$4,168.01)}{\$9,733.91} = .0214$$

and $IRR = .15 + X = .15 + .0214 = .1714$, or **17.14 percent.** (Solving for IRR by computer yields 17.04 percent, which in this case is very close to our approximate answer.)

If the cash-flow stream is a uniform series of inflows (an annuity) and the initial outflow occurs at time 0, there is no need for a trial-and-error approach. We simply divide the initial cash outflow by the periodic receipt and search for the nearest discount factor in a table of present value interest factors of an annuity ($PVIFAs$). This is because for a net cash-flow stream that is an annuity, we have

$$ICO = (PVIFA_{IRR,n}) \times (\text{periodic cash flow}) \tag{13-2}$$

And, rearranging terms reveals

$$(PVIFA_{IRR,n}) = ICO/(\text{periodic cash flow}) \tag{13-3}$$

Modifying our example, let's assume that the initial cash outflow of $100,000 was followed by four annual receipts of $36,000. We divide $100,000 by $36,000, obtaining 2.778. The nearest discount factor on the four-period row in Table IV in the Appendix at the end of the book is 2.798, and this figure corresponds to a discount rate of 16 percent. Inasmuch as 2.778 is less than 2.798, we know that the actual rate lies between 16 and 17 percent, and we would interpolate accordingly if a more precise answer were required. As we have seen, when the cash-flow stream is an uneven series the task is more difficult. In such a case we must resort to trial and error. With practice, a person can become surprisingly close in selecting discount rates from which to start.

Acceptance Criterion. The acceptance criterion generally employed with the internal rate of return method is to compare the internal rate of return to a required rate of return, known as the cutoff or **hurdle rate.** We assume for now that the required rate of return is given. If the internal rate of return exceeds the required rate, the project is accepted; if not, the project is rejected. If the required rate of return is 12 percent in our example problem and the internal rate of return method is employed, the investment proposal will be accepted. If the required rate of return is the return investors expect the firm to earn on the project, accepting a project with an internal rate of return in excess of the required rate of return should result in an increase in the market price of the stock. This is because the firm accepts a project with a return greater than that required to maintain the present market price per share. An example is Coca-Cola's acceptance criterion for investments. (See Coca-Cola's feature on the next page.)

Hurdle rate The minimum required rate of return on an investment in a discounted cash flow analysis; the rate at which a project is acceptable.

Net Present Value

Net present value (NPV) The present value of an investment project's net cash flows minus the project's initial cash outflow.

Like the internal rate of return method, the net present value method is a discounted cash flow approach to capital budgeting. The **net present value (NPV)** of an investment proposal is the present value of the proposal's net cash flows less the proposal's initial cash outflow. In formula form we have

Coca-Cola and Its Capital Investments

With a global business system that operates in nearly 200 countries and generates superior cash flows, our Company is uniquely positioned to capitalize on profitable new investment opportunities. Our criterion for investment is simple: New investments must directly enhance our existing operations and must be expected to provide cash returns that exceed our long-term, after-tax, weighted-average cost of capital, currently estimated at approximately 11 percent.

Source: The Coca-Cola Company, 1998 Annual Report, p. 27.
Reproduced with permission of The Coca-Cola Company.

$$NPV = \frac{CF_1}{(1 + k)^1} + \frac{CF_2}{(1 + k)^2} + \ldots + \frac{CF_n}{(1 + k)^n} - ICO \qquad \textbf{(13-4)}$$

where k is the required rate of return and all the other variables remain as previously defined.

Acceptance Criterion. If an investment project's net present value is zero or more, the project is accepted; if not, it is rejected. Another way to express the acceptance criterion is to say that the project will be accepted if the present value of cash inflows exceeds the present value of cash outflows. The rationale behind the acceptance criterion is the same as that behind the internal rate of return method. If the required rate of return is the return investors expect the firm to earn on the investment proposal and the firm accepts a proposal with a net present value greater than zero, the market value of the stock should rise. In fact, if the required rate of return, or discount rate, is chosen correctly, the total market price of the firm's stock should change by an amount equal to the net present value of the project. Thus, taking a project with a net present value equal to zero should leave the market price of the firm's stock unchanged.

If we assume a required rate of return of 12 percent after taxes, the net present value of our previous example is

$$NPV = \frac{\$34,432}{(1 + .12)^1} + \frac{\$39,530}{(1 + .12)^2} + \frac{\$39,359}{(1 + .12)^3} + \frac{\$32,219}{(1 + .12)^4} - \$100,000$$

or, alternatively,

$$NPV = \$34,432(PVIF_{12\%,1}) + \$39,530(PVIF_{12\%,2}) + \$39,359(PVIF_{12\%,3})$$
$$+ \$32,219(PVIF_{12\%,4}) - \$100,000$$

$$= \$30,748 + \$31,505 + \$28,024 + \$20,491 - \$100,000$$

$$= \mathbf{\$10,768}$$

Once again, the problem can be solved by computer, by calculator, or by reference to the appropriate present value table in the Appendix at the end of the book. Inasmuch as the net present value of this proposal is greater than zero, the proposal should be accepted, based on the net present value method.

NPV Profile. In general, the net present value and internal rate of return methods lead to the same acceptance or rejection decision. In Figure 13-1 we illustrate graphi-

FIGURE 13-1
NPV Profile for Fish-
Flaking Facility
Example Showing
the Project's Net Pre-
sent Value Calcu-
lated for a Wide
Range of Discount
Rates

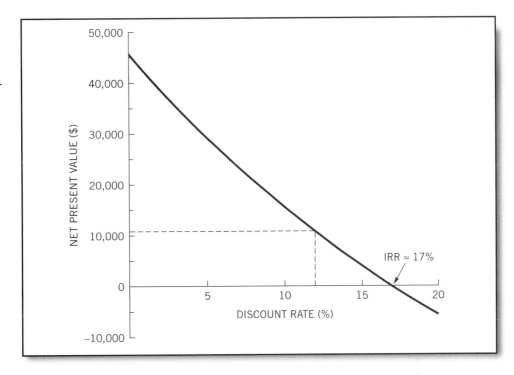

NPV profile A graph
showing the relationship
between a project's net
present value and the discount rate employed.

cally the two methods applied to our example project. The graph, called an **NPV profile,** shows the curvilinear relationship between the net present value for a project and the discount rate employed. When the discount rate is zero, net present value is simply the total cash inflows less the total cash outflows of the project. Assuming a *conventional project*—one where total inflows exceed total outflows and where the initial outflow(s) is (are) followed by inflows—the highest net present value will occur when the discount rate is zero. As the discount rate increases, the net present value profile slopes downward to the right. At the point where the NPV curve intersects the horizontal axis on the graph, the net present value of the project is zero. By definition, the discount rate at that point represents the internal rate of return—the discount rate at which the project's net present value equals zero. For discount rates greater than the internal rate of return, the net present value of the project is negative.

If the required rate of return is less than the internal rate of return, we would accept the project using either method. Suppose that the required rate of return was 12 percent. As seen in Figure 13-1, the net present value of the project is somewhat over $10,000. (From our previous net present value calculations, we know it to be $10,768.) Inasmuch as the net present value of the project is greater than zero, we would accept the project using the net present value method. Similarly, we would accept the project

TIP•TIP•TIP•TIP•TIP•TIP•TIP•TIP•TIP•TIP•TIP

The greater the number of data points plotted, the more accurate the resulting NPV profile. However, a useful rough approximation of a conventional project's NPV profile can often result from plotting and connecting as few as three data points—NPV at a 0 percent discount rate, NPV at the required rate of return, and NPV at the project's IRR.

using the internal rate of return method because the internal rate of return (roughly 17 percent) exceeds the required rate of return (12 percent). For required rates greater than the internal rate of return, we would reject the project under either method. Thus, we see that the internal rate of return and the net present value methods give us identical answers with respect to the acceptance or rejection of an investment project.

Profitability Index

Profitability index (PI) The ratio of the present value of a project's future net cash flows to the project's initial cash outflow.

The **profitability index (PI),** or benefit-cost ratio, of a project is the ratio of the present value of future net cash flows to the initial cash outflow. It can be expressed as

$$PI = \left[\frac{CF_1}{(1 + k)^1} + \frac{CF_2}{(1 + k)^2} + \cdots + \frac{CF_n}{(1 + k)^n} \right] / ICO \qquad \text{(13-5)}$$

For our example problem,

$$PI = (\$30{,}748 + \$31{,}505 + \$28{,}024 + \$20{,}491)/\$100{,}000$$
$$= \$110{,}768/\$100{,}000 = \mathbf{1.11}$$

Acceptance Criterion. As long as the profitability index is 1.00 or greater, the investment proposal is acceptable. For any given project, the net present value and the profitability index methods give the same accept-reject signals. (A profitability index greater than 1.00 implies that a project's present value is greater than its initial cash outflow which, in turn, implies that net present value is greater than zero.) The net present value method, however, is often preferred over the profitability index method. The reason for this is that the net present value tells you whether to accept a project or not and also expresses the absolute dollar economic contribution that the project makes to shareholder wealth. In contrast, the profitability index expresses only the relative profitability.

POTENTIAL DIFFICULTIES

Dependency and Mutual Exclusion

Independent project A project whose acceptance (or rejection) does not prevent the acceptance of other projects under consideration.

So far our analysis has shown that for a single, conventional, **independent project,** the IRR, NPV, and PI methods would lead us to make the same accept-reject decision. We must be aware, however, that several different types of projects pose potential difficulties for the capital budgeting analyst.

Dependent (or **contingent**) **project** A project whose acceptance depends on the acceptance of one or more other projects.

A **dependent** (or **contingent**) **project**—one whose acceptance depends on the acceptance of one or more other projects—deserves special attention. The addition of a large machine, for example, may necessitate construction of a new factory wing to house it. Any contingent proposals must be part of our thinking when we consider the original, dependent proposal.

Mutually exclusive project A project whose acceptance precludes the acceptance of one or more alternative projects.

In evaluating a group of investment proposals, some of them may be mutually exclusive. A **mutually exclusive project** is one whose acceptance precludes the acceptance of one or more alternative proposals. For example, if the firm is considering investment in one of two computer systems, acceptance of one system will rule out the acceptance of the other. Two mutually exclusive proposals cannot both be accepted. When faced with mutually exclusive projects, merely knowing whether each project is good or bad is not enough. We must be able to determine which one is best.

Ranking Problems

When two or more investment proposals are mutually exclusive, so that we can select only one, ranking proposals on the basis of the IRR, NPV, and PI methods *may* give contradictory results. If projects are ranked differently using these methods, the conflict in rankings will be due to one or a combination of the following three project differences:

1. *Scale of investment:* Costs of projects differ.
2. *Cash flow pattern:* Timing of cash flows differs. For example, the cash flows of one project increase over time whereas those of another decrease.
3. *Project life:* Projects have unequal useful lives.

It is important to remember that one or more of these project differences constitutes a necessary, but not sufficient, condition for a conflict in rankings. Thus, it is possible that mutually exclusive projects could differ on all these dimensions (scale, pattern, and life) and still not show any conflict between rankings under the IRR, NPV, and PI methods.

Scale Differences. A problem sometimes arises if the initial cash outflows are different for mutually exclusive investment projects. Suppose a firm had two mutually exclusive investment proposals that were expected to generate the following net cash flows:

	NET CASH FLOWS	
END OF YEAR	PROJECT S	PROJECT L
0	−$100	−$100,000
1	0	0
2	400	156,250

Internal rates of return for projects S and L are 100 percent and 25 percent, respectively. If the required rate of return is 10 percent, the net present value of project S is $231, while its profitability index is 3.31. For project L the net present value is $29,132 with a corresponding profitability index of 1.29. Summarizing our results, we have

	IRR	NPV AT 10%	PI AT 10%
Project S	100%	$ 231	3.31
Project L	25%	$29,132	1.29

Ranking the projects based on our results reveals

RANKINGS	IRR	NPV AT 10%	PI AT 10%
1st place project	S	L	S
2nd place project	L	S	L

Project S is preferred if we use either the internal rate of return or profitability index method. However, project L is preferred if we use the net present value method. If we can choose only one of these proposals, we obviously have a conflict.

Because the results of the internal rate of return method are expressed as a percent, the scale of investment is ignored. Likewise, because the profitability index method looks at relative profitability, scale of investment is ignored once again. Without allowance for this factor, a 100 percent return on a $100 investment would always be preferred to a 25 percent return on a $100,000 investment. In contrast, the results of the net present value method are expressed in terms of absolute dollar increase in value to the firm. With respect to absolute dollar returns, project L is clearly superior, despite the fact that its internal rate of return and profitability index are less than those for project S. The reason is that the scale of investment is greater, affording a greater net present value in this case.

Differences in Cash-Flow Patterns.   To illustrate the nature of the problem that may be caused by differences in cash-flow patterns, assume that a firm is facing two mutually exclusive investment proposals with the following cash-flow patterns:

	NET CASH FLOWS	
END OF YEAR	PROJECT D	PROJECT I
0	−$1,200	−$1,200
1	1,000	100
2	500	600
3	100	1,080

Notice that both projects, D and I, require the same initial cash outflow and have the same useful life. Their cash-flow patterns, however, are different. Project D's cash flows *decrease* over time, whereas project I's cash flows *increase*.

Internal rates of return for projects D and I are 23 percent and 17 percent, respectively. For every discount rate greater than 10 percent, project D's net present value and profitability index will be larger than those for project I. On the other hand, for every discount rate less than 10 percent, project I's net present value and profitability index will be larger than those for project D. If we assume a required rate of return (k) of 10 percent, each project will have identical net present values of $198 and profitability indexes of 1.17. Using these results to determine project rankings, we find the following:

		$K < 10\%$		$K > 10\%$	
RANKINGS	IRR	NPV	PI	NPV	PI
1st place project	D	I	I	D	D
2nd place project	I	D	D	I	I

The nature of the conflict in rankings can be more fully explored with the aid of Figure 13-2, where NPV profiles for the two projects are shown. The intercepts on the horizontal axis represent the internal rates of return for the two projects. The intercepts on the vertical axis represent total undiscounted cash inflows less cash outflows for the two projects. We see that project D ranks higher than project I on the basis of highest internal rate of return, regardless of the appropriate discount or hurdle rate. The net present value and profitability index rankings in this case, however, are sensitive to the discount rate chosen.

The discount rate associated with the intersection of the two NPV profiles, 10 percent, represents the rate at which the projects have identical net present values. It is referred to as *Fisher's rate of intersection* after the noted economist Irving Fisher. This discount rate is important because at required rates of return less than Fisher's rate, our net present value and profitability index rankings will conflict with those provided under the internal rate of return method.

In our example, the conflict in rankings under the alternative methods for discount rates less than Fisher's rate cannot be caused by scale or life problems. Remember, the initial cash outflow and useful life are identical for projects D and I. The

Part V Investment in Capital Assets

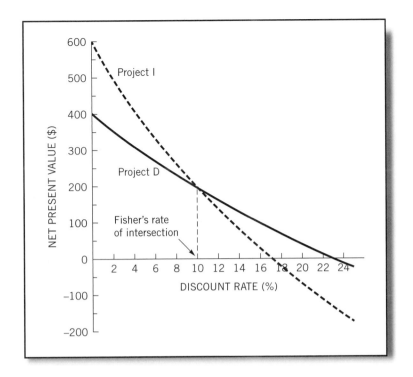

FIGURE 13-2
NPV Profiles for Mutually Exclusive Projects I and D

observed conflict among methods is due to different implicit assumptions with respect to the reinvestment rate on intermediate cash flows released from the projects. Each of the discounted cash flow methods implicitly assumes that the project's cash inflows can be reinvested at the rate employed by that method to discount cash flows. Thus, the internal rate of return method implicitly assumes that funds can be reinvested at the internal rate of return over the remaining life of the project. The net present value and profitability index methods, however, implicitly assume reinvestment at a rate equivalent to the required rate of return used as the discount rate.

With the internal rate of return method, then, the implicit reinvestment rate will differ from project to project depending on the pattern of the cash-flow stream for each proposal under consideration. For a project with a high internal rate of return, a high reinvestment rate is assumed. For a project with a low internal rate of return, a low reinvestment rate is inferred. Only if two projects had the same internal rate of return would the reinvestment rates be identical. With the net present value method, however, the implicit reinvestment rate—namely, the required rate of return—is the same for each project. In essence, this reinvestment rate represents the minimum return on opportunities available to the firm. This single rate more accurately reflects the marginal rate of return the firm can expect to earn on any marginal funds available to it. Thus, when mutually exclusive projects rank differently because of cash-flow-pattern differences, the net present value rankings should be used. In this fashion we can identify the project that adds most to shareholder wealth.

Differences in Project Lives. A final project difference that might lead to a conflict in project rankings concerns mutually exclusive projects with unequal useful lives. The key question here is, what happens at the end of the shorter-lived project? Most likely, the firm will either (1) replace the investment with an identical (or similar) project, or (2) reinvest in some other project or projects. We will explore the former situation in Appendix B at the end of this chapter. There we will view the choice as one involving a series of project replications—or a "replacement chain"—of the respective alternatives over some common investment horizon. The second situation, where alternative projects would not be replaced at the end of their useful lives, is considered here.

As an example, suppose that you are faced with choosing between two mutually exclusive investment projects, X and Y, that have the following patterns of cash flows:

END OF YEAR	NET CASH FLOWS	
	PROJECT X	PROJECT Y
0	−$1,000	−$1,000
1	0	2,000
2	0	0
3	3,375	0

Internal rates of return for projects X and Y are 50 percent and 100 percent, respectively. If the required rate of return is 10 percent, the net present value of project X is $1,536, and its profitability index is 2.54. For project Y the net present value is $818 with a corresponding profitability index of 1.82. Summarizing our results, we have

	IRR	NPV AT 10%	PI AT 10%
Project X	50%	$1,536	2.54
Project Y	100%	$ 818	1.82

Ranking the projects based on our results reveals

RANKINGS	IRR	NPV AT 10%	PI AT 10%
1st place project	Y	X	X
2nd place project	X	Y	Y

Once again we see a conflict in project rankings among the alternative methods. By now we hope that your inclination is to base your choice on the net present value method—that is, to choose the project that adds the greatest absolute increment in value to the firm. In that case you would choose project X. However, you may be bothered by the following facts: (1) project Y's IRR is twice that of project X, and yet it costs the same amount, namely, $1,000; (2) you have to wait three years to get any positive cash flow from project X, whereas project Y provides all of its cash flow after just one year; and (3) you could put project Y's positive cash flow to work for you all the while project X produced nothing.

To see that the net present value method will lead to the proper rankings even when faced with mutually exclusive projects possessing unequal lives, we can compare the projects as of a common termination date. To do so, we assume that the shorter-lived project's cash flows are reinvested up to the termination date of the longer-lived project at the firm's required rate of return. We use this reinvestment rate, as opposed to some higher rate, because this is the rate we assume that the firm would be able to earn on the next-best (marginal) project when additional funds are made available.

| | NET CASH FLOWS AT END OF YEAR | | | | |
	0	1	2	3	NPV AT 10%
Project X	−$1,000	0	0	$3,375	$1,536
Project Y	−$1,000	$2,000	0	0	$ 818
If project Y's cash flows are reinvested at 10%, then			Compounded 2 years		
	−$1,000	0	0	$2,420	$ 818

Because projects X and Y each require the same initial cash outlay, we can compare these two projects on the basis of terminal values. Notice that on this basis project X, the project with higher NPV, is preferred because its terminal value of $3,375 is higher than the $2,420 terminal value for project Y. Also, whether the projects had equivalent initial cash outlays or not, we could always rank the projects by net present values based on terminal values and initial cash outflows. Notice that project Y's net present value does not change when we switch from actual cash flows to imputed flows. This is because we have used the same required rate of return for both compounding and discounting. Thus, net present values based on actual cash flows for mutually exclusive projects with unequal lives will still produce correct project rankings. In this case, project X is preferred over project Y because it has a positive net present value and adds $718 ($1,536 − $818) more in present value to the firm.

Multiple Internal Rates of Return

A potential problem with the internal rate of return method that we have yet to mention is that multiple internal rates of return are possible. A necessary, but not sufficient, condition for this occurrence is that the cash-flow stream changes sign more than once. For example, the pattern −, +, +, − reveals two changes in sign—from minus to plus and from plus to minus. All of our examples so far depicted conventional cash-flow patterns, where a cash outflow was followed by one or more cash

Marketing and Finance Are Complementary: When the Analysis is Right

Harvard Business Review

From a financial perspective, a good investment is one with a positive net present value—that is, one whose value exceeds its costs. While marketers often think a project's NPV is merely the result of financial arithmetic, in reality, it is derived from strategic marketing issues. To have a positive NPV, a project must pass two tests: Does the product or service have enough value to enough customers to support prices and volumes that exceed the costs of supplying it—including the opportunity cost of capital? This question is central to post-

war marketing and the "marketing concept." Second, does the company have enough sources of sustainable competitive advantage to exploit, develop, and defend the opportunity? This reflects marketing's more recent emphasis on competitive strategy. The trick, then, is to encourage an investment decision-making process in which the financial analysis highlights rather than masks these two fundamental marketing questions.

Reprinted by permission of the Harvard Business Review. *Excerpt from "Must Finance and Strategy Clash?" by Patrick Barwise, Paul R. Marsh, and Robin Wensley (September–October 1989). Copyright © 1989 by the President and Fellows of Harvard College; all rights reserved.*

inflows. In other words, there was but one change in sign (from minus to plus), which ensured a unique internal rate of return. However, some projects, which we could label as *nonconventional*, involve multiple changes in sign. For example, at the end of a project there may be a requirement to restore the environment. This often happens in an extractive industry like strip mining where land must be reclaimed at the end of the project. Additionally, with a chemical plant there are often sizable dismantling costs. Whatever the cause, these costs result in a cash outflow at the end of the project and, hence, in more than one change in sign in the cash-flow stream.

Whether these changes in sign cause more than one internal rate of return also depends on the magnitudes of the cash flows. Because the relationship is complicated and requires illustration, we address the problem in detail in Appendix A at the end of the chapter. Most projects have only one change in sign in the cash-flow stream, but some have more. When this occurs, the financial manager must be alert to the possibility of multiple internal rates of return. As shown in Appendix A, no one internal rate of return makes sense economically when there are multiple internal rates of return. Therefore, an alternative method of analysis must be used.

When multiple IRR situations are analyzed, calculators and computer programs are often fooled and produce only one IRR. Perhaps the best way to determine if a problem exists is to calculate the net present value of a project at various discount rates. If the discount rate were increased from zero in small increments up to 1,000 percent, for instance, an NPV profile similar to that shown in Figure 13-2 could be plotted. If the NPV profile line connecting the dots crosses the horizontal axis more than once, you have a multiple IRR problem.

Summary of Shortcomings of the IRR Method.   We have seen that the net present value method always provides correct rankings of mutually exclusive investment projects, whereas the internal rate of return method sometimes does not. With the IRR method, the implicit reinvestment rate will differ depending on the cash-flow stream for each investment proposal under consideration. With the net present value method, however, the implicit reinvestment rate—namely, the required rate of return—is the same for each investment.

In addition, the net present value method takes into account differences in the scale and life of each investment. If our objective is truly value maximization, the only theoretically correct opportunity cost of funds is the required rate of return. It is consistently applied with the net present value method, thereby avoiding the reinvestment rate problem. Finally, the possibility of multiple rates of return hurts the case for the internal rate of return method.

With all these criticisms, why is the IRR method used at all? The reason is that many managers find the internal rate of return easier to visualize and interpret than they do the net present value measure. One does not have to initially specify a required rate of return in the calculations. To the extent that the required rate of return is but a rough estimate, the internal rate of return method may permit a more satisfying comparison of projects for the typical manager. Put another way, managers feel comfortable with a return measure as opposed to an absolute net present value figure. As long as the company is not confronted with many mutually exclusive projects or with unusual projects having multiple sign changes in the cash-flow stream, the internal rate of return method may be used with reasonable confidence. When this is not the case, the shortcomings just discussed must be borne in mind. Either modifications in the internal rate of return method (see Appendix A to this chapter for a discussion) or a switch to the net present value method (perhaps augmented by an NPV profile) needs to occur.

Capital Rationing

The final potential difficulty related to implementing the alternative methods of project evaluation and selection that we will discuss concerns **capital rationing.** Capital rationing occurs any time there is a budget ceiling, or constraint, on the amount of funds that can be invested during a specific period, such as a year. Such constraints are prevalent in a number of firms, particularly in those that have a policy of internally financing all capital expenditures. Another example of capital rationing occurs when a division of a large company is allowed to make capital expenditures only up to a specified budget ceiling, over which the division usually has no control. With a capital rationing constraint, the firm attempts to select the combination of investment proposals that will provide the greatest increase in the value of the firm subject to not exceeding the budget ceiling constraint.

When capital is rationed over multiple periods, several alternative (and rather complicated) methods of handling constrained maximization can be applied to the capital rationing problem. These methods make use of linear, integer, or goal programming.

If capital is to be rationed *for only the current period,* the problem is reduced to selecting those projects that add the greatest increment in value per dollar of investment without surpassing the budget ceiling. Assume, for example, that your firm faces the following investment opportunities:

PROJECT	INITIAL CASH OUTFLOW	IRR	NPV	PI
A	$50,000	15%	$12,000	1.24
B	35,000	19	15,000	1.43
C	30,000	28	42,000	2.40
D	25,000	26	1,000	1.04
E	15,000	20	10,000	1.67
F	10,000	37	11,000	2.10
G	10,000	25	13,000	2.30
H	1,000	18	100	1.10

If the budget ceiling for initial cash outflows during the present period is $65,000 and the proposals are independent of each other, you would want to select the combination of proposals that provides the greatest increase in firm value that $65,000 (or less) can provide. Selecting projects in descending order of profitability according to the various discounted cash flow methods until the $65,000 budget is exhausted reveals the following:

PROJECT	IRR	NPV	INITIAL OUTFLOW
F	37%	$11,000	$10,000
C	28	42,000	30,000
D	26	1,000	25,000
		$54,000	$65,000

PROJECT	NPV	INITIAL OUTFLOW
C	$42,000	$30,000
B	15,000	35,000
	$57,000	$65,000

PROJECT	PI	NPV	INITIAL OUTFLOW
C	2.40	$42,000	$30,000
G	2.30	13,000	10,000
F	2.10	11,000	10,000
E	1.67	10,000	15,000
		$76,000	$65,000

With capital rationing, you would accept projects C, E, F, and G, totaling $65,000 in initial outflows. No other mix of available projects will provide a greater total net present value than the $76,000 that these projects provide. Because of the budget constraint, you cannot necessarily invest in all proposals that increase the net present value of the firm; you invest in an acceptable proposal only if the budget constraint allows such an investment. As you can see, selecting projects by descending order of profitability index (the ratio of the present value of future net cash flows over the initial cash outflow) allows you to select the mix of projects that adds most to firm value when operating under a single-period budget ceiling. This is because the problem boils down to selecting that mix of projects that gives you "the biggest bang for the buck"—exactly what ranking projects by profitability index reveals.[1]

A budget ceiling carries a real cost when it bars us from taking advantage of any additional profitable opportunities. In our example, a number of opportunities were forgone by the imposition of the $65,000 budget ceiling. We were prohibited from taking projects A, B, D, and H even though they would have added $28,100 ($12,000 + $15,000 + $1,000 + $100) in value to the firm.

It should come as no surprise, then, that capital rationing usually results in an investment policy that is less than optimal. From a theoretical standpoint, a firm should accept all projects yielding more than the required rate of return. By doing so, it will increase the market price per share of its common stock because it is taking on projects that will provide a return higher than necessary to maintain the present market price per share. This proposition assumes that the firm actually can raise capital, within reasonable limits, at the required rate of return. Certainly, unlimited amounts of capital are not available at any one cost. However, most firms are involved in a more or less continuous process of making decisions to undertake capital expenditures and to finance these expenditures. Given these assumptions the firm should accept all proposals yielding more than the required rate of return and raise capital to

---

[1]Sometimes a firm may not be able to utilize its full capital budget by selecting projects on the basis of descending order of profitability index because the next best acceptable project is too large. When this situation occurs the firm *may* be better off searching for another combination of projects (perhaps including some smaller ones in place of a larger one) that will use up more of the capital budget while still increasing the net present value of the total group of projects accepted. (See end-of-chapter Problem 8 for an example.)

Georgia-Pacific and Project Monitoring

In addition to the preinvestment evaluations of capital projects, we review major investments during the course of the projects and/or after their completion. These reviews compare the actual timing and amounts of expenditures, product prices, raw material costs and other critical success factors to the assumptions made when the investments were proposed. These reviews (presented periodically to the Corporation's Board) are key to continually learning about and understanding the risks inherent in future investments. This knowledge is critical to our ability to employ shareholders' capital where it is most likely to create positive economic returns.

Source: Georgia-Pacific Corporation—Georgia-Pacific Group, 1998 Annual Report, pp. 27–28. © 1998 Georgia-Pacific Corporation—Georgia-Pacific Group. Used by permission. All rights reserved.

finance these proposals at that approximate real cost. Without doubt, there are circumstances that complicate the use of this rule. In general, however, this policy should tend to maximize the market price of the firm's stock over the long run. If the firm rations capital and rejects projects that yield more than the required return, the firm's investment policy is, by definition, less than optimal. Management could increase the value of the firm to the shareholders by accepting these rejected value-creating projects.

PROJECT MONITORING: PROGRESS REVIEWS AND POST-COMPLETION AUDITS

Post-completion audit A formal comparison of the actual costs and benefits of a project with original estimates. A key element of the audit is feedback; that is, results of the audit are given to relevant personnel so that future decision making can be improved.

The capital budgeting process should not end with the decision to accept a project. Continual monitoring of the project is the necessary next step to help ensure project success. Therefore, companies should perform progress reviews followed by **post-completion audits** for all large projects; strategically important projects, regardless of size; and a sample of smaller projects. Progress reviews, or status reports, can provide, especially during the implementation phase of a project, early warnings of potential cost overruns, revenue shortfalls, invalid assumptions, and outright project failure. Information revealed through progress reviews may lead to revised forecasts, remedial actions to improve performance, or project abandonment.

Post-completion audits allow management to determine how close the actual results of an implemented project have come to its original estimates. When they are used properly, progress reviews and post-completion audits can help identify forecasting weaknesses and any important factors that were omitted. With a good feedback system, any lessons learned can be used to improve the quality of future capital budgeting decision making.

Monitoring of a project can also have important psychological effects on managers. For example, if managers know in advance that their capital investment decisions will be monitored, they will be more likely to make realistic forecasts and to see that original estimates are met. In addition, managers may find it easier to abandon a failing project within the context of a formal review process.

SUMMARY

- We began our discussion of capital budgeting in Chapter 12 with the assumption that the acceptance of any investment proposal would not change the total business-risk complexion of the firm. This assumption allowed us to use a single required rate of return in judging whether or not to accept a project.
- Four alternative methods of project evaluation and selection were discussed. The first was a simple additive method for assessing the worth of a project called the payback period. The remaining three methods (internal rate of return, net present value, and profitability index) were all *discounted cash flow techniques.*

- The *payback period (PBP)* of an investment tells us the number of years required to recover our initial cash investment. Although this measure provides a rough guide to the liquidity of a project, it is a poor gauge of profitability. It falls short as a measure of profitability because it (1) ignores cash flows occurring after the expiration of the payback period, (2) ignores the time value of money, and (3) makes use of a crude acceptance criterion, namely, a subjectively determined cut-off point.
- The *internal rate of return (IRR)* for an investment proposal is the discount rate that equates the present value of the expected net cash flows with

the initial cash outflow. If a project's IRR is greater than or equal to a required rate of return, the project should be accepted.

- The *net present value (NPV)* of an investment proposal is the present value of the proposal's net cash flows less the proposal's initial cash outflow. If a project's NPV is greater than or equal to zero, the project should be accepted.

- The *profitability index (PI)*, or benefit-cost ratio, of a project is the ratio of the present value of future net cash flows to the initial cash outflow. If a project's PI is greater than or equal to 1.00, the project should be accepted.

- When two or more investment proposals are *mutually exclusive,* so that we can select only one, ranking proposals on the basis of the IRR, NPV, and PI methods *may* give contradictory results. If a conflict in rankings occurs, it will be due to one or a combination of the following three project differences: (1) scale of investment, (2) cash-flow pattern, and (3) project life. In every case, the net present value rankings can be shown to lead to the correct project selection. In short, if net present value rankings are used, projects that are expected to add the greatest increment in dollar value to the firm will be chosen.

- A potential problem with the internal rate of return method is that multiple internal rates of return *might* occur for *nonconventional* projects— projects whose cash-flow streams show multiple changes in sign. When there are multiple rates of return, an alternative method of analysis must be used.

- *Capital rationing* occurs any time there is a budget ceiling, or constraint, on the amount of funds that can be invested during a specific period, such as a year. When capital is rationed over multiple periods, several alternative (and rather complicated) methods can be applied to the capital rationing problem. If capital is to be rationed for only the current period, selecting projects by descending order of profitability index generally leads to a selection of a project mix that adds most to firm value.

- It is important to monitor projects continually to help ensure project success. Therefore, companies should perform progress reviews followed by *post-completion audits.*

Appendix A

Multiple Internal Rates of Return

Certain nonconventional cash-flow streams may have more than one internal rate of return. To illustrate the problem, suppose that we are considering an investment proposal consisting of a new, more effective, oil pump that will remove a fixed quantity of oil out of the ground more quickly than our existing pump.[2] This investment would require an initial cash outflow of $1,600 for the new pump. Our older, slower pump would provide cash flows of $10,000 in each of the next two years. However, our new pump would produce a cash flow of $20,000 in one year, after which our oil supply is exhausted. Salvage value for both pumps is negligible. The calculations necessary to determine the appropriate incremental net cash flows due to the pump replacement are as follows:

	END OF YEAR		
	0	1	2
(a) New pump's cash flows	−$1,600	$20,000	0
(b) Old pump's cash flows	0	$10,000	$10,000
(c) Net cash flows due to pump replacement Line (a)—Line (b)	**−$1,600**	**$10,000**	**−$10,000**

---

[2]This problem is adapted from James H. Lorie and Leonard J. Savage, "Three Problems in Rationing Capital." *Journal of Business* 28 (October 1955), 229–39.

Part V Investment in Capital Assets

On an incremental basis, then, the net cash flows resulting from the increased efficiency of the new pump are −$1,600, + $10,000, and −$10,000. When we solve for the internal rate of return for the cash-flow stream, we find that it is not one rate but two: 25 percent and 400 percent.

Take Note

$$\$1,600 = \frac{\$10,000}{(1 + IRR)^1} - \frac{\$10,000}{(1 + IRR)^2}$$

when $IRR = .25$ or 4.0

This unusual situation is illustrated in Figure 13A-1, which consists of this nonconventional proposal's NPV profile. At a 0 percent discount rate, the net present value of the project is simply the sum of all the cash flows. It is −$1,600 because total cash outflows exceed total cash inflows. As the discount rate increases, the present value of the second-year outflow diminishes with respect to the first-year inflow, and the net present value of the proposal becomes positive when the discount rate exceeds 25 percent. As the discount rate increases beyond 100 percent, the present value of all future cash flows (years 1 and 2) diminishes relative to the initial outflow of −$1,600. At 400 percent, the net present value again becomes zero.

This type of proposal differs from the usual case, shown previously in Figure 13-1, in which net present value is a decreasing function of the discount rate and in which there is but one internal rate of return that equates the present value of the future net cash flows with the initial cash outflow. A nonconventional proposal may have any number of internal rates of return depending on the cash-flow pattern. Consider the following series of cash flows:

	END OF YEAR			
	0	1	2	3
Cash flows	−$1,000	$6,000	−$11,000	$6,000

In this example, discount rates of 0, 100, and 200 percent result in the net present value of all cash flows equaling zero.

FIGURE 13A-1
NPV Profile for Pump Replacement Proposal Showing Two Internal Rates of Return

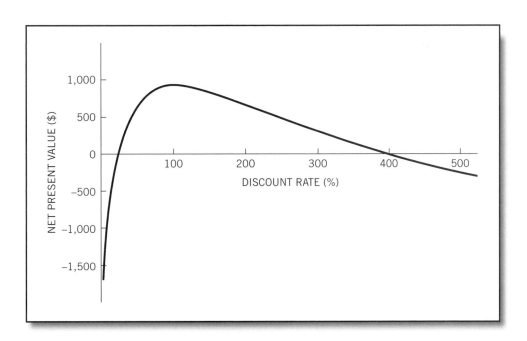

The number of possible internal rates of return has an upper limit equal to the number of reversals of sign in the cash-flow stream. In the example, we have three reversals and, it just so happens, three internal rates of return. Although a multiple reversal in signs is a necessary condition for multiple internal rates of return, it is not sufficient for such an occurrence. The occurrence of multiple internal rates of return also depends on the magnitude of cash flows. For the following series of cash flows, there is but one internal rate of return (32.5 percent), despite two reversals of sign:

| | END OF YEAR | | |
	0	1	2
Cash flows	−$1,000	$1,400	−$100

When confronted with a proposal having multiple rates of return, how does one decide which is the correct rate? In our first example, is the correct rate 25 percent or 400 percent? Actually, neither rate is correct, because neither is a measure of investment worth. If the firm's required rate of return is 20 percent, should the investment be accepted? Despite the fact that both internal rates of return are greater than the required rate of return, a glance at Figure 13A-1 is enough to reveal that at a 20 percent discount rate the project has a negative net present value (−$211) and, therefore, should not be accepted.

$$NPV = \frac{\$10,000}{(1 + .20)^1} - \frac{\$10,000}{(1 + .20)^2} - \$1,600$$

$$= \$8,333 - \$6,944 - \$1,600 = -\mathbf{\$211}$$

An alternative way to view the pump problem is that the firm is being offered the chance to accelerate the receipt of the cash flow of the second year by one year in exchange for paying a $1,600 fee. The relevant question then becomes, what is it worth to the firm to have the use of $10,000 for one year? This question, in turn, depends on the rate of return on investment opportunities available to the firm for that period of time. If the firm could earn 20 percent on the use of these funds and realize these earnings at the end of the period, the value of this opportunity would be $2,000, to be received at the end of the second year. The present value of this $2,000 at a 20 percent discount rate is $1,389 ($2,000/(1 + .20)^2)—which, when added to the $1,600 outflow, yields, once again, a net present value of −$211. Similarly, other projects having multiple rates of return are best evaluated using a net present value approach.

Appendix B

Replacement Chain Analysis

In this chapter we noted that it was possible to encounter a conflict in project rankings for mutually exclusive projects with unequal useful lives. The key question is, what happens at the end of the shorter-lived project? Most likely, the firm will either (1) replace the investment with an identical (or similar) project, or (2) reinvest in some other projects. We saw that, where alternative projects would not be replaced at the end of their useful lives (the latter situation), we do not need to take future investment decisions into account. In these cases we simply choose the project with the highest net present value.

We now turn our attention to the former situation. Here we are faced with a choice between mutually exclusive investments having unequal lives that will require replacements. For example, we may need to purchase one of two alternative machines—with one machine being more durable and, therefore, having a longer useful life than the other. Because subsequent decisions are affected by the initial investment, the sequence of decisions associated with each alternative must be evaluated. This evaluation generally views the choice as one involving a series of replications—or "replacement chain"—of respective alternatives over some common investment horizon.

REPLACEMENT CHAIN (COMMON LIFE) APPROACH

Repeating each project until the earliest date that we can terminate each project in the same year results in multiple like-for-like replacement chains covering the shortest common life. At the conclusion of each chain, the firm thus has identical options regardless of which choice was made initially.

Then, we solve for the net present value of each replacement chain, NPV_{chain}, according to the following formula:

$$NPV_{chain} = \sum_{t=1}^{R} \frac{NPV_n}{(1 + k)^{n(t-1)}} \qquad \text{(13B-1)}$$

where n = single-replication project life, in years
NPV_n = single-replication net present value for a project with an n-year useful life
R = number of replications needed to provide the shortest common life, $(R) \times (n)$, for all mutually exclusive alternatives under consideration
k = appropriate project-specific discount rate

In effect, the firm realizes a net present value at the beginning of each replacement. The value of each replacement chain, therefore, is simply the present value of the sequence of NPVs generated by that replacement chain.

AN ILLUSTRATION

Assume the following regarding mutually exclusive investment alternatives A and B, both of which require future replacements:

	PROJECT A	PROJECT B
Single-replication life (n)	5 years	10 years
Single-replication net present value calculated at project-specific required rate of return (NPV_n)	$5,328	$8,000
Number of replications needed to provide the shortest common life (R)	2	1
Project-specific discount rate (k)[a]	10%	10%

[a]Discount rates for alternative projects could differ.

At first glance, project B looks better. Its single-replication net present value of $8,000 is certainly higher than the $5,328 net present value provided by project A. However, the need to make future replacements dictates that we consider the value provided by both alternatives over the same common life—in this case, 10 years. Figure 13B-1 shows how to find the net present value for two replications of project A—a replacement chain 10 years in length.

FIGURE 13B-1
Time Line for Calculating the Replacement Chain NPV for Project A ($NPV_5 = \$5,328$; $k = 10\%$; and $R = 2$)

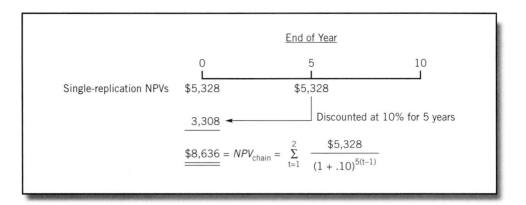

The net present value of the replacement chain for project B involves but a single replication and is, therefore, already known; that is, project B's $NPV_{chain} = \$8,000$. Since

$$\text{Project A's } NPV_{chain} = \$8,636 > \text{Project B's } NPV_{chain} = \$8,000$$

we prefer project A.[3]

QUESTIONS

1. Explain what is meant by the *time value of money*. Why is a bird in the hand worth two (or so) in the bush? Which capital budgeting approach ignores this concept? Is it optimal?
2. Why does the payback period bias the process of asset selection toward short-lived assets?
3. Why does the net present value method favor larger projects over smaller ones when used to choose between mutually exclusive projects? Is this a problem?
4. Contrast the internal rate of return method of project evaluation and selection with the net present value method. Why might these two discounted cash flow techniques lead to conflicts in project rankings?
5. Although it is conceptually unsound, the payback period is very popular in business as a criterion for assigning priorities to investment projects. Why is it unsound, and why is it popular?
6. What are *mutually exclusive* investment projects? What is a *dependent* project?
7. Is the economic efficiency of a country enhanced by the use of modern capital budgeting techniques? Why?
8. If *capital rationing* is not optimal, why would any company use it?
9. The internal rate of return method implies that intermediate cash flows are reinvested at the internal rate of return. Under what circumstances is this assump-

---

[3]Notice that we have just discounted the second single-replication NPV of project A at a "risky" 10 percent rate. The use of a *risky* project-specific rate is the procedure most commonly discussed. There may be instances, however, when discounting NPVs of future replications to the present at the risk-free rate will be more appropriate. The choice of the discount rate to be used in calculating the net present value of a chain of project replications should depend on the nature of uncertainty (risk) *between replications*. For a full discussion of this issue and alternative capital budgeting procedures that correctly reflect the nature of risk between replications, see Ronald E. Shrieves and John M. Wachowicz Jr., "Proper Risk Resolution in Replacement Chain Analysis," *The Engineering Economist* 34 (Winter 1989), 91–114.

tion likely to lead to a seriously biased measure of the economic return from the project?

10. Some people have suggested combining the payback period (PBP) method with present value analysis to calculate a *"discounted" payback period (DPBP)*. Instead of using cumulative inflows, cumulative *present values* of inflows (discounted at the cost of capital) are used to see how long it takes to "pay" for a project with discounted cash flows. For a firm not subject to a capital rationing restraint, if an independent project's "discounted" payback period is less than some maximum acceptable "discounted" payback period, the project would be accepted; if not, it would be rejected. Assume that an independent project's "discounted" payback period is greater than a company's maximum acceptable "discounted" payback period but less than the project's useful life; would rejection of this project cause you any concern? Why? Does the "discounted" payback period method overcome all the problems encountered when using the "traditional" payback period method? What advantages (if any) do you see the net present value method holding over a "discounted" payback period method?

SELF-CORRECTION PROBLEMS

1. Briarcliff Stove Company is considering a new product line to supplement its range line. It is anticipated that the new product line will involve cash investment of $700,000 at time 0 and $1.0 million in year 1. After-tax cash inflows of $250,000 are expected in year 2, $300,000 in year 3, $350,000 in year 4, and $400,000 each year thereafter through year 10. Though the product line might be viable after year 10, the company prefers to be conservative and end all calculations at that time.
   a. If the required rate of return is 15 percent, what is the net present value of the project? Is it acceptable?
   b. What is its internal rate of return?
   c. What would be the case if the required rate of return was 10 percent?
   d. What is the project's payback period?

2. Carbide Chemical Company is considering the replacement of two old machines with a new, more efficient machine. It has determined that the relevant after-tax incremental operating cash flows of this replacement proposal are as follows:

	END OF YEAR			
	0	1	2	3
Cash flows	−$404,424	$86,890	$106,474	$91,612

	END OF YEAR				
	4	5	6	7	8
Cash flows	$84,801	$84,801	$75,400	$66,000	$92,400

What is the project's net present value if the required rate of return is 14 percent? Is the project acceptable?

3. The Acme Blivet Company is evaluating three investment situations: (1) produce a new line of aluminum blivets, (2) expand its existing blivet line to include several new sizes, and (3) develop a new, higher quality line of blivet. If only the project in question is undertaken, the expected present values and the amounts of investment required are as follows:

PROJECT	INVESTMENT REQUIRED	PRESENT VALUE OF FUTURE CASH FLOWS
1	$200,000	$290,000
2	115,000	185,000
3	270,000	400,000

If projects 1 and 2 are jointly undertaken, there will be no economies; the investment required and present values will simply be the sum of the parts. With projects 1 and 3, economies are possible in investment because one of the machines acquired can be used in both production processes. The total investment required for projects 1 and 3 combined is $440,000. If projects 2 and 3 are undertaken, there are economies to be achieved in marketing and producing the products but not in investment. The expected present value of future cash flows for projects 2 and 3 combined is $620,000. If all three projects are undertaken simultaneously, the economies noted above will still hold. However, a $125,000 extension on the plant will be necessary, as space is not available for all three projects. Which project or projects should be chosen?

PROBLEMS

1. Lobers, Inc., has two investment proposals, which have the following characteristics:

	PROJECT A			PROJECT B		
PERIOD	COST	PROFIT AFTER TAXES	NET CASH FLOW	COST	PROFIT AFTER TAXES	NET CASH FLOW
0	$9,000	—	—	$12,000	—	—
1		$1,000	$5,000		$1,000	$5,000
2		1,000	4,000		1,000	5,000
3		1,000	3,000		4,000	8,000

For each project, compute its payback period, its net present value, and its profitability index using a discount rate of 15 percent.

2. In Problem 1, what criticisms may be offered against the payback method?

3. The following are exercises on internal rates of return:

   a. An investment of $1,000 today will return $2,000 at the end of 10 years. What is its internal rate of return?

   b. An investment of $1,000 will return $500 at the end of each of the next 3 years. What is its internal rate of return?

   c. An investment of $1,000 today will return $900 at the end of 1 year, $500 at the end of 2 years, and $100 at the end of 3 years. What is its internal rate of return?

   d. An investment of $1,000 will return $130 per year forever. What is its internal rate of return?

4. Two *mutually exclusive* projects have projected cash flows as follows:

	END OF YEAR				
	0	1	2	3	4
Project A	−$2,000	$1,000	$1,000	$1,000	$1,000
Project B	− 2,000	0	0	0	6,000

   a. Determine the internal rate of return for each project.

   b. Determine the net present value for each project at discount rates of 0, 5, 10, 20, 30, and 35 percent.

c. Plot a graph of the net present value of each project at the different discount rates.

d. Which project would you select? Why? What assumptions are inherent in your decision?

5. Zaire Electronics can make either of two investments at time 0. Assuming a required rate of return of 14 percent, determine for each project (a) the payback period, (b) the net present value, (c) the profitability index, and (d) the internal rate of return. Assume under MACRS the asset falls in the five-year property class and that the corporate tax rate is 34 percent. The initial investments required and yearly savings before depreciation and taxes are shown below:

		END OF YEAR						
PROJECT	INVESTMENT	1	2	3	4	5	6	7
A	$28,000	$8,000	$8,000	$8,000	$8,000	$8,000	$8,000	$8,000
B	20,000	5,000	5,000	6,000	6,000	7,000	7,000	7,000

6. Thoma Pharmaceutical Company may buy DNA testing equipment costing $60,000. This equipment is expected to reduce labor costs of clinical staff by $20,000 annually. The equipment has a useful life of five years but falls in the three-year property class for cost recovery (depreciation) purposes. No salvage value is expected at the end. The corporate tax rate for Thoma is 38 percent (combined federal and state), and its required rate of return is 15 percent. (If profits after taxes on the project are negative in any year, the firm will offset the loss against other firm income for that year.) On the basis of this information, what is the net present value of the project? Is it acceptable?

7. In Problem 6, suppose that 6 percent inflation in cost savings from labor is expected over the last four years, so that savings in the first year are $20,000, savings in the second year are $21,200, and so forth.

a. If the required rate of return is still 15 percent, what is the net present value of the project? Is it acceptable?

b. If a working capital requirement of $10,000 were required in addition to the cost of the equipment and this additional investment were needed over the life of the project, what would be the effect on net present value? (All other things are the same as in Problem 7, Part (a).)

8. The Lake Tahow Ski Resort is comparing a half dozen capital improvement projects. It has allocated $1 million for capital budgeting purposes. The following proposals and associated profitability indexes have been determined. The projects themselves are independent of one another.

PROJECT	AMOUNT	PROFITABILITY INDEX
1. Extend ski lift 3	$500,000	1.22
2. Build a new sports shop	150,000	.95
3. Extend ski lift 4	350,000	1.20
4. Build a new restaurant	450,000	1.18
5. Build addition to housing complex	200,000	1.19
6. Build an indoor skating rink	400,000	1.05

a. If strict capital rationing for only the current period is assumed, which of the investments should be undertaken? (*Tip:* If you didn't use up the entire capital budget, try some other combinations of projects, and determine the total net present value for each combination.)

b. Is this an optimal strategy?

9. The City of San Jose must replace a number of its concrete mixer trucks with new trucks. It has received two bids and has evaluated closely the performance characteristics of the various trucks. The Rockbuilt truck, which costs $74,000, is top-of-the-line equipment. The truck has a life of eight years, assuming that the engine is rebuilt in the fifth year. Maintenance costs of $2,000 a year are expected in the first four years, followed by total maintenance and rebuilding costs of $13,000 in the fifth year. During the last three years, maintenance costs are expected to be $4,000 a year. At the end of eight years the truck will have an estimated scrap value of $9,000.

A bid from Bulldog Trucks, Inc., is for $59,000 a truck. Maintenance costs for the truck will be higher. In the first year they are expected to be $3,000, and this amount is expected to increase by $1,500 a year through the eighth year. In the fourth year the engine will need to be rebuilt, and this will cost the company $15,000 in addition to maintenance costs in that year. At the end of eight years the Bulldog truck will have an estimated scrap value of $5,000.

a. If the City of San Jose's opportunity cost of funds is 8 percent, which bid should it accept? Ignore tax considerations, because the city pays no taxes.

b. If its opportunity cost were 15 percent, would your answer change?

SOLUTIONS TO SELF-CORRECTION PROBLEMS

1. a.

YEAR	CASH FLOW	PRESENT VALUE DISCOUNT FACTOR (15%)	PRESENT VALUE
0	$ (700,000)	1.000	$(700,000)
1	(1,000,000)	.870	(870,000)
2	250,000	.756	189,000
3	300,000	.658	197,400
4	350,000	.572	200,200
5–10	400,000	2.164*	865,600**
		Net present value =	**$(117,800)**

*PVIFA of 5.019 for 10 years minus PVIFA of 2.855 for 4 years.
**Total for years 5–10.

Because the net present value is negative, the project is *unacceptable*.

b. The internal rate of return is **13.21 percent.** If the trial-and-error method were used, we would have the following:

YEAR	CASH FLOW	14% DISCOUNT FACTOR	14% PRESENT VALUE	13% DISCOUNT FACTOR	13% PRESENT VALUE
0	$ (700,000)	1.000	$(700,000)	1.000	$(700,000)
1	(1,000,000)	.877	(877,000)	.885	(885,000)
2	250,000	.769	192,250	.783	195,750
3	300,000	.675	202,500	.693	207,900
4	350,000	.592	207,200	.613	214,550
5–10	400,000	2.302*	920,800**	2.452*	980,800**
	Net present value		$ (54,250)		$ 14,000

*PVIFA for 10 years minus PVIFA for 4 years.
**Total for years 5–10.

To approximate the actual rate, we **interpolate** between 13 and 14 percent as follows:

$$.01 \begin{bmatrix} X \begin{bmatrix} .13 & \$\,14{,}000 \\ IRR & 0 \\ .14 & \$(54{,}250) \end{bmatrix} \$14{,}000 \end{bmatrix} \$68{,}250$$

$$\frac{X}{.01} = \frac{\$14{,}000}{\$68{,}250} \qquad \text{Therefore,} \qquad X = \frac{(.01) \times (\$14{,}000)}{\$68{,}250} = .0021$$

and $IRR = .13 + X = .13 + .0021 = .1321$, or **13.21 percent.** Because the internal rate of return is less than the required rate of return, the project would not be acceptable.

c. The project would be *acceptable.*

d. Payback period = **6 years.** ($-\$700{,}000 - \$1{,}000{,}000 + \$250{,}000 + \$300{,}000 + \$350{,}000 + \$400{,}000 + \$400{,}000 = 0$)

2.

YEAR	CASH FLOW	PRESENT VALUE DISCOUNT FACTOR (14%)	PRESENT VALUE
0	$(404,424)	1.000	$(404,424)
1	86,890	.877	76,203
2	106,474	.769	81,879
3	91,612	.675	61,838
4	84,801	.592	50,202
5	84,801	.519	44,012
6	75,400	.456	34,382
7	66,000	.400	26,400
8	92,400	.351	32,432
		Net present value = $	2,924

Because the net present value is positive, the project is *acceptable.*

3.

PROJECT(S)	INVESTMENT REQUIRED	PRESENT VALUE OF FUTURE CASH FLOWS	NET PRESENT VALUE
1	$200,000	$290,000	$ 90,000
2	115,000	185,000	70,000
3	270,000	400,000	130,000
1, 2	315,000	475,000	160,000
1, 3	**440,000**	**690,000**	**250,000**
2, 3	385,000	620,000	235,000
1, 2, 3	680,000	910,000	230,000

Projects 1 and 3 should be chosen because they provide the highest net present value.

SELECTED REFERENCES

Aggarwal, Raj. *Capital Budgeting Under Uncertainty.* Englewood Cliffs, NJ: Prentice Hall, 1993.

Bacon, Peter W. "The Evaluation of Mutually Exclusive Investments." *Financial Management* 6 (Summer 1977), 55–58.

Barwise, Patrick, Paul R. Marsh, and Robin Wensley. "Must Finance and Strategy Clash?" *Harvard Business Review* 67 (September–October 1989), 85–90.

Bierman, Harold, Jr., and Seymour Smidt. *The Capital Budgeting Decision,* 8th ed. New York: Macmillan, 1993.

Gordon, Lawrence A., and Mary D. Myers. "Postauditing Capital Projects: Are You in Step with the Competition?" *Management Accounting* 72 (January 1991), 39–42.

Harris, Milton, and Arthur Raviv. "The Capital Budgeting Process: Incentives and Information." *Journal of Finance* 51 (September 1996), 1139–74.

Herbst, Anthony. "The Unique, Real Internal Rate of Return: Caveat Emptor!" *Journal of Financial and Quantitative Analysis* 13 (June 1978), 363–70.

Levy, Haim, and Marshall Sarnat. *Capital Investment and Financial Decisions*, 5th ed. Englewood Cliffs, NJ: Prentice Hall, 1994.

Logue, Dennis E., and T. Craig Tapley. "Performance Monitoring and the Timing of Cash Flows." *Financial Management* 14 (Autumn 1985), 34–39.

Lorie, James H., and Leonard J. Savage. "Three Problems in Rationing Capital." *Journal of Business* 28 (October 1955), 229–39.

McConnell, John J., and Chris J. Muscarella. "Corporate Capital Expenditure Decisions and the Market Value of the Firm." *Journal of Financial Economics* 14 (September 1985), 399–422.

Pinches, George E. "Myopia, Capital Budgeting and Decision Making." *Financial Management* 11 (Autumn 1982), 6–19.

Schwab, Bernhard, and Peter Lusztig. "A Comparative Analysis of the Net Present Value and the Benefit-Cost Ratios as Measures of the Economic Desirability of Investments." *Journal of Finance* 24 (June 1969), 507–16.

Seitz, Neil, and Mitch Ellison. *Capital Budgeting and Long-Term Financing Decisions*, 3rd ed. Forth Worth, TX: Dryden, 1998.

Shrieves, Ronald E., and John M. Wachowicz Jr. "Proper Risk Resolution in Replacement Chain Analysis." *Engineering Economist* 34 (Winter 1989), 91–114.

Smith, Kimberly J., "Postauditing Capital Investments." *Financial Practice and Education* 4 (Spring–Summer 1994), 129–37.

Smyth, David. "Keeping Control with Post Completion Audits." *Accountancy* 106 (August 1990), 163–64.

Van Horne, James C. "The Variation of Project Life as a Means for Adjusting for Risk." *The Engineering Economist* 21 (Spring 1976), 151–58.

Weingartner, H. Martin. "Capital Rationing: Authors in Search of a Plot." *Journal of Finance* 32 (December 1977), 1403–31.

Chapter 14

Risk and Managerial Options in Capital Budgeting

THE PROBLEM OF PROJECT RISK
 An Illustration • Expectation and Measurement of Dispersion:
  A Cash-Flow Example
TOTAL PROJECT RISK
 Probability Tree Approach • Simulation Approach • Use of
  Probability Distribution Information
CONTRIBUTION TO TOTAL FIRM RISK: FIRM-PORTFOLIO
  APPROACH
 Expectation and Measurement of Portfolio Risk • An Illustration
  • Correlation Between Projects • Combinations of Risky
  Investments
MANAGERIAL OPTIONS
 Valuation Implications • The Option to Expand (or Contract)
  • The Option to Abandon • The Option to Postpone • Some
  Final Observations
SUMMARY
QUESTIONS
SELF-CORRECTION PROBLEMS
PROBLEMS
SOLUTIONS TO SELF-CORRECTION PROBLEMS
SELECTED REFERENCES

> *"Risk? Risk is our business. That's what this starship is all about.
> That's why we're aboard her!"*
>
> —JAMES T. KIRK,
> CAPTAIN OF THE STARSHIP *ENTERPRISE*

In the preceding chapter, we assumed that the acceptance of any investment proposal would not alter the business-risk complexion of the firm as perceived by the suppliers of capital. This assumption allowed us to use a single required rate of return in determining which capital budgeting projects a firm should select. We know, however, that different investment projects often have different degrees of risk. The project that is expected to provide a high return may be so risky that it causes a significant increase in the perceived risk of the firm. In turn, this may cause a decrease in the firm's value, despite the project's considerable potential. In this chapter we consider various ways by which management can gauge the risk of a project or a group of projects. Our ultimate objective is to come to a better understanding of how risk affects value. However, to do so, we must first be able to measure project risk under a variety of circumstances.

Given information about the expected risk of an investment proposal or proposals, together with information about the expected return, management must evaluate this information and reach a decision. The decision to accept or reject an investment proposal will depend on the risk-adjusted return required by suppliers of capital. Because we consider required rates of return in the next chapter, we defer the actual evaluation of risky investments until that time.

In this chapter we develop the information necessary to evaluate risky investments. In addition to risk, investment projects sometimes embody options for management to make decisions at a later date. Once a project is accepted, management may have flexibility to make changes that will affect subsequent cash flows and/or the project's life. This flexibility is called a *managerial, or real, option.* This chapter begins with a general introduction to project risk and follows with the consideration of its specific measurement. Next, an investment project is examined with respect to its firm-portfolio risk—that is, the marginal risk of a project to the firm as a whole. Finally, the effect of managerial options on project desirability is studied.

THE PROBLEM OF PROJECT RISK

For now, we will define the "riskiness" of an investment project as the variability of its cash flows from those that are expected. The greater the variability, the riskier the project is said to be. For each project under consideration, we can make estimates of the future cash flows. Rather than estimate only the most likely cash-flow outcome for each year in the future as we did in Chapter 12, we estimate a number of possible outcomes. In this way we are able to consider the range of possible cash flows for a particular future period rather than just the most likely cash flow.

An Illustration

To illustrate the formulation of multiple cash-flow forecasts for a future period, suppose that we had two investment proposals under consideration. Suppose further that we were interested in making forecasts for the following alternative states of the economy: deep recession, mild recession, normal, minor boom, and major boom. After assessing the future under each of these possible states, we estimate the following net cash flows for the next year:

	ANNUAL CASH FLOWS: YEAR 1	
STATE OF THE ECONOMY	PROPOSAL A	PROPOSAL B
Deep recession	$3,000	$2,000
Mild recession	3,500	3,000
Normal	4,000	4,000
Minor boom	4,500	5,000
Major boom	5,000	6,000

We see that the dispersion of possible cash flows for proposal B is greater than that for proposal A. Therefore, we might say that it is riskier. To quantify our analysis of risk, however, we need additional information. More specifically, we need to know the likelihood of the occurrence of various states of the economy. Assume that our estimate of the probability of a deep recession occurring next year is 10 percent, of a mild recession 20 percent, of a normal economy 40 percent, of a minor boom 20 percent, and of a major economic boom 10 percent. Given this information, we are now able to formulate a probability distribution of possible cash flows for proposals A and B, as follows:

	PROPOSAL A		PROPOSAL B	
STATE OF THE ECONOMY	PROBABILITY	CASH FLOW	PROBABILITY	CASH FLOW
Deep recession	.10	$3,000	.10	$2,000
Mild recession	.20	3,500	.20	3,000
Normal	.40	4,000	.40	4,000
Minor boom	.20	4,500	.20	5,000
Major boom	.10	5,000	.10	6,000
	1.00		1.00	

We can graph the probability distributions, and the results are shown in Figure 14-1. As we see, the dispersion of cash flows is greater for proposal B than it is for proposal A, despite the fact that the most likely outcome is the same for both investment proposals—namely, $4,000. According to the discussion in Chapter 13 (and assuming equal initial outlays and one-year project lives), the firm would rank the proposals equally. The critical question is whether dispersion of cash flows should be considered. If risk is associated with the probability distribution of possible cash flows, such that the greater the dispersion, the greater the risk, proposal B would be the riskier investment. If management, stockholders, and creditors are averse to risk, proposal A would then be preferred to proposal B.

Expectation and Measurement of Dispersion: A Cash-Flow Example

The probability distributions shown in Figure 14-1 can be summarized in terms of two parameters of the distribution: (1) the *expected value* and (2) the *standard deviation*. You may remember that we discussed both of these parameters—as related to security returns—in Chapter 5. This time our focus is on cash flows as opposed to percentage returns. We will present the mathematical calculation of expected value and standard deviation, once again, as a review. Then we will illustrate these calculations with the previous cash-flow example.

FIGURE 14-1
Comparison of Two Proposals Using Probability Distributions of Possible Cash Flows

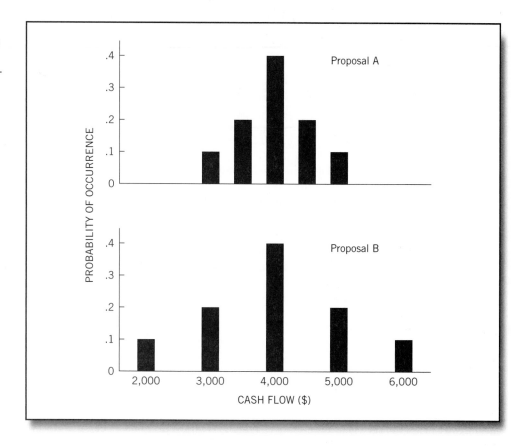

The **expected value** of a cash-flow probability distribution for time period t, $\overline{CF}_t$, is defined as

$$\overline{CF}_t = \sum_{x=1}^{n}(CF_{xt})(P_{xt})$$

(14-1)

where CF_{xt} is the cash flow for the xth possibility at time period t, P_{xt} is the probability of that cash flow occurring, and n is the total number of cash-flow possibilities occurring at time period t. Thus, the expected value of cash flow is simply a weighted average of the possible cash flows, with the weights being the probabilities of occurrence.

The conventional measure of dispersion is the **standard deviation,** which completes our two-parameter description of a cash-flow distribution. The tighter the distribution, the lower this measure will be; the wider the distribution, the greater it will be. The cash-flow standard deviation at time period t, σ_t, can be expressed mathematically as

$$\sigma_t = \sqrt{\sum_{x=1}^{n}(CF_{xt} - \overline{CF}_t)^2(P_{xt})}$$

(14-2)

where $\sqrt{}$ represents the square-root sign. The square of the standard deviation, σ_t^2, is known as the *variance* of the distribution. Though all of this looks rather formidable, in fact the standard deviation can be computed easily with the aid of a calculator.

The standard deviation is simply a measure of the tightness of a probability distribution. For a normal, bell-shaped distribution, approximately 68 percent of the

Part V Investment in Capital Assets

total area of the distribution falls within one standard deviation on either side of the expected value. This means that there is only a 32 percent chance that the actual outcome will be more than one standard deviation from the mean. The probability that the actual outcome will fall within two standard deviations of the expected value of the distribution is approximately 95 percent, and the probability that it will fall within three standard deviations is over 99 percent. Table V showing the area of a normal distribution that is so many standard deviations to the left or right of the expected value is given in the Appendix at the end of the book. As we shall review later in the chapter, the standard deviation can be used to assess the likelihood of an event's occurring.

An Illustration. To illustrate the derivation of the expected value and standard deviation of a probability distribution of possible cash flows, consider again our previous two-proposal example.

Proposal A

POSSIBLE CASH FLOW, CF_{X1}	PROBABILITY OF OCCURRENCE, P_{X1}	$(CF_{X1})(P_{X1})$	$(CF_{X1} - \overline{CF}_1)^2(P_X)$
$3,000	.10	$ 300	$(\$3,000 - \$4,000)^2(.10)$
3,500	.20	700	$(3,500 - 4,000)^2(.20)$
4,000	.40	1,600	$(4,000 - 4,000)^2(.40)$
4,500	.20	900	$(4,500 - 4,000)^2(.20)$
5,000	.10	500	$(5,000 - 4,000)^2(.10)$
	$\Sigma = 1.00$	$\Sigma = \mathbf{\$4,000} = \overline{CF}_1$	$\Sigma = \$300,000 = \sigma_1^2$
			$(\$300,000)^{.5} = \mathbf{\$548} = \sigma_1$

Proposal B

POSSIBLE CASH FLOW, CF_{X1}	PROBABILITY OF OCCURRENCE, P_{X1}	$(CF_{X1})(P_{X1})$	$(CF_{X1} - \overline{CF}_1)^2(P_X)$
$2,000	.10	$ 200	$(\$2,000 - \$4,000)^2(.10)$
3,000	.20	600	$(3,000 - 4,000)^2(.20)$
4,000	.40	1,600	$(4,000 - 4,000)^2(.40)$
5,000	.20	1,000	$(5,000 - 4,000)^2(.20)$
6,000	.10	600	$(6,000 - 4,000)^2(.10)$
	$\Sigma = 1.00$	$\Sigma = \mathbf{\$4,000} = \overline{CF}_1$	$\Sigma = \$1,200,000 = \sigma_1^2$
			$(\$1,200,000)^{.5} = \mathbf{\$1,095} = \sigma_1$

The expected value of the cash-flow distribution for proposal A is $4,000, the same as for proposal B. However, the standard deviation for proposal A is $548, whereas the standard deviation for proposal B is $1,095. Thus, proposal B has a higher standard deviation, indicating a greater dispersion of possible outcomes—so we would say that it has greater risk.

Coefficient of Variation. A measure of the relative dispersion of a distribution is the *coefficient of variation (CV)*. Mathematically it is defined as the ratio of the standard deviation of a distribution to the expected value of the distribution. Thus, it is simply a measure of risk per unit of expected value. For proposal A, the coefficient of variation is

$$CV_A = \$548/\$4,000 = \mathbf{.14}$$

and that for proposal B is

$$CV_B = \$1,095/\$4,000 = \mathbf{.27}$$

Because the coefficient of variation for proposal B exceeds that for proposal A, it has a greater degree of relative risk. Frequent reference to the expected value, the standard deviation, and the coefficient of variation will be made in the remainder of this chapter.[1]

TOTAL PROJECT RISK

If investors and creditors are risk averse—and all available evidence suggests that they are—it is necessary for management to incorporate the risk of an investment proposal into its analysis of the proposal's worth. Otherwise, capital budgeting decisions are unlikely to be in accord with the objective of maximizing share price. Having established the need for taking risk into account, we proceed to measure it for individual investment proposals. But remember that the riskiness of a stream of cash flows for a project can, and often does, change with the length of time in the future that the flows occur. In other words, the probability distributions are not necessarily the same from one period to the next.

This notion is illustrated in Figure 14-2 for a hypothetical investment project. The distributions are like those shown in Figure 14-1 except that they are *continuous* instead of *discrete*. This means that the cash-flow outcome for each period can take on any value within a given interval as opposed to taking on only certain values within

---

[1]We assume that risk can be judged solely in relation to the expected value and standard deviation of a probability distribution. Implied is that the shape of the distribution is unimportant. This holds when the distribution is relatively symmetric, or "bell-shaped." However, if it is significantly skewed to the left or right, management may wish to take account of this fact as well. Although it is possible to incorporate a skewness measure into our analysis of risk, it is difficult to do so mathematically. For simplicity, we shall deal with only the expected value and standard deviation of a normal probability distribution.

FIGURE 14-2
Probability Distributions of Possible Cash Flows Showing Changing Expected Value and Risk over Time

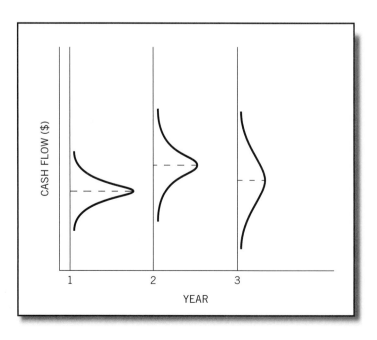

Part V Investment in Capital Assets

an interval. Thus, a continuous line is drawn for each graph in Figure 14-2 instead of a series of bars like those appearing in Figure 14-1. As before, the tighter and more peaked the distribution, the less risk. The expected value of each of the distributions is depicted by the horizontal dashed line. We see that both the expected value of cash flow and the dispersion of the probability distribution change over time. We must come to grips with this factor so that we can quantify the risk of a prospective investment proposal.

Probability Tree Approach

Probability tree A graphic or tabular approach for organizing the possible cash-flow streams generated by an investment. The presentation resembles the branches of a tree. Each complete branch represents one possible cash-flow sequence.

One way of approaching the problem is with a **probability tree.** A probability tree is a graphic or tabular approach for organizing the possible cash-flow streams generated by an investment. Here we specify the likely future cash flows of a project as they relate to the outcomes in previous periods. In this way we can build into our analysis how the cash flows are correlated over time. For example, if a project happens to have a good (high) cash flow in the first period, it may well have good cash flows in subsequent periods. Although there frequently is a link between what happens in one period and what happens in the next, this is not always the case. If cash flows are believed to be independent from period to period, we simply specify a probability distribution of cash-flow outcomes for each period. If there is a link, we should take this dependence into account.

With a probability tree we attempt to unfold future events as they might occur. Figure 14-3 shows a probability tree for a two-period project. Each complete branch represents one possible cash-flow sequence. For each of the nine branches in the figure, cash flows as well as probabilities are enumerated. Here we see that if the outcome in period 1 is very good (placing you on the $500 limb), it results in a different set of possible outcomes in period 2 ($800, $500, or $200) than if you had done very poorly in period 1 (placing you on the −$100 limb). Therefore, at time 0 the probability tree represents our best estimate of what is likely to occur in the future, contingent on what occurs before (in previous periods).

FIGURE 14-3
Graphic Illustration of a Probability Tree Showing How Flows in the Second Year Are Moderately Correlated with Those in the First Year; e.g., That It Is More Likely (But Not Guaranteed) You Will Have a Good Cash Flow in Year 2 if Year 1's Cash Flow Is Good.

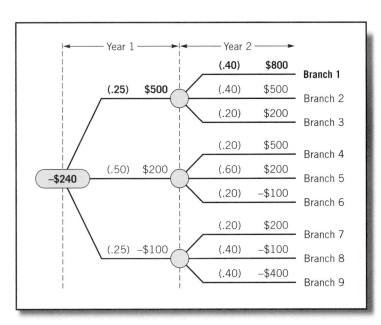

For the first period, the cash-flow outcome does not depend on what happened before. Therefore, the probability associated with the initial portion of each complete branch is said to be an *initial probability*. For the second period, however, cash-flow outcomes depend on what happened before. Therefore, the probabilities involved in succeeding periods are said to be *conditional probabilities*. Finally, the *joint probability* is the probability that a particular sequence of cash flows might occur. To illustrate, let us refer to our two-period example.

Suppose that we are considering the investment project described in Figure 14-3, which requires an initial investment outflow of $240. Given a resulting cash flow of $500 in year 1, the conditional probability is 40 percent that an $800 inflow will occur in year 2, 40 percent that the cash flow will be $500, and 20 percent that it will be $200. The joint probability that a $500 inflow in year 1 will be followed by an $800 cash flow in period 2 (that is, the probability of completing the path indicated by **boldfaced** branch 1) is simply the product of the initial probability and the conditional probability, or .25 × .40 = **.10**. (See Table 14-1.)

Similarly, the joint probability that a cash flow of $500 in year 1 will be followed by a cash flow of $500 in year 2 is .25 × .40 = **.10**, and the probability that a $500 cash flow in year 1 will be followed by a $200 cash flow in year 2 is .25 × .20 = **.05**. If the cash flow in year 1 turns out to be $200, there is a .20 probability that year 2's cash flow will be $500, .60 that it will be $200, and .20 that it will be −$100. In the same manner as before, we can calculate the joint probabilities for the three complete branches represented by these figures. They are found to be .10, .30, and .10, respectively. Likewise, the joint probabilities for the last set of three complete branches, where a −$100 net cash flow occurs in year 1, can be determined.

Discounting to Present Value at the Risk-Free Rate. In the last chapter we calculated a *single* net present value for each project by discounting cash flows at a

TABLE 14-1
Tabular illustration of a probability tree*

YEAR 1		YEAR 2		
INITIAL PROBABILITY $P(1)$	NET CASH FLOW	CONDITIONAL PROBABILITY $P(2\mid1)$	NET CASH FLOW	JOINT PROBABILITY $P(1,2)$
		.40	$800	.10
.25	$500	.40	500	.10
		.20	200	.05
		1.00		
		.20	500	.10
.50	200	.60	200	.30
		.20	−100	.10
		1.00		
		.20	200	.05
.25	−100	.40	−100	.10
		.40	−400	.10
1.00		1.00		1.00

*Initial investment at time 0 = $240.

required rate of return that "adjusted" future cash flows for both the time value of money and risk. Using a probability tree approach, however, we attempt to gather information on an entire probability distribution of net present values. We do not want to "adjust" for risk at this point, but rather to study it. Therefore, we discount the various cash flows to their present value *at the risk-free rate*. This rate is used because in this approach we attempt to isolate the time value of money by discounting and then analyze risk separately. To include a premium for risk in the discount rate would result in double counting risk with regard to this method. We would be compensating for risk in the discounting process and then again in our analysis of the dispersion of the probability distribution of possible net present values. For this reason, we use the risk-free rate for discounting purposes.

For our example problem, the expected value of the probability distribution of possible net present values is

$$\overline{NPV} = \sum_{i=1}^{z}(NPV_i)(P_i) \tag{14-3}$$

where NPV_i is the net present value calculated at the risk-free rate for cash-flow series i (complete cash-flow branch i), P_i is the joint probability of that cash-flow series occurring, and z is the total number of complete cash-flow series (or branches). For our example, there are nine possible series of net cash flows, so $z = 9$. The first series (branch) is represented by a net cash flow of −$240 at time 0, $500 in year 1, and $800 in year 2. The joint probability of that particular cash-flow sequence is .10. If the risk-free rate used as the discount rate is 8 percent, the net present value of this particular series is

$$NPV_1 = \frac{\$500}{(1 + .08)^1} + \frac{\$800}{(1 + .08)^2} - \$240 = \textbf{\$909}$$

The second cash-flow series is represented by a net cash flow of −$240 at time 0, $500 in year 1, and $500 in year 2. The net present value of this series is

$$NPV_2 = \frac{\$500}{(1 + .08)^1} + \frac{\$500}{(1 + .08)^2} - \$240 = \textbf{\$652}$$

In the same manner, the net present values for the seven other cash-flow series can be determined. When these values are multiplied by their respective joint probabilities of occurrence (the last column in Table 14-1) and summed, we obtain the expected value of net present value of the probability distribution of possible net present values (rounded to the nearest dollar). The calculations are shown in Table 14-2, and we see that the expected value of net present value is $116.

It is important to note that a positive expected value of net present value ($\overline{NPV}$) cannot be used as a clear-cut accept signal for the project. This is because we have not yet considered risk. By the same token, the expected value of net present value does *not* represent the increase in value of the firm if the project were to be accepted. The correct NPV to use for such a purpose would require that expected cash flows for each period be discounted at a risk-adjusted required rate of return.

Calculating the Standard Deviation. The standard deviation of the probability distribution of possible net present values, σ_{NPV}, can be determined by

$$\sigma_{NPV} = \sqrt{\sum_{i=1}^{z}(NPV_i - \overline{NPV})^2(P_i)} \tag{14-4}$$

TABLE 14-2
Calculation of expected value of net present value for example problem

(1) CASH FLOW SERIES	(2) NET PRESENT VALUE	(3) JOINT PROBABILITY OF OCCURRENCE	(4) (2) × (3)
1	$ 909	.10	$ 91
2	652	.10	65
3	394	.05	20
4	374	.10	37
5	117	.30	35
6	−141	.10	−14
7	−161	.05	− 8
8	−418	.10	−42
9	−676	.10	−68
		Weighted average	**$ 116** $= \overline{NPV}$

where our variables remain as previously defined. The standard deviation for our example problem is

$$\sigma_{NPV} = [\ (\ \$909 - \$116)^2(.10) \ + (-\$652 - \$116)^2(.10)$$
$$+ (\ 394 - \ 116)^2(.05) \ + (\ 374 - \ 116)^2(.10)$$
$$+ (\ 117 - \ 116)^2(.30) \ + (\ -141 - \ 116)^2(.10)$$
$$+ (-161 - \ 116)^2(.05) \ + (\ -418 - \ 116)^2(.10)$$
$$+ (-676 - \ 116)^2(.10)]^{.5} = [\$197.277]^{.5} = \textbf{\$444}$$

Rounding to the nearest dollar, the project has an expected value of net present value of $116 and a standard deviation of $444. Although the mathematical calculation of the standard deviation is feasible for simple cases, it is not for complex situations. Here, one should resort to simulation to approximate the standard deviation.

Simulation Approach

In considering risky investments, we can also use simulation to approximate the expected value of net present value, the expected value of internal rate of return, or the expected value of profitability index and the dispersion about the expected value. By *simulation*, we mean testing the possible results of an investment proposal before it is accepted. The testing itself is based on a model coupled with probabilistic information. Making use of a simulation model first proposed by David Hertz, we might consider, for example, the following factors in deriving a project's cash-flow stream:[2]

Market analysis

1. Market size
2. Selling price
3. Market growth rate
4. Share of market (which controls physical sales volume)

---

[2]David B. Hertz, "Risk Analysis in Capital Investment." *Harvard Business Review* 42 (January–February 1964), 95–106.

Investment cost analysis

5. Investment required
6. Useful life of facilities
7. Residual value of investment

Operating and fixed costs

8. Operating costs
9. Fixed costs

Probability distributions are assigned to each of these factors based on management's assessment of the probable outcomes. Thus, the possible outcomes are charted for each factor according to their probability of occurrence. Once the probability distributions are determined, the next step is to determine the internal rate of return (or net present value calculated at the risk-free rate) that will result from a random combination of the nine factors just listed.

To illustrate the simulation process, assume that the market-size factor has the following probability distribution:

Market size (in thousands of units)	450	500	550	600	650	700	750
Probability of occurrence	.05	.10	.20	.30	.20	.10	.05

Now suppose that we have a roulette wheel with 100 numbered slots, on which numbers 1 through 5 represent a market size of 450,000 units, 6 through 15 represent a market size of 500,000 units, 16 through 35 represent a market size of 550,000 units, and so on through 100. As in roulette, we spin the wheel, and the ball falls in one of the 100 numbered slots. Assume that the ball lands on number 26. For this trial, then, we simulate a market size of 550,000 units. Fortunately, we do not need a roulette wheel to undertake a simulation. The same type of operation can be carried out on a computer in a much more efficient manner.

Simulation trials are undertaken for each of the other eight factors. Jointly, the first four factors (market analysis) give us the annual sales per year. Factors 8 and 9 give us the operating and fixed costs per year. Together, these six factors enable us to calculate the annual incremental revenues. When trial values for these six factors are combined with trial values for the required investment, the useful life, and the residual value of the project, we have sufficient information to calculate the internal rate of return (or net present value) for that trial run. Thus, the computer simulates trial values for each of the nine factors and then calculates the internal rate of return based on the values simulated. The process is repeated many times. Each time we obtain a combination of values for the nine factors and the internal rate of return for that combination. When the process is repeated often enough, the internal rates of return can be plotted in a frequency distribution like that shown in Figure 14-4. From this frequency distribution we are able to identify the expected value of internal rate of return and the dispersion about this expected return.

Use of Probability Distribution Information

The expected value and standard deviation of the probability distribution of possible net present values (or alternatively, internal rates of return), whether derived by a probability tree, simulation, or some other means, give us a considerable amount of information by which to evaluate the risk of the investment proposal. For example, if

FIGURE 14-4
Probability Distribution for Internal Rate of Return

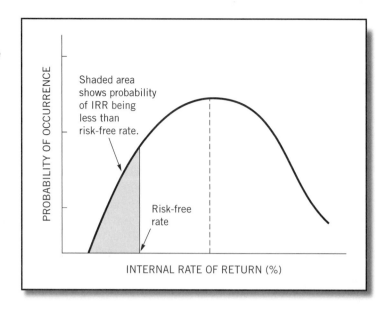

the probability distribution of net present values is approximately normal, we are able to calculate the probability of the proposal providing a net present value of less than (greater than) a specified amount. The probability is found by determining the area under the probability distribution curve to the left (to the right) of a particular point of interest.

Building on our previous probability tree results (but assuming a normal distribution), suppose that we wish to determine the probability that the net present value will be zero or less. To determine this probability, we first determine how many standard deviations zero is from the expected value of net present value for the project, $116. To do this we first take the difference between zero and $116, and standardize this difference by dividing it by the standard deviation of possible net present values. The general formula is

$$Z = \frac{NPV^* - \overline{NPV}}{\sigma_{NPV}}$$
(14-5)

where Z (the Z-score) tells us how many standard deviations NPV^*, the outcome in which we are interested, is from the expected value; $\overline{NPV}$ is the expected value of net present value; and σ_{NPV} is the standard deviation of the probability distribution. In our case

$$Z = \frac{0 - \$116}{\$444} = -.26$$

This figure tells us that a net present value of zero lies .26 standard deviations *to the left* of the expected value of the probability distribution of possible net present values. (The *negative* Z-score value reminds us that we are looking *to the left* of the mean.)

To determine the probability that the net present value of the project will be zero or less, we consult a normal probability distribution table found in Table V in the Appendix at the end of this book. We find that for a normal distribution there is a .4013 probability that an observation will be more than .25 standard deviations left of the expected value of that distribution. There is a .3821 probability that it will be more than .30 standard deviations from the expected value. Interpolating, we find that there is "approximately" a 40 percent probability that the net present value of the proposal will be zero or less. Thus, we also know that there is a 60 percent probability that the net present value of the project will be greater than zero. By expressing differences from the expected value in terms of standard deviations, we are able to determine the probability that the net present value for an investment will be greater or less than a particular amount.[3]

Problems with Interpretation.   Although the foregoing procedures allow us to calculate the probability that net present value might be less than some specific value (like zero), the results may be difficult to interpret. This is because net present value, you should remember, is now being calculated at the risk-free rate and not the project's required rate of return. Therefore, what does it really mean when we say, for example, that the probability of net present value being negative is 40 percent?

A key to answering this question lies in noting that the probability that a project's internal rate of return will be less than the risk-free rate is equal to the probability that the project's net present value will be less than zero, where the risk-free rate is used in discounting.[4] If we view an *opportunity loss* as any return less than the risk-free return, then the 40 percent likelihood of an NPV less than zero can be interpreted as a 40 percent chance at incurring an opportunity loss—earning a rate of return less than the risk-free rate—if the project is accepted. In short, there is a 40 percent chance that the firm would be better off by simply investing in Treasury securities than investing in this project. However, even with this added perspective on risk, namely, the likelihood of an opportunity loss, we still do not have a clear-cut accept-reject signal. Whether a 40 percent chance of an opportunity loss should rule out the project's acceptance remains a subjective management decision.

Probability Distribution Comparisons.   Knowledge of NPV or IRR probability distributions may prove especially useful in the assessment of risk for competing projects. Suppose that the firm is considering another investment proposal, called project Y. The probability distribution for this proposal is shown in Figure 14-5, as well as our probability tree proposal, which we call project X. We see that the expected value of net present value for project Y is $200, which is higher than the $116 figure for project X. Moreover, there is less dispersion with project Y than there is with project X. Therefore, we would say that project Y dominates project X on the basis of both total project risk and return. Whether project Y should be accepted depends on the risk tolerance of management. We address ourselves to that issue in the next chapter. In this chapter we focus on learning how to measure risk.

CONTRIBUTION TO TOTAL FIRM RISK: FIRM-PORTFOLIO APPROACH

In the last section we measured risk for a single, stand-alone investment proposal. When multiple investment projects are involved, we may want to study their combined risk. In that case, we need to use a measurement procedure that differs from

[3]In these examples we have assumed normal distributions. Although this property is very desirable for purposes of calculation, it is not necessary for use of the above approach. Even when the distribution is not normal, we are usually able to make relatively strong probability statements by using *Chebyshev's inequality*, which places an upper limit on the proportion of values falling in the tails of any distribution.
[4]Frederick S. Hillier, "The Derivation of Probabilistic Information for the Evaluation of Risky Investments." *Management Science* 9 (April 1963), 450.

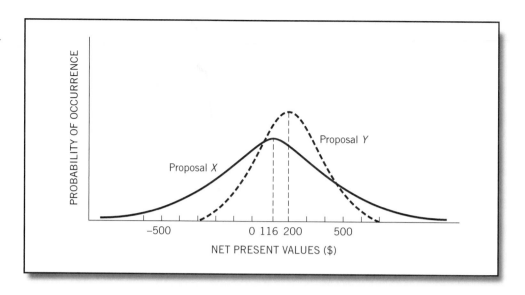

that for a single project. The approach we take corresponds to the portfolio approach in security analysis discussed in Chapter 5. Now, however, we apply that approach to capital investment projects. The limited circumstances under which the approach is feasible are covered in Chapter 15, when we examine the acceptance criteria for risky investments. Our purpose here is only to show how to measure risk for combinations of risky investments, assuming that such a measure is desired.

If a firm adds a project whose future cash flows are likely to be highly correlated with those of existing assets, the total risk of the firm will increase more than if it adds a project that has a low degree of correlation with existing assets. Given this reality, a firm might wish to seek out projects that could be combined to reduce relative firm risk.

Figure 14-6 shows the expected cash-flow patterns for two projects over time. Proposal A is cyclical, whereas proposal B is mildly countercyclical. By combining the two projects, we see that total cash-flow dispersion is reduced. The combining of projects in a way that will reduce risk is known as *diversification*, and the principle is the same as for diversification of securities. We attempt to reduce deviations in return from the expected value of return.

Expectation and Measurement of Portfolio Risk

The expected value of the net present value for a combination (portfolio) of investment projects, $\overline{NPV_p}$, is simply the sum of the separate expected values of net present value, where discounting takes place at the risk-free rate. The standard deviation of the probability distribution of the portfolio's net present values (σ_p), however, is *not* merely the summation of the standard deviations of the individual projects making up the portfolio. Instead, it is

$$\sigma_p = \sqrt{\sum_{j=1}^{m} \sum_{k=1}^{m} \sigma_{j,k}} \tag{14-6}$$

where m is the total number of projects in the portfolio, and $\sigma_{j,k}$ is the covariance between possible net present values for projects j and k. (This rather formidable expression will be illustrated shortly.)

FIGURE 14-6

Effect of Diversifica-
tion on Cash Flows

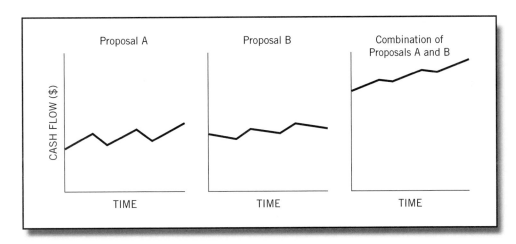

The covariance term in Eq. (14-6) is

$$\sigma_{j,k} = r_{j,k}\sigma_j\sigma_k \tag{14-7}$$

where $r_{j,k}$ is the expected correlation coefficient between possible net present values for projects j and k, σ_j is the standard deviation for project j, and σ_k is the standard deviation for project k. The standard deviations of the probability distributions of possible net present values for projects j and k are determined by the methods taken up in the previous section. When $j = k$ in Eq. (14-7), the correlation coefficient is 1, and $\sigma_j\sigma_k$ becomes σ_j^2 (that is, the covariance of project j's net present value with itself is its variance).

An Illustration

To illustrate these concepts, suppose that a firm has a single existing investment project, 1, and that it is considering investing in an additional project, 2. Assume further that the projects have the following expected values of net present value, standard deviations, and correlation coefficient:

	EXPECTED VALUE OF NET PRESENT VALUE	STANDARD DEVIATION	CORRELATION COEFFICIENT
Project 1	$12,000	$14,000	between 1 and 2 .40
Project 2	8,000	6,000	

The expected value of the net present value of the combination of projects is the sum of the two separate expected values of net present value.

$$\overline{NPV}_p = \$12,000 + \$8,000 = \mathbf{\$20,000}$$

The standard deviation for the combination, using Eqs. (14-6) and (14-7), is

$$
\begin{aligned}
\sigma_p &= \sqrt{\sum_{j=1}^{2}\sum_{k=1}^{2} r_{j,k}\sigma_j\sigma_k} \\
&= \sqrt{r_{1,1}\sigma_1^2 + 2(r_{1,2}\sigma_1\sigma_2) + r_{2,2}\sigma_2^2} \\
&= \sqrt{(1)(\$14,000)^2 + (2)(.40)(\$14,000)(\$6,000) + (1)(\$6,000)^2} \\
&= \mathbf{\$17,297}
\end{aligned}
$$

Thus, the expected value of net present value of the firm increases from $12,000 to $20,000, and the standard deviation of possible net present values increases from $14,000 to $17,297 with the acceptance of project 2. The firm's coefficient of variation—standard deviation over expected value of net present value—is $14,000/$12,000 = **1.17** without project 2 and $17,297/$20,000 = **.86** with the project. If we employ the coefficient of variation as a measure of relative firm risk, we conclude that acceptance of project 2 would lower the risk of the firm.

By accepting projects with relatively low degrees of correlation with existing projects, a firm diversifies and, in so doing, may be able to lower its overall risk. Note, the lower the degree of positive correlation between possible net present values for projects, the lower the standard deviation of possible net present values, all other things being equal. Whether the coefficient of variation declines when an investment project is added also depends on the expected value of net present value for the project.

Correlation Between Projects

Estimating the correlation between possible net present values for pairs of projects is called for in Eq. (14-7). These correlations prove to be the key ingredients in analyzing risk in a firm-portfolio context. When prospective projects are similar to projects with which the company has had experience, it may be feasible to compute the correlation coefficients using historical data. For other investments, estimates of the correlation coefficients must be based solely on an assessment of the future.

Management might have reason to expect only slight correlation between investment projects involving research and development for an electronic tester and a new food product. On the other hand, it might expect high positive correlation between investments in a milling machine and a turret lathe if both machines were used in the production of industrial lift trucks. The profit from a machine to be used in a production line will be highly, if not perfectly, correlated with the profit for the production line itself.

The correlation between expected net present values of various investments may be positive, negative, or 0, depending on the nature of the association. A correlation of 1 indicates that the net present values of two investments vary directly in the same proportional manner. A correlation coefficient of −1 indicates that they vary inversely in exactly the same proportional manner. And, a correlation of 0 indicates that they are independent or unrelated. For most pairs of investments, the correlation coefficient lies between 0 and 1. The reason for the lack of negatively correlated investment projects is that most investments are correlated positively with the economy and, thus, with each other.

Estimates of the correlation coefficients must be as objective as possible if the total standard deviation obtained in Eq. (14-6) is to be realistic. It is not unreasonable to expect management to make fairly accurate estimates of these coefficients. When actual correlation differs from expected correlation, the situation can be a learning process, and estimates on other projects can be revised.

Combinations of Risky Investments

We now have a procedure for determining the total expected value and the standard deviation of a probability distribution of possible net present values for a combination of investments. For our purposes, we define a *combination* as including all of the firm's existing investment projects plus one or more projects under consideration. We assume, then, that the firm has existing investment projects and that these projects are expected to generate future cash flows. Thus, existing projects constitute a subset that is included in all potential future combinations. We denote the portfolio of existing projects by the letter E.

Assume further that a firm is considering four new investment projects that are independent of one another. If these proposals are labeled 1, 2, 3, and 4, we have the following possible combinations of risky investments:

E	E + 1	E + 1 + 2	E + 1 + 2 + 3	E + 1 + 2 + 3 + 4
	E + 2	E + 1 + 3	E + 1 + 2 + 4	
	E + 3	E + 1 + 4	E + 1 + 3 + 4	
	E + 4	E + 2 + 3	E + 2 + 3 + 4	
		E + 2 + 4		
		E + 3 + 4		

Thus, 16 project combinations are possible. One of these possibilities consists of the rejection of all of the new projects under consideration, so that the firm is left with only its existing projects—combination E. The expected value of net present value, standard deviation, and coefficient of variation for each of these combinations can be computed in the manner described previously. The results can then be graphed.

Figure 14-7 is a scatter diagram of the 16 possible combinations. Here the expected value of net present value is measured along the vertical axis, while risk (standard deviation or, alternatively, coefficient of variation) is measured on the horizontal axis. Each dot represents a combination of projects. Collectively, these dots constitute the total set of feasible combinations of investment opportunities available to the firm.

We see that certain dots dominate others in the sense that they represent either (1) a higher expected value of net present value and the same level of risk, (2) a lower level of risk and the same expected value of net present value, or (3) both a higher

FIGURE 14-7
Scatter Diagram Showing the Set of Feasible Combinations (Portfolios) of Projects

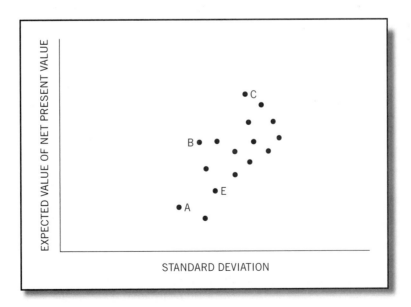

expected value of net present value and a lower level of risk. The dominating combinations have been specifically identified in Figure 14-7 as dots A, B, and C. (The dot E represents a portfolio consisting of all existing projects.)

Although the selection process itself is deferred until Chapter 15, we observe here that the combination ultimately chosen determines the new investment project(s) that will be accepted. If combination B were selected and it consisted of E plus projects 1 and 4, investment projects 1 and 4 would be accepted. Those investment proposals not in the combination finally selected would be rejected. In our example, projects 2 and 3 would be rejected. If the combination finally selected consisted of only existing investment projects (E), all new investment proposals under consideration would be rejected. The selection of any other combination implies acceptance of one or more of the investment proposals under consideration.

The incremental expected value of net present value and level of risk can be determined by measuring the horizontal and vertical distances from dot E to the dot representing the combination finally selected. These distances can be thought of as the incremental contribution of expected value of net present value and level of risk to the firm as a whole. In Chapter 15 we explore how the actual selection can be made and under what circumstances this approach is appropriate. Our purpose here has been to measure risk for combinations of risky investments in order to provide management with such information.

MANAGERIAL OPTIONS

Up to now, we have assumed that cash flows in a capital budgeting project occurred out to some horizon and then were discounted to obtain their present value. However, investment projects are not necessarily set in stone once they are accepted. Managers can, and often do, make changes that affect subsequent cash flows and/or the life of the project. Slavish devotion to traditional discounted cash flow (DCF) methods often ignores future managerial flexibility—that is, the flexibility to alter old decisions when conditions change.

Valuation Implications

Managerial (real) option
Management flexibility to make future decisions that affect a project's expected cash flows, life, or future acceptance.

The presence of **managerial,** or **real, options** enhances the worth of an investment project. The worth of a project can be viewed as its net present value, calculated in the traditional way, together with the value of any option(s).

$$\text{Project worth} = \text{NPV} + \text{Option(s) value} \tag{14-8}$$

The greater the number of options and the uncertainty surrounding their use, the greater the second term in Eq. (14-8), and the greater the project's worth. In Chapter 22 and its Appendix we consider option valuation more formally. For now, it is sufficient to say that the greater the uncertainty, the greater the chance that an option will be exercised, and hence, the greater the option's value.

The types of managerial options available include

1. *Option to expand (or contract)*—An important option is one that allows the firm to expand production if conditions become favorable and to contract production if conditions become unfavorable.
2. *Option to abandon*—If a project has abandonment value, this effectively represents a *put option* to the project's owner.

3. *Option to postpone*—For some projects there is the option to wait and thereby to obtain new information.

Sometimes these options are treated informally as qualitative factors when judging the worth of a project. The treatment given to these options may consist of no more than the recognition that "if such and such occurs, we will have the opportunity to do this and that."

Managerial options are more difficult to value than are financial options; you will find that the formulas for financial options taken up in the Appendix to Chapter 22 often do not work when applied to managerial options. Rather, we must resort to less precise approaches such as *decision trees* (i.e., diagrams of decision problems) and simulations.

The Option to Expand (or Contract)

In a project such as establishing a manufacturing plant, management often has the option to make a follow-up investment. For example, Gummy Glue Company is evaluating a new, revolutionary glue. The company can build a plant that is capable of producing 25,000 gallons of glue a month. That level of production is not economical, however, either from a manufacturing or from a marketing standpoint. As a result, the project's net present value is expected to be a negative $3 million. According to traditional DCF analysis, the project should be rejected.

However, the new glue could prove to be a winner. If sales were to increase dramatically, Gummy Glue Company could expand the new plant, say, in two years. With the expansion, output would triple, and the plant would be operating at a highly efficient scale. However, the opportunity to accommodate this higher level of demand will not be available unless a first-stage investment is made now. If Gummy Glue does not make the initial investment, the company will not have what business strategists refer to as the *first-mover* (i.e., first into a market) advantage.

Let's assume there is a fifty-fifty chance that the market will be much larger in two years. If it is, the net present value of the second-stage investment (expansion) *at the end of year 2* will be $15 million. When this value is discounted to the present at the required rate of return, the net present value at time 0 is $11 million. If the market falters over the next two years, the company will not invest further, and the incremental net present value at the end of year 2, by definition, is zero. The situation is depicted in a decision tree in Figure 14-8.

The mean of the distribution of possible net present values associated with the option is (.5)($11 million) + (.5)($0) = **$5.5 million.** Using Eq. (14-8), we determine the project's worth as follows:

$$\text{Project worth} = -\$3.0 \text{ million} + \$5.5 \text{ million}$$

$$= \$2.5 \text{ million}$$

Although our initial view of the project revealed a negative net present value, we find the option to expand more than offsets the negative NPV. Because the project embraces a valuable option, it should be accepted. For sequential decisions of this sort, a decision tree approach allows us to analyze subsequent chance events.

Abandonment value The value of a project if the project's assets were sold externally; or alternatively, its opportunity value if the assets were employed elsewhere in the firm.

The Option to Abandon

A second option is that of abandoning a project after it has been undertaken. This may consist of selling the project's assets or employing them in another area of the enterprise. In either case, an **abandonment value** can be estimated. Certain projects,

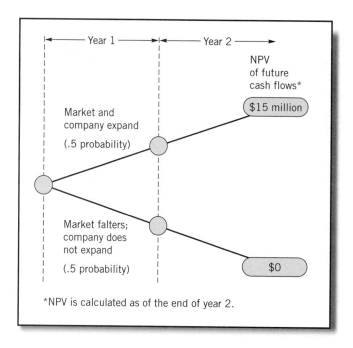

Year 1 — Year 2

NPV
of future
cash flows*

$15 million

Market and
company expand

(.5 probability)

Market falters;
company does
not expand

(.5 probability)

$0

*NPV is calculated as of the end of year 2.

however, have no external market value or alternative use, and for them abandonment value is zero.

The rationale used to determine whether to abandon a project is the same as that
used for capital budgeting. Funds should be removed or divested from a project
whenever the project does not economically justify their continued use. In general,
an investment project should be abandoned when (1) its abandonment value exceeds
the present value of the project's subsequent future cash flows, and (2) it is better to
abandon the project at that time than it is to abandon it at some future date. When the
ability to abandon exists, the worth of an investment project may be enhanced. Thus,
we can say that

$$\text{Project worth} = \begin{array}{c} \text{NPV without} \\ \text{abandonment} \\ \text{option} \end{array} + \begin{array}{c} \text{Value of} \\ \text{abandonment} \\ \text{option} \end{array} \qquad (14\text{-}9)$$

The recognition of an abandonment option may have a significant effect on project
selection.

To illustrate, we suppose Acme Tractor Company is considering establishing a
new facility to produce the Acme Mulchmaster III lawn tractor. This tractor will be
produced for only one or two years because the Acme Mulchmaster IV, now on the
drawing boards, will replace it. The proposal will cost $3 million, and the cash flows
and their probabilities of occurrence are shown as a series of conditional probabilities
in Table 14-3. For simplicity of illustration, we assume that after the second year, the
proposal is not expected to provide any cash flow or residual value. We also assume
an expected abandonment value of $1.5 million at the end of the first year. There are
nine possible series of cash flows over the two-year horizon. The first series (indicated by the **boldfaced** path) represents a cash flow of $1 million in the first year fol-
lowed by a cash flow of zero in year 2. The joint probability of each series of cash
flows is shown in the last column of the table. For the first series, the joint probability

TABLE 14-3
Probability distribution series for abandonment example—base case[a]

YEAR 1		YEAR 2		JOINT
INITIAL PROBABILITY $P(1)$	CASH FLOW (IN MILLIONS)	CONDITIONAL PROBABILITY $P(2 \mid 1)$	CASH FLOW (IN MILLIONS)	PROBABILITY $P(1,2)$
		.25	$ .0	.0625
.25	$1.0	.50	1.0	.1250
		.25	2.0	.0625
		1.00		
		.25	1.0	.1250
.50	2.0	.50	2.0	.2500
		.25	3.0	.1250
		1.00		
		.25	2.0	.0625
.25	3.0	.50	3.0	.1250
		.25	3.5	.0625
1.00		1.00		1.0000

Abandonment Value[b]   1.5

[a]Initial investment at time 0 is $3 million.

[b]If the project were to be abandoned, there would be an *additional* cash inflow at the end of the year 1 of $1.5 million.

is the product of the initial probability and the conditional probability, or .25 × .25 = .0625.

If we assume a required rate of return of 10 percent and use this rate in discounting, we are able to determine the expected net present value of the proposal without the abandonment option.[5] We do this by (1) computing the net present value for each possible cash-flow series, (2) weighting each series by multiplying the computed net present value by the (joint) probability of occurrence of that series, and (3) adding the probability-weighted net present values of all the possible sequences. Carrying out these computations for our example problem, we find the expected net present value to be $445,246.

When we allow for the possibility of abandoning the project at a later date, however, the results change dramatically. Following the abandonment rationale specified earlier, Acme Tractor would divest itself of the project if its abandonment value at the end of year 1 were to exceed the present value of the subsequent expected cash flows discounted at 10 percent. Because cash flows are expected for only two periods, the possibility of abandoning the project beyond year 1 does not exist. Consequently, we do not need to determine if it might be better to abandon the project at some date farther in the future. Referring again to Table 14-3, we find that we should abandon the project at the end of the first year if the cash flow in that year

---

[5]Earlier in this chapter we used a similar probability tree approach. There we discounted the various cash flows to their present value at the *risk-free rate*. We chose that rate because we wanted to isolate the time value of money by discounting and then analyze risk separately. Here we are discounting cash flows at a required rate of return that "adjusts" future cash flows for both the time value of money and risk.

turns out to be $1 million. The reason is that if the first-year cash flow is $1 million, the expected value of possible second-year cash flows is also $1 million (i.e., (.25)($.0) + (.50)($1.0) + (.25)($2.0) = $1 million). And, when this second-year $1 million expected value is discounted to the end of year 1, the present value is only $909,091, which is less than the $1.5 million abandonment value at the end of year 1. If the cash flow in year 1 turns out to be either $2 million or $3 million, however, abandonment would not be worthwhile because in both instances the expected values of possible cash flows in the second year discounted to the end of year 1 exceed $1.5 million.

When we allow for abandonment, we must revise the projected cash flows shown in Table 14-3. The revised figures are shown in Table 14-4. When we recalculate the expected net present value for the proposal based on the revised information, we find it to be $579,544. This significant improvement in expected net present value occurs relative to that in the base case because a portion of the base case's worst possible future cash-flow outcomes is eliminated if the project is abandoned when market conditions become unfavorable.

The greater the variability of possible cash flows for a project, the more valuable is the option to abandon. The abandonment option, like other managerial options, lets a firm benefit from good times, while it can mitigate the effect of bad times by exercising its option. To the extent that the option has value, recognizing its existence may change a signal to reject a project into a signal to accept.

In addition to being used to evaluate new investment proposals, the procedure outlined above can be used to evaluate existing investment projects on a continuing basis—that is, to decide whether it is better to continue with the project or to abandon it and employ released funds elsewhere. Thus, even though a project is profitable, it may make sense to abandon it if its abandonment value is sufficiently high. The optimal time to abandon is found by determining which combination of

TABLE 14-4
Probability distribution series for abandonment example—revised case[a]

YEAR 1		YEAR 2		
INITIAL PROBABILITY $P(1)$	CASH FLOW (IN MILLIONS)	CONDITIONAL PROBABILITY $P(2 \mid 1)$	CASH FLOW (IN MILLIONS)	JOINT PROBABILITY $P(1,2)$
.25	$2.5[b]	1.00	$ .0	.2500
		.25	1.0	.1250
.50	2.0	.50	2.0	.2500
		.25	3.0	.1250
		1.00		
		.25	2.0	.0625
.25	3.0	.50	3.0	.1250
		.25	3.5	.0625
1.00		1.00		1.0000

[a]Initial investment at time 0 is $3 million.

[b]If the project is abandoned after year 1, the cash flow in year 1 of $1 million increases to $2.5 million when the $1.5 million abandonment cash flow is added. Note also that the cash flow in year 2 falls to zero.

expected remaining future cash flows and future abandonment values has the highest present value. Through the continual assessment of projects, a company is able to weed out those that are no longer economically viable.

The Option to Postpone

For some investment projects, an option exists to wait; that is, the project does not have to be undertaken immediately. By waiting, a firm can obtain new information on the market, prices, costs, and perhaps other things as well. However, waiting causes a firm to give up the early cash flows and, possibly, a *first-mover* advantage as well. When it makes a decision regarding a new product, management has the option to launch the product now or to defer its introduction. If the product is launched now, the company will realize cash flows earlier than if it waits. But if it waits, the company may be able to execute the launch more advantageously. As with other managerial options, the greater the volatility of possible outcomes, the greater the value of the option to postpone.

One must, however, make sure that the option remains open. It is generally not good to wait for the last piece of information. By then, others will have exploited the opportunity, and profit margins will be unsatisfactory.

Some Final Observations

The managerial options discussed—expansion (or contraction), abandonment, and postponement—have a common thread. Because they limit the downside outcomes, the greater the uncertainty associated with the future, the more valuable these options become. Recognition of management flexibility can alter an initial decision to accept or reject a project. A decision to reject arrived at using traditional DCF analysis can be reversed if the option value is high enough. A decision to accept can be turned into a decision to postpone if the option value more than offsets that of missing out on the early cash flows. Though a DCF approach to determining net present value is an appropriate starting point, in many cases this approach needs to be modified to allow for managerial options.

SUMMARY

- The risk of an investment project can be viewed as the variability of its cash flows from those that are expected.
- The possible outcomes for an investment project can be expressed in the form of probability distributions of possible cash flows. Given a cash-flow probability distribution, we can express risk quantitatively as the *standard deviation* of the distribution.
- A measure of the relative risk of a distribution is the *coefficient of variation (CV)*. Mathematically, it is defined as the ratio of the standard deviation of a distribution to the expected value of the distribution.
- One approach to the evaluation of risky investments is the direct analysis of the probability distribution of possible net present values of a

project calculated at the risk-free rate. A *probability tree* or *simulation* method may be used to estimate the expected value and standard deviation of the distribution. Management can then use this information to determine the probability that the actual net present value will be lower than some amount, such as zero.
- The probability that a project's internal rate of return will be less than the risk-free rate is equal to the probability that the project's net present value will be less than zero, where the risk-free rate is used in discounting. If we view an *opportunity loss* as any return less than the risk-free return, then the likelihood of an NPV less than zero can be interpreted as the chance of incurring an opportunity loss if the project is accepted.

- Investment projects can also be judged with respect to their contribution to total firm risk, which implies a firm-portfolio approach to risk assessment.
- By diversifying into projects not having high degrees of correlation with existing assets, a firm is able to reduce the standard deviation of its probability distribution of possible net present values relative to the expected value of the distribution. The correlations between pairs of projects prove to be the key ingredients in analyzing risk in a firm-portfolio context.
- Often *managerial options* are important considerations in capital budgeting. The term simply means the flexibility that management has to alter a previously made decision.
- An investment project's worth can be viewed as its traditionally calculated net present value together with the value of any managerial option(s). The greater the uncertainty surrounding the use of an option, the greater its value.
- Managerial options include the option to expand (contract), the option to abandon, and the option to postpone. Consideration of these various options can sometimes turn a *reject decision* otherwise made in evaluating a capital budgeting project into an *accept decision* and an *accept decision* into a *decision to postpone*.

QUESTIONS

1. Why should we be concerned with risk in capital budgeting? Why not just work with the expected cash flows as we did in Chapter 13?
2. Is the standard deviation an adequate measure of risk? Can you think of a better measure?
3. How do you go about "standardizing" the dispersion of a probability distribution to make generalizations about the risk of a project?
4. Risk in capital budgeting can be judged by analyzing the probability distribution of possible returns. What shape distribution would you expect to find for a safe project whose returns were absolutely certain? For a very risky project?
5. If project A has an expected value of net present value of $200 and a standard deviation of $400, is it more risky than project B, whose expected value is $140 and standard deviation is $300? Explain.
6. In a *probability tree* approach to project risk analysis, what are *initial, conditional,* and *joint probabilities?*
7. Why should the risk-free rate be used for discounting cash flows to their present value when evaluating the risk of capital investments?
8. What are the benefits of using *simulation* to evaluate capital investment projects?
9. What role does the correlation between net present values play in the risk of a portfolio of investment projects?
10. What is meant by "dominance" in a portfolio sense?
11. Under a *portfolio approach* how would we know whether particular projects were accepted or rejected?
12. What are *managerial options* and why are they important?
13. In general terms, what determines the value of a managerial option?
14. Name the various types of managerial options, and describe how they differ from one another.

SELF-CORRECTION PROBLEMS

1. Naughty Pine Lumber Company is evaluating a new saw with a life of two years. The saw costs $3,000, and future after-tax cash flows depend on demand for the company's products. The tabular illustration of a probability tree of possible future cash flows associated with the new saw is as follows:

| YEAR 1 | | YEAR 2 | | |
INITIAL PROBABILITY $P(1)$	NET CASH FLOW	CONDITIONAL PROBABILITY $P(2 \mid 1)$	NET CASH FLOW	BRANCH
		.30	$1,000	1
.40	$1,500	.40	1,500	2
		.30	2,000	3
		1.00		
		.40	2,000	4
.60	2,500	.40	2,500	5
		.20	3,000	6
1.00		1.00		

    a. What are the *joint probabilities* of occurrence of the various branches?

    b. If the risk-free rate is 10 percent, what is (i) the net present value of each of the six complete branches, and (ii) the expected value and standard deviation of the probability distribution of possible net present values?

    c. Assuming a normal distribution, what is the probability that the actual net present value will be less than zero? What is the significance of this probability?

2. Zello Creamery Company would like to develop a new product line—puddings. The expected value and standard deviation of the probability distribution of possible net present values for the product line are $12,000 and $9,000, respectively. The company's existing lines include ice cream, cottage cheese, and yogurt. The expected values of net present value and standard deviation for these product lines are as follows:

	EXPECTED NET PRESENT VALUE	σ_{NPV}
Ice cream	$16,000	$8,000
Cottage cheese	20,000	7,000
Yogurt	10,000	4,000

The correlation coefficients between products are

	ICE CREAM	COTTAGE CHEESE	YOGURT	PUDDING
Ice cream	1.00			
Cottage cheese	.90	1.00		
Yogurt	.80	.84	1.00	
Pudding	.40	.20	.30	1.00

    a. Compute the expected value and the standard deviation of the probability distribution of possible net present values for a combination consisting of the three existing products.

    b. Compute the expected value and standard deviation for a combination consisting of existing products plus pudding. Compare your results in Parts (a) and (b). What can you say about the pudding line?

3. Zydeco Enterprises is considering undertaking a special project requiring an initial outlay of $90,000. The project would have a two-year life, after which there will be no expected salvage or terminal value. The possible incremental after-tax cash flows and associated probabilities of occurrence are as follows:

YEAR 1			YEAR 2		
INITIAL PROBABILITY $P(1)$	NET CASH FLOW		CONDITIONAL PROBABILITY $P(2\mid 1)$	NET CASH FLOW	BRANCH
.30	$60,000		.30	$20,000	1
			.50	30,000	2
			.20	40,000	3
			1.00		
.40	70,000		.30	40,000	4
			.40	50,000	5
			.30	60,000	6
			1.00		
.30	80,000		.20	60,000	7
			.50	70,000	8
			.30	80,000	9
1.00			1.00		

The company's required rate of return for this investment is 8 percent.

a. Calculate the expected net present value of this project.

b. Suppose that the possibility of abandonment exists and that the abandonment value of the project at the end of the first year is $45,000 after taxes. For this project, would abandonment after one year ever be the right choice? Calculate the new expected net present value, assuming that the company would abandon the project if it is worthwhile to do so. Compare your calculations with those in Part (a). What are the implications to you as a manager?

PROBLEMS

1. George Gau, Inc., can invest in one of two mutually exclusive, one-year projects requiring equal initial outlays. The two proposals have the following discrete probability distributions of net cash inflows for the first year:

PROJECT A		PROJECT B	
PROBABILITY	CASH FLOW	PROBABILITY	CASH FLOW
.20	$2,000	.10	$2,000
.30	4,000	.40	4,000
.30	6,000	.40	6,000
.20	8,000	.10	8,000
1.00		1.00	

a. Without calculating a mean and a coefficient of variation, can you select the better proposal, assuming a risk-averse management?

b. Verify your intuitive determination.

2. Smith, Jones, and Nguyen, Inc., is faced with several possible investment projects. For each, the total cash outflow required will occur in the initial period. The cash outflows, expected net present values, and standard deviations are given in the following table. All projects have been discounted at the risk-free rate, and it is assumed that the distributions of their possible net present values are normal.

PROJECT	COST	EXPECTED NET PRESENT VALUE	STANDARD DEVIATION
A	$100,000	$10,000	$20,000
B	50,000	10,000	30,000
C	200,000	25,000	10,000
D	10,000	5,000	10,000
E	500,000	75,000	75,000

a. Are there some projects that are clearly dominated by others with respect to expected value and standard deviation? With respect to expected value and coefficient of variation?

b. What is the probability that each of the projects will have a net present value less than zero?

3. The probability distribution of possible net present values for project X has an expected value of $20,000 and a standard deviation of $10,000. Assuming a normal distribution, calculate the probability that the net present value will be zero or less, that it will be greater than $30,000, and that it will be less than $5,000.

4. Xonics Graphics, Inc., is evaluating a new technology for its reproduction equipment. The technology will have a three-year life, will cost $1,000, and will have an impact on cash flows that is subject to risk. Management estimates that there is a fifty-fifty chance that the technology will either save the company $1,000 in the first year or save it nothing at all. If nothing at all, savings in the last two years would be zero as well. Even here there is some possibility that in the second year an additional outlay of $300 would be required to convert back to the original process, for the new technology may decrease efficiency. Management attaches a 40 percent probability to this occurrence if the new technology "bombs out" in the first year. If the technology proves itself in the first year, it is felt that second-year cash flows will be $1,800, $1,400, and $1,000, with probabilities of .20, .60, and .20, respectively. In the third year, cash flows are expected to be either $200 greater or $200 less than the cash flow in period 2, with an equal chance of occurrence. (Again, these cash flows depend on the cash flow in period 1 being $1,000.)

a. Set up a tabular version of a probability tree to depict the cash-flow possibilities, as well as the initial, conditional, and joint probabilities.

b. Calculate a net present value for each of the three-year possibilities (that is, for each of the eight complete branches in the probability tree) using a risk-free rate of 5 percent.

c. Calculate the expected value of net present value for the project represented in the probability tree.

d. What is the risk of the project?

5. The Flotsam and Jetsam Wreckage Company will invest in two of three possible proposals, the cash flows of which are normally distributed. The expected net present value (discounted at the risk-free rate) and the standard deviation for each proposal are given as follows:

	PROPOSAL		
	1	2	3
Expected net present value	$10,000	$8,000	$6,000
Standard deviation	4,000	3,000	4,000

Assuming the following correlation coefficients for each possible two-project combination, which combination dominates the others?

PROPOSAL COMBINATIONS	CORRELATION COEFFICIENTS
1 with 2	.60
1 with 3	.40
2 with 3	.50

6. The Plaza Corporation is confronted with various combinations of risky investments.

COMBINATION	EXPECTED NET PRESENT VALUE	STANDARD DEVIATION
A	$100,000	$200,000
B	20,000	80,000
C	75,000	100,000
D	60,000	150,000
E	50,000	20,000
F	40,000	60,000
G	120,000	170,000
H	90,000	70,000
I	50,000	100,000
J	75,000	30,000

   a. Plot the above portfolios.
   b. Which combinations dominate the others?

7. The Bertz Merchandising Company uses a simulation approach to judge investment projects. Three factors are employed: market demand, in units; price per unit minus cost per unit (on an after-tax basis); and investment required at time 0. These factors are felt to be independent of one another. In analyzing a new "fad" consumer product with a one-year product life, Bertz estimates the following probability distributions:

MARKET DEMAND		PRICE MINUS COST PER UNIT (AFTER-TAX)		INVESTMENT REQUIRED	
PROBABILITY	UNITS	PROBABILITY	DOLLARS	PROBABILITY	DOLLARS
.15	26,000	.30	$6.00	.30	$160,000
.20	27,000	.40	6.50	.40	165,000
.30	28,000	.30	7.00	.30	170,000
.20	29,000	1.00		1.00	
.15	30,000				
1.00					

   a. Using a table of random numbers or some other random process, simulate 20 or more trials of these three factors, and compute the internal rate of return on this one-year investment for each trial.
   b. Approximately, what is the most likely return? How risky is the project?

8. The Bates Pet Motel Company is considering opening a new branch location. If it constructs an office and 100 pet cages at its new location, the initial outlay will be $100,000, and the project is likely to produce net cash flows of $17,000 per year for fifteen years, after which the leasehold on the land expires and the project is left with no residual or salvage value. The company's required rate of return is 18 percent. If the location proves favorable, Bates Pet Motel will be able to expand

Part V Investment in Capital Assets

by another 100 cages at the end of four years. This second-stage expansion would require a $20,000 outlay. With the additional 100 cages installed, incremental net cash flows of $17,000 per year for years 5 through 15 would be expected. The company believes there is a fifty-fifty chance that the location will prove to be a favorable one.

a. Is the initial project acceptable? Why?

b. What is the value of the option to expand? What is the project worth with this option? Is the project now acceptable? Why?

SOLUTIONS TO SELF-CORRECTION PROBLEMS

1. a.

			BRANCH				
	1	2	3	4	5	6	TOTAL
Joint probability	.12	.16	.12	.24	.24	.12	1.00

b. At a risk-free rate of 10 percent (i) the net present value of each of the six complete branches, and (ii) the expected value and standard deviation of the probability distribution of possible net present values are as follows (with rounding):

YEAR 0	YEAR 1	YEAR 2	BRANCH	NPV
		$ 826	1	$ –810
	$1,364	1,240	2	–396
		1,653	3	17
–$3,000				
		1,653	4	926
	2,273	2,066	5	1,339
		2,479	6	1,752

$$\overline{NPV} = .12(-\$810) + .16(-\$396) + .12(\$17) + .24(\$926)$$
$$+ .24(\$1,339) + .12(\$1,752) = \mathbf{\$595}$$

$$\sigma_{NPV} = [.12(-\$810 - \$595)^2 + .16(-\$396 - \$595)^2 + .12(\$17 - \$595)^2$$
$$+ .24(\$926 - \$595)^2 + .24(\$1,339 - \$595)^2 + .12(\$1,752 - \$595)^2]^{.5}$$

$$= \mathbf{\$868}$$

c. Standardizing the difference from zero, we have $-\$595/\$868 = -.685$. Looking in Table V in the Appendix at the end of the book, we find that $-.685$ corresponds to an area of approximately .25. Therefore, there is approximately one chance out of four that the net present value will be zero or less.

2. a. Expected net present value = $16,000 + $20,000 + $10,000 = **$46,000**

$$\text{Standard deviation} = [(\$8,000)^2 + (2)(.9)(\$8,000)(\$7,000)$$
$$+ (2)(.8)(\$8,000)(\$4,000) + (\$7,000)^2$$
$$+ (2)(.84)(\$7,000)(\$4,000) + (\$4,000)^2]^{1/2}$$
$$= [\$328,040,000]^{.5} = \mathbf{\$18,112}$$

b. Expected net present value = $46,000 + $12,000 = **$58,000**

$$\text{Standard deviation} = [\$328,040,000 + (\$9,000)^2$$

$$+ \ (2)(.4)(\$9,000)(\$8,000)$$

$$+ \ (2)(.2)(\$9,000)(\$7,000)$$

$$+ \ (2)(.3)(\$9,000)(\$4,000)]^{1/2}$$

$$= [\$513,440,000]^{.5} = \textbf{\$22,659}$$

The coefficient of variation for existing projects $(\sigma / \overline{NPV}) = \$18,112/\$46,000$ = .39. The coefficient of variation for existing projects plus puddings = $\$22,659/\$58,000 = .39$. Though the pudding line has a higher coefficient of variation ($\$9,000/\$12,000 = .75$) than existing projects, indicating a higher degree of risk, the correlation of this product line with existing lines is sufficiently low as to bring the coefficient of variation for all products, including puddings, in line with that for only existing products.

3. a.

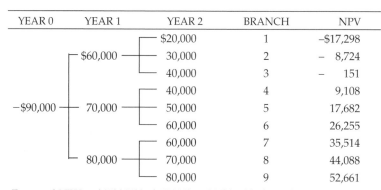

YEAR 0	YEAR 1	YEAR 2	BRANCH	NPV
		$20,000	1	−$17,298
	$60,000	30,000	2	− 8,724
		40,000	3	− 151
		40,000	4	9,108
−$90,000	70,000	50,000	5	17,682
		60,000	6	26,255
		60,000	7	35,514
	80,000	70,000	8	44,088
		80,000	9	52,661

Expected NPV = (.30)(.30)(−$17,298) + (.30)(.50)(−$8,724)
+ (.30)(.20)(−$151) + (.40)(.30)($9,108) + (.40)(.40)($17,682)
+ (.40)(.30)($26,255) + (.30)(.20)($35,514) + (.30)(.50)($44,088)
+ (.30)(.30)($52,661) = **$17,682**

b. We should abandon the project at the end of the first year if the cash flow in that year turns out to be $60,000. The reason is that given a $60,000 first-year cash flow, the $29,000 expected value of possible second-year cash flows (i.e., (.30)($20,000) + (.50)($30,000) + (.20)($40,000) = $29,000), when discounted to the end of year 1 is only $26,854, and this value is less than the $45,000 abandonment value at the end of year 1. If the cash flow in year 1 turns out to be either $70,000 or $80,000, however, abandonment would not be worthwhile because in both instances the expected values of possible cash flows in year 2 discounted to the end of year 1 exceed $45,000.

When we allow for abandonment, the original projected cash flows for branches 1, 2, and 3 are replaced by a single branch having a cash flow of $105,000 ($60,000 plus $45,000, the abandonment value) in year 1 and resulting NPV of $7,230. Recalculating the expected net present value for the proposal based upon revised information, we find it to be

(.30)($7,230) + (.40)(.30)($9,108) + (.40)(.40)($17,682) + (.40)(.30)($26,255)
+ (.30)(.20)($35,514) + (.30)(.50)($44,088) + (.30)(.30)($52,661) = **$22,725.**

Thus, the expected net present value is increased when the possibility of abandonment is considered in the evaluation. Part of the downside risk is eliminated because of the abandonment option.

SELECTED REFERENCES

Aggarwal, Raj, and Luc A. Soenen. "Project Exit Value as a Measure of Flexibility and Risk Exposure." *The Engineering Economist* 35 (Fall 1989), 39–54.

Amram, Martha, and Nalin Kulatilaka. *Real Options: Strategic Investments in an Uncertain World.* Boston, MA: Harvard Business School Press, 1999.

Berger, Philip G., Eli Ofek, and Itzhak Swarg. "Investor Valuation of the Abandonment Option." *Journal of Financial Economics* 42 (October 1996), 257–87.

Bey, Roger P. "Capital Budgeting Decisions When Cash Flows and Project Lives Are Stochastic and Dependent." *Journal of Financial Research* 6 (Fall 1983), 175–87.

Brennen, Michael J., and Eduardo S. Schwartz. "A New Approach to Evaluating Natural Resource Investments." *Midland Corporate Finance Journal* 3 (Spring 1985), 37–47.

Butler, J.S., and Barry Schachter. "The Investment Decision: Estimation Risk and Risk Adjusted Discount Rates." *Financial Management* 18 (Winter 1989), 13–22.

Cromwell, Nancy O., and Charles W. Hodges. "Teaching Real Options in Corporate Finance." *Journal of Financial Education* 24 (Spring 1998), 33–48.

Dixit, Avinash. "Entry and Exit Decisions Under Uncertainty." *Journal of Political Economy* 97 (June 1989), 620–38.

———, and Robert S. Pindyck. "The Options Approach to Capital Investment." *Harvard Business Review* 73 (May–June 1995), 105–15.

Hertz, David B. "Risk Analysis in Capital Investment." *Harvard Business Review* 42 (January–February 1964), 95–106.

———. "Investment Policies That Pay Off." *Harvard Business Review* 46 (January–February 1968), 96–108.

Hillier, Frederick S. "The Derivation of Probabilistic Information for the Evaluation of Risky Investments." *Management Science* 9 (April 1963), 443–57.

Ingersoll, Jonathan E., Jr., and Stephen A. Ross. "Waiting to Invest: Investment Under Uncertainty." *Journal of Business* 65 (1992), 1–29.

Kulatilaka, Nalin, and Alan J. Marcus. "Project Valuation Under Uncertainty: When Does DCF Fail?" *Journal of Applied Corporate Finance* 5 (Fall 1992), 92–100.

Kwan, Clarence C. Y., and Yufei Yuan. "Optimal Sequential Selection in Capital Budgeting: A Shortcut." *Financial Management* 17 (Spring 1988), 54–59.

Luehrman, Timothy A. "Investment Opportunities as Real Options: Getting Started on the Numbers." *Harvard Business Review* 76 (July–August 1998), 51–67.

Magee, J. F. "How to Use Decision Trees in Capital Investment." *Harvard Business Review* 42 (September–October 1964), 79–96.

Robichek, Alexander A. "Interpreting the Results of Risk Analysis." *Journal of Finance* 30 (December 1975), 1384–86.

———, and James Van Horne. "Abandonment Value and Capital Budgeting." *Journal of Finance* 22 (December 1967), 557–89; Edward A. Dyl and Hugh W. Long, "Comment," *Journal of Finance* 24 (March 1969), 88–95; and Robichek and Van Horne, "Reply," ibid., 96–97.

Ross, Stephen A. "Uses, Abuses, and Alternatives to the Net Present Value Rule." *Financial Management* 24 (Autumn 1995), 96–101.

Shrieves, Ronald E., and John M. Wachowicz Jr. "A Utility Theoretic Basis for 'Generalized' Mean-Coefficient of Variation (MCV) Analysis." *Journal of Financial and Quantitative Analysis* 16 (December 1981), 671–83.

Trigeorgis, Lenos. "Real Options and Interactions with Financial Flexibility." *Financial Management* 22 (Autumn 1993), 202–24.

———, and Scott P. Mason. "Valuing Managerial Flexibility." *Midland Corporate Finance Journal* 5 (Spring 1987), 14–21.

Van Horne, James. "Capital-Budgeting Decisions Involving Combinations of Risky Investments." *Management Science* 13 (October 1966), 84–92.

———. "The Analysis of Uncertainty Resolution in Capital Budgeting for New Products." *Management Science* 15 (April 1969), 376–86.

———. "Capital Budgeting Under Conditions of Uncertainty as to Project Life." *The Engineering Economist* 17 (Spring 1972), 189–99.

———. "Variation of Project Life as a Means of Adjusting for Risk." *The Engineering Economist* 21 (Summer 1976), 151–58.

Wachowicz, John M., Jr., and Ronald E. Shrieves. "An Argument for 'Generalized' Mean-Coefficient of Variation Analysis." *Financial Management* 9 (Winter 1980), 51–58.

Chapter

15

Required Returns and the Cost of Capital

CREATION OF VALUE
    Industry Attractiveness • Competitive Advantage
OVERALL COST OF CAPITAL OF THE FIRM
    Cost of Debt • Cost of Preferred Stock • Cost of Equity: Dividend
        Discount Model Approach • Cost of Equity: Capital-Asset
        Pricing Model Approach • Cost of Equity: Before-Tax Cost of
        Debt Plus Risk Premium Approach • Weighted Average Cost
        of Capital • Some Limitations • Rationale for a Weighted
        Average Cost • Economic Value Added (EVA)
THE CAPM: PROJECT-SPECIFIC AND GROUP-SPECIFIC REQUIRED
    RATES OF RETURN
    Capital-Asset Pricing Model Approach to Project Selection
        • Group-Specific Required Return • Some Qualifications
        • Ascribing Debt Funds to Groups
EVALUATION OF PROJECTS ON THE BASIS OF THEIR TOTAL RISK
    Risk-Adjusted Discount Rate Approach • Probability Distribution
        Approach • Contribution to Total Firm Risk: Firm-Portfolio
        Approach • Conceptual Implications
SUMMARY
APPENDIX A: ADJUSTING THE BETA FOR FINANCIAL LEVERAGE
APPENDIX B: ADJUSTED PRESENT VALUE
QUESTIONS
SELF-CORRECTION PROBLEMS
PROBLEMS
SOLUTIONS TO SELF-CORRECTION PROBLEMS
SELECTED REFERENCES

To guess is cheap. To guess wrong is expensive.

—CHINESE PROVERB

Having just considered risk in the capital budgeting process, we need to understand how risk affects the valuation of the enterprise. Its effect on value is shown through the returns that financial markets expect the corporation to provide on debt, equity, and other financial instruments. In general, the greater the risk, the higher the returns the financial markets expect from a capital investment. Thus, the link from a capital investment to valuation is the required return used to determine whether or not a capital budgeting project will be accepted.

The acceptance criterion for capital investments is perhaps the most difficult and controversial topic in finance. We know that in theory the minimum acceptable rate of return on a project should be the rate that will leave the market price of the company's common stock unchanged. The difficulty lies in determining this rate in practice. Because predicting the effect of capital investment decisions on stock prices is an inexact science (some would call it an art form), estimating the appropriate required rate of return is inexact as well. Rather than skirt the issue, we address it head on and propose a general framework for measuring the required rate of return. The idea is a simple one. We try to determine the opportunity cost of a capital investment project by relating it to a financial market investment with the same risk.

CREATION OF VALUE

If the return on a project exceeds what the financial markets require, it is said to earn an *excess return*. This excess return, as we define it, represents the creation of value. Simply put, the project earns more than its economic keep. Finding and undertaking these value-creating (positive NPV) projects increases a company's common stock share price.

Industry Attractiveness

Value creation has several sources, but perhaps the most important are industry attractiveness and competitive advantage. These are the things that give rise to projects with positive net present values—ones that provide expected returns in excess of what the financial markets require. Favorable industry characteristics include positioning in the growth phase of a product cycle, barriers to competitive entry, and other protective devices, such as patents, temporary monopoly power, and/or oligopoly pricing where nearly all competitors are profitable. In short, industry attractiveness has to do with the relative position of an industry in the spectrum of value-creating investment opportunities.

Competitive Advantage

Competitive advantage involves a company's relative position within an industry. The company could be multidivisional, in which case competitive advantage needs to be judged industry by industry. The avenues to competitive advantage are several: cost advantage, marketing and price advantage, perceived quality advantage, and superior organizational capability (corporate culture). Competitive advantage is eroded with competition. Relative cost, quality, or marketing superiority, for example, is conspicuous and will be attacked. A successful company is one that continually identifies and exploits opportunities for excess returns. Only with a sequence of short-run advantages can any overall competitive advantage be sustained.

FIGURE 15-1
Key Sources of Value
Creation

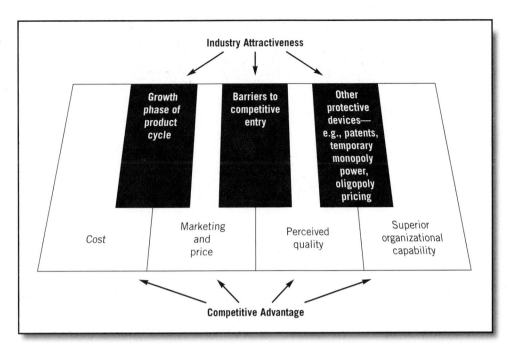

Thus, industry attractiveness and competitive advantage are principal sources of value creation. The more favorable these are, the more likely the company is to have expected returns in excess of what the financial markets require for the risk involved. These notions are illustrated in Figure 15-1.

OVERALL COST OF CAPITAL OF THE FIRM

Cost of capital The required rate of return on the various types of financing. The overall cost of capital is a weighted average of the individual required rates of return (costs).

Cost of equity capital The required rate of return on investment of the common shareholders of the company.

Cost of debt (capital) The required rate of return on investment of the lenders of a company.

Cost of preferred stock (capital) The required rate of return on investment of the preferred shareholders of the company.

A company can be viewed as a collection of projects. As a result, the use of an overall **cost of capital** as the acceptance criterion (hurdle rate) for investment decisions is appropriate only under certain circumstances. These circumstances are that the current projects of the firm are of similar risk and that investment proposals under consideration are of the same character. If investment proposals vary widely with respect to risk, the required rate of return for the company as a whole is not appropriate as the sole acceptance criterion. The advantage of using the firm's overall required rate of return is, of course, its simplicity. Once it is computed, projects can be evaluated using a single rate that does not change unless underlying business and financial market conditions change. Using a single hurdle rate avoids the problem of computing individual required rates of return for each investment proposal. It is important to note, however, that if the firm's overall required rate of return is used as an acceptance criterion, projects should generally correspond to the foregoing conditions. Otherwise, one should determine an individual acceptance criterion for each project, a topic that we take up in the latter part of this chapter.

The overall cost of capital of a firm is a proportionate average of the costs of the various components of the firm's financing. The **cost of equity capital** is the most difficult to measure, and it will occupy most of our attention. We also consider the component **costs of debt** and **preferred stock.** We will rely on return (yield) calculations to determine cost figures because "cost" and "return" are essentially two sides of the same coin.[1] Our concern throughout will be with the *marginal* cost of a specific source of financing. The use of marginal costs follows from the fact that we use the cost of capital to decide whether to invest in *new* projects. Past costs of financing have no bearing on this decision. All costs will be expressed on an after-tax basis, to conform to the expression of investment project cash flows on an after-tax basis. Once we have examined the explicit costs of the various sources of financing, we will assign weights to each source. Finally, we will compute a weighted average of the component costs of financing to obtain an overall cost of capital to the firm. We assume in the development of this chapter that the reader has covered the foundation materials in Chapters 3 and 4 on the mathematics of finance and on valuation.

QUESTION•ANSWER•QUESTION•ANSWER

The cost of capital—what is it, really?

It is the firm's required rate of return that will just satisfy *all* capital providers. To get some feel for what this *cost of capital* figure really means, let's look at a simple, personal example. Assume that you borrow some money from two friends (at two different costs), add some of your own money with the expectation of at least a certain minimum return, and seek out an investment. What is the minimum return you can earn that will just satisfy the return expectations of all capital providers (as listed in column number 2 of the table below)?

	(1)	(2)	(3)	(2) × (3)	(1) × (2)
CAPITAL PROVIDERS	INVESTED CAPITAL	PERCENTAGE ANNUAL COST (INVESTOR RETURN)	PROPORTION OF TOTAL FINANCING	WEIGHTED COST	DOLLAR ANNUAL COST (INVESTOR RETURN)
Bubba	$ 2,000	5%	20%	1.0%	$ 100
Dolly	3,000	10	30	3.0	300
You	5,000	15	50	7.5	750
	$10,000		100%	11.5%	$1,150

Assume that your "firm" earns a yearly 11.5 percent return (the weighted average cost of capital employed) on the $10,000 of invested capital. The $1,150 so provided will just satisfy the return requirements of all the capital providers. Now, replace "Bubba," "Dolly," and "You" with the terms "Debt," "Preferred Stock," and "Common Stock" (and yes, we still need to consider tax implications; but let's assume no taxes for the moment). With these new terms in place you should begin to understand the direction that we will be taking in finding the firm's required rate of return—*the cost of capital*—that will just satisfy all capital providers.

Cost of Debt

Although the liabilities of a company are varied, our focus is only on nonseasonal debt that bears an explicit interest cost. We ignore accounts payable, accrued expenses, and other obligations not having an explicit interest cost. For the most part, our concern is with long-term debt. However, continuous short-term debt, such as an

---

[1]For example, if we give you $10, you have just experienced a $10 return while we have experienced a $10 cost.

accounts-receivable-backed loan, also qualifies. (A bank loan to finance seasonal inventory requirements would not qualify.) The assumption is that the firm is following a **hedging (maturity matching approach)** to project financing. That is, the firm will finance a capital project, whose benefits extend over a number of years, with financing that is generally long term in nature.

The explicit cost of debt can be derived by solving for the discount rate, k_d, that equates the market price of the debt issue with the present value of interest plus principal payments and by then adjusting the explicit cost obtained for the tax deductibility of interest payments. The discount rate, k_d, known as the *yield to maturity*, is solved for by making use of the formula

$$P_0 = \sum_{t=1}^{n} \frac{I_t + P_t}{(1 + k_d)^t} \qquad \text{(15-1)}$$

where P_0 is the current market price of the debt issue; Σ denotes the summation for periods 1 through n, the final maturity; I_t is the interest payment in period t; and P_t is the payment of principal in period t. If principal payments occur only at final maturity, only P_n will occur. By solving for k_d, the discount rate that equates the present value of cash flows to the suppliers of debt capital with the current market price of the new debt issue, we obtain the required rate of return of the lenders to the company. This required return to lenders can be viewed as the issuing company's before-tax cost of debt. (Most of this should already be familiar to you from our discussion of yield to maturity (YTM) on bonds in Chapter 4.)

The after-tax cost of debt, which we denote by k_i, can be approximated by

$$k_i = k_d(1 - t) \qquad \text{(15-2)}$$

where k_d remains as previously stated and t is now defined as the company's marginal tax rate. Because interest charges are tax deductible to the issuer, the after-tax cost of debt is substantially less than the before-tax cost. If the before-tax cost, k_d, in Eq. (15-1) was found to be 11 percent and the marginal tax rate (federal plus state) was 40 percent, the after-tax cost of debt would be

$$k_i = 11.00(1 - .40) = \mathbf{6.60\%}$$

You should note that the 6.60 percent after-tax cost in our example represents the marginal, or incremental, cost of additional debt. It does not represent the cost of debt funds already employed.

Implied in the calculation of an after-tax cost of debt is the fact that the firm has taxable income. Otherwise, it does not gain the tax benefit associated with interest payments. The explicit cost of debt for a firm without taxable income is the before-tax cost, k_d.

Cost of Preferred Stock

The cost of preferred stock is a function of its stated dividend. As we discuss in Chapter 20, this dividend is not a contractual obligation of the firm but, rather, is payable at the discretion of the firm's board of directors. Consequently, unlike debt, it does not create a risk of legal bankruptcy. To the holders of common stock, however, preferred stock is a security that takes priority over their securities when it comes to the payment of dividends and to the distribution of assets if the company is dissolved. Most corporations that issue preferred stock fully intend to pay the stated dividend. The market-required return for this stock, or simply the yield on preferred stock, serves as our estimate of the cost of preferred stock. Because preferred stock has no maturity date, its cost, k_p, may be represented as

$$k_p = D_p / P_0 \tag{15-3}$$

where D_p is the stated annual dividend and P_0 is the current market price of the preferred stock.[2] If a company were able to sell a 10 percent preferred stock issue ($50 par value) at a current market price of $49 a share, the cost of preferred stock would be $5/$49 = **10.20%**. Note that this cost is not adjusted for taxes because the preferred stock dividend used in Eq. (15-3) is already an after-tax figure—preferred stock dividends being paid after taxes. Thus, the explicit cost of preferred stock is greater than that for debt.

However, the preferred stock offers a desirable feature to the corporate investor. The tax law provides that generally 70 percent of the dividends received by one corporation from another are exempt from federal taxation. This attraction on the demand side usually results in yields on preferred stock being slightly below those on bonds issued by the same company. It is only after taxes, then, that debt financing generally looks more attractive to the issuing firm.

Cost of Equity: Dividend Discount Model Approach

Take Note

The cost of equity capital is by far the most difficult cost to measure. Equity capital can be raised either internally by retaining earnings or externally by selling common stock. In theory, the cost of both may be thought of as the minimum rate of return that the company must earn on the equity-financed portion of an investment project in order to leave the market price of the firm's common stock unchanged. If the firm invests in projects having an expected return less than this required return, the market price of the stock will suffer over the long run.

In the context of the dividend discount valuation models presented in Chapter 4, the cost of equity capital, k_e, can be thought of as the discount rate that equates the present value of all expected future dividends per share, as perceived by investors at the margin, with the current market price per share. Recall from Chapter 4 that

$$P_0 = \frac{D_1}{(1 + k_e)^1} + \frac{D_2}{(1 + k_e)^2} + \cdots + \frac{D_\infty}{(1 + k_e)^\infty}$$

$$\tag{15-4}$$

$$= \sum_{t=1}^{\infty} \frac{D_t}{(1 + k_e)^t}$$

where P_0 is the market price of a share of stock at time 0, D_t is the dividend per share expected to be paid at the end of time period t, k_e is the appropriate discount rate, and Σ represents the sum of the discounted future dividends from period 1 through infinity, depicted by the symbol ∞.

---

[2]Virtually all preferred stock issues have a *call feature* (a provision that allows the company to force retirement). If the issuer anticipates retiring (calling) preferred stock at a particular date, we can apply a modified version of the formula used to solve for the yield on debt, Eq. (15-1), to find the yield (cost) of preferred stock that will be called. In Eq. (15-1) the periodic preferred dividend replaces the periodic interest payment, and the "call price" replaces the principal payment at final maturity (call date). The discount rate that equates all payments to the price of the preferred stock is the cost of the preferred stock.

Part VI The Cost of Capital, Capital Structure, and Dividend Policy

Estimating Future Dividends. If we accurately estimate the stream of future dividends that the market expects, it is an easy matter to solve for the discount rate that equates this cash stream with the current market price of the stock. Because expected future dividends are not directly observable, they must be estimated. Herein lies the major difficulty in estimating the cost of equity capital. Given reasonably stable patterns of past growth, one might project this trend into the future. However, we must temper our projection with current market sentiment. Insight into such sentiment can come from reviewing various analyses about the company in financial newspapers and magazines.

For example, if dividends are expected to grow at an 8 percent annual rate into the foreseeable future, the constant growth model presented in Chapter 4 might be used to determine the required rate of return. If the expected dividend in the first year were \$2 and the present market price were \$27, we would have

$$k_e = (D_1/P_0) + g \tag{15-5}$$

$$= (\$2/\$27) + .08 = \textbf{15.4\%}$$

This rate would then be used as an estimate of the firm's required return on equity capital. The key element in Eq. (15-5) is an accurate measurement of the growth in dividends per share, g, as perceived by investors at the margin.

Growth Phases. If the growth in dividends is expected to taper off in the future, the constant growth model will not do. As explained in Chapter 4, a modification of Eq. (15-4) is then in order. Frequently, the transition in dividend growth is from an above-normal growth rate to one that is considered normal. If dividends were expected to grow at a 15 percent compound rate for five years, at a 10 percent rate for the next five years, and then grow at a 5 percent rate, we would have

$$P_0 = \sum_{t=1}^{5} \frac{D_0(1.15)^t}{(1 + k_e)^t} + \sum_{t=6}^{10} \frac{D_5(1.10)^{t-5}}{(1 + k_e)^t} + \sum_{t=11}^{\infty} \frac{D_{10}(1.05)^{t-10}}{(1 + k_e)^t} \tag{15-6}$$

We see that the current dividend, D_0, is the base on which the expected growth in future dividends is built. By solving for k_e, we obtain the cost of equity capital. One would use the method illustrated in Chapter 4 to solve for k_e. For example, if the current dividend, D_0, were \$2 a share and the market price per share, P_0, were \$70, k_e in Eq. (15-6) would be 10.42 percent. For other patterns of expected future growth, Eq. (15-4) can easily be modified to deal with the particular situation.

The more growth segments that we specify, of course, the more the growth pattern will approximate a curvilinear relationship. From Chapter 4, we learned how to determine the present value of the last growth phase in Eq. (15-6). This last phase is nothing more than a constant growth model following periods of above-normal growth.

Cost of Equity: Capital-Asset Pricing Model Approach

Rather than estimating the future dividend stream of the firm and then solving for the cost of equity capital, we may approach the problem directly by estimating the required rate of return on the company's common stock. From our discussion of the capital-asset pricing model (CAPM) in Chapter 5, we know that the CAPM implies the following required rate of return, R_j, for a share of common stock:

$$R_j = R_f + (\bar{R}_m - R_f)\beta_j \tag{15-7}$$

where R_f is the risk-free rate, $\bar{R}_m$ is the expected return for the market portfolio, and β_j is the beta coefficient for stock j. From Chapter 5, we know that because of the market's aversion to systematic risk, the greater the beta of a stock, the greater its required return. The risk-return relationship is described by Eq. (15-7) and is known as the *security market line* (see Fig. 5-6 in Chapter 5). It implies that in market equilibrium, security prices will be such that there is a linear trade-off between the required rate of return and systematic risk, as measured by beta.

Beta. Beta is a measure of the responsiveness of the excess returns for a security (in excess of the risk-free rate) to those of the market, using some broad-based index, such as the S&P 500 Index as a surrogate for the market portfolio. If the historical relationship between security returns and those for the market portfolio is believed to be a reasonable proxy for the future, one can use past returns to compute beta for a stock. This was illustrated in Chapter 5, where a *characteristic line* was fitted to the relationship between returns in excess of the risk-free rate for a stock and those for the market index. *Beta* is defined as the slope of this line. To free us of the need to calculate beta information directly, several services (for example, Value Line Investment Survey, Standard & Poor's Stock Reports, and Market Guide [www.marketguide.com]) provide historical beta information on a large number of publicly traded stocks. These services allow us to obtain the beta for a stock with ease, thereby greatly facilitating the calculation of the cost of equity capital.

If the past is thought to be a good proxy for the future, we can use Eq. (15-7) to compute the cost of equity capital for a company. To illustrate, suppose that the beta for Schlosky's Paint Company was found to be 1.20, based on monthly excess return data over the last five years. This beta value tells us that the stock's excess return goes up or down by a somewhat greater percentage than does the excess return for the market. (A beta of 1.00 means that excess returns for the stock vary proportionally with excess returns for the market portfolio.) Thus, the stock of Schlosky's Paint Company has more unavoidable, or systematic, risk than does the market as a whole. Management believes that this past relationship is likely to hold in the future. Furthermore, assume that a rate of return of about 13 percent on stocks in general is expected to prevail and that a risk-free rate of 8 percent is expected.

This is all the information that we need to compute the required rate of return on equity for Schlosky's Paint Company. Using Eq. (15-7), the cost of equity capital would be

$$R_j = .08 + (.13 - .08)(1.20) = \mathbf{14\%}$$

Thus, the estimated required rate of return for Schlosky's Paint Company is approximately 14 percent. In essence, we are saying that this is the rate of return that investors expect the company to earn on its equity.

Risk-Free Rate and Market Return. In addition to beta, it is important that the numbers used for the risk-free rate and the expected market return in Eq. (15-7) be the best possible estimates of the future. The risk-free return estimate is controversial—not as to the type of security return that should be used but as to the security's relevant maturity. Most agree that a Treasury security, which is backed by the full faith and credit of the U.S. government, is the proper instrument to use in making a "risk-free" return estimate. But the choice of a proper maturity is another matter. As the CAPM is a one-period model, some contend that a short-term rate, such as that for three-month Treasury bills, is in order. Others argue that because capital investment projects are long-lived, a long-term Treasury bond rate should be used. Still others, the authors included, feel more comfortable with an intermediate-term rate, such as that on three-year Treasury securities. This is a middle position in a rather murky area. With an upward-sloping *yield curve* (graph of the relationship between yields and maturity), the longer the maturity, the higher the risk-free rate.

For the expected return on the market portfolio of stock, as usually depicted by the S&P 500 Index, one can use consensus estimates of security analysts, economists, and others who regularly predict such returns. Goldman Sachs, Merrill Lynch, and other investment banks make these predictions, often on a monthly basis. These estimated annual returns are for the immediate future. The expected return on the market portfolio has exceeded the risk-free rate by anywhere from 5 to 8 percent in recent years. Expressed differently, the "before-hand" or *ex ante* market risk premium has ranged from 5 to 8 percent. This is not the range of risk premiums actually realized over some holding period but rather the expected risk premium for investing in the market portfolio as opposed to the risk-free security. Due to changes in expected inflation, interest rates, and the degree of investor risk aversion in society, both the risk-free rate and the expected market return change over time. Therefore, the 14 percent figure that we computed earlier would be an estimate of the required return on equity at only a particular moment in time.

If measurements were exact and the assumption of a perfect capital market held,[3] the cost of equity determined by this method would be the same as that provided by a dividend discount model. Recall that the latter estimate is the discount rate that equates the present value of the stream of expected future dividends with the current market price of the stock. By now it should be apparent that we can only hope to approximate the cost of equity capital. We believe that the methods suggested enable such an approximation more or less accurately, depending on the situation. For a large company whose stock is actively traded on the New York Stock Exchange and whose systematic risk is close to that of the market as a whole, we can usually estimate more confidently than we can for a moderate-sized company whose stock is inactively traded in the over-the-counter market and whose systematic risk is very large. We must live with the inexactness involved in the measurement process and try to do as good a job as possible.

Cost of Equity: Before-Tax Cost of Debt Plus Risk Premium Approach

Rather than estimate the required return on equity capital using the sophisticated methods previously described, some people use a relatively simple, "quick and dirty," approach. Here the company's before-tax cost of debt forms the basis for estimating the firm's cost of equity. The firm's before-tax cost of debt will exceed the risk-free rate by a risk premium. The greater the risk of the firm, the greater this premium, and the more interest the firm must pay in order to borrow. The relationship is illustrated in Figure 15-2. On the horizontal axis, the firm's debt is shown to have

---

[3]As discussed in Chapter 5, the capital-asset pricing model assumes the presence of perfect capital markets. When this assumption is relaxed to take account of real-world conditions, the unsystematic risk of a stock may take on a degree of importance. We know that the total risk of a security is composed of its systematic as well as its unsystematic risk. The assumption of the capital-asset pricing model is that unsystematic risk can be completely diversified away, leaving us with only systematic risk.

If imperfections exist in the capital markets, these may impede efficient diversification by investors. (One example of an imperfection is the presence of significant bankruptcy costs.) The greater the imperfections that are believed to exist, the greater the allowance that must be made for the return on common stock to also provide compensation for unsystematic risk. As a result, it would be necessary to adjust upward the required rate of return on equity.

FIGURE 15-2
The Security Market
Line (SML) with Debt
and Stock Illustrated

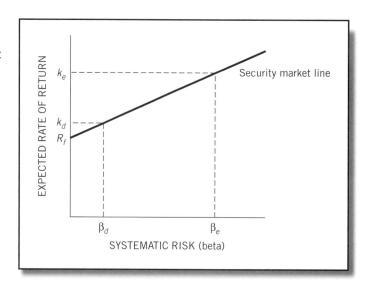

systematic risk equal to β_d. As a result, its required return is k_d, which exceeds the risk-free rate of R_f.

In addition to this risk premium, the common stock of a company must provide a higher expected return than the debt of the same company. The reason is that there is more systematic risk involved. This phenomenon is also illustrated in Figure 15-2. We see that for an equity beta of β_e, an expected return of k_e is required and that this percentage exceeds the company's before-tax cost of debt, k_d. The historical (modern era) risk premium in expected return for stocks over corporate bonds has been around 5 percent. If this seemed reasonable for a particular company, one could use the firm's before-tax cost of debt as a base and add to it a premium of around 5 percent to estimate its cost of equity capital.

To illustrate, suppose that Schlosky's Paint Company's bonds sell in the market to yield 9 percent. Using the approach just outlined, we find the company's approximate cost of equity would be

$$k_e = \begin{matrix} \text{Before-tax} \\ \text{cost of} \\ \text{debt } (k_d) \end{matrix} + \begin{matrix} \text{Risk premium in} \\ \text{expected return for} \\ \text{stock over debt} \end{matrix} \qquad \textbf{(15-8)}$$

$$= \quad 9\% \quad + \quad 5\% = \textbf{14\%}$$

This percentage would then be used as an estimate of the cost of equity capital. The advantage of this approach is that one does not have to use beta information and make the calculation involved in Eq. (15-7). One disadvantage is that it does not allow for changing risk premiums over time. Also, because the 5 percent risk premium is based on an average for companies overall, the approach is not as accurate as either of the other methods discussed for estimating the required return on equity capital for a specific company. It does, however, offer an alternative method of estimating the cost of equity capital that falls within the overall framework of the capital-asset pricing model. It also provides a ready check on the reasonableness of the answers we get from applying the more complicated estimation techniques.

Part VI The Cost of Capital, Capital Structure, and Dividend Policy

Weighted Average Cost of Capital

Once we have computed the costs of the individual components of the firm's financing,[4] we would assign weights to each financing source according to some standard and then calculate a weighted average cost of capital (WACC). Thus, the firm's overall cost of capital can be expressed as

$$\text{Cost of capital} = \sum_{x=1}^{n} k_x(W_x) \qquad \text{(15-9)}$$

where k_x is the after-tax cost of the xth method of financing, W_x is the weight given to that method of financing as a percentage of the firm's total financing, and Σ denotes the summation for financing methods 1 through n. To illustrate the calculations involved, suppose that a firm had the following financing at the latest balance sheet statement date, where the amounts shown in the table below represent market values.

	AMOUNT OF FINANCING	PROPORTION OF TOTAL FINANCING
Debt	$ 30 million	30%
Preferred stock	10 million	10
Common stock equity	60 million	60
	$100 million	100%

Take Note

> Remember, common stock equity on our books is the sum total of common stock at par, additional paid-in capital, and retained earnings. For market value purposes, however, it is represented by the current market price per share of common stock times the number of shares outstanding. In calculating proportions, it is important that we use *market value* as opposed to *book value* weights. Because we are trying to maximize the value of the firm to its shareholders, only market value weights are consistent with our objective. Market values are used in the calculation of costs of the various components of financing, so market value weights should be used in determining the weighted average cost of capital. (Also, we are implicitly assuming that the current financing proportions will be maintained into the future. We will have more to say on this issue a little later in the chapter.)

To continue with our illustration, suppose that the firm computed the following after-tax costs for the component sources of financing:

	COST
Debt	6.6%
Preferred stock	10.2
Common stock equity	14.0

---

[4]Debt, preferred stock, and equity are the major types of financing. So, generally we have

$$\text{Cost of capital} = k_i(W_i) + k_p(W_p) + k_e(W_e)$$

However, there are other types of financing, such as leasing and convertible securities. Because determining the costs of these other financing sources involves some special and rather complex issues, we treat them in individual chapters, where we are able to give such issues proper attention. For our purposes in this chapter, knowing the costs of debt, preferred stock, and equity financing is sufficient for illustrating the overall cost of capital for a company. When costs are determined for other types of financing, they can be inserted in the weighting scheme to be discussed now.

Again we emphasize that these costs must be present-day costs based on current financial market conditions. Past embedded costs of financing have no bearing on the required rate of return to be applied to new projects. Given the costs shown, the weighted average cost of capital for this example problem is determined as follows:

	(1) COST	(2) PROPORTION OF TOTAL FINANCING	(1) × (2) WEIGHTED COST
Debt	6.6%	30%	1.98%
Preferred stock	10.2	10	1.02
Common stock equity	14.0	60	8.40
		100%	**11.40%**

Thus, given the assumptions of this example, 11.4 percent represents the weighted average cost of the component sources of financing, where each component is weighted according to market value proportions.

Some Limitations

With the calculation of a weighted average cost of capital, the critical question is whether the figure represents the firm's real cost of capital. The answer depends on how accurately we have measured the individual marginal costs, on the weighting system, and on certain other assumptions. Assume for now that we are able to accurately measure the marginal costs of the individual sources of financing, and let us examine the importance of the weighting system.

Weighting System.   The critical assumption in any weighting system is that the firm will in fact raise capital in the proportions specified. Because the firm raises capital *marginally* to make *marginal* investments in new projects, we need to work with the marginal cost of capital for the firm as a whole. This rate depends on the package of funds employed to finance investment projects. In other words, our concern is with new or incremental capital, not with capital raised in the past. For the weighted average cost of capital to represent a marginal cost, the weights employed must be marginal. That is, the weights must correspond to the proportions of financing inputs the firm intends to employ. If they do not, capital is raised on a marginal basis in proportions other than those used to calculate this cost. As a result, the real weighted average cost of capital will differ from that calculated and used for capital investment decisions. If the real cost is greater than that which is measured, certain investment projects that will leave investors worse off than before will be accepted. On the other hand, if the real cost is less than the measured cost, projects that could increase shareholder wealth will be rejected. Therefore, the 11.4 percent weighted average cost of capital computed in our example is realistic only if the firm intends to finance in the future in the same proportions as its existing capital structure would imply.

Raising capital is "lumpy," and strict proportions cannot be maintained. For example, a firm would have difficulty financing each project with exactly 30 percent debt, 10 percent preferred stock, and 60 percent equity. In practice, it may finance with debt in one instance and with preferred stock or equity in another. Over time, however, most firms are able to finance in a roughly proportional manner. It is in this sense that we try to measure the marginal cost of capital for the package of financing employed.

Flotation Costs. Flotation costs involved in the sale of debt instruments, preferred stock, or common stock affect the profitability of a firm's investments. In many cases, the new issue must be priced below the market price of existing financing. In addition, there are out-of-pocket flotation costs. Owing to flotation costs, the amount of funds the firm receives is less than the price at which the issue is sold. The presence of flotation costs in financing requires that an adjustment be made in the evaluation of investment proposals.

One approach, which we refer to as the adjustment to initial outlay (AIO) method, treats the flotation costs of financing as an addition to the initial cash outlay for the project. According to this procedure, the net present value of a project is computed according to:[5]

$$NPV = \sum_{t=1}^{n} \frac{CF_t}{(1 + k)^t} - (ICO + \text{Flotation costs}) \qquad \textbf{(15-10)}$$

where CF_t is the project cash flow at time, t, ICO is the initial cash outlay required for the project, and k is the firm's cost of capital.

Suppose that an investment proposal costs $100,000 and that to finance the project the company must raise $60,000 externally. Both debt and common stock are involved, and after-tax flotation costs (in present value terms) come to $4,000.[6] Therefore, $4,000 should be added to $100,000, bringing the total initial outlay to $104,000. In this way, the proposal is properly "penalized" for the flotation costs associated with its financing. The expected future cash flows associated with the project are then discounted at the weighted average cost of capital. If the project were expected to provide annual after-tax cash inflows of $24,000 for 20 years and the weighted average cost of capital were 20 percent, the project's net present value would be

$$NPV = \sum_{t=1}^{20} \frac{\$24,000}{(1 + .20)^t} - (\$100,000 + \$4,000)$$

$$= \$24,000(PVIFA_{20\%,20}) - \$104,000$$

$$= \$116,870 - \$104,000 = \mathbf{\$12,870}$$

This amount contrasts with a net present value of $116,870 - $100,000 = **$16,870** if no adjustment is made for flotation costs.

A second, more traditional approach calls for an upward adjustment of the cost of capital when flotation costs are present. This method, which we refer to as the adjustment to discount rate (ADR) procedure, thus adjusts a project's discount rate

---

[5]Alternatively, expressing flotation costs as a percentage of the initial investment, f = flotation costs/ICO, we can rewrite Eq. (15-10) as follows

$$NPV = \sum_{t=1}^{n} \frac{CF_t}{(1 + k)^t} - ICO(1 + f)$$

This alternative formula may come in handy when trying to estimate actual future flotation costs proves difficult. One could use instead a flotation cost percentage based on past experience.

[6]Equity flotation costs are not tax deductible. Debt flotation costs, however, are a tax-deductible expense amortized over the life of the debt issue. Therefore, we reduce out-of-pocket total flotation costs by the present value of the debt flotation cost tax-shield benefits provided over the life of the debt issue.

for flotation costs and not the project's cash flows. Under this procedure each component cost of capital would be recalculated by finding the discount rate that equates the present value of cash flows to the suppliers of capital with the *net proceeds* of a security issue, rather than with the security's market price. The resulting "adjusted" component costs would then be weighted and combined to produce an overall "adjusted" cost of capital for the firm.

The "adjusted" cost of capital figure thus calculated will always be greater than the "unadjusted" cost of capital figure, which we have described in this chapter. However, NPVs calculated under the AIO and ADR methods will (with rare exceptions) have different numerical values and may, in fact, have opposite signs. Thus, the question of which method is "correct" is not a matter of indifference.

Advocates of the AIO method argue that it is superior to the ADR method because (1) it is simpler and/or (2) the discount rate derived under the ADR approach is not the "true" cost of capital and therefore does not give the "true" market value of a project's cash flows.[7] We tend to agree with both arguments and therefore favor the AIO method. We suggest that a flotation cost adjustment be made to the project's initial cash outlay and that the weighted average "unadjusted" cost of capital be used as the discount rate. However, we should point out that in many circumstances (for example, where external financing is a small proportion of total project financing) the differences in resulting NPVs under the two alternative methods will be small. In such cases, the ADR method is acceptable.

QUESTION•ANSWER•QUESTION•ANSWER

Some projects that a firm accepts will undoubtedly result in zero or negative returns. Therefore, shouldn't the firm adjust its hurdle rate upward to ensure that the weighted average return on its total new investments meets or exceeds the firm's cost of capital?

No. Arbitrarily raising the firm's hurdle rate means that the firm will be rejecting some projects with otherwise positive net present values. Only by accepting all positive net present value projects does the firm maximize its ability to offset any nonearning investments.

Rationale for a Weighted Average Cost

The rationale behind the use of a weighted average cost of capital is that by financing in the proportions specified and accepting projects yielding more than the weighted average required return, the firm is able to increase the market price of its stock. This increase occurs because investment projects are expected to return more on their equity-financed portions than the required return on equity capital, k_e. Once these expectations are apparent to the marketplace, the market price of the firm's stock should rise because expected future earnings per share (and dividends per share) are higher than those expected before the projects were accepted. The firm has accepted projects that are expected to provide a return greater than that required by investors at the margin, based on the risk involved.

---

[7]For a defense of the AIO procedure, see John R. Ezzell and R. Burr Porter, "Flotation Costs and the Weighted Average Cost of Capital," *Journal of Financial and Quantitative Analysis* 11 (September 1976), 403–13.

We must return to the critical assumption that over time the firm finances projects in the proportions specified. If it does so, the financial risk of the company remains roughly unchanged. As we shall see in Chapter 17, the "implicit" costs of financing are embodied in the weighted average cost of capital by virtue of the fact that a firm has to supplement nonequity financing with equity financing. It does not continually raise capital with supposedly cheaper debt funds without increasing its equity base. The firm's financing mix need not be optimal for the firm to employ the weighted average cost of capital for capital budgeting purposes. The important consideration is that the weights be based on the future financing plans of the company. If they are not, the weighted average cost of capital calculated does not correspond to the actual cost of funds obtained. As a result, capital budgeting decisions are likely to be suboptimal.

QUESTION•ANSWER•QUESTION•ANSWER

Felsham Industries plans on financing *all* of its new capital budgeting projects this year with long-term debt. Therefore, its cost of capital this year should be the after-tax cost of its new debt—right?

Wrong. Firms frequently finance new projects with long-term debt one year and equity the next. The firm's capital structure will thus vary somewhat year to year from its optimal level. It is the firm's long-term, target capital structure along with its associated component costs and market value weights that should be used to determine the firm's cost of capital. To do otherwise would cause the firm's cost of capital (hurdle rate) to be overly generous (low) in years when debt financing is primarily employed and unduly severe (high) in years when equity capital is primarily used to finance new projects.

The use of a weighted average cost of capital figure must also be qualified for the points raised earlier. It assumes that the investment proposals being considered do not differ in systematic, or unavoidable, risk from that of the firm and that the unsystematic risk of the proposals does not provide any diversification benefits to the firm. Only under these circumstances is the cost of capital figure obtained appropriate as an acceptance criterion. These assumptions are extremely limiting. They imply that the projects of a firm are completely alike with respect to risk and that only projects of the same risk will be considered.

In actual practice, however, the issue is one of degree. If the conditions noted are approximately met, then the company's weighted average cost of capital may be used as the acceptance criterion. If a firm produced only one product and all proposals considered were in conjunction with the marketing and production of the product, the use of the firm's overall cost of capital as the acceptance criterion would probably be appropriate. (Even here, however, there may be significant enough differences in risk among investment proposals to warrant separate consideration.) For a multiproduct firm with investment proposals of varying risk, the use of an overall required return is inappropriate. Here a required rate of return based on the risk characteristics of the specific proposal should be used. We will determine these project-specific required rates of return with the methods proposed in the next section. The key, then, to using the overall cost of capital as a project's required rate of return is the similarity of the project with respect to the risk of existing projects and investment proposals under consideration.

Economic Value Added (EVA)

Another way of expressing the fact that to create value a company must earn returns on invested capital greater than its cost of capital is through the concept of **economic value added (EVA).** EVA is the trademarked name for a specific approach to calculating *economic profit* developed by the consulting firm of Stern Stewart & Co. The concept of economic profit (or residual income) has been discussed in the economic literature for more than 100 years. EVA, however, was introduced in the late 1980s. Basically, EVA is the economic profit a company earns after all capital costs are deducted. More specifically, it is a firm's net operating profit after tax (NOPAT) minus a dollar-amount cost of capital charge for the capital employed. Although the basic EVA calculation appears quite simple, Stern Stewart's specific method of calculating EVA includes a long list of possible adjustments to the accounting figures. Adjustments are suggested to NOPAT to reflect more of a cash rather than accrual accounting approach to performance. And adjustments are suggested to the accounting book value of capital employed, such as capitalizing research and development (R&D) expenditures to better reflect the investment nature of these expenditures.

Briggs & Stratton Corporation follows a Stern Stewart & Co. approach to EVA (including making some minor adjustments to NOPAT and capital employed). Based on figures reported in Briggs & Stratton's 1998 Annual Report, here is a condensed version of their EVA calculation for 1998:

	(IN THOUSANDS)
Net (adjusted) operating profit after taxes	$90,444
Less: Capital employed × Cost of capital	
$716,112 × 10.0%	71,611
Economic value added	**$18,833**

This says that Briggs & Stratton earned roughly $18.8 million more in profit than is required to cover all costs, including the cost of capital.

EVA's strength comes from its explicit recognition that a firm is not really creating shareholder value until it is able to cover all of its capital costs. *Accounting profit* calculations explicitly consider debt financing charges but exclude the costs related to equity financing. *Economic profit,* and hence EVA, differs from accounting profit in that it includes a charge for *all* the company's capital—both debt and equity. In short, a firm showing a positive accounting profit could actually be destroying value because shareholders might not be earning their required return. Thus, a positive EVA value generally indicates that shareholder value is being created, whereas a negative EVA value suggests value destruction.

EVA enjoys growing popularity because it serves as a constant reminder to managers that they have not really done a good job unless and until they have earned a return that covers their cost of capital. To the extent a company finds that the EVA concept better links corporate strategy and investments with shareholder value, it is a useful device. It also helps underscore why it is so important for all managers to understand the concept of the cost of capital.

THE CAPM: PROJECT-SPECIFIC AND GROUP-SPECIFIC REQUIRED RATES OF RETURN

When the existing investment projects of the firm and investment proposals under consideration are not alike with respect to risk, the use of the firm's cost of capital as the sole acceptance criterion will not do. In such cases, we must formulate a specific acceptance criterion for the particular project involved. One means for so doing relies on the capital-asset pricing model (CAPM). This CAPM approach is described in this section.

Capital-Asset Pricing Model Approach to Project Selection

We assume initially that projects will be financed entirely by equity, that the firm considering projects is entirely equity financed, and that all beta information pertains to all-equity situations. Later we modify the approach for financial leverage, but our understanding of the basics is made much easier if we first ignore this consideration. This simplifying assumption results in the firm's overall cost of capital being simply its cost of equity. For such a firm, the CAPM approach to determining a required return is equivalent to determining the cost of equity capital of a firm. However, instead of the expected relationship between excess returns for common stock (returns in excess of the risk-free rate) and those for the market portfolio, one is concerned with the expected relationship of excess returns for a project and those for the market portfolio. The required return for an equity-financed project, therefore, would be

$$R_k = R_f + (\bar{R}_m - R_f)\beta_k \qquad \text{(15-11)}$$

where β_k is the slope of the *characteristic line* that describes the relationship between excess returns for project k and those for the market portfolio. As can be seen, the right-hand side of this equation is identical to that of Eq. (15-7) except for the substitution of the project's beta for that of the stock. R_k, then, becomes the required return for the project, which compensates for the project's systematic risk.

Assuming that the firm intends to finance a project entirely with equity, the acceptance criterion would then be to invest in the project if its expected return met or exceeded the required return, R_k, as determined by Eq. (15-11).[8] To illustrate the acceptance criterion for projects using this concept, see Figure 15-3. The line in the figure represents the security market line—the market-determined relationship

---

[8]Alternatively, the required rate of return, R_k, could be used as the appropriate discount rate for calculating the project's net present value, in which case the acceptance criterion would be to invest in the project if its net present value was greater than or equal to zero.

FIGURE 15-3
Creating Value by Accepting Projects Expected to Provide Returns Greater than their Respective Required Returns

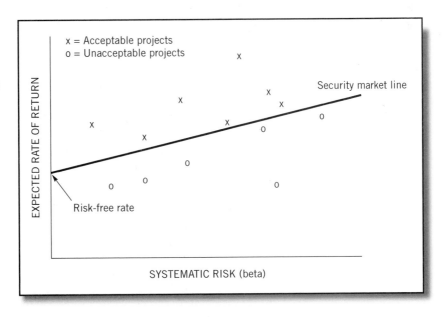

between required rate of return and systematic risk. All projects with internal rates of return lying on or above the line should be accepted, because they are expected to provide returns greater than or equal to their respective required returns. Acceptable projects are depicted by x's. All projects lying below the line, shown by the o's, would be rejected. Note that the greater the systematic risk of a project, the greater the return that is required. If a project had no systematic risk, only the risk-free rate would be required. For projects with more risk, however, a risk premium is demanded, and it increases with the degree of systematic risk of the project. The goal of the firm, in this context, is to search for investment opportunities lying above the line.

Application of the Model—the Use of Proxy Companies. The difficulty in applying the CAPM approach to project selection is in estimating the beta for a project. Recall from Chapter 5 that derivation of the *characteristic line* (whose slope equals beta) is based on a series of period returns for a stock and those for the market portfolio. It is therefore necessary to estimate a project's period returns in terms of its periodic cash flows and its change in value from the beginning of each period to the end of that period. The difficulty is in estimating the value of the project from period to period. Unfortunately, the values of assets that are not publicly traded are not directly observable, so we cannot calculate beta in the manner presented earlier for a publicly traded stock.

However, in many cases a project is sufficiently similar to a company whose stock is publicly held so that we can use that company's beta in deriving the required rate of return on equity for the project. For large projects one can frequently identify publicly traded companies that are engaged entirely, or almost entirely, in the same type of operation. The important thing is to identify a company or companies with systematic risk characteristics similar to those of the project in question.

Suppose that a chemical company is considering the formation of a real estate division. Because there are a number of real estate companies with publicly traded stock, one could simply determine the beta for one of those companies, or a group of them, and use it in Eq. (15-11) to derive the required rate of return for the project. Note that the relevant required rate of return is not that for the chemical company but that for other real estate firms. Stated differently, the market views the chemical company's potential real estate venture in the same way that it views other firms engaged solely in real estate. By concentrating on companies in the same line of business as the firm desires to enter, we can find surrogates that approximate the systematic risk of the project. An exact duplication of the project's risk is unlikely, but reasonable approximations are frequently possible.

To illustrate the calculations, suppose that the median beta for a sample of real estate companies whose stocks were publicly traded and whose basic businesses were similar to the venture contemplated by the chemical company was 1.6. We can use this beta as a surrogate for the beta of the project.[9] If we expect the average return on the market portfolio of stocks to be 13 percent and the risk-free rate to be 8 percent, the required return on equity for the project would be

$$R_k = .08 + (.13 - .08)1.6 = \mathbf{16\%}$$

Therefore, 16 percent would be used as the required equity return for the project.

Finding Proxy Companies. One should try to identify companies of a similar nature to the project in question. The search for these companies is usually industry

---

[9]If the proxy company did not have financing similar to our firm, we would need to adjust this company's beta for the difference in relative financial risk. We will have more to say on this later in the chapter.

North American Industry Classification System (NAICS, pronounced "nakes") **Codes** A standardized classification of businesses by types of economic activity developed jointly by Canada, Mexico, and the United States. A five- or six-digit code number is assigned depending on how a business is defined.

based. One option is to turn to the **North American Industry Classification System (NAICS,** pronounced "nakes") **Codes** to determine an initial sample.[10] When a project falls into a single industry classification, the job is relatively easy. The betas of the proxy companies should be rank ordered. Rather than computing an arithmetic average of the sample betas, we suggest taking a median or modal value from the rank-ordered array. This choice helps minimize the effects of any outliers in the group. The idea is to come up with a beta that broadly portrays the business risk of the investment project.

Unless one is able to find a company or companies whose stock is publicly traded to use as a proxy for the project, the derivation of a beta for a specific project is a difficult matter. For this reason, we will restrict our discussion to the use of proxy company information. Sometimes a mutual fund specializes in common stocks in a specific industry. In such a case, one might use the fund's beta and industry leverage ratio to measure the project's systematic risk.

The Required Return with Leverage.   If the firm consistently finances its projects only with equity, we would use the required return on equity, R_k, as the required rate of return for the project. If some debt financing is employed, however, we need to determine a weighted average required return. Here the weighting system is the same as that illustrated earlier for the firm's overall cost of capital. Rather than vary the proportion of debt financing project by project, a more consistent approach is to apply the same weights to all projects. Presumably these weights will correspond to the proportions with which the firm intends to finance over time. If, for example, the firm intends to finance with one part debt for every three parts equity, and the after-tax cost of debt is 6.60 percent and the required return on equity is 16 percent, the overall (weighted average) required return for the project is

$$\begin{array}{c}\text{Weighted average}\\\text{required return}\end{array} = \begin{bmatrix}\text{Cost of}\\\text{debt}\end{bmatrix}\begin{bmatrix}\text{Proportion}\\\text{of debt}\end{bmatrix} + \begin{bmatrix}\text{Cost of}\\\text{equity}\end{bmatrix}\begin{bmatrix}\text{Proportion}\\\text{of equity}\end{bmatrix}$$

$$= (.066)(.25) + (.16)(.75) = \textbf{13.65\%}$$

If the project were expected to provide an internal rate of return greater than or equal to this rate, the project would be accepted. If not, it would be rejected. Thus, even for a leveraged firm, the acceptance criterion remains specifically related to the systematic risk of the project through the cost of equity capital.

Group-Specific Required Return

Rather than determine project-specific required returns, some companies categorize projects into roughly risk-equivalent groups and then apply the same CAPM-determined required return to all projects included within that group. One advantage to this procedure is that it is not as time-consuming as computing required returns for each project. Another advantage is that it is often easier to find proxy companies for a group than it is for individual projects. By "group," we mean some subunit of the company that carries on a set of activities that can be differentiated from the other activities of the firm. Usually these activities are differentiated along product or service lines as well as along management lines. Frequently the subunits are divisions or **subsidiaries** of the company.

Subsidiary A company which has more than half of its voting shares owned by another company (the parent company).

If the products or services of the group are similar with respect to risk and new proposals are of the same sort, a group-specific required return is an appropriate

---

[10]NAICS replaces the older *Standard Industrial Classification (SIC) System.*

acceptance criterion. It represents the rate charged by the company against a group for capital employed. Stated differently, it is the rate of return the company expects the group to earn on its capital investments. The greater the systematic risk of the group, the greater its required return.

The computation of the required rate of return is the same as that for the specific project. For each group, proxy companies whose stocks are publicly traded are identified. Based on these surrogates, a beta is derived for each group, and a required return on equity capital is calculated from this. If debt is used, a weighted average required return for the group is derived in the same manner as in the previous section. Once group-specific required returns are computed, capital is allocated, or transferred, throughout the firm on the basis of each group's ability to earn its required rate of return. This approach provides a consistent framework for allocating capital among groups with greatly different risks.

The "group-specific required return approach" to project selection is illustrated in Figure 15-4. Here, the horizontal bars represent the required returns, or hurdles, for four different groups. The cost of capital for the firm as a whole is depicted by the dashed line. Projects from a group that provide expected returns above their group-specific bar should be accepted. Those below their respective bars should be rejected. This criterion means that for the two "lower-risk" groups, some accepted projects may provide expected returns below the firm's overall cost of capital but above the required return for the group. For the two "riskier" groups, rejected projects may have provided expected returns greater than the overall cost of capital but less than the group's required return. In short, capital is allocated on a risk-return basis specific to the systematic risk of the group. Otherwise, accept/reject decisions will be biased in favor of bad, high-risk projects and against good, low-risk projects.

Some Qualifications

Whether the required returns are project specific or group specific, there are certain problems in the application of the CAPM approach. For one thing, the amount of nonequity financing that is attributed to a project is an important consideration. For

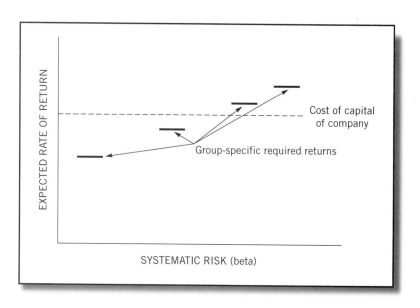

FIGURE 15-4
Comparison of a Company's Cost of Capital and Group-Specific Required Returns

Part VI The Cost of Capital, Capital Structure, and Dividend Policy

the procedure to hold, non-equity financing should approximate the same relative amount as that used by the proxy company. In other words, the proportion of non-equity financing allocated to a project should not be significantly out of line with that for the proxy company being used. Otherwise, one will not get a reasonable proxy for the systematic risk of the project. Where the proportions are not nearly the same, the proxy company's beta should be adjusted before it is used in determining the cost of equity capital for the project. A procedure for adjusting the beta is presented in Appendix A to this chapter. Using this procedure, one can derive an adjusted beta for the proxy company—a beta that assumes that the proxy company had the same relative proportion of nonequity financing as that contemplated for the project. Armed with this adjusted beta, the cost of equity capital for the project can then be determined in the same manner as before.

In addition to any practical problems encountered, there is an underlying assumption in the CAPM approach that must be questioned. As we know, the capital-asset pricing model assumes that only the systematic risk of the firm is important. However, the probability of a firm becoming insolvent depends on its total risk, not just its systematic risk. When insolvency or bankruptcy costs are significant, investors may be served by the firm paying attention to the impact of a project on the firm's total risk. The total risk is composed of both systematic and unsystematic risk. The variability of cash flows determines the possibility of a company becoming insolvent, and this variability depends on the firm's total risk, not just its systematic risk.[11] For this reason, a company may wish to estimate the impact of a new project on both systematic and total risk.

Ascribing Debt Funds to Groups

When determining the weighted average required return for a group, most analysts use the company's overall after-tax borrowing cost as the cost of debt component. However, the notion that equity costs differ according to a group's underlying risk also applies to the cost of debt funds. Both types of costs are determined in capital markets according to a risk-return trade-off. The greater the risk, the greater the interest rate that will be required on debt funds. Although a case can be made for differentiating debt costs among groups according to their systematic risks, few companies do it. For one thing, there are mechanical difficulties in computing the beta, because the market index must include debt instruments. Also, conceptually, the group itself is not ultimately responsible for its debt. The company as a whole is responsible. Because of the diversification of cash flows among groups, the probability of payment for the whole (the firm) may be greater than the sum of the parts (the groups). For these reasons, few companies have tried to apply the capital-asset pricing model to group debt costs as they have to equity costs. Still, it may be appropriate to vary debt costs for groups depending on their risk, even though the adjustment is partly subjective.

If a much higher than average proportion of debt is ascribed to one group, it will have a lower overall required return assigned to it than would otherwise be the case. But is that figure the "true" required return for that group? Should one group be allowed to significantly lower its required return simply by taking on more leverage?

---

[11]When there are significant bankruptcy costs, these costs work to the detriment of stockholders as the residual owners of the company. It therefore may be important for the firm to keep the probability of becoming bankrupt within reasonable bounds. To do so, the company must consider the impact of the project on the firm's total risk (systematic plus unsystematic). This approach is taken up in the last section of the chapter.

Is it fair to other groups? Apart from the incentive issue, what problems are created for the company as a whole by such a policy?

First, high leverage for one group may cause the cost of debt funds for the overall company to rise. This marginal increase should not be allocated across groups, but rather it should be pinpointed to the group responsible. Second, the high leverage incurred by one group may increase the uncertainty of the tax shield associated with debt for the company as a whole. Finally, high leverage for one group increases the volatility of returns to stockholders of the company, together with the possibility of insolvency and bankruptcy costs being incurred. In turn, this will cause investors to increase the required return on equity to compensate for the increased risk. (The way this comes about will be taken up in Chapter 17.)

For these reasons, the "true" cost of debt for the high-leverage group may be considerably greater than originally imagined. If this is the case, some type of premium should be added to the group's required return to reflect more accurately the "true" cost of capital for the group. The difficulty lies in deciding on what premium is appropriate to assign as an adjustment factor. Any adjustments are usually at least partly subjective. While only an approximation, it is best to make some adjustment in overall group required returns when significantly different debt costs and/or proportions of debt financing are involved.

EVALUATION OF PROJECTS ON THE BASIS OF THEIR TOTAL RISK

When either for theoretical or practical reasons it is not appropriate to compute a required rate of return for a project or group using a CAPM approach, or when we simply want to supplement that approach for the reasons just mentioned, we turn to more subjective means for evaluating risky investments. Many firms deal with the problem in very informal ways. Decision makers simply try to incorporate risk into their judgment on the basis of their "feel" for the projects being evaluated. This "feel" can be improved on by discussions with others familiar with the proposals and the risks inherent in them. Often, such discussions result in a "risk-adjusted discount rate" being applied to the project or group.

Risk-adjusted discount rate (RADR) A required return (discount rate) that is increased relative to the firm's overall cost of capital for projects or groups showing greater than "average" risk and decreased for projects or groups showing less than "average" risk.

Risk-Adjusted Discount Rate Approach

For investment proposals having risk similar to that of an "average" project for the firm, we have already seen that the firm's overall cost of capital can serve as the required rate of return. The **risk-adjusted discount rate (RADR)** approach to investment proposal selection pertains to projects or groups whose outcomes are considered to have greater or less risk than the "average" undertaking of the firm.

Take Note

The RADR approach calls for

- Adjusting the required return (discount rate) *upward* from the firm's overall cost of capital for projects or groups showing *greater* than "average" risk and
- Adjusting the required return (discount rate) *downward* from the firm's overall cost of capital for projects or groups showing *less* than "average" risk.

Thus, in the RADR method, the discount rate is "adjusted" for risk by increasing it relative to the overall cost of capital to compensate for greater risk and lowering it to account for less risk. The project- or group-specific required return then becomes the risk-adjusted discount rate.

If the RADR approach sounds familiar, it should. A CAPM-determined required return could be considered as simply a special type of risk-adjusted rate, but with any adjustment taking place relative to a risk-free return base. However, the RADR approach, unlike the CAPM approach, generally relies on relatively informal, subjective ways of determining the required risk adjustment. The problems with this approach, of course, are that the information used to make risk adjustments is often sketchy and the treatment applied to this information may not be consistent from project to project or over time.

Other project selection approaches try to make better, more consistent use of proposal information. We know from our discussion in Chapter 14 that expected return and risk can be quantified in a consistent manner. Given this information, the question becomes whether a project should be accepted or rejected. We begin to answer this question by examining how management might evaluate a single investment proposal and then move on to combinations of risky investments. The methods that we will employ are firm-risk-oriented in the sense that management does not explicitly consider the effect of the firm's project selection on investors' portfolios. The focus is on total risk, the sum of systematic and unsystematic risk. Management assesses the likely effect of project selection on the variability of cash flows and earnings of the firm. From this assessment, management can then estimate the likely effect on share price. The critical factor from the standpoint of stock valuation is how accurately management is able to link share price with risk-return information for an investment proposal. As we shall see, the linkage tends to be subjective, which detracts from the accuracy of these approaches.

Probability Distribution Approach

You will recall from Chapter 14 that one set of information that can be generated for an investment proposal is the probability distribution of possible net present values. (Remember, in a probability distribution approach we do not initially "adjust" for risk, but rather study it. Therefore, the various cash flows are discounted to their present value at the risk-free rate.) We also saw that by standardizing the dispersion in terms of so many standard deviations from the expected value of the distribution, we can determine the probability that the net present value of the project will be zero or less. In the evaluation of a single proposal, it is unlikely that management would accept an investment proposal having an expected value of net present value of zero unless the probability distribution had no dispersion. In this special case, we would have, by definition, a risk-free proposal providing a risk-free return. For risky investments, the expected net present value would have to exceed zero. How much it would have to exceed zero before acceptance were warranted depends on the amount of dispersion of the probability distribution and the utility preferences of management with respect to risk.

A real problem with this approach is that we cannot relate it directly with the effect of project selection on share price. Management is simply presented with information about the expected return and risk of a project. On the basis of this information it reaches a decision. However, there is no "direct" link between a decision based on this information and the likely reaction of well-diversified stockholders in the company. Thus, any success in using this method depends entirely on the perceptiveness of management in judging investors' trade-off between profitability and risk. Moreover, there is no analysis of the impact of the project on the overall risk of the firm. In essence, the project is evaluated in isolation—separate from the portfolios of the firm's shareholders and separate from the firm's already existing projects.

Contribution to Total Firm Risk: Firm-Portfolio Approach

From Chapter 14 we know that the marginal risk of an individual proposal to the firm as a whole depends on its correlation with existing projects as well as its correlation with proposals under consideration that might be accepted. The appropriate information is the expected value and standard deviation of the probability distribution of possible net present values for all feasible combinations of existing projects and investment proposals under consideration. Assume for now that management is interested only in the marginal impact of an investment proposal on the risk complexion of the firm as a whole.

The selection of the most desirable combination of investments will depend on management's risk preferences with respect to expected net present value and standard deviation. Figure 15-5 shows various combinations of risky investments available to the firm. This figure is the same as Figure 14-7 in Chapter 14 except that here we also superimpose a series of management's **indifference curves.** Management is indifferent to any combination of expected value of net present value and standard deviation on a particular curve. As we move to the left in Figure 15-5, each successive curve represents a greater level of satisfaction. Each dot represents a combination of all of the firm's existing investment projects plus one or more proposals under consideration. We see that certain dots dominate others in the sense that they represent a higher expected value of net present value and the same standard deviation, a lower standard deviation and the same expected value of net present value, or both a higher expected value and a lower standard deviation. The dots that dominate others are those that are located on the leftmost outer edge of the figure. With information of this sort before it, management can eliminate most combinations of risky investments simply because they are dominated by other combinations.

Indifference curve A line representing all combinations of expected return and risk that provide an investor with an equal amount of satisfaction.

FIGURE 15-5
Scatter Diagram Showing the Set of Feasible Combinations (Portfolios) of Projects with Management's Indifference Map Superimposed on This Scatter Diagram

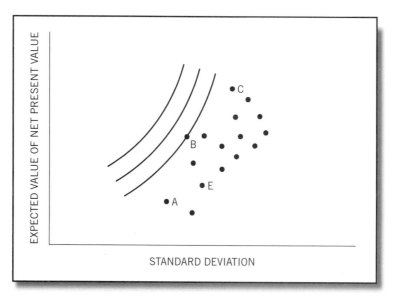

Part VI The Cost of Capital, Capital Structure, and Dividend Policy

In this case, management would probably consider only three combinations of risky investments—A, B, and C. From these it would choose the one that it felt offered the best combination of expected return and risk. If it were moderately averse to risk, as represented by the indifference map shown in Figure 15-5, it would probably choose combination B. This combination is determined by the intersection of a dot in the figure—point B—with the highest attainable indifference curve. Point B represents the portfolio of existing projects and proposals under consideration that possesses the most desirable combination of expected value of net present value and standard deviation. Though combination C provides a somewhat higher expected value of net present value, it also has a higher standard deviation. Combination A has lower risk but also lower expected value of net present value.

As discussed in Chapter 14, the final selection determines the new investment proposal or proposals that will be accepted. An exception would occur only when the combination selected was composed solely of existing projects. In this situation, no investment proposals under consideration would be accepted. If the portfolio of existing projects were represented by combination E in the figure, the selection of any of the three outlying combinations would imply the acceptance of one or more new investment proposals. Investment proposals under consideration that were not in the combination finally selected would, of course, be rejected.

Conceptual Implications

On the basis of the information just presented, management determines which investment proposals under consideration offer the best marginal contribution of expected value of net present value and standard deviation to the firm as a whole. In determining the standard deviation for a combination, management must consider the correlation between an investment proposal and the set of existing investments and other new proposed investments. This evaluation suggests that the total risk of the firm is what is important. Investment decisions would then be made in light of their marginal impact on total risk.

This approach implies that from the standpoint of stockholders, management should be concerned with the firm's solvency. As discussed, such solvency depends on the total risk of the firm. Owing to less than perfect correlation with each other, certain projects have diversification properties. As a result, the total risk of the firm will be less than the sum of the parts. Management will presumably endeavor to accept investment proposals in a way that will keep the probability of insolvency within reasonable bounds while providing the best combination of expected return and risk.

As indicated before, the problem with this approach is that it ignores the fact that investors can diversify the portfolios of common stocks that they hold. They are not dependent on the firm to diversify away risk. Therefore, diversification by the firm may not be a thing of value in the sense of doing something for investors that they cannot do for themselves. To the extent that investors are concerned only with the unavoidable or systematic risk of a project, the CAPM approach illustrated earlier should be used.

Dual Approach. It may be reasonable to use both approaches. The CAPM approach might serve as the foundation for judging the valuation implications of an investment project. To the extent that the possibility of insolvency exists and the bankruptcy costs that result are considerable, the project would also be judged in a total firm-risk context. If both approaches give clear accept or reject signals, those signals should be followed. An obvious problem occurs if one approach gives an accept signal while the other gives a reject signal. In this case, management should place more weight on one or the other signal, depending on which approach is more applicable.

If the stock of a large company is publicly held and if the possibility of insolvency is remote, a strong case can be made for using the signal given by the capital-asset pricing model. If the stock is traded in a market with high transactions and information costs, if the possibility of insolvency is significant, and if the expression of project returns in terms of market-based returns is crude, greater reliance should be placed on the total firm-risk approach. Even here, one should recognize that a portion of unsystematic risk can be diversified away.

SUMMARY

- In theory, the required rate of return for an investment project should be the rate that leaves the market price of the stock unchanged. If an investment project earns more than what financial markets require it to earn for the risk involved, value is created. The key sources of value creation are industry attractiveness and competitive advantage.
- If existing investment projects and investment proposals under consideration are similar with respect to risk, it is appropriate to use the overall *cost of capital* as the acceptance criterion.
- The overall *cost of capital* is a weighted average of the individual required rates of return (costs) for the various instruments with which the firm intends to finance.
- By far the most difficult component cost to measure is the *cost of equity capital*. Using a dividend discount model, this cost is the discount rate that equates the present value of the stream of expected future dividends with the market price of the common stock. Alternatively, we can estimate the cost of equity with the capital-asset pricing model or add a risk premium to the before-tax cost of the firm's debt.
- Once we have computed the marginal costs of the individual components of the firm's financing, we assign weights to each financing source and calculate a weighted average cost of capital. The weights employed should correspond to the proportions with which the firm intends to finance long-term.
- The presence of *flotation costs* in financing requires an adjustment in the evaluation of investment proposals. One approach treats the flotation costs of financing as an addition to the initial cash outlay for the project. A second approach calls for an upward adjustment of the cost capital when flotation costs are present. Theoretically, it is more

appropriate to make a flotation cost adjustment to the project's initial cash outlay and then use the weighted average "unadjusted" cost of capital as the discount rate.
- The key to using the overall cost of capital as a project's required rate of return is the similarity of the project with respect to the risk of existing projects and investments under consideration.
- When investment projects, both existing and new, vary widely with respect to risk, use of the company's overall cost of capital as an acceptance criterion is not appropriate. In such cases, we should determine an acceptance criterion for each investment project or group of projects under consideration.
- One means for computing a *project-specific required rate of return* for a proposal is with the capital-asset pricing model. Here the idea is to identify publicly traded companies whose line of business and systematic risk closely parallel the project in question. These companies serve as proxies for developing *beta* information, which may be adjusted for financial leverage. (See Appendix A to this chapter.) Once a representative beta is computed, the required return on equity can be determined. If debt financing is employed, a weighted average required return for the project is calculated, based on the proportions the firm uses in its financing.
- A *group-specific required rate of return* may also be determined for a division, a subsidiary, or some other subunit of the firm with the capital-asset pricing model. Certain problems may arise, however, due to the differential utilization of non-equity financing among various groups of a company.
- The *risk-adjusted discount rate (RADR)* method of investment selection calls for "adjusting" the required return, or discount rate, upward

(downward) from the firm's overall cost of capital for projects or groups showing greater (less) than "average" risk. The RADR approach, unlike the CAPM approach, generally relies on relatively informal, subjective ways of determining the required risk adjustment.

- A practical means for evaluating risky investments is to analyze the expected value and standard deviation of the probability distribution of possible returns for an investment proposal and, on the basis of this information, reach a decision. The greater the dispersion of the distribution, the greater the expected value that would presumably be required by management. The problem with this approach is that the link between the investment decision and anticipated share price reaction is not direct.

- Solvency depends on the total risk of the firm. When the possibility of firm insolvency is real and potentially costly, management may be concerned with the marginal impact of an investment project on the total risk of the firm. By analyzing the expected return and risk of various possible combinations of existing projects and investment proposals under consideration, management is able to select the best combination—often relying on dominance.

Appendix A

Adjusting the Beta for Financial Leverage

The common stock beta for a firm with financial leverage reflects both the *business risk* and the *financial risk* of the company. In attempting to indirectly calculate a project's (or group's) cost of equity capital, we need to use a proxy company that has business risk similar to that of our project. Unfortunately, the proxy firm may use a significantly different proportion of debt than that used by our firm. Therefore, it may be necessary to adjust the beta of the proxy company for this difference in capital structure.

In what follows, we present a way to adjust betas for capital structure differences. This adjustment is made under the assumptions of the capital-asset pricing model with taxes. At the end, we qualify the results somewhat due to considerations to be taken up in Chapter 17.

The required rate of return for common stock in a firm with financial leverage (a "levered" firm) is

$$R_j = R_f + (\bar{R}_m - R_f)\beta_j \qquad \text{(15A-1)}$$

where R_f = risk-free rate

$\bar{R}_m$ = expected return on the market portfolio

β_j = beta measuring the systematic risk of the equity of the levered firm

Equation (15A-1) can also be expressed as[12]

$$R_j = R_f + (\bar{R}_m - R_f)\beta_{ju}[1 + (B/S)(1 - T_c)] \qquad \text{(15A-2)}$$

where β_{ju} = beta measuring the systematic risk of the equity of the firm in the *absence of financial leverage* (the beta if the firm were all-equity-financed or "unlevered")

B/S = debt-to-equity ratio in market value terms

T_c = corporate tax rate

Rewriting Eq. (15A-2), we can clearly see that the required rate of return on equity is composed of the risk-free rate, plus a premium for business risk and a premium for financial risk:

---

[12]See Robert S. Hamada, "Portfolio Analysis, Market Equilibrium and Corporation Finance," *Journal of Finance* 24 (March 1969), 19–30.

$$
\begin{array}{ccccccc}
\text{Required} & & \text{Risk-} & & \text{Business-} & & \text{Finacial-} \\
\text{return} & = & \text{free} & + & \text{risk} & + & \text{risk} \\
& & \text{rate} & & \text{premium} & & \text{premium}
\end{array}
$$

$$
R_j = R_f + (\bar{R}_m - R_f)\beta_{ju} + (\bar{R}_m - R_f)\beta_{ju}(B/S)(1 - T_c)
$$

The measured beta for the stock, β_j, embodies both risks and is simply

$$
\beta_j = \beta_{ju}[1 + (B/S)(1 - T_c)] \tag{15A-3}
$$

Rearranging Eq. (15A-3), the unlevered beta for the stock can be expressed as follows:

$$
\beta_{ju} = \frac{\beta_j}{1 + (B/S)(1 - T_c)} \tag{15A-4}
$$

Given these expressions, we can derive the unlevered beta for a particular stock. Suppose that the measured (levered) beta, β_j, for security j is 1.4; the debt-to-equity ratio, B/S, is .70; and the tax rate is 40 percent. The unlevered beta would be

$$
\beta_{ju} = \frac{1.4}{1 + (.70)(.60)} = \mathbf{.99}
$$

If we now wish to determine the beta with a different amount of financial leverage employed, we would use Eq. (15A-3). Using security j as a proxy for the systematic business risk of our project, we require a debt-to-equity ratio of .30 instead of the .70 for adjusted security j. Therefore, the adjusted beta would be

$$
\text{Adjusted } \beta_j = \beta_{ju}[1 + (B/S)(1 - T_c)]
$$
$$
= (.99)[1 + (.30)(.60)] = \mathbf{1.17}
$$

This beta is higher than the .99 figure for an unlevered security j, but lower than the 1.40 figure for the actual, more highly levered, security j.

In summary, we are able to derive an adjusted beta for a security when the proxy firm uses a different proportion of debt than our own. We first estimate the beta for the stock in the absence of leverage and then adjust this figure for the proportion of leverage we wish to employ. The final result is an approximation of the beta that would prevail if the proxy company were to employ the desired proportion of debt.

Note that the adjustment procedure assumes that all the tenets of the capital-asset pricing model, except for the presence of corporate taxes, hold. With corporate taxes, value is assumed to increase in a linear manner with leverage. Chapter 17 introduces additional imperfections in an overall assessment of the impact of capital structure on valuation. Therefore, the adjustment procedure presented provides an approximate beta when the proportion of debt is varied, but it is only an approximation. For large beta adjustments, the procedure is crude.

Appendix B

Adjusted Present Value

In much of our discussion in Chapter 15, we have focused on the weighted average cost of capital (WACC) as an acceptance criterion. This, of course, is a blended cost of capital where all component costs are embraced. An alternative acceptance criterion is the **adjusted present value (APV)** method, first proposed by Stewart C. Myers.[13] With an APV approach, project

---

[13]Stewart C. Meyers, "Interactions of Corporate Financing and Investment Decisions—Implications for Capital Budgeting," *Journal of Finance* 29 (March 1974), 1–25.

Adjusted present value (APV) The sum of the discounted value of a project's operating cash flows (assuming equity financing) plus the value of any tax-shield benefits of interest associated with the project's financing minus any flotation costs.

cash flows are broken down into two components: operating cash flows and certain cash flows associated with financing the project. These components then are valued so that

$$APV = \frac{\text{Unlevered}}{\text{project value}} + \frac{\text{Value of project}}{\text{financing}} \qquad \text{(15B-1)}$$

The decomposition of cash flows is undertaken so that different discount rates may be used on the components. As operating cash flows are more risky than the financing-related cash flows, they are discounted at a higher rate.

More formally, the adjusted present value is

$$APV = \left[\sum_{t=1}^{n} \frac{CF_t}{(1 + k_{eu})^t} - ICO \right] + \left[\sum_{t=1}^{n} \frac{(I_t)(T_c)}{(1 + k_d)^t} - F \right] \qquad \text{(15B-2)}$$

where CF_t is the after-tax operating cash flow at time t; ICO is the initial cash outlay required for the project; k_{eu} is the required rate of return in the absence of financial leverage (the required rate of return if the firm were all-equity-financed or "unlevered"); I_t is the interest payment on debt at time t; T_c is the corporate tax rate; k_d is the before-tax cost of debt financing; and F is the after-tax flotation cost (in present value terms) associated with financing (debt or equity, or both). The first bracketed term on the right-hand side of Eq. (15B-2) represents the net present value of operating cash flows discounted at the unlevered cost of equity capital. The first component within the second bracketed term is the present value of the **tax-shield** benefits of interest on any debt employed to finance the project. The discount rate used on this component is the before-tax corporate cost of borrowing. This rate is used because the realization of the tax-shield benefits bears a risk comparable to that embraced in the cost of debt funds. Finally, any flotation costs are subtracted to arrive at the project's adjusted present value.

tax shield A tax-deductible expense. The expense protects (shields) an equivalent dollar amount of revenue from being taxed by reducing taxable income.

AN ILLUSTRATION

Tennessee-Atlantic Paper Company is considering a new linerboard machine costing $2 million. It is expected to produce after-tax savings of $400,000 per year for eight years. The required rate of return on unlevered equity is 13 percent. To an all-equity-financed firm, the net present value of the project would be

$$NPV = \sum_{t=1}^{8} \frac{\$400,000}{(1 + .13)^t} - \$2,000,000 = \textbf{-\$80,400}$$

Under these circumstances the project would be rejected. Wally Bord, plant manager at the linerboard mill, is heartbroken, because he really wanted the new machine.

But, all is not lost! After all, it is the policy of the company to finance capital investment projects with 50 percent debt, because that is the target debt to total capitalization of the company. Tennessee-Atlantic Paper Company is able to borrow $1 million at 10 percent interest to finance part of the new machine. (The balance will come from equity funds.) The principal amount of the loan will be repaid in equal year-end installments of $125,000 through the end of the eighth year. (In this way the amount borrowed declines over time along with, we would assume, the value of the depreciating asset.) If the company's tax rate (federal plus state) equals 40 percent, we now have enough information to compute the tax-shield benefits of interest and their present value. Our results are shown in Table 15B-1. We see in column (4) that the present value of the tax-shield benefits of interest totals $132,000.

The adjusted present value of the project is now

$$APV = -\$80,400 + \$132,000 = \textbf{\$51,600}$$

Wally Bord is happy because the project now appears to be acceptable and he can look forward to soon hearing the roar of the shiny, new linerboard machine.

But what about flotation costs? These are the legal, underwriting, printing, and other fees involved in issuing securities. These costs pertain both to new debt and equity, with those

TABLE 15B-1
Schedule for determining the present value of the tax-shield benefits of interest related to the new linerboard machine (in thousands)

END OF YEAR	(1) DEBT OWED AT YEAR END $(1)_{t-1} - \$125$	(2) ANNUAL INTEREST $(1)_{t-1} \times .10$	(3) TAX-SHIELD BENEFITS $(2) \times .40$	(4) PV OF BENEFITS AT 10%
0	$1,000	—	—	—
1	875	$100	$40	$ 36
2	750	88	35	29
3	625	75	30	23
4	500	62	25	17
5	375	50	20	12
6	250	38	15	8
7	125	25	10	5
8	0	12	5	2
				$132

belonging to issuance of new equity usually being higher. Suppose in our example that Tennessee-Atlantic incurs after-tax flotation costs (in present value terms) of $40,000. These costs reduce the company's cash flows such that the adjusted present value becomes

$$APV = -\$80,400 + \$132,000 - \$40,000 = \textbf{\$11,600}$$

The project is still acceptable but provides less benefit than it did when flotation costs were absent.

WACC VERSUS APV METHOD

We have examined two ways of determining the value of a project. One method makes use of the firm's weighted average cost of capital (WACC), and the other relies on finding the project's adjusted present value (APV). The APV is actually a general theoretical rule that can be shown to contain the WACC method as a subcase. In his original article advocating the APV method, Myers pointed to certain biases involved in the WACC method. His article has been followed by a number of challenges and counterchallenges.[14]

Whenever a capital investment occurs, there is an interaction of investment and financing. As a general rule, as long as the firm maintains a relatively constant debt ratio over time and it invests in projects like those it already owns, the WACC method gives a relatively accurate portrayal of a project's worth. This is merely to say that financial risk and business risk are relatively unchanging over time. If a company should depart radically from its previous financing patterns and/or invest in an entirely new line of business (like production of motion pictures by a soft-drink company), then the APV approach could theoretically provide a more accurate answer.

A major advantage of the WACC method is that it is easy to understand and widely used. The APV method is pleasing to many academics, but it is not widely used in business. Also, the APV method is not without its own difficulties. Implied is the assumption that there

---

[14]See James Miles and John R. Ezzell, "The Weighted Average Cost of Capital, Perfect Capital Markets, and Project Life: A Clarification," *Journal of Financial and Quantitative Analysis* 15 (September 1980), 719–30; Donald R. Chambers, Robert S. Harris, and John J. Pringle, "Treatment of Financing Mix in Analyzing Investment Opportunities," *Financial Management* 11 (Summer 1982), 24–41; and Robert A. Taggart Jr., "Consistent Valuation and Cost of Capital Expressions with Corporate and Personal Taxes," Working Paper, National Bureau of Economic Research (August 1989).

are no market imperfections other than corporate taxes and flotation costs. In other words, consideration of the tax-shield benefits of interest and flotation costs are all that matter when it comes to financing decisions. We explore other market imperfections in Chapter 17, when we evaluate capital structure decisions from a broader perspective. For now it is enough to recognize the differences in approach and that for most situations the two approaches (if properly applied) lead to identical accept or reject decisions.

QUESTIONS

1. Why is it important to use *marginal* weights in calculating a weighted average cost of capital?
2. Under what circumstances is it appropriate to use the weighted average cost of capital as an acceptance criterion?
3. Do the funds provided by sources such as accounts payable and accruals have a cost of capital? Explain.
4. What will happen to the cost of debt funds for cost of capital purposes if a company should go into a period when it has negligible profits and pays no taxes?
5. With a dividend discount model, how do you estimate the cost of equity capital? What is the critical variable in this model?
6. What is the critical assumption inherent in the capital-asset pricing model (CAPM) as it relates to the acceptance criterion for risky investments?
7. Instead of using the expected return on the market portfolio and the risk-free rate in a CAPM approach to estimating the required return on equity, how would one use the firm's debt cost in a CAPM-type approach to estimate the firm's required return on equity?
8. What is the purpose of proxy companies in the application of the capital-asset pricing model to estimating required returns?
9. Distinguish a project-specific required return from a group-specific required return.
10. When a project is evaluated on the basis of its total risk, who determines whether the project is acceptable? How? Is share price likely to be maximized?
11. What is the risk-adjusted discount rate (RADR) approach to project selection? How is it similar to the CAPM approach? How is it different from the CAPM approach?
12. What is the distinction between evaluating the expected value of net present value and standard deviation for an individual investment project and those for a group or combination of projects?
13. Should companies in the same industry have approximately the same required rates of return on investment projects? Why or why not?
14. If you use debt funds to finance a project, is the after-tax cost of debt the required return for the project? As long as the project earns more than enough to pay interest and service the principal, does it not benefit the firm?
15. If the cost of bankruptcy proceedings (attorney fees, trustee fees, delays, inefficiencies, and so on) were to rise substantially, would this occurrence have an effect on a company's required rate of return and on the way the firm looks at investment opportunities?
16. Should a company with multiple divisions establish separate required rates of return, or costs of capital, for each division as opposed to using the company's overall cost of capital? Explain.
17. For a corporation investing in capital projects, how is value created by using required return calculations?
18. What are the sources of value creation through capital investment decisions?

SELF-CORRECTION PROBLEMS

1. Silicon Wafer Company presently pays a dividend of $1 per share and has a share price of $20.
   a. If this dividend was expected to grow at a 12 percent rate forever, what is the firm's expected, or required, return on equity using a dividend discount model approach?
   b. Instead of the situation in Part (a), suppose that the dividend was expected to grow at a 20 percent rate for five years and at 10 percent per year thereafter. Now what is the firm's expected, or required, return on equity?
2. Using the capital-asset pricing model, determine the required return on equity for the following situations:

SITUATION	EXPECTED RETURN ON MARKET PORTFOLIO	RISK-FREE RATE	BETA
1	15%	10%	1.00
2	18	14	.70
3	15	8	1.20
4	17	11	.80
5	16	10	1.90

What generalizations can you make?
3. The Sprouts-N-Steel Company has two divisions: health foods and specialty metals. Each division employs debt equal to 30 percent and preferred stock equal to 10 percent of its total requirements, with equity capital used for the remainder. The current borrowing rate is 15 percent, and the company's tax rate is 40 percent. Presently, preferred stock can be sold yielding 13 percent.

   Sprouts-N-Steel wishes to establish a minimum return standard for each division based on the risk of that division. This standard then would serve as the transfer price of capital to the division. The company has thought about using the capital-asset pricing model in this regard. It has identified two samples of companies, with modal value betas of .90 for health foods and 1.30 for specialty metals. (Assume that the sample companies had similar capital structures to that of Sprouts-N-Steel.) The risk-free rate is presently 12 percent and the expected return on the market portfolio 17 percent. Using the CAPM approach, what weighted average required returns on investment would you recommend for these two divisions?
4. You are evaluating two independent projects as to their effect on the total risk and return of your corporation. The projects are expected to result in the following:

	EXPECTED VALUE OF NET PRESENT VALUE OF COMPANY (IN MILLIONS)	STANDARD DEVIATION OF NET PRESENT VALUE (IN MILLIONS)
Existing projects only	$6.00	$3.00
Plus project 1	7.50	4.50
Plus project 2	8.20	3.50
Plus projects 1 and 2	9.70	4.80

   a. In which of the new projects (if any) would you invest? Explain.
   b. What would you do if a CAPM approach to the problem suggested a different decision?

PROBLEMS

1. Zapata Enterprises is financed by two sources of funds: bonds and common stock. The cost of capital for funds provided by bonds is k_i, and k_e is the cost of capital for equity funds. The capital structure consists of B dollars worth of bonds and S dollars worth of stock, where the amounts represent market values. Compute the overall weighted average of cost of capital, k_o.

2. Assume that B (in Problem 1) is $3 million and S is $7 million. The bonds have a 14 percent yield to maturity, and the stock is expected to pay $500,000 in dividends this year. The growth rate of dividends has been 11 percent and is expected to continue at the same rate. Find the cost of capital if the corporation tax rate on income is 40 percent.

3. On January 1, 20X1, International Copy Machines (ICOM), one of the favorites of the stock market, was priced at $300 per share. This price was based on an expected dividend at the end of the year of $3 per share and an expected annual growth rate in dividends of 20 percent into the future. By January 20X2, economic indicators have turned down, and investors have revised their estimate for future dividend growth of ICOM downward to 15 percent. What should be the price of the firm's common stock in January 20X2? Assume the following:

   a. A constant dividend growth valuation model is a reasonable representation of the way the market values ICOM.

   b. The firm does not change the risk complexion of its assets nor its financial leverage.

   c. The expected dividend at the end of 20X2 is $3.45 per share.

4. K-Far Stores has launched an expansion program that should result in the saturation of the Bay Area marketing region of California in six years. As a result, the company is predicting a growth in earnings of 12 percent for three years and 6 percent for the fourth through sixth years, after which it expects constant earnings forever. The company expects to increase its annual dividend per share, most recently $2, in keeping with this growth pattern. Currently, the market price of the stock is $25 per share. Estimate the company's cost of equity capital.

5. The Manx Company was recently formed to manufacture a new product. It has the following capital structure in market value terms:

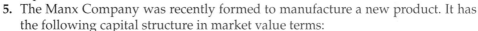

Debentures	$ 6,000,000
Preferred stock	2,000,000
Common stock (320,000 shares)	8,000,000
	$16,000,000

The company has a marginal tax rate of 40 percent. A study of publicly held companies in this line of business suggests that the required return on equity is about 17 percent. (The CAPM approach was used to determine the required rate of return.) The Manx Company's debt is currently yielding 13 percent, and its preferred stock is yielding 12 percent. Compute the firm's present weighted average cost of capital.

6. The R-Bar-M Ranch in Montana would like a new mechanized barn, which will require a $600,000 initial cash outlay. The barn is expected to provide after-tax annual cash savings of $90,000 indefinitely (for practical purposes of computation, forever). The ranch, which is incorporated and has a public market for its stock, has a weighted average cost of capital of 14.5 percent. For this project,

Mark O. Witz, the president, intends to provide $200,000 from a new debt issue and another $200,000 from a new issue of common stock. The balance of the financing would be provided internally by retaining earnings.

The present value of the after-tax flotation costs on the debt issue amount to 2 percent of the total debt raised, whereas flotation costs on the new common stock issue come to 15 percent of the issue. What is the net present value of the project after allowance for flotation costs? Should the ranch invest in the new barn?

7. Cohn and Sitwell, Inc., is considering manufacturing special drill bits and other equipment for oil rigs. The proposed project is currently regarded as complementary to its other lines of business, and the company has certain expertise by virtue of its having a large mechanical engineering staff. Because of the large outlays required to get into the business, management is concerned that Cohn and Sitwell earn a proper return. Since the new venture is believed to be sufficiently different from the company's existing operations, management feels that a required rate of return other than the company's present one should be employed.

The financial manager's staff has identified several companies (with capital structures similar to that of Cohn and Sitwell) engaged solely in the manufacture and sale of oil-drilling equipment whose common stocks are publicly traded. Over the last five years, the median average beta for these companies has been 1.28. The staff believes that 18 percent is a reasonable estimate of the average return on stocks "in general" for the foreseeable future and that the risk-free rate will be around 12 percent. In financing projects, Cohn and Sitwell uses 40 percent debt and 60 percent equity. The after-tax cost of debt is 8 percent.

   a. On the basis of this information, determine a required rate of return for the project, using the CAPM approach.
   b. Is the figure obtained likely to be a realistic estimate of the required rate of return on the project?

8. Acosta Sugar Company has estimated that the overall return for the S&P 500 Index will be 15 percent over the next 10 years. The company also feels that the interest rate on Treasury securities will average 10 percent over this interval. The company is thinking of expanding into a new product line—almonds.

It has no experience in this line but has been able to obtain information on various companies involved in producing and processing nuts. Although no company examined produces only almonds, Acosta's management feels that the beta for such a company would be 1.10, once the almond operation was ongoing. There is some uncertainty about the beta that will actually prevail. (Assume that Acosta and all proxy firms are all-equity-financed.) Management has attached the following probabilities to possible outcomes:

Probability	.2	.3	.2	.2	.1
Beta	1.00	1.10	1.20	1.30	1.40

   a. What is the required rate of return for the project using the mode-average *beta* of 1.10?
   b. What is the range of required rates of return?
   c. What is the expected value of required rate of return?

9. Able Elba Palindrome, Inc., is evaluating a capital investment project. The after-tax cash flows for the project are listed as follows:

YEAR	EXPECTED CASH FLOW
0	$-400,000
1	50,000
2	50,000
3	150,000
4	350,000

The risk-free rate is 8 percent, the firm's weighted average cost of capital is 10 percent, and the management-determined risk-adjusted discount rate appropriate to this project is 15 percent. Should the project be accepted? Explain.

10. The Totally Tubular Tube Company wishes to evaluate three new investment proposals. The firm is concerned with the impact of the proposals on its total risk. Consequently, it has determined expected values and standard deviations of the probability distributions of possible net present values for the possible combinations of existing projects, E, and investment proposals under consideration:

COMBINATION	EXPECTED VALUE OF NET PRESENT VALUE (IN MILLIONS)	STANDARD DEVIATION (IN MILLIONS)
E	$6.50	$5.25
E + 1	6.80	5.00
E + 2	7.60	8.00
E + 3	7.20	6.50
E + 1 + 2	7.90	7.50
E + 1 + 3	7.50	5.60
E + 2 + 3	8.30	8.50
E + 1 + 2 + 3	8.60	9.00

Which combination do you feel is most desirable? Which proposals should be accepted? Which should be rejected?

Appendix A Problem

11. Willie Sutton Bank Vault Company has a debt-to-equity ratio (in market value terms) of .75. Its present cost of debt funds is 15 percent, and it has a marginal tax rate of 40 percent. Willie Sutton Bank Vault is eyeing the automated bank teller business, a field that involves electronics and is considerably different from its own line of business, so the company is looking for a benchmark or proxy company. The Peerless Machine Company, whose stock is publicly traded, produces only automated teller equipment. Peerless has a debt-to-equity ratio (in market value terms) of .25, a beta of 1.15, and an effective tax rate of .40.
    a. If Willie Sutton Bank Vault Company wishes to enter the automated bank teller business, what systematic risk (beta) is involved if it intends to employ the same amount of leverage in the new venture as it presently employs?
    b. If the risk-free rate presently is 13 percent and the expected return on the market portfolio is 17 percent, what return should the company require for the project if it uses a CAPM approach?

Appendix B Problem

12. Aspen Plowing, Inc., is considering investing in a new snowplow truck costing $30,000. The truck is likely to provide after-tax incremental operating cash flows

of $10,000 per year for six years. The unlevered cost of equity capital for the firm is 16 percent. The company intends to finance the project with 60 percent debt, bearing an interest rate of 12 percent. The loan will be repaid in equal annual principal payments at the end of each of the six years. Flotation costs (in present value terms) on financing amount to $1,000, and the company is in a 30 percent tax bracket.

a. What is the adjusted present value (APV) of the project? Is the project acceptable?

b. What would happen if expected after-tax incremental operating cash flows were $8,000 per year instead of $10,000?

Solutions to Self-Correction Problems

1. a. $k_e = D_1/P_0 + g$ $D_1 = D_0(1.12) = \$1(1.12) = \$1.12$
$k_e = \$1.12/\$20 + 12\% = \mathbf{17.6\%}$

b. Through the trial-and-error approach illustrated in Chapters 3 and 4, one ends up determining that the discount rate necessary to discount the cash-dividend stream to $20 must fall somewhere between 18 and 19 percent as follows:

END OF YEAR	DIVIDEND PER SHARE	PRESENT VALUE AT 18%	PRESENT VALUE AT 19%
1	$1.20	$1.02	$1.01
2	1.44	1.03	1.02
3	1.73	1.05	1.03
4	2.07	1.07	1.03
5	2.49	1.09	1.04
Present value, years 1–5		$5.26	$5.13

Year 6 dividend = $2.49 (1.10) = $2.74
Market prices at the end of year 5 using a constant growth dividend valuation model: $P_5 = D_6/(k_e - g)$

$$P_5 = \$2.74/(.18 - .10) = \$34.25, \qquad P_5 = \$2.74/(.19 - .10) = \$30.44$$

Present value at time 0 for amounts received at end of year 5:

$$\$34.25 \text{ at } 18\% = \$14.97, \qquad \$30.44 \text{ at } 19\% = \$12.76$$

	18%	19%
Present value of years 1–5	$ 5.26	$ 5.13
Present value of years 6–∞	14.97	12.76
Present value of all dividends	$20.23	$17.89

Therefore, the discount rate is closer to 18 percent than it is to 19 percent. Interpolating, we get

$$.01 \begin{bmatrix} X \begin{bmatrix} .18 & \$20.23 \\ k_e & \$20.00 \\ .19 & \$17.89 \end{bmatrix} \$.23 \\ \end{bmatrix} \$2.34$$

$$\frac{X}{.01} = \frac{\$.23}{\$2.34} \qquad \text{Therefore,} \quad X = \frac{(.01)(\$.23)}{\$2.34} = .0010$$

and $k_e = .18 + X = .18 + .0010 = \mathbf{18.10\%},$ which is the estimated return on equity that the market requires.

2.

SITUATION	EQUATION: $R_f + (\bar{R}_M - R_f)\beta$	REQUIRED RETURN
1	$10\% + (15\% - 10\%)1.00$	**15.0%**
2	$14\% + (18\% - 14\%)\ .70$	**16.8**
3	$8\% + (15\% - \ 8\%)1.20$	**16.4**
4	$11\% + (17\% - 11\%)\ .80$	**15.8**
5	$10\% + (16\% - 10\%)1.90$	**21.4**

The greater the risk-free rate, the greater the expected return on the market portfolio; and the greater the beta, the greater will be the required return on equity, all other things being the same. In addition, the greater the market risk premium $(\bar{R}_m - R_f)$, the greater the required return, all other things being the same.

3. Cost of debt $= 15\%(1 - .4) = 9\%$

Cost of preferred stock $= 13\%$

Cost of equity for health foods division $= .12 + (.17 - .12).90 = 16.5\%$

Cost of equity for specialty metals division $= .12 + (.17 - .12)1.30 = 18.5\%$

Weighted average required return for health foods division
$= 9\%(.3) + 13\%(.1) + 16.5\%(.6) = \mathbf{13.9\%}$

Weighted average required return for specialty metals division
$= 9\%(.3) + 13\%(.1) + 18.5\%(.6) = \mathbf{15.1\%}$

As mentioned in the text, a conceptual case can be made for adjusting the non-equity costs of financing of the two divisions for differences in systematic risks. However, we have not done so.

4. **a.** The graphs of risk versus return and the coefficients of variation (standard deviation/NPV) for the alternatives are as follows:

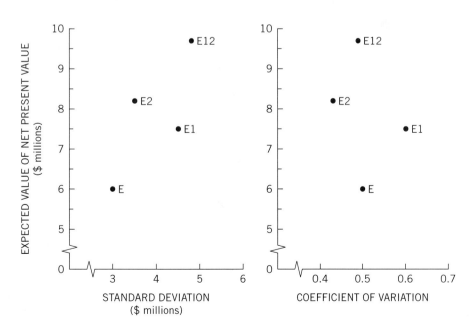

Existing projects (E)	.50
Plus project 1 (E1)	.60
Plus project 2 (E2)	.43
Plus projects 1 and 2 (E12)	.49

A moderately risk-averse decision maker will probably prefer the existing projects plus both new projects to any of the other three possible combinations. If this is the case, both new projects will be accepted. The actual decision will depend on your risk preferences. A very risk-averse individual might prefer the existing projects plus only project 2. Presumably, these preferences will be influenced by the presence of bankruptcy costs.

b. If the CAPM approach leads to a different decision, the key to deciding would be the importance of market imperfections. As indicated earlier, if a company's stock is traded in imperfect markets, if the possibility of insolvency is substantive, and if bankruptcy costs are significant, more reliance should be placed on a total variability approach because it recognizes unsystematic plus systematic risk. If things point to minimal market imperfections, more reliance should be placed on the CAPM results.

SELECTED REFERENCES

Arditti, Fred D., and Haim Levy. "The Weighted Average Cost of Capital as a Cutoff Rate: A Critical Analysis of the Classical Textbook Weighted Average." *Financial Management* 6 (Fall 1977), 24–34.

Ariel, Robert. "Risk Adjusted Discount Rates and the Present Value of Risky Costs." *The Financial Review* 33 (February 1998), 17–29.

Bruner, Robert F., Kenneth M. Eades, Robert S. Harris, and Robert C. Higgins. "Best Practices in Estimating the Cost of Capital: Survey and Synthesis." *Financial Practice and Education* 8 (Spring/Summer 1998), 13–28.

Chambers, Donald R., Robert S. Harris, and John J. Pringle. "Treatment of Financing Mix in Analyzing Investment Opportunities." *Financial Management* 11 (Summer 1982), 24–41.

Conine, Thomas E., Jr., and Maurry Tamarkin. "Division Cost of Capital Estimation: Adjusting for Leverage." *Financial Management* 14 (Spring 1985), 54–58.

Ehrhardt, Michael C., and Yatin N. Bhagwat. "A Full-Information Approach for Estimating Divisional Betas." *Financial Management* 20 (Summer 1991), 60–69.

Ezzell, John R., and R. Burr Porter. "Flotation Costs and the Weighted Average Cost of Capital." *Journal of Financial and Quantitative Analysis* 11 (September 1976), 403–13.

Fuller, Russell J., and Halbert S. Kerr. "Estimating the Divisional Cost of Capital: An Analysis of the Pure-Play Technique." *Journal of Finance* 36 (December 1981), 997–1009.

Greenfield, Robert L., Maury R. Randall, and John C. Woods. "Financial Leverage and Use of the Net Present Value Investment Criterion." *Financial Management* 12 (Autumn 1983), 40–44.

Gup, Benton E., and Samuel W. Norwood III. "Divisional Cost of Capital: A Practical Approach." *Financial Management* 11 (Spring 1982), 20–24.

Hamada, Robert S. "Portfolio Analysis, Market Equilibrium and Corporation Finance." *Journal of Finance* 24 (March 1969), 19–30.

Harrington, Diana R. "Stock Prices, Beta and Strategic Planning." *Harvard Business Review* 61 (May–June 1983), 157–64.

Harris, Robert S., Thomas J. O'Brien, and Doug Wakeman. "Divisional Cost-of-Capital Estimation for Multi-Industry Firms." *Financial Management* 18 (Summer 1989), 74–84.

Harris, Robert S., and John J. Pringle. "Risk-Adjusted Discount Rate—Extensions from the Average-Risk Case." *Journal of Financial Research* 8 (Fall 1985), 237–44.

Howe, Keith M. "A Note on Flotation Costs and Capital Budgeting." *Financial Management* 11 (Winter 1982), 30–33.

Lessard, Donald R., and Richard S. Bower. "An Operational Approach to Risk Screening." *Journal of Finance* 27 (May 1973), 321–38.

Lewellen, Wilbur G., and Douglas R. Emery. "Corporate Debt Management and the Value of the Firm." *Journal of Financial and Quantitative Analysis* 21 (December 1986), 415–25.

Miles, James A., and John R. Ezzell. "The Weighted Average Cost of Capital, Perfect Capital Markets, and Project Life: A Clarification." *Journal of Financial and Quantitative Analysis* 15 (September 1980), 719–30.

———. "Reforming Tax Shield Valuation: A Note." *Journal of Financial Economics* 40 (December 1985), 1485–92.

Myers, Stewart C. "Interactions of Corporate Financing and Investment Decisions—Implications for Capital Budgeting." *Journal of Finance* 29 (March 1974), 1–25.

———. "Determinants of Corporate Borrowing." *Journal of Financial Economics* 5 (November 1977), 147–75.

Porter, Michael E. *Competitive Advantage.* New York: Free Press, 1985.

Pratt, Shannon P. *Cost of Capital: Estimates and Applications.* New York: John Wiley & Sons, 1998.

Rosenburg, Barr, and Andrew Rudd. "The Corporate Use of Beta," *Issues in Corporate Finance.* New York: Stern, Stewart, Putnam & Macklis, Inc., 1983.

Shapiro, Alan C. "Corporate Strategy and the Capital Budgeting Decision." *Midland Corporate Finance Journal* 3 (Spring 1985), 22–36.

———, and Sheridan Titman. "An Integrated Approach to Corporate Risk Management." *Midland Corporate Finance Journal* 3 (Summer 1985), 41–56.

Stein, Jeremy C. "Rational Capital Budgeting in an Irrational World." *Journal of Business* 69 (1996), 429–55.

Stewart, G. Bennett. *The Quest for Value.* New York: Harper Collins, 1991.

Van Horne, James C. "An Application of the Capital Asset Pricing Model to Divisional Required Returns." *Financial Management* 9 (Spring 1980), 14–19.

Chapter 16

Operating and Financial Leverage

OPERATING LEVERAGE
> Break-Even Analysis • Degree of Operating Leverage (DOL)
>> • DOL and the Break-Even Point • DOL and Business Risk

FINANCIAL LEVERAGE
> EBIT-EPS Break-Even, or Indifference, Analysis • Degree
> of Financial Leverage (DFL) • DFL and Financial Risk

TOTAL LEVERAGE
> Degree of Total Leverage (DTL) • DTL and Total Firm Risk

CASH-FLOW ABILITY TO SERVICE DEBT
> Coverage Ratios • Probability of Cash Insolvency

OTHER METHODS OF ANALYSIS
> Comparison of Capital Structure Ratios • Surveying Investment
> Analysts and Lenders • Security Ratings

COMBINATION OF METHODS

SUMMARY

QUESTIONS

SELF-CORRECTION PROBLEMS

PROBLEMS

SOLUTIONS TO SELF-CORRECTION PROBLEMS

SELECTED REFERENCES

*It does not do to leave a live dragon out of your calculations,
if you live near him.*

—J. R. R. Tolkien, *The Hobbit*

Leverage The use of fixed costs in an attempt to increase (or lever up) profitability.

Operating leverage The use of fixed operating costs by the firm.

Financial leverage The use of fixed financing costs by the firm. The British expression is *gearing*.

When a lever is used properly, a force applied at one point is transformed, or magnified, into another, larger force or motion at some other point. This comes most readily to mind when considering *mechanical leverage*, such as that which occurs when using a crowbar. In a business context, however, **leverage** refers to the use of fixed costs in an attempt to increase (or lever up) profitability. In this chapter we explore the principles of both **operating leverage** and **financial leverage.** The former is due to fixed operating costs associated with the production of goods or services, whereas the latter is due to the existence of fixed financing costs—in particular, interest on debt. Both types of leverage affect the level and variability of the firm's after-tax earnings and, hence, the firm's overall risk and return.

OPERATING LEVERAGE

Operating leverage is present anytime a firm has fixed operating costs—regardless of volume. In the long run, of course, all costs are variable. Consequently, our analysis necessarily involves the short run. We incur fixed operating costs in the hope that sales volume will produce revenues more than sufficient to cover all fixed and variable operating costs. One of the more dramatic examples of an effect of operating leverage is the airline industry, where a large proportion of total operating costs is fixed. Beyond a certain break-even load factor, each additional passenger essentially represents straight operating profit (earnings before interest and taxes, or EBIT) to the airline.

It is essential to note that fixed operating costs do not vary as volume changes. These costs include such things as depreciation of buildings and equipment, insurance, part of the overall utility bills, and part of the cost of management. On the other hand, variable operating costs vary directly with the level of output. These costs include raw materials, direct labor costs, part of the overall utility bills, direct selling commissions, and certain parts of general and administrative expenses.

One interesting potential effect caused by the presence of fixed operating costs (operating leverage) is that a change in the volume of sales results in a *more than proportional* change in operating profit (or loss). Thus, like a lever used to magnify a force applied at one point into a larger force at some other point, the presence of fixed operating costs causes a percentage change in sales volume to produce a magnified percentage change in operating profit (or loss). [A note of caution: remember, leverage is a two-edged sword—just as a company's profits can be magnified, so too can the company's losses.]

This magnification effect is illustrated in Table 16-1. In Frame A we find three different firms possessing various amounts of operating leverage. Firm F has a heavy amount of fixed operating costs (FC) relative to variable costs (VC). Firm V has a greater dollar amount of variable operating costs than of fixed operating costs. Finally, Firm 2F has twice the amount of fixed operating costs as does Firm F. Notice that of the three firms shown, Firm 2F has (1) the largest *absolute* dollar amount of fixed costs and (2) the largest *relative* amount of fixed costs as measured by both the (FC/total costs) and (FC/sales) ratios.

Each firm is then subjected to an anticipated 50 percent increase in sales for next year. Before going any further, which firm do you think will be more sensitive to the change in sales; that is, for a given percentage change in sales, which firm will show the largest percentage change in operating profit (EBIT)? (Most people would pick Firm 2F—because it has either the largest absolute or the largest relative amount of fixed costs. Most people would be wrong.)

TABLE 16-1
Effect of operating leverage showing that changes in sales result in more than proportional changes in operating profit (EBIT)

Frame A: Three firms before changes in sales	Firm F	Firm V	Firm 2F
Sales	$10,000	$11,000	$19,500
Operating costs			
Fixed (FC)	7,000	2,000	14,000
Variable (VC)	2,000	7,000	3,000
Operating profit (EBIT)	$ 1,000	$ 2,000	$ 2,500
Operating leverage ratios			
FC/total costs	.78	.22	.82
FC/sales	.70	.18	.72

Frame B: Three firms after 50 percent increases in sales in following year	Firm F	Firm V	Firm 2F
Sales	$15,000	$16,500	$29,250
Operating costs:			
Fixed (FC)	7,000	2,000	14,000
Variable (VC)	3,000	10,500	4,500
Operating profit (EBIT)	$ 5,000	$ 4,000	$10,750
Percent change in EBIT			
$(EBIT_t - EBIT_{t-1})/EBIT_{t-1}$	400%	100%	330%

The results are shown in Frame B of Table 16-1. For each firm, sales and variable costs increase by 50 percent. Fixed costs do not change. All firms show the effects of operating leverage (that is, changes in sales result in more than proportional changes in operating profits). But, Firm F proves to be the most sensitive firm with a 50 percent increase in sales leading to a 400 percent increase in operating profit. As we have just seen, it would be an error to assume that the firm with the largest absolute or relative amount of fixed costs automatically shows the most dramatic effects of operating leverage. Later, we will come up with an easy way to determine which firm is most sensitive to the presence of operating leverage. But before we can do so, we need to learn how to study operating leverage by means of break-even analysis.

Break-Even Analysis

Break-even analysis A technique for studying the relationship among fixed costs, variable costs, profits, and sales volume.

Break-even chart A graphic representation of the relationship between total revenues and total costs for various levels of production and sales, indicating areas of profit and loss.

To illustrate **break-even analysis** as applied to the study of operating leverage, consider a firm that produces a high-quality child's bicycle helmet that sells for $50 a unit. The company has annual fixed operating costs of $100,000, and variable operating costs are $25 a unit regardless of the volume sold. We wish to study the relationship between total operating costs and total revenues. One means for doing so is with the **break-even chart** in Figure 16-1, which shows the relationship among total revenues, total operating costs, and profits for various levels of production and sales. As we are concerned only with operating costs at this point, we define *profits* here to mean operating profits before taxes. This definition purposely excludes interest on

FIGURE 16-1
Break-Even Chart
with the Break-Even
Point Expressed
in Units and Sales
Dollars

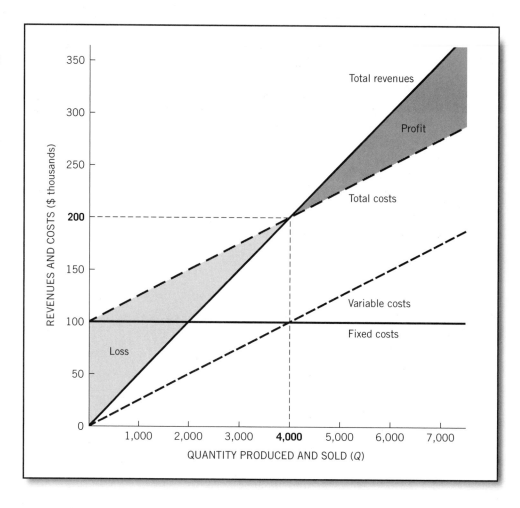

debt and preferred stock dividends. These costs are not part of the total fixed operating costs of the firm and have no relevance when it comes to analyzing operating leverage. They are taken into account, however, when we analyze financial leverage in the next section.

Break-even point The sales volume required so that total revenues and total costs are equal; may be expressed in units or in sales dollars.

Break-Even (Quantity) Point.   The intersection of the total costs line with the total revenues line determines the **break-even point.** The break-even point is the sales volume required for total revenues to equal total operating costs or for operating profit to equal zero. In Figure 16-1 this break-even point is 4,000 units of output (or $200,000 in sales). Mathematically, we find this point (in units) by first noting that operating profit (EBIT) equals total revenues minus variable and fixed operating costs:

$$EBIT = P(Q) - V(Q) - FC$$
$$= Q(P - V) - FC \qquad \textbf{(16-1)}$$

where $EBIT$ = earnings before interest and taxes (operating profit)
$\qquad P$ = price per unit
$\qquad V$ = variable costs per unit
$\qquad (P - V)$ = unit contribution margin
$\qquad Q$ = quantity (units) produced and sold
$\qquad FC$ = fixed costs

At the break-even point (Q_{BE}), EBIT is zero. Therefore,

$$0 = Q_{BE}(P - V) - FC \qquad \text{(16-2)}$$

Rearranging Eq. (16-2), the break-even point is

$$Q_{BE} = FC/(P - V) \qquad \text{(16-3)}$$

Thus, the break-even (quantity) point is equal to fixed costs divided by the unit contribution margin ($P - V$). In our example,

$$Q_{BE} = \$100,000/(\$50 - \$25) = \textbf{4,000 units}$$

For additional increments of volume above the break-even point, there are increases in profits, which are represented by the darker area in Figure 16-1. Likewise, as volume falls below the break-even point, losses increase, which are represented by the lighter area.

Break-Even (Sales) Point. Calculating a break-even point on the basis of dollar sales instead of units is often useful. Sometimes, as in the case of a firm that sells multiple products, it is a necessity. It would be impossible, for example, to come up with a meaningful break-even point in total units for a firm like General Electric, but a break-even point based on sales revenues could easily be imagined. When determining a general break-even point for a multiproduct firm, we assume that sales of each product are a constant proportion of the firm's total sales.

Recognizing that at the break-even (sales) point the firm is just able to cover its fixed and variable operating costs, we turn to the following formula:

$$S_{BE} = FC + VC_{BE} \qquad \text{(16-4)}$$

where S_{BE} = break-even sales revenues
  FC = fixed costs
  VC_{BE} = total variable costs at the break-even point

Unfortunately, we are now faced with a single equation containing two unknowns—S_{BE} and VC_{BE}. Such an equation is insolvable. Luckily, there is a trick that we can use in order to turn Eq. (16-4) into a single equation with a single unknown. First, we need to rewrite Eq. (16-4) as follows:

$$S_{BE} = FC + (VC_{BE}/S_{BE})S_{BE} \qquad \text{(16-5)}$$

Because the relationship between total variable costs and sales is assumed constant in linear break-even analysis, we can replace the ratio (VC_{BE}/S_{BE}) with the ratio of total variable costs to sales (VC/S) for *any* level of sales. For example, we can use the total variable costs and sales figures from the firm's most recent income statement to produce a suitable (VC/S) ratio. In short, after replacing the ratio (VC_{BE}/S_{BE}) with the "generic" ratio (VC/S) in Eq. (16-5), we get

$$S_{BE} = FC + (VC/S)S_{BE}$$
$$S_{BE}[1 - (VC/S)] = FC$$
$$S_{BE} = FC/[1 - (VC/S)] \qquad \text{(16-6)}$$

For our example bicycle-helmet manufacturing firm, the ratio of total variable costs to sales is .50 regardless of sales volume. Therefore, using Eq. (16-6) to solve for the break-even (sales) point, we get

$$S_{BE} = \$100,000/[1 - .50] = \textbf{\$200,000}$$

At \$50 a unit, this \$200,000 break-even (sales) point is consistent with the 4,000 unit break-even (quantity) point determined earlier [i.e., (4,000)(\$50) = \$200,000].

TIP•TIP•TIP•TIP•TIP•TIP•TIP•TIP•TIP•TIP•TIP

You can easily modify *break-even (quantity)* Eq. (16-3) and *break-even (sales) point* Eq. (16-6) to calculate the sales volume (in units or dollars) required to produce a "target" operating income (EBIT) figure. Simply add your target or minimum desired operating income figure to fixed costs (*FC*) in each equation. The resulting answers will be your target sales volume—in units and dollars, respectively—needed to produce your target operating income figure.

Degree of Operating Leverage (DOL)

Earlier, we said that one potential effect of operating leverage is that a change in the volume of sales results in a *more than proportional* change in operating profit (or loss). A quantitative measure of this sensitivity of a firm's operating profit to a change in the firm's sales is called the **degree of operating leverage (DOL).** The degree of operating leverage of a firm at a particular level of output (or sales) is simply the percentage change in operating profit over the percentage change in output (or sales) that causes the change in profits. Thus,

Degree of operating leverage (DOL) The percentage change in a firm's operating profit (EBIT) resulting from a 1 percent change in output (sales).

$$\text{Degree of operating leverage (DOL) at } Q \text{ units of output (or sales)} = \frac{\text{Percentage change in operating profit (EBIT)}}{\text{Percentage change in output (or sales)}} \quad (16\text{-}7)$$

The sensitivity of the firm to a change in sales as measured by DOL will be different at each level of output (or sales). Therefore, we always need to indicate the level of output (or sales) at which DOL is measured—as in *DOL at Q units.*

TIP•TIP•TIP•TIP•TIP•TIP•TIP•TIP•TIP•TIP•TIP

When you use Eq. (16-7) to describe DOL at the firm's current level of sales, remember that you are dealing with *future* percentage changes in EBIT and sales as opposed to *past* percentage changes. Using last period's percentage changes in the equation would give us what the firm's DOL *used to be* as opposed to *what it is* currently.

It is often difficult to work directly with Eq. (16-7) to solve for the DOL at a particular level of sales because an anticipated percentage change in EBIT (the numerator in the equation) will not be observable from historical data. Thus, although Eq. (16-7) is crucial for *defining* and *understanding* DOL, a few simple alternative formulas derived from Eq. (16-7) are more useful for actually *computing DOL* values:

$$DOL_{Q \text{ units}} = \frac{Q(P - V)}{Q(P - V) - FC} = \frac{Q}{(Q - Q_{BE})} \quad (16\text{-}8)$$

$$DOL_{S \text{ dollars of sales}} = \frac{S - VC}{S - VC - FC} = \frac{EBIT + FC}{EBIT} \quad (16\text{-}9)$$

Equation (16-8) is especially well suited for calculating the degree of operating leverage for a single product or a single-product firm.[1] It requires only two pieces of information,

---

[1]Self-correction Problem 4 at the end of this chapter asks you to mathematically derive Eq. (16-8) from Eq. (16-7).

Q and Q_{BE}, both of which are stated in terms of units. Equation (16-9), on the other hand, comes in very handy for finding the degree of operating leverage for a multi-product firm. It too requires only two pieces of information, $EBIT$ and FC, both of which are stated in dollar terms.

Suppose that we wish to determine the degree of operating leverage at 5,000 units of output and sales for our hypothetical example firm. Making use of Eq. (16-8), we have

$$DOL_{5,000 \text{ units}} = \frac{5,000}{(5,000 - 4,000)} = 5$$

For 6,000 units of output and sales, we have

$$DOL_{6,000 \text{ units}} = \frac{6,000}{(6,000 - 4,000)} = 3$$

Take Note

Notice that when output was increased from 5,000 to 6,000 units, the degree of operating leverage decreased from a value of 5 to a value of 3. Thus, the further the level of output is from the break-even point, the lower the degree of operating leverage. How close a firm operates to its break-even point—not its absolute or relative amount of fixed operating costs—determines how sensitive its operating profits will be to a change in output or sales.

QUESTION•ANSWER•QUESTION•ANSWER

What does "$DOL_{5,000 \text{ units}} = 5$" really mean?

It means that a 1 percent change in *sales* from the 5,000-unit sales position causes a 5 percent change in EBIT. In fact, any percentage change in sales from the 5,000-unit position causes a percentage change in EBIT that is five times as large. For example, a 3 percent *decrease* in sales causes a 15 percent *decrease* in EBIT, while a 4 percent *increase* in sales causes a 20 percent *increase* in EBIT.

DOL and the Break-Even Point

Table 16-2 shows us the operating profit and degree of operating leverage for various levels of output (sales). We see that the further we move from the firm's break-even point, the *greater* is the absolute value of the firm's operating profit or loss and the *lower* is the relative sensitivity of operating profit to changes in output (sales) as measured by DOL. The *linear* relationship between operating profits and output (sales) has previously been revealed with the break-even chart in Figure 16-1. In Figure 16-2 we plot the distinctly *nonlinear* relationship between DOL and output (sales).

Given the stable, linear cost and revenue functions of our example firm, we see that DOL approaches positive (or negative) infinity as sales approach the break-even point from above (or below) that point. DOL approaches 1 as sales grow beyond the break-even point. This implies that the magnification effect on operating profits caused by the presence of fixed costs diminishes toward a simple 1-to-1 relationship as sales continue to grow beyond the break-even point. Figure 16-2 demonstrates that even firms with large fixed costs will have a low DOL if they operate well above

TABLE 16-2
Operating profit and degree of operating leverage at various levels of output (sales) for our example firm

QUANTITY PRODUCED AND SOLD (Q)	OPERATING PROFIT (EBIT)	DEGREE OF OPERATING LEVERAGE (DOL)
0	$-100,000	.00
1,000	-75,000	-0.33
2,000	-50,000	-1.00
3,000	-25,000	-3.00
$Q_{BE} = 4,000$	0	Infinite
5,000	25,000	5.00
6,000	50,000	3.00
7,000	75,000	2.33
8,000	100,000	2.00

FIGURE 16-2
Plot of *DOL* versus Quantity Produced and Sold Showing that Closeness to the Break-Even Point Means Higher Sensitivity of Operating Profits to Changes in Quantity Produced and Sold

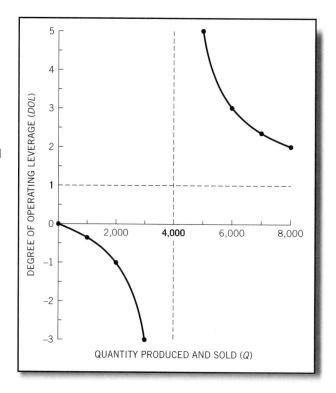

their break-even point. By the same token, a firm with very low fixed costs will have an enormous DOL if it operates close to its break-even point.[2]

---

[2]The graph in Fig. 16-2 is a rectangular hyperbola with *asymptotes* $Q = Q_{BE}$ and $DOL = 1$. All firms having stable, linear cost structures will have similar-looking graphs—but each firm's graph will be centered above its own respective break-even point. Plotting *DOL* versus dollar sales instead of unit sales would produce a similar-looking result.

Interestingly, one can produce a standardized graph that could serve for all firms if we plot *DOL* versus Q/Q_{BE} or S/S_{BE}—that is, *DOL* versus *relative* proximity to the break-even point. (The authors thank Professor James Gahlon for sharing this insight as well as other helpful leverage observations.) The interpretation here would be that a firm's relative proximity to its break-even point determines its *DOL*. Further, all firms operating at the same relative distance from their break-even points (1.5 times Q_{BE} or S_{BE}, for example) will have the same *DOL*.

How would knowledge of a firm's DOL be of use to a financial manager?

The manager would know *in advance* what impact a potential change in sales would have on operating profit. Sometimes, in response to this advance knowledge, the firm may decide to make some changes in its sales policy and/or cost structure. As a general rule, firms do not like to operate under conditions of a high degree of operating leverage because in that situation, a small drop in sales may lead to an operating loss.

DOL and Business Risk

Business risk The inherent uncertainty in the physical operations of the firm. Its impact is shown in the variability of the firm's operating income (EBIT).

It is important to recognize that the degree of operating leverage is only one component of the overall **business risk** of the firm. The other principal factors giving rise to business risk are variability or uncertainty of sales and production costs. The firm's degree of operating leverage magnifies the impact of these other factors on the variability of operating profits. However, the degree of operating leverage itself is not the source of the variability. A high DOL means nothing if the firm maintains constant sales and a constant cost structure. Likewise, it would be a mistake to treat the degree of operating leverage of the firm as a synonym for its business risk. Because of the underlying variability of sales and production costs, however, the degree of operating leverage will magnify the variability of operating profits and, hence, the company's business risk. The degree of operating leverage should thus be viewed as a measure of "potential risk" which becomes "active" only in the presence of sales and production cost variability.

Now that you have a better understanding of DOL, how can you tell from only the information in Frame A of Table 16-1 which firm—F, V, or 2F—will be more sensitive to the anticipated 50 percent increase in sales for the next year?

Simple. Calculate the DOL—using $[(EBIT + FC)/EBIT]$—for each firm, and then pick the firm with the largest DOL.

$$\text{Firm F: } DOL_{\$10,000 \text{ of sales}} = \frac{\$1,000 + \$7,000}{\$1,000} = 8$$

$$\text{Firm V: } DOL_{\$11,000 \text{ of sales}} = \frac{\$2,000 + \$2,000}{\$2,000} = 2$$

$$\text{Firm 2F: } DOL_{\$19,500 \text{ of sales}} = \frac{\$2,500 + \$14,000}{\$2,500} = 6.6$$

In short, Firm F—with a DOL of 8—is most sensitive to the presence of operating leverage. That is why a 50 percent increase in sales in the following year causes a 400 percent ($8 \times 50\%$) increase in operating profit.

FINANCIAL LEVERAGE

Financial leverage involves the use of fixed cost financing. Interestingly, financial leverage is acquired by choice, but operating leverage sometimes is not. The amount of operating leverage (the amount of fixed operating costs) employed by a firm is sometimes dictated by the physical requirements of the firm's operations. For example, a steel mill by way of its heavy investment in plant and equipment will have a large fixed operating cost component consisting of depreciation. Financial leverage, on the other hand, is always a choice item. No firm is required to have *any* long-term debt or preferred stock financing. Firms can, instead, finance operations and capital expenditures from internal sources and the issuance of common stock. Nevertheless, it is a rare firm that has no financial leverage. Why, then, do we see such reliance on financial leverage?

Financial leverage is employed in the hope of increasing the return to common shareholders. Favorable or positive leverage is said to occur when the firm uses funds obtained at a fixed cost (funds obtained by issuing debt with a fixed interest rate or preferred stock with a constant dividend rate) to earn more than the fixed financing costs paid. Any profits left after meeting fixed financing costs then belong to common shareholders. Unfavorable or negative leverage occurs when the firm does not earn as much as the fixed financing costs. The favorability of financial leverage, or "trading on the equity" as it is sometimes called, is judged in terms of the effect that it has on earnings per share to the common shareholders. In effect, financial leverage is the second step in a two-step profit-magnification process. In step one, operating leverage magnifies the effect of changes in sales on changes in operating profit. In step two, the financial manager has the option of using financial leverage to further magnify the effect of any resulting changes in operating profit on changes in earnings per share. In the next section we are interested in determining the relationship between earnings per share (EPS) and operating profit (EBIT) under various financing alternatives and the **indifference points** between these alternatives.

EBIT-EPS Break-Even, or Indifference, Analysis

Calculation of Earnings per Share. To illustrate an **EBIT-EPS break-even analysis** of financial leverage, suppose that Cherokee Tire Company with long-term financing of $10 million, consisting entirely of common stock equity, wishes to raise another $5 million for expansion through one of three possible financing plans. The company may gain additional financing with a new issue of (1) all common stock, (2) all debt at 12 percent interest, or (3) all preferred stock with an 11 percent dividend. Present annual earnings before interest and taxes (EBIT) are $1.5 million but with expansion are expected to rise to $2.7 million. The income tax rate is 40 percent, and 200,000 shares of common stock are now outstanding. Common stock can be sold at $50 per share under the first financing option, which translates into 100,000 additional shares of stock.

To determine the EBIT-EPS break-even, or indifference, points among the various financing alternatives, we begin by calculating earnings per share, *EPS*, for some hypothetical level of EBIT using the following formula:

$$EPS = \frac{(EBIT - I)(1 - t) - PD}{NS} \tag{16-10}$$

where I = annual interest paid
PD = annual preferred dividend paid
t = corporate tax rate
NS = number of shares of common stock outstanding

Suppose we wish to know what earnings per share would be under the three alternative additional-financing plans if EBIT were $2.7 million. The calculations are shown

Sidebar definitions:

Indifference point (EBIT-EPS indifference point) The level of EBIT that produces the same level of EPS for two (or more) alternative capital structures.

EBIT-EPS break-even analysis Analysis of the effect of financing alternatives on earnings per share. The break-even point is the EBIT level where EPS is the same for two (or more) alternatives.

TABLE 16-3

Calculations of earnings per share under three additional-financing alternatives

	COMMON STOCK	DEBT	PREFERRED STOCK
Earnings before interest and taxes (*EBIT*)	$2,700,000	$2,700,000	$2,700,000
Interest (*I*)	—	600,000	—
Earnings before taxes (*EBT*)	$2,700,000	$2,100,000	$2,700,000
Income taxes [(*EBT*) × (*t*)]	1,080,000	840,000	1,080,000
Earnings after taxes (*EAT*)	$1,620,000	$1,260,000	$1,620,000
Preferred stock dividends (*PD*)	—	—	550,000
Earnings available to common shareholders (*EACS*)	$1,620,000	$1,260,000	$1,070,000
Number of shares of common stock outstanding (*NS*)	300,000	200,000	200,000
Earnings per share (EPS)	**$5.40**	**$6.30**	**$5.35**

in Table 16-3. Note that interest on debt is deducted before taxes, while preferred stock dividends are deducted after taxes. As a result, earnings available to common shareholders (EACS) are higher under the debt alternative than they are under the preferred stock alternative, despite the fact that the interest rate on debt is higher than the preferred stock dividend rate.

EBIT-EPS Chart.   Given the information in Table 16-3, we are able to construct an *EBIT-EPS break-even chart* similar to the one for operating leverage. On the horizontal axis we plot earnings before interest and taxes, and on the vertical axis we plot earnings per share. For each financing alternative, we must draw a straight line to reflect EPS for all possible levels of EBIT. Because two points determine a straight line, we need two data points for each financing alternative. The first is the EPS calculated for some hypothetical level of EBIT. For the expected $2.7 million level of EBIT, we see in Table 16-3 that earnings per share are $5.40, $6.30, and $5.35 for the common stock, debt, and preferred stock financing alternatives. We simply plot these earnings per share levels to correspond with the $2.7 million level of EBIT. Technically, it does not matter which hypothetical level of EBIT we choose for calculating EPS. On good graph paper one EBIT level is as good as the next. However, it does seem to make common sense to choose the most likely, or expected, EBIT level rather than some level not too likely to occur.

The second data point—chosen chiefly because of its ease of calculation—is where EPS is zero. This is simply the EBIT necessary to cover all fixed financial costs for a particular financing plan, and it is plotted on the horizontal axis. We can make use of Eq. (16-10) to determine the horizontal axis intercept under each alternative. We simply set the numerator in the equation equal to zero and solve for *EBIT*. For the common stock alternative we have

$$0 = (EBIT - I)(1 - t) - PD \qquad \text{(16-11)}$$

$$= (EBIT - 0)(1 - .40) - 0$$

$$= (EBIT)(.60)$$

$$EBIT = 0/(.60) = \mathbf{0}$$

Notice there are no fixed financing costs whatsoever (either on old or new financing). Therefore, EPS equals zero at zero EBIT.[3] For the debt alternative we have

$$0 = (EBIT - I)(1 - t) - PD$$

$$= (EBIT - \$600,000)(1 - .40) - 0$$

$$= (EBIT)(.60) - \$360,000$$

$$EBIT = \$360,000/(.60) = \mathbf{\$600,000}$$

Thus, the after-tax interest charge divided by 1 minus the tax rate gives us the EBIT necessary to cover these interest payments. In short, we must have $600,000 to cover interest charges, so $600,000 becomes the horizontal axis intercept. Finally, for the preferred stock alternative we have

$$0 = (EBIT - I)(1 - t) - PD$$

$$= (EBIT - 0)(1 - .40) - \$550,000$$

$$= (EBIT)(.60) - \$550,000$$

$$EBIT = \$550,000/(.60) = \mathbf{\$916,667}$$

We divide total annual preferred dividends by 1 minus the tax rate to obtain the EBIT necessary to cover these dividends. Thus, we need $916,667 in EBIT to cover $550,000 in preferred stock dividends, assuming a 40 percent tax rate. Again, preferred dividends are deducted after taxes, so it takes more in before-tax earnings to cover them than it does to cover interest. Given the horizontal axis intercepts and earnings per share for some hypothetical level of EBIT (like the "expected" EBIT), we draw a straight line through each set of data points. The break-even, or indifference, chart for Cherokee Tire Company is shown in Figure 16-3.

---

[3]If some of the firm's pre-expansion financing had involved fixed costs, the horizontal intercept for the common stock financing alternative would not have been zero. It is only because I and PD are both zero in Eq. (16-11) that we get a zero value for EBIT.

FIGURE 16-3
EBIT-EPS Break-Even, or Indifference, Chart for Three Additional-Financing Alternatives

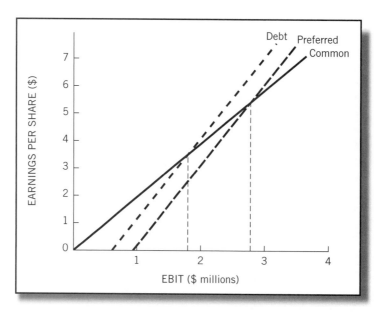

Part VI The Cost of Capital, Capital Structure, and Dividend Policy

We see from Figure 16-3 that the earnings per share indifference point between the debt and common stock additional-financing alternatives is $1.8 million in EBIT.[4] If EBIT is below that point, the common stock alternative will provide higher earnings per share. Above that point the debt alternative produces higher earnings per share. The indifference point between the preferred stock and the common stock alternative is $2.75 million in EBIT. Above that point, the preferred stock alternative produces more favorable earnings per share. Below that point, the common stock alternative leads to higher earnings per share. Note that there is no indifference point between the debt and preferred stock alternatives. The debt alternative dominates for all levels of EBIT and by a constant amount of earnings per share, namely 95 cents.

Indifference Point Determined Mathematically. The indifference point between two alternative financing methods can be determined mathematically by first using Eq. (16-10) to express *EPS* for each alternative and then setting these expressions equal to each other as follows:

$$\frac{(EBIT_{1,2} - I_1)(1 - t) - PD_1}{NS_1} = \frac{(EBIT_{1,2} - I_2)(1 - t) - PD_2}{NS_2} \qquad \textbf{(16-12)}$$

where $EBIT_{1,2}$ = EBIT indifference point between the two alternative financing methods that we are concerned with—in this case, methods 1 and 2
I_1, I_2 = annual interest paid under financing methods 1 and 2
PD_1, PD_2 = annual preferred stock dividend paid under financing methods 1 and 2
t = corporate tax rate
NS_1, NS_2 = number of shares of common stock to be outstanding under financing methods 1 and 2

Suppose that we wish to determine the indifference point between the common stock and debt-financing alternatives in our example. We would have

$$\overset{\textit{Common Stock}}{\frac{(EBIT_{1,2} - 0)(1 - .40) - 0}{300,000}} = \overset{\textit{Debt}}{\frac{(EBIT_{1,2} - \$600,000)(1 - .40) - 0}{200,000}}$$

Cross multiplying and rearranging, we obtain

$$(EBIT_{1,2})(.60)(200,000) = (EBIT_{1,2})(.60)(300,000) - (.60)(\$600,000)(300,000)$$

$$(EBIT_{1,2})(60,000) = \$108,000,000,000$$

$$EBIT_{1,2} = \textbf{\$1,800,000}$$

The EBIT-EPS indifference point, where earnings per share for the two methods of financing are the same, is $1.8 million. This amount can be verified graphically in Figure 16-3. Thus, indifference points can be determined both graphically and mathematically.

Effect on Risk. So far our concern with EBIT-EPS analysis has been only with what happens to the return to common shareholders as measured by earnings per share.

---

[4]Actually, $1.8 million in EBIT is more accurately referred to as a "break-even point" rather than an "indifference point." The financial manager will probably not be truly *indifferent* between the two alternative financing plans at that level of EBIT. Though both plans do produce the same level of EPS at $1.8 million in EBIT, they do not do so by incurring the same level of financial risk—an issue that we will take up shortly. However, "indifference point" is part of the terminology common to EBIT-EPS analysis, so we need to be familiar with it.

We have seen in our example that if EBIT is above $1.8 million, debt financing is the preferred alternative from the standpoint of earnings per share. We know from our earlier discussion, however, that the impact on expected return is only one side of the coin. The other side is the effect that financial leverage has on risk. An EBIT-EPS chart does not permit a precise analysis of risk. Nevertheless, certain generalizations are possible. For one thing, the financial manager should compare the indifference point between two alternatives, like debt financing versus common stock financing, with the most likely level of EBIT. The higher the expected level of EBIT, assuming that it exceeds the indifference point, the stronger the case that can be made for debt financing, all other things the same.

In addition, the financial manager should assess the likelihood of future EBITs actually falling below the indifference point. As before, our estimate of expected EBIT is $2.7 million. Given the business risk of the company and the resulting possible fluctuations in EBIT, the financial manager should assess the probability of EBITs falling below $1.8 million. If the probability is negligible, the use of the debt alternative will be supported. On the other hand, if EBIT is presently only slightly above the indifference point and the probability of EBITs falling below this point is high, the financial manager may conclude that the debt alternative is too risky.

This notion is illustrated in Figure 16-4, where two probability distributions of possible EBITs are superimposed on the indifference chart first shown in Figure 16-2. In Figure 16-4, however, we focus on only the debt and common stock alternatives. For the *safe* (peaked) distribution, there is virtually no probability that EBIT will fall below the indifference point. Therefore, we might conclude that debt should be used, because the effect on shareholder return is substantial, whereas risk is negligible. For the *risky* (flat) distribution, there is a significant probability that EBIT will

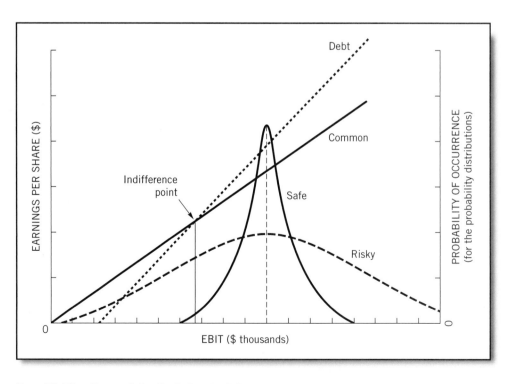

FIGURE 16-4
EBIT-EPS Break-Even, or Indifference, Chart and EBIT Probability Distributions for Debt and Common Stock Additional-Financing Alternatives

fall below the indifference point. In this case, the financial manager may conclude that the debt alternative is too risky.

In summary, the greater the level of expected EBIT above the indifference point and the lower the probability of downside fluctuation, the stronger the case that can be made for the use of debt financing. EBIT-EPS break-even analysis is but one of several methods used for determining the appropriate amount of debt a firm might carry. No one method of analysis is satisfactory by itself. When several methods of analysis are undertaken simultaneously, however, generalizations are possible.

Degree of Financial Leverage (DFL)

A quantitative measure of the sensitivity of a firm's earnings per share to a change in the firm's operating profit is called the **degree of financial leverage (DFL).** The degree of financial leverage at a particular level of operating profit is simply the percentage change in earnings per share over the percentage change in operating profit that causes the change in earnings per share. Thus,

Degree of financial leverage (DFL) The percentage change in a firm's earnings per share (EPS) resulting from a 1 percent change in operating profit (EBIT).

$$\text{Degree of financial leverage (DFL) at EBIT of X dollars} = \frac{\text{Percentage change in earnings per share (EPS)}}{\text{Percentage change in operating profit (EBIT)}} \qquad \text{(16-13)}$$

While Eq. (16-13) is useful for *defining DFL,* a simple alternative formula derived from Eq. (16-13) is more useful for actually *computing DFL* values:

$$DFL_{EBIT \text{ of } X \text{ dollars}} = \frac{EBIT}{EBIT - I - [PD/(1 - t)]} \qquad \text{(16-14)}$$

Equation (16-14) states that DFL at a particular level of operating profit is calculated by dividing operating profit by the dollar difference between operating profit and the amount of *before-tax* operating profit necessary to cover total fixed financing costs. (Remember, it takes more in before-tax earnings to cover preferred dividends than it does to cover interest; hence, we need to divide preferred dividends by 1 minus the tax rate in our formula.)

For our example firm, using the debt-financing alternative at $2.7 million in EBIT, we have

$$DFL_{EBIT \text{ of } \$2.7 \text{ million}} = \frac{\$2,700,000}{\$2,700,000 - \$600,000} = \textbf{1.29}$$

For the preferred stock financing alternative, the degree of financial leverage is

$$DFL_{EBIT \text{ of } \$2.7 \text{ million}} = \frac{\$2,700,000}{\$2,700,000 - [\$550,000/(.60)]} = \textbf{1.51}$$

Interestingly, although the stated fixed cost involved with the preferred stock financing alternative is lower than that for the debt alternative ($550,000 versus $600,000), the DFL is greater under the preferred stock option than under the debt option. This is because of the tax deductibility of interest and the nondeductibility of preferred dividends. It is often argued that preferred stock financing is of less risk than debt financing for the issuing firm. With regard to the risk of **cash insolvency,** this is probably true. But the DFL tells us that the relative variability of EPS will be greater under the preferred stock financing arrangement, everything else being equal. This discussion naturally leads us to the topic of financial risk and its relationship to the degree of financial leverage.

Cash insolvency Inability to pay obligations as they fall due.

DFL and Financial Risk

Financial risk The added variability in earnings per share (EPS)—plus the risk of possible insolvency— that is induced by the use of financial leverage.

Financial Risk. Broadly speaking, **financial risk** encompasses both the risk of possible insolvency and the *added* variability in earnings per share that is induced by the use of financial leverage. As a firm increases the proportion of fixed cost financing in its capital structure, fixed cash outflows increase. As a result, the probability of cash insolvency increases. To illustrate this aspect of financial risk, suppose that two firms differ with respect to financial leverage but are identical in every other respect. Each has expected annual cash earnings before interest and taxes of $80,000. Firm A has no debt. Firm B has $200,000 worth of 15 percent perpetual bonds outstanding. Thus, the total annual fixed financial charges for Firm B are $30,000, whereas Firm A has no fixed financial charges. If cash earnings for both firms happen to be 75 percent lower than expected, namely $20,000, firm B will be unable to cover its financial charges with cash earnings. We see, then, that the probability of cash insolvency increases with the financial charges incurred by the firm.

The second aspect of financial risk involves the relative dispersion of earnings per share. To illustrate, suppose that the expected future EBITs for firm A and firm B are random variables where the expected values of the probability distributions are each $80,000 and the standard deviations $40,000. As before, firm A has no debt but rather 4,000 shares of $10-par-value common stock outstanding. Firm B has $200,000 in 15 percent bonds and 2,000 shares of $10-par-value common stock outstanding.

Frame A in Table 16-4 shows that the expected earnings available to common shareholders for firm A equals $48,000, while for firm B this figure equals only $30,000.

TABLE 16-4
Effect of financial leverage example showing financial leverage affects both the level and variability of earnings per share

	FIRM A (100% EQUITY)	FIRM B (50% EQUITY)
Frame A: Forecast income statement information		
Expected earnings before interest and taxes [$E(EBIT)$]	$80,000	$80,000
Interest (I)	—	30,000
Expected earnings before taxes [$E(EBT)$]	$80,000	$50,000
Expected taxes [$E(EBT) \times t$]	32,000	20,000
Expected earnings available to common shareholders [$E(EACS)$]	$48,000	$30,000
Number of shares of common stock outstanding (NS)	4,000	2,000
Expected earnings per share [$E(EPS)$]	$12.00	$15.00
Frame B: Risk components		
Standard deviation of earnings per share (σ_{EPS})*	$6.00	$12.00
Coefficient of variation of earnings before interest and taxes [$\sigma_{EBIT}/E(EBIT)$]	.50	.50
$DFL_{\text{expected } EBIT \text{ of } \$800,000}$ $[E(EBIT)]/[E(EBIT) - I - PD/(1-t)]$	1.00	1.60
Coefficient of variation of earnings per share $[\sigma_{EPS}/E(EPS)]$ or $[\sigma_{EBIT}/E(EBIT)] \times [DFL_{E(EBIT)}]$	.50	.80

*For any random variable X, the $\sigma_{(a+bx)} = (b)(\sigma_x)$; therefore $\sigma_{EPS} = (1/\text{number of shares of common stock outstanding}) (1 - t)(\sigma_{EBIT})$. Example for 50% debt: $(1/2,000)(1 - .40)(\$40,000) = \$12.00$.

Dividing expected earnings available to common shareholders by the number of shares of common stock outstanding, however, reveals that firm B has a higher expected earnings per share than firm A, that is, $15 and $12, respectively. The standard deviation of earnings per share is determined to be $6 for firm A and $12 for firm B.

Total Firm Risk Equals Business Risk Plus Financial Risk.   The coefficient of variation of earnings per share, which is simply the standard deviation divided by the expected value, gives us a measure of the relative dispersion of earnings per share. We use this statistic as a measure of **total firm risk.** In frame B of Table 16-4 we see that for firm A, the 100-percent-equity situation, the coefficient of variation of earnings per share is .50. Notice that this figure is exactly equal to the firm's coefficient of variation of earnings before interest and taxes. What this says is that even in the absence of financial leverage, the firm's shareholders are still exposed to risk—business risk. A good quantitative measure of a firm's relative amount of business risk is thus the coefficient of variation of EBIT. For firm B, the 50-percent-debt situation, the coefficient of variation of earnings per share is .80. Because firm B is exactly like firm A except for the use of financial leverage, we can use the difference between the coefficients of variation of earnings per share for firm B and firm A; that is, .80 − .50 = **.30,** as a measure of the *added* variability in earnings per share for firm B that is induced by the use of leverage; in short, this *difference* is a measure of financial risk. Equivalently, this measure of financial risk equals the difference between firm B's coefficient of variation of earnings per share and its coefficient of variation of earnings before interest and taxes.

Total firm risk The variability in earnings per share (EPS). It is the sum of business plus financial risk.

> **Take Note**
>
> In summary, then
>
> - *Total firm risk = business risk + financial risk.*
> - The coefficient of variation of earnings per share, CV_{EPS}, is a measure of relative *total firm risk*: $CV_{EPS} = \sigma_{EPS}/E(EPS)$.
> - The coefficient of variation of earnings before interest and taxes, CV_{EBIT}, is a measure of relative *business risk*: $CV_{EBIT} = \sigma_{EBIT}/E(EBIT)$.
> - The difference, therefore, between the coefficient of variation of earnings per share (CV_{EPS}) and the coefficient of variation of earnings before interest and taxes (CV_{EBIT}) is a measure of relative *financial risk*: ($CV_{EPS} - CV_{EBIT}$).

We have seen from Table 16-4 that total firm risk in our example, as measured by the coefficient of variation of earnings per share, is higher under the 50-percent-bond financing than it is under the 100-percent-equity financing. However, the expected level of earnings per share is also higher. We witness, once again, the kind of risk-return trade-off that characterizes most financial leverage decisions.

DFL Magnifies Risk.   Our measure of relative total firm risk, the coefficient of variation of earnings per share, can be calculated directly by dividing the standard deviation of earnings per share by the expected earnings per share. However, given the assumptions behind our example, it can be shown that this measure is also equal to the coefficient of variation of earnings before interest and taxes times the degree of financial leverage at the expected EBIT level.[5] Firm A, in our example, has no financial leverage and a resulting DFL equal to 1; in short, there is no magnification of business risk as measured by the CV_{EBIT}. For firm A, then, CV_{EPS} equals CV_{EBIT} and, thus, its total firm risk is equal to its business risk. Firm B's CV_{EPS}, on the other hand, is equal to its CV_{EBIT} (its measure of business risk) times 1.6 (its DFL at the expected EBIT). Thus, for firms employing financial leverage, their DFL will act to magnify the impact of business risk on the variability of earnings per share. So, although DFL is not synonymous with financial risk, its magnitude does determine the relative amount of additional risk induced by the use of financial leverage. As a result, firms with high business risk will often employ a financing mix that entails a limited DFL, and vice versa.

TOTAL LEVERAGE

Total (or combined) leverage The use of both fixed operating and financing costs by the firm.

Degree of total leverage (DTL) The percentage change in a firm's earnings per share (EPS) resulting from a 1 percent change in output (sales). This is also equal to a firm's degree of operating leverage (DOL) times its degree of financial leverage (DFL) at a particular level of output (sales).

When financial leverage is combined with operating leverage, the result is referred to as **total (or combined) leverage.** The effect of combining financial and operating leverage is a two-step magnification of any change in sales into a larger relative change in earnings per share. A quantitative measure of this total sensitivity of a firm's earnings per share to a change in the firm's sales is called the **degree of total leverage (DTL).**

Degree of Total Leverage (DTL)

The degree of total leverage of a firm at a particular level of output (or sales) is equal to the percentage change in earnings per share over the percentage change in output (or sales) that causes the change in earnings per share. Thus,

$$\begin{array}{c} \text{Degree of total leverage (DTL)} \\ \text{at } Q \text{ units (or } S \text{ dollars)} \\ \text{of output (or sales)} \end{array} = \dfrac{\begin{array}{c}\text{Percentage change in} \\ \text{earnings per share (EPS)}\end{array}}{\begin{array}{c}\text{Percentage change in} \\ \text{output (or sales)}\end{array}} \qquad \textbf{(16-15)}$$

Computationally, we can make use of the fact that the degree of total leverage is simply the product of the degree of operating leverage and the degree of financial leverage as follows:

$$DTL_{Q \text{ units (or } S \text{ dollars)}} = DOL_{Q \text{ units (or } S \text{ dollars)}} \times DFL_{EBIT \text{ of X dollars}} \qquad \textbf{(16-16)}$$

In addition, multiplying alternative DOLs, Eqs. (16-8) and (16-9), by DFL, Eq. (16-14), gives us

---

[5]Proof:

$$\frac{\sigma_{EPS}}{E(EPS)} = \frac{(1/NS)(1-t)(\sigma_{EBIT})}{[E(EBIT)(1-t) - I(1-t) - PD]/NS}$$

$$= \frac{\sigma_{EBIT}}{E(EBIT) - I - [PD/(1-t)]}$$

$$= \frac{\sigma_{EBIT}}{E(EBIT)} \times \frac{E(EBIT)}{E(EBIT) - I - [PD/(1-t)]}$$

$$= CV_{EBIT} \times DFL_{E(EBIT)}$$

$$DTL_{Q\,units} = \frac{Q(P - V)}{Q(P - V) - FC - I - [PD/(1 - t)]} \qquad (16\text{-}17)$$

$$DTL_{S\,dollars\,of\,sales} = \frac{EBIT + FC}{EBIT - I - [PD/(1 - t)]} \qquad (16\text{-}18)$$

These alternative equations tell us that for a particular firm the greater the *before-tax* financial costs, the greater the degree of total leverage over what it would be in the absence of financial leverage.

Suppose that our bicycle-helmet manufacturing firm used to illustrate operating leverage has $200,000 in debt at 8 percent interest. Recall that the selling price is $50 a unit, variable operating costs are $25 a unit, and annual fixed operating costs are $100,000. Assume that the tax rate is 40 percent, and that we wish to determine the degree of total leverage at 8,000 units of production and sales. Therefore, using Eq. (16-17), we have

$$DTL_{8,000\,units} = \frac{8,000(\$50 - \$25)}{8,000(\$50 - \$25) - \$100,000 - \$16,000} = 2.38$$

Thus, a 10 percent increase in the number of units produced and sold would result in a 23.8 percent increase in earnings per share.

Stating the degree of total leverage for our example firm in terms of the product of its degree of operating leverage times its degree of financial leverage, we get

$$DOL_{8,000\,units} \qquad \times DFL_{EBIT\,of\,\$100,000} \qquad = DTL_{8,000\,units}$$

$$\frac{8,000(\$50 - \$25)}{8,000(\$50 - \$25) - \$100,000} \times \frac{\$100,000}{\$100,000 - \$16,000} = 2.38$$

$$2.00 \qquad \times \qquad 1.19 \qquad = 2.38$$

In the absence of financial leverage, our firm's degree of total leverage would have been equal to its degree of operating leverage for a value of 2 (remember, DFL for a firm with no financial leverage equals 1). We see, however, that the firm's financial leverage magnifies its DOL figure by a factor of 1.19 to produce a degree of total leverage equal to 2.38.

DTL and Total Firm Risk

Operating leverage and financial leverage can be combined in a number of different ways to obtain a desirable degree of total leverage and level of total firm risk. High business risk can be offset with low financial risk and vice versa. The proper overall level of firm risk involves a trade-off between total firm risk and expected return. This trade-off must be made in keeping with the objective of maximizing shareholder value. The discussion, so far, is meant to show how certain tools can be employed to provide information on the two types of leverage—operating and financial—and their combined effect.

CASH-FLOW ABILITY TO SERVICE DEBT

When trying to determine the appropriate financial leverage for a firm, we would also analyze the cash-flow ability of the firm to service fixed financial charges. The greater the dollar amount of senior securities that the firm issues and the shorter their maturity, the greater the fixed financial charges of the firm. These charges include principal and interest payments on debt, financial lease payments, and preferred stock dividends. Before taking on additional fixed financial charges, the firm should analyze its expected future cash flows, because fixed financial charges must be met with cash. The inability to meet these charges, with the exception of preferred stock dividends, may result in financial insolvency. The greater and more stable the expected future cash flows of the firm, the greater the **debt capacity** of the company.

Debt capacity The maximum amount of debt (and other fixed-charge financing) that a firm can adequately service.

Coverage Ratios

Among the ways in which we can gain knowledge about the debt capacity of a firm is through an analysis of *coverage ratios*. These ratios, as you may remember from Chapter 6, are designed to relate the financial charges of a firm to the firm's ability to service, or cover, them. In the computation of these ratios, one typically uses earnings before interest and taxes as a rough measure of the cash flow available to cover fixed financial charges. Perhaps the most widely used coverage ratio is the *interest coverage ratio*, or *times interest earned*. This ratio is simply earnings before interest and taxes for a particular period divided by interest charges for the period:

$$\frac{\text{Interest coverage}}{\text{(or times interest earned)}} = \frac{\text{Earnings before interest and taxes (EBIT)}}{\text{Interest expense}} \tag{16-19}$$

Suppose, for example, that the most recent annual earnings before interest and taxes for a company were $6 million and annual interest payments on all debt obligations were $1.5 million. Then, EBIT would "cover" interest charges four times. This tells us that EBIT can drop by as much as 75 percent and the firm will still be able to cover interest payments out of earnings.

An interest coverage ratio of only 1 indicates that earnings are just sufficient to satisfy the interest burden. Generalizations about what is a proper interest coverage ratio are inappropriate unless reference is made to the type of business in which the firm is engaged. In a highly stable business, a relatively low interest coverage ratio may be appropriate, whereas it may not be appropriate in a highly cyclical business.

Note that the interest coverage ratio tells us nothing about the firm's ability to meet principal payments on its debts. The inability to meet a principal payment constitutes the same legal default as failure to meet an interest payment. Therefore, it is useful to compute the coverage ratio for the full **debt-service burden.** This ratio is

Debt-service burden Cash required during a specific period, usually a year, to meet interest expenses and principal payments. Also called simply *debt service*.

$$\frac{\text{Debt-service}}{\text{coverage}} = \frac{\text{Earnings before interest and taxes (EBIT)}}{\text{Interest expense} + \dfrac{\text{Principal payments}}{1 - \text{Tax rate}}} \tag{16-20}$$

Here principal payments are adjusted upward for the tax effect. The reason is that EBIT represents earnings *before tax*. Because principal payments are not deductible for tax purposes, they must be paid out of *after-tax* earnings. Therefore, we must adjust principal payments so that they are consistent with EBIT. If principal payments in our previous example were $1 million per annum and the tax rate were 40 percent, the debt-service coverage ratio would be

$$\frac{\text{Debt-service}}{\text{coverage}} = \frac{\$6 \text{ million}}{\$1.5 \text{ million} + \dfrac{\$1 \text{ million}}{1 - .40}} = \mathbf{1.89}$$

A coverage ratio of 1.89 means that EBIT can fall by only 47 percent before earnings coverage is insufficient to service the debt.[6] Obviously, the closer the debt-service coverage ratio is to 1, the worse things are, all other things the same. However, even with this coverage ratio being less than 1, a company may still be able to meet its obligations if it can renew some of its debt when principal comes due or if assets are sold.

Part of the overall analysis of the financial risk associated with financial leverage should focus on the firm's ability to service total fixed charges. Lease financing is not debt per se, but its impact on cash flows is exactly the same as the payment of interest and principal on a debt obligation. (See Chapter 21 for an analysis of lease financing.) Annual financial lease payments, therefore, should be added to the numerator and denominator of Eq. (16-20) in order to properly reflect the total cash-flow burden associated with financing.

As with the interest coverage ratio, "rules of thumb" generalizations about what constitutes a good or bad debt-service ratio are often inappropriate. What constitutes a good or bad ratio varies according to the business risk of the firm. This fact is illustrated in Figure 16-5, which shows the probability distributions of EBIT for two hypothetical companies. The expected value of EBIT is the same for both companies, as is the debt-service burden as described by the denominator in Eq. (16-20). Therefore, the debt-service coverage ratios are also the same, namely $100,000/$60,000 = **1.67.** Company A, however, has much more business risk as shown in the greater variability of its EBIT. The probability that EBIT will fall below the debt-service burden is depicted by the shaded areas in the figure. We see that this probability is much greater for company A than it is for company B. Though a debt-service coverage ratio of 1.67 may be appropriate for company B, it may not be appropriate for company A. Simply put, a company with stable cash flows is better able to take on relatively more fixed charges.

---

[6]This percent is determined by $1 - (1/1.89) = .47$.

FIGURE 16-5
Possible EBITs in Relation to Debt-Service Burdens for Companies A and B

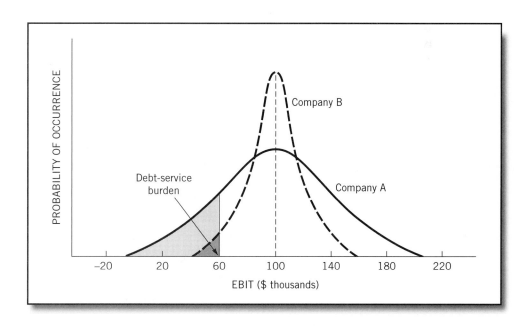

Ultimately, one wants to make generalizations about the appropriate amount of debt (and leases) for a firm to have in its financing mix. It is clear that the ability of a going-concern firm to service debt over the long run is tied to earnings. Therefore, coverage ratios are an important tool of analysis. However, they are but one tool by which a person is able to reach conclusions with respect to determining an appropriate financing mix for the firm. Coverage ratios, like all ratios, are subject to certain limitations and, consequently, cannot be used as a sole means for determining a firm's financing. The fact that EBIT falls below the debt-service burden does not spell immediate doom for the company. Often alternative sources of funds, including renewal of the loan, are available, and these sources must be considered.

Probability of Cash Insolvency

The vital question for the firm is not so much whether a coverage ratio will fall below 1 but rather, what are the chances of cash insolvency? Fixed-charge financing adds to the firm's danger of cash insolvency. Therefore, the answer depends on whether all sources of payment—earnings, cash, a new financing arrangement, or the sale of assets—are collectively deficient. A coverage ratio tells only part of the story. To address the broad question of cash insolvency, we must obtain information on the possible deviation of actual cash flows from those that are expected. As we discussed in Chapter 7, cash budgets can be prepared for a range of possible outcomes, with a probability attached to each outcome. This information is extremely valuable to the financial manager in evaluating the ability of the firm to meet fixed obligations. Not only expected earnings are taken into account in determining this ability, but other cash-flow factors as well—the purchase or sale of assets, the liquidity of the firm, dividend payments, and seasonal patterns. Given the probabilities of particular cash-flow sequences, the financial manager is able to determine the amount of fixed financing charges the company can undertake while still remaining within insolvency limits tolerable to management.

Management may feel that a 5 percent probability of being out of cash is the maximum that it can tolerate and that this probability corresponds to a cash budget prepared under pessimistic assumptions. In this case, debt might be undertaken up to the point where the cash balance under the pessimistic cash budget is just sufficient to cover the fixed charges associated with the debt. In other words, debt would be increased to the point at which the additional cash drain would cause the probability of cash insolvency to equal the risk tolerance specified by management. Note that the method of analysis simply provides a means for assessing the effect of increases in debt on the risk of cash insolvency. On the basis of this information, management would arrive at the most appropriate level of debt.

The analysis of the cash-flow ability of the firm to service fixed financial charges is perhaps the best way to analyze financial risk, but there is a real question as to whether all (or most) of the participants in the financial markets analyze a company in this manner. Sophisticated lenders and institutional investors certainly analyze the amount of fixed financial charges and evaluate financial risk in keeping with the ability of the firm to service these charges. However, individual investors may judge financial risk more by book value proportions of debt and equity. There may or may not be a reasonable correspondence between the ratio of debt to equity and the amount of fixed charges relative to the firm's cash-flow ability to service these charges. Some firms may have relatively high ratios of debt to equity but substantial cash-flow ability to service debt. Consequently, the analysis of debt-to-equity ratios alone can be deceiving, and an analysis of the magnitude and stability of cash flows relative to fixed financial charges is extremely important in determining the appropriate financing mix for the firm.

OTHER METHODS OF ANALYSIS

Comparison of Capital Structure Ratios

Capital structure The mix (or proportion) of a firm's permanent long-term financing represented by debt, preferred stock, and common stock equity.

Another method of analyzing the appropriate financing mix for a company is to evaluate the **capital structure** of other companies having similar business risk. Companies used in this comparison are most often those in the same industry. If the firm is contemplating a capital structure significantly out of line with that of similar companies, it is conspicuous in the marketplace. This is not to say that the firm is wrong. Other companies in the industry may be too conservative in their use of debt. The optimal capital structure for all companies in the industry might call for a higher proportion of debt to equity than the industry average. As a result, the firm may be able to justify more debt than the industry average. If the firm's financial leverage is noticeably out of line in either direction, it should be prepared to justify its position, because investment analysts and creditors tend to evaluate companies by industry.

There are wide variations in the use of financial leverage across business firms. A good deal of the variation is removed, however, if one groups firms by industry classification, because there is a tendency for the firms in an industry to cluster when it comes to debt ratios. For selected industries, the debt-to-net-worth ratios for a recent period looked as follows:

INDUSTRY	DEBT TO NET WORTH
Optical instruments (manufacturing)	1.0
Drugs (manufacturing)	1.0
Electrical components (manufacturing)	1.3
General merchandise stores (retail)	1.7
Dairy products (manufacturing)	1.9
Gasoline service stations	2.2
Air transportation (scheduled)	2.3
General building contractors (residential)	2.9

Whereas optical instruments manufacturers and drug companies do not employ much financial leverage, general building contractors make extensive use of debt in financing projects. So when making capital structure comparisons, look at other companies in the same industry. In short, compare apples with apples as opposed to apples with oranges.

Surveying Investment Analysts and Lenders

The firm may profit by also talking with investment analysts, institutional investors, and investment bankers to obtain their views on appropriate amounts of financial leverage. These analysts examine many companies and are in the business of recommending stocks. They, therefore, have an influence on the financial market. Their judgments with respect to how the market evaluates financial leverage may be very worthwhile. Similarly, a firm may wish to interview lenders to see how much debt it can undertake before the cost of borrowing is likely to rise. Finally, the management of a company may develop a "feel" for what has happened to the market price of the company's stock when it has issued debt in the past.

Security Ratings

The financial manager must consider the effect of a financing alternative on its security rating. Whenever a company sells a debt or preferred stock issue to public investors, as opposed to private lenders such as banks, it must have the issue rated by one or more rating services. The principal rating agencies are Moody's Investors Service and Standard & Poor's. The issuer of a new corporate security issue contracts with the agency to evaluate the issue as to quality, as well as to update the rating throughout the issue's life. For this service, the issuer pays a fee. In addition, the rating agency charges subscribers to its rating publications. While the assignment of a rating for a new issue is current, changes in ratings of existing securities tend to lag the events that prompt the changes.

Both agencies use much the same letter grading. The ratings used by Moody's and Standard & Poor's, as well as brief descriptions, are shown in Table 16-5. In their ratings, the agencies attempt to rank issues in order of their perceived probability of default. The highest grade securities, judged to have negligible default risk, are rated triple-A.

Credit ratings in the top four categories (for Moody's, Aaa to Baa; for Standard & Poor's, AAA to BBB) are considered "investment grade" quality, whereas ratings in the other categories signify "speculative grade." The ratings by the agencies are widely respected and are recognized by various government regulatory agencies as measures of default risk. In fact, many investors accept them without further investigation of the risk of default.

The rating agencies look at a number of things before assigning a grade: levels and trends in ratios of liquidity, debt, profitability, and coverage; the firm's business risk, both historical and expected; present and likely future capital requirements;

TABLE 16-5
Ratings by investment agencies

MOODY'S INVESTORS SERVICE		STANDARD & POOR'S	
Aaa	Best quality	AAA	Highest grade
Aa	High quality	AA	High grade
A	Upper medium grade	A	Higher medium grade
Baa	Medium grade	BBB	Medium grade
Ba	Possess speculative elements	BB	Speculative
B	Generally lack characteristics of desirable investment	B	Very speculative
Caa	Poor standing; may be in default	CCC-CC	Outright speculation
Ca	Highly speculative; often in default	C	Reserved for income bonds on which no interest is being paid
C	Lowest grade	D	In default

Note: The top four categories indicate "investment grade quality" securities; the categories below the dashed line are reserved for securities below investment grade.

specific features associated with the instrument being issued; and, perhaps most important, the cash-flow ability of the firm to service interest and principal payments. If a public security offering is contemplated, the financial manager must be mindful of ratings when determining how much financial leverage is appropriate. If taking on additional debt lowers a firm's security rating from an investment-grade to a speculative-grade category—thus making the security ineligible for investment by many institutional investors—the manager will want to factor this into account before making a decision.

COMBINATION OF METHODS

We have seen that the variability of sales and production costs, coupled with operating leverage, affect the variability of operating profit and, thus, a firm's business risk. In addition to incurring business risk, most firms consciously expose themselves to financial risk by employing financial leverage to greater or lesser degrees. Most of this chapter has been devoted to examining methods of analysis that can be brought to bear on the question: In light of the firm's business risk, what is the appropriate amount of financial leverage for a company? The methods studied include undertaking EBIT-EPS analysis, assessing the cash-flow ability of the firm to service fixed financial charges, comparing capital structure ratios of other companies having similar business risk, surveying investment analysts and lenders, and evaluating the effect of a financial leverage decision on a firm's security rating. In addition to the information provided by using these techniques, the financial manager will want to know the changing interest costs for various levels of debt. The maturity structure of debt is important as well, but we take this up later in the book. We focus here on only the broad issue of the amount of financial leverage to employ. All of the analyses should be guided by the conceptual framework presented in the next chapter.

The implicit cost of financial leverage—that is, the effect that financial leverage has on the value of the firm's common stock—is not easy to isolate and determine. Nevertheless, by undertaking a variety of analyses, the financial manager should be able to determine, within some range, the appropriate capital structure for the firm. By necessity, the final decision has to be somewhat subjective, but it should be based on the best information available. In this way, the firm is able to obtain the capital structure most appropriate for its situation—the one it hopes will maximize the market price of the firm's common stock.

SUMMARY

- *Leverage* refers to the use of fixed costs in an attempt to increase (or lever up) profitability. *Operating leverage* is due to fixed operating costs associated with the production of goods or services, while *financial leverage* is due to the existence of fixed financing costs—in particular, interest on debt. Both types of leverage affect the level and variability of the firm's after-tax earnings and, hence, the firm's overall risk and return.
- We can study the relationship between total operating costs and total revenues by using a *break-*

even chart, which shows the relationship among total revenues, total operating costs, and operating profits for various levels of production and sales.
- The *break-even point* is the sales volume required so that total revenues and total costs are equal. It may be expressed in units or in sales dollars.
- A quantitative measure of the sensitivity of a firm's operating profit to a change in the firm's sales is called the *degree of operating leverage (DOL)*. The DOL of a firm at a particular level of

output (or sales) is the percentage change in operating profit over the percentage change in output (or sales) that causes the change in profits. The closer a firm operates to its break-even point, the higher is the absolute value of its DOL.

- The degree of operating leverage contributes but one component of the overall business risk of the firm. The other principal factors giving rise to business risk are variability or uncertainty of sales and production costs. The firm's degree of operating leverage magnifies the impact of these other factors on the variability of operating profits.

- Financial leverage is the second step in a two-step profit-magnification process. In step one, operating leverage magnifies the effect of changes in sales on changes in operating profit. In step two, financial leverage can be used to further magnify the effect of any resulting changes in operating profit on changes in earnings per share.

- *EBIT-EPS break-even, or indifference, analysis* is used to study the effect of financing alternatives on earnings per share. The break-even point is the EBIT level where EPS is the same for two (or more) alternatives. The higher the expected level of EBIT, assuming that it exceeds the indifference point, the stronger the case that can be made for debt financing, all other things the same. In addition, the financial manager should assess the likelihood of future EBITs actually falling below the indifference point.

- A quantitative measure of the sensitivity of a firm's earnings per share to a change in the firm's operating profit is called the *degree of financial leverage (DFL)*. The DFL at a particular level of operating profit is the percentage change in earnings per share over the percentage change in operating profit that causes the change in earnings per share.

- *Financial risk* encompasses both the risk of possible insolvency and the "added" variability in earnings per share that is induced by the use of financial leverage.

- When financial leverage is combined with operating leverage, the result is referred to as *total (or combined) leverage*. A quantitative measure of the total sensitivity of a firm's earnings per share to a change in the firm's sales is called the *degree of total leverage (DTL)*. The DTL of a firm at a particular level of output (or sales) is equal to the percentage change in earnings per share over the percentage change in output (or sales) that causes the change in earnings per share.

- When trying to determine the appropriate financial leverage for a firm, the cash-flow ability of the firm to service debt should be evaluated. The firm's *debt capacity* can be assessed by analyzing coverage ratios and the probability of cash insolvency under various levels of debt.

- Other methods of analyzing the appropriate financing mix for a company include comparing capital structure ratios of other companies having similar business risk, surveying investment analysts and lenders, and evaluating the effect of a financial leverage decision on a firm's security rating. In deciding on an appropriate capital structure, all these factors should be considered. In addition, certain concepts involving valuation should guide the decision. These concepts are discussed in the next chapter.

QUESTIONS

1. Define *operating leverage* and the *degree of operating leverage (DOL)*. How are the two related?
2. Classify the following short-run manufacturing costs as either typically fixed or typically variable. Which costs are variable at management's discretion? Are any of these costs fixed in the long run?
   - a. Insurance
   - b. Direct labor
   - c. Bad-debt loss
   - d. R&D
   - e. Advertising
   - f. Raw materials
   - g. Depletion
   - h. Depreciation
   - i. Maintenance
3. What would be the effect on the firm's operating break-even point of the following individual changes?
   - a. An increase in selling price
   - b. An increase in the minimum wage paid to the firm's employees
   - c. A change from straight-line to accelerated depreciation

    d. Increased sales

    e. A liberalized credit policy to customers

4. Are there any businesses that are risk free?

5. Your friend, Jacques Fauxpas, suggests, "Firms with high fixed operating costs show extremely dramatic fluctuations in operating profits for any given change in sales volume." Do you agree with Jacques? Why or why not?

6. You can have a high degree of operating leverage (DOL) and still have low business risk. Why? By the same token, you can have a low DOL and still have high business risk. Why?

7. Define *financial leverage* and the *degree of financial leverage (DFL)*. How are the two related?

8. Discuss the similarities and differences between financial leverage and operating leverage.

9. Can the concept of financial leverage be analyzed quantitatively? Explain.

10. The EBIT-EPS chart suggests that the higher the debt ratio, the higher are the earnings per share for any level of EBIT above the indifference point. Why do firms sometimes choose financing alternatives that do not maximize EPS?

11. Why is the percentage of debt for an electric utility higher than that for the typical manufacturing company?

12. Is the debt-to-equity ratio a good proxy for financial risk as represented by the cash-flow ability of a company to service debt? Why or why not?

13. How can a company determine in practice if it has too much debt? Too little debt?

14. How can coverage ratios be used to determine an appropriate amount of debt to employ? Are there any shortcomings to the use of these ratios?

15. In financial leverage, why not simply increase leverage as long as the firm is able to earn more on the employment of the funds thus provided than they cost? Would not earnings per share increase?

16. Describe how a company could determine its debt capacity by increasing its debt hypothetically until the probability of running out of cash reached some degree of tolerance.

17. How might a company's bond rating influence a capital structure decision?

SELF-CORRECTION PROBLEMS

1. Stallings Specialty Paint Company has fixed operating costs of $3 million a year. Variable operating costs are $1.75 per half pint of paint produced, and the average selling price is $2 per half pint.

    a. What is the annual operating break-even point in half pints (Q_{BE})? In dollars of sales (S_{BE})?

    b. If variable operating costs decline to $1.68 per half pint, what would happen to the operating break-even point (Q_{BE})?

    c. If fixed costs increase to $3.75 million per year, what would be the effect on the operating break-even point (Q_{BE})?

    d. Compute the degree of operating leverage (DOL) at the current sales level of 16 million half pints.

    e. If sales are expected to increase by 15 percent from the current sales position of 16 million half pints, what would be the resulting percentage change in operating profit (EBIT) from its current position?

2. Gahlon Gearing, Ltd., has a DOL of 2 at its current production and sales level of 10,000 units. The resulting operating income figure is $1,000.

Chapter 16 Operating and Financial Leverage

a. If sales are expected to increase by 20 percent from the current 10,000-unit sales position, what would be the resulting operating profit figure?

b. At the company's new sales position of 12,000 units, what is the firm's "new" DOL figure?

3. David Ding Baseball Bat Company presently has $3 million in debt outstanding, bearing an interest rate of 12 percent. It wishes to finance a $4 million expansion program and is considering three alternatives: additional debt at 14 percent interest (option 1), preferred stock with a 12 percent dividend (option 2), and the sale of common stock at $16 per share (option 3). The company presently has 800,000 shares of common stock outstanding and is in a 40 percent tax bracket.

a. If earnings before interest and taxes are presently $1.5 million, what would be earnings per share for the three alternatives, assuming no immediate increase in operating profit?

b. Develop a break-even, or indifference, chart for these alternatives. What are the approximate indifference points? To check one of these points, mathematically determine the indifference point between the debt plan and the common stock plan. What are the horizontal axis intercepts?

c. Compute the degree of financial leverage (DFL) for each alternative at the expected EBIT level of $1.5 million.

d. Which alternative do you prefer? How much would EBIT need to increase before the next alternative would be "better" (in terms of EPS)?

4. Show how to derive Eq. (16-8),

$$DOL_{Q\text{ units}} = \frac{Q(P-V)}{Q(P-V)-FC} = \frac{Q}{Q-Q_{BE}}$$

from Eq. (16-7),

$$\text{Degree of operating leverage (DOL) at } Q \text{ units of output (or sales)} = \frac{\text{Percentage change in operating profit (EBIT)}}{\text{Percentage change in output (or sales)}}$$

5. Archimedes Torque and Gear Company has $7.4 million in long-term debt having the following payment schedule:

	AMOUNT
15% serial bonds, $100,000 payable annually in principal	$2,400,000
13% first-mortgage bonds, $150,000 payable annually in principal	3,000,000
18% subordinated debentures, interest only until maturity in 10 years	2,000,000
	$7,400,000

Archimedes' common stock has a book value of $8.3 million and a market value of $6 million. The corporate tax rate, federal plus state, is 50 percent. Archimedes is in a cyclical business; its expected EBIT is $2 million, with a standard deviation of $1.5 million. The average debt-to-equity ratio of other companies in the industry is .47.

a. Determine the interest coverage and the debt-service coverage ratios for the company.

b. What are the probabilities that these two ratios will go below 1:1?

c. Does Archimedes have too much debt?

6. Aberez Company and Vorlas Vactor, Inc., have the following financial characteristics:

	ABEREZ		VORLAS VACTOR	
	COMPANY	INDUSTRY NORM	COMPANY	INDUSTRY NORM
Debt to equity	1.10	1.43	.78	.47
Bond rating	Aa	A	Ba	Baa
Interest coverage	6.10	5.70	7.30	7.10
Cash and marketable securities to total assets	.08	.07	.10	.13

On the basis of these data, which company has the greater degree of financial risk? Why?

PROBLEMS

1. The Andrea S. Fault Seismometer Company is an all-equity-financed firm. It earns monthly, after taxes, $24,000 on sales of $880,000. The tax rate of the company is 40 percent. The company's only product, "The Desktop Seismometer," sells for $200, of which $150 is variable cost.
   a. What is the company's monthly fixed operating cost?
   b. What is the monthly operating break-even point in units? In dollars?
   c. Compute and plot the degree of operating leverage (DOL) versus quantity produced and sold for the following possible monthly sales levels: 4,000 units; 4,400 units; 4,800 units; 5,200 units; 5,600 units; and 6,000 units.
   d. What does the graph that you drew (see Part (c))—and especially the company's DOL at its current sales figure—tell you about the sensitivity of the company's operating profit to changes in sales?
2. What would be the effect of the following on the break-even point of the Andrea S. Fault Company (Problem 1)?
   a. An increase in selling price of $50 per unit (assume that sales volume remains constant)
   b. A decrease in fixed operating costs of $20,000 per month
   c. A decrease in variable costs of $10 per unit and an increase in fixed costs of $60,000 per month
3. The Crazy Horse Hotel has a capacity to stable 50 horses. The fee for stabling a horse is $100 per month. Maintenance, depreciation, and other fixed operating costs total $1,200 per month. Variable operating costs per horse are $12 per month for hay and bedding and $8 per month for grain.
   a. Determine the monthly operating break-even point (in horses stabled).
   b. Compute the monthly operating profit if an average of 40 horses are stabled.
4. Cybernauts, Ltd., is a new firm that wishes to determine an appropriate capital structure. It can issue 16 percent debt or 15 percent preferred stock. The total capitalization of the company will be $5 million, and common stock can be sold at $20 per share. The company is expected to have a 50 percent tax rate (federal plus state). Four possible capital structures being considered are as follows:

PLAN	DEBT	PREFERRED	EQUITY
1	0%	0%	100%
2	30	0	70
3	50	0	50
4	50	20	30

a. Construct an EBIT-EPS chart for the four plans. (EBIT is expected to be $1 million.) Be sure to identify the relevant indifference points and determine the horizontal-axis intercepts.

b. Using Eq. (16-12), verify the indifference point on your graph between plans 1 and 3 and between plans 3 and 4.

c. Compute the degree of financial leverage (DFL) for each alternative at an expected EBIT level of $1 million.

d. Which plan is best? Why?

5. Hi-Grade Regulator Company currently has 100,000 shares of common stock outstanding with a market price of $60 per share. It also has $2 million in 6 percent bonds. The company is considering a $3 million expansion program that it can finance with all common stock at $60 a share (option 1), straight bonds at 8 percent interest (option 2), preferred stock at 7 percent (option 3), and half common stock at $60 per share and half 8 percent bonds (option 4).

a. For an expected EBIT level of $1 million after the expansion program, calculate the earnings per share for each of the alternative methods of financing. Assume a tax rate of 50 percent.

b. Construct an EBIT-EPS chart. Calculate the indifference points between alternatives. What is your interpretation of them?

6. Hi-Grade Regulator Company (see Problem 5) expects the EBIT level after the expansion program to be $1 million, with a two-thirds probability that it will be between $600,000 and $1,400,000.

a. Which financing alternative do you prefer? Why?

b. Suppose that the expected EBIT level were $1.5 million and that there is a two-thirds probability that it would be between $1.3 million and $1.7 million. Which financing alternative would you prefer? Why?

7. Fazio Pump Corporation presently has 1.1 million shares of common stock outstanding and $8 million in debt bearing an interest rate of 10 percent on average. It is considering a $5 million expansion program financed with either common stock at $20 per share being realized (option 1), debt at an interest rate of 11 percent (option 2), or preferred stock with a 10 percent dividend rate (option 3). Earnings before interest and taxes (EBIT) after the new funds are raised are expected to be $6 million, and the company's tax rate is 35 percent.

a. Determine likely earnings per share after financing for each of the three alternatives.

b. What would happen if EBIT were $3 million? $4 million? $8 million?

c. What would happen under the original conditions if the tax rate were 46 percent? If the interest rate on new debt were 8 percent and the preferred stock dividend rate were 7 percent? If the common could be sold for $40 per share?

8. Boehm-Gau Real Estate Speculators, Inc., and the Northern California Electric Utility Company have the following EBIT and debt-servicing burden:

	BOEHM-GAU	NORTHERN CALIFORNIA
Expected EBIT	$5,000,000	$100,000,000
Annual interest	1,600,000	45,000,000
Annual principal payments on debt	2,000,000	35,000,000

The tax rate for Boehm-Gau is 40 percent, and for Northern California Electric Utility is 36 percent. Compute the interest coverage and the debt-service coverage ratios for the two companies. With which company would you feel more comfortable if you were a lender? Why?

9. The debt ratios of four companies are

COMPANY	TOTAL DEBT/ TOTAL ASSETS	LONG-TERM DEBT/ TOTAL CAPITALIZATION*
A	.56	.43
B	.64	.66
C	.47	.08
D	.42	.26

*Total capitalization represents all long-term debt plus shareholders' equity.

The companies are part of the following industries: supermarket, chemical, apparel making, and airline (not in order). Match the company with the industry.

SOLUTIONS TO SELF-CORRECTION PROBLEMS

1.

a. $Q_{BE} = \dfrac{\$3M}{(\$2.00 - \$1.75)} = $ **12 million half pints**

$S_{BE} = \dfrac{\$3M}{1 - (\$1.75/\$2.00)} = $ **$24 million in annual sales**

b. $Q_{BE} = \dfrac{\$3M}{(\$2.00 - \$1.68)} = $ **9.375 million half pints**

c. $Q_{BE} = \dfrac{\$3.75M}{(\$2.00 - \$1.75)} = $ **15 million half pints**

d. $DOL_{16 \text{ million units}} = \dfrac{16M}{(16M - 12M)} = $ **4**

e. (15 percent) $\times$ 4 = **60% increase in EBIT**

2.

a. (Percentage change in sales) $\times$ DOL = Percentage change in EBIT
(20 percent) $\times$ 2 = 40% change in EBIT
Therefore, $\$1,000 \times (1 + .40) = $ **$1,400**

b. $DOL_{10,000 \text{ units}} = \dfrac{10,000}{10,000 - Q_{BE}} = 2$

Therefore, Q_{BE} must equal 5,000 units.

$DOL_{12,000 \text{ units}} = \dfrac{12,000}{12,000 - 5,000} = $ **1.7**

3. a. (000s omitted)

	DEBT	PREFERRED STOCK	COMMON STOCK
Operating profit (EBIT)	$1,500	$1,500	$1,500
Interest on existing debt	360	360	360
Interest on new debt	560	—	—
Profit before taxes	$ 580	$1,140	$1,140
Taxes	232	456	456
Profit after taxes	$ 348	$ 684	$ 684
Preferred stock dividend	—	480	—
Earnings available to common shareholders	$ 348	$ 204	$ 684
Number of shares	800	800	1,050
Earnings per share	**$ .435**	**$ .255**	**$ .651**

b.

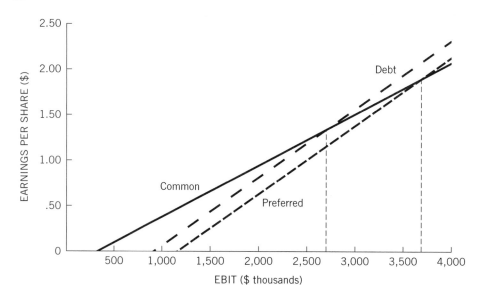

Approximate indifference points:

Debt (1) and common (3): **$2.7 million in EBIT**
Preferred (2) and common (3): **$3.7 million in EBIT**

Debt dominates preferred by the same margin throughout. There is no indifference point between these two alternative financing methods.

Mathematically, the indifference point between debt (1) and common (3), with 000s omitted, is

$$
\underset{\textit{Debt (1)}}{\frac{(EBIT_{1,3} - \$920)(1 - .40) - 0}{800}} = \underset{\textit{Common Stock (3)}}{\frac{(EBIT_{1,3} - \$360)(1 - .40) - 0}{1,050}}
$$

Cross multiplying and rearranging, we obtain

$$(EBIT_{1,3})(.60)(1,050) - (\$920)(.60)(1,050) = (EBIT_{1,3})(.60)(800) - (\$360)(.60)(800)$$

$$(EBIT_{1,3})(630) - (\$579,600) = (EBIT_{1,3})(480) - (\$172,800)$$

$$(EBIT_{1,3})(150) = \$406,800$$

$$(EBIT_{1,3}) = \textbf{\$2,712}$$

Note that for the debt alternative, the total before-tax interest is *$920,* and this is the intercept on the horizontal axis. For the preferred stock alternative, we divide $480 by $(1 - .4)$ to get $800. When this is added to $360 in interest on existing debt, the intercept becomes *$1,160.*

c.

Debt (1):

$$
DFL_{EBIT \text{ of } \$1.5 \text{ million}} = \frac{\$1,500,000}{\$1,500,000 - \$920,000} = \textbf{2.59}
$$

Preferred (2):

$$DFL_{EBIT\,of\,\$1.5\,million} = \frac{\$1,500,000}{\$1,500,000 - \$360,000 - [\$480,000/(1 - .40)]} = \textbf{4.41}$$

Common (3):

$$DFL_{EBIT\,of\,\$1.5\,million} = \frac{\$1,500,000}{\$1,500,000 - \$360,000} = \textbf{1.32}$$

    d. For the present EBIT level, common is clearly preferable. EBIT would need to increase by $2,712,000 − $1,500,000 = **$1,212,000** before an indifference point with debt is reached. One would want to be comfortably above this indifference point before a strong case for debt should be made. The lower the probability that actual EBIT will fall below the indifference point, the stronger the case that can be made for debt, all other things the same.

4.

$$DOL_{Q\,units} = \frac{\text{Percentage change in operating profit (EBIT)}}{\text{Percentage change in output (or sales)}} = \frac{\left[\dfrac{\Delta Q(P - V)}{Q(P - V) - FC}\right]}{\Delta Q/Q}$$

Which reduces to
$$DOL_{Q\,units} = \frac{Q(P - V)}{Q(P - V) - FC}$$

Dividing both the numerator and denominator by $(P - V)$ produces

$$DOL_{Q\,units} = \frac{Q}{Q - [FC/(P - V)]} = \frac{Q}{Q - Q_{BE}}$$

5. a. Total annual interest is determined as follows:

15% of $2.4 million =	$ 360,000
13% of $3.0 million =	390,000
18% of $2.0 million =	360,000
	$1,110,000

Interest coverage ratio = $2,000,000/$1,110,000 = **1.80**

Total annual principal payments = $100,000 + $150,000 = $250,000

$$\text{Debt-service coverage ratio} = \frac{\$2,000,000}{\$1,110,000 + [\$250,000/(1 - .50)]} = \textbf{1.24}$$

    b. Required deviation of EBIT from its mean value before ratio in question becomes 1:1:

Interest coverage: $1,110,000 − $2,000,000 = −$890,000

Debt-service coverage: $1,610,000 − $2,000,000 = −$390,000

Standardizing each deviation from the mean produces the following Z-scores:

Interest coverage: $\dfrac{-\$890,000}{\$1,500,000} =$ −.593 standard deviations (left of the mean)

Debt-service coverage: $\dfrac{-\$390,000}{\$1,500,000} =$ −.260 standard deviations (left of the mean)

Table V in the Appendix at the end of the book can be used to determine the proportion of the area under the normal curve that is Z standard deviations left of the mean. This proportion corresponds to the probability that an EBIT figure will occur that produces coverage ratios lower than 1:1. For interest coverage and debt-service coverage ratios less than 1:1, these probabilities are approximately 28 percent and 40 percent, respectively. These probabilities assume that the distribution of possible EBITs is normal.

c. There is a substantial probability, 40 percent, that the company will fail to cover its interest and principal payments. Its debt ratio (using either book or market values) is much higher than the industry norm of .47. Although the information is limited, based on what we have, it would appear that Archimedes has too much debt. However, other factors, such as liquidity, may mitigate against this conclusion.

6. Aberez has a lower debt ratio than its industry norm. Vorlas has a higher ratio relative to its industry. Both companies exceed modestly their industry norms with respect to interest coverage. The lower debt-to-equity ratio and higher interest coverage for Vorlas's industry suggests that its industry might have more business risk than the industry of which Aberez is a part. The liquidity ratio of Aberez is higher than the industry norm, whereas that for Vorlas is lower than the industry norm. Although all three financial ratios for Vorlas are better than are those for Aberez, they are lower relative to the industry norm. Finally, the bond rating of Aberez is much better than is that of Vorlas, being an Aa grade and higher than the industry norm. The bond rating of Vorlas is one grade below the very lowest grade for investment-grade bonds. It is also lower than the typical company's bond rating in the industry. If the industry norms are reasonable representations of underlying business and financial risk, we would say that Vorlas had the greater degree of risk.

SELECTED REFERENCES

Donaldson, Gordon. *Corporate Debt Capacity.* Boston: Division of Research, Harvard Business School, 1961.

———. "Strategy for Financial Emergencies." *Harvard Business Review* 47 (November–December 1969), 67–79.

Gahlon, James. "Operating Leverage as a Determinant of Systematic Risk." *Journal of Business Research* 9 (September 1981), 297–308.

———, and James Gentry. "On the Relationship Between Systematic Risk and the Degrees of Operating and Financial Leverage." *Financial Management* 11 (Summer 1982), 15–23.

Hong, Hai, and Alfred Rappaport. "Debt Capacity, Optimal Capital Structure, and Capital Budgeting." *Financial Management* 7 (Autumn 1978), 7–11.

Levy, Haim, and Robert Brooks. "Financial Break-Even Analysis and the Value of the Firm." *Financial Management* 15 (Autumn 1986), 22–26.

Myers, Stewart C. "Capital Structure Puzzle." *Journal of Finance* 39 (July 1984), 575–92.

Piper, Thomas R., and Wolf A. Weinhold. "How Much Debt Is Right for Your Company?" *Harvard Business Review* 60 (July–August 1982), 106–14.

Chapter 17

Capital Structure Determination

A CONCEPTUAL LOOK
  Net Operating Income Approach • Traditional Approach
THE TOTAL-VALUE PRINCIPLE
  Arbitrage Support Illustrated
PRESENCE OF MARKET IMPERFECTIONS AND INCENTIVE ISSUES
  Bankruptcy Costs • Agency Costs • Debt and the Incentive to
      Manage Efficiently • Institutional Restrictions • Transactions
      Costs
THE EFFECT OF TAXES
  Corporate Taxes • Uncertainty of Tax-Shield Benefits • Corporate
      Plus Personal Taxes
TAXES AND MARKET IMPERFECTIONS COMBINED
  Bankruptcy Costs, Agency Costs, and Taxes • Impact of
      Additional Imperfections
FINANCIAL SIGNALING
SUMMARY
QUESTIONS
SELF-CORRECTION PROBLEMS
PROBLEMS
SOLUTIONS TO SELF-CORRECTION PROBLEMS
SELECTED REFERENCES

> When you have eliminated the impossible, whatever remains, however
> improbable, must be the truth.

—SHERLOCK HOLMES
IN *THE SIGN OF THE FOUR*

Capital structure The mix (or proportion) of a firm's permanent long-term financing represented by debt, preferred stock, and common stock equity.

In the last chapter we approached the question of how much debt a company should have in its **capital structure.** The incremental expected return and risk to common shareholders are very much a part of the answer. Now we explore the valuation underpinnings to the question of capital structure. As we shall see, much controversy surrounds the issue. Despite the unsettled nature of the matter, we hope that this presentation will provide the conceptual backdrop necessary to guide the financial manager in capital structure decisions.

Throughout our discussion, we assume that the investment and asset management decisions of the firm are held constant. We do this in an attempt to isolate the effect of a change in financing mix on share price. The focus is different from before in that we are concerned with how security prices are determined in the financial markets. That is, how do suppliers of capital value a company in relation to other firms when the company changes its capital structure? We shall see that financial market imperfections play a major role in this valuation process. For simplicity, we consider only debt-versus-equity financing, though the principles discussed apply to preferred stock financing as well.

A CONCEPTUAL LOOK

The key question with which we are concerned is whether a firm can affect its total valuation (debt plus equity) and its cost of capital by changing its financing mix. We must be careful not to confuse any effects of a change in the financing mix with the results of investment or asset management decisions made by the firm. Therefore, changes in the financing mix are assumed to occur by issuing debt and repurchasing common stock or by issuing common stock and retiring debt. In what follows, our attention is directed to what happens to the total valuation of the firm and to its overall required return when the ratio of debt to equity, or the relative amount of financial leverage, is varied.

For ease of illustration, let us assume that we are concerned with a company whose earnings are not expected to grow and that pays out all of its earnings to shareholders in the form of dividends. Moreover, suppose that we live in a world where there are no income taxes. Later, this assumption will be relaxed to consider the very real-world issue of taxes. For now, the matter of capital structure can best be understood if we assume no taxes and later treat taxes as a financial market imperfection.

In the subsequent discussion we are concerned with three different rates of return. The first is

$$k_i = \frac{I}{B} = \frac{\text{Annual interest on debt}}{\text{Market value of debt outstanding}} \qquad \text{(17-1)}$$

In this equation, k_i is the yield on the company's debt, assuming this debt to be perpetual.[1] The second rate of return with which we are concerned is

$$k_e = \frac{E}{S} = \frac{\text{Earnings available to common shareholders}}{\text{Market value of common stock outstanding}} \qquad \text{(17-2)}$$

With our assumptions of a firm whose earnings are not expected to grow and that has a 100 percent dividend payout, the firm's earnings/price ratio represents the

---

[1] In Chapter 4 we saw that the price of a security expected to provide a fixed periodic receipt of R forever is $P = R/k$, where k is the yield on a perpetual investment. Rearranging, we have $k = R/P$, which is equivalent to Eq. (17-1).

market rate of discount that equates the present value of the perpetual stream of expected constant future dividends with the current market price of the common stock.[2] This is not to say that this particular equation should be used as a general rule to depict the required return on equity. (See Chapter 15.) We use it here only because it works for our example situation of zero growth—a situation chosen specifically for its simplicity in illustrating the theory of capital structure. The final rate we consider is

$$k_o = \frac{O}{V} = \frac{\text{Net operating income}}{\text{Total market value of the firm}} \qquad \text{(17-3)}$$

where $V = B + S$ (i.e., the total market value of the firm is the sum of the market value of its debt and equity), and $O = I + E$ (i.e., the firm's net operating income is equal to interest paid plus earnings available to common shareholders). Here, k_o is an overall **capitalization rate** for the firm. It is defined as the weighted average cost of capital and may also be expressed as

Capitalization rate The discount rate used to determine the present value of a stream of expected future cash flows.

$$k_o = k_i \left[\frac{B}{B + S} \right] + k_e \left[\frac{S}{B + S} \right] \qquad \text{(17-4)}$$

We want to know what happens to k_i, k_e, and k_o when the amount of financial leverage, as denoted by the ratio B/S, increases.

Net Operating Income Approach

Net operating income (NOI) approach (to capital structure) A theory of capital structure in which the weighted average cost of capital and the total value of the firm remain constant as financial leverage is changed.

One approach to the valuation of the earnings of a company is known as the **net operating income (NOI) approach.** To illustrate it, assume that a firm has $1,000 in debt at 10 percent interest, that the expected annual net operating income (NOI or EBIT) figure is $1,000, and that the overall capitalization rate, k_o, is 15 percent. Given this information, we may calculate the value of the firm as follows:

O	Net operating income	$1,000
k_o	Overall capitalization rate	÷ .15
V	Total value of the firm (O/k_o)	$6,667
B	Market value of debt	1,000
S	Market value of stock $(V - B)$	$5,667

The earnings available to common shareholders, E, is simply net operating income minus interest payments, $O - I$, or $1,000 - $100 = **$900.** The implied required return on equity is

$$k_e = \frac{E}{S} = \frac{\$900}{\$5,667} = \textbf{15.88\%}$$

With this approach, net operating income is capitalized (discounted) at the firm's overall capitalization rate to obtain the total market value of the firm. The market value of the debt is then deducted from the total market value to obtain the market value of the common stock. Note that with this approach the overall capitalization rate, k_o, as well as the cost of debt funds, k_i, stays the same regardless of the financial leverage employed. However, the required return on equity, k_e, increases linearly with financial leverage measured as B/S.

---

[2]Dividing both the numerator and denominator in Eq. (17-2) by the number of shares outstanding reveals that the market rate of discount, in this case, is equivalent to the earnings/price ratio.

To illustrate, suppose that the firm increases the amount of debt from $1,000 to $3,000 and uses the proceeds of the debt issue to repurchase common stock. The valuation of the firm would then proceed as follows:

O	Net operating income	$1,000
k_o	Overall capitalization rate	÷ .15
V	Total value of the firm (O/k_o)	$6,667
B	Market value of debt	3,000
S	Market value of stock $(V - B)$	$3,667

The earnings available to common shareholders, E, is equal to net operating income minus the now higher interest payments, or $1,000 − $300 = **$700.** The implied required return on equity is

$$k_e = \frac{E}{S} = \frac{\$700}{\$3,667} = \mathbf{19.09\%}$$

We see that the required return on equity, k_e, rises with increasing leverage. This approach implies that the total valuation of the firm is unaffected by its capital structure. The reason is that both net operating income and the capitalization rate applied to that income remain constant in the face of changing capital structure. Figure 17-1 shows the NOI approach graphically.

Importantly, not only is the total value of the firm unaffected by changes in financial leverage but so is share price. To illustrate, assume in our example that the firm with $1,000 in debt has 100 shares of common stock outstanding. Thus, the market price per share is $5,667/100 = **$56.67.** The firm then issues $2,000 in additional debt and at the same time repurchases $2,000 of stock at $56.67 per share, or

FIGURE 17-1
Capital Costs and the Net Operating Income (NOI) Approach to Capital Structure

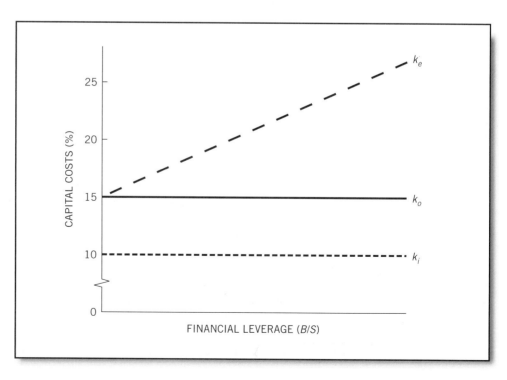

Part VI The Cost of Capital, Capital Structure, and Dividend Policy

The Coca-Cola Company Comments on Its Use of Debt Financing

Debt Financing—Our Company maintains prudent debt levels based on our cash flow, interest coverage and percentage of debt to capital. We use debt financing to lower our overall cost of capital, which increases our return on share-owners' equity.

Source: The Coca-Cola Company 1998 Annual Report, p. 29.
Reproduced with permission of The Coca-Cola Company.

Recapitalization An alteration of a firm's capital structure. For example, a firm may sell bonds to acquire the cash necessary to repurchase some of its outstanding common stock.

35.29 shares if we permit fractional shares. It now has $100 - 35.29 = $ **64.71** shares outstanding. We saw that the total market value of the firm's stock after the change in capital structure is $3,667. Therefore, the market price per share is $3,667/64.71 = **$56.67,** the same as before the increase in financial leverage resulting from **recapitalization.**

The critical assumption with this approach is that k_o is constant regardless of the amount of financial leverage. The market capitalizes the net operating income of the firm and thereby determines the value of the firm as a whole. As a result, the mix of debt and equity financing is unimportant. An increase in the supposedly "cheaper" debt funds is exactly offset by the increase in the required rate of return on equity, k_e. Thus, the weighted average of k_e and k_i remains constant as financial leverage is changed. As a firm increases its use of financial leverage, it becomes increasingly more risky. Investors penalize the stock by raising the required equity return directly in keeping with the increase in the debt-to-equity ratio. As long as k_i remains constant, k_e is a constant linear function of the debt-to-equity ratio (measured in market value terms). Because the cost of capital of the firm, k_o, cannot be altered through financial leverage, the net operating income approach implies that there is no one optimal capital structure.

So far, our discussion of the net operating income approach has been purely definitional. It lacks behavioral significance. Two Nobel Prize–winning finance theorists, Modigliani and Miller, offered behavioral support for the independence of the total valuation and cost of capital of the firm from its capital structure.[3] Before taking up the implications of their position, however, we examine what is called the **traditional approach** to capital structure and valuation.

Traditional approach (to capital structure) A theory of capital structure in which there exists an optimal capital structure and where management can increase the total value of the firm through the judicious use of financial leverage.

Traditional Approach

The traditional approach to capital structure and valuation assumes that there is an **optimal capital structure** and that management can increase the total value of the firm through the judicious use of financial leverage. This approach suggests that the firm can initially lower its cost of capital and raise its total value through increasing leverage. Although investors raise the required rate of return on equity, the increase in k_e does not entirely offset the benefit of using "cheaper" debt funds. As more and more financial leverage occurs, investors increasingly penalize the firm's required equity return until eventually this effect more than offsets the benefits of "cheaper" debt funds.

Optimal capital structure The capital structure that minimizes the firm's cost of capital and thereby maximizes the value of the firm.

In one variation of the traditional approach, shown in Figure 17-2, k_e is assumed to rise at an increasing rate with financial leverage, whereas k_i is assumed to rise only

---

[3]Franco Modigliani and Merton Miller, "The Cost of Capital, Corporation Finance and the Theory of Investment," *American Economic Review* 48 (June 1958), 261–97.

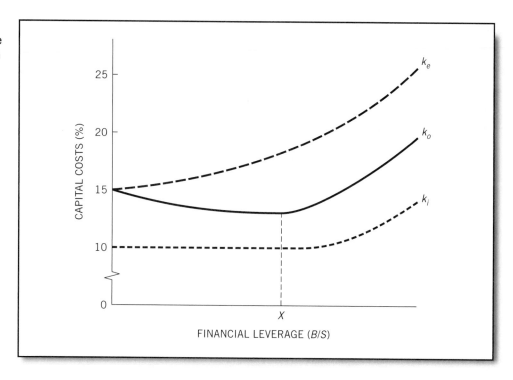

after a significant increase in financial leverage has occurred. At first, the weighted average cost of capital declines with leverage because the rise in k_e does not entirely offset the use of cheaper debt funds. As a result, the weighted average cost of capital, k_o, declines with the moderate use of financial leverage. After a point, however, the increase in k_e more than offsets the use of cheaper debt funds in the capital structure, and k_o begins to rise. The rise in k_o is supported further, once k_i begins to rise. The optimal capital structure is the point at which k_o bottoms out. In the figure, this optimal capital structure is represented by point X. At the optimal capital structure position represented by point X, not only will the firm's weighted average cost of capital be at its lowest point but the firm's total value will be at its highest point. This is because the lower the capitalization rate, k_o, applied to the firm's net operating income stream, the higher the present value of that stream. Thus, the traditional approach to capital structure implies that (1) the cost of capital is dependent on the capital structure of the firm, and (2) there is an optimal capital structure.

THE TOTAL-VALUE PRINCIPLE

Modigliani and Miller (M&M) in their original position advocate that the relationship between financial leverage and the cost of capital is explained by the net operating income approach. They make a formidable attack on the traditional position by offering behavioral justification for having the firm's overall capitalization rate, k_o, remain constant throughout the entire range of financial leverage possibilities.

M&M argue that the total risk for all security holders of a firm is not altered by changes in the firm's capital structure. Therefore, the total value of the firm must be

FIGURE 17-3
Illustration of the
Total-Value Principle
Showing the Value
of a Firm Is Indepen-
dent of Its Capital
Structure

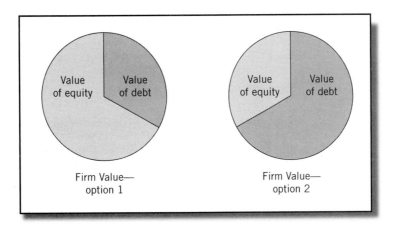

Firm Value—
option 1

Firm Value—
option 2

the same, regardless of the firm's financing mix. Simply put, the M&M position is based on the idea that no matter how you divide up the capital structure of a firm among debt, equity, and other claims, there is a conservation of investment value. That is, because the total investment value of a corporation depends on its underlying profitability and risk, firm value is unchanging with respect to changes in the firm's capital structure. Thus, in the absence of taxes and other market imperfections, the value of the total pie does not change as it is divided into debt, equity, and other securities. This idea is illustrated with the two pie graphs in Figure 17-3. Different mixes of debt and equity do not alter the overall size of the pie; in other words, the total value of the firm stays the same.

The support for this position rests on the idea that investors are able to substitute personal for corporate financial leverage. Thus, investors have the ability, through personal borrowing, to replicate any capital structure the firm might undertake. Because the firm is unable to do something for its shareholders (in terms of making use of financial leverage) that these shareholders cannot do for themselves, capital structure changes are not a thing of value in the world of perfect capital markets that M&M assume. Therefore, two firms alike in every respect except for capital structure must have the same total value. If not, **arbitrage** will be possible, and its occurrence will cause the two firms to sell in the market at the same total value. In other words, arbitrage precludes perfect substitutes from selling at different prices in the same market.

Arbitrage Finding two assets that are essentially the same, buying the cheaper, and selling the more expensive.

Arbitrage Support Illustrated

Consider two (zero-growth) companies identical in every respect except that Company NL has no financial leverage, whereas Company L has $30,000 of 12 percent bonds outstanding. According to the traditional approach to capital structure, Company L may have a higher total value and lower weighted average cost of capital than Company NL. For simplicity, we assume that Company L's debt has a market value equal to its par value (implying that the coupon rate on its debt equals the current market-required interest rate). We also assume that the required return on equity for Company L is 16 percent (slightly higher than that for company NL). The valuation of the two firms is assumed to proceed as follows:

		COMPANY NL	COMPANY L
O	Net operating income	$10,000	$10,000
I	Interest on debt	—	3,600
E	Earnings available to common shareholders $(O - I)$	$10,000	$ 6,400
k_e	Required return on equity	$\div.15$	$\div.16$
S	Market value of stock (E/k_e)	$66,667	$40,000
B	Market value of debt	—	30,000
V	Total value of firm $(B + S)$	$66,667	$70,000
k_o	Implied overall capitalization rate $[k_i(B/V) + k_e(S/V)]$	.15	.143
B/S	Debt-to-equity ratio	0	.75

M&M maintain that the situation just described cannot continue because arbitrage will drive the total values of the two firms together. Company L cannot command a higher total value simply because it has a financing mix different from Company NL's. M&M argue that Company L's investors would be able to maintain their same total dollar return for a smaller personal investment outlay and with no increase in financial risk by engaging in arbitrage. This would call for investors to sell their shares in Company L (the overvalued asset) and buy shares in Company NL (the undervalued asset). These arbitrage transactions would continue until Company L's shares declined in price and Company NL's shares increased in price enough to make the total value of the two firms identical.

For example, assume that you are a rational investor who owns 1 percent of the stock of Company L, the levered firm, with a market value of $40,000 × .01 = **$400.** You should

1. Sell the stock in Company L for $400.
2. Borrow $300 at 12 percent interest. This personal debt is equal to 1 percent of the debt of Company L—the same percentage as your previous ownership interest in Company L. (Your total capital available for investment is now $400 + $300 = **$700.**)
3. Buy 1 percent of the shares of Company NL, the unlevered firm, for $666.67 and still have $700 − $666.67 = **$33.33** left over for other investments.

Prior to this series of transactions, your expected return on investment in Company L's common stock was 16 percent on an investment of $400, or $64. Your return on investment in Company NL is 15 percent on a $666.67 investment, or $100. From this return, you must deduct the interest charges on your personal borrowings, so your net dollar return is determined as follows:

Return on investment in Company NL	$100
Less: Interest paid ($300 × .12)	36
Net return	$ 64

Your net dollar return, $64, is the same as it was for your investment in Company L. However, your personal cash outlay of $366.67 ($666.67 less personal borrowings of $300) is $33.33 less than the previous $400 investment in Company L, the levered firm. Because of the lower personal investment, you would prefer to invest in Company NL under the conditions we described. In essence, you "lever" the common stock of the unlevered firm by taking on personal debt.

The action of a number of investors undertaking similar arbitrage transactions will tend to (1) *drive up* Company NL's share price while *lowering* its required return on equity, and (2) *drive down* Company L's share price while *increasing* its required

Part VI The Cost of Capital, Capital Structure, and Dividend Policy

return on equity. This arbitrage process will continue until there is no further opportunity for reducing one's investment outlay and achieving the same dollar return. At this equilibrium, the total value of the two firms must be the same. As a result, the weighted average costs of capital for the two firms, the k_os, must also be the same.

The important element in this process is the presence of rational investors in the market who are willing to substitute personal, or "homemade," financial leverage for corporate financial leverage. On the basis of the arbitrage process illustrated, M&M conclude that a firm cannot change its total value or its weighted average cost of capital by using financial leverage. From our earlier discussion of the NOI approach—the approach advocated by M&M—we saw that not only is the total value of the firm unaffected by changes in financial leverage but so is share price. Consequently, the financing decision does not matter from the standpoint of our objective of maximizing market price per share. One capital structure is as good as the next.

PRESENCE OF MARKET IMPERFECTIONS AND INCENTIVE ISSUES

With perfect capital markets, the arbitrage argument ensures the validity of M&M's contention that the cost of capital and total valuation of a firm are independent of its capital structure. To dispute the M&M position, we need to look for reasons why the arbitrage process may not work perfectly. The following are the major arguments against the M&M arbitrage process.

Bankruptcy Costs

If there is a possibility of bankruptcy and if administrative and other costs associated with bankruptcy are significant, the levered firm may be less attractive to investors than the unlevered one. With perfect capital markets, zero bankruptcy costs are assumed. If the firm goes bankrupt, assets presumably can be sold at their economic values with no liquidating or legal costs involved. Proceeds from the sale are distributed according to the priority of claims on assets as described in the Appendix to Chapter 23. If capital markets are less than perfect, however, there may be administrative costs, and assets may have to be liquidated at less than their economic values. These administrative costs and the "shortfall" in liquidating value from economic value represent a drain on the system from the viewpoint of the debt and equity holders. (See the Appendix to Chapter 23 for a discussion of the administrative aspects of bankruptcy.)

In the event of bankruptcy, security holders as a whole receive less than they would have in the absence of bankruptcy costs. To the extent that the levered firm has a greater possibility of bankruptcy than the unlevered one, it would be a less attractive investment, all other things being the same. The possibility of bankruptcy is not a linear function of the debt-to-equity ratio but rather increases at an increasing rate beyond some threshold. As a result, the expected cost of bankruptcy also increases in this accelerating manner and would be expected to have a corresponding negative effect on the value of the firm.

Put another way, investors are likely to penalize the price of the stock as leverage increases. The nature of the penalty is illustrated in Figure 17-4 for the case of a no-tax world. Here the required rate of return for equity investors, k_e, is broken down

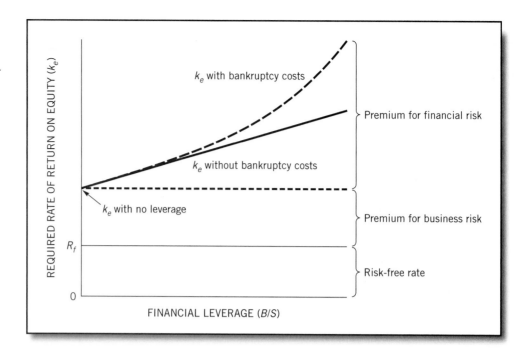

into its component parts. There is the risk-free rate, R_f, plus a premium for business risk. The premium is depicted on the vertical axis by the difference between the required rate of return for an all-equity capital structure and the risk-free rate. As debt is added, the required rate of return rises, and this increment represents a financial-risk premium. In the absence of bankruptcy costs, the required return would rise in a linear manner according to M&M, and this relationship is shown. However, allowing for bankruptcy costs and an increasing probability of bankruptcy with increasing financial leverage, the required rate of return on equity would be expected to rise at an increasing rate beyond some point. At first there might be a negligible probability of bankruptcy, so there would be little or no penalty. As financial leverage increases, so too does the penalty. For extreme leverage, the penalty becomes very substantial indeed.

Agency Costs

Agency costs Costs associated with monitoring management to ensure that it behaves in ways consistent with the firm's contractual agreements with creditors and share-holders.

Closely related to bankruptcy costs with respect to impact on capital structure and value are **agency costs.** We may think of management as *agents* of the owners of the company, the shareholders. These shareholders, hoping that the agents will act in the shareholders' best interests, delegate decision-making authority to them. For management to make optimal decisions in the shareholders' behalf, it is important that management not only have the correct incentives (salary, bonuses, stock options, and "perks") but that it be monitored as well. Monitoring can be done through such methods as bonding the agents, auditing financial statements, and explicitly restricting management decisions. Creditors monitor the behavior of management and shareholders by imposing protective covenants in loan agreements between the borrower and lenders. (See Chapter 20.) The monitoring activities mentioned necessarily involve costs.

Jensen and Meckling have developed a sophisticated theory of agency costs.[4] Among other things, they show that regardless of who makes the monitoring expenditures, the cost is ultimately borne by shareholders. For example, debt holders, anticipating monitoring expenditures, charge higher interest. The greater the probable monitoring costs, the higher the interest rate, and the lower the value of the firm to its shareholders, all other things staying the same. The presence of monitoring costs acts as a disincentive to the issuance of debt, particularly beyond a prudent amount. It is likely that the amount of monitoring required by debt holders increases with the amount of debt outstanding. When there is little or no debt, lenders may engage in only limited monitoring, whereas with a great deal of debt, they may insist on extensive monitoring. Monitoring costs, like bankruptcy costs, tend to rise at an increasing rate with financial leverage, as illustrated in Figure 17-4.

Debt and the Incentive to Manage Efficiently

Working in the opposite direction from bankruptcy and agency costs is the notion that high debt levels create incentives for management to be more efficient.[5] By taking on the cash-flow obligation to service debt, it is claimed that management's "feet are held close to the fire." As a result there is said to be an incentive not to squander funds in wasteful expenditures, whether it be for an investment, a "perk," a company plane, or whatever. The idea is that levered companies may be leaner because management cuts the fat. In contrast, the company with little debt and significant *free cash flow* (cash left over after investing in all worthwhile projects) may have a tendency to squander money. In the absence of other incentives, "running scared" to make debt payments may have a salutary effect on efficiency.

Institutional Restrictions

Restrictions on investment behavior may retard the arbitrage process. Many institutional investors, such as pension funds and life insurance companies, are not allowed to engage in the "homemade" leverage that was described earlier. Regulatory bodies often restrict stock and bond investments to a list of companies meeting certain quality standards such as exhibiting only a "safe" amount of financial leverage. If a company exceeds that amount, its securities may be removed from the *approved list,* thereby preventing certain institutions from investing in them. This reduction in institutional investor demand can have an adverse effect on the market value of the company's financial instruments.

Transactions Costs

Transactions costs tend to restrict the arbitrage process. Arbitrage will take place only up to the limits imposed by transactions costs, after which it is no longer profitable. As a result, the levered firm could have a slightly higher or slightly lower total value than theory might dictate. The direction of the net effect of this imperfection is not predictable.

---

[4]Michael C. Jensen and William H. Meckling, "Theory of the Firm: Managerial Behavior, Agency Costs and Ownership Structure," *Journal of Financial Economics* 3 (October 1976), 305–60.

[5]A number of people have made this argument, but it is perhaps articulated best in Michael C. Jensen, "The Takeover Controversy: Analysis and Evidence," *Midland Corporate Finance Journal* 4 (Summer 1986), 12–21.

With the exception of the incentive to manage efficiently and of transactions costs, the factors discussed above limit the amount of debt that the firm will want to issue. In particular, extreme financial leverage will be burdened by a number of costs and restrictions. If market imperfections systematically affect the arbitrage process, then capital structure decisions may matter. To develop a complete picture, we must include the important role of taxes, to which we now turn.

THE EFFECT OF TAXES

When we allow for taxes, most financial experts agree that the judicious use of financial leverage can have a favorable impact on a company's total valuation. We must consider two taxes—corporate and personal. Because their effects are different, we take them up separately. In the end, we will draw together their separate effects along with those of the market imperfections previously considered. For now, we assume that there are no market imperfections other than the presence of corporate taxes.

Corporate Taxes

The advantage of debt in a world of corporate taxes is that interest payments are a tax-deductible expense to the debt-issuing firm. However, dividends paid are not a tax-deductible expense to the dividend-paying corporation. Consequently, the total amount of funds available to pay both debt holders and shareholders is greater if debt is employed.

To illustrate, suppose that net operating income is $2,000 for Companies ND and D. These two companies are alike in every respect except for their use of financial leverage. Company D has $5,000 in debt at 12 percent interest, whereas Company ND has no debt. If the tax rate (federal plus state) is 40 percent for each company, we have

	COMPANY ND	COMPANY D
Net operating income	$2,000	$2,000
Interest on debt (also, income to debt holders)	—	600
Income before taxes	$2,000	$1,400
Taxes (at .40 rate)	800	560
Income available to common shareholders	$1,200	$ 840
Total income available to *all* (debt plus equity) security holders	$1,200	$1,440
Difference in income available to *all* (debt plus equity) security holders		$240

Thus, total income available to both debt holders and shareholders is larger for the levered Company D than it is for unlevered Company ND. The reason is that debt holders receive interest payments before the deduction of taxes at the corporate level, whereas income to shareholders is available only after corporate taxes have been paid. In essence, the government pays a subsidy to the levered firm for the firm's use of debt. Because interest on debt reduces taxable income, it is called a **tax shield.** Total income available to all investors increases by an amount equal to the interest tax shield times the corporate tax rate. In our example, this amounts to $600 × .40 = **$240.** This figure represents a tax-shield benefit that the government provides the levered company. If the debt employed by a company is permanent, the present value of the annual tax-shield benefit using the perpetual cash-flow formula is

Tax shield A tax-deductible expense. The expense protects (shields) an equivalent dollar amount of revenue from being taxed by reducing taxable income.

478   **Part VI The Cost of Capital, Capital Structure, and Dividend Policy**

$$\text{Present value of tax-shield benefits of debt} = \frac{(r)(B)(t_c)}{r} = (B)(t_c) \tag{17-5}$$

where r is the interest rate on the debt, B is the market value of the debt, and t_c is the corporate tax rate. For Company D in our example, we have

$$\text{Present value of tax-shield benefits of debt} = (\$5,000)(.40) = \mathbf{\$2,000}$$

The "bottom line" is that the interest tax shield is a thing of value and that the overall value of Company D is $2,000 higher because the company employed debt than it would be if the company had no debt. This increased valuation occurs because the stream of income to all investors is $240 per year greater than in the absence of debt. The present value of $240 per year discounted at 12 percent is $240/.12 = **$2,000.** Implied is that the risk associated with the tax-shield benefits is that of the stream of interest payments, so the appropriate discount rate is the interest rate on the debt. Thus, we have

$$\text{Value of levered firm} = \text{Value of firm if unlevered} + \text{Present value of tax-shield benefits of debt} \tag{17-6}$$

For our example situation, suppose that the equity capitalization rate for company ND, which has no debt, is 16 percent. Assuming zero growth and a 100 percent earnings payout, the value of the (unlevered) firm is $1,200/.16 = **$7,500.** The value of the tax-shield benefits is $2,000, so the total value of Company D, the levered firm, is $7,500 + $2,000 = **$9,500.**

We see in Eqs. (17-5) and (17-6) that the greater the amount of debt, the greater the tax-shield benefits and the greater the value of the firm, all other things staying the same. By the same token, the greater the financial leverage, the lower the cost of capital of the firm. Thus, the original M&M proposition as subsequently adjusted for corporate taxes suggests that an optimal strategy is to take on a maximum amount of financial leverage.[6] This implies a capital structure consisting almost entirely of debt. Because this is not consistent with the observed behavior of corporations, we must seek alternative explanations.

Uncertainty of Tax-Shield Benefits

The tax savings associated with the use of debt are not usually certain, as implied in the treatment above. If taxable income should be low or turn negative, the tax-shield benefits from debt are reduced or even eliminated. Moreover, if the firm should go bankrupt and liquidate, the future tax savings associated with debt would stop altogether. Not only is there uncertainty as to the tax-shield benefits associated with debt but those associated with other tax shields (e.g., lease payments) as well. This only compounds the overall uncertainty. Finally, there is uncertainty that Congress will change the corporate tax rate.

All of these things make the tax-shield benefits associated with debt financing less than certain. As financial leverage increases, the uncertainty associated with the interest tax-shield benefits becomes a more and more important issue. As a result,

---

[6]Franco Modigliani and Merton H. Miller, "Corporate Income Taxes and the Cost of Capital: A Correction," *American Economic Review* 64 (June 1963), 433–42.

this uncertainty may reduce the value of the corporate tax-shield benefits shown in Eq. (17-6). With extreme financial leverage, the lessening in value of the corporate tax-shield benefits may be rather significant.

Corporate Plus Personal Taxes

With the combination of corporate taxes and personal taxes on both debt and stock income, the present value of the interest tax-shield benefits shown in Eq. (17-5) will likely be lowered. The magnitude of the resulting tax-shield benefits is an empirical question subject to much debate. However, the general consensus is that personal taxes act to reduce but not eliminate the corporate tax advantage associated with debt. As a result, an optimal leverage strategy would still call for the corporation to have a large proportion of debt. This is despite the fact that tax-shield benefits uncertainty may lessen the "net" tax effect with extreme leverage. As corporations overall are not highly levered, we must search for other factors affecting the valuation of the corporation when it alters the proportion of debt in its capital structure.

TAXES AND MARKET IMPERFECTIONS COMBINED

Our last statement brings us back to the influence of various market imperfections considered earlier. Only if they in some way restrict the use of debt financing can the observed capital structure behavior of corporations be explained.

Bankruptcy Costs, Agency Costs, and Taxes

If one allows for bankruptcy costs and if the probability of bankruptcy increases at an increasing rate with the use of financial leverage, extreme leverage is likely to be penalized by lenders and investors. (As discussed earlier, bankruptcy costs represent a drain on the system to security holders.) In a world of both bankruptcy costs and taxes, an optimal capital structure would exist even if all of the other behavioral tenets of the M&M position held. The cost of capital of a firm would decline as financial leverage was first employed because of the net tax advantage of debt. Gradually, however, the prospect of bankruptcy would become increasingly important, causing the cost of capital to decrease at a decreasing rate as financial leverage increased. As financial leverage became extreme, the bankruptcy effect might more than offset the tax effect, causing the cost of capital of the firm to rise.

The presence of agency, or monitoring, costs accentuates this rise in the cost of capital. Again, with increases in financial leverage beyond some threshold, agency costs increase at an increasing rate. The combined influence of bankruptcy and agency costs serves to limit the range over which the net tax-shield benefits have a positive effect on share price. In short, we have

$$
\begin{array}{cccc}
\text{Value of} & \text{Value of} & \text{Present value of} & \text{Present value of} \\
\text{levered} = & \text{firm if} & + \text{ net tax-shield} & - \text{ bankruptcy and} \\
\text{firm} & \text{unlevered} & \text{benefits of debt} & \text{agency costs}
\end{array}
\qquad \textbf{(17-7)}
$$

As financial leverage is increased, the second term on the right increases so that the value of the firm also increases. With more and more financial leverage, the growing uncertainty surrounding tax-shield benefits gradually lessens the increment in value that occurs. Despite this occurrence, if we look only at the net tax effect, a high proportion of debt would be optimal.

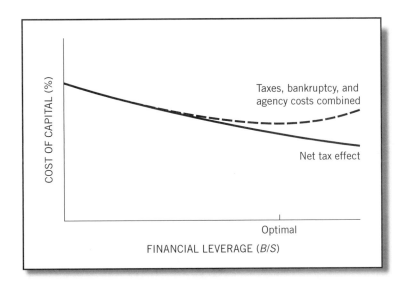

This effect is illustrated in Figure 17-5 by the solid line. We see that tax-shield benefit uncertainty causes the cost of capital line to curve up slightly as more and more financial leverage occurs. Still, the net tax effect (corporate plus personal) has a favorable impact on the cost of capital and on share value. When the firm has little debt, bankruptcy and agency costs are seen to be insignificant. As more debt is employed, these costs eventually become significant, as reflected by the dashed line. Increasingly, these costs offset the net tax-shield benefits. At the point where marginal bankruptcy/agency costs equal the marginal tax-shield benefits, the cost of capital is minimized and share price is maximized. By definition, this represents the optimal capital structure, as denoted by the mark along the horizontal axis in Figure 17-5. To visualize the effect of financial leverage on share price, substitute share value for cost of capital on the vertical axis and turn the figure upside down.

Impact of Additional Imperfections

If other imperfections and behavioral factors further dilute the M&M position, the point at which the cost of capital line turns up would be earlier than that depicted in the figure. Consider now the cost of borrowing. After some point of financial leverage, the interest rate charged by creditors usually rises. The greater the financial leverage, of course, the higher the interest rate charged. As a result, the cost of debt would turn up after a point. This phenomenon was illustrated earlier in Figure 17-2. In turn, this factor exerts upward influence on the overall cost of capital line. Institutional restrictions on lenders might also cause the cost of capital line to turn up sooner than it does in Figure 17-5. Because of extreme financial leverage a company may no longer be able to sell debt securities to institutions. In such a case, the company must seek out unrestricted investors, and these investors will demand even higher interest rates. If institutional imperfections are serious enough, debt funds may not be available beyond a particular point of financial leverage. In that case there would be a discontinuity in Figure 17-5.

Other capital market imperfections work to hamper the arbitrage process so that "homemade" financial leverage is not a perfect substitute for corporate financial leverage. Recall that these imperfections include institutional restrictions and transaction costs. The greater the importance attached to market imperfections, the less effective the arbitrage process becomes, and the stronger the case that can be made for an optimal capital structure.

There are a number of reasons for believing that an optimal capital structure exists in theory. Depending on one's view as to the strengths of the various capital market and behavioral imperfections, the expected optimal capital structure may occur earlier or later along the scale of possible debt-to-equity ratios.

FINANCIAL SIGNALING

Closely related to monitoring costs and agency relationships is the notion of *signaling*. Because strict managerial contracts are difficult to enforce, a manager may use capital structure changes to convey information about the profitability and risk of the firm. The implication is that insiders (managers) know something about the firm that outsiders (security holders) do not. As a manager, your pay and benefits may depend on the firm's market value, which gives you an incentive to let investors know when the firm is undervalued. You could make an announcement, "Our firm is undervalued," but you know that investors would probably be as convinced as if you were boasting about your child's intelligence. So, instead, you alter your firm's capital structure by issuing more debt. Increased leverage implies a higher probability of bankruptcy. Because you would be penalized contractually if bankruptcy occurred, investors conclude that you have good reason to believe that things are really better than the stock price reflects. Your actions speak louder than words. Increased leverage is a positive sign.

More formally, a signaling effect assumes that information asymmetry (unequalness) exists between management and shareholders. Assume that management is considering additional long-term financing and will issue either bonds or common stock. Management will want to choose the overvalued security if it is acting in the interests of current shareholders. That is, it will issue common stock if it believes the existing common stock is overvalued and debt if it believes the stock is undervalued. However, investors are aware of this phenomenon, so they regard debt issues as "good news" and common stock issues as "bad news."

This is not to say that capital structure changes necessarily cause changes in valuation. Rather, it is the signal conveyed by the change that is significant. This signal pertains to the underlying profitability and risk of the firm, because that is what is important when it comes to valuation. Financial signaling is a topic of considerable interest in finance research, but the various models that have been built around this topic are difficult to evaluate. Unless the managerial contract is very precise, the manager is tempted to give false signals. Moreover, there may simply be more effective and less costly ways to convey information than by altering the firm's capital structure. We will have more to say about financial signaling when we consider dividend policy in Chapter 18 and new security issues in Chapter 19.

SUMMARY

- Much controversy has developed over whether a firm can affect its total valuation (debt plus equity) and its cost of capital by changing its financing mix.
- The *traditional approach* to capital structure and valuation assumes that there is an *optimal capital*

structure and that management can increase the total value of the firm (and market value per share) through the judicious use of financial leverage.

- Modigliani and Miller (M&M), on the other hand, argue that in the absence of taxes and other market imperfections, the total value of the firm and its cost of capital are independent of capital structure.

- M&M's position, which is the same as the *net operating income (NOI) approach,* is based on the notion that there is a conservation of investment value. No matter how you divide the investment value pie between debt and equity claims, the total pie (or investment value of the firm) stays the same. Therefore, leverage is said to be irrelevant. Behavioral support for the M&M position is based on the *arbitrage* process.
- Bankruptcy and agency costs work to the disadvantage of financial leverage, particularly extreme financial leverage.
- In a world of corporate income taxes, there is a substantial advantage to the use of debt, and we can measure the present value of the tax-shield

benefits of debt. This advantage is lessened with tax-shield benefits uncertainty, particularly if financial leverage is high.
- When we allow for personal income taxes, we find the tax advantage of debt to be further reduced.
- A combination of the net tax effect with bankruptcy and agency costs will result in an optimal capital structure. Other market imperfections impede the equilibrium of security prices based on expected return and risk. As a result, financial leverage may affect the value of the firm.
- Financial *signaling* occurs when capital structure changes convey information to security holders. Management behavior results in new debt issues being regarded as "good news" by investors, whereas new stock issues are regarded as "bad news."

Questions

1. Contrast the net operating income (NOI) approach with the Modigliani and Miller (M&M) approach to the theory of the capital structure.
2. Why might you suspect that the optimal capital structure would differ significantly from one industry to another? Would the same factors produce differing optimal capital structures within all industry groupings?
3. What factors determine the interest rate a firm must pay for debt funds? Is it reasonable to expect this rate to rise with an increasing debt-to-equity ratio? Why?
4. What is the *total-value principle* as it applies to capital structure?
5. Define the notion of *arbitrage.* How does it affect the issue of capital structure?
6. If there were no imperfections in financial markets, what capital structure should the firm seek? Why are market imperfections important considerations in finance? Which imperfections are most important?
7. What are bankruptcy costs? What are agency costs? How do they affect the valuation of the firm when it comes to financial leverage?
8. Why do institutional lenders no longer lend money to a corporation when it takes on too much debt?
9. Suppose that a company were to earn negligible profits and pay no taxes. How would this affect the firm's optimal capital structure?
10. If the corporate tax rate were cut in half, what would be the effect on debt financing?
11. Dividends are currently taxed twice. The corporation must pay taxes on its earnings, and then shareholders must pay taxes on the dividends paid. What would be the effect on corporate financing if this double taxation were eliminated by permitting companies to deduct dividend payments as an expense?
12. Why might capital structure changes speak louder than words if management believed its stock were undervalued? What is the likely direction of the financial signal?

SELF-CORRECTION PROBLEMS

1. Qwert Typewriter Company and Yuiop Typewriters, Inc., are identical except for capital structures. Qwert has 50 percent debt and 50 percent equity financing, while Yuiop has 20 percent debt and 80 percent equity financing. (All percentages are in market value terms.) The borrowing rate for both companies is 13 percent in a no-tax world, and capital markets are assumed to be perfect. The earnings of both companies are not expected to grow, and all earnings are paid out to shareholders in the form of dividends.
   a. If you own 2 percent of the common stock of Qwert, what is your dollar return if the company has net operating income of $360,000 and the overall capitalization rate of the company, k_o, is 18 percent? What is the implied equity capitalization rate, k_e?
   b. Yuiop has the same net operating income as Qwert. What is the implied equity capitalization rate of Yuiop? Why does it differ from that of Qwert?
2. Enoch-Arden Corporation has earnings before interest and taxes of $3 million and a 40 percent tax rate. It is able to borrow at an interest rate of 14 percent, whereas its equity capitalization rate in the absence of borrowing is 18 percent. The earnings of the company are not expected to grow, and all earnings are paid out to shareholders in the form of dividends. In the presence of corporate but no personal taxes, what is the value of the company in an M&M world with no financial leverage? With $4 million in debt? With $7 million in debt?
3. L'Etoile du Nord Resorts is considering various levels of debt. Presently, it has no debt and a total market value of $15 million. By undertaking financial leverage, it believes that it can achieve a "net" corporate plus personal tax advantage (a positive present value of tax-shield benefits) equal to 20 percent of the market value of the debt. However, the company is concerned with bankruptcy and agency costs as well as with lenders increasing their required interest rate if the firm borrows too much. The company believes that it can borrow up to $5 million without incurring any of these additional costs. However, each additional $5 million increment in borrowing is expected to result in these three costs being incurred. Moreover, these costs are expected to increase at an increasing rate with financial leverage. The present value cost is expected to be the following for various levels of debt:

Debt (in millions)	$5	$10	$15	$20	$25	$30
Present value cost of bankruptcy, agency, and increased interest rate (in millions)	0	.6	1.2	2	3.2	5

Is there an optimal amount of debt for the company? If so, what is it?

PROBLEMS

1. The Lex I. Cographer Dictionary Company has net operating income of $10 million and $20 million of debt with a 7 percent interest rate. The earnings of the company are not expected to grow, and all earnings are paid out to shareholders in the form of dividends. In all cases, assume no taxes.
   a. Using the net operating income approach with an equity capitalization rate of 12.5 percent at the $20 million debt level, compute the total value of the firm and the implied overall capitalization rate, k_o.

b. Next, assume that the firm issues an additional $10 million in debt and uses the proceeds to retire common stock. Also, assume that the interest rate and overall capitalization rate remain the same as in Part (a). Compute the new total value of the firm and the new implied equity capitalization rate.

2. The Wannabee Company and the Gottahave Company are identical in every respect except that the Wannabee Company is not financially levered, whereas the Gottahave Company has $2 million in 12 percent bonds outstanding. There are no taxes, and capital markets are assumed to be perfect. The earnings of both companies are not expected to grow, and all earnings are paid out to shareholders in the form of dividends. The valuation of the two firms is shown as follows:

		WANNABEE	GOTTAHAVE
O	Net operating income	$ 600,000	$ 600,000
I	Interest on debt	0	240,000
E	Earnings available to common shareholders $(O - I)$	$ 600,000	$ 360,000
k_e	Equity capitalization rate	÷.15	÷.16
S	Market value of stock (E/k_e)	$4,000,000	$2,250,000
B	Market value of debt	0	2,000,000
V	Total value of firm $(B + S)$	$4,000,000	$4,250,000
k_o	Implied overall capitalization rate $[k_i(B/V) + k_e(S/V)]$	.15	.1412
B/S	Debt-to-equity ratio	0	.89

a. You own $22,500 worth of Gottahave stock. Show the process and the amount by which you could reduce your outlay through the use of arbitrage.

b. When will this arbitrage process cease?

3. The T. Boom Pickens Corporation has a $1 million capital structure and always maintains this book value amount. Pickens currently earns $250,000 per year before taxes of 50 percent, has an all-equity capital structure of 100,000 shares, and pays out all earnings in dividends. The company is considering issuing debt in order to retire common stock. The cost of the debt and the resulting price per share of the common stock at various levels of debt are given in the following table. It is assumed that the new capital structure would be reached all at once by purchasing common stock at the current price of $10 per share. In other words, the table below is a schedule of alternative conditions at a single point in time.

AMOUNT OF DEBT	AVERAGE PRE-TAX COST OF DEBT	RESULTING PRICE PER SHARE OF COMMON STOCK
$ 0	—	$10.00
100,000	10.0%	10.00
200,000	10.0	10.50
300,000	10.5	10.75
400,000	11.0	11.00
500,000	12.0	10.50
600,000	14.0	9.50

a. By observation, what do you think is the optimal capital structure (the capital structure that minimizes the firm's overall cost of capital)? Why?

b. Construct a graph that relates after-tax capital costs $(k_e, k_i,$ and $k_o)$ to financial leverage ratios (B/S) based on the data given above.

c. Are your feelings in Part (a) confirmed?

4. Gioanni Chantel Truffles, Inc., has $1 million in earnings before interest and taxes. Currently it is all-equity-financed. It may issue $3 million in perpetual debt at 15 percent interest in order to repurchase stock, thereby recapitalizing the corporation. There are no personal taxes.
    a. If the corporate tax rate is 40 percent, what is the income available to all security holders if the company remains all-equity-financed? If it is recapitalized?
    b. What is the present value of the debt tax-shield benefits?
    c. The equity capitalization rate for the company's common stock is 20 percent while it remains all-equity-financed. What is the value of the firm if it remains all-equity-financed? What is the firm's value if it is recapitalized?
5. Stinton Vintage Wine Company is presently family owned and has no debt. The Stinton family is considering going public by selling some of their stock in the company. Investment bankers tell them the total market value of the company is $10 million if no debt is employed. In addition to selling stock, the family wishes to consider issuing debt that, for computational purposes, would be perpetual. The debt would then be used to purchase and retire common stock, so that the size of the company would stay the same. Based on various valuation studies, the present value of the tax-shield benefits is estimated at 22 percent of the amount borrowed when both corporate and personal taxes are taken into account. The company's investment banker has estimated the following present values for bankruptcy costs associated with various levels of debt:

DEBT	PRESENT VALUE OF BANKRUPTCY COSTS
$1,000,000	$ 0
2,000,000	50,000
3,000,000	100,000
4,000,000	200,000
5,000,000	400,000
6,000,000	700,000
7,000,000	1,100,000
8,000,000	1,600,000

Given this information, what amount of debt should the family choose?

6. Rebecca Isbell Optical Corporation is trying to determine an appropriate capital structure. It knows that as its financial leverage increases, its cost of borrowing will eventually increase as will the required rate of return on its common stock. The company has made the following estimates for various financial leverage ratios.

DEBT DIVIDED BY (DEBT + EQUITY)	INTEREST RATE ON BORROWINGS	REQUIRED RATE OF RETURN ON EQUITY	
		WITHOUT BANKRUPTCY COSTS	WITH BANKRUPTCY COSTS
0	—	10.00%	10.00%
.10	8.0%	10.50	10.50
.20	8.0	11.00	11.25
.30	8.5	11.50	12.00
.40	9.0	12.25	13.00
.50	10.0	13.25	14.50
.60	11.0	14.50	16.25
.70	12.5	16.00	18.50
.80	15.0	18.00	21.00

    a. At a tax rate of 50 percent, what is the weighted average cost of capital of the company at various leverage ratios in the absence of bankruptcy costs?

b. With bankruptcy costs, what is the optimal capital structure?

7. Art Wyatt Pool Company wishes to finance a $15 million expansion program and is trying to decide between debt and external equity. Management believes that the market does not appreciate the company's profit potential and that the common stock is undervalued. What type of security (debt or common stock) do you suppose that the company will issue to provide financing, and what will be the market's reaction? What type of security do you think would be issued if management felt the stock were overvalued? Explain.

SOLUTIONS TO SELF-CORRECTION PROBLEMS

1. a. Qwert Typewriter Company:

O	Net operating income	$ 360,000
k_o	Overall capitalization rate	÷.18
V	Total value of the firm $(B + S)$	$2,000,000
B	Market value of debt (50%)	1,000,000
S	Market value of stock (50%)	$1,000,000
O	Net operating income	$ 360,000
I	Interest on debt (13%)	130,000
E	Earnings available to common shareholders $(O - I)$	$ 230,000
	2% of $230,000 = **$4,600**	

Implied equity capitalization rate, $k_e = E/S = \$230,000/\$1,000,000 = $ **23%**

b. Yuiop Typewriters, Inc.:

O	Net operating income	$ 360,000
k_o	Overall capitalization rate	÷.18
V	Total value of the firm $(B + S)$	$2,000,000
B	Market value of debt (20%)	400,000
S	Market value of stock (80%)	$1,600,000
O	Net operating income	$ 360,000
I	Interest on debt (13%)	52,000
E	Earnings available to common shareholders $(O - I)$	$ 308,000

Implied equity capitalization rate, $k_e = E/S = \$308,000/\$1,600,000 = $ **19.25%** Yuiop has a lower equity capitalization rate than Qwert because Yuiop uses less debt in its capital structure. As the equity capitalization rate is a linear function of the debt-to-equity ratio when we use the net operating income approach, the decline in the equity capitalization rate exactly offsets the disadvantage of not employing so much in the way of cheaper debt funds.

2. Value of firm if unlevered:

Earnings before interest and taxes	$ 3,000,000
Interest	0
Earnings before taxes	$ 3,000,000
Taxes (40 percent)	1,200,000
Earnings after taxes	$ 1,800,000
Equity capitalization rate, k_e	÷ .18
Value of the firm (unlevered)	**$10,000,000**

Value with $4 million in debt:

$$\frac{\text{Value of}}{\text{levered firm}} = \frac{\text{Value of firm}}{\text{if unlevered}} + \frac{\text{Present value of}}{\text{tax-shield benefits of debt}}$$

$$= \$10,000,000 + (\$4,000,000)(.40)$$

$$= \mathbf{\$11,600,000}$$

Value with $7 million in debt:

$$= \$10,000,000 + (\$7,000,000)(.40)$$

$$= \mathbf{\$12,800,000}$$

Due to the tax subsidy, the firm is able to increase its value in a linear manner with more debt.

3. (In millions):

(1) LEVEL OF DEBT	(2) FIRM VALUE UNLEVERED	(3) PV OF TAX-SHIELD BENEFITS OF DEBT (1) × .20	(4) PV OF BANKRUPTCY, AGENCY & INCREASED INTEREST COSTS	VALUE OF FIRM (2) + (3) − (4)
$ 0	$15	$0	$ .0	$15.0
5	15	1	.0	16.0
10	15	2	.6	16.4
15	15	3	1.2	16.8
20*	**15**	**4**	**2.0**	**17.0**
25	15	5	3.2	16.8
30	15	6	5.0	16.0

*The market value of the firm is maximized with $20 million in debt.

SELECTED REFERENCES

Arditti, Fred D. "The Weighted Average Cost of Capital: Some Questions on Its Definition, Interpretation, and Use." *Journal of Finance* 28 (September 1973), 1001–9.

Barclay, Michael J., and Clifford W. Smith Jr. "The Capital Structure Puzzle: Another Look at the Evidence." *Journal of Applied Corporate Finance* 12 (Spring 1999), 8–20.

Baxter, Nevins D. "Leverage, Risk of Ruin, and the Cost of Capital." *Journal of Finance* 22 (September 1967), 395–404.

Deangelo, Harry, and Ronald W. Masulis. "Optimal Capital Structure Under Corporate and Personal Taxation." *Journal of Financial Economics* 8 (March 1980), 3–29.

Harris, Milton, and Arthur Raviv. "The Theory of Capital Structure." *Journal of Finance* 46 (March 1991), 297–355.

Haugen, Robert A., and Lemma W. Senbet. "The Irrelevance of Bankruptcy Costs to the Theory of Optimal Capital Structure." *Journal of Finance* 33 (June 1978), 383–94.

———. "Corporate Finance and Taxes: A Review." *Financial Management* 15 (Autumn 1986), 5–21.

Jensen, Michael C. "The Takeover Controversy: Analysis and Evidence." *Midland Corporate Finance Journal* 4 (Summer 1986), 12–21.

———, and William E. Meckling. "Theory of the Firm: Managerial Behavior, Agency Cost and Ownership Structure." *Journal of Financial Economics* 3 (October 1976), 305–60.

Litzenberger, Robert H. "Some Observations on Capital Structure and the Impact of Recent Recapitalizations on Share Prices." *Journal of Financial and Quantitative Analysis* 21 (March 1986), 47–58.

———, and James C. Van Horne. "Elimination of the Double Taxation of Dividends and Corporate Financial Policy." *Journal of Finance* 33 (June 1978), 737–49.

Maloney, Michael T., Robert E. McCormick, and Mark L. Mitchell. "Managerial Decision Making and Capital Structure." *Journal of Business* 66, No. 2 (1993), 189–217.

Mello, Antonio S., and John E. Parsons. "Measuring the Agency Costs of Debt." *Journal of Finance* 47 (December 1992), 1887–904.

Miller, Merton H. "Debt and Taxes." *Journal of Finance* 32 (May 1977), 266–68.

———. "The Modigliani–Miller Propositions After Thirty Years." *Journal of Applied Corporate Finance* 2 (Spring 1989), 6–18.

Modigliani, Franco, and M. H. Miller. "The Cost of Capital, Corporate Finance, and the Theory of Investment." *American Economic Review* 48 (June 1958), 261–97.

———. "The Cost of Capital Corporation Finance, and the Theory of Investment: Reply." *American Economic Review* 51 (September 1959), 655–69; "Taxes and the Cost of Capital: A Correction." *American Economic Review* 53 (June 1963), 433–43; "Reply." *American Economic Review* 55 (June 1965), 524–27; "Reply to Heins and Sprenkle." *American Economic Review* 59 (September 1969), 592–95.

Myers, Stewart C. "Capital Structure Puzzle." *Journal of Finance* 39 (July 1984), 575–92.

———, and Nicholas S. Mujluf. "Corporate Financing and Investment Decisions When Firms Have Information That Investors Do Not Have." *Journal of Financial Economics* 13 (June 1984), 187–222.

Opler, Tim C., and Sheridan Titman. "Financial Distress and Corporate Performance." *Journal of Finance* 49 (July 1994), 1015–40.

Rajan, Raghuram G., and Luigi Zingales. "What Do We Know about Capital Structure: Some Evidence from International Data." *Journal of Finance* 50 (December 1995), 1421–60.

Ross, Stephen A. "The Determination of Financial Structure: The Incentive-Signalling Approach." *Bell Journal of Economics* 8 (Spring 1977), 23–40.

Van Horne, James C. "Optimal Initiation of Bankruptcy Proceedings by Debt Holders." *Journal of Finance* 31 (1976), 897–910.

Chapter 18

Dividend Policy

PASSIVE VERSUS ACTIVE DIVIDEND POLICIES
   Dividends as a Passive Residual • Irrelevance of Dividends
      • Arguments for Dividend Relevance • Empirical Testing
      of Dividend Policy • Implications for Corporate Policy
FACTORS INFLUENCING DIVIDEND POLICY
   Legal Rules • Funding Needs of the Firm • Liquidity • Ability to
      Borrow • Restrictions in Debt Contracts • Control • Some
      Final Observations
DIVIDEND STABILITY
   Valuation of Dividend Stability • Target Payout Ratios • Regular
      and Extra Dividends
STOCK DIVIDENDS AND STOCK SPLITS
   Stock Dividends • Stock Splits • Value to Investors of Stock
      Dividends and Stock Splits • Reverse Stock Split
STOCK REPURCHASE
   Method of Repurchase • Repurchasing as Part of Dividend
      Policy • Investment or Financing Decision? • Possible
      Signaling Effect
ADMINISTRATIVE CONSIDERATIONS
   Procedural Aspects • Dividend Reinvestment Plans
SUMMARY
QUESTIONS
SELF-CORRECTION PROBLEMS
PROBLEMS
SOLUTIONS TO SELF-CORRECTION PROBLEMS
SELECTED REFERENCES

> *"Contrariwise,"* continued Tweedledee, *"if it was so, it might be; and if it were so, it would be; but as it isn't, it ain't. That's logic."*

—LEWIS CARROLL,
THROUGH THE LOOKING GLASS

Dividend policy is an integral part of the firm's financing decision. The **dividend-payout ratio** determines the amount of earnings that can be retained in the firm as a source of financing. However, retaining a greater amount of current earnings in the firm means that fewer dollars will be available for current dividend payments. A major aspect, then, of the dividend policy of the firm is to determine the appropriate allocation of profits between dividend payments and additions to the firm's retained earnings. But also important are other issues pertaining to a firm's overall dividend policy: legal, liquidity, and control issues; stability of dividends; stock dividends and splits; stock repurchase; and administrative considerations.

PASSIVE VERSUS ACTIVE DIVIDEND POLICIES

Dividends as a Passive Residual

We focus first on a two-part question. Can the payment of cash dividends affect shareholder wealth and if so, what dividend-payout ratio will maximize shareholder wealth? As we did when studying the effects of financial leverage, we again assume that business risk is held constant. To evaluate the question of whether the dividend-payout ratio affects shareholder wealth, it is necessary to first examine the firm's dividend policy as solely a financing decision involving the retention of earnings. Each period, the firm must decide whether to retain its earnings or to distribute part or all of them to shareholders as cash dividends. (We rule out share repurchase for now.) As long as the firm is faced with investment projects having returns exceeding those that are required (i.e., positive-NPV projects), the firm will use earnings, plus the amount of senior securities the increase in the equity base will support, to finance these projects. If the firm has earnings left after financing all acceptable investment opportunities, these earnings would then be distributed to shareholders in the form of cash dividends. If not, there would be no dividends. If the number of acceptable investment opportunities involves a total dollar amount that exceeds the amount of retained earnings plus the senior securities these retained earnings will support, the firm would finance the excess needs with a combination of a new equity issue and senior securities.

When we treat dividend policy as strictly a financing decision, the payment of cash dividends is a passive residual. The percentage of earnings paid out as dividends will fluctuate from period to period in keeping with fluctuations in the amount of acceptable investment opportunities available to the firm. If these opportunities abound, the percentage of earnings paid out is likely to be zero. On the other hand, if the firm is unable to find profitable investment opportunities, dividends paid out will be 100 percent of earnings. For situations between these two extremes, the dividend-payout ratio will be a fraction between zero and one.

The treatment of dividend policy as a passive residual, determined solely by the availability of acceptable investment proposals, implies that dividends are irrelevant. Are dividends really just a means of distributing unused funds? Instead, should dividend payments be an active decision variable with earnings retentions as a residual? To answer these questions, we must examine the argument that dividends are irrelevant, which means that changes in the dividend-payout ratio (holding investment opportunities constant) do not affect shareholder wealth.

Irrelevance of Dividends

Modigliani and Miller (M&M) provide the most comprehensive argument for the irrelevance of dividends.[1] They assert that, given the investment decision of the firm, the dividend-payout ratio is a mere detail and that it does not affect the wealth of shareholders. M&M argue that the value of the firm is determined solely by the earning power of the firm's assets or its investment policy and that the manner in which the earnings stream is split between dividends and retained earnings does not affect this value. As we pointed out in the previous chapter, when we considered the capital structure decision, M&M assume perfect capital markets where there are no transactions costs, no flotation costs to companies issuing securities, and no taxes. Moreover, the future profits of the firm are assumed to be known with certainty. (Later this last assumption will be removed.)

Current Dividends versus Retention of Earnings.   The crux of M&M's position is that the effect of dividend payments on shareholder wealth is exactly offset by other means of financing. Let us first consider selling additional common stock to raise equity capital instead of simply retaining earnings. After the firm has made its investment decision, it must decide whether (1) to retain earnings or (2) to pay dividends and sell new stock in the amount of these dividends in order to finance the investments. M&M suggest that the sum of the discounted value per share of common stock after financing plus current dividends paid is exactly equal to the market value per share of common stock before the payment of current dividends. In other words, the common stock's decline in market price because of the dilution caused by external equity financing is exactly offset by the payment of the dividend. Thus, the shareholder is said to be indifferent between receiving dividends and having earnings retained by the firm.

Dilution A decrease in the proportional claim on earnings and assets of a share of common stock because of the issuance of additional shares.

Take Note

> At this point, one might rightfully ask, How does all of this relate to our earlier chapters, when we said that dividends are the foundation for the valuation of common stock? Is there some contradiction? Although it is still true that the market value of a share of common stock is the present value of all expected future dividends, the timing and magnitude of the dividends can vary. It is still true that a company that is expected *never* to pay a dividend—not even a liquidation dividend—should be worthless to an investor. The dividend-irrelevance position simply argues that the present value of future dividends remains unchanged even though dividend policy may change the timing and magnitude of dividends. It does not argue that dividends, including a liquidating dividend, are never paid. On the contrary, it argues only that dividend postponement (but where the future dividend magnitude is allowed to grow) is a matter of indifference when it comes to the market price of common stock.

Conservation of Value.   Given M&M's assumptions of certainty and perfect capital markets, the irrelevance of dividends naturally follows. As with our example for corporate financial leverage in the previous chapter, the *total-value principle* ensures that

---

[1]Merton H. Miller and Franco Modigliani, "Dividend Policy, Growth, and the Valuation of Shares," *Journal of Business* 34 (October 1961), 411–33.

the sum of market value plus current dividends of two firms identical in all respects other than dividend-payout ratios will be the same.

Investors are able to replicate any dividend stream the corporation might be able to pay but currently is not. If dividends are lower than desired, investors can sell some shares of stock to obtain their desired cash distribution. If dividends are higher than desired, investors can use dividends to purchase additional shares of stock in the company. Thus, investors are able to manufacture "homemade" dividends in the same way that they could devise "homemade" financial leverage if they were unhappy with a firm's current capital structure. For a corporate decision to have value, the company must be able to do something for shareholders that they cannot do for themselves. Because investors can manufacture homemade dividends, which are perfect substitutes for corporate dividends under the preceding assumptions, dividend policy is irrelevant. As a result, one dividend policy is as good as the next. The firm is unable to create value simply by altering the mix of dividends and retained earnings. As in capital structure theory, there is a conservation of value so that the sum of the parts is always the same. The total size of the pie is not changed by the slicing.

Arguments for Dividend Relevance

A number of arguments have been advanced in support of the contrary position, namely, that dividends are relevant under conditions of uncertainty. In other words, investors are not indifferent as to whether they receive returns in the form of dividend income or share price appreciation. We shall examine these arguments under conditions of uncertainty.

Preference for Dividends. Certain investors may have a preference for dividends over capital gains. The payment of dividends may resolve uncertainty in their minds concerning company profitability. Dividends are received on a current, ongoing basis, whereas the prospect of realizing capital gains is in the future. Therefore, investors in a dividend-paying company resolve their uncertainty earlier than those investing in a non-dividend-paying company. To the extent that investors prefer the early resolution of uncertainty, they may be willing to pay a higher price for the stock that offers the greater dividend, all other things held constant. If, in fact, investors can manufacture "homemade" dividends, such a preference is irrational. Nonetheless, sufficient statements from investors make it difficult to dismiss this argument. Perhaps, for either psychological reasons or reasons of inconvenience, investors prefer not to manufacture "homemade" dividends but to get the "real thing" directly from the company.

Taxes on the Investor. When we allow for taxes, there are a variety of effects. To the extent that the personal tax rate on capital gains is less than that on dividend income, there may be an advantage to the retention of earnings. In addition, the capital gains tax is deferred until the actual sale of stock (when any gain is then *realized*). Effectively, the shareholder is given a valuable timing option when the firm retains earnings as opposed to pays dividends. Also, the capital gains tax may be avoided altogether if appreciated securities are given as gifts to charitable causes or if the security owner dies. For these reasons, the effective tax on capital gains (in present value terms) is less than that on dividend income, even when the federal tax rate on the two types of income is the same. This would suggest that a dividend-paying stock will need to provide a higher expected before-tax return than a non-dividend-paying stock of the same risk. According to this notion, the greater the

Dividend yield Anticipated annual dividend
divided by the market
price of the stock.

dividend yield on a stock, the higher the required before-tax return, all other things being the same.

However, all investors do not experience the same taxation on the two types of income just discussed. Certain institutional investors, such as retirement and pension funds, pay no tax on either dividend income or realized capital gains. Such investors would be indifferent from a tax standpoint between a dollar of dividend income and a dollar of capital gains. For corporate investors intercompany dividends are taxed at an effective rate below that applicable to capital gains. For example, if Alpha Corporation owns 100 shares of Omega Corporation, which pays a $1 per share annual dividend, 70 percent of the dividend income to Alpha Corporation is tax exempt. In other words, Alpha Corporation would pay taxes on $30 of dividend income at the corporate tax rate. The overall tax effect will be less than if Omega Corporation had share appreciation of $100 and all of this were taxed at the capital gains rate. Accordingly, there may be a preference for current dividends on the part of corporate investors. Also, there are a growing number of institutional investors.

If there are clienteles of investors having different dividend preferences, corporations could adjust their dividend-payout ratio to take advantage of the situation. Suppose that two-fifths of all investors prefer a zero dividend-payout ratio, one-fifth prefer a 25 percent payout ratio, and the remaining two-fifths prefer a 50 percent payout ratio. If most companies pay out 25 percent of their earnings in dividends, there will be excess demand for the shares of companies paying zero dividends and for the shares of companies whose dividend-payout ratio is 50 percent. Presumably, a number of companies will recognize this excess demand and adjust their payout ratios to increase share price. The action of these companies will eliminate the excess demand. In equilibrium, the dividend-payout ratios of corporations will match the desires of investor groups. At this point, no company would be able to affect its share price by altering its dividend. As a result, even with taxes, the dividend-payout ratio would be irrelevant.

In actuality, we are left with an unsettled situation in which the effect of taxes on dividends is not clear. Before considering some of the empirical evidence on the effect that dividends have on share price, we must look at other factors that may influence the payment of dividends.

Flotation Costs. The irrelevance of the dividend payout is based on the idea that when favorable investment opportunities exist and yet dividends are paid, the funds paid out of the firm must be replaced by funds acquired through external financing. The introduction of flotation costs involved with external financing favors the retention of earnings in the firm. For each dollar paid out in dividends, the firm nets less than a dollar after flotation costs per dollar of external financing.

Transactions Costs and Divisibility of Securities. Transactions costs involved in the sale of securities tend to restrict the arbitrage process in the same manner as that described for debt. Shareholders who desire current income must pay brokerage fees on the sale of portions of their stock ownership if the dividend paid is not sufficient to satisfy their current desire for income. This fee, per dollar of shares sold, varies inversely with the size of the sale. For a small sale, the brokerage fee can be a rather significant percentage of the total sale. As a result of this fee, shareholders with consumption desires in excess of current dividends will prefer that the company pay additional dividends. Perfect capital markets also assume that securities are infinitely divisible. The fact that the smallest equity-security unit is one share may result in "lumpiness" with respect to selling shares for current income. This, too, acts as a deterrent to the sale of stock in lieu of dividends. On the other hand, shareholders not desiring dividends for current consumption purposes will need to reinvest their dividends. Here, again, transactions costs and divisibility problems work to the disadvantage of the shareholder, although this time as a deterrent to the purchase of stock. Thus, transactions costs and divisibility problems cut both ways, and one is not able to draw directional implications regarding paying dividends versus retaining earnings.

Institutional Restrictions.   Certain institutional investors are restricted in the types of common stock they can buy or in the portfolio percentages they can hold in various types of common stock. The prescribed list of eligible securities for these investors is determined in part by the length of time over which dividends have been paid. If a company does not pay dividends or has not paid them over a sufficiently long period, certain institutional investors are not permitted to invest in the stock of that company.

Universities, on the other hand, sometimes have restrictions on the expenditure of capital gains from their endowments. Also, a number of trusts have a prohibition against the liquidation of principal. In the case of common stocks, the trust beneficiary is entitled to dividend income but not to the proceeds from the sale of common stock. As a result of this stipulation, the trustee who manages the investments may feel constrained to pay particular attention to dividend yield and seek stocks paying reasonable dividends. Though the two influences described are small in aggregate, they work in the direction of a preference for dividends as opposed to earnings retention and capital gains.

Financial Signaling.   Financial signaling is different from the other arguments presented in this section in that it depends on imperfections in the market for financial information. It suggests that dividends have an impact on share price because they communicate information, or signals, about the firm's profitability. Presumably, firms with good news about their future profitability will want to tell investors. Rather than make a simple announcement, dividends may be increased to add conviction to the statement. When a firm has a target dividend-payout ratio that has been stable over time and the firm increases this ratio, investors may believe that management is announcing a positive change in the expected future profitability of the firm. The signal to investors is that management and the board of directors truly believe that things are better than the stock price reflects.

Accordingly, the price of the stock may react favorably to this increase in dividends. The idea here is that the reported accounting earnings of a company may not be a proper reflection of the company's economic earnings. To the extent that dividends provide information on economic earnings not provided by reported earnings, share price will respond. Put another way, cash dividends speak louder than words. Thus, dividends are said to be used by investors as predictors of the firm's future performance. Dividends convey management's expectations of the future.

Empirical Testing of Dividend Policy

Although there are a number of factors that may explain dividends' impact on valuation, many are difficult to test. Most empirical testing has concentrated on the tax effect and on financial signaling. This is not to say that such things as preference for dividends, flotation costs, transactions costs, and institutional restrictions have no effect. Rather, whatever result these factors may have is swamped by tax and financial signaling effects.

With a tax effect, where dividends are taxed more heavily (in present value terms) than are capital gains, stock prices and before-tax returns should reflect this differential taxation. Empirical results have been mixed as to whether high-dividend stocks provide higher expected before-tax returns than low-dividend stocks to offset the tax effect. In recent years, however, the evidence is largely consistent with dividend neutrality.

In contrast to the mixed results for a tax effect, the evidence on financial signaling is consistent in support of a dividend announcement effect: Increases in dividends lead to positive excess stock returns, whereas decreases in dividends lead to negative excess returns. Therefore, dividends would appear to convey information. Where does all this leave us with respect to directions for a corporation's dividend policy?

Implications for Corporate Policy

A company should endeavor to establish a dividend policy that will maximize shareholder wealth. Most everyone agrees that if a company does not have sufficiently profitable investment opportunities, it should distribute any excess funds to its shareholders. The firm need not pay out the exact unused portion of earnings each period. Indeed, it may wish to stabilize the absolute amount of dividends paid from period to period. But over the longer run the total earnings retained, plus the additional senior securities the increasing equity base will support, will correspond to the amount of new profitable investment opportunities. Dividend policy would still be a passive residual determined by the amount of investment opportunities.

For the firm to be justified in paying a dividend larger than that dictated by the amount of earnings left over after making all acceptable investment opportunities, there must be a net preference for dividends in the market. It is difficult to "net out" the arguments just discussed to arrive at the bottom line. Only institutional restrictions and some investors' preferences for dividends argue for dividends. The other arguments suggest either a neutral effect or a bias favoring earnings retention. There does appear to be some positive value associated with a modest dividend as opposed to none at all. This occurrence may be due to institutional restrictions and a signaling effect. Beyond that, the picture is cloudy, and some argue that even a modest dividend has no effect on valuation. Few academic scholars argue that dividends significantly in excess of what a passive policy would dictate will lead to share price improvement. With personal taxes and flotation costs, shareholders are "money behind" when a company issues stock to pay dividends. Before making a final observation, let us look at some practical things to consider in approaching a dividend policy decision.

FACTORS INFLUENCING DIVIDEND POLICY

So far we have discussed only the theoretical aspects of dividend policy. Yet when a company establishes a dividend policy, it looks at a number of other matters. These additional considerations should be related to the theoretical concepts surrounding dividend payout and the valuation of the firm. In what follows, we take up various practical factors that firms actually do (and should) analyze when approaching a dividend policy decision.

Legal Rules

The laws of a firm's state of incorporation decide the legality of any distribution to common shareholders. The legal rules that we discuss below are important in establishing the legal boundaries within which a firm's finalized dividend policy can operate. These legal rules have to do with capital impairment, insolvency, and undue retention of earnings.

Capital Impairment Rule.   Although state laws vary considerably, many states prohibit the payment of dividends if these dividends impair capital. Some states define *capital* as the total par value of the common stock. If a firm's shareholders' equity consists of $4 million in common stock (at par), $3 million in additional paid-in capital, and $2 million in retained earnings, total capital would be $4 million. This company could not pay a cash dividend totaling more than $5 million without impairing capital (i.e., reducing shareholders' equity below $4 million).

Other states define *capital* to include not only the total par value of the common stock but also the additional paid-in capital. Under such state statutes, dividends can be paid only "to the extent of retained earnings." Notice, we did not say that dividends can be paid "out of retained earnings." A company pays dividends "out of cash," while incurring a corresponding reduction in the retained earnings account.

Interestingly, in some states dividends to common shareholders can exceed not only the book value of a firm's retained earnings but also the total book value of shareholders' equity. For example, Holiday Corporation (the parent company of Holiday Inns of America) paid a one-time, $65-per-share dividend in 1987 as part of an antitakeover strategy. This $1.55 billion dividend created a $770 million negative book balance for Holiday's total common shareholders' equity. Under "traditional" capital impairment laws, this would not have been possible because the book value of *capital* was now negative. Holiday, a Delaware corporation, could make this huge dividend payment (legally, according to Delaware law) only if the dividend came from *surplus*. In Delaware, *capital* means the "par value" of a firm's common stock, and *surplus* is equal to the "fair value" (i.e., market value) of its assets minus the total of its debts plus *capital*. In short, in Delaware—and other like-minded states—the "fair value," rather than "book value," of a firm's assets can be used to judge whether a dividend payment impairs *capital*. By the way, we chose to highlight a Delaware company in our example for an important reason. Delaware is the state of incorporation for roughly 60 percent of the Fortune 500 firms and 50 percent of all companies listed on the New York Stock Exchange.

Insolvency Rule.   Some states prohibit the payment of cash dividends if the company is insolvent. *Insolvency* is defined either in a legal sense as total liabilities of a company exceeding its assets "at a fair valuation," or in an "equitable" (technical) sense as the firm's inability to pay its creditors as obligations come due. Because the firm's ability to pay its obligations is dependent on its liquidity rather than on its capital, the equitable (technical) insolvency restriction gives creditors a good deal of protection. When cash is limited, a company is restricted from favoring shareholders to the detriment of creditors.

Undue Retention of Earnings Rule.   The Internal Revenue Code prohibits the undue retention of earnings. Although *undue retention* is vaguely defined, it is usually thought to mean retention significantly in excess of the present and future investment needs of the company. The purpose of the law is to prevent companies from retaining earnings for the sake of avoiding taxes. For example, a company might retain all of its earnings and build up a substantial cash and marketable securities position. The entire company could then be sold, and shareholders would be subject to only a capital gains tax, which is postponed relative to what would occur if dividends were paid. If the Internal Revenue Service can prove unjustified retention, it can impose penalty tax rates on the earnings accumulation. Whenever a company does build up a substantial liquid position, it has to be sure that it can justify the retention of these funds to the IRS. Otherwise, it may be more prudent to pay the excess funds as dividends to shareholders.

Funding Needs of the Firm

Once the legal boundaries for the firm's dividend policy have been established, the next step involves an assessment of the funding needs of the firm. In this regard, cash budgets, projected sources and uses of funds statements, and projected cash flow statements (topics taken up in Chapter 7) are of particular use. The key is to determine the likely cash flows and cash position of the company in the absence of a change in dividend policy. In addition to looking at expected outcomes, we should factor in business risk, so that we may obtain a range of possible cash-flow outcomes, a procedure spelled out in Chapter 7.

In keeping with our earlier discussion of the theoretical aspects of dividend policy, the firm would wish to determine if anything is left over after servicing its funding needs, including funding acceptable investment projects. In this regard, the firm should look at its situation over a reasonable number of future years to iron out fluctuations. The likely ability of the firm to sustain a dividend should be analyzed relative to the probability distributions of possible future cash flows and cash balances. On the basis of this analysis, a company can determine its likely future residual funds.

Liquidity

The liquidity of a company is a prime consideration in many dividend decisions. Because dividends represent a cash outflow, the greater the cash position and overall liquidity of a company, the greater its ability to pay a dividend. A company that is growing and profitable may not be liquid because its funds may go into fixed assets and permanent working capital. Because the management of such a company usually desires to maintain some liquidity cushion to give it financial flexibility and protection against uncertainty, it may be reluctant to jeopardize this position to pay a large dividend.

Ability to Borrow

A liquid position is not the only way to provide for financial flexibility and thereby protect against uncertainty. If a firm has the ability to borrow on comparatively short notice, it may be relatively financially flexible. This ability to borrow can be in the form of a line of credit or a revolving credit agreement from a bank or simply the informal willingness of a financial institution to extend credit. In addition, financial flexibility can come from the ability of a firm to go to the capital market with a bond issue. The larger and more established a company, the better its access to the capital market. The greater the ability of the firm to borrow, the greater its financial flexibility, and the greater its ability to pay a cash dividend. With ready access to debt funds, management should be less concerned with the effect that a cash dividend has on its liquidity.

Restrictions in Debt Contracts

The protective covenants in a bond indenture or loan agreement often include a restriction on the payment of dividends. The restriction is employed by the lenders to preserve the company's ability to service debt. Usually it is expressed as a maximum percentage of cumulative earnings retained (reinvested) in the firm. When such a restriction is in force, it naturally influences the firm's dividend policy. Sometimes the management of a company welcomes a dividend restriction imposed by lenders, because then it does not have to justify the retention of earnings to its shareholders. It only needs to point to the restriction.

Control

If a company pays substantial dividends, it may need to raise capital at a later time through the sale of stock in order to finance profitable investment opportunities. Under such circumstances, the controlling interest of the company may be diluted if controlling shareholders do not or cannot subscribe for additional shares. These shareholders may prefer a low dividend payout and the financing of investment needs by retaining earnings. Such a dividend policy may not maximize overall shareholder wealth, but it still may be in the best interests of those in control.

Control can operate in another, very different, way. When a company is being sought for acquisition by another company or by individuals, a low dividend payout may work to the advantage of the "outsiders" seeking control. The outsiders may be able to convince shareholders that the company is not maximizing shareholder wealth and that they (the outsiders) can do a better job. Consequently, companies in danger of being acquired may establish a high dividend payout to please shareholders.

Some Final Observations

In determining a dividend payout, the typical company will analyze a number of the factors just described. These factors largely dictate the legal and other boundaries within which a dividend can be paid. When a company pays a dividend in excess of its residual funds, it implies that management and the board of directors believe that the payment has a favorable effect on shareholder wealth. The frustrating thing is that we have so little in the way of clear generalizations from the empirical evidence. The lack of a firm footing for predicting the long-run effect of a specific dividend policy on valuation makes the dividend choice a most difficult policy decision.

Considerations taken up in this section allow a company to determine with reasonable accuracy what would be an appropriate passive dividend strategy. An active dividend policy involves an act of faith, because it demands that a portion of the cumulative dividends paid out ultimately be replaced with common stock financing. Such a strategy is undertaken in a foggy area, but one in which most academics have difficulty believing that shareholder wealth will be enhanced. Notwithstanding, many companies profess a belief that dividend payout affects share price and behave in a manner consistent with dividend importance.

DIVIDEND STABILITY

Stability of dividend payments is an attractive feature to many investors. By *stability* we mean maintaining the position of the firm's dividend payments in relation to a trend line, preferably one that is upward sloping. All other things being the same, a share of stock may command a higher price if it pays a stable dividend over time than if it pays out a fixed percentage of earnings. Suppose that Company A has a long-run dividend-payout ratio of 50 percent of earnings. It pays out this percentage every year, despite the fact that its earnings are cyclical. The earnings and dividends per share of Company A are shown in Figure 18-1. Company B, on the other hand, has exactly the same earnings and a long-run dividend-payout ratio of 50 percent, but it maintains a relatively stable dividend over time. It changes the absolute amount of dividend payment only in keeping with the underlying trend of earnings. The earnings and dividends per share of Company B are shown in Figure 18-2.

Over the long run, the total amount of dividends paid by these two firms is the same. However, the market price per share of Company B may be higher than that of Company A, all other things being the same. Investors may well place a positive utility on dividend stability and pay a premium for the company that offers it. To the extent that investors value dividend stability, the overall dividend policy of Company B would be better than that of Company A. This policy encompasses not only the percentage of dividend payout in relation to earnings but also the manner in which the actual dividends are paid. Rather than vary dividends directly with changes in earnings per share, Company B raises the dividend only when reasonably confident a higher dividend can be maintained.

Valuation of Dividend Stability

Investors may be willing to pay a premium for stable dividends because of the informational content of dividends, the desire of investors for current income, and certain institutional considerations.

Informational Content. When earnings drop and a company does not cut its dividend, the market may have more confidence in the stock than it would have if the dividend were cut. The stable dividend may convey management's view that the future of the company is better than the drop in earnings suggests. Thus, management may be able to affect the expectations of investors through the informational content of

FIGURE 18-1
Dividend Policy of Company A Showing Strict Adherence to a Constant 50 Percent Dividend-Payout Ratio

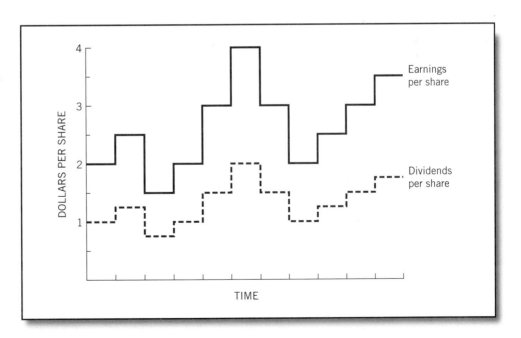

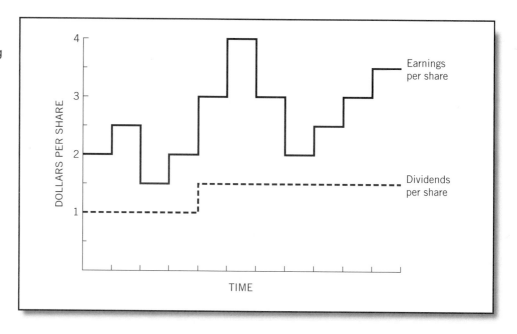

FIGURE 18-2
Dividend Policy of Company B Showing a Long-Run 50 Percent Dividend-Payout Ratio but Dividend Increases Only When Supported by Growth in Earnings

dividends. Management will not be able to fool the market permanently. If there is a downward trend in earnings, a stable dividend will not convey forever an impression of a promising future. Moreover, if a firm is in an unstable business with wide swings in earnings, a stable dividend cannot give the illusion of underlying stability.

Current Income Desires.   A second factor may favor stable dividends. Investors who desire a specific periodic income will prefer a company with stable dividends to one with unstable dividends, even though both companies may have the same pattern of earnings and long-run dividend payout. Although investors can always sell a portion of their common stock for income when the dividend is not sufficient to meet their current needs, many investors have an aversion to dipping into principal. Moreover, when a company reduces its dividend, earnings are usually down and the market price of the common stock depressed. Overall, income-conscious investors place a positive utility on stable dividends, even though they can always sell a few shares of stock for income.

Institutional Considerations.   A stable dividend may be advantageous from the legal standpoint of permitting certain institutional investors to buy the common stock. Various governmental bodies prepare *approved (or legal) lists* of securities in which pension funds, savings banks, trustees, insurance companies, and certain other institutions may invest. To qualify, a company often must have an uninterrupted pattern of dividends. A cut in dividends may result in the removal of a company from these approved lists.

The arguments presented in support of the notion that stable dividends have a positive effect on the market price of the stock are only suggestive. Little empirical evidence sheds light on the question. Although studies of individual stocks often suggest that stable dividends buffer the market price of the stock when earnings are down, there have been no comprehensive studies of a large sample of stocks dealing with the relationship between dividend stability and valuation. Nevertheless, most companies strive for stability in their dividend payments. This is consistent with a belief that stable dividends have a positive effect on value.

Part VI The Cost of Capital, Capital Structure, and Dividend Policy

Target Payout Ratios

A number of companies appear to follow the policy of a target dividend-payout ratio over the long run. John Lintner contends that dividends are adjusted to changes in earnings, but only with a lag.[2] When earnings increase to a new level, a company increases dividends only when it feels it can maintain the increase in earnings. Companies are also reluctant to cut the absolute amount of their cash dividend. Both of these factors help explain why dividend changes often lag behind changes in earnings. In an economic upturn, the lag relationship becomes visible when retained earnings increase in relation to dividends. In a contraction, retained earnings will decrease relative to dividends.

Regular and Extra Dividends

Extra dividend A nonrecurring dividend paid to shareholders in addition to the regular dividend. It is brought about by special circumstances.

Regular dividend The dividend that is normally expected to be paid by the firm.

One way for a company to increase its cash distribution to shareholders in periods of prosperity is to declare an **extra dividend** in addition to the **regular dividend** that is generally paid on a quarterly or semiannual basis. By declaring an extra dividend, the company warns investors that the dividend is not an increase in the established dividend rate. The declaration of an extra dividend is particularly suitable for companies with fluctuating earnings. The use of extra dividends enables the company to maintain a stable record of regular dividends and also to distribute some of the rewards of prosperity. If a company pays extra dividends continuously, it defeats its purpose. The extra dividend becomes expected. When properly labeled, however, an extra, or special, dividend still conveys positive information to the market concerning the firm's present and future performance.

STOCK DIVIDENDS AND STOCK SPLITS

Stock dividends and stock splits are often used for different purposes. In an economic sense, there is little difference between the two. Only from an accounting standpoint is there a significant difference.

Stock Dividends

Stock dividend A payment of additional shares of stock to shareholders. Often used in place of or in addition to a cash dividend.

A **stock dividend** is simply the payment of additional shares of common stock to shareholders. It represents nothing more than a bookkeeping shift within the shareholders' equity account on the firm's balance sheet. A shareholder's proportional ownership in the firm remains unchanged. Accounting authorities make a distinction between small-percentage stock dividends and large-percentage stock dividends.

Small-Percentage Stock Dividends. If a stock dividend represents an increase of less than (typically) 25 percent of the previously outstanding common stock, it is referred to as a *small-percentage stock dividend*. Accounting for this type of stock dividend entails transferring an amount from retained earnings to common stock and additional paid-in capital.

Suppose that Chen Industries had a total shareholders' equity account—before issuing a stock dividend—as shown on the left-hand side of Table 18-1. Chen Industries then pays a 5 percent stock dividend, amounting to 20,000 additional shares

[2]See John Lintner, "Distribution of Income of Corporations," *American Economic Review* 46 (May 1956), 97–113

TABLE 18-1
5% stock dividend
for Chen Industries

Before		After	
Common stock		Common stock	
($5 par; 400,000 shares)	$ 2,000,000	($5 par; **420,000** shares)	**$ 2,100,000**
Additional paid-in capital	1,000,000	Additional paid-in capital	**1,700,000**
Retained earnings	7,000,000	Retained earnings	**6,200,000**
Total shareholders' equity	$10,000,000	Total shareholders' equity	**$10,000,000**

Note: Current market price per share = $40.

(400,000 × .05) of stock. The fair market value of the stock is $40 per share. For each 20 shares of common stock owned, the shareholder receives an additional share. The total shareholders' equity account after the stock dividend is pictured on the right-hand side of Table 18-1.

With a 5 percent stock dividend, $800,000 ($40 × 20,000 shares) in market value of the additional shares is transferred (on paper) from retained earnings to the common stock and additional paid-in capital accounts. Because the par value per share stays the same, the increase in number of shares is reflected in a $100,000 ($5 × 20,000 shares) increase in the common stock account. The residual of $700,000 is entered into the additional paid-in capital account. The total shareholders' equity of the company remains the same, namely $10 million.

Because the number of shares of common stock outstanding is increased by 5 percent, earnings per share of the company are reduced proportionately. Assume that net profit after taxes for the period just ended is $1 million. Before the stock dividend, earnings per share were $2.50 ($1,000,000/400,000 shares). After the stock dividend, earnings per share would be $2.38 ($1,000,000/420,000 shares). Shareholders have more shares of stock but lower earnings per share. However, each shareholder's proportionate ownership claim against total earnings available to common shareholders remains unchanged.

Large-Percentage Stock Dividends. *Large-percentage stock dividends* (typically 25 percent or higher of previously outstanding common stock) must be accounted for differently. Though small-percentage stock dividends are not expected to have much effect on the market value per share of stock, large-percentage stock dividends are expected to materially reduce the market price per share of stock. In the case of large-percentage stock dividends, therefore, conservatism argues for reclassifying an amount limited to the par value of additional shares rather than an amount related to the pre-stock-dividend market value of the stock.

Suppose that Chen Industries decided to issue a 100 percent stock dividend instead of the 5 percent stock dividend originally discussed. In Table 18-2 we see what the total shareholders' equity section of Chen Industries' balance sheet looks like both before and after the 100 percent stock dividend.

Because of the 100 percent stock dividend, $2,000,000 ($5 × 400,000 shares) in par value of the additional 400,000 shares is transferred from retained earnings to the common stock (at par) account. The total shareholders' equity of the company remains unchanged at $10 million.

TABLE 18-2
100% stock dividend
for Chen Industries

Before		After	
Common stock		Common stock	
($5 par; 400,000 shares)	$ 2,000,000	($5 par; **800,000** shares)	**$ 4,000,000**
Additional paid-in capital	1,000,000	Additional paid-in capital	1,000,000
Retained earnings	7,000,000	Retained earnings	**5,000,000**
Total shareholders' equity	$10,000,000	Total shareholders' equity	$10,000,000

Stock Splits

Stock split An increase in the number of shares outstanding by reducing the par value of the stock; for example, a 2-for-1 stock split where par value per share is reduced by one-half.

With a **stock split** the number of shares is increased through a proportional reduction in the par value of the stock. In our last example, Chen Industries issued a 100 percent stock dividend. A 2-for-1 stock split would have similar economic consequences to a 100 percent stock dividend but would require different accounting treatment. Table 18-3 shows us the total shareholders' equity account for Chen Industries both before and after a 2-for-1 stock split.

With a stock dividend, the par value of common stock is not reduced, whereas with a stock split, it is. As a result, the common stock, additional paid-in capital, and retained earnings accounts remain unchanged with a stock split. The total shareholders' equity, of course, also stays the same. The only change is in the par value of the common stock which, on a per-share basis, is now half of what it once was. Except in accounting treatment, then, the stock dividend and stock split are very similar. A stock split (or alternatively, a large-percentage stock dividend) is usually reserved for occasions when a company wishes to achieve a substantial reduction in the market price per share of common stock. A principal purpose of a split is to place the stock in a more popular trading range, thereby (hopefully) attracting more buyers.

A company will seldom maintain the same cash dividend per share before and after a stock split. But it might increase the effective dividend to shareholders. For example, a company may split its common stock 2 for 1 and establish an annual dividend rate of $1.20 a share, whereas before the rate might have been $2 a share. A shareholder owning 100 shares before the stock split would receive $200 in cash dividends per year. After the stock split, the shareholder would own 200 shares and would receive $240 in dividends per year.

TABLE 18-3
2-for-1 stock split for
Chen Industries

Before		After	
Common stock		Common stock	
($5 par; 400,000 shares)	$ 2,000,000	(**$2.50** par; **800,000** shares)	$ 2,000,000
Additional paid-in capital	1,000,000	Additional paid-in capital	1,000,000
Retained earnings	7,000,000	Retained earnings	7,000,000
Total shareholders' equity	$10,000,000	Total shareholders' equity	$10,000,000

Value to Investors of Stock Dividends and Stock Splits

Theoretically, a stock dividend or stock split is not a thing of value to investors. They receive ownership of additional shares of common stock, but their proportionate ownership of the company is unchanged. The market price of the stock should decline proportionately, so that the total value of each shareholder's holdings stays the same. To illustrate with a stock dividend, suppose that you held 100 shares of common stock worth $40 per share or $4,000 in total. After a 5 percent stock dividend, share price should drop to $38.10 ($40/1.05). The total value of your holdings, however, would still be worth $4,000 ($38.10 × 105 shares). Under these conditions, the stock dividend does not represent a thing of value to you. You merely have a greater number of shares of stock evidencing the same ownership interest. In theory, the stock dividend or split is a purely cosmetic change.

To the extent that an investor wishes to sell a few shares of stock for income, the stock dividend/split may make it easier to do so. Without the stock dividend/split, of course, shareholders could also sell a few shares of their original holdings for income. In either case, the sale of stock represents the sale of principal and is subject to the capital gains tax. It is probable that certain investors do not look at the sale of additional stock resulting from a stock dividend/split as a sale of principal. To them, the stock dividend/split represents a windfall gain. They can sell the additional shares and still retain their original holdings. The stock dividend/split may have a favorable psychological effect on these shareholders.

Effect on Cash Dividends.   The stock dividend or stock split may be accompanied by an increased cash dividend. For the former, suppose that an investor owns 100 shares of a company paying a $1 annual dividend. The company declares a 10 percent stock dividend and, at the same time, announces that the cash dividend per share will remain unchanged. The investor will then have 110 shares, and total cash dividends will be $110 rather than $100, as before. In this case, a stock dividend increases the total cash dividends. Whether this increase in cash dividend has a positive effect on shareholder wealth will depend on the trade-off between current dividends and the retention of earnings, which we discussed earlier. Clearly, the stock dividend in this case represents a decision by the firm to moderately increase the amount of cash dividends. However, the firm does not need the stock dividend to do so. The firm could merely increase its cash dividend per share from $1 to $1.10.

Sometimes a stock dividend is employed to conserve cash. Instead of increasing the cash dividend as earnings rise, a company may desire to retain a greater portion of its earnings and declare a modest stock dividend. This decision effectively amounts to lowering the dividend-payout ratio: as earnings rise and the dividend remains approximately the same, the dividend-payout ratio will decline. Whether shareholder wealth is increased by this action will depend on considerations previously discussed. The decision to retain a higher proportion of earnings, of course, could be accomplished without a stock dividend. Although the stock dividend may tend to please certain investors by virtue of its psychological impact, the substitution of common stock for cash dividends involves a sizable administrative cost. Stock dividends are simply much more costly to administer than are cash dividends. This out-of-pocket expense works to the disadvantage of stock dividends.

More Popular Trading Range.   A stock split and, to a lesser extent, a stock dividend are used to place a stock in a lower, more popular trading range that may attract more buyers and may also affect the mix of stockholders as individual holdings are increased and institutional holdings are decreased.

Informational Content. The declaration of a stock dividend or a stock split may convey information to investors. As taken up earlier, there may be a situation in which management possesses more favorable information about the company than investors. Instead of simply issuing an announcement to the press, management may use a stock dividend or stock split to more convincingly state its belief about the favorable prospects of the company. Whether such a signal has a positive share price effect is an empirical question. Here the evidence is overwhelming. There is a statistically significant, positive stock price reaction around the announcement of a stock dividend or a stock split.[3] The information effect is that the stock is undervalued and should be higher priced. But we must be careful in how we interpret these results. As it turns out, stock dividends and stock splits generally precede cash dividend and earnings increases. The market appears to be viewing stock dividends and stock splits as leading indicators of greater cash dividends and earning power. Thus, it is not the stock dividend or stock split itself that causes a positive share price reaction, but rather it is the positive information that these signals convey. Also, the company must eventually deliver improved dividends and earnings if the stock price is to remain higher.

Reverse Stock Split

Reverse stock split A stock split in which the number of shares outstanding is decreased; for example, a 1-for-2 reverse stock split where each shareholder receives one new share in exchange for every two old shares held.

Rather than increase the number of shares of common stock outstanding, a company may want to reduce the number. It can accomplish this with a **reverse stock split.** If the firm in our previous examples, Chen Industries, had engaged in a 1-for-4 reverse stock split, for each four shares held, the shareholder would receive one new share in exchange. The new par value per share would become $20 ($5 × 4), and there would be 100,000 shares outstanding (400,000 shares/4) rather than 400,000. Reverse stock splits are employed to increase the market price per share when the stock is considered to be selling at too low a price.

As with stock dividends and straight stock splits, there is likely to be an information or signaling effect associated with the announcement of a reverse stock split. Usually the signal is negative, such as would accompany the admission by a company that it is in financial difficulty. However, financial difficulty need not be the underlying motivating factor for the reverse split. The company may simply want to move the stock price into a higher trading range where total trading costs and servicing expenses are lower. Nevertheless, the empirical evidence is consistent with a statistically significant decline in share price around the reverse stock split announcement date, holding other things constant.[4] The decline is tempered by the company's past earnings performance, but a healthy company should think twice before undertaking a reverse stock split. There are too many bad apples in the barrel to not be tainted by association.

---

[3]See Guy Charest, "Split Information, Stock Returns and Market Efficiency, *Journal of Financial Economics* 6 (June–September 1978), 265–96; Eugene F. Fama, Lawrence Fisher, Michael Jensen, and Richard Roll, "The Adjustment of Stock Prices to New Information," *International Economic Review* 10 (February 1969), 1–21; Mark S. Grinblatt, Ronald W. Masulis, and Sheridan Titman, "The Valuation Effects of Stock Splits and Stock Dividends," *Journal of Financial Economics* 13 (December 1984), 461–90; and J. Randall Woolridge, "Stock Dividends as Signals," *Journal of Financial Research* 6 (Spring 1983), 1–12.
[4]See J. Randall Woolridge and Donald R. Chambers, "Reverse Splits and Shareholder Wealth," *Financial Management* 12 (Autumn 1983), 5–15; and R. C. Radcliffe and W. Gillespie, "The Price Impact of Reverse Splits," *Financial Analysts Journal* 35 (January–February 1979), 63–67.

Ask the Fool

Q What are "stock splits?"

A Wondering whether to buy a stock before or after a split is like asking, "Should I eat this peanut-butter-and-jelly sandwich before or after Mom cuts it in half?

Stocks don't become more inexpensive when they split. True, you get more shares. But each is worth less. Imagine you own 100 shares of Sisyphus Transport Corp. (ticker: UPDWN). They're trading at $60 each and total $6,000. When Sisyphus splits 2-for-1, you'll own 200 shares, worth about $30 each. Total value: (drum roll, please) $6,000. Yawn.

Some people drool over stocks about to split, thinking the price will surge. Stock prices sometimes do pop a little on news of splits. But these are artificial moves, sustainable only if the businesses grow to jus-

tify them. The real reason to smile at a split announcement is because it signals that management is bullish. They're not likely to split their stock if they expect the price to go down.

Splits come in many varieties, such as 3-for-2 or 4-for-1. There's even a "reverse split," when you end up with fewer shares, with each worth more. Reverse splits are usually employed by companies in trouble, to avoid looking like the penny stocks they are. If a stock is trading at a red-flag-raising $2 per share and it does a reverse 1-for-10 split, the price will rise to $20 and those who held 100 shares will then own 10.

Companies often split their stock so that the price will remain psychologically appealing. Sometimes, not splitting would mean that few people could afford even a single share. If Microsoft hadn't split seven times in the last decade, each share would be worth more than $6,500.

With stocks, just as with any purchase, examine what you're getting for the price. Study the company and compare the stock price to other numbers, such as earnings. A low price might be inviting, but a $200 stock can be much more of a bargain than a $20 one. If your funds are limited, you can just buy fewer shares.

It's always fun to suddenly own more shares, but splits are like getting change for a dollar. They're not cause for celebration.

Source: The Motley Fool (www.fool.com). Reproduced with the permission of The Motley Fool.

STOCK REPURCHASE

Stock repurchase The repurchase (buyback) of stock by the issuing firm, either in the open (secondary) market or by *self-tender offer.*

In recent years, the repurchase of common stock by corporations has grown dramatically.[5] Some companies repurchase their common stock to have it available for management stock-option plans. In this way, the total number of shares is not increased with the exercise of the options. Another reason for **stock repurchase** is to have shares available for the acquisition of other companies. In certain cases, companies no longer wishing to be publicly owned "go private" by purchasing all of the stock of outside shareholders. In still other situations, stock is repurchased with the full intention of retiring it. When you look at the total cash distributed to shareholders by corporations—cash dividends, share repurchases, and cash tender offers in connection with acquisitions—dividends are simply one (and not always the primary) mechanism for cash distribution.

[5]Outside the United States, common stock repurchases are less common. In some countries share buybacks are not even legal. In other countries, the tax consequences to investors make them unpopular.

Method of Repurchase

The three most common methods of stock repurchase are through a *fixed-price* **self-tender offer**, a **Dutch-auction** *self-tender offer*, and an *open-market purchase*. With a fixed-price self-tender offer, the company makes a formal offer to shareholders to purchase a certain number of shares, typically at a set price. This bid price is above the current market price. Shareholders can elect either to sell their shares at the specified price or to continue to hold them. Usually, the tender-offer period is between two and three weeks. If shareholders tender more shares than originally sought by the company, the company may elect to purchase all or part of the excess. However, it is under no obligation to do so. In general, the transaction costs to the firm in making a self-tender offer are higher than those incurred in the purchase of stock in the open market.

With a Dutch-auction self-tender offer, the company specifies the number of shares it wishes to repurchase plus a minimum and maximum price it is willing to pay. Typically, the minimum price is slightly above the current market price. Shareholders then have the opportunity to submit to the company the number of shares each is willing to sell and their minimum acceptable selling price within the company's stated price range. Upon receipt of the tenders, the company arrays them from low to high. It then determines the lowest price that will result in the full repurchase of the shares specified. This price is paid to all shareholders who tendered shares at or below that price. If more shares than specified are tendered at or below the purchase price, the company will make purchases on a pro rata basis. If too few shares are tendered, the firm either cancels the offer or buys back all tendered shares at the stated maximum price.

Unlike a fixed-price self-tender offer, the company does not know in advance the eventual purchase price. In both types of self-tender offers, the firm is initially uncertain as to the number of shares that will be tendered. The Dutch-auction self-tender offer has become a popular means of repurchase, sometimes exceeding the number of fixed-price self-tender offers in a given year. Larger companies tend to use the Dutch-auction, versus the fixed-price, self-tender offer more than smaller companies do.

In open-market purchases, a company buys its stock as any other investor does—through a brokerage house. Usually, the brokerage fee is negotiated. Certain Securities and Exchange Commission rules restrict the manner in which a company bids for its own shares. As a result, it takes an extended period of time for a company to accumulate a relatively large block of stock. For this reason, the self-tender offer is more suitable when the company seeks a large amount of stock.

Before the company repurchases its stock, shareholders must be informed of the company's intentions. In a self-tender offer, these intentions are announced by the offer itself. Even here, the company must not withhold other information. It would be unethical for a mining company, for example, to withhold information of a substantial ore discovery while making a self-tender offer to repurchase shares. In open-market purchases, especially, it is necessary to disclose the company's repurchase intentions. Otherwise, shareholders may sell their stock not knowing about a repurchase program that will increase earnings per share. Given full information about the amount of repurchase and the objective of the company, the shareholders can sell their shares if they so choose. Without proper disclosure, the selling shareholder may be penalized. When the amount of the stock repurchase is substantial, a self-tender offer is particularly suitable, for it gives all shareholders equal treatment.

Self-tender offer An offer by a firm to repurchase some of its own shares.

Dutch-auction A procedure for buying (selling) securities named for a system used for flower auctions in Holland. A buyer (seller) seeks bids within a specified price range, usually for a large block of stock or bonds. After evaluating the range of bid prices received, the buyer (seller) accepts the lowest price that will allow it to acquire (dispose of) the entire block.

Repurchasing as Part of Dividend Policy

If a firm has excess cash and insufficient profitable investment opportunities to justify the use of these funds, it may be in the shareholders' interests to distribute the funds. The distribution can be accomplished either by the repurchase of stock or by paying the funds out in increased dividends. In the absence of personal income taxes and transactions costs, the two alternatives should theoretically make no difference to shareholders. With repurchase, fewer shares remain outstanding, and earnings per share and, ultimately, dividends per share rise. As a result, the market price per share should rise as well. In theory, the capital gain arising from repurchase should equal the dividend that otherwise would have been paid.

Suppose Deuce Hardware Company is considering the distribution of $1.5 million, either in cash dividends or in the repurchase of its own stock. Key company figures just prior to the $1.5 million distribution are as follows:

Earnings after taxes	$2,000,000
Number of common shares outstanding	÷ 500,000
Earnings per share (EPS)	$ 4
Current market price per share	$ 63
Expected dividend per share	$ 3

Because investors are expecting a $3-per-share cash dividend ($1,500,000/500,000 shares), the $63 value of a share of stock before the dividend is paid consists of the $3-per-share expected dividend plus the $60 market price expected to occur after the cash dividend distribution.

Alternatively, the firm could choose to repurchase some of its stock and make a self-tender offer to shareholders at $63 a share. It then would be able to repurchase 23,810 shares ($1,500,000/$63). Earnings per share after repurchase would be

$$EPS = \$2,000,000/(500,000 - 23,810) = \mathbf{\$4.20}$$

If the firm chooses to pay a cash dividend, its price/earnings ratio after the dividend would be 15 ($60/$4). If this price/earnings ratio stays at 15 after a stock repurchase, the total market price per share will be $63 ($4.20 × 15). The firm's shareholders are equally well off with either a cash dividend or stock repurchase. Under the cash dividend option, current shareholders end up with $3 in dividends per share plus stock worth $60 a share, while under the repurchase option, current shareholders have stock worth $63 a share. Thus, the amount of distribution to shareholders is $3 per share—either in the form of dividends or share price appreciation (and resulting capital gain).

To the extent that the personal tax rate on capital gains is less than that on dividend income, the repurchase of stock offers a tax advantage over the payment of dividends to the taxable investor. In addition, the capital gains tax is postponed until the stock is sold, whereas with dividends the tax must be paid on a current basis.

The repurchase of stock seems particularly appropriate when the firm has a large amount of excess cash to distribute. To pay these funds out through an extra dividend would result in a nonpostponable tax to shareholders. The tax effect could be alleviated somewhat by paying the funds out as extra dividends over a period of time, but this action might result in investors' counting on the extra dividend to be maintained continuously into the future. Also, the firm must be careful not to undertake a steady program of stock repurchase in lieu of paying dividends. The Internal Revenue Service may regard regularly occurring repurchases as the equivalent of cash dividends and not allow shareholders redeeming their shares any capital gains tax advantages.

Investment or Financing Decision?

Treasury stock Common stock that has been repurchased and is held by the issuing company.

Some regard the repurchase of stock as an investment decision instead of a financing decision. Indeed, in a strict sense, it is, even though shares held as **treasury stock** do not provide an expected return as do other investments. No company can exist by "investing" only in its own stock. The decision to repurchase stock should involve distribution of excess funds when the firm's investment opportunities are not sufficiently attractive to warrant employing those funds, either now or in the foreseeable future. Thus, the repurchase of stock cannot really be treated as an investment decision as we define the term.

Stock repurchase is best regarded as a type of financing decision possessing capital structure or dividend policy motivations. For example, sometimes the purpose of a stock repurchase is to alter the capital structure of the firm. By issuing debt and repurchasing stock, a firm can immediately change its debt-to-equity ratio toward a greater proportion of debt. At other times, when there is excess cash, the repurchase of stock can be viewed as part of the firm's overall dividend policy.

Possible Signaling Effect

Stock repurchases may also have a positive signaling effect. For example, suppose management believed that the firm's common stock was undervalued and that they were personally constrained in not being able to respond to a self-tender offer with shares that they owned individually. In such a case, the self-tender offer "premium" (amount by which the repurchase price exceeds the existing share price) would reflect management's belief about the degree of undervaluation. The idea is that concrete actions speak louder than words.[6]

---

[6]A number of empirical studies find evidence supporting the positive signaling effect of stock repurchases, particularly for self-tender offers as opposed to open-market purchases. See Larry Y. Dann, "Common Stock Repurchases: An Analysis of Returns to Bondholders and Stockholders," *Journal of Financial Economics* 9 (June 1981), 113–38; Theo Vermaelen, "Common Stock Repurchases and Market Signaling," *Journal of Financial Economics* 9 (June 1981), 139–83; and Theo Vermaelen, "Repurchase Tender Offers, Signaling, and Managerial Incentives," *Journal of Financial and Quantitative Analysis,* 19 (June 1984), 163–82.

Dividends and Share Repurchases at Georgia-Pacific

We believe a portion of our cash flows should be paid to shareholders as regular, sustainable quarterly dividends. Currently, the Group pays a $0.25 per share quarterly dividend. In the future, the dividend rate will depend on our cash flows, long-term capital requirements and overall capital structure.

As was the case in 1998, there likely will be periods when the Georgia-Pacific Group generates cash in excess of our opportunities for reinvestment and dividend requirements. Excess cash will be returned to our shareholders through share repurchases, so they can make their own reinvestment choices. We believe our long-term shareholders will benefit as their proportionate share of the Group grows.

Management is authorized to repurchase shares of the Georgia-Pacific Group when total corporate debt is below $5.75 billion and Georgia-Pacific Group debt is below $4.75 billion. During 1998, the Georgia-Pacific Group repurchased 7.7 million shares. This represents a tax-efficient distribution of $436 million to our shareholders and an 8 percent gross reduction from our January 1 share base.

Source: Georgia-Pacific Corporation—Georgia-Pacific Group, 1998 Annual Report, p. 28. © 1998 Georgia-Pacific Corporation—Georgia-Pacific Group. Used by permission. All rights reserved.

Interestingly, Dutch-auction self-tender offers appear to have a somewhat smaller positive signaling effect than fixed-price self-tender offers. One reason is that a Dutch auction usually results in a lower "premium" than does a fixed-price self-tender offer. Open-market purchase programs generally provide only a modest positive signaling effect. One explanation is that such programs often are instigated only after a period of share price decline, in contrast to the two types of self-tender offers.[7]

Although cash dividends and stock repurchases are similar in informational content in that they both use cash to send a positive signal, they also provide some dissimilar information. The regular cash dividend provides ongoing reinforcement of the underlying ability of the firm to generate cash. It is like a quarterly news release and can be habit-forming. In contrast, share repurchase is not a regular event. It may be viewed more as an "extra" news bulletin used on occasions when management believes that the firm's common stock is greatly undervalued.[8] Because both cash dividends and stock repurchases are done with money, management has a disincentive to give false signals and implicitly pledges itself to provide cash-flow results consistent with the signal.

ADMINISTRATIVE CONSIDERATIONS

Procedural Aspects

Record date The date, set by the board of directors when a dividend is declared, on which an investor must be a shareholder of record to be entitled to the upcoming dividend.

Ex-dividend date The first date on which a stock purchaser is no longer entitled to the recently declared dividend.

Declaration date The date that the board of directors announces the amount and date of the next dividend.

Payment date The date when the corporation actually pays the declared dividend.

When the board of directors of a corporation declares a cash dividend, it specifies a **record date.** At the close of business on that date, a list of shareholders is drawn up by the company from its stock-transfer books. Shareholders on the list are entitled to the dividend, whereas shareholders who come on the books after the record date are not entitled to the dividend. For example, suppose that when the board of directors of United Chemical Company met on May 8, it declared a dividend of $1 per share payable June 15 to shareholders of record on May 31. Beth Broach owns some United Chemical stock purchased well before May 31, so she is entitled to the dividend even though she might sell her stock prior to the dividend actually being paid on June 15.

A problem can develop in the sale of stock in the days immediately prior to the record date. The buyer and the seller of the stock have several days to *settle,* that is, to pay for the stock or to deliver it, in the case of the seller. To avoid confusion about which investors are entitled to dividends when shares are sold just prior to the record date, the brokerage community has a rule whereby new shareholders are entitled to dividends only if they purchase the stock at least two business days prior to the record date. If the stock is purchased after that time, the shareholder is not entitled to the dividend. The date itself is known as the **ex-dividend date.**

Figure 18-3 shows the important dividend dates in our example on a time line. May 8 was the date on which the board of directors declared a dividend (the **declaration date**), payable June 15 (the **payment date**) to shareholders of record as of May 31 (the record date). If May 31 were a Friday, two business days before would be May 29 (the ex-dividend date). To receive the dividend, a new shareholder must purchase

---

[7]Robert Comment and Gregg A. Jarrell, "The Relative Signalling Power of Dutch-Auction and Fixed-Price Self-Tender Offers and Open-Market Share Repurchases," *Journal of Finance* 46 (September 1991), 1243–71. See also Laurie Simon Bagwell, "Dutch Auction Repurchases: An Analysis of Shareholder Heterogeneity," *Journal of Finance* 47 (March 1992), 71–105.

[8]See Paul Asquith and David W. Mullins Jr., "Signalling with Dividends, Stock Repurchases, and Equity Issues," *Financial Management* 15 (Autumn 1986), 27–44.

FIGURE 18-3
Important Dividend
Dates for United
Chemical Company

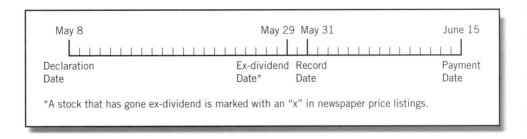

the stock on May 28 or before. If purchased on May 29 or after, the stock is said to be *ex-dividend*. That is, it trades without the right to the declared dividend.

Dividend Reinvestment Plans

Dividend reinvestment plan (DRIP) An optional plan allowing shareholders to automatically reinvest dividend payments in additional shares of the company's stock.

A number of large companies have established **dividend reinvestment plans (DRIPs).** Under these plans, shareholders have the option to reinvest their cash dividends in additional shares of the company's stock. There are two basic types of DRIPs, characterized by whether the additional shares come from already existing common stock or newly issued common stock. If existing common stock is used, the company transfers the cash dividends from all shareholders wishing to reinvest to a bank, which acts as a trustee. The bank then purchases shares of the company's common stock in the open market. Some companies even absorb any brokerage costs involved with purchasing the common stock required for reinvestment. For DRIPs in which the shareholder must bear the brokerage costs, these costs are relatively low, however, because the trustee buys stock in volume.

The other type of reinvestment plan involves having the firm issue new common stock. Only under this method can the firm actually raise new funds. This type of plan has proven especially popular with companies in need of new capital for construction and improvements. Effectively, such a plan reduces a firm's cash dividend payout. For example, suppose that a firm using a "new-stock" DRIP currently reports a 60 percent dividend-payout ratio. But after subtracting all cash dividends that are reinvested in new common stock, the "actual" payout may drop to only 40 percent. The cash savings to a large firm could easily amount to millions of dollars. With a new-stock DRIP the shares come directly from the company, so there are no brokerage costs involved. Some of these new-stock plans even allow participants to buy additional shares at a discount from the current market price of the stock. Commonly the discount is 3 to 5 percent, and it serves as an inducement for reinvestment. Even though reinvested, the dividend is taxable to the shareholder as ordinary income, and this is a major disadvantage to the taxable shareholder. Companies offering DRIPs range from utilities to banks to industrial concerns.

SUMMARY

- The critical question in dividend policy is, given the investment decision of the firm, do dividends have an influence on the value of the firm?
- If dividends are irrelevant, as argued by Modigliani and Miller (M&M), the firm should retain earnings only in keeping with the availability of acceptable investment proposals. If there are not sufficient investment opportunities to provide returns in excess of those that are required, the unused funds should be paid out as dividends.

- With perfect capital markets and an absence of taxes, shareholders can manufacture "home-made" dividends, making the firm's dividend payout irrelevant. With differential taxes (in present value terms) on cash dividends and capital gains, there seemingly is a bias in favor of earnings retention.

- The market imperfection of flotation costs biases things in favor of earnings retention because this "internal" equity financing is less expensive than "external" equity financing (issuance of new common stock) used to replace the funds lost to the cash dividend. On the other hand, restrictions on the investment behavior of financial institutions work in the direction of a preference for dividends. Other market imperfections are also part of the picture.

- Empirical testing of dividend policy has focused on whether there is a tax effect and whether dividends serve as a signal in conveying information. The evidence is conflicting with respect to the tax effect, ranging from a neutral effect to a negative (anti-dividend-paying) effect. However, there seems to be agreement that dividends provide financial signals.

- In the final analysis, finance experts are unable to state unequivocally whether the dividend payout of the firm should be more than a passive decision variable. Most academics think not. Admittedly, many companies behave as if dividend policy is relevant, but the case for it is not conclusive.

- When a company is faced with a dividend decision, managerial considerations include legal rules, the funding needs of the firm, business risk, liquidity, ability to borrow, assessment of any valuation information, control, and restrictions in debt contracts.

- Many people feel that the stability of dividends has a positive effect on the market price of the stock. Stable dividends may tend to resolve uncertainty in the minds of investors, particularly when earnings per share drop. Stable dividends may also have a positive utility to investors interested in current periodic income. Many companies appear to follow the policy of a target dividend-payout ratio, increasing dividends only when they feel that an increase in earnings can be maintained. The use of an *extra dividend* permits a cyclical company to maintain a stable record of *regular dividends* while paying additional dividends whenever earnings are unusually high.

- A *stock dividend* pays additional common stock to shareholders. It is frequently used to conserve cash and to reduce the cash-dividend-payout ratio of the firm. Theoretically, a stock dividend/split per se is not a thing of value to the shareholder unless total cash dividends paid increase.

- When the intent is to materially reduce the market price per share of stock, either a *stock split* or *large-percentage stock dividend* is used. With a split, the number of shares is increased by the terms of the split. For example, a 3-for-1 split means that the number of shares outstanding is tripled.

- Both stock dividends and stock splits appear to have an informational or signaling effect. Share price tends to rise around the time of a stock dividend/split announcement, consistent with a positive signal. The market appears to view the stock dividend/split as a leading indicator of greater cash dividends and earning power. In a *reverse stock split,* the number of shares outstanding is reduced, and the signal to the market usually is negative.

- A company's repurchase of its own stock should be treated as part of the firm's dividend policy when the firm has funds in excess of present and foreseeable future investment needs. The use of these excess funds to repurchase stock is an alternative to distributing them in the form of cash dividends.

- With a tax differential (in present value terms) between cash dividends and capital gains, there is a tax advantage to the repurchase of common stock. Because of objections by the Internal Revenue Service, regularly occurring repurchases of common stock cannot be used in lieu of regular dividends.

- The dividend payment process begins with the firm's board of directors, which on a particular date (the *declaration date*) declares a dividend, payable on a later date (the *payment date*) to shareholders of record as of a particular date (the *record date*). On the second business date before the record date (the *ex-dividend date*), the stock goes "ex-dividend"—meaning that the stock trades without the right to the declared dividend.

- *Dividend reinvestment plans (DRIPs)* allow shareholders to automatically reinvest dividend payments in additional shares of the company's stock.

QUESTIONS

1. Contrast a passive dividend policy with an active one.
2. How does an investor manufacture "homemade" dividends? What is the effect of the actions of a number of investors doing so, all other things held constant?
3. How do taxes affect the return to different investors? Are taxes a consideration in the dividend policy decision?
4. Why do companies with high growth rates tend to have low dividend-payout ratios and companies with low growth rates tend to have high dividend-payout ratios?
5. What is financial signaling as it relates to cash dividends, stock dividends/splits, and stock repurchase?
6. From a managerial standpoint, how does a firm's liquidity and ability to borrow affect its dividend-payout ratio?
7. As the firm's financial manager, would you recommend to the board of directors that the firm adopt as policy a stable dividend payment per share or a stable dividend-payout ratio? What are the disadvantages of each? Would the firm's industry influence your decision? Why?
8. What is a *target dividend-payout ratio?* An *extra cash dividend?*
9. Define a *stock dividend* and a *stock split.* What is the impact of each on share value?
10. Are *stock dividends* valuable to investors? Why or why not?
11. If we wish to raise share price, is it a good idea to have a *reverse stock split?* Explain.
12. As an investor, would you prefer the firm to repurchase its common stock by means of a *self-tender offer* or through open-market operations? Why?
13. If repurchase of stock has a favorable tax effect, why would a company ever want to pay a cash dividend?
14. When earnings falter, why are boards of directors of companies reluctant to reduce the dividend?
15. Why do lenders frequently place a formal restriction in the debt contract on the amount of dividends that can be paid?
16. What is a *dividend reinvestment plan (DRIP)* and how might it help shareholders?
17. Is dividend policy a type of financing decision or is it a type of investment decision? Explain.

SELF-CORRECTION PROBLEMS

1. The Borowiak Rose Water Company expects with some degree of certainty to generate the following net income and to have the following capital expenditures during the next five years (in thousands of dollars):

	YEAR				
	1	2	3	4	5
Net income	$2,000	$1,500	$2,500	$2,300	$1,800
Capital expenditures	1,000	1,500	2,000	1,500	2,000

The company currently has 1 million shares of common stock outstanding and pays annual dividends of $1 per share.

a. Determine dividends per share and external financing required in each year if dividend policy is treated as a residual decision.

b. Determine the amounts of external financing that will be necessary in each year if the present annual dividend per share is maintained.

c. Determine dividends per share and the amounts of external financing that will be necessary if a dividend-payout ratio of 50 percent is maintained.
d. Under which of the three dividend policies are aggregate dividends (total dividends over five years) maximized? External required financing (total financing over five years) minimized?

2. Dew Drop Inn, Inc.'s earnings per share over the last 10 years were the following:

					YEAR					
	1	2	3	4	5	6	7	8	9	10
EPS	$1.70	$1.82	$1.44	$1.88	$2.18	$2.32	$1.84	$2.23	$2.50	$2.73

a. Determine annual dividends per share under the following policies:
   (1) A constant dividend-payout ratio of 40 percent (to the nearest cent).
   (2) A regular dividend of 80 cents and an extra dividend to bring the payout ratio to 40 percent if it otherwise would fall below.
   (3) A stable dividend that is occasionally raised. The payout ratio may range between 30 percent and 50 percent in any given year, but it should average approximately 40 percent.
b. What are the valuation implications of each of these policies?

3. The Klingon Fastener Company has the following shareholders' equity account:

Common stock ($8 par value)	$ 2,000,000
Additional paid-in capital	1,600,000
Retained earnings	8,400,000
Total shareholders' equity	$12,000,000

The current market price of the stock is $60 per share.
a. What will happen to this account and to the number of shares outstanding with (1) a 10 percent stock dividend? (2) a 2-for-1 stock split? (3) a 1-for-2 reverse stock split?
b. In the absence of an informational or signaling effect, at what share price should the common stock sell after the 10 percent stock dividend? What might happen to stock price if there were a signaling effect?

PROBLEMS

1. The DeWitt Company's shareholders' equity account (book value) as of December 31, 20X1, is as follows:

Common stock ($5 par value; 1,000,000 shares)	$ 5,000,000
Additional paid-in capital	5,000,000
Retained earnings	15,000,000
Total shareholders' equity	$25,000,000

Currently, DeWitt is under pressure from shareholders to pay some dividends. DeWitt's cash balance is $500,000, all of which is needed for transactions purposes. The stock is trading for $7 a share.
a. Reformulate the shareholders' equity account if the company pays a 15 percent stock dividend.

    b. Reformulate the shareholders' equity account if the company pays a 25 percent stock dividend.

    c. Reformulate the shareholders' equity account if the company declares a 5-for-4 stock split.

2. Tijuana Brass Instruments Company treats dividends as a residual decision. It expects to generate $2 million in net earnings after taxes in the coming year. The company has an all-equity capital structure, and its cost of equity capital is 15 percent. The company treats this cost as the opportunity cost of "internal" equity financing (retained earnings). Because of flotation costs and underpricing, "external" equity financing (new common stock) is not relied on until internal equity financing is exhausted.

    a. How much in dividends (out of the $2 million in earnings) should be paid if the company has $1.5 million in projects whose expected returns exceed 15 percent?

    b. How much in dividends should be paid if it has $2 million in projects whose expected returns exceed 15 percent?

    c. How much in dividends should be paid if it has $3 million in projects whose expected returns exceed 16 percent? What else should be done?

3. For each of the companies described here, would you expect it to have a low, medium, or high dividend-payout ratio? Explain why.

    a. A company with a large proportion of inside ownership, all of whom are high-income individuals

    b. A growth company with an abundance of good investment opportunities

    c. A company that has high liquidity and much unused borrowing capacity and is experiencing ordinary growth

    d. A dividend-paying company that experiences an unexpected drop in earnings from an upward-sloping trend line

    e. A company with volatile earnings and high business risk

4. Jumbo Shrimp Corporation and Giant Shrimp Company are in the same industry; both are publicly held with a large number of shareholders; and they have the following characteristics:

	JUMBO	GIANT
Expected annual cash flow (in thousands)	$ 50,000	$35,000
Standard deviation of cash flow (in thousands)	30,000	25,000
Annual capital expenditures (in thousands)	42,000	40,000
Cash and marketable securities (in thousands)	5,000	7,000
Existing long-term debt (in thousands)	100,000	85,000
Unused short-term line of credit (in thousands)	25,000	10,000
Flotation costs on common stock issues as a percent of proceeds	.05	.08

On the basis of this information, which company is likely to have the higher dividend-payout ratio? Why?

5. The Oprah Corporation and the Harpo Corporation have had remarkably similar earnings patterns over the last five years. In fact, both firms have had identical earnings per share. Further, both firms are in the same industry, produce the same product, and face the same business and financial risks. In short, these firms are carbon copies of each other in every respect but one: Oprah paid out a

constant percentage of its earnings (50 percent) in dividends, while Harpo has paid a constant cash dividend. The financial manager of the Oprah Corporation has been puzzled by the fact that the price of her firm's stock has been generally lower than the price of Harpo's stock, even though in some years Oprah's dividend was substantially larger than Harpo's.

a. What might account for the condition that has been puzzling the financial manager of Oprah?

b. What might be done by both companies to increase the market prices of their stock?

	OPRAH			HARPO		
YEARS	EPS	DIVIDEND	MARKET PRICE	EPS	DIVIDEND	MARKET PRICE
1	$1.00	$.50	$6.00	$1.00	$.23	$4.75
2	.50	.25	4.00	.50	.23	4.00
3	−.25	nil	2.00	−.25	.23	4.25
4	.50	.25	3.50	.50	.23	4.50

6. The Chris Clapper Copper Company declared a 25 percent stock dividend on March 10 to shareholders of record on April 1. The market price of the stock is $50 per share. You own 160 shares of the stock.

a. If you sold your stock on March 20, what would be the price per share, all other things the same (no signaling effect)?

b. After the stock dividend is paid, how many shares of stock will you own?

c. At what price would you expect the stock to sell on April 2, all other things the same (no signaling effect)?

d. What will be the total value of your holdings before and after the stock dividend, all other things the same?

e. If there were an informational or signaling effect, what would be the effect on share price?

7.

SHERILL CORPORATION SHAREHOLDERS' EQUITY AS OF DECEMBER 30, 20X3	
Common stock ($1 par value; 1,000,000 shares)	$1,000,000
Additional paid-in capital	300,000
Retained earnings	1,700,000
Total shareholders' equity	$3,000,000

The firm earned $300,000 after taxes in 20X3 and paid out 50 percent of these earnings as cash dividends. The price on the firm's stock on December 30 was $5.

a. If the firm declared a stock dividend of 3 percent on December 31, what would be the reformulated shareholders' equity account?

b. Assuming the firm paid no stock dividend, how much would earnings per share be for 20X3? Dividends per share?

c. Assuming a 3 percent stock dividend, what would happen to earnings per share (EPS) and dividends per share (DPS) for 20X3?

d. What would the price of the stock be after the 3 percent stock dividend if there were no signaling or other effects?

8. Johore Trading Company has 2.4 million shares of common stock outstanding, and the present market price per share is $36. Its equity capitalization is as follows:

Common stock ($2.00 par; 2,400,000 shares)	$ 4,800,000
Additional paid-in capital	5,900,000
Retained earnings	87,300,000
Total shareholders' equity	$98,000,000

a. If the company were to declare a 12 percent stock dividend, what would happen to these accounts? A 25 percent stock dividend? A 5 percent stock dividend?

b. If, instead, the company declared a 3-for-2 stock split, what would happen to the accounts? A 2-for-1 stock split? A 3-for-1 split?

c. What would happen if there were a reverse stock split of 1 for 4? 1 for 6?

9. The H. M. Hornes Company is primarily owned by several wealthy Texans. The firm earned $3,500,000 after taxes this year. With 1 million shares outstanding, earnings per share were $3.50. The stock recently has traded at $72 per share, among the current shareholders. Two dollars of this value is accounted for by investor anticipation of a cash dividend. As financial manager of H. M. Hornes, you have contemplated the alternative of repurchasing some company common stock by means of a tender offer at $72 per share.

a. How much common stock could the firm repurchase if this alternative were selected?

b. Ignoring taxes, which alternative should be selected?

c. Considering taxes, which alternative should be selected?

SOLUTIONS TO SELF-CORRECTION PROBLEMS

1. a.

YEAR	INCOME AVAILABLE FOR DIVIDENDS (IN THOUSANDS)	DIVIDENDS PER SHARE	EXTERNAL FINANCING REQUIRED (IN THOUSANDS)
1	$1,000	$1.00	$ 0
2	0	0	0
3	500	.50	0
4	800	.80	0
5	0	0	200
	$2,300		$200

b. (in thousands)

	(1)	(2)	(3)	(4)
				EXTERNAL FINANCING
			CAPITAL	REQUIRED
YEAR	NET INCOME	DIVIDENDS	EXPENDITURES	(2) + (3) − (1)
1	$2,000	$1,000	$1,000	$ 0
2	1,500	1,000	1,500	1,000
3	2,500	1,000	2,000	500
4	2,300	1,000	1,500	200
5	1,800	1,000	2,000	1,200
		$5,000		$2,900

c.

YEAR	(1) NET INCOME (IN THOUSANDS)	(2) DIVIDENDS (IN THOUSANDS)	(3) DIVIDENDS PER SHARE	(4) CAPITAL EXPENDITURES (IN THOUSANDS)	(5) EXTERNAL FINANCING REQUIRED (2) + (4) − (1) (IN THOUSANDS)
1	$2,000	$1,000	$1.00	$1,000	$ 0
2	1,500	750	.75	1,500	750
3	2,500	1,250	1.25	2,000	750
4	2,300	1,150	1.15	1,500	350
5	1,800	900	.90	2,000	1,100
		$5,050			$2,950

d. Aggregate dividends are highest under Alternative C, which involves a 50 percent dividend-payout ratio. However, they are only slightly higher than that which occurs under Alternative B. External financing is minimized under Alternative A, the residual dividend policy.

2. a.

YEAR	POLICY 1	POLICY 2	POLICY 3
1	$ .68	$ .80	$ .68
2	.73	.80	.68
3	.58	.80	.68
4	.75	.80	.80
5	.87	.87	.80
6	.93	.93	.80
7	.74	.80	.80
8	.89	.89	1.00
9	1.00	1.00	1.00
10	1.09	1.09	1.00

Other dividend streams are possible under Policy 3. This solution is but one.

b. Policy 1 and, to a much lesser degree, Policy 2 result in fluctuating dividends over time, as the company is cyclical. Because of the $.80 minimum regular dividend, Policy 2 results in an average payout ratio in excess of 40 percent. Shareholders may come to count on the extra dividend and be disappointed when it is not paid, such as in year 7. To the extent that investors value stable dividends and periodic rising dividends over time and that 40 percent is an optimal average payout ratio, dividend Policy 3 would be preferred and would likely maximize share price.

3. a. Present number of shares = $2,000,000/$8 par value = 250,000.

	(1) STOCK DIVIDEND	(2) STOCK SPLIT	(3) REVERSE SPLIT
Common stock (par)	$ 2,200,000 ($8)	$ 2,000,000 ($4)	$ 2,000,000 ($16)
Additional paid-in capital	2,900,000	1,600,000	1,600,000
Retained earnings	6,900,000	8,400,000	8,400,000
Total shareholders' equity	$12,000,000	$12,000,000	$12,000,000
Number of shares	275,000	500,000	125,000

b. The total market value of the firm before the stock dividend is $60 \times 250,000$ shares = $15 million. With no change in the total value of the firm, market price per share after the stock dividend should be $15,000,000/275,000$ shares = **$54.55 per share.** If there is a signaling effect, the total value of the firm might rise and share price be somewhat higher than $54.55 per share. The magnitude of the effect would probably be no more than several dollars a share, based on empirical findings.

SELECTED REFERENCES

Asquith, Paul, and David W. Mullins Jr. "The Impact of Initiating Dividend Payments on Shareholders' Wealth." *Journal of Business* 56 (January 1983), 77–96.

———. "Signalling with Dividends, Stock Repurchases, and Equity Issues." *Financial Management* 15 (Autumn 1986), 27–44.

Bagwell, Laurie Simon. "Dutch Auction Repurchases: An Analysis of Shareholder Heterogeneity." *Journal of Finance* 47 (March 1992), 71–105.

———, and John B. Shoven. "Cash Distributions to Shareholders." *Journal of Economic Perspectives* 3 (Summer 1989), 129–40.

Baker, H. Kent, Aaron L. Phillips, and Gary E. Powell. "The Stock Distribution Puzzle: A Synthesis of the Literature on Stock Splits and Stock Dividends." *Financial Practice and Education* 5 (Spring/Summer 1995), 24–37.

Benartzi, Shlomo, Roni Michaely, and Richard Thaler. "Do Changes in Dividends Signal the Future or the Past?" *Journal of Finance* 52 (July 1997), 1007–34.

Black, Fischer. "The Dividend Puzzle." *Journal of Portfolio Management* 2 (Winter 1976), 5–8.

———, and Myron Scholes. "The Effects of Dividend Yield and Dividend Policy on Common Stock Prices and Returns." *Journal of Financial Economics* 1 (May 1974), 1–22.

Bline, Dennis M., and Charles P. Cullinan. "Distributions to Stockholders: Legal Distinctions and Accounting Implications for Classroom Discussion." *Issues in Accounting Education* 10 (Fall 1995), 307–16.

Brennan, Michael J., and Thomas E. Copeland. "Stock Splits, Stock Prices, and Transaction Costs." *Journal of Financial Economics* 22 (October 1988), 83–101.

Charest, Guy. "Split Information, Stock Returns and Market Efficiency." *Journal of Financial Economics* 6 (June–September 1978), 265–96.

Comment, Robert, and Gregg A. Jarrell. "The Relative Signalling Power of Dutch-Auction and Fixed-Price Self-Tender Offers and Open-Market Share Repurchases." *Journal of Finance* 46 (September 1991), 1243–71.

Dann, Larry Y. "Common Stock Repurchases: An Analysis of Returns to Bondholders and Stockholders." *Journal of Financial Economics* 9 (June 1981), 113–38.

Fama, Eugene F., Lawrence Fisher, Michael Jensen, and Richard Roll. "The Adjustment of Stock Prices to New Information." *International Economic Review* 10 (February 1969), 1–21.

Grinblatt, Mark S., Ronald W. Masulis, and Sheridan Titman. "The Valuation Effects of Stock Splits and Stock Dividends." *Journal of Financial Economics* 13 (December 1984), 461–90.

Healy, Paul M., and Krishna G. Palepu. "Earnings Information Conveyed by Dividend Initiations and Omissions." *Journal of Financial Economics* 21 (September 1988), 149–75.

Ikenberry, David L., Graeme Rankin, and Earl K. Stice. "What Do Stock Splits Really Signal?" *Journal of Financial and Quantitative Analysis* 31 (September 1996), 357–75.

Lakonishok, Josef, and Theo Vermaelen. "Anomalous Price Behavior Around Repurchase Tender Offers." *Journal of Finance* 45 (June 1990), 455–78.

Lintner, John. "Distribution of Income of Corporations Among Dividends, Retained Earnings, and Taxes." *American Economic Review* 46 (May 1956), 97–113.

Litzenberger, Robert H., and Krishna Ramiswamy. "Dividends, Short Selling Restrictions, Tax Induced Investor Clienteles and Market Equilibrium." *Journal of Finance* 35 (May 1980), 469–82.

———. "The Effects of Dividends on Common Stock Prices: Tax Effects or Information Effects?" *Journal of Finance* 37 (May 1982), 429–44.

Litzenberger, Robert H., and James C. Van Horne. "Elimination of the Double Taxation of Dividends and Corporate Financial Policy." *Journal of Finance* 33 (June 1978), 737–49.

Markese, John. "Common Stock Dividends: What Are They Worth?" *AAII Journal* 11 (July 1989), 29–33.

McNichols, Maureen, and Ajay Dravid. "Stock Dividends, Stock Splits, and Signaling." *Journal of Finance* 45 (July 1990), 857–79.

Miller, Merton H. "Behavioral Rationality in Finance: The Case of Dividends." *Midland Corporate Finance Journal* 4 (Winter 1987), 6–15.

————, and Franco Modigliani. "Dividend Policy, Growth, and the Valuation of Shares." *Journal of Business* 34 (October 1961), 411–33.

Miller, Merton H., and Kevin Rock. "Dividend Policy under Asymmetric Information." *Journal of Finance* 40 (September 1985), 1031–51.

Roberts, Michael, William D. Samson, and Michael T. Dugan. "The Stockholders' Equity Section: Form Without Substance?" *Accounting Horizons* 4 (December 1990), 35–46.

Szewczyk, Samuel H., and George P. Tsetsekos. "The Effect of Managerial Ownership on Stock Split-Induced Abnormal Returns." *Financial Review* 28 (August 1993), 351–70.

Van Horne, James C., and John G. McDonald. "Dividend Policy and New Equity Financing." *Journal of Finance* 26 (May 1971), 507–19.

Vermalelen, Theo. "Common Stock Repurchases and Market Signaling." *Journal of Financial Economics* 9 (June 1981), 139–83.

————. "Repurchase Tender Offers, Signaling, and Managerial Incentives." *Journal of Financial and Quantitative Analysis,* 19 (June 1984), 163–82.

Woolridge, J. Randall. "Stock Dividends as Signals." *Journal of Financial Research* 6 (Spring 1983), 1–12.

————, and Donald R. Chambers. "Reverse Splits and Shareholder Wealth." *Financial Management* 12 (Autumn 1983), 5–15.

Chapter 19

The Capital Market

DÉJÀ VU ALL OVER AGAIN

PUBLIC ISSUE
> Traditional Underwriting • Best Efforts Offering • Shelf
> Registration

PRIVILEGED SUBSCRIPTION
> Preemptive Right • Terms of Offering • Value of Rights • Standby
> Arrangement and Oversubscription Privilege • Privileged
> Subscription versus Public Issue

REGULATION OF SECURITY OFFERINGS
> Federal Regulation • State Regulation

PRIVATE PLACEMENT
> Features • Developments in the Market

INITIAL FINANCING
> Venture Capital • Initial Public Offerings

SIGNALING EFFECTS
> Expectations of Future Cash Flows • Asymmetric (Unequal)
> Information

THE SECONDARY MARKET

SUMMARY

QUESTIONS

SELF-CORRECTION PROBLEMS

PROBLEMS

SOLUTIONS TO SELF-CORRECTION PROBLEMS

SELECTED REFERENCES

> *"Mr. Morgan, will the market go up or down?"*
> *"Yes."*

—EXCHANGE BETWEEN A JOURNALIST AND J. P. MORGAN

In Chapters 17 and 18 we studied how business firms determine their mix of permanent long-term financing and how they finance "internally" by retaining earnings. We now need to find out how firms raise long-term financing "externally." More specifically, the purpose of this chapter is to observe the ways in which bond and stock issues are initially sold in the capital market. We shall get to know public issues of securities placed through investment bankers, privileged subscriptions to the company's own shareholders, and private placements by the firm to institutional investors. The presentation here draws on "The Financial Environment" section of Chapter 2. It was there that we first discussed financial markets in general.

DÉJÀ VU ALL OVER AGAIN

Capital market The market for relatively long-term (greater than one year original maturity) financial instruments (e.g., bonds and stocks).

Primary market A market where new securities are bought and sold for the first time (a "new issues" market).

Secondary market A market for existing (used) securities rather than new issues.

The **capital market,** you may remember, deals with bonds and stocks. Within the capital market there exist both a primary and a secondary market. A **primary market** is a "new issues" market. It is here that funds raised through the sale of new securities flow from the buyers of securities (the savings sector) to the issuers of securities (the investment sector). In a **secondary market,** existing securities are bought and sold. Transactions in these already existing securities do *not* provide additional funds to finance capital investment. In this chapter, we will focus chiefly on primary market activities within the capital market.

Figure 19-1 illustrates the capital market for corporate securities. From the figure, we can note the prominent position held by certain financial institutions in moving funds from the savings sector to the investment sector via three main avenues: a public issue, a privileged subscription, and a private placement. Investment bankers, financial intermediaries, and the secondary market are the key institutions that enhance the movement of funds. You may want to use Figure 19-1 as a "road map" for the unfolding discussion in this chapter.

PUBLIC ISSUE

Public issue Sale of bonds or stock to the general public.

A large company typically raises funds both publicly and privately. With a **public issue,** securities are sold to hundreds, and often thousands, of investors under a formal contract overseen by federal and state regulatory authorities. A *private placement,* on the other hand, is made to a limited number of investors, sometimes only one, and with considerably less regulation. An example of a private placement might be a loan by a small group of insurance companies to a corporation. Thus, the two types of security issues differ primarily in the number of investors involved and in the regulations governing issuance.

Investment banker A financial institution that underwrites (purchases at a fixed price on a fixed date) new securities for resale.

When a company issues securities to the general public, it usually uses the services of an **investment banker.** The investment banker acts as a middleman in bringing together parties who need funds with those who have savings. The principal function of the investment banker is to buy the new securities from the issuing company (at wholesale) and then resell them to investors (at retail). For this service, investment bankers receive the difference, or *underwriting spread,* between the price they pay for the security and the price at which the security is resold to the public. Because most companies make only occasional trips to the capital market, they are not specialists in the distribution of securities. On the other hand, investment banking

FIGURE 19-1
Capital Market for
Corporate Securities

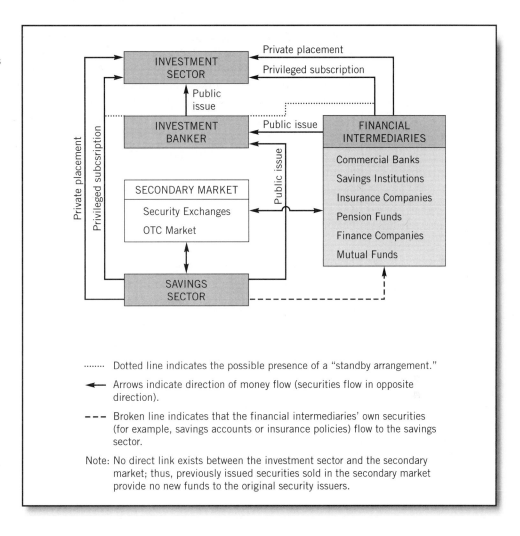

.... Dotted line indicates the possible presence of a "standby arrangement."

◄─── Arrows indicate direction of money flow (securities flow in opposite direction).

--- Broken line indicates that the financial intermediaries' own securities (for example, savings accounts or insurance policies) flow to the savings sector.

Note: No direct link exists between the investment sector and the secondary market; thus, previously issued securities sold in the secondary market provide no new funds to the original security issuers.

firms have the expertise, the contacts, and the sales organization necessary to do an efficient job of marketing securities to investors. Because they are continually in the business of buying securities from companies and selling them to investors, investment bankers can perform this service at a lower cost than can the individual firm.

There are three primary means by which companies offer securities to the general public: a traditional (or firm commitment) underwriting, a best efforts offering, and a shelf registration. In recent years, the shelf registration has come to dominate, at least for larger corporations. Let us explore these three methods for offering bonds and stock to investors.

Traditional Underwriting

Underwriting Bearing the risk of not being able to sell a security at the established price by virtue of purchasing the security for resale to the public; also known as *firm commitment underwriting*.

An investment banker or group of investment bankers buying a security issue **underwrites** the sale of the issue by giving the company a check for the purchase price. At that time, the issuing company is relieved of the risk of not being able to sell the issue to the general public at the established price. If the issue does not sell well, either because of an adverse turn in the market or because it is overpriced, the underwriter, not the company, takes the loss. Thus, the investment banker insures, or underwrites, the risk of adverse price fluctuations during the period of distribution.

Often, the investment banking institution with which a company discusses the offering does not handle the underwriting alone. To spread the risk and obtain better distribution, other investment bankers are invited to participate in the offering. The originating investment banker is usually the manager and has the largest participation. Other investment bankers are invited into the **underwriting syndicate,** and their participation is determined primarily on the basis of their ability to sell securities.

Competitive Bid versus Negotiated Offerings. A traditional underwriting can be on either a *competitive-bid* or *negotiated* basis. With a competitive bid, the issuing company specifies the date that sealed bids will be received, and competing syndicates submit bids at the specified time and place. The syndicate with the highest bid wins the security issue. With a negotiated offering, the issuing company selects an investment banking firm and works directly with that firm in determining the essential features of the issue. Together they discuss and negotiate a price for the security and the timing of the issue. Depending on the size of the issue, the investment banker may invite other firms to join in sharing the risk and selling the issue. In either case, the investment bankers are compensated for the risk-bearing function through the underwriting spread. The competitive-bid method frequently is used by municipalities and public utilities (often because required by law), whereas the negotiated method generally is used in corporate stock and most corporate bond issues.

Making a Market. On occasion, the underwriter will *make a market* for a security after it is issued. In a company's first public offering of common stock, making a market is especially important to investors. In making a market, the underwriter maintains an inventory in the stock, quotes a price at which the stock will be purchased (a bid price) and a price at which the stock will be sold (an ask price), and stands ready to buy and sell at those prices. With this secondary market activity provided by the investment banker, the stock has greater liquidity to investors. This added liquidity enhances the chances for success of the original offering.

Best Efforts Offering

Instead of underwriting a security issue, investment bankers may sell the issue on a **best efforts offering** basis. Under this arrangement, the investment bankers agree to sell only as many securities as they can at an established price. They have no responsibility for securities that remain unsold. In other words, they bear no risk. Investment bankers are often unwilling to underwrite security issues of small, nontechnological companies. For these companies, the only feasible means by which to place securities with the general public may be through a best efforts offering.

Shelf Registration

A distinguishing feature of public issues is that the registration process with the Securities and Exchange Commission (SEC) generally takes at least several weeks to complete. (The process itself is described later in the chapter.) Often two or more months elapse between the time a company decides to finance and the time the security offering actually takes place. As a result of this time lapse, as well as the fixed costs associated with a registration, there is an incentive for having a large, as opposed to a small, public offering.

Large, high-quality, well-known corporations as well as qualified medium-sized companies are able to shortcut the registration process by filing only a brief

Shelf registration A procedure whereby a company is permitted to register securities it plans to sell over the next two years; also called *SEC Rule 415*. These securities can then be sold piecemeal whenever the company chooses.

registration form under SEC Rule 415. This rule permits what is known as a **shelf registration.** Shelf registration allows a company to register a quantity of securities, "put them on the shelf," and then sell them in successive issues for up to two years. Little additional paperwork is required when the securities are sold "off the shelf." By using a shelf registration, a company is able to go to the market with a new issue in a matter of days as opposed to weeks or months. As a result, the firm has the flexibility to time issues to market conditions, and the individual issues themselves need not be large.

Flotation Costs and Other Advantages. The firm with securities sitting "on the shelf" can require that investment banking firms competitively bid for its underwriting business. Obviously, the company will either select the low-cost bidder or simply refuse to sell at all if the bids prove unacceptable. In this regard, large corporations are able to play investment bankers off against each other, and the resulting competition leads to reduced underwriting spreads. In addition, the total fixed costs (legal and administrative) of successive public debt issues are lower when accomplished with a single shelf registration than with a series of traditional registrations. Therefore, it is not surprising that large corporations have turned to shelf registrations.

Privileged subscription The sale of new securities in which existing shareholders are given a preference in purchasing these securities up to the proportion of common shares that they already own; also known as a *rights offering*.

Selling New Securities No Longer Is a Strictly Domestic Affair

A growing number of companies are looking to foreign capital markets to sell new issues of common stocks and bonds. Foreign sales may be for strategic as well as financial reasons. International equity sales can broaden a company's shareholder base. Raising capital abroad can also give a company greater visibility with foreign suppliers and customers.

The foreign sale of new, long-term securities takes the form of either an *international* or *global securities offering*. An international offering consists of the sale of

new securities outside the issuer's home country. A properly structured international offering by a U.S. firm would not be subject to the registration requirement of the 1933 Securities Act. A global offering consists of an international offering combined with an offering in the issuer's home country. For a U.S. firm making a global offering this would involve registration with the SEC, unless the U.S. "tranche" (French word for "slice") is structured as a *private placement*.

PRIVILEGED SUBSCRIPTION

Instead of selling a security issue to new investors, a number of firms offer the security first to existing shareholders on a **privileged subscription** basis. This method of issuance is also known as a *rights offering*. Frequently, the firm's corporate charter or state stature requires that a new issue of common stock or an issue of securities convertible into common stock be offered first to existing shareholders because of their preemptive right.

Preemptive right The privilege of shareholders to maintain their proportional company ownership by purchasing a proportionate share of any new issue of common stock, or securities convertible into common stock.

Preemptive Right

Under a **preemptive right,** existing common shareholders have the right to preserve their proportionate ownership in the corporation; if the corporation issues common stock, shareholders must be given the right to subscribe to the new stock so that they can maintain their pro rata interest in the company. Suppose that you own 100 shares of stock in a corporation that decides to make a new common stock offering that would increase outstanding shares by 10 percent. If you have a preemptive right, you must be given the option to buy 10 additional shares so that you can maintain your proportionate ownership in the company. Various states have different laws regarding preemptive rights. For example, some states provide that a shareholder has a preemptive right unless the corporate charter otherwise denies it, while other states deny that the preemptive right exists unless it is specified in the corporate charter.

Terms of Offering

When a company offers its securities for sale by privileged subscription (either because it "has to" under a preemptive right or because it simply "wants to"), it mails its shareholders one **right** for each share of common stock that they hold. With a common stock offering, the rights give shareholders the option to purchase additional shares according to the terms of the offering. The terms specify the number of rights required to subscribe for an additional share of stock, the subscription (purchase) price per share, and the expiration date of the offering. The holder of rights has three choices: (1) exercise the rights and subscribe for additional shares; (2) sell the rights, because they are transferable; or (3) do nothing and let the rights expire. With rational investors, the last option usually occurs only if the value of a right is negligible or if the shareholder owns only a few shares of stock. Generally, the subscription period is three weeks or less. A shareholder who wishes to buy a share of additional stock but does not have the necessary number of rights may purchase additional rights in the open market. If you now own 85 shares of stock in a company and the number of rights required to purchase 1 additional share is 10, your 85 rights would allow you to purchase only 8 full shares of stock. If you would like to buy the 9th share, you may do so by purchasing an additional 5 rights.

Companies follow a procedure for distributing rights that looks very much like that designed for cash dividends. The board of directors declares a record date and an **ex-rights date.** An investor who purchases the firm's stock prior to the ex-rights date receives the right to subscribe to additional stock. The stock is therefore said to trade "rights-on" prior to the ex-rights date. On or after the ex-rights date, the stock is said to trade "ex-rights." That is, the stock is traded without the rights attached.

Value of Rights

What gives a right its value is that it allows you to buy new stock at a discount from the current market price. The discount is given to ensure the successful sale of the new issue. For most rights offerings, the subscription price discount from the current market price ranges between 10 and 20 percent. Technically, the market value of a right is a function of the present market price of the stock, the subscription price, and the number of rights required to purchase an additional share of stock.

Suppose that a rights offering has been announced and that the stock is still selling "rights-on." An investor wishing to be sure of owning one share of stock trading "ex-rights" could buy one share of stock just before the stock went "ex-rights" for the "rights-on" market price of the stock and simply hold the stock. Alternatively, the investor could purchase the number of rights necessary to purchase one share, set aside an amount of money equal to the subscription price, and wait until the subscription date to purchase the stock. The difference between the two options is that the former gives the investor one right in addition to one share of stock. Therefore, the dollar difference between the two alternatives must equal the value of the right.

Mathematically, then, the theoretical market value of one right after the offering is announced but while the stock is still selling "rights-on" is

$$R_o = P_o - [(R_o)(N) + S]$$ (19-1)

where R_o = market value of one right when the stock is selling "rights-on"
P_o = market price of a share of stock selling "rights-on"
S = subscription price per share
N = number of rights required to purchase one share of stock

Rearranging Eq. (19-1), we get

$$R_o = \frac{P_o - S}{N + 1}$$ (19-2)

If the market price of a stock "rights-on" is $100 a share, the subscription price is $90 a share, and it takes four rights to buy an additional share of stock, the theoretical value of a right when the stock is selling "rights-on" is

$$R_o = \frac{\$100 - \$90}{4 + 1} = \$2$$

Note that the market value of the stock "rights-on" contains the value of one right.

When the stock goes "ex-rights," the market price theoretically declines, because investors no longer receive the right to subscribe to additional shares. The theoretical value of one share of stock when it goes "ex-rights," P_x, is

$$P_x = \frac{(P_o)(N) + S}{N + 1}$$ (19-3)

For our example,

$$P_x = \frac{(\$100)(4) + \$90}{4 + 1} = \$98$$

From this example, we see that, theoretically, the right does not provide additional value to the shareholder who either exercises the right or sells it. Notice, the shareholder's stock was worth $100 before the ex-rights date. After that date, it is worth $98 a share. The decline in market price is exactly offset by the value of the right. Thus, theoretically, the shareholder does not receive additional benefit from a rights offering. The right merely represents a return of capital.

The theoretical value of a right when the stock sells "ex-rights," R_x, is

$$R_x = \frac{P_x - S}{N}$$ (19-4)

If, in our example, the market price of the stock is $98 a share when it goes "ex-rights," then

$$R_x = \frac{\$98 - \$90}{4} = \$2$$

or the same value as before.

We should be aware that the actual value of a right may differ somewhat from its theoretical value because of transactions costs, speculation, and the irregular exercise and sale of rights over the subscription period. However, arbitrage acts to limit the deviation of the actual value from the theoretical value. If the price of a right is significantly higher than its theoretical value, shareholders will sell their rights and purchase the stock in the market. Such action will exert downward pressure on the market price of the right and upward pressure on its theoretical value. The latter occurs because of the upward pressure on the market price of the stock. If the price of the right is significantly lower than its theoretical value, arbitragers will buy the rights, exercise their option to buy stock, and then sell the stock in the market. This occurrence will exert upward pressure on the market price of the right and downward pressure on its theoretical value. These arbitrage actions will continue as long as they are profitable.

Standby Arrangement and Oversubscription Privilege

A company can ensure the complete success of a rights offering by having an investment banker or group of investment bankers "stand by" to underwrite any unsold portion of the issue. In fact, most companies use a **standby arrangement** in a rights offering. For this standby commitment, the underwriter charges a fee that varies with the risk involved in the offering. Often the fee consists of two parts: a flat fee and an additional fee for each unsold share of stock that the underwriter has to buy. From the standpoint of the company issuing the stock, the greater the risk of an unsuccessful rights offering, the more desirable a standby arrangement. However, the added cost must also be considered.

Another, less used means to increase the probability that the entire issue will be sold is through the use of an **oversubscription privilege.** This device gives shareholders not only the right to subscribe for their proportional share of the total rights offering but also the right to oversubscribe for any unsold shares. Oversubscriptions are then awarded on a pro rata basis relative to the number of unsold shares. For example, shareholders might subscribe to 460,000 shares of a 500,000-share rights offering. Perhaps some of them would like to purchase more shares, and their oversubscriptions total 100,000 shares. As a result, each shareholder oversubscribing is awarded four-tenths (40,000/100,000) of a share for each share oversubscribed. This results in the entire issue being sold. Although the use of oversubscriptions increases the chances that the issue will be entirely sold, it does not completely ensure this occurrence, as does the standby arrangement. It is always possible that the combination of subscriptions and oversubscriptions will still fall short of the amount of stock that the company desires to sell.

Privileged Subscription versus Public Issue

By offering new common stock first to existing shareholders, the company taps investors who are familiar with its operations. The principal sales tool is the discount from the current market price, whereas with a public issue, the major selling tool is the investment banking organization. Because the issue is not underwritten, the flotation costs of a rights offering are lower than the costs of an offering to the general public. Moreover, many shareholders feel that they should be given the first opportunity to buy new common shares.

Offsetting these advantages in the minds of some is that a rights offering will have to be sold at a lower price than will an issue to the general public. If a company goes to the equity market with reasonable frequency, this means that there will be somewhat more dilution with rights offerings than there will be with public issues. Even though this consideration is not relevant theoretically, many companies wish to minimize dilution. Also, a public offering will tend to result in a wider distribution of shares, which may be desirable to the company.

Although these factors may have an effect on shareholder wealth, we would expect their effect to be slight. The question remains as to why so many companies incur the costs associated with a public issue when they could sell securities through a privileged subscription (without a standby arrangement) at less cost. Several explanations have been offered. These include the concentration of stock ownership affecting the merchandising cost of a security and greater decline in share price associated with a rights offering.

REGULATION OF SECURITY OFFERINGS

Both the federal and state governments regulate the sale of new securities to the public, but federal authority is far more encompassing in its influence.

Federal Regulation

With the collapse of the stock market in 1929 and the subsequent Great Depression, there came a cry to protect investors from misinformation and fraud. Congress undertook extensive investigations and proposed federal regulation of the securities industry. The **Securities Act of 1933 (1933 Act)** deals with the sale of new securities to the public and requires full disclosure of material information to investors. The **Securities Exchange Act of 1934 (1934 Act)** deals with the regulation of securities already outstanding. It also established the **Securities and Exchange Commission (SEC)** to enforce the two Acts.

Registration of Securities. Because of the 1933 Act most corporations selling securities to the public must register with the SEC. There are some exemptions, and certain qualified "small business issuers" are required to file only a limited amount of information. Most security-issuing corporations, however, must file a detailed **registration statement**.

The registration statement generally consists of two parts: Part I is the **prospectus** (see Fig. 19-2), which will also be distributed as a separate booklet to underwriters and investors, and Part II is additional information required by the SEC. Part I (the prospectus) contains the more essential information, such as the nature and history of the company, the use of the proceeds of the security issue, certified financial statements, the names of management and directors and their security holdings, competitive conditions, risk factors, legal opinions, and a description of the security being registered. Part II contains miscellaneous information that, although available for public inspection, is not part of the printed prospectus that will be provided to investors once the registration statement is approved.

Because one of the basic purposes of the 1933 Act is that investors be provided with material information concerning securities offered for public sale, the SEC allows distribution of a preliminary prospectus, called a **red herring**, while it studies the registration statement. The preliminary prospectus is known as a "red herring" because it includes a statement in red ink on the cover stating that although the prospectus has been filed with the SEC, the registration statement is not yet effective and therefore subject to change.

The SEC reviews the registration statement to see that all the required information is presented and that it is not misleading. Any deficiencies are communicated to the issuing firm in the form of a *comment letter,* in response to which the firm may file an amended statement. Once the SEC is satisfied with the information, it approves the registration, and the company is then able to issue a final prospectus and sell the securities. If not, the SEC issues a *stop order,* which prevents the sale of the securities. Most deficiencies can be corrected by the company, and approval will usually be

Securities Act of 1933 (1933 Act) Generally requires that public offerings be registered with the federal government before they may be sold; also known as the *Truth in Securities Act.*

Securities Exchange Act of 1934 (1934 Act) Regulates the secondary market for long-term securities—the securities exchanges and the over-the-counter market.

Securities and Exchange Commission (SEC) The U.S. government agency responsible for administration of federal securities laws, including the 1933 and 1934 Acts.

Registration statement The disclosure document filed with the SEC to register a new securities issue. The registration statement includes the prospectus and other information required by the SEC.

Prospectus Part I of the registration statement filed with the SEC. It discloses information about the issuing company and its new offering and is distributed as a separate booklet to investors.

Red herring The preliminary prospectus. It includes a legend in red ink on the cover stating that the registration statement has not yet become effective.

FIGURE 19-2

Sample of Outside Front Cover of a Prospectus Showing Key Facts about the Security Offering, Including Members of the Underwriting Syndicate at the Bottom

$75,000,000

Acme Aglet Company

11% FIRST MORTGAGE BONDS DUE 2031

Interest payable September 1 and March 1. The bonds are redeemable on 30 days' notice at the option of the company at 111% to and including March 1, 2002, at decreasing prices thereafter to and including March 1, 2020, and thereafter at 100%. Due March 1, 2031.

Application will be made to list the bonds on the New York Stock Exchange.

THESE SECURITIES HAVE NOT BEEN APPROVED OR DISAPPROVED BY THE SECURITIES AND EXCHANGE COMMISSION NOR HAS THE COMMISSION PASSED UPON THE ACCURACY OR ADEQUACY OF THIS PROSPECTUS. ANY REPRESENTATION TO THE CONTRARY IS A CRIMINAL OFFENSE.

	Price to Public (1)	Underwriting Discounts and Commissions (2)	Proceeds to Company (1)(3)
Per unit.	99.750%	0.875%	98.875%
Total	$74,812,500	$656,250	$74,156,250

(1) Plus accrued interest from March 1, 2001 to date of delivery and payment.
(2) The company has agreed to indemnify the several purchasers against certain civil liabilities.
(3) Before deducting expenses payable by the company estimated at $200,000.

The new bonds are offered by the several purchasers named herein subject to prior sale, when, as and if issued and accepted by the purchasers and subject to their right to reject any orders for the purchase of the new bonds, in whole or in part. It is expected that the new bonds will be ready for delivery on or about March 12, 2001 in New York City.

Markese, Gau, Gahlon, and Cammack
Incorporated

Ding, Cyree, Woatich, Murphy, and Kuhlemeyer, Inc.

Nguyen-Barnaby & Co.

A. E. Winston & Sons

Harikumar, Proffitt, Banner, Davis, and Lawriwsky, Inc.

Collins Brothers, Inc.

Cohn, Gonzalez, DeGennaro, & Lindahl
Securities Corporation

The date of this prospectus is March 5, 2001.

given eventually, except in discovered cases of fraud or misrepresentation. For serious violations of the 1933 Act, the SEC is empowered to go to court and seek an injunction.

It should be pointed out that the SEC is not concerned with the investment value of the securities being issued, only with the presentation of complete and accurate information of all material facts regarding the security. Investors must make their own decisions based on the facts. A security undergoing registration may very well be issued by a risky, poorly managed, or unprofitable company. As long as the information in the registration statement is correct, the SEC will not prevent its sale. In short, the saying *caveat emptor*—let the buyer beware—definitely applies to registered securities.

The 1933 Act provides that most registration statements become effective on the 20th day after filing (or on the 20th day after filing the last amendment). The SEC, at its discretion, may advance the effective date if it wishes. As a practical matter, the usual time lapse from filing to approval is around 40 days. As we discussed earlier, large corporations are able to use shelf registrations. Once a statement is preapproved covering a block of securities, the company is able to sell "off the shelf" by filing a simple amendment and having the SEC accelerate the "normal" 20-day waiting period. The resulting time lapse in this case is very short—perhaps a day or two.

Once the registration statement becomes effective, final prospectuses are made available to interested investors. Also, the SEC allows the issuing firm to publish in the press a limited notice of the offering, including the company's name, a brief description of the security, the offering price, and the names of the investment bankers in the underwriting syndicate. These notices are known as **tombstone advertisements** (see Fig. 19-3) because of their stark, black-bordered appearance.

Tombstone advertisement An announcement placed in newspapers and magazines giving just the most basic details of a security offering. The term reflects the stark, black-bordered look of the ad.

Streamlining Registration Procedures. At the time of this writing, the SEC was proposing to make significant changes to the securities registration process discussed in this chapter. The suggested changes are contained in a document nicknamed the "Aircraft Carrier Proposal" because of its huge size and complexity. The SEC reforms are meant to help issuers sell securities faster and more simply while affording investors some additional benefits and protections. The proposals call for less SEC review of registration material, more information coming sooner for investors, and, in an attempt to enhance investor protection, greater liability than currently exists on issuers and underwriters. (For the latest information on these and other SEC proposals, visit the SEC's Web site at www.sec.gov.)

Secondary Market Regulation. The SEC regulates the sale of securities in the secondary market in addition to the sale of new issues. In this regard, it regulates the activities of the security exchanges, the over-the-counter market, investment bankers and brokers, the National Association of Securities Dealers, and investment companies. It requires monthly reports on inside stock transactions by officers, directors, and large shareholders. Whenever an investor group obtains 5 percent or more of a company's stock, it must file Form 13D, which alerts all to the accumulation and to possible subsequent changes in effective ownership. In its regulatory capacity, the SEC seeks to prevent manipulative practices by investment dealers and by officers and directors of companies, abuses by insiders (officers and directors) in transactions involving a company's stock, fraud by any party, and other abuses affecting the investing public.

State Regulation

Individual states have security commissions that regulate the offering and sale of new securities in their states. Like the SEC, these commissions seek to prevent the fraudulent sale of securities. The laws providing for state regulation are known as **blue sky laws,** in reference to various schemes common in the early 1900s promoting the sale of securities representing nothing more than a "piece of the blue sky." State regulations are particularly important when a security issue is sold entirely to people within the state and may therefore not be subject to SEC scrutiny. In addition, it can be important in other instances where the issue may be subject to only limited SEC review. Unfortunately, the laws of the individual states vary greatly in their effectiveness. Some states are strict, but others are fairly permissive. The result is that misrepresentative security promotions can sometimes occur.

Blue sky laws State laws regulating the offering and sale of securities.

FIGURE 19-3
Sample Tombstone
Advertisement

This announcement is neither an offer to sell nor a solicitation of an offer to buy these securities.
The offer is made only by the Prospectus Supplement and the related Prospectus.

New Issue/March 5, 2001

$75,000,000

Acme Aglet Company

11% FIRST MORTGAGE BONDS DUE MARCH 1, 2031

Price 99.75% and accrued interest, if any, from March 1, 2001

*Copies of the Prospectus Supplement and the related Prospectus may be obtained
in any State in which this announcement is circulated only from such of the
undersigned as may legally offer these securities in such State.*

Markese, Gau, Gahlon, and Cammack
Incorporated

Ding, Cyree, Woatich,   **Nguyen-Barnaby & Co.**
Murphy, and Kuhlemeyer, Inc.

         A. E. Winston & Sons

Harikumar, Proffitt, Banner,
Davis, and Lawriwsky, Inc.   **Collins Brothers, Inc.**

Cohn, Gonzalez, DeGennaro, & Lindahl
Securities Corporation

PRIVATE PLACEMENT

Private (or direct) placement The sale of an entire issue of unregistered securities (usually bonds) directly to one purchaser or a group of purchasers (usually financial intermediaries).

Rather than sell new securities to the general public or existing shareholders, a corporation can sell the entire issue to a single purchaser (generally a financial institution or wealthy individual) or a group of such purchasers. This type of sale is known as a **private (or direct) placement**, for the company negotiates directly with the investor(s) over the terms of the offering, eliminating the underwriting function of the investment banker. *Financial intermediaries* is the term that might best describe the many types of financial institutions that invest in private placements. Dominant private placement investors in this group include insurance companies, bank trust departments, and pension funds. In what immediately follows, we focus on the private placement of debt issues. Equity placements involving venture capitalists will be discussed shortly.

Features

One of the more frequently mentioned advantages of a private placement is the speed with which the private deal is transacted. A public issue must be registered with the SEC, red herrings and final prospectuses prepared and printed, and extensive negotiations undertaken. All this requires time. In addition, public issues always involve risks with respect to timing. Private placements, on the other hand, are not subject to SEC registration requirements, because it is felt that persons or institutions with enough capital to buy an entire security issue should be able to acquire on their own the kind of information that registration would disclose. Also, with private placements the terms can be tailored to the borrower's needs, and financing can be consummated quickly. However, we need to remember that the qualified large corporation can also tap the public market quickly, and with limited paperwork, through a shelf registration.

Because the private placement of debt is negotiated, the exact timing in the market is not a critical problem. The fact that there is most often only a single investor or small group of investors is attractive if it later becomes necessary to change any of the terms of the issue. It is much easier to deal with one investor (or a small group) than with a large number of security holders.

Another advantage of a privately placed debt issue is that the actual borrowing does not necessarily have to take place all at once. The company can enter an arrangement whereby it can borrow up to a fixed amount over a period of time. For this credit arrangement, the borrower will pay a commitment fee. This type of arrangement gives the company flexibility, allowing it to borrow only when it needs the funds. Also, because the private placement does not have to be registered with the SEC, the company avoids making public certain information that it may deem better left confidential, such as sources of raw materials, a unique manufacturing process, or executive compensation.

Developments in the Market

By selling new bonds to the general public, the issuing corporation can dramatically change its capital structure and thereby end up with much higher debt. Any bonds previously outstanding become less creditworthy and drop in price. Generally, this **event risk**—decline in creditworthiness brought on by increased financial leverage—cannot legally be prevented by the holders of the company's previously issued bonds. With a private placement, however, such event risk can be avoided with tightly written protective covenants. Under such covenants, should the corporation undergo a substantial change in capital structure, the bonds would become immediately payable at their face value. Thus, starting in the 1980s, private placements gained renewed importance as lenders sought to protect themselves from some of the adverse effects caused by prevalent corporate restructurings.

Another advantage to institutional investors is that the SEC (through Rule 144a) now permits them to resell securities generated in the private placement market to other large institutions. Thus, U.S. companies, as well as foreign companies, can issue bonds and stocks in the market without having to go through public market registration procedures. Then, *qualified institutional buyers (QIBs)* can sell the securities to other qualified institutional buyers, without waiting out any holding period and without subjecting the issuer or security holder to additional regulation by the SEC. As a result, the market becomes broader and more liquid.

Private Placement with Registration Rights. A *private placement with registration rights* is a novel twist on the familiar private placement of securities. It combines a standard private placement with a contract requiring the issuer to register the securities

Event risk The risk that existing debt will suffer a decline in creditworthiness because of the issuance of additional debt securities, usually in connection with corporate restructurings.

with the SEC for possible resale in the public market. Thirty days is the typical time frame, although some issuers have up to six months or a year before having to register. With *registration rights* purchasers are virtually guaranteed that they will have a publicly issued, more marketable security, usually within months. Penalty interest must be paid by the issuer for failing to meet registration deadlines. Another variation on this approach calls for the issuer to agree to exchange the privately placed securities for registered securities to be issued in the near future. The registered securities would have identical terms and features as the securities initially sold. What is the benefit to the issuer in all this? The issuer gets security sale proceeds right away, receives additional time to work out registration details, and has a lower interest cost than would be the case without registration.

Underwritten Rule 144a Private Placement.   The so-called *underwritten Rule 144a* transaction is another variation on the traditional private placement. In this arrangement, the issuer sells its securities initially to an investment bank. The investment bank then resells these securities to the same institutional buyers that are candidates for a regular private placement. In this way the issuer outsources the marketing and distribution of the securities. This method of sale is often combined with *registration rights*—thus providing the ultimate purchasers with the promise, once again, of greater marketability for their securities.

INITIAL FINANCING

When a company is formed, it obviously must be financed. Often the *seed money* (i.e., initial financing) comes from the founders and their families and friends. For some companies, this is sufficient to get things launched, and by retaining future earnings they need no more external equity financing. For others, infusions of additional external equity are necessary. In this section, we look at *venture capital* and *initial public offerings*.

Venture Capital

Venture capital represents funds invested in a new enterprise. Wealthy investors and financial institutions are the major sources of venture capital. Debt funds are sometimes provided, but it is mostly common stock that is involved. This stock is almost always initially placed privately. Rule 144 of the 1933 Act currently requires that newly issued, privately placed securities be held for at least two years or be registered before they can be resold without restriction. (Limited quantities of privately placed securities can be resold beginning one year after issuance.) The aim of this rule is to protect "unsophisticated" investors from being offered unproven securities. As a result, however, investors in these securities have no liquidity for a period of time. The hope of investors in privately placed stock (known as **letter stock**) is that the company will thrive and, after five years or so, be large and profitable enough to have the stock registered and sold in the public market. (*Note:* Under SEC Rule 144a, however, letter stock could be resold to qualified institutional buyers without a waiting period.)

Letter stock Privately placed common stock that cannot be immediately resold.

Initial Public Offerings

If the new enterprise is successful, the owners may want to "take the company public" with a sale of common stock to outsiders. Often this desire is prompted by venture capitalists, who want to realize a cash return on their investment. In another situation, the founders may simply want to establish a value, and liquidity, for their common stock. Whatever their motivations, the owners may decide to turn their firm into a public corporation. There are exceptions to this pattern of events; some large, successful companies choose to remain privately held. For example, Bechtel Corporation is one of the largest construction and engineering companies in the world, but its common stock is privately held.

Initial public offering (IPO) A company's first offering of common stock to the general public.

Most **initial public offerings (IPOs)** are accomplished through underwriters. In an IPO, because the common stock has not been previously traded in the public market, there is no stock price benchmark to use. Consequently, there is more price uncertainty than there is when a public company sells additional common stock. Empirical studies suggest that, on average, IPOs are sold at a significant discount (over 15 percent) from the prices that ultimately prevail in the after-issued market.[1] For the corporation, the implication is that the initial public stock offering will need to be priced significantly below what management believes it should be based on its true value. This difference is the price of admission to the public market. Any subsequent public offering will not need to be underpriced by as much, because a benchmark price will exist, and thus there will be less price uncertainty.

---

[1]For a synthesis of these studies, see Clifford W. Smith Jr., "Investment Banking and the Capital Acquisition Process," *Journal of Financial Economics* 15 (January–February 1986), 19–22.

Investment Banking Meets the Internet

After graduating from Harvard Law School, Andrew Klein practiced law at one of the most prestigious firms in New York City until he decided to open a microbrewery. Little did he know that his upstart Wit Beer would be the catalyst for a revolution on Wall Street. But then he launched the first initial public offering over the Internet, raising $1.6 million for Wit Beer, and at the same time etched his mark in financial history.

Suddenly, Klein found himself in the financial news all over the globe. More important, he found himself in touch with thousands of eager online investors. The entrepreneurial next step was obvious—at least to Klein.

Wit Capital Corporation, the world's first online investment banking firm was founded in 1996 with a mission: to empower investors and issuers alike by transforming the capital raising process through the use of the Internet. Wit Capital offers a modified first come, first served opportunity to participate directly in the capital raising process through initial public offerings (IPOs) as well as secondary and follow-on offerings.

To issuers, Wit Capital offers an expanding array of investment banking services. Wit Capital provides issuers the ability to build sustainable relationships with their shareholders through research and other after-market support published by a team of Internet analysts considered to be among the strongest in the securities industry.

Andrew Klein and Wit Capital believe that the digital economy offers investors and issuers alike a world of opportunity. Geography, time and access have always been barriers to the efficient flow of capital. The Internet changes all that. Today, Wit Capital is at the forefront of this revolution and expects to remain there for many years to come.

To learn more about Wit Capital, visit their Web site www.witcapital.com.

Source: Rhee Rosenman, Wit Capital Group, Inc. Reproduced with the permission of Wit Capital Group, Inc.

When a public company announces a security issue, there may be an information effect that causes a stock market reaction. In studies where other factors causing market movements have been held constant, scholars have found negative stock price reactions (or "abnormal returns") to common stock or convertible security issues.[2] Announcements regarding straight debt and preferred stock do not tend to show statistically significant effects. The typical reaction of returns to an announcement of a stock issue is shown in Figure 19-4. Time around the announcement event is shown on the horizontal axis, and the cumulative average abnormal return, after isolating overall market-movement effects, is along the vertical axis. As seen, a reduction in stock price occurs around the announcement date (day 0) and tends to average about 3 percent.

Expectations of Future Cash Flows

Several explanations have been offered for this phenomenon. For one thing, the announcement may tell investors something about cash flows expected in the future. When a company announces a security issue, it implies that the funds raised will go to one or more purposes, such as investment in assets, reduction of debt, stock repurchase or increased dividends, or offsetting of lower than expected operating cash flows. To the extent that an unexpected sale of securities is associated with the last situation, the event may be interpreted as bad news, and the stock price may suffer accordingly.

---

[2]For an excellent synthesis of the empirical evidence, see Clifford W. Smith Jr., "Investment Banking and the Capital Acquisition Process," *Journal of Financial Economics* 15 (January–February 1986), 3–29. See also Paul Asquith and David W. Mullins Jr., "Signalling with Dividends, Stock Repurchases, and Equity Issues," *Financial Management* 15 (Autumn 1986), 27–44.

FIGURE 19-4
Relative Abnormal Stock Returns (Calculated as the Difference Between Actual and Predicted Returns) in Connection with the Announcement of a New Equity Issue

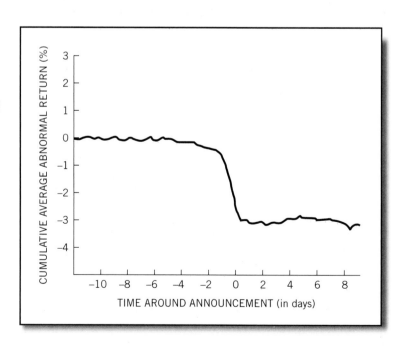

Asymmetric (Unequal) Information

A second effect relates to "asymmetric" (unequal) information possessed by investors and management. The idea is that potential investors in securities have less information than management and management tends to issue securities when the market's assessment of the company's value is higher than management's.[3] This would be particularly true for common stock, where investors have only a residual claim to income and assets. Because cash flows are affected when a new security is offered, the effect of asymmetric information is difficult to sort out using data about new issues.

When one security is exchanged for another, however, operating cash flows are not affected. When empirical studies on exchange offers are categorized into those that increase financial leverage and those that decrease financial leverage, the results are striking. Leverage-increasing transactions are accompanied by positive abnormal stock returns in the two days prior to the exchange announcement. Leverage-reducing transactions are accompanied by negative abnormal returns. The effects are greatest for debt-for-common-stock exchanges (positive return) and common-stock-for-debt exchanges (negative return). Thus, the evidence supports an asymmetric information effect. In other words, managers are more likely to issue debt when they believe the common stock is underpriced in the market and to issue common stock when they believe it is overpriced.

In summary, the issuance of new securities, as well as exchange offerings, appears to cause information effects that impact stock prices. The financial manager must be mindful of these potential effects before reaching a decision to issue securities.

THE SECONDARY MARKET

Purchases and sales of existing stocks and bonds occur in the *secondary market.* Transactions in this market do *not* provide firms with additional funds to buy new plants or buy new equipment. However, the presence of a viable secondary market increases the liquidity of securities already outstanding. Without this liquidity, firms issuing new securities would have to pay higher returns because investors would have trouble finding a resale market for their stocks and bonds. Thus, the ongoing trading of existing securities is crucial to the efficient operation of the primary or new-issues market for long-term securities.

The secondary market for long-term securities consists of the *organized exchanges,* such as the New York Stock Exchange, the American Stock Exchange, and the New York Bond Exchange. In addition, the over-the-counter (OTC) market serves as part of the secondary market for stocks and bonds not listed on an exchange as well as for a number of listed securities. It is composed of brokers and dealers who stand ready to buy and sell securities at quoted prices. Most corporate bonds and a growing number of stocks are traded OTC. Also, as we saw earlier, the advent of SEC Rule 144a allows qualified institutional buyers to trade privately placed securities among themselves.

---

[3]See Stewart C. Myers and Nicholas S. Majluf, "Corporate Financing and Investment Decisions When Firms Have Information That Investors Do Not Have," *Journal of Financial Economics* 13 (June 1984), 187–221.

Ask the Fool

Q What are OTC-issued stocks?

A OTC officially stands for "over the counter," but "over the computer" is more apt today. Long ago, to buy or sell a stock that didn't trade on an exchange, you would call your broker. He would call another broker and make the trade over the phone—not a terribly efficient system. Then, in 1971, Nasdaq was established, offering an automated system. Suddenly, it was much easier to get the best price on your transaction, and trading activity could be monitored.

Stocks that are listed on exchanges are traded face-to-face at one location, in "pits." All others are OTC stocks, traded electronically via a network of dealers across the country. The Nasdaq market is the main OTC system in the U.S., listing over 5,500 companies. It encompasses a range of firms, from young, relatively unknown enterprises to behemoths like Microsoft and Intel. Thousands of more obscure OTC companies which don't meet Nasdaq's requirements trade separately, often with their prices listed only once daily, on "pink sheets." Little information is often available about these companies, and they're frequently penny stocks, shunned by Fools.

Source: The Motley Fool (www.fool.com). Reproduced with the permission of The Motley Fool.

SUMMARY

- When companies finance their long-term needs externally, they may use three primary methods: a *public issue* of securities placed through investment bankers; a *privileged subscription* to the company's own shareholders; and a *private placement* to institutional investors.

- When a company issues securities to the general public, it usually uses the services of an *investment banker.* The investment banker's principal functions are risk bearing, or underwriting, and selling the securities. For performing these functions, investment bankers are compensated by the *spread* between the price they pay for the securities and the price at which they resell the securities to investors.

- A public issue can be either a *traditional (firm commitment) underwriting;* a *best efforts offering;* or, in the case of a large corporation, a *shelf registration.* With a shelf registration, a company sells securities "off the shelf" without the delays associated with a lengthy registration process. Instead, only an amendment to a pre-approved offering is filed with the SEC. Not only is the shelf registration faster, but the cost of the issue is a good deal less than otherwise.

- A company may give its existing shareholders the first opportunity to purchase a new security issue on a privileged subscription basis. This type of issue is also known as a *rights offering,* because existing shareholders receive one (subscription) right for each share of stock that they hold. A *right* represents a short-term option to buy the new security at the subscription price. It takes a certain number of rights to purchase the security.

- Security offerings to the general public and offerings on a privileged subscription basis must comply with federal and state regulations. The enforcement agency for the federal government is the *Securities and Exchange Commission (SEC),* whose authority encompasses both the sale of new securities and the trading of existing securities in the secondary market.

- Rather than sell new securities to the general public or to existing shareholders, a corporation can place them privately with an institutional investor or a group of such investors. With a private placement, the company negotiates directly with the investor(s). There is no underwriting and no registration of the issue with the SEC. The private placement has the virtue of flexibility, and it affords the medium-sized and even the small company the opportunity to sell its securities. As a result in part of large institutional investors being able to sell private placements to one another in the secondary market, such offerings have grown in importance in recent years.

- In its early stages, a company needs financing. One source is the *venture capitalist* who specializes in financing new enterprises. If the company is successful, it often will "go public" with an *initial public offering* of common stock.
- The announcement of a debt or stock issue may be accompanied by a stock market reaction. The announcement may connote information about the future cash flows of the company or information about whether management believes the common stock is under- or overvalued. Empirical evidence is consistent with both of these ideas, so the financial manager must be aware of information effects when issuing securities.
- Purchases and sales of existing stocks and bonds occur in the *secondary market*. The presence of a viable secondary market increases the liquidity of securities already outstanding. Without this liquidity, firms issuing new securities would have to pay higher returns because investors would have trouble finding a resale market for their stocks and bonds.

QUESTIONS

1. What is the difference between a public and a private issue of securities?
2. How does a traditional (firm commitment) underwriting differ from a shelf registration?
3. As a best efforts offering is "cheaper" than a traditional (firm commitment) underwriting, why don't more companies make use of it?
4. In offering a new bond issue, the firm may decide to sell the bonds through a private placement or through a public issue. Evaluate these two alternatives.
5. An inverse relationship exists between flotation costs and the size of the issue being sold. Explain the economic forces that cause this relationship.
6. Should the preemptive right be required of all companies that issue common stock or securities convertible into common stock?
7. Many major U.S. corporations have extensively used rights offerings in the past. Why do you feel these corporations have chosen to raise funds with a rights offering rather than a public equity issue, especially when a fair percentage of the rights (2 to 5 percent) is never exercised?
8. What role does the subscription price play in a rights offering?
9. Define a *standby arrangement* and an *oversubscription privilege*. Why are they used? Which do you think is used more often?
10. What is the principal regulatory authority when it comes to security offerings? What is its function?
11. Which of the following companies would you expect to use a private placement of long-term debt as opposed to a public offering?
    a. An electric utility serving Chicago
    b. A $13-million-annual-volume maker of electronic components
    c. A consortium of oil companies to finance an oil discovery in the Arctic
    d. A tennis-shoe-retreading company serving northern California
12. In general, how do the costs of a private placement of a debt issue differ from those of a traditional (firm commitment) underwriting?
13. Has the availability of shelf registrations reduced the importance of private placements? Why?
14. What does a venture capitalist hope to gain from an investment in a new enterprise? How liquid is the investment?
15. Why is a security offering of new common stock often accompanied by a stock price reaction around the time of the announcement?

SELF-CORRECTION PROBLEMS

1. The stock of the Ocean Specific Company is selling for $150 per share. The company issues rights that allow the holders to subscribe for one additional share of stock at a subscription price of $125 a share for each nine rights held. Compute the theoretical value of the following:
   a. A right when the stock is selling "rights-on"
   b. One share of stock when it goes "ex-rights"
   c. A right when the stock sells "ex-rights" and the actual market price goes to $143 per share

2. Dim-Sum Restaurants, Inc., must decide between a public issue of intermediate-term notes and the private placement of this debt with an insurance company. In both cases, the funds needed are $6 million for 6 years with no principal repayment until the final maturity of the notes. With a public issue, the interest rate will be 15 percent, the underwriting spread will be $10 per note, and the notes will be priced to the public at $1,000 apiece. To realize $6 million in proceeds, the company will need to issue some additional notes to offset the spread. Legal, printing, and other initial costs come to $195,000 with the public issue. For the private issue, the interest rate will be 15.5 percent, and initial costs will come to only $20,000.
   a. Ignoring the time value of money, which method has the higher total costs over the 6 years? In words, which method would be helped if we considered the time value of money?
   b. What if the maturity were 12 years and all other things stayed the same?

PROBLEMS

1. Tex Turner Telecommunications Company needs to raise $1.8 billion (face value) of debt funds over the next two years. If it were to use traditional (firm commitment) underwritings, the company would expect to have six underwritings over the two-year span. The underwriter spread would likely be $7.50 per bond, and out-of-pocket expenses paid by the company would total $350,000 per underwriting. With shelf registrations, the average size of offering would probably be $75 million. Here the estimated spread is $3 per bond, and out-of-pocket expenses of $40,000 per issue are expected.
   a. Ignoring interest costs and the time value of money, what are the total absolute costs of flotation over the two years for (1) the traditional underwriting method of offering securities? (2) the shelf registration method?
   b. Which method results in lower total costs?

2. The Cliff Claven Artists School will issue 200,000 shares of common stock at $40 per share through a privileged subscription. The 800,000 shares of stock currently outstanding have a "rights-on" market price of $50 per share.
   a. Compute the number of rights required to buy a share of stock at $40.
   b. Compute the value of a right.
   c. Compute the value of the stock "ex-rights."

3. The stock of the HAL Computer Corporation is selling for $50 per share. The company then issues rights which allow holders to subscribe for one new share at $40 for each five rights held.
   a. What is the theoretical value of a right if the stock is selling "rights-on"?
   b. What is the theoretical value of one share of stock when it goes "ex-rights"?
   c. What is the theoretical value of a right if the stock sells "ex-rights" at $50?

4. Two different companies are considering rights offerings. The current market price per share is $48 in both cases. To allow for fluctuations in market price, company X wants to set a subscription price of $42, while company Y feels a subscription price of $41.50 is in order. The number of rights necessary to purchase an additional share is 14 in the case of company X and 4 in the case of company Y.
   a. Which company (potentially) will have the greatest percentage increase in shares outstanding? Is it the larger stock issue in absolute terms?
   b. In which case is there less risk that the market price will fall below the subscription price?

5. Obtain a prospectus on a recent security issue of a corporation. Analyze it according to the following:
   a. *The type of security being offered.* Are there any special features? If a bond, is it secured? How is it secured?
   b. *The size of the issue and the type of company involved.* How financially sound is the company? How stable are its earnings? What is the growth potential? Is the size of the issue appropriate?
   c. *The flotation cost.* What is the underwriter spread? Is it too high a percentage of gross proceeds? What portion of the spread is in support of underwriting? What portion of the spread is in support of selling? What is the dealer concession? Under which conditions may it be earned?
   d. *The underwriting syndicate.* How many underwriters are there? What is the maximum participation? What is the minimum participation? Who is the manager? Are there provisions made for support of the price during the distribution period?
   e. *The pricing.* Is the issue priced properly from the standpoint of (1) the company? (2) the investor? (3) the underwriter? How successful was the issue?

SOLUTIONS TO SELF-CORRECTION PROBLEMS

1. a. $R_o = \dfrac{P_o - S}{N + 1} = \dfrac{\$150 - \$125}{9 + 1} = \dfrac{\$25}{10} = \mathbf{\$2.50}$

   b. $P_x = \dfrac{(P_o)(N) + S}{N + 1} = \dfrac{(\$150)(9) + \$125}{9 + 1} = \dfrac{\$1,475}{10} = \mathbf{\$147.50}$

   c. $R_x = \dfrac{P_x - S}{N} = \dfrac{\$143 - \$125}{9} = \dfrac{\$18}{9} = \mathbf{\$2}$

2. a. *Public issue:*
   Number of $1,000-face-value notes to be issued to raise $6 million (to nearest note) = $6,000,000/$990 = 6,061 or $6,061,000 in notes.

   Total interest cost = $6,061,000 × 15% × 6 years = $5,454,900
   Total costs = $5,454,900 + $195,000 = **$5,649,900**

   Private placement:

   Total interest cost = $6,000,000 × 15.5% × 6 years = $5,580,000
   Total costs = $5,580,000 + $20,000 = **$5,600,000**

   The public issue has the higher total costs. As the interest payments are spread out over the 6 years, the time value of money effect would act to enhance the private placement. The differential in out-of-pocket expense occurs at the beginning.

b. *Public issue:*

Total interest cost = $6,061,000 × 15% × 12 years = $10,909,800
Total costs = $10,909,800 + $195,000 = **$11,104,800**

Private placement:

Total interest cost = $6,000,000 × 15.5% × 12 years = $11,160,000
Total costs = $11,160,000 + $20,000 = **$11,180,000**

The private placement has the higher total costs. With a longer-term loan, the differential in interest rate becomes more important.

SELECTED REFERENCES

Admati, Anat R., and Paul Pfleiderer. "Robust Financial Contracting and the Role of Venture Capitalists." *Journal of Finance* 49 (June 1994), 371–402.

Allen, David S., Robert E. Lamy, and G. Rodney Thompson. "The Shelf Registration and Self Selection Bias." *Journal of Finance* 45 (March 1990), 275–87.

Asquith, Paul, and David Mullins Jr. "Equity Issues and Offering Dilution." *Journal of Financial Economics* 15 (January–February 1986), 61–90.

———. "Signalling with Dividends, Stock Repurchases, and Equity Issues." *Financial Management* 15 (Autumn 1986), 27–44.

Berlin, Mitchell. "That Thing Venture Capitalists Do." *Business Review of the Federal Reserve Bank of Philadelphia* (January/February 1998), 15–26 (available online at www.phil.frb.org/econ/br/brjf98mb.pdf).

Bethel, Jennifer E., and Erik R. Sirri. "Express Lane or Tollbooth in the Desert? The SEC's Framework for Security Issuance." *Journal of Applied Corporate Finance* 11 (Spring 1998), 25–38.

Carey, Mark S., Stephen D. Prowse, John D. Rea, and Gregory F. Udell. "Recent Developments in the Market for Privately Placed Debt." *Federal Reserve Bulletin* 79 (February 1993), 77–92.

Fung, W. K. H., and Andrew Rudd. "Pricing New Corporate Bond Issues: An Analysis of Issue Cost and Seasoning Effects." *Journal of Finance* 41 (July 1986), 633–42.

Gompers, Paul A. "Optimal Investment, Monitoring, and Staging of Venture Capital." *Journal of Finance* 50 (December 1995), 1461–89.

Hansen, Robert S. "The Demise of the Rights Issue." *Review of Financial Studies* 1 (Fall 1988), 289–309.

———, and John M. Pinkerton. "Direct Equity Financing: A Resolution of a Paradox." *Journal of Finance* 37 (June 1982), 651–65.

Hess, Alan C., and Peter A. Frost. "Tests for Price Effects of New Issues of Seasoned Securities." *Journal of Finance* 37 (March 1982), 11–26.

Ibbotson, Roger G., Jody L. Sindelar, and Jay R. Ritter. "The Market's Problems with the Pricing of Initial Public Offerings." *Journal of Applied Corporate Finance* 7 (Spring 1994), 66–74.

Johnson, Greg, Thomas Funkhouser, and Robertson Stephens. "Yankee Bonds and Cross-Border Private Placement." *Journal of Applied Corporate Finance* 10 (Fall 1997), 34–45.

Keane, Simon M. "The Significance of the Issue Price in Rights Issues." *Journal of Business Finance* 4 (1972), 40–45.

Loughran, Tim, and Jay R. Ritter. "The New Issues Puzzle." *Journal of Finance* 50 (March 1995), 23–51.

Myers, Stewart C., and Nicholas S. Majluf. "Corporate Financing and Investment Decisions When Firms Have Information That Investors Do Not Have." *Journal of Financial Economics* 13 (June 1984), 187–221.

Q&A: Small Business & the SEC. Washington, D.C.: U.S. Securities and Exchange Commission, 1997 (available online at www.sec.gov/smbus/qasbsec.htm).

Ritter, Jay R. "The Costs of Going Public." *Journal of Financial Economics* 19 (June 1987), 269–282.

Smith, Clifford W., Jr. "Investment Banking and the Capital Acquisition Process." *Journal of Financial Economics* 15 (January–February 1986), 3–29.

Tinic, Seha M. "Anatomy of Initial Public Offerings of Common Stock." *Journal of Finance* 43 (September 1988), 789–822.

Wilhelm, William J., Jr. "Internet Investment Banking: The Impact of Information Technology on Relationship Banking." *Journal of Applied Corporate Finance* 12 (Spring 1999), 21–27.

The Work of the SEC. Washington, D.C.: U.S. Securities and Exchange Commission, 1997 (available online at www.sec.gov/asec/wot.htm).

Wruck, Karen Hopper. "Equity Ownership Concentration and Firm Value: Evidence from Private Equity Financings." *Journal of Financial Economics* 23 (June 1989), 3–28.

Chapter 20

Long-Term Debt, Preferred Stock, and Common Stock

BONDS AND THEIR FEATURES
   Basic Terms • Trustee and Indenture • Bond Ratings
TYPES OF LONG-TERM DEBT INSTRUMENTS
   Debentures • Subordinated Debentures • Income Bonds • Junk
      Bonds • Mortgage Bonds • Equipment Trust Certificates
      • Asset Securitization
RETIREMENT OF BONDS
   Sinking Funds • Serial Payments • Call Provision
PREFERRED STOCK AND ITS FEATURES
   Cumulative Dividends Feature • Participating Feature • Voting
      Rights (in Special Situations) • Retirement of Preferred Stock
      • Use in Financing
COMMON STOCK AND ITS FEATURES
   Authorized, Issued, and Outstanding Shares • Par Value • Book
      Value and Liquidating Value • Market Value
RIGHTS OF COMMON SHAREHOLDERS
   Right to Income • Voting Rights • Rights to Purchase New
      Shares (Maybe)
DUAL-CLASS COMMON STOCK
SUMMARY
APPENDIX: REFUNDING A BOND ISSUE
QUESTIONS
SELF-CORRECTION PROBLEMS
PROBLEMS
SOLUTIONS TO SELF-CORRECTION PROBLEMS
SELECTED REFERENCES

An investment in knowledge always pays the best interest.

—BENJAMIN FRANKLIN

In Chapter 19 we explored the *capital market* for corporate securities—the market for relatively long-term financial instruments. In this chapter, we examine the major long-term securities issued by firms to provide for their long-term financing needs—long-term debt (bonds), preferred stock, and common stock—as well as evaluate their features. Also, in the Appendix to this chapter we analyze the potential profitability of a company refunding (replacing) an existing bond issue with a new one.

BONDS AND THEIR FEATURES

Bond A long-term debt instrument issued by a corporation or government.

A **bond** is a long-term debt instrument with a final maturity generally being 10 years or more. If the security has a final maturity shorter than 10 years, it is usually called a *note*. To fully understand bonds, we must be familiar with certain basic terms and common features.

Basic Terms

Par Value.   *Par value* for a bond represents the amount to be paid the lender at the bond's maturity. It is also called *face value* or *principal*. Par value is usually $1,000 per bond (or some multiple of $1,000). With the major exception of a zero-coupon bond, most bonds pay interest that is calculated on the basis of the bond's par value.

Coupon rate The stated rate of interest on a bond; the annual interest payment divided by the bond's face value.

Coupon Rate.   The stated rate of interest on a bond is referred to as the **coupon rate**. For example, a 13 percent coupon rate indicates that the issuer will pay bondholders $130 per annum for every $1,000-par-value bond that they hold.

Maturity.   Bonds almost always have a stated *maturity*. This is the time when the company is obligated to pay the bondholder the par value of the bond.

Trustee and Indenture

Trustee A person or institution designated by a bond issuer as the official representative of the bondholders. Typically, a bank serves as trustee.

A company issuing bonds to the public designates a qualified **trustee** to represent the interests of the bondholders. The obligations of a trustee are specified in the Trust Indenture Act of 1939, administered by the Securities and Exchange Commission. The trustee's responsibilities are to authenticate the bond issue's legality at the time of issuance, to watch over the financial condition and behavior of the borrower, to make sure that all contractual obligations are carried out, and to initiate appropriate actions if the borrower does not meet any of these obligations. The trustee is compensated directly by the corporation, a compensation that adds to the effective costs of borrowing.

Indenture The legal agreement, also called the *deed of trust*, between the corporation issuing bonds and the bondholders, establishing the terms of the bond issue and naming the trustee.

The legal agreement between the corporation issuing the bonds and the trustee, who represents the bondholders, is defined in the bond **indenture**. The indenture contains the terms of the bond issue as well as any restrictions placed on the company. These restrictions, known as *protective covenants*, are very similar to those contained in a term loan agreement. (Because we analyze protective covenants extensively in the next chapter, when we deal with term loans, we will not describe them here.) The terms contained in the indenture are established jointly by the borrower and the underwriter along with the trustee. If the corporation defaults under any of the provisions of the indenture, the trustee, on the behalf of the bondholders, can take action to correct the situation. If not satisfied, the trustee can then call for the immediate repayment of all outstanding bonds.

Bond Ratings

The creditworthiness of a publicly traded debt instrument is often judged in terms of the credit ratings assigned to it by investment rating agencies. The principal rating agencies are Moody's Investors Service (Moody's) and Standard & Poor's (S&P). The issuer of a new corporate bond contracts with the agency to evaluate and rate the bond, as well as to update the rating throughout the bond's life. For this service, the issuer pays a fee. In addition, the rating agency charges subscribers to its rating publications.

Based on their evaluations of a bond issue, the agencies give their opinion in the form of letter grades, which are published for use by investors. In their ratings, the agencies attempt to rank issues according to the perceived probability of default. The highest grade issues, whose risk of default is felt to be negligible, are rated triple-A, followed by double-A, single-A, B-double-A (Moody's) or triple-B (S&P), and so forth through C and D, which are the lowest grades of Moody's and S&P, respectively. The first four grades mentioned are considered to represent investment-quality issues, whereas the other rated bonds are considered speculative. (The ratings used by Moody's and S&P, as well as brief descriptions, are shown in Chapter 16's Table 16-5.) The ratings by the two agencies are widely respected as measures of default risk. In fact, many investors do not separately analyze the default risk of a company.

TYPES OF LONG-TERM DEBT INSTRUMENTS

Bonds can be issued on either an *unsecured* or *secured* (asset-backed) basis. Debentures, subordinated debentures, and income bonds form the major categories of unsecured bonds, whereas mortgage bonds represent the most common type of secured long-term debt instrument.

Debentures

Debenture A long-term, unsecured debt instrument.

The word **debenture** usually applies to the unsecured bonds of a corporation. Because debentures are not secured by any specific company property, the debenture holder becomes a general creditor of the firm in the event of company liquidation. Therefore, investors look to the earning power of the firm as their primary security. Although the bonds are unsecured, debenture holders are afforded some protection by the restrictions imposed in the bond indenture, particularly any *negative-pledge clause*, which precludes the corporation from pledging any of its assets (not already pledged) to other creditors. This provision safeguards the investor in that the borrower's assets will not be additionally restricted. Because debenture holders must look to the general credit of the borrower to meet principal and interest payments, typically only well-established and creditworthy companies are able to issue debentures.

Subordinated Debentures

Subordinated debenture A long-term, unsecured debt instrument with a lower claim on assets and income than other classes of debt; known as junior debt.

Subordinated debentures represent unsecured debt with a claim to assets that ranks behind all debt senior to these debentures. In the event of liquidation, subordinated debenture holders usually receive settlement only if all senior creditors are paid the full amount owed them. These subordinated debenture holders would still rank ahead of preferred and common stockholders in the event of liquidation. The existence of subordinated debt may work to the advantage of senior bondholders because senior holders are able to assume the claims of the subordinated holders. To illustrate, suppose that a corporation is liquidated for $600,000. It had $400,000 in straight debentures outstanding, $400,000 in subordinated debentures outstanding, and $400,000 in obligations owed to general creditors. One might suppose that the straight debenture holders and the general creditors would have an equal and prior claim in liquidation—that each would receive $300,000. The fact (of law) is that the straight debenture holders are entitled to use the subordinated debenture holders' claims, giving them $800,000 in total claims for purposes of determining a partial repayment. As a result they are entitled to two-thirds ($800,000/$1,200,000) of the liquidating value, or $400,000, whereas the general creditors are entitled to only one-third ($400,000/$1,200,000) of the liquidating value, or $200,000.

Because of the nature of the claim, a subordinated debenture issue has to provide a yield significantly higher than does a regular debenture issue in order to be attractive to investors. Frequently, subordinated debentures are convertible into common stock. Therefore, this added option feature may allow the convertible subordinated debenture to sell at a yield that is actually less than what the company would have to pay on an ordinary debenture.

Income Bonds

Income bond A bond where the payment of interest is contingent on sufficient earnings of the firm.

A company is obligated to pay interest on an **income bond** only when the interest is earned. There may be a *cumulative feature* where unpaid interest in a particular year accumulates. If the company does generate earnings in the future, it will have to pay the cumulative interest to the extent that earnings permit. However, the cumulative obligation is usually limited to no more than three years. As should be evident, this type of security offers the investor a rather weak promise of a fixed return. Nevertheless, the income bond is still senior to preferred and common stock, as well as to any subordinated debt. Unlike preferred stock dividends, the interest payment is deductible for tax purposes. Because income bonds are not popular with investors, their issuance has been primarily limited to situations involving reorganizations.

Junk Bonds

Junk bond A high-risk, high-yield (often unsecured) bond rated below investment grade.

During the 1980s an active market developed for non-investment-grade bonds. These are bonds with a rating of Ba (Moody's) or less, and they are called "junk" or "high-yield" bonds. The market for **junk bonds** was fostered by the investment banking firm of Drexel Burnham Lambert, which dominated this market until Drexel's demise in 1990. A number of companies used the market to raise billions of dollars, displacing what was previously bank and private placement financing. In addition, junk bonds were used in acquisitions and leveraged buyouts (topics taken up in Chapter 23).

Principal investors in junk bonds include pension funds, high-yield bond mutual funds, and some individuals who invest directly. A secondary market of sorts exists, but in any kind of financial panic or "flight to quality" by investors in the bond markets, such liquidity dries up. In the late 1980s, bonds issued in connection with highly levered transactions (leveraged buyouts) began to experience difficulty and many issues defaulted. Investors lost confidence and there was a sharp drop in new issues. The market recovered after the early 1990s, particularly for higher-quality issues. While junk bonds are a viable means of financing for some companies, it must be recognized that there are windows of opportunity. In an unstable market, few investors are to be found.

Mortgage Bonds

Mortgage bond A bond issue secured by a mortgage on the issuer's property.

A **mortgage bond** issue is secured by a *lien* (creditor claim) on specific assets of the corporation—usually fixed assets. The specific property securing the bonds is described in detail in the *mortgage,* which is the legal document giving the bondholder a lien on a property. As with other secured lending arrangements, the market value of the collateral should exceed the amount of the bond issue by a reasonable margin of safety. If the corporation defaults on any of the provisions in the bond indenture, the trustee, on behalf of the bondholders, has the power to *foreclose.* In a foreclosure, the trustee takes over the property and sells it, using the proceeds to pay the bondholders. If the proceeds are less than the amount of the bond issue outstanding, the bondholders become general creditors for the residual amount.

A company may have more than one bond issue secured by the same property. A bond issue may be secured by a *second mortgage* on property already used to secure another bond issue under a *first mortgage.* In the event of foreclosure, the first-mortgage bondholders must be paid the full amount owed them before there can be any distribution to the second-mortgage bondholders.

Equipment Trust Certificates

Equipment trust certificate An intermediate- to long-term security, usually issued by a transportation company, such as a railroad or airline, that is used to finance new equipment.

Although equipment trust financing is a form of lease financing, the **equipment trust certificates** themselves represent an intermediate- to long-term investment. This method of financing is used by railroads to finance the acquisition of rolling stock. Under this method, a railroad arranges with a trustee to purchase equipment from a manufacturer. The railroad signs a contract with the manufacturer for the construction of specific equipment. When the equipment is delivered, equipment trust certificates are sold to investors. The proceeds of this sale, together with the down payment by the railroad, are used to pay the manufacturer. Title to the equipment is held by the trustee, which in turn leases the equipment to the railroad. Lease payments are used by the trustee to pay a fixed return on the certificates outstanding— actually a dividend—and to retire a specified portion of the certificates at regular intervals. Upon the final lease payment by the railroad, the last of the certificates is retired, and title to the equipment passes to the railroad.

The life of the lease varies according to the equipment involved, but 15 years is rather common. Because rolling stock is essential to the operation of a railroad and has a ready market value, equipment trust certificates enjoy a very high standing as fixed-income investments. As a result, railroads are able to acquire cars and locomotives on favorable financing terms. Airlines, too, use a form of equipment trust certificate to finance aircraft. Although these certificates are usually sold to institutional investors, some issues are sold to the public.

Asset Securitization

Asset securitization The process of packaging a pool of assets and then selling interests in the pool in the form of *asset-backed securities (ABS).*

Asset securitization is the process of taking a cash-flow-producing asset, packaging it into a pool of similar assets, and then issuing securities backed by the asset pool. The purpose is to reduce financing costs. For example, the Acme Aglet Company needs cash but doesn't have a high enough credit rating to make a bond issue economical. So it picks assets to package, removes them from its balance sheet, and sells them to a special-purpose, bankruptcy-remote entity (called a *special-purpose vehicle).*

Asset-backed securities (ABS) Debt securities whose interest and principal payments are provided by the cash flows coming from a discrete pool of assets.

In this way, if Acme ever went bankrupt, its creditors could not seize the packaged assets. The special-purpose vehicle (SPV), in turn, raises money by selling **asset-backed securities (ABS)**—securities backed by the assets just purchased from Acme Aglet Company.

Interest and principal payments on the asset-backed securities are dependent on the cash flow coming from the specific package of assets. Thus asset-backed securities can be issued that are not tied to the Acme Aglet Company's low general credit rating. Instead, the securities' rating is now a function of the cash flow from the underlying assets. In this way, asset-backed securities are able to get a higher credit rating—and a lower interest rate—than could the Acme Aglet Company by itself.

A wide range of assets has been successfully *securitized* in the past, including trade receivables, car loans, credit card receivables, and leases. Ever more exotic assets have been recently showing up as securitized—royalty streams from films and music, electric utility bill receivables, health spa memberships, and security alarm contracts. What all these assets have in common is that they generate predictable cash flows.

Faced with Sky-High Capital Costs, Some CFOs in Asia Eye Asset-Backed Securitization (ABS)

Asset-backed securitization, in its bare bones, is the transformation of illiquid assets—such as receivables—into a security that is issued and traded in a capital market. Typically, mortgages, auto loans and utility payments are the most common types of revenue streams that can be used to create asset-linked securities, which are traded on markets in the U.S. and Europe.

Asset securitization differs from traditional asset-based lending in a number of ways, however. In an ABS deal, loans or other financial claims, such as receivables or future revenues, are assigned to a third party known as a special purpose vehicle (SPV). The SPV then issues debt instruments whose interest and principal repayments are derived from the cash flows generated by the underlying assets.

This separation of assets from the issuing company is crucial. Why? Because the quality of the assets is no longer tied to the creditworthiness of the originator. That would seem to be a big attraction for investors in Asia these days. It's certainly a plus for CFOs doing the deals. By offering high-quality assets—assets that are no longer tied to the financial health of the issuing company—finance managers can secure a lower cost of funding.

Depending on the quality of the assets, a degree of over-collateralization is usually required for ABS. This usually involves putting up additional assets or cash. The extra collateral is then used to service debt due the SPV when certain trigger events occur, such as an obligator's late or non-payment.

Residential mortgage loans constitute the core of the global asset-backed securities market. Other assets commonly securitized include credit card receivables, home equity loans, cellular phone receivables, heavy equipment loans, corporate loans and leases. Virtually any income-producing asset with an adequate performance record can be securitized.

Players in Asia's securitization game have much faith in ABS as both a source of funds and a vital first step in the creation of effective local capital markets. Their confidence is bolstered by the phenomenal growth in ABS activity in the U.S. and Europe. Between 1991 and 1996, ABS issues in the U.S. went from US$50 billion per annum to US$150 billion. Analysts say ABS issues by European corporates will reach US$1.8 trillion before 2003.

Source: Adapted from Simon Littlewood, "Tomorrow's Cash Today," CFO Asia (February 1999), pp. 70–73. Copyright © 1999 by CFO ASIA. (www.cfoasia.com) Used by permission. All rights reserved.

RETIREMENT OF BONDS

The *retirement* (repayment) of bonds may be accomplished in a number of different ways. For example, bonds may be retired by making a single-sum payment at final maturity, by *conversion* (an exchange for common stock) if the bonds are convertible, by calling the bonds if there is a call feature, or by periodic repayment. Periodic repayment of the debt is possible if either a sinking-fund or serial bond issue is involved. Conversion is taken up in Chapter 22, and the calling of bonds will be taken up shortly. But first we turn our attention to sinking-fund and serial bonds.

Sinking Funds

Sinking fund Fund established to periodically retire a portion of a security issue before maturity. The corporation is required to make periodic sinking-fund payments to a trustee.

The majority of corporate bond issues carry a provision for a **sinking fund** that requires the corporation to make periodic sinking-fund payments to a trustee in order to retire a specified face amount of bonds each period. The sinking-fund retirement of a bond issue can take two forms. The corporation can make a cash payment to the trustee, which in turn calls the bonds for redemption at the sinking-fund *call price*. (This is usually lower than the regular call price of a bond, which we discuss shortly.) The bonds themselves are called on a lottery basis by their serial numbers, which are published in the *Wall Street Journal* and other newspapers. The second option available to the issuing firm is to purchase bonds in the open market and to deliver a given number of bonds to the trustee.

The corporation should purchase the bonds in the open market as long as the market price is less than the sinking-fund call price. When the market price exceeds the call price, it should make cash payments to the trustee. If interest rates increase and/or credit quality deteriorates, the bond's price will decline in relation to the sinking-fund call price. As a result, the option of the corporation to deliver either cash or bonds to the trustee can have significant value. As with any option, the option feature works to the advantage of the holder—in this case the corporation—and to the disadvantage of the bondholders. The greater the volatility of interest rates and/or the volatility of the firm's value, the more valuable the option to the corporation.

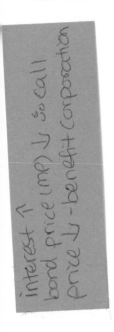

On the other hand, the sinking-fund provision may benefit the bondholder. By delivering bonds whose cost is lower than the call price, the company conserves cash, which may lower the probability of default. Because of the orderly retirement of sinking-fund debt, known as the *amortization effect,* some feel that this type of debt has less default risk than non-sinking-fund debt. In addition, steady repurchase activity adds liquidity to the market, which may be beneficial to the firm's bondholders.

Balloon payment A payment on debt that is much larger than other payments. The ultimate balloon payment is the entire principal at maturity.

The two factors discussed work in opposite directions. The "delivery" option works to the disadvantage of bondholders, but debt amortization and other things that reduce risk and/or increase liquidity work to the bondholders' advantage. The limited empirical evidence available supports both effects but the amortization effect somewhat more so. Also, sinking-fund payments do not necessarily retire the entire bond issue. There can be a **balloon payment** at final maturity.

Serial Payments

Serial bonds An issue of bonds with different maturities, as distinguished from an issue where all the bonds have identical maturities (term bonds).

All sinking-fund bonds in an issue mature on the same date, although specific bonds are retired before that date. **Serial bonds,** however, mature periodically until final maturity. For example, a $20 million issue of serial bonds might have $1 million of predetermined bonds maturing each year for 20 years. With a serial bond issue, the investor is able to choose the maturity that best suits his or her needs. Thus, a bond issue of this type might appeal to a wider group of investors than an issue in which all the bonds have the same maturity.

Call Provision

Corporate bond issues often provide for a **call provision,** which gives the corporation the option to buy back its bonds at a stated price (or series of stated prices) before their maturity. However, not all bond issues are callable. Particularly in times of low interest rates some corporations issue noncallable bonds. When a bond is callable, the **call price** is usually above the par value of the bond and often decreases over time. Frequently, the call price in the first year is established at 1 year's interest above the face value of the bond. If the coupon rate is 14 percent, the initial call price may be 114 ($1,140 per $1,000 face value).[1]

There are two types of call provisions, according to when they can be exercised. The security may be immediately callable, which simply means that the instrument may be bought back by the issuer at the call price at any time. Alternatively, the call provision may be deferred for a period of time. The most widely used deferred call periods are 5 years for public utility bonds and 10 years for industrial bonds. During this deferment period, the investor is protected from a call by the issuer. In recent years, virtually all issues of corporate bonds have involved a deferred call as opposed to an immediate call feature.

The call provision gives the company flexibility in its financing. If interest rates should decline significantly, it can call the bonds and refinance the issue at a lower interest cost. Thus, the company does not have to wait until the final maturity to refinance. In addition, the provision may be advantageous to the company if it finds any of the protective covenants in the bond indenture to be unduly restrictive.

Value of Call Privilege. Although the call privilege is beneficial to the issuing corporation, it works to the detriment of investors. If interest rates fall and the bond issue is called, the investors can invest in other bonds only at a sacrifice in yield to maturity. Consequently, the call privilege usually does not come free to the borrower. Its cost, or value, is measured at the time of bond issuance by the difference in yield on the callable bond and the yield that would be necessary if the security were noncallable. This value is determined by supply and demand forces in the market for callable securities.

One can think of the value of a callable bond as

$$\frac{\text{Callable-bond}}{\text{value}} = \frac{\text{Noncallable-bond}}{\text{value}} - \frac{\text{Call-option}}{\text{value}} \qquad \text{(20-1)}$$

where the noncallable bond is identical to the callable bond in all respects except for the call feature. The greater the value of the call feature, the lower the value of the callable bond relative to that of the noncallable one. The level and volatility of interest rates are key factors giving value to the call feature.

If interest rates are high and expected to fall, the call feature is likely to have significant value. Because the call price limits the upside potential in price movement, bondholders do not realize the full benefit of a significant interest-rate decline. Just as

---

[1]Among professionals (and in the newspaper bond quotations) bonds are always quoted as a percentage of their face value. For example, a bond callable at 105 would actually be callable at 105 percent of $1,000, or $1,050 per $1,000 face value.

Part VII Intermediate and Long-Term Financing

the bondholders' party gets going, the bonds are called, and they can invest in other bonds only at a lower coupon rate than the rate they currently enjoy. As a result, investors demand a significantly higher yield (and lower price) on the callable bond than they do on the noncallable one. In contrast, when interest rates are low and expected to rise, the threat of a call is negligible. As a result, the yields on the two bonds (callable and noncallable) may be nearly the same. The volatility of interest rates determines the magnitude of bond price movement. The greater the volatility, the greater the magnitude of *possible* interest-rate decline. As with any option, the greater the volatility of the associated asset, the more valuable the option. (See Chapter 21 and its Appendix for elaboration on this principle.)

In the Appendix to this chapter, we explore how a company decides whether or not calling its bonds will be a profitable undertaking. By refunding (replacing) the bonds with a bond issue with a lower coupon, certain costs may be more than offset, and the call would be worthwhile.

PREFERRED STOCK AND ITS FEATURES

Preferred stock A type of stock that promises a (usually) fixed dividend but at the discretion of the board of directors. It has preference over common stock in the payment of dividends and claims on assets.

Preferred stock is a hybrid form of financing, combining features of debt and common stock. In the event of liquidation, a preferred stockholder's claim on assets comes after that of creditors but before that of common stockholders. Usually, this claim is restricted to the par value of the stock. If the par value of a share of preferred stock is $100, the investor will be entitled to a maximum of $100 in settlement of the principal amount. Although preferred stock carries a stipulated dividend, the actual payment of a dividend is a discretionary rather than a fixed obligation of the company. The omission of a dividend will not result in a default of the obligation or insolvency of the company. The board of directors has full power to omit a preferred stock dividend if it so chooses.

The maximum return to preferred stockholders is usually limited to the specified dividend, and these stockholders do not share in the residual earnings of the company. Thus, if you own 100 shares of $10 \frac{1}{2}$ percent preferred stock, $50 par value, the maximum return you can expect in any year is $525, and this return is at the discretion of the board of directors. The corporation cannot deduct this dividend on its tax return. This fact is the principal shortcoming of preferred stock as a means of financing. In view of the fact that interest payments on debt are deductible for tax purposes, the company that treats a preferred stock dividend as a fixed obligation finds the explicit cost to be rather high.

Cumulative Dividends Feature

Cumulative dividends feature A requirement that all cumulative unpaid dividends on the preferred stock be paid before a dividend may be paid on the common stock.

Almost all preferred stocks have a **cumulative dividends feature,** providing for unpaid dividends in any single year to be carried forward. Before the company can pay a dividend on its common stock, it must pay dividends *in arrears* on its preferred stock. Suppose that a board of directors omits the preferred stock dividend on the company's 8 percent cumulative preferred stock for three consecutive years. If the stock has a $100 par value, the company is $24 per share in arrears on its preferred stock. Before it can pay a dividend to its common stockholders, it must pay preferred stockholders $24 for each share of preferred stock held. It should be emphasized that just because preferred stock dividends are in arrears, there is no guarantee that they will ever be paid. If the corporation has no intention of paying a common stock dividend, there is no need to clear up the **arrearage** on the preferred stock. The preferred stock dividend is typically omitted for lack of earnings, but the corporation does not have to pay a dividend even if earnings are restored.

Participating Feature

A *participating feature* allows preferred stockholders to participate in the residual earnings of the corporation according to some specified formula. The preferred stockholders might be entitled to share equally with common stockholders in any common stock dividend beyond a certain amount. Suppose that a 6 percent preferred issue ($100 par value) was **participating preferred stock,** so that the holders were entitled to share equally in any common stock dividends in excess of $6 a share. If the common stock dividend is $7, the preferred stockholders will receive $1 in extra dividends for each share of stock owned. The formula for participation can vary greatly. The essential feature is that preferred stockholders have a prior claim on income and an opportunity for additional return if the dividends to common stockholders exceed a certain amount. Unfortunately for the investor, practically all preferred stock issues are nonparticipating, with the maximum return limited to the specified dividend rate.

Voting Rights (in Special Situations)

Because of their "preferred" (prior) claim on assets and income, preferred stockholders are not normally given a voice in management unless the company is unable to pay preferred stock dividends during a specified period. Arrearages on four quarterly dividend payments might constitute such a default. Under such circumstances, preferred stockholders as a class would be entitled to elect a specific number of directors. Usually, the number of directors is rather small in relation to the total. Also, by the time the preferred stockholders obtain a voice in management, the company is probably in considerable financial difficulty. Consequently, the voting power that preferred stockholders are granted may be virtually meaningless.

Depending on the agreement between the preferred stockholders and the company, the preferred stockholders may obtain voting power under other conditions as well. The company may default under restrictions in the agreement that are similar to those found in a loan agreement or a bond indenture. One of the more frequently imposed restrictions is that dividends on common stock are prohibited if the company does not satisfy certain financial ratios. We note, however, that default under any of the provisions of the agreement between the corporation and its preferred stockholders does not result in the obligation's becoming immediately payable, as does default under a loan agreement or bond indenture. The preferred stockholders are merely given a voice in management and assurance that common stock dividends will not be paid during the period of default. Thus, preferred stockholders do not have nearly the same legal power in default as do debt holders.

Retirement of Preferred Stock

The fact that preferred stock, like common stock, has no maturity does not, however, mean that most preferred stock issues will remain outstanding forever. Provision for retirement of the preferred stock invariably is made.

Call Provision. Almost all preferred stock issues have a stated call price, which is above the original issuance price and may decrease over time. Like the call provision on bonds, the call provision on preferred stock affords the company flexibility.

Long-term debt, unlike preferred stock, has a final maturity that ensures the eventual retirement of the issue. Without a call feature on preferred stock, the corporation would be able to retire the issue only by the more expensive and less efficient methods of purchasing the stock in the open market, inviting tenders of the stock from preferred stockholders at a price above the market price, or offering the preferred stockholders another security in its place.

Sinking Fund.   Many preferred stock issues provide for a sinking fund, which partially ensures the orderly retirement of the stock. Like bond issues, a preferred stock sinking fund may be advantageous to investors because the retirement process exerts upward pressure on the market price of the remaining shares.

Conversion.   Certain preferred stock issues are convertible into common stock at the option of the holder. Upon conversion, of course, the preferred stock is retired. Because virtually all convertible securities have a call feature, the company can force conversion by calling the preferred stock if the market price of the preferred is significantly above the call price. Convertible preferred stock is used frequently in the acquisition of other companies. In part, its use in acquisitions stems from the fact that the transaction is not taxable for the company that is acquired or its stockholders at the time of the acquisition. It becomes a taxable transaction only when the preferred stock is sold. We shall examine convertible securities in much more detail in Chapter 22.

Use in Financing

Nonconvertible preferred stock is not used extensively as a means of long-term financing. One of its drawbacks is the fact that the preferred dividend is not tax deductible by the issuer. Public utilities, however, employ it with a certain degree of regularity. Why? Public utilities are allowed to take preferred dividends into account when they set their rates. Thus, these regulated monopolies can pass through the higher cost of preferred stock to their customers.

For the corporate investor, however, preferred stock may be more attractive than debt instruments because generally 70 percent of the dividends received by the corporation is not subject to taxation.[2] It is not surprising, then, that most preferred stock is held by corporate investors.

This attraction for corporate investors has given rise to floating-rate preferred stock. In one variation, *money market preferred stock (MMP)*, the dividend rate is set by auction every 49 days. Put another way, the dividend rate is established by the forces of supply and demand in keeping with money market rates in general. A typical rate might be .75 times the commercial paper rate, and more creditworthy issuers may command an even greater discount. As long as enough investors bid at each auction, the security's effective maturity date is 49 days. As a result, there is little variation in the market price of the investment over time. For the issuer, the relevant cost comparison is with the after-tax cost of other methods of short-term financing.

Apart from such short-term financing considerations, one advantage of regular (long-term) preferred stock financing is that it is a flexible financing arrangement. The dividend is not a legal obligation of the corporation issuing the securities. If earnings falter and the financial condition of the company deteriorates, the dividend

---

[2]Corporate investors receiving dividends from less-than-20-percent-owned corporations are allowed the 70 percent deduction. Dividends from 20-percent-or-more-owned corporations are subject to an 80 percent deduction.

can be omitted. With debt financing, interest must be paid regardless of whether earnings are good or bad. To be sure, companies that are accustomed to paying dividends on their common stock certainly regard the preferred dividend as a fixed obligation. Nevertheless, under dire circumstances, a company that omits its common stock dividend can also omit its preferred dividend.

Another advantage of a straight (nonconvertible) preferred stock issue is that it has no final maturity. In essence, it is a perpetual loan. From the standpoint of creditors, preferred stock adds to the equity base of the company and thereby strengthens its financial condition. The additional equity base enhances the ability of the company to borrow in the future. Although the explicit, after-tax cost of preferred stock is considerably higher than that of bonds, the implied benefits just discussed may offset this cost. In addition, the implicit cost of preferred stock financing, from the standpoint of penalizing the **price/earnings ratio** of the common stock, may be somewhat less than that of debt financing. To the extent that investors are apprehensive over legal bankruptcy, they would regard debt as a riskier form of leverage. Unlike creditors, preferred stockholders cannot force a company into legal bankruptcy.

Price/earnings ratio The market price per share of a firm's common stock divided by the most recent 12 months of earnings per share.

COMMON STOCK AND ITS FEATURES

The common stockholders of a company are its ultimate owners. Collectively, they own the company and assume the ultimate risk associated with ownership. Their liability, however, is restricted to the amount of their investment. In the event of liquidation, these stockholders have a residual claim on the assets of the company after the claims of all creditors and preferred stockholders are settled in full. **Common stock,** like preferred stock, has no maturity date. However, shareholders can still liquidate their investments by selling their stocks in the secondary market.

Common stock Securities that represent the ultimate ownership (and risk) position in a corporation.

Authorized, Issued, and Outstanding Shares

The corporate charter of a company specifies the number of *authorized shares* of common stock, the maximum that the company can issue without amending its charter. Although amending the charter is not a difficult procedure, it does require the approval of existing shareholders, which takes time. For this reason, a company usually likes to have a certain number of shares that are authorized but unissued. These unissued shares allow flexibility in granting stock options, pursuing merger targets, and splitting the stock. When authorized shares of common stock are sold, they become *issued shares*. *Outstanding shares* refers to the number of shares issued and actually held by the public. The corporation can buy back part of its issued stock and hold it as **treasury stock.**

Treasury stock Common stock that has been repurchased and is held by the issuing company.

Par Value

A share of common stock can be authorized either with or without **par value.** The par value of a share of stock is merely a recorded figure in the corporate charter and is of little economic significance. A company should not, however, issue common stock at a price less than par value, because any discount from par value (amount by which the issuing price is less than the par value) is considered a contingent liability of the owners to the creditors of the company. In the event of liquidation, the shareholders

Par value The face value of a stock or bond.

would be legally liable to the creditors for any discount from par value. Consequently, the par values of most stocks (if they have any par values at all) are set at fairly low figures relative to their market values. Suppose that Fawlty Pacemakers, Inc., is ready to start business for the first time after just having sold 10,000 shares of $5-par-value common stock at $45 a share. The shareholders' equity portion of the balance sheet would be

Common stock ($5 par value; 10,000 shares issued and outstanding)	$ 50,000
Additional paid-in capital	400,000
Total shareholders' equity	$450,000

Common stock that is authorized without par value (no-par stock) is carried on the books at the original market price or at some **assigned** (or **stated**) **value.** The difference between the issuing price and the par or stated value is reflected as **additional paid-in capital.**

Book Value and Liquidating Value

The *book value per share* of common stock is the shareholders' equity—total assets minus liabilities and preferred stock as listed on the balance sheet—divided by the number of shares outstanding. Suppose that Fawlty Pacemakers is now one year old, has generated $80,000 in after-tax profit, but pays no dividend. Thus, retained earnings are $80,000; the shareholders' equity is now $450,000 + $80,000 = **$530,000;** and the book value per share is $530,000/10,000 shares = **$53.**

Although one might expect the book value per share of stock to correspond to the *liquidating value (per share)* of the company, most frequently it does not. Often assets are sold for less than their book values, particularly when liquidating costs are involved. In some cases, certain assets—notably land and mineral rights—have book values that are modest in relation to their market values. For the company involved, liquidating value may be higher than book value. Thus, book value may not correspond to liquidating value, and, as we shall see, it often does not correspond to market value.

Market Value

Market value per share is the current price at which the stock is traded. For actively traded stocks, market price quotations are readily available. For the many inactive stocks that have thin markets, prices are difficult to obtain. Even when obtainable, the information may reflect only the sale of a few shares of stock and not typify the market value of the firm as a whole. For companies of this sort, care must be taken in interpreting market price information.

The market value of a share of common stock will usually differ from its book value and its liquidating value. Market value per share of common stock is a function of the current and expected future dividends of the company and the perceived risk of the stock on the part of investors. Because these factors bear only a partial relationship to the book value and liquidating value of the company, the market value per share may not be tied closely to these values.

Typically, the shares of a newer company are traded in the *over-the-counter (OTC) market,* where one or more security dealers maintain an inventory in the common stock and buy and sell it at the bid and ask prices that they quote. As a company grows in financial stature, number of shareholders, and volume of transactions, it may qualify for **listing** on a stock exchange, such as the New York Stock Exchange. However, many firms prefer to remain a part of the OTC marketplace. The National Association of Securities Dealers Automated Quotations (NASDAQ) system for many of these OTC stocks provides significant marketability to the investor.

RIGHTS OF COMMON SHAREHOLDERS

Right to Income

Common shareholders are entitled to share in the earnings of the company only if cash dividends are paid. Shareholders also prosper from the market value appreciation of their shares, but they are entirely dependent on the board of directors for the declaration of dividends that give them income from the company. Thus, we see that the position of a common shareholder differs markedly from that of a creditor. If the company fails to pay contractual interest and principal payments to creditors, the creditors are able to take legal action to ensure that payment is made or the company is liquidated. Common shareholders, on the other hand, have no legal recourse to a company for not distributing profits.

Voting Rights

Because the common shareholders of a company are its owners, they are entitled to elect a board of directors. In a large corporation, shareholders usually exercise only indirect control through the board of directors they elect. The board, in turn, selects the management, and management actually controls the operations of the company. In a sole proprietorship, partnership, or small corporation, the owners usually control the operation of the business directly. In a large corporation, there may be times when the goals of management differ from those of the common shareholders. One of the few recourses of a shareholder who wishes to affect management is through the board of directors.

Because common shareholders are often geographically widely dispersed and thus operatively disorganized, management can often exercise effective control of a large corporation if it controls only a small percentage of the outstanding common stock. By proposing a slate of directors that is favorable to its own interests, management is able to maintain control.

Proxies and Proxy Contests.   Voting can be done either in person at the shareholders' annual meeting or by proxy. A **proxy** is a form that a shareholder signs giving his or her right to vote to another person or persons. Because most shareholders do not attend the annual meeting, voting by proxy is the mechanism by which most votes are cast. The Securities and Exchange Commission (SEC) regulates the solicitation of proxies and also requires companies to disseminate information to their shareholders through proxy mailings. Prior to the annual meeting, management solicits proxies from shareholders to vote for the recommended slate of directors and for any other proposals requiring shareholder approval. If shareholders are satisfied with the company, they generally sign the proxy in favor of management, giving written authorization to management to vote their shares. If some shareholders do not vote their shares, the number of shares voted at the meeting and the number needed to constitute a majority are lower. Because of the proxy system and the fact that management is able to mail information to shareholders at the company's expense, management has a distinct advantage in the voting process.

But the fortress is not invulnerable. Outsiders can seize control of a company through a proxy contest. When an outside group undertakes a proxy raid, it is required to register its proxy statement with the SEC to prevent the presentation of misleading or false information. In a proxy contest, the odds favor existing management to win. Management has both the organization and the use of the company's resources to carry on the proxy fight. Insurgents are likely to be successful only when the earnings performance of the company has been bad and management obviously ineffective. Still, the undertaking of a proxy contest is often associated with a higher share price performance than would otherwise be the case. Apparently, the challenge itself is sufficient to change investor expectations about management in the future behaving more in keeping with maximizing shareholder wealth.

Majority-rule voting A method of electing corporate directors, where each common share held carries one vote for each director position that is open; also called *statutory voting*.

Cumulative voting A method of electing corporate directors, where each common share held carries as many votes as there are directors to be elected and each shareholder may accumulate these votes and cast them in any fashion for one or more particular directors.

Voting Procedures.   Depending on the corporate charter, the board of directors is elected under either a **majority-rule voting** system or a **cumulative voting** system. Under the majority-rule system, stockholders have one vote for each share of stock that they own, and they must vote for each director position that is open. A stockholder who owns 100 shares will be able to cast 100 votes for each director's position open. Because each person seeking a position on the board must win a majority of the total votes cast for that position, the system precludes minority interests from electing any of their own directors. If management can obtain proxies for over 50 percent of the shares voted, it can select the entire board of directors.

Under a cumulative voting system, a stockholder is able to accumulate votes and cast them for less than the total number of directors being elected. The total number of votes for each stockholder is equal to the number of shares the stockholder owns times the number of directors being elected. If you are a stockholder who owns 100 shares and 12 directors are to be elected, you may cast $100 \times 12 = \mathbf{1{,}200}$ votes. All 1,200 of your votes may be cast for one director, or these votes may be spread over whatever other number of directors you choose.

A cumulative voting system, in contrast to a majority-rule system, allows minority interests a greater chance to elect a certain number of directors. The minimum number of shares necessary to elect a specific number of directors is determined by the following equation:[3]

$$\frac{\text{Total number of voting shares} \times \text{Specific number of directors sought}}{\text{Total number of directors to be elected} + 1} + 1 \qquad \text{(20-2)}$$

If there are 3 million voting shares, if the total number of directors to be elected is 15, and if a minority group wishes to elect 2 directors, it will need at least the following number of shares:

$$\frac{3{,}000{,}000 \times 2}{15 + 1} + 1 = \mathbf{375{,}001}$$

In this example, $375{,}001/3{,}000{,}000 = \mathbf{12.5\%}$ of the voting shares has been sufficient to elect $2/15 = \mathbf{13.3\%}$ of the board of directors.

As you can see, cumulative voting gives minority interests a better opportunity to be represented on the board of directors of a corporation. Because this system is more democratic, a number of states require that companies chartered in their states elect directors in this way. Even with cumulative voting, however, management is

---

[3]This formula assumes that the minority votes are cast evenly for only the specific number of directors sought and that the majority votes are cast evenly for the majority's entire slate of directors.

able to take steps that may effectively preclude minority interests from obtaining a seat on the board. One method involves reducing the number of directors on the board. Suppose that the minority group actually owns the 375,001 shares mentioned earlier. With 15 directors to be elected the group can elect 2 directors. If the board is reduced to 6 members, however, the minority group can elect no directors because the minimum number of shares needed to elect a single director is

$$\frac{3,000,000 \times 1}{6 + 1} + 1 = \textbf{428,572}$$

Another method of thwarting a minority interest from obtaining representation is to stagger the terms of the directors so that only a portion of the board is elected each year. If a firm has 15 directors and the term is for 5 years, it is possible to have only 3 directors elected each year. As a result, a minority group needs considerably more shares voted in its favor—750,001 shares to be exact—to elect a director than it would if all 15 directors came up for election each year.

Right to Purchase New Shares (Maybe)

As discussed in Chapter 19, a firm's corporate charter or state statute may require that a new issue of common stock or an issue of securities convertible into common stock be offered first to existing common shareholders because of their *preemptive right*. If the preemptive right applies to a particular firm, existing common shareholders would have the right to preserve their proportionate ownership in the corporation. Thus, if the corporation issues common stock, the common shareholders must be given the right to subscribe to the new stock so that they can maintain their pro rata interest in the company.

DUAL-CLASS COMMON STOCK

To retain control for management, for company founders, or for some other group, a company may have more than one class of common stock. For example, common stock might be classified according to voting power and to the claim on income. Class A common stock of a company may have inferior voting privileges but may be entitled to a prior claim to dividends, whereas Class B common stock may have superior voting rights but a lower claim to dividends. Dual classes of common stock are common in new ventures where promotional common stock usually goes to the founders. Usually, the promoters of a corporation and its management hold the Class B common stock, while the Class A common stock is sold to the public.

Suppose that the Class A and Class B common shareholders of a company are entitled to one vote per share but that the Class A stock is issued at an initial price of $20 a share. If $2 million is raised in the original offering through the issuance of 80,000 shares of Class A common stock for $1.6 million and 200,000 shares of Class B common stock for $400,000, the Class B shareholders will have over twice as many votes as Class A holders have, although their original investment is only one-fourth as large. Thus, the Class B holders have effective control of the company. Indeed, this is the purpose of **dual-class common stock.**

For this control, the Class B holders must be willing to give up something in order to make Class A common stock attractive to investors. Usually, they take a lower claim both to dividends and assets. An appropriate balance must be struck

Dual-class common stock Two classes of common stock, usually designated Class A and Class B. Class A is usually the weaker voting or nonvoting class, and Class B is usually the stronger.

between voting power and the claim to dividends and assets if the company is to bargain effectively for Class A equity funds. Sometimes, the Class B common stock is simply given to the promoters of a corporation without any cash investment on their part. Perhaps the most famous example of a company with dual-class common stock is the Ford Motor Company. The Class B common stock is owned by members of the Ford family, and the Class A common stock is held by the general public. Regardless of the number of shares of Class A common stock issued, the Class B common stock constitutes 40 percent of the voting power of the Ford Motor Company. Thus, members of the Ford family retain substantial voting power in the company, despite the fact that they hold far fewer shares than does the general public.

SUMMARY

- A *bond* is a long-term debt instrument with a final maturity generally being 10 years or more. Basic terms related to bonds include par value, coupon rate, and maturity.
- A *trustee* is a person or institution designated by a bond issuer as the official representative of the bondholder, and an *indenture* is the legal agreement between the corporation issuing bonds and the bondholders establishing the terms of the bond issue and naming the trustee.
- Bonds can be issued on either an *unsecured* or *secured* (asset-backed) basis. *Debentures, subordinated debentures,* and *income bonds* form the major categories of unsecured bonds; *mortgage bonds* represent the most common type of secured long-term debt instrument.
- The *retirement* (repayment) of bonds may be accomplished in a number of different ways. For example, bonds may be retired by making a single-sum payment at final maturity, by conversion if the bonds are convertible, by calling the bonds, if there is a call feature, or by periodic repayment. Periodic repayment of the debt is possible if either a *sinking-fund* or *serial bond* issue is involved.
- Preferred stock is a hybrid form of security having characteristics of both debt and common stock. The payment of dividends is not a legal but rather a discretionary obligation, although many companies regard the obligation as fixed. Preferred stockholders' claims on assets and income come after those of creditors but before those of common shareholders.
- Preferred stock, like common stock, has no maturity. However, retirement of the preferred stock can occur through the use of a *call provision,* a *sinking fund,* or *a conversion.*
- Because of the generally 70 percent exemption of dividends to the corporate investor, preferred stock typically has a lower yield than corporate bonds. Particularly popular for marketable security portfolios of corporations is *money market preferred stock (MMP).* The principal disadvantage of preferred stock to the issuer is the nondeductibility for tax purposes of preferred dividends paid.
- The common stockholders of a company are its ultimate owners. As such they are entitled to share in the residual earnings of the company if cash dividends are paid. As owners, however, they have only a residual claim on assets in the event of liquidation.
- Common stockholders are also entitled to a voice in management through the board of directors that they elect. Many shareholders vote by means of a *proxy.* The directors are elected under either a *majority-rule voting* system or a *cumulative voting* system. The cumulative system allows minority interests a greater chance to obtain representation on the board of directors.
- The use of different classes of common stock allows the promoters and management of a corporation to retain voting control without having to make a large capital contribution.

Appendix

Refunding a Bond Issue

Refunding Replacing an old debt issue with a new one, usually to lower the interest cost.

In this Appendix, we analyze the profitability of a company's refunding a bond issue before its maturity. By **refunding,** we mean calling the issue and replacing it with a new issue of bonds. In this regard, we focus our attention on only one reason for refunding—profitability—which, in turn, is due to interest rates having declined since the bonds were issued.

A REFUNDING EXAMPLE

The refunding decision can be regarded as a form of capital budgeting. There is an initial cash outlay followed by future interest savings. These savings are represented by the difference between the annual net cash outflow required under the old bonds and the net cash outflow required on the new, or refunding, bonds. Calculating the initial cash outlay is more complex. Consequently, it is best to show an example of this method of evaluation.[4]

A company currently has a $20 million, 12 percent debenture issue outstanding, and the issue still has 20 years to final maturity. Because current interest rates are significantly lower than at the time of the original offering, the company can now sell a $20 million issue of 20-year bonds at a coupon rate of 10 percent that will net it $19,600,000 after the underwriting spread.

Call premium The excess of the call price of a security over its par value.

For federal income tax purposes, the unamortized (not-yet-written-off) issuing expense of the old bonds, the **call premium,** and the unamortized discount of the old bonds, if they were sold at a discount, are deductible as expenses in the year of the refunding. The old bonds were sold 5 years ago at a $250,000 discount from par value, so the unamortized portion now is $200,000. Moreover, the legal fees and other issuing expenses involved with the old bonds have an unamortized balance of $100,000. The call price on the old bonds is 109 ($1,090 per $1,000-face-value bond); issuing expenses on the new bonds are $150,000; the income tax rate is 40 percent; and there is a 30-day period of overlap. The period of overlap is the lag between the time the new bonds are sold and the time the old bonds are called. This lag occurs because most companies wish to have the proceeds from the new issue in hand before they call the old issue. Otherwise, there is a certain amount of risk associated with calling the old issue and being at the "mercy" of the bond market in raising new funds. During the period of overlap, the company pays interest on both bond issues.

Framework for Analysis. With this rather involved background information in mind, we can calculate the initial cash outflow and the future cash benefits. The net cash outflow at the time of the refunding is as follows:

Cost of calling old bonds (call price, 109)		$21,800,000
Net proceeds of new bond issue		19,600,000
Difference		$ 2,200,000
Expenses		
Issuing expense of new bonds	$150,000	
Interest expense on old bonds during overlap period	200,000	350,000
Gross cash outlay		$ 2,550,000

[4]This section draws upon Oswald D. Bowlin, "The Refunding Decision: Another Special Case in Capital Budgeting," *Journal of Finance* 21 (March 1966), 55–68. The development in this section assumes that the reader has covered Chapters 12 and 13.

Less: Tax savings		
Interest expense on old bonds during overlap period	$ 200,000	
Call premium	1,800,000	
Unamortized discount on old bonds	200,000	
Unamortized issuing expenses on old bonds	100,000	
Total	$2,300,000	
Tax savings (40% of $2,300,000)		920,000
Net cash outflow		$1,630,000

For ease of presentation, we ignore any interest that might be earned by investing the refunding bond proceeds in marketable securities during the 30-day period of overlap. The annual net cash benefits may be determined by calculating the difference between the net cash outflow required on the old bonds and the net cash outflow required on the new or refunding bonds. We assume for simplicity that interest is paid but once a year, at year end. The annual net cash outflow on the old bonds is

Interest expense, 12% coupon rate		$2,400,000
Less: Tax savings		
Interest expense	$2,400,000	
Amortization of bond discount ($200,000/20)	10,000	
Amortization of issuing costs ($100,000/20)	5,000	
Total	$2,415,000	
Tax savings (40% of $2,415,000)		966,000
Annual net cash outflow, old bonds		$1,434,000

For the new bonds, the bond discount as well as the issuing costs may be amortized for tax purposes in the same manner as were the old bonds. The annual net cash outflow on the new bonds is as follows:

Interest expense, 10% coupon rate		$2,000,000
Less: Tax savings		
Interest expense	$2,000,000	
Amortization of bond discount ($400,000/20)	20,000	
Amortization of issuing costs ($150,000/20)	7,500	
Total	$2,027,500	
Tax savings (40% of $2,027,500)		811,000
Annual net cash outflow, new bonds		$1,189,000
Difference between annual net cash outflows ($1,434,000 − $1,189,000)		$ 245,000

Discounting. Thus, for an initial net cash outflow of $1,630,000, the company can achieve annual net cash benefits of $1,434,000 − $1,189,000 = **$245,000** over the next 20 years. Because the net cash benefits occur in the future, they must be discounted back to present value. But what discount rate should be used? Certain individuals advocate the use of the cost of capital. However, a refunding operation differs from other investment proposals. Once the new bonds are sold, the net cash benefits are known with certainty. From the standpoint of the corporation, the refunding operation is essentially a riskless investment project. The only risk associated with the cash flows is that of the firm's defaulting in the payment of principal or interest. Because a premium for default risk is embodied in the market rate of interest the firm pays, a more appropriate discount might be the after-tax cost of borrowing on the refunding bonds.

Using this cost, $(.10) \times (1 - .40) = 6\%,$ as our discount factor, the refunding operation would be worthwhile if the net present value were positive.[5] For our example, the net present value is $1,180,131, indicating that the refunding operation is worthwhile. The internal rate of return is 13.92 percent, indicating again that the refunding is worthwhile, because the internal rate of return exceeds the required rate of 6 percent.[6]

OTHER CONSIDERATIONS

Just because a refunding operation is found to be worthwhile, it should not necessarily be undertaken right away. If interest rates are declining and this decline is expected to continue, management may prefer to delay the refunding. At a later date, the refunding bonds can be sold at an even lower rate of interest, making the refunding operation even more worthwhile. The decision concerning timing must be based on expectations of future interest rates.

Several points should be raised with respect to the calculations in our example. First, most firms refund an existing issue with a new bond issue of a longer maturity. In our example, we assumed that the new bond issue had the same final maturity date as that of the old bond issue. Our analysis needs to be modified slightly when the maturity dates are different. The usual procedure is to consider only the net cash benefits up to the maturity of the old bonds. A second assumption in our example was that neither issue involved sinking-fund bonds or serial bonds. If either issue calls for periodic reduction of the debt, we must adjust our procedure for determining future net cash benefits. Finally, the annual cash outflows associated with the refunded bonds are usually less than those associated with the original bond issue. As a result, there is a decrease in the degree of financial leverage of the firm. Though this effect is likely to be small, on occasion it can be a significant consideration.

---

[5]Recall from Chapter 13 that the net present value is the present value of net cash benefits less the initial cash outflow.

[6]An alternative method of analysis is to replicate the cash outflows of the old bond issue and then determine the present value of this stream using as the discount rate the interest rate at which new bonds could be sold in the current market. If this present value exceeds the call price of the old bonds, the refunding would be worthwhile. Among others using this approach are Jess B. Yawitz and James A. Anderson, "The Effect of Bond Refunding on Shareholder Wealth," *Journal of Finance* 32 (December 1979), 1738–46.

QUESTIONS

1. Contrast serial bonds and bonds requiring a sinking fund.
2. How does an income bond differ from a mortgage bond issue?
3. Explain why a commercial bank loan officer would be particularly concerned that debt owed by a corporate borrower to the principal stockholders or officers of the company be subordinated debt.
4. What are "junk bonds"? How might they be used in financing a corporation?
5. In issuing long-term debt, which types of debt instruments would most likely be used by (a) railroads? (b) public utilities? (c) strong industrial firms?
6. Why do callable bonds typically have a higher yield to maturity than noncallable bonds, holding all other things constant? Is the yield differential between callable and noncallable bonds likely to be constant over time? Why?
7. Because the dividend payments on preferred stock are not a tax-deductible expense, the explicit cost of this form of financing is high. What are some of the offsetting advantages to the issuing firm and to the investor that enable this type of security to be sold?
8. From the standpoint of the preferred stock issuer, why is it desirable to have a *call feature?*

9. How does a money market preferred (MMP) stock differ from regular preferred stock?
10. Why do most preferred stock issues have a cumulative feature? Would the company be better off with a noncumulative feature?
11. If not otherwise stated, what would you "typically" expect to find with respect to the following features for a preferred stock: cumulative feature, participation, voting rights, call feature, and claim on assets?
12. Why would a company ever wish to use dual-class common stock in its financing instead of straight common stock?
13. Why does most common stock have a low par value in relation to its market value?
14. The common stockholder is considered the residual owner of a corporation. What does this mean in terms of risk and return?
15. In any proxy attempt by an outside group to gain control of a company, the advantage lies with management. What are the reasons for this advantage?
16. If Congress were to eliminate the double taxation of dividends so that a company could deduct dividend payments in the same way it does interest payments for tax purposes, what would be the effect on preferred stock and common stock financing?

Appendix Questions

17. In the refunding decision, differential cash flows are discounted at the after-tax cost of debt. Explain why these cash flows are not discounted at the average cost of capital.
18. Are refundings by corporations likely to occur steadily over time? If not, when are waves of refundings likely to occur?

SELF-CORRECTION PROBLEMS

1. The Phelps Corporation has $8 million of 10 percent mortgage bonds outstanding under an open-end indenture. The indenture allows additional bonds to be issued as long as all of the following conditions are met:
   a. Pretax interest coverage [(income before taxes + bond interest)/bond interest] remains greater than 4.
   b. Net depreciated value of mortgage assets remains twice the amount of mortgage debt.
   c. Debt-to-equity ratio remains below .5.
   The Phelps Corporation has net income after taxes of $2 million and a 40 percent tax rate, $40 million in equity, and $30 million in depreciated assets, covered by the mortgage. Assuming that 50 percent of the proceeds of a new issue would be added to the base of mortgaged assets and that the company has no sinking-fund payments until next year, how much more 10 percent debt could be sold under each of the three conditions? Which protective covenant is binding?
2. Alvarez Apparel, Inc., could sell preferred stock with a dividend cost of 12 percent. If it were to sell bonds in the current market, the interest rate cost would be 14 percent. The company is in a 40 percent tax bracket.
   a. What is the after-tax cost of each of these methods of financing?
   b. Powder Milk Biscuits, Inc., holds a limited number of preferred stocks as investments. It is in a 40 percent tax bracket. If it were to invest in the preferred stock of Alvarez Apparel, what would be its after-tax return? What would be its after-tax return if it were to invest in the bonds?

3. Thousand Islands Resorts has 1,750,000 shares of authorized common stock, each having a $1 par value. Over the years, it has issued 1,532,000 shares, but presently 63,000 are held as treasury stock. The additional paid-in capital of the company is presently $5,314,000.

    a. How many shares are now outstanding?

    b. If the company were able to sell stock at $19 per share, what is the maximum amount it could raise under its existing authorization, including treasury shares?

    c. What would be its common stock and additional paid-in capital accounts after the financing?

4. Roy's Orbs & Sons, Inc., has a nine-person board and 2 million shares of common stock outstanding. It is chartered with a cumulative voting rule. Tammy Whynot, a granddaughter of the founder, directly or indirectly controls 482,000 shares. Because she disagrees with present management, she wants a slate of her own directors on the board.

    a. If all directors are elected once a year, how many directors can she elect?

    b. If directors' terms are staggered so that only three are elected each year, how many can she elect?

PROBLEMS

1. Gillis Manufacturing Company has in its capital structure $20 million of 13.5 percent sinking-fund debentures. The sinking-fund call price is $1,000 per bond, and sinking-fund payments of $1 million in face amount of bonds are required annually. Presently, the yield to maturity on the debentures in the market is 12.21 percent. To satisfy the sinking-fund payment, should the company deliver cash to the trustee or bonds? What if the yield to maturity were 14.60 percent?

2. Five years ago, Zapada International issued $50 million of 10 percent, 25-year debentures at a price of $990 per bond to the public. The call price was originally $1,100 per bond the first year after issuance, and this price declined by $10 each subsequent year. Zapada is now "calling" the bonds in order to refund them at a lower interest rate.

    a. Ignoring taxes, what is a bondholder's return on investment for the 5 years? (Assume that interest is paid once a year and that the investor owns one bond.)

    b. If the bondholder can now invest $1,000 in a 20-year security of equivalent risk that provides 8 percent interest, what is the overall return over the 25-year holding period? How does this compare with the return on the Zapada bonds had they not been called? (Assume again that interest is paid once a year. Both rates of return can be approximated using the present value tables at the end of the book.)

3. Crakow Machine Company wishes to borrow $10 million for 10 years. It can issue either a noncallable bond at 11.40 percent interest or a bond callable at the end of 5 years for 12 percent. For simplicity, we assume that the bond will be called only at the end of year 5. The interest rate that is likely to prevail 5 years hence for a 5-year straight bond can be described by the following probability distribution:

Interest rate	9%	10%	11%	12%	13%
Probability	.1	.2	.4	.2	.1

Issuing and other costs involved in selling a bond issue 5 years hence will total $200,000. The call price is assumed to be par.

a. What is the total absolute amount of interest payments for the noncallable issue over the 10 years? (Do not discount.) What is the expected value of total interest payments and other costs if the company issues callable bonds? (Assume that the company calls the bonds and issues new ones only if there is a savings in interest costs after issuing expenses.) On the basis of total costs, should the company issue noncallable or callable bonds?

b. What would be the outcome if the probability distribution of interest rates 5 years hence were the following?

Interest rate	7%	9%	11%	13%	15%
Probability	.2	.2	.2	.2	.2

Assume that all other conditions stay the same.

4. *Research Project:* Obtain copies of several bond indentures. Pay particular attention to the restrictive covenants concerning such things as dividends, working capital, additional debt, and nature of the business. Try to relate the cost of debt to the firm to the relative restrictiveness of these provisions. How would you go about finding a measure of the degree of restriction so that trade-offs with interest cost could be made?

5. The O.K. Railroad needs to raise $9.5 million for capital improvements. One possibility is a new preferred stock issue—8 percent dividend, $100 par value—stock that would yield 9 percent to investors. Flotation costs for an issue this size amount to 5 percent of the total amount of preferred stock sold. These costs are deducted from gross proceeds in determining the net proceeds to the company. (Ignore any tax considerations.)

a. At what price per share will the preferred stock be offered to investors? (Assume that the issue will never be called.)

b. How many shares must be issued to raise $9.5 million for the O.K. Railroad?

6. Lost Dutchman Silver Mining Company has 200,000 shares of $7 cumulative preferred stock outstanding, $100 par value. The preferred stock has a participating feature. If dividends on the common stock exceed $1 per share, preferred stockholders receive additional dividends per share equal to one-half of the excess. In other words, if the common stock dividend were $2, preferred stockholders would receive an additional dividend of $.50. The company has 1 million shares of common stock outstanding. What would dividends per share be on the preferred stock and on the common stock if earnings available for dividends in three successive years were (a) $1,000,000, $600,000, and $3,000,000? (b) $2,000,000, $2,400,000, and $4,600,000? (c) $1,000,000, $2,500,000, and $5,700,000? (Assume that all of the available earnings are paid in dividends, but nothing more is paid.)

7. Mel Content, a disgruntled stockholder of the Penultimate Corporation, desires representation on the board. The Penultimate Corporation, which has 10 directors, has 1 million shares outstanding.

a. How many shares would Mel have to control to be assured of 1 directorship under a majority-rule voting system?

b. Recompute Part (a), assuming a cumulative voting system.

c. Recompute Parts (a) and (b), assuming that the number of directors was reduced to 5.

Appendix Problem

8. The U.S. Zither Corporation has $50 million of 14 percent debentures outstanding, which are due in 25 years. USZ could refund these bonds in the current market with new 25-year bonds, sold to the public at par ($1,000 per bond) with a 12 percent coupon rate. The spread to the underwriter is 1 percent, leaving $990 per bond in proceeds to the company. The old bonds have an unamortized discount of $1 million, unamortized legal fees and other expenses of $100,000, and a call price of $1,140 per bond. The tax rate is 40 percent. There is a one-month overlap during which both issues are outstanding, and issuing expenses are $200,000. Compute the present value of the refunding, using the after-tax rate on the new bonds as the discount rate. Is the refunding worthwhile?

SOLUTIONS TO SELF-CORRECTION PROBLEMS

1. (dollars in millions) Let X = the number of millions of dollars of new debt that can be issued.

a.

$$\frac{[\$2/(1 - .40)] + [\$8(.10)]}{[\$8(.10)] + [(.10)X]} = 4$$

$$\frac{\$3.33 + \$.80}{\$.80 + (.10)X} = \frac{\$4.13}{\$.80 + (.10)X} = 4$$

$$4(\$.80) + (4)(.10)X = \$4.13$$

$$(.40)X = \$.93$$

$$X = \$.93/.40 = \mathbf{\$2.325}$$

b.

$$\frac{\$30 + (.5)X}{\$8 + X} = 2$$

$$2(\$8) = 2(X) = \$30 + (.5)X$$

$$(1.5)X = \$14$$

$$X = \$14/(1.5) = \mathbf{\$9.33}$$

c.

$$\frac{\$8 + X}{\$40} = .5$$

$$\$8 + X = (.5)(\$40)$$

$$X = \$20 - \$8 = \mathbf{\$12}$$

Condition (a) is binding, and it limits the amount of new debt to $2.325 million.

2. a. After-tax cost:

Preferred stock = **12%**

$$\text{Bonds} = 14\%(1 - .40) = \mathbf{8.40\%}$$

b. The dividend income to a corporate investor is generally either 70 or 80 percent exempt from taxation. With a corporate tax rate of 40 percent, we have for the preferred stock either

after-tax return = 12% (1 − [(.30)(.40)]) = **10.56%** or
12% (1 − [(.20)(.40)]) = **11.04%**

For the bonds,

after-tax return = 14%(1 − .40) = **8.40%**

3. a.

Issued shares	1,532,000
Treasury shares	63,000
Outstanding shares	**1,469,000**

b.

Authorized shares	1,750,000
Outstanding shares	1,469,000
Available shares	281,000
281,000 shares × $19 =	**$5,339,000**

c.

Common stock ($1 par)	$ 1,750,000
Additional paid-in capital*	10,372,000

*Consists of $18 × 281,000 shares plus $5,314,000

4. a. Number of shares necessary to elect one director =

$$\frac{2{,}000{,}000 \times 1}{(9 + 1)} + 1 = 200{,}001$$

Therefore, she can elect two directors.

b. Number of shares necessary to elect one director =

$$\frac{2{,}000{,}000 \times 1}{(3 + 1)} + 1 = 500{,}001$$

She can elect no directors.

SELECTED REFERENCES

Alderson, Michael J., and K. C. Chen. "Excess Asset Reversions and Shareholder Wealth." *Journal of Finance* 41 (March 1986), 225–42.

Anderson, James S. "Asset Securitization: An Overview for Issuers and Investors." *TMA Journal* 15 (November/December 1995), 38–42.

Ang, James S. "The Two Faces of Bond Refunding." *Journal of Finance* 30 (June 1975), 869–74.

Bowlin, Oswald D. "The Refunding Decision: Another Special Case in Capital Budgeting." *Journal of Finance* 21 (March 1966), 55–68.

Crabbe, Leland E., and Jean Helwege. "Alternative Tests of Agency Theories of Callable Corporate Bonds." *Financial Management* 23 (Winter 1994), 3–20.

DeAngelo, Harry, and Linda DeAngelo. "Managerial Ownership of Voting Rights: A Study of Public Corporations with Dual Classes of Common Stock." *Journal of Financial Economics* 14 (March 1985), 33–70.

———. "Proxy Contests and the Governance of Publicly Held Corporations." *Journal of Financial Economics* 23 (June 1989), 29–59.

Donaldson, Gordon. "In Defense of Preferred Stock." *Harvard Business Review* 40 (July–August 1962), 123–36.

———. "Financial Goals: Management vs. Stockholders." *Harvard Business Review* 41 (May–June 1963), 116–29.

Dyl, Edward A., and Michael D. Joehnk. "Sinking Funds and the Cost of Corporate Debt." *Journal of Finance* 34 (September 1979), 887–94.

Emerick, Dennis, and William White. "The Case for Private Placements: How Sophisticated Investors Add Value to Corporate Debt Issuers." *Journal of Applied Corporate Finance* 5 (Fall 1992), 83–91.

Fooladi, Iraj, and Gordon S. Roberts. "On Preferred Stock." *Journal of Financial Research* 9 (Winter 1986), 319–24.

Ho, Andrew, and Michael Zaretsky. "Valuation of Sinking Fund Bonds." *Journal of Fixed Income* 48 (March–April 1992), 59–67.

Kalotay, Andrew J. "On the Management of Sinking Funds." *Financial Management* 10 (Summer 1981), 34–40.

———, George O. Williams, and Frank J. Fabozzi. "A Model for Valuing Bonds and Embedded Options." *Financial Analysts Journal* 49 (May–June 1993), 35–46.

Khanna, Arun, and John J. McConnell. "MIPS, QUIPS, and TOPrS: Old Wine in New Bottles." *Journal of Applied Corporate Finance* 11 (Spring 1998), 39–44.

Markese, John. "Shareholder Voting Rights: Differences Among Classes." *AAII Journal* 11 (February 1989), 35–37.

McDaniel, Morey W. "Are Negative Pledge Clauses in Public Debt Issues Obsolete?" *Business Lawyer* 38 (May 1983), 867–81.

———. "Bondholders and Corporate Governance." *Business Lawyer* 41 (February 1986), 413–60.

Mitchell, Karlyn. "The Call, Sinking Fund, and Term-to-Maturity Features of Corporate Bonds: An Empirical Investigation." *Journal of Financial and Quantitative Analysis* 26 (June 1991), 201–22.

Ofer, Aharon R., and Robert A. Taggart Jr. "Bond Refunding: A Clarifying Analysis." *Journal of Finance* 32 (March 1977), 21–30.

Pound, John. "Proxy Contests and the Efficiency of Shareholder Oversight." *Journal of Financial Economics* 20 (January–March 1988), 237–65.

Van Horne, James C. "Implied Fixed Costs in Long-Term Debt Issues." *Journal of Financial and Quantitative Analysis* 8 (December 1973), 821–33.

———. *Financial Market Rates and Flows*, 6th ed. Upper Saddle River, NJ: Prentice Hall, 2001, Chaps. 7 and 11.

Chapter 21

Term Loans and Leases

TERM LOANS
   Costs and Benefits • Revolving Credit Agreements • Insurance
      Company Term Loans • Medium-Term Notes
PROVISIONS OF LOAN AGREEMENTS
   Formulation of Provisions • Negotiation of Restrictions
EQUIPMENT FINANCING
   Sources and Types of Equipment Financing
LEASE FINANCING
   Forms of Lease Financing • Accounting Treatment • Tax
      Treatment • Economic Rationale for Leasing
EVALUATING LEASE FINANCING IN RELATION TO DEBT FINANCING
   Example for Analysis • Present Value for Lease Alternative
      • Present Value for Borrowing Alternative • Other
      Considerations • The Importance of the Tax Rate
SUMMARY
APPENDIX: ACCOUNTING TREATMENT OF LEASES
QUESTIONS
SELF-CORRECTION PROBLEMS
PROBLEMS
SOLUTIONS TO SELF-CORRECTION PROBLEMS
SELECTED REFERENCES

> Rough winds do shake the darling buds of May,
> And summer's lease hath all too short a date. . . .
>
> —WILLIAM SHAKESPEARE, SONNET XVIII

The principal characteristic of short-term loans is that they are self-liquidating in less than a year. Frequently, they finance seasonal or temporary funds requirements. Term financing, on the other hand, finances more permanent funds requirements, such as those for fixed assets and underlying buildups in receivables and inventories. The loan is usually paid with the generation of cash flows over a period of years. As a result, most of these loans are paid in regular, periodic installments. We regard term financing as involving final maturities between 1 and 10 years. Although the 1-year boundary is rather commonly accepted, the 10-year upper limit is somewhat arbitrary. In this chapter we examine various types of term debt as well as lease financing.

TERM LOANS

Term loan Debt originally scheduled for repayment in more than 1 year, but generally in less than 10 years.

Commercial banks are a primary source of term financing. Two features of a bank **term loan** distinguish it from other types of business loans. First, a term loan has a final maturity of more than 1 year. Second, it most often represents credit extended under a formal loan agreement. For the most part, these loans are repayable in periodic installments—quarterly, semiannual, or annual—that cover both interest and principal. The payment schedule of the loan is usually geared to the borrower's cash-flow ability to service the debt. Typically, the repayment schedule calls for equal periodic installments, but it may specify irregular amounts or repayment in one lump sum at final maturity. Sometimes the loan is *amortized* (gradually extinguished) in equal periodic installments except for a final *balloon payment* (a payment much larger than any of the others). Most bank term loans are written with original maturities in the 3- to 5-year range.

Costs and Benefits

Generally, the interest rate on a term loan is higher than the rate on a short-term loan to the same borrower. If a firm could borrow at the prime rate on a short-term basis, it might pay .25 percent to .50 percent more on a term loan. The higher interest rate helps to compensate for the more prolonged risk exposure of the lender. The interest rate on a term loan is generally set in two ways: (1) a fixed rate established at the outset that remains effective over the life of the loan, or (2) a variable rate adjusted in keeping with changes in market rates. Sometimes a floor or a ceiling rate is established, limiting the range within which a variable rate may fluctuate.

Commitment fee A fee charged by the lender for agreeing to hold credit available.

In addition to interest costs, the borrower is required to pay the legal expenses that the bank incurs in drawing up the loan agreement. Also, a **commitment fee** may be charged for the time during the commitment period when the loan is not "taken down." For an ordinary term loan, these additional costs are usually rather small in relation to the total interest cost of the loan. Typically fees on the unused portion of a commitment range between .25 percent and .75 percent. Suppose, for example, that the commitment fee was .50 percent on a commitment of $1 million and a company took down all of the loan 3 months after the commitment. The firm would owe the bank a ($1 million) $\times$ (.005) $\times$ (3 months/12 months) = **$1,250** commitment fee.

The principal advantage of an ordinary bank term loan is flexibility. The borrower deals directly with the lender, and the loan can be tailored to the borrower's needs through direct negotiation. Should the firm's requirements change, the terms and conditions of the loan may be revised. In many instances, bank term loans are made to small businesses that do not have access to the capital markets and cannot readily float a public issue. The ability to float a public issue varies over time in keeping with the tone of the capital markets, whereas access to term loan financing is more dependable. Even large companies that are able to go to the public market may occasionally find it more convenient to seek a bank term loan than to float a public issue.

Revolving Credit Agreements

Revolving credit agreement A formal, legal commitment to extend credit up to some maximum amount over a stated period of time.

As we said in Chapter 11, a **revolving credit agreement** is a formal commitment by a bank to lend up to a certain amount of money to a company over a specified period of time. The actual notes evidencing debt are short term (usually 90 days), but the company may renew them or borrow additionally, up to the specified maximum, throughout the duration of the commitment. Many revolving credit commitments are for three years, although it is possible for a firm to obtain a shorter commitment. As with a term loan, the interest rate is usually .25 to .50 percent higher than the rate at which the firm could borrow on a short-term basis under a line of credit. When a bank makes a revolving credit commitment, it is legally bound under the loan agreement to have funds available whenever the company wants to borrow. The borrower usually must pay for this availability in the form of a commitment fee, perhaps .50 percent per annum, on the difference between the amount borrowed and the specified maximum.

This borrowing arrangement is particularly useful at times when the firm is uncertain about its funds requirements. The borrower has flexible access to funds over a period of uncertainty and can make more definite credit arrangements when the uncertainty is resolved. Revolving credit agreements can be set up so that at the maturity of the commitment, borrowings then owing can be converted into a term loan at the option of the borrower. Suppose that the company you work for is introducing a new product and is facing a period of uncertainty over the next several years. To provide maximum financial flexibility, you might arrange a three-year revolving credit agreement that is convertible into a five-year term loan at the expiration of the revolving credit commitment. At the end of three years, the company should know its funds requirements better. If these requirements are permanent, or nearly so, the firm might wish to exercise its option and take down the term loan.

Insurance Company Term Loans

In addition to banks, life insurance companies and certain other institutional investors lend money on a term basis but with differences in the maturity of the loan extended and in the interest rate charged. In general, life insurance companies are interested in term loans with final maturities in excess of seven years. Because these companies do not have the benefit of compensating balances or other business from the borrower and because their loans usually have a longer maturity than bank term loans, the rate of interest is typically higher than a bank would charge. To the insurance company, the term loan represents an investment and must yield a return commensurate with the costs involved in making the loan, as well as the risk and the maturity of the loan and the prevailing yields on alternative investments. Because an insurance company is interested in keeping its funds employed without interruption, it normally has a prepayment penalty, whereas the bank usually does not. Insurance company term loans are generally not competitive with bank term loans. Indeed, they are complementary, for they serve different maturity ranges.

Medium-Term Notes

Medium-term notes (MTNs) are a type of continuously offered debt obligation originally designed in the 1970s to fill the maturity gap between commercial paper and long-term bonds. Initially, MTNs were issued with maturities in the nine-month to two-year range. But now, maturities of up to 30 years or more are common (thus making "medium-term" a misnomer).

The coming of *shelf registration* gave MTNs their real start. SEC Rule 415 made it practical for corporate issuers to offer small amounts of medium-term debt to the public continuously without having to refile with the Securities and Exchange Commission after each sale.

Merrill Lynch pioneered the dealer-sponsored MTN market in the early 1980s. Today, several competitors—notably Goldman Sachs, Lehman Brothers, and CS First Boston—are also quite active and help support a secondary market. Issuers of MTNs include finance companies, banks or bank holding companies, and industrial companies.

MTNs were introduced internationally in the mid-1980s. **Euro medium-term notes (Euro MTNs)** are issued in a variety of currencies, amounts, maturities, and at fixed or floating rates of interest. Thus, from humble beginnings in the 1970s, the public MTN market has grown into a multibillion-dollar international funding vehicle.

PROVISIONS OF LOAN AGREEMENTS

When a lender makes a term loan or revolving credit commitment, it provides the borrower with available funds for an extended period. Much can happen to the financial condition of the borrower during that period. To safeguard itself, the lender requires the borrower to maintain its financial condition and, in particular, its current position at a level at least as favorable as when the commitment was made. The provisions for protection contained in a loan agreement are known as protective **covenants.**

The **loan agreement** itself simply gives the lender legal authority to step in should the borrower default under any of the loan provisions. Otherwise, the lender would be locked into a commitment and would have to wait until maturity before being able to take corrective actions. The borrower who suffers losses or other adverse developments will default under a well-written loan agreement—thus giving an "early warning" of potentially more serious problems ahead. The lender will then be able to act. The action usually takes the form of working with the company to straighten out its problems. Seldom will a lender demand immediate repayment, despite the legal right to do so in cases of default. More typically, the condition under which the borrower defaults is waived, or the loan agreement is amended. The point is that the lender has the authority to act.

Formulation of Provisions

The formulation of the different restrictive provisions should be tailored to the specific loan situation. The lender fashions these provisions for the overall protection of the loan. No one provision is able by itself to provide the necessary safeguard. Collectively, however, these provisions act to ensure the firm's overall liquidity and ability to repay a loan. The important protective covenants of a loan agreement may be classified as follows: (1) general provisions used in most loan agreements, which are usually variable to fit the situation; (2) routine provisions used in most agreements, which are usually not variable; and (3) specific provisions that are used according to the situation. Although we focus on a loan agreement, the protective covenants used and the philosophy underlying their use are the same for a bond indenture, which we described in Chapter 20.

General Provisions. The *working capital requirement* is probably the most commonly used and most comprehensive provision in a loan agreement. Its purpose is to preserve the company's current position and ability to repay the loan. Frequently, a straight dollar amount, such as $6 million, is set as the minimum working capital the company must maintain during the duration of the commitment. When the lender feels that it is desirable for a specific company to build working capital, it may increase the minimum working capital requirement throughout the duration of the loan. The establishment of a working capital minimum is normally based on the amount of present working capital and projected working capital, allowing for seasonal fluctuations. The requirement should not unduly restrict the company in the ordinary generation of profit. Should the borrower incur sharp losses or spend too much for fixed assets, common stock repurchases, dividends, redemption of long-term debt, and so forth, it would probably breach the working capital requirement.

The *cash dividend and repurchase of common stock restriction* is another major provision in this category. Its purpose is to limit cash going outside the business, thus preserving the liquidity of the company. Most often, cash dividends and repurchases of common stock are limited to a percentage of net profits on a cumulative basis after a certain base date, frequently the last fiscal year end prior to the date of the term loan agreement. A less flexible method is to restrict dividends and repurchases of common stock to an absolute dollar amount each year. In most cases the prospective borrower must be willing to restrict cash dividends and repurchases of common stock. If tied to earnings, this restriction will still allow adequate dividends as long as the company is able to generate satisfactory profits.

The *capital expenditures limitation* is third in the category of general provisions. Capital expenditures may be limited to a yearly fixed dollar amount or, more commonly, to an amount equal to current depreciation charges or to a certain percentage of current depreciation charges. The capital expenditures limitation is another tool the lender uses to ensure the maintenance of the borrower's current position. By directly limiting capital expenditures, the bank can be more sure that it will not have to look to liquidation of fixed assets for repayment of its loan. Again, the provision should not be so restrictive that it prevents adequate maintenance and improvement of facilities.

A *limitation on other indebtedness* is the last general provision. This limitation may take a number of forms, depending on the circumstances. Frequently, a loan agreement will prohibit a company from incurring any other long-term debt. This provision protects the lender, inasmuch as it prevents future lenders from obtaining a prior claim on the borrower's assets. Usually a company is permitted to borrow within reasonable limits for seasonal and other short-term purposes arising in the ordinary course of business.

Routine Provisions. The second category of restrictions includes routine, usually inflexible, provisions found in most loan agreements. Ordinarily, the loan agreement requires the borrower to furnish the bank with financial statements and to maintain adequate insurance. Additionally, the borrower normally must not sell a significant portion of its assets and must pay, when due, all taxes and other liabilities, except those it contests in good faith. A provision forbidding the future pledging or mortgaging of

Negative pledge clause
A protective covenant whereby the borrower agrees not to allow a lien on any of its assets.

any of the borrower's assets is almost always included in a loan agreement. This important provision is known as a **negative pledge clause.**

Ordinarily, the company is required not to discount or sell its receivables. Moreover, the borrower generally is prohibited from entering into any leasing arrangement of property, except up to a certain dollar amount of annual rental. The purpose of this provision is to prevent the borrower from taking on a substantial lease liability, which might endanger its ability to repay the loan. A lease restriction also prevents the firm from leasing property instead of purchasing it and thereby getting around the limitations on capital expenditures and debt. Usually there is a restriction on other contingent liabilities. In addition, there is typically a restriction on the acquisition of other companies. This restriction often takes the form of a prohibition on acquisitions unless specifically approved by the lender. The provisions in this category appear as a matter of routine in most loan agreements. Although somewhat mechanical, they close many loopholes and provide a tight, comprehensive loan agreement.

Special Provisions. In specific loan agreements, the lender uses special provisions to achieve a desired protection of its loan. A loan agreement may contain a definite understanding regarding the use of the loan proceeds, so that there will be no diversion of funds to purposes other than those contemplated when the loan was negotiated. If one or more key executives are essential to a firm's effective operation, a lender may insist that the company carry life insurance on them. Proceeds of the insurance may be payable to the company or directly to the lender, to be applied to the loan. An agreement may also contain a management clause, under which certain key individuals must remain actively employed in the company during the time the loan is outstanding. Aggregate executive salaries and bonuses are sometimes limited in the loan agreement to prevent excessive compensation of executives, which might reduce profits. This provision also closes another loophole. It prevents large shareholders who are officers of the company from increasing their own salaries in lieu of paying higher dividends, which are limited under the agreement.

Negotiation of Restrictions

The provisions just described represent the most frequently used protective covenants in a loan agreement. From the standpoint of the lender, the aggregate impact of these provisions should be to safeguard the financial position of the borrower and its ability to repay the loan. Under a well-written agreement, a borrower cannot get into serious financial difficulty without defaulting under an agreement, thereby giving the lender legal authority to take action. Although the lender is instrumental in establishing the restrictions, the restrictiveness of protective covenants is subject to negotiation between borrower and lender. The final result will depend on the bargaining power of each of the parties involved.

EQUIPMENT FINANCING

Equipment represents another asset that may be pledged to secure a loan. If the firm either has equipment that is marketable or is purchasing such equipment, it is usually able to obtain some sort of secured financing. Because the terms of such loans are usually more than a year, we take them up in this chapter rather than under short-term secured loans. As with other secured loans, the lender evaluates the marketability of the collateral and will advance a percentage of the market value, depending on the quality of the equipment. Frequently, the repayment schedule for the loan is set in keeping with the economic depreciation schedule of the equipment. In setting the repayment schedule, the lender wants to be sure that the market value of the equipment always exceeds the balance of the loan.

The excess of the expected market value of the equipment over the amount of the loan is the margin of safety, which will vary according to the specific situation. For example, the rolling stock of a trucking company is movable collateral and reasonably marketable. As a result, the advance may be as high as 80 percent. Less marketable equipment, such as that with a limited use, will not command as high an advance. A certain type of lathe may have a thin market, and a lender might not be willing to advance more than 40 percent of its reported market value. Some equipment is so specialized that it has no value as collateral.

Sources and Types of Equipment Financing

Commercial banks, finance companies, and the sellers of equipment are among the sources of equipment financing. The seller of the equipment may finance the purchase either by holding a secured note or by selling the note to its captive finance subsidiary or some third party. The interest charge will depend on the extent to which the seller uses financing as a sales tool. The seller who uses financing extensively may charge only a moderate interest rate but may make up for part of the cost of carrying the notes by charging higher prices for the equipment. The borrower must consider this possibility in judging the true cost of financing. Equipment loans may be secured either by a chattel mortgage or by a conditional sales contract arrangement.

Lien A legal claim on certain assets. A lien can be used to secure a loan.

Chattel Mortgage.   A *chattel mortgage* is a **lien** on property other than real estate. The borrower signs a security agreement that gives the lender a lien on the equipment specified in the agreement. To *perfect* (make legally valid) the lien, the lender files a copy of the security agreement or a financing statement with a public office of the state in which the equipment is located. Given a valid lien, the lender can sell the equipment if the borrower defaults in the payment of principal or interest on the loan.

Conditional sales contract A means of financing provided by the seller of equipment, who holds title to it until the financing is paid off.

Promissory note A legal promise to pay a sum of money to a lender.

Conditional Sales Contract.   With a **conditional sales contract** arrangement, the seller of the equipment retains the title to it until the purchaser has satisfied all the terms of the contract. The buyer signs a conditional sales contract security agreement to make periodic installment payments to the seller over a specified period of time. These payments are usually monthly or quarterly. Until the terms of the contract are completely satisfied, the seller retains title to the equipment. Thus, the seller receives a down payment and a **promissory note** for the balance of the purchase price on the sale of the equipment. The note is secured by the contract, which gives the seller the authority to repossess the equipment if the buyer does not meet all of the terms of the contract. The seller may either hold the contract or sell it, simply by endorsing it, to a commercial bank or finance company. The bank or finance company then becomes the lender and assumes the security interest in the equipment.

LEASE FINANCING

A lease is a contract. By its terms the owner of an asset (the lessor) gives another party (the lessee) the exclusive right to use the asset, usually for a specified period of time, in return for the payment of rent. Most of us are familiar with leases of houses, apartments, offices, or automobiles. Recent decades have seen an enormous growth

Lease A contract under which one party, the lessor (owner) of an asset, agrees to grant the use of that asset to another, the lessee, in exchange for periodic rental payments.

Net lease A lease where the lessee maintains and insures the leased asset.

Operating lease A short-term lease that is often cancellable.

Financial lease A long-term lease that is not cancellable.

Fair market value The price at which property can be sold in an arm's length transaction.

Residual value The value of a leased asset at the end of the lease period.

Sale and leaseback The sale of an asset with the agreement to immediately lease it back for an extended period of time.

in the leasing of business assets, such as cars and trucks, computers, machinery, and even manufacturing plants. An obvious advantage to the lessee is the use of an asset without having to buy it. For this advantage, the lessee incurs several obligations. First and foremost is the obligation to make periodic lease payments, usually monthly or quarterly. Also, the **lease** contract specifies who is to maintain the asset. Under a *full-service (or maintenance) lease,* the lessor pays for maintenance, repairs, taxes, and insurance. Under a **net lease,** the lessee pays these costs.

The lease may be cancellable or noncancellable. When cancellable, there sometimes is a penalty. An **operating lease** for office space, for example, is relatively short term and is often cancellable at the option of the lessee with proper notice. The term of this type of lease is shorter than the asset's economic life. It is only in leasing the space over and over, either to the same party or to others, that the lessor recovers its costs. Other examples of operating leases include the leasing of copying machines, certain computer hardware, word processors, and automobiles. In contrast, a **financial lease** is longer term in nature and is noncancellable. The lessee is obligated to make lease payments until the lease's expiration, which generally corresponds to the useful life of the asset. These payments not only amortize the cost of the asset but provide the lessor an interest return.

Finally, the lease contract typically specifies one or more options to the lessee at expiration. One option is to simply return the leased asset to the lessor. Another option may involve renewal, where the lessee has the right to renew the lease for another lease period, either at the same rent or at a different, usually lower, rent. A final option would be to purchase the asset at expiration. For tax reasons, the asset's purchase price must not be significantly lower than its **fair market value.** If the lessee does not exercise its option, the lessor takes possession of the asset and is entitled to any **residual value** associated with it. As we will see, the determination of the cost of lease financing and the return to the lessor depend importantly on the asset's assumed residual value. This is particularly true for operating leases.

Forms of Lease Financing

Virtually all financial lease arrangements fall into one of three main types of lease financing: a sale and leaseback arrangement, direct leasing, and leveraged leasing. In this section we briefly describe these categories. In the subsequent section we present a framework for the analysis of lease financing.

Sale and Leaseback.   Under a **sale and leaseback** arrangement a firm sells an asset to another party, and this party leases it back to the firm. Usually the asset is sold at approximately its market value. The firm receives the sales price in cash and the economic use of the asset during the basic lease period. In turn, it contracts to make periodic lease payments and give up title to the asset. As a result, the lessor realizes any residual value the asset might have at the end of the lease period, whereas before, this value would have been realized by the firm. The firm may realize an income tax advantage if the asset involves a building on owned land. Land is not depreciable if owned outright. However, because lease payments are tax deductible, the lessee is able to indirectly "depreciate" (or expense) the cost of the land. Lessors engaged in sale and leaseback arrangements include insurance companies, other institutional investors, finance companies, and independent leasing companies.

Direct Leasing.   Under *direct leasing,* a company acquires the use of an asset it did not own previously. A firm may lease an asset from the manufacturer. IBM leases computers. Xerox Corporation leases copiers. Indeed, many capital goods are available today on a lease-financed basis. The major lessors are manufacturers, finance companies, banks, independent leasing companies, special-purpose leasing companies, and partnerships. For leasing arrangements involving all but manufacturers, the vendor sells the asset to the lessor who, in turn, leases it to the lessee.

Leveraged leasing A lease arrangement in which the lessor provides an equity portion (usually 20 to 40 percent) of the leased asset's cost and third-party lenders provide the balance of the financing.

Leveraged Leasing.   A special form of leasing has become popular in the financing of big-ticket assets, such as aircraft, oil rigs, and railway equipment. This device is known as **leveraged leasing.** In contrast to the two parties involved in a sale and leaseback or direct leasing, there are three parties involved in leveraged leasing: (1) the lessee, (2) the lessor (or equity participant), and (3) the lender.

From the standpoint of the lessee, there is no difference between a leveraged lease and any other type of lease. The lessee contracts to make periodic payments over the basic lease period and, in return, is entitled to the use of the asset over that period of time. The role of the lessor, however, is changed. The lessor acquires the asset in keeping with the terms of the lease arrangement and finances the acquisition in part by an equity investment of, say, 20 percent (hence the term "equity participant"). The remaining 80 percent of the financing is provided by a long-term lender or lenders. Usually the loan is secured by a mortgage on the asset, as well as by the assignment of the lease and lease payments. The lessor, then, is itself a borrower.

As owner of the asset, the lessor is entitled to deduct all depreciation charges associated with the asset. The cash-flow pattern for the lessor typically involves (1) a cash outflow at the time the asset is acquired, which represents the lessor's equity participation; (2) a period of cash inflows represented by lease payments and tax benefits, less payments on the debt (interest and principal); and (3) a period of net cash outflows during which, because of declining tax benefits, the sum of lease payments and tax benefits falls below the debt payments due. If there is any *residual value* at the end of the lease period, this of course represents a cash inflow to the lessor. Although the leveraged lease may seem the most complicated of the three forms of lease financing we have described, it reduces to certain basic concepts. From the standpoint of the lessee, which is our stance, the leveraged lease can be analyzed in the same manner as any other lease.

Accounting Treatment

Accounting for leases has changed dramatically over time. A number of years ago lease financing was attractive to some because the lease obligation did not appear on the company's financial statements. As a result, leasing was regarded as a "hidden" or "off-balance-sheet" method of financing. However, accounting requirements have changed so that now many long-term leases must be shown on the balance sheet as a "capitalized" asset with an associated liability being shown as well. For these leases, the reporting of earnings is affected. Other leases must be fully disclosed in footnotes to the financial statements. Because the accounting treatment of leases is involved, we discuss it separately in the Appendix to this chapter to maintain the chapter's continuity. The main point is that it is no longer possible for a firm to "fool" informed investors and creditors by using a lease as opposed to debt financing. The full impact of the lease obligation is apparent to any supplier of capital who makes the effort to read the financial statements.

Tax Treatment

For tax purposes, the lessee can deduct the full amount of the lease payment in a properly structured (tax-oriented) lease. The Internal Revenue Service (IRS) wants to be sure that the lease contract truly represents a lease and not an installment purchase of the asset. To assure itself that a "true lease" is in fact involved, the IRS has established some guidelines. The most important is that the lessor have a minimum "at-risk" investment, both at lease inception and throughout the lease period, of 20 percent or more of the acquisition cost of the asset. This means that the asset must also have a residual value of at least 20 percent of initial cost. Another guideline is that the remaining life of the asset at the end of the lease period must be at least the longer of one year or 20 percent of the asset's original estimated life. There can be no bargain purchase option given to the lessee, nor can there be a loan from the lessee to the lessor. Last, there must be an expected profit to the lessor from the lease contract, apart from any tax benefits.

The IRS wants to assure itself that the lease contract is not, in effect, a purchase of the asset, for which the lease payments are much more rapid than would be allowed with depreciation under an outright purchase. Because lease payments are deductible for tax purposes, such a contract would allow the lessor effectively to "depreciate" the asset more quickly than allowed under a straight purchase. If the lease contract meets the conditions described, the full lease payment is deductible for tax purposes. If not, the lease is regarded as a conditional sales contract and the tax rules governing a depreciable asset hold.

With leasing, the cost of any land is amortized in the lease payments. By deducting the lease payments as an expense for federal income tax purposes, the lessee is able to effectively write off the original cost of the land. If, instead, the land is purchased, the firm cannot depreciate it for tax purposes. When the value of land represents a significant portion of the asset acquired, lease financing can offer a tax advantage to the firm. Offsetting this tax advantage is the likely residual value of land at the end of the basic lease period. The firm may also gain certain tax advantages in a sale and leaseback arrangement when the assets are sold for less than their depreciated value.

Economic Rationale for Leasing

The principal reason for the existence of leasing is that companies, financial institutions, and individuals derive different tax benefits from owning assets. The marginally profitable company may not be able to reap the full benefit of accelerated depreciation, whereas the high-income taxable corporation or individual is able to realize such. The former may be able to obtain a greater portion of the overall tax benefits by leasing the asset from the latter party as opposed to buying it. Because of competition among lessors, part of the tax benefits may be passed on to the lessee in the form of lower lease payments than would otherwise be the case.

Alternative minimum tax (AMT) An alternative, separate tax calculation based on the taxpayer's regular taxable income, increased by certain tax benefits, collectively referred to as "tax preference items." The taxpayer pays the larger of the regularly determined tax or the AMT.

Another tax disparity has to do with the **alternative minimum tax (AMT).** For a company subject to the AMT, accelerated depreciation is a "tax preference item," whereas a lease payment is not. Such a company may prefer to lease, particularly from another party that pays taxes at a higher effective rate. The greater the divergence in abilities of various parties to realize the tax benefits associated with owning an asset, the greater the attraction of lease financing overall. It is not the existence of taxes per se that gives rise to leasing but divergences in the abilities of various parties to realize the tax benefits.

Another consideration, albeit a minor one, is that lessors enjoy a somewhat superior position in bankruptcy proceedings over what would be the case if they were secured lenders. The riskier the firm that seeks financing, the greater the incentive for the supplier of capital to make the arrangement a lease rather than a loan.

In addition to these reasons, there may be others that explain the existence of lease financing. For one thing, the lessor may enjoy economies of scale in the purchase of assets that are not available to individual lessees. This is particularly true for the purchase of autos and trucks. Also, the lessor may have a different estimate of the life of the asset, its salvage value, or the opportunity cost of funds. Finally, the lessor may be able to provide expertise to its customers in equipment selection and maintenance. Though all of these factors may give rise to leasing, we would not expect them to be nearly as important as the tax reason.

EVALUATING LEASE FINANCING IN RELATION TO DEBT FINANCING

To evaluate whether or not a proposal for lease financing makes economic sense, one should compare the proposal with financing the asset with debt. Whether leasing or borrowing is best will depend on the patterns of cash flows for each financing method and on the opportunity cost of funds. To illustrate a method of analysis, we compare lease financing with debt financing using a hypothetical example.

Take Note

> We assume that the firm has decided to invest in a project on the basis of discounted-cash-flow and required rate of return considerations that were discussed in Part V. In other words, the investment worthiness of the project is evaluated separately from the specific method of financing to be employed. We also assume that the firm has determined an appropriate capital structure and has decided to finance the project with a fixed-cost type of instrument—either debt or lease financing. For our purposes, the relevant comparison is the after-tax cost of debt financing versus that of lease financing. The company will want to use the least costly alternative.

We turn now to examining the two alternatives.

Example for Analysis

Suppose that McNabb Electronics, Inc., wants to acquire a piece of equipment costing $148,000 for use in the fabrication of microprocessors. A leasing company is willing to finance the equipment with a 7-year "true" lease. The terms of the lease call for an annual payment of $26,000. The lease payments are made in advance—that is, at the beginning of each of the seven years. At the end of seven years, the equipment is expected to have a residual value of $30,000. The lessee is responsible for maintenance of the equipment, insurance, and taxes; in short, it is a *net lease*.

Embodied in the lease payments is an implied interest rate to the lessor. The before-tax return to the lessor can be found by solving the following for R:

$$\$148,000 = \sum_{t=0}^{6} \frac{\$26,000}{(1 + R)^t} + \frac{\$30,000}{(1 + R)^7} \tag{21-1}$$

$$= \$26,000 + \$26,000(PVIFA_{R,6}) + \$30,000(PVIF_{R,7}) \tag{21-2}$$

Because these lease payments are made in advance, we solve for the internal rate of return, R, that equates the cost of the asset with one lease payment at time 0, plus the present value of an annuity consisting of six lease payments at the end of each of the next six years, plus the present value of the residual value at the end of year 7. When we solve for R, we find it to be 11.61 percent. If, instead of this return, the lessor wishes a before-tax return of 13 percent, it would need to obtain annual lease payments of X in the following equation:

$$\$148{,}000 = \sum_{t=0}^{6} \frac{X}{(1 + .13)^t} + \frac{\$30{,}000}{(1 + .13)^7}$$

$$\$148{,}000 = X + X(PVIFA_{13\%,6}) + \$30{,}000(PVIF_{13\%,7})$$

$$\$148{,}000 = X + X(3.998) + \$30{,}000(.425)$$

$$\$148{,}000 = X(4.998) + \$12{,}750$$

$$X = (\$148{,}000 - \$12{,}750)/4.998$$

$$X = \mathbf{\$27{,}061}$$

Therefore, the annual lease payment would be $27,061.

If the asset is purchased, McNabb Electronics would finance it with a seven-year term loan at 12 percent. The company is in a 40 percent tax bracket. The asset falls in the five-year property class for modified accelerated cost recovery (depreciation) purposes. Accordingly, the depreciation schedule discussed in Chapter 2 is used:

	YEAR					
	1	2	3	4	5	6
Depreciation	20.00%	32.00%	19.20%	11.52%	11.52%	5.76%

The cost of the asset is then depreciated at these rates, so that first-year depreciation is $.20 \times \$148{,}000 = \mathbf{\$29{,}600}$ and so forth. At the end of the seven years, the equipment is expected to have a salvage value of $30,000. McNabb Electronics is entitled to this residual value, as it would be the owner of the asset under the purchase alternative.

A potential lessee will find it useful to first calculate the before-tax return to the lessor, as we did earlier. This allows you to make a quick comparison with interest rates for other methods of financing. Only if the before-tax return to the lessor is lower than the before-tax cost of borrowing is it usually worthwhile to go on to after-tax calculations. In our example, because the imputed return to the lessor is less than the lessee's borrowing rate (11.61 versus 12 percent), it is appropriate to bring in tax effects and consider alternative discounted after-tax cash flows.

Present Value for Lease Alternative

By comparing the present values of cash outflows for leasing and borrowing, we are able to tell which method of financing should be used. It is simply the one with the *lowest* present value of cash outflows less inflows. Remember that the company will make annual lease payments of $26,000 if the asset is leased. Because these "true" lease payments are an expense, they are deductible for tax purposes, but only in the year for which the payment applies. The $26,000 payment at the end of year 0 represents a prepaid expense and is not deductible for tax purposes until the end of year 1. Similarly, the other six payments are not deductible until the end of the following year.

As leasing is analogous to borrowing, an appropriate discount rate for discounting the after-tax cash flows might be the after-tax cost of borrowing. For our example, the after-tax cost of borrowing is 12 percent times $(1 - .40)$, or 7.2 percent. The reason for using this rate as our discount rate is that the difference in cash flows between lease financing and debt financing involves little risk. Therefore, it is not appropriate to use the company's overall cost of capital, which embodies a risk premium for the firm as a whole, as the discount rate.

Given the foregoing information, we are able to compute the present value of cash flows. The computed figures are shown in the last column of Table 21-1. We see that the present value of the total cash flows under the leasing alternative is $93,509. This figure must then be compared with the present value of cash flows under the borrowing alternative.

Present Value for Borrowing Alternative

If the asset is purchased, McNabb Electronics is assumed to finance it entirely with a 12 percent term loan with a payment schedule being of the same general configuration as the lease payment schedule. In other words, loan payments are assumed to be payable at the beginning, not the end, of each year. This assumption places the loan on a basis roughly equivalent with the lease in terms of the time pattern of cash flows. A loan of $148,000 is taken out at time 0 and is payable over seven years with annual payments of $28,955 at the beginning of each year. The proportion of interest in each payment depends on the unpaid principal amount owing during the year. The principal amount owing during the first year is $148,000 minus the payment at the very start of the year of $28,955, or **$119,045.** The annual interest for the first year is $119,045 × .12 = **$14,285.**[1] As subsequent payments are made, the interest component decreases. Table 21-2 shows these components over time.

To compute the cash outflows after taxes for the debt alternative, we must determine the tax effect.[2] This requires knowing the amounts of annual interest and annual depreciation. Using the modified accelerated cost recovery schedule for the five-year property class listed earlier, we show the annual depreciation charges in column (c) of Table 21-3. Because both depreciation and interest are deductible expenses for tax purposes, they provide tax-shield benefits equal to their sum times the assumed tax rate of 40 percent. This is shown in column (d) of the table. When

---

[1] For ease of illustration, we round to the nearest dollar throughout. This results in the final debt payment in Table 21-2 being slightly less than would otherwise be the case.

[2] We assume for ease of illustration that the firm's regularly determined tax is higher than its AMT. Therefore, the tax-shield benefits of depreciation (a "tax preference item") are not lost (or lowered) through a debt-financed purchase.

TABLE 21-1
Schedule of cash flows for the leasing alternative

END OF YEAR	(a) LEASE PAYMENT	(b) TAX-SHIELD BENEFITS $(a)_{t-1} \times (.40)$	(c) CASH OUTFLOW AFTER TAXES (a) − (b)	(d) PRESENT VALUE OF CASH OUTFLOWS (AT 7.2%)
0	$26,000	—	$26,000	$26,000
1–6	26,000	$10,400	15,600	73,901*
7	—	10,400	(10,400)	(6,392)
				$93,509

*Total for years 1–6.

TABLE 21-2
Schedule of debt payments

END OF YEAR	(a) LOAN PAYMENT	(b) PRINCIPAL AMOUNT OWING AT END OF YEAR $(b)_{t-1} - (a) + (c)$	(c) ANNUAL INTEREST $(b)_{t-1} \times (.12)$
0	$28,955	$119,045	—
1	28,955	104,375	$14,285
2	28,955	87,945	12,525
3	28,955	69,543	10,553
4	28,955	48,933	8,345
5	28,955	25,850	5,872
6	28,952*	0	3,102

*The last payment is slightly lower due to rounding throughout.

these benefits are deducted from the debt payment, we obtain the cash outflow after taxes at the end of each year, shown in column (e). At the end of the seventh year, the asset is expected to have a salvage value of $30,000. This *recapture of depreciation* is subject to the corporate tax rate of 40 percent for the company, which leaves an expected after-tax cash inflow of $18,000. Finally we compute the present value of all of these cash flows at a 7.2 percent discount rate and find that they total $87,952.

This present value of cash outflow for the debt alternative, $87,952, is less than that for the lease alternative, which is $93,509. Therefore, the analysis suggests that the company use debt as opposed to lease financing in acquiring the use of the asset.

TABLE 21-3
Schedule of cash flows for the debt alternative

END OF YEAR	(a) LOAN PAYMENT	(b) ANNUAL INTEREST	(c) ANNUAL DEPRECIATION	(d) TAX-SHIELD BENEFITS $[(b) + (c)] \times (.40)$	(e) CASH OUTFLOWS AFTER TAXES $(a) - (d)$	(f) PRESENT VALUE OF CASH OUTFLOWS (AT 7.2%)
0	$ 28,955	$ 0	$ 0	$ 0	$28,955	$28,955
1	28,955	14,285	29,600	17,554	11,401	10,635
2	28,955	12,525	47,360	23,954	5,001	4,352
3	28,955	10,553	28,416	15,588	13,367	10,851
4	28,955	8,345	17,050	10,158	18,797	14,233
5	28,955	5,872	17,050	9,169	19,786	13,976
6	28,952	3,102	8,524	4,650	24,303	16,013
7	(30,000)*	0	0	(12,000)**	(18,000)	(11,064)
			$148,000			$87,952

*Salvage value.
**Tax due to recapture of depreciation, $30,000 × .40 = $12,000.

This conclusion arises despite the fact that the implicit interest rate embodied in the lease payments, 11.61 percent, is less than the explicit cost of debt financing, 12 percent. However, if the asset is bought, the company is able to avail itself of modified accelerated cost recovery depreciation, and this helps the situation from a present value standpoint. Moreover, the residual value at the end of the project is a favorable factor, whereas this value goes to the lessor with lease financing.

Another factor that favors the debt alternative is the deductibility of interest payments for tax purposes. Because the amount of interest embodied in a "mortgage-type" debt payment is higher at first and declines with successive payments, the tax benefits associated with these payments follow the same pattern over time. From a present value standpoint, this pattern benefits the firm relative to the pattern of lease payments, which are typically constant over time.

Other Considerations

The decision to borrow rests on the relative timing and magnitude of cash flows under the two financing alternatives, as well as on the discount rate employed. We have assumed that the cash flows are known with relative certainty. This is reasonable for the most part, but there is some uncertainty that, on occasion, can be important. The estimated salvage (residual) value of an asset is usually subject to considerable uncertainty, for example.

Take Note

> Because of the uncertainty surrounding an asset's salvage value, one can make an argument for discounting the net salvage value at a rate higher than the firm's after-tax cost of debt. For example, some leasing experts suggest using the firm's cost of capital as a more appropriate discount rate for salvage value flows under the buy/borrow alternative.
>
> In our example (see Table 21-3), applying a discount rate higher than the firm's after-tax cost of debt (i.e., 7.2 percent) to the net salvage value would increase the present value of the net cash outflows for the debt alternative, making buy/borrow less attractive. However, we would prefer lease financing to debt financing in our example only if the discount rate chosen for the net salvage value exceeded roughly 18.4 percent.

As we can see, deciding between leasing and borrowing can involve some rather extensive calculations. Each situation requires a separate analysis. The analysis is complicated if the two alternatives involve different amounts of financing. If we finance less than the total cost of the asset by borrowing but finance 100 percent of the cost by leasing, we must consider the difference in the amount of financing, both from the standpoint of explicit as well as implicit costs. These considerations and the others mentioned throughout this chapter can make the evaluation of lease financing rather detailed.

The Importance of the Tax Rate

Lease-versus-borrow analyses are very sensitive to the tax rate of the potential lessee. If the effective tax rate is 20 percent instead of the 40 percent in our previous example, the present value comparison changes. The tax-shield benefits are lower and the discount rate—the after-tax cost of borrowing—higher, that is, $12\% (1 - .20) = \mathbf{9.6\%}.$

By reworking the figures in Tables 21-1 and 21-3, we can determine that these two changes result in the present value of cash outflows for the lease alternative being $114,924 and for the debt alternative $112,261. The debt alternative still dominates but by a lesser margin than before. At a zero tax rate and using the full 12 percent as the discount rate, the present value of cash outflows for the lease alternative is $132,897 versus $134,430 for the debt alternative. The lease alternative now dominates by a slight margin.

The important lesson of these examples is that the tax rate of the lessee matters a lot. In general, as the effective tax rate declines, the relative advantage of debt versus lease financing declines. This explains why lease financing usually is attractive only to those in low or zero tax brackets who are unable to enjoy the full tax benefits associated with owning an asset. By leasing from a party in a high tax bracket, the lessee may be able to get part of the tax benefits of ownership because lease payments are lower than they otherwise would be. How much lower depends on the supply and demand conditions in the leasing industry. The exact sharing of the tax benefits is negotiable, and it depends on the competitive situation at the time.

For all practical purposes, the leasing industry in the United States is an artifact of the tax laws. As these laws change, the industry is impacted, often in dramatic ways. Parties that financed via the leasing route may no longer do so, while others may find it attractive. Previous lessors may step out of the business, whereas others may be able to serve this role to advantage. The greater the change in laws affecting asset write-offs, tax rates, and alternative minimum taxes, the greater the disequilibrium, and the longer the equilibration process as parties exit or enter the market as either lessors or lessees. One thing is clear: Taxes have a dominant influence on the leasing industry.

SUMMARY

- A *term loan* represents debt originally scheduled for repayment in more than 1 year but generally in less than 10 years.
- Commercial banks, insurance companies, and other institutional investors make term loans to business firms. Banks also provide financing under a *revolving credit agreement,* which represents a formal commitment on the part of the bank to lend up to a certain amount of money over a specified period of time.
- Lenders who offer unsecured credit usually impose restrictions on the borrower. These restrictions are called protective *covenants* and are contained in a *loan agreement.* If the borrower defaults under any of the provisions of the loan agreement, the lender may initiate immediate corrective measures.
- On a secured basis, firms can obtain intermediate-term financing by pledging equipment that they own or are purchasing. Banks, finance companies, and sellers of the equipment are active in providing this type of secured financing.
- In lease financing, the lessee (the renter) agrees to pay the lessor (the owner), periodically, for eco-

nomic use of the lessor's asset. Because of this contractual obligation, leasing is regarded as a method of financing similar to borrowing.
- An *operating lease* is a short-term lease that is often cancellable; a *financial lease* is a long-term lease that is not cancellable.
- A financial lease can involve the acquisition of an asset under a *direct lease,* a *sale and leaseback* arrangement, or a *leveraged lease.*
- One of the principal economic reasons for leasing is the inability of a firm to utilize all the tax benefits associated with the ownership of an asset. This can arise because of (1) unprofitable operations, (2) the provisions of the alternative minimum tax (AMT), or (3) insufficient earnings to effectively utilize all of the possible tax benefits.
- A common means used for analyzing lease financing in relation to debt financing is to discount to present value the after-tax net cash flows under each alternative. The preferred financing alternative is the one that provides the lower present value of cash outflows.

Appendix

Accounting Treatment of Leases

FASB 13 Statement issued by the Financial Accounting Standards Board (FASB) establishing financial accounting standards for lessees and lessors.

The accounting treatment of leases has undergone sweeping change over the past three decades. At one time leases were not disclosed in financial statements at all. Gradually lease disclosure was required and appeared first in the footnotes to the financial statements. With only minimal disclosure, leasing was attractive to certain firms as an "off-balance-sheet" method of financing. There is, however, no evidence that such financing had a favorable effect on company valuation, all other things the same. Nevertheless, many companies proceeded on the assumption that "off-balance-sheet" financing was a good thing. Then came the Financial Accounting Standards Board Statement No. 13 (called **FASB 13**) in 1976 with an explicit ruling that called for the capitalization on the balance sheet of certain types of leases.[3] In essence, this statement says that if the lessee acquires essentially all of the economic benefits and risks of the leased property, then the value of the asset along with the corresponding lease liability must be shown on the lessee's balance sheet.

CAPITAL AND OPERATING LEASES

Leases that conform in principle to this definition are called *capital leases*. More specifically, a lease is regarded as a capital lease if it meets one or more of the following conditions:

1. The lease transfers ownership of the asset to the lessee by the end of the lease period.
2. The lease contains an option to purchase the asset at a bargain price.
3. The lease period equals 75 percent or more of the estimated economic life of the asset.
4. At the beginning of the lease, the present value of the minimum lease payments equals 90 percent or more of the fair market value of the leased asset.[4]

If any of these conditions is met, the lessee is said to have acquired most of the economic benefits and risks associated with the leased property. Therefore, a capital lease is involved. If a lease does not meet any of these conditions, it is classified (for accounting purposes) as an *operating lease*.[5] Essentially, operating leases give the lessee the right to use the leased property over a period of time, but they do not give the lessee all of the benefits and risks that are associated with the asset.

Recording the Value of a Capital Lease. With a capital lease, the lessee must report the value of the leased property on the asset side of the balance sheet. The amount reflected is the present value of the minimum lease payments over the lease period. If executory costs, such as insurance, maintenance, and taxes, are a part of the total lease payment, these are deducted, and only the remainder is used for purposes of calculating the present value. As required by the accounting rules, the discount rate employed is the lower of (1) the lessee's incremental borrowing rate, or (2) the rate of interest implicit in the lease if, in fact, that rate can be determined.

---

[3]*Statement of Financial Accounting Standards No. 13, Accounting for Leases* (Stamford, CT: Financial Accounting Standards Board, November 1976).

[4]The discount rate used to determine the present value is generally the *lessee's incremental borrowing rate.* The FASB defines this as the before-tax interest rate that the lessee would have incurred to borrow the funds necessary to buy the leased asset using a secured loan with repayment terms similar to the payment schedule called for in the lease.

[5]Earlier in this chapter, we used the term *operating lease* to describe a short-term lease. Accountants, however, would also apply this term to any (long-term) financial lease that did not technically qualify to be considered a capital lease.

The present value of the lease payments should be recorded as an asset on the lessee's balance sheet. (If the fair market value of the leased property is lower than the present value of the minimum lease payments, then the fair market value would be shown.) A corresponding liability is also recorded on the balance sheet, with the present value of payments due within one year being reflected as current liabilities and the present value of payments due after one year being shown as noncurrent liabilities. Information on leased property may be combined with similar information on assets that are owned, but there must be a disclosure in a footnote with respect to the value of the leased property and its amortization. The capital-lease-related portions of a hypothetical balance sheet might look like the following:

ASSETS		LIABILITIES	
Gross fixed assets[a]	$3,000,000	Current	
Less: accumulated depreciation and amortization	1,000,000	Obligations under capital leases	$ 90,000
		Noncurrent	
Net fixed assets	$2,000,000	Obligations under capital leases	$270,000

[a]Gross fixed assets include leased property of $500,000. Accumulated depreciation and amortization includes $140,000 in amortization associated with such property.

Here we see in the footnote to the balance sheet information that the capitalized value of leases of the company is $500,000 less $140,000 in amortization, or $360,000 in total. The liability is split between $90,000 in current liabilities and $270,000 due beyond one year. In addition to this information, more details are required in footnotes. Relevant information here includes the gross amounts of leased property by major property categories (these can be combined with categories of owned assets); the total future minimum lease payments; a schedule, by years, of future lease payments required over the next five years; the total minimum sublease rentals to be received; the existence and terms of purchase or renewal options and escalation clauses; rentals that are contingent on some factor other than the passage of time; and any restrictions imposed in the lease agreements.

Disclosure of Operating Leases.   For operating leases, as for capital leases, some of the same disclosure is required, but it can be in footnotes. For noncancellable leases having remaining terms in excess of one year, the lessee must disclose total future minimum lease payments; a schedule, by year, for the next five years plus a total figure for all years thereafter; the total sublease rentals to be received; the basis for contingent rental payments; the existence and terms of purchase and renewal options and escalation clauses; and any lease agreement restrictions. The last two categories are included in a general description of the leasing arrangement.

AMORTIZING THE CAPITAL LEASE AND REDUCING THE OBLIGATION

A capital lease must be amortized and the liability reduced over the lease period. The method of amortization can be the lessee's usual depreciation method for assets that are owned. It should be pointed out that the period of amortization is always the lease term even if the economic life of the asset is longer. If the economic life is longer, the asset would have an expected residual value, which would go to the lessor. FASB 13 also requires that the capital lease obligation be reduced and expensed over the lease period by the "interest method." Under this method, each lease payment is separated into two components—the payment of principal and the payment of interest. The obligation is reduced by just the amount of the principal payment.

Reporting Earnings. For income reporting purposes, FASB 13 requires that both the amortization of the leased property and the annual interest embodied in the capital lease payment be treated as an expense. This expense is then deducted in the same way that any expense is to obtain net income. As you can appreciate, the accounting for leases can become quite complicated.

QUESTIONS

1. What reasons can you cite for a firm's use of intermediate-term debt? Why isn't (a) long-term debt substituted in its place? (b) short-term debt substituted in its place?
2. Why do insurance companies not compete more actively with banks to provide short- and intermediate-term financing?
3. What is the purpose of protective covenants in a term loan agreement?
4. How does a *revolving credit agreement* differ from a *line of credit?*
5. How should a lender go about setting (a) the working capital protective covenant in a loan agreement? (b) the capital expenditure covenant in a loan agreement?
6. As a borrower, how would you approach negotiating the working capital and capital expenditure restrictions a lender wished to impose?
7. What are the key financial institutions that provide intermediate-term financing to business firms?
8. How does a *chattel mortgage* differ from a *conditional sales contract* when it comes to financing equipment?
9. Chapter 1 suggests that the decision-making processes of investing in assets (buying assets) and of financing assets (raising funds) are two separate and distinct functions of the financial manager. This chapter suggests that, at least in the case of leasing, the decision-making processes cannot be separated. Discuss the problems raised by this sort of situation.
10. How does a *financial lease* differ from an *operating lease?* How does a *full-service (or maintenance) lease* differ from a *net lease?*
11. Contrast a *sale and leaseback* with *direct leasing.*
12. In general, how is lease financing treated from an accounting standpoint versus debt financing?
13. Discuss the probable impact that a sale and leaseback arrangement will have on the following:
    a. Liquidity ratios
    b. Return on investment
    c. Return on equity
    d. The risk class of the corporation's common stock
    e. The price of the corporation's common stock
14. Some business people consider that the risk of obsolescence and inflexibility is being transferred from the lessee to the lessor. How is the lessor induced to accept higher risk and greater inflexibility?
15. In your opinion, would the following factors tend to favor borrowing or leasing as a financing alternative? Why?
    a. Increased corporate tax rate
    b. Faster accelerated depreciation
    c. Rising price level
    d. Increased residual value of the leased asset
    e. An increase in the risk-free interest rate

SELF-CORRECTION PROBLEMS

1. Burger Rex is expanding its chain of fast-food outlets. This program will require a capital expenditure of $3 million, which must be financed. The company has settled on a three-year revolving credit of $3 million, which may be converted into a three-year term loan at the expiration of the revolving credit commitment. The commitment fee for both credit arrangements is .5 percent of the unused portions. The bank has quoted Burger Rex an interest rate of 1 percent over prime for the revolving credit and 1.5 percent over prime for the term loan, if that option is taken. The company expects to borrow $1.4 million at the outset and another $1.6 million at the very end of the first year. At the expiration of the revolving credit, the company expects to take down the full-term loan. At the end of each of the fourth, fifth, and sixth years, it expects to make principal payments of $1 million.
   a. For each of the next six years, what is the expected commitment fee in dollars?
   b. What is the expected dollar interest cost above the prime rate?

2. Assuming that annual lease payments are made in advance (an annuity due) and that there is no residual value, solve for the unknown in each of the following situations:
   a. For a purchase price of $46,000, an implicit interest rate of 11 percent, and a 6-year lease period, solve for the annual lease payment.
   b. For a purchase price of $210,000, a five-year lease period, and annual lease payments of $47,030, solve for the implied interest rate.
   c. For an implied interest rate of 8 percent, a seven-year lease period, and annual lease payments of $16,000, solve for the purchase price.
   d. For a purchase price of $165,000, an implied interest rate of 10 percent, and annual lease payments of $24,412, solve for the lease period.

3. U.S. Blivet wishes to acquire a $100,000 blivet-degreasing machine, which it plans to use for eight years. At the end of this time, the machine's residual value will be $24,000. The asset falls into the five-year property class for cost recovery (depreciation) purposes. The company can use either a "true" lease or debt financing. Lease payments of $16,000 at the beginning of each of the eight years would be required. If debt financed, the interest rate would be 14 percent, and debt payments would be due at the beginning of each of the eight years. (Interest would be amortized as a mortgage-type of debt instrument.) The company is in a 40 percent tax bracket. Which method of financing has the lower present value of cash outflows?

PROBLEMS

1. Eva Forlines Fashions Corporation wishes to borrow $600,000 on a five-year term basis. Cattleperson's National Bank is willing to make such a loan at a 14 percent rate, provided the loan is completely amortized over the five-year period. Payments are due at the end of each of the five years. Set up an amortization schedule of equal annual loan payments that will satisfy these conditions. Be sure to show both the principal and interest components of each of the overall payments.

2. On January 1, Acme Aglet Corporation is contemplating a four-year, $3 million term loan from the Fidelity First National Bank. The loan is payable at the end of the fourth year and would involve a loan agreement that would contain a

number of protective covenants. Among these restrictions are that the company must maintain net working capital (current assets minus current liabilities) of at least $3 million at all times, that it cannot take on any more long-term debt, that its total liabilities cannot be more than .6 of its total assets, and that capital expenditures in any year are limited to depreciation plus $3 million. The company's balance sheet at December 31, before the term loan, is as follows (in millions):

Current assets	$ 7	Current liabilities	$ 3
Net fixed assets	10	Long-term debt (due in 8 years)	5
		Shareholders' equity	9
Total	$17	Total	$17

The proceeds of the term loan will be used to increase Acme Aglet's investment in inventories and accounts receivables in response to introducing a new "fit-to-be-tied" metal aglet. The company anticipates a subsequent need to grow at a rate of 24 percent a year, equally divided between current assets and net fixed assets. Profits after taxes of $1.5 million are expected this year, and these profits are expected to grow by $250,000 per year over the subsequent three years. The company pays no cash dividends and does not intend to pay any over the next four years. Depreciation in the past year was $2.5 million, and this is predicted to grow over the next four years at the same rate as the increase in net fixed assets.

Under the loan agreement, will the company be able to achieve its growth objective? Explain numerically.

3. Given the following information, compute the annual lease payment (paid in advance) that a lessor will require:

   a. Purchase price of $260,000, interest rate of 13 percent, 5-year lease period, and no residual value

   b. Purchase price of $138,000, interest rate of 6 percent, 9-year lease period, and a near-certain residual value of $20,000

   c. Purchase price of $773,000, interest rate of 9 percent, 10-year lease period, and no residual value

4. Volt Electronics Company is considering leasing one of its products in addition to selling it outright to customers. The product, the Volt Tester, sells for $18,600 and has an economic life of eight years.

   a. To earn 12 percent interest, what annual lease payment must Volt require as lessor? (Assume that lease payments are payable in advance.)

   b. If the product has a salvage value (known with relative certainty) of $4,000 at the end of eight years, what annual lease payment will be required?

5. Fez Fabulous Fabrics wishes to acquire a $100,000 multifacet cutting machine. The machine is expected to be used for eight years, after which there is a $20,000 expected residual value. If Fez were to finance the cutting machine by signing an eight-year "true" lease contract, annual lease payments of $16,000 would be required, payable in advance. The company could also finance the purchase of the machine with a 12 percent term loan having a payment schedule of the same general configuration as the lease payment schedule. The asset falls in the five-year property class for cost recovery (depreciation) purposes, and the company has a 35 percent tax rate. What is the present value of cash outflows for each of these alternatives, using the after-tax cost of debt as the discount rate? Which alternative is preferred?

6. Valequez Ranches, Inc., wishes to use a new truck fueled by compressed natural gas that costs $80,000. The ranch intends to operate the truck for five years, at the end of which time it is expected to have a $16,000 residual value. Assume that the asset falls in the three-year property class for modified accelerated cost recovery (depreciation) purposes, and that Valequez Ranches is in a 30 percent tax bracket. Two means of financing the new truck are available. A five-year, "net lease" arrangement calls for annual lease payments of $17,000, payable in advance. A debt alternative carries an interest cost of 10 percent. Debt payments will be made at the start of each of the five years using a mortgage-type of debt amortization. Using the present value of cash outflows method, determine the best financing alternative.

Appendix Problem

7. The Locke Corporation has just leased a metal-bending machine that calls for annual lease payments of $30,000 payable in advance. The lease period is six years, and the lease is classified as a capital lease for accounting purposes. The company's incremental borrowing rate is 11 percent, whereas the lessor's implicit interest rate is 12 percent. Amortization of the lease in the first year amounts to $16,332. On the basis of this information, compute the following:

   a. The accounting lease liability that will be shown on the balance sheet immediately after the first lease payment.

   b. The annual lease expense (amortization plus interest) in the first year as it will appear on the accounting income statement. [The interest expense is based on the accounting value determined in Part (a).]

SOLUTIONS TO SELF-CORRECTION PROBLEMS

1. a. b. (in thousands)

| | YEAR | | | | | |
| | REVOLVING CREDIT | | | TERM LOAN | | |
	1	2	3	4	5	6
Amount borrowed during year	$1,400	$3,000	$3,000	$3,000	$2,000	$1,000
Unused portion	1,600	0	0	0	1,000	2,000
Commitment fee (.005)	8	0	0	0	5	10
Interest cost above prime (1% first 3 years and 1.5% in last 3)	14	30	30	45	30	15

2. A generalized version of Eq. (21-2) as the formula is used throughout.

   a. $\$46,000 = X + X(PVIFA_{11\%,5})$

$$\$46,000 = X + X(3.696) = X(4.696)$$

$$X = \$46,000/4.696 = \mathbf{\$9,796}$$

   b. $\$210,000 = \$47,030/(1 + PVIFA_{X,5})$

$$\$210,000/\$47,030 = (1 + PVIFA_{X,5}) = 4.465$$

Subtracting 1 from this gives $PVIFA_{X,5} = 3.465$. Looking in Table IV (in the Appendix at the end of the book) across the *4-period row*, we find that 3.465 is the figure reported for 6 percent. Therefore, the implied interest rate, X, is *6 percent.*

c. $X = \$16,000(1 + PVIFA_{8\%,6})$
$X = \$16,000(1 + 4.623) = \textbf{\$89,968}$

d. $\$165,000 = \$24,412(1 + PVIFA_{10\%,X})$
$\$165,000/\$24,412 = (1 + PVIFA_{10\%,X}) = 6.759$

Subtracting 1 from this gives 5.759. Looking in Table IV in the *10% column,* we find that 5.759 corresponds to the *9-period row.* Therefore, the lease period is 9 + 1, or *10 years.*

3.

SCHEDULE OF CASH FLOWS FOR THE LEASING ALTERNATIVE

END OF YEAR	(a) LEASE PAYMENT	(b) TAX-SHIELD BENEFITS $(a)_{t-1} \times (.40)$	(c) CASH OUTFLOW AFTER TAXES $(a) - (b)$	(d) PRESENT VALUE OF CASH OUTFLOWS (AT 8.4%)
0	$16,000	—	$16,000	$16,000
1–7	16,000	$6,400	9,600	49,305*
8	—	6,400	(6,400)	(3,357)
				$61,948

*Total for years 1–7

The discount rate is the before-tax cost of borrowing times 1 minus the tax rate, or (14 percent)(1 − .40) = 8.4%.
Annual debt payment:

$$\$100,000 = X(1 + PVIFA_{14\%,7})$$

$$\$100,000 = X(1 + 4.288) = X(5.288)$$

$$X = \$100,000/5.288 = \$18,910$$

SCHEDULE OF DEBT PAYMENTS

END OF YEAR	(a) LOAN PAYMENT	(b) PRINCIPAL AMOUNT OWING AT END OF YEAR $(b)_{t-1} - (a) + (c)$	(c) ANNUAL INTEREST $(b)_{t-1} \times (.14)$
0	$18,910	$81,090	—
1	18,910	73,533	$11,353
2	18,910	64,917	10,295
3	18,910	55,096	9,088
4	18,910	43,899	7,713
5	18,910	31,135	6,146
6	18,910	16,584	4,359
7	18,906*	0	2,322

*The last payment is slightly lower due to rounding throughout.

SCHEDULE OF CASH FLOWS FOR THE DEBT ALTERNATIVE

	(a)	(b)	(c)	(d)	(e)	(f)
END OF YEAR	DEBT PAYMENT	ANNUAL INTEREST	ANNUAL DEPRECIATION	TAX-SHIELD BENEFITS (b + c).40	AFTER-TAX CASH FLOW (a) − (d)	PV OF CASH FLOWS (AT 8.4%)
0	$18,910	$ 0	$ 0	$ 0	$18,910	$18,910
1	18,910	11,353	20,000	12,541	6,369	5,875
2	18,910	10,295	32,000	16,918	1,992	1,695
3	18,910	9,088	19,200	11,315	7,595	5,962
4	18,910	7,713	11,520	7,693	11,217	8,124
5	18,910	6,146	11,520	7,066	11,844	7,913
6	18,910	4,359	5,760	4,048	14,862	9,160
7	18,906	2,322		929	17,977	10,222
8	(24,000)*			(9,600)**	(14,400)	(7,553)
			$100,000			$60,308

*Salvage value.
**Tax due to recapture of depreciation, ($24,000)(.40) = $9,600.

Because the lease alternative has the higher present value of cash outflows, it is preferred. However, some would argue that we should apply a discount rate higher than the lessee's after-tax cost of debt (i.e., 8.4 percent) to the residual value because of the greater uncertainty to this cash flow. A discount rate of roughly 11.8 percent* or more—applied to the residual value—would now make the present value of cash outflows greater for the debt alternative than for the leasing alternative. In this situation, we would prefer the leasing alternative.

---

*For the present value of cash outflows for the leasing alternative ($61,948) to be less than the present value of cash outflows for the debt alternative ([$60,309 + $7,553] − [$14,400/(1 + X)^8]), the discount rate (X) must be roughly 11.8 percent or more.

SELECTED REFERENCES

Arnold, Jasper H., III. "How to Negotiate a Term Loan." *Harvard Business Review* 60 (March–April, 1982), 131–38.

Bierman, Harold, Jr. "Buy Versus Lease with an Alternative Minimum Tax." *Financial Management* 20 (Autumn 1991), 96–107.

Bobsin, Janet L. "The Medium-Term Note Market Comes of Age." *Treasury & Risk Management* (January–February 1996), 6.

Bower, Richard S. "Issues in Lease Financing." *Financial Management* 2 (Winter 1973), 25–34.

———, and George S. Oldfield Jr. "Of Lessees, Lessors, and Discount Rates and Whether Pigs Have Wings." *Journal of Business Research* 9 (March 1981), 29–38.

Bower, Richard S., Frank C. Herringer, and J. Peter Williamson. "Lease Evaluation." *Accounting Review* 41 (April 1966), 257–65.

Crabbe, Leland. "Corporate Medium-Term Notes." *Journal of Applied Corporate Finance* 4 (Winter 1992), 90–102.

———. "Anatomy of the Medium-Term Note Market." *Federal Reserve Bulletin* 79 (August 1993), 751–68.

GE Capital: Our Business Is Helping Yours Find Its Way Through the Leasing Maze. Stamford, CT: General Electric Capital Corporation, 1999.

Gill, Richard C. "Term Loan Agreements." *Journal of Commercial Bank Lending* 62 (February 1980), 22–27.

Hull, John C. "The Bargaining Positions of the Parties to a Lease Agreement." *Financial Management* 11 (Autumn 1982), 71–79.

Lease, Ronald C., John J. McConnell, and James S. Shallheim. "Realized Returns and the Default and Prepayment Experience of Financial Leasing Contracts." *Financial Management* 19 (Summer 1990), 11–20.

Lummer, Scott L., and John J. McConnell. "Further Evidence on the Bank Lending Process and the Capital-Market Response to Bank Loan Agreements." *Journal of Financial Economics* 25 (November 1989), 99–122.

McConnell, John J., and James S. Schallheim. "Valuation of Asset Leasing Contracts." *Journal of Financial Economics* 12 (August 1983), 237–61.

McDaniel, Morey W. "Are Negative Pledge Clauses in Public Debt Issues Obsolete?" *Business Lawyer* 38 (May 1983), 867–81.

Miller, Merton H., and Charles W. Upton. "Leasing, Buying, and the Cost of Capital Services." *Journal of Finance* 31 (June 1976), 787–98.

Mukherjee, Tarun K. "A Survey of Corporate Leasing Analysis." *Financial Management* 20 (Autumn 1991), 96–107.

Myers, Stewart C., David A. Dill, and Alberto J. Bautista. "Valuation of Financial Lease Contracts." *Journal of Finance* 31 (June 1976), 799–820.

Schallheim, James S. *Lease or Buy? Principles for Sound Decision Making.* Boston, MA: Harvard Business School Press, 1994.

Slovin, Myron B., Marie E. Sushka, and John A. Polonchek. "Corporate Sale-and-Leasebacks and Shareholder Wealth." *Journal of Finance* 45 (March 1990), 289–99.

Van Horne, James. "A Linear-Programming Approach to Evaluating Restrictions under a Bond Indenture or Loan Agreement." *Journal of Financial and Quantitative Analysis* 1 (June 1966), 68–83.

———. "The Cost of Leasing with Capital Market Imperfections." *The Engineering Economist* 23 (Fall 1977), 1–12.

Weingartner, H. Martin. "Leasing, Asset Lives and Uncertainty: Guides to Decision Making." *Financial Management* 16 (Summer 1987), 5–12.

Chapter 22

Convertibles, Exchangeables, and Warrants

CONVERTIBLE SECURITIES
   Conversion Price and Conversion Ratio • Conversion Value and
      Premium Over Conversion Value • Other Features • Financing
      with Convertibles • Forcing or Stimulating Conversion
VALUE OF CONVERTIBLE SECURITIES
   Debt-Plus-Option Characteristic • Straight Bond Value
      • Premiums • Relationships Among Premiums
EXCHANGEABLE BONDS
   Features • Use in Financing • Valuation of an Exchangeable
WARRANTS
   Features • Valuation of a Warrant • Premium Over Theoretical
      Value • Relationship Between Values
SUMMARY
APPENDIX: OPTION PRICING
QUESTIONS
SELF-CORRECTION PROBLEMS
PROBLEMS
SOLUTIONS TO SELF-CORRECTION PROBLEMS
SELECTED REFERENCES

You pays your money and you takes your choice.

—PUNCH

Straight debt (or equity)

Debt (or equity) that cannot be exchanged for another asset.

In addition to **straight debt** and **equity** instruments, a company may finance with an *option,* a contract giving its holder the right to buy common stock or to exchange something for it within a specific period of time. As a result, the value of the option instrument is strongly influenced by changes in value of the stock. Options belong to a broad category of financial instruments known as **derivative securities.** In this chapter we consider three specific types of options employed by business firms in their financing—the convertible security, the exchangeable bond, and the warrant. In the Appendix to the chapter, a detailed discussion of option pricing theory appears.

CONVERTIBLE SECURITIES

Derivative security A financial contract whose value derives in part from the value and characteristics of one or more underlying assets (e.g., securities, commodities), interest rates, exchange rates, or indices.

Convertible security A bond or a preferred stock that is convertible into a specified number of shares of common stock at the option of the holder.

Conversion price The price per share at which common stock will be exchanged for a convertible security. It is equal to the face value of the convertible security divided by the conversion ratio.

Conversion ratio The number of shares of common stock into which a convertible security can be converted. It is equal to the face value of the convertible security divided by the conversion price.

Conversion value The value of the convertible security in terms of the common stock into which the security can be converted. It is equal to the conversion ratio times the current market price per share of the common stock.

A **convertible security** is a bond or share of preferred stock that can be converted at the option of the holder into common stock of the same corporation. The convertible security gives the investor a fixed return from a bond or a specified dividend from preferred stock. In addition, the investor receives an option on the common stock. Because of this option, the company can sell the convertible security at a lower yield than it would have to pay on a straight bond or preferred stock issue.

Conversion Price and Conversion Ratio

The ratio of exchange between the convertible security and the common stock can be stated in terms of either a **conversion price** or a **conversion ratio.** Suppose McKesson Corporation's 9.75 percent convertible subordinated debentures ($1,000 face value) have a conversion price of $43.75, meaning that each debenture is convertible into 22.86 shares of common stock. We simply divide the face value of the security ($1,000) by the conversion price ($43.75) to obtain the conversion ratio, **22.86 shares.** This is the number of shares of common stock an investor will receive upon converting each convertible debenture.

The conversion terms are not necessarily constant over time. Some convertible issues provide for increases or "step-ups" in the conversion price at periodic intervals. For example, a $1,000-face-value bond might have a conversion price of $40 a share for the first five years, $45 a share for the second five years, $50 for the third five years, and so on. In this way, the bond converts into fewer shares of common stock as time goes by. Usually, the conversion price is adjusted for any stock splits or stock dividends that occur after the securities are sold. If the common stock were split 2 for 1, the conversion price would be halved. This provision protects the convertible bondholder and is known as an *antidilution clause.*

Conversion Value and Premium Over Conversion Value

The **conversion value** of a convertible security is the conversion ratio of the security times the market price per share of the common stock. If McKesson stock were selling for $50, the conversion value of one convertible subordinated debenture would be $22.86 \times \$50 = \$1,143.$

At the time of issuance, the convertible security will be priced higher than its conversion value. The differential is known as the premium over conversion value. The McKesson convertible subordinated debentures were sold to the public for $1,000 a bond. The market price of the common stock at the time of issuance of the convertibles was approximately $38.50 per share. Therefore, the conversion value of

Part VIII Special Areas of Financial Management

Premium over conversion value The market price of a convertible security minus its conversion value; also called *conversion premium*.

each bond was 22.86 × $38.50 = **$880,** and the differential of $120 between this value and the $1,000 issuing price represented the **premium over conversion value**. Frequently, this premium is expressed as a percentage of the conversion value. In our example the conversion premium is $120 divided by $880, or **13.6 percent.** For most issues of convertibles, the conversion premium ranges from 10 to 20 percent. For a growth company, the conversion premium can be in the upper part of this range, or perhaps even higher in the case of "super-growth." For companies with more moderate growth, the conversion premium may be closer to 10 percent. The range itself is established mainly by market tradition, in keeping with the idea that the issuer should be in a position to force conversion within a reasonable period of time. (Forcing conversion will be illustrated shortly.)

Almost without exception, convertible securities provide for a *call price*. As was true with the straight bond or preferred stock, the call feature enables the corporation to call the security for redemption. Few convertible securities, however, are ever redeemed. Instead, the purpose of the call is usually to force conversion when the conversion value of the security is significantly above its call price.

Other Features

Almost all convertible bond issues are subordinated to other creditors. That fact permits the lender to treat convertible subordinated debt or convertible preferred stock as a part of the equity base when evaluating the financial condition of the issuer. In the event of liquidation, it makes no difference to the creditor if the issue is actually converted. In either case, the lender has a prior claim.

Dilution A decrease in the proportional claim on earnings and assets of a share of common stock because of the issuance of additional shares.

Investors in a company's common stock tend to recognize the potential **dilution** in their position before actual conversion takes place. For accounting reporting purposes, a company with convertible securities or warrants outstanding is required to report earnings per share in such a way that the reader of the financial statement can visualize the potential dilution. More specifically, it must report earnings per share on two bases. The first is *basic earnings per share,* where earnings per share is based on only outstanding common stock. The second is *diluted earnings per share,* where earnings per share is calculated "as if" all potentially dilutive securities were converted or exercised. For companies with sizable financing involving potentially dilutive securities, the difference between the two earnings per share figures can be substantial.

Financing with Convertibles

In many cases, convertible securities are employed as "deferred" common stock financing. Technically, these securities represent debt or preferred stock, but in essence they are delayed common stock. Companies that issue convertibles expect them to be converted in the future.

Dilution. By selling a convertible security instead of common stock, companies create less dilution in earnings per share, both now and in the future. The reason is that the conversion price on a convertible security is higher than the issuing price on a new issue of common stock.

The current market price of the common stock of the mythical ABC Corporation is $40 per share. If the company raises capital with an issue of common stock, it will have to underprice the issue to sell it in the market. The company can sell the stock through underwriters and thus realize net proceeds of $36 per share. If the company wishes to raise $18 million, the issue will involve 500,000 shares of additional stock.

On the other hand, if ABC Corporation sells a convertible issue, it is able to set the conversion price above the current market price per share. If the conversion premium is 15 percent, the conversion price will be $46 per share. Assuming an $18 million issue of convertibles, the number of shares of additional common stock after conversion will be

$$\frac{\$18 \text{ million}}{\$46} = \textbf{391,305}$$

We see that potential dilution with a convertible issue is less than that with a common stock issue because 500,000 minus 391,305 leaves **108,695** fewer shares to be added.

Financing Costs. Another advantage to the company in using convertible securities is that the interest rate or preferred dividend rate is lower than the rate the company would have to pay on a straight bond or a straight preferred stock issue. The conversion feature makes the issue more attractive to investors. The greater the value of the conversion feature to investors, the lower the yield the company will need to pay in order to sell the issue. The lower interest payments may be particularly useful to a company in a growth phase, because lower payments allow the firm to keep more cash for growth. Moreover, new companies or ones with relatively low credit ratings may find it extremely difficult to sell a straight issue of bonds or preferred stock. The market may respond favorably to convertible issues of these companies, not because of the quality of the convertible bonds or the convertible preferred stock per se but because of the quality of the underlying common stock.

Agency Problems. Finally, convertible securities may serve a useful role for the company when *agency problems* exist. Here straight debt holders are concerned about company actions that might result in wealth expropriation in favor of the equity holders. The convertible bond mitigates this problem by giving lenders a potential equity stake.

Forcing or Stimulating Conversion

Companies usually issue convertible securities with the expectation that these securities will be converted within a certain length of time. Investors can *exercise* (use) their options voluntarily at any time and exchange the convertible security for common stock. However, they may prefer to hold the security, for its price will increase if the price of the common stock increases. Also, during this time, they receive regular interest payments or preferred stock dividends. For the security convertible into common stock that pays no dividend, it is to the holder's advantage never to convert voluntarily. In other words, the investor should delay conversion as long as possible. (When a company pays a common stock dividend, it may be in the interest of the convertible security holder to convert voluntarily.) On the other hand, it is in the company's interest, on behalf of its current shareholders, to force conversion as soon as the conversion value exceeds the call price—thereby taking the option away from the option's holder. In doing so, the firm also eliminates the cost of paying interest on the convertible debentures or dividends on the convertible preferred stock. If the common dividend paid on conversion is more than the after-tax interest expense for the convertible, the issuing corporation has reason not to want to force conversion. It is cash flow ahead as long as the security stays unconverted.

Forcing Conversion. To force conversion, companies issuing convertible securities must usually call the issue. If the call is to succeed, the market price of the security must be significantly higher than the call price so that investors will convert rather than accept the lower call price. Many companies regard a 15 percent premium of conversion value over call price as a sufficient cushion for possible resulting declines in market price and for enticing investors to convert their securities. The conversion price of a convertible debenture ($1,000 face value) might be $50 and the call price $1,080. For the conversion value of the bond to equal the call price, the market price of the stock must be $1,080 divided by 20, or **$54** a share. If the bonds are called when the market price is $54, many investors might choose to accept the call price rather than convert. The company would then have to redeem many of the bonds for cash, in part defeating the purpose of the original financing. To ensure almost complete conversion, the company might wait to call the debentures until the conversion value of the bond was 15 percent above the call price, a value that corresponds to a common stock market price of approximately $62 a share. At this price, the investor who accepts the call price suffers a significant opportunity loss. Studies show that companies tend to call their convertibles after a period of rise in their common stock price relative to the market. As a result, the opportunity loss to the holder for not converting is pronounced.

Stimulating Conversion. Other means are available for a company to "stimulate," as opposed to "force," conversion. By establishing an acceleration or "step-up" in the conversion price at steady intervals in the future, the company places persistent pressure on bondholders to convert, assuming that the conversion value of the security is relatively high. If the conversion price is scheduled to increase from $50 to $56 at the end of next month, convertible bondholders have an incentive to convert prior to that time, all other things being the same. If the holders wait, they receive fewer shares of common stock. The step-up provision must be established at the time the convertible issue is sold. It cannot be used for purposes of stimulating conversion at a particular moment.

Another means for stimulating conversion is to increase the dividend on the common stock, thereby making the common stock more attractive. In certain cases, the dividend income available on the common stock may exceed interest income on the convertible security. Although these two stimulants enhance conversion, invariably a portion of the convertible bondholders will not convert, owing to the downside protection of the bond, the superior legal claim on assets, and other reasons. Consequently, calling the issue may be the only means for ensuring that the issue will be substantially converted.

VALUE OF CONVERTIBLE SECURITIES

The simplistic view that a convertible bond is the best of all possible worlds for the issuing firm—because it offers a lower interest cost than straight debt and less dilution than equity financing—overlooks the option nature of the contract.

Debt-Plus-Option Characteristic

The convertible bond may be viewed as straight debt plus an option to purchase common stock in the corporation. If the expiration of the option and the maturity of the convertible are the same, then the following relationship roughly holds

$$\text{Debt value} + \text{Option value} = \text{Convertible bond value}$$

Both the value of the debt and the value of the option components are affected by the volatility of the company's cash flows. The greater this volatility, the lower the value of the debt component but the higher the value of the option component.

Thus risk cuts both ways when it comes to convertibles. As its operating risk increases, a firm incurs higher interest costs on new straight debt. However, with convertible debt the option component becomes more valuable to the option holder as the firm's operating risk increases. This suggests that when a company's future is highly uncertain, a convertible security may be the financing method of choice. Whereas a high-risk company may be unable to sell straight debt at a reasonable price, the option characteristic in a convertible security makes the debt-plus-option characteristic attractive in the marketplace. Thus, the convertible security serves an important role for the company faced with operating uncertainty.

In the Appendix at the end of this chapter, we explore option characteristics in more detail. Next we look at convertible security valuation in more traditional ways.

Straight Bond Value

As we know, the value of a convertible security to an investor is twofold—its value as a bond or preferred stock and its potential value as common stock. (Because the principles of valuation of a convertible bond and of a convertible preferred stock are nearly the same, our subsequent discussion will refer to convertible bonds.) Investors obtain a **hedge** when they purchase a convertible bond. If the market price of the stock rises, the value of the convertible is determined largely by its conversion value. If the market for the stock turns down, the investor still holds a bond whose value provides a floor below which the price of the convertible is unlikely to fall.

The **straight bond value** of a convertible security is the price at which a similar but nonconvertible bond of the same company would sell in the open market. For semiannual compounding, it can be determined by solving the following equation for V_{SB}:

Hedge (Noun) Something that reduces the risk of future price movements.

Straight bond value The value of a convertible bond if the convertible feature were valueless; in other words, the value of a nonconvertible bond with the same coupon rate, maturity, and default risk as the convertible bond.

$$V_{SB} = \sum_{t=1}^{2n} \frac{I/2}{(1 + i/2)^t} + \frac{MV}{(1 + i/2)^{2n}} \qquad \text{(22-1)}$$

$$= (I/2)(PVIFA_{i/2,2n}) + MV(PVIF_{i/2,2n}) \qquad \text{(22-2)}$$

where V_{SB} = straight bond value of the convertible
$I/2$ = semiannual interest payments determined by the coupon rate
MV = maturity value of the bond
$2n$ = number of semiannual periods until final maturity
$i/2$ = market semiannual yield to maturity on a similar but nonconvertible bond of the same company

In Eqs. (22-1) and (22-2), we assume semiannual interest payments, which are typical with U.S. corporate bonds, so the total number of interest payments is 2 times the years to maturity.

Fawlty Food Company has outstanding a 9 percent convertible debenture with a final maturity 20 years hence. This corresponds to a semiannual coupon payment of 4.5 percent of the bond's face value of $1,000, or $45. If the company is to sell a straight 20-year debenture in the current market, the semiannual yield will have to be 6 percent to be attractive to investors. For a 20-year bond with a 9 percent coupon to provide a 6 percent semiannual yield to maturity, the bond has to sell at a discount. Using Eq. (22-2) and rounding, we have

$$V_{SB} = (\$45)(PVIFA_{6\%,40}) + \$1,000(PVIF_{6\%,40}) = \textbf{\$774}$$

Thus the straight bond floor value of Fawlty Food Company's convertible bonds would be $774. This floor value suggests that if the price of the common stock were to fall sharply so that the conversion feature had negligible value, the price of the convertible would fall only to $774. At that price, the security would sell as a straight bond in keeping with prevailing bond yields for that grade of security.

The straight bond value of a convertible is not constant over time. It varies with (1) interest-rate movements in the capital market and (2) changes in the financial risk of the company involved. If interest rates in general rise, the straight bond value of a convertible bond will decline. If the semiannual yield to maturity on a straight bond in our example increases from 6 to 7 percent, the straight bond value of the convertible will drop from $774 to $667. Moreover, the company's credit rating can either improve or deteriorate over time. If it improves and the company is able to sell a straight bond at a lower yield to maturity, the straight bond value of the convertible security will increase, all other things held constant. If the company's credit standing deteriorates and the yield on a straight bond increases, the straight bond value will decline. Unfortunately for the investor, when the market price of the stock falls because of poor earnings and/or increased risk, the company's credit standing may suffer. As a result, the straight bond value of the convertible may decline along with the decline in its conversion value, giving investors less downside protection than they might have originally expected.[1]

Premiums

Convertible securities frequently sell at premiums over both their straight bond value and their conversion value. Recall that the conversion value of a convertible is simply the current market price per share of the company's common stock times the number of shares into which the security is convertible. The fact that the convertible bond provides the investor with a degree of downside protection, given the qualifications mentioned, often results in its selling at a market price somewhat higher than its conversion value. In general, the more volatile the price movements of the stock, the more valuable is the downside protection afforded by the straight bond value floor. For this reason, as well as for additional reasons discussed later, the market price of a convertible security frequently is above its conversion value. The difference is known as the *premium over conversion value.*

Moreover, a convertible bond will typically sell at a **premium over straight bond value,** primarily because of the conversion feature. Unless the market price of the stock is very low relative to the conversion price, the conversion feature will usually have value, because investors may eventually find it profitable to convert the securities. To the extent that the conversion feature does have value, the convertible security will sell at a premium over its straight bond value. The higher the market price of the common stock relative to the conversion price, the greater this premium.

Relationships Among Premiums

The trade-off between the two premiums depicts the value of the option to investors and is illustrated in Figure 22-1. The market price of the common stock is on the horizontal axis. The value of the convertible security is on the vertical. It should be pointed out that the two axes are on different scales. The diagonal line, which starts

Premium over straight bond value Market price of a convertible bond minus its straight bond value.

---

[1]Mathematically, the straight bond value of a convertible will rise over time, all other things held constant, if the face value of the convertible is above the straight bond value at the time of issuance. At final maturity, the straight bond value will equal the face value of the convertible, assuming the company is not in default.

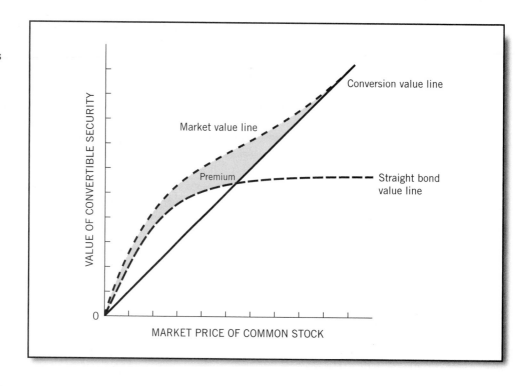

at the origin, represents the conversion value of the bond. It is linear, because the conversion ratio is unchanging with respect to the market price of the stock.

The straight bond value line, however, is related to the market price of the common stock. If a company is doing badly financially, the prices of both its common stock and its bonds are likely to be low. At the extreme, if the total value of the company were zero, both the bonds and the common stock would have a value of zero. As the company becomes sounder financially and the common stock increases in price, bond value increases but at a decreasing rate. After a point, the straight bond value line becomes flat, and further increases in common stock price are unrelated to it. At this point, the straight bond value is determined by what other similar high-grade bonds sell for in the market. The upper curved line in the figure represents the market price of the convertible security. The distance between this line and the straight bond value line is the premium over straight bond value, and the distance between the market value line and the conversion value line represents the premium over conversion value. Finally, if we consider the convertible bond's *floor value* to be the higher of its conversion value or straight bond value, the shaded area in Figure 22-1 represents the "overall" premium, or *premium over floor value*.

We see that at relatively high common stock price levels, the value of the convertible as a bond is insignificant. Consequently, its premium over straight bond value is high, whereas its premium over conversion value is negligible. The security sells mainly for its common stock equivalent. Investors are unwilling to pay a significant premium over conversion value for the following reasons. First, the greater the premium of market price of the convertible over its straight bond value, the less valuable the straight bond value protection is to the investor. Second, when the conversion value is high, the convertible may be called. If it is, the investor will want to convert rather than redeem the bond for the call price. Upon conversion, of course, the bond is worth only its conversion value.

On the other hand, when the market value of the convertible is close to its straight bond value, the conversion feature has little value. At this level, the convertible security is valued primarily as a straight bond. Under these circumstances, the market price of the convertible is likely to exceed its conversion value by a significant premium.

The principal reason for premiums in market price over both conversion value and straight bond value is the unusual appeal of a convertible as both a bond and an option on common stock. A convertible security offers the holder partial protection on the downside together with participation in upward movements in common stock price. Thus, the distribution of possible outcomes is skewed to the right, and this characteristic finds favor with investors. The greater the volatility of common stock price, the greater the potential for upside gain and the more valuable the option. In Figure 22-1, this greater volatility would be expressed as a larger shaded area in the figure. Lower volatility would cause the shaded area to be smaller. Option pricing theory allows for a deeper understanding of this characteristic, and that is the subject of the Appendix to this chapter.

EXCHANGEABLE BONDS

Exchangeable bond A bond that allows the holder to exchange the security for common stock of another company—generally, one in which the bond issuer has an ownership interest.

An **exchangeable bond** is like a convertible bond, but the common stock involved is that of another corporation. For example, National Distillers and Chemical Corporation issued $49 million in 6 percent subordinated debentures exchangeable into common stock of Cetus Corporation, a biotechnology firm.

Features

Like the conversion price and conversion ratio for a convertible security, the *exchange ratio* must be set at the time of issuance. The National Distillers debentures had an exchange price of $49, which translates into 20.41 shares of Cetus for each $1,000-face-value debenture. At the time of issuance, Cetus was selling for $37.50 per share. Therefore, the *exchange premium* was 30.7 percent, which is very high as conversion premiums go. This reflected the nature of Cetus—lots of potential but having little revenue and much uncertainty. The more variable the outcome, of course, the higher the option value. As with convertible bonds, there is typically a call feature with an exchangeable bond, and most issues are subordinated.

Use in Financing

Exchangeable bond issues usually occur only when the issuer owns common stock in the company in which the bonds can be exchanged. National Distillers, for example, owned 4 percent of the outstanding stock of Cetus Corporation. Exchange requests presumably would be satisfied from this holding, as opposed to acquiring stock in the open market. Therefore, the decision to go with an exchangeable bond issue may bring with it the reduction in or elimination of stock ownership in another company. A conscious decision of this sort is embodied in the financing.

As with a convertible security, interest costs of exchangeable bonds are lower because of the option value of the instrument. So far, most companies issuing exchangeables have been large and would not have experienced difficulty financing with a straight debt issue. The attraction is a lower interest cost together with the possibility of disposing of a common stock investment at a premium above the present price. Finally, some exchangeable issues of U.S. companies have been placed with investors outside the United States.

Valuation of an Exchangeable

The value of exchangeable debt can be viewed as

$$\text{Debt value} + \text{Option value} = \text{Exchangeable debt value}$$

where the call option is on the common stock of the company in which the debt is exchangeable. Therefore, the investor must analyze and track the bond of one company and the common stock of another.

One advantage with this arrangement is diversification. The straight bond value and the stock value are not directly linked. Poor earnings and financial performance in one company will not lead to a simultaneous decline in straight bond value and in the common stock value. If the companies are in unrelated industries, the investor achieves diversification. With market imperfections, this may lead to a higher valuation for an exchangeable than for a convertible, all other things the same.

Because option values are driven by the volatility of the associated asset, differences in volatility may affect the choice between an exchangeable and a convertible bond issue. If the common stock of the company in exchange is more volatile than that of the issuer, the option value will be greater with an exchangeable bond issue than it will with a convertible bond issue, all other things the same.

A relative disadvantage has to do with taxation. The difference between the market value of the common stock at the time of exchange and the cost of the bond is treated as a capital gain for tax purposes. In the case of a convertible, this gain goes unrecognized until the common stock is sold. The net effect of these factors is unclear.

WARRANTS

Warrant A relatively long-term option to purchase common stock at a specified exercise price over a specified period of time.

A **warrant** is an option to purchase common stock at a specified exercise price (usually higher than the market price at the time of warrant issuance) for a specified period (often lasting for years and, in some cases, in perpetuity). In contrast, a *right* is also an option to buy common stock, but normally it has a subscription price lower than the market value of the common stock and a very short life (often two to four weeks).

Warrants often are employed as "sweeteners" to a public issue of bonds or debt that is privately placed. As a result, the corporation should be able to obtain a lower interest rate than it would otherwise. For companies that are marginal credit risks, the use of warrants may spell the difference between being able and not being able to raise funds through a debt issue. Occasionally, warrants are sold directly to investors for cash. In addition, warrants are sometimes used in the founding of a company as compensation to underwriters and venture capitalists. Still, the origin of most warrants is in connection with a debt issue, often a *private placement*.

Features

The warrant itself contains the provisions of the option. It states the number of shares the holder can buy for each warrant. Frequently, a warrant will provide the option to purchase 1 share of common stock for each warrant held, but it might be 2 shares, 3 shares, or 2.54 shares. Another important provision is the price at which the warrant

Exercise price The price
at which the common stock
associated with a warrant
or call option can be purchased over a specified
period.

is exercisable, such as $12 a share. This means that in order to buy 1 share, the warrant holder must put up $12 a share. This **exercise price** may either be fixed or "stepped up" over time. For example, the exercise price might increase from $12 to $13 after three years and to $14 after another three years.

The warrant must specify the date that the option expires unless it is perpetual, having no expiration date. Because a warrant is only an option to purchase stock, warrant holders are not entitled to any cash dividends paid on the common stock, nor do they have voting power. If the common stock is split or a stock dividend is declared, the option price of the warrant is usually adjusted to take this change into account. Some warrants are callable after a period of time—provided that share price exceeds some minimum price.

As with convertibles, it is necessary for companies to report earnings per share on a diluted basis. Diluted earnings per share is calculated "as if" all convertible securities were converted into common stock and all warrants or options to purchase common stock were exercised. Because of this requirement, the common stock investor is not likely to overlook the potential dilution inherent in a company's financing with convertible securities and warrants.

Exercise of Warrants. When warrants are *exercised* (used), the common stock of the company is increased. Moreover, the debt that was issued in conjunction with the warrants remains outstanding. At the time of the issue of the warrants, the exercise price is usually set in excess of the market price of the common stock. The premium is often 15 percent or so above the stock's value. If the share price is $40, and the holder can purchase one share of common stock for each warrant held, this translates into an exercise price of $46.

To see how new capital can be infused with the exercise of warrants, let us take a look at a company we will call Black Shoals, Inc. It has just raised $25 million in debt funds with warrants attached. The debentures carry a 10 percent coupon rate. With each debenture ($1,000 face value) investors receive one warrant entitling them to purchase four shares of common stock at $30 a share. The capitalization of the company before financing, after financing, and after complete exercise of the warrant options is as follows (in millions):

	BEFORE FINANCING	AFTER FINANCING	AFTER EXERCISE
Debentures		$25	$25
Common stock ($10 par value)	$10	$10	$11
Additional paid-in capital			2
Retained earnings	40	40	40
Shareholders' equity	$50	$50	$53
Total capitalization	$50	$75	$78

The retained earnings of the company remain unchanged, and the debenture issue has neither matured nor been called. Exercising their warrant options, the warrant holders purchase 100,000 shares of stock at $30 a share, or $3 million in total. Consequently, the total capitalization of the company is increased by that amount.

Valuation of a Warrant

The theoretical value of a warrant can be determined by

$$\max[(N)(P_s) - E, 0] \tag{22-3}$$

where N is the number of shares that can be purchased with one warrant, P_s is the market price of one share of stock, E is the exercise price associated with the purchase of N shares, and max means the maximum value of $(N)(P_s) - E$, or zero, whichever is greater. The theoretical value of a warrant is the lowest level at which the warrant will generally sell. If, for some reason, the market price of a warrant were to go lower than its theoretical value, arbitragers would eliminate the differential by buying the warrants, exercising them, and selling the stock.

When the market value of the associated stock is less than the exercise price, the theoretical value of the warrant is zero, and it is said to be trading "out of the money." When the value of the associated common stock is greater than the exercise price, the theoretical value of the warrant is positive, as depicted by the solid diagonal line in Figure 22-2. Under these circumstances, the warrant is said to be trading "in the money."

Premium Over Theoretical Value

The primary reason that a warrant sells at a price higher than its theoretical value is the opportunity for leverage. To illustrate the concept of leverage, consider the Textron warrants. For each warrant held, one share of common stock can be purchased, and the exercise price is $10. If the common stock were selling at $12 a share, the theoretical value of the warrant would be $2. Suppose, however, that the common stock increased by 25 percent in price to $15 a share. The theoretical value of the warrant would go from $2 to $5, a gain of 150 percent.

The opportunity for increased gain is attractive to investors when the common stock is selling near its exercise price. For a particular dollar investment, the investor can buy more warrants than common stock. If the stock moves up in price, the investor will make more money on the warrants than on an equal dollar investment

FIGURE 22-2
Relationship Between the Theoretical Value and the Market Value of a Warrant

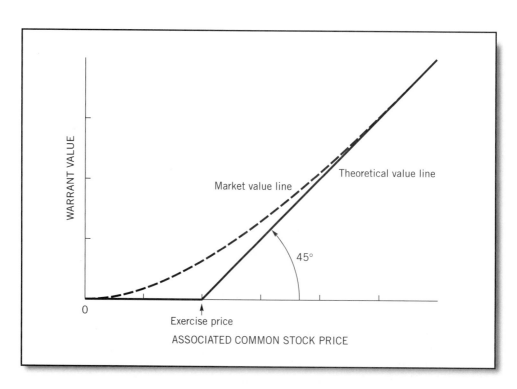

Part VIII Special Areas of Financial Management

in common stock. Of course, leverage works both ways. The percentage change can be almost as pronounced on the downside. However, there is a limit to how far the warrant can fall in price because it is bounded at zero. Moreover, for the market price to drop to zero, there would have to be no probability that the market price of the stock would exceed the exercise price during the exercise period. Usually there is some probability.

The market prices of many warrants are in excess of their theoretical values because of the potential for upside movements in the value of the warrant while, at the same time, downside movements are cushioned. In particular, this event occurs when the market price of the associated common stock is near the exercise price of the warrant.

Relationship Between Values

The typical relationship between the market value of a warrant and the price of the associated common stock is shown in Figure 22-2. The theoretical value of the warrant is represented by the solid line in the figure and the actual market value by the dashed line. One might think of the theoretical value line as representing the values a warrant might take with only a moment to expiration of the warrant. When there is a reasonable amount of time to expiration of the warrant, the relationship between warrant value and stock price is better depicted by the dashed line in Figure 22-2. The greater the length of time to expiration, the more time the investor has in which to exercise the warrant, and the more valuable it becomes. As a result, the further in the future the expiration date of the warrant, the higher the market value line tends to be in relation to the theoretical value line.

We note in the figure that when the market price of the associated common stock is low in relation to the exercise price, the actual market value of a warrant exceeds its theoretical value. As the market price of the associated stock rises, the market value of the warrant usually approaches its theoretical value. This simply suggests that a warrant has the greatest value, relative to its theoretical value, when it has the greatest potential in terms of percentage for upside movements and where the amount of funds invested is not all that great. The valuation of options, of which warrants are one form, is explored in more depth in the Appendix to this chapter.

SUMMARY

- Convertible securities, exchangeable securities, and warrants are options under which the holder can obtain common stock.
- A *convertible security* is a bond or a share of preferred stock that can be converted at the option of the holder into common stock of the same corporation. For the issuing corporation, convertibles often represent "delayed" common stock financing. For a given amount of financing, there will be less dilution with a convertible issue than with a common stock issue, assuming that the convertible is eventually converted and is not simply left "overhanging."
- As a hybrid security, a convertible bond has a straight bond value floor and a conversion, or

stock, value. As a result, the distribution of possible returns to the security holder is skewed to the right, and there is a trade-off between the two factors.
- An *exchangeable bond* may be exchanged for common stock in another corporation. It is like the convertible security in its valuation underpinnings with a couple of exceptions. This method of financing is applicable to companies that have stock holdings in another company.
- A *warrant* is an option to purchase common stock at a specified exercise price (usually higher than the market price at the time of warrant issuance) for a specified period (often lasting for years and, in some cases, in perpetuity).

- The conversion or exchange feature enables the investor to transfer a debt instrument or preferred stock into common stock, whereas a warrant attached to a bond enables the holder to purchase a specified number of shares at a specified price. With a warrant, the exercise of the option does not result in the elimination of the bonds.

- Normally, warrants are employed as a "sweetener" for a public or private issue of debt. The market price of a warrant is usually higher than its theoretical value when the market price of the stock is close to the exercise price. When the market price of the stock is high relative to the exercise price, warrants tend to sell at about their theoretical values.

Appendix

Option Pricing

Call option A contract that gives the holder the right to *purchase* a specified quantity of the underlying asset at a predetermined price (the *exercise price*) on or before a fixed expiration date.

Put option A contract that gives the holder the right to *sell* a specified quantity of the underlying asset at a predetermined price (the *exercise price*) on or before a fixed expiration date.

An *option* is simply a contract that gives the holder the right to buy or sell the common stock of a company at some specified price. Among a variety of option contracts, the most prevalent are the *call option* and the *put option*. The **call option** gives the holder the right to buy a share of stock at a specified price, known as the exercise price. We might have a call option to buy one share of ABC Corporation's common stock at $10 through December 31, which is the expiration date. The party that provides the option is known as the *option writer*. In the case of a call option, the writer must deliver stock to the option holder when the latter exercises the option.

As is evident from our discussions in the chapter, a warrant is a form of call option, as is a convertible security. Both give the holder an option on the company's stock. In contrast to a call option, a **put option** gives the holder the right to sell a share of stock at a specified price up to the expiration date. It is the mirror image of a call option. In what follows, we will focus only on the valuation of call options.

VALUATION ON EXPIRATION DATE

Suppose that we are concerned with the value of a call option (hereafter simply called an option) on its expiration date. The value of the option, V_o is simply

$$V_o = \max(P_s - E, 0) \tag{22A-1}$$

where P_s is the market price of one share of stock, E is the exercise price of the option, and max means the maximum value of $(P_s - E)$, or zero, whichever is greater. To illustrate the formula, suppose that one share of Lindahl Corporation's common stock is $25 at the expiration date and that the exercise price of an option is $15. The value of the option would be $25 − $15 = **$10.** Note that the value of the option is determined solely by the price of the common stock less the exercise price. However, the value of the option cannot have a negative value. When the exercise price exceeds the price of the common stock, the value of the option becomes zero.

This notion is illustrated graphically in Figure 22-2, where the theoretical value of a warrant is shown. The expiration value of the option lies along the theoretical value line. The horizontal axis represents the price of a share of common stock at the expiration date.

VALUATION PRIOR TO EXPIRATION

Consider now the value of the option with one period to expiration. For simplicity, let us assume that it can be exercised only on the expiration date. The price of the common stock at the expiration date is not known but rather is subject to probabilistic beliefs. As long as there is some time to expiration, it is possible for the market value of the option to be greater than its theoretical value. The reason is that the option *may* have value in the future. This idea was explored when we discussed warrants, so further discussion here is not necessary. The actual value of the option might be described by the dashed line in Figure 22-2.

The Effect of Time to Expiration.   In general, the longer the time to expiration, the greater the value of the option relative to its theoretical value. This makes sense in that there is more time in which the option may have value. Moreover, the further in the future one pays the exercise price, the lower its present value, and this too enhances the option's value. As the expiration date of an option approaches, the relationship between the option value and the common stock price becomes more convex (rounded outward). This is illustrated in Figure 22A-1. Market value line 1 represents an option with a shorter time to expiration than that for market value line 2, and market value line 2 represents an option with a shorter time to expiration than that for market value line 3.

The Interest Rate Employed.   Another feature crucial to option valuation is the time value of money. When an investor acquires a share of common stock by means of an option, he or she makes an initial "down payment" on the total price to be paid for the exercised option. The "final installment" (i.e., the exercise price) is not due until the option is exercised sometime in the future. The higher that interest rates are in the market, the more valuable this delay (until the time the exercise price is paid) is to the investor. Thus, an option will be more valuable the longer the time to its expiration and the higher the interest rate.

The Influence of Volatility.   Usually the most important factor in the valuation of options is the price volatility of the associated common stock. More specifically, the greater the possibility of extreme outcomes, the greater the value of the option to the holder, all other things the same. We may, at the beginning of a period, be considering options on two common stocks

FIGURE 22A-1
Relationship Between Common Stock Price and Option Value for Various Expiration Dates

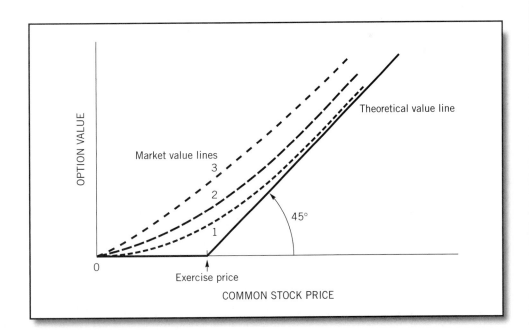

that have the following probability distributions of possible values at the expiration of the option:

PROBABILITY OF OCCURRENCE	PRICE OF COMMON STOCK A	PRICE OF COMMON STOCK B
.10	$30	$20
.25	36	30
.30	40	40
.25	44	50
.10	50	60
1.00		

The expected stock price at the end of the period is the same for both common stocks, namely $40. For common stock B, however, there is a much larger dispersion of possible outcomes. Suppose that the exercise prices of options to purchase common stock A and common stock B at the end of the period are also the same, say, $38. Thus, the two common stocks have the same expected values at the end of the period, and the options have the same exercise price. The expected value of the option, $\bar{V}_o$, for common stock A at the end of the period, however, is

(1) PROBABILITY OF OCCURRENCE	(2) PRICE OF COMMON STOCK A, P_s	(3) $\max(P_s - \$38, 0)$	(4) $(1) \times (3)$
.10	$30	$ 0	$ .00
.25	36	0	.00
.30	40	2	.60
.25	44	6	1.50
.10	50	12	1.20
1.00			$\bar{V}_o = \$3.30$

Whereas that for common stock B is

(1) PROBABILITY OF OCCURRENCE	(2) PRICE OF COMMON STOCK B, P_s	(3) $\max(P_s - \$38, 0)$	(4) $(1) \times (3)$
.10	$20	$ 0	$ .00
.25	30	0	.00
.30	40	2	.60
.25	50	12	3.00
.10	60	22	2.20
1.00			$\bar{V}_o = \$5.80$

Thus, the greater dispersion of possible outcomes for common stock B leads to a greater expected value of option price on the expiration date. The reason is that values for the option cannot be negative. As a result, the greater the dispersion, the greater the magnitude of favorable outcomes as measured by the common stock price minus the exercise price. Increases in the volatility of the common stock price therefore increase the magnitude of favorable outcomes for the option buyer and, hence, increase the value of the option.

This effect of stock price volatility on option value is illustrated in Figure 22A-2. Two common stocks with different end-of-period share price distributions are shown. The exercise price is the same for each stock, so the lower boundary for expiration-date option values (theoretical values) is also the same. This is shown by the hockey-stick-shaped portion of the line

Part VIII Special Areas of Financial Management

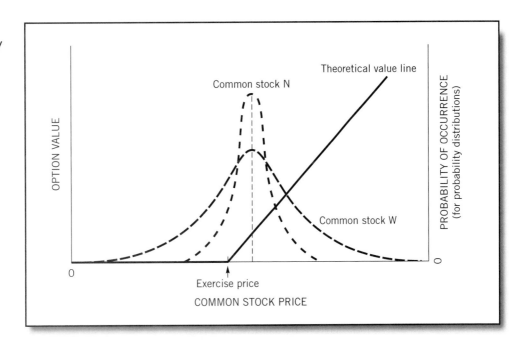

at the bottom of the figure. The probability distribution of end-of-period share price is wider for common stock W than it is for common stock N, reflecting greater price volatility for stock W. Because common stock W provides a greater chance for a big payoff (i.e., one that is far to the right of the exercise price), its option is worth more than that for common stock N.

To summarize where we are, we note that the value (or price) of a call option will change as follows when the variables listed below increase:

INCREASE IN VARIABLE	RESULTING CHANGE IN OPTION VALUE
Stock price volatility	Increase
Time to option expiration	Increase
Interest rate	Increase
Exercise price	Decrease
Current stock price	Increase

Keeping these relationships in mind will help us as we probe deeper into option valuation.

HEDGING WITH OPTIONS

Having two related financial assets—a common stock and an option on that common stock—we can set up a risk-free *hedged position*. Price movements in one of the financial assets will be offset by opposite price movements in the other. A hedged position can be established by buying the common stock (termed *holding it long*) and by writing options. If the common stock goes up in price, we gain in our long position, that is, in the value of the common stock we hold. We lose in the options we have written, because the price we must pay for the common stock to deliver to the person exercising the option is higher than it was when the option was written.

Thus when one holds a combination of common stock and options written, movements upward or downward in the price of the common stock are offset by opposite movements in the value of the option position written. If one does this properly, one can make the overall position (long in common stock coupled with options written) approximately risk free. In market equilibrium, one would expect to earn only the risk-free rate on a perfectly hedged position.

BLACK-SCHOLES OPTION MODEL

In a landmark paper, Fischer Black and Nobel laureate Myron Scholes developed a precise model for determining the equilibrium value of an option.[2] This model is based on the hedging notion just discussed. Black-Scholes assume an option that can be exercised only at maturity; no transactions costs or market imperfections; a common stock that pays no dividend; a known short-term interest rate at which market participants can both borrow and lend; and finally, changes to common stock prices that follow a random pattern.

Given these assumptions, we can determine the equilibrium value of an option. Should the actual price of the option differ from that given by the model, we could establish a riskless hedged position and earn a return in excess of the short-term interest rate. As arbitragers enter the scene, the excess return would eventually be driven out, and the price of the option would equal that value given by the model.

To illustrate a hedged position, suppose that the appropriate relationship between the option and the common stock of XYZ Corporation is that shown in Figure 22A-3. Suppose further that the current market price of the common stock is $20 and the price of the option $7. At $20 a share, the slope (rise over run) of the *market value line* in Figure 22A-3 is one-half, or 1 to 2. The slope determines the appropriate hedged position. Therefore, in this particular situation a hedged position could be undertaken by buying *one* share of stock for $20 and writing *two* options at $7 each. The "net money" invested in this position would be $20 − 2($7) = **$6.**

The combination of holding one share of common stock long and two options short leaves us essentially hedged with respect to risk. If the common stock drops slightly in price, the

---

[2]Fischer Black and Myron Scholes, "The Pricing of Options and Corporate Liabilities," *Journal of Political Economy* 81 (May–June 1973), 637–54.

FIGURE 22A-3
Relationship Between the Option Value and the Common Stock Price for XYZ Corporation

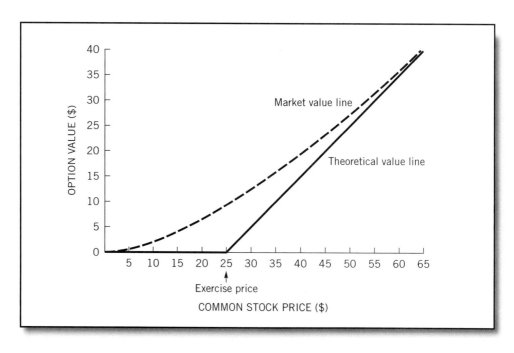

Part VIII Special Areas of Financial Management

value of the short position goes up by approximately an equal amount. We say *approximately* because with changes in the price of the common stock and with changes in time, the ideal hedge ratio changes. With a common stock price increase, for example, the slope of the market value line in Figure 22A-3 increases. Therefore, fewer options would need to be written. If the common stock price declines, the slope decreases, and more options would need to be written to maintain a hedge. In addition to modifications to the slope of the line caused by stock price changes, the line itself will shift downward as time goes on and the expiration date approaches. This is illustrated in Figure 22A-1.

Thus one's short position in options must be continually adjusted for changes in the common stock price and for changes in time if a riskless hedged position is to be maintained. The assumptions of the model make this possible. But in the real world, transactions costs make it impractical to adjust one's short position continuously. Even here, however, the risk that will appear as a result of moderate changes in common stock price or of the passage of time will be small. Moreover, it can be diversified away. For practical purposes, then, it is possible to maintain a hedged position that is approximately risk free. Arbitrage will ensure that the return on this position is approximately the short-term, risk-free rate.

The Exact Formula and Implications. In this context, the equilibrium value of the option, V_o, that entitles the holder to buy one share of stock is shown by Black and Scholes to be

$$V_o = (P_s)(N(d_1)) - (E/e^{rt})(N(d_2)) \qquad \text{(22A-2)}$$

where P_s = current price of the underlying common stock
$\qquad E$ = exercise price of the option
$\qquad e$ = 2.71828, the base of the natural system of logarithms
$\qquad r$ = short-term, risk-free annual interest rate, continuously compounded
$\qquad t$ = length of time in years to the expiration of the option
$\qquad N(d)$ = probability that a standardized, normally distributed random variable will have a value less than d

$$d_1 = \frac{\ln(P_s/E) + [r + (.5)\sigma^2]t}{\sigma\sqrt{t}}$$

$$d_2 = \frac{\ln(P_s/E) + [r - (.5)\sigma^2]t}{s\sqrt{t}}$$

$\qquad \ln$ = natural logarithm
$\qquad \sigma$ = standard deviation of the continuously compounded annual rate on the stock

The important implication of this formula is that the value of the option is a function of the short-term, risk-free interest rate; of the time to expiration; and of the variance of the rate of return on the stock but that it is *not* a function of the expected return on the stock. The value of the option in Eq. (22A-2) increases with the increase of the time to expiration, t, the standard deviation, σ, and the short-term, risk-free interest rate, r. The reasons for these relationships were discussed earlier in this Appendix.

In solving the formula, we know the current common stock price, the time to expiration, the exercise price, and the short-term interest rate. The key unknown, then, is the standard deviation of the annual rate of return on the common stock. This must be estimated. The usual approach is to use the past volatility of the common stock's return as a proxy for the future. Black and Scholes, as well as others, have tested the model using standard deviations estimated from past data with some degree of success. Given the valuation equation for options, Black and Scholes have derived the *hedge ratio* of shares of common stock to options necessary to maintain a fully hedged position. It is shown to be $N(d_1)$, which was defined earlier. Thus, the Black-Scholes model permits the quantification of the various factors that affect the value of an option. As we saw, the key factor is estimating the future volatility of the common stock.

A SUMMING UP

In summary, it is possible to establish a riskless hedged position by buying a common stock and by writing options. The hedge ratio determines the portion of stock held long in relation to the options that are written. In efficient financial markets, the rate of return on a perfectly hedged position would be the risk-free rate. If this is the case, it is possible to determine the appropriate value of the option at the beginning of the period. If the actual value is above or below this value, arbitrage should drive the price of the option toward the correct price.

The Black-Scholes option pricing model provides an exact formula for determining the value of an option based on the volatility of the common stock, the price of the common stock, the exercise price of the option, the time to expiration of the option, and the short-term, risk-free interest rate. The model is based on the notion that investors are able to maintain reasonably hedged positions over time and that arbitrage will drive the return on such positions to the risk-free rate. As a result, the option price will bear a precise relationship to the common stock price. The Black-Scholes model provides considerable insight into the valuation of options.

QUESTIONS

1. Define the *conversion price* of a convertible debenture, the *conversion ratio*, the *conversion value*, the *premium over conversion value*, and the *premium over straight bond value*.
2. This chapter argues that convertible securities are a form of delayed equity financing allowing the sale of equity at a 10 to 20 percent premium over current market price. Yet most convertibles are finally called only if the current market price is well in excess of the conversion price. Would the firm have been better off to simply wait and sell the common stock later? Explain your position.
3. If convertible securities can be issued at a lower effective interest rate than long-term bonds, why would a company ever issue straight debt?
4. Some warrants have a current theoretical value of zero and yet sell for positive prices. Explain why.
5. Suppose that you are the financial manager of a closely held (owned by few shareholders) small electronics firm. You have a favorable investment opportunity and are considering raising funds to finance it, using subordinated convertible debentures or straight bonds with warrants attached. Equity funds are not a possibility, as you feel the current stock price has been unnecessarily penalized for recent start-up expenses and the firm's high debt ratio (relative to the industry). If you expect additional large future funds requirements, which financing alternative would you adopt? Why?
6. Why might the holder of a convertible bond elect to convert voluntarily?
7. What reasons can you offer for the use of warrants by small, rapidly growing companies?
8. Why does the market price of an option such as a warrant usually exceed its value as common stock?
9. When a convertible security is converted into common stock, there is dilution in earnings per share. Would you expect the market price of the stock to decline as a result of this dilution? Explain.
10. If the desire of a company in selling convertible securities is delayed equity financing, would it be wise to establish at the time the security is initially sold a step-up in conversion price every few years?
11. Why would an investor want to invest in warrants as opposed to common stock?

12. As a lender, how attractive are warrants to you as a "sweetener"? Will you give terms more favorable than you otherwise would? Explain.

13. Why is unlimited upside potential and a lower (price) boundary of zero attractive to investors in a warrant? If the common stock were highly volatile, would this be a good or a bad thing?

14. With option financing, such as convertible securities and debt issues with warrants attached, does the company get something (a lower interest cost) for nothing?

15. How does an exchangeable bond differ from a convertible bond? How is the bond the same?

16. With respect to valuation, is the investor better off with an exchangeable bond or with a convertible bond?

SELF-CORRECTION PROBLEMS

1. The Barnaby Boat Company has current earnings of $3 a share with 500,000 shares of common stock outstanding. The company plans to issue 40,000 shares of 7 percent, $50-par-value convertible preferred stock at par. The preferred stock is convertible into two shares of common for each preferred share held. The common stock has a current market price of $21 per share.
   a. What is the preferred stock's conversion value?
   b. What is its premium over conversion value?
   c. Assuming that total earnings stay the same, what will be the effect of the issue on basic earnings per share (i) before conversion? (ii) on a *diluted* basis?
   d. If profits after taxes increase by $1 million, what will be basic earnings per share (i) before conversion? (ii) on a *diluted* basis?

2. Phlogiston Chemical Company plans to issue $10 million in 10 percent convertible subordinated debentures. Currently, the common stock price is $36 per share, and the company believes it could obtain a conversion premium (issuing price in excess of conversion value) of approximately 12 percent. The call price of the debenture in the first 10 years is $1,060 per bond, after which it drops to $1,030 in the next 10 years and to $1,000 in the last 10 years. To allow for fluctuations in the market price of the stock, the company does not want to call the debentures until their conversion value is at least 15 percent in excess of the call price. Earnings per share are expected to grow at an 8 percent compound annual rate in the foreseeable future, and the company envisions no change in its price/earnings ratio.
   a. Determine the expected length of time that must elapse before the company is in a position to force conversion.
   b. Is the issuance of a convertible security a good idea for the company?

3. Red Herring Pizza has outstanding warrants, where each warrant entitles the holder to purchase two shares of stock at $24 per share. The market price per share of stock and market price per warrant were the following over the last year:

	OBSERVATION					
	1	2	3	4	5	6
Stock price	$20	$18	$27	$32	$24	$38
Warrant price	5	3	12	20	8	29

Determine the theoretical value per warrant for each of these observations. Then plot the market value per warrant in relation to this theoretical value. At what price per common share is the warrant premium over theoretical value the greatest? Why?

PROBLEMS

1. The common stock of the Blue Sky Corporation earns $3 per share, has a 60 percent dividend payout, and sells at a P/E ratio of 8.333. Blue Sky wishes to offer $10 million of 9 percent, 20-year convertible debentures with an initial conversion premium of 20 percent and a call price of 105 ($1,050 per $1,000 face value). Blue Sky currently has 1 million common shares outstanding and has a 40 percent tax rate.
   a. What is the conversion price?
   b. What is the conversion ratio per $1,000 debenture?
   c. What is the initial conversion value of each debenture?
   d. How many new shares of common stock must be issued if all debentures are converted?
   e. If Blue Sky can increase operating earnings (before taxes) by $1 million per year with the proceeds of the debenture issue, compute the new earnings per share and earnings retained before and after conversion.

2. Assume that the Blue Sky Corporation (in Problem 1) could sell $10 million in straight debt at 12 percent as an alternative to the convertible issue. Compute the earnings per share and earnings retained after issuance of the straight debt under the assumption of a $1 million increase in operating earnings, and compare your answers with those obtained in Problem 1, Part (e).

3. Faversham Fish Farm has outstanding a 7.75 percent, 20-year convertible debenture issue. Each $1,000 debenture is convertible into 25 shares of common stock. The company also has a straight debt issue outstanding of the same approximate maturity, so it is an easy matter to determine the straight bond value of the convertible issue. The market price of Faversham common stock is volatile. Over the last year, the following was observed:

	OBSERVATION				
	1	2	3	4	5
Market price per share	$ 40	$ 45	$ 32	$ 23	$ 18
Straight bond value	690	700	650	600	550
Market price of convertible debenture	1,065	1,140	890	740	640

   a. Compute the premium over conversion value (in dollars) and the premium over straight bond value for each of the observations.
   b. Compare the two premiums either visually or by graph. What do the relationships tell you with respect to the valuation of the convertible debenture?

4. The following year, Faversham Fish Farm (see Problem 3) flounders. Its stock price drops to $10 per share and the market price of the convertible debentures to $440 per debenture. The straight bond value goes to $410. Determine the premium over conversion value and the premium over straight bond value. What can you say about the bond value floor?

5. The Rambutan Fruit Company needs to raise $10 million by means of a debt issue. It has the following two alternatives: a 20-year, 8 percent convertible debenture issue with a $50 conversion price and $1,000 face value; or a 20-year, 12 percent straight debt issue. Each $1,000 bond has a detachable warrant to

purchase four shares of stock for a total of $200. The company has a 40 percent tax rate, and its stock is currently selling at $40 per share. Its net income before interest and taxes is a constant 20 percent of its total capitalization, which currently appears as follows:

Common stock (par $5)	$ 5,000,000
Additional paid-in capital	10,000,000
Retained earnings	15,000,000
Total capitalization	$30,000,000

a. Show the capitalization from each alternative, both before and after conversion or exercise (a total of four different capitalizations).
b. Compute earnings per share currently and under each of the four capitalization determined in Part (a).
c. If the price of Rambutan stock went to $75, determine the theoretical value of each warrant issued under the second alternative.

6. Singapore Enterprise is considering an exchangeable bond issue where each bond can be exchanged for $16\frac{2}{3}$ shares of Malaysian Palm Oil Company. The latter company's stock is presently selling for $50 a share. At what premium over exchange value (expressed as a percentage) will the bonds be sold if they are sold for $1,000 a bond? Are there advantages to this type of financing versus a convertible issue?

7. Using Eq. (22-3), compute the theoretical value of each of the following warrants:

WARRANT	N	P_S	E
(a)	5	$100	$400
(b)	10	10	60
(c)	2.3	4	10
(d)	3.54	27.125	35.40

8. Alexander Zinc Company called its 7 percent convertible subordinated debentures for redemption at the end of last month. The call price was 106 ($1,060 per $1,000 face value). A holder of a $1,000 bond was entitled to convert into 34.7 shares of stock. At the time of the call announcement, the common stock of Alexander Zinc was selling at $43 per share.
a. What is the approximate market price at which the debentures would be selling at the time of the announcement?
b. By what percentage would market price per share need to drop before bondholders would rationally accept the call price?

9. Jenni Shover, Inc., has warrants outstanding that allow the holder to purchase three shares of common stock for a total $60 for each warrant that is held. Currently, the market price per share of Jenni Shover common stock is $18. However, investors hold the following probabilistic beliefs about the stock six months hence.

Market price per share	$16	$18	$20	$22	$24
Probability	.15	.20	.30	.20	.15

a. What is the present theoretical value of the warrant?
b. What is the expected value of stock price six months hence?
c. What is the expected theoretical value of the warrant six months hence?

d. Would you expect the present market price of the warrant to equal its theoretical value? If not, why not?

10. Suppose you have just bought a warrant that entitles you to purchase two shares of common stock for $45. The market price of the common stock is $26 per share, whereas the market price of the warrant is $10 in excess of its theoretical value. One year later the common stock has risen in price to $50 per share. The warrant now sells for $2 more than its theoretical value.

    a. If the common stock paid $1 in dividends for the year, what is the return on investment in the common stock?

    b. What is the return on investment in the warrant?

    c. Why do the two rates of return differ?

SOLUTIONS TO SELF-CORRECTION PROBLEMS

1. a. Conversion value = Conversion ratio × market price per share
$$= 2 \times \$21 = \mathbf{\$42}$$

    b. Premium over conversion value = $50 − $42 = **$8**
(or, expressed as a percentage = $8/$42 = 19.05%)

    c. Earnings per share:

Total after-tax earnings ($3 × 500,000 shares)	$1,500,000
Preferred stock dividend	140,000
Earnings available to common shareholders	$1,360,000
Number of shares	÷500,000
Basic earnings per share	**$2.72**
Total after-tax earnings	$1,500,000
Number of shares (500,000 + 80,000)	÷580,000
Diluted earnings per share	**$2.59**

    d. Earnings per share after profit increase:

Total after-tax earnings	$2,500,000
Preferred stock dividend	140,000
Earnings available to common shareholders	$2,360,000
Number of shares	÷500,000
Basic earnings per share	**$4.72**
Total after-tax earnings	$2,500,000
Number of shares (500,000 + 80,000)	÷580,000
Diluted earnings per share	**$4.31**

2. a. Conversion price = $36 × 1.12 = $40.32

Call price per share the first 10 years = $40.32 × 1.06 = $42.74

Price to which the common must rise before company will be in a position to force conversion = $42.74 × 1.15 = $49.15

Increase from present price = ($49.15/$36) − 1 = 36.5%

At an 8 percent compound growth rate, earnings per share will grow to 36 percent in 4 years—this is simply $(1.08)^4 - 1$. If the price/earnings ratio stays the same, it will take approximately *four years* before the company will be in a position to force conversion.

b. This period is somewhat longer than the two to three years that market participants have come to expect for the convertible security. Still, it is not far out of line, and the company may wish to go ahead. However, if uncertainty as to earnings per share increases with the length of time in the future, there may be considerable risk of an "overhanging" issue. This may cause the company to reconsider.

3. Market price of warrant and theoretical value at various common stock prices (in ascending order):

Common stock	$18	$20	$24	$27	$32	$38
Warrant price	3	5	8	12	20	29
Theoretical value	0	0	0	6	16	28

When plotted, the relationship is of the same pattern as shown in Figure 22-2. The maximum premium over theoretical value occurs when share price is $24 and the warrant has a theoretical value of zero. Here the greatest leverage occurs, and since volatility is what gives an option value, the premium over theoretical value tends to be greatest at this point.

SELECTED REFERENCES

Arditti, Fred D. *Derivatives: A Comprehensive Resource for Options, Futures, Interest Rate Swaps, and Mortgage Securities.* Boston: Harvard Business School Press, 1996.

Asquith, Paul. "Convertible Bonds Are Not Called Late." *Journal of Finance* 50 (September 1995), 1275–89.

———, and David W. Mullins Jr. "Convertible Debt: Corporate Call Policy and Voluntary Conversion." *Journal of Finance* 46 (September 1991), 1273–89.

Barber,Brad M. "Exchangeable Debt." *Financial Management* 22 (Summer 1993), 48–60.

Black, Fischer. "How to Use the Holes in Black-Scholes." *Journal of Applied Corporate Finance* 1 (Winter 1989), 67–73.

———, and Myron Scholes. "The Pricing of Options and Corporate Liabilities." *Journal of Political Economy* 81 (May–June 1973), 637–54.

Brennan, Michael J., and Eduardo S. Schwartz. "Convertible Bonds: Valuation and Optimal Strategies for Call and Conversion." *Journal of Finance* 32 (December 1977), 1699–1715.

———. "The Case for Convertibles." *Journal of Applied Corporate Finance* 1 (Summer 1988), 55–64.

Burney, Robert B., and William T. Moore. "Valuation of Callable Warrants." *Review of Quantitative Finance and Accounting* 8 (January 1997), 5–18.

Byrd, Anthony K., and William T. Moore. "On the Information Content of Calls of Convertible Securities." *Journal of Business* 69 (January 1996), 89–101.

Chen, Andrew H. "Uncommon Equity." *Journal of Applied Corporate Finance* 5 (Spring 1992), 36–43.

Ederington, Louis H., Gary L. Caton, and Cynthia J. Campbell. "To Call or Not to Call Convertible Debt." *Financial Management* 26 (Spring 1997), 22–31.

Finnerty, John D. "The Case for Issuing Synthetic Convertible Bonds." *Midland Corporate Finance Journal* 4 (Fall 1986), 73–82.

Green, Richard C. "Investment Incentives, Debt, and Warrants." *Journal of Financial Economics* 13 (March 1984), 115–36.

Haugen, Robert A. *Modern Investment Theory*, 4th ed. Upper Saddle River, NJ: Prentice Hall, 1997, Chaps. 17 and 18.

Hull, John C. *Options, Futures, and Other Derivatives*, 4th ed. Upper Saddle River, NJ: Prentice Hall, 1999.

Jen, Frank C., Dosoung Choi, and Seong-Hyo Lee. "Some New Evidence on Why Companies Use Convertible Bonds." *Journal of Applied Corporate Finance* 10 (Spring 1997), 44–53.

Jones, E. Philip, and Scott P. Mason. "Equity-Linked Debt." *Midland Corporate Finance Journal* 3 (Winter 1986), 47–58.

Lauterbach, Beni, and Paul Schultz. "Pricing Warrants: An Empirical Study of the Black-Scholes Model and Its Alternatives." *Journal of Finance* (September 1990), 1181–209.

Long, Michael S., and Stephen E. Sefcik. "Participation Financing: A Comparison of the Characteristics of Convertible Debt and Straight Bonds Issued in Conjunction with Warrants." *Financial Management* 19 (Autumn 1990), 23–34.

Marr, M. Wayne, and G. Rodney Thompson. "The Pricing of New Convertible Bond Issues." *Financial Management* 13 (Summer 1984), 31–37.

Mayers, David. "Why Firms Issue Convertible Bonds: The Matching of Financial and Real Investment Options." *Journal of Financial Economics* 47 (January 1998), 83–102.

Mikkelson, Wayne H. "Convertible Calls and Security Returns." *Journal of Financial Economics* 9 (September 1981), 237–64.

Sharpe, William F., Gordon J. Alexander, and Jeffrey V. Bailey. *Investments,* 6th ed. Upper Saddle River, NJ: Prentice Hall, 1999.

Tsiveriotis, Kostas, and Chris Fernandez. "Valuing Convertible Bonds with Credit Risk." *Journal of Fixed Income* 8 (September 1998), 95–102.

Van Horne, James C. "Warrant Valuation in Relation to Volatility and Opportunity Costs." *Industrial Management Review* 10 (Spring 1969), 19–32.

———. *Financial Market Rates and Flows,* 6th ed. Upper Saddle River, NJ: Prentice Hall, 2001.

Chapter 23

Mergers and Other Forms of Corporate Restructuring

SOURCES OF VALUE
Sales Enhancement and Operating Economies • Improved Management • Information Effect • Wealth Transfers • Tax Reasons • Leverage Gains • Hubris Hypothesis • Management's Personal Agenda
STRATEGIC ACQUISITIONS INVOLVING COMMON STOCK
Earnings Impact • Market Value Impact • Empirical Evidence on Mergers • Developments in Mergers and Acquisitions
ACQUISITIONS AND CAPITAL BUDGETING
Free Cash Flows and Their Value • Noncash Payments and Assumption of Liabilities • Estimating Cash Flows • Cash-Flow Approach versus Earnings Per Share Approach
CLOSING THE DEAL
Purchase of Assets or Common Stock • Taxable or Tax-Free Transaction • Alternative Accounting Treatments
TAKEOVERS, TENDER OFFERS, AND DEFENSES
Antitakeover Amendments and Other Devices • Empirical Evidence on Antitakeover Devices
STRATEGIC ALLIANCES
Joint Ventures • Virtual Corporations
DIVESTITURE
Voluntary Corporate Liquidation • Partial Sell-offs • Corporate Spin-offs • Equity Carve-outs • Empirical Evidence on Divestitures
OWNERSHIP RESTRUCTURING
Going Private • Motivations • Empirical Evidence on Going Private
LEVERAGED BUYOUTS
An Illustration in Detail • Arranging Debt Financing

SUMMARY
APPENDIX: REMEDIES FOR A FAILING COMPANY
QUESTIONS
SELF-CORRECTION PROBLEMS
PROBLEMS
SOLUTIONS TO SELF-CORRECTION PROBLEMS
SELECTED REFERENCES

In the takeover business, if you want a friend, you buy a dog.

—CARL ICAHN

Growth is an essential ingredient to the success and vitality of many companies. Without it, a company has difficulty generating dedication of purpose and attracting first-rate managers. Growth can be either internal or external. Up to now, we have considered only internal growth: a firm acquires specific assets and finances them by the retention of earnings or external financing. External growth, on the other hand, involves the acquisition of another company. In principle, growth by acquiring another company is little different from growth by acquiring a specific asset. Each requires an initial outlay, which is expected to be followed by future benefits.

Corporate restructuring embraces many things in addition to mergers. It can be construed as almost any change in capital structure, operations, or ownership that is outside the ordinary course of business. Such things as strategic alliances, sell-offs, spin-offs, and leveraged buyouts (LBOs) are some examples. In mergers and in other forms of restructuring the idea is to create value.

SOURCES OF VALUE

There are various reasons why a company would wish to engage in corporate restructuring. The foundation in all cases is to create value for the shareholders, a theme that runs throughout this book. In this section, we consider various reasons for a restructuring. But remember, these reasons must be considered collectively.

Sales Enhancement and Operating Economies

An important reason for some acquisitions is the enhancement of sales. By gaining market share, a firm may be able to increase sales continually and gain market dominance. Other marketing and strategic benefits may accrue as well. Perhaps the acquisition will bring technological advances to the product table; or it may be that an acquisition will fill a gap in the product line, thereby enhancing sales made throughout the firm. To be a thing of value, however, such an acquisition and corresponding enhancement of sales must be cost effective.

Operating economies can often be achieved through a combination of companies. Duplicate facilities can be eliminated. Marketing, accounting, purchasing, and

Merger The combination of two or more companies in which only one firm survives as a legal entity.

Synergy Economies realized in a merger where the performance of the combined firm exceeds that of its previously separate parts.

Economies of scale The benefits of size in which the average unit cost falls as volume increases.

other operations can be consolidated. The sales force may be reduced to avoid duplication of effort in a particular territory. In a railroad **merger,** the principal objective is to realize economies of operation through elimination of duplicate facilities and routes. When industrial companies merge, a firm with a product that complements an existing product line may fill out that line and increase the total demand for products of the acquiring company. The realization of such economies is known as **synergy.** The fused company is of greater value than the sum of its parts; that is, 2 + 2 = 5.

In addition to operating economies, **economies of scale** may be possible with a merger of two companies. Economies of scale occur when average cost declines as volume increases. Usually we think of economies of scale in production and overlook their possibilities in marketing, purchasing, distribution, accounting, and even finance. The idea is to concentrate a greater volume of activity into a given facility, into a given number of people, into a given distribution system, and so on. In other words, increases in volume permit a more efficient utilization of resources. Like anything else, economies of scale have limits. Beyond a point, increases in volume may cause more problems than they solve, and a company may actually become less efficient. Economists speak of an "envelope curve" (i.e., U-shaped average cost curve) with economies of scale possible up to some optimal point, after which diseconomies occur.

Economies can best be realized with a *horizontal merger,* combining two companies in the same line of business. The economies achieved by this means result primarily from eliminating duplicate facilities and offering a broader product line in the hope of increasing total demand. A *vertical merger,* whereby a company expands either forward toward the ultimate consumer or backward toward the source of raw material, may also bring about economies. This type of merger gives a company more control over its distribution and purchasing. There are few operating economies in a *conglomerate merger,* combining two companies in unrelated lines of business.

With a divestiture, such as a sell-off or spin-off, *reverse synergy* may occur, where 4 − 2 = 3. That is, the divested operation may be more valuable to someone else in generating cash flows and positive net present value. As a result, someone else is willing to pay a higher price for this operation than its present value to you. In some situations, the operation may be a chronic loser, and the present owner may be unwilling to commit the necessary resources to make it profitable.

Another reason for divestiture is a desire for a strategic change by the company. Periodically, most companies review their long-range plans in an effort to answer the eternal question, What businesses should we be in? Strategic considerations include internal capabilities (capital, plant, and people), the external product markets, and competitors. The market, as well as the competitive advantage of a company within a market, changes over time, sometimes very quickly. New markets emerge, as do new capabilities within the firm. What was once a good fit may no longer be a good fit. As a result, a decision may be reached to divest a particular operation. In the case of an acquisition of another company, not all of the acquired parts may fit the strategic plan of the acquiring company. As a result, a decision may be reached to divest one or more of the parts. Strategic realignment is the most cited reason chief executive officers give to justify a divestiture.

Improved Management

Some companies are inefficiently managed, with the result that profitability is lower than it might otherwise be. To the extent that restructuring can provide better management, it may make sense for this reason alone. Although a company can change management itself, the practical realities of entrenchment may be such that a pronounced restructuring is required for anything substantive to happen. This motivation would suggest that low-return companies whose earnings are poor are ripe acquisition candidates, and there appears to be some evidence in support of this contention. However, there must be the potential for significantly better earnings through improved management. Some products and companies simply have little potential, and poor performance is due to things other than inefficient management.

Information Effect

Value could also occur if new information is conveyed as a result of the corporate restructuring. This notion implies asymmetric (unequal) information possessed by management (or an acquirer) and the general market for the firm's common stock. To the extent that a stock is believed to be undervalued, a positive signal may occur via the restructuring announcement that causes share price to rise. The idea is that the merger/restructuring event provides information on underlying profitability that cannot otherwise be convincingly conveyed. This argument has been examined elsewhere in the book, and, in a nutshell, it is that specific actions speak louder than words.

In the case of a divestiture, its announcement may signal a change in investment strategy or in operating efficiency that, in turn, might have a positive effect on share price. On the other hand, if the announcement is interpreted as the sale of the most marketable subsidiary in order to deal with adversities elsewhere in the company, the signal will be negative. Whether a company is truly under- or overvalued is always questionable. Invariably, management believes it is undervalued, and in certain cases it has information that is not properly reflected in market price. There may be ways, however, to effectively convey value other than by an irreversible corporate restructuring.

Wealth Transfers

Another reason for shareholder wealth to change is wealth transfers from shareholders to debt holders, and vice versa. If a merger lowers the relative variability of cash flows, for example, debt holders benefit in having a more creditworthy claim. As a result, the market value of their claim should increase, all other things the same. If overall value does not change in other ways, their gain comes at the expense of shareholders.

In contrast, if a company divests a portion of the enterprise and distributes the proceeds to shareholders, there will be a wealth transfer from debt holders to shareholders. The transaction, by reducing the firm's earning assets, lowers the probability that the debt will be paid, and the debt will have a lesser value. If the value of the debt declines by virtue of more default risk, the value of the equity will increase, assuming the total value of the firm remains unchanged. In essence, the shareholders have stolen away part of the enterprise, thereby reducing its collateral value to debt holders.

In summary, any action that reduces the riskiness of cash flows, like a merger, may result in a wealth transfer from equity holders to debt holders. A restructuring that increases the relative riskiness, however, like a divestiture or increased financial leverage, may result in a wealth transfer from debt holders to equity holders.

Tax Reasons

A motivation in some mergers is a lower tax bill. In the case of a tax-loss carry-forward, a company with cumulative tax losses may have little prospect of earning enough in the future to fully utilize its tax-loss carryforward.[1] By merging with a profitable company, it may be possible for the surviving company to more effectively utilize the carryforward. However, there are restrictions that limit its utilization to a percentage of the fair market value of the acquired company. Still, there can be an economic gain—at the expense of the government—that cannot be realized by either company separately.

Leverage Gains

Value may also arise through the use of financial leverage. In many corporate restructurings, the amount of financial leverage often increases. When this occurs, value may be created for shareholders along the lines discussed in Chapter 17. There is a trade-off among the corporate tax effect, the personal tax effect, bankruptcy and agency costs, and incentive effects. Because the valuation implications were presented in the earlier chapter, we will not repeat the discussion here. However, recognize that value may change simply because the restructuring action results in a change in financial leverage.

Hubris Hypothesis

Richard Roll argues that takeovers are motivated by bidders who get caught up in believing that they can do no wrong and that their foresight is perfect.[2] *Hubris* refers to an overweening spirit of arrogant pride and self-confidence. Individuals possessing hubris are said not to have the rational behavior necessary to refrain from excessive bidding. They get caught up in the "heat of the hunt" where the prey must be grabbed regardless of cost. As a result, bidders pay too much for their targets. The hubris hypothesis suggests that the excess premium paid for the target company benefits the acquired firm's shareholders, but that shareholders of the acquiring company suffer a decrease in wealth.

Management's Personal Agenda

Rather than being the result of hubris, any overpayment made by the acquiring firm may be the result of its management pursuing personal goals rather than the goal of maximizing shareholder wealth. Sometimes management "chases growth." For example, going from a small company to a larger one may be viewed by management as more prestigious. Or management's goal may be diversification because, with diversification into unrelated businesses, a firm spreads out risk, and management jobs may be more secure.

When management considers selling the company, personal reasons also may come into play. In a privately held company, the individuals who have controlling interest may want their company acquired by another company that has an established market for its stock. For estate tax purposes, it may be desirable for these individuals to hold shares of stock that are readily marketable and for which market price quotations are available. The owners of a privately held company may have too

---

[1] A tax loss is generally carried back 2 years and forward up to 20 years to offset taxable income in those years. Any loss carried back must first be applied to the earliest preceding year and then to the next year in order. If the loss is not entirely offset by earnings in the 2 prior years, the residual is carried forward sequentially to reduce future profits and taxes in each year—up to the next 20 years. Prior to 1998, the loss carryback was 3 years and the carryforward was up to 15 years.

[2] Richard Roll, "The Hubris Hypothesis of Corporate Takeovers," *Journal of Business* 59 (April 1986), 197–216.

much of their wealth tied up in the company. By merging with a publicly held company, they obtain a marked improvement in their liquidity, enabling them to sell some of their stock and diversify their investments. All of these things are forms of *agency costs*, a concept explored in earlier chapters.

With these reasons in mind, let us consider various forms of corporate restructuring. We begin with mergers and then go on to divestitures and changes in ownership structure.

STRATEGIC ACQUISITIONS INVOLVING COMMON STOCK

A *strategic acquisition* occurs when one company acquires another as part of its overall business strategy. Achieving a cost advantage may be the desired result. For example, a brewing company in need of additional capacity may purchase another brewer that is suffering from overcapacity. Or, perhaps, the target company may be able to provide revenue enhancement through product extension or market dominance. The key is that a strategic reason exists for blending together two companies.

In contrast, a *financial acquisition* happens when a buyout firm, such as Kohlberg, Kravis, and Roberts (KKR), is the acquirer. The acquirer's motivation in this instance is to sell off assets, cut costs, and operate whatever remains more efficiently than before. Hopefully, these actions result in creating value in excess of the purchase price. The acquisition is not strategic, however, because the company acquired is operated as an independent, stand-alone entity. A financial acquisition invariably involves a cash exchange, and payment to the selling shareholders is financed largely with debt. Known as a *leveraged buyout (LBO)*, this type of acquisition is studied more closely later in the chapter.

Our focus here is on strategic acquisitions and, more narrowly, on those that are carried out with common stock as opposed to cash. When an acquisition is done for common stock, a "ratio of exchange," which denotes the relative weighting of the two companies with regard to certain key variables, results. In this section we consider two ratios of exchange, one for per-share earnings and the other for market price, of the two companies that are combined.

Earnings Impact

In evaluating a possible acquisition, the acquiring firm considers the effect that the merger will have on the earnings per share of the surviving corporation. Company A is considering the acquisition, by common stock, of Company B. The financial data on the potential acquisition at the time it is being considered are as follows:

	COMPANY A	COMPANY B
Present earnings	$20,000,000	$5,000,000
Shares outstanding	5,000,000	2,000,000
Earnings per share	$4.00	$2.50
Price per share	$64.00	$30.00
Price/earnings ratio	16	12

Company B has agreed to an offer of $35 a share to be paid in Company A's stock. The *exchange ratio*, then, is $35/$64, or about .547 of a share of Company A's stock for each share of Company's B's stock. In total, 1,093,750 shares of common stock in Company A will need to be issued to acquire Company B. Assuming that the earnings of the component companies stay the same after the acquisition, earnings per share of the surviving company would be

	SURVIVING COMPANY A
Total earnings	$25,000,000
Shares outstanding	6,093,750
Earnings per share	**$4.10**

Thus, there is an immediate improvement in earnings per share for Company A as a result of the merger. Company B's former shareholders experience a reduction in earnings per share, however. For each share of B's stock they had held, they now hold .547 of a share of A. Thus, the post-merger earnings per share related to each share of Company B's stock that they previously held is (.547)($4.10), or $2.24, compared with the pre-merger $2.50.

Suppose that the price agreed on for Company B's stock is $45 instead of $35 a share. The ratio of exchange would then be $45/$64, or about .703 of a share of Company A for each share of Company B. In total, 1,406,250 shares would have to be issued, and earnings per share after the merger would be

	SURVIVING COMPANY A
Total earnings	$25,000,000
Shares outstanding	6,406,250
Earnings per share	**$3.90**

In this case, there is an initial dilution in Company A's earnings per share on account of the acquisition of Company B.[3] Dilution in earnings per share will occur any time the price/earnings ratio paid for a company exceeds the price/earnings ratio of the company doing the acquiring. In our example, the price/earnings ratio in the first case was $35/$2.50, or 14. In the second case it was $45/$2.50, or 18. Because the price/earning ratio of Company A was 16, there was an increase in earnings per share in the first case and a decrease in the second.

Thus, both initial increases and decreases in earnings per share are possible for the surviving firm. The amount of increase or decrease is a function of (1) the ratio of pre-merger price/earnings multiples and (2) the relative size of the two pre-merger firms as measured by total earnings. The higher the pre-merger price/earnings ratio of the acquiring company in relation to that of the company being acquired and the larger the earnings of the acquired company in relation of those of the pre-merger acquiring company, the greater the increase in earnings per share of the surviving (acquiring) company.

Future Earnings. If the decision to acquire another company were based solely on the initial impact on earnings per share, an initial dilution in earnings per share would stop any company from acquiring another. This type of analysis, however, does not take into account the possibility of a future growth in earnings owing to the merger. This growth may be due to the expected growth in earnings of the acquired company as an independent entity and to any synergistic effects that result from the fusion of the two companies.

---

[3]Company B's former shareholders obtain an improvement in earnings per share. Post-merger earnings per share for each share of stock they had previously held is $2.74.

It is useful to graph likely future earnings per share with and without the acquisition. Figure 23-1 shows this for the acquiring firm in a hypothetical merger. The
graph tells us how long it will take for the dilution in earnings per share to be eliminated and for an increase to take place. In this example, it is 1.5 years. Earnings per
share drop $.30 initially, but this relative dilution is eliminated by the middle of the
second year. The greater the duration of the dilution, the less desirable the acquisition is said to be from the standpoint of the acquiring company. Some companies set
a ceiling on the number of years dilution will be tolerated.

Market Value Impact

The major emphasis in the acquisition bargaining process is on the ratio of exchange
of market price per share. The ratio of exchange of market price is simply

$$\frac{\text{Market price per share of the acquiring company} \times \begin{array}{c}\text{Number of shares offered by} \\ \text{the acquiring company for each} \\ \text{share of the acquired company}\end{array}}{\text{Market price per share of the acquired company}} \quad \textbf{(23-1)}$$

If the market price of Acquiring Company is $60 per share and that of Bought
Company is $30 and Acquiring Company offers a half share of its stock for each
share of Bought Company, the ratio of exchange of market prices will be

$$\frac{\$60 \times .5}{\$30} = \textbf{1.00}$$

FIGURE 23-1
Expected Earnings
Per Share of the
Acquiring Firm With
and Without the
Merger

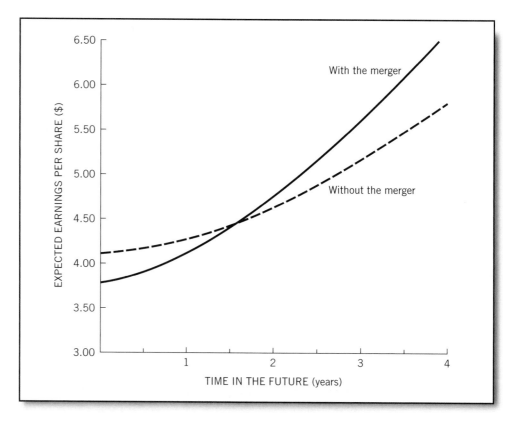

Part VIII Special Areas of Financial Management

In other words, the common stocks for the two companies will be exchanged 1 to 1 based on market price. If the market price of the surviving company is relatively stable at $60 a share, shareholders of both companies are as well off as before with respect to market value. The company being acquired finds little enticement to accept a market value ratio of exchange of 1 to 1, however. The acquiring company must usually offer a price in excess of the current market price per share of the company it wishes to acquire. Instead of a half share of stock, Acquiring Company might have to offer .667 of a share, or $40 a share in current market value.

"Bootstrapping" Earnings Per Share. In the absence of synergy, improved management, or the underpricing of Bought Company's stock in an inefficient market, we would not expect it to be in the interests of Acquiring's shareholders to offer a price in excess of Bought Company's current market price. Acquiring Company's shareholders could be better off, however, if their company's price/earnings ratio is higher than Bought Company's and if somehow the surviving company is able to keep that same higher price/earnings relationship after the merger. Suppose Bought Company has a price/earnings ratio of 10. Acquiring Company, on the other hand, has a price/earnings ratio of 18. Assume the following financial information:

	ACQUIRING COMPANY	BOUGHT COMPANY
Present earnings	$20,000,000	$6,000,000
Shares outstanding	6,000,000	2,000,000
Earnings per share	$3.33	$3.00
Market price per share	$60.00	$30.00
Price/earnings ratio	18	10

With an offer of .667 of a share of Acquiring Company for each share of Bought Company, or (.667) × ($60) = **$40** a share in value, the market price exchange ratio for Bought Company is

$$\frac{\$60 \times .667}{\$30} = \mathbf{1.33}$$

Shareholders of Bought Company are being offered $40 worth of stock for each share of stock that they own. Obviously, they benefit from the acquisition with respect to market price, because their stock was formerly worth only $30 a share. Altogether, 1,333,333 new Surviving Company shares (i.e., .667 × 2,000,000 Bought Company shares) would be issued to the shareholders of Bought Company. Shareholders of Acquiring Company also stand to benefit if the price/earnings ratio of the surviving company stays at 18. The market price per share of the surviving company after the acquisition, all other things held constant, would be

	SURVIVING COMPANY
Total earnings	$26,000,000
Shares outstanding	7,333,333
Earnings per share	$3.55
Price/earnings ratio	18
Market price per share	**$63.90**

The reason for this apparent bit of magic, whereby the shareholders of both companies benefit, is the difference in price/earnings ratios.

Thus, companies with high price/earnings ratios supposedly would be able to acquire companies with lower price/earnings ratios and obtain an immediate increase in earnings per share, despite the fact that they pay a premium with respect to the market value exchange ratio. The key factor is what happens to the surviving company's price/earnings ratio *after the merger.* If it stays the same, the market price of the stock will increase. As a result, an acquiring company would be able to show a steady growth in earnings per share if it acquired a sufficient number of companies over time in this manner. This increase is not the result of operating economies or underlying growth but is due to "bootstrapping" (pulling up as if by the bootstraps) its earnings per share through acquisitions. If the marketplace values this illusory growth in earnings per share, a company could presumably increase shareholder wealth through acquisitions alone.

In reasonably efficient capital markets, it is unlikely that the market will hold constant the price/earnings ratio of a company that cannot demonstrate growth potential in ways other than acquiring companies with lower price/earnings ratios. The acquiring company must be able to manage the companies it acquires and show some degree of synergy if the benefit of acquisitions is to be lasting. If the market is relatively free from imperfections and if synergy is not anticipated, we would expect the price/earnings ratio of the surviving firm to approach a weighted average of the pre-merger price/earnings ratios of the two firms. Under these circumstances, the acquisition of companies with lower price/earnings ratios would not enhance shareholder wealth. For the acquiring company, share price would actually decline if the market value exchange ratio were more than 1.00. If synergy and/or improved management were expected, however, shareholder wealth could be increased through the acquisition.

Empirical Evidence on Mergers

In recent years, there have been a number of empirical studies on acquisitions, and these studies provide a wealth of information. However, differences in samples, sample periods, and research methods render some of the valuation implications ambiguous. Nonetheless, with the ever-increasing number of studies certain patterns emerge that make generalizations possible.

For the successful, or completed, **takeover,** all studies show that the shareholders of the target or selling company realize appreciable increments in wealth relative to the market value of their holdings prior to any takeover activity. This wealth increment is due to the premium paid by the acquiring company, the size of which runs around 30 percent on average, though premiums as high as 80 percent occur. The market price of the target company's stock tends to rise once information about a potential takeover becomes available or rumors of such develop. Typically the stock price improvement begins prior to the takeover announcement, perhaps one month in advance. The return pattern usually observed for the target company is shown in Figure 23-2.

For the buying, or acquiring, company, the evidence is less clear. In all cases of a successful takeover, a premium is obviously paid, and its justification must be expected synergy and/or more efficient management of the resources of the target company. The question is whether likely synergy and/or improved management will result in a wealth increment sufficient to offset the premium. Answers from empirical studies to this question are mixed. Some studies suggest that shareholders of acquiring firms obtain a small improvement in share price, and others find no effect at all. The situation of no effect is illustrated in Figure 23-2. Still others find that

Takeover The acquisition of another company that may (from the viewpoint of the acquired firm's management) take the form of a "friendly" or "unfriendly" merger.

FIGURE 23-2
Relative Abnormal Stock Returns (Calculated as the Difference Between Actual and Predicted Returns) Around the Announcement Date of a Successful Takeover

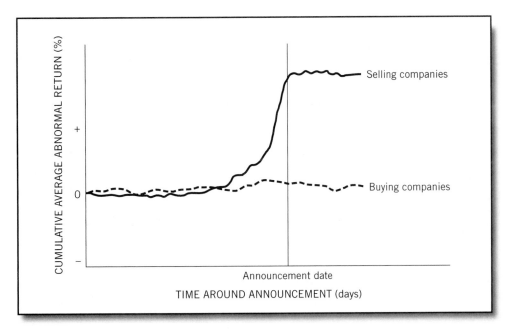

the shareholders of acquiring companies earn negative returns, holding constant other factors. In the year following a takeover, negative returns are particularly evident.

Another explanation, of course, is that acquiring companies simply pay too much. This would agree with the hubris hypothesis, which predicts a decrease in the value of the acquiring firm. In other words, potential synergy and management improvement are not enough to offset the premium paid. In certain bidding wars, the frenzy is such that rational decision making seems to disappear. In some takeover contests the quest of the prize is so important that the premium is bid up beyond what synergy and/or improved management will justify. This is fueled in part by investment bankers who earn ever more handsome fees, the greater the price paid.

One more cause for concern is that so many acquirers later divest themselves of the companies they acquired. More often than not the divestiture is of a diversifying acquisition as opposed to one in a related line of business. The invariable reason for the divestiture is that the target company did not live up to expectations. Often, the disposition involves a loss. The question remains as to why the acquirer was so eager and paid so much in the first place. Equally puzzling is why companies acquire firms in unrelated lines of business. On average, acquiring company shareholders experience negative returns in "conglomerate" types of acquisitions. The premium paid simply is not recovered given the limited possible synergy. Sometimes the acquiring company will get lucky and come across a truly undervalued firm, but this is usually not the case. An acquisition in a related line of business makes more sense.

In summary, the evidence on returns to shareholders of acquiring companies is mixed. It is difficult to make an overall case for takeovers being a thing of value to the shareholders of the acquiring company. Clearly, some acquisitions are worthwhile because of synergy and managerial improvement, and some are bad. The key for the financial manager is to be careful because, on average, a case cannot be made for corporations, overall, making consistently good acquisitions. For the acquired and the acquiring companies collectively, there is an increment in wealth associated with takeovers. This is primarily the result of the premium paid to the selling company's shareholders.

Developments in Mergers and Acquisitions

Roll-up The combining of multiple small companies in the same industry to create one larger company.

A number of industries are being transformed due to an increasingly popular merger and acquisition strategy—a multicompany union known as a **roll-up.** The roll-up trend is occurring within fragmented industries as a way to consolidate and gain economies of scale. Roll-ups have occurred for such companies as equipment rental firms, floral shops, travel agencies, and car dealerships.

Roll-up Transactions.   The idea behind a roll-up is to rapidly build a larger, more valuable company through multiple acquisitions of small- to medium-sized firms. Roll-ups carry the hope of cost savings due to volume purchasing and a centralized, lower-cost administration. Acquisitions are structured to provide the selling companies' owners with cash or stock. As a general rule, the owners of small independent companies that sold out stay on as managers in the new company. The new company, if privately owned, often uses roll-ups as a way to accelerate its growth and thus move more rapidly toward going public through an **initial public offering (IPO).**

Initial public offering (IPO) A company's first offering of common stock to the general public.

Industry Roll-Ups Continue Momentum

The "rolling up" of small companies into a larger entity through acquisitions doesn't attract the same attention as the megadeals that preoccupy the business press, but this investment strategy is rapidly changing the face of entire industries and generating some whopping profits for the companies involved. Ongoing roll-up acquisitions in industries dominated by scattered, independent small companies are creating some new contenders in industries as diverse as waste management and convenience stores. In the vast majority of cases, finance is leading the way from the earliest stages of targeting potential acquisitions to the rapid integration of the acquired companies.

KEY ELEMENTS

According to Rajesh U. Kothari, principal of GMA Capital in Farmington Hills, Mich., there are a number of key elements that are common to roll-ups. Most roll-ups occur in businesses where there are a large number of small players. A roll-up brings these competitors together under one umbrella and centralizes as much of the administrative process as possible into a corporate headquarters. "This accomplishes two important tasks," Kothari notes. "It reduces the expenses of all divisions, making the combined entity more profitable, and it allows the individual companies to focus on their core strength—manufacturing, design or sales, for example."

In most instances, Kothari says, the owner of the business being acquired stays in place and continues to run the operation, with potentially fewer administrative headaches. "The owner gets some money and some stock in the overall entity with a well-defined plan to reach an IPO," Kothari says. "Roll-ups are welcomed by business owners who recognize that it is better to have a small piece of a big pie than 100 percent of a small pie."

The growing number of roll-ups can be attributed to four main factors, Kothari says:

1. The increasing availability of capital from the banking and venture capital communities has made it easier to finance roll-ups.

2. The public marketplace has had a continuing appetite for IPOs at valuations that continue to climb with trends in the overall market.

3. The success of many roll-ups in the past has provided a framework that others are now following.

4. The growing drive for entrepreneurial spirit has pushed many executives to grow their businesses in new and different ways. "Roll-ups provide a vehicle that was not common 10 years ago that allows an aggressive CEO to take a small $30 million business to an IPO within three years," Kothari explains.

Source: Adapted from Fay Hansen, "Buy, Build and Improve," Business Finance *(May 1999), p. 23–24.* (*www.businessfinancemag.com*) *© Duke Communications International, 1999. Used by permission. All rights reserved.*

IPO roll-up An initial public offering (IPO) of independent companies in the same industry that merge into a single company concurrent with the stock offering. The funds from the IPO are used to finance the acquisition of the combining companies.

The ultimate consolidation tactic in accelerating growth and progress toward going public calls for combining roll-ups with an IPO—thus producing the **IPO roll-up**. In an IPO roll-up, privately owned companies in the same line of business simultaneously merge into a new company. At the time of the merger, the company undertakes an IPO. The newly formed company is sometimes called a "poof company," as in: "The multimillion-dollar public company appeared out of nowhere, as if—poof!—by magic!"

ACQUISITIONS AND CAPITAL BUDGETING

From the standpoint of the buying corporation, acquisitions can be treated as another aspect of capital budgeting. In principle, the prospective acquisition may be evaluated in much the same manner as any capital budgeting project. There is an initial outlay and expected future benefits. Whether the outlay is in cash or common stock, the firm should attempt to allocate capital optimally to increase shareholder wealth over the long run. Unlike traditional capital budgeting situations, however, there may be more uncertainty surrounding the initial outlay with an acquisition. Indeed, this outlay is usually subject to bargaining. Also, if it can be assumed that the acquiring company intends to maintain its existing capital structure over the long run, it is appropriate to evaluate the prospective acquisition without reference to the way it is financed.

Free Cash Flows and Their Value

In evaluating the prospective acquisition, the buying company should estimate the future cash flows that the acquisition is expected to add after taxes. We are interested in what is known as *free cash flows*. These are the cash flows that remain after we subtract from expected revenues any expected operating costs and the capital expenditures necessary to sustain, and hopefully improve, the cash flows. Expressed differently, free cash flow is the cash flow in excess of that required to finance all projects that have positive net present values when discounted at appropriate required rates of return.

The estimates of free cash flows should include consideration of any synergistic effects, for we are interested in the marginal impact of the acquisition. Moreover, the cash-flow estimates should be before any financial charges. The idea is to divorce the prospective acquisition's financial structure from its overall worth as an investment. Our concern is with after-tax operating cash flows that arise from operating the acquired company, not with prospective net income after financial changes. (Remember, these were exactly the same types of cash flows we were concerned with when we considered individual capital budgeting proposals.) On the basis of these considerations, suppose the following free cash flows are expected from a prospective acquisition:

	AVERAGE FOR YEARS (IN THOUSANDS)				
	1–5	6–10	11–15	16–20	21–25
Annual after-tax operating cash flows from acquisition	$2,000	$1,800	$1,400	$800	$200
Net investment	600	300	—	—	—
Cash flow after taxes	$1,400	$1,500	$1,400	$800	$200

The appropriate discount rate would be the cost of capital for the acquired firm. We use this rate to best reflect the riskiness of the acquired firm's cash flows. If this rate were 15 percent after taxes, the present value of the expected free cash flows shown would be $8,724,000. If the prospective acquisition has no debt, this figure suggests that the acquiring company can pay a maximum cash price of $8,724,000 for the acquisition and still be acting in the best interests of the company's shareholders. The actual price paid will be subject to negotiation. However, the present value of the prospective acquisition should represent an upper boundary for the acquiring company. Any price up to this amount should result in a worthwhile investment for the company. As a result, the market price per share of the firm's stock should increase. If the price paid is in excess of the acquisition's present value, this suggests that capital is less than optimally allocated.

Noncash Payments and Assumption of Liabilities

Now what if the acquisition were for something of value other than cash? Payment to the acquired company's shareholders may involve common stock, preferred stock, debt, cash, or some combination of these items. Moreover, in many cases, the buyer assumes the liabilities of the company it acquires. Do these matters complicate the acquisition analysis? They do. But we must keep our eye on the overriding valuation principle, that is, the value of the incremental cash flows. The present value figure obtained in our calculations, $8,724,000, represents the maximum "cash-equivalent" price to be paid. If securities other than cash are used in the acquisition, they should be converted to their cash-equivalent market value. If the acquiring firm assumes the liabilities of the acquired company, these too should be converted to their market value and subtracted from the cash-equivalent price. Thus, the present value of incremental cash flows (less the market value of any liabilities assumed in the acquisition) sets an upper limit on the market value of all securities, including cash, used in payment. In this way, we are able to separate the investment worth of an acquisition from the way it is financed.

Estimating Cash Flows

In an acquisition, there are the usual problems with estimating future cash flows. The process may be somewhat easier than for a capital budgeting proposal, however, because the company being acquired is a going concern. The acquiring company buys more than assets. It buys experience, an organization, and proven performance. The estimates of sales and costs are based on past results. Consequently, they are likely to be more accurate than the estimates for a new investment proposal. Less uncertainty involved in the estimates means less dispersion of expected outcomes and lower risk, all other things held constant. An additional problem, however, is introduced when the acquisition is to be integrated into the acquiring company. Under this circumstance, the acquisition cannot be evaluated as a separate operation. The synergistic effects must be considered. Estimates of these effects are difficult, particularly if the organization that results from the acquisition is complex.

Cash-Flow Approach versus Earnings Per Share Approach

The analysis of an acquisition on a free-cash-flow basis differs from that done on an earnings per share basis. With an earnings per share approach, assuming that an exchange of common stock for common stock were involved, the question is whether there would be an improvement in earnings per share now or in the future. In the cash-flow approach, the question is whether the expected net cash flows have a present value in excess of the acquisition's cost.

In general, the cash-flow approach looks at the valuation of an acquisition over the long run, whereas the earnings per share approach focuses on the short run. If a prospective acquisition does not result in a positive increment in earnings per share within a few years, it is usually ruled out if one relies only on the earnings per share approach. In contrast, the cash-flow approach looks at incremental cash flows likely to be generated from the acquisition for many years into the future. Thus, the earnings per share approach tends to bias the selection process in favor of companies with immediate growth prospects, but not necessarily long-term ones. Neither approach embodies in it a consideration for changes in business risk. However, this dimension can be incorporated into either method of analysis using the techniques discussed in Chapter 15.

Apart from risk, the question is which method should be used—the cash-flow or the earnings per share method. Probably the best answer is that both methods should be employed. The cash-flow method is more comprehensive and more theoretically correct with respect to the long-term economic worth of an acquisition. In practice, it is difficult to imagine management ignoring the effect of an acquisition on earnings per share, no matter how sound the cash-flow approach is conceptually. By the same token, an earnings per share approach by itself may be too shortsighted and may bias things away from solid long-term growth prospects. Therefore, a strong case can be made for using a free-cash-flow method of analysis *in addition* to an earnings per share one.

CLOSING THE DEAL

Consolidation The combination of two or more firms into an entirely new firm. The old firms cease to exist. Though technically different, the terms *merger* (where one firm survives) and *consolidation* tend to be used interchangeably.

A merger or **consolidation** often begins with negotiations between the management of the two companies. Usually, the boards of directors of the companies are kept up to date on the negotiations. The acquirer evaluates many facets of a target company. Terms are agreed on, ratified by the respective boards, then approved by the common shareholders of both companies. Depending on the corporate charter, an established majority—usually two-thirds—of the total shares is required. After approval by the common shareholders, the merger or consolidation can take place once the necessary papers are filed with the states in which the companies are incorporated.

Clayton Act A 1914 federal antitrust law designed to promote competition that addresses several antitrust matters, including interlocking directorates, race discrimination, exclusive dealing, and mergers.

One hurdle remains, however. The Antitrust Division of the Department of Justice or the Federal Trade Commission could bring suit to block the combination. To block a merger or consolidation, the government, under Section 7 of the **Clayton Act,** must prove that a "substantial lessening of competition" might occur because of it. Usually restraint of competition is interpreted as applying to either a geographic area, such as food stores in New Orleans, or to a line of commerce, such as aluminum ingot production. Broader interpretations are possible, and the combination of two large companies in unrelated lines of business and geographic areas is sometimes suspect simply because of "largeness" per se. Because the costs of executive time, legal expenses, and other expenses of waging an antitrust battle are so great, most companies want to be reasonably sure that they will not be challenged before going ahead with a consolidation.

Purchase of Assets or Common Stock

A company may be acquired either by the purchase of its assets or its common stock. The buying company may purchase all or a portion of the assets of another company and pay for them in cash or with its own common stock. Frequently, the buyer acquires only the assets of the other company and does not assume its liabilities.

When an acquiring company purchases the stock of another company, the latter is combined into the acquiring company. The company that is acquired ceases to exist, and the surviving company assumes all of the acquired firm's assets and liabilities. As with a purchase of assets, the means of payment to the shareholders of the company being acquired can be either cash or common stock.

Taxable or Tax-Free Transaction

If the acquisition is made with cash or with a debt instrument, the transaction is taxable to the selling company or to its shareholders at that time. This means that they must recognize any capital gain or loss on the sale of the assets or the sale of the stock at the time of the sale. If payment is made with voting preferred or common stock, the transaction is not taxable at the time of the sale. The capital gain or loss is recognized only when the newly received common stock is eventually sold. In addition to the requirement of voting stock, for a combination to be tax free, it must have a business purpose. In other words, it cannot be entirely for tax reasons. Moreover, in a purchase of assets the acquisition must involve substantially all of the assets of the selling company, and no less than 80 percent of those assets must be paid for with voting stock. In a purchase of stock, the buying company must own at least 80 percent of the selling company's stock immediately after the transaction.

Alternative Accounting Treatments

From an accounting standpoint, a combination of two companies is treated either as a **purchase** or as a **pooling of interests.** In a purchase, the buyer treats the acquired company as an investment. If the buyer pays a premium above the book value of the assets, this premium must be reflected on the buyer's balance sheet. The purchase method requires that tangible assets be reported at fair market value. As a result, it may be possible for the buyer to write up the acquired company's tangible assets. If such a write-up occurs, there are higher depreciation charges.

If the premium paid exceeds the write-up, however, the difference must be reflected as **goodwill** on the buyer's balance sheet. Moreover, goodwill must be written off against future income, the logic being that it will be reflected in such income. An estimate must be made of the life of goodwill, and goodwill is amortized over this period, which currently cannot exceed 40 years for "financial accounting purposes." Thus, accounting earnings are reduced by the amount of the charge. As a result of 1993 tax law changes, goodwill charges are generally deductible for "tax purposes" over 15 years for acquisitions occurring after August 10, 1993. Previously, goodwill charges were not deductible for tax purposes, which resulted in a tax disadvantage to firms acquiring goodwill in an asset purchase.

In a pooling of interests, the balance sheets of the two companies are combined, with the assets and liabilities simply being added together. As a result, write-ups of assets and/or goodwill are not reflected in the combination, and there are no charges against future income.

The choice of accounting treatment does not rest entirely with the acquiring company but rather is governed by the circumstances of the merger and the rules of the

Purchase (method) A method of accounting treatment for a merger based on the *market price* paid for the acquired company.

Pooling of interests (method) A method of accounting treatment for a merger based on the *net book value* of the acquired company's assets. The balance sheets of the two companies are simply combined.

Goodwill The intangible assets of the acquired firm arising from the acquiring firm paying more for them than their book value. Goodwill must be amortized.

accounting profession. Only under currently rather restricted conditions can a merger be treated as a pooling of interests.[4]

Proposed Accounting Changes. Because reported earnings are higher with the pooling-of-interests treatment than they are with the purchase treatment, many acquiring companies have preferred it. Widespread use of the pooling-of-interests method, however, has been largely a U.S. phenomenon. Most other major countries either ban the method outright or severely restrict its use. In 1999, the Financial Accounting Standards Board (FASB)—the professional group that writes accounting rules for U.S. businesses—took a big step toward harmonizing worldwide accounting standards. The FASB voted unanimously to eliminate pooling of interests as a method of accounting for business combinations. The tentative change would become effective for new business combinations only after the FASB issues a final standard on the issues, which is expected to occur late in 2000.[5]

Accounting Methods Illustrated. To illustrate both the purchase and pooling-of-interests accounting methods, let us take a look at a typical merger. ABC Company acquired XYZ Company in an exchange for ABC common stock valued at $2 million. XYZ Company had debt of $1 million and shareholders' equity of $1.2 million prior to the merger, the net book value of its assets being $2.2 million. On the other hand, ABC Company, the acquirer, has shareholders' equity of $10 million, debt of $5 million, and assets having a net book value of $15 million prior to the merger. The effects of the merger (in thousands) under the purchase and the pooling-of-interests methods of accounting are shown below:

	BEFORE MERGER		AFTER MERGER	
	ABC COMPANY	XYZ COMPANY	PURCHASE	POOLING
Net tangible assets	$15,000	$2,200	$17,200	$17,200
Goodwill	0	0	800	0
Total assets	$15,000	$2,200	$18,000	$17,200
Debt	$ 5,000	$1,000	$ 6,000	$ 6,000
Shareholders' equity	10,000	1,200	12,000	11,200
Total liabilities and shareholders' equity	$15,000	$2,200	$18,000	$17,200

With the purchase method, the total assets of the acquired company are written up by $800,000, which is the price paid in excess of the net book value of the acquired firm's assets. Moreover, this amount is reflected as goodwill and must be amortized in the manner described before. Under the pooling-of-interests accounting treatment, the assets shown for the surviving company are simply the sum of the net book values of assets shown for the two companies before the merger.

So far we have implicitly assumed that the fair market value of the assets of the acquired company was equal to their net book value. In many situations, the fair market value of the assets of the acquired company exceeds the net book value of those assets. Under the purchase method of accounting, the tangible assets of the acquired company are written up to their fair market value. This write-up reduces

---

[4]*Opinions of the Accounting Principles Board, No. 16* (New York: American Institute of Certified Public Accountants, August 1970).
[5]At the time of this writing there was still a lot of vocal opposition to the proposed accounting change coming from various industry groups that favored maintaining pooling of interests as an option. Most experts, however, were saying that the proposed change was all but a "done deal."

the amount of goodwill. In our example, had the fair market value of the assets of the acquired company been $2.5 million instead of $2.2 million, the net tangible assets of the surviving company would have been $17.5 million instead of $17.2 million, and goodwill would have been $500,000 instead of $800,000. If the purchase transaction is taxable, as defined in the previous section, the surviving company can claim a larger depreciation expense for tax purposes, which, in turn, enhances cash flows. This represents an advantage for purchase over pooling if the objective of the firm is to maximize the present value of after-tax cash flows. To the extent that the objective is maximizing accounting earnings, however, the purchase method loses its appeal as a greater amount of goodwill must be recorded.

TAKEOVERS, TENDER OFFERS, AND DEFENSES

Tender offer An offer to buy current shareholders' stock at a specified price, often with the objective of gaining control of the company. The offer is often made by another company and usually for more than the present market price.

In our hypothetical examples, negotiations were confined to the managements and boards of directors of the companies involved. However, the acquiring company can make a **tender offer** directly to the shareholders of the company it wishes to acquire. A *tender offer* is an offer to purchase shares of stock of another company at a fixed price per share from shareholders who "tender" (surrender) their shares. The tender price is usually set significantly above the present market price as an incentive to tender. Use of the tender offer allows the acquiring company to bypass the management of the company it wishes to acquire and therefore serves as a threat in any negotiations with that management.

The tender offer can also be used when there are no negotiations but when one company simply wants to acquire another. It is not possible to surprise another company with its acquisition, however, because the Securities and Exchange Commission requires rather extensive disclosure. The primary selling tool is the premium that is offered over the existing market price of the stock. In addition, brokers are often given attractive commissions for shares tendered through them. The tender offer itself is usually communicated through financial newspapers. Direct mailings are made to the shareholders of the company being bid for if the bidder is able to obtain a list of shareholders. Although a company is legally obligated to provide such a list, it is often able to delay delivery long enough to frustrate the bidder.

Two-tier tender offer
Tender offer in which the bidder offers a superior first-tier price (e.g., higher or all cash) for a specified maximum number (or percent) of shares and simultaneously offers to acquire the remaining shares at a second-tier price (e.g., lower and/or securities rather than cash).

Instead of one tender offer, some bidders make a **two-tier tender offer.** An example of this was the bid by CSX Corporation for Consolidated Rail Corporation (Conrail) in the late 1990s. With a two-tier offer, the first tier of stock usually represents control and, for example, might be 45 percent of the stock outstanding if the bidder already owned 5 percent. The first-tier offer is more attractive in terms of price and/or form of payment than is the second-tier offer for the remaining shares of stock. The differential is designed to increase the probability of successfully gaining control, by providing an incentive to tender early. The two-tier offer avoids the "free-rider" problem associated with a single tender offer where individual shareholders have an incentive to hold out in the hope of realizing a higher counteroffer by someone else.

The company being bid for may use a number of defensive tactics. Management may try to persuade shareholders that the offer is not in their best interests. Usually, the argument is that the bid is too low in relation to the true, long-run value of the firm. Hearing this, shareholders may look at an attractive premium and find the long run too long. Some companies raise the cash dividend or declare a stock split in hopes of gaining shareholder support. Legal actions are often undertaken, more to delay and frustrate the bidder than with the expectation of winning. When the two

Part VIII Special Areas of Financial Management

firms are competitors, an antitrust suit may prove a powerful deterrent to the bidder. As a last resort, management of the company being bid for may seek a merger with a "friendly" company, known as a **white knight.**

Antitakeover Amendments and Other Devices

In addition to defensive tactics, some companies use more formal methods that are put into place prior to an actual takeover attempt. Known as antitakeover devices or **shark repellent,** they are designed to make an unwanted takeover more difficult. Before describing them, it is useful to consider their motivation. The *managerial entrenchment hypothesis* suggests that the barriers erected are to protect management jobs and that such actions work to the detriment of shareholders. On the other hand, the *shareholders' interest hypothesis* implies that contests for corporate control are dysfunctional and take management time away from profit-making activities. Antitakeover devices ensure that more attention is paid by management to productive activities and are, therefore, in the interest of shareholders. Moreover, the barriers erected are said to cause individual shareholders not to accept a low offer price but to join other shareholders in a cartel response to any offer. Therefore, antitakeover devices actually enhance shareholder wealth, according to this hypothesis.

A handful of devices exist to make it more difficult for one party to take over another. As we know from Chapter 20, some companies *stagger the terms of their boards of directors* so that fewer directors stand for election each year and, accordingly, more votes are needed to elect a majority of directors sympathetic to a takeover. Sometimes, it is desirable to *change the state of incorporation.* Charter rules differ state by state, and many companies like to incorporate in a state with few limitations, such as Delaware. By so doing, it is easier for the corporation to install antitakeover amendments as well as defend itself legally if a takeover battle ensues. Some companies put into place a *supermajority merger approval provision.* Instead of an ordinary majority being needed for approval of a merger, a higher percentage, often two-thirds or three-fourths of the shareholder vote, is required.

Another antitakeover device is a *fair merger price provision.* Here the bidder must pay noncontrolling shareholders a price at least equal to a "fair price," which is established in advance. Usually, this minimum price is linked to earnings per share through a price/earnings ratio, but it may simply be a stated market price. Often the fair price provision is coupled with a supermajority provision. If the stated minimum price is not satisfied, the combination can only be approved if a supermajority of shareholders vote in favor of it. The fair price provision is also frequently accompanied by a *freeze-out provision,* under which the transaction is allowed to proceed at a "fair price" only after a delay of anywhere from two to five years.

Still another method used to thwart potential acquirers is the *leveraged recapitalization.* This calls for the current management to load the balance sheet with new debt and use the proceeds to pay a huge, one-time cash dividend to shareholders. Taking on all this debt acts to discourage the acquirer, who can no longer borrow against the firm's assets to help finance the acquisition. The company continues to be publicly held, because stockholders retain their common shares, known as "stub" shares. Obviously the shares now are worth much less because of the huge cash dividend. In this type of transaction, management and other insiders do not participate in the cash payout; instead, they take additional shares of common stock. As a result, their proportional ownership of the corporation increases substantially, which further discourages a potential acquirer. In effect, leveraged recapitalization allows a company to act as its own "white knight."

White knight A friendly acquirer who, at the invitation of a target company, purchases shares from the hostile bidder(s) or launches a friendly counterbid to frustrate the initial, unfriendly bidder(s).

Shark repellent Defenses employed by a company to ward off potential takeover bidders—the "sharks."

To discourage potential acquirers, some companies instigate a *distribution of rights to shareholders,* allowing them to purchase a new security, often convertible preferred stock. However, the security offering is triggered only if an outside party acquires some percentage, frequently 20 percent, of the company's stock. The idea is to have a security offering available that is unpalatable to the acquirer. This can be with respect to voting rights, with respect to a low (bargain) exercise price paid for the security, or with respect to precluding a control transaction unless a substantial premium, often several hundred percent, is paid. Known as a **poison pill,** the provision is meant to force the potential acquirer into negotiating directly with the board of directors. The board reserves the ability to redeem the rights at any time for a token amount. Thus, the poison pill puts power in the hands of the board of directors to dissuade a takeover, which may or may not be in the best interest of shareholders overall.

Poison pill A device used by a company to make itself less attractive as a takeover candidate. Its poison, so to speak, is released when the buyer takes a sufficient bite of the target firm.

A *lockup provision* is used in conjunction with other provisions. This provision requires supermajority shareholder approval to modify the corporate charter and any previously passed antitakeover provisions. In addition to these charter amendments, many companies enter into management contracts with their top management. Typically, high compensation is triggered if the company is taken over. Known as a "golden parachute," these contracts effectively increase the price the acquiring company must pay in an unfriendly takeover.

Despite these devices, outside groups do acquire blocks of stock in a corporation prior to either a takeover attempt or the sale of their stock to someone else who poses such a threat. Indication of unusual accumulation of stock comes from watching trading volume and stock transfers. If a group acquires more than 5 percent of a company, it is required to file *Form 13-D* with the Securities and Exchange Commission. This form describes the people involved with the group, its holdings, and its intention. The standard response to the last item is, "we bought it only as an investment," so little information is really conveyed. Each time the group acquires an additional 1 percent of the stock, it must file an amendment to its Form 13-D. Therefore, a company can accurately track the amount of its stock that is being accumulated.

Sometimes the company will negotiate a *standstill agreement* with the outside party. Such an agreement is a voluntary contract where, for a period of several years, the substantial shareholder group agrees not to increase its shareholdings. Often this limitation is expressed as a maximum percentage of stock the group may own. The agreement also specifies that the group will not participate in a control contest against management and that it gives the right of first refusal to the company if it should decide to sell its stock. The standstill agreement, together with the other provisions discussed, serves to reduce competition for corporate control.

As a last resort, some companies make a *premium buy-back offer* to the threatening party. As the name implies, the repurchase of stock is at a premium over its market price and is usually in excess of what the accumulator paid. Moreover, the offer is not extended to other shareholders. Known as "greenmail," the idea is to remove the threat by making it attractive for the party to leave. Of course the premium paid to one party may work to the disadvantage of shareholders left "holding the bag."

Empirical Evidence on Antitakeover Devices

Are antitakeover devices in the best interests of shareholders? The empirical results are mixed. For the most part, the evidence does not indicate that a significant share price effect occurs when various antitakeover amendments are adopted. However, standstill agreements appear to have a negative effect on shareholder wealth, as do stock repurchases by a company from the owner of a large block of stock. The latter are often associated with greenmail, where such an owner threatens the company with a hostile takeover and the company buys the owner's large block of stock at a favorable price to eliminate the threat. Unfortunately there is a wealth transfer away from nonparticipating shareholders. The use of a poison pill appears to have a negative, though modest, effect on share price, a finding consistent with the managerial entrenchment hypothesis. (See the Selected References at the end of the chapter for articles about actual studies.)

Strategic Alliances

Strategic alliance An agreement between two or more independent firms to cooperate in order to achieve some specific commercial objective.

Sometimes individual firms lack the resources to achieve all their strategic objectives through direct investment or acquisition. **Strategic alliances,** or cooperative arrangements between companies, offer a third option. Strategic alliances—distinct from mergers in that the members remain independent firms—can take many forms and involve a variety of partners. Collaboration can take place between suppliers and their customers (e.g., the cooperative agreements necessary to make "just-in-time" inventory systems work); between competitors in the same business (e.g., two auto firms sharing one assembly plant); or between noncompetitors with complementary strengths (e.g., health-care providers, hospitals, and physicians cooperating to reduce costs).

Joint Ventures

Joint venture A business venture jointly owned and controlled by two or more independent firms. Each venture partner continues to exist as a separate firm, and the joint venture represents a new business enterprise.

In one type of strategic alliance, the **joint venture,** two or more firms collaborate to such an extent that they jointly establish and control a separate company to meet their specific set of objectives. For example, NBC and Microsoft expanded a loose strategic alliance into a 50–50 joint venture. A major component of this joint venture was the creation of a global 24-hour news and information cable network called MSNBC.

Virtual Corporations

Outsourcing Subcontracting a certain business operation to an outside firm instead of doing it in house.

Virtual corporation A business organizational model that involves the large-scale outsourcing of business functions.

In recent years, **outsourcing** has become a widespread business tool. This shifting of what might ordinarily be an in-house operation to an outside firm has allowed firms to focus on the core competencies they possess that give them a competitive advantage. What happens when you take outsourcing to its limits and strip a company to only its bare-bones core competencies? You end up with what has been termed a **virtual corporation.** For such a firm, even the manufacture of its branded products might be outsourced. To survive, such firms would need to form alliances and/or joint ventures with suppliers and manufacturers.

Sara Lee, known for its baked goods as well as its Jimmy Dean sausages, Hanes T-shirts, and even the Wonderbra, made headlines when it sold off many of its bakeries, meat-processing plants, and textile factories to become a virtual corporation. John Bryan, CEO of Sara Lee, explained that he wanted to make his company "asset-less"—to outsource virtually everything and concentrate on marketing and managing Sara Lee's various brands.

Brand name recognition has become so valuable that a number of companies have outsourced their manufacturing processes so they could devote themselves entirely to brand management. Nike is a prime example. Nike manufactures no shoes—its strategic-partner suppliers (primarily in Asia) do that. Instead, Nike focuses on product design, marketing, and distribution; these are Nike's core competencies, not manufacturing.

For firms like Sara Lee and Nike, the virtual corporations, the strategic cooperative arrangements they form with their suppliers/manufacturers are crucial. These arrangements also give virtual corporations great flexibility and allow them to better control the risk surrounding new business initiatives. This is because the virtual corporation can experiment without overinvesting in activities that might not work out.

DIVESTITURE

In a merger, two or more enterprises are put together. With a strategic alliance, two or more independent firms agree to cooperate. However, sometimes value creation requires that corporate restructurings take on quite different aspects from either growth or cooperation. A company may decide to divest part of the enterprise or liquidate entirely. In this section, we consider various methods of **divestiture.**

Divestiture The divestment of a portion of the enterprise or the firm as a whole.

Voluntary Corporate Liquidation

The decision to sell a firm in its entirety should be rooted in value creation for the shareholders. Assuming the situation does not involve financial failure, which we address in the Appendix to this chapter, the idea is that the firm's assets may have a higher value in **liquidation** than the present value of the expected cash-flow stream emanating from them. By liquidating, the seller is able to sell the assets to multiple parties, which may result in a higher value being realized than if they had to be sold as a whole, as occurs in a merger. With a complete liquidation, the debt of the company must be paid off at its face value. If the market value of the debt was previously below this, debt holders realize a wealth gain, which ultimately is at the expense of equity holders.

Liquidation The sale of assets of a firm, either voluntarily or in bankruptcy.

Partial Sell-offs

Sell-off The sale of a division of a company, known as a partial sell-off, or the company as a whole, known as a voluntary liquidation.

In the case of a partial **sell-off,** only part of the company is sold. When a business unit is sold, payment is generally in the form of cash or securities. The decision should result in some positive net present value to the selling company. The key is whether the value received is more than the present value of the stream of expected future cash flows if the operation were to be continued.

Corporate Spin-offs

Spin-off A form of divestiture resulting in a subsidiary or division becoming an independent company. Ordinarily, shares in the new company are distributed to the parent company's shareholders on a pro rata basis.

Similar to a sell-off, a **spin-off** involves a decision to divest a business unit, such as a stand-alone subsidiary or division. In a spin-off, the business unit is not sold for cash or securities. Rather, common stock in the unit is distributed to the shareholders of the company on a pro rata basis, after which the unit operates as a completely separate company. For example, in 1997 Pepsico, Inc., "spun off" its restaurant holdings, KFC, Pizza Hut, and Taco Bell, into a $10 billion company called Tricon Global Restaurants. Physical assets as well as people were involved in the spin-off. There was no tax liability to the shareholders at the time of the spin-off because taxation occurs only when the common stock is sold. After the spin-off, Tricon operated independently with its common stock being traded under the **ticker symbol** YUM on the New York Stock Exchange.

The motivations for a spin-off are similar in some ways to those for a sell-off. In the case of a spin-off, however, another company will not operate the unit. Therefore, there is no opportunity for synergy in the usual sense of the term. It is possible that as an independent company with different management incentives, the operation will be better run. In this sense, an economic gain may be achieved from the transaction. However, costs are involved. New shares must be issued, and there are the ongoing costs of servicing shareholders, together with new agency costs in having two public companies as opposed to one. The case for economic net gain is not clear.

Other reasons for a spin-off would appear to have more substance. The previously cited argument of a wealth transfer from debt holders to equity holders might be applicable. Another factor from our earlier discussion is the information effect associated with the spin-off.

With a spin-off it may also be possible to obtain flexibility in contracting. With a separate operation, one can sometimes rearrange labor contracts, get out from under tax regulations, or skirt regulatory constraints that no longer are directly applicable. Another type of contract involves management. With a spin-off, there is a separation of the business unit's management from that of the parent. As a result, it may be possible to restructure incentives to gain improved managerial productivity. Finally, the spin-off may permit greater flexibility in debt contracts when it comes to imposed protective covenants.[6] All of these things may influence the decision to spin off a business unit and the valuation of the transaction.

Equity Carve-outs

An **equity carve-out** is similar in some ways to the two previously described forms of divestiture. However, common stock in the business unit is sold to the public. The initial public offering usually involves only some of the subsidiary's stock. Typically, the parent company continues to have an equity stake in the subsidiary and does not relinquish control. Under these circumstances, a minority interest is sold, and the carve-out represents a form of equity financing. The difference when it, rather than the parent company, sells stock under its own name is that the claim is on the subsidiary's cash flows and assets. For the first time, the value of the subsidiary becomes observable in the marketplace.

One motivation for the equity carve-out is that with a separate stock price and public trading, managers may have more incentive to perform well. For one thing, the size of the operation is such that their efforts will not go unnoticed as they sometimes do in a large, multibusiness company. With separate stock options, it may be possible to attract and retain better managers and to motivate them. Also, information about the subsidiary is more readily available. In turn, this may reduce asymmetric (unequal) information between managers and investors and cause the subsidiary's worth to be more accurately assessed by the marketplace.

Some suggest that the equity carve-out is a favorable means for financing growth. When the subsidiary is in leading-edge technology but not particularly profitable, the equity carve-out may be a more effective vehicle for financing than is financing through the parent. With a separate subsidiary, the market may become more complete because investors are able to obtain a **pure play** investment in the technology.

---

[6]For an analysis of these various reasons, see Katherine Schipper and Abbie Smith, "Effects of Recontracting on Shareholder Wealth: The Case of Voluntary Spin-Offs," *Journal of Financial Economics* 12 (December 1983), 437–68.

CORPORATE FINANCE

One of the textbook examples of how an equity carve-out—where a parent company makes an IPO of a piece of one of its subsidiaries—can be highly beneficial to all concerned is the separation, in two stages, of Associates First Capital from Ford Motor. The first stage was an IPO of 19.3% of Associates in May 1996, which raised $1.65 billion. In the second stage, Associates was spun off to shareholders in April 1998, in a deal valued at $23.69 billion.

According to Ford, the primary reasons for the carve-out were the usual corporate buzzwords—focus, global synergies, "concentrating on the fundamentals." Associates was—and is—a great consumer-finance company that was growing much faster than Ford itself. But it had little, if anything, to do with Ford's core business of cars and trucks. Once carved out, Associates could go it alone. In a fast-consolidating industry, it now had a valuable acquisition currency— its own stock—through which to expand. "It was necessary for Associates to separate so it could continue to grow," says a Ford spokesperson.

TAX MOTIVES

A big reason that carve-outs are so popular in the United States is their great tax-efficiency. Companies pay no tax on carve-outs of up to 20% of a subsidiary— hence the large number of deals in which just that amount is offered to investors. The only thing they have to be careful about is that the shares on offer are newly issued and not existing stock on which the parent company might have to pay capital gains tax. And if the rest of the subsidiary is subsequently spun off to shareholders, no cash accrues to the former parent, and therefore no tax has to be paid.

Source: Adapted from "Mega-mergers bring a new spate of carve-outs," Corporate Finance (September 1998), pp. 20–21. © Euromoney Publications plc, 1998. Used by permission. All rights reserved.

Empirical Evidence on Divestitures

As with mergers, the principal empirical tests on divestitures have involved event studies, where daily security return behavior, after isolating out general market effects, is studied around the time of the announcement. For liquidation of the entire company, the results indicate large gains to shareholders of the liquidating company, in the range of 12 to 20 percent. For partial sell-offs, shareholders of the selling company seem to realize a slight positive return (about 2 percent) around the time of the announcement. Shareholders of the buying company also experience small positive gains on average, consistent with the subsidiary or division sold being more valuable to the buyer in terms of economic efficiency than it is to the seller.

For the spin-off, somewhat higher shareholder excess returns (5 percent or more) were recorded on average than for sell-offs. The findings here are consistent with a positive information effect of the spin-off announcement. The evidence is not consistent with a wealth transfer from debt holders to equity holders. Finally, for equity carve-outs a modest gain (around 2 percent) to shareholders around the time of the announcement was found. On balance, then, divestitures seem to have a positive informational effect, with voluntary liquidations having the largest effect.

OWNERSHIP RESTRUCTURING

Other corporate restructurings are designed to change the ownership structure of a company. This is often accompanied by a dramatic change in the proportion of debt employed. In this section we explore *going private* and *leveraged buyouts*.

Going Private

Going private Making a public company private through the repurchase of stock by current management and/or outside private investors.

A number of well-known companies, such as Levi Strauss & Company, have "gone private." **Going private** simply means transforming a company whose stock is publicly held into a private one. The privately held stock is owned by a small group of investors, with incumbent management usually having a large equity stake. In this ownership change, a variety of vehicles are used to buy out the public shareholders. Probably the most common involves paying them cash and merging the company into a shell corporation owned solely by a private investor management group. Rather than being treated as a merger, the transaction may be treated as an asset sale to the private group. There are other ways, but the result is the same: the company ceases to exist as a publicly held entity, and the shareholders receive a valuable consideration for their shares. Though most transactions involve cash, noncash compensation, such as notes, is sometimes employed.

Motivations

A number of factors may prompt management to take a company private.[7] There are costs associated with being a publicly held company. The stock must be registered, and shareholders must be serviced. There are administrative expenses in paying dividends and sending out materials, and legal and administrative expenses are incurred in filing reports with the Securities and Exchange Commission and other regulators. In addition, there are annual shareholders meetings and meetings with security analysts leading to often embarrassing questions that most chief executive officers would rather do without. All of these things can be avoided by being a private company.

With a publicly held company, some feel there is a fixation on quarterly accounting earnings as opposed to long-run economic earnings. To the extent that decisions are directed more toward building economic value, going private may improve resource allocation decisions and, thereby, enhance value.

Another motivation for going private is to realign and improve management incentives. With increased equity ownership by management, there may be an incentive to work longer and more efficiently. The money saved and the profits generated through more effective management largely benefit the company's management as opposed to a wide group of shareholders. As a result, they may be more willing to make the tough decisions, to cut costs, to reduce management "perks," and simply to work harder. The rewards are linked more closely to their decisions. The greater the performance and profitability, the greater the reward. In a publicly held company, the compensation level is not so directly linked, particularly for decisions that produce high profitability. When compensation is high, there are always questions from security analysts, shareholders, and the press.

Although there are a number of reasons for going private, there are some offsetting arguments. For one thing, there are transactions costs to investment bankers, lawyers, and others that can be quite substantial. A private company gives little liquidity to its owners with respect to their stock ownership. A large portion of their wealth may be tied up in the company. Management, for example, may create value for the company but be unable to realize this value unless the company goes public in the future. If the company later goes public, transactions costs are repeated—wonderful for investment bankers and lawyers, but a sizable cost nonetheless.

---

[7]The major paper dealing with going private is by Harry DeAngelo, Linda DeAngelo, and Edward M. Rice, "Going Private: Minority Freezeouts and Stockholder Wealth," *Journal of Law and Economics* 27 (June 1984), 367–401, where most of these motivations are discussed.

Empirical Evidence on Going Private

There have been a few studies of the effect of going private on security holder wealth. The evidence we have suggests that shareholders realize sizable gains (about 12 to 22 percent in two studies) around the time of the announcement. In the case of a cash offer, the gain is much more, similar to the premiums realized in a merger. Shareholders clearly gain, but whether or not they are treated fairly cannot be stated.

LEVERAGED BUYOUTS

Leveraged buyout (LBO)
A primarily debt-financed purchase of all the stock or assets of a company, subsidiary, or division by an investor group.

Going private can be a straightforward transaction, where the investor group simply buys out the public shareholders, or it can be a **leveraged buyout (LBO),** where there are third- and sometimes fourth-party investors. As the name implies, a leveraged buyout represents an ownership transfer consummated primarily with debt. Sometimes called asset-based financing, the debt is secured by the assets of the enterprise involved. As a result, most leveraged buyouts involve capital-intensive businesses. Though some leveraged buyouts involve an entire company, most involve the purchase of a division of a company or some other subunit. Frequently, the sale is to the management of the division being sold, the company having decided that the division no longer fits its strategic objectives. This type of transaction is referred to as a **management buyout (MBO).** Another distinctive feature is that leveraged buyouts are cash purchases, as opposed to stock purchases. Finally, the business unit involved invariably becomes a privately held company.

Management buyout (MBO) A leverage buyout (LBO) in which prebuyout management ends up with a substantial equity position.

Desirable LBO candidates have certain common characteristics. Frequently the company in question enjoys a window of opportunity extending for several years and during which major expenditures can be deferred. Often the company has gone through a program of heavy capital expenditures, and, as a result, its plant is modern. The company may have subsidiary assets that can be sold without adversely impacting its core business, and such a sale can provide cash for debt service in the early years. In contrast, companies with high research and development (R&D) requirements, like drug companies, are not good candidates. For the first several years after an LBO, cash flows must be dedicated to debt service. Capital expenditures, R&D, advertising, and personnel development must take a back seat. Usually a service company, where people constitute the bulk of the franchise value, is not a good LBO candidate because if the people should leave, little of value remains.

Stable, predictable operating cash flows are prized in LBO candidates. In this regard, companies who produce consumer brands dominate "commodity-type" businesses. Proven historical performance, with an established market position, is also rated highly. Turnaround situations tend to be spurned. The less the products of the company or business are subject to cyclical demand, the better. As a rule, the company's assets must be physical assets and/or brand names. Management is also important in that the experience and quality of senior management are critical elements needed for success. While the characteristics just described are not all-inclusive, they give a flavor of the ingredients that make for desirable, and undesirable, LBO candidates.

An Illustration in Detail

To illustrate a typical leveraged buyout, suppose that Klim-On Corporation wishes to divest itself of its dairy products division. The assets of the division consist of plants, equipment, truck fleets, inventories, and receivables. These assets have a book value of $120 million. Their replacement value is $170 million, but if the division were to be liquidated, the assets would fetch only $95 million. Klim-On has decided to sell the division if it can obtain $110 million in cash, and it has enlisted an investment banker to assist it in the sale. After surveying the market for such a sale, the investment banker concludes that the best prospect is to sell the division to existing management. The four top divisional officers are interested and eager to pursue the opportunity. However, they are able to come up with only $2 million in personal capital among them. Obviously, more capital is needed.

The investment banker agrees to try to arrange a leveraged buyout. Financial projections and cash budgets are prepared for the division to determine how much debt can be serviced. On the basis of these forecasts, as well as the curtailment of certain capital expenditures, research and development expenses, and advertising expenses, it is felt that the likely cash thrown off is sufficient to service approximately $100 million in debt. The reduction in expenditures is regarded as temporary, for the company to service debt during the next several years. The investment banker has lined up a limited partnership to make an additional equity investment of $8 million, which will bring total equity to $10 million. For this cash contribution, the partnership receives 60 percent of the initial common stock, and management receives the remainder.

Arranging Debt Financing

With this equity capital commitment, the investment banker proceeds to arrange debt financing. In a leveraged buyout, two forms of debt are typically employed: senior debt and junior subordinated debt. For the senior debt, a large New York bank, through its asset-based lending subsidiary, has agreed to provide $75 million toward the cost plus an additional $8 million revolving credit for seasonal needs. The rate on both arrangements is 2 percent over the prime rate, and the loans are secured by liens on all of the assets—real estate, buildings, equipment, rolling stock, inventories, and receivables. The term of the $75 million loan is six years, payable in equal monthly installments of principal and with interest for the month being added on. All major banking will be done with the lending bank, and company receipts will be deposited into a special account at the bank for purposes of servicing the debt. In addition to the collateral, the usual protective covenants are imposed in a loan agreement.

Junior subordinated debt in the amount of $25 million has been arranged with the subsidiary of a large finance company funding the merger. This debt is sometimes referred to as "mezzanine" financing, because it falls between senior debt and the equity. The loan is for seven years with an interest rate of 13 percent being fixed throughout. Only monthly interest payments are required during the seven years, the full principal amount being due at the end. Because the senior lender will have liens on all assets, the debt is unsecured and subordinated to the senior debt as well as to all trade creditors. To help compensate for the greater risk faced by the provider of the subordinated financing, this lender receives an "equity kicker" in the form of warrants exercisable for 40 percent of the stock. These warrants may be exercised at any time throughout the seven years at a price of $1 per share, a price that is quite nominal. If the warrants are exercised, management's stock will go from 40 percent of the total outstanding to 24 percent. The ownership of the limited partnership will drop from 60 percent to 36 percent. The financing is summed up as follows (in millions):

Senior debt	$ 75
Junior subordinated debt	25
Equity	10
	$110

In addition, the company will have access to an $8 million revolving credit arrangement to meet seasonal needs.

We see that a leveraged buyout permits a company to go private with very little equity involved. The assets of the acquired company or division are used to secure a large amount of debt. The equity holders, as residual owners, may do very well if things go according to plan. However, with the thin equity cushion not much need go wrong for the owners' investment to be in jeopardy. Many investors found this out in the late 1980s and early 1990s, when numerous LBOs ran into difficulty. As we have cautioned before, leverage is a "two-edged sword!"

SUMMARY

- Corporate restructuring embraces many topics: *mergers; strategic alliances,* including *joint ventures; divestitures,* including *liquidation, sell-offs, spin-offs,* and *equity carve-outs; ownership restructuring,* such as taking a publicly owned company private; and *leveraged buyouts.* The motivation in all cases should be to enhance shareholder wealth.

- The sources of value creation in corporate restructuring include sales enhancement and operating economies, management improvements, information effects, wealth transfers from debt holders, and tax benefits. In takeovers, too-aggressive bidding (resulting from hubris and/or pursuit of management's personal agenda) often causes the shareholders of the acquiring company to suffer a decrease in wealth.

- A company may grow internally, or it may grow externally through acquisitions. The objective of the firm in either case is to maximize existing shareholder wealth. Both types of expansion can be regarded as special types of capital budgeting decisions. The criterion for acceptance is essentially the same—capital should be allocated to increase shareholder wealth.

- There are two common approaches to the analysis of an acquisition. With an *earnings per share approach,* the question is whether there would be an earnings per share improvement now or in the future. In the *free-cash-flow approach,* the question is whether the expected net cash flows have a present value in excess of the acquisition's cost. In general, the cash-flow approach looks at the valuation of an acquisition over the long run, whereas

- the earnings per share approach focuses on the short run. A strong case can be made for using both approaches.

- Empirical evidence on acquisitions indicates substantial excess returns to the shareholders of the selling company, owing to the substantial premium paid, and no excess returns on average to those of the buying company.

- Another company can be acquired through the purchase of either its assets or its common stock. In turn, the means of payment can be cash or common stock. From an accounting standpoint, a combination of two companies is treated as either a *purchase* or as a *pooling of interests.* With a purchase, any goodwill arising from the merger must be amortized against future earnings.

- Whether a combination is taxable or tax free is highly consequential to the selling company and its shareholders and, sometimes, to the buying company.

- The acquisition of another company can be negotiated with the management of the prospective acquisition, or the acquiring company can make its appeal directly to the shareholders through a *tender offer* to purchase their shares. These "unfriendly" takeovers are usually resisted by management. A number of antitakeover devices exist. Some appear to have a negative effect on shareholder wealth.

- A company may decide to restructure by divesting itself of a portion of the enterprise or liquidating entirely. *Voluntary liquidations, sell-offs, spin-offs,* and *equity carve-outs* are some of the major options open to the firm. In general, divestitures seem to have a positive informational effect, with voluntary liquidations having the largest.

- When a company *goes private,* it is transformed from public ownership to private ownership by a small group of investors, including management. The empirical evidence suggests sizable premiums, similar to those for mergers, being paid to the public shareholders.

- One means for going private is the *leveraged buyout (LBO).* Here a large amount of debt is used to finance a cash purchase of a division of a company or a company as a whole. Both senior debt secured by assets and junior subordinated debt are employed. Given the small equity base, leveraged buyouts are risky. It does not take a very large adverse change in operations or interest rates for default to occur.

Appendix

Remedies for a Failing Company

So far our discussion of corporate restructuring has assumed that the firm is a *going concern.* Nevertheless, we must not lose sight of the fact that some firms fail. Internal management must keep this in mind, and so must a creditor who has amounts due from a company in financial distress. The word "failure" is vague, partly because there are varying degrees of failure. Three terms are commonly used to give more precise meaning to the varying degrees of failure. *Equitable (technical) insolvency* is usually defined as a debtor's general inability to pay debts as they become due. However, such insolvency may be only temporary and subject to remedy. Equitable insolvency, then, denotes only a lack of liquidity. *Legal insolvency,* on the other hand, means that the liabilities of a company exceed its assets "at a fair valuation." *Financial failure* includes the entire range of situations between these two extremes.

The remedies for a failing company vary in harshness according to the degree of financial difficulty. If the outlook is sufficiently hopeless, liquidation may be the only feasible alternative. However, some failing companies can be rehabilitated to the gain of creditors, shareholders, and society. The purpose of this Appendix is to review the remedies available, beginning with those that are voluntary, and then to move on to examine legal actions.

VOLUNTARY SETTLEMENTS

An *extension* involves creditors postponing the maturity of their obligations. By not forcing legal proceedings, creditors avoid considerable legal expense and the possible shrinkage of value in liquidation. Because all creditors must agree to extend their obligations, the major creditors usually form a committee whose functions are to negotiate with the company and formulate a plan mutually satisfactory to all concerned.

A *composition* involves a pro rata settlement of creditors' claims in cash or in cash and promissory notes. All creditors must agree to accept this partial settlement in discharge of their entire claim. As with an extension, dissenting creditors must either be brought into the fold or paid in full.

Voluntary liquidation represents an orderly private liquidation of a company away from the bankruptcy courts. Not only is it likely to be more efficient than a court-imposed liquidation, but creditors are likely to receive a higher settlement as many of the costs of bankruptcy are avoided. However, the company and all creditors must go along. As a result, voluntary liquidations are usually restricted to companies with a limited number of creditors.

LEGAL PROCEEDINGS

Legal procedures undertaken in connection with a failing company fall under bankruptcy law as decreed through bankruptcy courts. Bankruptcy law is composed of many facets, but we are concerned with only two that pertain to business failure. Chapter 7 of the bankruptcy law deals with liquidation, and Chapter 11 deals with the rehabilitation of an enterprise through its reorganization.

In both cases, proceedings begin with the debtor or creditors filing a petition in the bankruptcy court. When the debtor initiates the petition, it is called a voluntary proceeding. If the initiative is taken by creditors, it is said to be involuntary. In a voluntary proceeding, merely filing the petition gives the debtor immediate protection from creditors. A *stay* restrains creditors from collecting their claims or taking actions until the court decides on the merit of the petition. The court can either accept the petition and order relief or dismiss it.

Three or more unsecured creditors with claims totaling $5,000 or more are required to initiate an involuntary bankruptcy. Here the petition must give evidence that the debtor firm has not paid debts on a timely basis (equitable insolvency) or has assigned possession of most of its property to someone else. The bankruptcy court then must decide whether the involuntary petition has merit. If the decision is negative, the petition is dismissed. If the petition is accepted, the court issues an order of relief pending a more permanent solution. The idea behind this stay of creditor action is to give the debtor breathing space to propose a solution to the problem. In what follows, we observe the solutions of liquidation and the reorganization of an enterprise.

LIQUIDATION

If there is no hope for the successful operation of a company, liquidation is the only feasible alternative. Upon petition of bankruptcy, the debtor obtains temporary relief from creditors until a decision is reached by the bankruptcy court. After issuing the order of relief, the court frequently appoints an interim trustee to take over the operation of the company and to call a meeting of creditors. The interim trustee is a "disinterested" private citizen who is appointed from an approved list and who serves until at least the first meeting of creditors. At the first meeting, claims are proven, and the creditors may then elect a new trustee to replace the interim trustee. Otherwise, the interim trustee serves as the regular trustee, continuing to function in that capacity until the case is completed. The trustee has responsibility for liquidating the property of the company and distributing liquidating dividends to creditors.

In distributing the proceeds of a liquidation to creditors with unsecured claims, the priority of claims must be observed. The order of distribution is as follows:

1. Administrative expenses associated with liquidating the property, including the trustee's fee and attorney fees
2. Creditor claims that arise in the ordinary course of the debtor's business from the time the case starts to the time a trustee is appointed
3. Wages earned by employees within 90 days of the bankruptcy petition (limited to $2,000 per employee)
4. Claims for contributions to employee benefit plans for services rendered within 180 days of the bankruptcy petition (limited to $2,000 per employee)
5. Claims of customers who make cash deposits for goods or services not provided by the debtor (limited to $900 per customer)
6. Taxes owed
7. Unsecured claims either filed on time or tardily filed if the creditor did not know of the bankruptcy
8. Unsecured claims filed late by creditors who had knowledge of the bankruptcy
9. Fines and punitive damages
10. Interest that accrues to claims after the date of the petition

Claims in each of these classes must be paid in full before any payment can be made to claims in the next class. If anything is left over after all of these claims are paid in full, liquidating dividends can then be paid to subordinated debt holders, to preferred stockholders, and, finally, to common stockholders. It is unlikely, however, that common stockholders will receive any distribution from a liquidation. Special provision is made in the Bankruptcy Act for damage claims by lessors to the debtor. In general, lessors are limited to the greater of one year of payments or 15 percent of the total remaining payments but not to exceed those for three years. Upon the payment of all liquidating dividends, the debtor is discharged and relieved of any further claims.

REORGANIZATION

It may be in the best interests of all concerned to reorganize a company rather than liquidate it. Conceptually, a firm should be reorganized if its economic worth as an operating entity is greater than its liquidation value. It should be liquidated if the converse is true, that is, if it is worth more "dead" than "alive." **Reorganization** is an effort to keep a company alive by changing its capital structure. The rehabilitation involves the reduction of fixed charges by substituting equity and limited-income securities for fixed-income securities.

Reorganization Recasting of the capital structure of a financially troubled company, under Chapter 11 of the Bankruptcy Act, in order to reduce fixed charges. Claim holders may be given substitute securities.

Procedures.   Reorganizations occur under Chapter 11 of the bankruptcy law and are initiated in the same general manner as liquidation in bankruptcy. Either the debtor or creditors file a petition, and the case begins. In most cases, the debtor will continue to run the business, although a trustee can assume operating responsibility of the company. One of the great needs in rehabilitation is interim credit. To provide inducements, Chapter 11 gives post-petition creditors priority over pre-petition creditors. If this inducement is not sufficient, the bankruptcy court is empowered to authorize new, or post-petition, creditors to obtain a lien on the debtor's property.

If a trustee is not appointed, the debtor has the sole right to draw up a reorganization plan and to file it within 120 days. Otherwise, the trustee has the responsibility of seeing that a plan is filed. It may be drawn up by the trustee, the debtor, the creditors' committee, or individual creditors, and more than one plan can be filed. All reorganization plans must be submitted to creditors and stockholders for approval. The role of the court is to review the information in the plan, to make sure disclosure is full.

In a reorganization, the plan should be *fair, equitable,* and *feasible.* This means that all parties must be treated fairly and equitably and that the plan must be workable with respect to the earning power and financial structure of the reorganized company as well as the ability of the company to obtain trade credit and, perhaps, short-term bank loans. Each class of claim holders must vote on a plan. More than one-half the number and two-thirds the amount of total claims in each class must vote in favor of the plan if it is to be accepted. If creditors reject the reorganization plan, the bankruptcy judge will try to get the various parties to negotiate another plan. If creditors reject such efforts, the judge may impose a plan, known as a *cram down,* on all claimholders. Upon confirmation of any plan by the bankruptcy court, the debtor must then perform according to the terms of the plan. Moreover, the plan binds all creditors and shareholders, including dissenters.

Reorganization Plan.   The difficult aspect of a reorganization is the recasting of the company's capital structure to reduce the amount of fixed charges. In formulating a reorganization plan, there are three steps. First, the total valuation of the reorganized company must be determined. This step is the most difficult and the most important. The technique favored by trustees is a capitalization of prospective earnings. If future annual earnings of the reorganized company are expected to be $2 million and the overall capitalization rate of similar companies averages 10 percent, a total valuation of ($2 million)/(.10) = **$20 million** would be set for the company. The valuation figure is subject to considerable variation, owing to the difficulty of estimating prospective earnings and determining an appropriate capitalization rate. Thus, the valuation figure represents nothing more than a best estimate of potential value. Although the capitalization of prospective earnings is the generally accepted approach of valuing a company in reorganization, the valuation may be adjusted upward if the assets have substantial liquidating value.

Once a valuation figure has been determined, the next step is to formulate a new capital structure for the company to reduce fixed charges, so that there will be an adequate coverage margin. To reduce these charges, the total debt of the firm is scaled down by being partly shifted to income bonds, preferred stock, and common stock. In addition to being scaled down, the terms of the remaining debt may be changed. The maturity of the debt can be extended to reduce the amount of annual sinking-fund obligation. If it appears that the reorganized company will need new financing in the future, the trustee may feel that a more conservative ratio of debt to equity is in order to provide for future financial flexibility.

Once a new capital structure is established, the last step involves the valuation of the old securities and their exchange for new securities. In general, all senior claims on assets must be settled in full before a junior claim can be settled. In the exchange process, bondholders must receive the par value of their bonds in another security before there can be any distribution to preferred stockholders. The total valuation figure arrived at in Step 1 sets an upper limit on the amount of securities that can be issued. The existing capital structure of a company undergoing reorganization may be as follows (in millions):

Debentures	$ 9
Subordinated debentures	3
Preferred stock	6
Common stock equity (at book value)	10
	$28

If the total valuation of the reorganized company is to be $20 million, the trustee might establish the following capital structure in step 2 (in millions):

Debentures	$ 3
Income bonds	6
Preferred stock	3
Common stock equity	8
	$20

Having established the "appropriate" capital structure for the reorganized company, the trustee must then allocate the new securities. In this regard, the trustee may propose that the debenture holders exchange their $9 million in debentures for $3 million in new debentures and $6 million in income bonds, that the subordinated debenture holders exchange their $3 million in securities for preferred stock, and that preferred stockholders exchange their securities for $6 million of common stock in the reorganized company. The common stockholders would then be entitled to $2 million in stock in the reorganized company, or 25 percent of the total common stock of the reorganized company.

Thus, each claim is settled in full before a junior claim is settled. The example represents a relatively mild reorganization. In a harsh reorganization, debt instruments may be exchanged entirely for common stock in the reorganized company, and the old common stock may be eliminated completely. Had the total valuation figure in the example been $12 million, the trustee might have proposed a new capital structure consisting of $3 million in preferred stock and $9 million in common stock. Only the straight and subordinated debenture holders would

Part VIII Special Areas of Financial Management

receive a settlement in this case. The preferred and the common stockholders of the old company would receive nothing.

These examples show that the common stockholders of a company undergoing reorganization suffer under an **absolute-priority rule,** whereby claims must be settled in the order of their legal priority. From their standpoint, they would much prefer to see claims settled on a *relative-priority basis*. Under this rule, new securities are allocated on the basis of the relative market prices of the securities. The common stockholders could never obtain senior securities in a reorganization, but they would be entitled to some common stock if their present stock had value. Because the company is not actually being liquidated, common stockholders argue that a rule of relative priority is really the fairest. The Supreme Court decided otherwise when it upheld the absolute-priority rule (*Case v. Los Angeles Lumber Products Company* 1939).

NEGOTIATED SETTLEMENTS

While the principle of absolute priority is used in reorganization cases, the Bankruptcy Reform Act of 1978 provided a degree of flexibility and shifted the focus in the direction of relative priority. During the late 1980s and early 1990s, when many companies experienced financial distress, negotiated settlements achieved even greater flexibility. The practical reality is that during often protracted reorganization proceedings, management still controls the company; put bluntly, management often wields a club over creditors. Parties willing to infuse new capital as equity participants have clout as well.

The problem for creditors is that bankruptcy proceedings are costly and time-consuming and that during the time taken in proceedings, corporate value often is destroyed. Management and equity participants are able to drive hard bargains, and creditors are asked to give significant ground in order to make the reorganization plan workable. If the "haircut" (i.e., reduction in the value of claims) is too severe, the creditors will rebel. So there is a delicate balance in negotiating a compromise between what the equity participants and management would like and what the creditors will begrudgingly accept. Various classes of creditors often battle with each other over sharing the corporate pie, and this sometimes gives equity participants and management a wedge they can use to extract concessions.

Prepackaged bankruptcy (prepack) is a device sometimes employed to avoid the legal delays inherent in a Chapter 11 reorganization. Here a company in financial distress devises a workout plan prior to filing under Chapter 11. The company seeks approval from a minimum of two-thirds of each class of claimants in advance. If the court approves the plan, the terms can be imposed on dissenting debt holders. For example, Resorts International and TWA used this method. The advantage of a prepackaged bankruptcy is that it takes a short time to implement. The delays involved in Chapter 11 proceedings often add up to years, but a prepackaged bankruptcy often takes six months or so to implement.

Whether voluntary or under Chapter 11, workouts help management and employees. But they are not always in the best interests of creditors, who are asked to accept less than the book value of their claims. For creditors, the trade-off is whether keeping the company running is better than "pulling the plug" and incurring the deadweight loss of bankruptcy proceedings.

Absolute-priority rule
The rule in bankruptcy or reorganization that claims of a set of claim holders must be paid, or settled, in full before the next, junior, set of claim holders may be paid anything.

Prepackaged bankruptcy (prepack) A reorganization that a majority of a company's creditors have approved prior to the beginning of a bankruptcy proceeding.

QUESTIONS

1. Explain the concept of *synergy*.
2. Illustrate and explain how the ratio of P/E multiples for two merged firms affects the earnings per share of the surviving firm.
3. With a common-stock-for-common-stock acquisition, is it better to analyze the situation on a cash-flow basis or to look more to the acquisition's effect on the surviving firm's earnings per share?

4. It has been noted that the number of mergers tends to vary directly with the level of relative business activity. Why would this be?

5. Both Company X and Company Y have considerable variability in their earnings, but they are in unrelated industries. Could a merger of the two companies reduce the risk for shareholders of both companies? Could investors lower the risk on their own?

6. Many a corporate merger is made with the motive of increasing "growth." What does this growth refer to? Can you increase growth without increasing the overall risk of the surviving company?

7. Why is it that so many acquisition opportunities look good before the merger but later prove to be "dogs"?

8. Is an acquisition-minded company consistently able to find bargains? If so, why is it that other companies do not discover these bargains?

9. When evaluating a potential acquisition's future, why penalize the prospect by deducting the capital expenditures that will need to be made when performing a cash-flow analysis? Are not future earnings what really matter?

10. How does a pooling-of-interests accounting treatment for an acquisition differ from the purchase method?

11. Why does it matter whether an acquisition is made with cash or with common stock?

12. As a shareholder in a company, would you like it to have antitakeover amendments? What are some of these devices?

13. In your opinion, does the threat of a tender offer lead to better management of corporations?

14. What is the purpose of a two-tier tender offer?

15. In corporate restructuring (broadly defined), what are the principal sources of value creation?

16. How does a *partial sell-off* differ from a *spin-off*? How does an *equity carve-out* differ from a *partial sell-off* and a *spin-off*?

17. Under what circumstances does liquidation of an entire company make sense?

18. What are the motivations of going private? Do the shareholders who are bought out gain anything?

19. Much has been written about leveraged buyouts (LBOs). Are they a good thing?

20. What is the incentive for senior lenders and junior subordinated lenders to finance a leveraged buyout? Are there risks to them?

SELF-CORRECTION PROBLEMS

1. Yablonski Cordage Company is considering the acquisition of Yawitz Wire and Mesh Corporation with common stock. Relevant financial information is as follows:

	YABLONSKI	YAWITZ
Present earnings (in thousands)	$4,000	$1,000
Common shares outstanding (in thousands)	2,000	800
Earnings per share	$2.00	$1.25
Price/earnings ratio	12	8

Yablonski plans to offer a premium of 20 percent over the market price of Yawitz stock.

a. What is the ratio of exchange of stock? How many new shares will be issued?

b. What are earnings per share for the surviving company immediately following the merger?

c. If the price/earnings ratio for Yablonski stays at 12, what is the market price per share of the surviving company? What would happen if the price/earnings ratio went to 11?

2. Tongue Company has merged into Groove Pharmacies, Inc., where 1.5 shares of Groove were exchanged for each share of Tongue. The balance sheets of the two companies before the merger were as follows (in millions):

	TONGUE	GROOVE
Current assets	$ 5	$20
Fixed assets	7	30
Goodwill	—	2
Total	$12	$52
Current liabilities	$ 3	$ 9
Long-term debt	2	15
Shareholders' equity	7	28
Total	$12	$52
Number of shares (in millions)	.2	1.4
Market value per share	$35	$28

The fair market value of Tongue's fixed assets is $400,000 higher than their book value. Construct the balance sheets for the company after the merger, using both the purchase and pooling-of-interests methods of accounting.

3. Hi-Tec Corporation is considering the acquisition of Lo-Tec, Inc., which is in a related line of business. Lo-Tec, an all-equity-financed firm, presently has an after-tax cash flow of $2 million per year. With a merger, synergy would be expected to result in a growth rate of this cash flow of 15 percent per year for 10 years, at the end of which time level cash flows would be expected. To sustain the cash-flow stream, Hi-Tec will need to invest $1 million annually. For purposes of analysis and to be conservative, Hi-Tec limits its calculations of cash flows to 25 years.

a. What expected annual cash flows would Hi-Tec realize from this acquisition?

b. If its required rate of return is 18 percent, what is the maximum price that Hi-Tec could pay?

4. Aggressive, Inc., wishes to make a tender offer for the Passive Company. Passive has 100,000 shares of common stock outstanding and earns $5.50 per share. If it were combined with Aggressive, total economies (in present value terms) of $1.5 million could be realized. Presently, the market price per share of Passive is $55. Aggressive makes a two-tier tender offer: $65 per share for the first 50,001 shares tendered and $50 per share for the remaining shares.

a. If successful, what will Aggressive end up paying for Passive? How much incrementally will shareholders of Passive receive for the economies?

b. Acting independently, what will each Passive shareholder do to maximize his or her wealth? What might they do if they could respond collectively as a cartel?

c. How can a target company increase the probability of individual shareholders resisting too low a tender offer?

d. What might happen if Aggressive offered $65 in the first tier and only $40 in the second tier?

5. McNabb Enterprises is considering going private through a leveraged buyout by management. Management presently owns 21 percent of the 5 million shares outstanding. Market price per share is $20, and it is felt that a 40 percent premium over the present price will be necessary to entice public shareholders to tender their shares in a cash offer. Management intends to keep its shares and to obtain senior debt equal to 80 percent of the funds necessary to consummate the buyout. The remaining 20 percent will come from junior subordinated debentures.

Terms on the senior debt are 2 percent above the prime rate with principal reductions of 20 percent of the initial loan at the end of each of the next five years. The junior subordinated debentures bear a 13 percent interest rate and must be retired at the end of six years with a single balloon payment. The debentures have warrants attached that enable the holders to purchase 30 percent of the stock at the end of the sixth year. Management estimates that earnings before interest and taxes will be $25 million per year. Because of tax-loss carryforwards, the company expects to pay no taxes over the next five years. The company will make capital expenditures in amounts equal to its depreciation.

   a. If the prime rate is expected to average 10 percent over the next five years, is the leveraged buyout feasible?

   b. What if the prime rate averages only 8 percent?

   c. What minimal EBIT is necessary to service the debt?

PROBLEMS

1. The following data are pertinent for Companies A and B:

	COMPANY A	COMPANY B
Present earnings (in millions)	$20	$ 4
Number of shares (in millions)	10	1
Price/earnings ratio	18	10

   a. If the two companies were to merge and the share exchange ratio were 1 share of Company A for each share of Company B, what would be the initial impact on earnings per share of the two companies? What is the market value exchange ratio? Is a merger likely to take place?

   b. If the share exchange ratio were 2 shares of Company A for each share of Company B, what would happen with respect to Part (a)?

   c. If the exchange ratio were 1.5 shares of Company A for each share of Company B, what would happen?

   d. What exchange ratio would you suggest?

2.

	EXPECTED EARNINGS	NUMBER OF SHARES	MARKET PRICE PER SHARE	TAX RATE
Schoettler Company	$5,000,000	1,000,000	$100	50%
Stevens Company	3,000,000	500,000	60	50%

The Schoettler Company wishes to acquire the Stevens Company. If the merger were effected through an exchange of stock, Schoettler would be willing to pay a 25 percent premium for the Stevens shares. If done for cash, the terms would have to be just as favorable to the Stevens shareholders. To obtain the cash, Schoettler would have to sell its own common stock in the market.

a. Compute the share exchange ratio and the combined expected earnings per share for Schoettler under an exchange of common stock.

b. If we assume that all Stevens shareholders have held their common stock for more than one year, have a 28 percent marginal capital gains tax rate, and have paid an average of $14 for their shares, what cash price would have to be offered to be just as attractive as the terms in Part (a)?

3. Assume the exchange of Schoettler shares for Stevens shares as outlined in Problem 2.

a. What is the share exchange ratio?

b. Compare the earnings per Stevens share before and after the merger. Compare the earnings per Schoettler share. On this basis alone, which merger group fared better? Why?

c. Why do you imagine that Schoettler commanded a higher P/E ratio than Stevens? What should be the change in P/E ratio resulting from the merger? Does this conflict with what you previously concluded? Why?

d. If the Schoettler Company were in a high-technology growth industry and Stevens made cement, would you revise your answers?

e. In determining the appropriate P/E ratio for Schoettler, should the increase in earnings resulting from this merger be added as a growth factor?

4. Copper Clapper Company presently has annual earnings of $10 million with 4 million shares of common stock outstanding and a market price per share of $30. In the absence of any mergers, Copper Clapper's annual earnings are expected to grow at a compound rate of 5 percent per annum. Brass Bell Company, whom Copper Clapper is seeking to acquire, has present annual earnings of $2 million, 1 million shares of common stock outstanding, and a market price per share of $36. Its annual earnings are expected to grow at a compound annual rate of 10 percent per annum. Copper Clapper will offer 1.2 shares of its stock for each share of Brass Bell Company.

a. What is the immediate effect on the surviving company's earnings per share?

b. Would you want to acquire Brass Bell Company? If it is not attractive now, when will it be attractive from the standpoint of earnings per share?

5. The Byer Corporation, which has a 16 percent after-tax cost of capital, is considering the acquisition of the Cellar Company, which has about the same degree of systematic risk. If the merger were effected, the incremental cash flows would be as follows:

	AVERAGE FOR YEARS (IN MILLIONS)			
	1–5	6–10	11–15	16–20
Annual cash income attributable to Cellar	$10	$15	$20	$15
Required new investment	2	5	10	10
Net after-tax cash flow	$ 8	$10	$10	$ 5

What is the maximum price that Byer should pay for Cellar, assuming the business-risk complexion of the company remains unchanged?

6. Valdez Coffee Company is considering the cash acquisition of Mountain Creamery, Inc., for $750,000. The acquisition is expected to result in incremental cash flows of $100,000 in the first year, and this amount is expected to grow at a 6 percent compound rate. In the absence of the acquisition, Valdez expects net cash flows (after capital expenditures) of $600,000 this year, and these are expected to grow at a 6 percent compound rate forever. Presently suppliers of capital require

a 14 percent overall rate of return for Valdez Coffee Company. However, Mountain Creamery is much more risky, and the acquisition of it will raise the company's overall required return to 15 percent.

a. Should Valdez Coffee Company acquire Mountain Creamery, Inc.?

b. Would your answer be the same if the overall required rate of return stayed the same?

c. Would your answer be the same if the acquisition increased the surviving company's growth rate to 8 percent forever?

7. Bigge Stores, Inc. (BSI), has acquired the L. Grande Company (LGC) for $4 million in stock and the assumption of $2 million in LGC liabilities. The balance sheets of the two companies before the merger revealed the following information (in millions):

	BSI	LGC
Tangible and total assets	$10.0	$5.0
Liabilities	4.0	2.0
Shareholders' equity	$ 6.0	$3.0

Determine the balance sheet of the combined company after the merger under both the purchase and pooling-of-interests methods of accounting. (Assume that the net book value of LGC assets represents their fair market value.)

8. Leonardo Company has three divisions, and the total market value (debt and equity) of the firm is $71 million. Its debt-to-market-value ratio is .40, and bond indentures provide the usual protective covenants. However, they do not preclude the sale of a division. Leonardo has decided to divest itself of its Raphael division for a consideration of $20 million. In addition to this payment to Leonardo, the buyer will assume $5 million of existing debt of the division. The full $20 million will be distributed to Leonardo Company shareholders. In words, explain whether the remaining debt holders of Leonardo Company are better or worse off. Why? In theory, are the equity holders better or worse off? Why?

9. Lorzo-Perez International has a subsidiary, the DelRay Sorter Company. The company believes the subsidiary on average will generate $1 million per year in annual net cash flows after necessary capital expenditures. These annual net cash flows are projected far into the future (assume infinity). The required rate of return for the subsidiary is 12 percent. If the company were to invest an additional $10 million now, it is believed that annual net cash flows could be increased from $1 to $2 million. Exson Corporation has expressed an interest in DelRay, because it is in the sorter business and believes it can achieve some economies. Accordingly, it has made a cash offer of $10 million for the subsidiary. Should Lorzo-Perez

a. Continue the business as is?

b. Invest the additional $10 million?

c. Sell the subsidiary to Exson? (Assume the subsidiary is entirely equity financed.)

10. Hogs Breath Inns, a chain of restaurants, is considering going private. The president, Clint Westwood, believes that with the elimination of shareholder servicing costs and other costs associated with public ownership, the company could save $800,000 per annum before taxes. In addition, the company believes management incentives and, hence, performance will be higher as a private company. As a result, annual profits are expected to be 10 percent greater than

present after-tax profits of $9 million. The effective tax rate is 30 percent; the price/earnings ratio of the stock is 12; and there are 10 million shares outstanding. What is the present market price per share? What is the maximum dollar premium above this price that the company could pay to take the company private?

11. Donatello Industries wishes to sell its sewer pipe division for $10 million. Management of the division wishes to buy it and has arranged a leveraged buyout. Management will put up $1 million in cash. A senior lender will advance $7 million secured by all the assets of the company. The rate on the loan is 2 percent above the prime rate, which is presently 12 percent. The loan is payable in equal annual principal installments over five years, with interest for the year payable at the end of each year. A junior subordinated loan of $2 million also has been arranged, and this loan is due at the end of six years. The interest rate is fixed at 15 percent, and interest payments *only* are due at the end of each of the first five years. Interest and the entire principal are due at the end of the sixth year. In addition, the lender has received warrants exercisable for 50 percent of the stock.

The sewer pipe division expects earnings before interest and taxes of $3.4 million in each of the first three years and $3.7 million in the last three years. The tax rate is $33\frac{1}{3}$ percent, and the company expects capital expenditures and investments in receivables and inventories to equal depreciation charges in each year. All debt servicing must come from profits. (Assume also that the warrants are not exercised and that there is no cash infusion as a result.)

If the prime rate stays at 12 percent on average throughout the six years, will the enterprise be able to service the debt properly? If the prime rate were to rise to 20 percent in the second year and average that for the second year through the sixth year, would the situation change?

Appendix Problems

12. Merry Land Company, an amusement park in Atlanta, has experienced increased difficulty in paying its bills. Although the park has been marginally profitable over the years, the current outlook is not encouraging, as profits during the last two years have been negative. The park is located on reasonably valuable real estate and has an overall liquidating value of $5 million. After much discussion with creditors, management has agreed to a voluntary liquidation. A trustee, who is appointed by the various parties to liquidate the properties, will charge $200,000 for her services. The Merry Land Company owes $300,000 in back property taxes. It has a $2 million mortgage on certain amusement park equipment that can be sold for only $1 million. Creditor claims are as follows:

PARTY	BOOK VALUE CLAIM
General creditors	$1,750,000
Mortgage bonds	2,000,000
Long-term subordinated debt	1,000,000
Common stock	5,000,000

What amount is each party likely to receive in liquidation?

13. The Fias Company is in Chapter 11. The trustee has estimated that the company can earn $1.5 million before interest and taxes (40 percent tax rate) in the future. In the new capitalization, the trustee feels that debentures should bear a coupon

of 10 percent and have a coverage ratio of 5, income bonds (12 percent) should have an overall coverage ratio of 2, preferred stock (10 percent) should have an after-tax coverage ratio of 3, and common stock should be issued on a price/earnings ratio basis of 12. Determine the capital structure that conforms to the trustee's criteria.

14. Facile Fastener Company had the following liabilities and equity position when it filed for bankruptcy under Chapter 11 (in thousands):

Accounts payable	$ 500
Accrued wages	200
Bank loan, 12% rate (secured by receivables)	600
Current liabilities	$1,300
13% First-mortgage bonds	500
15% Subordinated debentures	1,700
Total debt	$3,500
Common stock and additional paid-in capital	500
Retained earnings	420
Total liabilities and equity	$4,420

After straightening out some operating problems, the company is expected to be able to earn $800,000 annually before interest and taxes. Based on other going-concern values, it is felt that the company as a whole is worth five times its EBIT. Court costs associated with the reorganization will total $200,000, and the expected tax rate is 40 percent for the reorganized company. As trustee, suppose that you have the following instruments to use for the long-term capitalization of the company: 13 percent first-mortgage bonds, 15 percent capital notes, 13 percent preferred stock, and common stock.

With the new capitalization, the capital notes should have an overall coverage ratio, after bank loan interest, of 4, and preferred stock should have a coverage ratio after interest and taxes of 2. Moreover, it is felt that common stock equity should equal at least 30 percent of the total assets of the company.

a. What is the total valuation of the company after reorganization?

b. If the maximum amounts of debt and preferred stock are employed, what will be the new capital structure and current liabilities of the company?

c. How should these securities be allocated, assuming a rule of absolute priority?

SOLUTIONS TO SELF-CORRECTION PROBLEMS

1. a.

	YABLONSKI	YAWITZ
Earnings per share	$2.00	$1.25
Price/earnings ratio	12	8
Market price per share	$ 24	$ 10
Offer to Yawitz shareholders in Yablonski stock (including the premium) = $10 × 1.20 = $12 per share		

Exchange ratio = $12/24 = **.5**, or one-half share of Yablonski stock for every share of Yawitz stock.

Number of new shares issued = 800,000 shares × .5 = **400,000 shares.**

b.

Surviving company earnings (in thousands)	$5,000
Common shares outstanding (in thousands)	2,400
Earnings per share	**$2.0833**

There is an increase in earnings per share by virtue of acquiring a company with a lower price/earnings ratio.

c. Market price per share: $2.0833 × 12 = **$25.00**
Market price per share: $2.0833 × 11 = **$22.92**
In the first instance, share price rises, from $24, due to the increase in earnings per share. In the second case, share price falls owing to the decline in the price/earnings ratio. In efficient markets, we might expect some decline in the price/earnings ratio if there was not likely to be synergy and/or improved management.

2. With an exchange ratio of 1.5, Groove would issue 300,000 new shares of stock with a market value of $28 × 300,000 = **$8.4 million** for the common stock of Tongue. This exceeds the shareholders' equity of Tongue by $1.4 million. With the purchase method, Tongue's fixed assets will be written up by $400,000 and goodwill of Groove by $1 million. This does not happen, of course, with a pooling of interests. The balance sheets after the merger under the two methods of accounting are (in millions):

	PURCHASE	POOLING OF INTERESTS
Current assets	$25.0	$25.0
Fixed assets (net)	37.4	37.0
Goodwill	3.0	2.0
Total	$65.4	$64.0
Current liabilities	$12.0	$12.0
Long-term debt	17.0	17.0
Shareholders' equity	36.4	35.0
Total	$65.4	$64.0

3. a, b.

YEAR	CASH FLOW	INVESTMENT	NET CASH FLOW	PRESENT VALUE OF NET CASH FLOW (18%)
1	$2,300,000	$1,000,000	$1,300,000	$ 1,101,100
2	2,645,000	"	1,645,000	1,181,110
3	3,041,750	"	2,041,750	1,243,426
4	3,498,013	"	2,498,013	1,288,975
5	4,022,714	"	3,022,714	1,320,926
6	4,626,122	"	3,626,122	1,341,665
7	5,320,040	"	4,320,040	1,356,493
8	6,118,046	"	5,118,046	1,361,400
9	7,035,753	"	6,035,753	1,358,044
10–25	8,091,116	"	7,091,116	8,254,059*
			Total present value =	$19,807,198

*Total for years 10–25.

The maximum price that is justified is approximately **$19.81 million.** It should be noted that these calculations use present value tables. To arrive at the discount rate for cash flows going from years 10 to 25, we subtract the discount factor for 9 years of annuity payments, 4.303, from that for 25 years, 5.467. The difference, 5.467 − 4.303 = 1.164, is the discount factor for cash flows for an annuity starting in year 10 and going through year 25. If a present value function of a calculator is used, a slightly different total may be given due to our having rounded to three decimal points.

4. a.

$$
\begin{aligned}
50{,}001 \text{ shares} \times \$65 &= \$3{,}250{,}065 \\
49{,}999 \text{ shares} \times \$50 &= \underline{2{,}499{,}950} \\
\text{Total purchase price} &= \mathbf{\$5{,}750{,}015} \\
\text{Total value of stock before} = 100{,}000 \text{ shares} \times \$55 &= \underline{5{,}500{,}000} \\
\text{Increment to Passive shareholders} &= \mathbf{\$\ 250{,}015}
\end{aligned}
$$

The total value of the economies to be realized is $1,500,000. Therefore, Passive shareholders receive only a modest portion of the total value of the economies. In contrast, Aggressive shareholders obtain a large share.

b. With a two-tier offer, there is a great incentive for individual shareholders to tender early, thereby ensuring success for the acquiring firm. Collectively, Passive shareholders would be better off holding out for a larger fraction of the total value of the economies. They can do this only if they act as a cartel in their response to the offer.

c. By instigating antitakeover amendments and devices, some incentives may be created for individual shareholders to hold out for a higher offer. However, in practice it is impossible to achieve a complete cartel response.

d.

$$
\begin{aligned}
50{,}001 \text{ shares} \times \$65 &= \$3{,}250{,}065 \\
49{,}999 \text{ shares} \times \$40 &= \underline{1{,}999{,}960} \\
\text{Total purchase price} &= \$5{,}250{,}025
\end{aligned}
$$

This value is lower than the previous total market value of $5,500,000. Clearly, shareholders would fare poorly if in the rush to tender shares the offer were successful. However, other potential acquirers would have an incentive to offer more than Aggressive, even with no economies to be realized. Competition among potential acquirers should ensure counterbids, so that Aggressive would be forced to bid no less than $5,500,000 in total, the present market value.

5. a. Shares owned by outsiders = 5 million × .79 = 3,950,000

Price to be offered = $20 × 1.40 = $28 per share

Total buyout amount = 3,950,000 shares × $28 = $110,600,000

Senior debt = $110,600,000 × .80 = $88,480,000

Annual principal payment = $88,480,000/5 = $17,696,000

Junior debt = $110,600,000 × .20 = $22,120,000

Annual EBIT to service debt:

Senior debt interest: $88,480,000 × .12 =	$10,617,600
Senior debt principal:	17,696,000
Junior debt interest: $22,120,000 × .13 =	2,875,600
Total EBIT necessary:	$31,189,200

During the first five years, EBIT of $25 million will not be sufficient to service the debt.

b. $88,480,000 × .10 = $8,848,000, which, with the two other amounts above, comes to $29,419,600. *Expected EBIT will still not be sufficient to service the debt.*

c. *$31,189,200 is the minimal EBIT necessary to service the debt.*

SELECTED REFERENCES

Betker, Brian L. "An Empirical Examination of Prepackaged Bankruptcy." *Financial Management* 24 (Spring 1995), 3–18.

Black, Bernard S., and Joseph A. Gundfest. "Shareholder Gains from Takeovers and Restructurings." *Journal of Applied Corporate Finance* 1 (Spring 1988), 5–15.

Borokhovich, Kenneth A., Kelly R. Brunarski, and Robert Parrino. "CEO Contracting and Antitakeover Amendments." *Journal of Finance* 52 (September 1997), 1495–1517.

Bradley, Michael. "Interfirm Tender Offers and the Market for Corporate Control." *Journal of Business* 53 (October 1980), 345–76.

———, Anand Desai, and E. Han Kim. "The Rationale Behind Interfirm Tender Offers: Information or Synergy." *Journal of Financial Economics* 11 (April 1983), 183–206.

Chan, Su Han, John W. Kensinger, Arthur J. Keown, and John D. Martin. "When Do Strategic Alliances Create Shareholder Value?" *Journal of Applied Corporate Finance* 11 (Winter 1999), 82–87.

Chatterjee, Sris, Upinder S. Dhillon, and Gabriel G. Ramierez. "Resolution of Financial Distress: Debt Restructurings via Chapter 11, Prepackaged Bankruptcies, and Workouts." *Financial Management* 24 (Autumn 1995), 5–21.

DeAngelo, Harry, and Edward M. Rice. "Antitakeover Charter Amendments and Stockholder Wealth." *Journal of Financial Economics* 11 (April 1983), 329–60.

DeAngelo, Harry, Linda DeAngelo, and Edward M. Rice. "Going Private: Minority Freezeouts and Stockholder Wealth." *Journal of Law and Economics* 27 (June 1984), 367–401.

Dennis, Debra K., and John J. McConnell. "Corporate Mergers and Security Returns." *Journal of Financial Economics* 16 (June 1986), 143–87.

Donaldson, Gordon. *Corporate Restructuring.* Cambridge, MA: Harvard Business School Press, 1994.

Eberhart, Allan C., William T. Moore, and Rodney L. Roenfelt. "Security Pricing and Deviations from the Absolute Priority Rule in Bankruptcy Proceedings." *Journal of Finance* 45 (December 1990), 1457–69.

Fabozzi, Frank J., Jane Tripp Howe, Takashi Makabe, and Toshihide Sudo. "Recent Evidence on the Distribution Patterns in Chapter 11 Reorganizations." *Journal of Fixed Income* 2 (March 1993), 6–23.

Franks, Julian R., and Robert S. Harris. "Shareholder Wealth Effects of Corporate Takeovers: The UK Experience." *Journal of Financial Economics* 23 (August 1989), 225–50.

Halpern, Paul. "Corporate Acquisitions: A Theory of Special Cases? A Review of Event Studies Applied to Acquisitions." *Journal of Finance* 38 (May 1983), 297–317.

Hite, Gailen L., and James E. Owers. "Security Price Reactions Around Corporate Spin-Off Announcements." *Journal of Financial Economics* 12 (December 1983), 409–36.

———, and Ronald C. Rogers. "The Market for Interfirm Asset Sales: Partial Sell-Offs and Total Liquidations." *Journal of Financial Economics* 18 (June 1987), 229–52.

Hite, Gailen L., and Michael R. Vetsuypens. "Management Buyouts of Divisions and Shareholder Wealth." *Journal of Finance* 44 (June 1989), 953–80.

Hong, H., G. Mandelker, and R. S. Kaplan. "Pooling vs. Purchase: The Effects of Accounting for Mergers on Stock Prices." *Accounting Review* 53 (January 1978), 31–47.

Ikenberry, David, and Josef Lakonishok, "Corporate Governance Through the Proxy Contest: Evidence and Implications." *Journal of Business* 66 (July 1993), 405–35.

Jain, Prem C. "The Effect of Voluntary Sell-off Announcements on Shareholder Wealth." *Journal of Finance* 40 (March 1985), 209–24.

Jarrell, Greg A., and Annette B. Poulsen. "The Returns to Acquiring Firms in Tender Offers: Evidence from Three Decades." *Financial Management* 18 (Autumn 1989), 12–19.

Jensen, Michael C. "The Takeover Controversy: Analysis and Evidence." *Midland Corporate Finance Journal* 4 (Summer 1986), 6–32.

Kaplan, Steven. "Management Buyouts: Evidence on Taxes as a Source of Value." *Journal of Finance* 44 (July 1989), 611–32.

———. "The Effects of Management Buyouts on Operating Performance and Value." *Journal of Financial Economics* 24 (October 1989), 217–54.

Larson, Kermit D., and Nicholas J. Gonedes. "Business Combinations: An Exchange-Ratio Determination Model." *Accounting Review* 44 (October 1969), 720–28.

Lehn, Kenneth, and Annette Poulsen. "Free Cash Flow and Stockholder Gains in Going Private Transactions." *Journal of Finance* 44 (July 1989), 771–87.

Loughran, Tim, and Anand M. Vijh. "Do Long-Term Shareholders Benefit from Corporate Acquisitions?" *Journal of Finance* 52 (December 1997), 1765–90.

Marias, Laurentius, Katherine Schipper, and Abbie Smith. "Wealth Effects of Going Private for Senior Securities." *Journal of Financial Economics* 23 (June 1989), 155–91.

Michaely, Roni, and Wayne H. Shaw. "The Choice of Going Public: Spin-offs vs. Carve-outs." *Financial Management* 24 (Autumn 1995), 5–21.

Miles, James A., and James D. Rosenfeld. "The Effect of Voluntary Spin-off Announcements on Shareholder Wealth." *Journal of Finance* 38 (December 1983), 1597–1606.

Morck, Randall, Andrei Shleifer, and Robert W. Vishny. "Management Ownership and Market Valuation: An Empirical Analysis." *Journal of Financial Economics* 20 (January–March 1988), 293–316.

Nathan, Kevin S., and Terrence B. O'Keefe. "The Rise in Takeover Premiums: An Exploratory Study." *Journal of Financial Economics* 23 (June 1989), 101–20.

Opinions of the Accounting Principles Board, No. 16 (New York: American Institute of Certified Public Accountants, August 1970).

Roll, Richard. "The Hubris Hypothesis of Corporate Takeovers." *Journal of Business* 59 (April 1986), 197–216.

Rosenfeld, James D. "Additional Evidence on the Relation Between Divestiture Announcements and Shareholder Wealth." *Journal of Finance* 39 (December 1984), 1437–48.

Ryngaert, Michael. "The Effect of Poison Pill Securities on Shareholder Wealth." *Journal of Financial Economics* 20 (January–March 1988), 377–417.

Schipper, Katherine, and Abbie Smith. "A Comparison of Equity Carve-outs and Seasoned Equity Offerings: Share Price Effects and Corporate Restructuring." *Journal of Financial Economics* 15 (January–February 1986), 153–86.

———. "Effects of Recontracting on Shareholder Wealth: The Case of Voluntary Spin-offs." *Journal of Financial Economics* 12 (December 1983), 437–68.

Shleifer, Andrei, and Roberts W. Vishny. "Management Entrenchment: The Case of Manager-Specific Investments." *Journal of Financial Economics* 25 (November 1989), 123–39.

Sicherman, Neil W., and Richard H. Pettway. "Acquisition of Divested Assets and Shareholder Wealth." *Journal of Finance* 42 (December 1987), 1261–73.

Skantz, Terrance R., and Roberto Marchesini. "The Effect of Voluntary Corporate Liquidation on Shareholder Wealth." *Journal of Financial Research* 10 (Winter 1987), 65–76.

Stulz, Rene M., Ralph A. Walkling, and Moon H. Song. "The Distribution of Target Ownership and the Division of Gains in Successful Takeovers." *Journal of Finance* 45 (July 1990), 817–34.

Sullivan, Michael J., Marlin R. H. Jensen, and Carl D. Hudson. "The Role of Medium of Exchange in Merger Offers: Examination of Terminated Merger Proposals." *Financial Management* 23 (Autumn 1994), 51–62.

Weston, J. Fred. "Divestitures: Mistakes or Learning." *Journal of Applied Corporate Finance* (Summer 1989), 68–76.

———, Juan A. Siu, and Brian A. Johnson. *Takeovers, Restructuring, and Corporate Governance,* 3rd ed. Upper Saddle River, NJ: Prentice Hall, 2001.

Chapter 24

International Financial Management

SOME BACKGROUND
   International Capital Budgeting • Risk Factors • Taxation
      • Political Risk
TYPES OF EXCHANGE-RATE RISK EXPOSURE
   Translation Exposure • Transactions Exposure • Economic
   Exposure
MANAGEMENT OF EXCHANGE-RATE RISK EXPOSURE
   Natural Hedges • Cash Management and Adjusting Intracompany
      Accounts • International Financing Hedges • Currency Market
      Hedges • Hedging Exchange-Rate Risk Exposure: A Summing
      Up • Macro Factors Governing Exchange-Rate Behavior
STRUCTURING INTERNATIONAL TRADE TRANSACTIONS
   International Trade Draft • Bill of Lading • Letter of Credit
      • Countertrade • Export Factoring • Forfaiting
SUMMARY
QUESTIONS
SELF-CORRECTION PROBLEMS
PROBLEMS
SOLUTIONS TO SELF-CORRECTION PROBLEMS
SELECTED REFERENCES

Where profit is, loss is hidden nearby.

—JAPANESE PROVERB

Beginning in the 1980s, there has been an explosion in international investments, through mutual funds and other intermediaries by the individual and through direct investments by institutions. On the other side, capital raising increasingly is occurring across national boundaries. The financial manager must search for the "best price" in a global marketplace, sometimes while making use of currency and other hedges. To accommodate the underlying demands of investors and capital raisers, financial institutions and instruments have changed dramatically. Financial deregulation, first in the United States and then in Europe and in Asia, has prompted increased integration of world financial markets. As a result of the rapidly changing scene, the financial manager today must have a global perspective. Although the concepts developed earlier in this book are still applicable here, the environment in which decisions are made is different. In this chapter we develop an understanding of this environment and explore how a company goes about making decisions in an international setting.

SOME BACKGROUND

The motivation to invest capital in a foreign operation is, of course, to provide a return in excess of that required. There may be gaps in foreign markets where excess returns can be earned. Domestically, competitive pressures may be such that only a normal rate of return can be earned. Although expansion into foreign markets is the reason for most investment abroad, there are other reasons. Some firms invest in order to produce more efficiently. Another country may offer lower labor and other costs, and a company will choose to locate production facilities there in the quest for lower operating costs. The electronics industry has moved toward foreign production facilities for this saving. Finally, some companies invest abroad to secure necessary raw materials. Oil companies and mining companies in particular invest abroad for this reason. All of these pursuits—markets, production facilities, and raw materials—are in keeping with an objective of securing a higher rate of return than is possible through domestic operations alone.

International Capital Budgeting

The relevant cash inflows for a foreign investment are those that can be "repatriated" (returned) to the home-country parent. If the expected return on investment is based on nonremittable cash flows that build up in a foreign subsidiary, the investment is unlikely to be attractive. If cash flows can be freely repatriated, however, capital budgeting is straightforward. The U.S. firm would

Exchange rate The number of units of one currency that may be purchased with one unit of another currency.

1. Estimate expected cash flows in the foreign currency
2. Compute their U.S.-dollar equivalents at the expected **exchange rate** (foreign currency per dollar)
3. Determine the net present value of the project using the U.S. required rate of return, with the rate adjusted upward or downward for any risk premium effect associated with the foreign investment

Suppose that the Teasdale Company is considering an investment in the country of Freedonia costing 1.5 million Freedonian marks. The project has a short life—four years—and the required rate of return on repatriated U.S. dollars is 18 percent. The mark, now 2.50 to the dollar, is expected to "depreciate" over time. That is, a dollar is expected to be worth more marks in the future than it is now. Table 24-1 illustrates

TABLE 24-1
Expected cash flows for Teasdale Company's Freedonian project

END OF YEAR	(a) EXPECTED CASH FLOW (IN THOUSANDS OF MARKS)	(b) EXCHANGE RATE (MARKS:DOLLAR)	(c) EXPECTED CASH FLOW (IN THOUSANDS OF DOLLARS) (a)/(b)	(d) PRESENT VALUE OF DOLLAR CASH FLOWS AT 18% (IN THOUSANDS OF DOLLARS)
0	−1,500	2.50	−600	−600
1	500	2.54	197	167
2	800	2.59	309	222
3	700	2.65	264	161
4	600	2.72	221	114
			Net present value =	64

the three steps used to calculate dollar cash flows and their net present value, which we see to be approximately $64,000.

Although the calculations are straightforward, obviously much goes into the assumptions concerning projected cash flows, projected exchange rates, and the required rate of return. Learning about these things is the purpose of this chapter.

Risk Factors

With respect to required returns, international diversification is a consideration. Recall from our discussion of portfolio risk in Chapters 5 and 14 that the key element is the correlation among projects in the asset portfolio. By combining projects with low degrees of correlation with each other, a firm is able to reduce risk in relation to expected return. Because domestic investment projects tend to be correlated with each other, most being highly dependent on the state of the domestic economy, foreign investments have an advantage. The economic cycles of different countries do not tend to be completely synchronized, so it is possible to reduce risk relative to expected return by investing across countries. The idea is simply that returns on investment projects tend to be less correlated among countries than they are in any one particular country. By diversifying across countries, overall risk may be reduced.[1]

Taxation

Owing to different tax laws and different treatments of foreign investment, the taxation of a multinational firm is complex. Our purpose is to discuss some of the more prominent aspects of the problem.

Taxation by the U.S. Government. If a U.S. corporation carries on business abroad through a branch or division, the income from that operation is reported on the company's U.S. tax form and is taxed in the same way as domestic income. If business is

---

[1]We need to keep in mind that what is of more importance is not so much the physical location of the asset or investment but where the production of that investment is finally destined. For example, if a U.S. company produces goods in France that are ultimately sold in the United States and a competitive U.S. company produces the same product for sale in the United States, both companies' sales potential are equally impacted by ups and downs in the U.S. economy. However, many foreign investment projects are for local sales and thus may provide diversification benefits.

carried on through a foreign subsidiary, the income is normally not taxed in the United States until it is distributed to the parent in the form of dividends. The advantage here, of course, is that the tax is deferred until the parent receives a cash return. In the meantime, earnings are reinvested in the subsidiary to finance expansion. Unlike dividends received from a domestic corporation (generally 70 percent exempt to the receiving company), dividends received by a U.S. corporation from a foreign subsidiary are generally fully taxable.

Taxation by Foreign Governments. Every country taxes income of foreign companies doing business in that country. The type of tax imposed varies. Some of these countries differentiate between income distributed to shareholders and undistributed income, with a lower tax on distributed income. Less developed countries frequently have lower taxes and provide certain other tax incentives to encourage foreign investment.

The taxation policies of foreign governments are not only varied but also highly complex. The definition of what constitutes taxable income is different for different countries, and the tax rate varies among countries. Certain nations, such as Panama and the Bahamas, have low tax rates on corporate profits in order to encourage foreign investment, whereas the tax rates in most advanced industrial countries are high. The picture is further complicated by the numerous tax treaties that the United States has with other nations. Although the U.S. government restricts the use of a low-tax country as a tax haven, enough latitude remains so that companies still devise complicated legal structures to take advantage of such havens.

To avoid double taxation (by two different countries on the same income), the United States gives a federal income tax credit for foreign taxes paid by a U.S. corporation. If a foreign country has a tax rate that is lower than that applicable to the U.S. corporation, the firm will pay combined taxes at the full U.S. tax rate. Part of the taxes are paid to the foreign government, and the other part is paid to the U.S. government. Suppose that a foreign branch of a U.S. corporation operates in a country where the income tax rate is 27 percent. The branch earns $2 million and pays $540,000 in foreign income taxes. Assume further that the $2 million in earnings is subject to a 34 percent tax rate in the United States, or $680,000 in taxes. The company receives a tax credit of $540,000 for the foreign taxes paid. Thus, it pays only $140,000 in U.S. taxes on earnings of its foreign branch. If the foreign tax rate were 50 percent, the company would pay $1 million in foreign taxes on those earnings and nothing in U.S. taxes. Here, total taxes paid are obviously higher than they would be if only the U.S. tax rate applied.

Moreover, the size of the foreign tax credit may be constrained. The United States taxes companies on their worldwide income and permits a foreign tax credit only to the extent that the foreign source income would have been taxed in the United States. (Excess foreign tax credits can be carried forward, however.) Suppose that 30 percent of a multinational company's total income is attributable to foreign sources. If its pre-credit U.S. tax liability is $10 million, only $3 million in foreign tax credits may be used to offset the U.S. tax liability. If the company pays more in foreign taxes, it will be subject to double taxation on that portion. Some countries have withholding taxes on dividend distributions to foreign investors. To the extent that the investor pays little or no taxes domestically, such as occurs with institutional investors, there is no ability to neutralize the withholding tax. Thus, a withholding tax serves as a disincentive to foreign investment.

It is clear that tax planning for an international operation is both technical and complex. From time to time, various special tax incentives come into existence to help export industries. These tax provisions, both U.S. and foreign, are constantly changing. The advice of tax experts and legal counsel, both foreign and domestic, should be sought at the time the foreign operation is organized.

Political Risk

A **multinational company** faces political risks that can range from mild interference to complete confiscation of all assets. Interference includes laws that specify a minimum percentage of nationals who must be employed in various positions, required investment in environmental and social projects, and restrictions on the convertibility of currencies. The ultimate political risk is expropriation, such as that which occurred in Chile in 1971, when the country took over the copper companies. Between mild interference and outright expropriation, there may be discriminatory practices, such as higher taxes, higher utility charges, and the requirement to pay higher wages than a national company. In essence, these practices place the foreign operation of the U.S. company at a competitive disadvantage. However, the situation is not one directional. Certain developing countries give foreign companies concessions to invest such that they may have more favorable costs than a domestic company.

Because political risk has a serious influence on the overall risk of an investment project, it must be realistically assessed. Essentially, the job is one of forecasting political instability. How stable is the host government? What are the prevailing political winds? What is likely to be a new government's view of foreign investment? How efficient is the government in processing requests? How much inflation and economic stability are there? How strong and equitable are the courts? Answers to these questions should give considerable insight into the political risk involved in an investment. Some companies have categorized countries according to their political risk. If a country is classified in the undesirable category, probably no investment will be permitted, no matter how high its expected return.

Once a company decides to invest in a foreign country, it should take steps to protect itself. By cooperating with the host country in hiring local nationals, making

Foreign Currency Exchange

In order to buy foreign products or services, or to invest in other countries, companies and individuals may first have to buy the currency of the country with which they are doing business. Generally, exporters prefer to be paid for their goods and services either in their own currency (Japanese in yen and Germans in marks, for example) or in U.S. dollars, which are accepted all over the world. For example, when the French buy oil from Saudi Arabia, they may pay in U.S. dollars, not French francs or Saudi dinars, even though the United States is not involved in the transaction. The **foreign exchange market,** or "FX" market, is where the buying and selling of different currencies takes place. The price of one currency in terms of another country's currency is called an **exchange rate.**

The market itself is actually a worldwide network of traders, connected by telephone lines and computer screens—there is no central headquarters. The three major centers of trading, which handle more than half of all FX transactions, are Great Britain, the United States, and Japan. Transactions in Singapore, Switzerland, Hong Kong, Germany, France, and Australia account for most of the rest of the market. Trading goes on 24 hours a day; at 8 a.m. in London, the trading day is ending in Tokyo, Singapore, and Hong Kong. At 1 p.m. in London, the New York market opens for business. In the afternoon, traders in San Francisco can do business with their colleagues in the Far East.

Source: The Basics of Foreign Trade and Exchange, Federal Reserve Bank of New York, p. 28.

the "right" types of investment, and acting responsibly in other ways, political risk can be reduced. A joint venture with a company in the host country can improve the public image of the operation. Indeed, in some countries a joint venture may be the only way to do business, because direct ownership, particularly of manufacturing, is prohibited. The risk of expropriation also can be reduced by making the subsidiary dependent on the parent for technology, markets, and/or supplies. A foreign government is reluctant to expropriate when the enterprise is not self-sustaining. In addition, *political risk insurance* may be warranted. Insurance or guarantees against various political risks can be purchased from a number of private insurance companies, like Lloyds of London, and various governmental agencies, such as the Agency for International Development (AID), the Export-Import Bank of the United States (Eximbank), and the Overseas Private Investment Corporation (OPIC). The political risks covered may include expropriation, currency inconvertibility, war, and revolution. In any event, the time to look hardest at political risk is before the investment is made.

TYPES OF EXCHANGE-RATE RISK EXPOSURE

Spot exchange rate The rate today for exchanging one currency for another for immediate delivery.

The company with foreign operations is at risk in various ways. Apart from political danger, risk fundamentally emanates from changes in exchange rates. In this regard, the **spot exchange rate** represents the number of units of one currency that can be exchanged for another. Put differently, it is the price of one currency relative to another. The currencies of the major countries are traded in active markets, where rates are determined by the forces of supply and demand. Quotations can be in terms of the domestic currency or in terms of the foreign currency. If the U.S. dollar is the domestic currency and the British pound the foreign currency, a quotation might be .625 pounds per dollar or $1.60 per pound. The result is the same, for one is the reciprocal of the other (1/.625 = 1.60, while 1/1.60 = .625).

Currency risk can be thought of as the volatility of the exchange rate of one currency for another. In Figure 24-1, this risk is illustrated for the spot exchange rate of U.S. dollars per British pound. As shown, the dollar strengthened in value (fewer dollars per pound) from 1981 to 1985 and then weakened in value to 1988, after which it fluctuated until the 1992 European correction, when it fell in value. In recent years, it has fluctuated around $1.60 per pound.

Forward exchange rate The rate today for exchanging one currency for another at a specific future date.

We must distinguish a spot exchange rate from a **forward exchange rate.** Forward transactions involve an agreement today for settlement in the future. It might be the delivery of 1,000 British pounds 90 days hence, where the settlement rate is 1.59 U.S. dollars per pound. The forward exchange rate usually differs from the spot exchange rate for reasons we will explain shortly.

With these definitions in mind, there are three types of exchange-rate risk exposure with which we are concerned:

- Translation exposure
- Transactions exposure
- Economic exposure

The first, *translation exposure,* is the change in accounting income and balance sheet statements caused by changes in exchange rates. This will be illustrated in the next section. *Transactions exposure* has to do with settling a particular transaction, like a

Part VIII Special Areas of Financial Management

FIGURE 24-1
Exchange Rates
of U.S. Dollars per
British Pound
(January 1, 1980
to September 15,
1999).

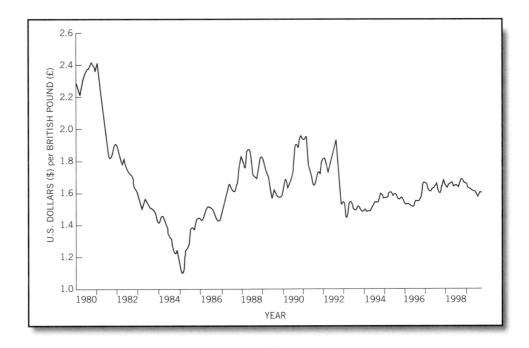

credit sale, at one exchange rate when the obligation was originally recorded at another. Finally, *economic exposure* involves changes in expected future cash flows, and hence economic value, caused by a change in exchange rates. For example, if we budget 1.3 million British pounds (£) to build an extension to our London plant and the exchange rate is now £.625 per U.S. dollar, this corresponds to £1.3 million/.625 = **$2,080,000.** When we pay for materials and labor, the British pound might strengthen, say to £.615 per dollar. The plant now has a dollar cost of £1.3 million/.615 = **$2,113,821.** The difference, $2,113,821 − $2,080,000 = **$33,821,** represents an economic loss.

Having briefly defined these three exchange-rate risk exposures, we investigate them in detail. This will be followed by a discussion of how exchange-rate risk exposure can be managed.

Translation Exposure

Financial Accounting Standards Board (FASB)

The rule-making body of the accounting profession that sets its standards.

Translation exposure relates to the accounting treatment of changes in exchange rates. Statement No. 52 of the **Financial Accounting Standards Board (FASB)** deals with the translation of foreign currency changes on the balance sheet and income statement. Under these accounting rules, a U.S. company must determine a "functional currency" for each of its foreign subsidiaries. If the subsidiary is a stand-alone operation that is integrated within a particular country, the functional currency may be the local currency—otherwise, it is the dollar.[2] Where high inflation occurs (over

---

[2]Various criteria are used to determine if the foreign subsidiary is self-contained. These include whether sales, labor, other costs, and debt are primarily denominated in the local currency. Also, the nature and magnitude of intracompany transactions are important. Under certain circumstances, it is possible for a foreign currency other than the local one to be used.

100 percent per annum), the functional currency must be the dollar regardless of the conditions given.

The functional currency used is important because it determines the translation process. If the local currency is used, all assets and liabilities are translated at the current rate of exchange. Moreover, **translation gains or losses** are not reflected in the income statement but rather are recognized in owners' equity as a translation adjustment. The fact that such adjustments do not affect accounting income is appealing to many companies. If the functional currency is the dollar, however, this is not the case. Gains or losses are reflected in the income statement of the parent company, using what is known as the *temporal method* (to be described shortly). In general, the use of the dollar as the functional currency results in greater fluctuations in accounting income but in smaller fluctuations in balance sheet items than does the use of the local currency. Let us examine the differences in accounting methods.

Differences in Accounting Methods.   With the dollar as the functional currency, balance sheet and income statement items are categorized as to historical exchange rates or as to current exchange rates. Cash, receivables, liabilities, sales, expenses, and taxes are translated using current exchange rates, whereas inventories, plant and equipment, equity, cost of goods sold, and depreciation are translated at the historical exchange rates existing at the time of the transactions. This differs from the situation where the local currency is used as the functional currency; in that situation, all items are translated at current exchange rates.

To illustrate, a company we shall call Woatich Precision Instruments has a subsidiary in the Kingdom of Spamany where the currency is the liso (L). At the first of the year, the exchange rate is 8 lisos to the dollar, and that rate has prevailed for many years. However, during 20X2, the liso declines steadily in value to 10 lisos to the dollar at year end. The average exchange rate during the year is 9 lisos to the dollar. Table 24-2 shows the foreign subsidiary's balance sheet at the beginning and end of the year, the income statement for the year, and the effect of the method of translation.

Taking the balance sheet first, we see the 12/31/X1 date serves as a base, and the dollar statement in column 3 is simply the liso amounts shown in column 1 divided by the exchange rate of 8 lisos to the dollar. For the two separate dollar statements at 12/31/X2, shown in the last two columns, we see that cash, receivables, current liabilities, and long-term debt are the same for both methods of accounting. These amounts are determined on a current exchange-rate basis by dividing the amounts shown in column 2 by the exchange rate at year end of 10 lisos to the dollar. For the local functional currency statement, column 4, inventories and fixed assets are determined in the same manner—by use of the current exchange rate. For the dollar functional currency statement, inventories and fixed assets are valued using historical exchange rates. Because the cost of goods sold figure equals beginning inventory, under the first-in, first-out (FIFO) inventory accounting method, the ending inventory represents items purchased throughout the year. Assuming steady purchases, we divided the ending liso amount by the average exchange rate (L9:$1) to obtain $500,000. Using historical exchange rates again, net fixed assets are determined by dividing the liso amount at year end by the earlier exchange rate of 8 lisos to the dollar. The common stock account is carried at the base amount under both methods.

Finally, the change in retained earnings is a residual. (We defer explaining the cumulative translation adjustment item until the discussion of the income statement.) Because of the upward adjustment in inventories and fixed assets, total assets are higher with the dollar functional currency (temporal method) than they are with the local functional currency (current method). The opposite would occur in our

TABLE 24-2
Foreign subsidiary
of Woatich Precision
Instruments

	(1)	(2)	(3)	(4)	(5)
				IN DOLLARS	
				LOCAL FUNCTIONAL CURRENCY	DOLLAR FUNCTIONAL CURRENCY
	IN LISOS				
	12/31/X1	12/31/X2	12/31/X1	12/31/X2	12/31/X2
Balance Sheets (in thousands)					
Cash	L 600	L 1,000	$ 75	$ 100	$ 100
Receivables	2,000	2,600	250	260	260
Inventories (FIFO)	4,000	4,500	500	450	500
Current Assets	L 6,600	L 8,100	$ 825	$ 810	$ 860
Net fixed assets	5,000	4,400	625	440	550
Total	L11,600	L12,500	$1,450	$1,250	$1,410
Current liabilities	L 3,000	L 3,300	$ 375	$ 330	$ 330
Long-term debt	2,000	1,600	250	160	160
Common stock	600	600	75	75	75
Retained earnings	6,000	7,000	750	861	845
Cumulative translation adjustment				−176	
Total	L11,600	L12,500	$1,450	$1,250	$1,410
Income Statements for the Years Ending (in thousands with rounding)					
Sales		L10,000		$1,111	$1,111
Cost of goods sold		4,000		444	500
Depreciation		600		67	75
Expenses		3,500		389	389
Taxes		900		100	100
Operating income		L 1,000		$ 111	$ 47
Translation					48
Net income		L 1,000		$ 111	$ 95
Translation adjustment				$−176	

example if the liso increased in value relative to the dollar. We see that there is substantially more change in total assets when a local functional currency is used than when a dollar functional currency is employed.

The opposite occurs for the income statement. Sales are adjusted by the average exchange rate that prevailed during the year (L9:$1) for both accounting methods. For the local functional currency statement, column 4, all cost and expense items are adjusted by this exchange rate. For the dollar functional currency statement, the last column, the cost of goods sold and depreciation are translated at historical exchange rates (L8:$1), whereas the other items are translated at the average rate (L9:$1). We see that operating income and net income are larger when the local functional currency is used than when the functional currency is the dollar. For the latter method, the translation gain is factored in, so that net income agrees with the change in retained earnings from 12/31/X1 to 12/31/X2. We see that this change is $845 − $750 = **$95.** In contrast, when the functional currency is local, the translation adjustment occurs after the income figure of $111 is calculated. The adjustment is that amount, namely −$176, that, together with net income, brings the liability and shareholders' equity part of the balance sheet into balance. This amount is then added to the sum of past translation adjustments to obtain the new cumulative translation adjustment figure that appears on the balance sheet. As we assume past adjustments total zero, this item becomes −$176.

Thus, the translation adjustments for the two methods are in opposite directions. Should the liso increase in value relative to the dollar, the effect would be the reverse of that illustrated. In this case, operating income would be higher if the functional currency were the dollar.

Because translation gains or losses are not reflected directly on the income statement, reported operating income tends to fluctuate less when the functional currency is local than when it is the dollar. However, the variability of balance sheet items is increased, owing to the translation of all items by the current exchange rate. Because many corporate executives are concerned with accounting income, the accounting method described in FASB No. 52 is popular as long as a subsidiary qualifies for a local functional currency. However, this accounting procedure also has its drawbacks. For one thing, it distorts the balance sheet and the historical cost numbers. Moreover, it may cause calculation of return on assets and other measures of return to be meaningless. It is simply inconsistent with the nature of other accounting rules, which are based on historical costs. Most financial ratios are affected by the functional currency employed, so the financial analyst must be very careful when foreign subsidiaries account for a sizable portion of a company's operations.[3] The method has also been criticized for not allowing proper assessment of the parent's likely future cash flows. In summary, there is no universally satisfactory way to treat foreign currency translations, and the accounting profession continues to struggle with the issue.

Transactions Exposure

Transactions exposure involves the gain or loss that occurs when settling a specific foreign transaction. The transaction might be the purchase or sale of a product, the lending or borrowing of funds, or some other transaction involving the acquisition of assets or the assumption of liabilities denominated in a foreign currency. While any transaction will do, the term "transactions exposure" is usually employed in connection with foreign trade, that is, specific imports or exports on open-account credit.

Suppose a British pound receivable of £680 is booked when the exchange rate is £.60 to the U.S. dollar. Payment is not due for two months. In the interim, the pound weakens (more pound per dollar), and the exchange rate goes to £.62 per $1. As a result, there is a transactions loss. Before, the receivable was worth £680/.60 = **$1,133.33.** When payment is received, the firm receives payment worth £680/.62 = **$1,096.77.** Thus, we have a transactions loss of $1,133.33 − $1,096.77 = **$36.56.** If instead the pound were to strengthen, for example, £.58 to the dollar, there would be a transactions gain. We would receive payment worth £680/.58 = **$1,172.41.** With this illustration in mind, it is easy to produce examples of other types of transactions gains and losses.

Economic Exposure

Perhaps the most important of the three exchange-rate risk exposures—translation, transactions, and economic—is the last. Economic exposure is the change in value of a company that accompanies an *unanticipated* change in exchange rates. Note that we

---

[3]See Thomas I. Selling and George H. Sorter, "FASB Statement No. 52 and Its Implications for Financial Statement Analysis," *Financial Analysts Journal* 39 (May–June 1983), 64–69.

distinguish anticipated from unanticipated. Anticipated changes in exchange rates are already reflected in the market value of the firm. If we do business with Spain, the anticipation might be that the peseta will weaken relative to the dollar. The fact that it weakens should not impact market value. However, if it weakens more or less than expected, this will affect value. Economic exposure does not lend itself to as precise a description and measurement as either translation or transactions exposure. Economic exposure depends on what happens to expected future cash flows, so subjectivity is necessarily involved.

MANAGEMENT OF EXCHANGE-RATE RISK EXPOSURE

There are a number of ways by which exchange-rate risk exposure can be managed. Natural hedges; cash management; adjusting of intracompany accounts; as well as international financing hedges and currency hedges, through forward contracts, futures contracts, currency options, and currency swaps, all serve this purpose.

Natural Hedges

The relationship between revenues (or pricing) and costs of a foreign subsidiary sometimes provides a *natural hedge*, giving the firm ongoing protection from exchange-rate fluctuations. The key is the extent to which cash flows adjust naturally to currency changes. It is not the country in which a subsidiary is located that matters, but whether the subsidiary's revenue and cost functions are sensitive to global or domestic market conditions. At the extremes there are four possible scenarios.[4]

	GLOBALLY DETERMINED	DOMESTICALLY DETERMINED
Scenario 1		
Pricing	X $]^*$	
Cost	X	
Scenario 2		
Pricing		X $]^*$
Cost		X
Scenario 3		
Pricing	X	
Cost		X
Scenario 4		
Pricing		X
Cost	X	

*There is a natural offsetting relationship provided by pricing and costs both occurring in similar market environments.

In the first category we might have a copper fabricator in Taiwan. Its principal cost is that for copper, the raw material, whose price is determined in the global market and quoted in U.S. dollars. Moreover, the fabricated product produced is sold in markets dominated by global pricing. Therefore, the subsidiary has little exposure to

---

[4]For further categorization and explanation, see Christine R. Hekman, "Don't Blame Currency Values for Strategic Errors," *Midland Corporate Finance Journal* 4 (Fall 1986), 45–55.

exchange-rate fluctuations. In other words, there is a "natural hedge," because protection of value follows from the natural workings of the global marketplace.

The second category might correspond to a cleaning service company in Switzerland. The dominant cost component is labor, and both it and the pricing of the service are determined domestically. As domestic inflation affects costs, the subsidiary is able to pass along the increase in its pricing to customers. Margins, expressed in U.S. dollars, are relatively insensitive to the combination of domestic inflation and exchange-rate changes. This situation also constitutes a natural hedge.

The third situation might involve a British-based international consulting firm. Pricing is largely determined in the global market, whereas costs, again mostly labor, are determined in the domestic market. If, due to inflation, the British pound should decrease in value relative to the dollar, costs will rise relative to prices, and margins will suffer. Here the subsidiary is exposed. Finally, the last category might correspond to a Japanese importer of foreign foods. Costs are determined globally, whereas prices are determined domestically. Here, too, the subsidiary would be subject to much exposure.

These simple notions illustrate the nature of natural hedging. A company's strategic positioning largely determines its natural exchange-rate risk exposure. However, such exposure can be modified. For one thing, a company can internationally diversify its operations when it is overexposed in one currency. It can also source differently in the production of a product. Any strategic decision that affects markets served, pricing, operations, or sourcing can be thought of as a form of natural hedging.

A key concern for the financial manager is the degree of exchange-rate risk exposure that remains *after* any natural hedging. This remaining risk exposure then can be hedged using operating, financing, or currency-market hedges. We explore each in turn.

Cash Management and Adjusting Intracompany Accounts

If a company knew that a country's currency, where a subsidiary was based, were going to fall in value, it would want to do a number of things. First, it should reduce its cash holdings in this currency to a minimum by purchasing inventories or other real assets. Moreover, the subsidiary should try to avoid extended trade credit (accounts receivable). Achieving as quick a turnover as possible of receivables into cash would thus be desirable. In contrast, it should try to obtain extended terms on its accounts payable. It may also want to borrow in the local currency to replace any advances made by the U.S. parent. The last step will depend on relative interest rates. If the currency were going to appreciate in value, opposite steps should be undertaken. Without knowledge of the future direction of currency value movements, aggressive policies in either direction are inappropriate. Under most circumstances we are unable to predict the future, so the best policy may be one of balancing monetary assets against monetary liabilities to neutralize the effect of exchange-rate fluctuations.

A company with multiple foreign operations can protect itself against exchange-rate risk by adjusting its commitments to transfer funds among companies. Accelerating the timing of payments made or received in foreign currencies is called *leading*, and decelerating the timing is called *lagging*. For example, assume that your company has foreign subsidiaries in Switzerland and the Czech Republic. You think that the Czech koruna will soon be revalued upward, but the Swiss franc will hold steady. The Swiss subsidiary purchases approximately $100,000 worth of goods each month from the Czech subsidiary. Normal billing calls for payment three months after delivery of the goods. Instead of this arrangement, you now instruct the Swiss subsidiary to *lead* by paying for the goods on delivery in view of the likely revaluation upward of the Czech koruna.

Some multinational companies establish a **reinvoicing center** to manage intracompany and third-party foreign trade. The multinational's exporting subsidiaries sell goods to the reinvoicing center, which resells (reinvoices) them to importing subsidiaries or third-party buyers. Title to the goods initially passes to the reinvoicing center, but the goods move directly from the selling unit to the buying unit or independent customer.

Tax implications form a large part of the incentive for reinvoicing. The location—especially the tax jurisdiction where revenue will be booked—is strategically important. Popular (i.e., tax-friendly) locations for reinvoicing centers include Hong Kong and the British Virgin Islands.

Generally, the reinvoicing center is billed in the selling unit's home currency and, in turn, bills the purchasing unit in that unit's home currency. In this way the reinvoicing center can then centralize and manage all intracompany transactions exposure. The reinvoicing center's centralized position also facilitates interunit **netting** of obligations so as to reduce the necessary volume of actual foreign exchange transactions. Also, this system allows for more coordinated control over any leading or lagging arrangements between affiliates.

In addition to these arrangements, the multinational company can also adjust intracompany dividends and royalty payments. Sometimes the currency in which a sale is billed is varied in keeping with anticipated foreign exchange movements. Transfer pricing of components or of finished goods, which are exchanged between the parent and various foreign affiliates, can be varied. (However, the tax authorities in most countries look very closely at transfer prices to ensure that taxes are not being avoided.) In all of these cases, as well as others, intracompany payments are arranged so that they fit into the company's overall management of its currency exposure.

International Financing Hedges

If a company is exposed in one country's currency and is hurt when that currency weakens in value, it can borrow in that country to offset the exposure. In the context of the framework presented earlier, asset-sensitive exposure would be balanced with borrowings. A wide variety of sources of external financing are available to the foreign affiliate. These range from commercial bank loans within the host country to loans from international lending agencies. In this section we consider the chief sources of external financing.

Commercial Bank Loans and Trade Bills. Foreign commercial banks are one of the major sources of financing abroad. They perform essentially the same financing function as domestic commercial banks. One subtle difference is that banking practices in Europe allow longer-term loans than are available in the United States. Another difference is that loans tend to be on an *overdraft* basis. That is, a company writes a check that overdraws its account and is charged interest on the overdraft. Many of these lending banks are known as *merchant banks,* which simply means that they offer a full menu of financial services to business firms. Corresponding to the growth in multinational companies, international banking operations of U.S. banks have grown accordingly. All the principal commercial cities of the world have branches or offices of U.S. banks.

In addition to commercial bank loans, "discounting" trade bills is a common method of short-term financing. Although this method of financing is not used extensively in the United States, it is widely used in Europe to finance both domestic and international trade. More will be said about the instruments involved later in the chapter.

Eurodollar Financing. **Eurodollars** are bank deposits denominated in U.S. dollars but not subject to U.S. banking regulations. Since the late 1950s an active market has developed for these deposits. Foreign banks and foreign branches of U.S. banks, mostly in Europe, actively bid for Eurodollar deposits, paying interest rates that fluctuate in keeping with supply and demand. The deposits are in large denominations, frequently $100,000 or more, and the banks use them to make dollar loans to quality borrowers. The loans are made at a rate in excess of the deposit rate. The rate differential varies according to the relative risk of the borrower. Essentially, borrowing and lending Eurodollars is a wholesale operation, with far fewer costs than are usually associated with banking. The market itself is unregulated, so supply and demand forces have free rein.

The Eurodollar market is a major source of short-term financing for the working capital requirements of the multinational company. The interest rate on loans is based on the Eurodollar deposit rate and bears only an indirect relationship to the U.S. prime rate. Typically, rates on loans are quoted in terms of the **London interbank offered rate (LIBOR).** The greater the risk, the greater the spread above LIBOR. A prime borrower will pay about one-half percent over LIBOR for an intermediate-term loan. One should realize that LIBOR is more volatile than the U.S. prime rate, owing to the sensitive nature of supply and demand for Eurodollar deposits.

We should point out that the Eurodollar market is part of a larger **Eurocurrency** market where deposit and lending rates are quoted on the stronger currencies of the world. The principles involved in this market are the same as for the Eurodollar market, so we do not repeat them. The development of the Eurocurrency market has greatly facilitated international borrowing and *financial intermediation* (the flow of funds through intermediaries like banks and insurance companies to ultimate borrowers).

International Bond Financing. The Eurocurrency market must be distinguished from the **Eurobond** market. The latter market is a more traditional one, with underwriters placing securities. Though a bond issue is denominated in a single currency, it is placed in multiple countries. Once issued, it is traded over the counter in multiple countries and by a number of security dealers. A Eurobond is different from a *foreign bond,* which is a bond issued by a foreign government or corporation in a local market. A foreign bond is sold in a single country and falls under the security regulations of that country. Foreign bonds have colorful nicknames. For example, *Yankee bonds* are issued by non-Americans in the U.S. market, and *Samurai bonds* are issued by non-Japanese in the Japanese market. Eurobonds, foreign bonds, and domestic bonds of different countries differ in terminology, in the way interest is computed, and in features. We do not address these differences, because that would require a separate book.

Many debt issues in the international arena are **floating-rate notes (FRNs).** These instruments have a variety of features, often involving multiple currencies. Some instruments are indexed to price levels or to commodity prices. Others are linked to an interest rate, such as LIBOR. The reset interval may be annual, semiannual, quarterly, or even more frequent. Still other instruments have option features.

Currency-Option and Multiple-Currency Bonds. Certain bonds provide the holder with the right to choose the currency in which payment is received, usually

Eurodollars A U.S. dollar-denominated deposit—generally in a bank located outside the United States—not subject to U.S. banking regulations.

London interbank offered rate (LIBOR) The interest rate that world-class banks in London pay each other for Eurodollars.

Eurocurrency A currency deposited outside its country of origin.

Eurobond A bond issue sold internationally outside of the country in whose currency the bond is denominated.

Floating-rate note (FRN) Debt issue with a variable interest rate.

prior to each coupon or principal payment. Typically, this option is confined to two currencies, although it can be more. For example, a company might issue $1,000-par-value bonds with an 8 percent coupon rate. Each bond might carry the option to receive payment in either U.S. dollars or in British pounds. The exchange rate between the currencies is fixed at the time of bond issue.

Bonds are sometimes issued with principal and interest payments being a weighted average, or "basket," of multiple currencies. Known as *currency cocktail bonds,* these securities provide a degree of exchange-rate stability not found in any one currency. In addition, *dual-currency bonds* have their purchase price and coupon payments denominated in one currency, whereas a different currency is used to make the principal payments. For example, a Swiss bond might call for interest payments in Swiss francs and principal payments in U.S. dollars.

Currency Market Hedges

Yet another means to hedge currency exposure is through devices of several currency markets—forward contracts, futures contracts, currency options, and currency swaps. Let us see how these markets and vehicles work to protect the multinational company.

Forward contract A contract for the delivery of a commodity, foreign currency, or financial instrument at a price specified now, with delivery and settlement at a specified future date. Although similar to a *futures contract,* it is not easily transferred or canceled.

Forward Exchange Market.   In the forward exchange market, one buys a **forward contract** for the exchange of one currency for another at a specific future date and at a specific exchange ratio. A forward contract provides assurance of being able to convert into a desired currency at a price set in advance.

The Fillups Electronics Company is hedging through the forward market. It sold equipment to a Swiss customer through its Zurich branch for 1 million francs with credit terms of "net 90." Upon payment, Fillups intends to convert the Swiss francs into U.S. dollars. The spot and 90-day forward rates of Swiss francs in terms of U.S. dollars were the following:

Spot rate	$.670
90-day forward rate	.665

The spot rate is simply the current market-determined exchange rate for Swiss francs. In our example, 1 franc is worth $.670, and $1 will buy $1.00/.670 = $ **1.493 francs.** A foreign currency sells at a *forward discount* if its forward price is less than its spot price. In our example, the Swiss franc sells at a discount. If the forward price exceeds the spot price, it is said to sell at a *forward premium*. For example, assume that the British pound sells at a forward premium. In that case, pounds buy more dollars for future delivery than they do for present delivery.

If Fillups wishes to avoid exchange-rate risk, it should sell 1 million Swiss francs forward 90 days. When it delivers the francs 90 days hence, it will receive $665,000 (1 million Swiss francs times the 90-day futures price of $.665). If the spot rate stays at $.670, of course, Fillups would have been better off not having sold francs forward. It could sell 1 million francs in the spot market for $670,000. In this sense, Fillups pays $.005 per franc, or $5,000 in total, to ensure its ability to convert Swiss francs to dollars. On an annualized basis, the cost of this protection is

$$(\$.005/\$.670) \times (365 \text{ days}/90 \text{ days}) = \mathbf{3.03\%}$$

For stable pairs of currencies, the discount or premium of the forward rate over the spot rate generally varies from 0 to 8 percent on an annualized basis. For somewhat less stable currencies, the discount may go as high as 20 percent. Much beyond this point of instability, the forward market for the currency ceases to exist. In summary, the forward exchange market allows a company to ensure against devaluation or market-determined declines in value. The forward market is particularly suited for hedging transactions exposure.

Quotations on selected foreign exchanges at a moment in time are shown in Table 24-3. The spot rates reported in the first column indicate the conversion rate into dollars. The exchange-rate quotations contained in newspapers such as the *Wall Street Journal* and the *New York Times* are for very large transactions. As a foreign traveler, you cannot buy or sell foreign currency at nearly as good a rate. Often you will pay several percent more when you buy and receive several percent less when you sell. Alas, the hardships of dealing in amounts less than $1 million!

In the first numerical column of Table 24-3, for each currency the conversion rate of one unit of a foreign currency into U.S. dollars is shown. Near the top, we see that the Australian dollar is worth .6447 U.S. dollars (U.S.$.6447). To determine how many Australian dollars (A$) one U.S. dollar will buy, we take the reciprocal, 1/.6447 = **A$1.5511.** Forward rates for 30, 90, and 180 days are shown for the British pound, Canadian dollar, Japanese yen, and Swiss franc. Comparing the forward rates to the spot rates for these four currencies, we find that all four currencies are at forward rate premiums relative to the U.S. dollar. That is, they are worth more dollars on future delivery than they are now. The reasons for premiums and discounts must await our discussion of *interest-rate parity*, which is coming up shortly.

Euro (EUR) The name given to the single European currency. Its official abbreviation is EUR. Like the dollar ($) and the British pound (£), the euro (€) has a distinctive symbol, which looks similar to a "C" with a "=" through it.

The Euro.   At the bottom of Table 24-3, we find the **euro.** This is the common currency for the European Monetary Union (EMU), which includes the following 11 European Union (EU) countries: Austria, Belgium, Finland, France, Germany, Ireland, Italy, Luxembourg, The Netherlands, Portugal, and Spain. (Four other EU countries—Denmark, Greece, Sweden, and the United Kingdom—at the time of this writing, have yet to adopt the common currency.) On January 1, 1999, currency conversion rates between the "legacy currencies" (i.e., former national currencies of the EMU member states) and the euro were established. Individuals in EMU countries can continue to use their national currencies alongside the euro until some time in 2002, when their national currencies will be retired. The euro was introduced amid much fanfare and began trading January 1, 1999 at 1.17 U.S. dollars to the euro, even getting as high as 1.19. However, there was a steady decline in value until it touched 1.01 in July 1999. From there, the euro gained strength against the U.S. dollar and is shown trading at 1.0624 in Table 24-3.

Futures contract A contract for the delivery of a commodity, foreign currency, or financial instrument at a specified price on a stipulated future date. Futures contracts are traded on organized exchanges.

Currency Futures.   Closely related to the use of a forward contract is a futures contract. A currency futures market exists for the major currencies of the world—for example, the Australian dollar, the Canadian dollar, the British pound, and the Swiss franc, and the yen. A **futures contract** is a standardized agreement that calls for delivery of a currency at some specified future date, either the third Wednesday of March, June, September, or December. Contracts are traded on an exchange, and the clearinghouse of the exchange interposes itself between the buyer and the seller. This means that all transactions are with the clearinghouse, not made directly between two parties. Very few contracts involve actual delivery at expiration. Rather, a buyer and a seller of a contract independently take offsetting positions to close out a contract. The seller cancels a contract by buying another contract, while the buyer cancels a contract by selling another contract.

Each day, the futures contract is *marked-to-market* in the sense that it is valued at the closing price. Price movements affect the buyer and seller in opposite ways. Every day there is a winner and a loser, depending on the direction of price movement. The

TABLE 24-3
Exchange rates on
July 27, 1999

	U.S. DOLLARS REQUIRED TO BUY ONE UNIT	UNITS REQUIRED TO BUY ONE U.S. DOLLAR
Argentina (peso)	$1.0005	0.9995
Australia (dollar)	.6447	1.5511
Brazil (real)	.5519	1.8120
Britain (pound)	1.5902	.6289
30-day forward	1.5903	.6288
90-day forward	1.5910	.6285
180-day forward	1.5925	.6279
Canada (dollar)	.6611	1.5127
30-day forward	.6613	1.5121
90-day forward	.6618	1.5111
180-day forward	.6625	1.5095
Chile (peso)	.0019	526.3158
China (renminbi)	.1208	8.2770
Czech Republic (koruna)	.0290	34.5290
Hong Kong (dollar)	.1288	7.7615
India (rupee)	.0231	43.3250
Japan (yen)	.0086	116.3300
30-day forward	.0086	115.8100
90-day forward	.0087	114.7900
180-day forward	.0088	113.0900
Malaysia (ringgit)	.2631	3.8005
Saudi Arabia (riyal)	.2666	3.7505
Singapore (dollar)	.5932	1.6859
Switzerland (franc)	.6635	1.5072
30-day forward	.6660	1.5016
90-day forward	.6706	1.4912
180-day forward	.6777	1.4756
Taiwan (dollar)	.0310	32.2650
Thailand (baht)	.0268	37.2800
Venezuela (bolivar)	.0016	625.0000
euro	1.0624	.9413

loser must come up with more margin (a deposit), whereas the winner can draw off excess margin. Futures contracts are different from forward contracts in this regard; forward contracts need to be settled only at expiration. Another difference is that only a set number of maturities are available for futures contracts. Finally, futures contracts come only in multiples of standard-size contracts—for example, multiples of 12.5 million yen. Forward contracts can be for most any size. However, the two instruments are used for the same hedging purpose.[5]

---

[5]See James C. Van Horne, *Financial Market Rates and Flows*, 6th ed. (Upper Saddle River, NJ: Prentice Hall, 2001) for a detailed discussion of futures markets.

Currency option A contract that gives the holder the right to buy (call) or sell (put) a specific amount of a foreign currency at some specified price until a certain (expiration) date.

Currency Options.   Forward and futures contracts provide a "two-sided" hedge against currency movements. That is, if the currency involved moves in one direction, the forward or futures position offsets it. **Currency options,** in contrast, enable the hedging of "one-sided" risk. Only adverse currency movements are hedged, either with a call option to buy the foreign currency or with a put option to sell it. The holder has the right, but not the obligation, to buy or sell the currency over the life of the contract. If not exercised, of course, the option expires. For this protection, one pays a premium.

There are both options on spot market currencies and options on currency futures contracts. Because currency options are traded on a number of exchanges throughout the world, one is able to trade with relative ease. The use of currency options and their valuation are largely the same as for stock options. (Since we described option valuation in the Appendix to Chapter 22 for stock options, we do not repeat that discussion.) The value of the option, and hence the premium paid, depends importantly on exchange-rate volatility.

Currency Swaps.   Yet another device for shifting risk is the *currency swap*. In a currency swap two parties exchange debt obligations denominated in different currencies. Each party agrees to pay the other's interest obligation. At maturity, principal amounts are exchanged, usually at a rate of exchange agreed to in advance. The exchange is *notional* in that only the cash-flow difference is paid. If one party should default, there is no loss of principal per se. There is, however, the opportunity cost associated with currency movements after the swap's initiation.

Currency swaps typically are arranged through an intermediary, such as a commercial bank. Many different arrangements are possible: a swap involving more than two currencies; a swap with option features; and a currency swap combined with an interest-rate swap, where the obligation to pay interest on long-term debt is swapped for that to pay interest on short-term, floating-rate, or some other type of debt. As can be imagined, things get complicated rather quickly. The point to keep in mind, however, is that currency swaps are widely used and serve as longer-term risk-shifting devices.

Hedging Exchange-Rate Risk Exposure: A Summing Up

We have seen that there are a number of ways that exchange-rate risk exposure can be hedged. The place to begin is to determine if your company has a natural hedge. If it does have a natural hedge, then to add a financing or a currency hedge actually increases your risk exposure. That is, you will have undone a natural hedge that your company has by virtue of the business it does abroad and the sourcing of such business. As a result, you will have created a net risk exposure where little or none existed before. Therefore, you need to carefully assess your exchange-rate risk exposure before taking any hedging actions.

The first step is to estimate your net, residual exchange-rate risk exposure after taking account of any natural hedges that your company may have. If you have a net exposure (a difference between estimated inflows and outflows of a foreign currency over a specified time), then the questions are whether you wish to hedge it and how. Cash management and intracompany account adjustments are only temporary measures, and they are limited in the magnitude of their effect. Financing hedges provide a means to hedge on a longer term basis, as do currency swaps. Currency forward contracts, futures, and options are usually available for up to one or two years. Though it is possible to arrange longer term contracts through a merchant bank, the cost is usually high, and there are liquidity problems. How you hedge your net exposure, if at all, should be a function of the suitability of the hedging device and its cost.

Macro Factors Governing Exchange-Rate Behavior

Fluctuations in exchange rates are continual and often defy explanation, at least in the short run. In the longer run, however, there are linkages between domestic and foreign inflation and between interest rates and exchange rates.

Purchasing-Power Parity. If product and financial markets are efficient internationally, we would expect certain relationships to hold. Over the long run, markets for tradeable goods and foreign exchange should move toward **purchasing-power parity (PPP).** The idea is that a basket of standardized goods should sell at the same price internationally.

> **Purchasing-power parity (PPP)** The idea that a basket of goods should sell for the same price in two countries, after exchange rates are taken into account.

If it is cheaper to buy wheat from Canada than it is from a U.S. producer, after accounting for transportation costs and after adjusting the Canadian price for the exchange rate, a rational U.S. buyer will purchase Canadian wheat. This action, together with commodity arbitrage, will cause the Canadian wheat price to rise relative to the U.S. price and, perhaps, for the Canadian-dollar exchange rate to strengthen. The combination of rising Canadian wheat prices and a changing Canadian-dollar value raises the U.S.-dollar price of Canadian wheat to the U.S. buyer. Theory would have it that these transactions would continue until the U.S.-dollar cost of wheat is the same as the Canadian. At that point, there would be purchasing-power parity for the U.S. buyer. That is, the buyer would be indifferent between U.S. and Canadian wheat. For that matter, a Canadian buyer of wheat should also be indifferent for purchasing-power parity works both ways.

How closely a country's exchange rate corresponds to purchasing-power parity depends on the price elasticity of exports and imports. To the extent that exports are traded in world competitive markets, there is usually close conformity to purchasing-power parity. Commodities and fabricated products like steel and clothing are highly price sensitive. In general, products in mature industries conform more closely to purchasing-power parity than products with emerging technology. To the extent that a country's inflation is dominated by services, there tends to be less conformity to purchasing-power parity. We also know that purchasing-power parity does not work well when a country intervenes in the exchange-rate market, either propping up its currency or keeping it artificially low. Because of frictions, trade barriers, government intervention in the exchange market, and other imperfections, purchasing-power parities between various tradeable goods generally do not hold in the short run. They are a long-run equilibration phenomenon, and they help us understand the likely direction of change.

The Coca-Cola Company and Foreign Currency Management

We manage most of our foreign currency exposures on a consolidated basis, which allows us to net certain exposures and take advantage of any natural offsets. With approximately 74 percent of 1998 operating income generated outside the United States, over time weakness in one particular currency is often offset by strengths in others. We use derivative financial instruments to further reduce our net exposure to currency fluctuations.

Source: The Coca-Cola Company 1998 Annual Report, p. 30. Reproduced with permission of The Coca-Cola Company.

Interest-Rate Parity. The second link in our equilibrium process concerns the interest-rate differential between two countries. *Interest-rate parity* suggests that if interest rates are higher in one country than they are in another, the former's currency will sell at a discount in the forward market. Expressed differently, interest-rate differentials and forward spot exchange-rate differentials are offsetting. How does it work? The starting point is the relationship between nominal (observed) interest rates and inflation. Recall from Chapter 2 that the *Fisher effect* implies that the nominal rate of interest is the sum of the real rate of interest (the interest rate in the absence of price-level changes) plus the rate of inflation *expected* to prevail over the life of the instrument.

Big Mac Purchasing-Power Parity

McDonald's Big Mac hamburgers are sold in more than 100 countries. Though standardized across countries, the product is produced locally with respect to both food materials and labor. If purchasing-power parity (PPP) were working perfectly, exchange rates would adjust so that Big Macs would cost the same in all countries. From time to time, *The Economist* publishes Big Mac price and exchange-rate comparisons, which suggest whether a currency is over- or undervalued relative to the U.S. dollar. This supposes, of course, that exchange rates can deviate significantly from purchasing-power parity in the short run. However, in the long run, economic forces will eventually equalize the purchasing power of currencies. A recent comparison showed the following:

COUNTRY	BIG MAC PRICE IN LOCAL CURRENCY	IMPLIED EXCHANGE RATE (TO BUY $1)	ACTUAL EXCHANGE RATE (TO BUY $1)	% OVER (+) OR UNDER (−) VALUATION AGAINST U.S. DOLLAR
United States	$2.43	—	—	—
Australia	A$2.65	1.09	1.59	−32
Britain	£1.90	.78	.62	+26
Japan	¥294	121.0	120.0	0
Malaysia	M$4.52	1.86	3.80	−51
Singapore	S$3.20	1.32	1.73	−24
Sweden	SKr24.0	9.88	8.32	+19
Switzerland	SFr5.90	2.43	1.48	+64

The implied exchange rate is simply the local price of a Big Mac divided by its U.S. dollar price. For Australia, it is A$2.65/$2.43 = **1.09.** As the actual exchange rate is 1.59, the Australian dollar is undervalued by (1.09 − 1.59)/1.59 = **−32%.** At the time, it was cheaper to eat Big Macs in Australia than in the United States. PPP theory implies that eventually undervalued currencies will *appreciate* (get stronger) against U.S. dollar, while overvalued currencies will *depreciate* (get weaker) against the U.S. dollar. If Big Macs are a reasonable approximation of a consumption basket, equilibrium suggests that the European currencies in our table will depreciate against the dollar, while the Asian-Pacific currencies—except for the yen, which is already showing "McParity"—will appreciate against the dollar.

In an international context, sometimes called the *international Fisher effect*, it is suggested that differences in interest rates between two countries serve as a proxy for differences in expected inflation. For example, if the nominal interest rate were 7 percent in the United States but 12 percent in Australia, the expected differential in inflation would be 5 percent. That is, inflation in Australia is expected to be 5 percent higher than in the United States. Does this hold exactly? Although there is disagreement as to the precise relationship between nominal interest rates and inflation, most people feel that expected inflation for a country has an important effect on interest rates in that country. The more open the capital markets, the closer the conformity to an international Fisher effect.

To illustrate interest-rate parity, consider the relationship between the U.S. dollar ($) and the British pound (£) both now and 90 days in the future. The international Fisher effect suggests that

$$\frac{F_£}{S_£} = \frac{1 + r_£}{1 + r_\$}$$ (24-1)

where $F_£$ = current 90-day forward exchange rate in pounds per dollar
   $S_£$ = current spot exchange rate in pounds per dollar
   $r_£$ = nominal British interbank Euromarket interest rate, expressed in terms of the 90-day return
   $r_\$$ = nominal U.S. interbank Euromarket interest rate, expressed in terms of the 90-day return

If the nominal interest rate in Britain were 8 percent and the nominal U.S. rate 6 percent, these annualized rates would translate into 90-day rates of 2 percent and 1.5 percent, respectively. If the current spot rate were .625 pounds per dollar, we would have

$$\frac{F_£}{.625} = \frac{1.020}{1.015}$$

Solving for the implied forward rate, we get

$$(1.015)F_£ = (.625)(1.020)$$
$$F_£ = .6375/1.015 = \textbf{.6281}$$

Thus the implied forward rate is .6281 British pounds per U.S. dollar. The British-pound forward rate is at a discount from the spot rate of .625 pounds to the dollar. That is, a pound is worth less in terms of dollars in the forward market, $1/.6281 =$ **$1.592,** than it is in the spot market, $1/.625 = $ **$1.60.** The discount is $(.6281 − .625)/.625 = \textbf{.005}.$ With interest-rate parity, the discount must equal the relative difference in interest rates, and, indeed, this is the case, for $(1.020 − 1.015)/1.015 = \textbf{.005}.$ If the interest rate in Britain were less than that in the United States, the implied forward rate in our example would be less than the spot rate. In this case, the British-pound forward rate is at a premium above the spot rate. For example, if the U.S. interest rate (annualized) were 8 percent and the British interest rate 6 percent, the implied 90-day forward rate for British pounds would be

$$\frac{F_£}{.625} = \frac{1.015}{1.020}$$

Solving for the implied forward rate, we get

$$(1.020)F_£ = (.625)(1.015)$$
$$F_£ = .6344/1.020 = \textbf{.6220}$$

Therefore, the forward rate is at a premium in the sense that it is worth more in terms of dollars in the forward market than in the spot market. If interest-rate parity did not occur, presumably arbitragers would be alert to the opportunity for profit.

Does this mean that interest-rate parity prevails between each set of currencies at all times? In the market for European and other currencies, which is largely free of imperfections, interest-rate parity generally holds within the limits of transactions costs. The relationship is strong for short-term interest rates, but it weakens for rates on investments with longer maturities. For countries with restrictions on exchange and where tax and other imperfections occur, interest-rate parity is not expected. To the extent that interest-rate parity is reasonable, however, one is able to determine the cost in dollars of a foreign sale or purchase where a future receipt or payment is involved.

STRUCTURING INTERNATIONAL TRADE TRANSACTIONS

Foreign trade differs from domestic trade with respect to the instruments and documents employed. Most domestic sales are on *open-account credit*. The customer is billed and has so many days to pay. In international trade, sellers are seldom able to obtain as accurate or as thorough credit information on potential buyers as they are in domestic sales. Communication is more cumbersome, and transportation of the goods slower and less certain. Moreover, the channels for legal settlement in cases of default are more complicated and more costly to pursue. For these reasons, procedures for international trade differ from those for domestic trade. There are three key documents in international trade: an order to pay, or draft; a bill of lading, which involves the physical movement of the goods; and a letter of credit, which guarantees the creditworthiness of the buyer. We examine each in turn. This is followed by a discussion of other means for facilitating international trade: countertrade, export factoring, and forfaiting.

International Trade Draft

The *international trade draft*, sometimes called a *bill of exchange*, is simply a written statement by the exporter ordering the importer to pay a specific amount of money at a specific time. Although the word "order" may seem harsh, it is the customary way of doing business internationally. The draft may be either a *sight draft* or a *time draft*. A sight draft is payable on presentation to the party to whom the draft is addressed. This party is known as the *drawee*. If the drawee, or importer, does not pay the amount specified on presentation of the draft, he or she defaults, and redress is achieved through the letter of credit arrangement (to be discussed later in this chapter).[6] A time draft is not payable until a specified future date.[6] For example, a time draft might be payable "90 days after sight." An example of such a time draft is shown in Figure 24-2.

Several features should be noted about the time draft. First, it is an unconditional order in writing signed by the drawer, the exporter. It specifies an exact amount of money that the drawee, the importer, must pay. Finally, it specifies the future date when this amount must be paid. Upon presentation of the time draft to the drawee, it is accepted. The *acceptance* can be by either the drawee or a bank. If the drawee accepts the draft, he or she acknowledges in writing on the back of the draft the obligation to pay the amount specified 90 days hence. The draft is then known as a *trade acceptance*. If a bank accepts the draft, it is known as a *banker's acceptance*. The bank accepts responsibility for payment and thereby substitutes its creditworthiness for that of the drawee.

---

[6]The draft itself can be either "clean" or "documentary." A clean draft is one to which documents of title are not attached. Documents of title are attached to a documentary draft and are delivered to the importer at the time the draft is presented. Clean drafts are usually used when there is no trade as such and the drawer is simply collecting a bill. Most drafts are documentary.

FIGURE 24-2
A Time Draft

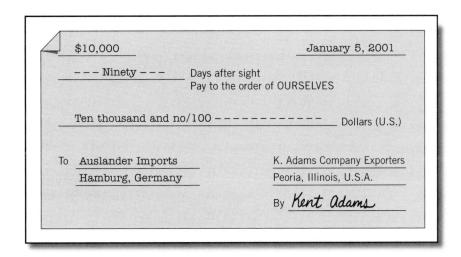

$10,000	January 5, 2001

– – – Ninety – – – Days after sight
Pay to the order of OURSELVES

Ten thousand and no/100 – – – – – – – – – – – Dollars (U.S.)

To   Auslander Imports   K. Adams Company Exporters
     Hamburg, Germany   Peoria, Illinois, U.S.A.

                                          By *Kent Adams*

If the bank is large and well known—and most banks accepting drafts are—the instrument becomes highly marketable on acceptance. As a result, the drawer, or exporter, does not have to hold the draft until the due date. He or she can sell it (at a discount from face) in the market. In fact, an active market exists for bankers' acceptances of well-known banks. For example, a 90-day draft for $10,000 may be accepted by a well-known bank. Say that 90-day interest rates in the bankers' acceptance market are 8 percent. The drawer could then sell the draft to an investor for $10,000 − [$10,000 × .08(90 days/360 days)] = **$9,800.** At the end of 90 days, the investor would present the acceptance to the accepting bank for payment and would receive $10,000. Thus, the existence of a strong secondary market for bankers' acceptances has facilitated international trade by providing liquidity to the exporter.

Bill of Lading

Bill of lading A shipping document indicating the details of the shipment and delivery of goods and their ownership.

A **bill of lading** is a shipping document used in the transportation of goods from the exporter to the importer. It has several functions. First, it serves as a receipt from the transportation company to the exporter, showing that specified goods have been received. Second, it serves as a contract between the transportation company and the exporter to ship the goods and deliver them to a specific party at a specific destination. Finally, the bill of lading can serve as a document of title. It gives the holder title to the goods. The importer cannot take title until it receives the bill of lading from the transportation company or its agent. This bill will not be released until the importer satisfies all the conditions of the draft.[7]

The bill of lading accompanies the draft, and the procedures by which the two are handled are well established. Banks and other institutions that are able to efficiently handle these documents exist in virtually every country. Moreover, the procedures by which goods are transferred internationally are well grounded in international law. These procedures allow an exporter in one country to sell goods to an unknown importer in another country and not release possession of the goods until paid if there is a sight draft or until the obligation is acknowledged if there is a time draft.

---

[7]The bill of lading can be negotiable if specified at the time it is made out. It can also be used as collateral for a loan.

Letter of Credit

A commercial *letter of credit* is issued by a bank on behalf of the importer. In the document, the bank agrees to honor a draft drawn on the importer, provided the bill of lading and other details are in order. In essence, the bank substitutes its credit for that of the importer. Obviously, the local bank will not issue a letter of credit unless it feels the importer is creditworthy and will pay the draft. The letter of credit arrangement almost eliminates the exporter's risk in selling goods to an unknown importer in another country.

Illustration of a Confirmed Letter. The letter of credit arrangement is further strengthened if a bank in the exporter's country confirms the letter of credit. For example, a New York exporter wishes to ship goods to a Brazilian importer located in Rio de Janeiro. The importer's bank in Rio regards the importer as a sound credit risk and is willing to issue a letter of credit guaranteeing payment for the goods when they are received. Thus, the Rio bank substitutes its credit for that of the importer. The contract is now between the Rio bank and the beneficiary of the letter of credit, the New York exporter. The exporter may wish to work through her bank, because she has little knowledge of the Rio bank. She asks her New York bank to confirm the Rio bank's letter of credit. If the New York bank is satisfied with the creditworthiness of the Rio bank, it will agree to do so. When it does, it obligates itself to honor drafts drawn in keeping with the letter of credit arrangement.

Thus, when the exporter ships the goods, she draws a draft in accordance with the terms of the letter of credit arrangement. She presents the draft to her New York bank, and the bank pays her the amount designated, assuming all the conditions of shipment are met. As a result of this arrangement, the exporter has her money, with no worries about payment. The New York bank then forwards the draft and other documents to the Rio bank. Upon affirming that the goods have been shipped in a proper manner, the Rio bank honors the draft and pays the New York bank. In turn, the Rio bank goes to the Brazilian importer and collects from him once the goods have arrived in Rio and are delivered.

Facilitation of Trade. From the description, it is easy to see why the letter of credit facilitates international trade. Rather than extending credit directly to an importer, the exporter relies on one or more banks, and their creditworthiness is substituted for that of the importer. The letter itself can be either irrevocable or revocable, but drafts drawn under an irrevocable letter must be honored by the issuing bank. This obligation can be neither canceled nor modified without the consent of all parties. On the other hand, a revocable letter of credit can be canceled or amended by the issuing bank. A revocable letter specifies an arrangement for payment but is no guarantee that the draft will be paid. Most letters of credit are irrevocable, and the process described assumes an irrevocable letter.

The three documents described—the draft, the bill of lading, and the letter of credit—are required in most international transactions. Established procedures exist for doing business on this basis. Together, they afford the exporter protection in selling goods to unknown importers in other countries. They also give the importer assurance that the goods will be shipped and delivered in a proper manner.

Countertrade

Countertrade Generic term for barter and other forms of trade that involve the international sale of goods or services that are paid for—in whole or in part—by the transfer of goods or services from a foreign country.

In addition to the documents used to facilitate a standard transaction, more customized means exist for financing international trade. One method is known as **countertrade.** In a typical countertrade agreement the selling party accepts payment

Part VIII Special Areas of Financial Management

in the form of goods instead of currency. When exchange restrictions or other difficulties prevent payment in *hard currencies* (i.e., currencies in which there is widespread confidence, such as dollars, British pounds, and yen), it may be necessary to accept goods instead. These goods may be produced in the country involved, but this need not be the case. A common form of countertrading is bartering. For example, a U.S. manufacturer of soft drinks may sell concentrates and syrups to a Russian bottling company in exchange for Russian vodka. One needs to be mindful that there are risks in accepting goods in lieu of a hard currency. Quality and standardization of goods that are delivered and accepted may differ from what was promised. In addition, there is then the added problem of having to resell the accepted goods for cash. Although countertrade carries risk, an infrastructure involving countertrade associations and specialized consultants has developed to facilitate this means of international trade.

Export Factoring

Factoring export receivables is similar to factoring domestic receivables, a topic discussed in Chapter 11. It involves the outright sale of the exporting firm's accounts receivable to a factoring institution, called a *factor*. The factor assumes the credit risk and services the export receivables. Typically, the exporter receives payment from the factor when the receivables are due. The usual commission fee is around 2 percent of the value of the overseas shipment. Before the receivable is collected, a cash advance is often possible for up to 90 percent of the shipment's value. For such an advance, the exporter pays interest, which is over and above the factor's fee. Due to the nature of the arrangement, most factors are primarily interested in exporters that generate large, recurring bases of export receivables. Also, the factor can reject certain accounts that it deems too risky. For accounts that are accepted, the main advantage to the exporter is the peace of mind that comes in entrusting collections to a factor with international contacts and experience.

Forfaiting

Forfaiting The selling "without recourse" of medium- to long-term export receivables to a financial institution, the *forfaiter*. A third party, usually a bank or governmental unit, guarantees the financing.

Forfaiting is a means of financing foreign trade that resembles export factoring. An exporter sells "without recourse" an export receivable, generally evidenced by a promissory note or bill of exchange from the importer, to a *forfaiter* at a discount. The forfaiter may be a subsidiary of an international bank or a specialized trade finance firm. The forfaiter assumes the credit risk and collects the amount owed from the importer. Additionally, forfaiting involves a guarantee of payment from a bank or an arm of the government of the importer's country. Usually the note or bill is for six months or longer and involves a large transaction. Forfaiting is especially useful to an exporter in a sales transaction involving an importer in a less-developed country (LDC) or in an Eastern European nation. It is the presence of a strong, third-party guarantee that makes the forfaiter willing to work with receivables from these countries.

SUMMARY

- Increasingly the financial manager is involved in global product and financial markets. The globalization movement means that investment and financing decisions must be made in an international arena. International capital budgeting, for example, embraces estimates of future rates of exchange between two currencies.

- Expansion abroad is undertaken to go into new markets, acquire less costly production facilities, and secure raw materials. Owing to market segmentation, foreign projects sometimes afford risk-reduction properties that are not available in domestic projects.

- A number of factors make foreign investment different from domestic investment. Taxation is different, and there are risks present in political conditions.
- A company faces three types of exchange-rate risk exposure in its foreign operations: translation exposure, transactions exposure, and economic exposure. *Translation exposure* is the change in accounting income and balance sheet statements caused by accounting treatment of a foreign subsidiary. *Transactions exposure* relates to settling a particular transaction, like open-account credit, at one exchange rate when the obligation was originally booked at another. *Economic exposure* has to do with the impact of unanticipated changes in exchange rates on expected future cash flows and, hence, on the economic value of the firm.
- There are a number of ways by which exchange-rate risk exposure can be managed. Natural hedges; cash management; adjusting of intracompany accounts; as well as international financing hedges and currency hedges, through forward contracts, futures contracts, currency options, and currency swaps, all serve this purpose.
- Natural hedges involve offsets between revenues and costs with respect to different sensitivities to exchange-rate changes. Natural hedges depend on the degree to which prices and costs are globally or domestically determined.
- A company can also protect itself by balancing monetary assets and liabilities and by adjusting intracompany accounts. It can hedge by financing in different currencies. The major sources of international financing are loans from commercial banks, discounted trade drafts, Eurodollar and Asiadollar loans, and international bonds.
- Currency hedges include forward contracts, futures contracts, currency options, and currency swaps. For the first, one buys a forward contract for the exchange of one currency for another at a specific future date and at an exchange ratio set in

advance. For this protection there is a cost that is determined by the difference in the forward and spot exchange rates. Currency futures contracts are like forward contracts in function, but there are differences in settlement and other features. Currency options afford protection against adverse currency movements, for which one pays a premium for the right, but not the obligation, to exercise the option. They are suited for hedging "one-sided" risk. Finally, currency swaps are an important longer term risk-shifting device. Here, two parties exchange debt obligations in different currencies.

- Two related theories provide a better understanding of the relationships among inflation, interest rates, and exchange rates. *Purchasing-power parity* is the idea that a basket of goods should sell at the same price internationally, after factoring into account exchange rates. *Interest-rate parity* suggests that the difference between forward and spot currency exchange rates can be explained by the difference in nominal interest rates between two countries.
- Three principal documents greatly facilitate international trade. The *international trade draft* is an order by the exporter to the importer to pay a specified amount of money either on presentation of the draft or a certain number of days after presentation. A *bill of lading* is a shipping document that can serve as a receipt, as a shipping contract, and as title to the goods involved. A *letter of credit* is an agreement by a bank to honor a draft drawn on the importer. It greatly reduces the risk to the exporter and may be confirmed by another bank.
- Additional means of financing international trade include *countertrade, export factoring,* and *forfaiting.* Countertrade involves the international trading of goods directly between two parties or through an intermediary. Export factoring involves the sale of receivables to a *factor* that assumes the credit risk. Forfaiting is similar to export factoring but involves high-value, medium- to long-term receivables (six months or longer) that are sold at a discount to a *forfaiter.* Additionally, a third-party guarantee is involved.

QUESTIONS

1. Is the risk-reward trade-off the same with an international investment as it is with a domestic investment?
2. Why would a company want to establish a joint foreign venture when it loses partial control over its foreign operations?

Part VIII Special Areas of Financial Management

3. Many countries require that nationals control more than 50 percent of the voting stock in any venture. Is this wise? Explain.
4. Do income taxes paid by a foreign branch work to the detriment of the U.S. parent company?
5. What are the various types of exchange-rate risk exposure to the corporation with operations abroad?
6. What difference does it make whether the dollar or the local currency is the "functional currency" when it comes to the accounting treatment of currency translations gains or losses?
7. *Natural hedges* sometimes exist for a company with an operation abroad. What is meant by this term, and why are natural hedges important?
8. With respect to foreign currency, what is a *forward discount?* What is a *forward premium?* Illustrate with an example. What is the purpose of forward exchange markets?
9. When it comes to currency hedges, how do *forward contracts, futures contracts, options contracts,* and *currency swaps* differ?
10. Should *purchasing-power parity* always hold in international markets? Explain.
11. What is meant by *interest-rate parity?* Does it work?
12. Why should a company manage its currency-risk exposure? Can the company "self-insure" at less cost?
13. Explain the function performed by the Eurodollar market.
14. What are the functions of the *bill of lading?*
15. In a *letter of credit* arrangement, who is the borrower? Who is the lender?
16. What is the creditworthiness of a bankers' acceptance? How does it differ from that of the international trade draft? What determines the face value of the acceptance?
17. In general, how does financing foreign trade differ from financing domestic trade?

SELF-CORRECTION PROBLEMS

1. The following exchange rates prevail in the foreign currency market:

CURRENCY	U.S. DOLLARS REQUIRED TO BUY ONE UNIT
Spamany (liso)	.100
Britland (ounce)	1.500
Chilaquay (peso)	.015
Trance (franc)	.130
Shopan (ben)	.005

Determine the number of:
   a. Spamany lisos that can be acquired for $1,000.
   b. U.S. dollars that 30 Britland ounces will buy.
   c. Chilaquay pesos that $900 will acquire.
   d. U.S. dollars that 100 Trench francs will purchase.
   e. Shopan bens that $50 will acquire.
2. Kingsborough Industries, Inc., has a subsidiary in Lolland where the currency is the guildnote. The exchange rate at the beginning of the year is 3 guildnotes to the

dollar. At the end of the year, the exchange rate is 2.5 guildnotes to the dollar, as the guildnote strengthens in value. The subsidiary's balance sheets at the two points in time and the income statement for the year are as follows (in thousands):

	IN GUILDNOTES	
	12/31/X1	12/31/X2
Balance Sheets		
Cash	300	400
Receivables	1,800	2,200
Inventories (FIFO)	1,500	2,000
Net fixed assets	2,100	1,800
Total	5,700	6,400
Current liabilities	2,000	1,900
Common stock	600	600
Retained earnings	3,100	3,900
Total	5,700	6,400
Income Statement		
Sales		10,400
Cost of goods sold		6,000
Depreciation		300
Expenses		2,400
Taxes		900
Operating income		800

The historical exchange rate for the fixed assets is 3 guildnotes to the dollar. The historical-cost exchange rate for inventories and cost of goods sold, using the dollar as the functional currency, is 2.70 guildnotes to the dollar. Using guild-notes as the functional currency, it is 2.60 guildnotes to the dollar for purposes of cost of goods sold. The average exchange rate for the year is 2.75 guildnotes to the dollar, and sales, depreciation, expenses, and taxes paid are steady through-out the year. Also assume no previous translation adjustments. On the basis of this information and assuming that the functional currency is the guildnote, determine the balance sheet for 12/31/X2 and income statement for the year (to the nearest thousand dollars). Now, reconstruct these statements assuming that the functional currency is the dollar. What differences do you observe?

3. Zike Athletic Shoe Company sells to a wholesaler in Freedonia. The purchase price of a shipment is 50,000 Freedonian marks with terms of 90 days. Upon pay-ment Zike will convert the marks to dollars. The present spot rate for marks per dollar is 1.71, whereas the 90-day forward rate is 1.70.

   a. If Zike were to hedge its exchange-rate risk, what would it do? What trans-actions are necessary?

   b. Is the mark at a *forward premium* or at a *forward discount*?

   c. What is the implied differential in interest rates between the two countries? (Use interest-rate parity assumptions.)

PROBLEMS

1. The following spot rates are observed in the foreign currency markets:

CURRENCY	UNITS REQUIRED TO BUY ONE U.S. DOLLAR
Britland (ounce)	.62
Spamany (liso)	1,300.00
Shopan (ben)	140.00
Lolland (guildnote)	1.90
Dweeden (corona)	6.40
Trance (franc)	1.50

On the basis of this information, compute to the nearest second decimal the number of
a. Britland ounces that can be acquired for $100
b. U.S. dollars that 50 Lolland guildnotes will buy
c. Dweedish corona that can be acquired for $40
d. U.S. dollars that 200 Trance francs can buy
e. Spamany lisos that can be acquired for $10
f. U.S. dollars that 1,000 Shopan bens will buy

2. The U.S. Imports Company purchased 100,000 Freedonian marks' worth of machinery from a firm in Zeppo, Freedonia. The value of the dollar in terms of the mark has been decreasing. The firm in Zeppo offered credit terms of "2/10, net 90." The spot rate for the mark is $.55, while the 90-day forward rate is $.56.
a. Compute the dollar cost of paying the account within the 10-day discount period.
b. Compute the dollar cost of buying a forward contract to liquidate the account in 90 days.
c. The differential between the correct answers to Parts (a) and (b) is the result of the time value of money (the discount for prepayment) and protection from currency value fluctuation. Determine the magnitude of each of these components.

3. Fuel-Guzzler Vehicles, Inc., is considering a new plant in Lolland. The plant will cost 26 million guildnotes. Incremental cash flows are expected to be 3 million guildnotes per year for the first 3 years, 4 million guildnotes for the next 3 years, 5 million guildnotes in years 7 through 9, and 6 million guildnotes in years 10 through 19, after which the project will terminate with no residual value. The present exchange rate is 1.90 guildnotes per dollar. The required rate of return on repatriated dollars is 16 percent.
a. If the exchange rate stays at 1.90, what is the project's net present value?
b. If the guildnote appreciates to 1.84 for years 1–3, to 1.78 for years 4–6, to 1.72 for years 7–9, and to 1.65 for years 10–19, what happens to the net present value?

4. Fleur du Lac, a Trance company, has shipped goods to an American importer under a letter of credit arrangement, which calls for payment at the end of 90 days. The invoice is for $124,000. Presently the exchange rate is 5.70 Trance francs to the dollar. If the Trance franc were to strengthen by 5 percent by the end of 90 days, what would be the transactions gain or loss in Trance francs? If the Trance franc were to weaken by 5 percent, what would happen? (*Note:* make all calculations in francs per dollar.)

5. Wheat sells for $4 a bushel in the United States. The price in Canada for a bushel of wheat is 4.56 Canadian dollars. The exchange rate is 1.2 Canadian dollars to $1 U.S. Does purchasing-power parity exist? If not, what changes would need to occur for it to exist?

6. Presently, the U.S. dollar is worth 140 yen in the spot market. The nominal Japanese interbank Euromarket interest rate, expressed in terms of the 90-day return is 4 percent, and for the United States this interest rate is 8 percent. If the interest-rate parity theorem holds, what is the implied 90-day forward exchange rate in yen per dollar? What would be implied if the U.S. interest rate mentioned above were 6 percent instead of 8 percent?

7. Cordova Leather Company is in a 38 percent U.S. tax bracket. It has sales branches in Algeria and in Switzerland, each of which generates earnings of $200,000 before taxes. If the effective income tax rate is 52 percent in Algeria and 35 percent in Switzerland, what total U.S. and foreign taxes will Cordova pay on the above earnings?

8. McDonnoughs Hamburger Company wishes to lend $500,000 to its Japanese subsidiary. At the same time, Tsunami Heavy Industries is interested in making a medium-term loan of approximately the same amount to its U.S. subsidiary. The two parties are brought together by an investment bank for the purpose of making *parallel loans* (a form of currency swap). McDonnoughs will lend $500,000 to the U.S. subsidiary of Tsunami for four years at 13 percent. Principal and interest are payable only at the end of the fourth year, with interest compounding annually. Tsunami will lend the Japanese subsidiary of McDonnoughs 70 million yen for four years at 10 percent. Again the principal and interest (annual compounding) are payable at the end. The current exchange rate is 140 yen to the dollar. However, the dollar is expected to decline by 5 yen to the dollar per year over the next four years.

   a. If these expectations prove to be correct, what will be the dollar equivalent of principal and interest payments to Tsunami at the end of four years?

   b. What total dollars will McDonnoughs receive at the end of four years from the payment of principal and interest on its loan by the U.S. subsidiary of Tsunami?

   c. Which party is better off with the parallel loan arrangement? What would happen if the yen did not change in value?

9. The government of Zwill presently encourages investment in the country. Comstock International Mining Corporation, a U.S. company, is planning to open a new copper mine in Zwill. The front-end investment is expected to be $25 million, after which cash flows are expected to be more than sufficient to cover further capital needs. Preliminary exploration findings suggest that the project is likely to be very profitable, providing an expected internal rate of return of 34 percent, based on business considerations alone.

   The government of Zwill, like that of many countries, is unstable. The management of Comstock, trying to assess this instability and its consequences, forecasts a 10 percent probability that the government will be overthrown and a new government will expropriate the property, with no compensation. The full $25 million would be lost, and the internal rate of return would be −100 percent. There also is a 15 percent probability that the government will be overthrown but that the new government will make a partial payment for the properties. This situation would result in an internal rate of return of −40 percent. Finally, there is a 15 percent probability that the present government will stay in power but that it will change its policy on repatriation of profits. More specifically, it will allow the

696   **Part VIII Special Areas of Financial Management**

corporation to repatriate its original investment, $25 million, but all other cash flows generated by the project would have to be reinvested in the host country forever. These probabilities still leave a 60 percent chance that a 34 percent internal rate of return will be achieved.

Given these political risks, approximate the likely return to Comstock. Should the mining venture be undertaken? Explain.

SOLUTIONS TO SELF-CORRECTION PROBLEMS

1. a. $1,000/.100 = **10,000 lisos**
    b. 30 × $1.500 = **$45**
    c. $900/.015 = **60,000 pesos**
    d. 100 × $.13 = **$13**
    e. $50/.005 = **10,000 ben**
2.

	IN DOLLARS 12/31/X2	
	GUILDNOTE FUNCTIONAL CURRENCY	DOLLAR FUNCTIONAL CURRENCY
Balance Sheets		
Cash	$ 160	$ 160
Receivables	880	880
Inventories	800	741
Net fixed assets	720	600
Total	$2,560	$2,381
Current liabilities	$ 760	$ 760
Common stock	200	200
Retained earnings ($1,033 at 12/31/X1)	1,198	1,421
Cumulative translation adjustment	402	
Total	$2,560	$2,381
Income Statements		
Sales	$3,782	$3,782
Cost of goods sold	2,308	2,222
Depreciation	109	100
Expenses	873	873
Taxes	327	327
Operating income	$ 165	$ 260
Translation gain		128
Net income	$ 165	$ 388
Translation adjustment	$ 402	

When the guildnote is used as the functional currency, all balance sheet items except common stock and retained earnings are translated at the current exchange rate, 2.50. All income statement items are translated at the average exchange rate for the year, 2.75, except cost of goods sold, which is translated at 2.60. Net income is a residual, after deducting costs and expenses from sales.

Retained earnings are net income, $165, plus retained earnings at the beginning of the year, $1,033, and total $1,198. The translation adjustment is that amount necessary to bring about an equality in the two totals on the balance sheet. It is $402. For the dollar as the functional currency, inventories and cost of goods sold are translated at the historical exchange rate of 2.70 and fixed assets and depreciation at the historical exchange rate of 3.00. Other items are translated in the same manner as they were with the other method. Retained earnings are a balancing factor to bring equality between the balance sheet totals. Operating income is a residual. The translation gain is that amount necessary to make net income equal to the change in retained earnings ($1,421 − $1,033 = $388) and therefore is $388 − $260 = $128. Depending on the accounting method, income is more variable with the dollar as the functional currency, whereas balance sheet totals are more variable with the guildnote as the functional currency.

3. **a.** It would hedge by selling marks forward 90 days. Upon delivery of 50,000 marks in 90 days, it would receive M50,000/1.70 = $29,412. If it were to receive payment today, Zike would get M50,000/1.71 = $29,240.

   b. The mark is at a *forward premium* because the 90-day forward rate of marks per dollar is less than the current spot rate. The mark is expected to strengthen (fewer marks to buy a dollar).

   c. $[(1.70 − 1.71)/1.71] \times [365 \text{ days}/90 \text{ days}] = r_M - r_\$ = -.0237$
   The differential in interest rates is −2.37 percent, which means if interest-rate parity holds, interest rates in the United States should be 2.37 percent higher than in Freedonia.

SELECTED REFERENCES

Abuaf, Niso, and Philippe Jorion. "Purchasing Power Parity in the Long-Run." *Journal of Finance* 45 (March 1990), 157–74.

Baker, James C. *International Finance: Management, Markets, and Institutions.* Upper Saddle River, NJ: Prentice Hall, 1998.

Baldwin, Carliss Y. "Competing for Capital in a Global Environment." *Midland Corporate Finance Journal* 5 (Spring 1987), 43–64.

Bhagwat, Yatin, Deborah L. Gunthorpe, and John M. Wachowicz Jr. "Creative Export Financing: Factoring and Forfaiting." *The Small Business Controller* 7 (Spring 1994), 51–55.

Black, Fischer. "Equilibrium Exchange Rate Hedging." *Journal of Finance* 45 (July 1990), 899–908.

Clarke, Roger G., and Mark P. Kritzman. *Currency Management: Concepts and Practices.* Charlottesville, VA: Research Foundation of the Institute of Chartered Financial Analysts, 1996.

Cross, Sam Y. *All About the Foreign Exchange Market in the United States.* Federal Reserve Bank of New York, 1998 (available online at www.ny.frb.org:80/pihome/addpub/usfxm/).

Errunza, Vihang R., and Lemma W. Senbet. "The Effects of International Operations on the Market Value of the Firm: Theory and Evidence." *Journal of Finance* 36 (May 1981), 401–18.

Eudey, Gwen. "Why Is Europe Forming a Monetary Union?" *Business Review,* Federal Reserve Bank of Philadelphia (November/December 1998), 13–21.

Fabozzi, Frank J., editor. *Perspectives on International Fixed Income Investing.* New Hope, PA: Frank J. Fabozzi Associates, 1998.

Hekman, Christine R. "Measuring Foreign Exchange Exposure: A Practical Theory and Its Application." *Financial Analysts Journal* 39 (September–October 1983), 59–65.

———. "Don't Blame Currency Values for Strategic Errors." *Midland Corporate Finance Journal* 4 (Fall 1986), 45–55.

Hill, Kendall P., and Murat N. Tanju. "Forfaiting: What Finance and Accounting Managers Should Know." *Financial Practice and Education* 8 (Fall/Winter 1998), 53–58.

Lessard, Donald. "International Portfolio Diversification: A Multivariate Analysis for a Group of Latin American Countries." *Journal of Finance* 28 (June 1973), 619–34.

Levy, Haim, and Marshall Sarnat. "International Diversification of Investment Portfolios." *American Economic Review* 60 (September 1970), 668–75.

Madura, Jeff. *International Financial Management,* 6th ed. Cincinnati, OH: South-Western, 1999.

Perold, Andre F., and Evan C. Schulman. "The Free Lunch in Currency Hedging: Implications for Investment Policy and Performance Standards." *Financial Analysts Journal* 44 (May–June 1988), 45–50.

Pringle, John J. "Managing Foreign Exchange Exposure." *Journal of Applied Corporate Finance* 3 (Winter 1991), 73–82.

Shapiro, Alan C. *Foundations of Multinational Financial Management*, 3rd ed. Upper Saddle River, NJ: Prentice Hall, 1998.

Solnick, Bruno. "Global Asset Management." *Journal of Portfolio Management* 24 (Summer 1998), 43–51.

Stulz, Rene M. "Globalization of Capital Markets and the Cost of Capital: The Case of Nestle." *Journal of Applied Corporate Finance* 8 (Fall 1995), 30–38.

Van Horne, James C. *Financial Market Rates and Flows*, 6th ed. Upper Saddle River, NJ: Prentice Hall, 2001.

Appendix

TABLE 1
Future value interest factor of $1 at **i**% at the end
of **n** periods (**FVIF**$_{i,n}$)

TABLE II
Present value interest factor of $1 at **i**% for **n** periods (**PVIF**$_{i,n}$)

TABLE III
Future value interest factor of an (ordinary) annuity
of $1 per period at **i**% for **n** periods (**FVIFA**$_{i,n}$)

TABLE IV
Present value interest factor of an (ordinary) annuity
of $1 per period at **i**% for **n** periods (**PVIFA**$_{i,n}$)

TABLE V
Area of normal distribution that is Z standard deviations
to the left or right of the mean

Now go, write it before them in a table, and note it in a book, that it may be for the time to come for ever and ever.

—Isaiah 30:8

TABLE I

Future value interest factor of $1 at i% at the end of n periods ($FVIF_{i,n}$)

$$(FVIF_{i,n}) = (1 + i)^n$$

PERIOD (n)	INTEREST RATE (i)												PERIOD (n)
	1%	2%	3%	4%	5%	6%	7%	8%	9%	10%	11%	12%	
1	1.010	1.020	1.030	1.040	1.050	1.060	1.070	1.080	1.090	1.100	1.100	1.120	1
2	1.020	1.040	1.061	1.082	1.102	1.124	1.145	1.166	1.188	1.210	1.232	1.254	2
3	1.030	1.061	1.093	1.125	1.158	1.191	1.225	1.260	1.295	1.331	1.368	1.405	3
4	1.041	1.082	1.126	1.170	1.216	1.262	1.311	1.360	1.412	1.464	1.518	1.574	4
5	1.051	1.104	1.159	1.217	1.276	1.338	1.403	1.469	1.539	1.611	1.685	1.762	5
6	1.062	1.126	1.194	1.265	1.340	1.419	1.501	1.587	1.677	1.772	1.870	1.974	6
7	1.072	1.149	1.230	1.316	1.407	1.504	1.606	1.714	1.828	1.949	2.076	2.211	7
8	1.083	1.172	1.267	1.369	1.477	1.594	1.718	1.851	1.993	2.144	2.305	2.476	8
9	1.094	1.195	1.305	1.423	1.551	1.689	1.838	1.999	2.172	2.358	2.558	2.773	9
10	1.105	1.219	1.344	1.480	1.629	1.791	1.967	2.159	2.367	2.594	2.839	3.106	10
11	1.116	1.243	1.384	1.539	1.710	1.898	2.105	2.332	2.580	2.853	3.152	3.479	11
12	1.127	1.268	1.426	1.601	1.796	2.012	2.252	2.518	2.813	3.138	3.498	3.896	12
13	1.138	1.294	1.469	1.665	1.886	2.133	2.410	2.720	3.066	3.452	3.883	4.363	13
14	1.149	1.319	1.513	1.732	1.980	2.261	2.579	2.937	3.342	3.797	4.310	4.887	14
15	1.161	1.346	1.558	1.801	2.079	2.397	2.759	3.172	3.642	4.177	4.785	5.474	15
16	1.173	1.373	1.605	1.873	2.183	2.540	2.952	3.426	3.970	4.595	5.311	6.130	16
17	1.184	1.400	1.653	1.948	2.292	2.693	3.159	3.700	4.328	5.054	5.895	6.866	17
18	1.196	1.428	1.702	2.026	2.407	2.854	3.380	3.996	4.717	5.560	6.544	7.690	18
19	1.208	1.457	1.754	2.107	2.527	3.026	3.617	4.316	5.142	6.116	7.263	8.613	19
20	1.220	1.486	1.806	2.191	2.653	3.207	3.870	4.661	5.604	6.727	8.062	9.646	20
25	1.282	1.641	2.094	2.666	3.386	4.292	5.427	6.848	8.623	10.835	13.585	17.000	25
30	1.348	1.811	2.427	3.243	4.322	5.743	7.612	10.063	13.268	17.449	22.892	29.960	30
35	1.417	2.000	2.814	3.946	5.516	7.686	10.677	14.785	20.414	28.102	38.575	52.800	35
40	1.489	2.208	3.262	4.801	7.040	10.286	14.974	21.725	31.409	45.259	65.001	93.051	40
50	1.645	2.692	4.384	7.107	11.467	18.420	29.457	46.902	74.358	117.391	184.565	289.002	50

TABLE I (cont.)

Future value interest factor of $1 at $i\%$ at the end of n periods ($FVIF_{i,n}$)

$$(FVIF_{i,n}) = (1 + i)^n$$

PERIOD (n)	13%	14%	15%	16%	17%	18%	19%	20%	25%	30%	40%	50%	PERIOD (n)
1	1.130	1.140	1.150	1.160	1.170	1.180	1.190	1.200	1.250	1.300	1.400	1.500	1
2	1.277	1.300	1.322	1.346	1.369	1.392	1.416	1.440	1.563	1.690	1.960	2.250	2
3	1.443	1.482	1.521	1.561	1.602	1.643	1.685	1.728	1.953	2.197	2.744	3.375	3
4	1.630	1.689	1.749	1.811	1.874	1.939	2.005	2.074	2.441	2.856	3.842	5.063	4
5	1.842	1.925	2.011	2.100	2.192	2.288	2.386	2.488	3.052	3.713	5.378	7.594	5
6	2.082	2.195	2.313	2.436	2.565	2.700	2.840	2.986	3.815	4.827	7.530	11.391	6
7	2.353	2.502	2.660	2.826	3.001	3.185	3.379	3.583	4.768	6.275	10.541	17.086	7
8	2.658	2.853	3.059	3.278	3.511	3.759	4.021	4.300	5.960	8.157	14.758	25.629	8
9	3.004	3.252	3.518	3.803	4.108	4.435	4.785	5.160	7.451	10.604	20.661	38.443	9
10	3.395	3.707	4.046	4.411	4.807	5.234	5.696	6.192	9.313	13.786	28.925	57.665	10
11	3.836	4.226	4.652	5.117	5.624	6.176	6.777	7.430	11.642	17.922	40.496	86.498	11
12	4.335	4.818	5.350	5.936	6.580	7.288	8.064	8.916	14.552	23.298	56.694	129.746	12
13	4.898	5.492	6.153	6.886	7.699	8.599	9.596	10.699	18.190	30.288	79.372	194.620	13
14	5.535	6.261	7.076	7.988	9.007	10.147	11.420	12.839	22.737	39.374	111.120	291.929	14
15	6.254	7.138	8.137	9.266	10.539	11.974	13.590	15.407	28.422	51.186	155.568	437.894	15
16	7.067	8.137	9.358	10.748	12.330	14.129	16.172	18.488	35.527	66.542	217.795	656.841	16
17	7.986	9.276	10.761	12.468	14.426	16.672	19.244	22.186	44.409	86.504	304.914	985.261	17
18	9.024	10.575	12.375	14.463	16.879	19.673	22.901	26.623	55.511	112.455	426.879	1477.892	18
19	10.197	12.056	14.232	16.777	19.748	23.214	27.252	31.948	69.389	146.192	597.630	2216.838	19
20	11.523	13.743	16.367	19.461	23.106	27.393	32.429	38.338	86.736	190.050	836.683	3325.257	20
25	21.231	26.462	32.919	40.874	50.658	62.669	77.388	95.396	264.698	705.641	4499.880	25251.168	25
30	39.116	50.950	66.212	85.850	111.065	143.371	184.675	237.376	807.794	2620.000	24201.432	191751	30
35	72.069	98.100	133.176	180.314	243.503	327.997	440.701	590.668	2465.190	9727.860	130161	1456110	35
40	139.782	188.884	267.864	378.721	533.869	750.378	1051.668	1469.772	7523.164	36118.865	700038	11057332	40
50	450.736	700.233	1083.657	1670.704	2566.215	3927.357	5988.914	9100.438	70064.923	497929.223	20248916	637621500	50

INTEREST RATE (i)

703

TABLE II

Present value interest factor of $1 at i% for n periods ($PVIF_{i,n}$)

$$(PVIF_{i,n}) = 1/(1 + i)^n$$

| PERIOD (n) | \multicolumn{12}{c}{INTEREST RATE (i)} | PERIOD (n) |

PERIOD (n)	1%	2%	3%	4%	5%	6%	7%	8%	9%	10%	11%	12%	PERIOD (n)
1	.990	.980	.971	.962	.952	.943	.935	.926	.917	.909	.901	.893	1
2	.980	.961	.943	.925	.907	.890	.873	.857	.842	.826	.812	.797	2
3	.971	.942	.915	.889	.864	.840	.816	.794	.772	.751	.731	.712	3
4	.961	.924	.888	.855	.823	.792	.763	.735	.708	.683	.659	.636	4
5	.951	.906	.863	.822	.784	.747	.713	.681	.650	.621	.593	.567	5
6	.942	.888	.837	.790	.746	.705	.666	.630	.596	.564	.535	.507	6
7	.933	.871	.813	.760	.711	.665	.623	.583	.547	.513	.482	.452	7
8	.923	.853	.789	.731	.677	.627	.582	.540	.502	.467	.434	.404	8
9	.914	.837	.766	.703	.645	.592	.544	.500	.460	.424	.391	.361	9
10	.905	.820	.744	.676	.614	.558	.508	.463	.422	.386	.352	.322	10
11	.896	.804	.722	.650	.585	.527	.475	.429	.388	.350	.317	.287	11
12	.887	.789	.701	.625	.557	.497	.444	.397	.356	.319	.286	.257	12
13	.879	.773	.681	.601	.530	.469	.415	.368	.326	.290	.258	.229	13
14	.870	.758	.661	.577	.505	.442	.388	.340	.299	.263	.232	.205	14
15	.861	.743	.642	.555	.481	.417	.362	.315	.275	.239	.209	.183	15
16	.853	.728	.623	.534	.458	.394	.339	.292	.252	.218	.188	.163	16
17	.844	.714	.605	.513	.436	.371	.317	.270	.231	.198	.170	.146	17
18	.836	.700	.587	.494	.416	.350	.296	.250	.212	.180	.153	.130	18
19	.828	.686	.570	.475	.396	.331	.277	.232	.194	.164	.138	.116	19
20	.820	.673	.554	.456	.377	.312	.258	.215	.178	.149	.124	.104	20
25	.780	.610	.478	.375	.295	.233	.184	.146	.116	.092	.074	.059	25
30	.742	.552	.412	.308	.231	.174	.131	.099	.075	.057	.044	.033	30
35	.706	.500	.355	.253	.181	.130	.094	.068	.049	.036	.026	.019	35
40	.672	.453	.307	.208	.142	.097	.067	.046	.032	.022	.015	.011	40
50	.608	.372	.228	.141	.087	.054	.034	.021	.013	.009	.005	.003	50

TABLE II (cont.)
Present value interest factor of \$1 at i% for n periods ($PVIF_{i,n}$)

$$PVIF_{i,n} = 1/(1 + i)^n$$

PERIOD (n)	13%	14%	15%	16%	17%	18%	19%	20%	25%	30%	40%	50%	PERIOD (n)
1	.885	.877	.870	.862	.855	.847	.840	.833	.800	.769	.714	.667	1
2	.783	.769	.756	.743	.731	.718	.706	.694	.640	.592	.510	.444	2
3	.693	.675	.658	.641	.624	.609	.593	.579	.512	.455	.364	.296	3
4	.613	.592	.572	.552	.534	.516	.499	.482	.410	.350	.260	.198	4
5	.543	.519	.497	.476	.456	.437	.419	.402	.328	.269	.186	.132	5
6	.480	.456	.432	.410	.390	.370	.352	.335	.262	.207	.133	.088	6
7	.425	.400	.376	.354	.333	.314	.296	.279	.210	.159	.095	.059	7
8	.376	.351	.327	.305	.285	.266	.249	.233	.168	.123	.068	.039	8
9	.333	.308	.284	.263	.243	.225	.209	.194	.134	.094	.048	.026	9
10	.295	.270	.247	.227	.208	.191	.176	.162	.107	.073	.035	.017	10
11	.261	.237	.215	.195	.178	.162	.148	.135	.086	.056	.025	.012	11
12	.231	.208	.187	.168	.152	.137	.124	.112	.069	.043	.018	.008	12
13	.204	.182	.163	.145	.130	.116	.104	.093	.055	.033	.013	.005	13
14	.181	.160	.141	.125	.111	.099	.088	.078	.044	.025	.009	.003	14
15	.160	.140	.123	.108	.095	.084	.074	.065	.035	.020	.006	.002	15
16	.141	.123	.107	.093	.081	.071	.062	.054	.028	.015	.005	.002	16
17	.125	.108	.093	.080	.069	.060	.052	.045	.023	.012	.003	.001	17
18	.111	.095	.081	.069	.059	.051	.044	.038	.018	.009	.002	.001	18
19	.098	.083	.070	.060	.051	.043	.037	.031	.014	.007	.002	.000	19
20	.087	.073	.061	.051	.043	.037	.031	.026	.012	.005	.001	.000	20
25	.047	.038	.030	.024	.020	.016	.013	.010	.004	.001	.000	.000	25
30	.026	.020	.015	.012	.009	.007	.005	.004	.001	.000	.000	.000	30
35	.014	.010	.008	.006	.004	.003	.002	.002	.000	.000	.000	.000	35
40	.008	.005	.004	.003	.002	.001	.001	.001	.000	.000	.000	.000	40
50	.002	.001	.001	.001	.000	.000	.000	.000	.000	.000	.000	.000	50

INTEREST RATE (i)

TABLE III

Future value interest factor of an (ordinary) annuity of $1 per period at $i\%$ for n periods ($FVIFA_{i,n}$)

$$(FVIFA_{i,n}) = \sum_{t=1}^{n}(1+i)^{n-t} = \frac{(1+i)^n - 1}{i}$$

PERIOD (n)	INTEREST RATE (i)												PERIOD (n)
	1%	2%	3%	4%	5%	6%	7%	8%	9%	10%	11%	12%	
1	1.000	1.000	1.000	1.000	1.000	1.000	1.000	1.000	1.000	1.000	1.000	1.000	1
2	2.010	2.020	2.030	2.040	2.050	2.060	2.070	2.080	2.090	2.100	2.110	2.120	2
3	3.030	3.060	3.091	3.122	3.153	3.184	3.215	3.246	3.278	3.310	3.342	3.374	3
4	4.060	4.122	4.184	4.246	4.310	4.375	4.440	4.506	4.573	4.641	4.710	4.779	4
5	5.101	5.204	5.309	5.416	5.526	5.637	5.751	5.867	5.985	6.105	6.228	6.353	5
6	6.152	6.308	6.468	6.633	6.802	6.975	7.153	7.336	7.523	7.716	7.913	8.115	6
7	7.214	7.434	7.662	7.898	8.142	8.394	8.654	8.923	9.200	9.487	9.783	10.089	7
8	8.286	8.583	8.892	9.214	9.549	9.897	10.260	10.637	11.028	11.436	11.859	12.300	8
9	9.369	9.755	10.159	10.583	11.027	11.491	11.978	12.488	13.021	13.579	14.164	14.776	9
10	10.462	10.950	11.464	12.006	12.578	13.181	13.816	14.487	15.193	15.937	16.722	17.549	10
11	11.567	12.169	12.808	13.486	14.207	14.972	15.784	16.645	17.560	18.531	19.561	20.655	11
12	12.683	13.412	14.192	15.026	15.917	16.870	17.888	18.977	20.141	21.384	22.713	24.133	12
13	13.809	14.680	15.618	16.627	17.713	18.882	20.141	21.495	22.953	24.523	26.212	28.029	13
14	14.947	15.974	17.086	18.292	19.599	21.015	22.550	24.215	26.019	27.975	30.095	32.393	14
15	16.097	17.293	18.599	20.024	21.579	23.276	25.129	27.152	29.361	31.772	34.405	37.280	15
16	17.258	18.639	20.157	21.825	23.657	25.673	27.888	30.324	33.003	35.950	39.190	42.753	16
17	18.430	20.012	21.762	23.698	25.840	28.213	30.840	33.750	36.974	40.545	44.501	48.884	17
18	19.615	21.412	23.414	25.645	28.132	30.906	33.999	37.450	41.301	45.599	50.396	55.750	18
19	20.811	22.841	25.117	27.671	30.539	33.760	37.379	41.446	46.018	51.159	56.939	63.440	19
20	22.019	24.297	26.870	29.778	33.066	36.786	40.995	45.762	51.160	57.275	64.203	72.052	20
25	28.243	32.030	36.459	41.646	47.727	54.865	63.249	73.106	84.701	98.347	114.413	133.334	25
30	34.785	40.568	47.575	56.085	66.439	79.058	94.461	113.283	136.308	164.494	199.021	241.333	30
35	41.660	49.994	60.462	73.652	90.320	111.435	138.237	172.317	215.711	271.024	341.590	431.663	35
40	48.886	60.402	75.401	95.026	120.800	154.762	199.635	259.057	337.882	442.593	581.826	767.091	40
50	64.463	84.579	112.797	152.667	209.348	290.336	406.529	573.770	815.084	1163.909	1668.771	2400.018	50

TABLE III (cont.)

Future value interest factor of an (ordinary) annuity of $1 per period at i% for n periods ($FVIFA_{i,n}$)

$$FVIFA_{i,n} = \sum_{t=1}^{n}(1+i)^{n-t} = \frac{(1+i)^n - 1}{i}$$

PERIOD (n)	13%	14%	15%	16%	17%	18%	19%	20%	25%	30%	40%	50%
1	1.000	1.000	1.000	1.000	1.000	1.000	1.000	1.000	1.000	1.000	1.000	1.000
2	2.130	2.140	2.150	2.160	2.170	2.180	2.190	2.200	2.250	2.300	2.400	2.500
3	3.407	3.440	3.473	3.506	3.539	3.572	3.606	3.640	3.813	3.990	4.360	4.750
4	4.850	4.921	4.993	5.066	5.141	5.215	5.291	5.368	5.766	6.187	7.104	8.125
5	6.480	6.610	6.742	6.877	7.014	7.154	7.297	7.442	8.207	9.043	10.946	13.188
6	8.323	8.536	8.754	8.977	9.207	9.442	9.683	9.930	11.259	12.756	16.324	20.781
7	10.405	10.730	11.067	11.414	11.772	12.142	12.523	12.916	15.073	17.583	23.853	32.172
8	12.757	13.233	13.727	14.240	14.773	15.327	15.902	16.499	19.842	23.858	34.395	49.258
9	15.416	16.085	16.786	17.519	18.285	19.086	19.923	20.799	25.802	32.015	49.153	74.887
10	18.420	19.337	20.304	21.321	22.393	23.521	24.709	25.959	33.253	42.619	69.814	113.330
11	21.814	23.045	24.349	25.733	27.200	28.755	30.404	32.150	42.566	56.405	98.739	170.995
12	25.650	27.271	29.002	30.850	32.824	34.931	37.180	39.581	54.208	74.327	139.235	257.493
13	29.985	32.089	34.352	36.786	39.404	42.219	45.244	48.497	68.760	97.625	195.929	387.239
14	34.883	37.581	40.505	43.672	47.103	50.818	54.841	59.196	86.949	127.913	275.300	581.859
15	40.417	43.842	47.580	51.660	56.110	60.965	66.261	72.035	109.687	167.286	386.420	873.788
16	46.672	50.980	55.717	60.925	66.649	72.939	79.850	87.442	138.109	218.472	541.988	1311.682
17	53.739	59.118	65.075	71.673	78.979	87.068	96.022	105.931	173.636	285.014	759.784	1968.523
18	61.725	68.394	75.836	84.141	93.406	103.740	115.266	128.117	218.045	371.518	1064.697	2953.784
19	70.749	78.969	88.212	98.603	110.285	123.414	138.166	154.740	273.556	483.973	1491.576	4431.676
20	80.947	91.025	102.444	115.380	130.033	146.638	165.418	186.688	342.945	630.165	2089.206	6648.513
25	155.620	181.871	212.793	249.214	292.105	342.603	402.042	471.981	1054.791	2348.803	11247.199	50500
30	293.199	356.787	434.745	530.312	647.439	790.948	966.712	1181.882	3227.174	8729.985	60501	383500
35	546.681	693.573	881.170	1120.713	1426.491	1816.652	2314.214	2948.341	9856.761	32423	325400	2912217
40	1013.704	1342.025	1779.090	2360.757	3134.522	4163.21	5529.829	7343.858	30089	120393	1750092	22114663
50	3459.507	4994.521	7217.716	10435.649	15089.502	21813.1	31515	45497	280256	1659761	50622288	127524998

TABLE IV

Present value interest factor of an (ordinary) annuity of $1 per period at i% for n periods ($PVIFA_{i,n}$)

$$(PVIFA_{i,n}) = \sum_{t=1}^{n} 1/(1+i)^t = \frac{1 - [1/(1+i)^n]}{i}$$

PERIOD (n)	1%	2%	3%	4%	5%	6%	7%	8%	9%	10%	11%	12%	PERIOD (n)
1	.990	.980	.971	.962	.952	.943	.935	.926	.917	.909	.901	.893	1
2	1.970	1.942	1.913	1.886	1.859	1.833	1.808	1.783	1.759	1.736	1.713	1.690	2
3	2.941	2.884	2.829	2.775	2.723	2.673	2.624	2.577	2.531	2.487	2.444	2.402	3
4	3.902	3.808	3.717	3.630	3.546	3.465	3.387	3.312	3.240	3.170	3.102	3.037	4
5	4.853	4.713	4.580	4.452	4.329	4.212	4.100	3.993	3.890	3.791	3.696	3.605	5
6	5.795	5.601	5.417	5.242	5.076	4.917	4.767	4.623	4.486	4.355	4.231	4.111	6
7	6.728	6.472	6.230	6.002	5.786	5.582	5.389	5.206	5.033	4.868	4.712	4.564	7
8	7.652	7.326	7.020	6.733	6.463	6.210	5.971	5.747	5.535	5.335	5.146	4.968	8
9	8.566	8.162	7.786	7.435	7.108	6.802	6.515	6.247	5.995	5.759	5.537	5.328	9
10	9.471	8.983	8.530	8.111	7.722	7.360	7.024	6.710	6.418	6.145	5.889	5.650	10
11	10.368	9.787	9.253	8.760	8.306	7.887	7.499	7.139	6.805	6.495	6.207	5.938	11
12	11.255	10.575	9.954	9.385	8.863	8.384	7.943	7.536	7.161	6.814	6.492	6.194	12
13	12.134	11.348	10.635	9.986	9.394	8.853	8.358	7.904	7.487	7.103	6.750	6.424	13
14	13.004	12.106	11.296	10.563	9.899	9.295	8.745	8.244	7.786	7.367	6.982	6.628	14
15	13.865	12.849	11.938	11.118	10.380	9.712	9.108	8.560	8.061	7.606	7.191	6.811	15
16	14.718	13.578	12.561	11.652	10.838	10.106	9.447	8.851	8.313	7.824	7.379	6.974	16
17	15.562	14.292	13.166	12.166	11.274	10.477	9.763	9.122	8.544	8.022	7.549	7.120	17
18	16.398	14.992	13.754	12.659	11.690	10.828	10.059	9.372	8.756	8.201	7.702	7.250	18
19	17.226	15.679	14.324	13.134	12.085	11.158	10.336	9.604	8.950	8.365	7.839	7.366	19
20	18.046	16.352	14.877	13.590	12.462	11.470	10.594	9.818	9.129	8.514	7.963	7.469	20
25	22.023	19.524	17.413	15.622	14.094	12.784	11.654	10.675	9.823	9.077	8.422	7.843	25
30	25.808	22.396	19.601	17.292	15.373	13.765	12.409	11.258	10.274	9.427	8.694	8.055	30
35	29.409	24.999	21.487	18.665	16.374	14.498	12.948	11.655	10.567	9.644	8.855	8.176	35
40	32.835	27.356	23.115	19.793	17.159	15.046	13.332	11.925	10.757	9.779	8.951	8.244	40
50	39.196	31.424	25.730	21.482	18.256	15.762	13.801	12.233	10.962	9.915	9.042	8.304	50

INTEREST RATE (i)

TABLE IV (cont.)

Present value interest factor of an (ordinary) annuity of $1 per period at i% for n periods ($PVIFA_{i,n}$)

$$(PVIFA_{i,n}) = \sum_{t=1}^{n} 1/(1+i)^t = \frac{1 - [1/(1+i)^n]}{i}$$

PERIOD (n)	13%	14%	15%	16%	17%	18%	19%	20%	25%	30%	40%	50%	PERIOD (n)
1	.885	.877	.870	.862	.855	.847	.840	.833	.800	.769	.714	.667	1
2	1.668	1.647	1.626	1.605	1.585	1.566	1.547	1.528	1.440	1.361	1.224	1.111	2
3	2.361	2.322	2.283	2.246	2.210	2.174	2.140	2.106	1.952	1.816	1.589	1.407	3
4	2.974	2.914	2.855	2.798	2.743	2.690	2.639	2.589	2.362	2.166	1.849	1.605	4
5	3.517	3.433	3.352	3.274	3.199	3.127	3.058	2.991	2.689	2.436	2.035	1.737	5
6	3.998	3.889	3.784	3.685	3.589	3.498	3.410	3.326	2.951	2.643	2.168	1.824	6
7	4.423	4.288	4.160	4.039	3.922	3.812	3.706	3.605	3.161	2.802	2.263	1.883	7
8	4.799	4.639	4.487	4.344	4.207	4.078	3.954	3.837	3.329	2.925	2.331	1.922	8
9	5.132	4.946	4.772	4.607	4.451	4.303	4.163	4.031	3.463	3.019	2.379	1.948	9
10	5.426	5.216	5.019	4.833	4.659	4.494	4.339	4.192	3.571	3.092	2.414	1.965	10
11	5.687	5.453	5.234	5.029	4.836	4.656	4.486	4.327	3.656	3.147	2.438	1.977	11
12	5.918	5.660	5.421	5.197	4.988	4.793	4.611	4.439	3.725	3.190	2.456	1.985	12
13	6.122	5.842	5.583	5.342	5.118	4.910	4.715	4.533	3.780	3.223	2.469	1.990	13
14	6.302	6.002	5.724	5.468	5.229	5.008	4.802	4.611	3.824	3.249	2.478	1.993	14
15	6.462	6.142	5.847	5.575	5.324	5.092	4.876	4.675	3.859	3.268	2.484	1.995	15
16	6.604	6.265	5.954	5.668	5.405	5.162	4.938	4.730	3.887	3.283	2.489	1.997	16
17	6.729	6.373	6.047	5.749	5.475	5.222	4.990	4.775	3.910	3.295	2.492	1.998	17
18	6.840	6.467	6.128	5.818	5.534	5.273	5.033	4.812	3.928	3.304	2.494	1.999	18
19	6.938	6.550	6.198	5.877	5.584	5.316	5.070	4.843	3.942	3.311	2.496	1.999	19
20	7.025	6.623	6.259	5.929	5.628	5.353	5.101	4.870	3.954	3.316	2.497	1.999	20
25	7.330	6.873	6.464	6.097	5.766	5.467	5.195	4.948	3.985	3.329	2.499	2.000	25
30	7.496	7.003	6.566	6.177	5.829	5.517	5.235	4.979	3.995	3.332	2.500	2.000	30
35	7.586	7.070	6.617	6.215	5.858	5.539	5.251	4.992	3.998	3.333	2.500	2.000	35
40	7.634	7.105	6.642	6.233	5.871	5.548	5.258	4.997	3.999	3.333	2.500	2.000	40
50	7.675	7.133	6.661	6.246	5.880	5.554	5.262	4.999	4.000	3.333	2.500	2.000	50

INTEREST RATE (i)

TABLE V
Area of normal distribution that is Z standard deviations to the left or right of the mean

NUMBER OF STANDARD DEVIATIONS FROM MEAN (Z)	AREA TO THE LEFT OR RIGHT (ONE TAIL)	NUMBER OF STANDARD DEVIATIONS FROM MEAN (Z)	AREA TO THE LEFT OR RIGHT (ONE TAIL)
.00	.5000	1.55	.0606
.05	.4801	1.60	.0548
.10	.4602	1.65	.0495
.15	.4404	1.70	.0446
.20	.4207	1.75	.0401
.25	.4013	1.80	.0359
.30	.3821	1.85	.0322
.35	.3632	1.90	.0287
.40	.3446	1.95	.0256
.45	.3264	2.00	.0228
.50	.3085	2.05	.0202
.55	.2912	2.10	.0179
.60	.2743	2.15	.0158
.65	.2578	2.20	.0139
.70	.2420	2.25	.0122
.75	.2264	2.30	.0107
.80	.2119	2.35	.0094
.85	.1977	2.40	.0082
.90	.1841	2.45	.0071
.95	.1711	2.50	.0062
1.00	.1577	2.55	.0054
1.05	.1469	2.60	.0047
1.10	.1357	2.65	.0040
1.15	.1251	2.70	.0035
1.20	.1151	2.75	.0030
1.25	.1056	2.80	.0026
1.30	.0968	2.85	.0022
1.35	.0885	2.90	.0019
1.40	.0808	2.95	.0016
1.45	.0735	3.00	.0013
1.50	.0668		

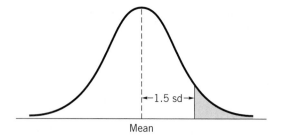

Mean

Table V shows the area of the normal distribution that is Z standard deviations to the left or to the right of the mean. The test is "one tail" in the sense that we are concerned with one side of the distribution or the other. If we wished to know the area of the curve, or probability, that was 1.5 standard deviations or more from the arithmetic mean on the right, it would be depicted by the colored area in the figure to the left. In Table V we see that this corresponds to 6.68 percent of the total area of the normal distribution. Thus, we could say that there was a 6.68 percent probability that the actual outcome would exceed the mean by 1.5 standard deviations.

GLOSSARY

Abandonment value The value of a project if the project's assets were sold externally; or alternatively, its opportunity value if the assets were employed elsewhere in the firm. [Chapter 14]

ABC method of inventory control Method that controls expensive inventory items more closely than less expensive items. [Chapter 10]

Absolute-priority rule The rule in bankruptcy or reorganization that claims of a set of claim holders must be paid, or settled, in full before the next, junior, set of claim holders may be paid anything. [Chapter 23 Appendix]

Accelerated depreciation Methods of depreciation that write off the cost of a capital asset faster than under straight-line depreciation. [Chapter 2]

Accounts receivable Amounts of money owed to a firm by customers who have bought goods or services on credit. A current asset, the accounts receivable account is also called *receivables*. [Chapter 10]

Accrued expenses Amounts owed but not yet paid for wages, taxes, interest, and dividends. The accrued expenses account is a short-term liability. [Chapter 11]

Acid-test (quick) ratio Current assets less inventories divided by current liabilities. It shows a firm's ability to meet current liabilities with its most liquid (quick) assets. [Chapter 6]

Activity ratios Ratios that measure how effectively the firm is using its assets. [Chapter 6]

Additional paid-in capital Funds received by a company in a sale of common stock that are in excess of the par or stated value of the stock. [Chapter 20]

Adjusted present value (APV) The sum of the discounted value of a project's operating cash flows (assuming equity financing) plus the value of any tax-shield benefits of interest associated with the project's financing minus any flotation costs. [Chapter 15 Appendix B]

Agency costs Costs associated with monitoring management to ensure that it behaves in ways consistent with the firm's contractual agreements with creditors and shareholders. [Chapter 17]

Agency (theory) A branch of economics relating to the behavior of principals (such as owners) and their agents (such as managers). [Chapter 1]

Agent(s) Individual(s) authorized by another person, called the principal, to act in the latter's behalf. [Chapter 1]

Aging accounts receivable The process of classifying accounts receivable by their age outstanding as of a given date. [Chapter 6]

Alternative minimum tax (AMT) An alternative, separate tax calculation based on the taxpayer's regular taxable income, increased by certain tax benefits, collectively referred to as "tax preference items." The taxpayer pays the larger of the regularly determined tax or the AMT. [Chapter 21]

Amortization schedule A table showing the repayment schedule of interest and principal necessary to pay off a loan by maturity. [Chapter 3]

Annuity A series of equal payments or receipts occurring over a specified number of periods. In an *ordinary annuity*, payments or receipts occur at the end of each period; in an *annuity due*, payments or receipts occur at the beginning of each period. [Chapter 3]

Arbitrage Finding two assets that are essentially the same, buying the cheaper, and selling the more expensive. [Chapter 17]

Arbitrage pricing theory (APT) A theory where the price of an asset depends on multiple factors and arbitrage efficiency prevails. [Chapter 5 Appendix B]

Arrearage A late or overdue payment, which may be cumulative. [Chapter 20]

Asset-backed securities (ABS) Debt securities whose interest and principal payments are provided by the cash flows coming from a discrete pool of assets. [Chapter 20]

Asset securitization The process of packaging a pool of assets and then selling interests in the pool in the form of *asset-backed securities (ABS)*. [Chapter 20]

Assigned (or stated) value A nominal value assigned to a share of no-par common stock that is usually far below the actual issuing price. [Chapter 20]

Automated clearinghouse (ACH) electronic transfer This is essentially an electronic version of the depository transfer check. [Chapter 9]

Balance sheet A summary of a firm's financial position on a given date that shows total assets = total liabilities + owners' equity. [Chapter 6]

Balloon payment A payment on debt that is much larger than other payments. The ultimate balloon payment is the entire principal at maturity. [Chapter 20]

***Bankers' acceptances (BAs)** Short-term promissory trade notes for which a bank (by having "accepted" them) promises to pay the holder the face amount at maturity. [Chapters 9 and 11]

Best efforts offering A security offering in which the investment bankers agree to use only their best efforts to sell the issuer's securities. The investment bankers do not commit to purchase any unsold securities. [Chapter 19]

Beta An index of systematic risk. It measures the sensitivity of a stock's returns to changes in returns on the market portfolio. The beta of a portfolio is simply a weighted average of the individual stock betas in the portfolio. [Chapter 5]

Bill of lading A shipping document indicating the details of the shipment and delivery of goods and their ownership. [Chapter 24]

Blue sky laws State laws regulating the offering and sale of securities. [Chapter 19]

***Bond** A long-term debt instrument issued by a corporation or government [Chapters 4 and 20]

Bond discount The amount by which the face value of a bond exceeds its current price. [Chapter 4]

Bond premium The amount by which the current price of a bond exceeds its face value. [Chapter 4]

Book value (1) An *asset:* the accounting value of an asset—the asset's cost minus its accumulated depreciation; (2) a *firm:* total assets minus liabilities and preferred stock as listed on the balance sheet. [Chapter 4]

Break-even analysis A technique for studying the relationship among fixed costs, variable costs, profits, and sales volume. [Chapter 16]

Break-even chart A graphic representation of the relationship between total revenues and total costs for various levels of production and sales, indicating areas of profit and loss. [Chapter 16]

Break-even point The sales volume required so that total revenues and total costs are equal; may be expressed in units or in sales dollars. [Chapter 16]

Business risk The inherent uncertainty in the physical operations of the firm. Its impact is shown in the variability of the firm's operating income (EBIT). [Chapter 16]

Call option A contract that gives the holder the right to *purchase* a specified quantity of the underlying asset at a predetermined price (the *exercise price*) on or before a fixed expiration date. [Chapter 22 Appendix]

Call premium The excess of the call price of a security over its par value. [Chapter 20 Appendix]

Call price The price at which a security with a call provision can be repurchased by the issuer prior to the security's maturity. [Chapter 20]

Call provision A feature in an indenture that permits the issuer to repurchase securities at a fixed price (or a series of fixed prices) before maturity; also called *call feature*. [Chapter 20]

Capital-asset pricing model (CAPM) A model that describes the relationship between risk and expected (required) return; in this model, a security's expected (required) return is the risk-free rate plus a premium based on the systematic risk of the security. [Chapter 5]

Capital budgeting The process of identifying, analyzing, and selecting investment projects whose returns (cash flows) are expected to extend beyond one year. [Chapter 12]

Capital gain (loss) The amount by which the proceeds from the sale of a capital asset exceeds (is less than) the asset's original cost. [Chapter 2]

Capitalization rate The discount rate used to determine the present value of a stream of expected future cash flows. [Chapter 17]

Capitalized expenditures Expenditures that may provide benefits into the future and therefore are treated as capital outlays and not as expenses of the period in which they were incurred. [Chapter 12]

***Capital market** The market for relatively long-term (greater than one year original maturity) financial instruments (e.g., bonds and stocks). [Chapters 2 and 19]

Capital rationing A situation where a constraint (or budget ceiling) is placed on the total size of capital expenditures during a particular period. [Chapter 13]

***Capital structure** The mix (or proportion) of a firm's permanent long-term financing represented by debt, preferred stock, and common stock equity. [Chapters 16 and 17]

Cash budget A forecast of a firm's future cash flows arising from collections and disbursements, usually on a monthly basis. [Chapter 7]

Cash concentration The movement of cash from lockbox or field banks into the firm's central cash pool residing in a concentration bank. [Chapter 9]

Cash cycle The length of time from the *actual outlay* of cash for purchases until the collection of receivables resulting from the sale of goods or services. [Chapter 6]

Cash discount A percent (%) reduction in sales or purchase price allowed for early payment of invoices. It is an incentive for credit customers to pay invoices in a timely fashion. [Chapter 10]

Cash discount period The period of time during which a cash discount can be taken for early payment. [Chapter 10]

Cash dividend Cash distribution of earnings to stockholders, usually on a quarterly basis. [Chapter 2]

Cash equivalents Highly liquid, short-term marketable securities that are readily convertible to known amounts of cash and generally have remaining maturities of three months or less at the time of acquisition. [Chapter 6]

Cash insolvency Inability to pay obligations as they fall due. [Chapter 16]

Certainty equivalent (CE) The amount of cash someone would require with certainty at a point in time to make the individual indifferent between that certain amount and an amount expected to be received with risk at the same point in time. [Chapter 5]

Characteristic line A line that describes the relationship between an individual security's returns and returns on the market portfolio. The slope of this line is *beta*. [Chapter 5]

Chattel mortgage A lien on specifically identified *personal property* (assets other than real estate) backing a loan. [Chapter 11]

Clayton Act A 1914 federal antitrust law designed to promote competition that addresses several antitrust matters, including interlocking directorates, race discrimination, exclusive dealing, and mergers. [Chapter 23]

Clearing House Interbank Payments System (CHIPS) An automated clearing system used primarily for international payments. The British counterpart is known as CHAPS. [Chapter 9]

Coefficient of variation (CV) The ratio of the standard deviation of a distribution to the mean of that distribution. It is a measure of *relative* risk. [Chapter 5]

*Commercial paper Short-term, unsecured promissory notes, generally issued by large corporations (unsecured corporate IOUs). [Chapters 9 and 11]

*Commitment fee A fee charged by the lender for agreeing to hold credit available. [Chapters 11 and 21]

Common-size analysis An analysis of *percentage* financial statements where all balance sheet items are divided by *total assets* and all income statement items are divided by *net sales* or *revenues*. [Chapter 6]

*Common stock Securities that represent the ultimate ownership (and risk) position in a corporation. [Chapters 4 and 20]

*Compensating balance Non-interest-bearing demand deposits maintained by a firm to compensate a bank for services provided, credit lines, or loans. [Chapters 9 and 11]

Compound interest Interest paid (earned) on any previous interest earned, as well as on the principal borrowed (lent). [Chapter 3]

Conditional sales contract A means of financing provided by the seller of equipment, who holds title to it until the financing is paid off. [Chapter 21]

Consol A bond that never matures; a perpetuity in the form of a bond. [Chapter 4]

Consolidation The combination of two or more firms into an entirely new firm. The old firms cease to exist. Though technically different, the terms *merger* (where one firm survives) and *consolidation* tend to be used interchangeably. [Chapter 23]

Controlled disbursement A system in which the firm directs checks to be drawn on a bank (or branch bank) that is able to give early or mid-morning notification of the total dollar amount of checks that will be presented against its account that day. [Chapter 9]

Conversion price The price per share at which common stock will be exchanged for a convertible security. It is equal to the face value of the convertible security divided by the conversion ratio. [Chapter 22]

Conversion ratio The number of shares of common stock into which a convertible security can be converted. It is equal to the face value of the convertible security divided by the conversion price. [Chapter 22]

Conversion value The value of the convertible security in terms of the common stock into which the security can be converted. It is equal to the conversion ratio times the current market price per share of the common stock. [Chapter 22]

Convertible security A bond or a preferred stock that is convertible into a specified number of shares of common stock at the option of the holder. [Chapter 22]

Corporation A business form legally separate from its owners. Its distinguishing features include limited liability, easy transfer of ownership, unlimited life, and an ability to raise large sums of capital. [Chapter 2]

Correlation coefficient A standardized statistical measure of the linear relationship between two variables. Its range is from -1.0 (perfect negative correlation), through 0 (no correlation), to $+1.0$ (perfect positive correlation). [Chapter 5 Appendix A]

Cost of capital The required rate of return on the various types of financing. The overall cost of capital is a weighted average of the individual required rates of return (costs). [Chapter 15]

Cost of debt (capital) The required rate of return on investment of the lenders of a company. [Chapter 15]

Cost of equity capital The required rate of return on investment of the common shareholders of the company. [Chapter 15]

Cost of goods sold Product costs (inventoriable costs) that become period expenses only when the products are sold; equals *beginning inventory* plus *cost of goods purchased* or *manufactured* minus *ending inventory*. [Chapter 6]

Cost of preferred stock (capital) The required rate of return on investment of the preferred shareholders of the company. [Chapter 15]

Countertrade Generic term for barter and other forms of trade that involve the international sale of goods or services that are paid for—in whole or in part—by the transfer of goods or services from a foreign country. [Chapter 24]

***Coupon rate** The stated rate of interest on a bond; the annual interest payment divided by the bond's face value. [Chapters 4 and 20]

Covariance A statistical measure of the degree to which two variables (e.g., securities' returns) move together. A positive value means that, on average, they move in the same direction. [Chapter 5]

Covenant A restriction on a borrower imposed by a lender; for example, the borrower must maintain a minimum amount of working capital. [Chapter 21]

Coverage ratios Ratios that relate the financial charges of a firm to its ability to service, or cover, them. [Chapter 6]

Credit period The total length of time over which credit is extended to a customer to pay a bill. [Chapter 10]

Credit-scoring system A system used to decide whether to grant credit by assigning numerical scores to various characteristics related to creditworthiness. [Chapter 10]

Credit standard The minimum quality of creditworthiness of a credit applicant that is acceptable to the firm. [Chapter 10]

Cumulative dividends feature A requirement that all cumulative unpaid dividends on the preferred stock be paid before a dividend may be paid on the common stock. [Chapter 20]

Cumulative voting A method of electing corporate directors, where each common share held carries as many votes as there are directors to be elected and each shareholder may accumulate these votes and cast them in any fashion for one or more particular directors. [Chapter 20]

Currency option A contract that gives the holder the right to buy (call) or sell (put) a specific amount of a foreign currency at some specified price until a certain (expiration) date. [Chapter 24]

Current ratio Current assets divided by current liabilities. It shows a firm's ability to cover its current liabilities with its current assets. [Chapter 6]

Debenture A long-term, unsecured debt instrument. [Chapter 20]

Debt capacity The maximum amount of debt (and other fixed-charge financing) that a firm can adequately service. [Chapter 16]

Debt ratios Ratios that show the extent to which the firm is financed by debt. [Chapter 6]

Debt-service burden Cash required during a specific period, usually a year, to meet interest expenses and principal payments. Also called simply *debt service*. [Chapter 16]

Declaration date The date that the board of directors announces the amount and date of the next dividend. [Chapter 18]

Declining-balance depreciation Methods of depreciation calling for an annual charge based on a fixed percentage of the asset's depreciated book value at the beginning of the year for which the depreciation charge applies. [Chapter 2]

Default The failure to meet the terms of a contract, such as failure to make interest or principal payments when due on a loan. [Chapter 2]

Deferred taxes A "liability" that represents the accumulated difference between the income tax expense reported on the firm's books and the income tax actually paid. It arises principally because depreciation is calculated differently for financial reporting than for tax reporting. [Chapter 6 Appendix]

Degree of financial leverage (DFL) The percentage change in a firm's earnings per share (EPS) resulting from a 1 percent change in operating profit (EBIT). [Chapter 16]

Degree of operating leverage (DOL) The percentage change in a firm's operating profit (EBIT) resulting from a 1 percent change in output (sales). [Chapter 16]

Degree of total leverage (DTL) The percentage change in a firm's earnings per share (EPS) resulting from a 1 percent change in output (sales). This is also equal to a firm's degree of operating leverage (DOL) times its degree of financial leverage (DFL) at a particular level of output (sales). [Chapter 16]

Dependent (or contingent) project A project whose acceptance depends on the acceptance of one or more other projects. [Chapter 13]

Depository transfer check (DTC) A non-negotiable check payable to a single company account at a concentration bank. [Chapter 9]

Depreciable basis In tax accounting, the fully installed cost of an asset. This is the amount that, by law, may be written off over time for tax purposes. [Chapter 12]

Depreciation The systematic allocation of the cost of a capital asset over a period of time for financial reporting purposes, tax purposes, or both. [Chapter 2]

Derivative security A financial contract whose value derives in part from the value and characteristics of one or more underlying assets (e.g., securities, commodities), interest rates, exchange rates, or indices. [Chapter 22]

*Dilution A decrease in the proportional claim on earnings and assets of a share of common stock because of the issuance of additional shares. [Chapters 18 and 22]

Disbursement float Total time between the mailing of a check by a firm and the check's clearing the firm's checking account. [Chapter 9]

Discounted cash flow (DCF) Any method of investment project evaluation and selection that adjusts cash flows over time for the time value of money. [Chapter 13]

Discount rate (capitalization rate) Interest rate used to convert *future values* to *present values*. [Chapter 3]

Divestiture The divestment of a portion of the enterprise or the firm as a whole. [Chapter 23]

Dividend-payout ratio Annual cash dividends divided by annual earnings; or alternatively, dividends per share divided by earnings per share. The ratio indicates the percentage of a company's earnings that is paid out to shareholders in cash. [Chapter 18]

Dividend reinvestment plan (DRIP) An optional plan allowing shareholders to automatically reinvest dividend payments in additional shares of the company's stock. [Chapter 18]

Dividend yield Anticipated annual dividend divided by the market price of the stock. [Chapter 18]

Draft A signed, written order by which the first party (drawer) instructs a second party (drawee) to pay a specified amount of money to a third party (payee). The drawer and payee are often one and the same. [Chapter 11]

Dual-class common stock Two classes of common stock, usually designated Class A and Class B. Class A is usually the weaker voting or nonvoting class, and Class B is usually the stronger. [Chapter 20]

Dutch auction A procedure for buying (selling) securities named for a system used for flower auctions in Holland. A buyer (seller) seeks bids within a specified price range, usually for a large block of stock or bonds. After evaluating the range of bid prices received, the buyer (seller) accepts the lowest price that will allow it to acquire (dispose of) the entire block. [Chapter 18]

Earnings per share (EPS) Earnings after taxes (EAT) divided by the number of common shares outstanding. [Chapter 1]

EBIT-EPS break-even analysis Analysis of the effect of financing alternatives on earnings per share. The break-even point is the EBIT level where EPS is the same for two (or more) alternatives. [Chapter 16]

Economic order quantity (EOQ) The quantity of an inventory item to order so that total inventory costs are minimized over the firm's planning period. [Chapter 10]

Economic value added (EVA) A measure of business performance. It is a type of economic profit that is equal to a company's after-tax net operating profit minus a dollar cost of capital charge (and possibly including some adjustments). [Chapter 15]

Economies of scale The benefits of size in which the average unit cost falls as volume increases. [Chapter 23]

Effective annual interest rate The actual rate of interest earned (paid) after adjusting the *nominal rate* for factors such as the number of compounding periods per year. [Chapter 3]

Efficient financial market A financial market in which current prices fully reflect all available relevant information. [Chapter 5]

Electronic commerce (EC) The exchange of business information in an electronic (nonpaper) format, including over the Internet. [Chapter 9]

Electronic data interchange (EDI) The movement of business data electronically in a structured, computer-readable format. [Chapter 9]

Electronic funds transfer (EFT) The electronic movements of information between two depository institutions resulting in a value (money) transfer. [Chapter 9]

Equipment trust certificate An intermediate- to long-term security, usually issued by a transportation company, such as a railroad or airline, that is used to finance new equipment. [Chapter 20]

Equity carve-out The public sale of stock in a subsidiary in which the parent usually retains majority control. [Chapter 23]

Euro (EUR) The name given to the single European currency. Its official abbreviation is EUR. Like the dollar (\$) and the British pound (£), the euro (€) has a distinctive symbol, which looks similar to a "C" with a "=" through it. [Chapter 24]

Eurobond A bond issue sold internationally outside of the country in whose currency the bond is denominated. [Chapter 24]

Eurocurrency A currency deposited outside its country of origin. [Chapter 24]

*Eurodollars A U.S. dollar-denominated deposit—generally in a bank located outside the United States—not subject to U.S. banking regulations. [Chapters 9 and 24]

Euro medium-term note (Euro MTN) An MTN issue sold internationally outside the country in whose currency the MTN is denominated. [Chapter 21]

Event risk The risk that existing debt will suffer a decline in creditworthiness because of the issuance of additional debt securities, usually in connection with corporate restructurings. [Chapter 19]

Exchangeable bond A bond that allows the holder to exchange the security for common stock of another company—generally, one in which the bond issuer has an ownership interest. [Chapter 22]

Exchange rate The number of units of one currency that may be purchased with one unit of another currency. [Chapter 24]

Ex-dividend date The first date on which a stock purchaser is no longer entitled to the recently declared dividend. [Chapter 18]

Exercise price The price at which the common stock associated with a warrant or call option can be purchased over a specified period. [Chapter 22]

Expected return The weighted average of possible returns, with the weights being the probabilities of occurrence. [Chapter 5]

Expected value The weighted average of possible outcomes, with the weights being the probabilities of occurrence. [Chapter 14]

Ex-rights date The first date on which a stock purchaser no longer receives the right to subscribe to additional shares through the recently announced rights offering. [Chapter 19]

Extra dividend A nonrecurring dividend paid to shareholders in addition to the regular dividend. It is brought about by special circumstances. [Chapter 18]

Face value The stated value of an asset. In the case of a bond, the face value is usually $1,000. [Chapter 4]

Factoring The selling of receivables to a financial institution, the *factor*, usually "without recourse." [Chapter 11]

Fair market value The price at which property can be sold in an arm's length transaction. [Chapter 21]

FASB 13 Statement issued by the Financial Accounting Standards Board (FASB) establishing financial accounting standards for lessees and lessors. [Chapter 21 Appendix]

Federal agency An executive department, an independent federal establishment, a corporation, or other entity established by Congress that is owned in whole or in part by the United States. [Chapter 9]

Field warehouse receipt A receipt for goods segregated and stored on the borrower's premises (but under the control of an independent warehousing company) that a lender holds as collateral for a loan. [Chapter 11]

Financial Accounting Standards Board (FASB) The rule-making body of the accounting profession that sets its standards. [Chapter 24]

Financial EDI (FEDI) The movement of financially related electronic information between a company and its bank or between banks. [Chapter 9]

Financial intermediaries Financial institutions that accept money from savers and use those funds to make loans and other financial investments in their own name. They include commercial banks, savings institutions, insurance companies, pension funds, finance companies, and mutual funds. [Chapter 2]

Financial lease A long-term lease that is not cancellable. [Chapter 21]

Financial leverage The use of fixed financing costs by the firm. The British expression is *gearing*. [Chapter 16]

Financial management Concerns the acquisition, financing, and management of assets with some overall goal in mind. [Chapter 1]

Financial markets All institutions and procedures for bringing buyers and sellers of financial instruments together. [Chapter 2]

Financial ratio An index that relates two accounting numbers and is obtained by dividing one number by the other. [Chapter 6]

Financial risk The added variability in earnings per share (EPS)—plus the risk of possible insolvency—that is induced by the use of financial leverage. [Chapter 16]

Floating lien A general, or blanket, lien against a group of assets, such as inventory or receivables, without the assets being specifically identified. [Chapter 11]

Floating-rate note (FRN) Debt issue with a variable interest rate. [Chapter 24]

Flotation costs The costs associated with issuing securities, such as underwriting, legal, listing, and printing fees. [Chapter 15]

Flow of funds statement A summary of a firm's changes in financial position from one period to another; it is also called a *sources and uses of funds statement* or a *statement of changes in financial position*. [Chapter 7]

Forecast financial statements Expected future financial statements based on conditions that management expects to exist and actions it expects to take. [Chapter 7]

Forfaiting The selling "without recourse" of medium- to long-term export receivables to a financial institution, the *forfaiter*. A third party, usually a bank or governmental unit, guarantees the financing. [Chapter 24]

Forward contract A contract for the delivery of a commodity, foreign currency, or financial instrument at a price specified now, with delivery and settlement at a specified future date. Although similar to a *futures contract*, it is not easily transferred or canceled. [Chapter 24]

Forward exchange rate The rate today for exchanging one currency for another at a specific future date. [Chapter 24]

Future value (terminal value) The value at some future time of a present amount of money, or a series of payments, evaluated at a given interest rate. [Chapter 3]

Futures contract A contract for the delivery of a commodity, foreign currency, or financial instrument at a specified price on a stipulated future date. Futures contracts are traded on organized exchanges. [Chapter 24]

General partner Member of a partnership with unlimited liability for the debts of the partnership. [Chapter 2]

Going-concern value The amount a firm could be sold for as a continuing operating business. [Chapter 4]

Going private Making a public company private through the repurchase of stock by current management and/or outside private investors. [Chapter 23]

Goodwill The intangible assets of the acquired firm arising from the acquiring firm paying more for them than their book value. Goodwill must be amortized. [Chapter 23]

Gross working capital The firm's investment in current assets (like cash and marketable securities, receivables, and inventory). [Chapter 8]

Hedge (Noun) Something that reduces the risk of future price movements. [Chapter 22]

*Hedging (maturity matching) approach A method of financing where each asset would be offset with a financing instrument of the same approximate maturity. [Chapters 8 and 15]

Hurdle rate The minimum required rate of return on an investment in a discounted cash flow analysis; the rate at which a project is acceptable. [Chapter 13]

Income bond A bond where the payment of interest is contingent on sufficient earnings of the firm. [Chapter 20]

Income statement A summary of a firm's revenues and expenses over a specified period, ending with net income or loss for the period. [Chapter 6]

Indenture The legal agreement, also called the *deed of trust*, between the corporation issuing bonds and the bondholders, establishing the terms of the bond issue and naming the trustee. [Chapter 20]

Independent project A project whose acceptance (or rejection) does not prevent the acceptance of other projects under consideration. [Chapter 13]

Index analysis An analysis of *percentage* financial statements where all balance sheet or income statement figures for a base year equal 100.0 (percent) and subsequent financial statement items are expressed as percentages of their values in the base year. [Chapter 6]

Indifference curve A line representing all combinations of expected return and risk that provide an investor with an equal amount of satisfaction. [Chapter 15]

Indifference point (EBIT-EPS indifference point) The level of EBIT that produces the same level of EPS for two (or more) alternative capital structures. [Chapter 16]

Inflation A rise in the average level of prices of goods and services. [Chapter 2]

*Initial public offering (IPO) A company's first offering of common stock to the general public. [Chapters 19 and 23]

Interest Money paid (earned) for the use of money. [Chapter 3]

Interest coverage ratio Earnings before interest and taxes divided by interest charges. It indicates a firm's ability to cover interest charges. [Chapter 6]

*Interest-rate (or yield) risk The variability in the market price of a security caused by changes in interest rates. [Chapters 4 and 9]

Internal rate of return (IRR) The discount rate that equates the present value of the future net cash flows from an investment project with the project's initial cash outflow. [Chapter 13]

*Interpolate Estimate an unknown number that lies somewhere between two known numbers. [Chapters 4 and 13]

Intrinsic value The price a security "ought to have" based on all factors bearing on valuation. [Chapter 4]

*Investment banker A financial institution that underwrites (purchases at a fixed price on a fixed date) new securities for resale. [Chapters 2 and 19]

Invoice Bill prepared by a seller of goods or services and submitted to the purchaser. It lists the items bought, prices, and terms of sale. [Chapter 9]

IPO roll-up An initial public offering (IPO) of independent companies in the same industry that merge into a single company concurrent with the stock offering. The funds from the IPO are used to finance the acquisition of the combining companies. [Chapter 23]

Joint venture A business venture jointly owned and controlled by two or more independent firms. Each venture partner continues to exist as a separate firm, and the joint venture represents a new business enterprise. [Chapter 23]

Junk bond A high-risk, high-yield (often unsecured) bond rated below investment grade. [Chapter 20]

Just-in-time (JIT) An approach to inventory management and control in which inventories are acquired and inserted in production at the exact times they are needed. [Chapter 10]

Lead time The length of time between the placement of an order for an inventory item and when the item is received in inventory. [Chapter 10]

Lease A contract under which one party, the lessor (owner) of an asset, agrees to grant the use of that asset to another, the lessee, in exchange for periodic rental payments. [Chapter 21]

Letter of credit (L/C) A promise from a third party (usually a bank) for payment in the event that certain conditions are met. It is frequently used to guarantee payment of an obligation. [Chapter 11]

Letter stock Privately placed common stock that cannot be immediately resold. [Chapter 19]

Leverage The use of fixed costs in an attempt to increase (or lever up) profitability. [Chapter 16]

Leveraged buyout (LBO) A primarily debt-financed purchase of all the stock or assets of a company, subsidiary, or division by an investor group. [Chapter 23]

Leveraged leasing A lease arrangement in which the lessor provides an equity portion (usually 20 to 40 percent) of the leased asset's cost and third-party lenders provide the balance of the financing. [Chapter 21]

Lien A legal claim on certain assets. A lien can be used to secure a loan. [Chapter 21]

Limited liability company (LLC) A business form that provides its owners (called "members") with corporate-style limited personal liability and the federal-tax treatment of a partnership. [Chapter 2]

Limited partner Member of a limited partnership not personally liable for the debts of the partnership. [Chapter 2]

Line of credit A limit to the amount of credit extended to an account. Purchaser can buy on credit up to that limit. [Chapter 10]

Line of credit (with a bank) An informal arrangement between a bank and its customer specifying the maximum amount of unsecured credit the bank will permit the firm to owe at any one time. [Chapter 11]

Liquidation The sale of assets of a firm, either voluntarily or in bankruptcy. [Chapter 23]

Liquidation value The amount of money that could be realized if an asset or a group of assets (e.g., a firm) is sold separately from its operating organization. [Chapter 4]

Liquidity The ability of an asset to be converted into cash without a significant price concession. [Chapter 6]

Liquidity ratios Ratios that measure a firm's ability to meet short-term obligations. [Chapter 6]

Listing Admission of a security for trading on an organized exchange. A security so admitted is referred to as a *listed security*. [Chapter 20]

Loan agreement A legal agreement specifying the terms of a loan and the obligations of the borrower. [Chapter 21]

Lockbox A post office box maintained by a firm's bank that is used as a receiving point for customer remittances. *Retail lockbox* systems cater to the receipt and processing of low- to moderate-dollar, high-volume remittances, whereas *wholesale lockbox* systems are designed to handle high-dollar, low-volume remittances. [Chapter 9]

*London interbank offered rate (LIBOR) The interest rate that world-class banks in London pay each other for Eurodollars. [Chapters 11 and 24]

Majority-rule voting A method of electing corporate directors, where each common share held carries one vote for each director position that is open; also called *statutory voting*. [Chapter 20]

Management buyout (MBO) A leveraged buyout (LBO) in which prebuyout management ends up with a substantial equity position. [Chapter 23]

Managerial (real) option Management flexibility to make future decisions that affect a project's expected cash flows, life, or future acceptance. [Chapter 14]

*Marketability (or liquidity) The ability to sell a significant volume of securities in a short period of time in the secondary market without significant price concession. [Chapters 2 and 9]

Market value The market price at which an asset trades. [Chapter 4]

Maturity The life of a security; the amount of time before the principal amount of a security becomes due. [Chapter 2]

Medium-term note (MTN) A corporate or government debt instrument that is offered to investors on a continuous basis. Maturities range from nine months to 30 years (or more). [Chapter 21]

Merger The combination of two or more companies in which only one firm survives as a legal entity. [Chapter 23]

Money market The market for short-term (less than one year original maturity) government and corporate debt securities. It also includes government securities originally issued with maturities of more than one year but that now have a year or less until maturity. [Chapter 2]

Money market instruments (Broadly defined). All government securities and short-term corporate obligations. [Chapter 9]

Money market mutual funds (MMFs) Mutual funds that utilize pools of investors' funds to invest in large-denomination money market instruments. [Chapter 9]

Money market preferred stock (MMP) Preferred stock having a dividend rate that is reset at auction every 49 days. [Chapter 9]

Mortgage banker A financial institution that originates (buys) mortgages primarily for resale. [Chapter 2]

Mortgage bond A bond issue secured by a mortgage on the issuer's property. [Chapter 20]

Multinational company A company that does business and has assets in two or more countries. [Chapter 24]

Mutually exclusive project A project whose acceptance precludes the acceptance of one or more alternative projects. [Chapter 13]

Negative pledge clause A protective covenant whereby the borrower agrees not to allow a lien on any of its assets. [Chapter 21]

Negotiable certificate of deposit (CD) A large-denomination investment in a negotiable time deposit at a commercial bank or savings institution paying a fixed or variable rate of interest for a specified time period. [Chapter 9]

Net float The dollar difference between the balance shown in a firm's (or individual's) checkbook balance and the balance on the bank's books. [Chapter 9]

Net lease A lease where the lessee maintains and insures the leased asset. [Chapter 21]

Net operating income (NOI) approach (to capital structure) A theory of capital structure in which the weighted average cost of capital and the total value of the firm remain constant as financial leverage is changed. [Chapter 17]

Net present value (NPV) The present value of an investment project's net cash flows minus the project's initial cash outflow. [Chapter 13]

Netting System in which cross-border purchases among participating subsidiaries of the same company are netted so that each participant pays or receives only the net amount of its intracompany purchases and sales. [Chapter 24]

Net working capital Current assets minus current liabilities. [Chapter 8]

Nominal (stated) interest rate A rate of interest quoted for a year that has not been adjusted for frequency of compounding. If interest is compounded more than once a year, the *effective interest rate* will be higher than the *nominal rate*. [Chapter 3]

North American Industry Classification System (NAICS, pronounced "nakes") Codes A standardized classification of businesses by types of economic activity developed jointly by Canada, Mexico, and the United States. A five- or six-digit code number is assigned depending on how a business is defined. [Chapter 15]

NPV profile A graph showing the relationship between a project's net present value and the discount rate employed. [Chapter 13]

Operating cycle The length of time from the *commitment* of cash for purchases until the collection of receivables resulting from the sale of goods or services. [Chapter 6]

Operating lease A short-term lease that is often cancellable. [Chapter 21]

Operating leverage The use of fixed operating costs by the firm. [Chapter 16]

Opportunity cost What is lost by not taking the next-best investment alternative. [Chapter 12]

Optimal capital structure The capital structure that minimizes the firm's cost of capital and thereby maximizes the value of the firm. [Chapter 17]

Order point The quantity to which inventory must fall in order to signal that an order must be placed to replenish an item. [Chapter 10]

*Outsourcing Subcontracting a certain business operation to an outside firm instead of doing it in house. [Chapters 9 and 23]

Oversubscription privilege The right to purchase, on a pro rata basis, any unsubscribed shares in a rights offering. [Chapter 19]

Participating preferred stock Preferred stock where the holder is allowed to participate in increasing dividends if the common stockholders receive increasing dividends. [Chapter 20]

Partnership A business form in which two or more individuals act as owners. In a *general partnership* all partners have unlimited liability for the debts of the firm; in a *limited partnership* one or more partners may have limited liability. [Chapter 2]

Par value The face value of a stock or bond. [Chapter 20]

Payable through draft (PTD) A check-like instrument that is drawn against the payor and not against a bank, as is a check. After a PTD is presented to a bank, the payor gets to decide whether to honor or refuse payment. [Chapter 9]

Payback period (PBP) The period of time required for the cumulative expected cash flows from an investment project to equal the initial cash outflow. [Chapter 13]

Payment date The date when the corporation actually pays the declared dividend. [Chapter 18]

Permanent working capital The amount of current assets required to meet a firm's long-term minimum needs. [Chapter 8]

Perpetuity An *ordinary annuity* whose payments or receipts continue forever. [Chapter 3]

Poison pill A device used by a company to make itself less attractive as a takeover candidate. Its poison, so to speak, is released when the buyer takes a sufficient bite of the target firm. [Chapter 23]

Pooling of interests (method) A method of accounting treatment for a merger based on the *net book value* of the acquired company's assets. The balance sheets of the two companies are simply combined. [Chapter 23]

Portfolio A combination of two or more securities or assets. [Chapter 5]

Post-completion audit A formal comparison of the actual costs and benefits of a project with original estimates. A key element of the audit is feedback; that is, results of the audit are given to relevant personnel so that future decision making can be improved. [Chapter 13]

Preauthorized debit The transfer of funds from a payor's bank account on a specified date to the payee's bank account; the transfer is initiated by the payee with the payor's advance authorization. [Chapter 9]

Preemptive right The privilege of shareholders to maintain their proportional company ownership by purchasing a proportionate share of any new issue of common stock, or securities convertible into common stock. [Chapter 19]

*Preferred stock A type of stock that promises a (usually) fixed dividend but at the discretion of the board of directors. It has preference over common stock in the payment of dividends and claims on assets. [Chapters 4 and 20]

Premium over conversion value The market price of a convertible security minus its conversion value; also called *conversion premium*. [Chapter 22]

Premium over straight bond value Market price of a convertible bond minus its straight bond value. [Chapter 22]

Prepackaged bankruptcy (prepack) A reorganization that a majority of a company's creditors have approved prior to the beginning of a bankruptcy proceeding. [Chapter 23]

Present value The current value of a future amount of money, or a series of payments, evaluated at a given interest rate. [Chapter 3]

Price/earnings ratio The market price per share of a firm's common stock divided by the most recent 12 months of earnings per share. [Chapter 20]

*Primary market A market where new securities are bought and sold for the first time (a "new issues" market). [Chapters 2 and 19]

Prime rate Short-term interest rate charged by banks to large, creditworthy customers. It is also called simply *prime*. [Chapter 11]

Private (or direct) placement The sale of an entire issue of unregistered securities (usually bonds) directly to one purchaser or a group of purchasers (usually financial intermediaries). [Chapter 19]

Privileged subscription The sale of new securities in which existing shareholders are given a preference in purchasing these securities up to the proportion of common shares that they already own; also known as a *rights offering*. [Chapter 19]

Probability distribution A set of possible values that a random variable can assume and their associated probabilities of occurrence. [Chapter 5]

Probability tree A graphic or tabular approach for organizing the possible cash-flow streams generated by an investment. The presentation resembles the branches of a tree. Each complete branch represents one possible cash-flow sequence. [Chapter 14]

Profitability index (PI) The ratio of the present value of a project's future net cash flows to the project's initial cash outflow. [Chapter 13]

Profitability ratios Ratios that relate profits to sales and investment. [Chapter 6]

Profit maximization Maximizing a firm's earnings after taxes (EAT). [Chapter 1]

Promissory note A legal promise to pay a sum of money to a lender. [Chapter 21]

Prospectus Part I of the registration statement filed with the SEC. It discloses information about the issuing company and its new offering and is distributed as a separate booklet to investors. [Chapter 19]

Proxy A legal document giving one person the authority to act for another. In business, it generally refers to the instructions given by a shareholder with regard to voting shares of common stock. [Chapter 20]

Public issue Sale of bonds or stock to the general public. [Chapter 19]

Purchase (method) A method of accounting treatment for a merger based on the *market price* paid for the acquired company. [Chapter 23]

Purchasing-power parity (PPP) The idea that a basket of goods should sell for the same price in two countries, after exchange rates are taken into account. [Chapter 24]

Pure play An investment concentrated in one line of business. The extreme opposite of a pure play would be an investment in a *conglomerate*. [Chapter 23]

Put option A contract that gives the holder the right to *sell* a specified quantity of the underlying asset at a predetermined price (the *exercise price*) on or before a fixed expiration date. [Chapter 22 Appendix]

Recapitalization An alteration of a firm's capital structure. For example, a firm may sell bonds to acquire the cash necessary to repurchase some of its outstanding common stock. [Chapter 17]

Record date The date, set by the board of directors when a dividend is declared, on which an investor must be a shareholder of record to be entitled to the upcoming dividend. [Chapter 18]

Red herring The preliminary prospectus. It includes a legend in red ink on the cover stating that the registration statement has not yet become effective. [Chapter 19]

Refunding Replacing an old debt issue with a new one, usually to lower the interest cost. [Chapter 20 Appendix]

Registration statement The disclosure document filed with the SEC to register a new securities issue. The registration statement includes the prospectus and other information required by the SEC. [Chapter 19]

Regular dividend The dividend that is normally expected to be paid by the firm. [Chapter 18]

Reinvoicing center A company-owned financial subsidiary that purchases exported goods from company affiliates and resells (reinvoices) them to other affiliates or independent customers. [Chapter 24]

Remote disbursement A system in which the firm directs checks to be drawn on a bank that is geographically remote from its customer so as to maximize check-clearing time. [Chapter 9]

Reorganization Recasting of the capital structure of a financially troubled company, under Chapter 11 of the Bankruptcy Act, to reduce fixed charges. Claim holders may be given substitute securities. [Chapter 23 Appendix]

Repurchase agreements (RPs; repos) Agreements to buy securities (usually Treasury bills) and to resell them at a specified higher price at a later date. [Chapter 9]

Residual value The value of a leased asset at the end of the lease period. [Chapter 21]

Return Income received on an investment plus any change in market price, usually expressed as a percent of the beginning market price of the investment. [Chapter 5]

Reverse stock split A stock split in which the number of shares outstanding is decreased; for example, a 1-for-2 reverse stock split where each shareholder receives one new share in exchange for every two old shares held. [Chapter 18]

*Revolving credit agreement A formal, legal commitment to extend credit up to some maximum amount over a stated period of time. [Chapters 11 and 21]

Right A short-term option to buy a certain number (or fraction) of securities from the issuing corporation; also called a *subscription right*. [Chapter 19]

Risk The variability of returns from those that are expected. [Chapter 5]

Risk-adjusted discount rate (RADR) A required return (discount rate) that is increased relative to the firm's overall cost of capital for projects or groups showing greater than "average" risk and decreased for projects or groups showing less than "average" risk. [Chapter 15]

Risk averse Term applied to an investor who demands a higher expected return, the higher the risk. [Chapter 5]

Roll-up The combining of multiple small companies in the same industry to create one larger company. [Chapter 23]

Safety (of principal) Refers to the likelihood of getting back the same number of dollars you originally invested (principal). [Chapter 9]

Safety stock Inventory stock held in reserve as a cushion against uncertain demand (or usage) and replenishment lead time. [Chapter 10]

Sale and leaseback The sale of an asset with the agreement to immediately lease it back for an extended period of time. [Chapter 21]

Seasonal dating Credit terms that encourage the buyer of seasonal products to take delivery before the peak sales period and to defer payment until after the peak sales period. [Chapter 10]

*Secondary market A market for existing (used) securities rather than new issues. [Chapters 2 and 19]

Secured loans A form of debt for money borrowed in which specific assets have been pledged to guarantee payment. [Chapter 11]

Securities Act of 1933 (1933 Act) Generally requires that public offerings be registered with the federal government before they may be sold; also known as the *Truth in Securities Act*. [Chapter 19]

Securities and Exchange Commission (SEC) The U.S. government agency responsible for administration of federal securities laws, including the 1933 and 1934 Acts. [Chapter 19]

Securities Exchange Act of 1934 (1934 Act) Regulates the secondary market for long-term securities—the securities exchanges and the over-the-counter market. [Chapter 19]

Security (collateral) Asset(s) pledged by a borrower to ensure repayment of a loan. If the borrower defaults, the lender may sell the security to pay off the loan. [Chapter 11]

Security market line (SML) A line that describes the linear relationship between expected rates of return for individual securities (and portfolios) and systematic risk, as measured by beta. [Chapter 5]

Self-tender offer An offer by a firm to repurchase some of its own shares. [Chapter 18]

Sell-off The sale of a division of a company, known as a partial sell-off, or the company as a whole, known as a voluntary liquidation. [Chapter 23]

Serial bonds An issue of bonds with different maturities, as distinguished from an issue where all the bonds have identical maturities (term bonds). [Chapter 20]

Shareholders' equity *Total assets* minus *total liabilities*. Alternatively, the book value of a company's common stock (at par) plus additional paid-in capital and retained earnings. [Chapter 6]

Shark repellent Defenses employed by a company to ward off potential takeover bidders—the "sharks." [Chapter 23]

Shelf registration A procedure whereby a company is permitted to register securities it plans to sell over the next two years; also called *SEC Rule 415*. These securities can then be sold piecemeal whenever the company chooses. [Chapter 19]

Simple interest Interest paid (earned) on only the original amount, or principal, borrowed (lent). [Chapter 3]

Sinking fund Fund established to periodically retire a portion of a security issue before maturity. The corporation is required to make periodic sinking-fund payments to a trustee. [Chapter 20]

Society for Worldwide Interbank Financial Telecommunication (SWIFT) The major international financial telecommunications network that transmits international payment instructions as well as other financial messages. [Chapter 9]

Sole proprietorship A business form for which there is one owner. This single owner has unlimited liability for all debts of the firm. [Chapter 2]

Spin-off A form of divestiture resulting in a subsidiary or division becoming an independent company. Ordinarily, shares in the new company are distributed to the parent company's shareholders on a pro rata basis. [Chapter 23]

Spontaneous financing Trade credit, and other payables and accruals, that arise spontaneously in the firm's day-to-day operations. [Chapter 8]

Spot exchange rate The rate today for exchanging one currency for another for immediate delivery. [Chapter 24]

Stakeholders All constituencies with a stake in the fortunes of the company. They include shareholders, creditors, customers, employees, suppliers, and local communities. [Chapter 1]

Standard & Poor's 500 Stock Index (S&P 500 Index) A market-value-weighted index of 500 large-capitalization common stocks selected from a broad cross section of industry groups. It is used as a measure of overall market performance. [Chapter 5]

*Standard deviation A statistical measure of the variability of a distribution around its mean. It is the square root of the *variance*. [Chapters 5 and 14]

Standby arrangement A measure taken to ensure the complete success of a rights offering in which an investment banker or group of investment bankers agrees to "stand by" to underwrite any unsubscribed (unsold) portion of the issue. [Chapter 19]

Statement of cash flows A summary of a firm's cash receipts and cash payments during a period of time. [Chapter 7]

Stock dividend A payment of additional shares of stock to shareholders. Often used in place of or in addition to a cash dividend. [Chapter 18]

Stockout Not having enough items in inventory to fill an order. [Chapter 6]

Stock repurchase The repurchase (buyback) of stock by the issuing firm, either in the open (secondary) market or by *self-tender offer*. [Chapter 18]

Stock split An increase in the number of shares outstanding by reducing the par value of the stock; for example, a 2-for-1 stock split where par value per share is reduced by one-half. [Chapter 18]

Straight bond value The value of a convertible bond if the convertible feature were valueless; in other words, the value of a nonconvertible bond with the same coupon rate, maturity, and default risk as the convertible bond. [Chapter 22]

Straight debt (or equity) Debt (or equity) that cannot be exchanged for another asset. [Chapter 22]

Straight-line depreciation A method of depreciation that allocates expenses evenly over the depreciable life of the asset. [Chapter 2]

Strategic alliance An agreement between two or more independent firms to cooperate in order to achieve some specific commercial objective. [Chapter 23]

Subordinated debenture A long-term, unsecured debt instrument with a lower claim on assets and income than other classes of debt; known as junior debt. [Chapter 20]

Subsidiary A company that has more than half of its voting shares owned by another company (the parent company). [Chapter 15]

Sunk costs Unrecoverable past outlays that, because they cannot be recovered, should not affect present actions or future decisions. [Chapter 12]

Synergy Economies realized in a merger where the performance of the combined firm exceeds that of its previously separate parts. [Chapter 23]

Systematic risk The variability of return on stocks or portfolios associated with changes in return on the market as a whole. [Chapter 5]

Takeover The acquisition of another company that may (from the viewpoint of the acquired firm's management) take the form of a "friendly" or "unfriendly" merger. [Chapter 23]

*Tax shield A tax-deductible expense. The expense protects (shields) an equivalent dollar amount of revenue from being taxed by reducing taxable income. [Chapter 15 Appendix B and Chapter 17]

Temporary working capital The amount of current assets that varies with seasonal requirements. [Chapter 8]

Tender offer An offer to buy current shareholders' stock at a specified price, often with the objective of gaining control of the company. The offer is often made by another company and usually for more than the present market price. [Chapter 23]

Terminal warehouse receipt A receipt for the deposit of goods in a public warehouse that a lender holds as collateral for a loan. [Chapter 11]

Term loan Debt originally scheduled for repayment in more than 1 year, but generally in less than 10 years. [Chapter 21]

Term structure of interest rates The relationship between yield and maturity for securities *differing only in the length of time (or term) to maturity.* [Chapter 2]

*Ticker symbol A unique, letter-character code name assigned to securities and mutual funds. It is often used in newspapers and price-quotation services. This shorthand method of identification was originally developed in the 1800s by telegraph operators. [Chapters 5 and 23]

Tombstone advertisement An announcement placed in newspapers and magazines giving just the most basic details of a security offering. The term reflects the stark, black-bordered look of the ad. [Chapter 19]

Total firm risk The variability in earnings per share (EPS). It is the sum of business plus financial risk. [Chapter 16]

Total (or combined) leverage The use of both fixed operating and financing costs by the firm. [Chapter 16]

Trade credit Credit granted from one business to another. [Chapter 11]

Trade liabilities Money owed to suppliers. [Chapter 11]

Traditional approach (to capital structure) A theory of capital structure in which there exists an optimal capital structure and where management can increase the total value of the firm through the judicious use of financial leverage. [Chapter 17]

Translation gain or loss An accounting gain or loss arising from the translation of the assets and liabilities of a foreign subsidiary into the parent company's currency. [Chapter 24]

Treasury bills (T-bills) Short-term, non-interest-bearing obligations of the U.S. Treasury issued at a discount and redeemed at maturity for full face value. [Chapter 9]

Treasury bonds Long-term (more than 10 years' original maturity) obligations of the U.S. Treasury. [Chapter 9]

Treasury notes Medium-term (2–10 years' original maturity) obligations of the U.S. Treasury. [Chapter 9]

*Treasury stock Common stock that has been repurchased and is held by the issuing company. [Chapters 18 and 20]

Trustee A person or institution designated by a bond issuer as the official representative of the bondholders. Typically, a bank serves as trustee. [Chapter 20]

Trust receipt A security device acknowledging that the borrower holds specifically identified inventory and proceeds from its sale in trust for the lender. [Chapter 11]

Two-tier tender offer Tender offer in which the bidder offers a superior first-tier price (e.g., higher or all cash) for a specified maximum number (or percent) of shares and simultaneously offers to acquire the remaining shares at a second-tier price (e.g., lower and/or securities rather than cash). [Chapter 23]

Underwriting Bearing the risk of not being able to sell a security at the established price by virtue of purchasing the security for resale to the public; also known as *firm commitment underwriting*. [Chapter 19]

Underwriting syndicate A temporary combination of investment banking firms formed to sell a new security issue. [Chapter 19]

Uniform Commercial Code Model state legislation related to many aspects of commercial transactions that went into effect in Pennsylvania in 1954. It has been adopted with limited changes by most state legislatures. [Chapter 11]

Unsecured loans A form of debt for money borrowed that is not backed by the pledge of specific assets. [Chapter 11]

Unsystematic risk The variability of return on stocks or portfolios not explained by general market movements. It is avoidable through diversification. [Chapter 5]

Virtual corporation A business organizational model that involves the large-scale outsourcing of business functions. [Chapter 23]

Warrant A relatively long-term option to purchase common stock at a specified exercise price over a specified period of time. [Chapter 22]

White knight A friendly acquirer who, at the invitation of a target company, purchases shares from the hostile bidder(s) or launches a friendly counterbid in order to frustrate the initial, unfriendly bidder(s). [Chapter 23]

Wire transfer A generic term for electronic funds transfer using a two-way communications system, like Fedwire. [Chapter 9]

Working capital management The administration of the firm's current assets and the financing needed to support current assets. [Chapter 8]

Yield curve A graph of the relationship between yields and term to maturity for particular securities. [Chapter 2]

Yield to maturity (YTM) The expected rate of return on a bond if bought at its current market price and held to maturity. [Chapter 4]

Zero balance account (ZBA) A corporate checking account in which a zero balance is maintained. The account requires a master (parent) account from which funds are drawn to cover negative balances or to which excess balances are sent. [Chapter 9]

Zero-coupon bond A bond that pays no interest but sells at a deep discount from its face value; it provides compensation to investors in the form of price appreciation. [Chapter 4]

COMMONLY USED SYMBOLS

ACH	Automated clearinghouse
AMT	Alternative minimum tax
A/P	Accounts payable
APR	Annual percentage rate
APT	Arbitrage pricing theory
APY	Annual percentage yield
A/R	Accounts receivable
BAs	Bankers' acceptances
β	Beta
CAPM	Capital-asset pricing model
CD	Negotiable certificate of deposit
CE	Certainty equivalent
CF_t	Cash flow at time t
CML	Capital market line
COD	Cash on delivery
CV	Coefficient of variation
D_p	Dividend on preferred stock
D_t	Dividend at time t
DCF	Discounted cash flow
DFL	Degree of financial leverage
DOL	Degree of operating leverage
DRIP	Dividend reinvestment plan
DTC	Depository transfer check
DTL	Degree of total leverage
EAT	Earnings after taxes
EBIT	Earnings before interest and taxes
EBT	Earnings before tax
EC	Electronic commerce
EDI	Electronic data interchange
EFT	Electronic funds transfer
EOM	End of month
EOQ	Economic order quantity
EPS	Earnings per share
EVA™	Economic value added
FASB	Financial Accounting Standards Board
FEDI	Financial EDI
FRN	Floating-rate note
FV	Future value
FVA	Future (compound) value of an (ordinary) annuity

FVIF	Future value interest factor
FVIFA	Future value interest factor of an (ordinary) annuity
g	Growth rate
i	Interest rate per time period
IPO	Initial public offering
IRR	Internal rate of return
IRS	Internal Revenue Service
JIT	Just-in-time
k_d	Before-tax cost of debt
k_e	Cost of equity capital
k_i	After-tax cost of debt
k_o	Overall cost of capital
k_p	Cost of preferred stock
LBO	Leveraged buyout
L/C	Letter of credit
LIBOR	London interbank offered rate
LLC	Limited liability company
MACRS	Modified Accelerated Cost Recovery System
MMFs	Money market mutual funds
MMP	Money market preferred stock
MTN	Medium-term note
n	Number of periods
NOI	Net operating income
NPV	Net present value
NWC	Net working capital
OP	Order point
P_t	Market price at time t
PBP	Payback period
P/E	Price/earnings ratio
PI	Profitability index
PPP	Purchasing-power parity
PTD	Payable through draft
PV	Present value
PVA	Present value of an (ordinary) annuity
PVIF	Present value interest factor
PVIFA	Present value interest factor of an (ordinary) annuity
Q_{BE}	Break-even sales quantity

r	Interest rate or return	S&P	Standard & Poor's
R_f	Risk-free rate	SWIFT	Society for Worldwide Interbank Financial Telecommunication
$\bar{R}_j$	Expected return on security j		
$\bar{R}_m$	Expected return on market portfolio	σ	Standard deviation
RADR	Risk-adjusted discount rate	σ^2	Variance
ROE	Return on equity	Σ	Summation sign
ROI	Return on investment	t	Time period
RPs	Repurchase agreements (repos)	UCC	Uniform commercial code
S_{BE}	Break-even sales revenue	WC	Working capital
SEC	Securities and Exchange Commission	YTM	Yield to maturity
SML	Security market line	ZBA	Zero balance account

INDEX

Abandonment value, 379–83
ABC method of inventory control, 269
Absolute-priority rule, 654
Accelerated collection, 227–30, 258
Accelerated Cost Recovery System (ACRS), 19*n*
Accelerated depreciation, 18, 319–20, 580
Acceptance criterion (hurdle rate), 337, 394, 395, 407
  with internal rate of return method, 337
  with net present value method, 338
  with payback period method, 335
  with profitability index method, 340
Accounting profit, 408
Accounting treatment
  of convertible securities or warrants outstanding, 599
  of leases, 579, 587–89
  of marketable securities, 238
  of merger or consolidation, 638–40
  standardizing data, for comparison, 133
  of stock dividends, 503–5
  of stock split, 505
  translation exposure and, 673–76
  value of fixed assets and, 127, 128
Accounts payable (trade credit), 176, 266, 288–93
  aging of, 141
  delaying payment of, 214*n*
  stretching, 290–92
Accounts receivable-backed loans, 301–2
Accounts receivable management, 127, 254–67
  aging accounts receivable, 140–41, 301
  analyzing credit applicant, 262–67
  collection policy and procedures, 259–62
  credit policies, 254–59
  default risk, 259
  defining accounts receivable, 254
  factoring accounts receivable, 305–7
"Accrual" method of recognizing sales, 129
Accrued expenses, 293
Acid-test ratio, 136, 154
Acquisitions. *See* Mergers

Activity ratios, 139–46, 155
Additional paid-in capital, 127, 557
Adjusted present value (APV), 420–23
  weighted average cost of capital vs., 422–23
Adjustment to discount rate (ADR) procedure, 405–6
Adjustment to initial outlay (AIO) method, 405, 406
Advertisement, tombstone, 533, 534
Agency costs, 476–77, 480–81, 601, 628
Agency for International Development (AID), 672
Agency theory, 5
Agents, management as, 5
Aggressive financing, 217–18
"Aggressive" investment, 105
Aging accounts receivable, 140–41, 301
Aging of accounts payable, 141
Aging schedule, 301
"Aircraft Carrier Proposal," 533
Alliances, strategic, 643–44
Allied Crude Vegetable Refining Corporation, 305
Allocation of funds in economy, 28–32
Almanac of Business and Industrial Financial Ratios, 131
Alternative Depreciation System (ADS), 319
Alternative minimum taxable income (AMTI), 18
Alternative minimum tax (AMT), 17–18, 580
American Stock Exchange, 27, 539
Amortization, 50, 51, 59–60, 572, 588–89
Amortization effect, 551
Amortization schedule, 60
Annual percentage rate (APR), 58
Annual percentage yield (APY), 58
Annuities, 46–53
  annuity due, 51–53
  consolidated (consol), 71
  ordinary, 46–50
    future value interest factor of, 47–49, 706–7
    present value interest factor of, 49–50, 52, 53, 708–9

  perpetuity, 51–53
Antidilution clause, 598
Antitakeover amendments and devices, 641–42
Antitrust Division of Department of Justice, 637
Arbitrage, 473–78, 529–30, 614, 616
  defined, 116, 473
  market imperfections and incentive issues and, 475–78
  reasons for imperfect process of, 475–78
  total-value principle and, 473–75
Arbitrage pricing theory (APT), 111, 116–18
Arrearage, 554
Asia, asset securitization in, 550
Asquith, Paul, 512*n*, 538*n*
Asset(s). *See also* Valuation of long-term securities
  acquisition by purchase of, 638
  book value of, 70
  current, 211–19
    combining liability structure and decisions about, 219–20
    financing, 214–19
    optimal amount of, 211–13
  debt-to-total assets ratio, 137–38, 154
  financial, 23–24, 26
  fixed, 127, 128, 174–75
  forecasting, 189–90, 191
  real, 23
  return on. *See* Return on investment (ROI)
  sale or disposal of depreciable, 320–21
  total assets-to-sales ratio, 193, 195–96
  total asset turnover ratio, 145–46, 155
Asset-backed securities (ABS), 550
Asset-based financing
  leveraged buyouts, 548, 648–50
  secured loans, 300–305
Asset expansion, after-tax incremental cash flows for, 323–24. *See also* Capital budgeting
Asset management decision, 3
Asset replacement, after-tax incremental cash flows for, 324–26

Asset securitization, 549–50
Assigned (stated) value, 557
Associates First Capital, 646
Astor, John Jacob, 43
Asymmetric (unequal) information, 482, 539, 626
Asymptotes, 440n
AT&T, 79n
Attitudes toward risk, 98–99
Audits, post-completion, 349
Authorized shares of common stock, 556
Automated clearinghouse (ACH) electronic transfer, 231
Availability float, 228, 229
Average collection period, 140, 145, 155, 183, 254, 255, 261
Average payable period, 141
Average tax rate, 171

Bacon, Francis, 225
Bad-debt losses, 254, 259, 260, 261
Bagwell, Laurie Simon, 512n
Balance
    cash, 185–86, 187, 237–38
    compensating, 230, 238, 299
Balance sheet, 126, 127–28
    capital lease on, 587–88
    common-size, 150, 151
    deferred taxes on, 156–57
    footnotes to, 588
    forecast, 170, 189–91
    of foreign subsidiary, 674, 675
    indexed, 152, 153
    information on, 127–28
    sources and uses of funds based on, 171–73
Balance sheet ratios, 133, 134–38
    financial leverage (debt) ratios, 136–38, 154, 193–94
    liquidity ratios, 134–36, 154
Balloon payment, 551, 572
Bankers
    investment, 27, 524–27, 633, 647, 649
    mortgage, 27
Bankers' acceptances (BAs), 242, 245, 294–95, 688
Bankruptcy
    costs of, 413, 475–76, 480–81
    insolvency in, 651
    lease financing and, 580
    liquidation and, 642
    prepackaged, 655
Bankruptcy law, 652–55
Bankruptcy Reform Act of 1978, 653, 655
Banks and banking
    commercial, 26, 295–97, 679
    compensating balance requirements of, 230, 238, 299
    concentration banking, 230–31
    cost of borrowing from, 297–99
    credit check through, 263

letter of credit issued by, 294, 690
    merchant, 679
    mutual savings, 26
    operations centers, 231
    outsourced operations management by, 236–37
"Bank-supported" commercial paper, 294
Bartering, 691
Barwise, Patrick, 345
Basic earnings per share, 599
Bearer bond, 71n
Before-tax cost of debt plus risk premium approach to cost of equity, 401–2
Benchmarking, 133
Benefit-cost ratio (profitability index), 340, 341–44
Best efforts offering, 526
Beta, 105–6, 107, 108, 110, 111, 400, 409, 410
    adjusting, for financial leverage, 413, 419–20
    of proxy companies, 411, 413
Bierce, Ambrose, 13
Billing, earlier, 228–29
Bill of exchange, 688–89
Bill of lading, 689
Black, Fischer, 614–15, 616
Black-Scholes option model, 614–15, 616
"Blanket" pledge of receivables, 301–2
Blue-sky laws, 533
Board of directors, 553, 554, 558–60, 637, 641
Bond(s), 546–53
    bearer, 71n
    behavior of prices of, 82–83
    convertible, 598–605
    coupon, zero and non-zero, 72–74, 85
    currency-option, 680–81
    defined, 71
    exchangeable, 605–6
    features of, 71, 546–47
    international bond financing, 680
    long-term, types of, 547–50
    maturity, 71, 72–74, 546
    multiple-currency, 680–81
    perpetual, 71–72
    registered, 71n
    retirement of, 551–53
    Treasury, 241
    valuation of, 71–74, 85
    yield to maturity on, 80–84
Bond discount, 82
Bond-equivalent yield, 83
Bond issue, refunding a, 562–64
Bond premium, 82
Bond ratings, 547
Bond rating services, 138
Book value, 70, 557
Book value weights, 403
"Bootstrapping" earnings per share, 631–32

Borrowing. See also Financing; Short-term financing
    ability, dividend policy and, 499
    costs of, 297–99, 481
Brand name recognition, outsourcing and, 643
Break-even analysis, 435–38
    EBIT-EPS, 442–47
Break-even chart, 435–36
Break-even point, 439–40, 445n
Break-even (quantity) point, 436–37, 438
Break-even (sales) point, 437, 438
Briggs & Stratton Corporation, 408
Brilloff, Abraham, 125
Brokerage fee, 495, 509
Brokers, financial, 27
Bryan, John, 643
Budget, cash, 170, 181, 186, 226, 454
Budget ceiling, capital rationing and, 347–49
Budgeting, capital. See Capital budgeting
Business environment, 14–16
Business process outsourcing (BPO), 237
Business risk, 131, 441, 449, 450, 451
    premium for, 476
Buyout
    leveraged, 548, 648–50
    management (MBO), 648

Call feature, 31, 398n
    on preferred stock, 75n, 398n, 552–53
Call option, 610–16. See also Warrants
Call premium, 562
Call price, 75n, 551, 552, 599, 600–601
Call provision
    on bonds, 552–53
    for preferred stock, 398n, 554–55
Campbell Soup Company, 4
Capital
    additional paid-in, 127, 557
    cost of. See Cost of capital
    defined, 498
    suppliers of, negotiation with, 131
    venture, 536
Capital-asset pricing model (CAPM), 103–11, 399–401, 408–14
    beta in, 105–6, 107, 108
    challenges to, 110–11
    characteristic line on, 104, 105, 106, 400, 409, 410
    cost of equity capital in, 399–401
    as foundation for judging valuation implications of project, 417–18
    group-specific required returns and, 411–12
    project selection and, 409–11
    required return, 106–8
    returns and stock prices in, 108–10
    security market line, 107, 400, 402, 409–10
Capital budgeting, 315–91

acquisitions and, 635–37
defined, 316
estimating project after-tax incremental operating cash flows, 317–26
  asset expansion example, 323–24
  asset replacement example, 324–26
  calculating incremental cash flows, 321–26
  cash flow checklist, 317–18, 319
  tax considerations, 318–21
generating investment project proposals, 316–17
international, 668–69
investment project evaluation and selection, alternative methods of, 334–40
managerial options in, 378–83
  option to abandon, 378, 379–83
  option to expand (or contract), 378, 379
  option to postpone, 379, 383
  valuation implications, 378–79
monitoring with progress reviews and post-completion audits, 348, 349
potential difficulties in, 340–49
  capital rationing, 347–49
  dependency and mutual exclusion, 340, 353–54
  multiple internal rates of return, 345–46, 350–52
  ranking problems, 341–45
process, overview of, 316
refunding as form of, 562
risk and, 361–91
  contribution to total firm risk, 373–78
  project risk, problem of, 362–66
  total project risk, 366–73, 414–18
Capital expenditures
  forecasting, 184, 185
  limitation in loan agreement, 575
Capital gains and losses, 22, 494–95, 638
Capital gains tax, 23, 494–95
Capital gains yield, 84
Capital impairment rule, 498
Capitalization of prospective earnings, 653–54
Capitalization rate. *See* Discount rate (capitalization rate)
Capitalized expenditures, 320
Capital leases, 587–88
Capital market, 24, 523–44
  defined, 524
  initial financing in, 536–37
  primary market, 24, 524
  private placement in, 524, 534–36, 606
  privileged subscription, 527–31
  public issue, 524–27
  regulation of security offerings in, 531–34, 558–59
  secondary market, 24, 25, 27–28, 524, 533, 539

signaling effects in, 538–39
Capital rationing, 347–49
Capital structure determination, 467–89
  conceptual look at, 468–72
  defining capital structure, 468
  financial signaling, 482, 496, 507, 511–12
  net operating income approach, 469–71
  optimal capital structure, 471–72
  presence of market imperfections and incentive issues, 475–78, 480–82
  reorganization plan and, 654
  taxes, effect of, 478–82
    and market imperfections combined, 480–82
  total-value principle and, 472–75, 493–94
  traditional approach, 471–72
Capital structure ratios, comparison of, 455
Capital turnover ratio, 145–46, 155
Carroll, Lewis, 491
Carryback and carryforward, 22, 626–27
Carrying costs per unit, 270–71
Case v. Los Angeles Lumber Products Company, 655
Cash, increase in, as use of funds, 172
Cash balance, 185–86, 187, 237–38
Cash before delivery (CBD), 289
Cash budget, 170, 181, 186, 226, 454
Cash concentration, 230
Cash cycle, 143–44
Cash disbursements, forecasting, 184–85
Cash discount, 258, 290
  net period with, 289, 290
Cash discount period, 257–58
Cash dividend, 21, 76, 506
  and repurchase of common stock restriction in loan agreement, 575
Cash equivalents, 127
Cash flow(s). *See also* Internal rate of return (IRR); Net present value (NPV); Profitability index (PI)
  in acquisition, 635–37
  discounted, 334
  diversification and, 374
  estimating project after-tax incremental operating, 317–26
  financing, 317
  free, 477, 635–36
  international capital budgeting and, 668–69
  in leasing vs. borrowing, 582–85
  net, 185–86
  pattern of
    leveraged leasing and, 579
    mixed (uneven), 54–56
    ranking problems due to differences in, 342–43
  probability tree approach to, 367–70
  project risk and possible, 362–67

security issue and expectations of future, 538
Cash-flow ability to service debt, 451–55
Cash flow analysis, 170, 177–88
  forecasting cash flow, 181–86
  range of cash-flow estimates, 186–88
  statement of cash flows, 170, 177–81
Cash insolvency, 447, 454–55
Cash management, 226–38. *See also* Marketable securities management
  cash balances to maintain, 185–86, 187, 237–38
  electronic data interchange (EDI) and, 234–35
  estimating cash receipts, 183–84
  exchange-rate risk exposure and, 678–79
  motives for holding cash, 226–27
  outsourcing and, 235–37
  slowing down cash payouts, 232–34
  speeding up cash receipts, 227–31
  system of, 226–27
Certainty equivalent (CE), 99
Certificates of deposit (CDs), 243–44, 245
Cetus Corporation, 605
Chambers, Donald R., 422n, 507n
Chapter 11 of bankruptcy law, 653–55
Charest, Guy, 507n
Charter rules, 641
Chattel mortgage, 303, 577
Chebyshev's inequality, 373n
Chemical Corporation, 605
Chief executive officer (CEO), 6
  incentives for, 6
Chief financial officer (CFO), 6
Claims, creditor, 547–48, 652, 654–55
Clayton Act, 637
Clean draft, 688n
"Cleanup" provision, 296
Clearing House Interbank Payments System (CHIPS), 235
Closing the deal, 637–40
Coca-Cola Company, 4, 338, 471, 685
COD (cash on delivery), 289
Coefficient of variation (CV), 97–98, 365–66
  of earnings before interest and taxes (EBIT), 449–50
  of earnings per share, 449–50
Collateral, 300–305
  asset securitization and, 550
Collect basis, interest paid on, 298
Collection agency, 261
Collection float, 228
Collections
  average collection period, 140, 145, 155, 183, 254, 255, 261
  estimating, 183–84
  policy and procedures for, 259–62
  speeding up, 227–30, 258

Combinations of risky investments, 376–78

Combined leverage. *See* Total (combined) leverage

Comment, Robert, 512*n*

Comment letter, 531

Commercial banks, 26, 295–97, 679

Commercial paper, 243, 245, 293–94

Commitment fee, 296, 299, 572

Common shareholders, rights of, 558–60

Common-size analysis, 150–52

Common stock, 3
  acquisition by purchase of, 638
  on balance sheet, 127
  convertible securities as deferred, 599–600
  dilution of, 493, 599–600
  dual-class, 560–61
  exercise of warrants and increase in, 607
  features of, 556–58
  one-period return on, 94
  stock dividends and stock splits, 503–8
  stock repurchase, 508–12
  strategic acquisitions involving, 628–35
  valuation of, 75–80, 85
  yield on, 84

Compensating balances, 230, 238, 299

Compensation programs, incentive, 5, 6

Competition, restraint of, 637

Competitive advantage, 394–95

Competitive bid, 526

Composition, 651

Compound growth, 42–43

Compound interest, 39–59
  annuities, 46–53
  compounding more than once a year, 56–59, 74, 83
  defined, 40
  formulas, summary table of, 60
  mixed flows, 54–56
  single amounts, 40–46

Compound value. *See* Future value

Computerized billing, 229

Computer spreadsheet program, 26–27, 186

Concentration banking, 230–31

Conditional probabilities, 368, 380, 381, 382

Conditional sales contract, 577

Confirmed letter of credit, 690

Conglomerate merger, 625

Conservation of value, 493–94

Conservative financing, 217

Consol, British (consolidated annuities), 71

Consolidation, closing the deal for, 637–40. *See also* Corporate restructuring

Constant growth dividend discount model, 77–78

Consumer credit, 266–67

Contingencies, range of cash-flow estimates for, 186

Contingent (dependent) project, 340

Continuous compounding, 57–58

Continuous form of credit, accounts payable as, 292

Continuous probability distribution of returns, 96–97

Contract
  bill of lading as, 689
  debt, restrictions in, 500
  forward, 681–82
  futures, 682–83

Contraction, managerial option for, 378, 379

Contribution margin per unit, 255

Control
  of disbursements, 232–33
  dividend policy and, 500

Controllable cash segment of marketable securities portfolio, 239, 245

Controlled disbursement, 234

Controller, 6, 7

Conventional project, 339

Conversion price, 598, 601

Conversion privilege, 30–31

Conversion ratio, 598

Conversion value, 598–99, 600, 601

Convertible securities, 403*n*, 555, 598–605, 642
  debt-plus-option characteristic, 601–2
  defined, 598
  features of, 598–99
  forcing or stimulating conversion, 600–601
  use of, 599–601
  value of, 602–5

Core competencies, 235

Corporate income taxes, 17–22, 478–79

Corporate investors, 555
  dividend relevance for, 495

Corporate restructuring, 623–66
  acquisitions and capital budgeting, 635–37
  closing the deal, 637–40
    alternative accounting treatments, 638–40
    by purchase of assets or common stock, 638
    taxable or tax-free transaction, 626–27, 638
  defensive tactics, 640–41
  divestiture, 625, 626, 644–46
  leveraged buyouts, 548, 648–50
  merger terms, impact of, 628–32
    on earnings, 628–30
    on market value, 630–32
  ownership restructuring, 646–48
  remedies for failing company, 651–55
  sources of value for, 624–28

strategic alliances, 643–44
tender offers, 640

Corporations, 15–16. *See also* Multinational company
  S corporation, 16*n*, 23
  virtual, 643–44

Correlation between investment projects, 376

Correlation coefficient, 115, 374, 376

Cost(s). *See also* Interest rate
  agency, 476–77, 480–81, 601, 628
  bankruptcy, 413, 475–76, 480–81
  of being publicly held company, 647
  of borrowing, 297–99, 481
  of carrying inventory, 270–71, 275–76
  factoring, 306–7
  flotation, 405–6, 421–22, 423, 495, 527, 530
  insolvency, 413
  marginal, 396, 404–5
  operating, 434–35
  opportunity, 237, 255, 275, 276, 278, 290, 318
  ordering, 270
  of relaxing credit standards, 255–56
  of running out of stock, 275
  sunk, 318
  of trade credit, 292–93
  transaction, 477–78, 495–96, 647

Cost of capital, 395–408. *See also* Capital structure determination
  debt, 395, 396–97
  equity capital, 395, 398–402
  preferred stock, 395, 397–98
  with taxes and market imperfections combined, 480–82
  weighted-average, 403–7, 420, 469
    adjusted present value method vs., 422–23

Cost of goods sold, 128–29, 188
  in inventory turnover ratio, 141–42

Cost recovery period, 19

Countertrade, 690–91

Coupon bonds, 72–74, 85

Coupon effect, 82

Coupon rate, 71, 546

Covariance, 100, 114, 115, 116
  portfolio risk and importance of, 100–101

Covenants, protective, 546, 574–76

Coverage ratios, 138–39, 154, 452–54

Cram down, 653

Creation of value, 3–5, 8, 394–95

Credit. *See also* Short-term financing
  consumer, 266–67
  letter of, 294, 690
  line of, 218*n*, 220, 267, 295–96, 297
  money-market, 293–95
  open-account, 288, 289–93, 688
  revolving credit agreement, 220, 296, 573

trade, 176, 214*n*, 266, 288–93
Credit applicant, analyzing, 262–67
  credit analysis, 265–67
  credit decision and line of credit, 267,
    295–96
  sources of information, 262–65
Credit department, company, 264–65
Creditors
  claims of, 547–48, 652, 654–55
  financial analysis by, 126
  reorganization and, 653
Credit period, 256–57
Credit policies, 254–59
Credit ratings, 29, 30, 138, 263, 264, 291,
  456–57, 547
Credit reports, 263
Credit-scoring systems, 266–67
Credit standards, 254–56, 259, 261
Credit terms, 256–59
Credit unions, 26
Creditworthiness
  asset securitization and, 550
  event risk and, 535
  interest rate and, 297–98
CS First Boston, 77, 574
CSX Corporation, 4
Cumulative dividends feature, 553–54
Cumulative obligation of income bond,
  548
Cumulative voting system, 559–60
Currencies
  hard, 691
  translation of foreign, 673–76
Currency cocktail bonds, 681
Currency futures, 682–83
Currency market hedges, 681–84
Currency-option bonds, 680–81
Currency options, 684
Currency risk. *See* Exchange-rate risk
  exposure
Currency swaps, 684
Current assets, 211–19
  combining liability structure and deci-
    sions about, 219–20
  financing, 214–19
  optimal amount (level) of, 211–13
Current ratio, 132, 135–36, 145, 154

Dann, Larry Y., 511*n*
Dartmouth College decision, 15
Data interchange, electronic (EDI), 234–35
Date
  dividend declaration, 512–13
  ex-dividend, 512
  expiration, value of call option on and
    before, 610–13
  ex-rights, 528
  record, 512
Dating, seasonal, 258–59, 289, 291–92
Deal, closing the, 637–40
Dealer market for commercial paper, 294

DeAngelis, Antonio "Tino," 305
DeAngelo, Harry, 647*n*
DeAngelo, Linda, 647*n*
Debentures, 547–48
Debit, preauthorized, 229
Debt. *See also* Leverage; Loan(s)
  ascribing debt funds to groups, 413–14
  business risk and, 131
  cash-flow ability to service, 451–55
  cost of, 395, 396–97
  incentive to manage efficiently and, 477
  junior subordinated, 649–50
  lease financing vs., 581–86
  leveraged buyouts, 548, 648–50
  private placement of issues of, 534–36
  senior, 649–50
  straight debt instruments, 598
  term, 572–77
Debt capacity, 452
Debt contracts, restrictions in, 500
Debt flotation costs, 405*n*
Debt-plus-option characteristic of con-
  vertible security, 601–2
Debt-service burden, 452, 453
Debt-service coverage ratio, 452–53
Debt-to-equity ratio, 136–37, 154, 193–94,
  196
Debt-to-net worth ratios, 455
Debt-to-total assets ratio, 137–38, 154
Decisions
  credit, 267
  major financial, 2–3
Decision trees, 379, 380
Declaration date, dividend, 512–13
Declining-balance depreciation, 19–20
Default, 554, 574
Default risk, 28–29, 259
"Defensive" investment, 105
Defensive tactics against takeovers,
  640–41
Deferred call periods, 552
Deferred taxes, 156–57
Degree of financial leverage (DFL),
  447–50
Degree of operating leverage (DOL),
  438–41
Degree of total leverage (DTL), 450–51
Dell Computers, 236
Department of Justice, 637
Dependent (contingent) project, 340
Deposit float, 228
Deposit institutions, 26
Depository transfer check (DTC), 230–31
Depreciable asset, sale or disposal of,
  320–21
Depreciable basis, 320
Depreciation, 18–20
  accelerated, 18, 319–20, 580
  declining-balance, 19–20
  deferred taxes and, 156, 157
  equipment financing based on, 577

estimating capital project operating
  cash flows and, 318–20
  in flow of funds statement, 174–75
  on income statement, 130
  modified accelerated cost recovery, 19,
    20–21, 319–20, 582
  recapture of, 320, 584
  straight-line, 18, 19
Derivative securities, 598. *See also*
  Option(s)
Differential from prime, 298
Dilution, 493, 599–600, 607
Direct leasing, 578–79
Direct method of cash flow statement
  presentation, 177–80
Directors, board of, 553, 554, 558–60, 637,
  641
Direct-placement market for commercial
  paper, 294
Direct (primary) securities, 25
Direct (private) placement, 524, 534–36
Disbursement float, maximizing, 234
Disbursements, 232–34. *See also* Cash
  management
  outsourcing, 236–37
Disclosure, lease, 587–89
Discount
  bond, 82
  cash, 258
    net period with, 289, 290
  forward, 681
  quantity, 289
  trade, 289–90
Discount basis, interest paid on, 298
Discounted cash flow (DCF), 334. *See also*
  Internal rate of return (IRR); Net
  present value (NPV); Profitability
  index (PI)
Discount rate (capitalization rate),
  43–44, 469–70. *See also* Required
  return
  adjustment to discount rate procedure,
    405–6
  bond valuation and, 71–74
  Fisher's rate of intersection, 342
  on free cash flows, 636
  interpolation, 81, 336–37
  lease-versus-borrow analyses and,
    582–83
  nominal, 59
  for recording value of capital lease, 587
  refunding a bond issue, 563–64
  risk-adjusted, 414–15
Discrete (non-continuous) probability
  distribution, 96
Disinvestment, 2
Distribution at liquidation, 652–53
Diversification, 101–3, 374, 401*n*, 417, 606,
  669. *See also* International financial
  management
Divestiture, 625, 626, 644–46

Dividend(s)
  adjusting intracompany, 679
  cash, 21, 76, 506
    leveraged recapitalization through
      one-time, 641
  common shareholders' rights concern-
    ing, 558
  common stock valuation by, 76–80
  cost of preferred stock and, 397–98
  cumulative dividends feature, 553–54
  declaration date, 512
  disbursements, 233
  estimating future, 185, 399
  extra, 503
  in flow of funds statement, 174
  growth phases, 79–80, 399
  "homemade," 494
  payment date, 512
  preference for, 494
  preferred stock, 555
  present value of, 79
  record date and entitlement to, 512
  regular, 503
  stimulation of conversion using, 601
  stock, 503–7
  taxes and, 21–22, 23
Dividend discount valuation models,
  77–80, 108–9, 398–99
Dividend-payout ratio, 3, 78, 492, 493,
  495, 501, 502
  stock dividend or stock split and, 506
  target, 503
Dividend policy, 491–522
  administrative considerations in,
    512–13
  dividend relevance vs. irrelevance,
    arguments for, 493–96
  dividend stability and, 500–503
  earnings per share and, 4
  empirical testing of, 496–97
  factors influencing, 497–500
  passive vs. active, 492–97
  repurchasing as part of, 510
  stock dividends, 503–7
  stock repurchase, 508–12
  stock splits, 505–8
Dividend reinvestment plans (DRIPs),
  513
Dividend yield, 84, 494–95
Divisibility of securities, 495–96
Documentary draft, 688n
Domestic CDs, 244
Double-declining-balance (DDB) method,
  19–20
Double taxation, 16, 18, 23
"Downside" risk, 97
Draft, 288–89, 294–95
  international-trade, 688–89
Drawee, 688
Drexel Burnham Lambert, 548
Dual-class common stock, 560–61

Dual-currency bonds, 681
Duff & Phelps, 294
Dun & Bradstreet (D&B), 132, 263, 264,
  265, 267, 291
DuPont Company approach
  to ratio analysis, 147–48
  to return on equity, 148–49
Dutch-auction self-tender offer, 509, 512

E. F. Hutton, 234
Earning power, 147
Earning retention rate, 193–94
Earnings, merger terms and, 628–30
Earnings before interest and taxes (EBIT;
  operating profit), 138, 434, 435
  at break-even point, 436–37
  coefficient of variation of, 449–50
  debt service burden and, 452, 453
  degree of financial leverage and,
    447–50
  degree of operating leverage and,
    438–39
  EBIT-EPS break-even analysis, 442–47
  net operating income approach and,
    469–71
Earnings multiplier approach, dividend
  valuation based on, 78
Earnings per share (EPS), 3–4. See also
  Retained earnings
  basic, 599
  "bootstrapping," 631–32
  calculation of, 442–43
  coefficient of variation of, 449–50
  degree of financial leverage and,
    447–50
  degree of total leverage and, 450–51
  dilution of, 599–600, 607
  EBIT-EPS break-even analysis of,
    442–47
  mergers and acquisitions and, 628–30,
    636–37
  stock dividends and, 504
  after stock repurchase, 510
EBIT. See Earnings before interest and
  taxes (EBIT; operating profit)
EBIT-EPS break-even analysis, 442–47
EBIT-EPS chart, 443–45
Economic exposure, 672, 673, 676–77
Economic order quantity (EOQ), 269–72
  in JIT world, 276
  order point and, 273, 274–75
Economic profit, 408
Economic value added (EVA), 408
Economies
  operating, 624–25
  of scale, 581, 625
Economy
  allocation of funds in, 28–32
  contribution of financial manager to, 2
  flow of funds in, 24–27
  industry sales and predictions of, 182

Effective annual interest rate (APR),
  58–59, 84
Effective periodic interest rate, 58
Efficiency, debt as incentive for, 477
Efficiency (activity) ratios, 139–46, 155
Efficiency gains, 625
Efficient financial markets, 112–13
Electronic commerce (EC), 234–35
Electronic data interchange (EDI), 234–35
Electronic funds transfer (EFT), 235
"Envelope curve," economies of scale on,
  625
Environment, 2
  business, 14–16
  financial, 23–32
  tax, 17–23
EOQ. See Economic order quantity (EOQ)
Equifax, 4
Equilibrium, market, arbitrage pricing
  theory and, 118
Equilibrium price of stock, 109
Equilibrium value of option, determin-
  ing, 614–15
Equipment financing, 576–77
Equipment trust certificates, 549
Equitable (technical) insolvency, 651
Equity. See also Shareholders' equity
  convertible securities as part of, 599
  debt-to-equity ratio, 136–37, 154,
    193–94, 196
  return on, 148–49, 155
  straight, 598
Equity capital, cost of, 395, 398–402
Equity carve-outs, 645–46
Equity financing, business risk and, 131
Equity flotation costs, 405n
Equity multiplier, 149
Euro, 682
Eurobond market, 680
Euro-commercial paper (Euro CP), 243
Eurocurrency, 680
Eurodollar certificates of deposit (Euro
  CDs), 244
Eurodollar financing, 680
Eurodollars, 244, 245
Eurodollar time deposits (Euro TDs),
  244
Euro medium-term notes (Euro MTNs),
  574
European Monetary Union (EMU), 682
Event risk, 535
Excess return, 394–95
Exchange, bill of, 688–89
Exchangeable bonds, 605–6
Exchange premium, 605
Exchange price, 605
Exchange rate, 668, 671, 685–88
  forward, 672
  spot, 672, 681–82
Exchange-rate risk exposure, 672–88
  management of, 677–88

cash management and adjusting intercompany accounts, 678–79
currency market hedges, 681–84
international financing hedges, 679–81
macro factors governing exchange-rate behavior and, 685–88
natural hedges, 677–78, 684
types of, 672–77
Exchange ratio, 605
in merger, 628–35
Exchanges, organized, 27, 539
Ex-dividend date, 512
Exercise of warrants, 607
Exercise price, 606, 607, 609
Expansion, managerial option for, 378, 379
Expected cash flows, deviations from, 186
Expected return, 28–29, 95, 96, 99–100. See also Required return
of portfolio, 99–100
Expected value, 363–66, 374–76
Expenditures
capital, 184, 185, 575
capitalized, 320
Expenses
accrued, 293
interest, 21
operating, 184
Expiration date, value of call option on and before, 610–13
Export factoring, 306, 691
Export-Import Bank of the United States (Eximbank), 672
Exports, price elasticity of imports and, 685. See also International financial management
Expropriation, 671, 672
Ex-rights date, 528
Extension, 651
External sales forecast, 182
Extra dividend, 503
Ezzell, John R., 406n, 422n

Face value, bond, 71, 546
Factor, 691
Factor analysis, 117
Factoring
accounts receivable, 305–7
export, 306, 691
Failing company, remedies for, 651–55
Fair market value, 578
Fair merger price provision, 641
Fama, Eugene, 111, 112, 507n
FASB No. 13, 587, 588
FASB No. 52, 673, 676
Federal agency securities, 242
Federal Farm Credit Banks (FFCBs), 242
Federal Financing Bank, 242
Federal Home Loan Mortgage Corporation (FHLMC, Freddie Mac), 242

Federal Housing Administration, 242
Federal National Mortgage Association (FNMA, Fannie Mae), 242
Federal regulation of securities, 531–33, 558–59
Federal Reserve System, 228
Federal Reserve Wire System (Fedwire), 231
Federal Trade Commission, 132, 637
Fees. See also Cost(s)
for bank services, compensating balances vs., 238
brokerage, 495, 509
commitment, 296, 299, 572
Field warehouse receipt, 304–5
Finance companies, 27, 294, 303
Financial Accounting Standards Board (FASB), 177
defined, 673
proposed accounting changes, 639
Statement No. 13 of, 587, 588
Statement No. 52 of, 673, 676
Financial acquisition, 628
Financial assets, 23, 26
Financial brokers, 27
Financial EDI (FEDI), 235
Financial environment, 23–32
Financial failure, 651
Financial flexibility, 499
Financial institutions, 25–27
Financial intermediaries, 25–27, 534, 680
Financial intermediation, defined, 25–26
Financial lease, 578
Financial leverage, 434, 441–50
cash-flow ability to service debt and, 451–55
degree of (DFL), 447–50
EBIT-EPS break-even or indifference analysis, 442–47
effect on risk, 445–47
"homemade," 477, 481–82, 494
taxes and, 478–82
Financial leverage (debt) ratios, 136–38, 154, 193–94
Financial management
defined, 2–3
goal of firm and, 3–6
organization of function of, 6–7
reasons for understanding, 9
Financial manager, 2, 254, 276–78, 441
Financial markets, 23–25. See also Capital market
efficient, 112–13
Financial operations, funds statement analysis for evaluation of, 176
Financial planning
cash-flow estimates, range of, 186–88
cash-flow forecasting, 181–86
forecast financial statements, 170, 188–92
Financial ratios. See Ratios

Financial risk, 448–50, 454
Financial-risk premium, 476
Financial signaling, 482, 496, 497, 507, 511–12
of stock issue, 538–39
Financial statement analysis, 125–67. See also Cash flow analysis; Financial planning; Ratios; Funds analysis
common-size and index analysis, 150–53
credit analysis and, 263, 265
deferred taxes and, 156–57
information for, 127–30
parties using, 126
possible framework for, 130–34
trend analysis, 149–50
Financing. See also Debt; Loan(s)
aggressive, 217–18
asset-based (leveraged buyout), 548, 648–50
cash inflow and outflow for, 177, 178, 181, 182
conservative, 217
current assets, 214–19
equipment, 576–77
Eurodollar, 680
funds statement analysis for evaluation of, 176
hedging approach to, 215–16, 397
initial, 536–37
international bonds, 680
international financing hedges, 679–81
of international trade, 688–91
lease, 549, 577–86
evaluating debt financing vs., 581–86
long-term vs. short-term, 216–19
"mezzanine," 649
short-term. See Short-term financing
spontaneous, 214–15, 288–93
trade credit, 289
Financing cash flows, 317
Financing decision, 3
Financing mix, analyzing. See also Capital structure determination; Financial leverage; Operating leverage
cash-flow ability to service debt, 451–55
combination of methods, 457
other methods of analysis, 455–57
total leverage, 450–51
Finished-goods inventory, 268
Firm
book value of, 70
goal of, 3–6
Firm-portfolio approach, 373–78, 416–17
Firm risk, total, 449–50, 451
contribution of project to, 373–78, 416–17
First-mover advantage, 379, 383
First Tennessee, Wholesale Lockbox service of, 230

Fisher, Irving, 31, 342
Fisher, Lawrence, 507n
Fisher effect, 686
    international, 686–87
Fisher's rate of intersection, 342
Fitch's, 294
Fixed assets, 127, 128, 174–75
Fixed operating costs, 434, 435. *See also*
        Operating leverage
Fixed-price self-tender offer, 509
Flexibility, 307–8, 499
    managerial options in capital budget-
        ing, 378–83
    of term loan, 572–73
Float
    collection, 228
    disbursement, maximizing, 234
    electronic funds transfer and, 235
    net, 232
    "playing the," 232
Floating lien, 303
Floating-rate notes (FRNs), 680
Floor planning, 303
Floor value of convertible security, 604
Flotation costs, 405–6, 421–22, 423, 495,
        527, 530
Flow of funds in economy, 24–27
Flow of funds statement, 170–76
Footnotes to balance sheet, 588
Ford Motor Company, 561, 646
Ford Motor Credit Company, 243
Forecast financial statements, 170, 188–92
    balance sheet, 170, 189–91
    income statement, 170, 188–89
    use of ratios and implication of, 191–92
Forecasting cash flow, 181–86
Foreclosure, 549
Foreign bonds, 680
Foreign currency, translation of, 673–76
Foreign exchange market (FX market),
        671
Foreign governments, taxation by, 670–71
Foreign investment. *See* International
        financial management
Foreign tax credit, 670
Foreign trade, financing, 688–91
Forfaiting, 691
Form 13D, 533, 642
Forward contract, 681–82
    futures contract vs., 682–83
Forward discount, 681
Forward-exchange market, 681–82
Forward exchange rate, 672
Forward premium, 681
Franklin, Benjamin, 287, 545
Fraud, warehouse receipt, 305
Free cash flow, 477, 635–36
Free cash segment of marketable securi-
        ties portfolio, 239–40, 245–46
"Free-rider" problem, 640
Freeze-out provision, 641

French, Kenneth, 111
Full-service (maintenance) lease, 578
Funds
    allocation of, in economy, 28–32
    alternative definitions of, 171
    dividend policy and firm's need for,
        499
    provided by operations, 174
    transfer of, 230–31
        electronic, 235
Funds analysis, 170–71
Funds requirements, 130, 131
Futures contract, 682–83
Future value
    of annuity, 47–49
    with compound interest, 40–42, 46
        continuous compounding, 57
        semiannual compounding, 56–57, 74,
            83–84
    effective annual interest rate and, 59
    with simple interest, 39
Future value interest factor (FVIF), 41–42,
        44, 46
    of annuity (FVIFA), 47–49, 706–7
Future Value Interest Factor Tables, 41,
        702–3
Future value of annuity due (FVAD),
        51–52

Gahlon, James, 440n
Gardner, David and Tom, 18
General Electric Capital Corporation, 243
General Motors Acceptance Corporation
        (GMAC), 243, 294
General partner, defined, 15
General partnership, 15
Georgia-Pacific Corporation, 4, 348, 511
Gillespie, W., 507n
Globalization of business activity. *See*
        International financial manage-
        ment
Global securities offering, 527
Glossary, 711–23
Goal of firm, 3–6
Going-concern value, 70
Going private, 647–48
Goizueta, Roberto, 1
"Golden parachute," 642
Goldman Sachs, 401, 574
Goodwill, 638, 640
Gordon, Myron J., 77n
Gordon Dividend Valuation Model, 77n
Government National Mortgage Associa-
        tion (GNMA, Ginnie Mae), 242
Government regulation, 531–34, 558–59
Government-sponsored enterprises
        (GSEs), 242
Great Salad Oil Swindle, 305
"Greenmail," 642, 643
Grinblatt, Mark S., 507n
Gross profit margin, 146

Gross working capital, 210
Group-specific required returns, 411–12
Growth
    compound, 42–43
    sustainable growth modeling, 170,
        193–96
Growth phases, dividend, 79–80, 399

Half-year convention, 20, 319
Hamada, Robert S., 419n
Handicapping, process of, 44
Hard currencies, 691
Harris, Robert S., 422n
Hedge ratio, 615, 616
Hedges, 602, 677–84
    currency market, 681–84
    international financing, 679–81
    natural, 677–78, 684
Hedging approach to financing, 215–16,
        397
    with options, 613–15
Hertz, David, 370
Hillier, Frederick S., 373n
Historical beta, 107
Holding it long, 613
Holiday Corporation, 498
Horizontal merger, 625
Hubris hypothesis, 627, 633
Hurdle rate (acceptance criterion), 337,
        394, 395, 407
    with internal rate of return method, 337
    with net present value method, 338
    with payback period method, 335
    with profitability index method, 340

IBM, 578
Icahn, Carl, 624
Imperfections, market, 475–78, 480–82
    effect of taxes combined with, 480–82
Imports, price elasticity of exports and,
        685. *See also* International financial
        management
Incentives for management, 5, 6, 477, 645,
        647
Income
    alternative minimum taxable, 18
    common shareholders' right to, 558
    dividend stability and desired current,
        502
    net operating income approach, 469–71
Income bonds, 548
Income statement, 126, 128–30
    common-size, 150–52
    deferred taxes on, 156
    forecast, 170, 188–89
    foreign subsidiary, 675–76
    indexed, 152, 153
    information on, 128–30
Income statement and income state-
        ment/balance sheet ratios, 133,
        138–49

activity ratios, 139–46, 155
coverage ratios, 138–39, 154, 452–54
profitability ratios, 146–49, 155
Income taxes
corporate, 17–22, 478–79
personal, 22–23
on securities, 30
Incorporation, state of, 641
Incremental operating cash flows, estimating, 317–26
Indenture, 546
Independent project, 340
Index. *See* Financial ratios
Index analysis, 150, 152–53
Indifference analysis, 442–47
Indifference curves, 416–17
Indifference points, EBIT-EPS, 442–47
Indirect method of cash flow statement presentation, 177–80
Indirect (secondary) securities, 25
Industry attractiveness, 394
Industry ratios, external comparisons and sources of, 132–33
Industry roll-ups, 634
Industry sales, economic predictions and, 182
Inflation, 31, 318
Information
asymmetric (unequal), 482, 539, 626
from corporate restructuring, 626
on credit applicant, sources of, 262–65
declaration of stock dividend or stock split as, 507
for financial statement analysis, 127–30
from stable dividends, 501–2
Initial cash outflow, 321, 323, 325
Initial financing, 536–37
Initial probability, 368
Initial public offerings (IPO), 536–37
roll-ups and, 634–35
Insolvency, 413, 447, 454–55, 498, 651
Insolvency rule, 498
Institutional investors, 535
dividend relevance for, 495
restrictions on investment behavior, 477, 496, 502
Institutions, financial, 25–27
Insurance, political risk, 672
Insurance companies, 26
Insurance company term loans, 573
Intercompany accounts, adjusting, 678–79
Interest
compound, 39–59
annuities, 46–53
compounding more than once a year, 56–59, 74, 83–84
defined, 40
mixed flows, 54–56
single amounts, 40–46
defined, 38
income taxes on, 21, 23

simple, 39
Interest costs of exchangeable bonds, 605–6
Interest coverage ratio (times interest earned), 138, 154, 452
Interest expense, 21
"Interest method," 588
Interest payments, lease vs. borrow analyses and, 585
Interest rate, 24, 38
allocation of funds and, 28–32
on commercial paper, 294
on convertible securities, 600, 603
decline of, refunding bond issue and, 562–64
effective annual, 58–59, 84
leveraged buyout risk and, 649
market imperfections and, 481
methods of computing, 298–99
nominal (stated), 56, 297
opportunity cost of cash balances and, 237
option valuation and, 611
for short-term vs. long-term financing, 216, 297–98
on term loan, 572
term structure of, 30
Interest-rate parity, 682, 686–88
Interest rate (yield) risk, 82, 240–41
Interest tax shield, 478–79
Interim incremental net cash flows, 321–22, 324, 326
Interim trustee, 652–53
Intermediaries, financial, 25–27, 534, 680
Internal comparisons, financial ratios for, 132
Internal rate of return (IRR), 80–84, 94n, 335–37
multiple, 345–46, 350–52
probability distribution for, 371, 372
ranking investment proposals using, problems with, 341–44
Internal Revenue Code, 23, 498
Internal Revenue Service (IRS), 14, 16, 17–18, 499, 510, 579–80
Internal sales forecast, 182
International bond financing, 680
International financial management, 667–99
capital budgeting, 668–69
exchange-rate risk exposure, 672–88
management of, 677–88
types of, 672–77
political risk and, 671–72
risk factors in, 669
structuring international trade transactions, 688–91
taxation and, 669–71
International financing hedges, 679–81
International Fisher effect, 686–87
International offering, 527

International trade draft, 688–89
Internet
initial public offering on, 537
selling direct on, 236
Interpolation, 81, 336–37
Intrinsic value, 70–71, 80, 108–9, 112
Inventories, 127
Inventory-backed loans, 302–5
Inventory in transit, 268
Inventory management, 267–78
classification of inventory, 268–69
economic order quantity (EOQ), 269–72, 276
financial manager and, 276–78
inventory activities, 141–42
Just-in-Time (JIT), 268, 276, 277
order point, 273, 274–75
safety stock, 273–76
types of inventory, 267–68
Inventory turnover in days (ITD), 142, 144, 145, 155
Inventory turnover (IT) ratio, 141–42, 155, 190
Investigation process in credit analysis, 265–66
Investment
"aggressive," 105
capital. *See* Capital budgeting
cash inflow and outflow for, 177, 178, 181, 182
"defensive," 105
foreign. *See* International financial management
in marketable securities, 238–46
profitability in relation to, 147
pure play, 645
return on, 147–48, 155, 212
Investment analysts, surveying, 455–56
Investment bankers, 27, 524–27, 633, 647, 649
Investment decision, 2
Investment-grade bonds, 547
"Investment grade quality," 29, 456
Investment project proposals. *See also* Capital budgeting
correlation between, 376
estimating "after-tax incremental operating cash flows," 317–26
evaluation and selection of
alternative methods of, 334–40
on basis of total risk, 414–18
capital-asset pricing model and, 409–11
ranking problems, 341–45
generating, 316–17
risk, 361–91
contribution to total firm risk, 373–78, 416–17
problem of, 362–66
total project risk, 366–73
Investment sector, 24, 524

Investors
  asymmetric information and, 539
  corporate, 495, 555
  financial analysis by, 126
  institutional, 477, 495, 496, 502, 535
  taxes on dividends vs. capital gains
    and, 494–95
  value of stock dividends and stock
    splits to, 506–7
Invoice, 227
Involuntary bankruptcy, 652
IPO roll-up, 635
Irrevocable letter of credit, 690
Issued shares, 556

January effect, 111
Jarrell, Gregg A., 512n
Jensen, Michael C., 5, 6, 477, 507n
Joint probability, 368, 369, 380–81, 382
Joint venture, 643, 672
Junior subordinated debt, 649–50
Junk bonds, 548–49
Just-in-Time (JIT) inventory method, 268,
    276, 277

Keynes, John Maynard, 226
Klein, Andrew, 537
Kohlberg, Kravis, and Roberts (KKR), 628
Kothari, Rajesh U., 634

Labor market, managerial, 5
Lading, bill of, 689
Lagging, 678
Large, Jack, 236
Large-percentage stock dividends, 504–5
Laughlin, Eugene J., 143n
Law
  bankruptcy, 652–55
  dividend policy and, 498–99
  government regulation, 531–34, 558–59
Lazere, Monroe R., 305
Leading, 678–79
Lead time, 273, 274, 275, 278
Lease
  defined, 578
  types of, 578
Lease disclosure, 587–89
Lease financing, 403n, 549, 577–86
  accounting treatment of, 579, 587–89
  economic rationale for, 580–81
  evaluating debt financing vs., 581–86
  forms of, 578–79, 587–88
  tax treatment of, 579–80, 583–84, 585–86
Legal insolvency, 651
Lehman Brothers, 574
Lenders, surveying, 455–56
Letter of credit, 294, 690
Letter stock, 536
Leverage. See also Capital structure deter-
    mination; Debt
  adjusting beta for financial, 413, 419–20

in corporate restructuring, 627
defined, 434
degree of total, 450–51
financial, 434, 441–50
  cash-flow ability to service debt and,
    451–55
  degree of (DFL), 447–50
  EBIT-EPS break-even analysis,
    442–47
  taxes and, 478–82
operating, 434–41
required return with, 411
value of warrant and opportunity for,
    608–9
Leveraged buyout (LBO), 548, 628, 648–50
Leveraged leasing, 579
Leveraged recapitalization, 641
Leverage ratios, 136–38, 154, 193–94
Levi Strauss & Company, 647
Liabilities
  assumption of, in acquisition, 636
  on balance sheet, 127
  corporation and, 15
  forecasting, 190–91
  partnerships and, 15
  trade, 288
Liability structure, combining current
    asset decisions and, 219–20
LIBOR, 298, 680
Liens, 303, 549, 577
Life insurance companies, 26
Limited liability companies (LLCs), 16,
    22, 23
Limited liability partnership (LLP), 16
Limited partners, defined, 15
Limited partnerships, 15
Line of credit, 218n, 220, 267, 295–96, 297
Lintner, John, 503
Liquidating value per share, 557
Liquidation, 644, 646
  bankruptcy and, 652
  convertible securities and, 599
  priority of claims in, 652–53
  subordinated debenture holders and,
    547–48
  voluntary, 644, 651
Liquidation value, 70
Liquidity
  activity ratios and, 144, 145
  defined, 136
  dividend policy and, 499
  marketability, 29, 240
  optimal level of current assets and,
    211–12
  for privately placed securities, Rule
    144a and, 535
  profitability and, 213
Liquidity ratios, 134–36, 154
Listing, 558
Littlewood, Simon, 550
Lloyds of London, 672

Lloyds TSB, 8
Loan(s). See also Amortization; Leverage;
    Short-term financing
  for international financing, 679
  secured (asset-based), 300–305
  term, 572–77
  unsecured, 295–97
Loan agreement, 574–76
Lock-box system of collections, 229–30,
    235, 236
Lockup provision, 642
London interbank offered rate (LIBOR),
    298, 680
Long-term debt instruments. See Bond(s)
Long-term debt-to-total capitalization
    ratio, 137
Long-term financing, 216–19
  external. See Capital market
Long-term securities, valuation of. See
    Valuation of long-term securities
Lorie, James H., 351n
Loss(es)
  bad-debt, 254, 259, 260, 261
  opportunity, 373
  in sale of disposal of depreciable asset,
    320

McDonald's, 686
Mailbox rule, 232n
Mail float, 228, 229
Maintenance lease, 578
Majluf, Nicholas S., 539n
Majority-rule voting, 559
Management
  as agents, 5
  corporate restructuring for improved,
    625–26
  financial analysis by, 126
  goals of firm for, 5
  incentives for, 5, 477, 645, 647
  monitoring of managers, 5, 476–77,
    480–81
  personal agenda, corporate restructur-
    ing based on, 627–28
  separation of ownership from, 5
Management buyout (MBO), 648
Management clause in loan agreement,
    576
Managerial entrenchment hypothesis of
    antitakeover defenses, 641, 643
Managerial labor market, 5
Managerial options in capital budgeting,
    378–83
  option to abandon, 378, 379–83
  option to expand (or contract), 378, 379
  option to postpone, 379, 383
  valuation implications, 378–79
Marginal cost, 396, 404–5
Marginal tax rate, 17
Margin of safety, 216, 217–18, 219–20, 300,
    577

Marked-to-market, 682

Market(s). *See also* Capital market
  Eurobond, 680
  financial, 23–25
    efficient, 112–13
  forward-exchange, 681–82
  making a, 526
  over-the-counter (OTC), 27–28, 539, 540, 557–58
  primary, 24, 524
  secondary, 24, 25, 27–28, 524, 533, 539
Marketability, 29, 240. *See also* Liquidity
Marketable securities management, 238–46
  common money-market instruments, 241–45
  key variables in, 240–41
  segments of portfolio, 239–40
  selecting securities for, 245–46
Market efficiency, 112, 113
Market equilibrium, arbitrage pricing theory and, 118
Market Guide, 107
Market imperfections, 475–78, 480–82
  effect of taxes combined with, 480–81
Marketing, finance and, 345
Marketing manager, credit and collection policies and, 254
Market portfolio, 103, 105
Market price, calling of convertible security and, 600–601
Market price per share, 3, 4, 470
Market required rate of return, 80, 82
Market return, 400–401
Market risk premium, 108
Market share, estimating, 182
Market-to-book-value ratios, low, 111
Market value, 70
  fair, 578
  merger terms and, 630–32
  per share, 557–58
Market value line, 614
Market value weights, 403
Marsh, Paul R., 345
Marshall, T., 15
Masulis, Ronald W., 507n
Maturity, 29–30, 241
  bond, 71, 72–74, 546
  yield to (YTM), 80–84, 397
Maturity matching approach. *See* Hedging approach to financing
Meckling, William H., 5, 477
Medium-term notes (MTNs), 574
Mehta, Dileep, 265n
Mencken, H.L., 37
Merchant banking, 679
Mergers
  capital budgeting, acquisitions and, 635–37
  closing the deal for, 637–40
  defined, 625

economies of scale from, 625
empirical evidence on, 632–33
fair merger price provision, 641
impact of terms of, 628–32
  on earnings, 628–30
  on market value, 630–32
information effect of, 626
roll-up transactions, 634–35
supermajority merger approval provision, 641
tax-motivated, 627
types of, 625
wealth transfer in, 626
Merrill Lynch, 77, 401, 574
Metastasio, Pietro, 209
"Mezzanine" financing, 649
Microsoft, 508, 643
Miles, James, 422n
Miller, Merton H., 471, 472–75, 479, 480, 493
Miller, N.C., 305
Minority interest, voting procedures and power of, 559–60
Mixed (uneven) pattern of cash flows, 54–56
Modified Accelerated Cost Recovery System (MACRS), 19, 20–21, 319–20, 582
Modigliani, Franco, 471, 472–75, 479, 480, 481, 493
Money market, 24
Money-market credit, 293–95
Money market instruments, 241–45
Money market mutual funds (MMFs), 246
Money-market preferred stock (MMP), 244–45, 555
Monitoring costs, 476–77, 480–81
Monitoring of capital budgeting, 348, 349
Moody's Investor Service, 29, 30, 138, 294, 456, 547
Morgan, J.P., 523
Mortgage, chattel, 303, 577
Mortgage bankers, 27
Mortgage bonds, 549
MSNBC, 643
Mullins, David W., Jr., 512n, 538n
Multifactor models of pricing, 111, 117–18
Multinational company. *See also* International financial management
  defined, 671
  political risks faced by, 671–72
  reinvoicing center of, 679
  taxation of, 669–71
Multiple-currency bonds, 680–81
Multiple internal rates of return, 345–46, 350–52
Multiplier, equity, 149
Municipals, short-term, 244
Murphy, Kevin J., 6
Mutual funds, money market, 246

Mutual investment funds, 26–27
Mutually exclusive project, 340, 353–54
  ranking problems with, 341–45
Mutual savings banks, 26
Myers, Stewart C., 420, 539n

National Association of Securities Dealers, 533
National Association of Securities Dealers Automated Quotations (NASDAQ), 28, 540, 558
National Distillers, 605
Natural hedges, 677–78, 684
NBC, 643
Negative-pledge clause, 547, 576
Negotiable certificate of deposit (CD), 243–44, 245
Negotiated offerings, 526
Negotiated reorganization settlements, 655
Negotiated short-term financing, 293–305
  money-market credit, 293–95
  secured (asset-based) loans, 300–305
  unsecured loans, 295–97
Net cash flow, 185–86
Net float, 232
Net lease, 578, 581
"Net-of-tax" approach to deferred taxes, 157
Net operating income (NOI) approach, 469–71
Net period, 289
  with cash discount, 289, 290
Net present value (NPV), 337–40, 345
  of each replacement chain, 353–54
  expected value of project portfolio, 374–76
  multiple internal rates of return and, 351–52
  NPV profile, 338–40, 351
  probability distribution of, 368–73, 415–16
  ranking problems using, 341–45
Net profit margin, 146, 147, 155, 193, 194, 196
Netting, 679
Net working capital, 210
Net worth. *See* Shareholders' equity
New-stock dividend reinvestment plan, 513
New York Bond Exchange, 27, 539
New York Stock Exchange, 27, 112, 401, 539, 558
Nike, 644
No growth dividend discount model, 78–79
Nominal discount rate, 59
Nominal (stated) interest rate, 56, 297
Noncash payments in acquisition, 636
Nonnotification arrangement, receivables-backed loan with, 302

Non-zero coupon bonds, 72–73, 85
Normal probability distribution, 96–97, 372–73
    area of, Z standard deviations to left or right of mean, 710
North American Industry Classification System (NAICS) Codes, 411
Note(s), 546. *See also* Promissory notes
    Euro medium-term (Euro MTNs), 574
    floating-rate (FRNs), 680
    medium-term (MTNs), 574
Notes payable, 288
Notification arrangement, receivables-backed loan with, 302
NPV profile, 338–40, 351

Offering. *See also* Capital market
    best efforts, 526
    global securities, 527
    negotiated, 526
    regulation of, 531–34
    rights, 527–31
Open-account credit, 288, 289–93, 688
Open-market purchases, 509
Operating cash flows, 177, 178, 181, 182
    project after-tax incremental, estimating, 317–26
Operating costs, 434–35
Operating cycle, 143–44
Operating economies, 624–25
Operating efficiency, 193
Operating expenses, schedule of projected, 184
Operating lease, 578, 587, 588
Operating leverage, 434–41
    break-even analysis, 435–38
    defined, 434
    degree of (DOL), 438–41
    magnification effect of, 434, 435
Operating profit. *See* Earnings before interest and taxes (EBIT; operating profit)
Operations, funds provided by, 174
Opportunity cost, 237, 255, 275, 276, 278, 290, 318
Opportunity loss, 373
Optimal amount of current assets, 211–13
Optimal capital structure, 471–72, 482
Optimal order quantity of inventory, 270, 271–72, 276
Option(s), 598. *See also* Convertible securities; Exchangeable bonds; Warrants
    call, valuation of, 610–16
    currency, 684
    defined, 610
    hedging with, 613–15
    managerial. *See* Managerial options in capital budgeting
    put, 378, 610
Option pricing, 610–16

Option writer, 610
Ordering costs, 270
Order point, 273, 274–75
Order quantity, optimal, 270, 271–72
Ordinary annuity, 46–50
Organization chart, 6, 7
Organization of financial management function, 6–7
Organized exchanges, 27, 539
Outsourcing, 235–37, 305, 643–44
Outsourcing Institute, 236
Outstanding shares, 556
Overdraft, 679
Overpriced stock, 109–10
Overseas Private Investment Corporation (OPIC), 672
Oversubscription privilege, 530
Over-the-counter (OTC) market, 27–28, 539, 540, 557–58
Ownership
    corporate, 15–16
    separation of management from, 5
Ownership restructuring, 646–48

Partial sell-offs, 644
Participating preferred stock, 554
Partnerships, 14–15, 22
    limited liability (LLP), 16
Par value, 127
    for bond, 71n, 546
    of common stock, 504, 505, 556–57
    of preferred stock, 553
Passive residual, dividends as, 492
Payables, outsourcing, 236–37
Payables activity, 141
Payables turnover (PT) ratio, 141
Payable through draft (PTD), 232–33
Payable turnover in days (PTD), 141, 143
Payback period (PBP), 334–35
Payment date, dividend, 512
Payroll disbursements, 233
Pension funds, 26
Pepsico, Inc., 644
Permanent working capital, 213–14
Perpetual bonds, 71–72, 85
Perpetual growth dividend discount model, 77–78, 109
Perpetuity, 51–53
Perquisites ("perks"), 5
Personal income taxes, 22–23, 480
Pitman, Brian, 8
Planning. *See* Financial planning
"Playing the float," 232
Poison pill, 642, 643
Political risk, 671–72
"Poof company," 635
Pooling of interests, 638–39
Porter, R. Burr, 406n
Portfolio, 99–101
    expected return of, 99–100
    market, 103, 105

marketable securities, 238–46
    risk, 100–103, 114–16
    standard deviation, 100–101, 114, 115–16, 374–75
Portfolio approach to capital investment projects, 373–76
Portfolio management, 246
Post-completion audits, 349
Preauthorized debit, 229
Precautionary motive for holding cash, 226
Preemptive right, 527–28, 560
Preferred stock, 74
    convertible, 555, 598–605, 642
    cost of, 395, 397–98
    in debt-to-equity ratio, 137
    features of, 398n, 553–56
    money-market, 244–45, 555
    retirement of, 554–55
    valuation of, 74–75, 85
    yield on, 84
Preferred stock financing, 555–56
Premium
    bond, 82
    call, 562
    convertible security, 603–5
    exchange, 605
    financial-risk, 476
    forward, 681
    risk, 28–29, 99, 106, 108, 401–2
    self-tender offer bid, 511–12
    for stable dividends, 501
Premium buy-back offer, 642
Premium over conversion value, 598–99, 603, 604, 605
Premium-over-floor value, 604
Premium over straight bond value, 603, 604, 605
Prentice Hall, 132
Prepackaged bankruptcy, 655
Present value, 39
    adjusted (APV), 420–23
    with compound interest, 43–45
        continuous, 57–58
        semiannual, 56–57
    discounting to, at risk-free rate, 368–69
    of dividend, 79
    internal rate of return and, 335–37
    for lease vs. borrowing, 582–85, 587, 588
    net. *See* Net present value (NPV)
    of perpetual bond, 72
    of preferred stock, 75
Present value interest factor (PVIF), 44
    of annuity (PVIFA), 49–50, 52, 53, 708–9
Present value interest factor table, 704–5
Present value of annuity due (PVAD), 52–53
Present value of annuity (PVA), 49
Present value of mixed cash flows, 55

Price
  bond, 82–83, 551
  call, 75n, 551, 552, 599, 600–601
  conversion, 598, 601
  elasticity of export and import, 685
  exchange, 605
  exercise, 606, 607, 609
  market, calling of convertible security
      and, 600–601
  market price per share, 3, 4, 470
  options and volatility of associated
      common stock, 611–13
  stock, returns and, 108–10
  subscription, 528–29
  tender, 640
Price/earnings ratio, 556, 629, 631–32
  low, 111
PricewaterhouseCoopers, 237
Pricing
  arbitrage pricing theory, 111, 116–18
  multifactor model of, 111, 117–18
  natural hedges, 677–78, 684
  option, 610–16
  two-factor model of, 116–17
Primary market, 24, 524
Prime rate, 297–98
Principal, 39, 71n
  bond, 546
  safety of, 240
Pringle, John J., 422n
Private, going, 647–48
Private placement, 524, 534–36, 606
Privileged subscription, 527–31
Probability distribution
  for abandonment example, 380–81, 382
  comparisons, 373
  defined, 95
  evaluating total project risk and, 415–16
  information, use of, 371–73
  for internal rate of return, 371, 372
  to measure risk, 95–98
  of net present values, 368–73, 415–16
  of possible cash flows
      for project proposals, 363–67
      range of cash-flow estimates, 186–88
  in simulation model, 371
  skewed, 366n
Probability of cash insolvency, 454–55
Probability tree, 367–70, 381n
Processing float, 228, 229
Production outlays, 184
Professional LLC (PLLC), 16
Profit
  accounting, 408
  economic, 408
  in flow of funds statement, 174
  gross profit margin, 146
  net profit margin, 146, 147, 155, 193,
      194, 196
  operating. See Earnings before interest
      and taxes (EBIT; operating profit)

value creation vs. maximization of, 3–5
Profitability. See also Income statement;
      Working capital
  financial signaling about, 482, 496
  liquidity and, 213
  optimal level of current assets and,
      211–13
  payback period as poor gauge of, 335
  refunding bond issue and, 562–64
  in relation to investment, 147
  in relation to sales, 146–47
  required return vs.
      credit period change and, 256–57
      credit policy changes and, 259
      credit standard changes and,
          255–56
  trade-off between risk and, 210–11,
      216–19, 220
Profitability index (PI), 340, 341–44
Profitability ratios, 146–49, 155
Progress reviews, 349
Project lives, ranking problems due to
      differences in, 343–45
Project monitoring, 348, 349
Project proposals. See Investment project
      proposals
Promissory notes, 242–43, 288, 577
  bankers' acceptances, 242, 245, 294–95,
      688
  commercial paper, 243, 245, 293–94
  unsecured loans, 295–97
Property and casualty companies, 26
Property classes under MACRS, 19, 21
  depreciation percentages for, 319–20
Proprietorship, sole, 14, 16, 22
Prospectus, 531–33
Protective covenants, 546, 574–76
Proxy, 558
Proxy companies, 410–11, 413, 419, 420
Proxy contest, 559
Public issue, 524–27
  equity carve-out, 645
  initial public offerings (IPO), 536–37
Publicly held company, costs associated
      with, 647
Public utilities, 555
Purchase method of accounting, 638
Purchasing-power parity (PPP), 685, 686
Pure play investment, 645
Put option, 378, 610

Quaker Oats Company, 4
Qualified institutional buyers (QIBs), 535
Quantity discount, 289
Quarterly Financial Report for Manufac-
      turing Corporations, 132n
Quarterly tax payments, 18
Quick ratio, 136, 154

Radcliffe, R.C., 507n
Railroads, financing used by, 549

Ranking of capital projects, problems
      with, 341–45
Rating agencies, 138, 294, 456–57
Ratings, credit, 29, 30, 138, 263, 264, 291,
      456–57, 547
Rationing, capital, 347–49
Ratio of exchange in merger, 628–35
Ratios, 132–50
  balance sheet, 133, 134–38
      financial leverage (debt) ratios,
          136–38, 154, 193–94
      liquidity ratios, 134–36, 154
  credit analysis using, 265
  defined, 132
  forecast financial statements and use
      of, 191–92
  income statement and income state-
      ment/balance sheet, 133, 138–49
      activity ratios, 139–46, 155
      coverage ratios, 138–39, 154, 452–54
      profitability ratios, 146–49, 155
  summary of key, 154–55
  trend analysis using, 149–50
  use of, 132–33
Raw-materials inventory, 268
Ready cash segment of marketable secu-
      rities portfolio, 239, 245
Real assets, 23
Real options. See Managerial options in
      capital budgeting
Recapitalization, 471
  leveraged, 641
Recapture of depreciation, 320, 584
Receipt, bill of lading as, 689
Receivables activity, 139–40
Receivable turnover in days (RTD), 140,
      143, 144, 155
Receivable turnover (RT) ratio, 139, 155,
      189
Record date, 512
Red herring, 531
Refunding bond issue, 562–64
Registered bonds, 71n
Registration, shelf, 526–27
Registration rights, private placement
      with, 535–36
Registration statement, 531–33
Regular dividend, 503
Regulation, government, 531–34, 558–59
Reinvoicing center, 679
Relative dispersion (risk), 98
Relative-priority basis, 654
Remedies for failing company, 651–55
Remote disbursement, 234
Reorganization, 653–55
Replacement chain analysis, 352–54
Repurchase, stock, 508–12
Repurchase agreements (RPs; repos), 242,
      245
Required return, 80, 106–8
  bankruptcy costs and, 476

Required return (*continued*)
  evaluation of projects on basis of their total risk, 414–18
  group-specific, 411–12
  with leverage, 411
  market, 80, 82
  profitability and
    credit period change and, 256–57
    credit policy changes and, 259
    credit standard changes and, 255–56
  project-specific and group-specific, 408–14
  trade-off between systematic risk and, 400
  weighted-average, 411
Residual (salvage) value, 578, 579, 580, 585
Resnick, Rosalind, 306
Resorts International, 655
Responsibility, social, 5–6
Restructuring. *See* Corporate restructuring
Retail lockbox systems, 229
Retained earnings, 127
  passive vs. active dividend policies and, 492–97
  statement of, 130
  undue retention of earnings rule, 498–99
Retirement funds, 26
Return, 240–41. *See also* Risk; Yield
  capital-asset pricing model and, 103–11, 399–400, 408–14
  defining, 94
  excess, 394–95
  expected, 28–29, 95, 96, 99–100
  market, 400–401
  minimum acceptable rate of, 394
  portfolio, 99–100
  standard deviation of, 95–97
Return on equity (ROE), 148–49, 155
Return on investment (ROI), 147–48, 155, 212
Revenue Reconciliation Act of 1993, 22
Reverse stock split, 507, 508
Reverse synergy, 625
Revocable letter of credit, 690
Revolving credit agreement, 220, 296, 573
Rice, Edward M., 647*n*
Richards, Verlyn D., 143*n*
Rights
  of common shareholders, 558–60
  preemptive, 527–28, 560
  registration, private placement with, 535–36
  subscription, 528
  value of, 528–30
  voting, 554, 558–60
Rights offering (privileged subscription), 527–31
Risk
  attitudes toward, 98–99

business, 131, 441, 449, 450, 451
  premium for, 476
  capital budgeting and, 361–91
    contribution to total firm risk, 373–78, 416–17
    project risk, problem of, 362–66
    total project risk, 366–73, 414–18
  convertible securities and, 602
  currency. *See* Exchange-rate risk exposure
  currency options and, 684
  currency swaps and, 684
  default, 28–29, 259
  defining, 94–95
  diversification and, 101–3
  "downside," 97
  earnings per share and, 4
  event, 535
  exchange-rate, 672–88
    management of, 677–88
    types of, 672–77
  expected return and, 28–29
  financial, 448–50, 454
    premium for, 476
  financial leverage, effect on, 445–47
  interest rate (yield), 82, 240–41
  in leveraged buyout, 649
  optimal level of current assets and, 211–13
  political, 671–72
  portfolio, 100–103, 114–16
  probability distributions to measure, 95–98
  between replications, 354*n*
  of short-term vs. long-term financing, 216–19
  standby arrangement and, 530
  systematic, 102, 105–6, 400, 413
    capital-asset pricing model and, 103–11
    security market line and, 107
  total firm, 449–50, 451
  trade-off between profitability and, 210–11, 216–19, 220
  unsystematic, 102–3, 106, 117, 401*n*
Risk-adjusted discount rate (RADR), 414–15
Risk aversion, 99
Risk factors
  arbitrage pricing theory and, 111, 117–18
  international diversification and, 669
Risk-free rate, 103, 104, 107, 108, 368–69, 381*n*
Risk-free return estimate, 400–401
Risk premium, 28–29, 99, 106, 108, 401–2
Robert Morris Associate (RMA), 132, 135
Roll, Richard, 117, 507*n*, 627
Roll-up, 634–35
Ross, Stephen A., 116, 117
Royalty payments, adjusting intracompany, 679

Rule 144, 536
Rule 144a, 535, 539
  underwritten Rule 144a private placement, 536
Rule 415, 574
"Rule of 72," 47

Safety
  margin of, 216, 217–18, 219–20, 300, 577
  of principal, 240
Safety stock, 273–76
Sale(s)
  "accrual" method of recognizing, 129
  break-even point
    for revenue, 437, 438
    for volume, 436–37
  corporate restructuring and enhancement of, 624–25
  credit policy and, 254–55
  degree of total leverage and, 450–51
  of depreciable asset, 320–21
  profitability in relation to, 146–47
  terms of, 289
  total assets-to-sales ratio, 193, 195–96
Sale and leaseback, 578
Sales contract, conditional, 577
Sales forecast, 181–83, 189
Sales receipts, schedule of expected, 183
Sales-to-total-assets ratio, 195
Salvage (residual) value, 578, 579, 580, 585
Samurai bonds, 680
Sara Lee, 643
Savage, Leonard J., 351*n*
Savings, 23–24
Savings and loan association, 26
Savings sector, 24, 25, 524
Scale differences, ranking problems due to, 341–42
Scale economies, 581, 625
Scholes, Myron, 614–15, 616
S corporation, 16*n*, 23
Sears, Roebuck Acceptance Corporation, 243
Seasonal dating, 258–59, 289, 291–92
Seasonality, 130, 131
Secondary market, 24, 25, 27–28, 524, 533, 539
Secured (asset-based) loans, 300–305, 308
Secured loans, 295
Secured long-term debt instruments, 547, 549
Securities. *See also* Capital market; Marketable securities management
  asset-backed (ABS), 550
  characteristic line of, 104, 105, 400, 409, 410
  convertible, 403*n*, 555, 598–605, 642
  derivative, 598. *See also* Option(s)
  direct (primary), 25
  divisibility of, 495–96

exchangeable, 605–6
indirect (secondary), 25
initial financing of, 536–37
intrinsic value of, 112
long-term. *See* Bond(s); Common stock; Preferred stock; Valuation of long-term securities
marketability of, 29, 240
maturity of, 29–30, 71, 72–74, 241, 546
option features of, 30–31
private placement of, 524, 534–36, 606
privileged subscription offer, 527–31
public issue of, 524–27
ratings of, 29, 30, 138, 456–57, 547
regulation of offerings, 531–34
signaling effects of issuing, 538–39
taxability of, 30
"trade-off" between risk and return for, 28, 29
Treasury, 28, 30, 31, 240, 241–42
yields on corporate, 31–32, 84
Securities Act of 1933 (1933 Act), 531, 533, 536
Securities and Exchange Act of 1934 (1934 Act), 531
Securities and Exchange Commission (SEC), 132, 509, 535, 546, 574, 640, 642
defined, 531
reforms, 533
registration process, 526–27
regulation by, 531–33, 558–59
Rule 415, 527
Securitization, asset, 549–50
Security agreement (security device), 301
Security (collateral), 300–305
accounts receivable as, 301–2
inventory as, 302–5
Security interest, 301
Security market line (SML), 107, 400, 402, 409–10
Self-liquidating principle, 216, 295
Self-tender offer, 509
Self-tender offer bid premium, 511–12
Selling, Thomas I., 676*n*
Sell-off, 625, 644, 646
Semiannual compounding, 56, 74, 83–84
Semistrong-form efficiency, 112
Senior debt, 649–50
Serial bonds, 551–52
Shakespeare, William, 571
Shareholders
antitakeover devices and interests of, 642–43
goals of firm for, 5
maximizing wealth of, 5–6
rights of common, 558–60
Shareholders' equity, 127, 128
debt-to-equity ratio, 136–37, 154, 193–94, 196
forecasting, 191–92

return of, 155
return on, 148–49
Shareholders' interest hypothesis of antitakeover defenses, 641
"Shark-repellent" devices, 641–42
Sharpe, William, 103
Shelf registration, 526–27, 574
Short-term, inherently self-liquidating (STISL) loan, 216
Short-term financing, 216–19, 287–314
composition of, 307–8
factoring accounts receivable, 305–7
hedging approach to, 215–16
interest rate on, 216, 297–98
long-term vs., 216–19
negotiated, 293–305
money-market credit, 293–95
secured (asset-based) loans, 300–305
unsecured loans, 295–97
spontaneous, 214–15, 288–93
accounts payable (trade credit), 266, 288–93
accrued expenses, 293
Short-term municipals, 244
Shrieves, Ronald E., 354*n*
Sight draft, 288*n*, 688
Signaling, financial, 482, 496, 497, 507, 511–12
of stock issue, 538–39
Simple interest, 39
Simulation
of total project risk, 370–71
using sustainable growth modeling, 196–97
Sinking fund, 551, 555
calculating periodic payment in, 50, 51
Sinking-fund provision, 31
Size effect, 111
Smaller companies, debt financing by, 218*n*
Small-firm effect, 111
Small-percentage stock dividends, 503–4
Smith, Clifford W., Jr., 537*n*, 538*n*
Social responsibility, 5–6
Society, value creation and, 8
Society of Worldwide Interbank Financial Telecommunications (SWIFT), 235
Sole proprietorship, 14, 16, 22
Sorter, George H., 676*n*
Sources and uses of funds statement, 170–76
Special-purpose vehicle, 549, 550
Speculative bonds, 547
"Speculative grade quality," 29, 456
Speculative motive for holding cash, 226
Spin-off, 625, 644–45, 646
Splits, stock, 505–8
Spontaneous financing, 214–15, 288–93
accounts payable (trade credit), 266, 288–93
accrued expenses, 293

Spot exchange rate, 672, 681–82
Spreadsheet program, computer, 126–27, 186
Stability of dividend payments, 500–503
Stakeholders, 6
Stancill, James M., 239*n*
Standard deviation, 95–97
of annual rate of return on common stock, estimating, 615
cash flow, 363, 364–65
portfolio, 100–101, 114, 115–16, 374–75
of probability distribution of possible net present values, calculating, 369–70
Standard Industrial Classification (SIC) code, 411*n*
Standard & Poor's, 29, 30, 138, 294, 456, 547
S&P 500 Stock Index, 103, 108, 400
Stock Reports, 107, 400
Standards, credit, 254–56, 259, 261–62
Standby arrangement, 530
Standstill agreement, 642
Statement of cash flows, 170, 177–81
analyzing, 180–81, 182
Statement of changes in financial position, 170–76
Statement of Financial Accounting Standards (SFAS) No. 95, 177
Statement of retained earnings, 130
State of incorporation, 641
State regulation, 533
Status reports, 349
Stay, 652
Steady-state model of sustainable growth, 193–95
Stern Stewart & Co., 408
Stock, "ex-rights," 528–29. *See also* Common stock; Preferred stock
Stock dividends, 503–7
Stock market crash (October 19, 1987), 113
Stock market efficiency, 112
Stockouts, 142
Stock prices, returns and, 108–10
Stock repurchase, 508–12
Stock splits, 505–8
Stop order, 531
Straight-bond value of convertible security, 602–3
Straight debt (equity), 598
Straight-line depreciation, 18, 19
Strategic acquisitions involving common stock, 628–35
Strategic alliances, 643–44
Strategic realignment, divestiture and, 625
Stretching accounts payable, 290–92
Strong-form efficiency, 112
"Stub" shares, 641
Subchapter S of Internal Revenue Code, 23

Subordinated debentures, 547–48
Subscription price, 528–29
Subscription right, 528
Subsidiaries, 411, 645, 646, 673–76
Sunk costs, 318
Supermajority merger approval provision, 641
Suppliers
  of capital, negotiation with, 131
  trade credit from, 266, 288–93
Supreme Court, 655
Sustainable growth modeling, 170, 193–96
  under changing assumptions, 195–96
  implications of, 196–97
  solving for other variables, 196–97
  steady-state model, 193–95
Sustainable growth rate (SGR), 193–96
Swaps, currency, 684
Symbols
  commonly used, 725–26
  ticker, 107, 645
Synergy, 625
  reverse, 625
Systematic risk, 102, 413
  beta as index of, 105–6, 107, 110, 111
  capital-asset pricing model and, 103–11
  security market line and, 107
  trade-off between required rate of return and, 400

Taggart, Robert A., Jr., 422n
Takeovers. See also Corporate restructuring
  defenses against, 640–41
  empirical evidence on, 632–33
  hubris hypothesis of, 627, 633
  tender offers and, 640
Target dividend-payout ratio, 503
Taxability of security, 30
Tax environment, 17–23
Taxes
  as accrued expenses, 293
  adjusting intercompany accounts and, 679
  alternative minimum tax, 17–18, 580
  capital gains, 23, 494–95
  capital structure determination and, 478–82
    combined with market imperfections, 480–81
  corporate restructuring and, 626–27, 638
  cost of preferred stock and, 398
  deferred, 156–57
  on dividends, 21–22, 23
  double taxation, 16, 18, 23
  equity carve-outs and, 646
  estimating capital project operating cash flows and, 318–21
  exchangeable bonds and, 606

forecast income statement and, 188
foreign tax credit, 670
income
  corporate, 17–22, 478–79
  personal, 22–23, 480
  on securities, 30
on investor, dividend relevance and, 494–95, 496–97
leasing vs. borrowing and, 579–80, 583–84, 585–86
market imperfections combined with, 480–81
on multinational firm, 669–71
sole proprietorship and, 14, 16
stock repurchase and, 510
withholding, 670
Taxes payable, 156n
Tax-loss carryforward, 626–27
Tax rate, 17
Tax Reform Act of 1986, 19, 319
Tax shield, 420, 422, 423, 478–80, 583, 585
Technical insolvency, 651
Temporal method, 674
Temporary working capital, 213, 214
Tender offer, 640
Tender price, 640
Tennessee Valley Authority (TVA), 242
Terminal value. See Future value
Terminal Value Interest Factor Tables, 41
Terminal warehouse receipt, 304
Terminal year incremental net cash flow, 321, 322–23, 324, 326
Term loans, 572–77
Terms, credit, 256–59
Terms of sale, 289
Term structure of interest rates, 30
Thomas, Mike, 231
Thrift CDs, 244
Ticker symbols, 107, 645
Time deposits, Eurodollar, 244
Time draft, 288, 294–95, 688–89
Time line, 47, 48, 49, 52, 53, 55
Times interest earned, 138, 154, 452
Time value of money, 37–68. See also Interest rate
  amortizing a loan, 59–60
  compound interest, 39–59
    annuities, 46–53
    compounding more than once a year, 56–59, 74, 83–84
    mixed flows, 54–56
    single amounts, 40–46
  simple interest, 39
Timing, mix of short-term financing and, 307
Title, bill of lading as document of, 689
Titman, Sheridan, 507n
Tolkien, J.R., 433
Tombstone advertisements, 533, 534
Total asset (capital) turnover ratio, 145–46, 155

Total assets-to-sales ratio, 193, 195–96
Total (combined) leverage, 450–51
Total firm risk, 449–50
  contribution of investment project to, 373–78, 416–17
  degree of total leverage and, 451
Total project risk, 366–73
Total-value principle, 472–75, 493–94
Trade
  credit checking through the, 263
  structuring international transactions, 688–91
Trade acceptance, 288–89, 688
Trade bills, 680
Trade credit (accounts payable), 176, 214n, 266, 288–93
Trade discount, 289–90
Trade liabilities, 288
Trading on the equity. See Financial leverage
Traditional approach to capital structure, 471–72
Tranche, international, 527
Transaction loan, 296
Transactions costs, 477–78, 495–96, 647
Transactions exposure, 672–73, 676
Transactions motive for holding cash, 226
Transfer of funds, concentration services for, 230–31
Translation exposure, 672, 673–76
Translation gains or losses, 674
Treasurer, 6, 7
Treasury bill (T-bill), 95, 241, 245
Treasury bonds, 241
Treasury notes, 241
Treasury securities, 28, 240, 241–42
  yield curve for, 30, 31
Treasury stock, 511, 556
Trend analysis, 149–50
Trial-and-error method, 336
Tricon Global Restaurants, 644–45
Trust certificates, equipment, 549
Trustee, 546
  interim, 652
Trustees of Dartmouth College v. *Woodward*, 15
Trust Indenture Act of 1939, 546
Trust receipt, 303–4
Truth-in-Lending Act, 58
Turnover (activity) ratios, 139–46, 155
TWA, 655
Two-factor model of pricing, 116–17
Two-tier offer, 640

Unavoidable risk. See Systematic risk
Uncertainty. See also Risk
  convertible securities and, 602
  margin of safety and, 219–20, 577
  relevance of dividends under conditions of, 494–96
  safety stock amount and, 273–74, 275

of tax-shield benefits, 479–81
Underpriced stock, 109–10
Underwriter, standby arrangement with, 530
Underwriting, 525–26, 530
Underwriting spread, 524
Underwriting syndicate, 526
Underwritten Rule 144a private placement, 536
Undue retention of earnings rule, 498–99
Unequal (asymmetric) information, 482, 539, 626
Uniform Commercial Code, 301, 303
Unisys Corporation, 231
Unsecured loans, 295–97
Unsecured long-term debt instruments, 547–49
Unsystematic risk, 102–3, 106, 117, 401n
Uses of funds, 171–73
Utilities, public, 555

Valuation of long-term securities, 69–92
    bonds, 71–74, 85
    common stock, 75–80, 85
    dividend discount valuation models, 77–80, 108–9, 398–99
    preferred stock, 74–75, 85
    rates of return (yields), 80–84
Value. *See also* Future value; Market value; Present value
    abandonment, 379–83
    book, 70, 557
    of call option, 610–16
        on its expiration date, 610
        prior to expiration, 610–13
    of call privilege, 552–53
    concepts of, 70–71
    conservation of, 493–94
    conversion, 598–99, 600, 601
    of convertible securities, 602–5
    creation of, 3–5, 8, 394–95
    of exchangeable bonds, 606
    expected, 363–66, 374–76
    intrinsic, 70–71, 80, 108–9, 112
    liquidating, per share, 557
    liquidation, 70

residual, 578, 579, 580, 585
    of rights, 528–30
    sources of corporate, 624–28
    total-value principle, 472–75, 493–94
    of warrant, 607–9
Value Line Investment Survey, 107, 400
Van Horne, James C., 83n, 237n, 683n
Variable operating costs, 434, 435
Variance, 364
Variance-covariance matrix, 115, 116
Variance of distribution, 95–96
Veeck, Bill, 47
Venture capital, 536
Vermaelen, Theo, 511n
Vertical merger, 625
Virtual corporations, 643–44
Viscione, Jerry A., 218n
Volatility, influence on option pricing of, 611–13
Voluntary bankruptcy proceeding, 652
Voluntary liquidation, 644, 651
Voluntary settlements for failing company, 651
Voting procedures, 559–60
Voting rights
    of common shareholders, 558–60
    dual-class common stock and, 560, 561
    for preferred stockholders, 554

Wachowicz, John M., Jr., 93, 354n
Wages, 184, 293
Warehouse receipts, 304–5
Warrants, 30–31, 599, 606–9, 649
Weak-form efficiency, 112
Wealth transfer, 626
Weighted-average cost of capital (WACC), 403–7, 420, 469
    adjusted present value method vs., 422–23
Weighted-average required return, 411
Weighting system, 404–5
Wensley, Robin, 345
"White knight," 641
Wholesale lockbox systems, 229, 230
Wilde, Oscar, 69
Williams, John B., 76n, 77n

Williams, Kathy, 237
Wire transfer, 231
Wit Capital Corp., 537
Withholding taxes, 670
Woolridge, J. Randall, 507n
Working capital, 209–24
    classification of, 213–14
    combining liability structure and current asset decisions, 219–20
    concepts of, 210
    financing current assets, 214–19
    net, decreased (increased) level of, 322
    optimal level of current assets, 211–13
    profitability and risk in, 210–11, 216–19
    requirement in loan agreement, 575
Working capital management, 210. *See also* Accounts receivable management; Cash management; Inventory management; Marketable securities management; Short-term financing
    significance of, 210
Work-in-process, 268

Xerox Corporation, 578

Yankee bonds, 680
Yankee CDs, 244
Yankee commercial paper, 243
Yankelovich Partners, 237
Yield, 80–84, 94n, 240–41. *See also* Return
    annual percentage, 58
    bond-equivalent, 83
    capital gains, 84
    on corporate securities, behavior of, 31–32, 84
    dividend, 84, 494–95
Yield curve, 30, 31, 401
Yield risk, 82, 240–41
Yield to maturity (YTM), 80–84, 397. *See also* Internal rate of return (IRR)

Zero balance account (ZBA), 233
Zero-coupon bonds, 73–74, 85
Z standard deviations (Z-score), 97, 372